MICROPROCESSORS AND INTERFACING

MICROPROCESSORS AND INTERFACING
PROGRAMMING AND HARDWARE

SECOND EDITION **DOUGLAS V. HALL**

GLENCOE
Macmillan/McGraw-Hill

Lake Forest, Illinois   Columbus, Ohio   Mission Hills, California   Peoria, Illinois

IBM PC, IBM PC/XT, IBM PC/AT, IBM PS/2, and MicroChannel Architecture are registered trademarks of IBM Corporation. The following are registered trademarks of Intel Corporation: i486™, i860™, ICE, iRMX. Borland, Sidekick, Turbo Assembler, TASM, Turbo Debugger, and Turbo C++ are registered trademarks of Borland International, Inc. Microsoft, MS, MS DOS, Windows 3.0, Codeview, and MASM are registered trademarks of Microsoft Corporation. Other product names are registered trademarks of the companies associated with the product name reference in the text or figure.

Hall, Douglas V.
    Microprocessors and interfacing : programming and hardware /
Douglas V. Hall.—2nd ed.
        p.   cm.
    Includes bibliographical references and index.
    ISBN 0-07-025742-6 (text).—ISBN 0-07-025743-4 (experiments
manual).—ISBN 0-07-025744-2 (instructor's manual)
    1. Microprocessors—Programming. 2. Microprocessors. 3. Computer
interfaces. I. Title
QA76.6.H2994   1991
005.26—dc20   91-14526
                                                                     CIP

Send all inquiries to:
GLENCOE DIVISION
Macmillan/McGraw-Hill
936 Eastwind Drive
Westerville, OH 43081

ISBN 0-07-025742-6

Printed in the United States of America

2 3 4 5 6 7 8 9 RRDW 99 98 97 96 95 94 93 92

TO MY STUDENTS

Let us go forward together into the future.

CONTENTS

PREFACE

This book is written for a wide variety of introductory microprocessor courses. The only prerequisite for this book is some knowledge of diodes, transistors, and simple digital devices.

My experience as an engineer and as a teacher indicates that it is much more productive to first learn one microprocessor family very thoroughly and from that strong base learn others as needed. For this book I chose the Intel 8086/80186/80286/80386/80486 family of microprocessors. Devices in this family are used in millions and millions of personal computers, including the IBM PC/AT, the IBM PS/2 models, and many "clones." The 8086 was the first member of this family, and although it has been superseded by newer processors, the 8086 is still an excellent entry point for learning about microprocessors. You don't need to know about the advanced features of the newer processors until you learn about multiuser/multitasking systems. Therefore, the 8086 is used for most of the hardware and programming examples until Chapter 15, which discusses the features of the newer processors and how these features are used in multiuser/multitasking systems.

CONTENT AND ORGANIZATION

All chapters begin with fundamental objectives and conclude with a review of important terms and concepts. Each chapter also concludes with a generous supply of questions and problems that reinforce both the theory and applications presented in the chapters.

To help refresh your memory, Chapter 1 contains a brief review of the digital concepts needed for the rest of the book. It also includes an overview of basic computer mathematics and arithmetic operations on binary, HEX, and BCD numbers.

Chapters 2–10

Chapters 2–10 provide you with a comprehensive introduction to microprocessors, including interrupt applications, digital and analog interfacing, and industrial controls. These chapters include an overview of the 8086 microprocessor family and its architecture, programming language, and systems connections and troubleshooting.

Because I came into the world of electronics through the route of vacuum tubes, my first tendency in teaching microprocessors was to approach them from a hardware direction. However, the more I designed with microprocessors and taught microprocessor classes, the more I became aware that the real essence of a microprocessor is what you can program it to do. Therefore, Chapters 2–5 introduce you to writing structured assembly language programs for the 8086 microprocessor. The approach taken in this programming section is to solve the problem, write an algorithm for the solution, and then simply translate the algorithm to assembly language. Experience has shown that this approach is much more likely to produce a working program than just writing down assembly language instructions. The 8086 instruction set is introduced in Chapters 2–5 as needed to solve simple programming problems, but for reference Chapter 6 contains a dictionary of all 8086 instructions with examples for each.

Chapter 7 discusses the signals, timing, and system connections for a simple 8086-based microcomputer. Also discussed in Chapter 7 is a systematic method for troubleshooting a malfunctioning 8086-based microcomputer system and the use of a logic analyzer to observe microcomputer bus signals. Chapter 8 discusses how the 8086 responds to interrupts, how interrupt-service procedures are written, and the operation of a peripheral device called a priority-interrupt controller.

Chapters 9 and 10 show how a microprocessor is interfaced with a wide variety of low-level input and output devices. Chapter 9 shows how a microprocessor is interfaced with digital devices such as keyboards, displays, and relays. Chapter 10 shows how a microprocessor is interfaced with analog input/output devices such as A/Ds, D/As, and a variety of sensors. Chapter 10 also shows how all the "pieces" are put together to produce a microprocessor-based scale and a simple microprocessor-based process control system. Chapter 10 concludes with a discussion of how microprocessors can be used to implement digital filters.

Chapters 11–15

Chapters 11–15 are devoted to the hardware, software, and peripheral interfacing for a microcomputer such as those in the IBM PC and the IBM PS/2 families. Chapter 11 discusses motherboard circuitry, including DRAM systems, caches, math coprocessors, and peripheral interface buses. Chapter 11 also shows how to use a schematic capture program to draw the schematic, a simulator program to verify the logic and timing of the design, and a layout program to design a printed-circuit board for the system. Knowledge of these electronic design automation tools is essential for anyone developing high-speed microprocessor systems.

At the request of many advisors from industry, Chapter 12 introduces you to the C programming language, which is used to write a large number of system-level programs. This chapter takes advantage of the fact that it is very easy to learn C if you are already familiar with 8086-type assembly language. A section in this chapter also shows you how to write simple programs which contain both C and assembly language modules.

Chapter 13 describes the operation and interfacing of common peripherals such as CRT displays, magnetic disks, and printers. Chapter 14 shows how a microcomputer is interfaced with communication systems such as modems and networks.

Finally, Chapter 15 starts with a discussion of the needs that must be met by a multiuser/multitasking operating system and then describes how the protected-mode features of the 80286, 80386, and 80486 processors meet these needs. This section of the book also includes discussions of how to develop programs for the 386 in a variety of environments. The chapter and the book conclude with introductions to parallel processors, neural networks, and fuzzy logic. I think you will find these newly developing areas as fascinating as I have.

SUGGESTIONS FOR ASSIGNMENTS

Flexible Organization

The text is comprehensive, yet flexible in its organization. Chapter 1 could be easily omitted if students have a solid background in basic binary mathematics and digital fundamentals.

Chapters 2–10

I suggest following Chapters 2–10 as an instructional block as each chapter builds on the preceding chapter. These nine chapters represent ideal coverage for a "short course" in microprocessors. The remaining chapters represent an opportunity for the instructor to tailor assignments for the students' needs or perhaps to give an individual student added study in recent developments in the architecture of microprocessors.

Chapter 11

Individual topics from Chapter 11 could be selected for study as students gain knowledge of the "tools available for designing computer based systems The DRAM section is very important.

Chapter 12

You may wish to assign or leave for outside reading Chapter 12 on programming in C, a new chapter. At the very least you should take a careful look at the simple programming examples and the development of tools for C. If class time does not permit assigning this chapter, you may wish to use selected examples and programs in your lecture presentations. This chapter should be included in any course sequence which does not have a separate class in C programming.

Chapter 13

Portions of the peripherals chapter may be assigned as required, depending upon the course syllabus. The CRT, disk, and printer sections are highly recommended.

Chapter 14

This is an important chapter, given the ever-expanding use of data communications. It should be assigned, if at all possible, unless the curriculum includes a separate course in data communications. Of primary importance are the sections on modems and LANs.

Chapter 15

The final chapter is on the cutting edge of the development of new microprocessors. It is my hope that all students will have the opportunity to read this chapter. At the very least students should read the section on the 386. This is a final chapter, yet it is only the beginning of their study of microprocessors.

NEW FEATURES IN THIS EDITION

In response to feedback from industry and from a variety of electronics instructors, the second edition of *Microprocessors and Interfacing: Programming and Hardware* contains the following new or enhanced features.

1. The order of the topics in Chapters 4 and 5 has been improved, based on instructor feedback.
2. A greatly expanded section on digital signal processing hardware and software has been added to Chapter 10.
3. A section in Chapter 11 describes and shows an example of how electronic design automation tools such as schematic capture programs, simulator programs, and PC board layout programs are used to develop the hardware for a microcomputer system.
4. At the request of industry advisors, Chapter 12 is a completely new chapter which contains a solid introduction to the C programming language, including examples of programs with C and assembly language modules.
5. Chapters 13 and 14, the systems peripherals chapters, have been updated to reflect advances in technology such as VGA graphics, optical-disk storage, laser printers, and digital video interactive. The chapters now include both assembly language and C interface program examples.
6. The network section of Chapter 14 has been expanded to reflect the current importance of networks.

7. Chapter 15 now contains an extensive description of the features of the 386 and 486 processors and a discussion of how these features are used in multitasking environments such as Microsoft's OS/2 and Windows 3.0.
8. Introductions to neutral network computers and to fuzzy logic have been added to Chapter 15.

SPECIAL FEATURES AND SUPPLEMENTS

This book and the Experiments Manual written to accompany it contain many hardware and software exercises students can do to solidify their knowledge of microprocessors. An IBM PC or IBM PC-compatible computer can be used to edit, assemble, link/locate, run, and debug many of the 8086 assembly language programs.

The Experiments Manual contains 40 laboratory exercises that are directly coordinated to the text. Each experiment includes chapter references, required equipment, objectives, and experimental procedures.

The Instructor's Manual contains answers to the review questions. It also includes experimental notes and answers to selected questions for the Experiments Manual.

The Instructor's Manual includes disk directories. There are two disks available. This set of disks contains the source code for all the programs in the text and Experiments Manual.

ADDITIONAL GOALS

One of the main goals of this book is to teach you how to decipher manufacturers' data sheets for microprocessor and peripheral devices, so the book contains relevant parts of many data sheets. Because of the large number of devices discussed, however, it was not possible to include complete data sheets. If you are doing an in-depth study, it is suggested that you acquire or gain access to the latest editions of Intel Microprocessors and Peripherals handbooks. These are available free of charge to colleges and universities from the Academic Relations Department of Intel. The bibliography at the end of the book contains a list of other books and periodicals you can refer to for further details on the topics discussed in the book.

ACKNOWLEDGMENTS

I wish to express my profound thanks to the people around me who helped make this book a reality. Thanks to Pat Hunter, whose cheerful encouragement helped me through seemingly endless details. She proofread and coded the manuscript, worked out the answers to the end-of-chapter problems to verify that they are solvable, and made suggestions and contributions too numerous to mention. Thanks to Richard Cihkey of New England Technical Institute in New Britain, Connecticut, who meticulously worked his way through the manuscript and made many valuable suggestions. Thanks to Mike Olisewski of Instant Information, Inc., who helped me "C the light" in Chapter 12 and contributed his industry perspective on the topics that should be included in the book. Thanks to Dr. Michael A. Driscoll of Portland State University, who helped me fine-tune Chapter 15. Thanks to Intel Corporation for letting me use many drawings from their data books so that this book could lead readers into the real world of data books. Finally, thanks to my wife, Rosemary, my children Linda, Brad, Mark, Lee, and Kathryn, and to the rest of my family for their patience and support during the long effort of rewriting this book.

If you have suggestions for improving the book or ideas that might clarify a point for someone else, please communicate with me through the publisher.

Douglas V. Hall

MICROPROCESSORS
AND
INTERFACING

CHAPTER 1

Computer Number Systems, Codes, and Digital Devices

Before starting our discussion of microprocessors and microcomputers, we need to make sure that some key concepts of the number systems, codes, and digital devices used in microcomputers are fresh in your mind. If the short summaries of these concepts in this chapter are not enough to refresh your memory, then you may want to consult some of the chapters in *Digital Circuits and Systems*, McGraw-Hill, 1989, before going on in this book.

OBJECTIVES

At the conclusion of this chapter you should be able to:

1. Convert numbers between the following codes: binary, hexadecimal, and BCD.

2. Define the terms *bit, nibble, byte, word, most significant bit,* and *least significant bit.*

3. Use a table to find the ASCII or EBCDIC code for a given alphanumeric character.

4. Perform addition and subtraction of binary, hexadecimal, and BCD numbers.

5. Describe the operation of gates, flip-flops, latches, registers, ROMs, PALs, dynamic RAMs, static RAMs, and buses.

6. Describe how an arithmetic logic unit can be instructed to perform arithmetic or logical operations on binary words.

COMPUTER NUMBER SYSTEMS AND CODES

Review of Decimal System

To understand the structure of the binary number system, the first step is to review the familiar decimal or base-10 number system. Here is a decimal number with the value of each place holder or digit expressed as a power of 10.

$$5 \quad 3 \quad 4 \quad 6 \quad . \quad 7 \quad 2$$
$$10^3 \quad 10^2 \quad 10^1 \quad 10^0 \quad \quad 10^{-1} \quad 10^{-2}$$

The digits in the decimal number 5346.72 thus tell you that you have 5 thousands, 3 hundreds, 4 tens, 6 ones, 7 tenths, and 2 hundredths. The number of symbols needed in any number system is equal to the base number. In the decimal number system, then, there are 10 symbols, 0 through 9. When the count in any digit position passes that of the highest-value symbol, the digit rolls back to 0 and the next higher digit is incremented by 1. A car odometer is a good example of this.

A number system can be built using powers of any number as place holders or digits, but some bases are more useful than others. It is difficult to build electronic circuits which can store and manipulate 10 different voltage levels but relatively easy to build circuits which can handle two levels. Therefore, a *binary*, or *base-2*, number system is used to represent numbers in digital systems.

The Binary Number System

Figure 1-1a, p. 2, shows the value of each digit in a binary number. Each binary digit represents a power of 2. A binary digit is often called a *bit*. Note that digits to the right of the *binary point* represent fractions used for numbers less than 1. The binary system uses only two symbols, zero (0) and one (1), so in binary you count as follows: 0, 1, 10, 11, 100, 101, 110, 111, 1000, etc. For reference, Figure 1-1b shows the powers of 2 from 2^1 to 2^{32}.

Binary numbers are often called *binary words* or just *words*. Binary words with certain numbers of bits have also acquired special names. A 4-bit binary word is called a *nibble*, and an 8-bit binary word is called a *byte*. A 16-bit binary word is often referred to just as a *word*, and a 32-bit binary word is referred to as a *doubleword*. The rightmost or *least significant bit* of a binary word is usually referred to as the LSB. The leftmost or *most significant bit* of a binary word is usually called the MSB.

To convert a binary number to its equivalent decimal number, multiply each digit times the decimal value of the digit and just add these up. The binary number 101, for example, represents: $(1 \times 2^2) + (0 \times 2^1) + (1 \times 2^0)$,

$$2^7 \quad 2^6 \quad 2^5 \quad 2^4 \; 2^3 \, 2^2 \, 2^1 \, 2^0 \quad 2^{-1} \, 2^{-2}$$

$$\text{1 0 1 1 0 . 1 1}$$

128 64 32 16 8 4 2 1 $\quad \frac{1}{2} \quad \frac{1}{4}$

(a)

2^1 =	2	2^9 =	512	2^{17} =	131,072	2^{25} =	33,554,432
2^2 =	4	2^{10} =	1,024	2^{18} =	262,144	2^{26} =	67,108,864
2^3 =	8	2^{11} =	2,048	2^{19} =	524,288	2^{27} =	134,217,728
2^4 =	16	2^{12} =	4,096	2^{20} =	1,048,576	2^{28} =	268,435,456
2^5 =	32	2^{13} =	8,192	2^{21} =	2,097,152	2^{29} =	536,870,912
2^6 =	64	2^{14} =	16,384	2^{22} =	4,194,304	2^{30} =	1,073,741,824
2^7 =	128	2^{15} =	32,768	2^{23} =	8,388,608	2^{31} =	2,147,483,648
2^8 =	256	2^{16} =	65,536	2^{24} =	16,777,216	2^{32} =	4,294,967,296

(b)

FIGURE 1-1 (a) Digit values in binary. (b) Powers of 2.

or $4 + 0 + 1 = $ decimal 5. For the binary number 10110.11, you have:

$$(1 \times 2^4) + (0 \times 2^3) + (1 \times 2^2) + (1 \times 2^1) + (0 \times 2^0)$$
$$+ (1 \times 2^{-1}) + (1 \times 2^{-2^2}) =$$
$$16 + 0 + 4 + 2 + 0 + 0.5 + 0.25 = \text{decimal } 22.75$$

To convert a decimal number to binary, there are two common methods. The first (Figure 1-2a) is simply a reverse of the binary-to-decimal method. For example, to convert the decimal number 21 (sometimes written as 21_{10}) to binary, first subtract the largest power of 2 that will fit in the number. For 21_{10} the largest power of 2 that will fit is 16 or 2^4. Subtracting 16 from 21 gives a remainder of 5. Put a 1 in the 2^4 digit position and see if the next lower power of 2 will fit in the remainder. Since 2^3 is 8 and 8 will not fit in the remainder of 5, put a 0 in the 2^3 digit position. Then try the next lower power of 2. In this case the next is 2^2 or 4, which will fit in the remainder of 5. A 1 is therefore put in the 2^2 digit position. When 2^2 or 4 is subtracted from the old remainder of 5, a new remainder of 1 is left. Since 2^1 or 2 will not fit into this remainder, a 0 is put in that position. A 1 is put in the 2^0 position because 2^0 is equal to 1 and this fits exactly into the remainder of 1. The result shows that 21_{10} is equal to 10101 in binary. This conversion process is somewhat messy to describe but easy to do. Try converting 46_{10} to binary. You should get 101110.

Another method of converting a decimal number to binary is shown in Figure 1-2b. Divide the decimal number by 2 and write the quotient and remainder as shown. Divide this quotient and following quotients by 2 until the quotient reaches 0. The column of remainders will be the binary equivalent of the given decimal number. Note that the MSD is on the bottom of the column and the LSD is on the top of the column if you perform the divisions in order from the top to the bottom of the page. You can demonstrate that the binary number is correct by reconverting from binary to decimal, as shown in the right-hand side of Figure 1-2b.

You can convert decimal numbers less than 1 to binary by successive multiplication by 2, recording carries until the quantity to the right of the decimal point becomes zero, as shown in Figure 1-2c. The carries represent the binary equivalent of the decimal number, with the *most significant bit* at the top of the column. Decimal 0.625 equals 0.101 in binary. For decimal values that do not convert exactly the way this one did (the quantity to the right of the decimal never becomes zero), you can continue the conversion process until you get the number of binary digits desired.

At this point it is interesting to compare the number of digits required to express numbers in decimal with the number required to express them in binary. In

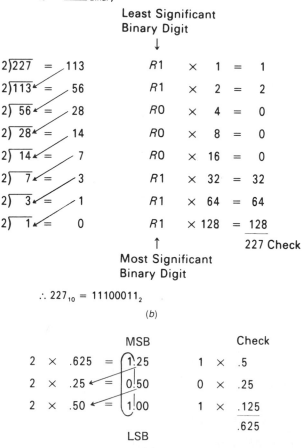

(a)

(b)

(c)

FIGURE 1-2 Converting decimal to binary. (a) Digit value method. (b) Divide by 2 method. (c) Decimal fraction conversion.

decimal, one digit can represent 10^1 numbers, 0 through 9; two digits can represent 10^2 or 100 numbers, 0 through 99; and three digits can represent 10^3 or 1000 numbers, 0 through 999. In binary, a similar pattern exists. One binary digit can represent 2 numbers, 0 and 1; two binary digits can represent 2^2 or 4 numbers, 0 through 11; and three binary digits can represent 2^3 or 8 numbers, 0 through 111. The pattern, then, is that N decimal digits can represent 10^N numbers and N binary digits can represent 2^N numbers. Eight binary digits can represent 2^8 or 256 numbers, 0 through 255 in decimal.

Hexadecimal

Binary is not a very compact code. This means that it requires many more digits to express a number than does, for example, decimal. Twelve binary digits can only describe a number up to 4095_{10}. Computers require binary data, but people working with computers have trouble remembering long binary words. One solution to the problem is to use the *hexadecimal* or base-16 number system.

Figure 1-3*a* shows the digit values for hexadecimal, which is often just called *hex*. Since hex is base 16, you have to have 16 possible symbols, one for each digit. The table of Figure 1-3*b* shows the symbols for hex code.

$$16^3 \quad 16^2 \quad 16^1 \quad 16^0 \,.\, 16^{-1} \quad 16^{-2} \quad 16^{-3}$$

$$4096 \quad 256 \quad 16 \quad 1 \qquad \tfrac{1}{16} \quad \tfrac{1}{256} \quad \tfrac{1}{4096}$$

(a)

Dec		Hex	Dec		Hex
0	=	0	8	=	8
1	=	1	9	=	9
2	=	2	10	=	A
3	=	3	11	=	B
4	=	4	12	=	C
5	=	5	13	=	D
6	=	6	14	=	E
7	=	7	15	=	F

(b)

$227_D = \underline{\quad ? \quad}_{Hex}$ LSD

$16\overline{)227} = 14$ $R3 \times 1 = 3$

$16\overline{)14} = 0$ $RE \times 16 = \underline{224}$

           MSD   227

$227_{10} = E3_{16}$

(c)

FIGURE 1-3 Hexadecimal numbers. (*a*) Value of place holders. (*b*) Symbols. (*c*) Decimal-to-hexadecimal conversion.

After the decimal symbols 0 through 9 are used up, you use the letters A through F for values 10 through 15.

As mentioned above, each hex digit is equal to four binary digits. To convert the binary number 11010110 to hex, mark off the binary bits in groups of 4, moving to the left from the binary point. Then write the hex symbol for the value of each group of 4.

Binary	1101	0110
Hex	D	6

The 0110 group is equal to 6 and the 1101 group is equal to 13. Since 13 is D in hex, 11010110 binary is equal to D6 in hex. "H" is usually used after a number to indicate that it is a hexadecimal number. For example, D6 hex is usually written D6H. As you can see, 8 bits can be represented with only 2 hex digits.

If you want to convert a number from decimal to hexadecimal, Figure 1-3*c* shows a familiar trick for doing this. The result shows that 227_{10} is equal to E3H. As you can see, hex is an even more compact code than decimal. Two hexadecimal digits can represent a decimal number up to 255. Four hex digits can represent a decimal number up to 65,535.

To illustrate how hexadecimal numbers are used in digital logic, a service manual tells you that the 8-bit-wide data bus of an 8088A microprocessor should contain 3FH during a certain operation. Converting 3FH to binary gives the pattern of 1's and 0's (0011 1111) you would expect to find with your oscilloscope or logic analyzer on the parallel lines. The 3FH is simply a shorthand which is easier to remember and less prone to errors than the binary equivalent.

BCD Codes

STANDARD BCD

In applications such as frequency counters, digital voltmeters, or calculators, where the output is a decimal display, a *binary-coded decimal* or *BCD* code is often used. BCD uses a 4-bit binary code to individually represent each decimal digit in a number. As you can see in Table 1-1, p. 4, the simplest BCD code uses the first 10 numbers of standard binary code for the BCD numbers 0 through 9. The hex codes A through F are invalid BCD codes. To convert a decimal number to its BCD equivalent, just represent each decimal digit by its 4-bit binary equivalent, as shown here.

Decimal	5	2	9
BCD	0101	0010	1001

To convert a BCD number to its decimal equivalent, reverse the process.

GRAY CODE

Gray code is another important binary code; it is often used for encoding shaft position data from machines such as computer-controlled lathes. This code has the same possible combinations as standard binary, but as you can see in the 4-bit example in Table 1-1, they are

TABLE 1-1
COMMON NUMBER CODES

Decimal	Binary	Octal	Hex	Binary-Coded Decimal 8421	BCD	EXCESS-3	Reflected Gray Code	7-Segment Display (1 = on) a b c d e f g	Display
0	0000	0	0		0000	0011 0011	0000	1 1 1 1 1 1 0	0
1	0001	1	1		0001	0011 0100	0001	0 1 1 0 0 0 0	1
2	0010	2	2		0010	0011 0101	0011	1 1 0 1 1 0 1	2
3	0011	3	3		0011	0011 0110	0010	1 1 1 1 0 0 1	3
4	0100	4	4		0100	0011 0111	0110	0 1 1 0 0 1 1	4
5	0101	5	5		0101	0011 1000	0111	1 0 1 1 0 1 1	5
6	0110	6	6		0110	0011 1001	0101	1 0 1 1 1 1 1	6
7	0111	7	7		0111	0011 1010	0100	1 1 1 0 0 0 0	7
8	1000	10	8		1000	0011 1011	1100	1 1 1 1 1 1 1	8
9	1001	11	9		1001	0011 1100	1101	1 1 1 0 0 1 1	9
10	1010	12	A	0001	0000	0100 0011	1111	1 1 1 1 1 0 1	A
11	1011	13	B	0001	0001	0100 0100	1110	0 0 1 1 1 1 1	B
12	1100	14	C	0001	0010	0100 0101	1010	0 0 0 1 1 0 1	C
13	1101	15	D	0001	0011	0100 0110	1011	0 1 1 1 1 0 1	D
14	1110	16	E	0001	0100	0100 0111	1001	1 1 0 1 1 1 1	E
15	1111	17	F	0001	0101	0100 1000	1000	1 0 0 0 1 1 1	F

arranged in a different order. Notice that only one binary digit changes at a time as you count up in this code.

If you need to construct a Gray-code table larger than that in Table 1-1, a handy way to do so is to observe the pattern of 1's and 0's and just extend it. The least significant digit column starts with one 0 and then has alternating groups of two 1's and two 0's as you go down the column. The second most significant digit column starts with two 0's and then has alternating groups of four 1's and four 0's. The third column starts with four 0's, then has alternating groups of eight 1's and eight 0's. By now you should see the pattern. Try to figure out the Gray code for the decimal number 16. You should get 11000.

7-Segment Display Code

Figure 1-4a shows the segment identifiers for a 7-segment display such as those commonly used in digital instruments. Table 1-1 shows the logic levels required to display 0 to 9 and A to F on a common-cathode LED display such as that shown in Figure 1-4b. For a common-anode LED display such as that in Figure 1-4c, simply invert the segment codes shown in Table 1-1.

Alphanumeric Codes

When communicating with or between computers, you need a binary-based code which can represent letters of the alphabet as well as numbers. Common codes used for this have 7 or 8 bits per word and are referred to as *alphanumeric codes*. To detect possible errors in these codes, an additional bit, called a *parity bit*, is often added as the most significant bit.

Parity is a term used to identify whether a data word has an odd or even number of 1's. If a data word contains an odd number of 1's, the word is said to have *odd parity*. The binary word 0110111 with five 1's has odd parity. The binary word 0110000 has an even number of 1's (two), so it has *even parity*.

In practice the parity bit is used as follows. The system that is sending a data word checks the parity of the word. If the parity of the data word is odd, the system will set the parity bit to a 1. This makes the parity of the data word plus parity bit even. If the parity of the data word is even, the sending system will reset the parity bit to a 0. This again makes the parity of the data word plus parity even. The receiving system checks the

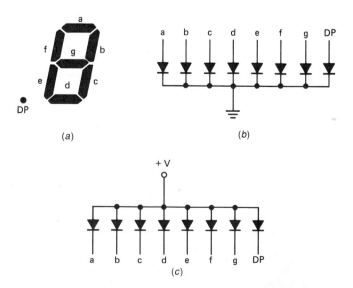

FIGURE 1-4   7-segment LED display. (a) Segment labels. (b) Schematic of common-cathode type. (c) Schematic of common-anode type.

parity of the data word plus parity bit that it receives. If the receiving system detects odd parity in the received data word plus parity, it assumes an error has occurred and tells the sending system to send the data again. The system is then said to be using even parity. The system could have been set up to use (maintain) odd parity in a similar manner.

ASCII

Table 1-2 shows several alphanumeric codes. The first of these is ASCII, or American Standard Code for Information Interchange. This is shown in the table as a 7-bit code. With 7 bits you can code up to 128 characters, which is enough for the full upper- and lowercase

TABLE 1-2
COMMON ALPHANUMERIC CODES

ASCII Symbol	HEX Code for 7-Bit ASCII	EBCDIC Symbol	HEX Code for EBCDIC	ASCII Symbol	HEX Code for 7-Bit ASCII	EBCDIC Symbol	HEX Code for EBCDIC	ASCII Symbol	HEX Code for 7-Bit ASCII	EBCDIC Symbol	HEX Code for EBCDIC
NUL	00	NUL	00	*	2A	*	5C	T	54	T	E3
SOH	01	SOH	01	+	2B	+	4E	U	55	U	E4
STX	02	STX	02	,	2C	,	6B	V	56	V	E5
ETX	03	ETX	03	-	2D	-	60	W	57	W	E6
EOT	04	EOT	37	.	2E	.	4B	X	58	X	E7
ENQ	05	ENQ	2D	/	2F	/	61	Y	59	Y	E8
ACK	06	ACK	2E	0	30	0	F0	Z	5A	Z	E9
BEL	07	BEL	2F	1	31	1	F1	[	5B	[	AD
BS	08	BS	16	2	32	2	F2	\	5C	NL	15
HT	09	HT	05	3	33	3	F3	]	5D	[	DD
LF	0A	LF	25	4	34	4	F4	^	5E	⌐	5F
VT	0B	VT	0B	5	35	5	F5	—	5F	—	6D
FF	0C	FF	0C	6	36	6	F6	`	60	RES	14
CR	0D	CR	0D	7	37	7	F7	a	61	a	81
SO	0E	SO	0E	8	38	8	F8	b	62	b	82
S1	0F	S1	0F	9	39	9	F9	c	63	c	83
DLE	10	DLE	10	:	3A	:	7A	d	64	d	84
DC1	11	DC1	11	;	3B	;	5E	e	65	e	85
DC2	12	DC2	12	—	3C	—	4C	f	66	f	86
DC3	13	DC3	13	=	3D	=	7E	g	67	g	87
DC4	14	DC4	35	\	3E	\	6E	h	68	h	88
NAK	15	NAK	3D	?	3F	?	6F	i	69	i	89
SYN	16	SYN	32	@	40	@	7C	j	6A	j	91
ETB	17	EOB	26	A	41	A	C1	k	6B	k	92
CAN	18	CAN	18	B	42	B	C2	l	6C	l	93
EM	19	EM	19	C	43	C	C3	m	6D	m	94
SUB	1A	SUB	3F	D	44	D	C4	n	6E	n	95
ESC	1B	BYP	24	E	45	E	C5	o	6F	o	96
FS	1C	FLS	1C	F	46	F	C6	p	70	p	97
GS	1D	GS	1D	G	47	G	C7	q	71	q	98
RS	1E	RDS	1E	H	48	H	C8	r	72	r	99
US	1F	US	1F	I	49	I	C9	s	73	s	A2
SP	20	SP	40	J	4A	J	D1	t	74	t	A3
!	21	!	5A	K	4B	K	D2	u	75	u	A4
"	22	"	7F	L	4C	L	D3	v	76	v	A5
#	23	#	7B	M	4D	M	D4	w	77	w	A6
$	24	$	5B	N	4E	N	D5	x	78	x	A7
%	25	%	6C	O	4F	O	D6	y	79	y	A8
&	26	&	50	P	50	P	D7	z	7A	z	A9
'	27	'	7D	Q	51	Q	D8	{	7B	{	8B
(	28	(	4D	R	52	R	D9			7C			4F
)	29	)	5D	S	53	S	E2	}	7D	}	9B
								~	7E	¢	4A
								DEL	7F	DEL	07

TABLE 1-3
DEFINITIONS OF CONTROL CHARACTERS

NULL	Null	DC1	Direct control 1
SOH	Start of heading	DC2	Direct control 2
STX	Start text	DC3	Direct control 3
ETX	End text	DC4	Direct control 4
EOT	End of transmission	NAK	Negative acknowledge
ENQ	Enquiry	SYN	Synchronous idle
ACK	Acknowledge	ETB	End transmission block
BEL	BS		
BS	Backspace	CAN	Cancel
HT	Horizontal tab	EM	End of medium
LF	Line feed	SUB	Substitute
VT	Vertical tab	ESC	Escape
FF	Form feed	FS	Form separator
CR	Carriage return	GS	Group separator
SO	Shift out	RS	Record separator
SI	Shift in	US	Unit separator
DLE	Data link escape		

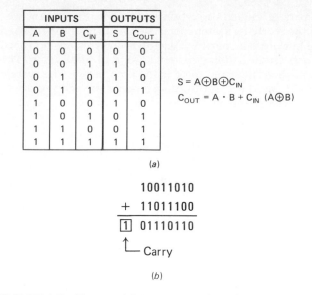

FIGURE 1-5 Binary addition. (*a*) Truth table for 2 bits plus carry. (*b*) Addition of two 8-bit words.

alphabet, numbers, punctuation marks, and control characters. The code is arranged so that if only uppercase letters, numbers, and a few control characters are needed, the lower 6 bits are all that are required. If a parity check is wanted, a parity bit is added to the basic 7-bit code in the MSB position. The binary word 1100 0100, for example, is the ASCII code for uppercase D with odd parity. Table 1-3 gives the meanings of the control character symbols used in the ASCII code table.

EBCDIC

Another alphanumeric code commonly encountered in IBM equipment is the Extended Binary-Coded Decimal Interchange Code or *EBCDIC*. This is an 8-bit code without parity. A ninth bit can be added for parity. To save space in Table 1-2, the eight binary digits of EBCDIC are represented by their 2-digit hex equivalent.

ARITHMETIC OPERATIONS ON BINARY, HEX, AND BCD NUMBERS

Binary Arithmetic

ADDITION

Figure 1-5*a* shows the truth table for addition of two binary digits and a carry in (C_{IN}) from addition of previous digits. Figure 1-5*b* shows the result of adding two 8-bit binary numbers together using these rules. Assuming that $C_{IN} = 1$, $1 + 0 + C_{IN} =$ a sum of 0 and a carry into the next digit, and $1 + 1 + C_{IN} =$ a sum of 1 and a carry into the next digit because the result in any digit position can only be a 1 or a 0.

2'S-COMPLEMENT SIGNS-AND-MAGNITUDE BINARY

When you handwrite a number that represents some physical quantity such as temperature, you can simply put a + sign in front of the number to indicate that the

number is positive, or you can write a − sign to indicate that the number is negative. However, if you want to store values such as temperatures, which can be positive or negative, in a computer memory, there is a problem. Since the computer memory can store only 1's and 0's, some way must be established to represent the sign of the number with a 1 or a 0.

A common way to represent signed numbers is to reserve the most significant bit of the data word as a *sign bit* and to use the rest of the bits of the data word to represent the size (magnitude) of the quantity. A computer that works with 8-bit words will use the MSB (bit 7) as the sign bit and the lower 7 bits to represent the magnitude of the numbers. The usual convention is to represent a positive number with a 0 sign bit and a negative number with a 1 sign bit.

To make computations with signed numbers easier, the magnitude of negative numbers is represented in a special form called *2's complement*. The 2's complement of a binary number is formed by inverting each bit of the data word and adding 1 to the result. Some examples should help clarify all of this.

The number $+7_{10}$ is represented in 8-bit sign-and-magnitude form as 00000111. The sign bit is 0, which indicates a positive number. The magnitude of positive numbers is represented in straight binary, so 00000111 in the least significant bits represents 7_{10}.

To represent $−7_{10}$ in 8-bit 2's-complement sign-and-magnitude form, start with the 8-bit code for +7, 0000 0111. Invert each bit, including the MSB, to get 1111 1000. Then add 1 to get 11111001. This result is the correct representation of $−7_{10}$. Figure 1-6 shows some more examples of positive and negative numbers expressed in 8-bit sign-and-magnitude form. For practice, try generating each of these yourself to see if you get the same result.

To reverse this procedure and find the magnitude of a number expressed in sign-and-magnitude form, proceed as follows. If the number is positive, as indicated

	Sign bit	
	↓	
+ 7	0	0000111
+ 46	0	0101110
+105	0	1101001
− 12	1	1110100
− 54	1	1001010
−117	1	0001011
− 46	1	1010010

Sign and two's complement of magnitude

FIGURE 1-6 Positive and negative numbers represented with a sign bit and 2's complement.

by the sign bit being a 0, then the least significant 7 bits represent the magnitude directly in binary. If the number is negative, as indicated by the sign bit being a 1, then the magnitude is expressed in 2's complement. To get the magnitude of this negative number expressed in standard binary, invert each bit of the data word, including the sign bit, and add 1 to the result. For example, given the word 11101011, invert each bit to get 00010100. Then add 1 to get 00010101. This equals 21_{10}, so you know that the original numbers represent $−21_{10}$. Again, try reconverting a few of the numbers in Figure 1-6 for practice.

Figure 1-7 shows some examples of addition of signed binary numbers of this type. Sign bits are added together just as the other bits are. Figure 1-7a shows the results of adding two positive numbers. The sign bit of the result is zero, so the result is positive. The second example, in Figure 1-7b, adds a −9 to a +13 or, in effect, subtracts 9 from 13. As indicated by the zero sign bit, the result of 4 is positive and in true binary form.

Figure 1-7c shows the result of adding a −13 to a smaller positive number, +9. The sign bit of the result is a 1. This indicates that the result is negative and the magnitude is in 2's-complement form. To reconvert a 2's complement result to a signed number in true binary form:

1. Invert each bit to produce the 1's complement.

2. Add 1.

3. Put a minus sign in front to indicate that the result is negative.

The final example, in Figure 1-7d, shows the result of adding two negative numbers. The sign bit of the result is a 1, so the result is negative and in 2's-complement form. Again, inverting each bit, adding 1, and prefixing a minus sign will put the result in a more recognizable form.

Now let's consider the range of numbers that can be represented with 8 bits in sign-and-magnitude form. Eight bits can represent a maximum of 2^8 or 256 numbers. Since we are representing both positive and negative numbers, half of this range will be positive and half negative. Therefore, the range is −128 to +127. Here are the sign-and-magnitude binary representations for these values:

```
0 1 1 1 1 1 1 1     +127
       ⋮
0 0 0 0 0 0 0 1     + 1
0 0 0 0 0 0 0 0     zero
1 1 1 1 1 1 1 1     − 1
       ⋮
1 0 0 0 0 0 0 1     − 127
1 0 0 0 0 0 0 0     − 128
```

If you like number patterns, you might notice that this scheme shifts the normal codes for 128 to 255 downward to represent −128 to −1.

If a computer is storing signed numbers as 16-bit words, then a much larger range of numbers can be represented. Since 16 bits gives 2^{16} or 65,536 possible values, the range for 16-bit sign-and-magnitude numbers is −32,768 to +32,767. Operations with 16-bit sign-and-magnitude numbers are done the same way as operations with 8-bit sign-and-magnitude numbers.

```
+13    00001101
+ 9    00001001
+22    00010110
         └─Sign bit is 0
           so result is positive
            (a)
```

```
+13        00001101
− 9        11110111 2's complement for −9 with sign bit
+ 4    1│ 00000100
            └─Sign bit is 0
              so result is positive
         └─ Ignore carry
            (b)
```

```
+ 9        00001001
−13        11110011 2's complement for −13 with sign bit
− 4        11111100 Sign bit is 1
           00000011 So invert each bit
         +        1 Add 1
equals  −00000100 Prefix with minus sign
            (c)
```

```
− 9        11110111 ⎫ 2's complement,
−13        11110011 ⎭ sign-and-magnitude form
−22        11101010 Sign bit is 1
           00010101 So invert each bit
         +        1 Add 1
equals  −00010110 Prefix with minus sign
            (d)
```

FIGURE 1-7 Addition of signed binary numbers. (a) +9 and +13. (b) −9 and +13. (c) +9 and −13. (d) −9 and −13.

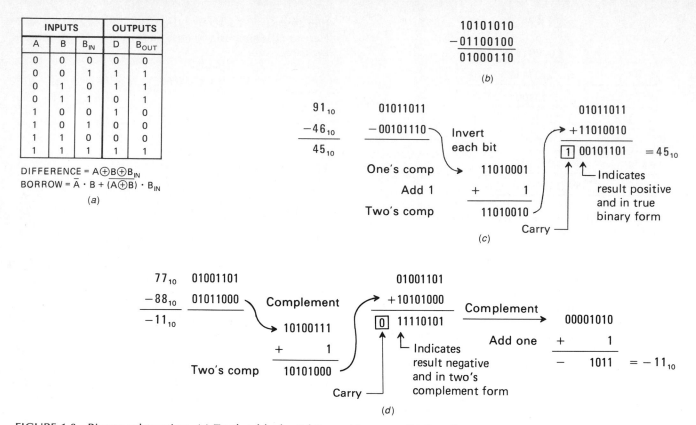

INPUTS			OUTPUTS	
A	B	B_{IN}	D	B_{OUT}
0	0	0	0	0
0	0	1	1	1
0	1	0	1	1
0	1	1	0	1
1	0	0	1	0
1	0	1	0	0
1	1	0	0	0
1	1	1	1	1

DIFFERENCE = $A \oplus B \oplus B_{IN}$
BORROW = $\bar{A} \cdot B + \overline{(A \oplus B)} \cdot B_{IN}$

(a)

FIGURE 1-8 Binary subtraction. (a) Truth table for 2 bits and borrow. (b) Pencil method. (c) 2's-complement positive result. (d) 2's-complement negative result.

SUBTRACTION

There are two common methods for doing binary subtraction. These are the pencil method and the 2's-complement add method. Figure 1-8a shows the truth table for binary subtraction of two binary digits A and B. Also included in the truth table is the effect of a borrow-in, B_{IN}, from subtracting previous digits. Figure 1-8b shows an example of the "pencil" method of subtracting two 8-bit numbers. Using the truth table, this method is done the same way that you do decimal subtraction.

A second method of performing binary subtraction is by adding the 2's-complement representation of the bottom number (subtrahend) to the top number (minuend). Figure 1-8c shows how this is done. First represent the top number in sign-and-magnitude form. Then form the 2's-complement sign-and-magnitude representation for the negative of the bottom number. Finally, add the two parts formed. For the example in Figure 1-8c, the sign of the result is a 0, which indicates that the result is positive and in true form. The final carry produced by the addition can be ignored. Figure 1-8d shows another example of this method of subtraction. In this case the bottom number is larger than the top number. Again, represent the top number in sign-and-magnitude form, produce the 2's-complement sign-and-magnitude form for the negative of the bottom number, and add the two together. The sign bit of the result is a 1 for this example. This indicates that the result is negative and its magnitude is represented in 2's-complement form. To

get the result into a form that is more recognizable to you, invert each bit of the result, add 1 to it, and put a minus sign in front of it as shown in Figure 1-8d.

Problems that may occur when doing signed addition or subtraction are *overflow* and *underflow*. If the magnitude of the number produced by adding two signed numbers is larger than the number of bits available to represent the magnitude, the result will "overflow" into the sign bit position and give an incorrect result. For example, if the signed positive number 01001001 is added to the signed positive number 01101101, the result is 10110110. The 1 in the MSB of this result indicates that it is negative, which is obviously incorrect for the sum of two positive numbers. In a similar manner, doing an 8-bit signed subtraction that produces a magnitude greater than -128 will cause an "underflow" into the sign bit and produce an incorrect result.

For simplicity the examples shown use 8 bits, but the method works for any number of bits. This method may seem awkward, but it is easy to do in a computer or microprocessor because it requires only the simple operations of inverting and adding.

MULTIPLICATION

There are several methods of doing binary multiplication. Figure 1-9 shows what is called the *pencil method* because it is the same way you learned to multiply decimal numbers. The top number, or multiplicand, is multiplied by the least significant digit of the bottom number, or multiplier. The partial product is written

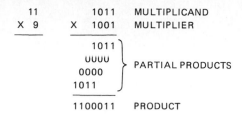

```
    11          1011    MULTIPLICAND
  X  9        X 1001    MULTIPLIER
  ___         _____
              1011  ⎫
              0000  ⎪
              0000  ⎬  PARTIAL PRODUCTS
              1011  ⎭
              _____
              1100011   PRODUCT
```

FIGURE 1-9   Binary multiplication.

down. The top number is then multiplied by the next digit of the multiplier. The resultant partial product is written down under the last, but shifted one place to the left. Adding all the partial products gives the total product. This method works well when doing multiplication by hand, but it is not practical for a computer because the type of shifts required makes it awkward to implement.

One of the multiplication methods used by computers is repeated addition. To multiply 7×55, for example, the computer can just add up seven 55's. For large numbers, however, this method is slow. To multiply 786×253, for example, requires 252 add operations.

Most computers use an add-and-shift-right method. This method takes advantage of the fact that for binary multiplication, the partial product can only be either the top number exactly if the multiplier digit is a 1 or a 0 if the multiplier digit is a 0. The method does the same thing as the pencil method, except that the partial products are added as they are produced and the sum of the partial products is shifted right rather than each partial product being shifted left.

A point to note about multiplying numbers is the number of bits the product requires. For example, multiplying two 4-bit numbers can give a product with as many as 8 bits, and two 8-bit numbers can give a 16-bit product.

DIVISION

Binary division can also be performed in several ways. Figure 1-10 shows two examples of the pencil method. This is the same process as decimal long division. However, it is much simpler than decimal long division

because the digits of the result (quotient) can only be 0 or 1. A division is attempted on part of the dividend. If this is not possible because the divisor is larger than that part of the dividend, a 0 is entered in the quotient. Another attempt is then made to divide using one more digit of the dividend. When a division is possible, a 1 is entered in the quotient. The divisor is then subtracted from the portion of the dividend used. As with standard long division, the process is continued until all the dividend is used. As shown in Figure 1-10b, 0's can be added to the right of the binary point and division continued to convert a remainder to a binary equivalent.

Another method of division that is easier for computers and microprocessors to perform uses successive subtractions. The divisor is subtracted from the dividend and from each successive remainder until a borrow is produced. The desired quotient is 1 less than the number of subtractions needed to produce a borrow. This method is simple, but for large numbers it is slow.

For faster division of large numbers, computers use a subtract-and-shift-left method that is essentially the same process you go through with a pencil long division.

Hexadecimal Addition and Subtraction

People working with computers or microprocessors often use hexadecimal as a shorthand way of representing long binary numbers such as memory addresses. It is therefore useful to be able to add and subtract hexadecimal numbers.

ADDITION

As shown in Figure 1-11a, one way to add two hexadecimal numbers is to convert each hexadecimal number to its binary equivalent, add the two binary numbers, and convert the binary result back to its hex equivalent. For converting to binary, remember that each hex digit represents 4 binary digits.

A second method, shown in Figure 1-11b, works directly with the hex numbers. When adding hex digits, a carry is produced whenever the sum is 16 decimal or greater. Another way of saying this is that the value of a carry in hex is 16 decimal. For the least significant digits in Figure 1-11b, an A in hex is 10 in decimal and an F is 15 in decimal. These add to give 25 decimal. This is greater than 16, so mentally subtract 16 from the 25 to give a carry and a remainder of 9. The 9 is written down and the carry is added to the next digit column. In this column 7 plus 3 plus a carry gives a decimal 11, or B in hex.

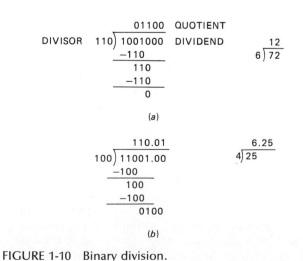

(a)

(b)

FIGURE 1-10   Binary division.

```
                         Carry
                           ↓
 7A     0111  1010      7  ¹  A₁₆
+3F    +0011  1111     + 3     F₁₆
___    _____      _____
 B9     1011  1001     11₁₀   25₁₀

         B     9        B₁₆    9₁₆

       (a)               (b)
```

FIGURE 1-11   Hexadecimal addition.

$$77_{16} = 119_{10}$$
$$-3B_{16} = -59_{10}$$
$$3C_{16} \qquad 60_{10}$$

FIGURE 1-12   Hexadecimal subtraction.

SUBTRACTION

You may use whichever method seems easier to you and gives you consistently right answers. If you are doing a great deal of hexadecimal arithmetic, you might buy an electronic calculator specifically designed to do decimal, binary, and hexadecimal arithmetic.

SUBTRACTION

Hexadecimal subtraction is similar to decimal subtraction except that when a borrow is needed, 16 is borrowed from the next most significant digit. Figure 1-12 shows an example of this. It may help you to follow the example if you do partial conversions to decimal in your head. For example, 7 plus a borrowed 16 is 23. Subtracting B or 11 leaves 12 or C in hexadecimal. Then 3 from the 6 left after a borrow leaves 3, so the result is 3CH.

BCD Addition and Subtraction

In systems where the final result of a calculation is to be displayed, such as a calculator, it may be easier to work with numbers in a BCD format. These codes, as shown in Table 1-1, represent each decimal digit, 0 through 9, by its 4-bit binary equivalent.

ADDITION

BCD can have no digit-word with a value greater than 9. Therefore, a carry must be generated if the result of a BCD addition is greater than 1001 or 9. Figure 1-13

```
           BCD
  35    0011  0101
 +23   +0010  0011
 ----   ----------
  58    0101  1000
          (a)

           BCD
   7       0111
 + 5     + 0101
 ----   ----------
  12       1100    INCORRECT BCD
         + 0110    ADD 6
        ----------
        0001  0010  CORRECT BCD 12
          (b)

           BCD
   9       1001
 + 8     + 1000
 ----   ----------
  17    0001  0001  INCORRECT BCD
        0000  0110  ADD 6
        ----------
        0001  0111  CORRECT BCD 17
          (c)
```

FIGURE 1-13   BCD addition. (a) No correction needed. (b) Correction needed because of illegal BCD result. (c) Correction needed because of carry-out of BCD digit.

```
  17    0001  0111
 - 9    0000  1001
 ----   ----------
   8    0000  1110    ILLEGAL BCD
         -0110        SUBTRACT 6
        ----------
        0000  1000    CORRECT BCD
```

FIGURE 1-14   BCD subtraction.

shows three examples of BCD addition. The first, in Figure 1-13a, is very straightforward because the sum for each BCD digit is less than 9. The result is the same as it would be for adding standard binary.

For the second example, in Figure 1-13b, adding BCD 7 to BCD 5 produces 1100. This is a correct binary result of 12, but it is an illegal BCD code. To convert the result to BCD format, a correction factor of 6 is added. The result of adding 6 is 0001 0010, which is the legal BCD code for 12.

Figure 1-13c shows another case where a correction factor must be added. The initial addition of 9 and 8 produces 0001 0001. Even though the lower four digits are less than 9, this is an incorrect BCD result because a carry out of bit 3 of the BCD digit-word was produced. This carry out of bit 3 is often called an *auxiliary carry.* Adding the correction factor of 6 gives the correct BCD result of 0001 0111 or 17.

To summarize, a correction factor of 6 must be added if the result in the lower 4 bits is greater than 9 or if the initial addition produces a carry out of bit 3 of any BCD digit-word. This correction is sometimes called a *decimal adjust operation.*

The reason for the correction factor of 6 is that in BCD we want a carry into the next digit after 1001 or 9, but in binary a carry out of the lower 4 bits does not occur until after 1111 or 15. The difference between the two carry points is 6, so you have to add 6 to produce the desired carry if the result of an addition in any BCD digit is more than 1001.

SUBTRACTION

Figure 1-14 shows a subtraction, BCD 17 (0001 0111) minus BCD 9 (0000 1001). The initial result, 0000 1110, is not a legal BCD number. Whenever this occurs in BCD subtraction, 6 must be *subtracted* from the initial result to produce the correct BCD result. For the example shown in Figure 1-14, subtracting 6 gives a correct BCD result of 0000 1000 or 8.

The correction factor of 6 must be subtracted from any BCD digit-word if that digit-word is greater than 1001, or if a borrow from the next higher digit was required to do the subtraction.

BASIC DIGITAL DEVICES

Microcomputers such as those we discuss throughout this book often contain basic logic gates as "glue" between LSI (large-scale integration) devices. For troubleshooting these systems, it is important to be able to predict logic levels at any point directly from the schematic rather than having to work your way through a truth table for each gate. This section should help refresh your memory of basic logic functions and help you remember how to quickly analyze logic gate circuits.

Inverting and Noninverting Buffers

Figure 1-15 shows the schematic symbols and truth tables for simple buffers and logic gates. The first thing to remember about these symbols is that the shape of the symbol indicates the logic function performed by the device. The second thing to remember about these symbols is that a bubble or no bubble indicates the *assertion* level for an input or output signal. Let's review how modern logic designers use these symbols.

The first symbol for a *buffer* in Figure 1-15a has no bubbles on the input or output. Therefore, the input is active high and the output is active high. We read this symbol as follows: If the input A is asserted high, then the output Y will be asserted high. The rest of the truth table is covered by the assumption that if the A input is not asserted high, then the Y output will not be asserted high.

The next two symbols for a buffer each contain a bubble. The bubble on the output of the first of these indicates that the output is active low. The input has no bubble, so it is active high. You can read the function of the device directly from the schematic symbol as follows. If the A input is asserted high, then the Y output will be asserted low. This device simply changes the assertion level of a signal. The output Y will always have a logic state which is the complement or inverse of that on the input, so the device is usually referred to as an *inverter*.

The second schematic symbol for an inverter in Figure 1-15a has the bubble on the input. We draw the symbol this way when we want to indicate that we are using the device to change an asserted-low signal to an asserted-high signal. For example, if we pass the signal $\overline{CS}$ through this device, it becomes CS. The symbol tells you directly that if the input is asserted low, then the output will be asserted high. Now let's review how you express the functions of logic gates using this approach.

Logic Gates

Figure 1-15b shows the symbols and truth tables for simple logic gates. A symbol with a flat back and a round front indicates that the device performs the logical *AND* function. This means that the output will be asserted if the A input is asserted *and* the B input is asserted. Again, bubbles or no bubbles are used to indicate the assertion level of each input and output. The first AND symbol in Figure 1-15b has no bubbles, so the inputs and the output are active high. The output then will be asserted high if the A input is asserted high *and* the B input is asserted high. The bubble on the output of the second AND symbol in Figure 1-15b indicates that this device, commonly called a *NAND* gate, has an active low output. If the A input is asserted high *and* the B input is asserted high, then the Y output will be asserted low. Look at the truth table in Figure 1-15b to see if you agree with this.

Figure 1-15c shows the other two possible cases for the AND symbol. The first of these has bubbles on the inputs and on the output. If you see this symbol in a schematic, you should immediately see that the output will be asserted low if the A input is asserted low *and* the B input is asserted low. The second AND symbol in Figure 1-15c has no bubble on the output, so the output will be asserted high if the A *and* B inputs are both asserted low.

A logic symbol with a curved back indicates that the output of the device will be asserted if the A input is asserted *or* the B input of the device is asserted. Again, bubbles or no bubbles are used to indicate the assertion level for inputs and outputs. Note in Figure 1-15b and c that each of the AND symbol forms has an equivalent OR symbol form. An AND symbol with active high inputs and an active high output, for example, represents the same device (a 74LS08 perhaps) as an OR symbol with active low inputs and an active low output. Use the truth table in Figure 1-15b to convince yourself of this. The bubbled-OR representation tells you that if one input is asserted low, the output will be low, regardless of the state of the other input. As we will show later in this chapter, this is often a useful way to think of the operation of an AND gate.

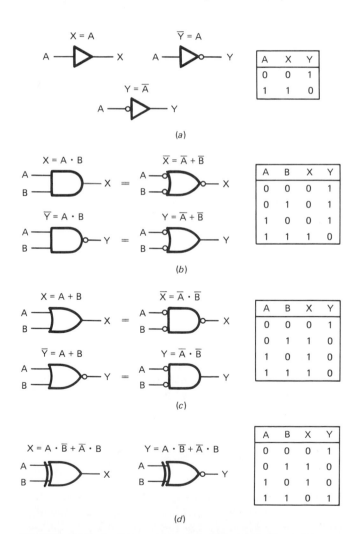

(a)

A	X	Y
0	0	1
1	1	0

(b)

A	B	X	Y
0	0	0	1
0	1	0	1
1	0	0	1
1	1	1	0

(c)

A	B	X	Y
0	0	0	1
0	1	1	0
1	0	1	0
1	1	1	0

(d)

A	B	X	Y
0	0	0	1
0	1	1	0
1	0	1	0
1	1	0	1

FIGURE 1-15 Buffers and logic gates. (a) Buffers. (b) AND-NAND. (c) OR-NOR. (d) Exclusive OR.

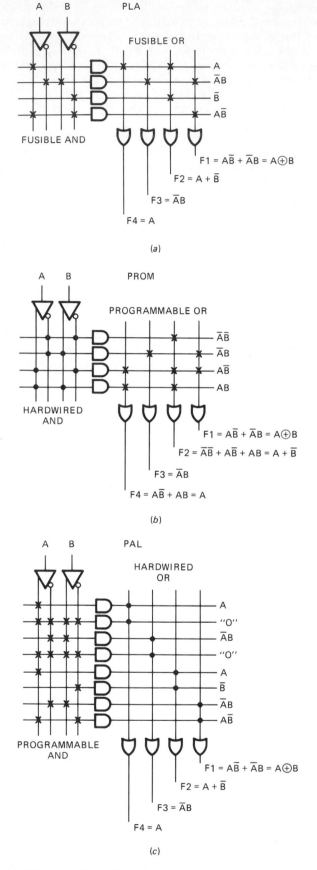

FIGURE 1-16 FPLA, PROM, and PAL programmed to implement some simple logic functions. (a) FPLA. (b) PROM. (c) PAL.

Figure 1-15d shows the symbol and truth table for an *exclusive* OR gate and for an *exclusive* NOR gate. The output of an exclusive OR gate will be high if the logic levels on the two inputs are different. The output of an exclusive NOR gate will be high if the logic levels on the two inputs are the same.

You need to be familiar with all these symbols, because most logic designers will use the symbol that best describes the function they want a device to perform in a particular circuit.

Programmable Logic Devices

Instead of using discrete gates, modern microcomputer systems usually use *programmable logic devices* such as PLAs, PROMs, or PALs to implement the "glue" logic between LSI devices. To refresh your memory, Figure 1-16 shows the internal structure of each of these devices. As you can see, they all consist of a programmable AND-OR matrix, so they can easily implement any sum-of-products logic expression. Each AND gate in these figures has up to four inputs, but to simplify the drawing only a single input line is shown. Likewise, the OR gates have several inputs, but are shown with a single input line to simplify the drawing. These devices are programmed by blowing out fuses, which are represented in the figure by Xs. An X in the figure indicates that the fuse is intact and makes a connection between, for example, the output of an AND gate and one of the inputs of an OR gate. A dot at the intersection of two wires indicates a hard-wired connection implemented during manufacture.

In a *programmable logic array* (PLA) or *field programmable logic array* (FPLA), both the AND matrix and the OR matrix are programmable by leaving in fuses or blowing them out. The two programmable matrixes make FPLAs very flexible, but difficult to program.

In a *programmable read-only memory* or *PROM*, the AND matrix is fixed and just the OR matrix is programmable by leaving in fuses or blowing them out. PROMs implement all the possible product terms for the input variables, so they are useful as code converters.

In a *programmable array logic* device or *PAL*, the connections in the OR matrix are fixed and the AND matrix connections are programmable. PALs are often used to implement combinational logic and address decoders in microcomputer systems.

A computer program is usually used to develop the fuse map for an FPLA, PROM, or PAL. Once developed, the fuse-map file is downloaded to a programmer which blows fuses or stores charges to actually program the device.

Latches, Flip-Flops, Registers, and Counters

THE D LATCH

A *latch* is a digital device that stores a 1 or a 0 on its output. Figure 1-17a shows the schematic symbol and truth table for a D latch. The device functions as follows. If the *enable* input CK is low, the logic level present on the D input will have no effect on the Q and $\overline{Q}$ outputs.

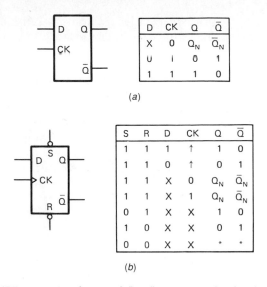

D	CK	Q	$\bar{Q}$
X	0	Q_N	$\bar{Q}_N$
U	l	0	1
1	1	1	0

(a)

S	R	D	CK	Q	$\bar{Q}$
1	1	1	↑	1	0
1	1	0	↑	0	1
1	1	X	0	Q_N	$\bar{Q}_N$
1	1	X	1	Q_N	$\bar{Q}_N$
0	1	X	X	1	0
1	0	X	X	0	1
0	0	X	X	*	*

(b)

FIGURE 1-17 Latches and flip-flops. (a) D latch. (b) D flip-flop.

This is indicated in the truth table by an X in the D column. If the enable input is high, a high or a low on the D input will be passed to the Q output. In other words, the Q output will follow the D input as long as the enable input is high. The $\bar{Q}$ output will contain the complement of the logic state on Q. When the enable input is made low again, the state on Q at that time will be latched there. Any changes on D will have no effect on Q until the enable input is made high again. When the enable input goes low, then, the state present on D just before the enable goes low will be stored on the Q output. Keep this operation in mind as you read about the D flip-flop in the next section.

THE D FLIP-FLOP

Figure 1-17b shows the schematic symbol and the truth table for a typical D flip-flop. The small triangle next to the CK input of this device tells you that the Q and $\bar{Q}$ outputs are updated when a rising signal edge is applied to the CK input. The up arrows in the clock column of the truth table also indicate that a 1 or 0 on the D input will be copied to the Q output when the clock input goes from low to high. In other words, the D flip-flop takes a snapshot of whatever state is on the D input when the clock goes high, and displays the "photo" on the Q output. If the clock input is low, a change on D will have no effect on the output. Likewise, if the clock input is high, a change on D will have no effect on the Q output. Contrast this operation with that of the D latch to make sure you understand the difference between the two devices.

The D flip-flop in Figure 1-17b also has direct *set* (S) and *reset* (R) inputs. A flip-flop is considered *set* if its Q output is a 1. It is *reset* if its Q output is a 0. The bubbles on the set and reset inputs tell you that these inputs are active low. The truth table for the D flip-flop in Figure 1-17b indicates that the set and reset inputs are *asynchronous*. This means that if the set input is asserted low, the output will be set, regardless of the states on the D and the clock inputs. Likewise, if the reset input is asserted low, the Q output will be reset, regardless of the state of the D and clock inputs. The Xs in the D and CK columns of the truth table remind you that these inputs are "don't cares" if set or reset is asserted. The condition indicated by the asterisks (*) is a nonstable condition; that is, it will not persist when reset or clear inputs return to their inactive (high) level.

REGISTERS

Flip-flops can be used individually or in groups to store binary data. A *register* is a group of D flip-flops connected in parallel, as shown in Figure 1-18a. A binary word applied to the data inputs of this register will be transferred to the Q outputs when the clock input is made high. The binary word will remain stored on the Q outputs until a new binary word is applied to the D inputs and a low-to-high signal is applied to the clock input. Other circuitry can read the stored binary word from the Q outputs at any time without changing its value.

If the Q output of each flip-flop in the register is connected to the D input of the next as shown in Figure 1-18b, then the register will function as a *shift register*. A 1 applied to the first D input will be shifted to the first Q output by a clock pulse. The next clock pulse will shift this 1 to the output of the second flip-flop. Each additional clock pulse will shift the 1 to the next flip-flop in the register. Some shift registers allow you to load a binary word into the register and shift the loaded word left or right when the register is clocked. As we will show later, the ability to shift binary numbers is very useful.

COUNTERS

Flip-flops can also be connected to make devices whose outputs step through a binary or other count sequence

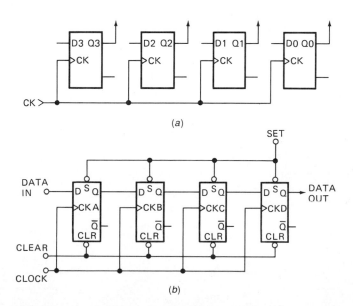

(a)

(b)

FIGURE 1-18 Registers. (a) Simple data storage. (b) Shift register.

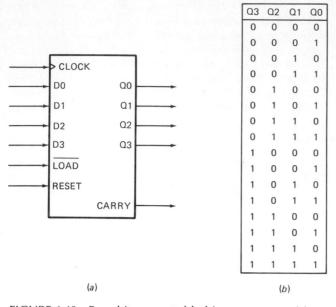

Q3	Q2	Q1	Q0
0	0	0	0
0	0	0	1
0	0	1	0
0	0	1	1
0	1	0	0
0	1	0	1
0	1	1	0
0	1	1	1
1	0	0	0
1	0	0	1
1	0	1	0
1	0	1	1
1	1	0	0
1	1	0	1
1	1	1	0
1	1	1	1

(a)

(b)

FIGURE 1-19 Four-bit, presettable binary counter. (a) Schematic symbol. (b) Count sequence.

when they are clocked. Figure 1-19a shows a schematic symbol and count sequence for a presettable 4-bit binary counter. The main point we want to review here is how a presettable counter functions, so there is no need to go into the internal circuitry of the device. If the reset input is asserted, the Q outputs will all be made 0's. After the reset signal is unasserted, each clock pulse will cause the binary count on the outputs to be incremented by 1. As shown in Figure 1-19b, the count sequence will go from 0000 to 1111. If the outputs are at 1111, then the next clock pulse will cause the outputs to "roll over" to 0000 and a carry pulse to be sent out the carry output.

This carry pulse can be used as the clock input for another counter. Counters can be cascaded to produce as large a count sequence as is needed for a particular application. The maximum count for a binary counter is $2^N - 1$, where N is the number of flip-flops.

Now, suppose that we want the counter to start counting from some number other than 0000. We can do this by applying the desired number to the four data inputs and asserting the load input. For example, if we apply a binary 6, 0110, to the data inputs and assert the load input, this value will be transferred to the Q outputs. After the load signal is unasserted, the next clock signal will increment the Q outputs to 0111 or 7.

ROMs, RAMs, and Buses

The next topics we need to review are the devices that store large numbers of binary words and how several of these devices can be connected on common data lines.

ROMS

The term *ROM* stands for *read-only memory*. There are several types of ROM that can be written to, read, erased, and written to with new data, but the main feature of ROMs is that they are *nonvolatile*. This means that the information stored in them is not lost when the power is removed from them.

Figure 1-20a shows the schematic symbol of a common ROM. As indicated by the eight *data* outputs, D0 to D7, this ROM stores 8-bit data words. The data outputs are *three-state* outputs. This means that each output can be at a logic low state, a logic high state, or a high-impedance floating state. In the high-impedance state an output is essentially disconnected from anything connected to it. If the $\overline{CE}$ input of the ROM is not asserted, then all the outputs will be in the high-

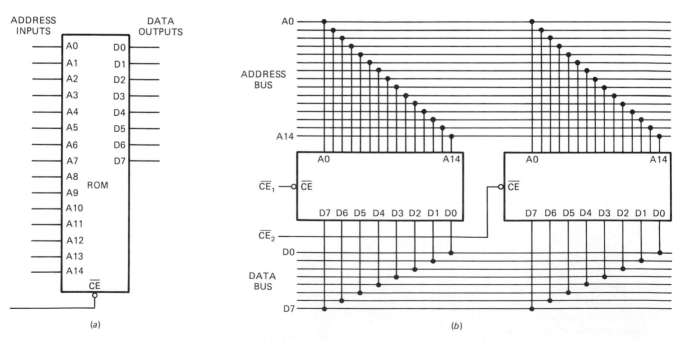

FIGURE 1-20 ROMs. (a) Schematic symbol. (b) Connection in parallel.

impedance state. Most ROMs also switch to a lower-power-consumption standby mode if $\overline{CE}$ is not asserted. If the $\overline{CE}$ input is asserted, the device will be powered up, and the output buffers will be enabled. Therefore, the outputs will be at a normal logic low or logic high state. If you don't happen to remember, you will soon see why this is important.

You can think of the binary words stored in the ROM as being in a long, numbered list. The number that identifies the location of each stored word in the list is called its *address.* You can tell the number of binary words stored in the ROM by the number of address inputs. The number of words is equal to 2^N, where N is the number of address lines. The device in Figure 1-20*a* has 15 address lines, A0 to A14, so the number of words is 2^{15} or 32,768. In a data sheet this device would be referred to as a 32K × 8 ROM. This means it has 32K addresses with 8 bits per address.

In order to get a particular word onto the outputs of the ROM, you have to do two things. You have to apply the address of that word to the address inputs, A0 to A14, and you have to assert the $\overline{CE}$ input to power up the device and to enable the three-state outputs.

Now, let's see why we want three-state outputs on this ROM. Suppose that we want to store more than 32K data words. We can do this by connecting two or more ROMs in parallel, as shown in Figure 1-20*b*. The address lines connect to each device in parallel, so we can address one of the 32,768 words in each. A set of parallel lines used to send addresses or data to several devices in this way is called a *bus.* The data outputs of the ROMs are likewise connected in parallel so that any one of the ROMs can output data on the common data bus. If these ROMs had standard two-state outputs, a serious problem would occur when both ROMs tried to output data words on the bus. The resulting argument between data outputs would probably destroy some of the outputs and give meaningless information on the data bus. Since the ROMs have three-state outputs, however, we can use external circuitry to make sure that only one ROM at a time has its outputs enabled. The very important principle here is that whenever several outputs are connected on a bus, the outputs should all be three-state, and only one set of outputs should be enabled at a time.

At the beginning of this section we mentioned that some ROMs can be erased and rewritten or reprogrammed with new data. Here's a summary of the different types of ROMs.

Mask-programmed ROM—Programmed during manufacture; cannot be altered.

PROM—User programs by blowing fuses; cannot be altered except to blow additional fuses.

EPROM—Electrically programmable by user; erased by shining ultraviolet light on quartz window in package.

EEPROM—Electrically programmable by user; erased with electrical signals, so it can be reprogrammed in circuit.

Flash EPROM—Electrically programmable by user; erased electrically, so it can be reprogrammed in circuit.

STATIC AND DYNAMIC RAMS

The name RAM stands for *random-access memory,* but since ROMs are also random access, the name probably should be *read-write memory.* RAMs are also used to store binary words. A *static RAM* is essentially a matrix of flip-flops. Therefore, we can write a new data word in a RAM location at any time by applying the word to the flip-flop data inputs and clocking the flip-flops. The stored data word will remain on the flip-flop outputs as long as the power is left on. This type of memory is *volatile* because data is lost when the power is turned off.

Figure 1-21 shows the schematic symbol for a common RAM. This RAM has 12 address lines, A0 to A11, so it stores 2^{12} (4096) binary words. The eight data lines tell you that the RAM stores 8-bit words. When we are reading a word from the RAM, these lines function as outputs. When we are writing a word to the RAM, these lines function as inputs. The *chip enable* input, $\overline{CE}$, is used to enable the device for a read or for a write. The R/$\overline{W}$ input will be asserted high if we want to read from the RAM or asserted low if we want to write a word to the RAM. Here's how all these lines work for reading from and writing to the device.

To write to the RAM, we apply the desired address to the address inputs, assert the $\overline{CE}$ input low to turn on the device, and assert the R/$\overline{W}$ input low to tell the RAM we want to write to it. We then apply the data word we want to store to the data lines of the RAM for a specified time. To read a word from the RAM, we address the desired word, assert $\overline{CE}$ low to turn on the device, and assert R/$\overline{W}$ high to tell the RAM we want to read from it. For a read operation the output buffers on the data lines will be enabled and the addressed data word will be present on the outputs.

The static RAMs we have just reviewed store binary words in a matrix of flip-flops. In *dynamic RAMs* (*DRAMs*), binary 1's and 0's are stored as an electric charge or no charge on a tiny capacitor. Since these tiny capacitors take up less space on a chip than a flip-flop

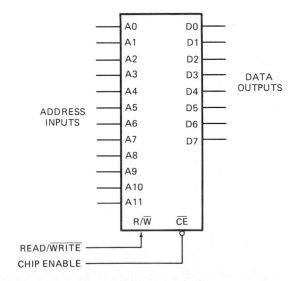

FIGURE 1-21   RAM schematic symbol.

would, a dynamic RAM chip can store many more bits than the same size static RAM chip. The disadvantage of dynamic RAMs is that the charge leaks off the tiny capacitors. The logic state stored in each capacitor must be *refreshed* every 2 milliseconds (ms) or so. A device called a *dynamic RAM refresh controller* can be used to refresh a large number of dynamic RAMs in a system. Some newer dynamic RAM devices contain built-in refresh circuitry, so they appear static to external circuitry.

Arithmetic Logic Units

An *arithmetic logic unit,* or *ALU,* is a device that can AND, OR, add, subtract, and perform a variety of other operations on binary words. Figure 1-22a shows a block diagram for the 74LS181, which is a 4-bit ALU. This device can perform any one of 16 logic functions or any one of 16 arithmetic functions on two 4-bit binary words. The function performed on the two words is determined by the logic level applied to the mode input M and by the 4-bit binary code applied to the select inputs S0 to S3.

Figure 1-22b shows the truth table for the 74LS181. In this truth table, A represents the 4-bit binary word applied to the A0 to A3 inputs, and B represents the 4-bit binary word applied to the B0 to B3 inputs. F represents the 4-bit binary word that will be produced on the F0 to F3 outputs. If the mode input M is high,

the device will perform one of 16 logic functions on the two words applied to the A and B inputs. For example, if M is high and we make S3 high, S2 low, S1 high, and S0 high, the 4-bit word on the A inputs will be ANDed with the 4-bit word on the B inputs. The result of this ANDing will appear on the F outputs. Each bit of the A word is ANDed with the corresponding bit of the B word to produce the result on F. Figure 1-22c shows an example of ANDing two words with this device. As you can see in this example, an output bit is high only if the corresponding bit is high in both the A word and the B word.

For another example of the operation of the 74LS181, suppose that the M input is high, S3 is high, S2 is high, S1 is high, and S0 is low. According to the truth table, the device will now OR each bit in the A word with the corresponding bit in the B word and give the result on the corresponding F output. Figure 1-22c shows the result that will be produced by ORing two 4-bit words. Figure 1-22c also shows for your reference the result that would be produced by exclusive ORing these two 4-bit words together.

If the M input of the 74LS181 is low, then the device will perform one of 16 arithmetic functions on the A and B words. Again, the result of the operation will be put on the F outputs. Several 74LS181s can be cascaded to operate on words longer than 4 bits. The ripple-carry input, $\overline{C}_N$, allows a carry from an operation on previous words to be included in the current operation. If the $\overline{C}_N$

```
           74LS181
 ──────── A0
 ──────── A1
 ──────── A2
 ──────── A3        F0 ────────
                    F1 ────────
 ──────── B0        F2 ────────
 ──────── B1        F3 ────────
 ──────── B2         P ────────
 ──────── B3      C_{N+4} ──────
 ──────── C̄_N     A = B ──────
 ──────── M
          S3 S2 S1 S0
```

(a)

SELECTION				M = H LOGIC FUNCTIONS	ACTIVE–HIGH DATA	
					M = L; ARITHMETIC OPERATIONS	
S3	S2	S1	S0		$\overline{C}_N$ = H (NO CARRY)	$\overline{C}_N$ = L (WITH CARRY)
L	L	L	L	$F = \overline{A}$	$F = A$	$F = A$ PLUS 1
L	L	L	H	$F = \overline{A + B}$	$F = A + B$	$F = (A + B)$ PLUS 1
L	L	H	L	$F = \overline{A}B$	$F = A + \overline{B}$	$F = (A + \overline{B})$ PLUS 1
L	L	H	H	$F = 0$	$F =$ MINUS 1 (2's COMPL)	$F = 0$
L	H	L	L	$F = \overline{AB}$	$F = A$ PLUS $A\overline{B}$	$F = A$ PLUS $A\overline{B}$ PLUS 1
L	H	L	H	$F = \overline{B}$	$F = (A + B)$ PLUS $A\overline{B}$	$F = (A + B)$ PLUS $A\overline{B}$ PLUS 1
L	H	H	L	$F = A \oplus B$	$F = A$ MINUS B MINUS 1	$F = A$ MINUS B
L	H	H	H	$F = A\overline{B}$	$F = A\overline{B}$ MINUS 1	$F = A\overline{B}$
H	L	L	L	$F = \overline{A} + B$	$F = A$ PLUS AB	$F = A$ PLUS AB PLUS 1
H	L	L	H	$F = A \oplus B$	$F = A$ PLUS B	$F = A$ PLUS B PLUS 1
H	L	H	L	$F = B$	$F = (A + \overline{B})$ PLUS AB	$F = (A + \overline{B})$ PLUS AB PLUS 1
H	L	H	H	$F = AB$	$F = AB$ MINUS 1	$F = AB$
H	H	L	L	$F = 1$	$F = A$ PLUS A*	$F = A$ PLUS A PLUS 1
H	H	L	H	$F = A + \overline{B}$	$F = (A + B)$ PLUS A	$F = (A + B)$ PLUS A PLUS 1
H	H	H	L	$F = A + B$	$F = (A + \overline{B})$ PLUS A	$F = (A + \overline{B})$ PLUS A PLUS 1
H	H	H	H	$F = A$	$F = A$ MINUS 1	$F = A$

*EACH BIT IS SHIFTED TO THE NEXT MORE SIGNIFICANT BIT POSITION

(b)

```
A =  A3  A2  A1  A0          A = 1 0 1 0          A = 1 0 1 0              A = 1 0 1 0
B =  B3  B2  B1  B0          B = 0 1 1 0          B = 0 1 1 0              B = 0 1 1 0
                            ─────────────        ─────────────            ─────────────
F =  F3  F2  F1  F0      F = A + B = 1 1 1 0   F = A · B = 0 0 1 0   F = A ⊕ B = 1 1 0 0
```

(c)

FIGURE 1-22 Arithmetic logic unit (ALU). (a) Schematic symbol. (b) Truth table. (c) Sample AND, OR, and XOR operations.

input is asserted low, then a carry will be added to the results of the operation on A and B. For example, if the M input is low, S3 is high, S2 is low, S1 is low, S0 is high, and $\overline{C}_N$ is low, the F outputs will have the sum of A plus B plus a carry.

The real importance of an ALU such as the 74LS181 is that it can be programmed with a binary instruction applied to its mode and select inputs to perform many different functions on two binary words applied to its data inputs. In other words, instead of having to build a different circuit to perform each of these functions, we have one programmable device. We can perform any of the operations that we want in a computer with a sequence of simple operations such as those of the 74LS181. Therefore, an ALU is a very important part of the microprocessors and microcomputers that we discuss in the next chapter.

CHECKLIST OF IMPORTANT TERMS AND CONCEPTS IN THIS CHAPTER

If you do not remember any of the terms or concepts in this list, use the index to find them in the chapter.

Binary, bit, nibble, byte, word, doubleword

LSB, MSB, LSD, MSD

Hexadecimal, standard BCD, Gray code

7-segment display code

Alphanumeric codes: ASCII, EBCDIC

Parity bit, odd parity, even parity

Converting between binary, decimal, hexadecimal, BCD

Arithmetic with binary, hexadecimal, BCD

BCD decimal adjust operation

Signed numbers, sign bit

2's complement sign-and-magnitude form

Signal assertion level

Inverting and noninverting buffers

Symbols and truth tables for AND, NAND, OR, NOR, XOR logic gates

FPLA, PROM, PAL

D latch, D flip-flop

Register, shift register, binary counter

ROM: address lines, data lines, bus lines, three-state outputs and enable input

PROM, EPROM, EEPROM, flash EPROM

RAM: static, dynamic

ALU

REVIEW QUESTIONS AND PROBLEMS

1. Write the decimal equivalent for each integral power of 2 from 2^0 to 2^{20}.

2. Convert the following decimal numbers to binary:
   a. 22
   b. 76
   c. 500

3. Convert the following binary numbers to decimal:
   a. 1011
   b. 11010001
   c. 1110111001011001

4. Convert to hexadecimal:
   a. 53 decimal
   b. 756 decimal
   c. 01101100010 binary
   d. 11000010111 binary

5. Convert to decimal:
   a. D3H
   b. 3FEH
   c. 44H

6. Convert the following decimal numbers to BCD:
   a. 86
   b. 62
   c. 33

7. The L key is depressed on an ASCII-encoded keyboard. What pattern of 1's and 0's would you expect to find on the seven parallel data lines coming from the keyboard? What pattern would a carriage return, CR, give?

8. Define *parity* and describe how it is used to detect an error in transmitted data.

9. Show addition of:
   a. 10011_2 and 1011_2 in binary
   b. 37_{10} and 25_{10} in BCD
   c. 4AH and 77H

10. Express the following decimal numbers in 8-bit sign-and-magnitude form:
    a. $+26$
    b. -7
    c. -26
    d. -125

11. Show the subtraction, in binary, of the following decimal numbers using both the pencil method and the 2's-complement addition method:
    a. $7 - 4$
    b. $37 - 26$
    c. $125 - 93$

12. Show the multiplication of 1001 and 011 by the pencil method. Do the same for 11010 and 101.

13. Show the division of 1100100 by 1010 using the pencil method.

14. Perform the indicated operations on the following numbers:
    a. 3AH + 94H
    b. 17AH − 4CH
    c.   0101 1001 BCD
       + 0100 0010 BCD

    d.   0111 1001 BCD
       + 0100 1001 BCD

    e.   0101 1001 BCD
       − 0010 0110 BCD

    f.   0110 0111 BCD
       − 0011 1001 BCD

15. For the circuit in Figure 1-23:
    a. Is the Y output active high or active low?
    b. Is the C signal active high or active low?
    c. What input conditions on A, B, and C will cause the Y output to be asserted?

16. Describe how a D latch responds to a positive pulse on its CK input and how a D flip-flop responds to a positive pulse on its CK input.

17. The National Semiconductor INS8298 is a 65,536-bit ROM organized as 8192 words or bytes of 8 bits. How many address lines are required to address one of the 8192 bytes?

18. Why do most ROMs and RAMs have three-state outputs?

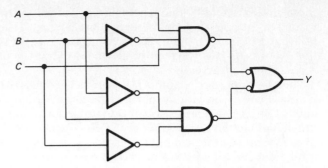

FIGURE 1-23   Circuit for problem 15.

19. Using Figure 1-22b, show the programming of the select and mode inputs the 74181 requires to perform the following arithmetic functions:
    a. A + B
    b. A − B − 1
    c. AB + A

20. Show the output word produced when the following binary words are ANDed with each other and when they are ORed with each other:
    a. 1010 and 0111
    b. 1011 and 1100
    c. 11010111 and 111000
    d. ANDing an 8-bit binary number with 1111 0000 is sometimes referred to as "masking" the lower 4 bits. Why?

CHAPTER 2

Computers, Microcomputers, and Microprocessors—An Introduction

We live in a computer-oriented society, and we are constantly bombarded with a multitude of terms relating to computers. Before getting started with the main flow of the book, we will try to clarify some of these terms and to give an overview of computers and computer systems.

OBJECTIVES

At the conclusion of this chapter, you should be able to:

1. Define the terms *microcomputer, microprocessor, hardware, software, firmware, timesharing, multitasking, distributed processing,* and *multiprocessing.*

2. Describe how a microcomputer fetches and executes an instruction.

3. List the registers and other parts in the 8086/8088 execution unit and bus interface unit.

4. Describe the function of the 8086/8088 queue.

5. Demonstrate how the 8086/8088 calculates memory addresses.

TYPES OF COMPUTERS

Mainframes

Computers come in a wide variety of sizes and capabilities. The largest and most powerful are often called *mainframes.* Mainframe computers may fill an entire room. They are designed to work at very high speeds with large data words, typically 64 bits or greater, and they have massive amounts of memory. Computers of this type are used for military defense control, for business data processing (in an insurance company, for example), and for creating computer graphics displays for science fiction movies. Examples of this type of computer are the IBM 4381, the Honeywell DPS8, and the Cray Y-MP/832. The fastest and most powerful mainframes are called *supercomputers.* Figure 2-1a, p. 20, shows a photograph of a Cray Y-MP/832 supercom-

puter, which contains eight central processors and 32 million 64-bit words of memory.

Minicomputers

Scaled-down versions of mainframe computers are often called *minicomputers.* The main unit of a minicomputer usually fits in a single rack or box. A minicomputer runs more slowly, works directly with smaller data words (often 32-bit words), and does not have as much memory as a mainframe. Computers of this type are used for business data processing, industrial control (for an oil refinery, for example), and scientific research. Examples of this type of computer are the Digital Equipment Corporation VAX 6360 and the Data General MV/8000II. Figure 2-1b shows a photograph of a Digital Equipment Corporation's VAX 6360 minicomputer.

Microcomputers

As the name implies, *microcomputers* are small computers. They range from small controllers that work directly with 4-bit words and can address a few thousand bytes of memory to larger units that work directly with 32-bit words and can address billions of bytes of memory. Some of the more powerful microcomputers have all or most of the features of earlier minicomputers. Therefore, it has become very hard to draw a sharp line between these two types. One distinguishing feature of a microcomputer is that the CPU is usually a single integrated circuit called a *microprocessor.* Older books often used the terms *microprocessor* and *microcomputer* interchangeably, but actually the microprocessor is the CPU to which you add ROM, RAM, and ports to make a microcomputer. A later section in this chapter discusses the evolution of different types of microprocessors. Microcomputers are used in everything from smart sewing machines to computer-aided design systems. Examples of microcomputers are the Intel 8051 single-chip controller; the SDK-86, a single-board computer design kit; the IBM Personal Computer (PC); and the Apple Macintosh computer. The Intel 8051 microcontroller is contained in a single 40-pin chip. Figure 2-2a, p. 21, shows the SDK-86 board, and Figure 2-2b shows the Compaq 386/25 system.

19

(a)

(b)

FIGURE 2-1 (a) Photograph of Cray Y-MP/832 computer. (*Courtesy Cray Research, Inc., and photographer, Paul Shambroom.*) (b) Photograph of VAX 6360 minicomputer. (*Courtesy Digital Equipment Corp.*)

HOW COMPUTERS AND MICROCOMPUTERS ARE USED—AN EXAMPLE

The following sections are intended to give you an overview of how computers are interfaced with users to do useful work. These sections should help you understand many of the features designed into current microprocessors and where this book is heading.

Computerizing an Electronics Factory—Problem

Now, suppose that we want to "computerize" an electronics company. By this we mean that we want to make computer use available to as many people in the company as possible as cheaply as possible. We want the engineers to have access to a computer which can help them design circuits. People in the drafting department should have access to a computer which can be used for computer-aided drafting. The accounting department should have access to a computer for doing all the financial bookkeeping. The warehouse should have access to a computer to help with inventory control. The manufacturing department should have access to a computer for controlling machines and testing finished products. The president, vice presidents, and supervisors should have access to a computer to help them with long-range planning. Secretaries should have access to a computer for word processing. Salespeople should have access to a computer to help them keep track of current pricing, product availability, and commissions. There are several ways to provide all the needed computer power. One solution is to simply give everyone an individual personal computer. The problem with this approach is that it makes it difficult for different people to access commonly needed data. In the next sections we show you two ways to provide computer power and common data to many users.

TIMESHARING AND MULTITASKING SYSTEMS

One common method of providing computer access is a *timesharing* system such as shown in Figure 2-3, p. 22. Several video terminals are connected to the computer through direct wires or through telephone lines. The terminal can be on the user's desk or even in the user's home. The rate at which a user usually enters data is very slow compared with the rate at which a computer can process the data. Therefore, the computer can serve many users by dividing its time among them in small increments. In other words, the computer works on user 1's program for perhaps 20 milliseconds (ms), then works on user 2's program for 20 ms, then works on user 3's program for 20 ms, and so on, until all the users have had a turn. In a few milliseconds the computer will get back to user 1 again and repeat the cycle. To each user it will appear as if he or she has exclusive use of the computer because the computer processes data as fast as the user enters it. A timesharing system such as this allows several users to interact with the computer at the same time. Each user can get information from or store information in the large memory attached to the computer. Each user can have an inexpensive printer attached to the terminal or can direct program or data output to a high-speed printer attached directly to the computer.

An airline ticket reservation computer might use a timesharing system such as this to allow users from all over the country to access flight information and make reservations. A time-multiplexed or time-sliced system such as this can also allow a computer to control many machines or processes in a factory. A computer is much faster than the machines or processes. Therefore, it can

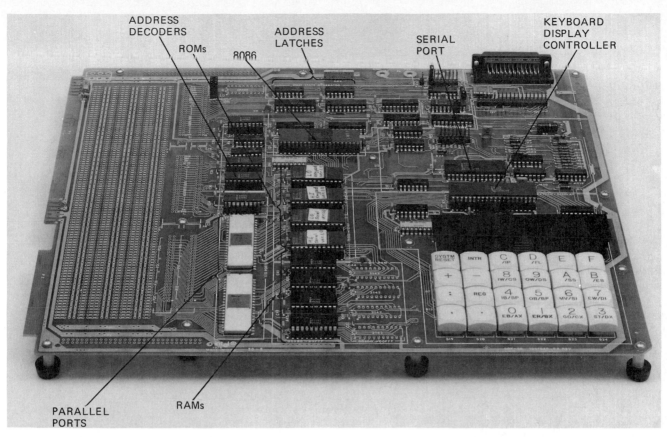

ADDRESS DECODERS ROMs 8086 ADDRESS LATCHES SERIAL PORT KEYBOARD DISPLAY CONTROLLER

PARALLEL PORTS RAMs

(a)

(b)

FIGURE 2-2 (a) Photograph of Intel SDK-86 board. (*Intel Corp.*) (b) Photograph of Compaq 386/25. (*Compaq Corp.*)

check and adjust many pressures, temperatures, motor speeds, etc., before it needs to get back and recheck the first one. A system such as this is often called a *multitasking system* because it appears to be doing many tasks at the same time.

Now let's take another look at our problem of computerizing the electronics company. We could put a powerful computer in some central location and run wires from it to video display terminals on users' desks. Each user could then run the program needed to do a particular task. The accountant could run a ledger program, the secretary could run a word processing program, etc. Each user could access the computer's large data memory. Incidentally, a large collection of data stored in a computer's memory is often referred to as a *data base*. For a small company a system such as this might be adequate. However, there are at least two potential problems.

The first potential problem is, "What happens if the computer is not working?" The answer to this question is that everything grinds to a halt. In a situation where people have become dependent on the computer, not much gets done until the computer is up and running again. The old saying about putting all your eggs in one basket comes to mind here.

The second potential problem of the simple timesharing system is saturation. As the number of users increases, the time it takes the computer to do each user's task increases also. Eventually the computer's response time to each user becomes unreasonably long. People get very upset about the time they have to wait.

DISTRIBUTED PROCESSING OR MULTIPROCESSING

A partial solution for the two potential problems of a simple timesharing system is to use a *distributed*

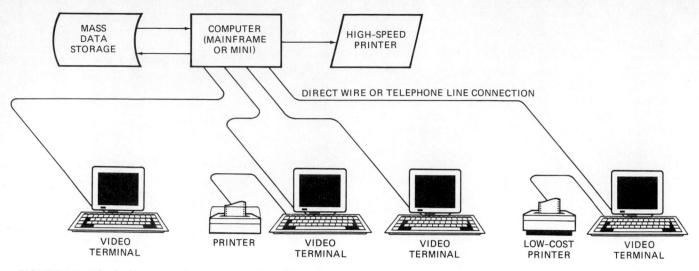

FIGURE 2-3 Block diagram of a computer timesharing system.

processing system. Figure 2-4 shows a block diagram for such a system. The system has a powerful central computer with a large memory and a high-speed printer, as does the simple timesharing system described previously. However, in this system each user has a microcomputer instead of simply a video display terminal. In other words, each user station is an independently functioning microcomputer with a CPU, ROM, RAM, and probably magnetic or optical disk memory. This means that a person can do many tasks locally on the microcomputer without having to use the large computer at all. Since the microcomputers are connected to the large computer through a network, however, a user can access the computing power, memory, or other resources of the large computer when needed.

Distributing the processing to multiple computers or processors in a system has several advantages. First, if the large computer goes down, the local microcomputers can continue working until they need to access the large computer for something. Second, the burden on the

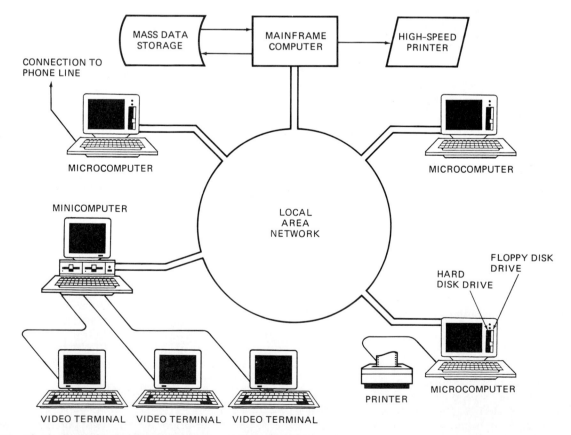

FIGURE 2-4 Block diagram of a distributed processing computer system.

large computer is reduced greatly, because much of the computing is done by the local microcomputers. Finally, the distributed processing approach allows the system designer to use a local microcomputer that is best suited to the task it has to do.

COMPUTERIZED ELECTRONICS COMPANY OVERVIEW

Distributed processing seems to be the best way to go about computerizing our electronics factory. Engineers can have personal computers or engineering workstations on their desks. With these they can use available programs to design and test circuits. They can access the large computer if they need data from its memory. Through the telephone lines, the engineer with a personal computer can access data in the memory of other computers all over the world. The drafting people can have personal computers for simple work, or large computer-aided design systems for more complex work. Completed work can be stored in the memory of the large computer. The production department can have networked computers to keep track of product flow and to control the machines which actually mount components on circuit boards, etc. The accounting department can use personal computers with spreadsheet programs to work with financial data kept in the memory of the large computer. The warehouse supervisor can likewise use a personal computer with an inventory program to keep personal records and those in the large computer's memory updated. Corporate officers can have personal computers tied into the network. They then can interact with any of the other systems on the network. Salespeople can have portable personal computers that they can carry with them in the field. They can communicate with the main computer over the telephone lines using a modem. Secretaries doing word processing can use individual word processing units or personal computers. Users can also send messages to one another over the network. The specifics of a computer system such as this will obviously depend on the needs of the individual company for which the system is designed.

SUMMARY AND DIRECTION FROM HERE

The main concepts that you should take with you from this section are timesharing or multitasking and distributed processing or multiprocessing. As you work your way through the rest of this book, keep an overview of the computerized electronics company in the back of your mind. The goal of this book is to teach you how the microcomputers and other parts of a system such as this work, how the parts are connected together, and how the system is programmed at different levels.

OVERVIEW OF MICROCOMPUTER STRUCTURE AND OPERATION

Figure 2-5 shows a block diagram for a simple microcomputer. The major parts are the *central processing unit* or CPU, *memory,* and the *input and output* circuitry or I/O. Connecting these parts are three sets of parallel lines called *buses.* The three buses are the *address bus,* the *data bus,* and the *control bus.* Let's take a brief look at each of these parts.

Memory

The memory section usually consists of a mixture of RAM and ROM. It may also have magnetic floppy disks, magnetic hard disks, or optical disks. Memory has two purposes. The first purpose is to store the binary codes for the sequences of instructions you want the computer to carry out. When you write a computer program, what you are really doing is writing a sequential list of instructions for the computer. The second purpose of the memory is to store the binary-coded data with which the computer is going to be working. This data might be the inventory records of a supermarket, for example.

Input/Output

The input/output or I/O section allows the computer to take in data from the outside world or send data to the outside world. Peripherals such as keyboards, video display terminals, printers, and modems are connected to the I/O section. These allow the user and the computer to communicate with each other. The actual physical devices used to interface the computer buses to external systems are often called *ports.* Ports in a computer function just as shipping ports do for a country. An *input port* allows data from a keyboard, an A/D converter, or some other source to be read into the computer under control of the CPU. An *output port* is used to send data from the computer to some peripheral, such as a video display terminal, a printer, or a D/A converter. Physically,

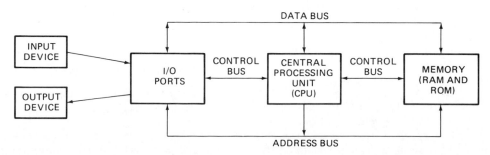

FIGURE 2-5   Block diagram of a simple microcomputer.

the simplest type of input or output port is just a set of parallel D flip-flops. If they are being used as an input port, the D inputs are connected to the external device, and the Q outputs are connected to the data bus which runs to the CPU. Data will then be transferred through the latches when they are enabled by a control signal from the CPU. In a system where they are being used as an output port, the D inputs of the latches are connected to the data bus, and the Q outputs are connected to some external device. Data sent out on the data bus by the CPU will be transferred to the external device when the latches are enabled by a control signal from the CPU.

Central Processing Unit

The central processing unit or CPU controls the operation of the computer. In a microcomputer the CPU is a microprocessor, as we discussed in an earlier section of the chapter. The CPU fetches binary-coded instructions from memory, decodes the instructions into a series of simple actions, and carries out these actions in a sequence of steps.

The CPU also contains an *address counter* or *instruction pointer* register, which holds the address of the next instruction or data item to be fetched from memory; general-purpose registers, which are used for temporary storage of binary data; and circuitry, which generates the control bus signals.

Address Bus

The address bus consists of 16, 20, 24, or 32 parallel signal lines. On these lines the CPU sends out the address of the memory location that is to be written to or read from. The number of memory locations that the CPU can address is determined by the number of address lines. If the CPU has N address lines, then it can directly address 2^N memory locations. For example, a CPU with 16 address lines can address 2^{16} or 65,536 memory locations, a CPU with 20 address lines can address 2^{20} or 1,048,576 locations, and a CPU with 24 address lines can address 2^{24} or 16,777,216 locations. When the CPU reads data from or writes data to a port, it sends the port address out on the address bus.

Data Bus

The data bus consists of 8, 16, or 32 parallel signal lines. As indicated by the double-ended arrows on the data bus line in Figure 2-5, the data bus lines are *bidirectional*. This means that the CPU can read data in from memory or from a port on these lines, or it can send data out to memory or to a port on these lines. Many devices in a system will have their outputs connected to the data bus, but only one device at a time will have its outputs enabled. Any device connected on the data bus must have *three-state outputs* so that its outputs can be disabled when it is not being used to put data on the bus.

Control Bus

The control bus consists of 4 to 10 parallel signal lines. The CPU sends out signals on the control bus to enable the outputs of addressed memory devices or port devices. Typical control bus signals are *Memory Read, Memory Write, I/O Read,* and *I/O Write*. To read a byte of data from a memory location, for example, the CPU sends out the memory address of the desired byte on the address bus and then sends out a Memory Read signal on the control bus. The Memory Read signal enables the addressed memory device to output a data word onto the data bus. The data word from memory travels along the data bus to the CPU.

Hardware, Software, and Firmware

When working around computers, you hear the terms hardware, software, and firmware almost constantly. *Hardware* is the name given to the physical devices and circuitry of the computer. *Software* refers to the programs written for the computer. *Firmware* is the term given to programs stored in ROMs or in other devices which permanently keep their stored information.

Summary of Important Points So Far

- A computer or microcomputer consists of memory, a CPU, and some input/output circuitry.

- These three parts are connected by the address bus, the data bus, and the control bus.

- The sequence of instructions or program for a computer is stored as binary numbers in successive memory locations.

- The CPU fetches an instruction from memory, decodes the instruction to determine what actions must be done for the instruction, and carries out these actions.

EXECUTION OF A THREE-INSTRUCTION PROGRAM

To give you a better idea of how the parts of a microcomputer function together, we will now describe the actions a simple microcomputer might go through to carry out (execute) a simple program. The three instructions of the program are

1. Input a value from a keyboard connected to the port at address 05H.

2. Add 7 to the value read in.

3. Output the result to a display connected to the port at address 02H.

Figure 2-6 shows in diagram form and sequential list form the actions that the computer will perform to execute these three instructions.

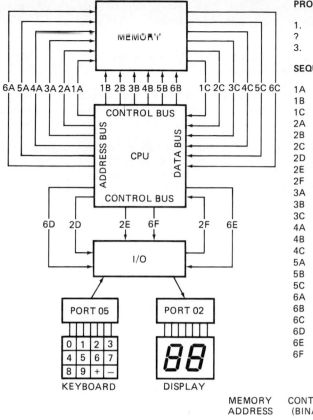

PROGRAM

1. INPUT A VALUE FROM PORT 05.
2. ADD 7 TO THIS VALUE.
3. OUTPUT THE RESULT TO PORT 02.

SEQUENCE

1A CPU SENDS OUT ADDRESS OF FIRST INSTRUCTION TO MEMORY.
1B CPU SENDS OUT MEMORY READ CONTROL SIGNAL TO ENABLE MEMORY.
1C INSTRUCTION BYTE SENT FROM MEMORY TO CPU ON DATA BUS.
2A ADDRESS NEXT MEMORY LOCATION TO GET REST OF INSTRUCTION.
2B SEND MEMORY READ CONTROL SIGNAL TO ENABLE MEMORY.
2C PORT ADDRESS BYTE SENT FROM MEMORY TO CPU ON DATA BUS.
2D CPU SENDS OUT PORT ADDRESS ON ADDRESS BUS.
2E CPU SENDS OUT INPUT READ CONTROL SIGNAL TO ENABLE PORT.
2F DATA FROM PORT SENT TO CPU ON DATA BUS.
3A CPU SENDS ADDRESS OF NEXT INSTRUCTION TO MEMORY.
3B CPU SENDS MEMORY READ CONTROL SIGNAL TO ENABLE MEMORY.
3C INSTRUCTION BYTE FROM MEMORY SENT TO CPU ON DATA BUS.
4A CPU SENDS NEXT ADDRESS TO MEMORY TO GET REST OF INSTRUCTION.
4B CPU SENDS MEMORY READ CONTROL SIGNAL TO ENABLE MEMORY.
4C NUMBER 07H SENT FROM MEMORY TO CPU ON DATA BUS.
5A CPU SENDS ADDRESS OF NEXT INSTRUCTION TO MEMORY.
5B CPU SENDS MEMORY READ CONTROL SIGNAL TO ENABLE MEMORY.
5C INSTRUCTION BYTE FROM MEMORY SENT TO CPU ON DATA BUS.
6A CPU SENDS OUT NEXT ADDRESS TO GET REST OF INSTRUCTION.
6B CPU SENDS OUT MEMORY READ CONTROL SIGNAL TO ENABLE MEMORY.
6C PORT ADDRESS BYTE SENT FROM MEMORY TO CPU ON DATA BUS.
6D CPU SENDS OUT PORT ADDRESS ON ADDRESS BUS.
6E CPU SENDS OUT DATA TO PORT ON DATA BUS.
6F CPU SENDS OUT OUTPUT WRITE SIGNAL TO ENABLE PORT.

(a)

MEMORY ADDRESS	CONTENTS (BINARY)	CONTENTS (HEX)	OPERATION	
00100H	11100100	E4	INPUT FROM	
00101H	00000101	05	PORT 05H	
00102H	00000100	04	ADD	
00103H	00000111	07	07H	
00104H	11100110	E6	OUTPUT TO	
00105H	00000010	02	PORT 02	

(b)

FIGURE 2-6 *(a)* Execution of a three-step computer program. *(b)* Memory addresses and memory contents for a three-step program.

For this example, assume that the CPU fetches instructions and data from memory 1 byte at a time, as is done in the original IBM PC and its clones. Also assume that the binary codes for the instructions are in sequential memory locations starting at address 00100H. Figure 2-6b shows the actual binary codes that would be required in successive memory locations to execute this program on an IBM PC-type microcomputer.

The CPU needs an instruction before it can do anything, so its first action is to fetch an instruction byte from memory. To do this, the CPU sends out the address of the first instruction byte, in this case 00100H, to memory on the address bus. This action is represented by line 1A in Figure 2-6a. The CPU then sends out a Memory Read signal on the control bus (line 1B in the figure). The Memory Read signal enables the memory to output the addressed byte on the data bus. This action is represented by line 1C in the figure. The CPU reads in this first instruction byte (E4H) from the data bus and *decodes* it. By *decode* we mean that the CPU determines from the binary code read in what actions it is supposed to take. If the CPU is a microprocessor, it selects the sequence of microinstructions needed to

carry out the instruction read from memory. For the example instruction here, the CPU determines that the code read in represents an Input instruction. From decoding this instruction byte, the CPU also determines that it needs more information before it can carry out the instruction. The additional information the CPU needs is the address of the port that the data is to be input from. This port address part of the instruction is stored in the next memory location after the code for the Input instruction.

To fetch this second byte of the instruction, the CPU sends out the next sequential address (00101H) to memory, as shown by line 2A in the figure. To enable the addressed memory device, the CPU also sends out another Memory Read signal on the control bus (line 2B). The memory then outputs the addressed byte on the data bus (line 2C). When the CPU has read in this second byte, 05H in this case, it has all the information it needs to execute the instruction.

To execute the Input instruction, the CPU sends out the port address (05H) on the address bus (line 2D) and sends out an I/O Read signal on the control bus (line 2E). The I/O Read signal enables the addressed port

COMPUTERS, MICROCOMPUTERS, AND MICROPROCESSORS—AN INTRODUCTION **25**

device to put a byte of data on the data bus (line 2F). The CPU reads in the byte of data and stores it in an internal register. This completes the fetching and execution of the first instruction.

Having completed the first instruction, the CPU must now fetch its next instruction from memory. To do this, it sends out the next sequential address (00102H) on the address bus (line 3A) and sends out a Memory Read signal on the control bus (line 3B). The Memory Read signal enables the memory device to put the addressed byte (04H) on the data bus (line 3C). The CPU reads in this instruction byte from the data bus and decodes it. From this instruction byte the CPU determines that it is supposed to add some number to the number stored in the internal register. The CPU also determines from decoding this instruction byte that it must go to memory again to get the next byte of the instruction, which contains the number that it is supposed to add. To get the required byte, the CPU will send out the next sequential address (00103H) on the address bus (line 4A) and another Memory Read signal on the control bus (line 4B). The memory will then output the contents of the addressed byte (the number 07H) on the data bus (line 4C). When the CPU receives this number, it will add it to the contents of the internal register. The result of the addition will be left in the internal register. This completes the fetching and executing of the second instruction.

The CPU must now fetch the third instruction. To do this, it sends out the next sequential address (00104H) on the address bus (line 5A) and sends out a Memory Read signal on the control bus (line 5B). The memory then outputs the addressed byte (E6H) on the data bus (line 5C). From decoding this byte, the CPU determines that it is now supposed to do an Output operation to a port. The CPU also determines from decoding this byte that it must go to memory again to get the address of the output port. To do this, it sends out the next sequential address (00105H) on the address bus (line 6A), sends out a Memory Read signal on the control bus (line 6B), and reads in the byte (02H) put on the data bus by the memory (line 6C). The CPU now has all the information that it needs to execute the Output instruction.

To output a data byte to a port, the CPU first sends out the address of the desired port on the address bus (line 6D). Next it outputs the data byte from the internal register on the data bus (line 6E). The CPU then sends out an I/O Write signal on the control bus (line 6F). This signal enables the addressed output port device so that the data from the data bus lines can pass through it to the LED displays. When the CPU removes the I/O Write signal to proceed with the next instruction, the data will remain latched on the output pins of the port device. The data will remain latched on the port until the power is turned off or until a new data word is output to the port. This is important because it means that the computer does not have to keep outputting a value over and over in order for it to remain on the output.

All the steps described above may seem like a great deal of work just to input a value from a keyboard, add 7 to it, and output the result to a display. Even a simple microcomputer, however, can run through all these steps in a few microseconds.

Summary of Simple Microcomputer Bus Operation

1. A microcomputer fetches each program instruction in sequence, decodes the instruction, and executes it.

2. The CPU in a microcomputer fetches instructions or reads data from memory by sending out an address on the address bus and a Memory Read signal on the control bus. The memory outputs the addressed instruction or data word to the CPU on the data bus.

3. The CPU writes a data word to memory by sending out an address on the address bus, sending out the data word on the data bus, and sending a Memory Write signal to memory on the control bus.

4. To read data from a port, the CPU sends out the port address on the address bus and sends an I/O Read signal to the port device on the control bus. Data from the port comes into the CPU on the data bus.

5. To write data to a port, the CPU sends out the port address on the address bus, sends out the data to be written to the port on the data bus, and sends an I/O Write signal to the port device on the control bus.

MICROPROCESSOR EVOLUTION AND TYPES

As we told you in the preceding section, a microprocessor is used as the CPU in a microcomputer. There are now many different microprocessors available, so before we dig into the details of a specific device, we will give you a short microprocessor history lesson and an overview of the different types.

Microprocessor Evolution

A common way of categorizing microprocessors is by the number of bits that their ALU can work with at a time. In other words, a microprocessor with a 4-bit ALU will be referred to as a 4-bit microprocessor, regardless of the number of address lines or the number of data bus lines that it has. The first commercially available microprocessor was the Intel 4004, produced in 1971. It contained 2300 PMOS transistors. The 4004 was a 4-bit device intended to be used with some other devices in making a calculator. Some logic designers, however, saw that this device could be used to replace PC boards full of combinational and sequential logic devices. Also, the ability to change the function of a system by just changing the programming, rather than redesigning the hardware, is very appealing. It was these factors that pushed the evolution of microprocessors.

In 1972 Intel came out with the 8008, which was capable of working with 8-bit words. The 8008, however, required 20 or more additional devices to form a functional CPU. In 1974 Intel announced the 8080, which had a much larger instruction set than the 8008 and required only two additional devices to form a functional CPU. Also, the 8080 used NMOS transistors, so it operated much faster than the 8008. The 8080 is referred to as a *second-generation microprocessor.*

Soon after Intel produced the 8080, Motorola came out with the MC6800, another 8-bit general-purpose CPU. The 6800 had the advantage that it required only a +5-V supply rather than the −5-V, +5-V, and +12-V supplies required by the 8080. For several years the 8080 and the 6800 were the top-selling 8-bit microprocessors. Some of their competitors were the MOS Technology 6502, used as the CPU in the Apple II microcomputer, and the Zilog Z80, used as the CPU in the Radio Shack TRS-80 microcomputer.

As designers found more and more applications for microprocessors, they pressured microprocessor manufacturers to develop devices with architectures and features optimized for doing certain types of tasks. In response to the expressed needs, microprocessors have evolved in three major directions during the last 15 years.

Dedicated or Embedded Controllers

One direction has been *dedicated or embedded controllers.* These devices are used to control "smart" machines, such as microwave ovens, clothes washers, sewing machines, auto ignition systems, and metal lathes. Texas Instruments has produced millions of their TMS-1000 family of 4-bit microprocessors for this type of application. In 1976 Intel introduced the 8048, which contains an 8-bit CPU, RAM, ROM, and some I/O ports all in one 40-pin package. Other manufacturers have followed with similar products. These devices are often referred to as *microcontrollers.* Some currently available devices in this category—the Intel 8051 and the Motorola MC6801, for example—contain programmable counters and a serial port (UART) as well as a CPU, ROM, RAM, and parallel I/O ports. A more recently introduced single-chip microcontroller, the Intel 8096, contains a 16-bit CPU, ROM, RAM, a UART, ports, timers, and a 10-bit analog-to-digital converter.

Bit-Slice Processors

A second direction of microprocessor evolution has been *bit-slice processors.* For some applications, general-purpose CPUs such as the 8080 and 6800 are not fast enough or do not have suitable instruction sets. For these applications, several manufacturers produce devices which can be used to build a custom CPU. An example is the Advanced Micro Devices 2900 family of devices. This family includes 4-bit ALUs, multiplexers, sequencers, and other parts needed for custom-building a CPU. The term *slice* comes from the fact that these parts can be connected in parallel to work with 8-bit words, 16-bit words, or 32-bit words. In other words, a designer can add as many slices as needed for a particu-

lar application. The designer not only custom-designs the hardware of the CPU, but also custom-makes the instruction set for it using "microcode."

General-Purpose CPUs

The third major direction of microprocessor evolution has been toward general-purpose CPUs which give a microcomputer most or all of the computing power of earlier minicomputers. After Motorola came out with the MC6800, Intel produced the 8085, an upgrade of the 8080 that required only a +5-V supply. Motorola then produced the MC6809, which has a few 16-bit instructions, but is still basically an 8-bit processor. In 1978 Intel came out with the 8086, which is a full 16-bit processor. Some 16-bit microprocessors, such as the National PACE and the Texas Instruments 9900 family of devices, had been available previously, but the market apparently wasn't ready. Soon after Intel came out with the 8086, Motorola came out with the 16-bit MC68000, and the 16-bit race was off and running. The 8086 and the 68000 work directly with 16-bit words instead of with 8-bit words, they can address a million or more bytes of memory instead of the 64 Kbytes addressable by the 8-bit processors, and they execute instructions much faster than the 8-bit processors. Also, these 16-bit processors have single instructions for functions such as *multiply* and *divide*, which required a lengthy sequence of instructions on the 8-bit processors.

The evolution along this last path has continued on to 32-bit processors that work with gigabytes (10^9 bytes) or terabytes (10^{12} bytes) of memory. Examples of these devices are the Intel 80386, the Motorola MC68020, and the National 32032.

Since we could not possibly describe in this book the operation and programming of even a few of the available processors, we confine our discussions primarily to one group of related microprocessors. The family we have chosen is the Intel 8086, 8088, 80186, 80188, 80286, 80386, 80486 family. Members of this family are very widely used in personal computers, business computer systems, and industrial control systems. Our experience has shown that learning the programming and operation of one family of microcomputers very thoroughly is much more useful than looking at many processors superficially. If you learn one processor family well, you will most likely find it quite easy to learn another when you have to.

THE 8086 MICROPROCESSOR FAMILY—OVERVIEW

The Intel 8086 is a 16-bit microprocessor that is intended to be used as the CPU in a microcomputer. The term *16-bit* means that its arithmetic logic unit, its internal registers, and most of its instructions are designed to work with 16-bit binary words. The 8086 has a 16-bit data bus, so it can read data from or write data to memory and ports either 16 bits or 8 bits at a time. The 8086 has a 20-bit address bus, so it can address any one of 2^{20}, or 1,048,576, memory locations.

Each of the 1,048,576 memory addresses of the 8086 represents a byte-wide location. Sixteen-bit words will be stored in two consecutive memory locations. If the first byte of a word is at an even address, the 8086 can read the entire word in one operation. If the first byte of the word is at an odd address, the 8086 will read the first byte with one bus operation and the second byte with another bus operation. Later we will discuss this in detail. The main point here is that if the first byte of a 16-bit word is at an even address, the 8086 can read the entire word in one operation.

The Intel 8088 has the same arithmetic logic unit, the same registers, and the same instruction set as the 8086. The 8088 also has a 20-bit address bus, so it can address any one of 1,048,576 bytes in memory. The 8088, however, has an 8-bit data bus, so it can only read data from or write data to memory and ports 8 bits at a time. The 8086, remember, can read or write either 8 or 16 bits at a time. To read a 16-bit word from two successive memory locations, the 8088 will always have to do two read operations. Since the 8086 and the 8088 are almost identical, any reference we make to the 8086 in the rest of the book will also pertain to the 8088 unless we specifically indicate otherwise. This is done to make reading easier. The Intel 8088, incidentally, is used as the CPU in the original IBM Personal Computer, the IBM PC/XT, and several compatible personal computers.

The Intel 80186 is an improved version of the 8086, and the 80188 is an improved version of the 8088. In addition to a 16-bit CPU, the 80186 and 80188 each have programmable peripheral devices integrated in the same package. In a later chapter we will discuss these integrated peripherals. The instruction set of the 80186 and 80188 is a *superset* of the instruction set of the 8086. The term *superset* means that all the 8086 and 8088 instructions will execute properly on an 80186 or an 80188, but the 80186 and the 80188 have a few additional instructions. In other words, a program written for an 8086 or an 8088 is *upward-compatible* to an 80186 or an 80188, but a program written for an 80186 or an 80188 may not execute correctly on an 8086 or an 8088. In the instruction set descriptions in Chapter 6, we specifically indicate which instructions work only with the 80186 or 80188.

The Intel 80286 is a 16-bit, advanced version of the 8086 which was specifically designed for use as the CPU in a multiuser or multitasking microcomputer. When operating in its *real address mode,* the 80286 functions mostly as a fast 8086. Most programs written for an 8086 can be run on an 80286 operating in its real address mode. When operating in its *virtual address mode,* an 80286 has features which make it easy to keep users' programs separate from one another and to protect the system program from destruction by users' programs. In Chapter 15 we discuss the operation and use of the 80286. The 80286 is the CPU used in the IBM PC/AT personal computer.

The Intel 80386 is a 32-bit microprocessor which can directly address up to 4 gigabytes of memory. The 80386 contains more sophisticated features than the 80286 for use in multiuser and multitasking microcomputer

systems. In Chapter 15 we discuss the features of the 80386 and the 80486, which is an evolutionary step up from the 80386.

8086 INTERNAL ARCHITECTURE

Before we can talk about how to write programs for the 8086, we need to discuss its specific internal features, such as its ALU, flags, registers, instruction byte queue, and segment registers.

As shown by the block diagram in Figure 2-7, the 8086 CPU is divided into two independent functional parts, the *bus interface unit* or BIU, and the *execution unit* or EU. Dividing the work between these two units speeds up processing.

The BIU sends out addresses, fetches instructions from memory, reads data from ports and memory, and writes data to ports and memory. In other words, the BIU handles all transfers of data and addresses on the buses for the execution unit.

The execution unit of the 8086 tells the BIU where to fetch instructions or data from, decodes instructions, and executes instructions. Let's take a look at some of the parts of the execution unit.

The Execution Unit

CONTROL CIRCUITRY, INSTRUCTION DECODER, AND ALU

As shown in Figure 2-7, the EU contains *control circuitry* which directs internal operations. A *decoder* in the EU translates instructions fetched from memory into a series of actions which the EU carries out. The EU has a 16-bit *arithmetic logic unit* which can add, subtract, AND, OR, XOR, increment, decrement, complement, or shift binary numbers.

FLAG REGISTER

A *flag* is a flip-flop which indicates some condition produced by the execution of an instruction or controls certain operations of the EU. A 16-bit *flag register* in the EU contains nine active flags. Figure 2-8 shows the location of the nine flags in the flag register. Six of the nine flags are used to indicate some *condition* produced by an instruction. For example, a flip-flop called the *carry flag* will be set to a 1 if the addition of two 16-bit binary numbers produces a carry out of the most significant bit position. If no carry out of the MSB is produced by the addition, then the carry flag will be a 0. The EU thus effectively runs up a "flag" to tell you that a carry was produced.

The six conditional flags in this group are the *carry flag* (CF), the *parity flag* (PF), the *auxiliary carry flag* (AF), the *zero flag* (ZF), the *sign flag* (SF), and the *overflow flag* (OF). The names of these flags should give you hints as to what conditions affect them. Certain 8086 instructions check these flags to determine which of two alternative actions should be done in executing the instruction.

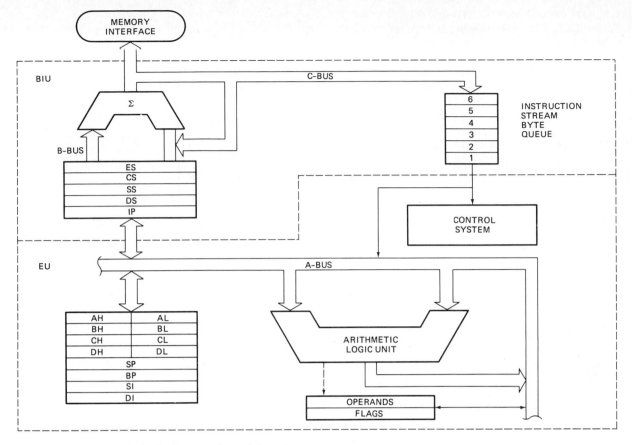

FIGURE 2-7   8086 internal block diagram. (*Intel Corp.*)

The three remaining flags in the flag register are used to *control* certain operations of the processor. These flags are different from the six conditional flags described above in the way they are set or reset. The six conditional flags are set or reset by the EU on the basis of the results of some arithmetic or logic operation. The *control flags* are deliberately set or reset with specific instructions you put in your program. The three control flags are the *trap flag* (TF), which is used for single stepping through a program; the *interrupt flag* (IF), which is used to allow or prohibit the interruption of a program; and the *direction flag* (DF), which is used with string instructions.

Later we will discuss in detail the operation and use of the nine flags.

GENERAL-PURPOSE REGISTERS

Observe in Figure 2-7 that the EU has eight *general-purpose registers*, labeled AH, AL, BH, BL, CH, CL, DH, and DL. These registers can be used individually for temporary storage of 8-bit data. The AL register is also called the *accumulator*. It has some features that the other general-purpose registers do not have.

Certain pairs of these general-purpose registers can be used together to store 16-bit data words. The acceptable

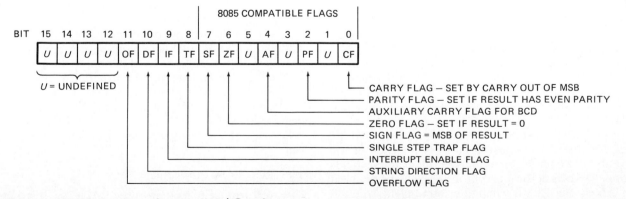

FIGURE 2-8   8086 flag register format. (*Intel Corp.*)

register pairs are AH and AL, BH and BL, CH and CL, and DH and DL. The AH–AL pair is referred to as the *AX register*, the BH–BL pair is referred to as the *BX register*, the CH–CL pair is referred to as the *CX register*, and the DH–DL pair is referred to as the *DX register*.

The 8086 general-purpose register set is very similar to those of the earlier-generation 8080 and 8085 microprocessors. It was designed this way so that the many programs written for the 8080 and 8085 could easily be translated to run on the 8086 or the 8088. The advantage of using internal registers for the temporary storage of data is that, since the data is already in the EU, it can be accessed much more quickly than it could be accessed in external memory. Now let's look at the features of the BIU.

The BIU

THE QUEUE

While the EU is decoding an instruction or executing an instruction which does not require use of the buses, the BIU fetches up to six instruction bytes for the following instructions. The BIU stores these prefetched bytes in a first-in–first-out register set called a *queue*. When the EU is ready for its next instruction, it simply reads the instruction byte(s) for the instruction from the queue in the BIU. This is much faster than sending out an address to the system memory and waiting for memory to send back the next instruction byte or bytes. The process is analogous to the way a bricklayer's assistant fetches bricks ahead of time and keeps a queue of bricks lined up so that the bricklayer can just reach out and grab a brick when necessary. Except in the cases of JMP and CALL instructions, where the queue must be dumped and then reloaded starting from a new address, this prefetch-and-queue scheme greatly speeds up processing. Fetching the next instruction while the current instruction executes is called *pipelining*.

SEGMENT REGISTERS

The 8086 BIU sends out 20-bit addresses, so it can address any of 2^{20} or 1,048,576 bytes in memory. However, at any given time the 8086 works with only four 65,536-byte (64-Kbyte) segments within this 1,048,576-byte (1-Mbyte) range. Four *segment registers* in the BIU are used to hold the upper 16 bits of the starting addresses of four memory segments that the 8086 is working with at a particular time. The four segment registers are the *code segment* (CS) register, the *stack segment* (SS) register, the *extra segment* (ES) register, and the *data segment* (DS) register.

Figure 2-9 shows how these four segments might be positioned in memory at a given time. The four segments can be separated as shown, or, for small programs which do not need all 64 Kbytes in each segment, they can overlap.

To repeat, then, a segment register is used to hold the upper 16 bits of the starting address for each of the segments. The code segment register, for example, holds the upper 16 bits of the starting address for the segment from which the BIU is currently fetching instruction code bytes. The BIU always inserts zeros for the lowest

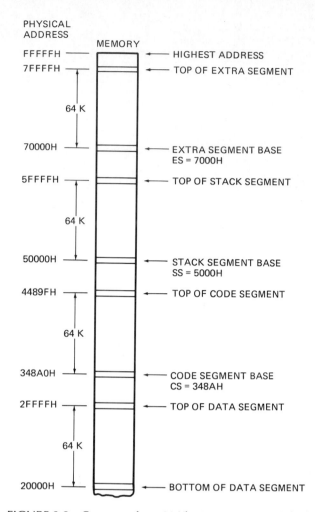

FIGURE 2-9   One way four 64-Kbyte segments might be positioned within the 1-Mbyte address space of an 8086.

4 bits (nibble) of the 20-bit starting address for a segment. If the code segment register contains 348AH, for example, then the code segment will start at address 348A0H. In other words, a 64-Kbyte segment can be located anywhere within the 1-Mbyte address space, but the segment will always start at an address with zeros in the lowest 4 bits. This constraint was put on the location of segments so that it is only necessary to store and manipulate 16-bit numbers when working with the starting address of a segment. The part of a segment starting address stored in a segment register is often called the *segment base*.

A *stack* is a section of memory set aside to store addresses and data while a *subprogram* executes. The stack segment register is used to hold the upper 16 bits of the starting address for the program stack. We will discuss the use and operation of a stack in detail later.

The extra segment register and the data segment register are used to hold the upper 16 bits of the starting addresses of two memory segments that are used for data.

INSTRUCTION POINTER

The next feature to look at in the BIU is the *instruction pointer* (IP) register. As discussed previously, the code

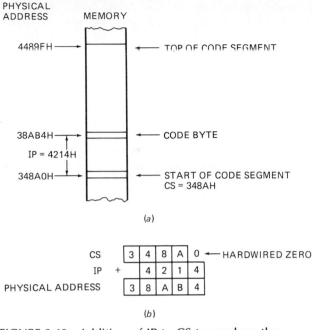

FIGURE 2-10 Addition of IP to CS to produce the physical address of the code byte. (a) Diagram. (b) Computation.

tells where in that 64-Kbyte code segment the next instruction byte is to be fetched from. The actual physical address sent to memory is produced by adding the offset contained in the IP register to the segment base represented by the upper 16 bits in the CS register.

Any time the 8086 accesses memory, the BIU produces the required 20-bit physical address by adding an offset to a segment base value represented by the contents of one of the segment registers. As another example of this, let's look at how the 8086 uses the contents of the stack segment register and the contents of the stack pointer register to produce a physical address.

STACK SEGMENT REGISTER AND STACK POINTER REGISTER

A stack, remember, is a section of memory set aside to store addresses and data while a subprogram is executing. The 8086 allows you to set aside an entire 64-Kbyte segment as a stack. The upper 16 bits of the starting address for this segment are kept in the stack segment register. The *stack pointer* (SP) register in the execution unit holds the 16-bit offset from the start of the segment to the memory location where a word was most recently stored on the stack. The memory location where a word was most recently stored is called the *top of stack*. Figure 2-11*a* shows this in diagram form.

The physical address for a stack read or a stack write is produced by adding the contents of the stack pointer register to the segment base address represented by the upper 16 bits of the base address in SS. Figure 2-11*b* shows an example. The 5000H in SS represents a segment base address of 50000H. When the FFE0H in the SP is added to this, the resultant physical address for the top of the stack will be 5FFE0H. The physical address can be represented either as a single number, 5FFE0H, or in SS:SP form as 5000:FFE0H.

segment register holds the upper 16 bits of the starting address of the segment from which the BIU is currently fetching instruction code bytes. The instruction pointer register holds the 16-bit address, or *offset*, of the next code byte *within* this code segment. The value contained in the IP is referred to as an *offset* because this value must be offset from (added to) the segment base address in CS to produce the required 20-bit physical address sent out by the BIU. Figure 2-10*a* shows in diagram form how this works. The CS register points to the *base* or start of the current code segment. The IP contains the distance or offset from this base address to the next instruction byte to be fetched. Figure 2-10*b* shows how the 16-bit offset in IP is added to the 16-bit segment base address in CS to produce the 20-bit *physical* address. Notice that the two 16-bit numbers are not added directly in line, because the CS register contains only the upper 16 bits of the base address for the code segment. As we said before, the BIU automatically inserts zeros for the lowest 4 bits of the segment base address.

If the CS register, for example, contains 348AH, you know that the starting address for the code segment is 348A0H. When the BIU adds the offset of 4214H in the IP to this segment base address, the result is a 20-bit physical address of 38AB4H.

An alternative way of representing a 20-bit physical address is the *segment base:offset form*. For the address of a code byte, the format for this alternative form will be CS:IP. As an example of this, the address constructed in the preceding paragraph, 38AB4H, can also be represented as 348A:4214.

To summarize, then, the CS register contains the upper 16 bits of the starting address of the code segment in the 1-Mbyte address range of the 8086. The instruction pointer register contains a 16-bit offset which

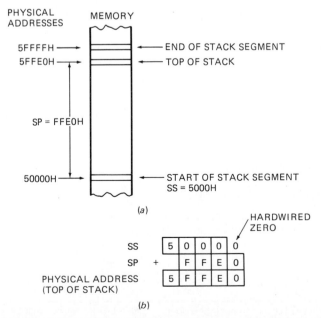

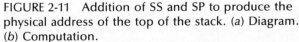

FIGURE 2-11 Addition of SS and SP to produce the physical address of the top of the stack. (a) Diagram. (b) Computation.

The operation and use of the stack will be discussed in detail later as need arises.

POINTER AND INDEX REGISTERS IN THE EXECUTION UNIT

In addition to the stack pointer register (SP), the EU contains a 16-bit *base pointer* (BP) register. It also contains a 16-bit *source index* (SI) register and a 16-bit *destination index* (DI) register. These three registers can be used for temporary storage of data just as the general-purpose registers described above. However, their main use is to hold the 16-bit offset of a data word in one of the segments. SI, for example, can be used to hold the offset of a data word in the data segment. The physical address of the data in memory will be generated in this case by adding the contents of SI to the segment base address represented by the 16-bit number in the DS register. After we give you an overview of the different levels of languages used to program a microcomputer, we will show you some examples of how we tell the 8086 to read data from or write data to a desired memory location.

INTRODUCTION TO PROGRAMMING THE 8086

Programming Languages

Now that you have an overview of the 8086 CPU, it is time to start thinking about how it is programmed. To run a program, a microcomputer must have the program stored in binary form in successive memory locations, as shown in Figure 2-12. There are three language levels that can be used to write a program for a microcomputer.

MACHINE LANGUAGE

You can write programs as simply a sequence of the binary codes for the instructions you want the microcomputer to execute. The three-instruction program in Figure 2-6*b* is an example. This binary form of the program is referred to as *machine language* because it is the form required by the machine. However, it is difficult, if not impossible, for a programmer to memorize the thousands of binary instruction codes for a CPU such as the 8086. Also, it is very easy for an error to occur when working with long series of 1's and 0's. Using hexadecimal representation for the binary codes might help some, but there are still thousands of instruction codes to cope with.

ASSEMBLY LANGUAGE

To make programming easier, many programmers write programs in *assembly language*. They then translate the assembly language program to machine language so that it can be loaded into memory and run. Assembly language uses two-, three-, or four-letter *mnemonics* to represent each instruction type. A mnemonic is just a device to help you remember something. The letters in an assembly language mnemonic are usually initials or a shortened form of the English word(s) for the operation performed by the instruction. For example, the mnemonic for subtract is SUB, the mnemonic for Exclusive OR is XOR, and the mnemonic for the instruction to copy data from one location to another is MOV.

Assembly language statements are usually written in a standard form that has four *fields*, as shown in Figure 2-12. The first field in an assembly language statement is the *label field*. A *label* is a symbol or group of symbols used to represent an address which is not specifically known at the time the statement is written. Labels are usually followed by a colon. Labels are not required in a statement, they are just inserted where they are needed. We will show later many uses of labels.

The *opcode field* of the instruction contains the mnemonic for the instruction to be performed. Instruction mnemonics are sometimes called *operation codes*, or *opcodes*. The ADD mnemonic in the example statement in Figure 2-12 indicates that we want the instruction to do an addition.

The *operand field* of the statement contains the data, the memory address, the port address, or the name of the register on which the instruction is to be performed. *Operand* is just another name for the data item(s) acted on by an instruction. In the example instruction in Figure 2-12, there are two operands, AL and 07H, specified in the operand field. AL represents the AL register, and 07H represents the number 07H. This assembly language statement thus says, "Add the number 07H to the contents of the AL register." By Intel convention, the result of the addition will be put in the register or the memory location specified *before* the comma in the operand field. For the example statement in Figure 2-12, then, the result will be left in the AL register. As another example, the assembly language statement ADD BH, AL, when converted to machine language and run, will add the contents of the AL register to the contents of the BH register. The results will be left in the BH register.

The final field in an assembly language statement such as that in Figure 2-12 is the *comment field*, which starts with a semicolon. Comments do not become part of the machine language program, but they are very important. You write *comments* in a program to remind you of the function that an instruction or group of instructions performs in the program.

To summarize why assembly language is easier to use than machine language, let's look a little more closely at the assembly language ADD statement. The general format of the 8086 ADD instruction is

ADD destination, source

The *source* can be a number written in the instruction, the contents of a specified register, or the contents of a memory location. The *destination* can be a specified register or a specified memory location. However, the

LABEL FIELD	OP CODE FIELD	OPERAND FIELD	COMMENT FIELD
NEXT:	ADD	AL, 07H	; ADD CORRECTION FACTOR

FIGURE 2-12 Assembly language program statement format.

source and the destination in an instruction cannot both be memory locations.

A later section on 8086 addressing modes will show all the ways in which the source of an operand and the destination of the result can be specified. The point here is that the single mnemonic ADD, together with a specified source and a specified destination, can represent a great many 8086 instructions in an easily understandable form.

The question that may occur to you at this point is, "If I write a program in assembly language, how do I get it translated into machine language which can be loaded into the microcomputer and executed?" There are two answers to this question. The first method of doing the translation is to work out the binary code for each instruction a bit at a time using the templates given in the manufacturer's data books. We will show you how to do this in the next chapter, but it is a tedious and error-prone task. The second method of doing the translation is with an *assembler.* An assembler is a program which can be run on a personal computer or *microcomputer development system.* It reads the file of assembly language instructions you write and generates the correct binary code for each. For developing all but the simplest assembly language programs, an assembler and other program development tools are essential. We will introduce you to these program development tools in the next chapter and describe their use throughout the rest of this book.

HIGH-LEVEL LANGUAGES

Another way of writing a program for a microcomputer is with a *high-level language,* such as BASIC, Pascal, or C. These languages use program statements which are even more English-like than those of assembly language. Each high-level statement may represent many machine code instructions. An *interpreter program* or a *compiler program* is used to translate higher-level language statements to machine codes which can be loaded into memory and executed. Programs can usually be written faster in high-level languages than in assembly language because the high-level language works with bigger building blocks. However, programs written in a high-level language and interpreted or compiled almost always execute more slowly and require more memory than the same programs written in assembly language. Programs that involve a lot of hardware control, such as robots and factory control systems, or programs that must run as quickly as possible are usually best written in assembly language. Complex data processing programs that manipulate massive amounts of data, such as insurance company records, are usually best written in a high-level language. The decision concerning which language to use has recently been made more difficult by the fact that current assemblers allow the use of many high-level language features, and the fact that some current high-level languages provide assembly language features.

OUR CHOICE

For most of this book we work very closely with hardware, so assembly language is the best choice. In later chapters, however, we do show you how to write programs which contain modules written in assembly language and modules written in the high-level language C. In the next chapter we introduce you to assembly language programming techniques. Before we go on to that, however, we will use a few simple 8086 instructions to show you more about accessing data in registers and memory locations.

How the 8086 Accesses Immediate and Register Data

In a previous discussion of the 8086 BIU, we described how the 8086 accesses code bytes using the contents of the CS and IP registers. We also described how the 8086 accesses the stack using the contents of the SS and SP registers. Before we can teach you assembly language programming techniques, we need to discuss some of the different ways in which an 8086 can access the data that it operates on. The different ways in which a processor can access data are referred to as its *addressing modes.* In assembly language statements, the addressing mode is indicated in the instruction. We will use the 8086 MOV instruction to illustrate some of the 8086 addressing modes.

The MOV instruction has the format

MOV destination, source

When executed, this instruction *copies* a word or a byte from the specified source location to the specified destination location. The source can be a number written directly in the instruction, a specified register, or a memory location specified in 1 of 24 different ways. The destination can be a specified register or a memory location specified in any 1 of 24 different ways. The source and the destination cannot both be memory locations in an instruction.

IMMEDIATE ADDRESSING MODE

Suppose that in a program you need to put the number 437BH in the CX register. The MOV CX, 437BH instruction can be used to do this. When it executes, this instruction will put the *immediate* hexadecimal number 437BH in the 16-bit CX register. This is referred to as *immediate addressing mode* because the number to be loaded into the CX register will be put in the two memory locations immediately following the code for the MOV instruction. This is similar to the way the port address was put in memory immediately after the code for the input instruction in the three-instruction program in Figure 2-6b.

A similar instruction, MOV CL, 48H, could be used to load the 8-bit immediate number 48H into the 8-bit CL register. You can also write instructions to load an 8-bit immediate number into an 8-bit memory location or to load a 16-bit number into two consecutive memory locations, but we are not yet ready to show you how to specify these.

REGISTER ADDRESSING MODE

Register addressing mode means that a register is the source of an operand for an instruction. The instruction

MOV CX, AX, for example, copies the contents of the 16-bit AX register into the 16-bit CX register. Remember that the destination location is specified in the instruction before the comma, and the source is specified after the comma. Also note that the contents of AX are just *copied* to CX, not actually moved. In other words, the previous contents of CX are written over, but the contents of AX are not changed. For example, if CX contains 2A84H and AX contains 4971H before the MOV CX, AX instruction executes, then after the instruction executes, CX will contain 4971H and AX will still contain 4971H. You can MOV any 16-bit register to any 16-bit register, or you can MOV any 8-bit register to any 8-bit register. However, you cannot use an instruction such as MOV CX, AL because this is an attempt to copy a *byte-type* operand (AL) into a *word-type* destination (CX). The byte in AL would fit in CX, but the 8086 would not know which half of CX to put it in. If you try to write an instruction like this and you are using a good assembler, the assembler will tell you that the instruction contains a *type error*. To copy the byte from AL to the high byte of CX, you can use the instruction MOV CH, AL. To copy the byte from AL to the low byte of CX, you can use the instruction MOV CL, AL.

Accessing Data in Memory

OVERVIEW OF MEMORY ADDRESSING MODES

The addressing modes described in the following sections are used to specify the location of an operand in memory. To access data in memory, the 8086 must also produce a 20-bit physical address. It does this by adding a 16-bit value called the *effective address* to a segment base address represented by the 16-bit number in one of the four segment registers. The effective address (EA) represents the *displacement* or *offset* of the desired operand from the segment base. In most cases, any of the segment bases can be specified, but the data segment is the one most often used. Figure 2-13a shows in graphic form how the EA is added to the data segment base to point to an operand in memory. Figure 2-13b shows how the 20-bit physical address is generated by the BIU. The starting address for the data segment in Figure 2-13b is 20000H, so the data segment register will contain 2000H. The BIU adds the effective address, 437AH, to the data segment base address of 20000H to produce the physical address sent out to memory. The 20-bit physical address sent out to memory by the BIU will then be 2437AH. The physical address can be represented either as a single number 2437AH or in the segment base:offset form as 2000:437AH.

The execution unit calculates the effective address for an operand using information you specify in the instruction. You can tell the EU to use a number in the instruction as the effective address, to use the contents of a specified register as the effective address, or to compute the effective address by adding a number in the instruction to the contents of one or two specified registers. The following section describes one way you can tell the execution unit to calculate an effective address. In later chapters we show other ways of specifying the effective address. Later we also show how the

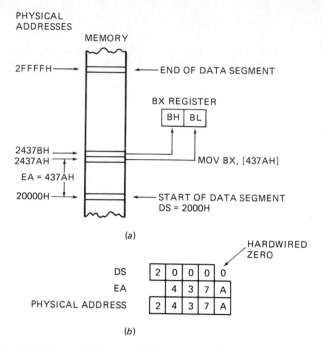

FIGURE 2-13 Addition of data segment register and effective address to produce the physical address of the data byte. (a) Diagram. (b) Computation.

addressing modes this provides are used to solve some common programming problems.

DIRECT ADDRESSING MODE

For the simplest memory addressing mode, the effective address is just a 16-bit number written directly in the instruction. The instruction MOV BL, [437AH] is an example. The square brackets around the 437AH are shorthand for "the contents of the memory location(s) at a displacement from the segment base of." When executed, this instruction will copy "the contents of the memory location at a displacement from the data segment base of " 437AH into the BL register, as shown by the rightmost arrow in Figure 2-13a. The BIU calculates the 20-bit physical memory address by adding the effective address 437AH to the data segment base, as shown in Figure 2-13b. This addressing mode is called *direct* because the displacement of the operand from the segment base is specified directly in the instruction. The displacement in the instruction will be added to the data segment base in DS unless you tell the BIU to add it to some other segment base. Later we will show you how to do this.

Another example of the direct addressing mode is the instruction MOV BX, [437AH]. When executed, this instruction copies a 16-bit word from memory into the BX register. Since each memory address of the 8086 represents a byte of storage, the word must come from two memory locations. The byte at a displacement of 437AH from the data segment base will be copied into BL, as shown by the right arrow in Figure 2-13a. The contents of the next higher address, displacement 437BH, will be copied into the BH register, as shown by the left arrow in Figure 2-13a. From the instruction coding, the 8086 will automatically determine the number of bytes that it must access in memory.

An important point here is that an 8086 always stores the low byte of a word in the lower of the two addresses and stores the high byte of a word in the higher address. To stick this in your mind, remember:

Low byte–low address, high byte–high address

The previous two examples showed how the direct addressing mode can be used to specify the source of an operand. Direct addressing can also be used to specify the destination of an operand in memory. The instruction MOV [437AH], BX, for example, will copy the contents of the BX register to two memory locations in the data segment. The contents of BL will be copied to the memory location at a displacement of 437AH. The contents of BH will be copied to the memory location at a displacement of 437BH. This operation is represented by simply reversing the direction of the arrows in Figure 2-13a.

NOTE: When you are *hand-coding* programs using direct addressing of the form shown above, make sure to put in the square brackets to remind you how to code the instruction. If you leave the brackets out of an instruction such as MOV BX, [437AH], you will code it as if it were the instruction MOV BX, 437AH. This second instruction will load the immediate number 437AH into BX, rather than loading a word from memory at a displacement of 437AH into BX. Also note that if you are writing an instruction using direct addressing such as this for an assembler, you must write the instruction in the form MOV BL, DS:BYTE PTR [437AH] to give the assembler all the information it needs. As we will show you in the next chapter, when you are using an assembler, you usually use a name to represent the direct address rather than the actual numerical value.

A FEW WORDS ABOUT SEGMENTATION

At this point you may be wondering why Intel designed the 8086 family devices to access memory using the segment:offset approach rather than accessing memory directly with 20-bit addresses. The segment:offset scheme requires only a 16-bit number to represent the base address for a segment, and only a 16-bit offset to access any location in a segment. This means that the 8086 has to manipulate and store only 16-bit quantities instead of 20-bit quantities. This makes for an easier interface with 8- and 16-bit-wide memory boards and with the 16-bit registers in the 8086.

The second reason for segmentation has to do with the type of microcomputer in which an 8086-family CPU is likely to be used. A previous section of this chapter described briefly the operation of a timesharing microcomputer system. In a timesharing system, several users share a CPU. The CPU works on one user's program for perhaps 20 ms, then works on the next user's program for 20 ms. After working 20 ms for each of the other users, the CPU comes back to the first user's program again. Each time the CPU switches from one user's program to the next, it must access a new section of code and new sections of data. Segmentation makes this switching quite easy. Each user's program can be assigned a separate set of logical segments for its code and data. The user's program will contain offsets or displacements from these segment bases. To change from one user's program to a second user's program, all that the CPU has to do is to reload the four segment registers with the segment base addresses assigned to the second user's program. In other words, segmentation makes it easy to keep users' programs and data separate from one another, and segmentation makes it easy to switch from one user's program to another user's program. In Chapter 15 we tell you much more about the use of segmentation in multiuser systems.

CHECKLIST OF IMPORTANT TERMS AND CONCEPTS IN THIS CHAPTER

If you do not remember any of the terms or concepts in the following list, use the index to find them in the chapter.

Microcomputer, microprocessor

Hardware, software, firmware

Timesharing computer system

Multitasking computer system

Distributed processing system

Multiprocessing

CPU

Memory, RAM, ROM

I/O ports

Address, data, and control buses

Control bus signals

ALU

Segmentation

Bus interface unit (BIU)
    Instruction byte queue, pipelining,
    ES, CS, SS, DS registers, IP register

Execution unit (EU)
    AX, BX, CX, DX registers, flag register,
    ALU, SP, BP, SI, DI registers

Machine language, assembly language, high-level language

Mnemonic, opcode, operand, label, comment

Assembler, compiler

Immediate address mode, register address mode, direct address mode

Effective address

REVIEW QUESTIONS AND PROBLEMS

1. Describe the main advantages of a distributed processing computer system over a simple time-sharing system.

2. Describe the sequence of signals that occurs on the address bus, the control bus, and the data bus when a simple microcomputer fetches an instruction.

3. What determines whether a microprocessor is considered an 8-bit, a 16-bit, or a 32-bit device?

4. a. How many address lines does an 8086 have?
    b. How many memory addresses does this number of address lines allow the 8086 to access directly?
    c. At any given time, the 8086 works with four segments in this address space. How many bytes are contained in each segment?

5. What is the main difference between the 8086 and the 8088?

6. a. Describe the function of the 8086 queue.
    b. How does the queue speed up processing?

7. a. If the code segment for an 8086 program starts at address 70400H, what number will be in the CS register?
    b. Assuming this same code segment base, what physical address will a code byte be fetched from if the instruction pointer contains 539CH?

8. What physical address is represented by:
    a. 4370:561EH
    b. 7A32:0028H

9. What is the advantage of using a CPU register for temporary data storage over using a memory location?

10. If the stack segment register contains 3000H and the stack pointer register contains 8434H, what is the physical address of the top of the stack?

11. a. What is the advantage of using assembly language instead of writing a program directly in machine language?
    b. Describe the operation an 8086 will perform when it executes ADD AX, BX.

12. What types of programs are usually written in assembly language?

13. Describe the operation that an 8086 will perform when it executes each of the following instructions:
    a. MOV BX, 03FFH
    b. MOV AL, 0DBH
    c. MOV DH, CL
    d. MOV BX, AX

14. Write the 8086 assembly language statement which will perform the following operations:
    a. Load the number 7986H into the BP register.
    b. Copy the BP register contents to the SP register.
    c. Copy the contents of the AX register to the DS register.
    d. Load the number F3H into the AL register.

15. If the 8086 execution unit calculates an effective address of 14A3H and DS contains 7000H, what physical address will the BIU produce?

16. If the data segment register (DS) contains 4000H, what physical address will the instruction MOV AL, [234BH] read?

17. If the 8086 data segment register contains 7000H, write the instruction that will copy the contents of DL to address 74B2CH.

18. Describe the difference between the instructions MOV AX, 2437H and MOV AX, [2437H].

## CHAPTER 3

8086 Family Assembly Language Programming — Introduction

The last chapter showed you the format for assembly language instructions and introduced you to a few 8086 instructions. Developing a program, however, requires more than just writing down a series of instructions. When you want to build a house, it is a good idea to first develop a complete set of plans for the house. From the plans you can see whether the house has the rooms you need, whether the rooms are efficiently placed, and whether the house is structured so that you can easily add on to it if you have more kids. You have probably seen examples of what happens when someone attempts to build a house by just putting pieces together without a plan.

Likewise, when you write a computer program, it is a good idea to start by developing a detailed plan or outline for the entire program. A good outline helps you to break down a large and seemingly overwhelming programming job into small . modules which can easily be written, tested, and debugged. The more time you spend organizing your programs, the less time it will take you to write and debug them. You should *never* start writing an assembly language program by just writing down instructions! In this chapter we show you how to develop assembly language programs in a systematic way.

OBJECTIVES

At the conclusion of this chapter, you should be able to:

1. Write a task list, flowchart, or pseudocode for a simple programming problem.

2. Write, code or assemble, and run a very simple assembly language program.

3. Describe the use of program development tools such as editors, assemblers, linkers, locators, debuggers, and emulators.

4. Properly document assembly language programs.

PROGRAM DEVELOPMENT STEPS

Defining the Problem

The first step in writing a program is to think very carefully about the problem that you want the program

to solve. In other words, ask yourself many times, "What do I really want this program to do?" If you don't do this, you may write a program that works great but does not do what you need it to do. As you think about the problem, it is a good idea to write down exactly what you want the program to do and the order in which you want the program to do it. At this point you do not write down program statements, you just write the operations you want in general terms. An example for a simple programming problem might be

1. Read temperature from sensor.

2. Add correction factor of $+7$.

3. Save result in a memory location.

For a program as simple as this, the three actions desired are very close to the eventual assembly language statements. For more complex problems, however, we develop a more extensive outline before writing the assembly language statements. The next section shows you some of the common ways of representing program operations in a program outline.

Representing Program Operations

The formula or sequence of operations used to solve a programming problem is often called the *algorithm* of the program. The following sections show you two common ways of representing the algorithm for a program or program segment.

FLOWCHARTS

If you have done any previous programming in BASIC or in FORTRAN, you are probably familiar with *flowcharts.* Flowcharts use graphic shapes to represent different types of program operations. The specific operation desired is written in the graphic symbol. Figure 3-1, p. 38, shows some of the common flowchart symbols. Plastic templates are available to help you draw these symbols if you decide to use them for your programs.

Figure 3-2, p. 38, shows a flowchart for a program to read in 24 data samples from a temperature sensor at 1-hour intervals, add 7 to each, and store each result in a memory location. A racetrack- or circular-shaped symbol labeled START is used to indicate the *beginning*

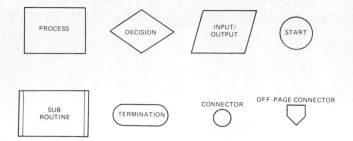

FIGURE 3-1 Flowchart symbols.

of the program. A parallelogram is used to represent an *input* or an *output* operation. In the example, we use it to indicate reading data from the temperature sensor. A rectangular box symbol is used to represent *simple operations* other than input and output operations. The box containing "add 7" in Figure 3-2 is an example.

A rectangular box with double lines at each end is often used to represent a *subroutine* or *procedure* that will be written separately from the main program. When a set of operations must be done several times during a program, it is usually more efficient to write the series of operations once as a separate subprogram, then just "call" this subprogram each time it is needed. For example, suppose that there are several places in a program where you need to compute the square root of a number. Instead of writing the series of instructions for computing a square root each time you need it in

the program, you can write the instruction sequence once as a separate procedure and put it in memory after the main program. A special instruction allows you to call this procedure each time you need to compute a square root. Another special instruction at the end of the procedure program returns execution to the main program. In the flowchart in Figure 3-2, we use the double-ended box to indicate that the "wait 1 hour" operation will be programmed as a procedure. Incidentally, the terms *subprogram*, *subroutine*, and *procedure* all have the same meaning. Chapter 5 shows how procedures are written and used.

A diamond-shaped box is used in flowcharts to represent a *decision* point or crossroad. Usually it indicates that some condition is to be checked at this point in the program. If the condition is found to be *true*, one set of actions is to be done; if the condition is found to be *false*, another set of actions is to be done. In the example flowchart in Figure 3-2, the condition to be checked is whether 24 samples have been read in and processed. If 24 samples have not been read in and processed, the arrow labeled NO in the flowchart indicates that we want the computer to jump back and execute the read, add, store, and wait steps again. If 24 samples have been read in, the arrow labeled YES in the flowchart of Figure 3-2 indicates that all the desired operations have been done. The racetrack-shaped symbol at the bottom of the flowchart indicates the *end* of the program.

The two additional flowchart symbols in Figure 3-1 are *connectors*. If a flowchart column gets to the bottom of the paper, but not all the program has been represented, you can put a small circle with a letter in it at the bottom of the column. You then start the next column at the top of the same paper with a small circle containing the same letter. If you need to continue a flowchart to another page, you can end the flowchart on the first page with the five-sided off-page connector symbol containing a letter or number. You then start the flowchart on the next page with an off-page connector symbol containing the same letter or number.

For simple programs and program sections, flowcharts are a graphic way of showing the operational flow of the program. We will show flowcharts for many of the program examples throughout this book. Flowcharts, however, have several disadvantages. First, you can't write much information in the little boxes. Second, flowcharts do not present information in a very compact form. For more complex problems, flowcharts tend to spread out over many pages. They are very hard to follow back and forth between pages. Third, and most important, with flowcharts the overall structure of the program tends to get lost in the details. The following section describes a more clearly *structured* and *compact* method of representing the algorithm of a program or program segment.

STRUCTURED PROGRAMMING AND PSEUDOCODE OVERVIEW

In the early days of computers, a single brilliant person might write even a large program single-handedly. The main concerns in this case were, "Does the program work?" and "What do we do if this person leaves the

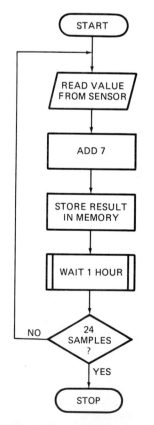

FIGURE 3-2 Flowchart for program to read in 24 data samples from a port, correct each value, and store each in a memory location.

company?" As the number of computers increased and the complexity of the programs being written increased, large programming jobs were usually turned over to a team of programmers. In this case the compatibility of parts written by different programmers became an important concern. During the 1970s it became obvious to many professional programmers that in order for team programming to work, a systematic approach and standardized tools were absolutely necessary.

One suggested systematic approach is called *top-down design.* In this approach, a large programming problem is first divided into major *modules.* The top level of the outline shows the relationship and function of these modules. This top level then presents a one-page overview of the entire program. Each of the major modules is broken down into still smaller modules on following pages. The division is continued until the steps in each module are clearly understandable. Each programmer can then be assigned a module or set of modules to write for the program. Another advantage of this approach is that people who later want to learn about the program can start with the overview and work their way down to the level of detail they need. This approach is the same as drawing the complete plans for a house before starting to build it.

The opposite of top-down design is *bottom-up design.* In this approach, each programmer starts writing low-level modules and hopes that all the pieces will eventually fit together. When completed, the result should be similar to that produced by the top-down design. Most modern programming teams use a combination of the two techniques. They do the top-down design first, then build, test, and link modules starting from the smallest and working upward.

The development of standard programming methods was helped by the discovery that any desired program operation could be represented by three basic types of operation. The first type of operation is *sequence,* which means simply doing a series of actions. The second basic type of operation is *decision,* or *selection,* which means choosing between two alternative actions. The third basic type of operation is *repetition,* or *iteration,* which means repeating a series of actions until some condition is or is not present.

On the basis of this observation, the suggestion was made that programmers use a set of three to seven standard *structures* to represent all the operations in their programs. Actually, only three structures, SEQUENCE, IF-THEN-ELSE, and WHILE-DO, are required to represent any desired program action, but three or four more structures derived from these often make programs clearer. If you have previously written programs in a structured language such as Pascal, then these structures are probably already familiar to you. Figure 3-3, p. 40, uses flowchart symbols to represent the commonly used structures so that you can more easily visualize their operation. In actual program documentation, however, English-like statements called *pseudocode* are used rather than the space-consuming flowchart symbols. Figure 3-3 also shows the pseudocode format and an example for each structure.

Each structure has only *one entry point* and *one exit point.* As you will see later, this feature makes debugging

the final program much easier. The output of one structure is connected to the input of the next structure. Program execution then proceeds through a series of these structures.

Any structure can be used within another. An IF-THEN-ELSE structure, for example, can contain a sequence of statements. Any place that the term *statement(s)* appears in Figure 3-3, one of the other structures could be substituted for it. The term *statement(s)* can also represent a subprogram or procedure that is called to do a series of actions. Now, let's look more closely at these structures.

STANDARD PROGRAMMING STRUCTURES

The structure shown in Figure 3-3*a* is an example of a simple sequence. In this structure, the actions are simply written down in the desired order. An example is

Read temperature from sensor.

Add correction factor of +7.

Store corrected value in memory.

Figure 3-3*b* shows an IF-THEN-ELSE example of the decision operation. This structure is used to direct operation to one of two different actions based on some condition. An example is

IF temperature less than 70 degrees THEN
    Turn on heater
ELSE
    Turn off heater

The example says that if the temperature is below the thermostat setting, we want to turn the heater on. If the temperature is equal to or above the thermostat setting, we want to turn the heater off.

The IF-THEN structure shown in Figure 3-3*c* is the same as the IF-THEN-ELSE except that one of the paths contains no action. An example of this is

IF hungry THEN
    Get food

The assumption for this example is that if you are not hungry, you will just continue on with your next task.

To represent a situation in which you want to select one of several actions based on some condition, you can use a nested IF-THEN-ELSE structure such as that shown in Figure 3-3*d*. This everyday example describes the thinking a soup cook might go through. Note that in this example the last IF-THEN has no ELSE after it because all the possible days have been checked. You can, if you want, add the final ELSE to the IF-THEN-ELSE chain to send an error message if the data does not match any of the choices.

The CASE structure shown in Figure 3-3*e* is really just a compact way to represent a complex IF-THEN-ELSE structure. The choice of action is determined by testing some quantity. The cook or the computer checks the value of the variable called "day" and selects the

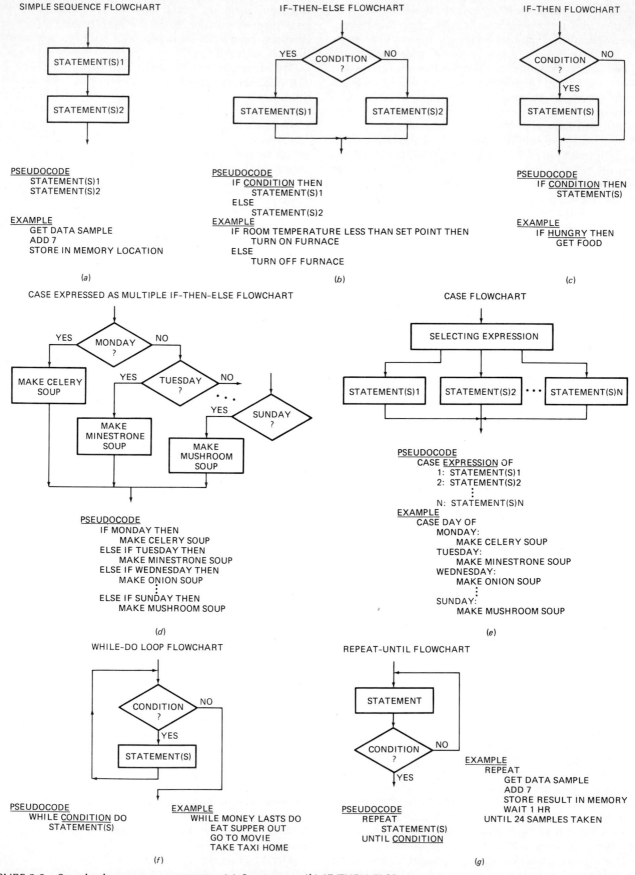

FIGURE 3-3 Standard program structures. (a) Sequence. (b) IF-THEN-ELSE.
(c) IF-THEN. (d) CASE expressed as nested IF-THEN-ELSE. (e) CASE. (f) WHILE-DO.
(g) REPEAT-UNTIL.

appropriate actions for that day. Each of the indicated actions, such as "Make celery soup," is itself a sequence of actions which could be represented by the structures we have described. Note that the CASE structure does not contain the final ELSE for an error.

The CASE form is more compact for documentation purposes, and some high-level languages such as Pascal allow you to implement it directly. However, the nested IF-THEN-ELSE structure gives you a much better idea of how you write an assembly language program section to choose between several alternative actions.

The WHILE-DO structure in Figure 3-3*f* is one form of repetition. It is used to indicate that you want to do some action or sequence of actions as long as some condition is present. This structure represents a *program loop*. The example in Figure 3-3*f* is

WHILE money lasts DO
   Eat supper out.
   Go to movie.
   Take a taxi home.

This example shows a sequence of actions you might do each evening until you ran out of money. Note that in this structure, the condition is checked *before* the action is done the first time. You certainly want to check how much money you have before eating out.

Another useful repetition structure is the REPEAT-UNTIL structure shown in Figure 3-3*g*. You use this structure to indicate that you want the program to repeat some action or series of actions until some condition is present. A good example of the use of this structure is the programming problem we used in the discussion of flowcharts. The example is

REPEAT
   Get data sample from sensor.
   Add correction of + 7.
   Store result in a memory location.
   Wait 1 hour.
UNTIL 24 samples taken.

Note that in a REPEAT-UNTIL structure, the action(s) is done once before the condition is checked. If you want the condition to be checked before any action is done, then you can write the algorithm with a WHILE-DO structure as follows:

WHILE NOT 24 samples DO
   Read data sample from temperature sensor.
   Add correction factor of + 7.
   Store result in memory location.
   Wait 1 hour.

Remember, a REPEAT-UNTIL structure indicates that the condition is first checked *after* the statement(s) is performed, so the action or series of actions will always be done at least once. If you don't want this to happen, then use the WHILE-DO, which indicates that the condition is checked *before* any action is taken. As we will show later, the structure you use makes a difference in the actual assembly language program you write to implement it.

The WHILE-DO and REPEAT-UNTIL structures contain a simple IF-THEN-ELSE decision operation. However, since this decision is an implied part of these two structures, we don't indicate the decision separately in them.

Another form of the repetition operation that you might see in high-level language programs is the FOR-DO loop. This structure has the form

FOR count = 1 TO n DO
   statement
   statement

This FOR-DO loop, as it is often called, simply repeats the sequence of actions n times, so for assembly language algorithms we usually implement this type of operation with a REPEAT-UNTIL structure.

Incidentally, if you compare the space required by the pseudocode representation for a program structure with the space required by the flowchart representation for the same structure, the space advantage of pseudocode should be obvious.

Throughout the rest of this book, we show you how to use these structures to represent program actions and how to implement these structures in assembly language.

SUMMARY OF PROGRAM STRUCTURE REPRESENTATION FORMS

Writing a successful program does not consist of just writing down a series of instructions. You must first think carefully about what you want the program to do and how you want the program to do it. Then you must represent the structure of the program in some way that is very clear both to you and to anyone else who might have to work on the program.

One way of representing program operations is with flowcharts. Flowcharts are a very graphic representation, and they are useful for short program segments, especially those that deal directly with hardware. However, flowcharts use a great deal of space. Consequently, the flowchart for even a moderately complex program may take up several pages. It often becomes difficult to follow program flow back and forth between pages. Also, since there are no agreed-upon structures, a poor programmer can write a flowchart which jumps all over the place and is even more difficult to follow. The term "logical spaghetti" comes to mind here.

A second way of representing the operations you want in a program is with a top-down design approach and standard program structures. The overall program problem is first broken down into major functional modules. Each of these modules is broken down into smaller and smaller modules until the steps in each module are obvious. The algorithms for the whole program and for each module are expressed with a standard structure. Only three basic structures, SEQUENCE, IF-THEN-ELSE, and WHILE-DO, are needed to represent any needed program action or series of actions. However, other useful structures such as IF-THEN, REPEAT-UNTIL, FOR-DO, and CASE can be derived from these basic three. A structure can contain another structure of the same type or one of the other types. Each structure has only one entry point and one exit point. These programming structures may seem restrictive, but using them usually results in algorithms which are easy to follow. Also, as we will show you soon, if you write the algorithm for a program carefully with these standard structures, it is relatively easy to translate the algorithm to the equivalent assembly language instructions.

Finding the Right Instruction

After you get the structure of a program worked out and written down, the next step is to determine the instruction statements required to do each part of the program. Since the examples in this book are based on the 8086 family of microprocessors, now is a good time to give you an overview of the instructions the 8086 has for you to use. First, however, is a hint about how to approach these instructions.

You do not usually learn a new language by memorizing an entire dictionary of the language. A better way is to learn a few useful words and practice putting these words together in simple sentences. You can then learn more words as you need them to express more complex thoughts. Likewise, you should not try to memorize all the instructions for a microprocessor at once.

For future reference, Chapter 6 contains a dictionary of all the 8086 instructions with detailed descriptions and examples of each. As an introduction, however, the few pages here contain a list of all the 8086 instructions with a short explanation of each. Skim through the list and pick out a dozen or so instructions that seem useful and understandable. As a start, look for move, input, output, logical, and arithmetic instructions. Then look through the list again to see if you can find the instructions that you might use to do the "read temperature sensor value from a port, add +7, and store result in memory" example program.

You can use Chapter 6 as a reference as you write programs. Here we simply list the 8086 instructions in *functional* groups with single-sentence descriptions so that you can see the types of instructions that are available to you. As you read through this section, do not expect to understand all the instructions. When you start writing programs, you will probably use this section to determine the type of instruction and Chapter 6 to get the instruction details as you need them. After you have written a few programs, you will remember most of the basic instruction types and will be able to simply look up an instruction in Chapter 6 to get any additional details you need. Chapter 4 shows you in detail how to use the move, arithmetic, logical, jump, and string instructions. Chapter 5 shows how to use the call instructions and the stack.

DATA TRANSFER INSTRUCTIONS

General-purpose byte or word transfer instructions:

MNEMONIC	DESCRIPTION
MOV	Copy byte or word from specified source to specified destination.
PUSH	Copy specified word to top of stack.
POP	Copy word from top of stack to specified location.
PUSHA	(80186/80188 only) Copy all registers to stack.
POPA	(80186/80188 only) Copy words from stack to all registers.
XCHG	Exchange bytes or exchange words.
XLAT	Translate a byte in AL using a table in memory.

Simple input and output port transfer instructions:

IN	Copy a byte or word from specified port to accumulator.
OUT	Copy a byte or word from accumulator to specified port.

Special address transfer instructions:

LEA	Load effective address of operand into specified register.
LDS	Load DS register and other specified register from memory.
LES	Load ES register and other specified register from memory.

Flag transfer instructions:

LAHF	Load (copy to) AH with the low byte of the flag register.
SAHF	Store (copy) AH register to low byte of flag register.
PUSHF	Copy flag register to top of stack.
POPF	Copy word at top of stack to flag register.

ARITHMETIC INSTRUCTIONS

Addition instructions:

ADD	Add specified byte to byte or specified word to word.
ADC	Add byte + byte + carry flag or word + word + carry flag.
INC	Increment specified byte or specified word by 1.
AAA	ASCII adjust after addition.
DAA	Decimal (BCD) adjust after addition.

Subtraction instructions:

SUB	Subtract byte from byte or word from word.
SBB	Subtract byte and carry flag from byte or word and carry flag from word.
DEC	Decrement specified byte or specified word by 1.

NEG	Negate — invert each bit of a specified byte or word and add 1 (form 2's complement).
CMP	Compare two specified bytes or two specified words.
AAS	ASCII adjust after subtraction.
DAS	Decimal (BCD) adjust after subtraction.

Multiplication instructions:

MUL	Multiply unsigned byte by byte or unsigned word by word.
IMUL	Multiply signed byte by byte or signed word by word.
AAM	ASCII adjust after multiplication.

Division instructions:

DIV	Divide unsigned word by byte or unsigned double word by word.
IDIV	Divide signed word by byte or signed double word by word.
AAD	ASCII adjust before division.
CBW	Fill upper byte of word with copies of sign bit of lower byte.
CWD	Fill upper word of double word with sign bit of lower word.

BIT MANIPULATION INSTRUCTIONS

Logical instructions:

NOT	Invert each bit of a byte or word.
AND	AND each bit in a byte or word with the corresponding bit in another byte or word.
OR	OR each bit in a byte or word with the corresponding bit in another byte or word.
XOR	Exclusive OR each bit in a byte or word with the corresponding bit in another byte or word.
TEST	AND operands to update flags, but don't change operands.

Shift instructions:

SHL/SAL	Shift bits of word or byte left, put zero(s) in LSB(s).
SHR	Shift bits of word or byte right, put zero(s) in MSB(s).
SAR	Shift bits of word or byte right, copy old MSB into new MSB.

Rotate instructions:

ROL	Rotate bits of byte or word left, MSB to LSB and to CF.
ROR	Rotate bits of byte or word right, LSB to MSB and to CF.
RCL	Rotate bits of byte or word left, MSB to CF and CF to LSB.
RCR	Rotate bits of byte or word right, LSB to CF and CF to MSB.

STRING INSTRUCTIONS

A *string* is a series of bytes or a series of words in sequential memory locations. A string often consists of ASCII character codes. In the list, a "/" is used to separate different mnemonics for the same instruction. Use the mnemonic which most clearly describes the function of the instruction in a specific application. A "B" in a mnemonic is used to specifically indicate that a string of bytes is to be acted upon. A "W" in the mnemonic is used to indicate that a string of words is to be acted upon.

REP	An instruction prefix. Repeat following instruction until CX = 0.
REPE/REPZ	An instruction prefix. Repeat instruction until CX = 0 or zero flag ZF ≠ 1.
REPNE/REPNZ	An instruction prefix. Repeat until CX = 0 or ZF = 1.
MOVS/MOVSB/MOVSW	Move byte or word from one string to another.
COMPS/COMPSB/COMPSW	Compare two string bytes or two string words.
INS/INSB/INSW	(80186/80188) Input string byte or word from port.
OUTS/OUTSB/OUTSW	(80186/80188) Output string byte or word to port.
SCAS/SCASB/SCASW	Scan a string. Compare a string byte with a byte in AL or a string word with a word in AX.
LODS/LODSB/LODSW	Load string byte into AL or string word into AX.
STOS/STOSB/STOSW	Store byte from AL or word from AX into string.

PROGRAM EXECUTION TRANSFER INSTRUCTIONS

These instructions are used to tell the 8086 to start fetching instructions from some new address, rather than continuing in sequence.

Unconditional transfer instructions:

CALL	Call a procedure (subprogram), save return address on stack.
RET	Return from procedure to calling program.
JMP	Go to specified address to get next instruction.

Conditional transfer instructions:

A "/" is used to separate two mnemonics which represent the same instruction. Use the mnemonic which most clearly describes the decision condition in a specific program. These instructions are often used after a compare instruction. The terms *below* and *above* refer to unsigned binary numbers. *Above* means larger in magnitude. The terms *greater than* or *less than* refer to signed binary numbers. *Greater than* means more positive.

JA/JNBE	Jump if above/Jump if not below or equal.
JAE/JNB	Jump if above or equal/Jump if not below.
JB/JNAE	Jump if below/Jump if not above or equal.
JBE/JNA	Jump if below or equal/Jump if not above.
JC	Jump if carry flag CF = 1.
JE/JZ	Jump if equal/Jump if zero flag ZF = 1.
JG/JNLE	Jump if greater/Jump if not less than or equal.
JGE/JNL	Jump if greater than or equal/Jump if not less than.
JL/JNGE	Jump if less than/Jump if not greater than or equal.
JLE/JNG	Jump if less than or equal/Jump if not greater than.
JNC	Jump if no carry (CF = 0).
JNE/JNZ	Jump if not equal/Jump if not zero (ZF = 0).
JNO	Jump if no overflow (overflow flag OF = 0).
JNP/JPO	Jump if not parity/Jump if parity odd (PF = 0).
JNS	Jump if not sign (sign flag SF = 0).
JO	Jump if overflow flag OF = 1.
JP/JPE	Jump if parity/Jump if parity even (PF = 1).
JS	Jump if sign (SF = 1).

Iteration control instructions:

These instructions can be used to execute a series of instructions some number of times. Here mnemonics separated by a "/" represent the same instruction. Use the one that best fits the specific application.

LOOP	Loop through a sequence of instructions until CX = 0.
LOOPE/LOOPZ	Loop through a sequence of instructions while ZF = 1 and CX ≠ 0.
LOOPNE/LOOPNZ	Loop through a sequence of instructions while ZF = 0 and CX ≠ 0.
JCXZ	Jump to specified address if CX = 0.

If you aren't tired of instructions, continue skimming through the rest of the list. Don't worry if the explanation is not clear to you because we will explain these instructions in detail in later chapters.

Interrupt instructions:

INT	Interrupt program execution, call service procedure.
INTO	Interrupt program execution if OF = 1.
IRET	Return from interrupt service procedure to main program.

High-level language interface instructions:

ENTER	(80186/80188 only) Enter procedure.
LEAVE	(80186/80188 only) Leave procedure.
BOUND	(80186/80188 only) Check if effective address within specified array bounds.

PROCESSOR CONTROL INSTRUCTIONS

Flag set/clear instructions:

STC	Set carry flag CF to 1.
CLC	Clear carry flag CF to 0.
CMC	Complement the state of the carry flag CF.
STD	Set direction flag DF to 1 (decrement string pointers).
CLD	Clear direction flag DF to 0.
STI	Set interrupt enable flag to 1 (enable INTR input).
CLI	Clear interrupt enable flag to 0 (disable INTR input).

External hardware synchronization instructions:

HLT	Halt (do nothing) until interrupt or reset.
WAIT	Wait (do nothing) until signal on the TEST pin is low.
ESC	Escape to external coprocessor such as 8087 or 8089.

LOCK
An instruction prefix. Prevents another processor from taking the bus while the adjacent instruction executes.

No operation instruction:

NOP
No action except fetch and decode.

Now that you have skimmed through an overview of the 8086 instruction set, let's see whether you found the instructions needed to implement the "read sensor, add +7, and store result in memory" example program. The IN instruction can be used to read the temperature value from an A/D converter connected to a port. The ADD instruction can be used to add the correction factor of +7 to the value read in. Finally, the MOV instruction can be used to copy the result of the addtion to a memory location. A major point here is that breaking down the programming problem into a sequence of steps makes it easy to find the instruction or small group of instructions that will perform each step. The next section shows you how to write the actual program using the 8086 instructions.

Writing a Program

INITIALIZATION INSTRUCTIONS

After finding the instructions you need to do the main part of your program, there are a few additional instructions that you need to determine before you actually write your program. The purpose of these additional instructions is to *initialize* various parts of the system, such as segment registers, flags, and programmable port devices. Segment registers, for example, must be loaded with the upper 16 bits of the address in memory where you want the segment to begin. For our "read temperature sensor, add +7, and store result in memory" example program, the only part we need to initialize is the data segment register. The data segment register must be initialized so that we can copy the result of the addition to a location in memory. If, for example, we want to store data in memory starting at address 00100H, then we want the data segment register to contain the upper 16 bits of this address, 0010H. The 8086 does not have an instruction to move a number directly into a segment register. Therefore, we move the desired number into one of the 16-bit general-purpose registers, then copy it to the desired segment register. Two MOV instructions will do this.

If you are using the stack in your program, then you must include instructions to load the stack segment register and an instruction to load the stack pointer register with the offset of the top of the stack. Most microcomputer systems contain several programmable peripheral devices, such as ports, timers, and controllers. You must include instructions which send control words to these devices to tell them the function you want them to perform. Also, you usually want to include instructions which set or clear the control flags, such as the interrupt enable flag and the direction flag.

The best way to approach the initialization task is to make a checklist of all the registers, programmable devices, and flags in the system you are working on. Then you can mark the ones you need for a specific program and determine the instructions needed to initialize each part. An initialization list for an 8086-based system, such as the SDK-86 prototyping board, might look like the following.

INITIALIZATION LIST

Data segment register DS

Stack segment register SS

Extra segment register ES

Stack pointer register SP

8255 programmable parallel port

8259A priority interrupt controller

8254 programmable counter

8251A programmable serial port

Initialize data variables

Set interrupt enable flag

As you can see, the list can become quite lengthy even though we have not included all the devices a system might commonly have. Note that initializing the code segment register CS is absent from this list. The code segment register is loaded with the correct starting value by the system command you use to run the program. Now let's see how you put all these parts together to make a program.

A STANDARD PROGRAM FORMAT

In this section we show you how to format your programs if you are going to construct the machine codes for each instruction by *hand*. A later section of this chapter will show you the additional parts you need to add to the program if you are going to use a computer program called an *assembler* to produce the binary codes for the instructions.

To help you write your programs in the correct format, *assembly language coding sheets* such as that shown in Figure 3-4 are available. The ADDRESS column is used for the address or the offset of a code byte or data byte. The actual code bytes or data bytes are put in the DATA/CODE column. A *label* is a name which represents an address referred to in a jump or call instruction; labels are put in the LABELS column. A label is followed by a colon (:) if it is used by a jump or call instruction in the same code segment. The MNEM column contains the opcode mnemonics for the instructions. The OPERAND(S) column contains the registers, memory locations, or data acted upon by the instructions. A COMMENTS column gives you space to describe the function of the instruction for future reference.

Figure 3-4, p. 46, shows how instructions for the "read temperature, add +7, store result in memory" program can be written in sequence on a coding sheet. We will discuss here the operation of these instructions

PROGRAM TITLE   READ TEMPERATURE & CORRECT   DATE: 1/1/XX

ABSTRACT: This program reads in a temperature value from a sensor connected to port 05H, adds a correction
                             factor of +7 to the value read in, and then stores the result in a reserved memory location.
PROCEDURES: None called.
REGISTERS USED: Ax
FLAGS AFFECTED: All conditional
PORTS: Uses 05 as input port
MEMORY: 00100H-DATA; 00200H-0020CH, CODE

ADDRESS	DATA or CODE	LABELS	MNEM.	OPERAND(S)	COMMENTS
00100	XX				Reserve memory location to store
00101					result. This location will be loaded
00102					with a data byte as read in
00103					& corrected by the program.
00104					XX means "don't care" about
00105					contents of location.
00106					
00107					
00108					
00109					
0010A					
0010B					
0010C					
0010D					
0010E					Code starts here
0010F					Note break in address
200	B8		MOV	AX, 0010H	Initialize DS to point to start of
01	10				memory set aside for storing data
02	00				
03	8E		MOV	DS, AX	
04	D8				
05	E4		IN	AL, 05H	Read temperature from
06	05				port 05H
07	04		ADD	AL, 07H	Add correction factor
08	07				of +07
09	A2		MOV	[0000], AL	Store result in reserved
0A	00				memory
0B	00				
0C	CC		INT	3	Stop, wait for command
0D					from user
0E					
0F					

FIGURE 3-4 Assembly language program on standard coding form.

to the extent needed. If you want more information, detailed descriptions of the *syntax* (assembly language grammar) and operation of each of these instructions can be found in Chapter 6.

The first line at the top of the coding form in Figure 3-4 does not represent an instruction. It simply indicates that we want to set aside a memory location to store the result. This location must be in available RAM so that we can write to it. Address 00100H is an available RAM location on an SDK-86 prototyping board, so we chose it for this example. Next, we decide where in memory we want to start putting the code bytes for the instructions of the program. Again, on an SDK-86 prototyping board, address 00200H and above is available RAM, so we chose to start the program at address 00200H.

The first operation we want to do in the program is to initialize the data segment register. As discussed previously, two MOV instructions are used to do this. The MOV AX, 0010H instruction, when executed, will load the upper 16 bits of the address we chose for data storage into the AX register. The MOV DS, AX instruction will copy this number from the AX register to the data segment register. Now we get to the instructions that do the input, add, and store operations. The IN AL, 05H instruction will copy a data byte from the port 05H to the AL register. The ADD AL, 07 instruction will add 07H to the AL register and leave the result in the AL register. The MOV [0000], AL instruction will copy the byte in AL to a memory location at a displacement of 0000H from the data segment base. In other words, AL will be copied to a physical address computed by adding 0000 to the segment base address represented by the 0010H in the DS register. The result of this addition is a physical address of 00100H, so the result in AL will be copied to physical address 00100H in memory. This is an example of the direct addressing mode described near the end of the previous chapter.

The INT 3 instruction at the end of the program functions as a *breakpoint*. When the 8086 on an SDK-86 board executes this instruction, it will cause the 8086 to stop executing the instructions of your program and return control to the *monitor* or *system program.* You can then use *system commands* to look at the contents of registers and memory locations, or you can run another program. Without an instruction such as this at the end of the program, the 8086 would fetch and execute the code bytes for your program, then go on fetching meaningless bytes from memory and trying to execute them as if they were code bytes.

The next major section of this chapter will show you how to construct the binary codes for these and other 8086 instructions so that you can assemble and run the programs on a development board such as the SDK-86. First, however, we want to use Figure 3-4 to make an important point about writing assembly language programs.

DOCUMENTATION

In a previous section of this chapter, we stressed the point that you should do a lot of thinking and carefully write down the algorithm for a program before you start writing instruction statements. You should also document the program itself so that its operation is clear to you and to anyone else who needs to understand it.

Each page of the program should contain the name of the program, the page number, the name of the programmer, and perhaps a version number. Each program or procedure should have a heading block containing an *abstract* describing what the program is supposed to do, which procedures it calls, which registers it uses, which ports it uses, which flags it affects, the memory used, and any other information which will make it easier for another programmer to interface with the program.

Comments should be used generously to describe the specific *function* of an instruction or group of instructions in this particular program. Comments should not be just an expansion of the instruction mnemonic. A comment of ";add 7 to AL" after the instruction ADD AL, 07H, for example, would not tell you much about the function of the instruction in a particular program. A more enlightening comment might be ";Add altitude correction factor to temperature." Incidentally, not every statement needs an individual comment. It is often more useful to write a comment which explains the function of a group of instructions.

We cannot overemphasize the importance of clear, concise documentation in your programs. Experience has shown that even a short program you wrote without comments a month ago may not be at all understandable to you now.

CONSTRUCTING THE MACHINE CODES FOR 8086 INSTRUCTIONS

This section shows you how to construct the binary codes for 8086 instructions. Most of the time you will probably use an assembler program to do this for you, but it is useful to understand how the codes are constructed. If you have an 8086-based prototyping board such as the Intel SDK-86 available, knowing how to hand code instructions will enable you to code, enter, and run simple programs.

Instruction Templates

To code the instructions for 8-bit processors such as the 8085, all you have to do is look up the hexadecimal code for each instruction on a one-page chart. For the 8086, the process is not quite as simple. Here's why. There are 32 ways to specify the source of the operand in an instruction such as MOV CX, source. The source of the operand can be any one of eight 16-bit registers, or a memory location specified by any one of 24 memory addressing modes. Each of the 32 possible instructions requires a different binary code. If CX is made the source rather than the destination, then there are 32 ways of specifying the destination. Each of these 32 possible instructions requires a different binary code. There are thus 64 different codes for MOV instructions using CX as a source or as a destination. Likewise, another 64 codes are required to specify all the possible MOVs using

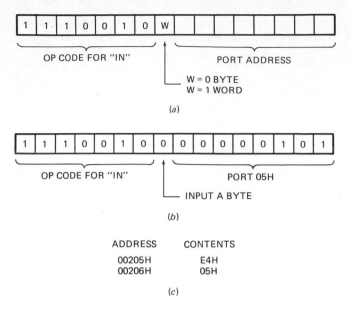

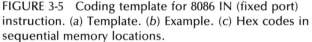

ADDRESS	CONTENTS
00205H	E4H
00206H	05H

(c)

FIGURE 3-5 Coding template for 8086 IN (fixed port) instruction. (a) Template. (b) Example. (c) Hex codes in sequential memory locations.

CL as a source or a destination, and 64 more are required to specify all the possible MOVs using CH as a source or a destination. The point here is that, because there is such a large number of possible codes for the 8086 instructions, it is impractical to list them all in a simple table. Instead, we use a *template* for each basic instruction type and fill in bits within this template to indicate the desired addressing mode, data type, etc. In other words, we build up the instruction codes on a bit-by-bit basis.

Different Intel literature shows two slightly different formats for coding 8086 instructions. One format is shown at the end of the 8086 data sheet in Appendix A. The second format is shown along with the 8086 instruction timings in Appendix B. We will start by showing you how to use the templates shown in the 8086 data sheet.

As a first example of how to use these templates, we will build the code for the IN AL, 05H instruction from our example program. To start, look at the template for this instruction in Figure 3-5a. Note that two bytes are

required for the instruction. The upper 7 bits of the first byte tell the 8086 that this is an "input from a fixed port" instruction. The bit labeled "W" in the template is used to tell the 8086 whether it should input a byte to AL or a word to AX. If you want the 8086 to input a byte from an 8-bit port to AL, then make the W bit a 0. If you want the 8086 to input a word from a 16-bit port to the AX register, then make the W bit a 1. The 8-bit port address, 05H or 00000101 binary, is put in the second byte of the instruction. When the program is loaded into memory to be run, the first instruction byte will be put in one memory location, and the second instruction byte will be put in the next. Figure 3-5c shows this in hexadecimal form as E4H, 05H.

To further illustrate how these templates are used, we will show here several examples with the simple MOV instruction. We will then show you how to construct the rest of the codes for the example program in Figure 3-4. Other examples will be shown as needed in the following chapters.

MOV Instruction Coding Format and Examples

FORMAT

Figure 3-6 shows the coding template or format for 8086 instructions which MOV data from a register to a register, from a register to a memory location, or from a memory location to a register. Note that at least two code bytes are required for the instruction.

The upper 6 bits of the first byte are an opcode which indicates the general type of instruction. Look in the table in Appendix A to find the 6-bit opcode for this MOV register/memory to/from register instruction. You should find it to be 100010.

The W bit in the first word is used to indicate whether a byte or a word is being moved. If you are moving a byte, make W = 0. If you are moving a word, make W = 1.

In this instruction, one operand must always be a register, so 3 bits in the second byte are used to indicate which register is involved. The 3-bit codes for each register are shown in the table at the end of Appendix A and in Figure 3-7. Look in one of these places to find the code for the CL register. You should get 001.

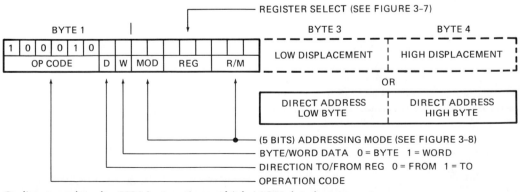

FIGURE 3-6 Coding template for 8086 instructions which MOV data between registers or between a register and a memory location.

```
         REGISTER              CODE
                W=1            W=0
         AL     AX            000
         BL     BX            011
         CL     CX            001
         DL     DX            010
         AH     SP            100
         BH     DI            111
         CH     BP            101
         DH     SI            110

                SEGREG        CODE
                CS            01
                DS            11
                ES            00
                SS            10
```

FIGURE 3-7   Instruction codes for 8086 registers.

The D bit in the first byte of the instruction code is used to indicate whether the data is being moved *to* the register identified in the REG field of the second byte or *from* that register. If the instruction is moving data *to* the register identified in the REG field, make D = 1. If the instruction is moving data *from* that register, make D = 0.

Now remember that in a MOV instruction, one operand must be a register and the other operand may be a register or a memory location. The 2-bit field labeled MOD and the 3-bit field labeled R/M in the second byte of the instruction code are used to specify the desired addressing mode for the other operand. Figure 3-8 shows the MOD and R/M bit patterns for each of the 32

possible addressing modes. Here's an overview of how you use this table.

1. If the other operand in the instruction is also one of the eight registers, then put in 11 for the MOD bits in the instruction code. In the R/M bit positions in the instruction code, put the 3-bit code for the other register.

2. If the other operand is a memory location, there are 24 ways of specifying how the execution unit should compute the effective address of the operand in memory. Remember from Chapter 2 that the effective address can be specified directly in the instruction, it can be contained in a register, or it can be the sum of one or two registers and a displacement. The MOD bits are used to indicate whether the address specification in the instruction contains a displacement. The R/M code indicates which register(s) contain part(s) of the effective address. Here's how it works:

If the specified effective address contains no displacement, as in the instruction MOV CX, [BX] or in the instruction MOV [BX][SI], DX, then make the MOD bits 00 and choose the R/M bits which correspond to the register(s) containing the effective address. For example, if an instruction contains just [BX], the 3-bit R/M code is 111. For an instruction which contains [BX][SI], the R/M code is 000. Note that for direct addressing, where the displacement of the operand from the segment base is specified directly in the instruction, MOD is 00 and R/M is

R/M \ MOD	00	01	10	11 W = 0	11 W = 1
000	[BX] + [SI]	[BX] + [SI] + d8	[BX] + [SI] + d16	AL	AX
001	[BX] + [DI]	[BX] + [DI] + d8	[BX] + [DI] + d16	CL	CX
010	[BP] + [SI]	[BP] + [SI] + d8	[BP] + [SI] + d16	DL	DX
011	[BP] + [DI]	[BP] + [DI] + d8	[BP] + [DI] + d16	BL	BX
100	[SI]	[SI] + d8	[SI] + d16	AH	SP
101	[DI]	[DI] + d8	[DI] + d16	CH	BP
110	d16 (direct address)	[BP] + d8	[BP] + d16	DH	SI
111	[BX]	[BX] + d8	[BX] + d16	BH	DI

MEMORY MODE   REGISTER MODE

d8 = 8-bit displacement   d16 = 16-bit displacement

FIGURE 3-8   MOD and R/M bit patterns for 8086 instructions. The effective address (EA) produced by these addressing modes will be added to the data segment base to form the physical address, except for those cases where BP is used as part of the EA. In that case the EA will be added to the stack segment base to form the physical address. You can use a segment-override prefix to indicate that you want the EA to be added to some other segment base.

110. For an instruction using direct addressing, the low byte of the direct address is put in as a third instruction code byte of the instruction, and the high byte of the direct address is put in as a fourth instruction code byte.

3. If the effective address specified in the instruction contains a displacement less than 256 along with a reference to the contents of a register, as in the instruction MOV CX, 43H[BX], then code in MOD as 01 and choose the R/M bits which correspond to the register(s) which contain the part(s) for the effective address. For the instruction MOV CX, 43H[BX], MOD will be 01 and R/M will be 111. Put the 8-bit value of the displacement in as the third byte of the instruction.

4. If the expression for the effective address contains a displacement which is too large to fit in 8 bits, as in the instruction MOV DX, 4527H[BX], then put in 10 for MOD and choose the R/M bits which correspond to the register(s) which contain the part(s) for the effective address. For the instruction MOV DX, 4527H[BX], the R/M bits are 111. The low byte of the displacement is put in as a third byte of the instruction. The high byte of the displacement is put in as a fourth byte of the instruction. The examples which follow should help clarify all this for you.

MOV Instruction Coding Examples

All the examples in this section use the MOV instruction template in Figure 3-6. As you read through these examples, it is a good idea to keep track of the bit-by-bit development on a separate piece of paper for practice.

CODING MOV SP, BX

This instruction will copy a word from the BX register to the SP register. Consulting the table in Appendix A, you find that the 6-bit opcode for this instruction is 100010. Because you are moving a word, W = 1. The D bit for this instruction may be somewhat confusing, however. Since two registers are involved, you can think of the move as either *to* SP or *from* BX. It actually does not matter which you assume as long as you are consistent in coding the rest of the instruction. If you think of the instruction as moving a word *to* SP, then make D = 1 and put 100 in the REG field to represent the SP register. The MOD field will be 11 to represent

register addressing mode. Make the R/M field 011 to represent the other register, BX. The resultant code for the instruction MOV SP, BX will be 10001011 11100011. Figure 3-9a shows the meaning of all these bits.

If you change the D bit to a 0 and swap the codes in the REG and R/M fields, you will get 10001001 11011100, which is another equally valid code for the instruction. Figure 3-9b shows the meaning of the bits in this form. This second form, incidentally, is the form that the Intel 8086 Macroassembler produces.

CODING MOV CL, [BX]

This instruction will copy a byte to CL from the memory location whose effective address is contained in BX. The effective address will be added to the data segment base in DS to produce the physical address.

To find the 6-bit opcode for byte 1 of the instruction, consult the table in Appendix A. You should find that this code is 100010. Make D = 1 because data is being moved *to* register CL. Make W = 0 because the instruction is moving a byte into CL. Next you need to put the 3-bit code which represents register CL in the REG field of the second byte of the instruction code. The codes for each register are shown in Figure 3-7. In this figure you should find that the code for CL is 001. Now, all you need to determine is the bit patterns for the MOD and R/M fields. Again use the table in Figure 3-8 to do this. In the table, first find the box containing the desired addressing mode. The box containing [BX], for example, is in the lower left corner of the table. Read the required MOD-bit pattern from the top of the column. In this case, MOD is 00. Then read the required R/M-bit pattern at the left of the box. For this instruction you should find R/M to be 111. Assembling all these bits together should give you 10001010 00001111 as the binary code for the instruction MOV CL, [BX]. Figure 3-10 summarizes the meaning of all the bits in this result.

CODING MOV 43H[SI], DH

This instruction will copy a byte from the DH register to a memory location. The BIU will compute the effective address of the memory location by adding the indicated displacement of 43H to the contents of the SI register. As we showed you in the last chapter, the BIU then produces the actual physical address by adding this effective address to the data segment base represented by the 16-bit number in the DS register.

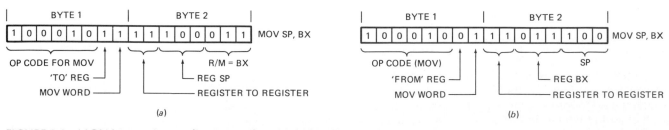

FIGURE 3-9   MOV instruction coding examples. (a) MOV SP, BX. (b) MOV SP, BX alternative.

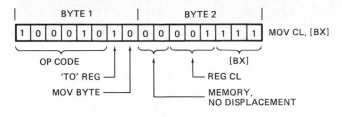

FIGURE 3-10   MOV CL, [BX].

The 6-bit opcode for this instruction is again 100010. Put 110 in the REG field to represent the DH register. D = 0 because you are moving data *from* the DH register. W = 0 because you are moving a byte. The R/M field will be 100 because SI contains part of the effective address. The MOD field will be 01 because the displacement contained in the instruction, 43H, will fit in 1 byte. If the specified displacement had been a number larger than FFH, then MOD would be 10. Putting all these pieces together gives 10001000 01110100 for the first two bytes of the instruction code. The specified displacement, 43H or 01000011 binary, is put after these two as a third instruction byte. Figure 3-11 shows this. If an instruction specifies a 16-bit displacement, then the low byte of the displacement is put in as byte 3 of the instruction code, and the high byte of the displacement is put in as byte 4 of the instruction code.

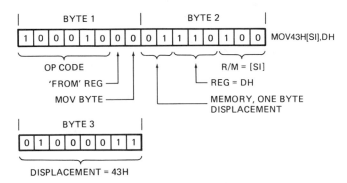

FIGURE 3-11   MOV 43H[SI], DH.

CODING MOV CX, [437AH]

This instruction copies the contents of two memory locations into the CX register. The direct address or displacement of the first memory location from the start of the data segment is 437AH. As we showed you in the last chapter, the BIU will produce the physical memory address by adding this displacement to the data segment base represented by the 16-bit number in the DS register.

The 6-bit opcode for this instruction is again 100010. Make D = 1 because you are moving data *to* the CX register, and make W = 1 because the data being moved is a word. Put 001 in the REG field to represent the CX register, then consult Figure 3-8 to find the MOD and R/M codes. In the first column of the figure, you should find a box labeled "direct address," which is the name given to the addressing mode used in this instruction. For direct addressing, you should find MOD to be 00

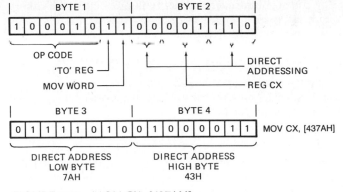

FIGURE 3-12   MOV CX, [437AH].

and R/M to be 110. The first two code bytes for the instruction, then, are 10001011 00001110. These two bytes will be followed by the low byte of the direct address, 7AH (01111010 binary), and the high byte of the direct address, 43H (01000011 binary). The instruction will be coded into four successive memory addresses as 8BH, 0EH, 7AH, and 43H. Figure 3-12 spells this out in detail.

CODING MOV CS:[BX], DL

This instruction copies a byte from the DL register to a memory location. The effective address for the memory location is contained in the BX register. Normally an effective address in BX will be added to the data segment base in DS to produce the physical memory address. In this instruction, the CS: in front of [BX] indicates that we want the BIU to add the effective address to the code segment base in CS to produce the physical address. The CS: is called a *segment override prefix.*

When an instruction containing a segment override prefix is coded, an 8-bit code for the segment override prefix is put in memory *before* the code for the rest of the instruction. The code byte for the segment override prefix has the format 001XX110. You insert a 2-bit code in place of the X's to indicate which segment base you want the effective address to be added to. As shown in Figure 3-7, the codes for these 2 bits are as follows: ES = 00, CS = 01, SS = 10, and DS = 11. The segment override prefix byte for CS, then, is 00101110. For practice, code out the rest of this instruction. Figure 3-13 shows the result you should get and how the code

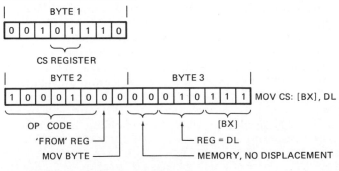

FIGURE 3-13   MOV CS:[BX], DL.

for the segment override prefix is put before the other code bytes for the instruction.

Coding the Example Program in Figure 3-4

Again, as you read through this section, follow the bit-by-bit development of the instruction codes on a separate piece of paper for practice.

MOV AX, 0010H

This instruction will load the immediate word 0010H into the AX register. The simplest code template to use for this instruction is listed in the table in Appendix A under the "MOV — Immediate to register" heading. The format for this instruction is 1011 W REG, data byte low, data byte high. W = 1 because you are moving a word. Consult Figure 3-7 to find the code for the AX register. You should find this to be 000. Put this 3-bit code in the REG field of the instruction code. The completed instruction code byte is 10111000. Put the low byte of the immediate number, 10H, in as the second code byte. Then put the high byte of the immediate data, 00H, in as the third code byte. The resultant sequence of code bytes, then, will be B8H, 10H, 00H.

MOV DS, AX

This instruction copies the contents of the AX register into the data segment register. The template to use for coding this instruction is found in the table in Appendix A under the heading "MOV — Register/memory to segment register." The format for this template is 10001110 MOD 0 segreg R/M. Segreg represents the 2-bit code for the desired segment register, as shown in Figure 3-7. These codes are also found in the table at the end of Appendix A. The segreg code for the DS register is 11. Since the other operand is a register, MOD should be 11. Put the 3-bit code for the AX register, 000, in the R/M field. The resultant codes for the two code bytes should then be 10001110 11011000, or 8EH D8H.

IN AL, 05H

This instruction copies a byte of data from port 05H to the AL register. The coding for this instruction was described in a previous section. The code for the instruction is 11100100 00000101 or E4H 05H.

ADD AL, 07H

This instruction adds the immediate number 07H to the AL register and puts the result in the AL register. The simplest template to use for coding this instruction is found in the table in Appendix A under the heading "ADD — Immediate to accumulator." The format is 0000010 W, data byte, data byte. Since you are adding a byte, W = 0. The immediate data byte you are adding will be put in the second code byte. The third code byte will not be needed because you are adding only a byte. The resultant codes, then, are 00000100 00000111 or 04H 07H.

MOV [0000], AL

This instruction copies the contents of the AL register to a memory location. The direct address or displacement of the memory location from the start of the data segment is 0000H. The code template for this instruction is found in the table in Appendix A under the heading "MOV — Accumulator to memory." The format for the instruction is 1010001 W, address low byte, address high byte. Since the instruction moves a byte, W = 0. The low byte of the direct address is written in as the second instruction code byte, and the high byte of the direct address is written in as the third instruction code byte. The codes for these 3 bytes, then, will be 10100010 00000000 00000000 or A2H 00H 00H.

INT 3

In some 8086 systems this instruction causes the 8086 to stop executing your program instructions, return to the monitor program, and wait for your next command. According to the format table in Appendix A, the code for a type 3 interrupt is the single byte 11001100 or CCH.

SUMMARY OF HAND CODING THE EXAMPLE PROGRAM

Figure 3-4 shows the example program with all the instruction codes in sequential order as you would write them so that you could load the program into memory and run it. Codes are in HEX to save space.

A Look at Another Coding Template Format

As we mentioned previously, Intel literature shows the 8086 instruction coding templates in two different forms. The preceding sections have shown you how to use the templates found at the end of the 8086 data sheet in Appendix A. Now let's take a brief look at the second form, which is shown along with the instruction clock cycles in Appendix B.

The only difference between the second form for the templates and the form we discussed previously is that the D and W bits are not individually identified. Instead, the complete opcode bytes are shown for each version of an instruction. For example, in Appendix B, the opcode byte for the MOV memory 8, register 8 instruction is shown as 88H, and the opcode byte for the MOV memory 16, register 16 instruction is shown as 89H. If you compare these codes with those derived from Appendix A, you will see that the only difference between the two codes is the W bit. For the 8-bit move, W = 0, and for the 16-bit move, W = 1.

One important point to make about using the templates in Appendix B is that for operations involving two registers, the register identified in the REG field is not consistent from instruction to instruction. For the MOV instructions, the templates in Appendix B assume that the 3-bit code for the source register is put in the REG field of the MOD/RM instruction byte, and the 3-bit code for the destination register is put in the R/M field of the MOD/RM instruction byte. According to Appendix B, the template for a 16-bit register-to-register move is 89H followed by the MOD reg R/M byte. In this template, D = 0, so the 3-bit code for the source register will be put in the reg field. Using this template, then, the instruction MOV BX, CX is coded as 10001001 11001011 or 89H CBH.

For the ADD, ADC, SUB, SBB, AND, OR, and XOR instructions which involve two registers, the templates in Appendix B show D = 1. To be consistent with these templates, then, you have to put the 3-bit code for the destination register in the reg field in the instruction.

It really doesn't matter whether you use the templates in Appendix A or those in Appendix B, as long as you are consistent in coding each instruction.

A Few Words about Hand Coding

If you have to hand code 8086 assembly language programs, here are a few tips to make your life easier. First, check your algorithm very carefully to make sure that it really does what it is supposed to do. Second, initially write down just the assembly language statements and comments for your program. You can check the table in the appendix to determine how many bytes each instruction takes so that you know how many blank lines to leave between instruction statements. You may find it helpful to insert three or four NOP instructions after every nine or ten instructions. The NOP instruction doesn't do anything but kill time. However, if you accidentally leave out an instruction in your program, you can replace the NOPs with the needed instruction(s). This way you don't have to rewrite the entire program after the missing instruction.

After you have written down the instruction statements, recheck very carefully to make sure you have the right instructions to implement your algorithm. Then work out the binary codes for each instruction and write them in the appropriate places on the coding form.

Hand coding is laborious for long programs. When writing long programs, it is much more efficient to use an assembler. The next section of this chapter shows you how to write your programs so that you can use an assembler to produce the machine codes for the instructions.

WRITING PROGRAMS FOR USE WITH AN ASSEMBLER

If you have an 8086 assembler available, you should learn to use it as soon as possible. Besides doing the tedious task of producing the binary codes for your instruction statements, an assembler also allows you to refer to data items by name rather than by their numerical offsets. As you should soon see, this greatly reduces the work you have to do and makes your programs much more readable. In this section we show you how to write your programs so that you can use an assembler on them.

NOTE: The assembly language programs in the rest of this book were assembled with TASM 1.0 from Borland International or MASM 5.1 from Microsoft Corp. TASM is faster, but the program format for these two assemblers is essentially the same. If you are using some other assembler, check the manual for it to determine any differences in syntax from the examples in this book.

Program Format

The best way to approach this section seems to be to show you a simple, but complete, program written for an assembler and explain the function of the various parts of the program. By now you are probably tired of the "read temperature, add +7, and store result in memory" program, so we will use another example.

Figure 3-14, p. 54, shows an 8086 assembly language program which multiplies two 16-bit binary numbers to give a 32-bit binary result. If you have a microcomputer development system or a microcomputer with an 8086 assembler to work on, this is a good program for you to key in, assemble, and run to become familiar with the operation of your system. (A sequence of exercises in the accompanying lab manual explains how to do this.) In any case, you can use the structure of this example program as a model for your own programs.

In addition to program instructions, the example program in Figure 3-14 contains directions to the assembler. These directions to the assembler are commonly called *assembler directives* or *pseudo operations*. A section at the end of Chapter 6 lists and describes for your reference a large number of the available assembler directives. Here we will discuss the basic assembler directives you need to get started writing programs. We will introduce more of these directives as we need them in the next two chapters.

SEGMENT and ENDS Directives

The SEGMENT and ENDS directives are used to identify a group of data items or a group of instructions that you want to be put together in a particular segment. These directives are used in the same way that parentheses are used to group like terms in algebra. A group of data statements or a group of instruction statements contained between SEGMENT and ENDS directives is called a *logical segment.* When you set up a logical segment, you give it a name of your choosing. In the example program, the statements DATA_HERE SEGMENT and DATA_HERE ENDS set up a logical segment named DATA_HERE. There is nothing sacred about the name DATA_HERE. We simply chose this name to help us remember that this logical segment contains data statements. The statements CODE_HERE SEGMENT and CODE_HERE ENDS in the example program set up a logical segment named CODE_HERE which contains instruction statements. Most 8086 assemblers, incidentally, allow you to use names and labels of up to 31 characters. You can't use spaces in a name, but you can

```
                    ; 8086 PROGRAM F3-14.ASM
    ;ABSTRACT    : This program multiplies the two 16-bit words in the memory
                    ; locations called MULTIPLICAND and MULTIPLIER. The result
                    ; is stored in the memory location, PRODUCT
    ;REGISTERS   : Uses CS, DS, AX, DX
    ;PORTS       : None used

    DATA_HERE       SEGMENT
                    MULTIPLICAND  DW 204AH        ; First word here
                    MULTIPLIER    DW 3B2AH        ; Second word here
                    PRODUCT       DW 2 DUP(0)     ; Result of multiplication here
    DATA_HERE       ENDS

    CODE_HERE       SEGMENT
                    ASSUME    CS:CODE_HERE, DS:DATA_HERE
    START:          MOV  AX, DATA_HERE           ; Initialize DS register
                    MOV  DS, AX
                    MOV  AX, MULTIPLICAND        ; Get one word
                    MUL  MULTIPLIER              ; Multiply by second word
                    MOV  PRODUCT, AX             ; Store low word of result
                    MOV  PRODUCT+2, DX           ; Store high word of result
                    INT  3                       ; Wait for command from user
    CODE_HERE       ENDS
                    END START

    ;      Programs to be run using a debugger in DOS must include the START: label and the
    ; START after the END followed by a carriage return. Programs to be downloaded and run need
    ; only the END directive followed by a carriage return.
```

FIGURE 3-14   Assembly language source program to multiply two 16-bit binary numbers to give a 32-bit result.

use an underscore as shown to separate words in a name. Also, you can't use instruction mnemonics as segment names or labels. Throughout the rest of the program you will refer to a logical segment by the name that you give it when you define it.

A logical segment is not usually given a physical starting address when it is declared. After the program is assembled and perhaps linked with other assembled program modules, it is then assigned the physical address where it will be loaded in memory to be run.

Naming Data and Addresses — EQU, DB, DW, and DD Directives

Programs work with three general categories of data: constants, variables, and addresses. The value of a constant does not change during the execution of the program. The number 7 is an example of a constant you might use in a program. A variable is the name given to a data item which can change during the execution of a program. The current temperature of an oven is an example of a variable. Addresses are referred to in many instructions. You may, for example, load an address into a register or jump to an address.

Constants, variables, and addresses used in your programs can be given names. This allows you to refer to them by name rather than having to remember or calculate their value each time you refer to them in an instruction. In other words, if you give names to constants, variables, and addresses, the assembler can

use these names to find a desired data item or address when you refer to it in an instruction. Specific directives are used to give names to constants and variables in your programs. Labels are used to give names to addresses in your programs.

THE EQU DIRECTIVE

The EQU, or *equate*, directive is used to assign names to constants used in your programs. The statement CORRECTION_FACTOR EQU 07H, in a program such as our previous example, would tell the assembler to insert the value 07H every time it finds the name CORRECTION_FACTOR in a program statement. In other words, when the assembler reads the statement ADD AL, CORRECTION_FACTOR, it will automatically code the instruction as if you had written it ADD AL, 07H. Here's the advantage of using an EQU directive to declare constants at the start of your program. Suppose you use the correction factor of +07H 23 times in your program. Now the company you work for changes the brand of temperature sensor it buys, and the new correction factor is +09H. If you used the number 07H directly in the 23 instructions which contain this correction factor, then you have to go through the entire program, find each instruction that uses the correction factor, and update the value. Murphy's law being what it is, you are likely to miss one or two of these, and the program won't work correctly. If you used an EQU at the start of your program and then referred to CORREC-TION_FACTOR by name in the 23 instructions, then all you do is change the value in the EQU statement from 07H to 09H and reassemble the program. The assembler automatically inserts the new value of 09H in all 23 instructions.

DB, DW, AND DD DIRECTIVES

The DB, DW, and DD directives are used to assign names to variables in your programs. The DB directive after a name specifies that the data is of *type byte*. The program statement OVEN_TEMPERATURE DB 27H, for example, declares a variable of type byte, gives it the name OVEN_TEMPERATURE, and gives it an initial value of 27H. When the binary code for the program is loaded into memory to be run, the value 27H will be loaded into the memory location identified by the name OVEN_TEMPERATURE DB 27H.

As another example, the statement CONVERSION_FACTORS DB 27H, 48H, 32H, 69H will declare a data structure (array) of 4 bytes and initialize the 4 bytes with the specified 4 values. If you don't care what value a data item is initialized to, then you can indicate this with a "?," as in the statement TARE_WEIGHT DB ?.

NOTE: Variables which are changed during the operation of a program should also be initialized with program instructions so that the program can be rerun from the start without reloading it to initialize the variables.

DW is used to specify that the data is of *type word* (16 bits), and DD is used to specify that the data is of *type doubleword* (32 bits). The example program in Figure 3-14 shows three examples of naming and initializing word-type data items.

The first example, MULTIPLICAND DW 204AH, declares a data word named MULTIPLICAND and initializes that data word with the value 204AH. What this means is that the assembler will set aside two successive memory locations and assign the name MULTIPLICAND to the first location. As you will see, this allows us to access the data in these memory locations by name. The MULTIPLICAND DW 204AH statement also indicates that when the final program is loaded into memory to be run, these memory locations will be loaded with (initialized to) 204AH. Actually, since this is an Intel microprocessor, the first address in memory will contain the low byte of the word, 4AH, and the second memory address will contain the high byte of the word, 20H.

The second data declaration example in Figure 3-14, MULTIPLIER DW 3B2AH, sets aside storage for a word in memory and gives the starting address of this word the name MULTIPLIER. When the program is loaded, the first memory address will be initialized with 2AH, and the second memory location with 3BH.

The third data declaration example in Figure 3-14, PRODUCT DW 2 DUP(0), sets aside storage for two words in memory and gives the starting address of the first word the name PRODUCT. The DUP(0) part of the statement tells the assembler to initialize the two words to all zeros. When we multiply two 16-bit binary numbers, the product can be as large as 32 bits, so we must set aside this much space to store the product. We could

have used the DD directive to declare PRODUCT a doubleword, but since in the program we move the result to PRODUCT one word at a time, it is more convenient to declare PRODUCT 2 words.

Figure 3-15 shows how the data for MULTIPLICAND, MULTIPLIER, and PRODUCT will actually be arranged in memory starting from the base of the DATA_HERE segment. The first byte of MULTIPLICAND, 4AH, will be at a displacement of zero from the segment base, because MULTIPLICAND is the first data item declared in the logical segment DATA_HERE. The displacement of the second byte of MULTIPLICAND is 0001. The displacement of the first byte of MULTIPLIER from the segment base is 0002H, and the displacement of the second byte of MULTIPLIER is 0003H. These are the displacements that we would have to figure out for each data item if we were not using names to refer to them.

If the logical segment DATA_HERE is eventually put in ROM or EPROM, then MULTIPLICAND will function as a constant, because it cannot be changed during program execution. However, if DATA_HERE is eventually put in RAM, then MULTIPLICAND can function as a variable because a new value could be written in those memory locations during program execution.

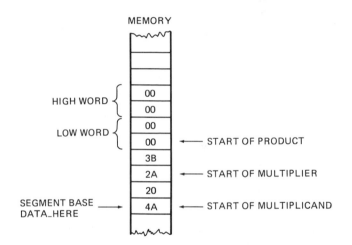

FIGURE 3-15   Data arrangement in memory for multiply program.

Types of Numbers Used in Data Statements

All the previous examples of DB, DW, and DD declarations use hexadecimal numbers, as indicated by an "H" after the number. You can, however, put in a number in any one of several other forms. For each form you must tell the assembler which form you are using.

BINARY

For example, when you use a binary number in a statement, you put a "B" after the string of 1's and 0's to let the assembler know that you want the number to be treated as a binary number. The statement TEMP_MAX DB 01111001B is an example. If you want to put in a negative binary number, write the number in its 2's complement sign-and-magnitude form.

DECIMAL

The assembler treats a number with no identifying letter after it as a decimal number. The assembler automatically converts a decimal number in a statement to binary so that the value can be loaded into memory. Given the statement TEMP_MAX DB 49, for example, the assembler will automatically convert the 49 decimal to its binary equivalent, 00110001. If you indicate a negative number in a data declaration statement, the assembler will convert the number to its 2's complement sign-and-magnitude form. For example, given the statement TEMP_MIN DB −20, the assembler will insert the value 11101100, which is the 2's complement representation for −20 decimal.

NOTE: If you forget to put an H after a number that you want the assembler to treat as hexadecimal, the assembler will treat it as a decimal number. You can put a D after the decimal values if you want to indicate more clearly that the value is decimal.

HEXADECIMAL

As shown in several previous examples, a hexadecimal number is indicated by an H after the hexadecimal digits. The statement MULTIPLIER DW 3B2AH is an example. A zero must be placed in front of a hex number that starts with a letter; for example, the number AH must be written 0AH.

BCD

Remember from Chapter 1 that in BCD each decimal digit is represented by its 4-bit binary equivalent. The decimal number 37, for example, is represented in BCD as 00110111. As you can see, this number is equal to 37H. The only way you can tell whether the number 00110111 represents BCD 37 or hexadecimal 37 is by how it is used in the program! The point here is that if you want the assembler to initialize a variable with the value 37 BCD, you put an H after the number. The statement SECONDS DB 59H, for example, will initialize the variable SECONDS with 01011001, the BCD representation of 59.

ASCII

You can declare a data structure (array) containing a sequence of ASCII codes by enclosing the letters or numbers after a DB in single quotation marks. The statement BOY1 DB 'ALBERT', for example, tells the assembler to declare a data item named BOY1 that has six memory locations. It also tells the assembler to put the ASCII code for A in the first memory location, the ASCII code for L in the second, the ASCII code for B in the third, etc. The assembler will automatically determine the ASCII codes for the letters or numbers within the quotes. Note that this ASCII trick can be used only with the DB directive.

Accessing Named Data with Program Instructions

Now that we have shown you how a data structure can be set up, let's look at how program instructions access this data. Temporarily skipping over the first two instructions in the CODE_HERE section of the program in Figure 3-16, find the instruction MOV AX, MULTIPLICAND. This instruction, when executed, will copy a word from the memory location named MULTIPLICAND to the AX register. Here's how this works.

When the assembler reads through this program the first time, it automatically calculates the offset of each of the named data items from the segment base DATA_HERE. In Figure 3-15 you can see that the displacement of MULTIPLICAND from the segment base is 0000. This is because MULTIPLICAND is the first data item declared in the segment. The assembler, then, will find that the displacement of MULTIPLICAND is 0000H. When the assembler reads the program the second time to produce the binary codes for the instructions, it will insert this displacement as part of the binary code for the instruction MOV AX, MULTIPLICAND. Since we know that the displacement of MULTIPLICAND is 0000, we could have written the instruction as MOV AX, [0000]. However, there would be a problem if we later changed the program by adding another data item before MULTIPLICAND in DATA_HERE. The displacement of MULTIPLICAND would be changed. Therefore, we would have to remember to go through the entire program and correct the displacement in all instructions that access MULTIPLICAND. If you use a name to refer to each data item as shown, the assembler will automatically calculate the correct displacement of that data item for you and insert this displacement each time you refer to it in an instruction.

To summarize how this works, then, the instruction MOV AX, MULTIPLICAND is an example of direct addressing where the direct address or displacement of the desired data word in the data segment is represented by the name MULTIPLICAND. For instructions such as this, the assembler will automatically calculate the displacement of the named data item from the start of the segment and insert this value as part of the binary code for the instruction. This can be seen on line 18 of the assembler listing shown in Figure 3-16. When the instruction executes, the BIU will add the displacement contained in the instruction to the data segment base in DS to produce the 20-bit physical address of the data word named MULTIPLICAND.

The next instruction in the program in Figure 3-16 is another example of direct addressing using a named data item. The instruction MUL MULTIPLIER multiplies the word from the memory location named MULTIPLIER in DATA_HERE by the word in the AX register. When the assembler reads through this program the first time, it will find that the displacement of MULTIPLIER in DATA_HERE is 0002H. When it reads through the program the second time, it inserts this displacement as part of the binary code for the MUL instruction, as shown on line 19 in Figure 3-16. When the MUL MULTIPLIER instruction executes, the BIU will add the displacement contained in the instruction to the data

```
Turbo Assembler  Version 1.0                                  Page 1

      1                                   ; 8086 PROGRAM F3-14.ASM
      2                         ,ABSTRACT . This program multiplies the two 16-bit words in the memory
      3                                   ; locations called MULTIPLICAND and MULTIPLIER. The result
      4                                   ; is stored in the memory location, PRODUCT
      5                         ;REGISTERS : Uses CS, DS, AX, DX
      6                         ;PORTS     : None used
      7
      8 0000                    DATA_HERE   SEGMENT
      9 0000  204A                          MULTIPLICAND  DW 204AH       ; First word here
     10 0002  3B2A                          MULTIPLIER    DW 3B2AH       ; Second word here
     11 0004  02*(0000)                     PRODUCT       DW 2 DUP(0)    ; Result of multiplication here
     12 0008                    DATA_HERE   ENDS
     13
     14 0000                    CODE_HERE   SEGMENT
     15                                     ASSUME   CS:CODE_HERE, DS:DATA_HERE
     16 0000  B8 0000s          START:      MOV  AX, DATA_HERE          ; Initialize DS register
     17 0003  8E D8                         MOV  DS, AX
     18 0005  A1 0000r                      MOV  AX, MULTIPLICAND       ; Get one word
     19 0008  F7 26 0002r                   MUL  MULTIPLIER             ; Multiply by second word
     20 000C  A3 0004r                      MOV  PRODUCT, AX            ; Store low word of result
     21 000F  89 16 0006r                   MOV  PRODUCT+2, DX          ; Store high word of result
     22 0013  CC                            INT  3                      ; Wait for command from user
     23 0014                    CODE_HERE   ENDS
     24                                     END START

Turbo Assembler  Version 1.0                                  Page 2
Symbol Table


Symbol Name                       Type    Value

??DATE                            Text    "04-06-89"
??FILENAME                        Text    "F3-14   "
??TIME                            Text    "07:41:58"
??VERSION                         Number  0100
@CPU                              Text    0101H
@CURSEG                           Text    CODE_HERE
@FILENAME                         Text    F3-14
@WORDSIZE                         Text    2
MULTIPLICAND                      Word    DATA_HERE:0000
MULTIPLIER                        Word    DATA_HERE:0002
PRODUCT                           Word    DATA_HERE:0004
START                             Near    CODE_HERE:0000

Groups & Segments                 Bit Size Align  Combine Class

CODE_HERE                         16  0014 Para   none
DATA_HERE                         16  0008 Para   none
```

FIGURE 3-16 Assembler listing for example program in Figure 3-14.

segment base in DS to address MULTIPLIER in memory. After the multiplication, the low word of the result is left in the AX register, and the high word of the result is left in the DX register.

The next instruction, MOV PRODUCT, AX, in the program in Figure 3-16 copies the low word of the result from AX to memory. The low byte of AX will be copied to a memory location named PRODUCT. The high byte of AX will be copied to the next higher address, which we can refer to as PRODUCT + 1. As you can see on line 20 in Figure 3-16, the displacement of PRODUCT, 0004H, is inserted in the code for the MOV PRODUCT, AX instruction.

The following instruction in the program, MOV PRODUCT + 2, DX, copies the high word of the multiplication result from DX to memory. When the assembler reads this instruction, it will add the indicated "2" to the displacement it calculated for PRODUCT and insert the result as part of the binary code for the instruction, as shown on line 21 in Figure 3-16. Therefore, when the instruction executes, the low byte of DX will be copied to memory at a displacement of PRODUCT + 2. The high byte of DX will be copied to a memory location which we can refer to as PRODUCT + 3. Figure 3-15 shows how the two words of the product are put in memory. Note that the lower byte of a word is always put in the lower memory address.

This example program should show you that if you are using an assembler, names are a very convenient way of specifying the direct address of data in memory. In the next section we show you how to refer to addresses by name.

Naming Addresses — Labels

One type of name used to represent addresses is called a *label*. Labels are written in the label field of an instruction statement or a directive statement. One major use of labels is to represent the destination for jump and call instructions. Suppose, for example, we want the 8086 to jump back to some previous instruction over and over. Instead of computing the numerical address that we want the 8086 to jump to, we put a label in front of the destination instruction and write the jump instruction as JMP label:. Here is a specific example.

```
NEXT:   IN AL, 05H  ;   Get data sample from port 05H
.                   ;   Process data value read in
.
        JMP NEXT    ;   Get  next  data  value  and
                        process
```

If you use a label to represent an address, as shown in this example, the assembler will automatically calculate the address that needs to be put in the code for the jump instruction. The next two chapters show many examples of the use of labels with jump and call instructions.

Another example of using a name to represent an address is in the SEGMENT directive statement. The name DATA_HERE in the statement DATA_HERE SEGMENT, for example, represents the starting address of a segment named DATA_HERE. Later we show you how we use this name to initialize the data segment register, but first we will discuss some other parts you need to know about in the example program in Figure 3-14.

The ASSUME Directive

An 8086 program may have several logical segments that contain code and several that contain data. However, at any given time the 8086 works directly with only four physical segments: a *code segment*, a *data segment*, a *stack segment*, and an *extra segment*. The ASSUME directive tells the assembler which logical segment to use for each of these physical segments at a given time.

In Figure 3-14, for example, the statement ASSUME CS:CODE_HERE, DS:DATA_HERE tells the assembler that the logical segment named CODE_HERE contains the instruction statements for the program and should be treated as a code segment. It also tells the assembler

that it should treat the logical segment DATA_HERE as the data segment for this program. In other words, the DS:DATA_HERE part of the statement tells the assembler that for any instruction which refers to data in the data segment, data will be found in the logical segment DATA_HERE. The ASSUME . . . DS:DATA_HERE, for example, tells the assembler that a named data item such as MULTIPLICAND is contained in the logical segment called DATA_HERE. Given this information, the assembler can construct the binary codes for the instruction. As we explained before, the displacement of MULTIPLICAND from the start of the DATA_HERE segment will be inserted as part of the instruction by the assembler.

If you are using the stack segment and the extra segment in your program, you must include terms in the ASSUME statement to tell the assembler which logical segments to use for each of these. To do this, you might add terms such as SS:STACK_HERE, ES:EXTRA_HERE. As we will show later, you can put another ASSUME directive later in the program to tell the assembler to use different logical segments from that point on.

If the ASSUME directive is not completely clear to you at this point, don't worry. We show many more examples of its use throughout the rest of the book. We introduced the ASSUME directive here because you need to put it in your programs for most 8086 assemblers. You can use the ASSUME statement in Figure 3-14 as a model of how to write this directive for your programs.

Initializing Segment Registers

The ASSUME directive tells the assembler the names of the logical segments to use as the code segment, data segment, stack segment, and extra segment. The assembler uses displacements from the start of the specified logical segment to code out instructions. When the instructions are executed, the displacements in the instructions will be added to the segment base addresses represented by the 16-bit numbers in the segment registers to produce the actual physical addresses. The assembler, however, cannot directly load the segment registers with the upper 16 bits of the segment starting addresses as needed.

The segment registers other than the code segment register must be initialized by program instructions before they can be used to access data. The first two instructions of the example program in Figure 3-14 show how you initialize the data segment register. The name DATA_HERE in the first instruction represents the upper 16 bits of the starting address you give the segment DATA_HERE. Since the 8086 does not allow us to move this immediate number directly into the data segment register, we must first load it into one of the general-purpose registers, then copy it into the data segment register. MOV AX, DATA_HERE loads the upper 16 bits of the segment starting address into the AX register. MOV DS, AX copies this value from AX to the data segment register. This is the same operation we described for hand coding the example program in Figure 3-4, except that here we use the segment name instead of a number to refer to the segment base address. In this example we used the AX register to pass the value, but any 16-bit register other than a segment register can be used. If you are hand coding your program, you can just insert the upper 16 bits of the 20-bit segment starting address in place of DATA_HERE in the instruction. For example, if in your particular system you decide to locate DATA_HERE at address 00300H, DS should be loaded with 0030H. If you are using an assembler, you can use the segment name to refer to the segment base address, as shown in the example.

If you use the stack segment and the extra segment in a program, the stack segment register and the extra segment register must be initialized by program instructions in the same way.

When the assembler reads through your assembly language program, it calculates the displacement of each named variable from the start of the logical segment that contains it. The assembler also keeps track of the displacement of each instruction code byte from the start of a logical segment. The CS:CODE_HERE part of the ASSUME statement in Figure 3-14 tells the assembler to calculate the displacements of the following instructions from the start of the logical segment CODE_HERE. In other words, it tells the assembler that when this program is run, the code segment register will contain the upper 16 bits of the address where the logical segment CODE_HERE was located in memory. The instruction byte displacements that the assembler is keeping track of are the values that the 8086 will put in the instruction pointer (IP) to fetch each instruction byte.

There are several ways in which the CS register can be loaded with the code segment base address and the instruction pointer can be loaded with the offset of the instruction byte to be fetched next. The first way is with the command you give your system to execute a program starting at a given address. A typical command of this sort is G = 0010:0000 <CR>. (<CR> means "press the return key.") This command will load CS with 0010 and load IP with 0000. The 8086 will then fetch and execute instructions starting from address 00100, the address produced when the BIU adds IP to the code segment base in the CS register.

As we will show you in the next two chapters, jump and call instructions load new values in IP, and in some cases they load new values in the CS register.

The END Directive

The END directive, as the name implies, tells the assembler to stop reading. Any instructions or statements that you write after an END directive will be ignored.

ASSEMBLY LANGUAGE PROGRAM DEVELOPMENT TOOLS

Introduction

For all but the very simplest assembly language programs, you will probably want to use some type of

FIGURE 3-17   Applied Microsystems ES 1800 16-bit emulator. *(Applied Microsystems Corp.)*

microcomputer development system and *program development tools* to make your work easier. A typical system might consist of an IBM PC-type microcomputer with at least several hundred kilobytes of RAM, a keyboard and video display, floppy and/or hard disk drives, a printer, and an emulator. Figure 3-17 shows an Applied Microsystems ES 1800 16-bit emulator which can be added to an IBM PC/AT or compatible computer to produce a complete 8086/80186/80286 development system.

The following sections give you an introduction to several common program development tools which you use with a system such as this. Most of these tools are programs which you run to perform some function on the program you are writing. You will have to consult the manuals for your system to get the specific details, but this section should give you an overview of the steps involved in developing an assembly language program. An accompanying lab manual takes you through the use of all these tools with the SDK-86 board and an IBM PC-type computer.

Editor

An *editor* is a program which allows you to create a file containing the assembly language statements for your program. Examples of suitable editors are PC Write, Wordstar, and the editor that comes with some assemblers.

Figure 3-14 shows an example of the format you should use when typing in your program. The actual position of each field on a line is not important, but you must put the fields of each statement in the correct order, and you must leave at least one blank between fields. Whenever possible, we like to line the fields up in columns so that it is easier to read the program.

As you type in your program, the editor stores the ASCII codes for the letters and numbers in successive RAM locations. If you make a typing error, the editor will let you back up and correct it. If you leave out a program statement, the editor will let you move everything down and insert the line. This is much easier than working with pencil and paper, even if you type as slowly as I do.

When you have typed in all of your program, you then save the file on a floppy or hard disk. This file is called a *source file.* The next step is to process the source file with an assembler. Incidentally, if you are going to use the TASM or MASM assembler, you should give your source file name the extension .ASM. You might, for instance, give the example source program in Figure 3-14 a name such as MULTIPLY.ASM.

Assembler

As we told you earlier in the chapter, an *assembler* program is used to translate the assembly language mnemonics for instructions to the corresponding binary codes. When you run the assembler, it reads the source file of your program from the disk where you saved it after editing. On the first pass through the source program, the assembler determines the displacement of named data items, the offset of labels, etc., and puts this information in a *symbol table.* On the second pass through the source program, the assembler produces the binary code for each instruction and inserts the offsets, etc., that it calculated during the first pass.

The assembler generates two files on the floppy or hard disk. The first file, called the *object file,* is given the extension .OBJ. The object file contains the binary codes for the instructions and information about the addresses of the instructions. After further processing, the contents of this file will be loaded into memory and run. The second file generated by the assembler is called the *assembler list file* and is given the extension .LST. Figure 3-16 shows the assembler list file for the source program in Figure 3-14. The list file contains your assembly language statements, the binary codes for each instruction, and the offset for each instruction. You usually send this file to a printer so that you will have a printout of the entire program to work with when you are testing and troubleshooting the program. The assembler listing will also indicate any typing or syntax (assembly language grammar) errors you made in your source program.

To correct the errors indicated on the listing, you use the editor to reedit your source program and save the corrected source program on disk. You then reassemble the corrected source program. It may take several times through the edit-assemble loop before you get all the syntax errors out of your source program.

NOTE: The assembler only finds syntax errors; it will not tell you whether your program does what it is supposed to do. To determine whether your program works, you have to run the program and test it.

Now let's take a closer look at some of the information given on the assembler listing in Figure 3-16. The leftmost column in the listing gives the offsets of data items from the start of the data segment and the offsets of code bytes from the start of the code segment. Note that the assembler generates only offsets, not absolute physical addresses. A linker or locator will be used to assign the physical starting addresses for the segments.

As evidence of this, note that the MOV AX, DATA_HERE statement is assembled with some blanks after the basic instruction code because the start of DS is not known at the time the program is assembled.

The trailer section of the listing in Figure 3-16 gives some additional information about the segments and names used in the program. The statement CODE_ HERE 16 0014 Para none, for example, tells you that the segment CODE_HERE is 14H bytes long. The statement MULTIPLIER Word DATA_HERE:0002 tells you that MULTIPLIER is a variable of type word and that it is located at an offset of 0002 in the segment DATA_HERE.

Linker

A *linker* is a program used to join several object files into one large object file. When writing large programs, it is usually much more efficient to divide the large program into smaller *modules.* Each module can be individually written, tested, and debugged. Then, when all the modules work, their object modules can be linked together to form a large, functioning program. Also, the object modules for useful programs — a square root program, for example — can be kept in a *library file* and linked into other programs as needed.

NOTE: On IBM PC-type computers, you must run the LINK program on your .OBJ file, even if it contains only one assembly module.

The linker produces a *link file* which contains the binary codes for all the combined modules. The linker also produces a *link map* file which contains the address information about the linked files. The linker, however, does not assign absolute addresses to the program; it assigns only relative addresses starting from zero. This form of the program is said to be *relocatable* because it can be put anywhere in memory to be run. The linkers which come with the TASM or MASM assemblers produce link files with the .EXE extension.

If your program does not require any external hardware, you can use a program called a *debugger* to load and run the .EXE file. We will tell you more about debuggers later. The debugger program which loads your program into memory automatically assigns physical starting addresses to the segments.

If you are going to run your program on a system such as an SDK-86 board, then you must use a *locator program* to assign physical addresses to the segments in the .EXE file.

Locator

A *locator* is a program used to assign the specific addresses of where the segments of object code are to be loaded into memory. A locator program called EXE2BIN comes with the IBM PC Disk Operating System (DOS). EXE2BIN converts a .EXE file to a .BIN file which has physical addresses. You can then use the SDKCOM1 program from Chapter 13 to download the .BIN file to the SDK-86 board. The SDKCOM1 program can also be used to run the program and debug it on the SDK-86 board.

Debugger

If your program requires no external hardware or requires only hardware accessible directly from your microcomputer, then you can use a *debugger* to run and debug your program. A debugger is a program which allows you to load your object code program into system memory, execute the program, and troubleshoot or "debug" it. The debugger allows you to look at the contents of registers and memory locations after your program runs. It allows you to change the contents of registers and memory locations and rerun the program. Some debuggers allow you to stop execution after each instruction so that you can check or alter memory and register contents. A debugger also allows you to set a *breakpoint* at any point in your program. If you insert a breakpoint, the debugger will run the program up to the instruction where you put the breakpoint and then stop execution. You can then examine register and memory contents to see whether the results are correct at that point. If the results arc corrcct, you can move the breakpoint to a later point in the program. If the results are not correct, you can check the program up to that point to find out why they are not correct.

The point here is that the debugger commands help you to quickly find the source of a problem in your program. Once you find the problem, you can then cycle back and correct the algorithm if necessary, use the editor to correct your source program, reassemble the corrected source program, relink, and run the program again.

A basic debugger comes with the DOS for most IBM PC-type computers, but more powerful debuggers such as Borland's Turbo Debugger and Microsoft's Codeview debugger make debugging much easier because they allow you to directly see the contents of registers and memory locations change as a program executes. In a later chapter we show you how to use one of these debuggers.

Microprocessor prototyping boards such as the SDK-86 contain a debugger program in ROM. On boards such as this, the debugger is commonly called a *monitor program* because it lets you monitor program activity. The SDK-86 monitor program, for example, lets you enter and run programs, single-step through programs, examine register and memory contents, and insert breakpoints.

Emulator

Another way to run your program is with an *emulator,* such as that shown in Figure 3-17. An emulator is a mixture of hardware and software. It is usually used to test and debug the hardware and software of an external system, such as the prototype of a microprocessor-based instrument. Part of the hardware of an emulator is a multiwire cable which connects the host system to the system being developed. A plug at the end of the cable is plugged into the prototype system in place of its microprocessor. Through this connection the software of the emulator allows you to download your object code program into RAM in the system being tested and run

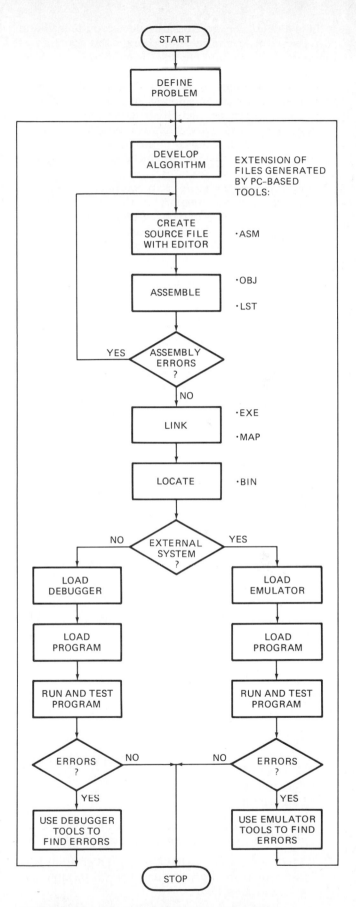

FIGURE 3-18   Program development algorithm (see p. 62).

it. Like a debugger, an emulator allows you to load and run programs, examine and change the contents of registers, examine and change the contents of memory locations, and insert breakpoints in the program. The emulator also takes a "snapshot" of the contents of registers, activity on the address and data bus, and the state of the flags as each instruction executes. The emulator stores this *trace data*, as it is called, in a large RAM. You can do a printout of the trace data to see the results that your program produced on a step-by-step basis.

Another powerful feature of an emulator is the ability to use either system memory or the memory on the prototype for the program you are debugging. In a later chapter we discuss in detail the use of an emulator in developing a microprocessor-based product.

Summary of the Use of Program Development Tools

Figure 3-18 (p. 61) summarizes the steps in developing a working program. This may seem complicated, but if you use the accompanying lab manual to go through the process a couple of times, you will find that it is quite easy.

The first and most important step is to think out very carefully what you want the program to do and how you want the program to do it. Next, use an editor to create the source file for your program. Assemble the source file. If the assembler list file indicates any errors in your program, use the editor to correct these errors. Cycle through the edit-assemble loop until the assembler tells you on the listing that it found no errors. If your program consists of several modules, then use the linker to join their object modules into one large object module. If your system requires it, use a locate program to specify where you want your program to be put in memory. Your program is now ready to be loaded into memory and run. Note that Figure 3-18 also shows the extensions for the files produced by each of the development programs.

If your program does not interact with any external hardware other than that connected directly to the system, then you can use the system debugger to run and debug your program. If your program is intended to work with external hardware, such as the prototype of a microprocessor-based instrument, then you will probably use an emulator to run and debug your pro-

gram. We will be discussing and showing the use of these program development tools throughout the rest of this book.

CHECKLIST OF IMPORTANT TERMS AND CONCEPTS IN THIS CHAPTER

If you do not remember any of the terms or concepts in the following list, use the index to find them in the chapter.

Algorithm

Flowcharts and flowchart symbols

Structured programming

Pseudocode

Top-down and bottom-up design methods

Sequence, repetition, and decision operations

SEQUENCE, IF-THEN-ELSE, IF-THEN, nested IF-THEN-ELSE, CASE, WHILE-DO, REPEAT-UNTIL programming structures

8086 instructions: MOV, IN, OUT, ADD, ADC, SUB, SBB, AND, OR, XOR, MUL, DIV

Instruction mnemonics

Initialization list

Assembly language program format

Instruction template: W bit, MOD, R/M, D bit

Segment-override prefix

Assembler directives: SEGMENT, ENDS, END, DB, DW, DD, EQU, ASSUME

Accessing named data items

Editor

Assembler

Linker: library file, link files, link map, relocatable

Locator

Debugger, monitor program

Emulator, trace data

REVIEW QUESTIONS AND PROBLEMS

1. List the major steps in developing an assembly language program.

2. What is the main advantage of a top-down design approach to solving a programming problem?

3. Why should you develop a detailed algorithm for a program before writing down any assembly language instructions?

4. *a.* What are the three basic structure types used to write the algorithm for a program?

   b. What is the advantage of using only these structures when writing the algorithm for a program?

5. A program is like a recipe. Use a flowchart or pseudocode to show the algorithm for the following recipe. The operations in it are sequence and repetition. Instead of implementing the resulting algorithm in assembly language, implement it in your microwave and use the result to help you get through the rest of the book.

Peanut Brittle:

1 cup sugar   1 teaspoon butter
0.5 cup white corn syrup   1 teaspoon vanilla
1 cup unsalted peanuts   1 teaspoon baking soda

   i. Put sugar and syrup in 1.5-quart casserole (with handle) and stir until thoroughly mixed.

   ii. Microwave at HIGH setting for 4 minutes.

   iii. Add peanuts and stir until thoroughly mixed.

   iv. Microwave at HIGH setting for 4 minutes. Add butter and vanilla, stir until well mixed, and microwave at HIGH setting for 2 more minutes.

   v. Add baking soda and gently stir until light and foamy. Pour mixture onto nonstick cookie sheet and let cool for 1 hour. When cool, break into pieces. Makes 1 pound.

6. Use a flowchart or pseudocode to show the algorithm for a program which gets a number from a memory location, subtracts 20H from it, and outputs 01H to port 3AH if the result of the subtraction is greater than 25H.

7. Given the register contents in Figure 3-19, answer the following questions:
   a. What physical address will the next instruction be fetched from?
   b. What is the physical address for the top of the stack?

```
                              DATA SEGMENT
          ES   6000           5000CH   D7
          CS   4000           5000BH   9A
          SS   7000           5000AH   7C
          DS   5000           50009H   DB
          IP   43E8           50008H   C3
          SP   0000           50007H   B2
          BP   2468           50006H   49
          SI   4C00           50005H   21
          DI   7D00           50004H   89
                              50003H   71
                              50002H   22
                              50001H   4A
                              50000H   3B

             AH  AL                 BH  BL
        AX   42  35          BX     07  5A

             CH  CL                 DH  DL
        CX   00  04          DX     33  02
```

FIGURE 3-19   8086 register and memory contents for Problems 7, 8, and 10.

8. Describe the operation and results of each of the following instructions, given the register contents shown in Figure 3-19. Include in your answer the physical address or register that each instruction will get its operands from and the physical address or register in which each instruction will put the result. Use the instruction descriptions in Chapter 6 to help you. Assume that the following instructions are independent, not sequential, unless listed together under a letter.

   a. MOV AX, BX   *k.* OR CL, BL
   b. MOV CL, 37H   *l.* NOT AH
   c. INC BX   *m.* ROL BX, 1
   d. MOV CX, [246BH]   *n.* AND AL, CH
   e. MOV CX, 246BH   *o.* MOV DS, AX
   f. ADD AL, DH   *p.* ROR BX, CL
   g. MUL BX   *q.* AND AL, 0FH
   h. DEC BP   *r.* MOV, AX, [BX]
   i. DIV BL   *s.* MOV [BX] [SI], CL
   j. SUB AX, DX

9. See if you can spot the grammatical (syntax) errors in the following instructions (use Chapter 6 to help you):
   a. MOV BH, AX   *d.* MOV 7632H, CX
   b. MOV DX, CL   *e.* IN BL, 04H
   c. ADD AL, 2073H

10. Show the results that will be in the affected registers or memory locations after each of the following groups of instructions executes. Assume that each group of instructions starts with the register and memory contents shown in Figure 3-19. (Use Chapter 6.)
    a. ADD BL, AL   *d.* MOV BX, 000AH
        MOV [0004], BL   MOV AL, [BX]
    b. MOV CL, 04   SUB AL, CL
        ROR DI, CL   INC BX
    c. ADD AL, BH   MOV [BX], AL
        DAA

11. Write the 8086 instruction which will perform the indicated operation. Use the instruction overview in this chapter and the detailed descriptions in Chapter 6 to help you.
    a. Copy AL to BL.
    b. Load 43H into CL.
    c. Increment the contents of CX by 1.
    d. Copy SP to BP.
    e. Add 07H to DL.
    f. Multiply AL times BL.
    g. Copy AX to a memory location at offset 245AH in the data segment.
    h. Decrement SP by 1.
    i. Rotate the most significant bit of AL into the least significant bit position.
    j. Copy DL to a memory location whose offset is in BX.
    k. Mask the lower 4 bits of BL.
    l. Set the most significant bit of AX to a 1, but do not affect the other bits.
    m. Invert the lower 4 bits of BL, but do not affect the other bits.

12. Construct the binary code for each of the following 8086 instructions.
    a. MOV BL, AL   *f.* ROR AX, 1
    b. MOV [BX], CX   *g.* OUT DX, AL
    c. ADD BX, 59H[DI]   *h.* AND AL, 0FH
    d. SUB [2048], DH   *i.* NOP
    e. XCHG CH, ES:[BX]   *j.* IN AL, DX

13. Describe the function of each assembler directive and instruction statement in the short program shown in Figure 3-20.

```
;PRESSURE READ PROGRAM

DATA_HERE SEGMENT
    PRESSURE  DB  0          ;storage for pressure
DATA_HERE ENDS

PRESSURE_PORT      EQU 04H  ;Pressure sensor connected
                           ; to port 04H
CORRECTION_FACTOR EQU 07H  ;Current correction factor
                           ; of 07
CODE_HERE SEGMENT
    ASSUME CS:CODE_HERE, DS:DATA_HERE
    MOV  AX, DATA_HERE
    MOV  DS, AX
    IN   AL, PRESSURE_PORT
    ADD  AL, CORRECTION_FACTOR
    MOV  PRESSURE, AL
CODE_HERE ENDS
        END
```

FIGURE 3-20   Program for Problem 13.

14. Describe how an assembly language program is developed and debugged using system tools such as editors, assemblers, linkers, locators, emulators, and debuggers.

15. Write the pseudocode representation for the flowchart in Figure 3-18, p. 61.

CHAPTER 4

Implementing Standard Program Structures in 8086 Assembly Language

In Chapter 3 we worked very hard to convince you that you should not try to write programs directly in assembly language. The analogy of building a house without a plan should come to mind here. When faced with a programming problem, you should solve the problem and write the algorithm for the solution using the standard program structures we described. Then you simply translate each step in the flowchart or pseudocode to a group of one to four assembly language instructions which will implement that step. The comments in the assembly language program should describe the functions of each instruction or group of instructions, so you essentially write the comments for the program, then write the assembly language instructions which implement those comments. Once you learn how to implement each of the standard programming structures, you should find it quite easy to translate algorithms to assembly language. Also, as we will show you, the standard structure approach makes debugging relatively easy.

The purposes of this chapter are to show you how to write the algorithms for some common programming problems, how to implement these algorithms in 8086 assembly language, and how to systematically debug assembly language programs. In the process you will also learn more about how some of the 8086 instructions work.

OBJECTIVES

At the conclusion of this chapter, you should be able to:

1. Write flowcharts or pseudocode for simple programming problems.

2. Implement SEQUENCE, IF-THEN-ELSE, WHILE-DO, and REPEAT-UNTIL program structures in 8086 assembly language.

3. Describe the operation of selected data transfer, arithmetic, logical, jump, and loop instructions.

4. Use based and indexed addressing modes to access data in your programs.

5. Describe a systematic approach to debugging a simple assembly language program using debugger, monitor, or emulator tools.

6. Write a delay loop which produces a desired amount of delay on a specific 8086 system.

SIMPLE SEQUENCE PROGRAMS

Finding the Average of Two Numbers

DEFINING THE PROBLEM AND WRITING THE ALGORITHM

A common need in programming is to find the average of two numbers. Suppose, for example, we know the maximum temperature and the minimum temperature for a given day, and we want to determine the average temperature. The sequence of steps we go through to do this might look something like the following.

Add maximum temperature and minimum temperature.

Divide sum by 2 to get average temperature.

This sequence doesn't look much like an assembly language program, and it shouldn't. The algorithm at this point should be general enough that it could be implemented in any programming language, or on any machine. Once you are reasonably sure of your algorithm, then you can start thinking about the architecture and instructions of the specific microcomputer on which you plan to run the program. Now let's show you how we get from the algorithm to the assembly language program for it.

SETTING UP THE DATA STRUCTURE

One of the first things for you to think about in this process is the data that the program will be working with. You need to ask yourself questions such as:

1. Will the data be in memory or in registers?

2. Is the data of type byte, type word, or perhaps type doubleword?

3. How many data items are there?

4. Does the data represent only positive numbers, or does it represent positive and negative (signed) numbers?

5. For more complex problems, you might ask how the data is structured. For example, is the data in an array or in a record?

Let's assume for this example that the data is all in memory, that the data is of type byte, and that the data represents only positive numbers in the range 0 to 0FFH. The top part of Figure 4-1, between the DATA SEGMENT and the DATA ENDS directives, shows how you might set up the data structure for this program. It is very similar to the data structure for the multiplication example in the last chapter. In the logical segment called DATA, HI_TEMP is declared as a variable of type byte and initialized with a value of 92H. In an actual application, the value in HI_TEMP would probably be put there by another program which reads the output from a temperature sensor. The statement LO_TEMP DB 52H declares a variable of type byte and initializes it with the value 52H. The statement AV_TEMP DB ? sets aside a byte location to store the average temperature, but does not initialize the location to any value. When the program executes, it will write a value to this location.

INITIALIZATION CHECKLIST

Although it does not show in the algorithm, you know from the discussion in Chapter 3 that most programs start with a series of initialization instructions. For this example program, all you have to initialize is the data segment register. The MOV AX,DATA and MOV DS,AX instructions at the start of the program in Figure 4-1 do this.

These instructions load the DS register with the upper 16 bits of the starting address for the data segment. If you are using an assembler, you can use the name DATA in the instruction to refer to this address. If you are not using an assembler, then just put the hex for the upper 16 bits of the address in the MOV AX,DATA instruction in place of the name.

CHOOSING INSTRUCTIONS TO IMPLEMENT THE ALGORITHM

The next step is to look at the algorithm to determine the major actions that you want the program to perform. If you have written the algorithm correctly, then all you should have to do is translate each step in the algorithm to one to four assembly language instructions which will implement that step.

You want the program to add two byte-type numbers together, so scan through the instruction groups in Chapter 3 to determine which 8086 instruction will do this for you. The ADD instruction is the obvious choice in this case.

Next, find and read the detailed discussion of the ADD instruction in Chapter 6. From the discussion there, you can determine how the instruction works and see if it will do the necessary job. From the discussion of the ADD instruction, you should find that the ADD instruction has the format ADD destination,source. A byte from the specified source is added to a byte in the specified destination, or a word from the specified source is added to a word in the specified destination. (Note that you cannot directly add a byte to a word.) The result in either case is put in the specified destination. The source can be an immediate number, a register, or a memory location. The destination can be a register or a

```
 1                                    ; 8086 PROGRAM     F4-01.ASM
 2                         ;ABSTRACT  : This program averages two temperatures
 3                                    ; named HI_TEMP and LO_TEMP and puts the
 4                                    ; result in the memory location AV_TEMP.
 5                         ;REGISTERS : Uses DS, CS, AX, BL
 6                         ;PORTS     : None used
 7
 8 0000                   DATA    SEGMENT
 9 0000  92                       HI_TEMP DB  92H      ; Max temp storage
10 0001  52                       LO_TEMP DB  52H      ; Low temp storage
11 0002  ??                       AV_TEMP DB  ?        ; Store average here
12 0003                   DATA    ENDS
13
14 0000                   CODE    SEGMENT
15                                ASSUME CS:CODE, DS:DATA
16 0000  B8 0000s         START:  MOV  AX, DATA        ; Initialize data segment
17 0003  8E D8                    MOV  DS, AX
18 0005  A0 0000r                 MOV  AL, HI_TEMP     ; Get first temperature
19 0008  02 06 0001r              ADD  AL, LO_TEMP     ; Add second to it
20 000C  B4 00                    MOV  AH, 00H         ; Clear all of AH register
21 000E  80 D4 00                 ADC  AH, 00H         ; Put carry in LSB of AH
22 0011  B3 02                    MOV  BL, 02H         ; Load divisor in BL register
23 0013  F6 F3                    DIV  BL              ; Divide AX by BL. Quotient in AL,
24                                                     ; and remainder in AH
25 0015  A2 0002r                 MOV  AV_TEMP, AL     ; Copy result to memory
26 0018                   CODE    ENDS
27                                END  START
```

FIGURE 4-1 8086 program to average two temperatures.

memory location. However, in a single instruction the source and the destination cannot both be memory locations. This means that you have to move one of the operands from memory to a register before you can do the ADD.

Another point to consider here is that if you add two 8-bit numbers, the sum can be larger than 8 bits. Adding F0H and 40H, for example, gives 130H. The 8-bit destination will contain 30H, and the carry will be held in the carry flag. This means that to have the complete sum, you must collect the parts of the result in a location large enough to hold all 9 bits. A 16-bit register is a good choice.

To summarize, then, you need to move one of the numbers you want to add into a register, such as AL, add the other number from memory to it, and move any carry produced by the addition to the upper half of the 16-bit register which contains the sum in its lower 8 bits. Now let's take another look at Figure 4-1 to see how you implement this step in the algorithm with 8086 instructions.

The instruction MOV AL,HI_TEMP copies one of the temperatures from a memory location to the AL register. The name HI_TEMP in the instruction represents the direct address or displacement of the variable in the logical segment DATA. The ADD AL,LO_TEMP instruction adds the specified byte from memory to the contents of the AL register. The lower 8 bits of the sum are left in the AL register. If the addition produces a result greater than FFH, the carry flag will be set to a 1. If the addition produces a result less than or equal to FFH, the carry flag will be a 0. In either case, we want to get the contents of the carry flag into the least significant bit of the AH register, so that the entire sum is in the AX register.

The MOV AH,00H instruction clears all the bits of AH to 0's. The ADC AH,00H instruction adds the immediate number 00H plus the contents of the carry flag to the contents of the AH register. The result will be left in the AH register. Since we cleared AH to all 0's before the add, what we are really adding is 00H + 00H + CF. The result of all this is that the carry bit ends up in the least significant bit of AH, which is what we set out to do.

The next major action in our algorithm is to divide the sum of the two temperatures by 2. To determine how this step can be translated to assembly language instructions, look at the instruction groups in the last chapter to see if the 8086 has a Divide instruction. You should find that it has two Divide instructions, DIV and IDIV. DIV is for dividing unsigned numbers, and IDIV is used for dividing signed binary numbers. Since in this example we are dividing unsigned binary numbers, look up the DIV instruction in Chapter 6 to find out how it works.

The DIV instruction can be used to divide a 16-bit number in AX by a specified byte in a register or in a memory location. After the division, an 8-bit quotient is left in the AL register, and an 8-bit remainder is left in the AH register. The DIV instruction can also be used to divide a 32-bit number in the DX and AX registers by a 16-bit number from a specified register or memory

location. In this case, a 16-bit quotient is left in the AX register, and a 16-bit remainder is left in the DX register. In either case, there is a problem if the quotient is too large to fit in AX for a 32-bit divide or AL for a 16-bit divide. Fortunately, the data in the example here is such that the problem will not arise. In a later chapter we discuss what to do about this problem.

Remember from the previous discussion that the sum of the two temperatures is already positioned in the AX register as required by the DIV operation. Before we can do the DIV operation, however, we have to get the divisor, 02H, into a register or memory location to satisfy the requirements of the DIV instruction. A simple way to do this is with the MOV BL,02H instruction, which loads the immediate number 02H into the BL register. Now you can do the divide operation with the instruction DIV BL. The 8-bit quotient from the division will be left in the AL register.

The algorithm doesn't show it, but in our discussion of the data structure we said that the minimum, maximum, and average temperatures were all in memory locations. Therefore, to complete the program, you have to copy the quotient in AL to the memory location we set aside for the average temperature. As shown in Figure 4-1, the instruction MOV AV_TEMP,AL will copy AL to this memory location.

NOTE: We could have used the remainder from the division in AH to round off the average temperature to the nearest degree, but that would have made the program more complex than we wanted for this example.

SUMMARY OF CONVERTING AN ALGORITHM TO ASSEMBLY LANGUAGE

The first step in converting an algorithm to assembly language is to set up the data structure that the algorithm will be working with. The next step is to write at the start of the code segment any instructions required to initialize variables, segment registers, peripheral devices, etc. Then determine the instructions required to implement each of the major actions in the algorithm, and decide how the data must be positioned for these instructions. Finally, insert the MOV or other instructions required to get the data into the correct position for these instructions.

A Few Comments about the 8086 Arithmetic Instructions

The 8086 has instructions to add, subtract, multiply, and divide. It can operate on signed or unsigned binary numbers, BCD numbers, or numbers represented in ASCII. Rather than put a lot of arithmetic examples at this point in the book, we show arithmetic examples with each arithmetic instruction description in Chapter 6. The description of the MUL instruction in Chapter 6, for example, shows how unsigned binary numbers are multiplied. Also we show other arithmetic examples as needed throughout the rest of the book. If you need to do some arithmetic operations with an 8086, there are a few instructions in addition to the basic add, subtract, multiply, and divide instructions that you need to look up in Chapter 6.

If you are adding BCD numbers, you need to also look up the Decimal Adjust for Addition (DAA) instruction. If you are subtracting BCD numbers, then you need to look up the Decimal Adjust for Subtraction (DAS) instruction. If you are working with ASCII numbers, then you need to look up the ASCII Adjust after Addition (AAA) instruction, the ASCII Adjust after Subtraction (AAS) instruction, the ASCII Adjust after Multiply (AAM) instruction, and the ASCII Adjust before Division (AAD) instruction.

Debugging Assembly Language Programs

By now you should be writing some programs of your own, so we need to give you a few hints on how to debug them if they don't work correctly the first time you try to run them.

The first technique you use when you hit a difficult-to-find problem in either hardware or software is the *5-minute rule.* This rule says, "You get 5 minutes to freak out and mumble about changing vocations, then you have to cope with the problem in a systematic manner." What this means is step back from the problem, collect your wits, and think out a systematic series of steps to find the solution. Random poking and probing wastes a lot of valuable time and seldom finds the problem. Here is a list of additional techniques you may find useful in writing and debugging your programs.

1. Very carefully define the problem you are trying to solve with the program and work out the best algorithm you can.

2. Write and test each section of a program as you go, instead of writing a large program all at once.

3. If a program or program section does not work, first recheck the algorithm to make sure it really does what you want it to. You might have someone else look at it also. Another person may quickly spot an error you have overlooked 17 times.

4. If the algorithm seems correct, check to make sure that you have used the correct instructions to implement the algorithm. It is very easy to accidentally switch the operands in an instruction. You might, for example, write down the instruction MOV AX,DX when the instruction you really want is MOV DX,AX. Sometimes it helps to work out on paper the effect that a series of instructions will have on some sample numbers. These predictions can later be compared with the actual results produced when the program section runs.

5. If you are hand coding your programs, this is the next place to check. It is very easy to get a bit wrong when you construct the 8086 instruction codes. Also remember, when constructing instruction codes which contain addresses or displacements, that the low byte of the address or displacement is coded in before the high byte.

6. If you don't find a problem in the algorithm, instructions, or coding, now is the time to use debugger, monitor, or emulator tools to help you localize the problem. You could use these tools right from the start, but if you do, it is easy to get lost in chasing bits and not see the bigger picture of what is causing the program to fail. When debugging short program sections on an SDK-86 board, for example, you might use the *single-step* command to help you determine why the program is not doing what you want it to do. The SDK-86 board's single-step command executes one instruction and then stops execution. You can then use the Examine Register and Examine Memory commands to see if registers and memory contain the correct data. If the results are correct at that point, you can use the single-step command to execute the next instruction. You keep stepping through the program until you reach a point where the results are not what you predicted they should be at that point. Once you have localized the problem to one or two instructions, it is usually not too hard to find the error. An exercise in the accompanying lab manual shows you how to use the single-step command on an SDK-86 board.

7. For longer programs, the single-step approach can be somewhat tedious. *Breakpoints* are often a faster technique to narrow the source of a problem down to a small region. Most debuggers, monitors, and emulators allow you to specify both a starting address and an ending address in their GO command. The SDK-86 monitor GO command, for example, has the format GO address,breakpoint address. When you enter one of these commands, execution will start at the address specified first in the command and stop when it reaches the address specified in the second position in the command. After the program runs to a breakpoint, you can use the Examine Register and Examine Memory commands to check the results at that point.

Here's how you use breakpoints. Instead of running the entire program, specify a breakpoint so that execution stops some distance into the program. You can then check to see if the results are correct at this point. If they are, you can run the program again with the breakpoint at a later address and check the results at that point. If the results are not correct, you can move the breakpoint to an earlier point in the program, run it again, and check whether the results in registers and memory are correct.

Suppose, for example, you write a program such as the averaging program in Figure 4-1, and it does not give the correct results. The first place to put a breakpoint might be at the address of the MOV AH,00 instruction. Incidentally, in most systems the instruction at the address where you put the breakpoint does not get executed. After the program runs to this breakpoint, you check to see if the data segment register was initialized correctly and if the basic addition was performed correctly. If the program works correctly to this point, you can run it again with the breakpoint at the address of the MOV AV_TEMP,AL instruction. After the program executes to this breakpoint, you can check AL to see if the division produced the results you predicted. If the 8086 is working at all, it will almost always do operations such as this correctly, so recheck your predictions if you disagree with it.

It helps your frustration level if you make a game of thinking where to put breakpoints to track down the little bug that is messing up your program. With a little practice you should soon develop an efficient debugging algorithm of your own using the specific tools available on your system. In the next chapter we show you how to use a more powerful debugger to run and debug programs in an IBM PC-type computer.

Converting Two ASCII Codes to Packed BCD

DEFINING THE PROBLEM AND WRITING THE ALGORITHM

Computer data is often transferred as a series of 8-bit ASCII codes. If, for example, you have a microcomputer connected to an SDK-86 board and you type a 9 on an ASCII-encoded computer terminal keyboard, the 8-bit ASCII code sent to the SDK-86 will be 00111001 binary, or 39H. If you type a 5 on the keyboard, the code sent to the computer will be 00110101 binary or 35H, the ASCII code for 5. As shown in Table 1-2, the ASCII codes for the numbers 0 through 9 are 30H through 39H. The lower nibble of the ASCII codes contains the 4-bit BCD code for the decimal number represented by the ASCII code.

For many applications, we want to convert the ASCII code to its simple BCD equivalent. We can do this by simply replacing the 3 in the upper nibble of the byte with four 0's. For example, suppose we read in 00111001 binary or 39H, the ASCII code for 9. If we replace the upper 4 bits with 0's, we are left with 00001001 binary or 09H. The lower 4 bits then contain 1001 binary, the BCD code for 9. Numbers represented as one BCD digit per byte are called *unpacked BCD*.

For applications in which we are going to perform mathematical operations on the BCD numbers, we usually combine two BCD digits in a single byte. This form is called *packed BCD*. Figure 4-2 shows examples of ASCII, unpacked BCD, and packed BCD. The problem we are going to work on here is how to convert two numbers from ASCII code form to unpacked BCD form and then pack the two BCD digits into one byte. Figure 4-2 shows in numerical form the steps we want the program to perform. When you are writing a program

```
ASCII                 5    0011  0101 = 35H
ASCII                 9    0011  1001 = 39H

UNPACKED BCD          5    0000  0101 = 05H
UNPACKED BCD          9    0000  1001 = 09H

UNPACKED BCD 5             0101  0000 = 50H
MOVED TO UPPER NIBBLE

PACKED BCD           59    0101  1001 = 59H
```

FIGURE 4-2 ASCII, unpacked BCD, and packed BCD examples.

which manipulates data such as this, a numerical example will help you visualize the algorithm.

The algorithm for this problem can be stated simply as

Convert first ASCII number to unpacked BCD.

Convert second ASCII number to unpacked BCD.

Move first BCD nibble to upper nibble position in byte.

Pack two BCD nibbles in one byte.

Now let's see how you can implement this algorithm in 8086 assembly language.

THE DATA STRUCTURE AND INITIALIZATION LIST

For this example program, let's assume that the ASCII code for 5 was received and put in the BL register, and the second ASCII code was received and left in the AL register. Since we are not using memory for data in this program, we do not need to declare a data segment or initialize the data segment register. Incidentally, in a real application this program would probably be a procedure or a part of a larger program.

MASKING WITH THE AND INSTRUCTION

The first operation in the algorithm is to convert a number in ASCII form to its unpacked BCD equivalent. This is done by replacing the upper 4 bits of the ASCII byte with four 0's. The 8086 AND instruction can be used to do this operation. Remember from basic logic or from the review in Chapter 1 that when a 1 or a 0 is ANDed with a 0, the result is always a zero. ANDing a bit with a 0 is called *masking* that bit because the previous state of the bit is hidden or masked. To mask 4 bits in a word, then, all you do is AND each bit you want to mask with a 0. A bit ANDed with a 1, remember, is not changed.

According to the description of the AND instruction in Chapter 6, the instruction has the format AND destination,source. The instruction ANDs each bit of the specified source with the corresponding bit of the specified destination and puts the result in the specified destination. The source can be an immediate number, a register, or a memory location specified in one of those 24 different ways. The destination can be a register or a memory location. The source and the destination must both be bytes, or they must both be words. The source and the destination cannot both be memory locations in an instruction.

For this example the first ASCII number is in the BL register, so we can just AND an immediate number with this register to mask the desired bits. The upper 4 bits of the immediate number should be 0's because these correspond to the bits we want to mask in BL. The lower 4 bits of the immediate number should be 1's because we want to leave these bits unchanged. The immediate number, then, should be 00001111 binary or 0FH. The instruction to convert the first ASCII number is AND BL,0FH. When this instruction executes, it will leave the desired unpacked BCD in BL. Figure 4-3 shows how this will work for an ASCII number of 35H initially in BL.

```
ASCII 5           0011  0101
MASK              0000  1111
RESULT            0000  0101
```

FIGURE 4-3 Effects of ANDing with 1's and 0's.

For the next action in the algorithm, we want to perform the same operation on a second ASCII number in the AL register. The instruction AND AL,0FH will do this for us. After this instruction executes, AL will contain the unpacked BCD for the second ASCII number.

MOVING A NIBBLE WITH THE ROTATE INSTRUCTION

The next action in the algorithm is to move the 4 BCD bits in the first unpacked BCD byte to the upper nibble position in the byte. We need to do this so that the 4 BCD bits are in the correct position for packing with the second BCD nibble. Take another look at Figure 4-2 to help you visualize this. What we are effectively doing here is swapping or exchanging the top nibble with the bottom nibble of the byte. If you check the instruction groups in Chapter 3, you will find that the 8086 has an Exchange instruction, XCHG, which can be used to swap two bytes or to swap two words. The 8086 does not have a specific instruction to swap the nibbles in a byte. However, if you think of the operation that we need to do as shifting or rotating the BCD bits 4 bit positions to the left, this will give you a good idea which instruction will do the job for you. The 8086 has a wide variety of rotate and shift instructions. For now, let's look at the rotate instructions. There are two instructions, ROL and RCL, which rotate the bits of a specified operand to the left. Figure 4-4 shows in diagram form how these two instructions work. For ROL, each bit in the specified register or memory location is rotated 1 bit position to the left. The bit that was the MSB is rotated around into the LSB position. The old MSB is also copied to the carry flag. For the RCL instruction, each bit of the specified register or memory location is also rotated 1 bit position to the left. However, the bit that was in the MSB position is moved to the carry flag, and the bit that was in the carry flag is moved into the LSB position. The C in the middle of the mnemonic

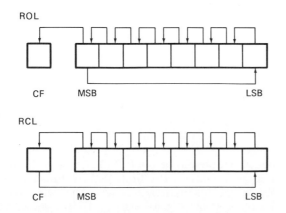

FIGURE 4-4 ROL instruction and RCL instruction operations for byte operands.

should help you remember that the carry flag is included in the rotated loop when the RCL instruction executes.

In the example program we really don't want the contents of the carry flag rotated into the operand, so the ROL instruction seems to be the one we want. If you consult the ROL instruction description in Chapter 6, you will find that the instruction has the format ROL destination,count. The destination can be a register or a memory location. It can be a byte location or a word location. The count can be the immediate number 1 specified directly in the instruction, or it can be a number previously loaded into the CL register. The instruction ROL AL,1, for example, will rotate the contents of AL 1 bit position to the left. We could repeat this instruction four times to produce the shift of 4 bit positions that we need for our BCD packing problem. However, there is an easier way to do it. We first load the CL register with the number of times we want to rotate AL. The instruction MOV CL,04H will do this. Then we use the instruction ROL BL,CL to do the rotation. When it executes, this instruction will automatically rotate BL the number of bit positions loaded into CL. Note that for the 80186 you can write the single instruction ROL BL,04H to do this job.

Now that we have determined the instructions needed to mask the upper nibbles and the instructions needed to move the first BCD digit into position, the only thing left is to pack the upper nibble from BL and the lower nibble from AL into a single byte.

COMBINING BYTES OR WORDS WITH THE ADD OR THE OR INSTRUCTION

You can't use a standard MOV instruction to combine two bytes into one as we need to do here. The reason is that the MOV instruction copies an operand from a specified source to a specified destination. The previous contents of the destination are lost. You can, however, use an ADD or an OR instruction to pack the two BCD nibbles.

As described in the previous program example, the ADD instruction adds the contents of a specified source to the contents of a specified destination and leaves the result in the specified destination. For the example program here, the instruction ADD AL,BL can be used to combine the two BCD nibbles. Take a look at Figure 4-2 to help you visualize this addition.

Another way to combine the two nibbles is with the OR instruction. If you look up the OR instruction in Chapter 6, you will find that it has the format OR destination,source. This instruction ORs each bit in the specified source with the corresponding bit in the specified destination. The result of the ORing is left in the specified destination. Remember from basic logic or the review in Chapter 1 that ORing a bit with a 1 always produces a result of 1. ORing a bit with a 0 leaves the bit unchanged. To set a bit in a word to a 1, then, all you have to do is OR that bit with a word which has a 1 in that bit position and 0's in all the other bit positions. This is similar to the way the AND instruction is used to clear bits in a word to 0's. See the OR instruction description in Chapter 6 for examples of this.

```
1                                      ;  8086 PROGRAM F4-05.ASM
2                        ;ABSTRACT    :  Program produces a packed BCD byte from 2 ASCII-encoded digits
3                                      ;  The first ASCII digit (5) is loaded in BL.
4                                      ;  The second ASCII digit (9) is loaded in AL.
5                                      ;  The result (packed BCD) is left in AL
6                        ;REGISTERS   :  Uses CS, AL, BL, CL
7                        ;PORTS       :  None used
8
9  0000                 CODE    SEGMENT
10                               ASSUME CS:CODE
11 0000   B3 35          START:  MOV  BL, '5'   ; Load first ASCII digit into BL
12 0002   B0 39                  MOV  AL, '9'   ; Load second ASCII digit into AL
13 0004   80 E3 0F               AND  BL, 0FH   ; Mask upper 4 bits of first digit
14 0007   24 0F                  AND  AL, 0FH   ; Mask upper 4 bits of second digit
15 0009   B1 04                  MOV  CL, 04H   ; Load CL for 4 rotates required
16 000B   D2 C3                  ROL  BL, CL    ; Rotate BL 4 bit positions
17 000D   0A C3                  OR   AL, BL    ; Combine nibbles, result in AL
18 000F                 CODE    ENDS
19                               END START
```

FIGURE 4-5   List file of 8086 assembly language program to produce packed
BCD from two ASCII characters.

For the example program here, we use the instruction OR AL,BL to pack the two BCD nibbles. Bits ORed with 0's will not be changed. Bits ORed with 1's will become or stay 1's. Again look at Figure 4-2 to help you visualize this operation.

SUMMARY OF BCD PACKING PROGRAM

If you compare the algorithm for this program with the finished program in Figure 4-5, you should see that each step in the algorithm translates to one or two assembly language instructions. As we told you before, developing the assembly language program from a good algorithm is really quite easy because you are simply translating one step at a time to its equivalent assembly language instructions. Also, debugging a program developed in this way is quite easy because you simply single-step or breakpoint your way through it and check the results after each step. In the next section we discuss the 8086 JMP instructions and flags so we can show you how you implement some of the other programming structures in assembly language.

JUMPS, FLAGS, AND CONDITIONAL JUMPS

Introduction

The real power of a computer comes from its ability to choose between two or more sequences of actions based on some condition, repeat a sequence of instructions *as long as* some condition exists, or repeat a sequence of instructions *until* some condition exists. *Flags* indicate whether some condition is present or not. *Jump* instructions are used to tell the computer the address to fetch its next instruction from. Figure 4-6 shows in diagram form the different ways a Jump instruction can direct the 8086 to fetch its next instruction from some place in memory other than the next sequential location.

The 8086 has two types of Jump instructions, conditional and unconditional. When the 8086 fetches and decodes an Unconditional Jump instruction, it always goes to the specified jump destination. You might use this type of Jump instruction at the end of a program so that the entire program runs over and over, as shown in Figure 4-6.

When the 8086 fetches and decodes a Conditional Jump instruction, it evaluates the state of a specified flag to determine whether to fetch its next instruction from the jump destination location or to fetch its next instruction from the next sequential memory location.

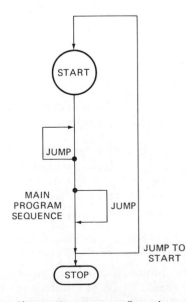

FIGURE 4-6   Change in program flow that can be caused by jump instructions.

Let's start by taking a look at how the 8086 Unconditional Jump instruction works.

The 8086 Unconditional Jump Instruction

INTRODUCTION

As we said before, Jump instructions can be used to tell the 8086 to start fetching its instructions from some new location rather than from the next sequential location. The 8086 JMP instruction always causes a jump to occur, so this is referred to as an *unconditional* jump.

Remember from previous discussions that the 8086 computes the physical address from which to fetch its next code byte by adding the offset in the instruction pointer register to the code segment base represented by the 16-bit number in the CS register. When the 8086 executes a JMP instruction, it loads a new number into the instruction pointer register, and in some cases it also loads a new number into the code segment register.

If the JMP destination is in the same code segment, the 8086 only has to change the contents of the instruction pointer. This type of jump is referred to as a *near*, or *intrasegment*, jump.

If the JMP destination is in a code segment which has a different name from the segment in which the JMP instruction is located, the 8086 has to change the contents of both CS and IP to make the jump. This type of jump is referred to as a *far*, or *intersegment*, jump.

Near and far jumps are further described as either *direct* or *indirect*. If the destination address for the jump is specified directly as part of the instruction, then the jump is described as *direct*. You can have a direct near jump or a direct far jump. If the destination address for the jump is contained in a register or memory location, the jump is referred to as *indirect*, because the 8086 has to go to the specified register or memory location to get the required destination address. You can have an indirect near jump or an indirect far jump.

Figure 4-7 shows the coding templates for the four basic types of unconditional jumps. As you can see, for the direct types, the destination offset, and, if necessary, the segment base are included directly in the instruction. The indirect types of jumps use the second byte of the instruction to tell the 8086 whether the destination offset (and segment base, if necessary) is contained in a register or in memory locations specified with one of the 24 address modes we introduced you to in the last chapter.

The JMP instruction description in Chapter 6 shows examples of each type of jump instruction, but in most of your programs you will use a direct near-type JMP instruction, so in the next section we will discuss in detail how this type works.

UNCONDITIONAL JUMP INSTRUCTION TYPES—OVERVIEW

The 8086 Unconditional Jump instruction, JMP, has five different types. Figure 4-7 shows the names and instruction coding templates for these five types. We will first summarize how these five types work to give you

JMP = Jump

Within segment or group, IP relative—near and short

Opcode	DispL	DispH

Opcode	Clocks	Operation
E9	15	IP ← IP + Disp16
EB	15	IP ← IP + Disp8 (Disp8 sign-extended)

Within segment or group, Indirect

Opcode	mod 100 r/m	mem-low	mem-high

Opcode	Clocks	Operation
FF	11	IP ← Reg16
FF	18+EA	IP ← Mem16

Inter-segment or group, Direct

Opcode	offset-low	offset-high	seg-low	seg-high

Opcode	Clocks	Operation
EA	15	CS ← segbase IP ← offset

Inter-segment or group, Indirect

Opcode	mod 101 r/m			

Opcode	Clocks	Operation
FF	24+EA	CS ← segbase IP ← offset

FIGURE 4-7 8086 Unconditional Jump instructions. (*Intel Corporation*)

an overview; then we will describe in detail the two types you need for your programs at this point. The JMP instruction description in Chapter 6 shows examples of each of the five types.

THE DIRECT NEAR- AND SHORT-TYPE JMP INSTRUCTIONS

As we described previously, a near-type jump instruction can cause the next instruction to be fetched from anywhere in the current code segment. To produce the new instruction fetch address, this instruction adds a 16-bit signed displacement contained in the instruction to the contents of the instruction pointer register. A 16-bit signed displacement means that the jump can be to a location anywhere from +32,767 to −32,768 bytes from the current instruction pointer location. A positive displacement usually means you are jumping ahead in the program, and a negative displacement usually means that you are jumping "backward" in the program.

A special case of the direct near-type jump instruction is the direct short-type jump. If the destination for the jump is within a displacement range of +127 to −128 bytes from the current instruction pointer location, the destination can be reached with just an 8-bit displacement. The coding for this type of jump is shown on the second line of the coding template for the direct near JMP in Figure 4-7. Only one byte is required for the displacement in this case. Again the 8086 produces the new instruction fetch address by adding the signed 8-bit displacement, contained in the instruction, to the contents of the instruction pointer register. Here are some examples of how you use these JMP instructions in programs.

DIRECT WITHIN-SEGMENT NEAR AND DIRECT WITHIN-SEGMENT SHORT JMP EXAMPLES

Suppose that we want an 8086 to execute the instructions in a program over and over. Figure 4-8 shows how the JMP instruction can be used to do this. In this program, the label BACK followed by a colon is used to give a name to the address we want to jump back to. When the assembler reads this label, it will make an entry in its symbol table indicating where it found the label. Then, when the assembler reads the JMP instruction and finds the name BACK in the instruction, it will be able to calculate the displacement from the jump instruction to the label. This displacement will be inserted as part of the code for the instruction. Even if you are not using an assembler, you should use labels to indicate jump destinations so that you can easily see them. The NOP instructions used in the program in Figure 4-8 do nothing except fill space. We used them in this example to represent the instructions that we want to loop through over and over. Once the 8086 gets into the JMP-BACK loop, the only ways it can get out are if the power is turned off, an interrupt occurs, or the system is reset.

Now let's see how the binary code for the JMP instruction in Figure 4-8 is constructed. The jump is to a label in the same segment, so this narrows our choices down to the first three types of JMP instruction shown in Figure 4-7. For several reasons, it is best to use the direct-type JMP instruction whenever possible. This narrows our choices down to the first two types in Figure 4-7. The choice between these two is determined by whether you need a 1-byte or a 2-byte displacement to reach the JMP destination address. Since for our example program the destination address is within the range of −128 to +127 bytes from the instruction after the JMP instruction, we can use the direct within-segment short type of JMP. According to Figure 4-7, the instruction template for this instruction is 11101011 (EBH) followed by a displacement. Here's how you calculate the displacement to put in the instruction.

NOTE: An assembler does this for you automatically, but you should still learn how it is done to help you in troubleshooting.

The numbers in the left column of Figure 4-8 represent the offset of each code byte from the code segment base. These are the numbers that will be in the instruction pointer as the program executes. After the 8086 fetches an instruction byte, it automatically increments the instruction pointer to point to the next instruction byte. The displacement in the JMP instruction will then be added to the offset of the next in-line instruction after the JMP instruction. For the example program in Figure 4-8, the displacement in the JMP instruction will be added to offset 0006H, which is in the instruction pointer after the JMP instruction executes. What this means is that when you are counting the number of bytes of displacement, you always start counting from the address of the instruction immediately after the JMP instruction. For the example program, we want to jump from offset 0006H back to offset 0000H. This is a displacement of −6H.

You can't, however, write the displacement in the instruction as −6H. Negative displacements must be expressed in 2's complement, sign-and-magnitude form. We showed how to do this in Chapter 1. First, write the number as an 8-bit positive binary number. In this case, that is 00000110. Then, invert each bit of this, including the sign bit, to give 11111001. Finally, add 1 to that result to give 11111010 binary or FAH, which is the correct 2's complement representation for −6H. As shown on line 11 in the assembler listing for the program in Figure 4-8, the two code bytes for this JMP instruction then are EBH and FAH.

To summarize this example, then, a label is used to give a name to the destination address for the jump. This name is used to refer to the destination address in the JMP instruction. Since the destination in this example is within the range of −128 to +127 bytes from the address after the JMP instruction, the instruction can be coded as a direct within-segment short-type

```
1                               ; 8086 PROGRAM    F4-08.ASM
2                        ;ABSTRACT  : This program illustrates a "backwards" jump
3                        ;REGISTERS : Uses CS, AL
4                        ;PORTS     : None used
5
6  0000                 CODE    SEGMENT
7                                ASSUME  CS:CODE
8  0000   04 03         BACK:   ADD AL, 03H  ; Add 3 to total
9  0002   90                    NOP          ; Dummy instructions to represent those
10 0003   90                    NOP          ; Instructions jumped back over
11 0004   EB FA                 JMP BACK     ; Jump back over instructions to BACK label
12 0006                 CODE    ENDS
13                              END
```

FIGURE 4-8   List file of program demonstrating "backward" JMP.

```
1                                       ; 8086 PROGRAM       F4-09.ASM
2                         ;ABSTRACT  : This program illustrates a "forwards" jump
3                         ;REGISTERS : Uses CS, AX
4                         ;PORTS     : None used
5
6 0000                    CODE    SEGMENT
7                                 ASSUME CS:CODE
8 0000  EB 03 90                  JMP THERE        ; Skip over a series of instructions
9 0003  90                        NOP              ; Dummy instructions to represent those
10 0004 90                        NOP              ; Instructions skipped over
11 0005 B8 0000           THERE:  MOV AX, 0000H    ; Zero accumulator before addition instructions
12 0008 90                        NOP              ; Dummy instruction to represent continuation of execution
13 0009                   CODE    ENDS
14                                 END
```

FIGURE 4-9   List file of program demonstrating "forward" JMP.

JMP. The displacement is calculated by counting the number of bytes from the next address after the JMP instruction to the destination. If the displacement is negative (backward in the program), then it must be expressed in 2's complement form before it can be written in the instruction code template.

Now let's look at another simple example program, in Figure 4-9, to see how you can jump ahead over a group of instructions in a program. Here again we use a label to give a name to the address that we want to JMP to. We also use NOP instructions to represent the instructions that we want to skip over and the instructions that continue after the JMP. Let's see how this JMP instruction is coded.

When the assembler reads through the source file for this program, it will find the label "THERE" after the JMP mnemonic. At this point the assembler has no way of knowing whether it will need 1 or 2 bytes to represent the displacement to the destination address. The assembler plays it safe by reserving 2 bytes for the displacement. Then the assembler reads on through the rest of the program. When the assembler finds the specified label, it calculates the displacement from the instruction after the JMP instruction to the label. If the assembler finds the displacement to be outside the range of −128 bytes to +127 bytes, then it will code the instruction as a direct within-segment near JMP with 2 bytes of displacement. If the assembler finds the displacement to be within the −128- to +127- byte range, then it will code the instruction as a direct within-segment short-type JMP with a 1-byte displacement. In the latter case, the assembler will put the code for a NOP instruction, 90H, in the third byte it had reserved for the JMP instruction. The instruction codes for the JMP THERE instruction on line 8 of Figure 4-9 demonstrate this. As shown in the instruction template in Figure 4-7, EBH is the basic opcode for the direct within-segment short JMP. The 03H represents the displacement to the JMP destination. Since we are jumping forward in this case, the displacement is a positive number. The 90H in the next memory byte is the code for a NOP instruction. The displacement is calculated from the offset of this NOP instruction, 0002H, to the offset of the destination label, 0005H. The difference of 03H between these two is the displacement you see coded in the instruction.

If you are hand coding a program such as this, you will probably know how far it is to the label, and you can leave just 1 byte for the displacement if that is enough. If you are using an assembler and you don't want to waste the byte of memory or the time it takes to fetch the extra NOP instruction, you can write the instruction as JMP SHORT label. The SHORT operator is a promise to the assembler that the destination will not be outside the range of −128 to +127 bytes. Trusting your promise, the assembler then reserves only 1 byte for the displacement.

Note that if you are making a JMP from an address near the start of a 64-Kbyte segment to an address near the end of the segment, you may not be able to get there with a jump of +32,767. The way you get there is to JMP backward around to the desired destination address. An assembler will automatically do this for you.

One advantage of the direct near- and short-type JMPs is that the destination address is specified *relative* to the address of the instruction after the JMP instruction. Since the JMP instruction in this case does not contain an absolute address or offset, the program can be loaded anywhere in memory and still run correctly. A program which can be loaded anywhere in memory to be run is said to be *relocatable*. You should try to write your programs so that they are relocatable.

Now that you know about unconditional JMP instructions, we will discuss the 8086 flags, so that we can show how the 8086 Conditional Jump instructions are used to implement the rest of the standard programming structures.

The 8086 Conditional Flags

The 8086 has six *conditional flags*. They are the *carry* flag (CF), the *parity* flag (PF), the *auxiliary carry* flag (AF), the *zero* flag (ZF), the *sign* flag (SF), and the *overflow* flag (OF). Chapter 1 shows numerical examples of some of the conditions indicated by these flags. Here we review these conditions and show how some of the important 8086 instructions affect these flags.

THE CARRY FLAG WITH ADD, SUBTRACT, AND COMPARE INSTRUCTIONS

If the addition of two 8-bit numbers produces a sum greater than 8 bits, the carry flag will be set to a 1 to indicate a carry into the next bit position. Likewise, if the addition of two 16-bit numbers produces a sum greater than 16 bits, then the carry flag will be set to a 1 to indicate that a final carry was produced by the addition.

During subtraction, the carry flag functions as a borrow flag. If the bottom number in a subtraction is larger than the top number, then the carry/borrow flag will be set to indicate that a borrow was needed to perform the subtraction.

The 8086 compare instruction has the format CMP destination,source. The source can be an immediate number, a register, or a memory location. The destination can be a register or a memory location. The comparison is done by subtracting the contents of the specified source from the contents of the specified destination. Flags are updated to reflect the result of the comparison, but neither the source nor the destination is changed. If the source operand is greater than the specified destination operand, then the carry/borrow flag will be set to indicate that a borrow was needed to do the comparison (subtraction). If the source operand is the same size as or smaller than the specified destination operand, then the carry/borrow flag will not be set after the compare. If the two operands are equal, the zero flag will be set to a 1 to indicate that the result of the compare (subtraction) was all 0's. Here's an example and summary of this for your reference.

CMP BX, CX

condition	CF	ZF
CX > BX	1	0
CX < BX	0	0
CX = BX	0	1

The compare instruction is very important because it allows you to easily determine whether one operand is greater than, less than, or the same size as another operand.

THE PARITY FLAG

Parity is a term used to indicate whether a binary word has an even number of 1's or an odd number of 1's. A binary number with an even number of 1's is said to have *even parity*. The 8086 parity flag will be set to a 1 after an instruction if the lower 8 bits of the destination operand has an even number of 1's. Probably the most common use of the parity flag is to determine whether ASCII data sent to a computer over phone lines or some other communications link contains any errors. In Chapter 14 we describe this use of parity.

THE AUXILIARY CARRY FLAG

This flag has significance in BCD addition or BCD subtraction. If a carry is produced when the least significant nibbles of 2 bytes are added, the auxiliary carry flag will be set. In other words, a carry out of bit 3 sets the auxiliary carry flag. Likewise, if the subtraction of the least significant nibbles requires a borrow, the auxiliary carry/borrow flag will be set. The auxiliary carry/borrow flag is used only by the DAA and DAS instructions. Consult the DAA and DAS instruction descriptions in Chapter 6 and the BCD operation exam-

ples section of Chapter 1 for further discussion of addition and subtraction of BCD numbers.

THE ZERO FLAG WITH INCREMENT, DECREMENT, AND COMPARE INSTRUCTIONS

As the name implies, this flag will be set to a 1 if the result of an arithmetic or logic operation is zero. For example, if you subtract two numbers which are equal, the zero flag will be set to indicate that the result of the subtraction is zero. If you AND two words together and the result contains no 1's, the zero flag will be set to indicate that the result is all 0's.

Besides the more obvious arithmetic and logic instructions, there are a few other very useful instructions which also affect the zero flag. One of these is the compare instruction CMP, which we discussed previously with the carry flag. As shown there, the zero flag will be set to a 1 if the two operands compared are equal.

Another important instruction which affects the zero flag is the decrement instruction, DEC. This instruction will decrement (or, in other words, subtract 1 from) a number in a specified register or memory location. If, after decrementing, the contents of the register or memory location are zero, the zero flag will be set. Here's a preview of how this is used. Suppose that we want to repeat a sequence of actions nine times. To do this, we first load a register with the number 09H and execute the sequence of actions. We then decrement the register and look at the zero flag to see if the register is down to zero yet. If the zero flag is not set, then we know that the register is not yet down to zero, so we tell the 8086, with a Jump instruction, to go back and execute the sequence of instructions again. The following sections will show many specific examples of how this is done.

The increment instruction, INC destination, also affects the zero flag. If an 8-bit destination containing FFH or a 16-bit destination containing FFFFH is incremented, the result in the destination will be all 0's. The zero flag will be set to indicate this.

THE SIGN FLAG—POSITIVE AND NEGATIVE NUMBERS

When you need to represent both positive and negative numbers for an 8086, you use 2's complement sign-and-magnitude form as described in Chapter 1. In this form, the most significant bit of the byte or word is used as a sign bit. A 0 in this bit indicates that the number is positive. A 1 in this bit indicates that the number is negative. The remaining 7 bits of a byte or the remaining 15 bits of a word are used to represent the magnitude of the number. For a positive number, the magnitude will be in standard binary form. For a negative number, the magnitude will be in 2's complement form. After an arithmetic or logic instruction executes, the sign flag will be a copy of the most significant bit of the destination byte or the destination word. In addition to its use with signed arithmetic operations, the sign flag can be used to determine whether an operand has been decremented beyond zero. Decrementing 00H, for example, will give FFH. Since the MSB of FFH is a 1, the sign flag will be set.

THE OVERFLOW FLAG

This flag will be set if the result of a signed operation is too large to fit in the number of bits available to represent it. To remind you of what *overflow* means, here is an example. Suppose you add the 8-bit signed number 01110101 (+117 decimal) and the 8-bit signed number 00110111 (+55 decimal). The result will be 10101100 (+172 decimal), which is the correct binary result in this case, but is too large to fit in the 7 bits allowed for the magnitude in an 8-bit signed number. For an 8-bit signed number, a 1 in the most significant bit indicates a negative number. The overflow flag will be set after this operation to indicate that the result of the addition has overflowed into the sign bit.

The 8086 Conditional Jump Instructions

As we stated previously, much of the real power of a computer comes from its ability to choose between two courses of action depending on whether some condition is present or not. In the 8086 the six conditional flags indicate the conditions that are present after an instruction. The 8086 Conditional Jump instructions look at the state of a specified flag(s) to determine whether the jump should be made or not.

Figure 4-10 shows the mnemonics for the 8086 Conditional Jump instructions. Next to each mnemonic is a brief explanation of the mnemonic. Note that the terms *above* and *below* are used when you are working with unsigned binary numbers. The 8-bit unsigned number 11000110 is above the 8-bit unsigned number 00111001, for example. The terms *greater* and *less* are used when you are working with signed binary numbers. The 8-bit signed number 00111001 is greater (more

positive) than the 8-bit signed number 11000110, which represents a negative number. Also shown in Figure 4-10 is an indication of the flag conditions that will cause the 8086 to do the jump. If the specified flag conditions are not present, the 8086 will just continue on to the next instruction in sequence. In other words, if the jump condition is not met, the Conditional Jump instruction will effectively function as a NOP. Suppose, for example, we have the instruction JC SAVE, where SAVE is the label at the destination address. If the carry flag is set, this instruction will cause the 8086 to jump to the instruction at the SAVE: label. If the carry flag is not set, the instruction will have no effect other than taking up a little processor time.

All conditional jumps are *short-type* jumps. This means that the destination label must be in the same code segment as the jump instruction. Also, the destination address must be in the range of −128 bytes to +127 bytes from the address of the instruction after the Jump instruction. As we show in later examples, it is important to be aware of this limit on the range of conditional jumps as you write your programs.

The Conditional Jump instructions are usually used after arithmetic or logic instructions. They are very commonly used after Compare instructions. For this case, the Compare instruction syntax and the Conditional Jump instruction syntax are such that a little trick makes it very easy to see what will cause a jump to occur. Here's the trick. Suppose that you see the instruction sequence

CMP BL, DH
JAE HEATER_OFF

in a program, and you want to determine what these instructions do. The CMP instruction compares the byte

MNEMONIC	CONDITION TESTED	"JUMP IF . . ."
JA/JNBE	(CF or ZF)=0	above/not below nor equal
JAE/JNB	CF=0	above or equal/not below
JB/JNAE	CF=1	below/not above nor equal
JBE/JNA	(CF or ZF)=1	below or equal/not above
JC	CF=1	carry
JE/JZ	ZF=1	equal/zero
JG/JNLE	((SF xor OF) or ZF)=0	greater/not less nor equal
JGE/JNL	(SF xor OF)=0	greater or equal/not less
JL/JNGE	(SF xor OF)=1	less/not greater nor equal
JLE/JNG	((SF xor OF) or ZF)=1	less or equal/not greater
JNC	CF=0	not carry
JNE/JNZ	ZF=0	not equal/not zero
JNO	OF=0	not overflow
JNP/JPO	PF=0	not parity/parity odd
JNS	SF=0	not sign
JO	OF=1	overflow
JP/JPE	PF=1	parity/parity equal
JS	SF=1	sign

Note: "above" and "below" refer to the relationship of two unsigned values;
"greater" and "less" refer to the relationship of two signed values.

FIGURE 4-10   8086 Conditional Jump instructions.

in the DH register with the byte in the BL register and sets flags according to the result. A previous section showed you how the carry and zero flags are affected by a Compare instruction. According to Figure 4-10, the JAE instruction says, "Jump if above or equal" to the label HEATER_OFF. The question now is, will it jump if BL is above DH, or will it jump if DH is above BL? You could determine how the flags will be affected by the comparison and use Figure 4-10 to answer the question, but an easier way is to mentally read parts of the Compare instruction between parts of the Jump instruction. If you read the example sequence as "Jump if BL is above or equal to DH," the meaning of the sequence is immediately clear. As you write your own programs, thinking of a conditional sequence in this way should help you to choose the right Conditional Jump instruction. The next sections show you how we use Conditional and Unconditional Jump instructions to implement some of the standard program structures and solve some common programming problems.

IF-THEN, IF-THEN-ELSE, AND MULTIPLE IF-THEN-ELSE PROGRAMS

IF-THEN Programs

Remember from Chapter 2 that the IF-THEN structure has the format

```
IF condition THEN
    action
    action
```

This structure says that IF the stated condition is found to be true, the series of actions following THEN will be executed. If the condition is false, execution will skip over the actions after the THEN and proceed with the next mainline instruction.

The simple IF-THEN is implemented with a Conditional Jump instruction. In some cases an instruction to set flags is needed before the Conditional Jump instruction. Figure 4-11a shows, with a program frag-

```
        CMP AX, BX    ; Compare to set flags
        JE  THERE     ; If equal then skip correction
        ADD AX, 0002H ; Add correction factor
THERE:  MOV CL, 07H   ; Load count
```

(a)

```
        CMP AX, BX    ; Compare to set flags
        JNE FIX       ; If not equal do correction
        JMP THERE     ; If equal then skip correction
FIX:    ADD AX, 0002H ; Add correction factor

THERE:  MOV CL, 07H ; Load count
```

(b)

FIGURE 4-11 Programming conditional jumps. (a) Destinations closer than ±128 bytes. (b) Destinations further than ±128 bytes.

ment, one way to implement the simple IF-THEN structure. In this program we first compare BX with AX to set the required flags. If the zero flag is set after the comparison, indicating that AX = BX, the JE instruction will cause execution to jump to the MOV CL,07H instruction labeled THERE. If AX ≠ BX, then the ADD AX,0002H instruction after the JE instruction will be executed before the MOV CL,07H instruction.

The implementation in Figure 4-11a will work well for a short sequence of instructions after the Conditional Jump instruction. However, if the sequence of instructions is lengthy, there is a potential problem. Remember from the discussion of conditional jumps in the last section that a conditional jump can only be to a location in the range of −128 bytes to +127 bytes from the address after the Conditional Jump instruction. A long sequence of instructions after the Conditional Jump instruction may put the label out of range of the instruction. If you are absolutely sure that the destination label will not be out of range, then use the instruction sequence shown in Figure 4-11a to implement an IF-THEN structure. If you are not sure whether the destination will be in range, the instruction sequence shown in Figure 4-11b will always work. In this sequence, the Conditional Jump instruction only has to jump over the JMP instruction. The JMP instruction used to get to the label THERE can jump to anywhere in the code segment, or even to another code segment. Note that you have to change the Conditional Jump instruction from JE to JNE for this second version. The price you pay for not having to worry whether the destination is in range is an extra jump instruction. Incidentally, some assemblers now automatically code Conditional Jump instructions in this way if necessary.

IF-THEN-ELSE Programs

OVERVIEW

The IF-THEN-ELSE structure is used to indicate a choice between two alternative courses of action. Figure 3-3b shows the flowchart and pseudocode for this structure. Basically the structure has the format

```
IF condition THEN
    action
ELSE
    action
```

This is a different situation from the simple IF-THEN, because here either one series of actions or another series of actions is done before the program goes on with the next mainline instruction. An example will show how we implement this structure.

Suppose that in the computerized factory we discussed in Chapter 2, we have an 8086 microcomputer which controls a printed-circuit-board-making machine. Part of the job of this 8086 is to check a temperature sensor and turn on a green lamp or a yellow lamp depending on the value of the temperature it reads in. If the temperature is below 30°C, we want to turn on a yellow lamp to tell the operator that the solution is not up to temperature. If the temperature is greater than or equal to 30°C, we want to light a green lamp. With a system such as this, the operator can visually scan all the lamps on the control panel until all the green lamps are lit. When all the lamps are green, the operator can push the GO button to start making boards. The reason that we have the yellow lamp is to let the operator know that this part of the machine is working, but that the temperature is not yet up to 30°C.

Figure 4-12 shows with flowcharts and with pseudocode two ways we can represent the algorithm for this problem. The difference between the two is simply a matter of whether we make the decision based on the temperature being below 30°C or based on the temperature being above or equal to 30°C. The two approaches are equally valid, but your choice determines which Conditional Jump instruction you use to implement the algorithm. Since this program involves reading data in from a port and writing data out to a port, we need to talk briefly about the 8086 IN and OUT instructions before we discuss the details of how these two algorithms can be implemented in assembly language.

THE 8086 IN AND OUT INSTRUCTIONS

The 8086 has two types of input instruction, *fixed*-port and *variable*-port. The fixed-port instruction has the format IN AL,port or IN AX,port. The term *port* in these instructions represents an 8-bit port address to be put directly in the instruction. The instruction IN AX,04H, for example, will copy a word from port 04H to the AX register. The 8-bit port address in this type of IN instruction allows you to address any one of 256 possible input ports, but the port address is fixed. The program cannot change the port address as it executes. Keep this in mind as we discuss the variable-port IN instruction.

The variable-port input instruction has the format IN AL,DX or IN AX,DX. When using the variable-port input instruction, you must first put the address of the desired port in the DX register. If, for example, you load DX with FFF8H and then do an IN AL,DX, the 8086 will copy a byte of data from port FFF8H to the AL register. The variable-port input instruction has two major advantages. First, up to 65,536 different input ports can be specified with the 16-bit port address in DX. Second, the port address can be changed as a program executes by simply putting a different number in DX. This is handy in a case where you want the computer to be able to input from 15 different terminals, for example. Instead of writing 15 different input programs, you can write one input program which simply changes the contents of DX to input from each of the different terminals.

The 8086 also has a fixed-port output instruction and a variable-port output instruction. The fixed-port output instruction has the form OUT port,AL or OUT port,AX. Here again the term *port* represents an 8-bit port address written in the instruction. OUT 0AH,AL, for example, will copy the contents of the AL register to port 0AH.

The format for the variable-port output instruction is OUT DX,AL or OUT DX,AX. To use this type of instruction, you have to first put the 16-bit port address in the DX register. If, for example, you load DX with FFFAH and then do an OUT DX,AL instruction, the 8086 will copy the contents of the AL register to port FFFAH.

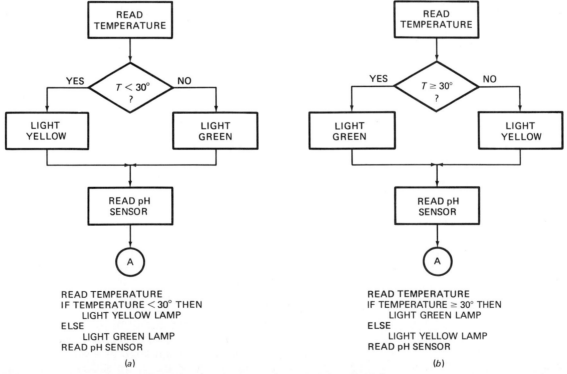

READ TEMPERATURE
IF TEMPERATURE < 30° THEN
    LIGHT YELLOW LAMP
ELSE
    LIGHT GREEN LAMP
READ pH SENSOR

(a)

READ TEMPERATURE
IF TEMPERATURE ≥ 30° THEN
    LIGHT GREEN LAMP
ELSE
    LIGHT YELLOW LAMP
READ pH SENSOR

(b)

FIGURE 4-12 Flowcharts and pseudocode for two ways of expressing algorithm for printed-circuit-board-making machine. (a) Temperature below 30° test. (b) Temperature above 30° test.

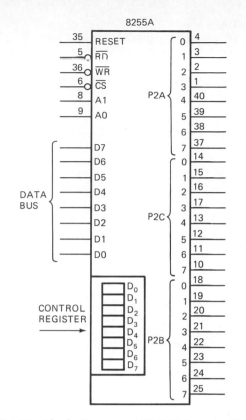

FIGURE 4-13   Block diagram of SDK-86 board's 8255A port.

The device used for parallel input and output ports on the SDK-86 board and in many microcomputers is the Intel 8255. As shown in the block diagram in Figure 4-13, the 8255 basically contains three 8-bit ports and a control register. Each of the ports and the control register will have a separate address, so you can write to them or read from them. The addresses for the ports and control registers for the two 8255s on an SDK-86 board, for example, are as follows:

PORT 2A	FFF8H	PORT 1A	FFF9H
PORT 2B	FFFAH	PORT 1B	FFFBH
PORT 2C	FFFCH	PORT 1C	FFFDH
CONTROL2	FFFEH	CONTROL1	FFFFH

The ports in an 8255 can be individually programmed to operate as input or output ports. When the power is first applied to an 8255, the ports are all configured as input ports. If you want to use any of the ports as an output port, you must write a control word to the control register to initialize that port for operation as an output. Chapter 9 and later chapters describe in detail how to initialize an 8255 for a variety of applications, but we show you here how to initialize one of the ports in an 8255 device on an SDK-86 microcomputer for use as an output port.

You initialize an 8255 by sending a control word to the control register address for that device. As we showed above, the control register address for one of the 8255s on an SDK-86 board is FFFEH. In order to write a control

word to this address, you first point DX at the address with the instruction MOV DX,0FFFEH.

The control word needed to make port P2B of this 8255 an output, and P2A and P2C inputs, is 99H. (In Chapter 9 we show how we determined this control word.) You load this control word into AL with MOV AL,99H and send it to the 8255 control register with OUT DX,AL. Now that port 2B is initialized as an output, you can output a byte to that port of the device any time you need to in the program.

IF-THEN-ELSE ASSEMBLY LANGUAGE PROGRAM EXAMPLE

Figure 4-14a, p. 80, shows the list file of the 8086 assembly language implementation of the algorithm in Figure 4-12a. The first three instructions in this program initialize port 2B at address FFFAH as an output port, so we can output values to it to turn on LEDs. Assume that the driver for the yellow lamp is connected to bit 0 of port FFFAH, and the driver for the green lamp is connected to bit 1 of port FFFAH. A 1 sent to a bit position of port FFFAH turns on the lamp connected to that line.

The next two instructions in the example program read the temperature in from an analog-to-digital converter connected to input port FFF8H.

After we read the data in from the port, we compare it with our set-point value of 30°C. If the input value is below 30°C, then we jump to the instructions which turn on the yellow lamp. If the temperature is above or equal to 30°C, we jump to the instructions which turn on the green lamp. Note that we have implemented this algorithm in such a way that the JB instruction will always be able to reach the label YELLOW.

To actually turn on a lamp, we load a 1 in the appropriate bit of the AL register with a MOV instruction and send the byte to the lamp control port, FFFAH. The instruction sequence MOV AL,01H—OUT DX,AL, for example, will light the yellow lamp by sending a 1 to bit 0 of port FFFAH.

The instruction sequence MOV AL,02H—OUT DX,AL will light the green lamp by sending a 1 to bit 1 of port FFFAH. Note that control words are sent to the control register address in an 8255 and data words are read from or written to the individual port addresses. Here's another way to implement this program in assembly language.

Figure 4-14b shows another equally valid assembly language program segment to solve our problem. This one uses a Jump if Above or Equal instruction, JAE, at the decision point and switches the order of the actions. This program more closely follows the second algorithm statement in Figure 4-12b. Perhaps you can see from these examples why two programmers may write very different programs to solve even very simple programming problems.

Multiple IF-THEN-ELSE Assembly Language Programs

In the preceding section we showed how to implement and use the IF-THEN-ELSE structure, which chooses between two alternative courses of action. In

```
 1                                   ; 8086 PROGRAM    F4-14A.ASM
 2                      ;ABSTRACT : Program section for PC board making machine.
 3                                  ; This program section reads the temperature of a cleaning bath
 4                                  ; solution and lights one of two lamps according to the
 5                                  ; temperature read. If the temp <30°C, a yellow lamp will be
 6                                  ; turned on. If the temp is ≥30°C, a green lamp will be turned on.
 7                      ;REGISTERS: Uses CS, AL, DX
 8                      ;PORTS    : Uses FFF8H - temperature input
 9                                  ; FFFAH - lamp control output (yellow=bit 0, green=bit 1)
10
11 0000                CODE    SEGMENT
12                              ASSUME CS:CODE
13                      ;initialize SDK-86 port FFFAH as output port, FFF8H as input port
14 0000 BA FFFE                 MOV DX, 0FFFEH      ; Point DX to port control register
15 0003 B0 99                   MOV AL, 99H         ; Load control word to initialize ports
16 0005 EE                      OUT DX, AL          ; Send control word to port control register
17
18 0006 BA FFF8                 MOV DX, 0FFF8H      ; Point DX at input port
19 0009 EC                      IN  AL, DX          ; Read temp from sensor on input port
20 000A 3C 1E                   CMP AL, 30          ; Compare temp with 30°C
21 000C 72 03                   JB  YELLOW          ; IF temp <30 THEN light yellow lamp
22 000E EB 0A 90                JMP GREEN           ; ELSE light green lamp
23 0011 B0 01          YELLOW: MOV AL, 01H          ; Load code to light yellow lamp
24 0013 BA FFFA                 MOV DX, 0FFFAH      ; Point DX at output port
25 0016 EE                      OUT DX, AL          ; Send code to light yellow lamp
26 0017 EB 07 90                JMP EXIT            ; Go to next mainline instruction
27 001A B0 02          GREEN:  MOV AL, 02H          ; Load code to light green lamp
28 001C BA FFFA                 MOV DX, 0FFFAH      ; Point DX at output port
29 001F EE                      OUT DX, AL          ; Send code to light green lamp
30 0020 BA FFFC        EXIT:   MOV DX, 0FFFCH       ; Next mainline instruction
31 0023 EC                      IN  AL, DX          ; Read ph sensor
32 0024                CODE    ENDS
33                              END
```

(a)

```
20 000A 3C 1E                   CMP AL, 30          ; Compare temp with 30°C
21 000C 73 03                   JAE GREEN           ; IF temp ≥30 THEN light green lamp
22 000E EB 0A 90                JMP YELLOW          ; ELSE light yellow lamp
23 0011 B0 02          GREEN:  MOV AL, 02H          ; Load code to light green lamp
24 0013 BA FFFA                 MOV DX, 0FFFAH      ; Point DX at output port
25 0016 EE                      OUT DX, AL          ; Send code to light green lamp
26 0017 EB 07 90                JMP EXIT            ; Go to next mainline instruction
27 001A B0 01          YELLOW: MOV AL, 01H          ; Load code to light yellow lamp
28 001C BA FFFA                 MOV DX, 0FFFAH      ; Point DX at output port
29 001F EE                      OUT DX, AL          ; Send code to light yellow lamp
30 0020 BA FFFC        EXIT:   MOV DX, 0FFFCH       ; Next mainline instruction
31 0023 EC                      IN  AL, DX          ; Read ph sensor
32 0024                CODE    ENDS
33                              END
```

(b)

FIGURE 4-14   List file for printed-circuit-board-making machine program.
(a) Below 30° version. (b) Program section for above 30° version.

many situations we want a computer to choose one of several alternative actions based on the value of some variable read in or on a command code entered by a user. To choose one alternative from several, we can *nest* IF-THEN-ELSE structures. The result has the form

IF condition THEN
    action
ELSE IF condition THEN
        action
    ELSE
        action

It is important to note that in this structure the last ELSE is part of the IF-THEN just before it. Figure 3-3d showed a flowchart and pseudocode for a "soup cook" example using this structure, but the soup cook example is too messy to implement here. Therefore, while the printed-circuit-board-making machine from the last section is still fresh in your mind, we will expand that example to show you how a multiple IF-THEN-ELSE is implemented.

Suppose that we want to have three lamps on our printed-circuit-board-making machine. We want a yellow lamp to indicate that the temperature is below 30°C, a green lamp to indicate that the temperature is above or equal to 30°C but below 40°C, and a red lamp to indicate that the temperature is at or above 40°C. Figure 4-15 shows three ways to indicate what we want to do here. The first way, in Figure 4-15a, simply indicates the desired action next to each temperature range. You may find this form very useful in visualizing problems where the alternatives are based on the range of a variable. Don't miss the ASCII-to-hexadecimal problem at the end of the chapter for some practice with this.

Once you get a problem such as this defined in list form, you can easily convert it to a flowchart or pseudocode. When writing the flowchart or the pseudocode, it is best to start at one end of the overall range and work your way to the other. For example, in the flowchart in Figure 4-15c, start by checking whether the temperature is below 30°. If the temperature is not below 30°, then it must be above or equal to 30°, and you do not have to do another test to determine this. You then check whether the temperature is below 40°. If the temperature is above or equal to 30°, but below 40°, then you know that the temperature is in the green lamp range. If the temperature is not below 40°, then you know that the temperature must be above or equal to 40°. In other words, two carefully chosen tests will direct execution to one of the three alternatives.

Figure 4-16, p. 82, shows how we can write a program for this algorithm in 8086 assembly language. In the program, we first initialize port FFFAH as an output port. We then read in the temperature from an A/D converter connected to port FFF8H. We compare the temperature read in with the first set-point value, 30°. If the temperature is below 30°, the Jump if Below instruction, JB, will cause a jump to the label YELLOW. If the jump is not taken, we know the temperature is above or equal to 30°, so we go on to the CMP AL,40 instruction to see whether the temperature is below the second set point, 40°. The JB GREEN instruction will cause a jump to the label GREEN if the temperature is less than 40°. If the jump is not taken, we know that the temperature must be at or above 40°C, so we just go ahead and turn on the red lamp.

For this program, we assume that the lines which control the three lamps are connected to port FFFAH. The yellow lamp is connected to bit 0, the green is connected to bit 1, and the red is connected to bit 2. We turn on a lamp by outputting a 1 to the appropriate bit of port FFFAH. The instruction sequence MOV AL,04H—OUT DX,AL, for example, will turn on the red lamp by sending a 1 to bit 2 of port FFFAH.

Summary of IF-THEN-ELSE Implementation

From the preceding examples, you should see that you can implement IF-THEN-ELSE structures in your programs by using Compare or other instructions to set the appropriate flag(s) and Conditional Jump instructions to go to the desired sequence of actions.

A single IF-THEN-ELSE structure is used to choose one of two alternative series of actions. IF-THEN-ELSE structures can be linked to choose one of three or more alternative series of actions. As shown in Figure 3-3d, linked IF-THEN-ELSE structures are one way to implement the CASE structure. The algorithm for the printed-circuit-board-making machine lamps program in the preceding section's example could have been expressed as

CASE temperature OF
< 30   :   light yellow lamp
≥ 30 and <40   :   light green lamp
≥ 40   :   light red lamp

This CASE structure would be implemented in the same way as the program in Figure 4-16. However, expressing

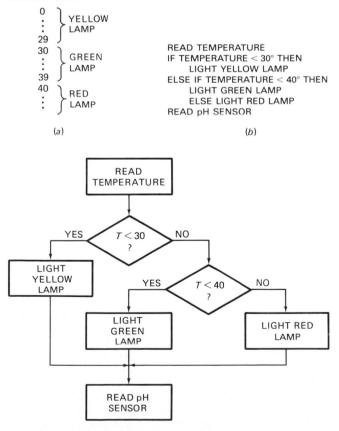

TEMPERATURE

```
0
: } YELLOW
:   LAMP
29
30            READ TEMPERATURE
: } GREEN     IF TEMPERATURE < 30° THEN
:   LAMP          LIGHT YELLOW LAMP
39            ELSE IF TEMPERATURE < 40° THEN
40 } RED          LIGHT GREEN LAMP
:    LAMP         ELSE LIGHT RED LAMP
:             READ pH SENSOR
```

(a)   (b)

FIGURE 4-15   Algorithm for three-lamp printed-circuit-board-making machine. (a) Condition list. (b) Pseudocode. (c) Flowchart.

```
 1                               ; 8086 PROGRAM F4-16.ASM
 2              ;ABSTRACT   : This program section reads the temperature of a cleaning bath
 3                          ; solution and lights one of three lamps according to the
 4                          ; temperature read. If the temp < 30°C, a yellow lamp will be
 5                          ; turned on. If the temp ≥ 30° and < 40°, a green lamp will be
 6                          ; turned on. Temperatures ≥ 40° will turn on a red lamp.
 7              ;REGISTERS  : Uses CS, AL, DX
 8              ;PORTS      : Uses FFF8H - temperature input
 9                          ;       FFFAH - lamp control output, yellow=bit 0, green=bit 1, red=bit 2
10 0000         CODE    SEGMENT
11                         ASSUME CS:CODE
12              ;initialize port FFFAH for output and port FFF8H for input
13 0000  BA FFFE            MOV DX, 0FFFEH      ; Point DX to port control register
14 0003  B0 99              MOV AL, 99H         ; Load control word to set up output port
15 0005  EE                 OUT DX, AL          ; Send control word to control register
16
17 0006  BA FFF8            MOV DX, 0FFF8H      ; Point DX at input port
18 0009  EC                 IN  AL, DX          ; Read temp from sensor on input port
19 000A  BA FFFA            MOV DX, 0FFFAH      ; Point DX at output port
20 000D  3C 1E              CMP AL, 30          ; Compare temp with 30°C
21 000F  72 0A              JB  YELLOW          ; IF temp < 30 THEN light yellow lamp
22 0011  3C 28              CMP AL, 40          ; ELSE compare with 40°
23 0013  72 0C              JB  GREEN           ;  IF temp < 40 THEN light green lamp
24 0015  B0 04      RED:    MOV AL, 04H         ;  ELSE temp ≥ 40 so light red lamp
25 0017  EE                 OUT DX, AL          ; Send code to light red lamp
26 0018  EB 0A 90           JMP EXIT            ; Go to next mainline instruction
27 001B  B0 01      YELLOW: MOV AL, 01H         ; Load code to light yellow lamp
28 001D  EE                 OUT DX, AL          ; Send code to light yellow lamp
29 001E  EB 04 90           JMP EXIT            ; Go to next mainline instruction
30 0021  B0 02      GREEN:  MOV AL, 02H         ; Load code to light green lamp
31 0023  EE                 OUT DX, AL          ; Send code to light green lamp
32 0024  BA FFFC    EXIT:   MOV DX, 0FFFCH      ; Next mainline instruction
33 0027  EC                 IN  AL, DX          ; Read ph sensor
34 0028         CODE    ENDS
35                     END
```

FIGURE 4-16   List file for three-lamp printed-circuit-board-making machine program.

the algorithm for the problem as linked IF-THEN-ELSE structures makes it much easier to see how to implement the algorithm in assembly language. In Chapter 10 we show you another way to implement a CASE situation using a *jump table*.

WHILE-DO PROGRAMS

Overview

Remember from the discussion in Chapter 3 that the WHILE-DO structure has the form

WHILE some condition is present DO
    action
    action

An important point about this structure is that the condition is checked *before* any action is done. In industrial control applications of microprocessors, there are many cases where we want to do this. The following very simple example will show you how to implement this structure in 8086 assembly language.

Defining the Problem and Writing the Algorithm

Suppose that, in controlling a chemical process, we want to bring the temperature of a solution up to 100°C before going on to the next step in the process. If the solution temperature is below 100°, we want to turn on a heater and wait for the temperature to reach 100°. If the solution temperature is at or above 100°, then we want to go on with the next step in the process. The WHILE-DO structure fits this problem because we want to check the condition (temperature) before we turn on the heater. We don't want to turn on the heater if the temperature is already high enough because we might overheat the solution.

Figure 4-17 shows a flowchart and the pseudocode of an algorithm for this problem. The first step in the algorithm is to read in the temperature from a sensor connected to a port. The temperature read in is then compared with 100°. These two parts represent the condition-checking part of the structure. If the temperature is at or above 100°, execution will exit the structure and do the next mainline action, turn off the heater. If the temperature is less than 100°, the heater is turned on and the temperature rechecked. Execution will stay in this loop while the temperature is below 100°. Inciden-

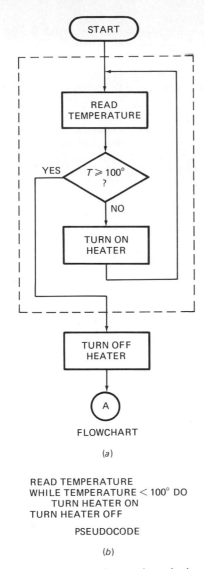

START

READ
TEMPERATURE

YES

$T \geqslant 100°$
?

NO

TURN ON
HEATER

TURN OFF
HEATER

A

FLOWCHART

(a)

READ TEMPERATURE
WHILE TEMPERATURE < 100° DO
    TURN HEATER ON
TURN HEATER OFF

PSEUDOCODE

(b)

FIGURE 4-17   Flowchart and pseudocode for heater control program.

tally, it will not do any harm to turn the heater on if it is already on.

When the temperature reaches 100°, execution will exit the structure and go on to the next mainline action, turn off the heater.

Implementing the Algorithm in Assembly Language

We have assumed for this example that the temperature sensor inputs an 8-bit binary value for the Celsius temperature to port FFF8H. We have also assumed that the heater control output is connected to the most significant bit of port FFFAH. As we showed previously, the actual address of port P2B on the SDK-86 board is FFFAH. It is to this address that we will output a byte to turn the heater on or off.

Figure 4-18a, p. 84, shows one way to implement our algorithm. After initializing the heater control port for output, we read in the temperature, and compare the

value read with 100. The JAE instruction after the compare can be read as "jump to the label HEATER_OFF if AL is above or equal to 100." Note that we used the Jump if Above or Equal instruction rather than a Jump if Equal instruction. Can you see why? To see the answer, visualize what would happen if we had used a JE instruction and the temperature of the solution were 101°. On the first check, the temperature would not be equal to 100°, so the 8086 would turn on the heater. The heater would not get turned off until meltdown.

If the heater temperature is below 100°, we turn on the heater by loading a 1 in the most significant bit of AL and outputting this value to the most significant bit of port FFFAH. Then we do an unconditional JMP to loop back and check the temperature again.

When the temperature is at or above 100°, we load a 0 in the most significant bit of AL and output this to port FFFAH to turn off the heater. Note that the action of turning off the heater is outside the basic WHILE-DO structure. The WHILE-DO structure is shown by the dotted box in the flowchart in Figure 4-17a and by the indentation in the pseudocode in Figure 4-17b.

Solving a Potential Problem of Conditional Jump Instructions

In the example program in Figure 4-18a, we used the Conditional Jump instruction JAE to implement the WHILE-DO structure. Remember that all the Conditional Jump instructions are short-type jumps. This means that a conditional jump can only be to a location within the range of −128 to +127 bytes from the instruction after the Conditional Jump instruction. This limit on the range of the jump posed no problem for the example program in Figure 4-18a because we were only jumping to a location 8 bytes ahead in the program. Suppose, however, that the instructions for turning on the heater required 220 bytes of memory. The HEATER_OFF label would then be outside the range of the JAE instruction.

We showed you how to solve this problem in Figure 4-11. To refresh your memory, Figure 4-18b shows how you can change the instructions in this program slightly to solve the problem without changing the basic WHILE-DO overall structure. In this example, we read the temperature in as before and compare it to 100. We then use the Jump if Below instruction to jump to the program section which turns on the heater. This instruction, together with the CMP instruction, says, "Jump to the label HEATER_ON if AL is below 100." If the temperature is at or above 100, the JB instruction will act like a NOP, and the 8086 will go on to the JMP HEATER_OFF instruction. Changing the Conditional Jump instruction and writing the program in this way means that the destination for the Conditional Jump instruction is always just two instructions away. Therefore, you know that the destination will always be reachable. Except for very time-critical program sections, you should always write Conditional Jump instruction sequences in this way so that you don't have to worry about the potential problem. The disadvantages of this approach are the time and memory space required by the extra JMP instruction.

```
 1                                      ; 8086 PROGRAM     F4-18A.ASM
 2                        ;ABSTRACT  : Program turns heater off if temperature ≥ 100°C
 3                                    ; and turns heater on if temperature < 100°C.
 4                        ;REGISTERS : Uses CS, DX, AL
 5                        ;PORTS     : Uses FFF8H - temperature data input
 6                        ;            FFFAH - MSB for heater control output, 0=off, 1=on
 7 0000                   CODE    SEGMENT
 8                                ASSUME  CS:CODE
 9                        ; Initialize port FFFAH for output, and port FFF8H for input
10 0000  BA FFFE                      MOV DX, 0FFFEH   ; Point DX to port control register
11 0003  B0 99                        MOV AL, 99H      ; Control word to set up output port
12 0005  EE                           OUT DX, AL       ; Send control word to port
13
14 0006  BA FFF8         TEMP_IN:     MOV DX, 0FFF8H   ; Point at input port
15 0009  EC                           IN  AL, DX       ; Input temperature data
16 000A  3C 64                        CMP AL, 100      ; If temp ≥ 100 then
17 000C  73 08                        JAE HEATER_OFF   ; turn heater off
18 000E  B0 80                        MOV AL, 80H      ; else load code for heater on
19 0010  BA FFFA                      MOV DX, 0FFFAH   ; Point DX to output port
20 0013  EE                           OUT DX, AL       ; Turn heater on
21 0014  EB F0                        JMP TEMP_IN      ; WHILE temp < 100 read temp again
22 0016  B0 00          HEATER_OFF:MOV AL, 00          ; Load code for heater off
23 0018  BA FFFA                      MOV DX, 0FFFAH   ; Point DX to output port
24 001B  EE                           OUT DX, AL       ; Turn heater off
25 001C                 CODE    ENDS
26                              END
```

(a)

```
14 0006  BA FFF8         TEMP_IN:     MOV DX, 0FFF8H   ; Point DX at input port
15 0009  EC                           IN  AL, DX       ; Read in temperature data
16 000A  3C 64                        CMP AL, 100      ; If temp < 100° then
17 000C  72 03                        JB  HEATER_ON    ; turn heater on
18 000E  EB 09 90                     JMP HEATER_OFF   ; else temp ≥100 so turn heater off
19 0011  B0 80          HEATER_ON:  MOV AL, 80H        ; Load code for heater on
20 0013  BA FFFA                      MOV DX, 0FFFAH   ; Point DX at output port
21 0016  EE                           OUT DX, AL       ; Turn heater on
22 0017  EB ED                        JMP TEMP_IN      ; WHILE temp < 100° read temp again
23 0019  B0 00          HEATER_OFF:MOV AL, 00          ; Load code for heater off
24 001B  BA FFFA                      MOV DX, 0FFFAH   ; Point DX at output port
25 001E  EE                           OUT DX, AL       ; Turn heater off
26 001F                 CODE    ENDS
27                              END
```

(b)

FIGURE 4-18   List file for heater control program. (a) First approach. (b) Improved version of WHILE-DO section of program.

REPEAT-UNTIL PROGRAMS

Overview

Remember from the discussion in Chapter 3 that the REPEAT-UNTIL structure has the form

REPEAT
    action
     .
     .
UNTIL some condition is present

An important point about this structure is that the action or series of actions is done once *before* the condition is checked. This is different from the WHILE-DO structure, where the condition is checked before any action(s).

The following examples will show you how you can implement the REPEAT-UNTIL with 8086 assembly language and introduce you to some more assembly language programming techniques.

Defining the Problem and Writing the Algorithm

Many systems that interface with a microcomputer output data on parallel-signal lines and then output a separate signal to indicate that valid data is on the parallel lines. The data-ready signal is often called a

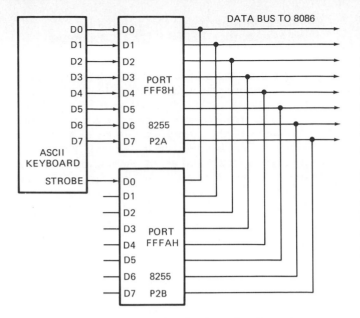

FIGURE 4-19   ASCII-encoded keyboard with strobe connected to microcomputer port.

strobe. An example of a strobed data system such as this is an ASCII-encoded computer-type keyboard. Figure 4-19 shows how the parallel data lines and the strobe line from such a keyboard are connected to ports of a microcomputer. When a key is pressed on the keyboard, circuitry in the keyboard detects which key is pressed and sends the ASCII code for that key out on the eight data lines connected to port FFF8H. After the data has had time to settle on these lines, the circuitry in the keyboard sends out a key-pressed strobe, which lets you know that the data on the eight lines is valid. A strobe can be an active high signal or an active low signal. For the example here, assume that the strobe signal goes high when a valid ASCII code is on the parallel data lines. As you can see in Figure 4-19, we have connected this strobe line to the least significant bit of port FFFAH so that we can input the strobe signal.

If we want to read the data from this keyboard, we can't do it at just any time. We must wait for the strobe to go high so that we know that the data we read will be valid. Basically, what we have to do is look at the strobe signal and test it over and over until it goes high. Figure 4-20*a*, p. 86, shows how we can represent this operation with a flowchart, and Figure 4-20*b* shows the pseudocode. We want to repeat the read-strobe-and-test loop until the strobe is found to be high. Then we want to exit the loop and read in the ASCII code byte. The basic REPEAT-UNTIL structure is shown by the indentation in the pseudocode. Note that the read ASCII data action is not part of this structure and is therefore not indented.

Implementing the Algorithm with Assembly Language

Figure 4-20*c* shows the 8086 assembly language to implement this algorithm. To read in the key-pressed strobe signal, we first load the address of the port to

which it is connected into the DX register. Then we use the variable-port input instruction, IN AL,DX, to read the strobe data to AL. This input instruction copies a byte of data from port FFFAH to the AL register. We care about only the least significant bit of the byte read in from the port, however, because that is where the strobe is connected. To determine whether the strobe is present, we need to check just this bit and determine whether it is a 1. Here are three different ways you can do this.

The first way, shown in Figure 4-20*c*, is to AND the byte in AL with the immediate number 01H. Remember that a bit ANDed with a 0 becomes a 0 (is masked). A bit ANDed with a 1 is not changed. If the least significant bit is a 0, then the result of the ANDing will be all 0's. The zero flag ZF will be set to a 1 to indicate this. If the least significant bit is a 1, the zero flag will not be set to a 1 because the result of the ANDing will still have a 1 in the least significant bit. The Jump if Zero instruction, JZ, will check the state of the zero flag; if it finds the zero flag set, it will jump to the label LOOK_AGAIN. If the JZ instruction finds the zero flag not set (indicating that the LSB was a 1), it passes execution on to the instructions which read in the ASCII data.

Another way to check the least significant bit of the strobe word is with the TEST instruction instead of the AND instruction. The 8086 TEST instruction has the format TEST destination,source. The TEST instruction ANDs the contents of the specified source with the contents of the specified destination and sets flags according to the result. However, the TEST instruction does not change the contents of either the source or the destination. The AND instruction, remember, puts the result of the ANDing in the specified destination. The TEST instruction is useful if you want to set flags without changing the operands. In the example program in Figure 4-20*c*, the AND AL,01H instruction could be replaced with the TEST AL,01H instruction.

Still another way to check the least significant bit of the strobe byte is with a Rotate instruction. If you rotate the least significant bit into the carry flag, you can use a Jump if Carry or Jump if Not Carry instruction to control the loop. For this example program, you could use either the ROR instruction or the RCR instruction. To verify this, take a look at the discussions of these instructions in Chapter 6. Assuming that you use the ROR instruction, the check and jump instruction sequence would look like this:

```
LOOK_AGAIN:IN AL, DX
           ROR AL, 1        ; Rotate LSB into carry
           JNC LOOK_AGAIN; If LSB = 0, keep looking
```

For your programs you can use the way of checking a bit that seems easiest in a particular situation.

To read the ASCII data, we first have to load the port address, FFF8H, into the DX register. We then use the variable-port input instruction IN AL,DX to copy the ASCII data byte from the port to the AL register.

The main purpose of the preceding section was to show you how you can use a Conditional Jump instruction to make the 8086 REPEAT a series of actions UNTIL the flags indicate that some condition is present. The following section shows another example of implementing the REPEAT-UNTIL structure. This example also shows you how a register-based addressing mode is used to access data in memory.

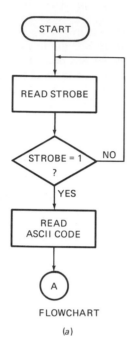

FLOWCHART

(a)

```
REPEAT
       READ KEYPRESSED STROBE
UNTIL STROBE = 1
READ ASCII CODE FOR KEY PRESSED

       PSEUDOCODE
```

(b)

Operating on a Series of Data Items in Memory—Another REPEAT-UNTIL Example

In many programming situations we want to perform some operation on a series of data items stored in successive memory locations. We might, for example, want to read in a series of data values from a port and put the values in successive memory locations. A series of data values of the *same type* stored in successive memory locations is often called an *array*. Each value in the array is referred to as an *element* of the array. For our example program here, we want to add an inflation factor of 03H to each price in an eight-element array of prices. Each price is stored in a byte location as packed BCD (two BCD digits per byte). The prices then are in the range of 1 cent to 99 cents. Figure 4-21a shows a flowchart and Figure 4-21b shows a pseudocode algorithm for the operations that we want to perform. Follow through whichever form you feel more comfortable with.

We read one of the BCD prices from memory, add the inflation factor to it, and adjust the result to keep it in BCD format. The new value is then copied back to the array, replacing the old value. After that, a check is made to see whether all the prices have been operated on. If they haven't, then we loop back and operate on the next price. The two questions that may occur to you at this point are, "How are we going to indicate in the program which price we want to operate on, and how are we going to know when we have operated on all of the prices?" To indicate which price we are operating on at a particular time, we use a register as a *pointer*. To keep track of how many prices we have operated on, we use another register as a *counter*. The example program in Figure 4-21c shows one way in which the algorithm for this problem can be implemented in assembly language.

The example program in Figure 4-21c uses several assembler directives. Let's review the function of these

```
1                                  ; 8086 PROGRAM F4-20C.ASM
2                       ;ABSTRACT : Program to read ASCII code after a strobe signal
3                                  ; is sent from a keyboard
4                       ;REGISTERS : Uses CS, DX, AL
5                       ;PORTS     : Uses FFFAH - strobe signal input on LSB
6                                  ;          FFF8H - ASCII data input port
7
8  0000                 CODE       SEGMENT
9                                  ASSUME CS:CODE
10 0000  BA FFFA                   MOV DX, OFFFAH      ; Point DX at strobe port
11 0003  EC            LOOK_AGAIN: IN  AL, DX          ; Read keyboard strobe
12 0004  24 01                     AND AL, 01          ; Mask extra bits and set flags
13 0006  74 FB                     JZ  LOOK_AGAIN      ; If strobe is low then keep looking
14 0008  BA FFF8                   MOV DX, OFFF8H      ; else point DX at data port
15 000B  EC                        IN  AL, DX          ; Read in ASCII code
16 000C                 CODE       ENDS
17                                 END
```

(c)

FIGURE 4-20 Flowchart, pseudocode, and assembly language for reading ASCII code when a strobe is present. (a) Flowchart. (b) Pseudocode. (c) List file of program.

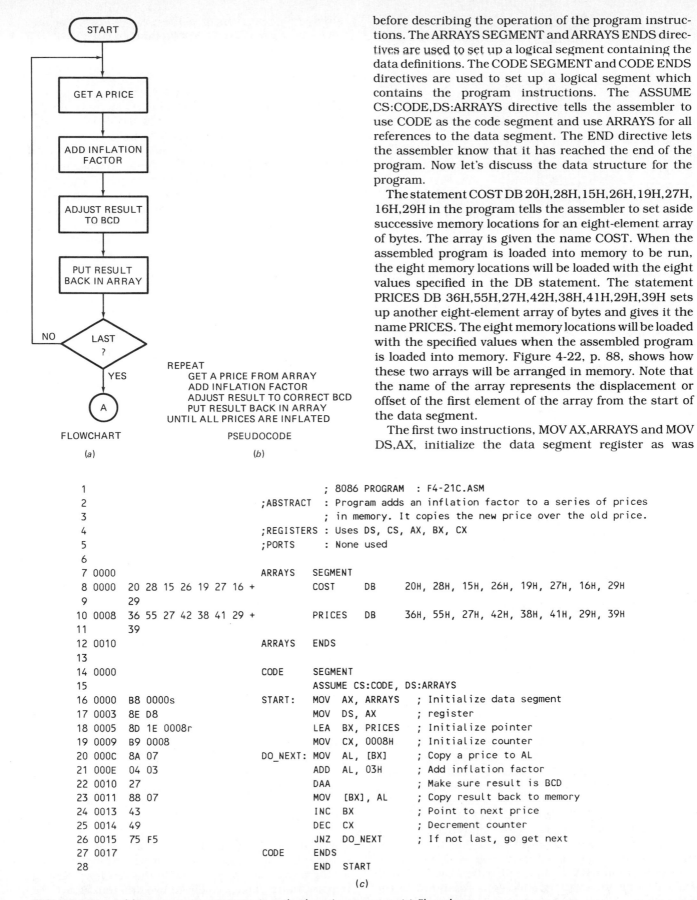

before describing the operation of the program instructions. The ARRAYS SEGMENT and ARRAYS ENDS directives are used to set up a logical segment containing the data definitions. The CODE SEGMENT and CODE ENDS directives are used to set up a logical segment which contains the program instructions. The ASSUME CS:CODE,DS:ARRAYS directive tells the assembler to use CODE as the code segment and use ARRAYS for all references to the data segment. The END directive lets the assembler know that it has reached the end of the program. Now let's discuss the data structure for the program.

The statement COST DB 20H,28H,15H,26H,19H,27H, 16H,29H in the program tells the assembler to set aside successive memory locations for an eight-element array of bytes. The array is given the name COST. When the assembled program is loaded into memory to be run, the eight memory locations will be loaded with the eight values specified in the DB statement. The statement PRICES DB 36H,55H,27H,42H,38H,41H,29H,39H sets up another eight-element array of bytes and gives it the name PRICES. The eight memory locations will be loaded with the specified values when the assembled program is loaded into memory. Figure 4-22, p. 88, shows how these two arrays will be arranged in memory. Note that the name of the array represents the displacement or offset of the first element of the array from the start of the data segment.

The first two instructions, MOV AX,ARRAYS and MOV DS,AX, initialize the data segment register as was

FLOWCHART
(a)

REPEAT
    GET A PRICE FROM ARRAY
    ADD INFLATION FACTOR
    ADJUST RESULT TO CORRECT BCD
    PUT RESULT BACK IN ARRAY
UNTIL ALL PRICES ARE INFLATED

PSEUDOCODE
(b)

```
1                                           ; 8086 PROGRAM   : F4-21C.ASM
2                            ;ABSTRACT   : Program adds an inflation factor to a series of prices
3                                           ; in memory. It copies the new price over the old price.
4                            ;REGISTERS : Uses DS, CS, AX, BX, CX
5                            ;PORTS      : None used
6
7  0000                      ARRAYS     SEGMENT
8  0000  20 28 15 26 19 27 16 +    COST    DB     20H, 28H, 15H, 26H, 19H, 27H, 16H, 29H
9        29
10 0008  36 55 27 42 38 41 29 +    PRICES  DB     36H, 55H, 27H, 42H, 38H, 41H, 29H, 39H
11       39
12 0010                      ARRAYS     ENDS
13
14 0000                      CODE       SEGMENT
15                                      ASSUME CS:CODE, DS:ARRAYS
16 0000  B8 0000s            START:  MOV  AX, ARRAYS   ; Initialize data segment
17 0003  8E D8                       MOV  DS, AX       ; register
18 0005  8D 1E 0008r                 LEA  BX, PRICES   ; Initialize pointer
19 0009  B9 0008                     MOV  CX, 0008H    ; Initialize counter
20 000C  8A 07              DO_NEXT: MOV  AL, [BX]     ; Copy a price to AL
21 000E  04 03                       ADD  AL, 03H      ; Add inflation factor
22 0010  27                          DAA               ; Make sure result is BCD
23 0011  88 07                       MOV  [BX], AL     ; Copy result back to memory
24 0013  43                          INC  BX           ; Point to next price
25 0014  49                          DEC  CX           ; Decrement counter
26 0015  75 F5                       JNZ  DO_NEXT      ; If not last, go get next
27 0017                      CODE       ENDS
28                                      END  START
```
(c)

FIGURE 4-21 Adding a constant to a series of values in memory. (a) Flowchart. (b) Pseudocode. (c) List file of program.

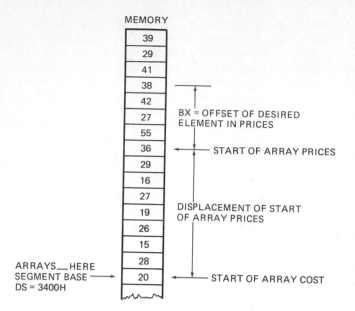

MEMORY

| 39 |
| 29 |
| 41 |
| 38 |
| 42 |
| 27 | ← BX = OFFSET OF DESIRED ELEMENT IN PRICES
| 55 |
| 36 | ← START OF ARRAY PRICES
| 29 |
| 16 |
| 27 | DISPLACEMENT OF START OF ARRAY PRICES
| 19 |
| 26 |
| 15 |
| 28 |
| 20 | ← START OF ARRAY COST

ARRAYS__HERE
SEGMENT BASE →
DS = 3400H

FIGURE 4-22 Data arrangement in memory for "inflate prices" program.

described for the example program in Figure 3-14. The LEA mnemonic in the next instruction stands for Load Effective Address. An effective address, remember, is the number of bytes from the start of a segment to the desired data item. The instruction LEA BX,PRICES loads the displacement of the first element of PRICES into the BX register. A displacement contained in a register is usually referred to as an *offset*. If you take another look at the data structure for this program in Figure 4-22, you should see that the offset of PRICES is 0008H. Therefore, the LEA BX,PRICES instruction will load BX with 0008H. We are using BX as a *pointer* to an element in PRICES. We will soon show you how this pointer is used to indicate which price we want to operate on at a given time in the program.

The next instruction, MOV CX,0008H, loads the CX register with the number of prices in the array. We use this register as a *counter* to keep track of how many prices we have operated on. After we operate on each price, we decrement the counter by 1. When the counter reaches 0, we know that we have operated on all the prices.

The MOV AL,[BX] instruction copies one of the prices from memory to the AL register. Here's how it works. Remember, the 8086 produces the physical address for accessing data in memory by adding an effective address to the segment base represented by the 16-bit number in a segment register. A section in Chapter 3 showed you how the effective address could be specified directly in the instruction with either a name or a number. The instructions MOV AX,MULTIPLICAND and MOV AX,DS:WORD PTR[0000H] are examples of this addressing mode. We also showed you that the effective address can be contained in a register. The square brackets around BX in the instruction MOV AL,[BX] indicate that the effective address is contained in the BX register. In our example program, we used the LEA BX,PRICES instruction to load the BX register with the

offset of the first element in the array PRICES. The first time the MOV AL,[BX] instruction executes, BX will contain 0008H, the effective address or offset of the first price in the array. Therefore, the first price will be copied into AL.

The next instruction, ADD AL,03H, adds the immediate number 03H to the contents of the AL register. The binary result of the addition will be left in AL. We want the prices in the array to be in BCD form, so we have to make sure the result is adjusted to be a legal BCD number. For example, if we add 03 to 29, the result in AL will be 2C. Most people would not understand this as a price, so we have to adjust the result to the desired BCD number. The Decimal Adjust after Addition instruction DAA will automatically make this adjustment for us. DAA will adjust the 2CH by adding 6 to the lower nibble and the carry produced to the upper nibble. The result of this in AL will be 32H, which is the result we want from adding 03 to 29. Note that the DAA instruction works only on the AL register. For further examples of DAA operation, consult the DAA instruction description in Chapter 6.

The INC BX instruction adds 1 to the number in BX. BX now contains the effective address or offset of the next price in the array. We like to say that BX now points to the next element in the array.

The DEC CX instruction decrements the count we set up in the CX register by 1. If CX contains 0 after this decrement, the zero flag will be set to a 1. The JNZ DO__NEXT checks the zero flag. If it finds the zero flag set, it just passes execution out of the structure to the next mainline instruction. If it finds the zero flag not set, the JNZ instruction will cause a jump to the label DO__NEXT. In other words, the 8086 will repeat the sequence of instructions between the label and the JNZ instruction until CX is counted down to zero. Each time through the loop, BX will be incremented to point to the next price in the array.

Still Another REPEAT-UNTIL Example

Using a pointer to access data items in memory is a powerful technique that you will want to use in many of your programs, so Figure 4-23 shows still another example. In this example, we want to add a profit of 15 cents to each element of an array called COST and put the result in the corresponding element of an array called PRICES. The algorithm for this example is

REPEAT
    Get an item from cost array
    Add profit factor
    Adjust result to correct BCD
    Put result into price array
UNTIL all prices are calculated

The assembly language implementation of this algorithm is very similar to that for the last example, except for the way we use the pointers. In this example we need to point to the same element in two different arrays. To do this, we use the BX register to keep track of which element we are currently accessing in the arrays. At the

```
1                                      ; 8086 PROGRAM F4-23.ASM
2                           ;ABSTRACT  : Program adds a profit factor to each element in a
3                                      ; COST array and puts the result in an PRICES array.
4                           ;REGISTERS : Uses DS, CS, AX, BX, CX
5                           ;PORTS     : None used
6
7         = 0015           PROFIT     EQU      15H        ; profit = 15 cents
8 0000                     ARRAYS     SEGMENT
9 0000  20 28 15 26 19 27 16 +         COST      DB   20H, 28H, 15H, 26H, 19H, 27H, 16H, 29H
10       29
11 0008  08*(00)                       PRICES    DB   8 DUP(0)
12 0010                    ARRAYS     ENDS
13
14 0000                    CODE       SEGMENT
15                                     ASSUME  CS:CODE, DS:ARRAYS
16 0000  B8 0000s          START:     MOV  AX, ARRAYS     ; Initialize data segment
17 0003  8E D8                         MOV  DS, AX         ; register
18 0005  B9 0008                       MOV  CX, 0008H      ; Initialize counter
19 0008  BB 0000                       MOV  BX, 0000H      ; Initialize pointer
20 000B  8A 87 0000r       DO_NEXT: MOV  AL, COST[BX]    ; Get element [BX] from COST
21 000F  04 15                         ADD  AL, PROFIT     ; Add the profit to value
22 0011  27                            DAA                 ; Decimal adjust result
23 0012  88 87 0008r                   MOV  PRICES[BX], AL ; Store result in PRICES at [BX]
24 0016  43                            INC  BX             ; Point to next element in arrays
25 0017  49                            DEC  CX             ; Decrement the counter
26 0018  75 F1                         JNZ  DO_NEXT        ; If not last element, do again
27 001A                    CODE       ENDS
28                                     END  START
```

FIGURE 4-23   List file of "price-calculating" program.

start of the program, then, we initialize BX as a pointer to the first element of each array with MOV BX,0000H. The instruction MOV AL,COST[BX] then will copy the first value from the array COST into AL. The effective address for this instruction will be produced by adding the displacement represented by the name COST to the contents of BX.

After the Addition and Decimal Adjust instructions, the instruction MOV PRICES[BX],AL copies the result of the addition to the first element of PRICES. The 8086 computes the effective address for this instruction by adding the contents of BX to the displacement represented by the name PRICES.

The BX register is incremented, so that if CX has not been decremented to zero, COST[BX] and PRICES[BX] will each access the next element in the array when execution goes through the DO_NEXT loop again. A programmer familiar with higher-level languages would probably say that BX is being used as an array index in this example.

Another Look at 8086 Addressing Modes

The preceding examples showed you how a register can be used as a pointer or index to access a sequence of data items in memory. While these examples are fresh in your mind, we want to show you more about the 8086 addressing modes we introduced you to in Chapter 3.

Figure 4-24, p. 90, summarizes all the ways you can tell the 8086 to calculate an effective address and a physical address for accessing data in memory. In all cases, the physical address is generated by adding an effective address to one of the segment bases, CS, SS, DS, or ES. The effective address can be a direct displacement specified directly in the instruction, as, for example, MOV AX,MULTIPLIER. The effective address or offset can be specified to be in a register, as in the instruction MOV AL,[BX]. Also, the effective address can be specified to be the contents of a register plus a displacement included in the instruction. The instruction MOV AX,PRICES[BX] is an example of this addressing mode. For this example, PRICES represents the displacement of the start of the array from the segment base, and BX represents the number of the element in the array that we want to access. The effective address of the desired element, then, is the sum of these two.

For working with more complex data structures such as the array of records shown in Figure 4-25, p. 90, you can tell the 8086 to compute an effective address by adding the contents of BX or BP plus the contents of SI or DI plus an 8-bit or a 16-bit displacement contained in the instruction. You can, for example, use an instruction such as MOV AL, PATIENTS[BX][SI] to access the balance due field in the array of medical records shown in Figure 4-25. The name PATIENTS in this instruction represents the displacement of the array PATIENTS from the start of the data segment. The BX register holds the offset of the start of the desired record in the array. The SI register holds the offset of the start of the desired field in the record. To access the next record in the array, you simply add a number equal to the length of the record to the BX register. To access another field in a record, you just change the value in the SI register.

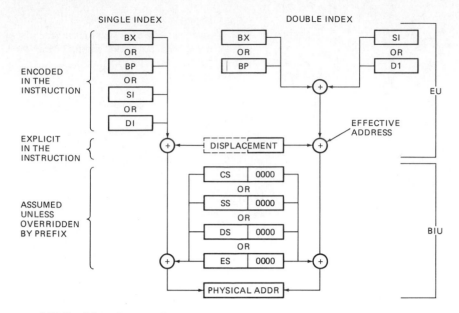

FIGURE 4-24   Summary of 8086 addressing modes.

When BX, SI, or DI is used to contain all or part of the effective address, the physical address will be produced by adding the effective address to the data segment base in DS. When BP is used to contain all or part of the effective address, the physical address will be produced by adding the effective address to the stack segment base in SS. For any of these four, you can use a segment override prefix to tell the 8086 to add the effective address to some other segment base. The instruction MOV AL,CS:[BX] tells the 8086 to produce a physical memory address by adding the offset in BX to the code segment base instead of adding it to the data segment base. An exception to this is that with a special group of instructions called *string instructions,* an offset

in DI will always be added to the extra segment base in ES to produce the physical address.

The 8086 LOOP Instructions

In the second REPEAT-UNTIL example, we showed you how to make a program repeat a sequence of instructions a specific number of times. To do this, you load the desired number of repeats in a register or memory location. Each time the sequence of instructions executes, the count value in the register or memory location is decremented by 1. When the count is decremented to zero, the zero flag will be set. You use a Conditional Jump instruction to check this flag and to decide whether to repeat the instruction sequence in the loop again.

The need to perform a sequence of actions a specified number of times in a program is so common that some programming languages use a specific structure to express it. This structure, derived from the basic WHILE-DO, is called the FOR-DO loop. It has the form

```
FOR count = 1 to count = n DO
    action
    action
```

where n is the number of times we want to do the sequence of actions.

The common need to repeat a sequence of actions a specified number of times led the designers of the 8086 to give it a group of instructions which make this easier for you. These instructions are the LOOP instructions.

INSTRUCTION OPERATION

The LOOP instructions are basically Conditional Jump instructions which have the format LOOP label. LOOP instructions, however, combine two operations in each instruction. The first operation is to decrement the CX

```
SEGMENT BASE
    .           Name PATIENTS represents displacement of
    .           start of array of records from segment base
    .
PATIENTS    ; array of patient records start here


                            RECORD 1
                            TV N. BEER
                            1324 Down Street
                            PORTLAND, OR 97219
                            2/15/45
                            247 lb
                            $327.56

BX holds offset of -------▶ RECORD 2
desired record  in array    IM A. RUNNER
                            17197 Hatton Road
                            Oregon City, OR 97045
                            6/30/41
SI holds offset of -------▶ 145 lb
desired field in record     $0.00

                            RECORD 3
```

FIGURE 4-25   Use of double indexed addressing mode.

LOOP	Loop until CX = 0
LOOPE/LOOPZ	Loop if zero flag set and CX $\neq$ 0
LOOPNE/LOOPNZ	Loop if zero flag not set and CX $\neq$ 0
JCXZ	Jump if CX = 0

FIGURE 4-26   8086 LOOP instructions.

register by 1. The second operation is to check the CX register and, in some cases, also the zero flag to decide whether to do a jump to the specified label. The simple LOOP label instruction then can be used in place of the DEC CX—JNZ label instruction sequence we used in Figure 4-21c.

As with the previously described Conditional Jump instructions, the LOOP instructions can do only short jumps. This means that the destination label must be in the range of -128 bytes to $+127$ bytes from the instruction after the LOOP instruction.

As shown in Figure 4-26, there are two additional forms of LOOP instructions. These instructions check the state of the zero flag as well as the value in the CX register to determine whether to take the jump or not. Shown in Figure 4-26 are the condition(s) checked by each instruction to determine whether it should do the jump. NE in the mnemonics stands for "not equal," and NZ in the mnemonics stands for "not zero." Instruction mnemonics separated by a "/" in Figure 4-26 represent the same instruction.

The LOOP instructions decrement the CX register but do not affect the zero flag. This leaves the zero flag available for other tests. The LOOPE/LOOPZ label instruction will decrement the CX register by 1 and jump to the specified label if CX $\neq$ 0 and ZF = 1. In other words, program execution will exit from the repeat loop if CX has been decremented to zero or the zero flag is not set. This instruction might be used after a Compare instruction, for example, to continue a sequence of operations for a specified number of times or until compared values were no longer equal.

The LOOPNE/LOOPNZ label instruction decrements the CX register by 1. If CX $\neq$ 0 and ZF = 0, this instruction will cause a jump to the specified label. In other words, execution will exit from the loop if CX is equal to zero or the zero flag is set. This instruction is useful when you want to execute a sequence of instructions a fixed number of times or until two values are equal. An example might be a program to read data from a disk. We typically write this type of program so that it attempts to read the data until the checksums are equal or until 10 unsuccessful attempts have been made to read the disk. Consult the descriptions for these instructions in Chapter 6 for specific examples of how the LOOPE and LOOPNE instructions are used.

In summary, then, the LOOP instructions are useful for implementing the REPEAT-UNTIL structure for those special cases where we want to do a series of actions a fixed number of times or until the zero flag changes state. LOOP instructions incorporate two operations in each instruction; therefore, they are somewhat more efficient than single instructions to do the same job. In the next section we introduce you to instruction timing and show you how the LOOP instruction can be used to produce a delay between the execution of two instructions.

INSTRUCTION TIMING AND DELAY LOOPS

The rate at which 8086 instructions are executed is determined by a crystal-controlled clock with a frequency of a few megahertz. Each instruction takes a certain number of clock cycles to execute. The MOV register, register instruction, for example, requires 2 clock cycles to execute, and the DAA instruction requires 4 clock cycles. The JNZ instruction requires 16 clock cycles if it does the jump, but it requires only 4 clock cycles if it doesn't do the jump. A table in Appendix B shows the number of clock cycles required by each instruction. Using the numbers in this table, you can calculate how long it takes to execute an instruction or series of instructions. For example, if you are running an 8086 with a 5-MHz clock, then each clock cycle takes 1/(5 MHz) or 0.2 μs. An instruction which takes 4 clock cycles, then, will take 4 clock cycles $\times$ 0.2 μs/clock cycle or 0.8 μs to execute.

A common programming problem is the need to introduce a delay between the execution of two instructions. For example, we might want to read a data value from a port, wait 1 ms, and then read the port again. A later chapter will show how you can use interrupts to mark off time intervals such as this, but for now we will show you how to use a program loop to do it.

The basic principle is to execute an instruction or series of instructions over and over until the desired time has elapsed. Figure 4-27a shows a program we might use to do this. The MOV CX,N instruction loads the CX register with the number of times we want to repeat the delay loop. The NOP instructions next in the program are not required; the KILL_TIME label could be right in front of the LOOP instruction. In this case, only the LOOP instruction would be repeated. However, we put the NOPs in to show you how you can get more delay by extending the time it takes to execute the loop.

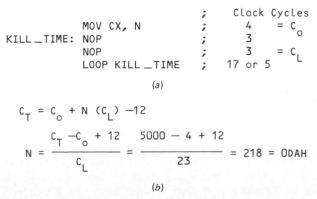

FIGURE 4-27   Delay loop program and calculations. (a) Program. (b) Calculations.

The LOOP KILL_TIME instruction will decrement CX and, if CX is not down to zero yet, do a jump to the label KILL_TIME. The program then will cause the 8086 to execute the two NOP instructions and the LOOP instruction over and over until CX is counted down to zero. The number in CX will determine how long this takes. Here's how you determine the value to put in CX for a given amount of delay.

First you calculate the number of clock cycles needed to produce the desired delay. If you are running your 8086 with a 5-MHz clock, then the time for each clock cycle is 1/(5 MHz) or 0.2 μs. Now, suppose that you want to create a delay of 1 ms or 1000 μs with a delay loop. If you divide the 1000 μs desired by the 0.2 μs per clock cycle, you get the number of clock cycles required to produce the desired delay. For this example you need a total of 1000/0.2 or 5000 processor clock cycles to produce the desired delay. We will call this number C_T for future reference.

The next step is to write the number of clock cycles required for each instruction next to that instruction, as shown in Figure 4-27a. Then you look at the program to determine which instructions get executed only once. The number of clock cycles for the instructions which execute only once will only contribute to the total once. Instructions which only enter the calculation once are often called *overhead*. We will represent the number of cycles of overhead with the symbol C_o. In Figure 4-27a, the only instruction which executes just once is MOV CX,N, which takes 4 clock cycles. For this example, then, $C_o = 4$.

Next you determine how many clock cycles are required for the loop. The two NOPs in the loop require a total of 6 clock cycles. The LOOP instruction requires 17 clock cycles if it does the jump back to KILL_TIME, but it requires only 5 clock cycles when it exits the loop. The jump takes longer because the instruction byte queue has to be reloaded starting from the new address. For all but the very last time through the loop, it will require 17 clock cycles for the LOOP instruction. Therefore, you can use 17 as the number of cycles for the LOOP instruction and compensate later for the fact that the last time it takes 12 cycles less. For the example program, the number of cycles per loop $C_L = 6 + 17$ or 23.

The total number of clock cycles delayed by the loop is equal to the number of times the loop executes multiplied by the time per loop. To be somewhat more accurate, you can subtract the 12 cycles that were not used when the last LOOP instruction executed. The total number of clock cycles required for the example program to execute is

$$C_T = C_o + N(C_L) - 12$$

To find the value for N for a desired amount of delay, put in the required C_T, 5000 for this example, and solve the result for N. Figure 4-27b shows how this is done. The resultant value for N is 218 decimal or 0DAH. This is the number of times you want the loop to repeat, so this is the value of N that you will load into CX before entering the loop.

With the simple relationship shown in Figure 4-27b,

you can determine the value of N to put in a delay loop you write, or you can determine the time a delay loop written by someone else will take to execute.

If you can't get a long enough delay by counting down a single register or memory location, you can nest delay loops. An example of this nesting is

```
                       ; number of states
        MOV BX, COUNT1; 4
CNTDN1:MOV CX, COUNT2; 4(COUNT1)
CNTDN2:LOOP CNTDN2   ; ((17 × COUNT2) − 12)COUNT1
        DEX BX       ; 2(COUNT1)
        JNZ CNTDN1   ; 16(COUNT1) − 12
```

The principle here is to load CX with COUNT2 and count CX down COUNT1 times. To determine the number of states that this program section will take to execute, observe that the LOOP instruction will execute COUNT2 times for each time CX is loaded with COUNT1. The total number of states, then, is COUNT1 times the number of states for the last four instructions plus 4, for the MOV BX,COUNT1 instruction. The best way to approach getting values for the two unknowns, COUNT1 and COUNT2, is to choose a value such as FFFFH for COUNT2 and then solve for the value of COUNT1. A couple of tries should get reasonable values for both COUNT1 and COUNT2.

Notes about Using Delay Loops for Timing

There are several additional factors you have to take into account when determining the time that a sequence of instructions will require to execute.

1. The BIU and the EU are asynchronous, so for some instruction sequences an extra clock cycle may be required. For a given sequence of instructions the added cycles are always the same, but obviously these cycles are not included in the numbers given in Appendix B.

2. The number of clock cycles required to read a word from memory or write a word to memory depends on whether the first byte of the word is at an even address or at an odd address. The 8086 will require 4 additional clock cycles to read or write a word located on an odd address.

3. The number of clock cycles required to read a byte from memory or write a byte to memory depends on the addressing mode used to access that byte. A table at the start of Appendix B shows the number of clock cycles that must be added for each addressing mode. According to Appendix B, the basic mem 8 to reg 8 instruction requires 8 + EA clock cycles. The [BX] addressing mode requires 5 clock cycles, so the instruction MOV AL,[BX] requires 8 + 5 or 13 clock cycles to execute.

4. If a given microcomputer system is designed to insert WAIT states during each memory access, this will increase the number of clock cycles required for each memory access. In Chapter 7 we discuss the use of WAIT states.

In summary, the calculations we showed you how to do in the preceding section give you the approximate time it will take a sequence of instructions to execute. If you really need to know the precise time a sequence of instructions requires to execute, the only way to determine it is to use a logic analyzer or emulator to measure the actual number of clock cycles.

CHECKLIST OF IMPORTANT TERMS AND CONCEPTS IN THIS CHAPTER

If you do not remember any of the terms or concepts in the following list, use the index to find them in the chapter.

Defining a problem

Setting up a data structure

Making an initialization checklist

Masking using the AND instruction

Packed and unpacked BCD numbers

Debugging—breakpoints, trace, single step

Conditional flags: CF, PF, AF, ZF, SF, OF

Unconditional JMP instructions
    Direct and indirect near (intrasegment) jumps
    Direct and indirect far (intersegment) jumps
    Short jumps

Conditional jumps

Fixed- and variable-port input/output instructions

Based and indexed addressing modes

Loop instruction

Processor clock cycles

Delay loops

REVIEW QUESTIONS AND PROBLEMS

1. Describe the operation and results of each of the following instructions, given the register contents shown in Figure 4-28 (below question 3). Include in your answer the physical address or register that each instruction will get its operands from and the physical address or register that each instruction will put the result in. Use the instruction descriptions in Chapter 6 to help you. Assume that the instructions below are independent, not sequential, unless listed together under a letter.
   a. ROL AX,CL
   b. IN AL,DXP
   c. MOV CX,[BX]
   d. ADD AX,[BX][SI]
   e. JMP 023AH
   f. JMP BX

2. Construct the binary codes for the instructions of Questions 1a through 1f.

3. Predict the state of the six 8086 conditional flags after each of the following instructions or group of instructions executes. Use the register contents shown in Figure 4-28. Assume that all flags are reset before the instructions execute. Use the detailed instruction descriptions in Chapter 6 to help you.
   a. MOV AL,AH
   b. ADD BL,CL
   c. ADD CL,DH
   d. OR CX,BX

```
CS = 2000      AX = A407
DS = 3000      BX = 24B3
SS = 4000      CX = 0002
ES = 3000      DX = FFFA
SP = FFFF
BP = 0009
SI = 4200
DI = 4300
```

FIGURE 4-28   Figure for Chapter 4 problems.

4. See if you can find any errors in the following instructions or groups of instructions.

   a. CNTDOWN: MOV BL, 72H
                  DEC BL
                  JNZ CNTDOWN
   b. ADD CX,AL
   c. JMP BL
   d. JNZ [BX]

5. a. Write an algorithm for a program which adds a byte number from one memory location to a byte from the next memory location, puts the sum in a third memory location, and saves the state of the carry flag in the least significant bit of a fourth memory location. Mask the upper 7 bits of the memory location where the carry is stored.
   b. Write an 8086 assembly language program for this algorithm. *Hints:* Set up data declarations similar to those in Figure 3-14. Use a Rotate instruction to get the carry flag state into the LSB of a register or memory location.
   c. What additional instructions would you have to add to this program so that it correctly adds 2 BCD bytes?

   For each of the following programming problems, draw a flowchart or write the pseudocode for an algorithm to solve the problem. Then write an 8086 assembly language program to implement the algorithm. If you have an 8086 system available, enter and assemble your source program, then load the object code for the program into memory so that you can run and test it. If the program does not work correctly, use the single-step or breakpoint approaches described earlier in this chapter to help you debug it.

6. Convert a packed BCD byte to two ASCII characters for the two BCD digits in the byte. For example, given a BCD byte containing 57H (01010111 binary), produce the two ASCII codes 35H and 37H.

7. In order to avoid hand keying programs into an SDK-86 board, we wrote a program to send machine code programs from an IBM PC to an SDK-86 board through a serial link. As part of this program, we had to convert each byte of the machine code program to ASCII codes for the two nibbles in the byte. In other words, a byte of 7AH has to be sent as 37H, the ASCII code for 7, and 41H, the ASCII code for A. Once you separate the nibbles of the byte, this conversion is a simple IF-THEN-ELSE situation. Write an algorithm and assembly language program section which does the needed conversion.

8. A common problem when reading a series of ASCII characters from a keyboard is the need to filter out those codes which represent the hex digits 0 to 9 and A to F, and convert these ASCII codes to the hex digits they represent. For example, if we read in 34H, the ASCII code for 4, we want to mask the upper 4 bits to leave 04, the 8-bit hex code for 4. If we read in 42H, the ASCII code for B, we want to add 09 and mask the upper 4 bits to leave 0B, the 8-bit code for hex B. If we read in an ASCII code that is not in the range of 30H to 39H or 41H to 46H, then we want to load an error code of FFH instead of the hex value of the entered character. Figure 4-29 shows the desired action next to each range of ASCII values. Write an algorithm and an assembly language program which implements these actions. *Hint:* A nested IF-THEN-ELSE structure might be useful.

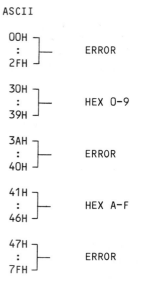

FIGURE 4-29   ASCII chart for Problem 8.

9. Compute the average of 4 bytes stored in an array in memory.

10. Compute the average of any number of bytes in an array in memory. The number of bytes to be added is in the first byte of the array.

11. Add a 5-byte number in one array to a 5-byte number in another array. Put the sum in another array. Put the state of the carry flag in byte 6 of the array that contains the sum. The first value in each array is the least significant byte of that number. *Hint:* See Figure 4-23.

12. An 8086-based process control system outputs a measured Fahrenheit temperature to a display on its front panel. You need to write a short program which converts the Fahrenheit temperature to Celsius so that the system can be sold in Europe. The relationship between Fahrenheit and Celsius is $C = (F - 32)5/9$. The Fahrenheit temperature will always be in the range of 50° to 250°. Round the Celsius value to the nearest degree.

13. An ASCII keyboard outputs parallel ASCII + parity to port FFF8H of an SDK-86 board. The keyboard also outputs a strobe to the least significant bit (D0) of port FFFAH. (See Figure 4-19.) When you press a key, the keyboard outputs the ASCII code for the pressed key on the eight parallel lines and outputs a strobe pulse high for 1 ms. You want to poll the strobe over and over until you find it high. Then you want to read in the ASCII code, mask the parity bit (D7), and store the ASCII code in an array in memory. Next, you want to poll the strobe over and over again until you find it low. When you find the strobe has gone low, check to see if you have read in 10 characters yet. If not, then go back and wait for the strobe to go high again. If 10 characters have been read in, stop.

14. *a.* Write a delay loop which produces a delay of 500 μs on an 8086 with a 5-MHz clock.
    b. Write a short program which outputs a 1-kHz square wave on D0 of port FFFAH. The basic principle here is to output a high, wait 500 μs (0.5 ms), output a low, wait 500 μs, output a high, etc. Remember that, before you can output to a port device, you must first initialize it as in Figure 4-18a. If you connect a buffer such as that shown in Figure 8-23 and a speaker to D0 of the port, you will be able to hear the tone produced.

CHAPTER 5

Strings, Procedures, and Macros

The last chapter showed you how quite a few of the 8086 instructions work and how jump instructions are used to implement IF-THEN-ELSE, WHILE-DO, and REPEAT-UNTIL program structures. The first section of this chapter introduces you to the 8086 string instructions, which can be used to repeat some operations on a sequence of data words in memory. The major point of this chapter, however, is to show you how to write and use subprograms called *procedures*. A final section of the chapter shows you how to write and use assembler *macros*.

OBJECTIVES

At the conclusion of this chapter, you should be able to:

1. Use the 8086 string instructions to perform a variety of operations on a sequence of data words in memory.

2. Describe how a stack is initialized and used in 8086 assembly language programs which call procedures.

3. Write an 8086 assembly language program which calls a near procedure.

4. Write an 8086 assembly language program which calls a far procedure.

5. Write, assemble, link, and run a program which consists of more than one assembly module.

6. Write and use an assembler macro.

THE 8086 STRING INSTRUCTIONS

Introduction and Operation

A *string* is a series of bytes or words stored in successive memory locations. Often a string consists of a series of ASCII character codes. When you use a word processor or text editor program, you are actually creating a string of this sort as you type in a series of characters. One important feature of a word processor is the ability to move a sentence or group of sentences from one place in the text to another. Doing this involves moving a string of ASCII characters from one place in memory to another. The 8086 Move String instruction, MOVS, allows you to do operations such as this very easily.

Another important feature of most word processors is the ability to search through the text looking for a given word or phrase. The 8086 Compare String instruction, CMPS, can be used to do operations of this type. In a similar manner, the 8086 SCAS instruction can be used to search a string to see whether it contains a specified character. A couple of examples should help you see how these instructions work.

MOVING A STRING

Suppose that you have a string of ASCII characters in successive memory locations in the data segment, and you want to move the string to some new sequence of locations in the data segment. To help you visualize this, take a look at the strings we set up in the data segment in Figure 5-1*b*, p. 96, to test our program.

The statement TEST_MESS DB 'TIS TIME FOR A NEW HOME' sets aside 23 bytes of memory and gives the first memory location the name TEST_MESS. This statement will also cause the ASCII codes for the letters enclosed in the single quotes to be written in the reserved memory locations when the program is loaded in memory to be run. This array or string then will contain 54H, 49H, 53H, 20H, etc. The statement DB 100 DUP(?) will set aside 100 memory locations, but the DUP(?) in the statement tells the assembler not to initialize these 100 locations. We put these bytes in to represent the block of text that we are going to move our string over. The statement NEW_LOC DB 23 DUP(0) sets aside 23 memory locations and gives the first byte the name NEW_LOC. When this program is loaded in memory to be run, the 23 locations will be loaded with 00 as specified by the DUP(0) in the statement. To help you visualize this, Figure 5-1*a* shows a memory map for this data segment. Now that you understand the data structure for the problem, the next step is to write an algorithm for the program.

The basic pseudocode algorithm shown here for the operations you want to perform doesn't really help you see how you might implement the algorithm in assembly language.

```
REPEAT
MOVE BYTE FROM SOURCE STRING
        TO DESTINATION STRING
UNTIL ALL BYTES MOVED
```

In Chapter 3 we introduced you to the use of pointers to access data in sequential memory locations, so your next thought might be to expand the algorithm as shown next:

INITIALIZE SOURCE POINTER, SI
INITIALIZE DESTINATION POINTER, DI
INITIALIZE COUNTER, CX

REPEAT
  COPY BYTE FROM SOURCE TO DESTINATION
  INCREMENT SOURCE POINTER
  INCREMENT DESTINATION POINTER
  DECREMENT COUNTER
UNTIL COUNTER = 0

We often describe an algorithm in general terms at first and then expand sections as needed to help us see how the algorithm is implemented in a specific language. In the expanded algorithm you can see that as part of the initialization list you need to initialize the two pointers and a counter. The REPEAT-UNTIL loop then consists of moving a byte, incrementing the pointers to point to the source and destination for the next byte, and decrementing the counter to determine whether all the bytes have been moved.

As it turns out, the single 8086 string instruction, MOVSB, will perform all the actions in the REPEAT-UNTIL loop. The MOVSB instruction will copy a byte from the location pointed to by the SI register to a location pointed to by the DI register. It will then automatically increment SI to point to the next source location, and increment DI to point to the next destination location. Actually, as we will show you soon, we can specify whether we want SI and DI to increment or decrement. If you add a special prefix called the *repeat*

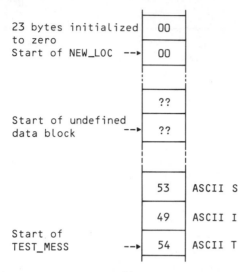

(a)

```
 1                                      ; 8086 PROGRAM F5-01.ASM
 2                        ;ABSTRACT  : Program moves a string from the location TEST_MESS
 3                                    ; to the location NEW_LOC.
 4                        ;REGISTERS ; Uses CS, DS, ES, SI, DI, AX, CX
 5                        ;PORTS     ; None used
 6
 7 0000                  DATA  SEGMENT
 8 0000  54 49 53 20 54 49 4D +       TEST_MESS DB 'TIS TIME FOR A NEW HOME' ; String to move
 9        45 20 46 4F 52 20 41 +
10        20 4E 45 57 20 48 4F +
11        4D 45
12 0017  64*(??)                                DB  100 DUP(?)           ; Stationary block of text
13 007B  17*(00)                      NEW_LOC   DB  23 DUP(0)            ; String destination
14 0092                  DATA  ENDS
15
16 0000                  CODE  SEGMENT
17                              ASSUME CS:CODE, DS:DATA, ES:DATA
18
19 0000  B8 0000s        START:MOV AX, DATA      ; Initialize data segment register
20 0003  8E D8                 MOV DS, AX
21 0005  8E C0                 MOV ES, AX        ; Initialize extra segment register
22 0007  8D 36 0000r            LEA SI, TEST_MESS ; Point SI at source string
23 000B  8D 3E 007Br            LEA DI, NEW_LOC   ; Point DI at destination location
24 000F  B9 0017               MOV CX, 23        ; Use CX register as counter
25 0012  FC                    CLD               ; Clear direction flag so pointers autoincrement
26                                               ; after each string element is moved
27 0013  F3> A4          REP   MOVSB             ; Move string bytes until all moved
28
29 0015                  CODE ENDS
30                              END START
```

(b)

FIGURE 5-1 Program for moving a string from one location to another in memory. (a) Memory map. (b) Assembly language program.

prefix in front of the MOVSB instruction, the MOVSB instruction will be repeated and CX decremented until CX is counted down to zero. In other words, the REP MOVSB instruction will move the entire string from the source location to the destination location if the pointers are properly initialized.

In order for the MOVSB instruction to work correctly, the source index register, SI, must contain the offset of the start of the source string, and the destination index register, DI, must contain the offset of the start of the destination location. Also, the number of string elements to be moved must be loaded into the CX register.

As we said previously, the string instructions will automatically increment or decrement the pointers after each operation, depending on the state of the direction flag DF. If the direction flag is cleared with a CLD instruction, then the pointers in SI and DI will automatically be incremented after each string operation. If the direction flag is set with an STD instruction, then the pointers in SI and DI will be automatically decremented after each string operation. For this example, it is easier to initialize the pointers to the starting offsets of each string and increment the pointers after each operation, so you will include the CLD instruction as part of the initialization.

Figure 5-1*b* shows how this algorithm can be implemented in assembly language. The first two MOV instructions in the program initialize the data segment register. The next instruction initializes the extra segment register. This is necessary because for string instructions, an offset in DI is added to the segment base represented by the number in the ES register to produce a physical address. If DS and ES are initialized with the same value, as we did with the first three instructions in this program, then SI and DI will point to locations in the same segment.

The next step in the program is to load SI with the effective address or offset of the first element in the source string. In the example we used the LEA instruction, but an alternative way to do this is with the instruction MOV SI,OFFSET TEST_MESS. The DI register is then initialized to contain the effective address or offset of the first destination location.

Next we load the CX register with the number of bytes in the string. Remember, CX functions as a counter to keep track of how many string bytes have been moved at any given time. Finally, we make the direction flag a zero with the Clear Direction Flag instruction, CLD. This will cause both SI and DI to be automatically incremented after a string byte is moved.

When the Move String Byte instruction, MOVSB, executes, a byte pointed to by SI will be copied to the location pointed to by DI. SI and DI will be automatically incremented to point to the next source and the next destination locations. The count register will be automatically decremented. The MOVSB instruction by itself will just copy one byte and update SI and DI to point to the next locations. However, as we said before, the repeat prefix, REP, will cause the MOVSB to be executed and the CX to be decremented over and over again until the CX register is counted down to zero. Incidentally, when the program is coded, the 8-bit code for the REP prefix,

11110011, is put in the memory location before the code for the MOVSB instruction.

After the MOVSB instruction is finished, SI will be pointing to the location after the last source string byte, DI will be pointing to the location after the last destination address, and CX will be zero.

The MOVSW instruction can be used to move a string of words. Depending on the state of the direction flag, SI and DI will automatically be incremented or decremented by 2 after each word move. If the REP prefix is used, CX will be decremented by 1 after each word move, so CX should be initialized with the number of words in the string.

As you can see from this example, a single MOVSB instruction can cause the 8086 to move up to 65,536 bytes from one location in memory to another. The string instruction is much more efficient than using a sequence of standard instructions, because the 8086 only has to fetch and decode the REP MOVSB instruction once! A standard instruction sequence such as MOV, MOV, INC, INC, LOOP, etc., would have to be fetched and decoded each time around the loop.

USING THE COMPARE STRING BYTE TO CHECK A PASSWORD

For this program example, suppose that we want to compare a user-entered password with the correct password stored in memory. If the passwords do not match, we want to sound an alarm. If the passwords match, we want to allow the user access to the computer and continue with the mainline program. Figure 5-2, p. 98, shows how we might represent the algorithm for this with a flowchart and with pseudocode. Note that we want to terminate the REPEAT-UNTIL when either the compared bytes do not match or we are at the end of the string. We then use an IF-THEN-ELSE structure to sound the alarm if the compared strings were not equal at any point. If the strings match, the IF-THEN-ELSE just directs execution on to the main program.

To implement this algorithm in assembly language, we probably would first expand the basic structures as shown in Figure 5-2*c*. The first action in the expanded algorithm is to initialize the port device for output. We need to have an output port because we will turn on the alarm by outputting a 1 to the alarm control circuit. Next we need to initialize a pointer to each string and a counter to keep track of how many string elements have been compared. The REPEAT-UNTIL shows how we will use the pointer and counter to do the compare.

Figure 5-3, p. 99, shows how the Compare String instruction, CMPS, can be used to help translate this algorithm to assembly language. As a review, first let's look at the data structure for this program. The statement PASSWORD DB'FAIL-SAFE' sets aside 8 bytes of memory and gives the first memory location the name PASSWORD. This statement also initializes the eight memory locations with the ASCII codes for the letters FAILSAFE. The ASCII codes will be 46H, 41H, 49H, 4CH, 53H, 41H, 46H, 45H.

When an assembler reads through the source code for a program, it uses a *location counter* to keep track of the offset of each item in a segment. A $ is used to symbolically represent the current value of the location

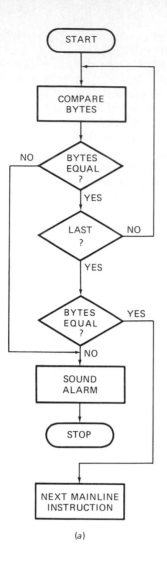

START

COMPARE
BYTES

BYTES
EQUAL
?
NO
YES

LAST
?
NO
YES

BYTES
EQUAL
?
YES

NO

SOUND
ALARM

STOP

NEXT MAINLINE
INSTRUCTION

(a)

```
REPEAT
        COMPARE SOURCE BYTE WITH DESTINATION BYTE
UNTIL (BYTES NOT EQUAL) OR (END OF STRING)
IF BYTES NOT EQUAL THEN
        SOUND ALARM
        STOP
ELSE DO NEXT MAINLINE INSTRUCTION
```

(b)

```
INITIALIZE PORT DEVICE FOR OUTPUT
INITIALIZE SOURCE POINTER — SI
INITIALIZE DESTINATION POINTER — DI
INITIALIZE COUNTER — CX
REPEAT
        COMPARE SOURCE BYTE WITH DESTINATION BYTE
        INCREMENT SOURCE POINTER
        INCREMENT DESTINATION POINTER
        DECREMENT COUNTER
UNTIL (STRING BYTES NOT EQUAL) OR (CX = 0)
IF STRING BYTES NOT EQUAL THEN
        SOUND ALARM
        STOP
ELSE DO NEXT MAINLINE INSTRUCTION
```

(c)

FIGURE 5-2   Flowchart and pseudocode for comparing strings program. (a) Flowchart. (b) Initial pseudocode. (c) Expanded pseudocode.

counter at any point. The statement STR_LENGTH EQU ($-PASSWORD) in the data segment then tells the assembler to compute the value for a constant called STR_LENGTH by subtracting the offset of PASSWORD from the current value in the location counter. The value of STR_LENGTH will be the length of the string PASSWORD. Note that the EQU statement must be in the data segment immediately after the password array so that the location counter contains the desired value. As you will see later, this trick with the $ sign allows you to load the number of string elements in CX symbolically, rather than having to manually count the number. This trick has the further advantage that if the password is changed and the program reassembled, the instruction that loads CX with the string length will automatically use the new value.

The statement INPUT_WORD DB 8 DUP(0) will set aside eight memory locations and assign the name INPUT_WORD to the first location. The DUP(0) in the statement tells the assembler to put 00H in each of these locations. We assume that a keyboard interface program section will load these locations with ASCII codes read from the keyboard as a user enters a password. We like to initialize locations such as this with zeros, so that during debugging we can more easily tell if the keyboard section correctly loaded the ASCII codes for the pressed keys in these locations.

Now let's look at the code segment section of the program. The ASSUME statement tells the assembler that the instructions will be in the segment CODE. It also tells the assembler that any references to the data segment or to the extra segment will mean the segment DATA. Remember that when you are using string instructions, you have to tell the assembler what to assume about the extra segment, because with string instructions an offset in DI is added to the extra segment base to produce the physical address.

The first three MOV statements in the program initialize the data and extra segment registers. Since we initialize DS and ES with the same values, both SI and DI will point to locations in the segment DATA. The next three instructions initialize port P2B of an SDK-86 board as an output port.

LEA SI,PASSWORD loads the effective address or offset of the start of the FAILSAFE string into the SI register. Since PASSWORD is the first data item in the segment DATA, SI will be loaded with 0000H. LEA DI,IN-PUT_WORD loads the effective address or offset of the start of the INPUT_WORD string into the DI register. Since the offset of INPUT_WORD is 0008H, DI will be loaded with this value. The MOV CX,STR_LENGTH statement uses the EQU we defined previously to initialize CX with the number of bytes in the string. The Clear Direction flag instruction tells the 8086 to automatically increment SI and DI after two string bytes are compared.

The CMPSB instruction will compare the byte pointed to by SI with the byte pointed to by DI and set the flags according to the result. It will also increment the pointers, SI and DI, to point to the next string elements. The REPE prefix in front of this instruction tells the 8086 to decrement the CX register after each compare, and repeat the CMPSB instruction if the compared bytes

The secon[...]
change the [...]
some cases, [...]
to contain th[...]
second func[...]
to the opera[...]
in Chapter 4[...]

For most [...]
dures by nam[...]
The DELAY [...]
put next to [...]
form of CALl[...]
the destinat[...]
struction. A [...]
destination [...]
different wa[...]
coding form[...]
instruction. [...]
in the way t[...]
for the proc[...]

DIRECT WI[...]

The first for[...]
8086 to prc[...]
by adding a [...]
instruction[...]
This is the [...]
within-segr[...]
With this ir[...]
dure can be[...]
+32,767 by[...]
the CALL. [...]
calculate th[...]
of the instr[...]
of the proc[...]
the CALL [...]
negative. I[...]
16-bit, 2's [...]
as you do[...]
using an [...]
calculate t[...]
the CALL t[...]

THE INDI[...]

The indire[...]
near call. \[...]
tion point[...]
specified [...]
the MOD-[...]
the value [...]
memory l[...]
dressing [...]
CALL inst[...]
procedure[...]
CALL BP, [...]
contained[...]
put in th[...]
WORD PT[...]
pointer fr[...]

```
  1                                       ; 8086 PROGRAM F5-03.ASM
  2                               ;ABSTRACT  : This program inputs a password and sounds an alarm
  3                                         ;            if the password is incorrect
  4                               ;REGISTERS : Uses CS, DS, ES, AX, DX, CX, SI, DI
  5                               ;PORTS     : Uses FFFAH - Port 2B on SDK-86 for alarm output
  6
  7 0000                          DATA  SEGMENT
  8 0000  46 41 49 4C 53 41 46 +        PASSWORD    DB    'FAILSAFE'     ; Password
  9        45
 10        = 0008                       STR_LENGTH  EQU   ($ - PASSWORD) ; Compute length of string
 11 0008  08*(00)                       INPUT_WORD  DB    8 DUP(0)       ; Space for user password input
 12 0010                          DATA  ENDS
 13
 14 0000                          CODE  SEGMENT
 15                                     ASSUME CS:CODE, DS:DATA, ES:DATA
 16 0000  B8 0000s                      MOV  AX, DATA
 17 0003  8E D8                         MOV  DS, AX          ; Initialize data segment register
 18 0005  8E C0                         MOV  ES, AX          ; Initialize extra segment register
 19 0007  BA FFFE                       MOV  DX, OFFFEH      ; These next three instructions
 20 000A  B0 99                         MOV  AL, 99H         ; set up an output port on
 21 000C  EE                            OUT  DX, AL          ; the SDK-86 board
 22 000D  8D 36 0000r                   LEA  SI, PASSWORD    ; Load source pointer
 23 0011  8D 3E 0008r                   LEA  DI, INPUT_WORD  ; Load destination pointer
 24 0015  B9 0008                       MOV  CX, STR_LENGTH  ; Load counter with password length
 25 0018  FC                            CLD                  ; Increment DI & SI
 26 0019  F3> A6          REPE          CMPSB                ; Compare the two string bytes
 27 001B  75 03                         JNE  SOUND_ALARM     ; If not equal, sound alarm
 28 001D  EB 08 90                      JMP  OK              ;  else continue
 29 0020  B0 01          SOUND_ALARM:MOV  AL, 01            ; To sound alarm, send a 1
 30 0022  BA FFFA                       MOV  DX, OFFFAH      ; to the output port whose
 31 0025  EE                            OUT  DX, AL          ; address is in DX
 32 0026  F4                            HLT                  ; and HALT.
 33 0027  90             OK:            NOP                  ; Program continues if password is OK
 34 0028                          CODE  ENDS
 35                                     END
```

FIGURE 5-3   Assembly language program for comparing strings.

were equal *and* CX is not yet decremented down to zero. As we mentioned before, when this instruction is coded, the code for the prefix will be put in memory before the code for the CMPSB instruction.

If the zero flag is not set when execution leaves the repeat loop, then we know that the two strings are not equal. This means that the password entered was not valid, so we want to sound an alarm. The JNE SOUND_ ALARM will check the zero flag and, if it is not set, do a jump to the specified label. If the zero flag is set, indicating a valid password, then execution falls through to the JMP OK instruction. This JMP instruction simply jumps over the instructions which sound the alarm and stop the computer.

For this example, we assume that the alarm control is connected to the least significant bit of port FFFAH and that a 1 output to this bit turns on the alarm. The MOV AL,01 instruction loads a 1 in the LSB of AL. The MOV DX,0FFFAH instruction points DX at the port that the alarm is connected to, and the OUT DX,AL instruction copies this byte to port FFFAH. Finally, the HLT instruction stops the computer. An interrupt or reset will be required to get it started again.

As the preceding examples show, the string instructions make it very easy to implement some commonly needed REPEAT-UNTIL algorithms. Some of the programming problems at the end of the chapter will give you practice with MOVS, CMPS, and SCAS instructions.

WRITING AND USING PROCEDURES

Introduction

Often when writing programs you will find that you need to use a particular sequence of instructions at several different points in a program. To avoid writing the sequence of instructions in the program each time you need them, you can write the sequence as a separate "subprogram" called a *procedure*. Each time you need to execute the sequence of instructions contained in the procedure, you use the CALL instruction to send the 8086 to the starting address of the procedure in memory. Figure 5-4*a*, p. 100, shows in diagram form how a CALL instruction causes execution to go from the mainline program to a procedure. A RET instruction at the end of the procedure returns execution to the next instruction in the mainline. As shown in Figure 5-4*b*, procedures can even be "nested." This means that one procedure calls another procedure as part of its instruction sequence. Follow the arrows in Figure 5-4*b*

```
 1                                              ; 8086 PROGRAM F5-14.ASM
 2                             ;ABSTRACT  : BCD to BINARY conversion program that uses a
 3                                         ; procedure to convert BCD numbers to binary.
 4                                         ; Program uses the AL register to pass parameters
 5                                         ; to the procedure
 6                             ;REGISTERS : Uses CS, DS, SS, SP, AX
 7                             ;PORTS     : None Used
 8                             ;PROCEDURES: BCD_BIN
 9
10 0000                       DATA        SEGMENT
11 0000   17                              BCD_INPUT    DB 17H        ; storage for BCD value
12 0001   ??                              BIN_VALUE    DB ?          ; storage for binary value
13 0002                       DATA        ENDS
14
15 0000                       STACK_SEG   SEGMENT      STACK
16 0000   64*(0000)                                    DW 100 DUP(0)    ; stack of 100 words
17                                        TOP_STACK    LABEL    WORD
18 00C8                       STACK_SEG   ENDS
19
20 0000                       CODE        SEGMENT
21                                        ASSUME CS:CODE, DS:DATA, SS:STACK_SEG
22 0000   B8 0000s            START:      MOV  AX, DATA              ; Initialize data segment
23 0003   8E D8                           MOV  DS, AX                ; register
24 0005   B8 0000s                        MOV  AX, STACK_SEG         ; Initialize stack segment
25 0008   8E D0                           MOV  SS, AX                ; register
26 000A   BC 00C8r                        MOV  SP, OFFSET TOP_STACK  ; Initialize stack pointer
27
28 000D   A0 0000r                        MOV  AL, BCD_INPUT
29 0010   E8 0005                         CALL BCD_BIN               ; Do the conversion
30 0013   A2 0001r                        MOV  BIN_VALUE, AL         ; Store the result
31 0016   90                              NOP                        ; Continue with program here
32 0017   90                              NOP                        ;
33
34                           ;PROCEDURE:  BCD_BIN - Converts BCD numbers to binary.
35                           ;INPUT    :  AL with BCD value
36                           ;OUTPUT   :  AL with binary value
37                           ;DESTROYS :  AX
38
39 0018                       BCD_BIN     PROC  NEAR
40 0018   9C                              PUSHF                      ; Save flags
41 0019   53                              PUSH BX                    ; and registers used in procedure
42 001A   51                              PUSH CX                    ; before starting the conversion
43                           ;Do the conversion
44 001B   8A D8                           MOV  BL, AL                ; Save copy of BCD in BL
45 001D   80 E3 0F                        AND  BL, 0FH               ; and mask
46 0020   24 F0                           AND  AL, 0F0H              ; Separate upper nibble
47 0022   B1 04                           MOV  CL, 04                ; Move upper BCD digit to low
48 0024   D2 C8                           ROR  AL, CL                ; nibble position for múltiply
49 0026   B7 0A                           MOV  BH, 0AH               ; Load conversion factor in BH
50 0028   F6 E7                           MUL  BH                    ; Multiply upper BCD digit in AL
51                                                                   ; by 0AH in BH, leave result in AL
52 002A   02 C3                           ADD  AL, BL                ; Add lower BCD digit to MUL result
53                           ;End of conversion, binary result in AL
54 002C   59                              POP  CX                    ; Restore registers
55 002D   5B                              POP  BX
56 002E   9D                              POPF
57 002F   C3                              RET                        ; and return to mainline
58 0030                       BCD_BIN     ENDP
59
60 0030                       CODE        ENDS
61                                        END      START
```

FIGURE 5-14   Example program passing parameters in registers.

```
  1                                        ; 8086 PROGRAM F5-15.ASM
  2                       ;ABSTRACT  : BCD to BINARY conversion program that uses a
  3                                  ; procedure to convert BCD numbers to binary.
  4                                  ; Program uses dedicated memory locations to
  5                                  ; pass parameters to the procedure.
  6                       ;REGISTERS : Uses CS, DS, SS, SP, AX
  7                       ;PORTS     : None used
  8                       ;PROCEDURES: Uses BCD_BIN

     SAME DATA STRUCTURE AND INITIALIZATION AS FIGURE 5-14 LINES 9 THROUGH 27

 28 000D  E8 0002                   CALL BCD_BIN            ; Do the conversion
 29 0010  90                        NOP                     ; Continue with program here
 30 0011  90                        NOP                     ;
 31
 32
 33
 34                       ;PROCEDURE:  BCD_BIN - Converts BCD numbers to binary.
 35                       ;INPUT    :  Data from dedicated memory location BCD_INPUT
 36                       ;OUTPUT   :  Data to dedicated memory location BIN_VALUE
 37                       ;DESTROYS :  Nothing
 38
 39 0012              BCD_BIN     PROC     NEAR
 40 0012  9C                       PUSHF                   ; Save flags
 41 0013  50                       PUSH AX                 ; and registers
 42 0014  53                       PUSH BX
 43 0015  51                       PUSH CX
 44 0016  A0 0000r                 MOV  AL, BCD_INPUT ; Get BCD value from memory
 45                       ;Do the conversion
 46 0019  8A D8                    MOV  BL, AL             ; Save copy of BCD in BL
 47 001B  80 E3 0F                 AND  BL, 0FH            ; and mask
 48 001E  24 F0                    AND  AL, 0F0H           ; Separate upper nibble
 49 0020  B1 04                    MOV  CL, 04             ; Move upper BCD digit to low
 50 0022  D2 C8                    ROR  AL, CL             ; nibble position for multiply
 51 0024  B7 0A                    MOV  BH, 0AH            ; Load conversion factor in BH
 52 0026  F6 E7                    MUL  BH                 ; Multiply upper BCD digit in AL
 53                                                        ; by 0AH in BH, leave result in AL
 54 0028  02 C3                    ADD  AL, BL             ; Add lower BCD digit to MUL result
 55                       ;End of conversion, binary value in AL
 56 002A  A2 0001r                 MOV  BIN_VALUE, AL ; Store binary value in memory
 57 002D  59                       POP  CX                 ; Restore flags and
 58 002E  5B                       POP  BX                 ; registers
 59 002F  58                       POP  AX
 60 0030  9D                       POPF
 61 0031  C3                       RET
 62 0032              BCD_BIN     ENDP
 63
 64 0032              CODE        ENDS
 65                               END     START
```

FIGURE 5-15   Example program passing parameters in named memory locations.

The approach used in Figure 5-15 works in this case, but it has a severe limitation. Can you see what it is? The limitation is that this procedure will always look to the memory location named BCD_INPUT to get its data and will always put its result in the memory location called BIN_VALUE. In other words, the way it is written, we can't easily use this procedure to convert a BCD number in some other memory location. As we explain in detail later, this method has the further problem that it makes the procedure *nonreentrant*.

PASSING PARAMETERS USING POINTERS

A parameter-passing method which overcomes the disadvantage of using data item names directly in a procedure is to use registers to pass the procedure pointers to the desired data. Figure 5-16, p. 112, shows one way to do this. In the main program, before we call the procedure, we use the MOV SI,OFFSET BCD_INPUT instruction to set up the SI register as a pointer to the memory location BCD_INPUT. We also use the MOV DI,OFFSET

```
 1                                      ; 8086 PROGRAM F5-16.ASM
 2                           ;ABSTRACT  : BCD to BINARY conversion program that uses a
 3                                      ; procedure to convert BCD numbers to binary.
 4                                      ; Program shows how to use pointers to pass
 5                                      ; parameters to a procedure.
 6                           ;REGISTERS : Uses CS, DS, SS, SP, AX, SI, DI
 7                           ;PORTS     : Uses none
 8                           ;PROCEDURES: Uses BCD_BIN

    SAME DATA STRUCTURE AND INITIALIZATION AS FIGURE 5-14 LINES 9 THROUGH 27

28                           ;Put pointer to BCD storage in SI and pointer to binary storage in DI
29 000D  BE 0000r                       MOV  SI, OFFSET BCD_INPUT   ; Create pointers to BCD and
30 0010  BF 0001r                       MOV  DI, OFFSET BIN_VALUE   ; binary storage
31 0013  E8 0001                        CALL BCD_BIN               ; Do the conversion
32 0016  90                             NOP                        ; Continue with program here
33
34                           ;PROCEDURE:  BCD_BIN - Converts BCD numbers to binary.
35                           ;INPUT    :  SI, points to location in memory of data
36                           ;OUTPUT   :  DI, points to location in memory for result
37                           ;DESTROYS :  Nothing
38
39 0017                      BCD_BIN     PROC      NEAR
40 0017  9C                              PUSHF                      ; Save flags
41 0018  50                              PUSH AX                    ; and registers
42 0019  53                              PUSH BX
43 001A  51                              PUSH CX
44 001B  8A 04                           MOV  AL, [SI]              ; Get BCD value from memory
45                           ;Do the conversion
46 001D  8A D8                           MOV  BL, AL                ; Save copy of BCD in BL
47 001F  80 E3 0F                        AND  BL, OFH               ; and mask
48 0022  24 F0                           AND  AL, OFOH              ; Separate upper nibble
49 0024  B1 04                           MOV  CL, 04                ; Move upper BCD digit to low
50 0026  D2 C8                           ROR  AL, CL                ; nibble position for multiply
51 0028  B7 0A                           MOV  BH, OAH               ; Load conversion factor in BH
52 002A  F6 E7                           MUL  BH                    ; Multiply upper BCD digit in AL
53                                                                  ; by OAH in BH, leave result in AL
54 002C  02 C3                           ADD  AL, BL                ; Add lower BCD digit to MUL result
55                           ;End of conversion, binary value in AL
56 002E  88 05                           MOV  [DI], AL              ; Store binary value in memory
57 0030  59                              POP  CX                    ; Restore flags and
58 0031  5B                              POP  BX                    ; registers
59 0032  58                              POP  AX
60 0033  9D                              POPF
61 0034  C3                              RET
62 0035                      BCD_BIN     ENDP
63
64 0035                      CODE        ENDS
65                                       END       START
```

FIGURE 5-16   Example program passing parameters using pointers to named memory locations.

BIN_VALUE instruction to set up the DI register as a pointer to the memory location named BIN_VALUE.

In the procedure, the MOV AL,[SI] instruction will copy the byte pointed to by SI into AL. Likewise, the MOV [DI],AL instruction later in the procedure will copy the byte from AL to the memory location pointed to by DI.

This pointer approach is more versatile because you can pass the procedure pointers to data anywhere in memory. You can pass pointers to individual values or pointers to arrays or strings. To access complex data structures, you can use registers to pass the segment base and the offset of a table of pointers in memory. The procedure then can read in a pointer from the table and use the pointer to access the desired data.

For many of your programs, you will probably use registers to pass data parameters or pointers to procedures. As we show you in Chapter 8, this is the method you use when you call procedures in the *Basic Input/ Output System* or *BIOS* of a computer. However, as we show you in later chapters, for programs which allow several users to timeshare a system or those which consist of a mixture of high-level languages and assembly language, we usually use the stack to pass parameters to and from procedures.

PASSING PARAMETERS USING THE STACK

To pass parameters to a procedure using the stack, we push the parameters on the stack somewhere in the mainline program before we call the procedure. Instructions in the procedure then read the parameters from the stack as needed. Likewise, parameters to be passed back to the calling program are written to the stack by instructions in the procedure and read off the stack by instructions in the mainline program. A simple example will best show you how this works.

Figure 5-17, p. 114, shows a version of our BCD_BIN procedure which uses the stack for passing the BCD number to the procedure and for passing the binary value back to the calling program. To save space here, we assume that previous instructions in the mainline program set up a stack segment, initialized the stack segment register, and initialized the stack pointer. Now in the mainline fragment in Figure 5-17, we copy the BCD number into AL. We then copy AX to the stack with the PUSH AX instruction. In a more complex example, the BCD number or a pointer to it would probably be put on the stack by a different mechanism, but the important point for now is that the BCD value is on the stack for the procedure to access.

The CALL instruction in the mainline program decrements the stack pointer by 2, copies the return address onto the stack, and loads the instruction pointer with the starting address of the procedure. PUSH instructions at the start of the procedure save the flags and all the registers used in the procedure on the stack. Before discussing any more instructions, let's take a look at the contents of the stack after these pushes.

Figure 5-18, p. 115, shows how the values pushed on the stack will be arranged. Note that the BCD value is in the stack at a higher address than the return address. After the registers are pushed onto the stack, the stack pointer is left pointing to the stack location where BP is stored. Now, the question is, how can we easily access the parameter that seems buried in the stack? One way is to add 12 to the stack pointer with an ADD SP,12 instruction so that the stack pointer points to the word we want from the stack. A POP AX instruction could then be used to copy the desired word from the stack to AX. However, for a variety of reasons, which we will explain later, we would like to be able to access the parameter without changing the contents of the stack pointer.

An alternative to using the SP register is to use the BP register to access the parameters in the stack. Remember from Chapter 2 that an offset in the BP register will be added to the stack segment register to produce a physical memory address. This means that the BP register can easily be used as a second pointer to a location in the stack. Here's how we use it this way in our example program.

After pushing all the registers at the start of the procedure, we copy the contents of the stack pointer register to the BP register with the MOV BP,SP instruc-

tion. BP then points to the same location as the stack pointer. Then we use the MOV AX,[BP + 12] instruction to copy the desired word from the stack to AX. The 8086 will produce the effective address for this instruction by adding the displacement of 12, specified in the instruction, to the contents of the BP register. As you can see in Figure 5-18, the effective address produced by adding 12 to the contents of BP will be that of the desired parameter. Note that the MOV AX,[BP + 12] instruction does not change the contents of BP. BP can then be used to access other parameters on the stack by simply specifying a different displacement in the instruction used to access the parameter.

Once we have the BCD number copied from the stack into AL, the instructions which convert it to binary are the same as those in the previous versions. When we want to put the binary value back in the stack to return it to the calling program, we again use BP as a pointer to the stack. The instruction MOV [BP + 12],AX will copy AX to a stack location 12 addresses higher than that to which BP is pointing. This, of course, is the same location we used to pass the BCD number to the procedure. After we pop the registers and return to the calling program, the registers will all have the values they had before the CALL instruction executed. AX will contain the original BCD number, and the stack pointer will be pointing to the binary value, now at the top of the stack. In the mainline program we can now pop this hex value into a register with an instruction such as POP CX.

Whenever you are using the stack to pass parameters, it is very important to keep track of what you have pushed on the stack and where the stack pointer is at each point in a program. We have found that diagrams such as the one in Figure 5-18 are very helpful in doing this. One potential problem to watch for when using the stack to pass parameters is *stack overflow*. Stack overflow means that the stack fills up and overflows the memory space you set aside for it. To see how this can easily happen if you don't watch for it, consider the following. Suppose that we use the stack to pass four word parameters to a procedure, but that we pass only one word parameter back to the calling program on the stack. Figure 5-19, p. 115, shows a stack diagram for this situation. Before a CALL instruction, the four parameters to be passed to the procedure are pushed on the stack. During the procedure, the parameter to be returned is put in the stack location previously occupied by the fourth input parameter. After the RET instruction at the end of the procedure executes, the stack pointer will be left pointing at this value. Now assume that we pop this value into a register. The POP instruction will copy the value to a register and increment the stack pointer by 2. The stack pointer now points to the third word we pushed to pass to the procedure. In other words the stack pointer is six addresses lower than it was when we started this process. Now suppose that we call this procedure many times in the course of the mainline program. Each time we push four words on the stack but only pop one word off, the stack pointer will be left six addresses lower than it was before the process. The top of the stack will keep moving downward. When the

```
      1                                                 ; 8086 PROGRAM F5-17.ASM
      2                            ;ABSTRACT   : BCD to BINARY conversion program that uses a
      3                                        ; procedure to convert BCD numbers to binary.
      4                                        ; Program shows how to use the stack to pass
      5                                        ; parameters to a procedure.
      6                            ;REGISTERS  : Uses CS, DS, SS, SP, AX
      7                            ;PORTS      : Uses none
      8                            ;PROCEDURES: Uses BCD_BIN

      SAME DATA STRUCTURE AND INITIALIZATION AS FIGURE 5-14 LINES 9 THROUGH 27

     28 000D   A0 0000r                        MOV  AL, BCD_INPUT       ; Move BCD value into AL
     29 0010   50                              PUSH AX                  ; and push it onto onto stack
     30 0011   E8 0005                         CALL BCD_BIN             ; Do the conversion
     31 0014   58                              POP  AX                  ; Get the binary value
     32 0015   A2 0001r                        MOV  BIN_VALUE, AL       ; and save it
     33 0018   90                              NOP                      ; Continue with program here
     34
     35                            ;PROCEDURE:  BCD_BIN - Converts BCD numbers to binary.
     36                            ;INPUT     :  None - BCD value assumed to be on stack before call
     37                            ;OUTPUT    :  None - Binary value on top of stack after return
     38                            ;DESTROYS  :  Nothing
     39
     40 0019                       BCD_BIN      PROC      NEAR
     41 0019   9C                               PUSHF                   ; Save flags
     42 001A   50                               PUSH AX                 ; and registers
     43 001B   53                               PUSH BX
     44 001C   51                               PUSH CX
     45 001D   55                               PUSH BP
     46 001E   8B EC                            MOV  BP, SP             ; Make a copy of the stack pointer
     47 0020   8B 46 0C                         MOV  AX, [BP+12]        ; Get BCD number from stack
     48                            ;Do the conversion
     49 0023   8A D8                            MOV  BL, AL             ; Save copy of BCD in BL
     50 0025   80 E3 0F                         AND  BL, 0FH            ; and mask
     51 0028   24 F0                            AND  AL, 0F0H           ; Separate upper nibble
     52 002A   B1 04                            MOV  CL, 04             ; Move upper BCD digit to low
     53 002C   D2 C8                            ROR  AL, CL             ; nibble position for multiply
     54 002E   B7 0A                            MOV  BH, 0AH            ; Load conversion factor in BH
     55 0030   F6 E7                            MUL  BH                 ; Multiply upper BCD digit in AL
     56                                                                 ; by 0AH in BH, leave result in AL
     57 0032   02 C3                            ADD  AL, BL             ; Add lower BCD digit to MUL result
     58                            ;End of conversion, binary value in AL
     59 0034   89 46 0C                         MOV  [BP+12], AX        ; Put binary value on stack
     60 0037   5D                               POP  BP                 ; Restore flags and
     61 0038   59                               POP  CX                 ; registers
     62 0039   5B                               POP  BX
     63 003A   58                               POP  AX
     64 003B   9D                               POPF
     65 003C   C3                               RET
     66 003D                       BCD_BIN      ENDP
     67
     68 003D                       CODE         ENDS
     69                                         END       START
```

FIGURE 5-17   Example program passing parameters on the stack.

stack pointer gets down to 0000H, the next push will roll it around to FFFEH and write a word at the very top of the 64-Kbyte stack segment. If you overlapped segments as you usually do in a small system, the word may get written in a memory location that you are using for data or your program code, and your data or code will be lost! This is what we mean by the term *stack overflow*.

The cure for this potential problem is to use stack diagrams to help you keep the stack balanced. You need to keep the number of pops equal to the number of pushes or in some other way make sure the stack pointer gets back to its initial location.

For this example, we could use an ADD SP,06H instruction after the POP instruction to get the stack pointer back up the additional six addresses to where it

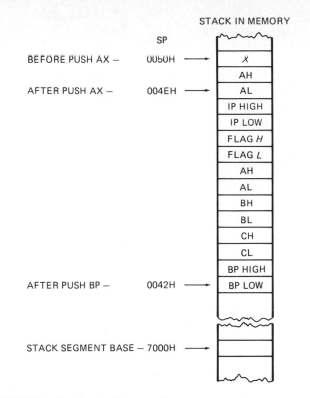

STACK IN MEMORY

	SP		
BEFORE PUSH AX —	0050H →		X
			AH
AFTER PUSH AX —	004EH →		AL
			IP HIGH
			IP LOW
			FLAG H
			FLAG L
			AH
			AL
			BH
			BL
			CH
			CL
			BP HIGH
AFTER PUSH BP —	0042H →		BP LOW
STACK SEGMENT BASE — 7000H →			

FIGURE 5-18   Stack diagram for program in Figure 5-17.

was before we pushed the four parameters onto the stack.

For other cases such as this, the 8086 RET instruction has two forms which help you to keep the stack balanced. Remember from a previous section of this chapter that the 8086 has four forms of the RET instruction. The regular near RET instruction copies the return address from the stack to the instruction pointer and increments the stack pointer by 2. The regular far RET instruction copies the return IP and CS values from the stack to IP and CS, and increments the stack pointer by 4. The other two forms of RET instruction perform the same functions, but they also add a number specified in the instruction to the stack pointer. The near RET 6

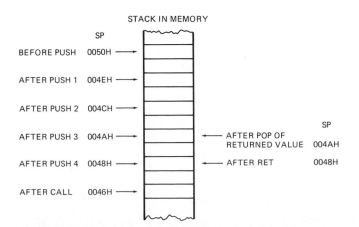

STACK IN MEMORY

	SP	
BEFORE PUSH	0050H →	
AFTER PUSH 1	004EH →	
AFTER PUSH 2	004CH →	
AFTER PUSH 3	004AH →	← AFTER POP OF RETURNED VALUE 004AH SP
AFTER PUSH 4	0048H →	← AFTER RET 0048H
AFTER CALL	0046H →	

FIGURE 5-19   Stack diagram showing cause of stack overflow.

instruction, for example, will first copy a word from the stack to the instruction pointer and increment the stack pointer by 2. It will then add 6 more to the stack pointer. This is a quick way to skip the stack pointer up over some old parameters on the stack.

SUMMARY OF PASSING PARAMETERS TO AND FROM PROCEDURES

You can pass parameters between a calling program and a procedure using registers, dedicated memory locations, or the stack. The method you choose depends largely on the specific program. There are no hard rules, but here are a few guidelines. For simple programs with just a few parameters to pass, registers are usually the easiest to use. For passing arrays or other data structures to and from procedures, you can use registers to pass pointers to the start of these data structures. As we explained previously, passing pointers to the procedure is a much more versatile method than having the procedure access the data structure directly by name.

For procedures in a multiuser-system program, procedures that will be called from a high-level language program, or procedures that call themselves, parameters should be passed on the stack. When writing programs which pass parameters on the stack, you should use stack diagrams such as the one in Figure 5-18 to help you keep track of where everything is in the stack at a particular time. The following section will give you some additional guidance as to when to use the stack to pass parameters, and it will give you some additional practice following the stack and stack pointer as a program executes.

Writing and Debugging Programs Containing Procedures

The most important point in writing a program containing procedures is to approach the overall job very systematically. You carefully work out the overall structure of the program and break it down into modules which can easily be written as procedures. You then set up the data structures and write the mainline program so that you know what each procedure has to do and how parameters can be most easily passed to each procedure.

To test this mainline program, you can simulate each procedure with a few instructions which simply pass test values back to the mainline program. Some programmers refer to these "dummy" procedures as *stubs*. If the structure of the mainline program seems reasonable, you then develop each procedure and replace the dummy with it. The advantage of this approach is that you have a structure to hang the procedures on. If you write the procedures first, you have the messy problem of trying to write a mainline program to connect all the pieces together.

Now, suppose that you have approached a program as we suggested, and the program doesn't work. After you have checked the algorithm and instructions, you should check that the number of PUSH and POP instructions are equal in each procedure. If none of the checks turns up anything, you can use the system debugging tools to track down the problem. Probably the best tools to help you localize a problem to a small area are breakpoints. Run the program to a breakpoint just before a CALL instruction to see whether the correct parameters are being passed to the procedure. Put a breakpoint at the start of the procedure to see if execution ever gets to the procedure. If execution gets to the procedure, move the breakpoint to a later point in the procedure to determine whether the procedure found the parameters passed from the mainline. Use a breakpoint just before the RET instruction to see whether the procedure produced the correct results and put these results in the correct locations to pass them back to the mainline program. Inserting breakpoints at key points in your program and checking the results at those points is much more effective in locating a problem than random poking and experimenting.

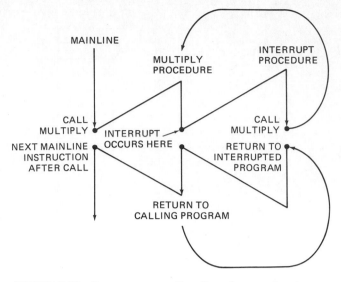

FIGURE 5-20 Program execution flow for reentrant procedure.

Reentrant and Recursive Procedures

The terms *reentrant* and *recursive* are often used in microprocessor manufacturers' literature, but seldom illustrated with examples. Here we try to give these terms some meaning for you. You should make almost all the procedures you write reentrant, so read that section carefully. You will seldom have to write a recursive procedure, so the main points to look for in that section are the definition of the term and the operation of the stack as a recursive procedure operates.

REENTRANT PROCEDURES

The 8086 has a signal input which allows a signal from some external device to interrupt the normal program execution sequence and call a specified procedure. In our electronics factory, for example, a temperature sensor in a flow-solder machine could be connected to the interrupt input. If the temperature gets too high, the sensor sends an interrupting signal to the 8086. The 8086 will then stop whatever it is doing and go to a procedure which takes whatever steps are necessary to cool down the solder bath. This procedure is called an *interrupt service procedure.* Chapter 8 discusses 8086 interrupts and interrupt service procedures in great detail, but it is appropriate to introduce the concept here.

Now, suppose that the 8086 was in the middle of executing a multiply procedure when the interrupt signal occurred, and that we also need to use the multiply procedure in the interrupt service subroutine. Figure 5-20 shows the program execution flow we want for this situation. When the interrupt occurs, execution goes to the interrupt service procedure. The interrupt service procedure then calls the multiply procedure when it needs it. The RET instruction at the end of the multiply procedure returns execution to the interrupt service procedure. A special return instruction at the end of the interrupt service procedure returns execution to the multiply procedure where it was executing when the interrupt occurred.

In order for the program flow in Figure 5-20 to work

correctly, the multiply procedure must be written in such a way that it can be interrupted, used, and "reentered" without losing or writing over anything. A procedure which can function in this way is said to be *reentrant.*

To be reentrant, a procedure must first of all push the flags and all registers used in the procedure. Also, to be reentrant, a program should use only registers or the stack to pass parameters. To see why this second point is necessary, let's take another look at the program in Figure 5-15. This program uses the named variables BCD_INPUT and BIN_VALUE. The procedure BCD_BIN accesses these two directly by name.

Now, suppose that the 8086 is in the middle of executing the BCD_BIN procedure and an interrupt occurs. Further suppose that the interrupt service procedure loads some new value in the memory location named BCD_INPUT, and calls the BCD_BIN procedure again. The initial value in BCD_INPUT has now been written over. If the interrupt occurred before the first execution of the procedure had a chance to read this value in, the value will be lost forever. When execution returns to BCD_BIN after the interrupt service procedure, the value used for BCD_INPUT will be that put there by the interrupt service routine instead of the desired initial value. There are several ways we can handle the parameters so that the procedure BCD_BIN is reentrant.

The first is to simply pass the parameters in registers, as we did in the program in Figure 5-14. If the interrupt procedure and the BCD_BIN procedure each push and pop all the registers they use, all the parameters from the interrupted execution will be saved and restored. When execution returns to BCD_BIN again, the registers will contain the same data they did when the interrupt occurred. The interrupted execution will then complete correctly.

A second method of making the BCD_BIN procedure reentrant is to pass pointers to the data items in registers, as we did in the program in Figure 5-16.

Again, if the interrupt procedure and the BCD_BIN procedure each push and pop the registers they use, execution will return to the interrupted procedure with data intact.

The third way to make the BCD_BIN procedure reentrant is by passing parameters or pointers on the stack, as we did in the version in Figure 5-17. In this version, the mainline program pushes the BCD number onto the stack and then calls the procedure. The procedure pushes registers on the stack and uses BP to access the BCD number relative to where the stack pointer ended up. If an interrupt occurs, the interrupt service procedure will push on the stack the BCD number it wishes to convert and call BCD_BIN. This second BCD number will be pushed on the stack at a different location from the first BCD number that was pushed.

The BCD_BIN procedure will use BP to access the new BCD value and pass the binary value back on the stack. If the BCD_BIN and interrupt procedure each save and restore the registers they use, the first execution of the procedure will produce correct results when it is reentered.

If you are writing a procedure that you may want to call from a program written in a high-level language such as Pascal or C, then you should definitely use the stack for passing parameters because that is how these languages do it. In a later chapter we show you how to pass parameters between C programs and assembly language programs.

RECURSIVE PROCEDURES

A *recursive procedure* is a procedure which calls itself. This seems simple enough, but the question you may be thinking is, "Why would we want a procedure to call itself?" The answer is that certain types of problems, such as choosing the next move in a computer chess program, can best be solved with a recursive procedure. Recursive procedures are often used to work with complex data structures called *trees*.

We usually write recursive procedures in a high-level language such as C or Pascal, except in those cases where we need the speed gained by writing in assembly language. However, the assembly language example in the following sections should help you understand how recursion works and how the stack is used by recursive and other nested procedures.

Recursive Procedure Example

ALGORITHM

Most of the examples of recursive procedures that we could think of are too complex to show here. Therefore, we have chosen a simple problem which could be solved without recursion.

The problem we have chosen to solve is to compute the factorial of a given number in the range of 1 to 8. The factorial of a number is the product of the number and all the positive integers less than the number. For example, 5 factorial is equal to $5 \times 4 \times 3 \times 2 \times 1$.

The word "factorial" is often represented with "!." For example, 5! is another way to represent 5 factorial.

What we want here is a recursive procedure which will compute the factorial of a number N which we pass to it on the stack, then pass the factorial back to the calling program on the stack. The basic algorithm can be expressed very simply as

IF N = 1 THEN factorial = 1,
ELSE factorial = N × (factorial of N − 1)

This says that if the number we pass to the procedure is 1, the procedure should return the factorial of 1, which is 1. If the number we pass is not 1, then the procedure should multiply this number by the factorial of the number minus 1.

Now here's where the recursion comes in. Suppose we pass a 3 to the procedure. When the procedure is first called, it has the value of 3 for N, but it does not have the value for the factorial of N − 1 that it needs to do the multiplication indicated in the algorithm. The procedure solves this problem by calling itself to compute the needed factorial of N − 1. It calls itself over and over until the factorial of N − 1 that it has to compute is the factorial of 1.

Figure 5-21, p. 118, shows several ways in which we can represent this process. In the program flow diagram in Figure 5-21*a*, you can see that if the value of N passed to the procedure is 1, then the procedure simply loads 1 into the stack location reserved for N! and returns to the calling program. Figure 5-21*b* shows the program flow that will occur when the number passed to the procedure is some number other than 1. If we call the procedure with N = 3, the procedure will call itself to compute (N − 1)! or 2!. It will then call itself again to compute the value of the next (N − 1)! or 1!. Since 1! = 1, the procedure will return this value to the program that called it. In this case the program that called it was a previous execution of the same procedure that needed this value to compute 2!. Given this value, it will compute 2! and return the value to the program that called it. Here again, the program that called it was a previous execution of the same procedure that needed 2! to compute the factorial of 3. Given the factorial of 2, this call of the procedure can now compute 3! and return to the program that called it. For the example here, the return now will be to the mainline program.

Figure 5-21*c* shows how we can represent this algorithm in slightly expanded pseudocode. Use the program flow diagram in Figure 5-21*b* to help you see how execution continues after the return when N = 1 and N = 3. Can you see that if N is initially 1, the first return will return execution to the instruction following CALL FACTO in the mainline program? If the initial N was 3, for example, this return will return execution to the instruction after the call in the procedure. Likewise, the return after the multiply can send execution back to the next instruction after the call or back to the mainline program if the final result has been computed.

Figure 5-21*d* shows a flowchart for this algorithm. Note that the flowchart shows the same ambiguity about where the return operations send execution to.

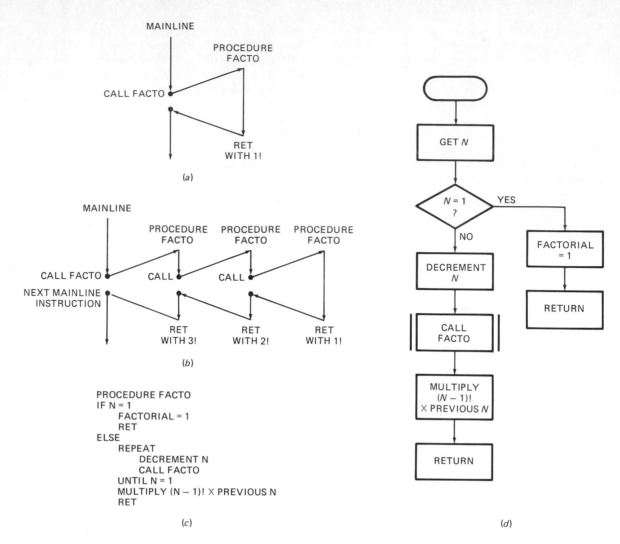

FIGURE 5-21 Algorithm for program to compute factorial for a number N between 1 and 8. (a) Flow diagram for N = 1. (b) Flow diagram for N = 3. (c) Pseudocode. (d) Flowchart.

ASSEMBLY LANGUAGE RECURSIVE FACTORIAL PROCEDURE

Figure 5-22 shows an 8086 assembly language procedure which computes the factorial of a number in the range of 1 to 8. To save space, we have not included instructions to return an error message if the number passed to the procedure is out of this range. Figure 5-23, p. 120, shows, with a stack diagram, how the stack will be affected if this procedure is called with N = 3. When working your way through a recursive procedure or any procedure which uses the stack extensively, a stack diagram such as this is absolutely necessary to keep track of everything.

The first parts of the program are housekeeping chores. We start the mainline program by declaring a stack segment and setting aside a stack of 200 words with a label at the top of the stack. The first three instructions in the code segment of the mainline program initialize the stack segment register and the stack pointer register. The SUB SP,04 instruction after this

will decrement the stack pointer register by 4. In other words, we skip the stack pointer down over 2 words in the stack. These two word locations will be used to pass the computed factorial from the procedure back to the mainline program. Next we load the number whose factorial we want into AX and push the value on the stack where the procedure will access it. Now we are ready to call the procedure. The procedure is near because it is in the same code segment as the instruction which calls it.

At the start of the procedure, we save the flags and all the registers used in the procedure on the stack. Let's take a look at Figure 5-23 to see what is on the stack at this point. As you can see, the stack now has the space for the result, the passed value, the return address, and the pushed registers. Unfortunately, the value of N is buried 10 addresses up the stack from where the stack pointer was left after BP was pushed. To access this buried value, we first copy SP to BP with the MOV BP,SP instruction so that BP points to the top of the stack. Then we use the MOV AX,[BP + 10] instruction to copy

```
  1                                           ; 8086 PROGRAM F5-22.ASM
  2                           ;ABSTRACT   : Program computes the factorial of a number between 1 and 8
  3                           ;REGISTERS  : Uses CS, SS, SP, AX, DX
  4                           ;PORTS      : None used
  5                           ;PROCEDURES: Uses FACTO
  6
  7 0000                      STACK_SEG   SEGMENT    STACK
  8 0000 C8*(0000)                        DW         200 DUP(0)     ; Set aside 200 words for stack
  9                           STACK_TOP   LABEL      WORD           ; Assign name to word above stack top
 10 0190                      STACK_SEG   ENDS
 11
 12      = 0008                  NUMBER      EQU        08           ; 8! = 40320 = 9D80H
 13
 14 0000                      CODE        SEGMENT
 15                                       ASSUME CS:CODE, SS:STACK_SEG
 16 0000 B8 0000s             START:      MOV  AX, STACK_SEG         ; Initialize stack segment register
 17 0003 8E D0                            MOV  SS, AX
 18 0005 BC 0190r                         MOV  SP, OFFSET STACK_TOP  ; Initialize stack pointer
 19 0008 83 EC 04                         SUB  SP, 0004H             ; Make space in stack for factorial
 20 000B B8 0008                          MOV  AX, NUMBER            ; to be returned and put number
 21 000E 50                               PUSH AX                    ; to be passed on stack
 22 000F E8 0009                          CALL FACTO                 ; Compute factorial of number
 23 0012 83 C4 02                         ADD  SP, 2                 ; Get over original number in stack
 24 0015 58                               POP  AX                    ; Get low word of the result
 25 0016 5A                               POP  DX                    ; Get high word of the result
 26 0017 90                               NOP                        ; Simulate next mainline instruction
 27 0018 EB 3A 90                         JMP  FIN                   ; Or EXIT program
 28
 29                           ;PROCEDURE: FACTO: Recursive procedure that computes the factorial of a number
 30                           ;INPUT     : Takes data (number = N) from the stack
 31                           ;OUTPUT    : Returns with result on stack above original data
 32                           ;DESTROYS  : Nothing
 33
 34 001B                      FACTO       PROC       NEAR
 35 001B 9C                               PUSHF                       ; Save flags and registers
 36 001C 50                               PUSH AX                     ; on the stack
 37 001D 52                               PUSH DX
 38 001E 55                               PUSH BP
 39 001F 8B EC                            MOV  BP, SP                 ; Point BP at top of stack
 40 0021 8B 46 0A                         MOV  AX,[BP+10]             ; Copy number from stack to AX
 41 0024 3D 0001                          CMP  AX, 0001H              ; If N not = 1 THEN
 42 0027 75 0D                            JNE  GO_ON                  ;   compute factorial
 43 0029 C7 46 0C 0001                    MOV  WORD PTR [BP+12], 0001H ; ELSE load 1! on stack
 44 002E C7 46 0E 0000                    MOV  WORD PTR [BP+14], 0000H ; and return to calling program
 45 0033 EB 1A 90                         JMP  EXIT
 46 0036 83 EC 04             GO_ON:      SUB  SP, 0004H              ; Make space in stack for
 47                                                                    ;   preliminary factorial
 48 0039 48                               DEC  AX                     ; Decrement number now in AX
 49 003A 50                               PUSH AX                     ; Save N-1 on stack
 50 003B E8 FFDD                          CALL FACTO                  ; Compute factorial of N-1
 51 003E 8B EC                            MOV  BP, SP                 ; Point BP at top of stack
 52 0040 8B 46 02                         MOV  AX, [BP+2]             ; Last (N-1)! from stack to AX
 53 0043 F7 66 10                         MUL  WORD PTR [BP+16]       ; Multiply by previous N
 54 0046 89 46 12                         MOV  [BP+18], AX            ; Copy new factorial to stack
 55 0049 89 56 14                         MOV  [BP+20], DX
 56 004C 83 C4 06                         ADD  SP, 0006H             ; Point SP at pushed register
 57 004F 5D                  EXIT:        POP  BP                     ; Restore registers
 58 0050 5A                               POP  DX
 59 0051 58                               POP  AX
 60 0052 9D                               POPF
 61 0053 C3                               RET
 62 0054                      FACTO       ENDP
 63 0054 90                   FIN:        NOP
 64 0055                      CODE        ENDS
 65                                       END      START
```

FIGURE 5-22   Program which uses a recursive procedure to calculate the factorial of a number between 1 and 8.

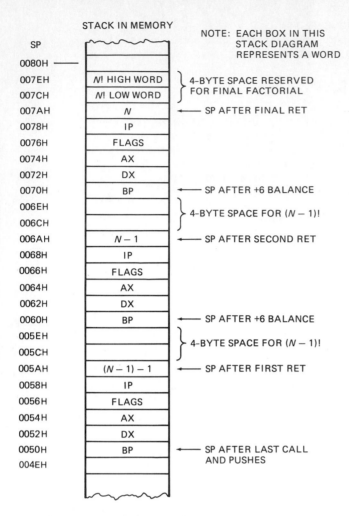

STACK IN MEMORY

NOTE: EACH BOX IN THIS STACK DIAGRAM REPRESENTS A WORD

SP		
0080H		
007EH	N! HIGH WORD	} 4-BYTE SPACE RESERVED FOR FINAL FACTORIAL
007CH	N! LOW WORD	
007AH	N	← SP AFTER FINAL RET
0078H	IP	
0076H	FLAGS	
0074H	AX	
0072H	DX	
0070H	BP	← SP AFTER +6 BALANCE
006EH		} 4-BYTE SPACE FOR (N − 1)!
006CH		
006AH	N − 1	← SP AFTER SECOND RET
0068H	IP	
0066H	FLAGS	
0064H	AX	
0062H	DX	
0060H	BP	← SP AFTER +6 BALANCE
005EH		} 4-BYTE SPACE FOR (N − 1)!
005CH		
005AH	(N − 1) − 1	← SP AFTER FIRST RET
0058H	IP	
0056H	FLAGS	
0054H	AX	
0052H	DX	
0050H	BP	← SP AFTER LAST CALL AND PUSHES
004EH		

FIGURE 5-23   Stack diagram for program in Figure 5-22 showing contents of stack for N = 3.

N from the stack to AX. Now that the procedure has the value of N, let's work through how it gets processed.

If the value of N read in is 1, then the factorial is 1. We want to put 00000001H in the stack locations we reserved for the result, restore the registers, and return to the mainline program. Follow this path through the program in Figure 5-22. Note how the MOV WORD PTR [BP + 12],0001H instruction is used to load a value to a location buried in the stack. The WORD PTR directives tell the assembler that you want to move a word to the specified memory location. Without these directives, the assembler will not know whether to code the instruction for moving a byte or for moving a word. The MOV WORD PTR [BP + 14],0000H instruction is likewise used to move a word value to the stack location reserved for the high word of the factorial.

Now let's see what happens if the number passed to FACTO is a 3. The CMP AX,0001H instruction and the JNE GO_ON instructions determine that N is not 1 and send execution to the SUB SP,04H instruction. According to the algorithm, we are going to find the value of N! by multiplying N times the value of (N − 1)!. We will be calling FACTO again to find the value of (N − 1)!. The SUB SP,04H instruction skips the stack pointer

down over four addresses in the stack to offset 006CH for our example. The value of (3 − 1)! will be returned in these locations.

The next step in the program is to decrement N by 1 and push the value of N − 1 on the stack at offset 006AH, where it can be accessed during the next call of FACTO.

Next we call FACTO again to compute the value of (N − 1)!. The IP flags and registers will again be pushed on the stack. As shown in Figure 5-23, the stack pointer is now pointing at offset 0060H, and the value of N − 1 that we need is again buried 10 addresses up in the stack. This is no problem, because the MOV BP,SP and MOV AX,[BP + 10] instructions will allow us to access the value. We started with N = 3 for this example, so the value of N − 1 that we read in at this point is equal to 2. Since this value is not 1, execution will again go to the label GO_ON. The SUB SP,04 instruction will again skip the stack pointer down over four addresses to offset 005CH. This leaves space for (2 − 1)!, which will be returned by the next call of FACTO. We decrement N − 1 by 1 to give a result of 1 and then push this value on the stack at offset 005AH. We then call FACTO to compute the factorial of 1.

After calling FACTO again and pushing all the registers on the stack, the stack pointer now points to offset 0050H. FACTO then reads N = 1 from the stack with the MOV AX,[BP + 10] instruction. When the CMP AX,0001H instruction in FACTO finds that the number passed to it is 1, FACTO loads a factorial value of 1 into the four memory locations we most recently set aside for a returned factorial at offsets 005CH to 005FH. The MOV WORD PTR [BP + 12],0001 and MOV WORD PTR [BP + 14],0000 instructions do this. Since N was a 1, execution will go to the EXIT label. The registers will then be popped and execution returned to the next instruction after the CALL instruction that last called FACTO.

Now in this case FACTO was called from a previous execution of FACTO, so the return will be to the MOV BP,SP instruction after CALL FACTO. The MOV BP,SP instruction points BP at the top of the stack at 005AH, so that we can access data on the stack without affecting the stack pointer. The MOV AX,[BP + 2] instruction after this copies the low word of (N − 1 − 1)! or 1 from the stack to AX so that we can multiply it by N − 1. We need only the lower word of the two we set aside for the factorial, because for an N of 8 or less, only the lower word will contain data. Restricting the allowed range of N for this example means that we only have to do a 16-bit by 16-bit multiplication. We could increase the allowed range of N by simply setting aside larger spaces in the stack for factorials and including instructions to multiply larger numbers.

In this example, the MUL WORD PTR [BP + 16] instruction multiplies the (N − 1 − 1)! in AX by the previous N from the stack. The low word of the product is left in AX, and the high word of the product is left in DX. The MOV [BP + 18],AX and the MOV [BP + 20],DX instructions copy these two words to the stack locations we reserved for the next factorial result at offsets 006CH to 006FH.

The next operation we would like to do in the program is pop the registers and return. As you can see from Figure 5-23, however, the stack pointer is now pointing at some old data on the stack at offset 005AH, not at the first register we want to pop. To get the stack pointer pointing where we want it, we add 6 to it with the ADD SP,06H instruction. Then we pop the registers and return.

After the pops and return, the stack pointer will be pointing at N − 1 at offset 006AH, and the value for 2! will be in the stack at offsets 006AH to 006FH in the stack. We still have one more computation to produce the desired 3!. Therefore, the return is again to the MOV BP,SP instruction after CALL in FACTO. The instructions after this will multiply 2! times 3 to produce the desired 3!, and copy 3! to the stack as described in the preceding paragraph. The ADD SP,06H instruction will again adjust the stack pointer so that we can pop the registers and return. Since we have done all the required computations, this time the return will be to the mainline program. The desired result, 3!, will be in the memory locations we reserved for it in the stack at offsets 007AH to 007FH.

After the final return, the stack pointer will be pointing at offset 007AH in the stack. We add 2 to the stack pointer so that it points to the factorial result and pop the result into the DX and AX registers. This brings the stack pointer back to its initial value.

If you work your way through the flow of the stack and the stack pointer in this example program, you should have a good understanding of how the stack functions during nested procedures.

Writing and Calling Far Procedures

INTRODUCTION AND OVERVIEW

A *far procedure* is one that is located in a segment which has a different name from the segment containing the CALL instruction. To get to the starting address of a far procedure, the 8086 must change the contents of both the code segment register and the instruction pointer.

```
CODE   SEGMENT
       ASSUME CS:CODE, DS:DATA, SS:STACK_SEG
       :
       :
       CALL MULTIPLY_32
       :
CODE   ENDS

PROCEDURES SEGMENT
  MULTIPLY_32 PROC FAR
       ASSUME CS:PROCEDURES
       :
       :
  MULTIPLY_32 ENDP
  PROCEDURES    ENDS
```

FIGURE 5-24   Program additions needed for a far procedure.

Therefore, if you are hand coding a program which calls a far procedure, make sure to use one of the intersegment forms of the CALL instruction shown in Figure 5-6. Likewise, at the end of a far procedure, both the contents of the code segment register and the contents of the instruction pointer must be popped off the stack to return to the calling program, so make sure to use one of the intersegment forms of the RET instruction to do this.

If you are using an assembler to assemble a program containing a far procedure, there are a few additional directives you have to give the assembler. The following sections show you how to put these needed additions into your programs. The first case we will describe is one in which the procedure is in the same assembly module, but it is in a segment with a different name from the segment that contains the CALL instruction.

ACCESSING A PROCEDURE IN ANOTHER SEGMENT

Suppose that in a program you want to put all of the mainline program in one logical segment and you want to put several procedures in another logical segment to keep them separate from the mainline program. Figure 5-24 shows some program fragments which illustrate this situation. For this example, our mainline instructions are in a segment named CODE. A procedure called MULTIPLY_32 is in a segment named PROCEDURES. Since the procedure is in a different segment from the CALL instruction, the 8086 must change the contents of the code segment register to access it. Therefore, the procedure is far.

You let the assembler know that the procedure is far by using the word FAR in the MULTIPLY_32 PROC FAR statement. When the assembler finds that the procedure is declared as far, it will automatically code the CALL instruction as an intersegment call and the RET instruction as an intersegment return.

Now the remaining thing you have to do, so that the program gets assembled correctly, is to make sure that the assembler uses the right code segment for each part of the program. You use the ASSUME directive to do this. At the start of the mainline program, you use the statement ASSUME CS:CODE to tell the assembler to compute the offsets of the following instructions from the segment base named CODE. At the start of the procedure, you use the ASSUME CS:PROCEDURES statement to tell the assembler to compute the offsets for the instructions in the procedure starting from the segment base named PROCEDURES.

When the assembler finally codes the CALL instruction, it will put the value of PROCEDURES in for CS in the instruction. It will put the offset of the first instruction of the procedure in PROCEDURES as the IP value in the instruction.

To summarize, then, if a procedure is in a different segment from the CALL instruction, you must declare it far with the FAR directive. Also, you must put an ASSUME statement in the procedure to tell the assembler what segment base to use when calculating the offsets of the instructions in the procedure.

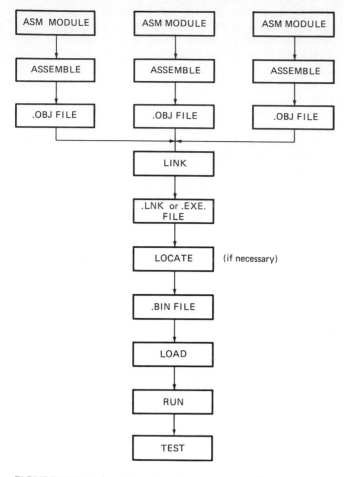

FIGURE 5-25 Chart showing the steps needed to run a program that has been written in modular form.

ACCESSING A PROCEDURE AND DATA IN A SEPARATE ASSEMBLY MODULE

As we have discussed previously, the best way to write a large program is to divide it into a series of modules. Each module can be individually written, assembled, tested, and debugged as shown in Figure 5-25. The object code files for the modules can then be linked together. Finally, the resulting link file can be located, run, and tested.

As we said earlier in this chapter, the individual modules of a large program are often written as procedures and called from a mainline or executive program. In the preceding section we showed you how to access a procedure in a different segment from the CALL instruction. Here we show you how to access a procedure or data in a different assembly module.

In order for a linker to be able to access data or a procedure in another assembly module correctly, there are two directives that you must use in your modules. We will give you an overview of these two and then show with an example how they are used in a program.

1. In the module where a variable or procedure is declared, you must use the PUBLIC directive to let the linker know that the variable or procedure can be accessed from other modules. The statement

PUBLIC DISPLAY, for example, tells the linker that a procedure or variable named DISPLAY can be legally accessed from another assembly module.

2. In a module which calls a procedure or accesses a variable in another module, you must use the EXTRN directive to let the assembler know that the procedure or variable is not in this module. The EXTRN statement also gives the linker some needed information about the procedure or variable. As an example of this, the statement EXTRN DISPLAY:FAR, SECONDS:BYTE tells the linker that DISPLAY is a far procedure and SECONDS is a variable of type byte located in another assembly module.

To summarize, a procedure or variable declared PUBLIC in one module will be declared EXTRN in modules which access the procedure or variable. Now let's see how these directives are used in an actual program.

PROBLEM DEFINITION AND ALGORITHM DISCUSSION

The procedure in the following example program was written to solve a small problem we encountered when writing the program for a microprocessor-controlled medical instrument. Here's the problem.

In the program we add up a series of values read in from an A/D converter. The sum is an unsigned number of between 24 and 32 bits. We needed to scale this value by dividing it by 10. This seems easy because the 8086 DIV instruction will divide a 32-bit unsigned binary number by a 16-bit binary number. The quotient from the division, remember, is put in AX, and the remainder is put in DX. However, if the quotient is larger than 16 bits, as it will often be for our scaling, the quotient will not fit in AX. In this case the 8086 will automatically respond in the same way that it would if you tried to divide a number by zero. We will discuss the details of this response in Chapter 8. For now, it is enough to say that we don't want the 8086 to make this response. The simple solution we came up with is to do the division in two steps in such a way that we get a 32-bit quotient and a 16-bit remainder.

Our algorithm is a simple sequence of actions very similar to the way you were probably taught to do long division. We will first describe how this works with decimal numbers, and then we will show how it works with 32-bit and 16-bit binary numbers.

Figure 5-26a shows an example of long division of the decimal number 433 by the decimal number 9. The 9 won't divide into the 4, so we put a 0 or nothing into this digit position of the quotient. We then see if 9 divides into 43. It fits 4 times, so we put a 4 in this digit position of the quotient and subtract 4 × 9 from the 43. The remainder of 7 now becomes the high digit of the 73, the next number we try to divide the 9 into. After we find that the 9 fits 8 times and subtract 9 × 8 from the 73, we are left with a final remainder of 1. Now let's see how we do this with large binary numbers.

As shown in Figure 5-26b, we first divide the 16-bit divisor into a 32-bit number made up of a word of all 0's and the high word of the dividend. This division

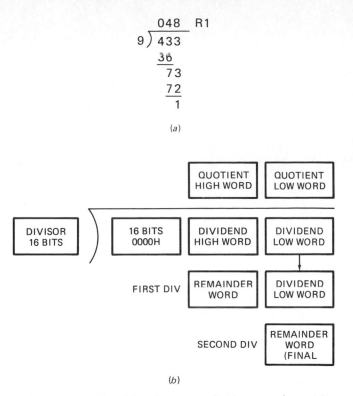

$$
\begin{array}{r}
048 R1 \\
9\overline{\smash{\big)}\,433} \\
\underline{36} \\
73 \\
\underline{72} \\
1
\end{array}
$$

(a)

	QUOTIENT HIGH WORD	QUOTIENT LOW WORD

| DIVISOR 16 BITS | 16 BITS 0000H | DIVIDEND HIGH WORD | DIVIDEND LOW WORD |

FIRST DIV | REMAINDER WORD | DIVIDEND LOW WORD |

SECOND DIV | | REMAINDER WORD (FINAL |

(b)

FIGURE 5-26 Algorithm for smart divide procedure. (a) Decimal analogy. (b) 8086 approach.

gives us the high word of the quotient and a remainder. The remainder becomes the high word of the dividend for the next division, just as it did for the decimal division. We move the low word of the original dividend in as the low word of this dividend and divide by the 16-bit divisor again. The 16-bit quotient from this division is the low word of the 32-bit quotient we want. The 16-bit final remainder can be used to round off the quotient or be discarded, depending on the application.

THE ASSEMBLY LANGUAGE PROGRAM

Figure 5-27*a*, pp. 124-5, shows the mainline of a program which calls the procedure shown in Figure 5-27*b*, p. 126, which implements our division algorithm. We wrote these two as separate assembly modules to show you how to add PUBLIC and EXTRN statements so that the modules are linkable. Let's look closely at these added parts before we discuss the actual division procedure.

The first added part of the program to look at is in the statement DATA SEGMENT WORD PUBLIC. The word PUBLIC in this statement tells the linker that this segment can be combined (concatenated) with segment(s) that have the same name but are located in other modules. In other words, if two or more assembly modules have PUBLIC segments named DATA, their contents will be pulled together in successive memory locations when the program modules are linked. You should then declare a segment PUBLIC anytime you want it to be linked with other segments of the same name in other modules.

The next addition to look at is the statement PUBLIC DIVISOR in the mainline module in Figure 5-27*a*. This

statement is necessary to tell the assembler and the linker that it is legal for the data item named DIVISOR to be accessed from other assembly modules. Essentially what we are doing here is telling the assembler to put the offset of DIVISOR in a special table where it can be accessed when the program modules are linked. Whenever you want a named data item or a label to be accessible from another assembly module, you must declare it as PUBLIC.

The other side of this coin is that, when you need to access a label, procedure, or variable in another module, you must use the EXTRN directive to tell the assembler that the label or data item is not in the present module. If you don't do this, the assembler will give you an error message because it can't find the label or variable in the current module. In the example program, the statement EXTRN SMART_DIVIDE:FAR tells the assembler that we will be accessing a label or procedure of type FAR in some other assembly module. For this example, we will be accessing our procedure, SMART_DIVIDE. We enclose the EXTRN statement with the PROCEDURES SEGMENT PUBLIC and the PROCEDURES ENDS statements to tell the assembler and linker that the procedure SMART_DIVIDE is located in the segment PROCEDURES. There are some cases in which these statements are not needed, but we have found that bracketing the EXTRN statement with SEGMENT-ENDS directives in this way is the best way to make sure that the linker can find everything when it links modules. As you can see in the table at the end of the assembler listing in Figure 5-27*a*, SMART_DIVIDE is identified as an external label of type FAR, found in a segment named PROCEDURES.

Now let's see how we handle EXTRN and PUBLIC in the procedure module in Figure 5-27*b*. The procedure accesses the data item named DIVISOR, which is defined in the mainline module. Therefore, we must use the statement EXTRN DIVISOR:WORD to tell the assembler that DIVISOR, a data item of type word, will be found in some other module. Furthermore, we enclose the EXTRN statement with the DATA SEGMENT PUBLIC and DATA ENDS statements to tell the assembler that DIVISOR will be found in a segment named DATA.

The procedure SMART_DIVIDE must be accessible from other modules, so we declare it public with the PUBLIC SMART_DIVIDE statement in the procedure module. If we needed to make other labels or data items public, we could have listed them separated by commas after PUBLIC SMART_DIVIDE. An example is PUBLIC SMART_DIVIDE, EXIT.

NOTES:

1. If we had needed to access DIVIDEND also, we could have written the EXTRN statement as EXTRN DIVISOR:WORD,DIVIDEND:WORD. To add more terms, just separate them with a comma.

2. Constants defined with an EQU directive in one module can be imported to another module by identifying them as EXTRN of type ABS. For example, if you declare CORRECTION_FAC-

```
 1                                              ; 8086 PROGRAM F5-27A.ASM
 2                                   ;ABSTRACT  : Program divides a 32-bit number by a 16-bit number
 3                                              ; to give a 32-bit quotient and a 16-bit remainder.
 4                                   ;REGISTERS : Uses CS, DS, SS, AX, SP, BX, CX
 5                                   ;PORTS     : None used
 6                                   ;PROCEDURES: Far procedure SMART_DIVIDE
 7
 8 0000                             DATA       SEGMENT     WORD  PUBLIC
 9 0000   403B 8C72                            DIVIDEND    DW    403BH, 8C72H   ; Dividend = 8C72403BH
10 0004   5692                                 DIVISOR     DW    5692H          ; 16-bit divisor
11 0006                             DATA       ENDS
12
13 0000                             MORE_DATA  SEGMENT     WORD
14 0000   02*(0000)                            QUOTIENT    DW    2 DUP(0)
15 0004   0000                                 REMAINDER   DW    0
16 0006                             MORE_DATA  ENDS
17
18 0000                             STACK_SEG  SEGMENT     STACK
19 0000   64*(0000)                            DW          100 DUP(0)    ; Stack of 100 words
20                                             TOP_STACK   LABEL  WORD   ; Name pointer to top of stack
21 00C8                             STACK_SEG  ENDS
22
23                                  PUBLIC     DIVISOR
24
25 0000                             PROCEDURES SEGMENT      PUBLIC        ; Let assembler know that SMART_DIVIDE
26                                      EXTRN SMART_DIVIDE : FAR          ; is a label of type FAR and is located
27 0000                             PROCEDURES ENDS                      ; in the segment PROCEDURES
28
29 0000                             CODE       SEGMENT    WORD    PUBLIC
30                                             ASSUME     CS:CODE, DS:DATA, SS:STACK_SEG
31 0000   B8 0000s                  START:     MOV  AX, DATA            ; Initialize data segment
32 0003   8E D8                                MOV  DS, AX              ; register
33 0005   B8 0000s                             MOV  AX, STACK_SEG       ; Initialize stack segment
34 0008   8E D0                                MOV  SS, AX              ; register
35 000A   BC 00C8r                             MOV  SP, OFFSET TOP_STACK ; Initialize stack pointer
36 000D   A1 0000r                             MOV  AX, DIVIDEND        ; Load low  word of dividend
37 0010   8B 16 0002r                          MOV  DX, DIVIDEND + 2    ; Load high word of dividend
38 0014   8B 0E 0004r                          MOV  CX, DIVISOR         ; Load divisor
39 0018   9A 00000000se                        CALL SMART_DIVIDE        ; Quotient returned in DX:AX
40                                  ; Remainder returned in CX, carry set if result invalid
41 001D   73 03                                JNC  SAVE_ALL            ; IF carry = 0, result valid
42 001F   EB 13 90                             JMP  STOP                ; ELSE carry set, don't save result
43                                     ASSUME DS:MORE_DATA              ; Change data segment
44 0022   1E                        SAVE_ALL: PUSH DS                   ; Save old DS
45 0023   BB 0000s                             MOV  BX, MORE_DATA       ; Load new data segment
46 0026   8E DB                                MOV  DS, BX              ; register
47 0028   A3 0000r                             MOV  QUOTIENT, AX        ; Store low  word of quotient
48 002B   89 16 0002r                          MOV  QUOTIENT + 2, DX    ; Store high word of quotient
49 002F   89 0E 0004r                          MOV  REMAINDER, CX       ; Store remainder
50                                     ASSUME DS:DATA
51 0033   1F                                   POP  DS                  ; Restore initial DS
52 0034   90                        STOP:      NOP
53 0035                             CODE       ENDS
54                                             END     START
```

FIGURE 5-27   Assembly language program to divide a 32-bit number by a 16-bit
number and return a 32-bit quotient. (a) Mainline program module (continued
on p. 125). (b) Procedure module (p. 126).

Symbol Name	Type	Value
??DATE	Text	"05-05-89"
??FILENAME	Text	"F5-27A "
??TIME	Text	"13:09:05"
??VERSION	Number	0100
@CPU	Text	0101H
@CURSEG	Text	CODE
@FILENAME	Text	F5-27A
@WORDSIZE	Text	2
DIVIDEND	Word	DATA:0000
DIVISOR	Word	DATA:0004
QUOTIENT	Word	MORE_DATA:0000
REMAINDER	Word	MORE_DATA:0004
SAVE_ALL	Near	CODE:0022
SMART_DIVIDE	Far	PROCEDURES:---- Extern
START	Near	CODE:0000
STOP	Near	CODE:0034
TOP_STACK	Word	STACK_SEG:00C8

Groups & Segments	Bit	Size	Align	Combine Class
CODE	16	0035	Word	Public
DATA	16	0006	Word	Public
MORE_DATA	16	0006	Word	none
PROCEDURES	16	0000	Para	Public
STACK_SEG	16	00C8	Para	Stack

(a)

FIGURE 5-27   (continued)

TOR EQU 07 in one module, you can import CORRECTION_FACTOR to another module with the statement
EXTRN CORRECTION_FACTOR:ABS.

Now that we have explained the use of PUBLIC and EXTRN, let's work our way through the rest of the program. At the start of the mainline, the ASSUME statement tells the assembler which logical segments to use as code, data, and stack. We then initialize the data segment, stack segment, and stack pointer registers as described in previous example programs. Now, before calling the SMART_DIVIDE procedure, we copy the dividend and divisor from memory to some registers. The dividend and the divisor are passed to the procedure in these registers. As we explained in a previous section, if we pass parameters to a procedure in registers, the procedure does not have to refer to specific named memory locations. The procedure is then more general and can more easily be called from any place in the mainline program. However, in this example we referenced the named memory location, DIVISOR, from the procedure just to show you how it can be done using the EXTRN and PUBLIC directives. The procedure is of type FAR, so when we call it, both the code segment register and the instruction pointer contents will be changed.

In the procedure shown in Figure 5-27b, we first check to see if the divisor is zero with a CMP DIVISOR,0 instruction. If the divisor is zero, the JE instruction will send execution to the label ERROR_EXIT. There we set the carry flag with STC as an error indicator and return to the mainline program. If the divisor is not zero, then we go on with the division. To understand how we do the division, remember that the 8086 DIV instruction divides the 32-bit number in DX and AX by the 16-bit number in a specified register or memory location. It puts a 16-bit quotient in AX and a 16-bit remainder in DX. Now, according to our algorithm in Figure 5-26b, we want to put 0000H in DX and the high word of the dividend in AX for our first DIV operation. MOV BX,AX saves a copy of the low word of the dividend for future reference. MOV AX,DX copies the high word of the dividend into AX where we want it, and MOV DX,0000H puts all 0's in DX. After the first DIV instruction executes, AX will contain the high word of the 32-bit quotient we want as our final answer. We save this in BP with the MOV BP,AX instruction so that we can use AX for the second DIV operation.

The remainder from the first DIV operation was left in the DX register. As shown by the diagram in Figure 5-26b, this is right where we want it for the second DIV operation. All we have to do now, before we do the second DIV operation, is to get the low word of the original dividend back into AX with the MOV AX,BX instruction. After the second DIV instruction executes, the 16-bit quotient will be in AX. This word is the low word of our

```
 1                                              ; 8086 PROCEDURE F5-27B.ASM called by program F5-27A.ASM
 2                              ;ABSTRACT  : PROCEDURE SMART_DIVIDE.
 3                                          ; This procedure divides a 32-bit number by a 16-bit number
 4                                          ; to give a 32-bit quotient and a 16-bit remainder.
 5                              ;INPUT     : Dividend - low word in AX, high word in DX, Divisor in CX
 6                              ;OUTPUT    : Quotient - low word in AX, high word in DX. Remainder in CX
 7                                          ; Carry     - carry flag set if try to divide by zero
 8                              ;DESTROYS  : AX, BX, CX, DX, BP, FLAGS
 9                              ;PORTS     : None used
10
11 0000                        DATA      SEGMENT  PUBLIC ; This block tells the assembler that
12                                EXTRN   DIVISOR:WORD    ; the divisor is a word variable found
13 0000                        DATA      ENDS            ; in the external segment named DATA
14
15                             PUBLIC  SMART_DIVIDE       ; Make SMART_DIVIDE available to other modules
16
17 0000                        PROCEDURES   SEGMENT   PUBLIC
18 0000                        SMART_DIVIDE PROC      FAR
19                               ASSUME CS:PROCEDURES, DS:DATA
20 0000  83 3E 0000e 00                    CMP  DIVISOR, 0     ; Check for illegal divide
21 0005  74 17                             JE   ERROR_EXIT     ; IF divisor = 0, exit procedure
22 0007  8B D8                             MOV  BX, AX         ; Save low order of dividend
23 0009  8B C2                             MOV  AX, DX         ; Position high word for 1st divide
24 000B  BA 0000                           MOV  DX, 0000H      ; Zero DX
25 000E  F7 F1                             DIV  CX             ; DX:AX/CX, quotient in AX, remainder in DX
26 0010  8B E8                             MOV  BP, AX         ; Save high order of final result
27 0012  8B C3                             MOV  AX, BX         ; Get back low order of dividend
28 0014  F7 F1                             DIV  CX             ; DX:AX/CX, quotient in AX, remainder in DX
29 0016  8B CA                             MOV  CX, DX         ; Pass remainder back in CX
30 0018  8B D5                             MOV  DX, BP         ; Pass high order result back in DX
31 001A  F8                                CLC                 ; Clear carry to indicate valid result
32 001B  EB 02 90                          JMP  EXIT           ; Finished
33 001E  F9              ERROR_EXIT: STC                       ; Set carry to indicate divide by zero
34 001F  CB              EXIT:       RET
35 0020                  SMART_DIVIDE ENDP
36 0020                  PROCEDURES   ENDS
37                                   END
```

Symbol Name	Type	Value
??DATE	Text	"05-05-89"
??FILENAME	Text	"F5-27B "
??TIME	Text	"13:09:19"
??VERSION	Number	0100
@CPU	Text	0101H
@CURSEG	Text	PROCEDURES
@FILENAME	Text	F5-27B
@WORDSIZE	Text	2
DIVISOR	Word	DATA:---- Extern
ERROR_EXIT	Near	PROCEDURES:001E
EXIT	Near	PROCEDURES:001F
SMART_DIVIDE	Far	PROCEDURES:0000

Groups & Segments	Bit Size Align	Combine Class
DATA	16 0000 Para	Public
PROCEDURES	16 0020 Para	Public

(b)

FIGURE 5-27 (continued)

desired 32-bit quotient. We just leave this word in AX to be passed back to the mainline program. The DX register was left with the final remainder. We copy this remainder to CX with the MOV CX,DX instruction to be passed back to the mainline program. After the first DIV operation, we saved the high word of our 32-bit quotient in BP. We now use the MOV DX,BP instruction to copy this word back to DX, where we want it to be when we return to the mainline program. You really don't have to shuffle the results around the way we did with these last three instructions, but we like to pass parameters to and from procedures in as systematic a way as possible so that we can more easily keep track of everything. After the shuffling, we clear the carry flag with CLC before returning to indicate that the result in DX and AX is valid.

Back in the mainline program, we check the carry flag with the JNC instruction. If the carry flag is set, we know that the divisor was 0, no division was done, and there is no result to put in memory. If the carry flag is not set, then we know that a valid 32-bit quotient was returned in DX and AX and a 16-bit remainder was returned in CX. We now want to copy this quotient and this remainder to some named memory locations we set aside for them.

If you look at some earlier lines in the program, you will see that the memory locations called QUOTIENT and REMAINDER are in a segment called MORE_DATA. At the start of the mainline program, we tell the assembler to ASSUME that we will be using DATA as the data segment. Now, however, we want to access some data items in MORE_DATA using DS. To do this, we have to do two things. First, we have to tell the assembler to ASSUME DS:MORE_DATA. Second, we have to load the segment base of MORE_DATA into DS. In our program we save the old value of DS by pushing it on the stack. We do this so that we can easily reload DS with the base address of DATA later in the program. The MOV BX,MORE_DATA and MOV DS,BX instructions load the base address of MORE_DATA into DS. The three MOV instructions after this copy the quotient and the remainder into the named memory locations.

Finally, in the program we point DS back at DATA so that later instructions can access data items in the DATA segment. To do this, we first tell the assembler to ASSUME DS:DATA. Then we pop the base address of DATA off the stack into DS. As you write more complex programs, you will often want to access different segments at different times in the program, so we wrote this example to show you how to do it. Remember, when you change segments, you have to do a new ASSUME statement and include instructions which initialize the segment register to the base address of the new segment.

WRITING AND USING ASSEMBLER MACROS

Macros and Procedures Compared

Whenever we need to use a group of instructions several times throughout a program, there are two ways we can avoid having to write the group of instructions each time we want to use it. One way is to write the group of instructions as a separate procedure. We can then just call the procedure whenever we need to execute that group of instructions. A big advantage of using a procedure is that the machine codes for the group of instructions in the procedure only have to be put in memory once. Disadvantages of using a procedure are the need for a stack, and the overhead time required to call the procedure and return to the calling program.

When the repeated group of instructions is too short or not appropriate to be written as a procedure, we use a macro. A *macro* is a group of instructions we bracket and give a name to at the start of our program. Each time we "call" the macro in our program, the assembler will insert the defined group of instructions in place of the "call." In other words, the macro call is like a shorthand expression which tells the assembler, "Every time you see a macro name in the program, replace it with the group of instructions defined as that macro at the start of the program." An important point here is that the assembler generates machine codes for the group of instructions each time the macro is called. Replacing the macro with the instructions it represents is commonly called "expanding" the macro. Since the generated machine codes are right *in-line* with the rest of the program, the processor does not have to go off to a procedure and return. Therefore, using a macro avoids the overhead time involved in calling and returning from a procedure. A disadvantage of generating in-line code each time a macro is called is that this will make the program take up more memory than using a procedure.

The examples which follow should help you see how to define and call macros. For these examples we use the syntax of MASM and TASM. If you are developing your programs on some other machine, consult the assembly language programming manual for your machine to find the macro definition and calling formats for it.

Defining and Calling a Macro Without Parameters

For our first example, suppose that we are writing an 8086 program which has many complex procedures. At the start of each procedure, we want to save the flags and all the registers by pushing them on the stack. At the end of each procedure, we want to restore the flags and all the registers by popping them off the stack. Each procedure would normally contain a long series of PUSH instructions at the start and a long series of POP instructions at the end. Typing in these lists of PUSH and POP instructions is tedious and prone to errors. We could write a procedure to do the pushing and another procedure to do the popping. However, this adds more complexity to the program and is therefore not appropriate. Two simple macros will solve the problem for us.

Here's how we write a macro to save all the registers.

```
PUSH_ALL MACRO
         PUSHF
         PUSH AX
         PUSH BX
```

```
        PUSH CX
        PUSH DX
        PUSH BP
        PUSH SI
        PUSH DI
        PUSH DS
        PUSH ES
        PUSH SS
ENDM
```

The PUSH_ALL MACRO statement identifies the start of the macro and gives the macro a name. The ENDM identifies the end of the macro.

Now, to call the macro in one of our procedures, we simply put in the name of the macro just as we would an instruction mnemonic. The start of the procedure which does this might look like this:

```
BREATH_RATE      PROC FAR
ASSUME CS:PROCEDURES, DS:PATIENT_PARAMETERS
    PUSH_ALL                    ; Macro call
    MOV AX, PATIENT_PARAMETERS ; Initialize data
    MOVE DS, AX                 ; segment reg
            .
            .
```

When the assembler assembles this program section, it will replace PUSH_ALL with the instructions that it represents and insert the machine codes for these instructions in the object code version of the program. The assembler listing tells you which lines were inserted by a macro call by putting a + in each program line inserted by a macro call. As you can see from the example here, using a macro makes the source program much more readable because the source program does not have the long series of push instructions cluttering it up.

The preceding example showed how a macro can be used as simple shorthand for a series of instructions. The real power of macros, however, comes from being able to pass parameters to them when you call them. The next section shows you how and why this is done.

Passing Parameters to Macros

Most of us have received computer printed letters of the form:

Dear MR. HALL,
    We are pleased to inform you that you may have won up to $1,000,000 in the *Reader's Weekly* sweepstakes. To find out if you are a winner, MR. HALL, return the gold card to *Reader's Weekly* in the enclosed envelope before OCTOBER 22, 1991. You can take advantage of our special offer of three years of *Reader's Weekly* for only $24.95 by putting an X in the YES box on the gold card. If you do not wish to take advantage of this offer, which is one third off the newsstand price, mark the no box on the gold card.
                                        Thank you,

A letter such as this is an everyday example of the macro with parameters concept. The basic letter "macro" is written with dummy words in place of the addressee's name, the reply date, and the cost of a three-year subscription. Each time the macro which prints the letter is called, new values for these parameters are passed to the macro. The result is a "personal"-looking letter.

In assembly language programs, we likewise can write a generalized macro with dummy parameters. Then, when we call the macro, we can pass it the actual parameters needed for the specific application. Suppose, for example, we are writing a word processing program. A frequent need in a word processing program is to move strings of ASCII characters from one place in memory to another. The 8086 MOVS instruction is intended to do this. Remember from the discussion of the string instructions at the beginning of this chapter, however, that in order for the MOVS instruction to work correctly, you first have to load SI with the offset of the source start, DI with the offset of the destination start, and CX with the number of bytes or words to be moved. We can define a macro to do all of this as follows:

```
MOVE_ASCII MACRO NUMBER, SOURCE, DESTINATION
    MOV CX, NUMBER       ; Number of characters to be moved in CX
    LEA SI, SOURCE       ; Point SI at ASCII source
    LEA DI, DESTINATION  ; Point DI at ASCII destination
    CLD                  ; Autoincrement pointers after move
REP MOVSB                ; Copy ASCII string to new location
    ENDM                 ;
```

The words NUMBER, SOURCE, and DESTINATION in this macro are called *dummy variables*. When we call the macro, values from the calling statement will be put in the instructions in place of the dummies. If, for example, we call this macro with the statement MOVE_ASCII 03DH,BLOCK_START,BLOCK_DEST, the assembler will expand the macro as follows.

```
    MOV CX, 03DH          ; Number of characters to be moved in CX
    LEA SI, BLOCK_START   ; Point SI at ASCII destination
    LEA DI, BLOCK_DEST    ; Point DI at ASCII destination
    CLD                   ; Autoincrement pointers after move
REP MOVSB                 ; Copy ASCII string to new location
```

We do not have space here to show you very much of what you can do with macros. Read through the assembly language programming manual for your system to find more details about working with macros. To help stick in your mind the differences between procedures and macros, here is a comparison between the two.

Summary of Procedures Versus Macros

PROCEDURE

Accessed by CALL and RET mechanism during program execution. Machine code for instructions only put in memory once. Parameters passed in registers, memory locations, or stack.

MACRO

Accessed during assembly with name given to macro when defined. Machine code generated for instructions each time called. Parameters passed as part of statement which calls macro.

CHECKLIST OF IMPORTANT TERMS AND CONCEPTS IN THIS CHAPTER

If you do not remember any of the terms in the following list, use the index to help you find them in the chapter for review.

Strings and 8086 string instructions

Procedures and nested procedures

CALL and RET instructions

Near and far procedures

Direct intersegment far call

Indirect intersegment far call

Direct intrasegment near call

Indirect intrasegment near call

Stack: top of stack, stack pointer

PUSH and POP instructions

Parameter, parameter passing methods

Stack overflow

Reentrant and recursive procedures

Interrupt

Interrupt service procedure

Separate assembly modules

PUBLIC and EXTRN directives

Macro

REVIEW QUESTIONS AND PROBLEMS

1. *a.* Given the following data structure, use the 8086 string instructions to help you write a program which moves the string "Charlie T. Tuna" from OLD_HOME to NEW_HOME, which is just above the initial location.

```
NAMES_HERE   SEGMENT
   OLD_HOME   DB 'CHARLIE T. TUNA'
   NEW_HOME   DB 15 DUP(0)
NAMES_HERE   ENDS
```

   b. Use the string instructions to write a simple program to move the string "Charlie T. Tuna" up four addresses in memory. Consider whether the pointers should be incremented or decremented after each byte is moved in order to keep any needed byte from being written over. *Hint:* Initialize DI with the value of SI + 4.

2. Use the 8086 string instructions to write a program which scans a string of 80 characters looking for a carriage return (0DH). If a carriage return is found, put the length of the string up to the carriage return in AL. If no carriage return is found, put 50H (80 decimal) in AL.

3. Show the 8086 instruction or group of instructions which will:
   a. Initialize the stack segment register to 4000H and the stack pointer register to 8000H.
   b. Call a near procedure named FIXIT.
   c. Save BX and BP at the start of a procedure and restore them at the end of the procedure.
   d. Return from a procedure and automatically increment the stack pointer by 8.

4. *a.* Use a stack map to show the effect of each of the following instructions on the stack pointer and on the contents of the stack.

```
         MOV SP,4000H
         PUSH AX
         CALL MULTO
         POP AX
MULTO PROC NEAR
         PUSHF
         PUSH BX
           ·
           ·
           ·
         POP BX
         POPF
         RET
MULTO ENDP
```

   b. What effect would it have on the execution of this program if the POPF instruction in the procedure was accidentally left out? Describe the steps you would take in tracking down this problem if you did not notice it in the program listing.

5. Show the binary codes for the following instructions.
   a. The instruction which will call a procedure which is 97H addresses higher in memory than the instruction after a call instruction.
   b. An instruction which returns execution from a far procedure to a mainline program and increments the stack pointer by 4.

6. *a.* List three methods of passing parameters to a procedure and give the advantages and disadvantages of each method.
   b. Define the term *reentrant* and explain how you must pass parameters to a procedure so that it is reentrant.

7. *a.* Write a procedure which produces a delay of

3.33 ms when run on an 8086 with a 5-MHz clock.

b. Write a mainline program which uses this procedure to output a square wave on bit D0 of port FFFAH.

8. Write a procedure which converts a four-digit BCD number passed in AX to its binary equivalent. Use the algorithm in Figure 5-13.

9. The 8086 MUL instruction allows you to multiply a 16-bit number by a 16-bit binary number to give a 32-bit result. In some cases, however, you may need to multiply a 32-bit number by a 32-bit number to give a 64-bit result. With the MUL instruction and a little adding, you can easily do this. Figure 5-28 shows in diagram form how to do it. Each letter in the diagram represents a 16-bit number. The principle is to use MUL to form partial products and add these partial products together as shown. Write an algorithm for this multiplication and then write the 8086 assembly language program for the algorithm.

10. Calculating the factorial of a number, which we did with a recursive procedure in Figure 5-22, can easily be done with a simple REPEAT-UNTIL structure of the form

```
IF N = 1 THEN
    FACTORIAL = 1
ELSE
    FACTORIAL = 1
    REPEAT
        FACTORIAL = FACTORIAL × N
        DECREMENT N
    UNTIL N = 0
```

Write an 8086 procedure which implements this algorithm for an N between 1 and 8.

11. a. Show the statement you would use to tell the assembler to make the label BINADD available to other assembly modules.

b. Show how you would tell the assembler to look for a byte type data item named CONVERSION_FACTOR in a segment named FIXUPS.

12. a. Write an assembler macro which will restore, in the correct order, the registers saved by the macro PUSH_ALL in this chapter.

b. Write the statement you would use to call the macro you wrote in part a.

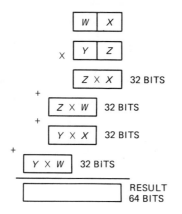

FIGURE 5-28   32-bit by 32-bit multiply method for Problem 9.

This chapter consists of two major sections. The first section is a dictionary of all the 8086/8088 instructions. For each instruction, we give a detailed description of its operation, the correct syntax for the instruction, and the flags affected by the instruction. Numerical examples are shown for those instructions for which they are appropriate. Instead of putting the binary codes for the instructions here, we have listed them alphabetically in Appendixes A and B. Putting the codes together in a table makes them easier to find if you are hand coding a program.

The second major section of this chapter is a dictionary of commonly used 8086 assembler directives. The directives described here are those defined for the Intel 8086 macro assembler, the Microsoft macro assembler (MASM), and the Borland Turbo Assembler (TASM). If you are using some other assembler, it probably has similar capabilities, but the names may be different.

You will probably use this chapter mostly as a reference to get the details of an instruction or directive as you write programs of your own or decipher someone else's programs. However, you should skim through the chapter at least once to give yourself an overview of the material it contains. You should not try to absorb all of this chapter at once. Many of the instructions described are used and discussed in various example programs throughout the book. For these instructions, we have included references to the appropriate sections in the text.

INSTRUCTION DESCRIPTIONS

AAA—ASCII Adjust for Addition

Numerical data coming into a computer from a terminal is usually in ASCII code. In this code, the numbers 0 to 9 are represented by the ASCII codes 30H to 39H. The 8086 allows you to add the ASCII codes for two decimal digits without masking off the "3" in the upper nibble of each. After the addition, the AAA instruction is used to make sure the result is the correct unpacked BCD. A simple numerical example will show how this works.

EXAMPLE:

```
; Assume AL = 0011 0101, ASCII 5
; BL = 0011 1001, ASCII 9
```

```
ADD AL, BL   ; Result: AL = 0110 1110 = 6EH, which
             ; is incorrect BCD
AAA          ; Now AL = 00000100, unpacked BCD 4.
             ; CF = 1 indicates answer is 14 decimal
```

NOTE: OR AL with 30H to get 34H, the ASCII code for 4, if you want to send the result back to a CRT terminal. The 1 in the carry flag can be rotated into the low nibble of a register, ORed with 30H to give the ASCII code for 1, and then sent to the terminal.

The AAA instruction works only on the AL register.
The AAA instruction updates AF and CF, but OF, PF, SF, and ZF are left undefined.

AAD—BCD-to-Binary Convert before Division

AAD converts two unpacked BCD digits in AH and AL to the equivalent binary number in AL. This adjustment must be made before dividing the two unpacked BCD digits in AX by an unpacked BCD byte. After the division, AL will contain the unpacked BCD quotient and AH will contain the unpacked BCD remainder. PF, SF, and ZF are updated. AF, CF, and OF are undefined after AAD.

EXAMPLE:

```
         ; AX = 0607H unpacked BCD for 67 decimal
         ; CH = 09H, now adjust to binary
AAD      ; Result: AX = 0043 = 43H = 67 decimal
DIV CH   ; Divide AX by unpacked BCD in CH
         ; Quotient: AL = 07 unpacked BCD
         ; Remainder: AH = 04 unpacked BCD
         ; Flags undefined after DIV
```

NOTE: If an attempt is made to divide by 0, the 8086 will do a type 0 interrupt. The type 0 interrupt response is described in Chapter 8.

AAM—BCD Adjust after Multiply

Before you can multiply two ASCII digits, you must first mask the upper 4 bits of each. This leaves unpacked BCD (one BCD digit per byte) in each byte. After the two unpacked BCD digits are multiplied, the AAM instruction is used to adjust the product to two unpacked BCD digits in AX.

AAM works only after the multiplication of two unpacked BCD bytes, and it works only on an operand in AL. AAM updates PF, SF, and ZF, but AF, CF, and OF are left undefined.

EXAMPLE:

```
              ; AL = 00000101 = unpacked BCD 5
              ; BH = 00001001 = unpacked BCD 9
MUL BH        ; AL × BH; result in AX
              ; AX = 00000000 00101101 = 002DH
AAM           ; AX = 00000100 00000101 = 0405H,
              ; which is unpacked BCD for 45.
              ; If ASCII codes for the result are
              ; desired, use next instruction
OR AX,3030H   ; Put 3 in upper nibble of each byte.
              ; AX = 00110100 00110101 = 3435H,
              ; which is ASCII code for 45
```

AAS—ASCII Adjust for Subtraction

Numerical data coming into a computer from a terminal is usually in ASCII code. In this code the numbers 0 to 9 are represented by the ASCII codes 30H to 39H. The 8086 allows you to subtract the ASCII codes for two decimal digits without masking the "3" in the upper nibble of each. The AAS instruction is then used to make sure the result is the correct unpacked BCD. Some simple numerical examples will show how this works.

EXAMPLE:

```
              ; ASCII 9–ASCII 5 (9–5)
              ; AL = 00111001 = 39H = ASCII 9
              ; BL = 00110101 = 35H = ASCII 5
SUB AL, BL    ; Result: AL = 00000100 = BCD 04
              ; and CF = 0
AAS           ; Result: AL = 00000100 = BCD 04
              ; and CF = 0; no borrow required

              ; ASCII 5–ASCII 9 (5–9)
              ; Assume AL = 00110101 = 35H =
              ;   ASCII 5
              ; and BL = 00111001 = 39H = ASCII 9
SUB AL, BL    ; Result: AL = 11111100 = − 4
              ; in 2's complement and CF = 1
AAS           ; Result: AL = 00000100 = BCD 04
              ; and CF = 1; borrow needed
```

The AAS instruction leaves the correct unpacked BCD result in the low nibble of AL and resets the upper nibble of AL to all 0's. If you want to send the result back to a CRT terminal, you can OR AL with 30H to produce the correct ASCII code for the result. If multiple-digit numbers are being subtracted, the CF can be taken into account by using the SBB instruction when subtracting the next digits.

The AAS instruction works only on the AL register. It updates AF and CF, but OF, PF, SF, and ZF are left undefined.

ADC—Add with Carry—ADC Destination,Source
ADD—Add—ADD Destination,Source

These instructions add a number from some source to a number from some destination and put the result in the specified destination. The Add with Carry instruction, ADC, also adds the status of the carry flag into the result. The source may be an immediate number, a register, or a memory location specified by any one of the 24 addressing modes shown in Figure 3-8. The destination may be a register or a memory location specified by any one of the 24 addressing modes in Figure 3-8. The source and the destination in an instruction cannot both be memory locations. The source and the destination must be of the same type. In other words, they must both be byte locations, or they must both be word locations. If you want to add a byte to a word, you must copy the byte to a word location and fill the upper byte of the word with 0's before adding. Flags affected: AF, CF, OF, PF, SF, ZF.

EXAMPLES (CODING):

```
ADD AL,74H        ; Add immediate number 74H to
                  ; contents of AL. Result in AL

ADC CL,BL         ; Add contents of BL plus carry
                  ;   status
                  ; to contents of CL.

ADD DX,BX         ; Add contents of BX
                  ; to contents of DX

ADD DX,[SI]       ; Add word from memory at offset
                  ;   [SI]
                  ; in DS to contents of DX

ADC AL,PRICES[BX] ; Add byte from effective
                  ; address PRICES[BX] plus carry
                  ; status to contents of AL

ADD PRICES[BX],AL ; Add contents of AL to
                  ; contents of memory location at
                  ; effective address PRICES[BX]
```

EXAMPLES (NUMERICAL):

```
              ; Addition of unsigned numbers
              ; CL = 01110011 = 115 decimal
              ; + BL = 01001111 = 79 decimal
ADD CL,BL     ; Result in CL
              ; CL = 11000010 = 194 decimal


              ; Addition of signed numbers
              ; CL = 01110011 = + 115 decimal
              ; + BL = 01001111 = + 79 decimal
ADD CL,BL     ; Result in CL
              ; CL = 11000010 = − 62 decimal—
              ; incorrect because result too large to fit
              ; in 7 bits
```

FLAG RESULTS FOR SIGNED ADDITION EXAMPLE

CF = 0   No carry out of bit 7.

PF = 0   Result has odd parity.

AF = 1   Carry was produced out of bit 3.

ZF = 0   Result in destination was not 0.

SF = 1   Copies most significant bit of result; indicates negative result if you are adding signed numbers.

OF = 1   Set to indicate that the result of the addition was too large to fit in the lower 7 bits of the destination used to represent the magnitude of a signed number. In other words, the result was greater than +127 decimal, so the result overflowed into the sign bit position and incorrectly indicated that the result was negative. If you are adding two signed 16-bit values, the OF will be set if the magnitude of the result is too large to fit in the lower 15 bits of the destination.

NOTE: PF is meaningful only for an 8-bit result. AF is set only by a carry out of bit 3. Therefore, the DAA instruction cannot be used after word additions to convert the result to correct BCD.

AND—AND Corresponding Bits of Two Operands—AND Destination,Source

This instruction ANDs each bit in a source byte or word with the same number bit in a destination byte or word. The result is put in the specified destination. The contents of the specified source will not be changed. The result for each bit position will follow the truth table for a two-input AND gate. In other words, a bit in the specified destination will be a 1 only if that bit is a 1 in both the source and the destination operands. Therefore, a bit can be masked (reset) by ANDing it with 0.

The source operand can be an immediate number, the contents of a register, or the contents of a memory location specified by one of the 24 addressing modes shown in Figure 3-8. The destination can be a register or a memory location. The source and the destination cannot both be memory locations in the same instruction. CF and OF are both 0 after AND. PF, SF, and ZF are updated by AND. AF is undefined. Note that PF has meaning only for an 8-bit operand.

EXAMPLES (CODING):

```
                 ; AND word in DS at offset [SI]
                   with word in CX register
AND CX,[SI]      ; Result in CX register

AND BH,CL        ; AND byte in CL with byte in BH
                 ; Result in BH

                 ; AND word in BX with immediate
AND BX,00FFH     ; 00FFH. Masks upper byte, leaves
                 ; lower byte unchanged
```

EXAMPLE (NUMERICAL):

```
              ; BX = 10110011 01011110
AND BX,00FFH  ; Mask out upper 8 bits of BX
              ; Result: BX = 00000000 01011110
              ; CF, OF, PF, SF, ZF = 0
```

CALL—Call a Procedure

The CALL instruction is used to transfer execution to a subprogram or procedure. There are two basic types of calls, *near* and *far*. A near call is a call to a procedure which is in the same code segment as the CALL instruction. When the 8086 executes a near CALL instruction, it decrements the stack pointer by 2 and copies the offset of the next instruction after the CALL onto the stack. This offset saved on the stack is referred to as the *return address*, because this is the address that execution will return to after the procedure executes. A near CALL instruction will also load the instruction pointer with the offset of the first instruction in the procedure. A RET instruction at the end of the procedure will return execution to the instruction after the call by copying the offset saved on the stack back to IP.

A far call is a call to a procedure which is in a different segment from the one that contains the CALL instruction. When the 8086 executes a far call, it decrements the stack pointer by 2 and copies the contents of the CS register to the stack. It then decrements the stack pointer by 2 again and copies the offset of the instruction after the CALL instruction to the stack. Finally, it loads CS with the segment base of the segment which contains the procedure, and loads IP with the offset of the first instruction of the procedure in that segment. A RET instruction at the end of the procedure will return execution to the next instruction after the CALL by restoring the saved values of CS and IP from the stack.

EXAMPLES:

CALL MULTO ; A direct within-segment (near or intrasegment) call. MULTO is the name of the procedure. The assembler determines the displacement of MULTO from the instruction after the CALL and codes this displacement in as part of the instruction.

CALL BX ; An indirect within-segment near or intrasegment call. BX contains the offset of the first instruction of the procedure. Replaces contents of IP with contents of register BX.

CALL WORD PTR [BX] ; An indirect within-segment near or intrasegment call. Offset of first instruction of procedure is in two memory addresses in DS. Replaces contents of IP with contents of word memory location in DS pointed to by BX.

CALL SMART_DIVIDE ; A direct call to another segment—far or intersegment call. SMART_DIVIDE is the name of the procedure. The procedure must be declared far with SMART_DIVIDE PROC FAR at its start (see

Chapter 5). The assembler will determine the code segment base for the segment which contains the procedure and the offset of the start of the procedure. It will put these values in as part of the instruction code.

CALL DWORD PTR[BX] ; An indirect call to another segment—far or intersegment call. New values for CS and IP are fetched from four memory locations in DS. The new value for CS is fetched from [BX] and [BX + 1]; the new IP is fetched from [BX + 2] and [BX + 3].

CBW—Convert Signed Byte to Signed Word

This instruction copies the sign of a byte in AL to all the bits in AH. AH is then said to be the *sign extension* of AL. The CBW operation must be done before a signed byte in AL can be divided by another signed byte with the IDIV instruction. CBW affects no flags.

EXAMPLE:

```
    ; AX = 00000000 10011011 =  - 155 decimal
CBW ; Convert signed byte in AL to signed word in AX
    ; Result: AX = 11111111 10011011 =  - 155
    ; decimal
```

For further examples of the use of CBW, see the IDIV instruction description.

CLC—Clear the Carry Flag (CF)

This instruction resets the carry flag to 0. No other flags are affected.

EXAMPLE:

CLC

CLD—Clear Direction Flag

This instruction resets the direction flag to 0. No other flags are affected. If the direction flag is reset, SI and DI will automatically be incremented when one of the string instructions, such as MOVS, CMPS, or SCAS, executes. Consult the string instruction descriptions for examples of the use of the direction flag.

EXAMPLE:

CLD ; Clear direction flag so that string pointers
    ; autoincrement after each string operation

CLI—Clear Interrupt Flag

This instruction resets the interrupt flag to 0. No other flags are affected. If the interrupt flag is reset, the 8086 will not respond to an interrupt signal on its INTR input. The CLI instruction, however, has no effect on the nonmaskable interrupt input, NMI.

CMC—Complement the Carry Flag

If the carry flag (CF) is a 0 before this instruction, it will be set to a 1 after the instruction. If the carry flag is 1 before this instruction, it will be reset to a 0 after the instruction executes. CMC affects no other flags.

EXAMPLE:

CMC   ; Invert the carry flag

CMP—Compare Byte or Word—CMP Destination,Source

This instruction compares a byte from the specified source with a byte from the specified destination, or a word from the specified source with a word from the specified destination. The source can be an immediate number, a register, or a memory location specified by one of the 24 addressing modes shown in Figure 3-8. The destination can be a register or a memory location. However, the source and the destination cannot both be memory locations in the same instruction. The comparison is actually done by subtracting the source byte or word from the destination byte or word. The source and the destination are not changed, but the flags are set to indicate the results of the comparison. AF, OF, SF, ZF, PF, and CF are updated by the CMP instruction. For the instruction CMP CX,BX, CF, ZF, and SF will be left as follows:

```
         CF ZF SF
CX = BX   0  1  0   ; Result of subtraction is 0
CX > BX   0  0  0   ; No borrow required, so CF = 0
CX < BX   1  0  1   ; Subtraction required
                    ; borrow, so CF = 1
```

EXAMPLES:

```
                 ; Compare immediate number
CMP AL,01H       ; 01H with byte in AL

                 ; Compare byte in CL with
CMP BH,CL        ; byte in BH

                 ; Compare word in DS at
                 ; displacement TEMP_MIN
CMP CX,TEMP_MIN  ; with word in CX

                 ; Compare CX with word in DS
CMP TEMP_MAX,CX  ; at displacement TEMP_MAX

                 ; Compare immediate 49H
CMP PRICES[BX],49H ; with byte at offset
                 ; [BX] in array PRICES
```

NOTE: The Compare instructions are often used with the Conditional Jump instructions, described in a later section. Having the Compare instructions formatted the way they are makes this use very easy to understand. For example, given the instruction sequence

CMP BX,CX
JAE TARGET

you can mentally read it as "jump to target if BX is above or equal to CX." In other words, just mentally insert the first operand after the J for jump and the second operand after the condition.

CMPS/CMPSB/CMPSW—Compare String Bytes or String Words

A string is a series of the same type of data items in sequential memory locations. The CMPS instruction can be used to compare a byte in one string with a byte in another string or to compare a word in one string with a word in another string. SI is used to hold the offset of a byte or word in the source string, and DI is used to hold the offset of a byte or a word in the other string. The comparison is done by subtracting the byte or word pointed to by DI from the byte or word pointed to by SI. The AF, CF, OF, PF, SF, and ZF flags are affected by the comparison, but neither operand is affected. After the comparison, SI and DI will automatically be incremented or decremented to point to the next elements in the two strings. If the direction flag has previously been set to a 1 with an STD instruction, then SI and DI will automatically be decremented by 1 for a byte string or by 2 for a word string. If the direction flag has previously been reset to a 0 with a CLD instruction, then SI and DI will automatically be incremented after the compare. They will be incremented by 1 for byte strings and by 2 for word strings.

The string pointed to by DI must be in the extra segment. The string pointed to by SI must be in the data segment.

The CMPS instruction can be used with a REPE or REPNE prefix to compare all the elements of a string. For further discussion of strings, see the discussion at the start of Chapter 5.

EXAMPLE:

```
MOV SI,OFFSET FIRST_STRING
              ; Point SI at source string

MOV DI,OFFSET SECOND_STRING
              ; Point DI at destination string
CLD           ; DF cleared, so SI and DI will
              ; autoincrement after compare
MOV CX,100    ; Put number of string elements
              ; in CX
REPE CMPSB    ; Repeat the comparison of
              ; string bytes
              ; until end of string or until
              ; compared bytes are not equal
```

NOTE: CX functions as a counter which the REPE prefix will cause to be decremented after each compare. The B attached to CMPS tells the assembler that the strings are of type byte. If you want to tell the assembler that the strings are of type

word, write the instruction as CMPSW. The REPE CMPSW instruction will cause the pointers in SI and DI to be incremented by 2 after each compare if the direction flag is cleared or decremented by 2 if the direction flag is set.

CWD—Convert Signed Word to Signed Doubleword

CWD copies the sign bit of a word in AX to all the bits of the DX register. In other words, it extends the sign of AX into all of DX. The CWD operation must be done before a signed word in AX can be divided by another signed word with the IDIV instruction. CWD affects no flags.

EXAMPLE:

```
      ; DX = 00000000 00000000
      ; AX = 11110000 11000111 = − 3897 decimal
CWD   ; Convert signed word in AX to signed
      ; doubleword in DX:AX
      ; Result: DX = 11111111 11111111
      ; AX = 11110000 11000111 = − 3897 decimal
```

For a further example of the use of CWD, see the IDIV instruction description.

DAA—Decimal Adjust AL after BCD Addition

This instruction is used to make sure the result of adding two packed BCD numbers is adjusted to be a legal BCD number. The result of the addition must be in AL for DAA to work correctly. If the lower nibble in AL after an addition is greater than 9 or AF was set by the addition, then the DAA instruction will add 6 to the lower nibble in AL. If the result in the upper nibble of AL is now greater than 9 or if the carry flag was set by the addition or correction, then the DAA instruction will add 60H to AL. A couple of simple examples should clarify how this works.

EXAMPLES:

```
          ; AL = 0101 1001 = 59 BCD
          ; BL = 0011 0101 = 35 BCD
ADD AL,BL ; AL = 1000 1110 = 8EH
DAA       ; Add 0110 because 1110 > 9
          ; AL = 1001 0100 = 94 BCD

          ; AL = 1000 1000 = 88 BCD
          ; BL = 0100 1001 = 49 BCD
ADD AL,BL ; AL = 1101 0001, AF = 1
DAA       ; Add 0110 because AF = 1
          ; AL = 1101 0111 = D7H
          ; 1101 > 9 so add 0110 0000
          ; AL = 0011 0111 = 37 BCD, CF = 1
```

The DAA instruction updates AF, CF, PF, and ZF. OF is undefined after a DAA instruction.

A decimal up counter can be implemented using the DAA instruction as follows:

```
MOV COUNT,00H    ; Initialize count in memory
                 ; location to 0
                 ; Other instructions here
MOV AL, COUNT    ; Bring count into AL to work on
ADD AL,01H       ; Can also count up by 2, by 3, or
                 ; by some other number using the
                 ; ADD instruction
DAA              ; Decimal adjust the result
MOV COUNT,AL     ; Put decimal result back
                 ; in memory
```

DAS—Decimal Adjust after BCD Subtraction

This instruction is used after subtracting two packed BCD numbers to make sure the result is correct packed BCD. The result of the subtraction must be in AL for DAS to work correctly. If the lower nibble in AL after a subtraction is greater than 9 or the AF was set by the subtraction, then the DAS instruction will subtract 6 from the lower nibble of AL. If the result in the upper nibble is now greater than 9 or if the carry flag was set, the DAS instruction will subtract 60 from AL. A couple of simple examples should clarify how this works.

EXAMPLES:

```
                 ; AL = 1000 0110 = 86 BCD
                 ; BH = 0101 0111 = 57 BCD

SUB AL,BH        ; AL = 0010 1111 = 2FH, CF = 0
DAS              ; Lower nibble of result is 1111,
                 ; so DAS automatically subtracts
                 ; 0000 0110 to give AL = 00101001
                 ; = 29 BCD


                 ; AL = 0100 1001 = 49 BCD
                 ; BH = 0111 0010 = 72 BCD
SUB AL,BH        ; AL = 1101 0111 = D7H, CF = 1
DAS              ; Subtracts 0110 0000 (− 60H)
                 ; because 1101 in upper nibble > 9
                 ; AL = 01110111 = 77 BCD, CF = 1
                 ; CF = 1 means borrow was needed
```

The DAS instruction updates AF, CF, SF, PF, and ZF, but OF is undefined.

A decimal down counter can be implemented using the DAS instruction as follows:

```
MOV AL,COUNT     ; Bring count into AL to work on
SUB AL,01H       ; Decrement. Can also count down
                 ; by 2, 3, etc., using SUB instruction
DAS              ; Keep results in BCD format
MOV COUNT,AL     ; Put new count back in memory
```

DEC—Decrement Destination Register or Memory—DEC Destination

This instruction subtracts 1 from the destination word or byte. The destination can be a register or a memory location specified by any one of the 24 addressing modes shown in Figure 3-8. AF, OF, PF, SF, and ZF are updated, but CF is not affected. This means that if an 8-bit destination containing 00H or a 16-bit destination containing 0000H is decremented, the result will be FFH or FFFFH with no carry (borrow).

EXAMPLES

DEC CL   ; Subtract 1 from contents of CL register

DEC BP   ; Subtract 1 from contents of BP register

DEC BYTE PTR [BX]; Subtract 1 from byte at offset [BX] in DS. The BYTE PTR directive is necessary to tell the assembler to put in the correct code for decrementing a byte in memory, rather than decrementing a word. The instruction essentially says, "Decrement the byte in memory pointed to by the offset in BX."

DEC WORD PTR [BP] ; Subtract 1 from a word at offset [BP] in SS. The WORD PTR directive tells the assembler to put in the code for decrementing a word pointed to by the contents of BP. An offset in BP will be added to the SS register contents to produce the physical address.

DEC TOMATO_CAN_COUNT ; Subtract 1 from byte or word named TOMATO_CAN_COUNT in DS. If TOMA-TO_CAN_COUNT was declared with a DB, then the assembler will code this instruction to decrement a byte. If TOMATO_CAN_COUNT was declared with a DW, then the assembler will code this instruction to decrement a word.

DIV—Unsigned Divide—DIV Source

This instruction is used to divide an unsigned word by a byte or to divide an unsigned doubleword (32 bits) by a word.

When a word is divided by a byte, the word must be in the AX register. The divisor can be in a register or a memory location. After the division, AL will contain an 8-bit result (quotient), and AH will contain an 8-bit remainder. If an attempt is made to divide by 0 or if the quotient is too large to fit in AL (greater than FFH), the 8086 will automatically do a type 0 interrupt. Interrupts are explained in Chapter 8.

When a doubleword is divided by a word, the most significant word of the doubleword must be in DX, and the least significant word of the doubleword must be in AX. After the division, AX will contain the 16-bit result (quotient), and DX will contain a 16-bit remainder. Again, if an attempt is made to divide by 0 or if the quotient is too large to fit in AX (greater than FFFFH), the 8086 will do a type 0 interrupt.

For a DIV, the dividend (numerator) must always be in AX or DX and AX, but the source of the divisor (denominator) can be a register or a memory location specified by any one of the 24 addressing modes shown in Figure 3-8. If the divisor does not divide an integral number of times into the dividend, the quotient is truncated, not rounded. The example below will illustrate this. All flags are undefined after a DIV instruction.

If you want to divide a byte by a byte, you must first put the dividend byte in AL and fill AH with all 0's. The SUB AH,AH instruction is a quick way to do this. Likewise, if you want to divide a word by a word, put the dividend word in AX and fill DX with all 0's. The SUB DX,DX instruction does this quickly.

EXAMPLES (SYNTAX):

DIV BL	; Divide word in AX by byte in BL. Quotient in AL, remainder in AH
DIV CX	; Divide doubleword in DX and AX by word in CX. Quotient in AX, remainder in DX.
DIV SCALE[BX]	; AX/(byte at effective address SCALE[BX]) if SCALE[BX] is of type byte or (DX and AX)/(word at effective address SCALE [BX]) if SCALE[BX] is of type word

EXAMPLE (NUMERICAL):

	; AX = 37D7H = 14,295 decimal
	; BH = 97H = 151 decimal
DIV BH	; AX/BH. AL = quotient = 5EH = 94 decimal
	; AH = remainder = 65H = 101 decimal

Since the remainder is greater than half of the divisor, the actual quotient is closer to 5FH than to the 5EH produced. However, as indicated before, the quotient is always truncated to the next lower integer rather than rounded to the closest integer. If you want to round the quotient, you can compare the remainder with (divisor/2) and add 1 to the quotient if the remainder is greater than (divisor/2).

ESC—Escape

This instruction is used to pass instructions to a coprocessor, such as the 8087 math coprocessor which shares the address and data bus with an 8086. Instructions for the coprocessor are represented by a 6-bit code embedded in the escape instruction. As the 8086 fetches instruction bytes, the coprocessor also catches these bytes from the data bus and puts them in its queue. However, the coprocessor treats all the normal 8086 instructions as NOPs. When the 8086 fetches an ESC instruction, the coprocessor decodes the instruction and carries out the action specified by the 6-bit code specified in the instruction. In most cases the 8086 treats the ESC instruction as a NOP. In some cases the 8086 will access a data item in memory for the coprocessor. A section in Chapter 11 describes the operation and use of the ESC instruction.

HLT—Halt Processing

The HLT instruction will cause the 8086 to stop fetching and executing instructions. The 8086 will enter a halt state. The only ways to get the processor out of the halt state are with an interrupt signal on the INTR pin, an interrupt signal on the NMI pin, or a reset signal on the RESET input. See Chapter 7 for further details about the halt state.

IDIV—Divide by Signed Byte or Word—IDIV Source

This instruction is used to divide a signed word by a signed byte, or to divide a signed doubleword (32 bits) by a signed word.

When dividing a signed word by a signed byte, the word must be in the AX register. The divisor can be in an 8-bit register or a memory location. After the division, AL will contain the signed result (quotient), and AH will contain the signed remainder. The sign of the remainder will be the same as the sign of the dividend. If an attempt is made to divide by 0, the quotient is greater than 127 (7FH), or the quotient is less than −127 (81H), the 8086 will automatically do a type 0 interrupt. Interrupts are discussed in Chapter 8. For the 80186, 80286, etc., this range is −128 to +127.

When dividing a signed doubleword by a signed word, the most significant word of the dividend (numerator) must be in the DX register, and the least significant word of the dividend must be in the AX register. The divisor can be in any other 16-bit register or memory location. After the division, AX will contain a signed 16-bit quotient, and DX will contain a signed 16-bit remainder. The sign of the remainder will be the same as the sign of the dividend. Again, if an attempt is made to divide by 0, the quotient is greater than +32,767 (7FFFH), or the quotient is less than −32,767 (8001H), the 8086 will automatically do a type 0 interrupt. For the 80186, 80286, etc., this range is −32,768 to +32,767.

If the divisor does not divide evenly into the dividend, the quotient will be truncated, not rounded. An example below illustrates this. All flags are undefined after an IDIV.

If you want to divide a signed byte by a signed byte, you must first put the dividend byte in AL and fill AH with copies of the sign bit from AL. In other words, if AL is positive (sign bit = 0), then AH should be filled with 0's. If AL is negative (sign bit = 1), then AH should be filled with 1's. The 8086 Convert Byte to Word instruction, CBW, does this by copying the sign bit of AL to all the bits of AH. AH is then said to contain the "sign extension of AL." Likewise, if you want to divide a signed word by a signed word, you must put the dividend word in AX and extend the sign of AX to all the bits of DX. The 8086 Convert Word to Doubleword instruction, CWD, will copy the sign bit of AX to all the bits of DX.

EXAMPLES (CODING):

| IDIV BL | ; Signed word in AX/signed byte in BL |

```
IDIV BP              ; Signed doubleword in DX and
                     ;   AX/signed word
                     ; in BP

IDIV BYTE PTR [BX]   ; AX/byte at offset [BX] in DS

MOV AL,DIVIDEND      ; Position byte dividend
CBW                  ; Extend sign of AL into AH
IDIV DIVISOR         ; Divide by byte divisor
```

EXAMPLES (NUMERICAL):

```
              ; A signed word divided by a signed byte
              ; AX = 00000011 10101011 = 03ABH
              ; = 39 decimal
              ; BL = 11010011 = D3H = − 2DH
              ; = − 45 decimal
IDIV BL       ; Quotient: AL = ECH = − 14H = − 20
              decimal
              ; Remainder: AH = 27H = + 39 decimal
```

NOTE: The quotient is negative because positive was divided by negative. The remainder has same sign as dividend (positive).

```
              ; A signed byte divided by a signed byte
              ; AL = 11011010 = − 26 H = − 38 decimal
              ; CH = 00000011 = + 3H = + 3 decimal
CBW           ; Extend sign of AL through AH,
              ; AX = 11111111 11011010
IDIV CH       ; Divide AX by CH
              ; AL = 11110100 = − 0CH = − 12 decimal
              ; AH = 11111110 = − 2H = − 2 decimal
```

Although the quotient is actually closer to 13 (12.666667) than to 12, the 8086 truncates it to 12 rather than rounding it to 13. If you want to round the quotient, you can compare the magnitude of the remainder with (divisor/2) and add 1 to the quotient if the remainder is greater than (divisor/2). Note that the sign of the remainder is the same as the sign of the dividend (negative). All flags are undefined after IDIV.

IMUL—Multiply Signed Numbers—IMUL Source

This instruction multiplies a signed byte from some source times a signed byte in AL or a signed word from some source times a signed word in AX. The source can be another register or a memory location specified by any one of the 24 addressing modes shown in Figure 3-8. When a byte from some source is multiplied by AL, the signed result (product) will be put in AX. A 16-bit destination is required because the result of multiplying two 8-bit numbers can be as large as 16 bits. When a word from some source is multiplied by AX, the result can be as large as 32 bits. The high-order (most significant) word of the signed result is put in DX, and the low-order (least significant) word of the signed result is put in AX. If the magnitude of the product does not require all the bits of the destination, the unused bits will be filled with copies of the sign bit. If the upper byte

of a 16-bit result or the upper word of a 32-bit result contains only copies of the sign bit (all 0's or all 1's), then CF and the OF will both be 0. If the upper byte of a 16-bit result or the upper word of a 32-bit result contains part of the product, CF and OF will both be 1. You can use the status of these flags to determine whether the upper byte or word of the product needs to be kept. AF, PF, SF, and ZF are undefined after IMUL.

If you want to multiply a signed byte by a signed word, you must first move the byte into a word location and fill the upper byte of the word with copies of the sign bit. If you move the byte into AL, you can use the 8086 Convert Byte to Word instruction, CBW, to do this. CBW extends the sign bit from AL into all the bits of AH. Once you have converted the byte to a word, you can do word times word IMUL. The result of this multiplication will be in DX and AX.

EXAMPLES (CODING):

```
IMUL BH ; Signed byte in AL times signed byte in BH,
        result in AX
```

```
IMUL AX                  ; AX times AX, result in DX
                         ; and AX

                         ; Multiplying a signed byte
                         ; by a signed word
MOV CX,MULTIPLIER        ; Load signed word in CX
MOV AL,MULTIPLICAND      ; Load signed byte in AL
CBW                      ; Extend sign of AL into AH
IMUL CX                  ; Result in DX and AX
```

EXAMPLES (NUMERICAL):

```
              ; 69 × 14
              ; AL = 01000101 = 69 decimal
              ; BL = 00001110 = 14 decimal
IMUL BL       ; AX = 03C6H = + 966 decimal
              ; MSB = 0, positive result magnitude
              ; in true form. SF = 0, CF,OF = 1

              ; − 28 × 59
              ; AL = 11100100 = − 28 decimal
              ; BL = 00111011 = + 59 decimal
IMUL BL       ; AX = F98CH = − 1652 decimal
              ; MSB = 1, negative result magnitude
              ; in 2's complement. SF,CF,OF = 1
```

IMUL—80186/80188 Only—Integer (Signed) Multiply Immediate—IMUL Destination Register,Source,Immediate Byte or Word

This version of the IMUL instruction functions in the same way as the IMUL instruction described in the preceding section, except that this version allows you to multiply an immediate byte or word by a byte or word in a specified register and put the result in a specified general-purpose register. If the immediate number is a byte, it will be automatically sign-extended to 16 bits. The source of the other operand for the multiplication can be a register or a memory location specified by any one of the 24 addressing modes shown in Figure 3-8. Since the result is put in a 16-bit general-purpose register, only the lower 16 bits of the product are saved!

EXAMPLE:

IMUL CX,BX,07H   ; Multiply contents of BX by 07H
                 ; CX = lower 16 bits of result

IN—Copy Data from a Port—IN Accumulator,Port

The IN instruction will copy data from a port to the AL or AX register. If an 8-bit port is read, the data will go to AL. If a 16-bit port is read, the data will go to AX. The IN instruction has two possible formats, fixed port and variable port.

For the fixed-port type, the 8-bit address of a port is specified directly in the instruction.

EXAMPLES:

IN AL,0C8H   ; Input a byte from port 0C8H to AL

IN AX,34H   ; Input a word from port 34H to AX

A_TO_D EQU 4AH
IN AX,A_TO_D   ; Input a word from port 4AH to AX

For the variable-port-type IN instruction, the port address is loaded into the DX register before the IN instruction. Since DX is a 16-bit register, the port address can be any number between 0000H and FFFFH. Therefore, up to 65,536 ports are addressable in this mode.

EXAMPLES:

MOV DX,0FF78H   ; Initialize DX to point to port
IN AL,DX   ; Input a byte from 8-bit port
                ; 0FF78H to AL

IN AX,DX   ; Input a word from 16-bit port
                ; 0FF78H to AX

The variable-port IN instruction has the advantage that the port address can be computed or dynamically determined in the program. Suppose, for example, that an 8086-based computer needs to input data from 10 terminals, each having its own port address. Instead of having a separate procedure to input data from each port, we can write one generalized input procedure and simply pass the address of the desired port to the procedure in DX. The IN instructions do not change any flags.

INC—Increment—INC Destination

The INC instruction adds 1 to a specified register or to a memory location specified in any one of the 24 ways

shown in Figure 3-8. AF, OF, PF, SF, and ZF are affected (updated) by this instruction. Note that the carry flag (CF) is not affected. This means that if an 8-bit destination containing FFH or a 16-bit destination containing FFFFH is incremented, the result will be all 0's with no carry.

EXAMPLES:

INC BL   ; Add 1 to contents of BL register
INC CX   ; Add 1 to contents of CX register

INC BYTE PTR [BX] ; Increment byte in data segment at offset contained in BX. The BYTE PTR directive is necessary to tell the assembler to put in the right code to indicate that a byte in memory, rather than a word, is to be incremented. The instruction essentially says, "Increment the byte pointed to by the contents of BX."

INC WORD PTR [BX] ; Increment the word at offset of [BX] and [BX + 1] in the data segment. In other words, increment the word in memory pointed to by BX.

INC MAX_TEMPERATURE ; Increment byte or word named MAX_TEMPERATURE in data segment. Increment byte if MAX_TEMPERATURE declared with DB. Increment word if MAX_TEMPERATURE declared with DW.

INC PRICES [BX] ; Increment element pointed to by [BX] in array PRICES. Increment a word if PRICES was defined as an array of words with a DW directive. Increment a byte if PRICES was defined as an array of bytes with a DB directive.

> NOTE: The PTR operator is not needed in the last two examples because the assembler knows the type of the operand from the DB or DW used to declare the named data initially.

INT—Interrupt Program Execution—INT Type

The term *type* in the instruction format refers to a number between 0 and 255 which identifies the interrupt. When an 8086 executes an INT instruction, it will:

1. Decrement the stack pointer by 2 and push the flags onto the stack.

2. Decrement the stack pointer by 2 and push the contents of CS onto the stack.

3. Decrement the stack pointer by 2 and push the offset of the next instruction after the INT number instruction on the stack.

4. Get a new value for IP from an absolute memory address of 4 times the type specified in the instruction. For an INT 8 instruction, for example, the new IP will be read from address 00020H.

5. Get a new value for CS from an absolute memory address of 4 times the type specified in the instruc-

tion plus 2. For an INT 8 instruction, for example, the new value of CS will be read from address 00022H.

6. Reset both IF and TF. Other flags are not affected.

Chapter 8 further describes the use of this instruction.

EXAMPLES:

INT 35 ; New IP from 0008CH, new CS from 0008EH

INT 3 ; This is a special form which has the single-byte code of CCH. Many systems use this as a breakpoint instruction. New IP from 0000CH, new CS from 0000EH.

INTO—Interrupt on Overflow

If the overflow flag (OF) is set, this instruction will cause the 8086 to do an indirect far call to a procedure you write to handle the overflow condition. Before doing the call, the 8086 will:

1. Decrement the stack pointer by 2 and push the flags onto the stack.

2. Decrement the stack pointer by 2 and push CS onto the stack.

3. Decrement the stack pointer by 2 and push the offset of the next instruction after the INTO instruction onto the stack

4. Reset TF and IF. Other flags are not affected. To do the call, the 8086 will read a new value for IP from address 00010H and a new value of CS from address 00012H.

Chapter 8 further describes the 8086 interrupt system.

EXAMPLE:

INTO ; Call interrupt procedure if OF = 1

IRET—Interrupt Return

When the 8086 responds to an interrupt signal or to an interrupt instruction, it pushes the flags, the current value of CS, and the current value of IP onto the stack. It then loads CS and IP with the starting address of the procedure which you write for the response to that interrupt. The IRET instruction is used at the end of the interrupt service procedure to return execution to the interrupted program. To do this return, the 8086 copies the saved value of IP from the stack to IP, the stored value of CS from the stack to CS, and the stored value of the flags back to the flag register. Flags will have the values they had before the interrupt, so any flag settings from the procedure will be lost unless they are specifically saved in some way.

NOTE: The RET instruction should not normally be used to return from interrupt procedures be-

cause it does not copy the flags from the stack back to the flag register. See Chapter 8 for further discussion of interrupts and the use of IRET.

JA/JNBE—Jump if Above/Jump if Not Below or Equal

These two mnemonics represent the same instruction. The terms *above* and *below* are used when referring to the magnitude of unsigned numbers. The number 0111 is above the number 0010. If, after a compare or some other instruction which affects flags, the zero flag and the carry flag are both 0, this instruction will cause execution to jump to a label given in the instruction. If CF and ZF are not both 0, the instruction will have no effect on program execution. The destination label for the jump must be in the range of −128 bytes to +127 bytes from the address of the instruction after the JA. JA/JNBE affects no flags. For further explanation of Conditional Jump instructions, see Chapter 4.

EXAMPLES:

CMP AX,4371H	; Compare by subtracting 4371H ; from AX
JA RUN_PRESS	; Jump to label RUN_PRESS if AX ; above 4371H
CMP AX,4371H	; Compare (AX − 4371H)
JNBE RUN_PRESS	; Jump to label RUN_PRESS if AX ; not below or equal to 4371H

JAE/JNB/JNC—Jump if Above or Equal/Jump if Not Below/Jump if No Carry

These three mnemonics represent the same instruction. The terms *above* and *below* are used when referring to the magnitude of unsigned numbers. The number 0111 is above the number 0010. If, after a compare or some other instruction which affects flags, the carry flag is 0, this instruction will cause execution to jump to a label given in the instruction. If CF is 1, the instruction will have no effect on program execution. The destination label for the jump must be in the range of −128 bytes to +127 bytes from the address of the instruction after the JAE. JAE/JNB/JNC affects no flags. For further explanation of Conditional Jump instructions, see Chapter 4.

EXAMPLES:

CMP AX,4371H	; Compare (AX − 4371H)
JAE RUN_PRESS	; Jump to label RUN_PRESS if AX ; above or equal to 4371H
CMP AX,4371H	; Compare (AX − 4371H)
JNB RUN_PRESS	; Jump to label RUN_PRESS if AX ; not below 4371H
ADD AL,BL	; Add two bytes. If result within
JNC OK	; acceptable range, continue

JB/JC/JNAE—Jump if Below/Jump if Carry/Jump if Not Above or Equal

These three mnemonics represent the same instruction. The terms *above* and *below* are used when referring to the magnitude of unsigned numbers. The number 0111 is above the number 0010. If, after a compare or some other instruction which affects flags, the carry flag is a 1, this instruction will cause execution to jump to a label given in the instruction. If CF is 0, the instruction will have no effect on program execution. The destination label for the jump must be in the range of -128 bytes to $+127$ bytes from the address of the instruction after the JB. JB/JC/JNAE affects no flags. For further explanation of Conditional Jump instructions, see Chapter 4.

EXAMPLES:

```
CMP AX,4371H     ; Compare (AX − 4371H)
JB RUN_PRESS     ; Jump to label RUN_PRESS if
                 ; AX below 4371H

ADD BX,CX        ; Add two words and jump
JC ERROR_FIX     ; to label ERROR_FIX if CF = 1

CMP AX,4371H     ; Compare (AX − 4371H)
JNAE RUN_PRESS   ; Jump to label RUN_PRESS if
                 ; AX not above or equal to 4371H
```

JBE/JNA—Jump if Below or Equal/Jump if Not Above

These two mnemonics represent the same instruction. The terms *above* and *below* are used when referring to the magnitude of unsigned numbers. The number 0111 is above the number 0010. If, after a compare or some other instruction which affects flags, either the zero flag or the carry flag is 1, this instruction will cause execution to jump to a label given in the instruction. If CF and ZF are both 0, the instruction will have no effect on program execution. The destination label for the jump must be in the range of -128 bytes to $+127$ bytes from the address of the instruction after the JBE. JBE/JNA affects no flags. For further explanation of Conditional Jump instructions, see Chapter 4.

EXAMPLES:

```
CMP AX,4371H     ; Compare (AX − 4371H)
JBE RUN_PRESS    ; Jump to label RUN_PRESS if AX
                 ; below or equal to 4371H

CMP AX,4371H     ; Compare (AX − 4371H)
JNA RUN_PRESS    ; Jump to label RUN_PRESS if AX
                 ; not above 4371H
```

JCXZ—Jump if the CX Register Is Zero

This instruction will cause a jump to a label given in the instruction if the CX register contains all 0's. If CX does not contain all 0's, execution will simply proceed to the next instruction. Note that this instruction does not look at the zero flag when it decides whether to jump or not. The destination label for this instruction must be in the range of -128 to $+127$ bytes from the address of the instruction after the JCXZ instruction. JCXZ affects no flags.

EXAMPLE:

```
JCXZ SKIP_LOOP   ; If CX = 0, skip the process
NXT:SUB [BX],07H ; Subtract 7 from data value
    INC BX       ; Point to next value
    LOOP NXT     ; Loop until CX = 0
    SKIP_LOOP:   ; Next instruction
```

JE/JZ—Jump if Equal/Jump if Zero

These two mnemonics represent the same instruction. If the zero flag is set, then this instruction will cause execution to jump to a label given in the instruction. If the zero flag is not 1, then execution will simply go on to the next instruction after JE or JZ. The destination label for the JE/JZ instruction must be in the range of -128 to $+127$ bytes from the address of the instruction after the JE/JZ instruction. JE/JZ affects no flags.

EXAMPLES:

```
NXT:CMP BX,DX     ; Compare (BX-DX)
    JE DONE       ; Jump to DONE if BX = DX
    SUB BX,AX     ; Else subtract AX
    INC CX        ; Increment counter
    JMP NXT       ; Check again
DONE:MOV AX,CX    ; Copy count to AX

IN AL,8FH         ; Read data from port 8FH
SUB AL,30H        ; Subtract minimum value
JZ START_MACHINE  ; Jump to label if result of
                  ; subtraction was 0
```

JG/JNLE—Jump if Greater/Jump if Not Less Than or Equal

These two mnemonics represent the same instruction. The terms *greater* and *less* are used to refer to the relationship of two signed numbers. Greater means more positive. The number 00000111 is greater than the number 11101010, because in signed notation the second number is negative. This instruction is usually used after a Compare instruction. The instruction will cause a jump to a label given in the instruction if the zero flag is 0 and the carry flag is the same as the overflow flag. The destination label must be in the range of -128 bytes to $+127$ bytes from the address of the instruction after the JG/JNLE instruction. If the jump is not taken, execution simply goes on to the next instruction after the JG or JNLE instruction. JG/JNLE affects no flags.

EXAMPLES:

```
CMP BL,39H    ; Compare by subtracting 39H from BL
JG NEXT_1     ; Jump to label if BL more positive
              ; than 39H
CMP BL,39H    ; Compare by subtracting
              ; 39H from BL
JNLE NEXT_1   ; Jump to label if BL not less than
              ; or equal to 39H
```

JGE/JNL—Jump if Greater Than or Equal/Jump if Not Less Than

These two mnemonics represent the same instruction. The terms *greater* and *less* are used to refer to the relationship of two signed numbers. Greater means more positive. The number 00000111 is greater than the number 11101010, because in signed notation the second number is negative. This instruction is usually used after a Compare instruction. The instruction will cause a jump to a label given in the instruction if the sign flag is equal to the overflow flag. The destination label must be in the range of -128 bytes to $+127$ bytes from the address of the instruction after the JGE/JNL instruction. If the jump is not taken, execution simply goes on to the next instruction after the JGE or JNL instruction. JGE/JNL affects no flags.

EXAMPLES:

```
CMP BL,39H    ; Compare by subtracting 39H from BL
JGE NEXT_1    ; Jump to label if BL more positive
              ; than 39H or equal to 39H

CMP BL,39H    ; Compare by subtracting 39H from BL
JNL NEXT_1    ; Jump to label if BL not less than 39H
```

JL/JNGE—Jump if Less Than/Jump if Not Greater Than or Equal

These two mnemonics represent the same instruction. The terms *greater* and *less* are used to refer to the relationship of two signed numbers. Greater means more positive. The number 00000111 is greater than the number 11101010, because in signed notation the second number is negative. This instruction is usually used after a Compare instruction. The instruction will cause a jump to a label given in the instruction if the sign flag is not equal to the overflow flag. The destination label must be in the range of -128 bytes to $+127$ bytes from the address of the instruction after the JL/JNGE instruction. If the jump is not taken, execution simply goes on to the next instruction after the JL or JNGE instruction. JL/JNGE affects no flags.

EXAMPLES:

```
CMP BL,39H    ; Compare by subtracting 39H from BL
JL AGAIN      ; Jump to label if BL more negative
              ; than 39H
```

```
CMP BL,39H    ; Compare by subtracting 39H from BL
JNGE AGAIN    ; Jump to label if BL not more positive
              ; than 39H or BL not equal to 39H
```

JLE/JNG—Jump if Less Than or Equal/Jump if Not Greater

These two mnemonics represent the same instruction. The terms *greater* and *less* are used to refer to the relationship of two signed numbers. Greater means more positive. The number 00000111 is greater than the number 11101010, because in signed notation the second number is negative. This instruction is usually used after a Compare instruction. The instruction will cause a jump to a label given in the instruction if the zero flag is set, or if the sign flag is not equal to the overflow flag. The destination label must be in the range of -128 bytes to $+127$ bytes from the address of the instruction after the JLE/JNG instruction. If the jump is not taken, execution simply goes on to the next instruction after the JLE/JNG instruction. JLE/JNG affects no flags.

EXAMPLES:

```
CMP BL,39H    ; Compare by subtracting 39H from BL
JLE NXT_1     ; Jump to label if BL more negative
              ; than 39H or equal to 39H

CMP BL,39H    ; Compare by subtracting 39H from BL
JNG PRINTER   ; Jump to label if BL not more
              ; positive than 39H
```

JMP—Unconditional Jump to Specified Destination

This instruction will always cause the 8086 to fetch its next instruction from the location specified in the instruction rather than from the next location after the JMP instruction. If the destination is in the same code segment as the JMP instruction, then only the instruction pointer will be changed to get to the destination location. This is referred to as a *near jump*. If the destination for the jump instruction is in a segment with a name different from that of the segment containing the JMP instruction, then both the instruction pointer and the code segment register contents will be changed to get to the destination location. This is referred to as a *far jump*. The JMP instruction affects no flags. Refer to Chapter 4 for a detailed discussion of the different forms of the unconditional JMP instruction.

EXAMPLES:

JMP CONTINUE ; Fetch next instruction from address at label CONTINUE. If the label is in the same segment, an offset coded as part of the instruction will be added to the instruction pointer to produce the new fetch address. If the label is in another segment, then IP and CS will be replaced with values coded in as part of the instruction. This type of jump is referred to as direct because the displacement of the destination or the destination itself is specified directly in the instruction.

JMP BX ; Replace the contents of IP with the contents of BX. BX must first be loaded with the offset of the destination instruction in CS. This is a near jump. It is also referred to as an indirect jump because the new value for IP comes from a register rather than from the instruction itself, as in a direct jump.

JMP WORD PTR [BX] ; Replace IP with a word from a memory location pointed to by BX in DS. This is an indirect near jump.

JMP DWORD PTR [SI] ; Replace IP with a word pointed to by SI in DS. Replace CS with a word pointed to by SI + 2 in DS. This is an indirect far jump.

JNA—See Heading JBE

JNAE—See Heading JB

JNB—See Heading JAE

JNBE—See Heading JA

JNC—See Heading JAE

JNE/JNZ—Jump if Not Equal/Jump if Not Zero

These two mnemonics represent the same instruction. If the zero flag is 0, then this instruction will cause execution to jump to a label given in the instruction. If the zero flag is 1, then execution will simply go on to the next instruction after JNE or JNZ. The destination label for the JNE/JNZ instruction must be in the range of −128 to +127 bytes from the address of the instruction after the JNE/JNZ instruction. JNE/JNZ affects no flags.

EXAMPLES:

```
NXT: IN AL,0F8H      ; Read data value from port
     CMP AL,72        ; Compare (AL-72)
     JNE NXT          ; Jump to NXT if AL ≠ 72
     IN AL,0F9H       ; Read next port when
                      ;   AL = 72

        MOV BX,2734H  ; Load BX as counter
NXT_1: ADD AX,0002H   ; Add count factor to AX
       DEC BX         ; Decrement BX
       JNZ NXT_1:     ; Repeat until BX = 0
```

JNG—See Heading JLE

JNGE—See Heading JL

JNL—See Heading JGE

JNLE—See Heading JG

JNO—Jump if No Overflow

The overflow flag will be set if the result of some signed arithmetic operation is too large to fit in the destination

register or memory location. The JNO instruction will cause the 8086 to jump to a destination given in the instruction if the overflow flag is not set. The destination must be in the range of −128 bytes to +127 bytes from the address of the instruction after the JNO instruction. If the overflow flag is set, execution will simply continue with the next instruction after JNO. JNO affects no flags.

EXAMPLE:

```
      ADD AL,BL    ; Add signed bytes in AL and BL
      JNO DONE     ; Process done if no overflow
      MOV AL,00H   ; Else load error code in AL
DONE: OUT 24H,AL   ; Send result to display
```

JNP/JPO—Jump if No Parity/Jump if Parity Odd

If the number of 1's left in the lower 8 bits of a data word after an instruction which affects the parity flag is odd, then the parity flag will be 0. The JNP/JPO instruction will cause execution to jump to a specified destination address if the parity flag is 0. The destination address must be in the range of −128 bytes to +127 bytes from the address of the instruction after the JNP/JPO instruction. If the parity flag is set, execution will simply continue on to the instruction after the JNP/JPO instruction. The JNP/JPO instruction affects no flags.

EXAMPLE:

```
IN AL,0F8H    ; Read ASCII character from UART
OR AL,AL      ; Set flags
JPO ERROR1    ; Even parity expected, send error
              ; message if parity found odd
```

JNS—Jump if Not Signed (Jump if Positive)

This instruction will cause execution to jump to a specified destination if the sign flag is 0. Since a 0 in the sign flag indicates a positive signed number, you can think of this instruction as saying "jump if positive." If the sign flag is set, indicating a negative signed result, execution will simply go on to the next instruction after JNS. The destination for the jump must be in the range of −128 bytes to +127 bytes from the address of the instruction after the JNS. JNS affects no flags.

EXAMPLE:

```
DEC AL        ; Decrement counter
JNS REDO      ; Jump to label REDO if counter has not
              ; decremented to FFH
```

JNZ—See Heading JNE

JO—Jump if Overflow

The JO instruction will cause the 8086 to jump to a destination given in the instruction if the overflow flag is set. The overflow flag will be set if the magnitude of the result produced by some signed arithmetic operation is too large to fit in the destination register or memory location. The destination for the JO instruction must be in the range of −128 bytes to +127 bytes from the address of the instruction after the JO instruction. If the overflow flag is not set, execution will simply continue with the next instruction after JO. JO affects no flags.

EXAMPLE:

```
ADD AL,BL    ; Add signed bytes in AL and BL
JO ERROR     ; Jump to label ERROR if overflow
             ; from add
MOV SUM,AL   ; Else put result in memory location
             ; named SUM
```

JP/JPE—Jump if Parity/Jump if Parity Even

If the number of 1's left in the lower 8 bits of a data word after an instruction which affects the parity flag is even, then the parity flag will be set. If the parity flag is set, the JP/JPE instruction will cause execution to jump to a specified destination address. If the parity flag is 0, execution will simply continue on to the instruction after the JP/JPE instruction. The destination address must be in the range of −128 bytes to +127 bytes from the address of the instruction after the JP/JPE instruction. The JP/JPE instruction affects no flags.

EXAMPLE:

```
IN AL,F8H     ; Read ASCII character from UART
OR AL,AL      ; Set flags
JPE ERROR2    ; Odd parity expected, send error
              ; message if parity found even
```

JPE—See Heading JP

JPO—See Heading JNP

JS—Jump if Signed (Jump if Negative)

This instruction will cause execution to jump to a specified destination if the sign flag is set. Since a 1 in the sign flag indicates a negative signed number, you can think of this instruction as saying "jump if negative" or "jump if minus." If the sign flag is 0, indicating a positive signed result, execution will simply go on to the next instruction after JS. The destination for the jump must be in the range of −128 bytes to +127 bytes from the address of the instruction after the JS. JS affects no flags.

EXAMPLE:

```
ADD BL,DH      ; Add signed byte in DH to signed
               ; byte in BL
JS TOO_COLD    ; Jump to label TOO_COLD if result
               ; of addition is negative number
```

JZ—See Heading JE

LAHF—Copy Low Byte of Flag Register to AH

The lower byte of the 8086 flag register is the same as the flag byte for the 8085. LAHF copies these 8085 equivalent flags to the AH register. They can then be pushed onto the stack along with AL by a PUSH AX instruction. An LAHF instruction followed by a PUSH AX instruction has the same effect as the 8085 PUSH PSW instruction. The LAHF instruction was included in the 8086 instruction set so that the 8085 PUSH PSW instruction could easily be simulated on an 8086. LAHF changes no flags.

LDS—Load Register and DS with Words from Memory—LDS Register, Memory Address of First Word

This instruction copies a word from two memory locations into the register specified in the instruction. It then copies a word from the next two memory locations into the DS register. LDS is useful for pointing SI and DS at the start of a string before using one of the string instructions. LDS affects no flags.

EXAMPLES:

LDS BX, [4326] ; Copy contents of memory at displacement 4326H in DS to BL, contents of 4327H to BH. Copy contents at displacement of 4328H and 4329H in DS to DS register.

LDS SI,STRING_POINTER ; Copy contents of memory at displacements STRING_POINTER and STRING_ POINTER + 1 in DS to SI register. Copy contents of memory at displacements STRING_POINTER + 2 and STRING POINTER + 3 in DS to DS register. DS:SI now points at start of desired string.

LEA—Load Effective Address—LEA Register,Source

This instruction determines the offset of the variable or memory location named as the source and puts this offset in the indicated 16-bit register. LEA changes no flags.

EXAMPLES:

```
LEA BX,PRICES          ; Load BX with offset of
                       ; PRICES in DS

LEA BP,SS:STACK_TOP    ; Load BP with offset of
                       ; STACK_TOP in SS

LEA CX,[BX][DI]        ; Load CX with EA =
                       ; (BX) + (DI)
```

A program example will better show the context in which this instruction is used. If you look at the program in Figure 4-21c, you will see that PRICES is an array of bytes in a segment called ARRAYS. The instruction LEA BX, PRICES will load the displacement of the first element of PRICES directly into BX. The instruction MOV AL, [BX] can then be used to bring an element from the array into AL. After one element in the array is processed, BX is incremented to point to the next element in the array.

LES—Load Register and ES with Words from Memory—LES Register, Memory Address of First Word

This instruction loads new values into the specified register and into the ES register from four successive memory locations. The word from the first two memory locations is copied into the specified register, and the word from the next two memory locations is copied into the ES register. LES can be used to point DI and ES at the start of a string before a string instruction is executed. LES affects no flags.

EXAMPLES:

LES BX,[789AH] ; Contents of memory at displacements 789AH and 789BH in DS copied to BX. Contents of memory at displacements 789CH and 789DH in DS copied to ES register.

LES DI,[BX] ; Copy contents of memory at offset [BX] and offset [BX + 1] in DS to DI register. Copy contents of memory at offsets [BX + 2] and [BX + 3] to ES register.

LOCK—Assert Bus Lock Signal

Many microcomputer systems contain several microprocessors. Each microprocessor has its own local buses and memory. The individual microprocessors are connected together by a system bus so that each can access system resources such as disk drives or memory. Each microprocessor takes control of the system bus only when it needs to access some system resource. The LOCK prefix allows a microprocessor to make sure that another processor does not take control of the system bus while it is in the middle of a critical instruction which uses the system bus. The LOCK prefix is put in front of the critical instruction. When an instruction with a LOCK prefix executes, the 8086 will assert its bus lock signal output. This signal is connected to an external bus controller device, which then prevents any other processor from taking over the system bus. LOCK affects no flags. See Chapter 11 for further discussion of this.

EXAMPLE:

LOCK XCHG SEMAPHORE,AL ; The XCHG instruction requires two bus accesses. The LOCK prefix prevents another processor from taking control of the system bus between the two accesses.

LODS/LODSB/LODSW—Load String Byte into AL or Load String Word into AX

This instruction copies a byte from a string location pointed to by SI to AL, or a word from a string location pointed to by SI to AX. If the direction flag is cleared (0), SI will automatically be incremented to point to the next element of the string. For a string of bytes, SI will be incremented by 1. For a string of words, SI will be incremented by 2. If the direction flag (DF) is set (1), SI will be automatically decremented to point to the next string element. For a byte string, SI will be decremented by 1, and for a word string, SI will be decremented by 2. LODS affects no flags.

EXAMPLE:

CLD	; Clear direction flag so SI
	; is autoincremented

MOV SI, OFFSET SOURCE_STRING	
	; Point SI at start
	; of string
LODS SOURCE_STRING	; Copy byte or word from
	; string to AL or AX

NOTE: The assembler uses the name of the string to determine whether the string is of type byte or type word. Instead of using the string name to do this, you can use the mnemonic LODSB to tell the assembler that the string is of type byte or the mnemonic LODSW to tell the assembler that the string is of type word.

LOOP—Jump to Specified Label if CX ≠ 0 after Autodecrement—LOOP Label

This instruction is used to repeat a series of instructions some number of times. The number of times the instruction sequence is to be repeated is loaded into CX. Each time the LOOP instruction executes, CX is automatically decremented by 1. If CX is not 0, execution will jump to a destination specified by a label in the instruction. If CX = 0 after the autodecrement, execution will simply go on to the next instruction after LOOP. The destination address for the jump must be in the range of −128 bytes to +127 bytes from the address of the instruction after the LOOP instruction. LOOP affects no flags. See Chapter 4 for further discussion and examples of the LOOP instruction.

EXAMPLE:

	MOV BX, OFFSET PRICES	
		; Point BX at
		; first element in array
	MOV CX,4	; Load CX with number of
		; elements in array
NEXT:	MOV AL,[BX]	; Get element from array
	ADD AL,07H	; Add correction factor
	DAA	; Decimal adjust result

```
MOV [BX],AL        ; Put result back in array
INC BX
LOOP NEXT          ; Repeat until all elements
                   ; adjusted
```

LOOPE/LOOPZ—Loop While CX ≠ 0 and ZF = 1

LOOPE and LOOPZ are two mnemonics for the same instruction. This instruction is used to repeat a group of instructions some number of times or until the zero flag becomes 0. The number of times the instruction sequence is to be repeated is loaded into CX. Each time the LOOP instruction executes, CX is automatically decremented by 1. If CX ≠ 0 and ZF = 1, execution will jump to a destination specified by a label in the instruction. If CX = 0 after the autodecrement or if ZF = 0, execution will simply go on to the next instruction after LOOPE/LOOPZ. In other words, the two ways to exit the loop are CX = 0 or ZF = 0. The destination address for the jump must be in the range of −128 bytes to +127 bytes from the address of the instruction after the LOOPE/LOOPZ instruction. LOOPE/LOOPZ affects no flags. See Chapter 4 for further discussion and examples of the LOOPE/LOOPZ instruction.

EXAMPLE:

```
        MOV BX,OFFSET ARRAY ; Point BX to just
        DEC BX              ; before start of array
        MOV CX,100          ; Put number of array
                            ; elements in CX
NEXT: INC BX                ; Point to next
                            ; element in array
        CMP [BX],0FFH       ; Compare array
                            ; element with FFH
        LOOPE NEXT
```

NOTE: The next element is checked if the element equals FFH and the element was not the last one in the array. If CX = 0 and ZF = 1 on exit, all elements were equal to FFH. If CX ≠ 0 on exit from the loop, then BX points to the first element that was not FFH. If CX = 0 and ZF = 0 on exit, then the last element was not FFH.

LOOPNE/LOOPNZ—Loop While CX ≠ 0 and ZF = 0

LOOPNE and LOOPNZ are two mnemonics for the same instruction. This instruction is used to repeat a group of instructions some number of times or until the zero flag becomes a 1. The number of times the instruction sequence is to be repeated is loaded into the count register CX. Each time the LOOPNE/LOOPNZ instruction executes, CX is automatically decremented by 1. If CX ≠ 0 and ZF = 0, execution will jump to a destination specified by a label in the instruction. If CX = 0 after the autodecrement or if ZF = 1, execution will simply go on to the next instruction after LOOPNE/LOOPNZ. In other words, the two ways to exit the loop are CX = 0

and ZF = 1. The destination address for the jump must be in the range of −128 bytes to +127 bytes from the address of the instruction after the LOOPNE/LOOPNZ instruction. LOOPNE/LOOPNZ affects no flags. See Chapter 4 for further discussion and examples of the LOOPNE/LOOPNZ instruction.

EXAMPLE:

```
        MOV BX,OFFSET ARRAY ; Point BX to just
        DEC BX              ; before start of array
        MOV CX,100          ; Put number of array
                            ; elements in CX
NEXT: INC BX                ; Point to next
                            ; element in array
        CMP [BX],0DH        ; Compare array
                            ; element with 0DH
        LOOPNE NEXT
```

NOTE: When the LOOPNE instruction executes, CX will be decremented by 1. If CX ≠ 0 and ZF = 0, execution will go to the label NEXT. If CX = 0 or ZF = 1, execution will go on to the next instruction after LOOPNE. If CX = 0 and ZF = 0 on exit, 0DH was not found in the array. If CX ≠ 0 on exit from the loop, then BX points to the first element which contains 0DH. If CX = 0 and ZF = 1 on exit from the loop, the last array element was 0DH.

LOOPNZ—See Heading LOOPNE

LOOPZ—See Heading LOOPE

MOV—Copy a Word or Byte—MOV Destination,Source

The MOV instruction copies a word or byte of data from a specified source to a specified destination. The destination can be a register or a memory location. The source can be a register, a memory location, or an immediate number. The source and destination in an instruction cannot both be memory locations. The source and destination in a MOV instruction must both be of type byte, or they must both be of type word. MOV instructions do not affect any flags.

EXAMPLES:

```
MOV CX,037AH    ; Put the immediate number
                ; 037AH in CX

MOV BL,[437AH]  ; Copy byte in DS at offset
                ; 437AH to BL

MOV AX,BX       ; Copy contents of register BX to AX

MOV DL,[BX]     ; Copy byte from memory at [BX]
                ; to DL
                ; BX contains offset of byte in DS

MOV DS,BX       ; Copy word from BX to DS register
```

MOV RESULTS[BP],AX; Copy AX to two memory locations—AL to the first location, AH to the second. EA of the first memory location is the sum of the displacement represented by RESULT3 and contents of BP. Physical address = EA + SS.

MOV CS:RESULTS[BP],AX ; Same as the above instruction, but physical address = EA + CS because of the segment override prefix CS.

MOVS/MOVSB/MOVSW—Move String Byte or String Word—MOVS Destination String Name,Source String Name

This instruction copies a byte or a word from a location in the data segment to a location in the extra segment. The offset of the source byte or word in the data segment must be in the SI register. The offset of the destination in the extra segment must be contained in the DI register. For multiple-byte or multiple-word moves, the number of elements to be moved is put in the CX register so that it can function as a counter. After the byte or word is moved, SI and DI are automatically adjusted to point to the next source and the next destination. If the direction flag is 0, then SI and DI will be incremented by 1 after a byte move and incremented by 2 after a word move. If the DF is a 1, then SI and DI will be decremented by 1 after a byte move and decremented by 2 after a word move. MOVS affects no flags.

When using the MOVS instruction, you must in some way tell the assembler whether you want to move a string as bytes or as words. There are two ways to do this. The first way is to indicate the names of the source and destination strings in the instruction, as, for example, MOVS STRING_DUMP,STRING_CREATE. The assembler will code the instruction for a byte move if STRING_DUMP and STRING_CREATE were declared with a DB. It will code the instruction for a word move if they were declared with a DW. Note that this reference to the source and destination strings does not load SI and DI. This must be done with separate instructions. The second way to tell the assembler whether to code the instruction for a byte or word move is to add a "B" or a "W" to the MOVS mnemonic. MOVSB, for example, says move a string as bytes. MOVSW says move a string as words.

EXAMPLE:

```
MOV SI,OFFSET SOURCE_STRING
                    ; Load offset of start of source
                    ; string in DS into SI
MOV DI,OFFSET DESTINATION_STRING
                    ; Load offset of start of
                      destination
                    ; string in ES into DI
CLD                 ; Clear direction flag to auto-
                    ; increment SI & DI after move
MOV CX,04H          ; Load length of string into CX
                    ; as counter
REP MOVSB           ; Decrement CX and copy
                    ; string bytes until CX = 0
```

After the move, SI will be 1 greater than the offset of the last byte in the source string. DI will be 1 greater than the offset of the last byte in the destination string. CX will be 0.

MUL—Multiply Unsigned Bytes or Words—MUL Source

This instruction multiplies an unsigned byte from some source times an unsigned byte in the AL register or an unsigned word from some source times an unsigned word in the AX register. The source can be a register or a memory location specified by any one of the 24 addressing modes shown in Figure 3-8. When a byte is multiplied by the contents of AL, the result (product) is put in AX. A 16-bit destination is required because the result of multiplying an 8-bit number by an 8-bit number can be as large as 16 bits. The most significant byte of the result is put in AH, and the least significant byte of the result is put in AL. When a word is multiplied by the contents of AX, the product can be as large as 32 bits. The most significant word of the result is put in the DX register, and the least significant word of the result is put in the AX register. If the most significant byte of a 16-bit result or the most significant word of a 32-bit result is 0, CF and OF will both be 0's. Checking these flags, then, allows you to detect and perhaps discard unnecessary leading 0's in a result. AF, PF, SF, and ZF are undefined after a MUL instruction.

If you want to multiply a byte by a word, you must first move the byte to a word location such as an extended register and fill the upper byte of the word with all 0's.

NOTE: You cannot use the 8086 Convert Byte to Word instruction, CBW, to do this. The CBW instruction fills the upper byte of AX with copies of the MSB of AL. If the number in AL is 80H or greater, CBW will fill the upper half of AX with 1's instead of with 0's. Once you get the byte converted correctly to a word with 0's in the upper byte, you can then do a word times word multiply. The 32-bit result will be in DX and AX.

EXAMPLES:

MUL BH   ; AL times BH, result in AX

MUL CX   ; AX times CX, result high word
                      in DX,
                    ; low word in AX

MUL BYTE PTR [BX]   ; AL times byte in DS pointed
                    ; to by [BX]

MUL CONVERSION_FACTOR[BX] ; Multiply AL times byte at effective address CONVERSION_FACTOR[BX] if it was declared as type byte with DB. Multiply AX times word at effective address CONVERSION_FACTOR[BX] if it was declared as type word with DW.

; Example showing a byte multiplied by a word

```
MOV AX,MULTIPLICAND_16    ; Load 16-bit
                         ; multiplicand into AX
MOV CL,MULTIPLIER_8      ; Load 8-bit multiplier
                         ; into CL
MOV CH,00H               ; Set upper byte of CX
                         ; to all 0's
MUL CX                   ; AX times CX, 32-bit
                         ; result in DX and AX
```

NEG—Form 2's Complement—NEG Destination

This instruction replaces the number in a destination with the 2's complement of that number. The destination can be a register or a memory location specified by any one of the 24 addressing modes shown in Figure 3-8. This instruction forms the 2's complement by subtracting the original word or byte in the indicated destination from zero. You may want to try this with a couple of numbers to convince yourself that it gives the same result as the invert each bit and add 1 algorithm. As shown in some of the following examples, the NEG instruction is useful for changing the sign of a signed word or byte. An attempt to NEG a byte location containing -128 or a word location containing $-32,768$ will produce no change in the destination contents because the maximum positive signed number in 8 bits is $+127$ and the maximum positive signed number in 16 bits is $+32,767$. OF will be set to indicate that the operation could not be done. The NEG instruction updates AF, CF, SF, PF, ZF, and OF.

EXAMPLES:

```
NEG AL               ; Replace number in AL with its
                     ; 2's complement

NEG BX               ; Replace word in BX with its
                     ; 2's complement

NEG BYTE PTR [BX]    ; Replace byte at offset [BX] in
                     ; DS with its 2's complement

NEG WORD PTR [BP]    ; Replace word at offset [BP] in
                     ; SS with its 2's complement
```

NOTE: The BYTE PTR and WORD PTR directives are required in the last two examples to tell the assembler whether to code the instruction for a byte operation or a word operation. The [BP] reference by itself does not indicate the type of the operand.

NOP—Perform No Operation

This instruction simply uses up three clock cycles and increments the instruction pointer to point to the next instruction. NOP affects no flags. The NOP instruction can be used to increase the delay of a delay loop, as shown in Figure 4-27a. When hand coding, a NOP can

also be used to hold a place in a program for an instruction that will be added later.

NOT—Invert Each Bit of Operand—NOT Destination

The NOT instruction inverts each bit (forms the 1's complement) of the byte or word at the specified destination. The destination can be a register or a memory location specified by any one of the 24 addressing modes shown in Figure 3-8. No flags are affected by the NOT instruction.

EXAMPLES:

```
NOT BX              ; Complement contents of
                    ; BX register

NOT BYTE PTR [BX]   ; Complement memory byte at
                    ; offset [BX] in data segment
```

OR—Logically OR Corresponding Bits of Two Operands—OR Destination,Source

This instruction ORs each bit in a source byte or word with the corresponding bit in a destination byte or word. The result is put in the specified destination. The contents of the specified source will not be changed. The result for each bit will follow the truth table for a two-input OR gate. In other words, a bit in the destination will become a 1 if that bit is a 1 in the source operand *or* that bit is a 1 in the original destination operand. Therefore, a bit in the destination operand can be set to a 1 by simply ORing that bit with a 1 in the same bit of the source operand. A bit ORed with 0 is not changed.

The source operand can be an immediate number, the contents of a register, or the contents of a memory location specified by one of the 24 addressing modes shown in Figure 3-8. The destination can be a register or a memory location. The source and the destination cannot both be memory locations in the same instruction. CF and OF are both 0 after OR. PF, SF, and ZF are updated by the OR instruction. AF is undefined after OR. Note that PF has meaning only for the lower 8 bits of a result.

EXAMPLES (SYNTAX):

```
OR AH,CL            ; CL ORed with AH, result in AH.
                    ; CL not changed

OR BP,SI            ; SI ORed with BP, result in BP.
                    ; SI not changed

OR SI,BP            ; BP ORed with SI, result in SI.
                    ; BP not changed

OR BL,80H           ; BL ORed with immediate 80H.
                    ; Set MSB of BL to a 1
```

OR CX, TABLE[BX][SI]
                    ; CX ORed with word from
                    ; effective address TABLE[BX][SI]
                    ; in data segment. Word in
                    ; memory is not changed

EXAMPLE (NUMERICAL):

                    ; CX = 00111101 10100101
ORCX,0FF00H   ; OR CX with immediate FF00H
                    ; Result in CX = 11111111 10100101
                    ; Note upper byte now all 1's, lower
                    ; byte unchanged
                    ; CF = 0, OF = 0, PF = 1, SF = 1,
                    ; ZF = 0

OUT—Output a Byte or Word to a Port—OUT Port,Accumulator AL or AX

The OUT instruction copies a byte from AL or a word from AX to the specified port. The OUT instruction has two possible forms, fixed port and variable port.

For the fixed-port form, the 8-bit port address is specified directly in the instruction. With this form, any one of 256 possible ports can be addressed.

EXAMPLES:

OUT 3BH,AL   ; Copy the contents of AL to port 3BH

OUT 2CH,AX   ; Copy the contents of AX to port 2CH

For the variable-port form of the OUT instruction, the contents of AL or AX will be copied to the port at an address contained in DX. Therefore, the DX register must always be loaded with the desired port address before this form of the OUT instruction is used. The advantage of the variable-port form of addressing is described in the discussion of the IN instruction. The OUT instruction does not affect any flags.

EXAMPLES:

MOV DX,0FFF8H   ; Load desired port address in DX
OUT DX,AL   ; Copy contents of AL to port FFF8H
OUT DX,AX   ; Copy contents of AX to port FFF8H

POP—POP Destination

The POP instruction copies a word from the stack location pointed to by the stack pointer to a destination specified in the instruction. The destination can be a general-purpose register, a segment register, or a memory location. The data in the stack is not changed. After the word is copied to the specified destination, the stack pointer is automatically incremented by 2 to point to the next word on the stack. No flags are affected by the POP instruction.

NOTE: POP CS is illegal.

EXAMPLES:

POP DX   ; Copy a word from top of stack to DX
              ; Increment SP by 2

POP DS   ; Copy a word from top of stack to DS
              ; Increment SP by 2

POP TABLE [BX] ; Copy a word from top of stack to
                ; memory in DS with EA =
                ; TABLE + [BX]

POPF—Pop Word from Top of Stack to Flag Register

This instruction copies a word from the two memory locations at the top of the stack to the flag register and increments the stack pointer by 2. The stack segment register and the word on the stack are not affected. All flags are affected.

PUSH—PUSH Source

The PUSH instruction decrements the stack pointer by 2 and copies a word from a specified source to the location in the stack segment where the stack pointer then points. The source of the word can be a general-purpose register, a segment register, or memory. The stack segment register and the stack pointer must be initialized before this instruction can be used. PUSH can be used to save data on the stack so that it will not be destroyed by a procedure. It can also be used to put data on the stack so that a procedure can access it there as needed. No flags are affected by this instruction. Refer to Chapter 5 for further discussion of the stack and the PUSH instruction.

EXAMPLES:

PUSH BX   ; Decrement SP by 2, copy BX
                  to stack

PUSH DS   ; Decrement SP by 2, copy DS
                  to stack

PUSH AL   ; Illegal, must push a word

PUSH TABLE [BX] ; Decrement SP by 2, copy word
                ; from memory in DS at
                ; EA = TABLE + [BX] to stack

PUSHF—Push Flag Register on the Stack

This instruction decrements the stack pointer by 2 and copies the word in the flag register to the memory location(s) pointed to by the stack pointer. The stack segment register is not affected. No flags are changed.

RCL—Rotate Operand Around to the Left through CF—RCL Destination,Count

This instruction rotates all the bits in a specified word or byte some number of bit positions to the left. The operation is circular because the MSB of the operand is rotated into the carry flag and the bit in the carry flag is rotated around into the LSB of the operand. See the following diagram.

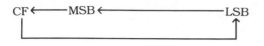

The "C" in the middle of the mnemonic should help you remember that CF is in the rotated loop and help distinguish this instruction from the ROL instruction. For multibit rotates, CF will contain the bit most recently rotated out of the MSB.

The destination operand can be in a register or in a memory location specified by any one of the 24 addressing modes shown in Figure 3-8. If you want to rotate the operand one bit position, you can specify this by putting a 1 in the count position of the instruction. To rotate more than one bit position, load the desired number into the CL register and put "CL" in the count position of the instruction.

> NOTE: The 80186, 80286, 80386, etc., allow you to specify a rotate of up to 32 bit positions with either an immediate number in the instruction or a number in CL.

RCL affects only CF and OF. After RCL, CF will contain the bit most recently rotated out of the MSB. OF will be a 1 after a single-bit RCL if the MSB was changed by the rotate. OF is undefined after a multibit rotate.

The RCL instruction is a handy way to move CF into the LSB of a register or memory location to save it after addition or subtraction.

EXAMPLES (SYNTAX):

```
RCL DX,1          ; Word in DX 1 bit left, MSB to
                  ; CF, CF to LSB

MOV CL,4          ; Load number of bit positions to
                  ; rotate into CL
RCL SUM[BX],CL    ; Rotate byte or word at effective
                  ; address SUM[BX] 4 bits left
                  ; Original bit 4 now in CF, original
                  ; CF now in bit 3
```

EXAMPLES (NUMERICAL):

```
            ; CF = 0, BH = 10110011
RCL BH,1    ; Result: BH = 01100110
            ; CF = 1, OF = 1 because MSB changed

            ; CF = 1, AX = 00011111 10101001
MOV CL,2    ; Load CL for rotating 2 bit positions
RCL AX,CL   ; Result: CF = 0, OF undefined
            ; AX = 01111110 10100110
```

RCR—Rotate Operand Around to the Right through CF—RCR Destination,Count

This instruction rotates all the bits in a specified word or byte some number of bit positions to the right. The operation is circular because the LSB of the operand is rotated into the carry flag and the bit in the carry flag is rotated around into the MSB of the operand. See the following diagram.

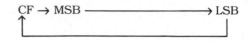

The "C" in the middle of the mnemonic should help you remember that CF is in the rotated loop and should help distinguish this instruction from the ROR instruction. For multibit rotates, CF will contain the bit most recently rotated out of the LSB.

The destination operand can be in a register or in a memory location specified by any one of the 24 addressing modes shown in Figure 3-8. If you want to rotate the operand one bit position, you can specify this by putting a 1 in the count position of the instruction. To rotate more than one bit position, load the desired number into the CL register and put "CL" in the count position of the instruction.

> NOTE: The 80186, 80286, 80386, etc., allow you to specify a rotate of up to 32 bit positions with either an immediate number in the instruction or a number in CL.

RCR affects only CF and OF. After RCR, CF will contain the bit most recently rotated out of the MSB. OF will be a 1 after a single-bit RCR if the MSB was changed by the rotate. OF will be undefined after multibit rotates.

EXAMPLES (CODING):

```
RCR BX,1          ; Word in BX right 1 bit
                  ; CF to MSB, LSB to CF

MOV CL,04H        ; Load CL for rotating
                  ; 4 bit positions
RCR BYTE PTR [BX] ; Rotate byte at offset [BX] in
                  ; DS 4 bit positions right
                  ; CF = original bit 3. Bit 4
                  ; = original CF
```

EXAMPLES (NUMERICAL):

```
            ; CF = 1, BL = 00111000
RCR BL,1    ; Result: BL = 10011100, CF = 0
            ; OF = 1 because MSB
            ; changed to 1

            ; CF = 0, WORD PTR [BX]
            ; = 01011110 00001111
MOV CL,02H  ; Load CL for rotate 2 bit
            ; positions
```

```
RCR WORD PTR [BX], CL    ; Rotate word in DS at
                         ; offset [BX] 2 bits right
                         ; CF = original bit 1.
                         ; Bit 14 = original CF
                         ; WORD PTR [BX] =
                         ; 10010111 10000011
```

REP/REPE/REPZ/REPNE/REPNZ—(Prefix) Repeat String Instruction until Specified Conditions Exist

REP is a prefix which is written before one of the string instructions. It will cause the CX register to be decremented and the string instruction to be repeated until CX = 0. The instruction REP MOVSB, for example, will continue to copy string bytes until the number of bytes loaded into CX has been copied.

REPE and REPZ are two mnemonics for the same prefix. They stand for Repeat if Equal and Repeat if Zero, respectively. You can use whichever prefix makes the operation clearer to you in a given program. REPE or REPZ is often used with the Compare String instruction or with the Scan String instruction. REPE or REPZ will cause the string instruction to be repeated as long as the compared bytes or words are equal (ZF = 1) *and* CX is not yet counted down to zero. In other words, there are two conditions that will stop the repetition: CX = 0 or string bytes or words *not* equal.

EXAMPLE:

REPE CMPSB ; Compare string bytes until end of string or until string bytes not equal. See the discussion of the CMPS instruction for a more detailed example of the use of REPE.

REPNE and REPNZ are also two mnemonics for the same prefix. They stand for Repeat if Not Equal and Repeat if Not Zero, respectively. REPNE or REPNZ is often used with the Scan String instruction. REPNE or REPNZ will cause the string instruction to be repeated until the compared bytes or words are equal (ZF = 1) *or* until CX = 0 (end of string).

EXAMPLE:

REPNE SCASW ; Scan a string of words until a word in the string matches the word in AX or until all of the string has been scanned. See the discussion of SCAS for a more detailed example of the use of this prefix

The string instruction used with the prefix determines which flags are affected. See the individual instructions for this information. Also see Chapter 5 for further examples of the REP instruction with string instructions.

NOTE: Interrupts should be disabled when multiple prefixes are used, such as LOCK, segment override, and REP with string instructions on the 8086/8088. This is because, during an interrupt response, the 8086 can remember only the prefix

just before the string instruction. The 80186, 80286, etc., will remember all the prefixes and start up correctly after an interrupt during a string instruction.

RET—Return Execution from Procedure to Calling Program

The RET instruction will return execution from a procedure to the next instruction after the CALL instruction which was used to call the procedure. If the procedure is a near procedure (in the same code segment as the CALL instruction), then the return will be done by replacing the instruction pointer with a word from the top of the stack. The word from the top of the stack is the offset of the next instruction after the CALL. This offset was pushed onto the stack as part of the operation of the CALL instruction. The stack pointer will be incremented by 2 after the return address is popped off the stack.

If the procedure is a far procedure (in a different code segment from the CALL instruction which calls it), then the instruction pointer will be replaced by the word at the top of the stack. This word is the offset part of the return address put there by the CALL instruction. The stack pointer will then be incremented by 2. The code segment register is then replaced with a word from the new top of the stack. This word is the segment base part of the return address that was pushed onto the stack by a far call operation. After the code segment word is popped off the stack, the stack pointer is again incremented by 2.

A RET instruction can be followed by a number, for example, RET 6. In this case the stack pointer will be incremented by an additional six addresses after the IP or the IP and CS are popped off the stack. This form is used to increment the stack pointer over parameters passed to the procedure on the stack.

The RET instruction affects no flags.

Please refer to Chapter 5 for further discussion of the CALL and RET instructions.

ROL—Rotate All Bits of Operand Left, MSB to LSB—ROL Destination,Count

This instruction rotates all the bits in a specified word or byte to the left some number of bit positions. The operation can be thought of as circular, because the data bit rotated out of the MSB is circled back into the LSB. The data bit rotated out of the MSB is also copied to CF during ROL. In the case of multiple bit rotates, CF will contain a copy of the bit most recently moved out of the MSB. See the following diagram.

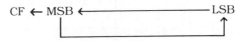

The destination operand can be in a register or in a memory location specified by any one of the 24 addressing modes shown in Figure 3-8. If you want to rotate the operand one bit position, you can specify this by putting a 1 in the count position of the instruction. To rotate more than one bit position, load the desired number in the CL register and put "CL" in the count position of the instruction.

NOTE: The 80186, 80286, 80386, etc., allow you to specify a rotate of up to 32 bit positions with either an immediate number in the instruction or a number in CL.

ROL affects only CF and OF. After ROL, CF will contain the bit most recently rotated out of the MSB. OF will be a 1 after a single bit ROL if the MSB was changed by the rotate.

The ROL instruction can be used to swap the nibbles in a byte or to swap the bytes in a word. It can also be used to rotate a bit into CF, where it can be checked and acted upon by the Conditional Jump instructions JC (Jump if Carry) and JNC (Jump if No Carry).

EXAMPLES (SYNTAX):

ROL AX,1   ; Word in AX 1 bit position left,
                  ; MSB to LSB and CF

MOV CL,04H   ; Load number of bits to rotate in CL
ROL BL,CL   ; Rotate BL 4 bit positions
                  ; (swap nibbles)

ROL FACTOR[BX],1 ; MSB of word or byte in DS at
                  ; EA = FACTOR[BX]
                  ; 1 bit position left into CF
JC ERROR   ; Jump if CF = 1 to error routine

EXAMPLES (NUMERICAL):

                  ; CF = 0, BH = 10101110
ROL BH,1   ; Result: CF,OF = 1, BH = 01011101

                  ; BX = 01011100 11010011
                  ; CL = 8, set for 8-bit rotate
ROL BX,CL   ; Rotate BX 8 times left (swap bytes)
                  ; CF = 0, BX = 11010011 01011100,
                  ; OF undefined

ROR—Rotate All Bits of Operand Right, LSB to MSB—ROR Destination,Count

This instruction rotates all the bits of the specified word or byte some number of bit positions to the right. The operation is described as a rotate rather than a shift because the bit moved out of the LSB is rotated around into the MSB. To help visualize the operation, think of the operand as a loop with the LSB connected around to the MSB. The data bit moved out of the LSB is also copied to CF during ROR. See the following diagram. In the case of multiple-bit rotates, CF will contain a copy of the bit most recently moved out of the LSB.

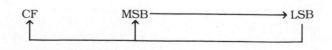

The destination operand can be in a register or in a memory location specified by any one of the 24 addressing modes shown in Figure 3-8. If you want to rotate the operand one bit position, you can specify this by putting a 1 in the count position of the instruction. To rotate more than one bit position, load the desired number in the CL register and put "CL" in the count position of the instruction.

NOTE: The 80186, 80286, 80386, etc., allow you to specify a rotate of up to 32 bit positions with either an immediate number or a number in CL.

ROR affects only CF and OF. After ROR, CF will contain the bit most recently rotated out of the LSB. For a single-bit rotate, OF will be a 1 after ROR if the MSB is changed by the rotate.

The ROR instruction can be used to swap the nibbles in a byte or to swap the bytes in a word. It can also be used to rotate a bit into CF, where it can be checked and acted upon by the Conditional Jump instructions JC (Jump if Carry) and JNC (Jump if No Carry).

EXAMPLES (SYNTAX):

ROR BL,1   ; Rotate all bits in BL right 1 bit position
           ; LSB to MSB and to CF

MOV CL,08H   ; Load CL with number of bit
                     ; positions to be rotated
ROR WORD PTR [BX],CL ; Rotate word in DS at offset
                     ; [BX] 8 bit positions right
                     ; (swap bytes in word)

EXAMPLES (NUMERICAL):

           ; CF = 0, BX = 00111011 01110101
ROR BX,1   ; Rotate all bits of BX 1 bit position right
           ; CF = 1, BX = 10011101 10111010

           ; CF = 0, AL = 10110011, OF = 1
MOV CL,04H ; Load CL for rotate 4 bit positions
ROR AL,CL ; Rotate all bits of AL 4 bits right
           ; CF = 0, AL = 00111011, OF = ?

SAHF—Copy AH Register to Low Byte of Flag Register

The lower byte of the 8086 flag regsiter corresponds exactly to the 8085 flag byte. SAHF replaces this 8085 equivalent flag byte with a byte from the AH register. SAHF is used with the POP AX instruction to simulate the 8085 POP PSW instruction. As described under the heading LAHF, an 8085 PUSH PSW instruction will be translated to an LAHF—PUSH AX sequence to run on an 8086. An 8085 POP PSW instruction will be translated to a POP AX—SAHF sequence to run on an 8086. SAHF changes the flags in the lower byte of the flag register.

SAL/SHL—Shift Operand Bits Left, Put Zero in LSB(s)—SAL/SHL Destination,Count

SAL and SHL are two mnemonics for the same instruction. This instruction shifts each bit in the specified destination some number of bit positions to the left. As a bit is shifted out of the LSB position, a 0 is put in the LSB position. The MSB will be shifted into CF. In the case of multiple-bit shifts, CF will contain the bit most recently shifted in from the MSB. Bits shifted into CF previously will be lost. See the following diagram.

$$CF \leftarrow MSB \longleftarrow LSB \leftarrow 0$$

The destination operand can be a byte or a word. It can be in a register or in a memory location specified by any one of the 24 addressing modes shown in Figure 3-8.

If the desired number of shifts is one, this can be specified by putting a 1 in the count position of the instruction. For shifts of more than 1 bit position, the desired number of shifts is loaded into the CL register, and CL is put in the count position of the instruction. The advantage of using the CL register is that the number of shifts can be dynamically calculated as the program executes.

> NOTE: The 80186, 80286, 80386, etc., allow you to specify a shift of up to 32 bit positions with either an immediate number in the instruction or a number in CL.

The flags are affected as follows: CF contains the bit most recently shifted in from MSB. For a count of one, OF will be 1 if CF and the current MSB are not the same. For multiple-bit shifts, OF is undefined. SF and ZF will be updated to reflect the condition of the destination. PF will have meaning only for an operand in AL. AF is undefined.

The SAL or SHL instruction can also be used to multiply an unsigned binary number by a power of 2. Shifting a binary number one bit position to the left and putting a 0 in the LSB multiplies the number by 2. Shifting the number two bit positions multiplies it by 4. Shifting the number three bit positions multiplies it by 8, etc. For this specific type of multiply, the SAL method is faster than using MUL, but you must make sure that the result does not become too large for the destination.

EXAMPLES (SYNTAX):

```
SAL BX,1          ; Shift word in BX 1 bit
                    position left,
                  ; 0 in LSB

MOV CL,02H        ; Load desired number of
                    shifts in CL
SAL BP,CL         ; Shift word in BP left (CL)
                    bit
                  ; positions, 0's in 2 LSBs
```

```
SAL BYTE PTR [BX],1   ; Shift byte in DS at offset
                        [BX]
                      ; 1 bit position left, 0 in
                        LSB

                      ; Example of SAL
                        instruction's
                      ; use to help pack BCD
IN AL,COUNTER_DIGIT   ; Unpacked BCD from
                      ; counter to AL
MOV CL,04H            ; Set count for 4 bit
                        positions
SAL AL,CL             ; Shift BCD to upper
                        nibble,
                      ; 0's in lower nibble. Ready
                        to OR
                      ; another BCD digit into
                      ; lower nibble of AL
```

EXAMPLE (NUMERICAL):

```
            ; CF = 0, BX = 11100101 11010011
SAL BX,1    ; Shift BX register contents 1 bit position left
            ; CF = 1, BX = 11001011 10100110
            ; OF = 0, PF = ?, SF = 1, ZF = 0
```

SAR—Shift Operand Bits Right, New MSB = Old MSB—SAR Destination,Count

This instruction shifts each bit in the specified destination some number of bit positions to the right. As a bit is shifted out of the MSB position, a copy of the old MSB is put in the MSB position. In other words, the sign bit is copied into the MSB. The LSB will be shifted into CF. In the case of multiple bit shifts, CF will contain the bit most recently shifted in from the LSB. Bits shifted into CF previously will be lost. See the following diagram.

$$MSB \rightarrow MSB \longrightarrow LSB \rightarrow CF$$

The destination operand can be a byte or a word. It can be in a register or in a memory location specified by any one of the 24 addressing modes shown in Figure 3-8.

If the desired number of shifts is one, this can be specified by putting a 1 in the count position of the instruction. For shifts of more than one bit position, the desired number of shifts is loaded into the CL register, and CL is put in the count position of the instruction.

> NOTE: The 80186, 80286, 80386, etc., allow you to specify a shift of up to 32 bit positions with either an immediate number in the instruction or a number in CL.

The flags are affected as follows: CF contains the bit most recently shifted in from the LSB. For a count of one, OF will be a 1 if the two MSBs are not the same. After a multibit SAR, OF will be 0. SF and ZF will be updated to show the condition of the destination. PF will have meaning only for an 8-bit destination. AF will be undefined after SAR.

The SAR instruction can be used to divide a signed byte or word by a power of 2. Shifting a binary number right one bit position divides it by 2. Shifting a binary number right two bit positions divides it by 4. Shifting it right three positions divides it by 8, etc. For unsigned numbers, a 0 is put in the MSB after the old MSB is shifted right. (See discussion of SHR instruction.) For signed binary numbers, the sign bit must be copied into the new MSB as the old sign bit is shifted right. This is necessary to retain the correct sign in the result. SAR shifts the operand right and copies the sign bit into the MSB as required for this operation. Using SAR to do a divide by 2, however, gives slightly different results than using the IDIV instruction to do the same job. IDIV always truncates a signed result toward 0. For example, an IDIV of 7 by 2 gives 3, and an IDIV of −7 by 2 gives −3. SAR always truncates a result in a downward direction. Using SAR to divide 7 by 2 gives 3, but using SAR to divide −7 by 2 gives −4.

EXAMPLES (SYNTAX):

SAR DI,1 ; Shift word in DI one bit position right,
         ; new MSB = old MSB

MOV CL,02H   ; Load desired number of
                   ; shifts in CL
SAR WORD PTR [BP],CL ; Shift word at offset [BP]
                   ; in stack segment right
                   ; two bit positions. Two MSBs
                   ; are now copies of
                   ; original MSB

EXAMPLES (NUMERICAL):

         ; AL = 00011101 = + 29 decimal CF = 0
SAR AL,1 ; Shift signed byte in AL right
         ; to divide by 2
         ; AL = 00001110 = + 14 decimal. CF = 1,
         ; OF = 0, PF = 0, SF = 0, ZF = 0

         ; BH = 11110011 = − 13 decimal
SAR BH, 1 ; Shift signed byte in BH right to
         ; divide by 2
         ; BH = 11111001 = − 7 decimal. CF = 1,
         ; OF = 0, PF = 1, SF = 1, ZF = 0

SBB—Subtract with Borrow—SBB Destination,Source

SUB—Subtract—SUB Destination,Source

These instructions subtract the number in the indicated source from the number in the indicated destination and put the result in the indicated destination. For subtraction, the carry flag (CF) functions as a borrow flag. The carry flag will be set after a subtraction if the number in the specified source is larger than the number in the specified destination. In other words, the carry/

borrow flag will be set if a borrow was required to do the subtraction. The Subtract instruction, SUB, subtracts just the contents of the specified source from the contents of the specified destination. The Subtract with Borrow instruction, SBB, subtracts the contents of the source and the contents of CF from the contents of the indicated destination. The source may be an immediate number, a register, or a memory location specified by any of the 24 addressing modes shown in Figure 3-8. The destination can also be a register or a memory location. However, the source and the destination cannot both be memory locations in an instruction. The source and the destination must both be of type byte or both be of type word. If you want to subtract a byte from a word, you must first move the byte to a word location such as a 16-bit register and fill the upper byte of the word with 0's. AF, CF, OF, PF, SF, and ZF are updated by the SUB instruction.

EXAMPLES (SYNTAX):

SUB CX,BX   ; CX − BX. Result in CX

SBB CH,AL   ; Subtract contents of AL and
                 ; contents of CF from
                 ; contents of CH. Result in CH

SUB AX,3427H   ; Subtract immediate number
                 ; 3427H from AX

SBB BX,[3427H]   ; Subtract word at displacement
                 ; 3427H in DS and contents
                 ; of CF from BX

SUB PRICES[BX],04H ; Subtract 04 from byte at effective address PRICES[BX] if PRICES declared with DB. Subtract 04 from word at effective address PRICES[BX] if PRICES declared with DW.

SBB CX,TABLE[BX] ; Subtract word from effective address TABLE[BX] and status of CF from CX.

SBB TABLE[BX],CX ; Subtract CX and status of CF from word in memory at effective address TABLE[BX].

EXAMPLES (NUMERICAL):

          ; Example subtracting unsigned numbers
          ; CL = 10011100 = 156 decimal
          ; BH = 00110111 = 55 decimal
SUB CL, BH ; Result: CF,AF,SF,ZF = 0, OF,PF = 1
          ; CL = 01100101 = 101 decimal

          ; First example subtracting signed numbers
          ; CL = 00101110 = + 46 decimal
          ; BH = 01001010 = + 74 decimal
SUB CL, BH ; Results: AF,ZF = 0, PF = 1
          ; CL = 11100100 = − 28 decimal
          ; CF = 1, borrow required
          ; SF = 1, result negative
          ; OF = 0, magnitude of result fits in 7 bits

```
                    ; Second example subtracting
                    ; signed numbers
                    ; CL = 10100001 = − 95 decimal
                    ; DII = 01001100 = + 76 decimal
SUB CL, BH          ; Results: CF,ZF = 0, AF,PF = 1
                    ; CL = 01010101 = + 85 decimal
                    ; SF = 0, result positive !
                    ; OF = 1, invalid result
```

The overflow flag being set indicates that the magnitude of the expected result, − 171 decimal, is too large to fit in the 7 bits used for the magnitude in an 8-bit signed number. If the Interrupt on Overflow instruction, INTO, has been executed previously, this error will cause the 8086 to perform a software interrupt procedure. Part of this procedure is a user-written subroutine to handle the error.

> NOTE: The SBB instruction allows you to subtract two multibyte numbers because any borrow produced by subtracting less significant bytes is included in the result when the SBB instruction executes. Although the preceding examples were for 8-bit numbers to save space, the principles are the same for 16-bit numbers. For 16-bit signed numbers, however, SF is a copy of bit 15, and the least significant 15 bits of the number are used to represent the magnitude. Also, PF and AF function only for the lower 8 bits.

SCAS/SCASB/SCASW—Scan a String Byte or a String Word

SCAS compares a byte in AL or a word in AX with a byte or word pointed to by DI in ES. Therefore, the string to be scanned must be in the extra segment, and DI must contain the offset of the byte or the word to be compared. If the direction flag is cleared (0), then DI will be incremented after SCAS. If the direction flag is set (1), then DI will be decremented after SCAS. For byte strings, DI will be incremented or decremented by 1, and for word strings, DI will be incremented or decremented by 2. SCAS affects AF, CF, OF, PF, SF, and ZF, but it does not change either the operand in AL (AX) or the operand in the string. This instruction is often used with a repeat prefix to find the first occurrence of a specified byte or word in a string.

EXAMPLE:

```
                    ; Scan a text string of 80 characters
                    ; for a carriage return, 0DH.
                    ; Put offset of string into DI
MOV DI,OFFSET TEXT_STRING
MOV AL,0DH          ; Byte to be scanned for into AL
MOV CX,80           ; CX used as element counter
CLD                 ; Clear DF so DI autoincrements
REPNE SCAS TEXT_STRING
                    ; Compare byte in string with
                    ; byte in AL
```

> NOTE: Scanning is repeated as long as the bytes are not equal and the end of the string has not been reached. If a carriage return 0DH is found, ZF = 1, and DI will point at the next byte after the carriage return in the string. If a carriage return is not found, then CX = 0 and ZF = 0. The assembler uses the name of the string to determine whether the string is of type byte or type word. Instead of using the name, you can tell the assembler the type of string directly by using the mnemonic SCASB for a byte string and SCASW for a word string.

SHL—See Heading SAL

SHR—Shift Operand Bits Right, Put Zero in MSB(s)—SHR Destination,Count

This instruction shifts each bit in the specified destination some number of bit positions to the right. As a bit is shifted right out of the MSB position, a 0 is put in its place. The bit shifted out of the LSB position goes to CF. In the case of a multiple-bit shift, CF will contain the bit most recently shifted in from the LSB. Bits shifted into CF previously will be lost. See the following diagram.

$$0 \rightarrow \text{MSB} \longrightarrow \text{LSB} \rightarrow \text{CF}$$

The destination operand can be a byte or a word in a register or in a memory location specified by any one of the 24 addressing modes shown in Figure 3-8.

If the desired number of shifts is one, this can be specified by putting a 1 in the count position of the instruction. For shifts of more than one bit position, the desired number of shifts is loaded into the CL register, and CL is put in the count position of the instruction.

> NOTE: The 80186, 80286, 80386, etc., allow you to specify a shift of up to 32 bit positions with either an immediate number in the instruction or a number in CL.

The flags are affected by SHR as follows: CF contains the bit most recently shifted in from the LSB. For a count of one, OF will be a 1 if the two MSBs are not both 0's. For multiple-bit shifts, OF is meaningless. SF and ZF will be updated to show the condition of the destination. PF will have meaning only for the lower 8 bits of the destination. AF is undefined.

The SHR instruction can be used to divide an unsigned binary number by a power of 2. Shifting a binary number one bit position to the right and putting 0 in the MSB divides the number by 2. Shifting the number two bit positions to the right divides it by 4. Shifting it three bit positions to the right divides it by 8, etc. When an odd number is divided with this method, the result will be truncated. In other words, dividing 7 by 2 will give a result of 3.

EXAMPLES (SYNTAX):

```
SHR BP,1    ; Shift word in BP one bit position right,
            ; 0 in MSB

MOV CL,03H        ; Load desired number of shifts into CL
SHR BYTE PTR [BX] ; Shift byte in DS at offset
                  ; [BX] 3 bits right.
                  ; 0's in 3 MSBs

                  ; Example of SHR used to help unpack
                  ; two BCD digits in AL to BH and BL
MOV BL,AL         ; Copy packed BCD to BL
AND BL,0FH        ; Mask out upper nibble. Low BCD
                  ; digit now in BL
MOV CL,04H        ; Load count for shift in CL
SHR AL,CL         ; Shift AL four bit positions right and
                  ; put 0's in upper 4 bits
MOV BH,AL         ; Copy upper BCD nibble to BH
```

EXAMPLES (NUMERICAL):

```
          ; SI = 10010011 10101101, CF = 0
SHR SI,1  ; Result: SI = 01001001 11010110
          ; CF = 1, OF = 1, PF = ?, SF = 0, ZF = 0
```

STC—Set the Carry Flag to a 1

STC does not affect any other flags.

STD—Set the Direction Flag to a 1

STD is used to set the direction flag to a 1 so that SI and/or DI will automatically be decremented to point to the next string element when one of the string instructions executes. If the direction flag is set, SI and/or DI will be decremented by 1 for byte strings, and by 2 for word strings. STD affects no other flags. Please refer to Chapter 5 and the discussion of the REP prefix in this chapter for examples of the use of this instruction.

STI—Set Interrupt Flag (IF)

Setting the interrupt flag to a 1 enables the INTR interrupt input of the 8086. The instruction will not take effect until after the next instruction after STI. When the INTR input is enabled, an interrupt signal on this input will then cause the 8086 to interrupt program execution, push the return address and flags on the stack, and execute an interrupt service procedure. An IRET instruction at the end of the interrupt service procedure will restore the flags which were pushed onto the stack, and return execution to the interrupted program. STI does not affect any other flags.

Please refer to Chapter 8 for a thorough discussion of interrupts.

STOS/STOSB/STOSW—Store Byte or Word in String

The STOS instruction copies a byte from AL or a word from AX to a memory location in the extra segment

pointed to by DI. In effect, it replaces a string element with a byte from AL or a word from AX. After the copy, DI is automatically incremented or decremented to point to the next string element in memory. If the direction flag (DF) is cleared, then DI will automatically be incremented by 1 for a byte string or incremented by 2 for a word string. If the direction flag is set, DI will be automatically decremented by 1 for a byte string or decremented by 2 for a word string. STOS does not affect any flags.

EXAMPLES:

```
; Point DI at start of destination string
MOV DI,OFFSET TARGET_STRING
STOS TARGET_STRING
  ; Assembler uses string name to determine
    whether string is of type byte or type word. If
    byte string, then string byte replaced with
    contents of AL. If word string, then string word
    replaced with contents of AX
  ; Point DI at start of destination string.

MOV DI,OFFSET TARGET_STRING
STOSB
  ; "B" added to STOS mnemonic directly tells
    assembler to replace byte in string with byte
    from AL. STOSW would tell assembler directly to
    replace a word in the string with a word from AX.
```

SUB—See Heading SBB

TEST—AND Operands to Update Flags—TEST Destination,Source

This instruction ANDs the contents of a source byte or word with the contents of the specified destination word. Flags are updated, but neither operand is changed. The TEST instruction is often used to set flags before a Conditional Jump instruction.

The source operand can be an immediate number, the contents of a register, or the contents of a memory location specified by one of the 24 addressing modes shown in Figure 3-8. The destination operand can be in a register or in a memory location. The source and the destination cannot both be memory locations in an instruction. CF and OF are both 0's after TEST. PF, SF, and ZF will be updated to show the results of the ANDing. PF has meaning only for the lower 8 bits of the destination. AF will be undefined.

EXAMPLES (SYNTAX):

```
TEST AL,BH      ; AND BH with AL, no result stored.
                ; Update PF, SF, ZF

TEST CX,0001H   ; AND CX with immediate number
                ; 0001H, no result stored.
                ; Update PF, SF, ZF

TEST BP,[BX][DI] ; AND word at offset [BX][DI] in
                 ; DS with word in BP, no result
                 ; stored. Update PF, SF, and ZF
```

```
                    ; Example of a polling sequence
                    ; using TEST
AGAIN; IN AL,2AH    ; Read port with strobe
                    ; connected to LSB
TEST AL,01H         ; AND immediate 01H with AL
                    ; to test if LSB of AL is 1 or 0
                    ; ZF = 1 if LSB of result is 0
                    ; No result stored
JZ AGAIN            ; Read port again if LSB = 0
```

EXAMPLES (NUMERICAL):

```
                ; AL = 01010001
TEST AL,80H     ; AND immediate 80H with AL to test
                ; if MSB of AL is 1 or 0
                ; ZF = 1 if MSB of AL = 0.
                ; AL = 01010001 (unchanged)
                ; PF = 0, SF = 0,
                ; ZF = 1 because ANDing produced 00
```

WAIT—Wait for Test Signal or Interrupt Signal

When this instruction executes, the 8086 enters an idle condition in which it is doing no processing. The 8086 will stay in this idle state until the 8086 TEST input pin is made low or until an interrupt signal is received on the INTR or the NMI interrupt input pins. If a valid interrupt occurs while the 8086 is in this idle state, the 8086 will return to the idle state after the interrupt service procedure executes. It returns to the idle state because the address of the WAIT instruction is the address pushed on the stack when the 8086 responds to the interrupt request. WAIT affects no flags. The WAIT instruction is used to synchronize the 8086 with external hardware such as the 8087 math coprocessor. In Chapter 11 we describe how this works.

XCHG—XCHG Destination,Source

The XCHG instruction exchanges the contents of a register with the contents of another register or the contents of a register with the contents of a memory location(s). The XCHG cannot directly exchange the contents of two memory locations. A memory location can be specified as the source or as the destination by any of the 24 addressing modes summarized in Figure 3-8. The source and destination must both be words, or they must both be bytes. The segment registers cannot be used in this instruction. No flags are affected by this instruction.

EXAMPLES:

```
XCHG AX,DX  ; Exchange word in AX with word in DX

XCHG BL,CH  ; Exchange byte in BL with byte in CH

XCHG AL,PRICES [BX]  ; Exchange byte in AL with
                     ; byte in memory at
                     ; EA = PRICES [BX] in DS
```

XLAT/XLATB—Translate a Byte in AL

The XLATB instruction is used to translate a byte from one code to another code. The instruction replaces a byte in the AL register with a byte pointed to by BX in a lookup table in memory. Before the XLATB instruction can be executed, the lookup table containing the values for the new code must be put in memory, and the offset of the starting address of the lookup table must be loaded in BX. The code byte to be translated is put in AL. To point to the desired byte in the lookup table, the XLATB instruction adds the byte in AL to the offset of the start of the table in BX. It then copies the byte from the address pointed to by (BX + AL) back into AL. XLATB changes no flags. The section "Converting One Keyboard Code to Another" in Chapter 9 should clarify the use of the XLATB instruction.

EXAMPLE:

```
                ; 8086 routine to convert ASCII code
                ; byte to EBCDIC equivalent.
                ; ASCII code byte is in AL at start.
                ; EBCDIC code in AL at end
MOV BX,OFFSET EBCDIC_TABLE
                ; Point BX at start of EBCDIC
                ; table in DS
XLATB           ; Replace ASCII in AL with
                ; EBCDIC from table
```

The XLATB instruction can be used to convert any code of 8 bits or less to any other code of 8 bits or less.

XOR—Exclusive OR Corresponding Bits of Two Operands—XOR Destination,Source

This instruction Exclusive-ORs each bit in a source byte or word with the same number bit in a destination byte or word. The result replaces the contents of the specified destination. The contents of the specified source will not be changed. The result for each bit position will follow the truth table for a two-input Exclusive OR gate. In other words, a bit in the destination will be set to a 1 if that bit in the source and that bit in the original destination were not the same. A bit Exclusive-ORed with a 1 will be inverted. A bit Exclusive-ORed with a 0 will not be changed. Because of this, you can use the XOR instruction to selectively invert or not invert bits in an operand.

The source operand can be an immediate number, the contents of a register, or the contents of a memory location specified by any one of the addressing modes shown in Figure 3-8. The destination can be a register or a memory location. The source and destination cannot both be memory locations in the same instruction. CF and OF are both 0 after XOR. PF, SF, and ZF are updated. PF has meaning only for an 8-bit operand. AF is undefined after XOR.

EXAMPLES (SYNTAX):

```
XOR CL,BH  ; Byte in BH Exclusive-ORed with byte
           ; in CL. Result in CL. BH not changed
```

```
XOR BP,DI   ; Word in DI Exclusive-ORed with word
            ; in BP. Result in BP. DI not changed

XOR WORD PTR [BX],00FFH
   ; Exclusive-OR immediate number 00FFH with
   ; word at offset [BX] in data segment. Result in
   ; memory location [BX]

   EXAMPLE (NUMERICAL):

            ; BX = 00111101 01101001
            ; CX = 00000000 11111111
XOR BX,CX   ; Result: BX = 00111101 10010110
            ; Note bits in lower byte are inverted
            ; CF,OF,SF,ZF = 0, PF = 1, AF = ?
```

ASSEMBLER DIRECTIVES

The words defined in this section are directions to the assembler, not instructions for the 8086. The assembler directives described here are those for the Intel 8086 macro assembler (ASM86), the Borland Turbo Assembler (TASM), and the IBM macro assembler (MASM). If you are using some other assembler, consult the manual for it to find the corresponding directives.

ASSUME

The ASSUME directive is used to tell the assembler the name of the logical segment it should use for a specified segment. The statement ASSUME CS:CODE, for example, tells the assembler that the instructions for a program are in a logical segment named CODE. The statement ASSUME DS:DATA tells the assembler that for any program instruction which refers to the data segment, it should use the logical segment called DATA. If, for example, the assembler reads the statement MOV AX,[BX] after it reads this ASSUME, it will know that the memory location referred to by [BX] is in the logical segment DATA. You must tell the assembler what to assume for any segment you use in a program. If you use a stack in your program, you must tell the assembler the name of the logical segment you have set up as a stack with a statement such as ASSUME SS:STACK_HERE. For a program with string instructions which use DI, the assembler must be told what to assume for the extra segment with a statement such as ASSUME ES:STRING_DESTINATION. For further discussion of the ASSUME directive, refer to the appropriate section of Chapter 3.

DB—Define Byte

The DB directive is used to declare a byte-type variable, or to set aside one or more storage locations of type byte in memory. The statement CURRENT_TEMPERATURE DB 42H, for example, tells the assembler to reserve 1 byte of memory for a variable named CURRENT_TEMPERATURE and to put the value 42H in that memory location when the program is loaded into RAM to be

run. Refer to Chapter 3 for further discussion of the DB directive and to Chapter 4 for a discussion of how you can access variables named with a DB in your programs. Here are a few more examples of DB statements.

PRICES DB 49H,98H,29H ; Declare array of 3 bytes named PRICES and initialize 3 bytes as shown.

NAME_HERE DB 'THOMAS' ; Declare array of 6 bytes and initialize with ASCII codes for letters in THOMAS.

TEMPERATURE_STORAGE DB 100 DUP(?) ; Set aside 100 bytes of storage in memory and give it the name TEMPERATURE_STORAGE, but leave the 100 bytes uninitialized. Program instructions will load values into these locations.

PRESSURE_STORAGE DB 20H DUP(0) ; Set aside 20H bytes of storage in memory, give it the name PRESSURE_STORAGE, and put 0 in all 20H locations.

DD—Define Doubleword

The DD directive is used to declare a variable of type doubleword or to reserve memory locations which can be accessed as type doubleword. The statement ARRAY_POINTER DD 25629261H, for example, will define a doubleword named ARRAY_POINTER and initialize the doubleword with the specified value when the program is loaded into memory to be run. The low word, 9261H, will be put in memory at a lower address than the high word. A declaration of this type is often used with the LES or LDS instruction. The instruction LES DI,ARRAY_POINTER, for example, will copy the low word of this doubleword, 9261H, into the DI register and the high word of the doubleword, 2562H, into the extra segment register.

DQ—Define Quadword

This directive is used to tell the assembler to declare a variable 4 words in length or to reserve 4 words of storage in memory. The statement BIG_NUMBER DQ 243598740192A92BH, for example, will declare a variable named BIG_NUMBER and initialize the 4 words set aside with the specified number when the program is loaded into memory to be run. The statement STORAGE DQ 100 DUP(0) reserves 100 quadwords of storage and initializes them all to 0 when the program is loaded into memory to be run.

DT—Define Ten Bytes

DT is used to tell the assembler to define a variable which is 10 bytes in length or to reserve 10 bytes of storage in memory. The statement PACKED_BCD DT 11223344556677889900 will declare an array named PACKED_BCD which is 10 bytes in length. It will initialize the 10 bytes with the values 11223344556677889900 when the program is loaded into memory to be run. This directive is often used when declaring data arrays for the 8087 math coprocessor, discussed in Chapter 11. The statement RESULTS DT 20H DUP(0) will declare an array of 20H blocks of 10 bytes each and initialize all 320 bytes to 00 when the program is loaded into memory to be run.

DW—Define Word

The DW directive is used to tell the assembler to define a variable of type word or to reserve storage locations of type word in memory. The statement MULTIPLIER DW 437AH, for example, declares a variable of type word named MULTIPLIER. The statement also tells the assembler that the variable MULTIPLIER should be initialized with the value 437AH when the program is loaded into memory to be run. Refer to Chapter 3 for further discussion of the DW directive and how you can access variables named with a DW in your programs. Here are a few more examples of DW statements.

THREE_LITTLE_WORDS   DW   1234H,3456H,5678H
;Declare array of 3 words and initialize with specified values.

STORAGE DW 100 DUP(0) ; Reserve an array of 100 words of memory and initialize all 100 words with 0000. Array is named STORAGE.

STORAGE DW 100 DUP(?) ; Reserve 100 words of storage in memory and give it the name STORAGE, but leave the words uninitialized.

END—End Program

The END directive is put after the last statement of a program to tell the assembler that this is the end of the program module. The assembler will ignore any statements after an END directive, so you should make sure to use only one END directive at the very end of your program module. A carriage return is required after the END directive.

ENDP—End Procedure

This directive is used along with the name of the procedure to indicate the end of a procedure to the assembler. This directive, together with the procedure directive, PROC, is used to "bracket" a procedure. Here's an example.

SQUARE_ROOT PROC   ; Start of procedure
                   ; Procedure instruction
                   ; statements
SQUARE_ROOT ENDP   ; End of procedure

Chapter 5 shows more examples and describes how procedures are written and called.

ENDS—End Segment

This directive is used with the name of a segment to indicate the end of that logical segment. ENDS is used with the SEGMENT directive to "bracket" a logical segment containing instructions or data. Here's an example.

CODE SEGMENT   ; Start of logical segment
               ; containing code
               ; Instruction statements
CODE ENDS   ; End of segment named
               ; CODE

EQU—Equate

EQU is used to give a name to some value or symbol. Each time the assembler finds the given name in the program, it will replace the name with the value or symbol you equated with that name. Suppose, for example, you write the statement CORRECTION_FACTOR EQU 03H at the start of your program, and later in the program you write the instruction statement ADD AL,CORRECTION_FACTOR. When it codes this instruction statement, the assembler will code it as if you had written the instruction ADD AL,03H. The advantage of using EQU in this manner is that if CORRECTION_FACTOR is used 27 times in a program, and you want to change the value, all you have to do is change the EQU statement and reassemble the program. The assembler will automatically put in the new value each time it finds the name CORRECTION_FACTOR. If you had used 03H instead of the EQU approach, then you would have had to try to find all 27 instructions and change them yourself. Here are some more examples.

CONTROL_WORD EQU 11001001 ; Replacement
MOV AL,CONTROL_WORD   ; assignment

DECIMAL_ADJUST EQU DAA   ; Create clearer
                         ; mnemonic for DAA
ADD AL,BL   ; Add BCD numbers
DECIMAL_ADJUST   ; Keep result in BCD format

STRING_START EQU [BX]   ; Give name to [BX]

EVEN—Align on Even Memory Address

As the assembler assembles a section of data declarations or instruction statements, it uses a location counter to keep track of how many bytes it is from the start of a segment at any time. The EVEN directive tells the assembler to increment the location counter to the next even address if it is not already at an even address. The 8086 can read a word from memory in one bus cycle if the word is at an even address. If the word starts at an odd address, the 8086 must do two bus cycles to get the 2 bytes of the word. Therefore, a series of words can be read much more quickly if they are at even addresses. When EVEN is used in a data segment, the location counter will simply be incremented to the next even address if necessary. When EVEN is used in a code segment, the location counter will be incremented to the next even address if necessary. A NOP instruction will be inserted in the location incremented over. Here's an example which shows why you might want to use EVEN in a data segment.

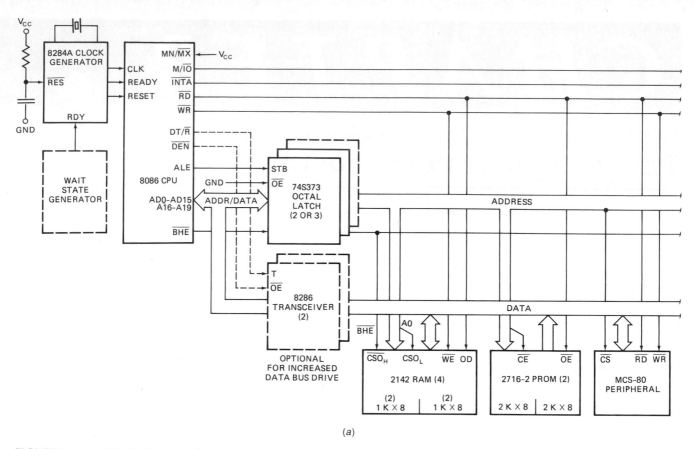

(a)

FIGURE 7-1 (a) Block diagram of a simple 8086-based microcomputer. (*See also next page.*)

Another section of Figure 7-1a to look at briefly is the block labeled 8286 Transceiver. This block represents bidirectional three-state buffers. For a very small system these buffers are not needed, but as more devices are added to a system, they become necessary. Here's why. Most of the devices—such as ROMs, RAMs, and ports—connected on microprocessor buses have MOS inputs, so on a dc basis they don't require much current. However, each input or output added to the system data bus, for example, acts like a capacitor of a few picofarads connected to ground. In order to change the logic state on these signal lines from low to high, all this added capacitance must be charged. To change the logic state to a low, the capacitance must be discharged. If we connect more than a few devices on the data bus lines, the 8086 outputs cannot supply enough current drive to charge and discharge the circuit capacitance fast enough. Therefore, we add external high-current drive buffers to do the job.

Buffers used on the data bus must be bidirectional because the 8086 sends data out on the data bus and also reads data in on the data bus. The *Data Transmit/ Receive signal*, DT/R̄, from the 8086 sets the direction in which data will pass through the buffers. When DT/R̄ is asserted high, the buffers will be set up to transmit data from the 8086 to ROM, RAM, or ports. When DT/R̄ is asserted low, the buffers will be set up to allow data to come into the 8086 from ROM, RAM, or ports.

The buffers used on the data bus must have three-state outputs so the outputs can be floated when the

bus is being used for other operations. For example, you certainly don't want data bus buffer outputs enabled onto the data bus while the 8086 is putting out the lower 16 bits of an address on these lines. The 8086 asserts the DEN signal to enable the three-state outputs on data bus buffers at the appropriate time in an operation.

The final section of Figure 7-1a to look at is the 8284A clock generator in the upper left corner. This device uses a crystal to produce the stable-frequency clock signal which steps the 8086 through execution of its instructions in an orderly manner. The 8284A also synchronizes the RESET signal and the READY signal with the clock so that these signals are applied to the 8086 at the proper times. When the RESET input is asserted, the 8086 goes to address FFFF0H to get its next instruction. The first instruction of the system start-up program is usually located at this address, so asserting this signal is a way to *boot*, or start, the system. We will discuss the use of the READY input in the next section.

Now that you have an overview of the basic system connections for an 8086 microcomputer, let's take a look at the signal present on the buses as an 8086 reads data from memory or from a port.

8086 Bus Activities During a Read Machine Cycle

Figure 7-1b shows the signal activities on the 8086 microcomputer buses during simple read and write

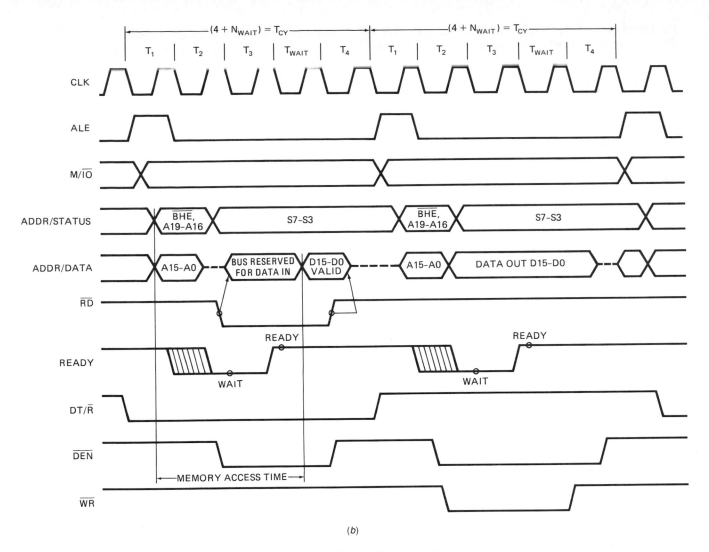

(b)

FIGURE 7-1 (*continued*) (*b*) Basic 8086 system timing. (*Intel Corporation*)

operations. Don't be overwhelmed by all the lines on this diagram. Their meanings should become clear to you as we work through the diagram.

The first line to look at in Figure 7-1*b* is the *clock waveform*, CLK, at the top. This represents the crystal-controlled clock signal sent to the 8086 from an external clock generator device such as the 8284 shown in the top left corner of Figure 7-1*a*. One cycle of this clock is called a *state*. For reference purposes, a state is measured from the falling edge of one clock pulse to the falling edge of the next clock pulse. The time interval labeled T_1 in the figure is an example of a state. Different versions of the 8086 have maximum clock frequencies of between 5 MHz and 10 MHz, so the minimum time for one state will be between 100 and 200 ns, depending on the part used and the crystal used.

A basic microprocessor operation such as reading a byte from memory or writing a byte to a port is called a *machine cycle*. The times labeled T_{CY} in Figure 7-1*b* are examples of machine cycles. As you can see in the figure, a machine cycle consists of several states.

The time a microprocessor requires to fetch and execute an entire instruction is referred to as an *instruc-*

tion cycle. An instruction cycle consists of one or more machine cycles.

To summarize this, an instruction cycle is made up of machine cycles, and a machine cycle is made up of states. The time for a state is determined by the frequency of the clock signal. In this section we discuss the activities that occur on the 8086 microcomputer buses during a read machine cycle.

The best way to analyze a timing diagram such as the one in Figure 7-1*b* is to think of time as a vertical line moving from left to right across the diagram. With this technique you can easily see the sequence of activities on the signal lines as you move your imaginary time line across the waveforms.

During T_1 of a read machine cycle the 8086 first asserts the M/$\overline{\text{IO}}$ signal. It will assert this signal high if it is going to do a read from memory during this cycle, and it will assert M/$\overline{\text{IO}}$ low if it is going to do a read from a port during this cycle. The timing diagram in Figure 7-1*b* shows two crossed waveforms for the M/$\overline{\text{IO}}$ signal because the signal may be going low or going high for a read cycle. The point where the two waveforms cross indicates the time at which the signal becomes valid for

IC	+5 V VCC	GND
8Ø86	4Ø	1, 2Ø
8255A	26	7
8251A	26	4
8284	18	9
8279	4Ø	2Ø
2716	24	12
2142	2Ø	1Ø
3625	18	9
8286	2Ø	1Ø
74LSØØ	14	7
74LSØ4	14	7
74LS1Ø	14	7
74LS14	14	7
74LS2Ø	14	7
74S3Ø	14	7
74LS74	14	7
74LS156	16	8
74LS164	14	7
74LS244	2Ø	1Ø
74LS393	14	7
7445	16	8
74S133	16	8
74S373	2Ø	1Ø
ULN2ØØ3A	9	8

4. ALL DIODES 1N914B.
3. ALL TRANSISTORS Q2T2905.
2. ALL CAPACITANCE VALUES ARE IN UF, +80 –20%, 50 V.
1. ALL RESISTANCE VALUES ARE IN OHMS, ± 5%, 1/4 WATT.
NOTES: UNLESS OTHERWISE SPECIFIED,

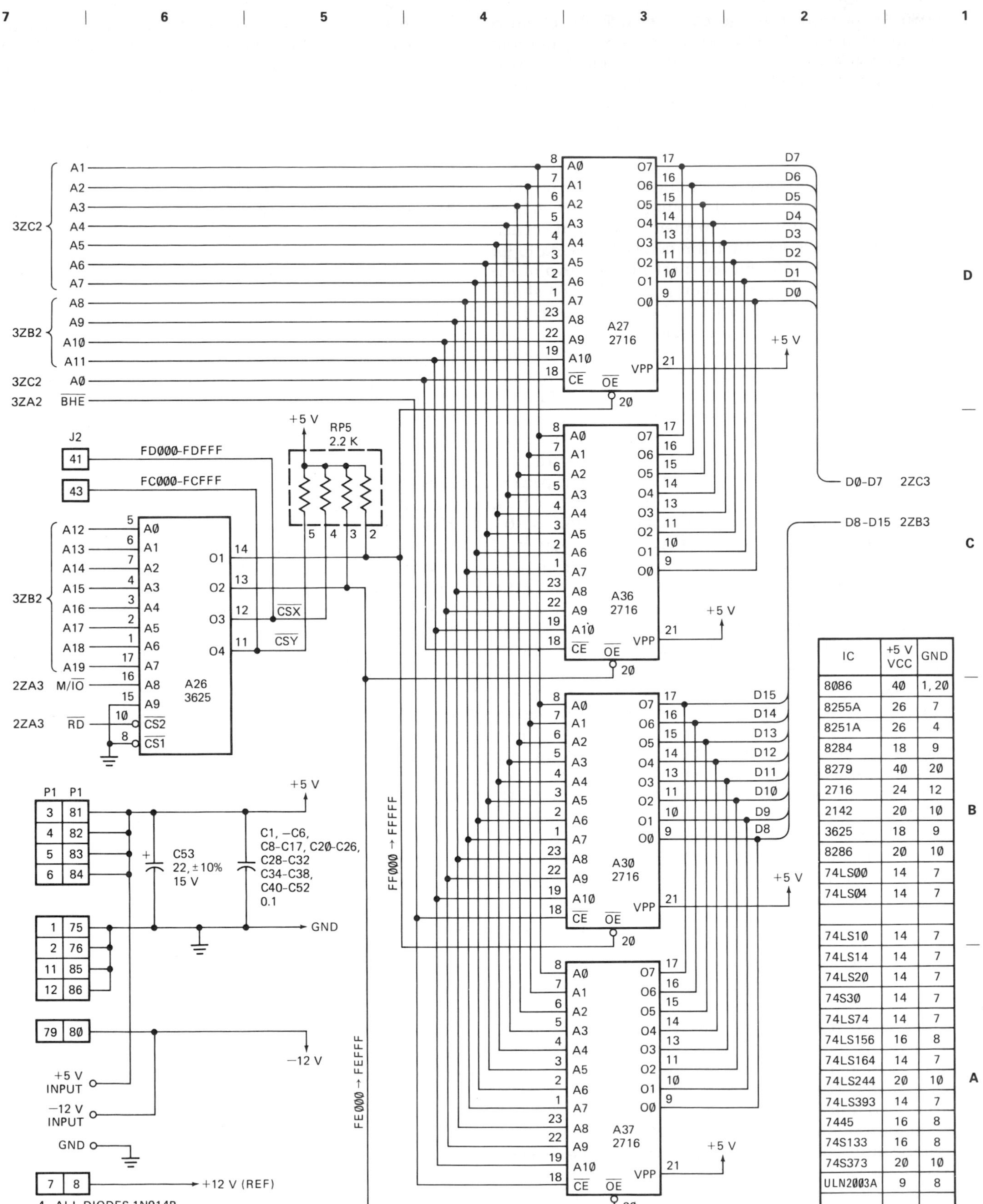

FIGURE 7-8 SDK-86 complete schematics; see also pages 177–184. Sheet 1 of 9. (*Intel Corporation*)

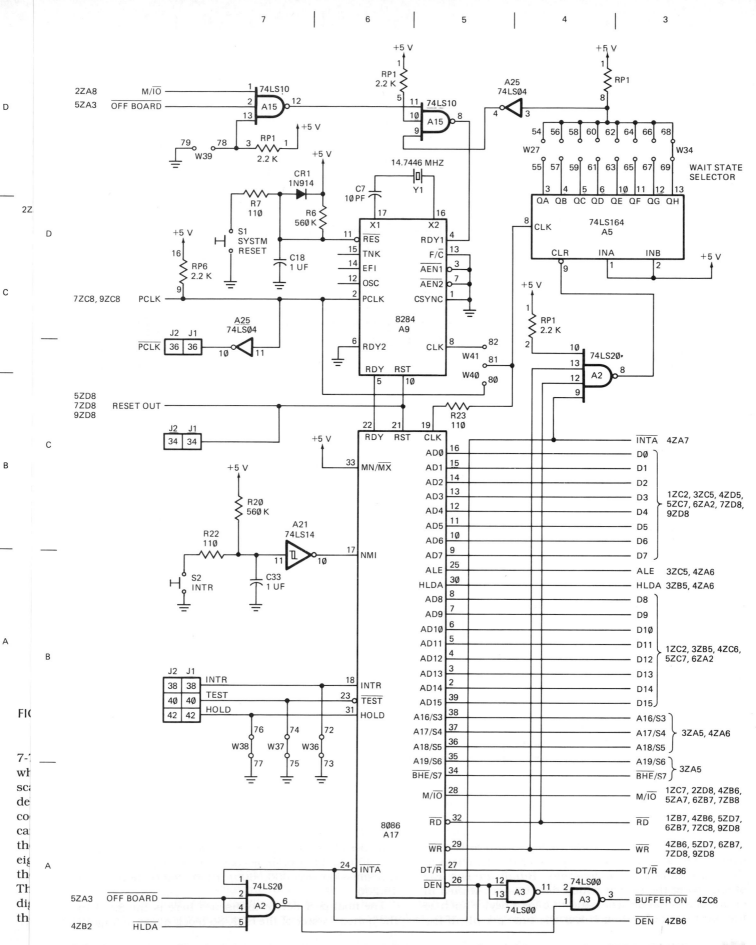

FIGURE 7-8 (*continued*) Sheet 2 of 9.   8086 SYSTEM CONNECTIONS, TIMING, AND TROUBLESHOOTING   **177**

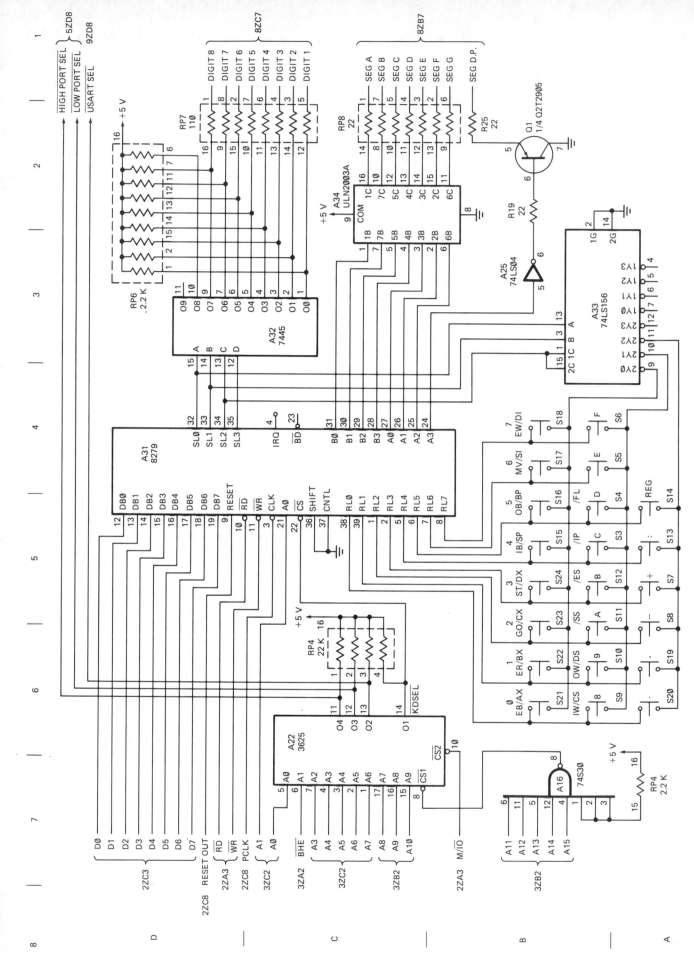

FIGURE 7-8 (continued) Sheet 7 of 9.

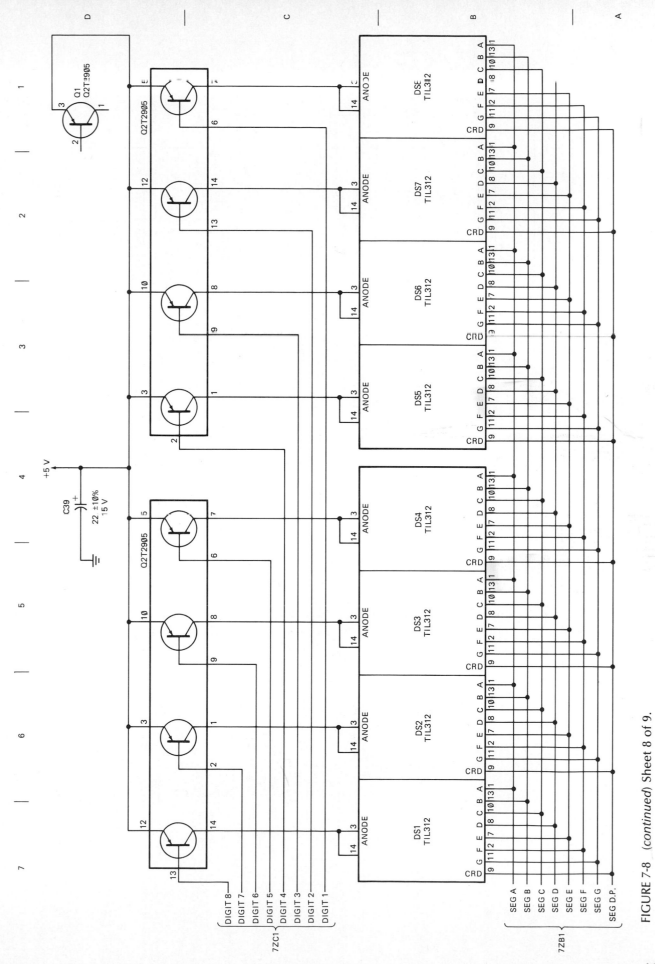

FIGURE 7-8 (continued) Sheet 8 of 9.

183

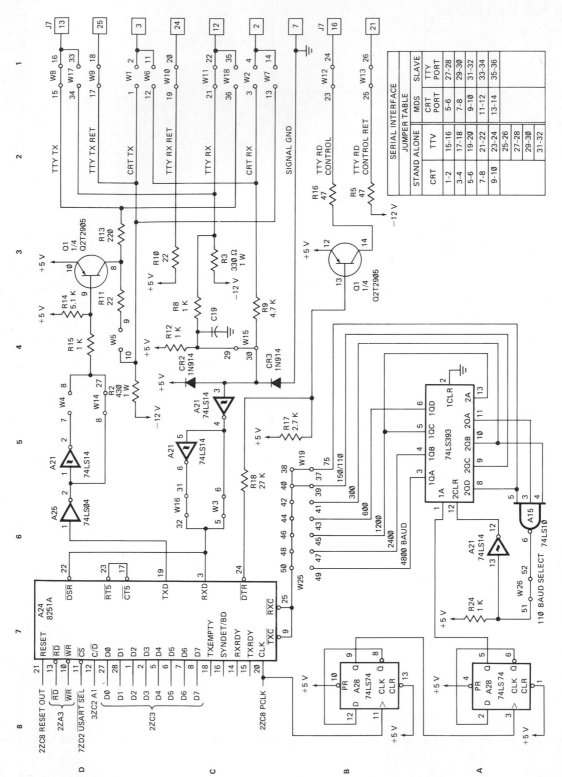

FIGURE 7-8 (continued) Sheet 9 of 9.

184

produces the port select signals from a port address sent out by the 8086.

The final parts of the SDK-86 block diagram to take a look at are the buffers along the right-hand edge. The purpose of these devices is to buffer the data and control bus lines so that they can drive additional ROM, RAM, or ports that you might add to the expansion area of the board. Note that the address lines are already buffered by the 74S373 address latches.

A First Look at the SDK-86 Schematics

Now that you have seen an overview of the SDK-86, the next step is to take a first look at Figure 7-8, which shows the actual schematics for the board. At first the many pages of schematics may seem overwhelming to you, but if you use the *5-minute freak-out rule* and then approach the schematics one part at a time, you should have no trouble understanding them. The schematics simply show greater detail for each of the parts of the block diagram that we discussed in the preceding sections of the chapter.

At this point we want to make clear that it is not the purpose of this chapter to make you an expert on the circuit connections of an SDK-86 board. We use parts of these schematics to demonstrate some major concepts, such as address decoding, and to show how the parts are connected together to form a small but real system. Even if you do not have an SDK-86 board, you can learn a great deal from these schematics about how an 8086 system functions. Multipage schematics such as these are typical for any microprocessor-based board or product, so you need to get used to working with them.

Before getting started on the next major concept, we will discuss some of the symbols commonly used on microprocessor system schematics. First, take a look at the numbers across the top and bottom of each schematic and the letters along the sides of each. These are called *zone coordinates*. You use these coordinates to identify the location of a part or connection on the schematic, just as you might use similar coordinates on a road map to help you locate Bowers Avenue. For example, on sheet 1 of the schematics, find the lines labeled A1 through A7 in the upper left corner. Next to these lines you should see 3ZC2. This indicates that these address lines come from zone C2 on sheet 3. To see what the lines actually connect to, first find schematic sheet 3. Then move across the row of the schematic labeled C until you come to the column labeled 2. This zone is small enough that you should easily be able to find where these lines come from. The zone coordinates next to these lines on sheet 3 indicate the other schematic sheets and zones that these lines go to. For practice, try finding where a few more lines connect from and to.

The next points to look at on the schematics are the numbers on the ICs. In addition to a part number such as 2716, each IC has a number of the form A36. This second number is used to help locate the IC on the printed circuit board. The number is commonly silk-screened on the board next to the corresponding IC. Usually IC numbers are sequential and start from the upper left corner of the component side of a board. There may be several 2716s on the board, but only one will be labeled A36.

In addition to ICs, another type of device often found on microprocessor boards is a *resistor pack*. You can find an example in zone C5 of schematic sheet 1. As you can see from the schematic, this device contains four 2.2-kΩ resistors. Resistor packs may physically be thin, vertical, rectangular wafers, or they may be in packages similar to small ICs. The advantages of resistor packs are that they take up less printed-circuit-board space and that they are easier to install than individual resistors.

Some other symbols to look at in the schematics are the structures with labels such as J2 and P1. You can find examples of these in zones C7 and B7 of schematic sheet 1. These symbols are used to indicate *connectors*. The number in the rectangular box specifies the pin number on the connector that a signal goes to. The letter P stands for *plug*. A connector is considered a plug if it plugs into something else. In the case of the SDK-86, the connector labeled P1 is the printed-circuit-board edge connector. The letter J next to a connector stands for *jack*. A connector is considered a jack if something else plugs into it. On the SDK-86 board the jacks J1 through J6 are 50-pin connectors that you can plug ribbon cable connectors into. These jacks allow the address bus, data bus, control bus, and parallel ports to be connected to additional circuitry.

One more point to notice on the SDK-86 schematics is the capacitors on the power supply inputs shown in zone B6 of sheet 1. As you can see there, the schematic shows a large number of 0.1-μF capacitors in parallel with a 22-μF capacitor. Most systems have *filtering* such as this on their power lines. You may wonder what is the use of putting all these small capacitors in parallel with one which is obviously many times larger. The point of this is that the large capacitor filters out, or *bypasses*, low-frequency noise on the power lines, and the small capacitors, spread around the board, bypass high-frequency noise on the power supply lines. Noise is produced on the power supply lines by devices switching from one logic state to another. If this noise is not filtered out with bypass capacitors, it may become great enough to disturb system operation.

Glance through the SDK-86 schematics to get an idea of where various parts are located and to see what additional information you can pick up from the notes on them. In the next section of this chapter, we discuss how microcomputer systems address memory and ports. As part of the discussion, we cycle back to these schematics to see how the SDK-86 does it.

Addressing Memory and Ports in Microcomputer Systems

ADDRESS DECODER CONCEPT

While discussing the block diagram of the SDK-86 board earlier in this chapter, we mentioned that the 3625 devices on the board serve as *address decoders*. One function of an address decoder is to produce a signal

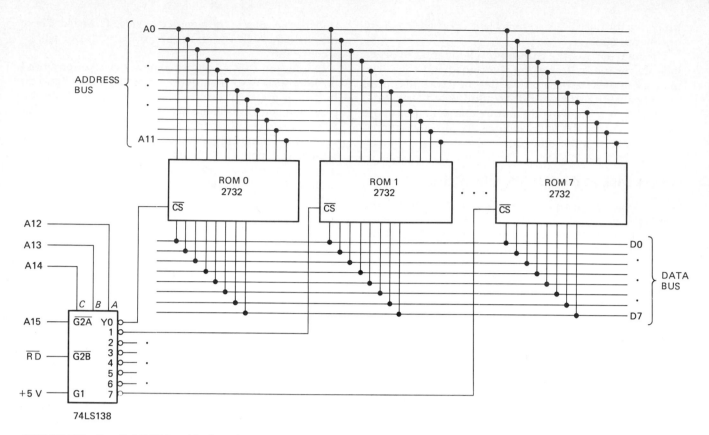

FIGURE 7-9   Parallel ROMs with decoder.

which enables the ROM, RAM, or port device that you want enabled for a particular address. A second, related function of an address decoder is to make sure that only one device at a time is enabled to put data on the data bus lines.

It seems that every microcomputer system does address decoding in a different way from every other system. Therefore, instead of memorizing the method used in one particular system, it is important that you understand the concept of address decoding. You can then figure out any system you have to work on.

AN EXAMPLE ROM DECODER

To start, look at Figure 7-9. This figure shows how eight EPROMs can be connected in parallel on a common address bus and common data bus. Just by looking at the schematic you can see that these EPROMs output bytes of data because each has eight outputs connected to the system data bus. The number of address lines connected to each device gives you an indication of how many bytes are stored in it. Each EPROM has 12 address lines (A0–A11) connected to it. Therefore, the number of bytes stored in the device is 2^{12} or 4096. If you have trouble with this, think of how many bits a counter has to have to count the 4096 states from 0 to 4095 decimal, or 0000H to 0FFFH.

Note that each 2732 in Figure 7-9 has a Chip Select, $\overline{CS}$, input. When this input is asserted low, the addressed byte in a device will be output on the data bus. The 74LS138 in Figure 7-9 makes sure that the $\overline{CS}$ input of only one ROM device at a time is low.

If the 74LS138 is enabled by making its $\overline{G2A}$ and $\overline{G2B}$ inputs low and its G1 input high, then only one output of the device will be low at a time. The output that will be low is determined by the 3-bit address applied to the C, B, and A select inputs. For example, if CBA is 000, then the Y0 output will be low, and all the other outputs will be high. This will assert the $\overline{CS}$ input of ROM 0. If CBA is 001, the Y1 output will be low and the ROM 1 will be selected. If CBA is 111, then Y7 will be low, and only ROM 7 will be enabled. Now let's see what address range these connections on the 74LS138 will give each of these ROMs in the system.

To determine the addresses of ROMs, RAMs, and ports in a system, a good approach in many cases is to use a worksheet such as that in Figure 7-10. To make one of these worksheets, you start by writing the address bits and the binary weight of each address bit across the top of the paper, as shown in the figure. To make it easier to convert binary addresses to hex, it helps if you mark off the address lines in groups of four, as shown. Next, draw vertical lines which mark off the three address lines that connect to the decoder select inputs (C, B, and A). For the decoder in Figure 7-9, address lines A14, A13, and A12 are connected to the C, B, and A inputs of the decoder, respectively. Then write under each address bit the logic level that must be on that line to address the first location in the first EPROM.

To address the first location in any of the EPROMs, the A0 through A11 address lines must all be low, so put a 0 under each of these address bits on the worksheet. To enable EPROM 0, the select inputs of the decoder must

		HEX DIGIT				HEX DIGIT				HEX DIGIT				HEX DIGIT				HEX EQUIVALENT ADDRESS
		2^{15} A15	2^{14} A14	2^{13} A13	2^{12} A12	2^{11} A11	2^{10} A10	2^9 A9	2^8 A8	2^7 A7	2^6 A6	2^5 A5	2^4 A4	2^3 A3	2^2 A2	2^1 A1	2^0 A0	
BLOCK 1	START	0	0	0	0	0	0	0	0	0	0	0	0	0	0	0	0	= 0000
	END	0	0	0	0	1	1	1	1	1	1	1	1	1	1	1	1	= 0FFF
BLOCK 2	START	0	0	0	1	0	0	0	0	0	0	0	0	0	0	0	0	= 1000
	END	0	0	0	1	1	1	1	1	1	1	1	1	1	1	1	1	= 1FFF
BLOCK 3	START	0	0	1	0	0	0	0	0	0	0	0	0	0	0	0	0	= 2000
	END	0	0	1	0	1	1	1	1	1	1	1	1	1	1	1	1	= 2FFF
BLOCK 4	START	0	0	1	1	0	0	0	0	0	0	0	0	0	0	0	0	= 3000
	END	0	0	1	1	1	1	1	1	1	1	1	1	1	1	1	1	= 3FFF
BLOCK 5	START	0	1	0	0	0	0	0	0	0	0	0	0	0	0	0	0	= 4000
	END	0	1	0	0	1	1	1	1	1	1	1	1	1	1	1	1	= 4FFF
BLOCK 6	START	0	1	0	1	0	0	0	0	0	0	0	0	0	0	0	0	= 5000
	END	0	1	0	1	1	1	1	1	1	1	1	1	1	1	1	1	= 5FFF
BLOCK 7	START	0	1	1	0	0	0	0	0	0	0	0	0	0	0	0	0	= 6000
	END	0	1	1	0	1	1	1	1	1	1	1	1	1	1	1	1	= 6FFF
BLOCK 8	START	0	1	1	1	0	0	0	0	0	0	0	0	0	0	0	0	= 7000
	END	0	1	1	1	1	1	1	1	1	1	1	1	1	1	1	1	= 7FFF

DECODER ADDRESS INPUTS

FIGURE 7-10 Address decoder worksheet showing address decoding for eight 2732s in Figure 7-9.

be all 0's. Since address lines A14, A13, and A12 are connected to these select inputs, they must then all be 0's to enable EPROM 0. Write a 0 under each of these address bits on the worksheet. Since address line A15 is connected to the $\overline{G2A}$ enable input of the decoder, it must be asserted low in order for the decoder to work at all. Write a 0 under the A15 bit on your worksheet. Note that the $\overline{RD}$ signal from the microprocessor control bus is connected to the $\overline{G2B}$ enable input of the decoder. The decoder then will only be enabled during a read operation. This is done to make sure that data cannot accidentally be written to ROM. The G1 enable input of the decoder is permanently asserted by tying it to +5 V because we don't need it for anything else in this circuit.

You can now read the starting address of EPROM 0 directly from the worksheet as 0000H. The highest address in EPROM 0 is that address where A0–A11 are all 1's. If you put a 1 under each of these bits as shown on the worksheet, you can see that the ending address for EPROM 0 is 0FFFH. Remember that A12–A14 have to be low to select EPROM 0. A15 has to be low to enable the decoder. The address range of EPROM 0 is said to be 0000H to 0FFFH, a 4-Kbyte block.

Now let's use the worksheet to determine the address range for EPROM 1. EPROM 1 is enabled when A15 is 0, A14 is 0, A13 is 0, and A12 is 1. For the first address in EPROM 1, address lines A0 through A11 must all be low. Therefore, the starting address of EPROM 1 is 1000H. Its ending address, when A0 through A11 are all 1's, is 1FFFH. If you look at the worksheet in Figure 7-10, you should see that the address ranges for the other six EPROMs in the system are 2000H to 2FFFH, 3000H to 3FFFH, 4000H to 4FFFH, 5000H to 5FFFH, 6000H to 6FFFH, and 7000H to 7FFFH. In this system, then, we use address lines A14, A13, and A12 to select one of eight EPROMs in the overall address range of 0000H to 7FFFH. Some people like to think of address lines A14, A13, and A12 as "counting off" 4096-byte

blocks of memory. If you think of the address lines as the outputs of a 16-bit counter, you can see how this works. The end address for each EPROM has all 1's in address bits A0–A11. When you increment the address to access the next byte in memory, these bits all go to 0, and a 1 rolls over into bits A14, A13, and A12. This increments the count in these 3 bits by 1 and enables the next highest 4096-byte EPROM. The count in these bits goes from binary 000 to 111.

AN EXAMPLE RAM DECODER

The system in Figure 7-9 contains only ROM. In most systems, you want to have ROM, RAM, and ports. To give you more practice with basic address decoding, we will show you now how you can add a decoder for RAM to the system.

Suppose that you want to add eight 2K × 8 RAMs to the system, and you want the first RAM to start at address 8000H, just above the EPROMs, which end at address 7FFFH.

To start, make a worksheet similar to the one in Figure 7-10. Addressing one of the 2048 bytes (2^{11}) in each RAM requires 11 address lines, A0 through A10. These lines will be connected directly to the address inputs on each RAM, so draw a vertical line on the worksheet to indicate this.

The three address lines A11, A12, and A13 will be used to select one of the eight RAMS, so write a 3-bit binary count sequence under these three columns in your worksheet.

We want the RAM to start at address 8000H. For this address, A15 is a 1 and A14 is a 0, so mark these values in the appropriate columns in your worksheet. Your completed worksheet should look like the one in Figure 7-11a, p. 188. Now, let's see how you can implement this truth table with hardware.

Since you want to select one of eight RAM devices, you can use another 74LS138 such as the one we used for

HEX DIGIT				HEX DIGIT				HEX DIGIT				HEX DIGIT				HEX EQUIVALENT ADDRESS	START OF BLOCK
A15	A14	A13	A12	A11	A10	A9	A8	A7	A6	A5	A4	A3	A2	A1	A0		
1	0	0	0	0	0	0	0	0	0	0	0	0	0	0	0	= 8000H	1
1	0	0	0	1	0	0	0	0	0	0	0	0	0	0	0	= 8800H	2
1	0	0	1	0	0	0	0	0	0	0	0	0	0	0	0	= 9000H	3
1	0	0	1	1	0	0	0	0	0	0	0	0	0	0	0	= 9800H	4
1	0	1	0	0	0	0	0	0	0	0	0	0	0	0	0	= A000H	5
1	0	1	0	1	0	0	0	0	0	0	0	0	0	0	0	= A800H	6
1	0	1	1	0	0	0	0	0	0	0	0	0	0	0	0	= B000H	7
1	0	1	1	1	0	0	0	0	0	0	0	0	0	0	0	= B800H	8

DECODER ADDRESS INPUTS

(a)

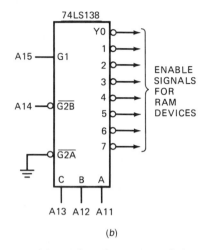

(b)

FIGURE 7-11   Address decoder. (a) Worksheet for eight 2-Kbyte RAMs starting at address 8000H. (b) Schematic for 74LS138 connections.

the EPROMs. You want to select 2048-byte blocks of memory, so address line A11 will be connected to the A input of the decoder, A12 will be connected to the B input of the decoder, and A13 will be connected to the C input of the decoder.

You want the block of RAM selected by the outputs of this decoder to start at address 8000H. For this, address A15 is high and A14 is low. The G1 enable input of the decoder is active high, so you connect it to the A15 address line. This input will then be asserted when A15 is high. You connect the A14 address line to the $\overline{G2A}$ input of the decoder so that this input will be asserted when A14 is low. Because you don't need to use it in this circuit, you can simply tie the $\overline{G2B}$ input of the decoder to ground so that it will be asserted all the time. Figure 7-11b shows the connections for this decoder. Note that you don't connect the 8086 $\overline{RD}$ signal to an enable input on a RAM decoder, because you want to enable the RAMs for both read and write operations.

From the worksheet or truth table in Figure 7-11a, you can quickly determine the address range for each of the RAMs. The first RAM will start at address 8000H. The ending address for this RAM will be at the address where bits A0–A10 are all 1's. If you put 1's under these bits on your worksheet, you should see that the ending address for the first RAM is 87FFH. For practice, work

out the hexadecimal addresses for each of the other seven RAMs. When you finish, compare your results with those in Figure 7-11a. The eight RAMs occupy the address space from 8000H to BFFFH.

AN EXAMPLE PORT DECODER

Figure 7-12a shows how another 74LS138 can be connected in a system to produce chip select signals for some port devices. The truth table or address decoder worksheet in Figure 7-12b shows the system address which corresponds to each of the decoder outputs.

First, note that A15 and A14 must be high to enable the decoder, so these bits are 1's in the worksheet. Then notice that A13 and A12 must be low to enable the decoder, so these columns on the worksheet contain 0's. Finally, address lines A3, A4, and A5 are connected to the decoder select inputs, so we wrote a 3-bit binary count sequence in these columns in the worksheet.

Address lines A0, A1, and A2 will be connected directly to the port devices to address individual ports and control registers in the devices. This is the same idea as connecting the lower address lines directly to a ROM so that we can address one of the bytes stored there.

Address lines A6 through A11 are not connected to the port devices or to the decoder, so they have no effect on selecting a port. We don't care then whether these bits are 1's or 0's. As you will see, these "don't care" bits mean that there are many addresses which will turn on one of the port devices. To give the simplest address for each device, however, we assume that each of these don't care bits is 0. Write 0's under each of these bits on your worksheet. You should now see that the address C000H will cause the Y0 output of the decoder to be asserted. The address C008H will cause the Y1 output of the decoder to be asserted. Using address lines A3, A4, and A5 on the decoder select inputs, then, leaves eight address spaces for each port device.

To see that any one of several different addresses can select one of these port devices, replace the 0 you put under A6 on the first line of your worksheet with a 1. This represents a system address of C040H. A15 and A14 are 1's and A13, A12, A5, A4, and A3 are 0's for this address. Therefore, this address will also cause the Y0 output of the decoder to be asserted. You can try other combinations of 1's and 0's on A6 through A11 if you need to further convince yourself that these bits

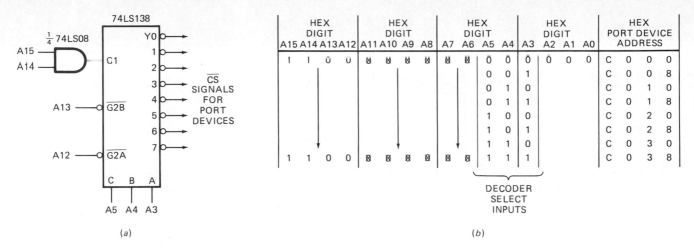

FIGURE 7-12 Adding a port device decoder. (a) Schematic for 74LS138 connections. (b) Address decoder worksheet.

HEX DIGIT A15 A14 A13 A12	HEX DIGIT A11 A10 A9 A8	HEX DIGIT A7 A6 A5 A4	HEX DIGIT A3 A2 A1 A0	HEX PORT DEVICE ADDRESS
1 1 0 0	X X X X	X X 0 0	0 0 0 0	C 0 0 0
		0 0 1		C 0 0 8
		0 1 0		C 0 1 0
		0 1 1		C 0 1 8
		1 0 0		C 0 2 0
		1 0 1		C 0 2 8
		1 1 0		C 0 3 0
1 1 0 0	X X X X	X X 1 1	1 1 1	C 0 3 8

(decoder select inputs = A5 A4 A3)

don't matter when addressing ports. Again, we usually use 0's for these bits to give the simplest address.

Using a decoder which translates memory addresses to chip select signals for port devices is called *memory-mapped I/O*. In this system a port will be written to or read from in the same way as any other memory location. In other words, if this were an 8088 system, you would use an instruction such as MOV AL,DS:BYTE PTR 0C000H to read a byte of data from the first port to the AL register instead of using the MOV DX,0C000H and IN AL,DX instructions. The advantage of memory-mapped I/O is that any instruction which references memory can be used to input data from or output data to ports. In a system such as this, for example, the single instruction ADD AL,DS:BYTE PTR[0C000H] could be used to input a byte of data from the port at address C000H and add the byte to the AL register. The disadvantage of memory-mapped I/O is that some of the system memory address space is used up for ports and is therefore not available for memory.

You can use memory-mapped I/O with any microprocessor, but some microprocessors, such as those of the 8086 family, allow you to set up separate address spaces for input ports and for output ports. You access ports in these separate address spaces directly with the IN and OUT instructions. Having separate address spaces for input and output ports is called *direct I/O*. The advantage of direct I/O is that none of the system memory space is used for ports. The disadvantage is that only the specialized IN and OUT instructions can be used to input or output data.

In a later section of this chapter, we show how direct I/O is done with the 8086, but first we will discuss how the 8086 addresses memory.

8086 and 8088 Addressing and Address Decoding

8086 MEMORY BANKS

The 8086 has a 20-bit address bus, so it can address 2^{20} or 1,048,576 addresses. Each address represents a stored byte. As you know from previous chapters, when you write a word to memory with an instruction such as MOV DS:WORD PTR[437AH],BX, the word is actually written into two consecutive memory addresses. Assuming that DS contains 0000, the low byte of the word is written into the specified memory address, 0437AH, and the high byte of the word is written into the next-higher address, 0437BH. To make it possible to read or write a word with one machine cycle, the memory for an 8086 is set up as two "banks" of up to 524,288 bytes each. Figure 7-13a, p. 190, shows this in diagram form.

One memory bank contains all the bytes which have even addresses such as 00000, 00002, and 00004. The data lines of this bank are connected to the lower eight data lines, D0 through D7, of the 8086. The other memory bank contains all the bytes which have odd addresses such as 00001, 00003, and 00005. The data lines of this bank are connected to the upper eight data lines, D8 through D15, of the 8086. Address line A0 is used as part of the enabling for memory devices in the lower bank. An addressed memory device in this bank will be enabled when address line A0 is low, as it will be for any even address. Address lines A1 through A19 are used to select the desired memory device in the bank and to address the desired byte in that device.

Address lines A1 through A19 are also used to select a desired memory device in the upper bank and to address the desired byte in that bank. An additional part of the enabling for memory devices in the upper bank is a separate signal called *bus high enable*, BHE. BHE is multiplexed out from the 8086 on a signal line at the same time as an address is sent out. An external latch, strobed by ALE, grabs the BHE signal and holds it stable for the rest of the machine cycle, just as is done with addresses. Figure 7-13b shows you the logic level that will be on the BHE and A0 lines for different types of memory accesses.

If you read a byte from or write a byte to an even address such as 00000H, A0 will be low and BHE will be high. The lower bank will be enabled, and the upper bank will be disabled. A byte will be transferred to or from the addressed location in the low bank on D0—

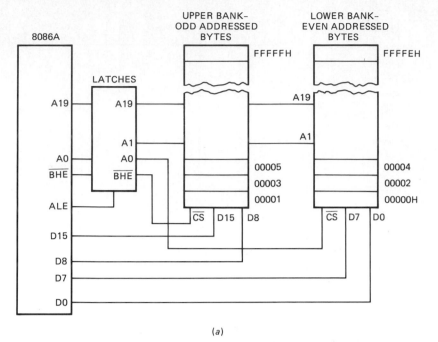

FIGURE 7-13   8086 memory banks. (a) Block diagram. (b) Signals for byte and word operations.

ADDRESS	DATA TYPE	$\overline{\text{BHE}}$	A0	BUS CYCLES	DATA LINES USED
0000	BYTE	1	0	ONE	D0–D7
0000	WORD	0	0	ONE	D0–D15
0001	BYTE	0	1	ONE	D7–D15
0001	WORD	0	1	FIRST	D0–D7
		1	0	SECOND	D7–D15

(b)

D7. For an instruction such as MOV AH,DS:BYTE PTR[0000], the 8086 will automatically transfer the byte of data from the lower data bus lines to AH, the upper byte of the AX register. You just write the instruction and the 8086 takes care of getting the data in the right place.

Now, if the DS register contains 0000H and you use an instruction such as MOV AX,DS:WORD PTR[0000] to read a word from memory into AX, both A0 and $\overline{\text{BHE}}$ will be asserted low. Therefore, both banks will be enabled. The low byte of the word will be transferred from address 00000H to the 8086 on D0–D7. The high byte of the word will be transferred from address 00001H to the 8086 on D8–D15. The 8086 memory, remember, is set up in banks so that words, which have their low byte at an even address, can be transferred to or from the 8086 in one bus cycle. When programming an 8086, then, it is important to start an array of words on an even address for most efficient operation. If you are using an assembler, the EVEN directive is used to do this.

When you use an instruction such as MOV AL,DS: BYTE PTR[0001] to access just a byte at an odd address, A0 will be high and $\overline{\text{BHE}}$ will be asserted low. Therefore, the low bank will be disabled, and the high bank will be

enabled. The byte will be transferred from memory address 00001H in the high bank to the 8086 on lines D8–D15. The 8086 will automatically transfer the byte of data from the higher eight data lines to AL, the low byte of the AX register. Note that address 00001H is actually the first location in the upper bank.

The final case in Figure 7-13b is the one where you want to read a word from or write a word to an odd address. The instruction MOV AX,DS:WORD PTR[0001H] copies the low byte of a word from address 00001 to AL and the high byte from address 00002H to AH. In this case, the 8086 requires two machine cycles to copy the two bytes from memory. During the first machine cycle the 8086 will output address 00001H, assert $\overline{\text{BHE}}$ low, and assert A0 high. The byte from address 00001H will be read into the 8086 on lines D8–D15 and put in AL. During the second machine cycle the 8086 will send out address 00002H. Since this is an even address, A0 will be low. However, since we are accessing only a byte, $\overline{\text{BHE}}$ will be high. The second byte will be read into the 8086 on lines D0–D7 and put in AH. Note that the 8086 automatically takes care of getting a byte to the correct register regardless of which data lines the byte comes in on.

The main reason that the A0 and $\overline{\text{BHE}}$ signals function the way they do is to prevent the writing of an unwanted byte into an adjacent memory location when the 8086 writes a byte. To understand this, think what would happen if both memory banks were turned on for all write operations and you wrote a byte to address 00002 with the instruction MOV DS:BYTE PTR[0002],AL. The data from AL would be written to address 00002 as desired. However, if the upper bank were also enabled, the random data on D8–D15 would be written into address 00003. Since the 8086 is designed so that $\overline{BHE}$ is high during this byte write, the upper bank of memory is not enabled. This prevents the random data on D8–D15 from being written to address 00003.

Now that you have an overview of address decoding and of the 8086 memory banks, let's look at some examples of how all this is put together in a small system.

ROM ADDRESS DECODING ON THE SDK-86

Sheet 1 of the SDK-86 schematics in Figure 7-8 shows the circuit connections for the EPROMs and EPROM decoder. The 2716 EPROMs there are 2K × 8 devices. Two of the EPROMs have their eight data outputs connected in parallel to system data lines D0–D7. These two EPROMs then give 4 Kbytes of storage in the lower memory bank. The other two EPROMs have their data outputs connected in parallel to system data lines D8–D15 to give 4 Kbytes of storage in the upper bank of ROM.

Eleven address lines are needed to address the 2 Kbytes in each device. Therefore, system address lines A1–A11 are connected to all the EPROMs in parallel. Remember that A0 cannot be used to select a byte in the EPROMs because, as we described in the last section, it is used to enable or disable the lower bank.

A 2716 has two enable inputs, $\overline{CE}$ and $\overline{OE}$. In order for the 2716 to output an addressed byte, both of these enable inputs must be asserted low. The $\overline{CE}$ inputs of the two devices in the lower bank are connected to system address line A0, so the $\overline{CE}$ inputs of these devices will be asserted if A0 is low. The $\overline{CE}$ inputs of the two 2716s in the upper bank are connected to the $\overline{BHE}$ line. The $\overline{CE}$ inputs of these devices then will be asserted whenever $\overline{BHE}$ is asserted low. To summarize, then, the two devices labeled A27 and A36 form the lower bank of EPROMs and the two devices labeled A30 and A37 form the upper bank of EPROMs in this system. To see how the $\overline{OE}$ enable input of each of these devices gets asserted and to determine the address that each device will have

in the system, you need to look next at the 3625 address decoder labeled A26 on sheet 1 of Figure 7-8.

A 3625 is a 1K × 4 bipolar PROM which functions as an address decoder, just as the 74LS138 performs in Figures 7-9 and 7-11. Since a 3625 has open collector outputs, a pull-up resistor to +5 V is required on each output. The dotted box around the four resistors on the schematic indicates the four are all contained in one package, resistor pack 5 (RP5). The 3625 translates an address to a signal which is used as part of the enabling of the desired device. Using a PROM as an address decoder, however, is for several reasons much more powerful than using a simple decoder such as the 74LS138. In the first place, the 3625 is programmable, which means that you can move the memory devices to new addresses in memory by simply programming a new PROM. Second, the large number of inputs on the PROM allows you to select a specific area of memory without using external gates. If, for example, you wanted the G2A input of a 74LS138 to be asserted if A11–A15 were all high, you would have to use an external NAND gate to detect this condition. With a PROM, you can just make this condition part of the truth table you use to burn the PROM.

Now, to analyze any address decoder circuit, first determine what signals are required to enable the decoder. The $\overline{CS1}$ enable input of the 3625 EPROM decoder is tied to ground, so it is permanently enabled. The $\overline{CS2}$ enable input is tied to the $\overline{RD}$ signal from the 8086, so that the decoder will only be enabled if the 8086 is doing a read operation. As explained previously, you don't want to accidentally enable a ROM if you send out a wrong address during a write operation.

The next step in analyzing a decoder circuit using a PROM is to consult the manufacturer's manual for the system. You have to do this because, for a PROM, the relationship between the inputs and the outputs cannot be determined directly from the schematic.

Figure 7-14 shows the truth table for the PROM from the SDK-86 manual. This truth table is just a compressed form of writing an address decoder worksheet such as those we used in the previous discussion of address decoding. From the truth table you can see that in order for the O1 output of the 3625 to be asserted low, M/$\overline{IO}$ has to be high. This is reasonable, since this decoder is enabling memory devices, not port devices. Also, address lines A12 through A19 have to be high in order for the O1 output of the PROM to be asserted low. Since the upper eight address bits must all be 1's for the O1 output to be asserted, the lowest address which

PROM INPUTS				PROM OUTPUTS				PROM ADDRESS BLOCK SELECTED
M/$\overline{IO}$	A14–A19	A13	A12	O4	O3	O2	O1	
1	1	1	1	1	1	1	0	FF000H–FFFFFH
1	1	1	0	1	1	0	1	FE000H–FEFFFH
1	1	0	1	1	0	1	1	FD000H–FDFFFH ($\overline{CSX}$)
1	1	0	0	0	1	1	1	FC000H–FCFFFH ($\overline{CSY}$)
ALL OTHER STATES				1	1	1	1	NONE

FIGURE 7-14 Truth table for an SDK-86 ROM decoder PROM (A26).

will cause this is FF000H. If you refer to sheet 1 of the SDK-86 schematics in Figure 7-8, you will see that the O1 output of the decoder PROM connects to the $\overline{OE}$ enable inputs of two of the 2716 EPROMs, A27 and A30. These $\overline{OE}$ outputs then will be enabled whenever the 8086 sends out an address in the range of FF000H to FFFFFH. To fully enable these devices, however, their $\overline{CE}$ inputs must also be asserted.

The $\overline{CE}$ input of the A27 EPROM is connected to system address line A0, so this device will be enabled whenever the 8086 does a memory read from an even address (A0 = 0) in the range FF000H to FFFFEH.

The $\overline{CE}$ enable input of A30 is connected to the system $\overline{BHE}$ line. As shown in Figure 7-13, $\overline{BHE}$ will be asserted low whenever the 8086 accesses a byte at an odd address or a word at an even address. Therefore, the A30 EPROM will be enabled when the 8086 reads a byte from an odd address in the range FF000H to FFFFFH. A30 will also be enabled when the 8086 asserts both A0 and $\overline{BHE}$ low to read a word that starts on an even address in the range FF000H to FFFFFH.

Note in Figure 7-14 and the first sheet of Figure 7-8 that the O2 output of the 3625 decoder PROM will be asserted for addresses in the range of FE000H to FEFFFH. This signal is used as part of the enabling for the A36 and A37 EPROMS. A0 and $\overline{BHE}$ provide the rest of the enabling for these devices, just as we described previously for A27 and A30 devices. For practice, trace these signals on the first sheet of Figure 7-8.

Also note in the first sheet of Figure 7-8 that the 3625 ROM decoder has two unused outputs which can be used as part of the enabling for EPROMs you add to the prototyping section of the board. As shown in Figure 7-14, the address ranges for these two outputs are FD000H to FDFFFH and FC000H to FCFFFH.

The four SDK-86 EPROMs actually contain two monitor programs. One monitor, in devices A27 and A30, allows you to use the hex keypad for entering and running programs. The other monitor, in devices A36 and A37, allows you to use an external CRT terminal to enter and run programs. The EPROMs are put at this high address in memory on the SDK-86 board because, after a RESET, the 8086 goes to address FFFF0H to get its first instruction. Since we want the SDK-86 to execute its monitor program after we press the RESET button, we locate the EPROM containing the monitor program such that this address is in it. You can interchange the actual EPROM devices so that either the keypad monitor or the serial monitor executes when you press the RESET button.

RAM ADDRESS DECODING ON THE SDK-86

To give you another example of memory address decoding in a real system, we now discuss the RAM decoding of the SDK-86 board. Sheet 6 of the SDK-86 schematics in Figure 7-8 shows the circuit for the system RAM and RAM decoder. Let's look at this schematic to see what we can learn from it.

First, take a look at the input and output lines on the 2142 static RAM devices. From the fact that each device has four data I/O lines, you can conclude that the devices store 4-bit words. The fact that each device has 10

address inputs, A0–A9, indicates that each one stores 2^{10} or 1024 of these 4-bit words. To store bytes, two 2142s are enabled in parallel. Devices A38 and A41, for example, are enabled together to store bytes from the lower eight data lines, and devices A43 and A45 are enabled together to store bytes from the upper eight data lines. Note next that the control bus signals $\overline{RD}$, $\overline{WR}$, and M/$\overline{IO}$ are connected to all the 2142s. $\overline{RD}$ is connected to the *output disable*, OD, pin on the 2142s. When the $\overline{RD}$ signal is high or when the device is not enabled, the output buffers will be disabled. During a read operation the $\overline{RD}$ signal is asserted low. If a 2142 is enabled and its OD input is low, the output buffers will be turned on so that an addressed word is output onto the data bus.

$\overline{WR}$ from the 8086 is connected to the *write enable*, $\overline{WE}$, input of the 2142s. If a 2142 is enabled, data on the data bus will be written into the addressed location in the RAM when the 8086 asserts $\overline{WR}$ low.

The 2142s have two *enable* inputs, $\overline{CS1}$ and CS2. The M/$\overline{IO}$ signal from the 8086 is connected to the CS2 input of all the 2142s. Since the CS2 input is active high, it will be asserted whenever the 8086 is doing a memory operation. The $\overline{CS1}$ inputs of the 2142s are connected in pairs to the outputs of a 3625 PROM which functions as an address decoder.

In order to assert any of its outputs and enable some RAM, the 3625 must itself be enabled. Since the $\overline{CS2}$ enable input of the 3625 PROM is tied to ground, it is permanently enabled. The $\overline{CS1}$ enable input will be asserted when system address line A19 is low. To determine any more information about this PROM, you need to look at the truth table for the device. Before we go on to that, however, note that A0 and $\overline{BHE}$ are connected to two of the address inputs on the 3625 PROM. Knowing what you do about 8086 memory banks, why do you think we want A0 and $\overline{BHE}$ to be part of what determines the outputs for this decoder? If you don't have the answer to this question, a look at the truth table for the device in Figure 7-15 should help you.

According to the third line of the truth table/address decoder worksheet in Figure 7-15, the O1 output of the PROM will be asserted low if A12 through A18 are low, A11 is low, $\overline{BHE}$ is high, and A0 is low. The O1 output then will be asserted for even system addresses starting with 00000H. A low on the O1 output will enable the A38 and A41 RAMs, which are connected to the lower half of the data bus. These two devices are part of the lower bank of RAM.

Next, look at the second line of the PROM truth table in Figure 7-15. From this line you should see that the O2 output of the PROM will be asserted low if A12 through A18 are low, A11 is low, $\overline{BHE}$ is low, and A0 is high. The O2 output will then be asserted for odd system addresses starting with 00001H. A low on the O2 output will enable the A43 and A45 RAMs, which are connected on the upper half of the data bus. These two devices are part of the upper bank of RAM.

Now, suppose we want to write a 16-bit word to RAM at an even address. To do this, we want both O1 and O2 to be asserted low so that both the lower-bank RAMs

PROM INPUTS				PROM OUTPUTS				BYTE(S) SELECTED (ADDRESS BLOCK)
A12–A18	A11	$\overline{BHE}$	A0	O4	O3	O2	O1	
0	0	0	0	1	1	0	0	BOTH BYTES (0H–07FFH)
0	0	0	1	1	1	0	1	HIGH BYTE (0H–07FFH)
0	0	1	0	1	1	1	0	LOW BYTE (0H–07FFH)
0	1	0	0	0	0	1	1	BOTH BYTES (0800H–0FFFH)
0	1	0	1	0	1	1	1	HIGH BYTE (0800H–0FFFH)
0	1	1	0	1	0	1	1	LOW BYTE (0800H–0FFFH)
ALL OTHER STATES				1	1	1	1	NONE

FIGURE 7-15   Truth table for an SDK-86 RAM decoder PROM (A29).

and the upper-bank RAMs are enabled. According to the first line of the PROM truth table in Figure 7-15, O1 and O2 will both be asserted low if $\overline{BHE}$ and A0 are both low. Remember from Figure 7-13 that $\overline{BHE}$ and A0 will both be low whenever you write a word to an even address or read a word from an even address. This last case gives the answer to the question we asked earlier about why A0 and $\overline{BHE}$ are connected to the address decoder PROM inputs. The two inputs are required to tell the PROM decoder to assert both O1 and O2 for a word read or write operation.

The address range for the A38, A41, A43, and A45 RAMs is 00000H to 007FFH. Another look at the PROM truth table in Figure 7-15 should show you that RAMS A39, A42, A44, and A46 contain 2 Kbytes more in the range 00800H to 00FFFH. Again, both banks of this additional RAM will be enabled if A0 and $\overline{BHE}$ are both low, as they are for reading or writing a word to an even address.

SDK-86 PORT ADDRESSING AND PORT DECODING

In a previous section of this chapter we described *memory-mapped input/output*. In a system with memory-mapped I/O, port devices are addressed and selected by decoders as if they were memory devices. The main advantage of memory-mapped I/O is that any instruction which refers to memory can theoretically be used to read from or write to a port. The single instruction ADD BH,DS:BYTE PTR[437AH] could be used to read a byte from a memory-mapped port and add the byte read in to the BH register. The disadvantage of memory-mapped I/O is that the ports occupy part of the system memory space. This space is then not available for storing data or instructions.

To avoid having to use part of the system memory space for ports, 8086 family microprocessors have a separate address space for ports. Having a separate address space for ports is called *direct I/O* because this separate address space is accessed directly with the IN and the OUT instructions.

Remember from previous chapters that the 8086 IN and OUT instructions each have two forms, *fixed* port and *variable* port. For fixed-port instructions, an 8-bit port address is written as part of the instruction. The instruction IN AL,38H, for example, copies a byte from port 38H to the AL register. For variable-port input or

output operations, the 16-bit port address is first loaded into the DX register with an instruction such as MOV DX,0FFF8H. The instruction IN AL,DX is then used to copy a byte from port FFF8H to the AL register. MOV DX,0038H followed by IN AL,DX has the same effect as IN AL,38H.

Whenever the 8086 executes an IN or OUT instruction to access a port, none of the segment registers are involved in producing the physical address sent out by the 8086. The port address is sent out directly from the 8086 on lines AD0–AD15, and 0's are output on lines A16–A19.

In an 8086 system which uses direct I/O, the $\overline{M/IO}$ signal is used to enable a memory decoder or a port decoder. Remember that the $\overline{M/IO}$ signal being high was one of the enabling conditions for the SDK-86 ROM and RAM decoders we discussed in previous sections. As you will see, a low on $\overline{M/IO}$ is used to enable a port decoder.

During the execution of an IN instruction, the $\overline{RD}$ signal from the 8086 will be low. This signal can be used to enable an addressed input port device. During execution of an OUT instruction the $\overline{WR}$ signal from the 8086 will be low. This signal can be used to enable an addressed output port device. Since the 8086 outputs up to a 16-bit address for direct I/O operations, it can address any one of 2^{16} or 65,536 input ports and any one of 65,536 output ports.

For an example of how direct I/O ports are addressed and selected in a real system, we will again look at the SDK-86 schematics in Figure 7-8, sheet 7. Here another 3625 PROM, A22, is used to produce the chip select signals for four I/O devices. The O1 output of the PROM is used to enable the 8279 keyboard/display interface device, which we discuss in a section of Chapter 9. The O2 output of the PROM is used to enable the 8251A USART shown on sheet 9 of the schematics. The 8251A allows communication with other systems in serial form. A section in Chapter 14 discusses the operation of this device. The O3 and O4 outputs are connected to two 8255A parallel port devices, shown on sheet 5 of the schematics. These devices can be enabled individually to input or output bytes. They can also be enabled together to input or output words. A section in Chapter 9 shows you how to tell each port in these devices whether you want it to be an input or an output.

Take a look now at the 3625 decoder PROM to determine what conditions enable it. You should find that

PROM INPUTS						PROM OUTPUTS*			
A11–A15	A5–A10	A4	A3	BHE	A0	O4 HIGH PORT SELECT	O3 LOW PORT SELECT	O2 USART SELECT	O1 KDSEL
1	1	0	1	0	0	1	1	1	0
1	1	0	1	1	0	1	1	1	0
1	1	1	0	0	0	1	1	0	1
1	1	1	0	1	0	1	1	0	1
1	1	1	1	0	0	0	0	1	1
1	1	1	1	0	1	0	1	1	1
1	1	1	1	1	0	1	0	1	1
ALL OTHER STATES						1	1	1	1

(a)

PORT ADDRESS	PORT FUNCTION
0000 to FFDF	OPEN
FFE8 E9	READ/WRITE 8279 DISPLAY RAM OR READ 8279 FIFO
EA EB	READ 8279 STATUS OR WRITE 8279 COMMAND
EC ED	RESERVED
EE FFEF	RESERVED
FFF0 F1	READ/WRITE 8251A DATA
F2 F3	READ 8251A STATUS OR WRITE 8251A CONTROL
F4 F5	RESERVED
F6 FFF7	RESERVED
FFF8	READ/WRITE 8255A PORT P2A
F9	READ/WRITE 8255A PORT P1A
FA	READ/WRITE 8255A PORT P2B
FB	READ/WRITE 8255A PORT P1B
FC	READ/WRITE 8255A PORT P2C
FD	READ/WRITE 8255A PORT P1C
FE	WRITE 8255A P2 CONTROL
FFFF	WRITE 8255A P1 CONTROL

(b)

FIGURE 7-16 Truth table and map for SDK-86 port decoder. (a) Truth table. (b) Map.

the $\overline{CS2}$ enable input of the PROM will be asserted when $M/\overline{IO}$ is low, as it is during an input or output operation. Furthermore, you should see that the $\overline{CS1}$ input will be asserted when A11 to A15 are all high. Now, to see what addresses cause each of the PROM outputs to be asserted, refer to the truth table for the PROM in Figure 7-16a. From this figure you can see that to assert the O1 output low, A5 through A15 have to be high, A4 has to be low, A3 has to be high, and A0 has to be low. BHE can be either high or low. Note, however, that only the lower eight data lines, D0–D7, are connected to the 8279. Therefore, data must be sent to or read from the 8279 at an even byte address. In other words, data must be sent as a byte to an even address or as the lower byte of a word to an even address.

The system base address for this device then is FFE8H. System address line A1 is connected to the 8279 to select one of two internal addresses in the device. A1 low

selects one internal address, and A1 high selects the other internal address. A1 low gives system address FFE8H, and A1 high gives system address FFEAH. These are then the two addresses for the 8279 in this system.

According to the truth table in Figure 7-16a, the O2 output of the decoder PROM will be asserted low when A4 through A15 are high and A3 and A0 are low. BHE can be either low or high, but, since only the lower eight data lines are connected to the 8251A USART, data must be sent to or read from the device as bytes at an even address. Again, system address line A1 is used to select one of two internal addresses in the 8251A (Figure 7-8, sheet 9). A1 low selects one internal address and A1 high selects the other internal address. Therefore, the two system addresses for this device are FFF0H and FFF2H.

Now, before discussing the O3 and O4 outputs of the decoder PROM, we will take a brief look at the two 8255 parallel port devices they enable. These devices are shown on sheet 5 of the schematics in Figure 7-8. Each of these devices contains three 8-bit parallel ports and a control register. System address lines A1 and A2 are used to address the desired port or register in the device, just as lower address lines are used to address the desired internal location in a memory device. Note that the lower eight data lines, D0–D7, are connected to the A40 device, and the upper eight data lines are connected to the A35 device. This is done so that you have several input or output possibilities. You can read a byte from or write a byte to an even-addressed port in device A40. You can read a byte from or write a byte to an odd-addressed port in device A35. You can read a word from or write a word to a 16-bit port made up from an 8-bit port from device A40 and an 8-bit port from device A35. To input or output a word, both devices have to be enabled. Now let's look at the decoder truth table to determine what addresses enable the various ports in these devices.

The A40 device will be enabled by the O3 output of the 3625 decoder PROM if address lines A3 through A15 are high and A0 is low. A1 and A2 are used to select internal ports of the 8255A. Let's assume that these two bits are 0 for the first address in the device. To select the A port in the A40 8255A, address lines A1 and A2 have to be low. The system address that will enable this device and select the A port within it is FFF8H. Other values of A2 and A1 will select one of the other ports or the control register in this device. Figure 7-16b shows the system addresses for the ports and control register in this 8255. Note that the ports in this device (A40) are identified as port 2A, port 2B, and port 2C. These all have even addresses because A0 must be low for this device to be selected.

The A35 8255A, which contains port 1A, port 1B, and port 1C, will be enabled by the O4 output of the decoder PROM if A3 through A15 are high and the BHE line is low. If this 8255A is being enabled for a byte read or write, then the A0 line will also be high. A2 and A1 are again used to address one of the ports or the control register within the 8255A. A2 = 0 and A1 = 1 will select port 1A in this 8255A. As shown in Figure 7-16b, then, the system address for port 1A is FFF9H. Port 1B will be accessed with a system address of FFFBH, port 1C will be accessed with a system address of FFFDH, and the internal control register will be accessed with a system address of FFFFH.

As we said before, the 8086 can input a 16-bit value in one operation by enabling a port device on the lower half of the data bus and a port device on the upper half

of the data bus at the same time. When the 8086 on an SDK-86 board executes the instruction sequence MOV DX,FFF8H–IN AX,DX, both A0 and BHE will be low during the IN instruction. As shown by the fifth line in the truth table, this will cause both the O3 and the O4 outputs of the port decoder to be low. These signals will enable both the A40 and A35 port devices. The byte of data on port 2A will be input to the 8086 on the lower half of the data bus, and the byte of data on port 1A will be input to the 8086 on the upper half of the data bus.

Note in the truth table in Figure 7-16a that the 3625 PROM decoder will enable a port device only when the specific address assigned to that device is sent out by the 8086. This is sometimes called *complete decoding* because all the address lines play a part in selecting a device and one of its internal ports or registers. As we show in Chapter 8, adding another decoder to produce enable signals for more port devices is very easy in a system which uses this complete decoding.

THE SDK-86 "OFF-BOARD" DECODER

Take a look at the *off-board circuitry* in zone A5 on sheet 5 of the SDK-86 schematics. The purpose of this circuitry is to produce the signal OFF BOARD whenever the 8086 sends out a memory or port address which does not correspond to a device decoded on the board. The OFF BOARD signal will be asserted low if pin 4 of the A3 NAND gate is low or if pin 5 of the A3 NAND gate is low. According to the truth table for the A12 PROM in Figure 7-17, the O1 output will be low if the 8086 is doing a memory operation and the address sent out is not in one of the ranges decoded for the onboard RAM or ROM.

In order for pin 4 of the A3 NAND gate to be low, both pin 9 and pin 10 of the A3 NAND gate must be high. Pin 10 will be high if the 8086 is doing an input or output operation (IO/M from the 8286 inverting buffer equals 1). Pin 9 of the A3 NAND gate will be high if any one of the A19 NAND gate inputs is low. Since system address lines A5 through A15 are connected to the inputs of the 74LS133 NAND gate, the signal to pin 9 of A3 will be high for any address less than FFE0H. In other words, pin 4 of the A3 NAND gate will be asserted low for any I/O operation in an address range not selected by the A22 port decoder.

The OFF BOARD signal produced by the previously discussed PROM and logic gates is connected to an input of a NAND gate labeled A2 on sheet 2 of the schematics. If OFF BOARD is asserted low, or INTA is asserted low, or HLDA is asserted low, the output of this gate will be high. For now, all we are interested in is the fact that if OFF BOARD is asserted low, a high will be applied to

PROM INPUTS									PROM OUTPUT (O1)	CORRESPONDING ADDRESS BLOCK
M/IO	A19	A18	A17	A16	A15	A14	A13	A12		
1	0	0	0	0	0	0	0	0	1 (INACTIVE)	0H–0FFFH (ON-BOARD RAM)
1	1	1	1	1	1	1	1	0	1 (INACTIVE)	FE000H–FEFFFH (ON-BOARD PROM)
1	1	1	1	1	1	1	1	1	1 (INACTIVE)	FF000H–FFFFFH (ON-BOARD PROM)
ALL OTHER STATES									0 (ACTIVE)	01000H–FDFFFH (OFF-BOARD)

FIGURE 7-17   SDK-86 off-board decoder PROM truth table.

pin 1 of the A3 NAND gate in zone A4 of the schematic. If the $\overline{\text{DEN}}$ signal from the 8086 is also asserted low, the signal labeled $\overline{\text{BUFFER ON}}$ will be asserted low. The $\overline{\text{DEN}}$ signal from the 8086 will be asserted whenever the 8086 reads in data from a memory location or a port or when it writes data to a memory location or a port. The $\overline{\text{BUFFER ON}}$ signal produced here is used to enable the 8286 data bus buffers (A6 and A7) shown on sheet 4 of the schematics. Now here's the point of all this.

In the next chapter we show you how to add another I/O decoder and some other devices to the prototyping area of an SDK-86 board. To drive these additional devices, the address, data, and control buses must all be buffered. The address bus on the SDK-86 board is buffered by the 74S373 address latches shown on sheet 3 of the schematics. Data bus and control bus buffers are not needed to drive the ROM, RAM, and port devices that come with the SDK-86 board. To read data from or write data to external devices, however, the data bus is buffered by two 8286s, shown as A7 and A6 on sheet 4 of the SDK-86 schematics. These two buffers are turned on when the $\overline{\text{BUFFER ON}}$ signal, described in the preceding paragraph, is asserted low. The 8286 buffers are bidirectional. When these buffers are enabled, the *Data Transmit/Receive* signal, DT/$\overline{\text{R}}$, from the 8086 will determine in which direction the buffers are pointed. If DT/$\overline{\text{R}}$ is high, the buffers will be enabled to write data to some external device. If DT/$\overline{\text{R}}$ is low, the buffers will be enabled to read data in from some external device.

The control bus signals are buffered by an 8286 labeled A11 and a 74LS244 labeled A8 on sheet 4 of the SDK-86 schematics. These buffers are permanently enabled to send out the control bus signals except during a HOLD state, which we will explain later.

THE SDK-86 WAIT-STATE GENERATOR CIRCUITRY

Now that you know how the $\overline{\text{OFF BOARD}}$ signal is produced on the SDK-86 board, we can explain the operation of the *WAIT-state generator circuitry* shown on sheet 2 of the schematics.

In a previous section of the chapter we showed you that if the RDY input of the 8086 is asserted low, the 8086 will insert one or more WAIT states in the machine cycle it is currently executing. Figure 7-1b shows how a WAIT state is inserted in an 8086 machine cycle. During a WAIT state, the information on the buses is held constant. The signal levels on the buses at the start of the WAIT state remain there throughout the WAIT state. The main purpose of inserting one or more WAIT states in a machine cycle is to give an addressed memory device or I/O device more time to accept or output data. In the next major section of the chapter, we show you how to determine whether a WAIT state is needed for a given device with a given 8086 clock frequency. For now, however, let's just see how the circuitry on the SDK-86 board causes the 8086 to insert a selected number of WAIT states.

WAIT states are inserted by pulling the RDY1 input of the 8284 clock generator IC low (Figure 7-8, sheet 2, zone D5). The 8284 internally synchronizes the RDY1 input signal with the clock signal and sends the resultant signal to the RDY input of the 8086. For the SDK-86,

the RDY1 input will be asserted low if all three inputs of the A15 NAND gate shown in zone D5 of the schematic are high. Pin 10 of this device is tied to $+5$ V, so it is permanently high. Pin 11 of A15 will be high if any of the inputs of the NAND gate in zone D7 are asserted low. Pin 1 of gate A15 will be low whenever the 8086 does an input or output operation. Pin 2 of gate A15 will be low whenever the 8086 accesses a port or memory location which is not decoded on the board. In other words, with these connections, the selected number of WAIT states will be inserted in each machine cycle when the 8086 does a read from or a write to an on-board I/O device or when the 8086 does a read from or a write to any device not decoded on the board. If jumper W39 is installed on pin 13 of A15, pin 11 of A15 will always be high. The number of WAIT states selected by the W27–W34 jumpers will be inserted for all read and write operations.

The desired number of WAIT states to be inserted is selected by putting a jumper between two pins in the W27–W34 matrix shown in zone D3 (sheet 2) of the schematic. If a jumper is installed in the W27 position, for example, no WAIT states will be inserted. If a jumper is installed in the W28 position, one WAIT state will be inserted. The pattern continues to jumper W34, which will cause seven WAIT states to be inserted in each machine cycle. Here's how the WAIT-state generator itself works.

The 74LS164 WAIT-state generator is an 8-bit shift register. At the start of a machine cycle, the $\overline{\text{RD}}$, $\overline{\text{WR}}$, and $\overline{\text{INTA}}$ signals from the 8086 are all high. These three signals being high will cause the A2 NAND gate in zone C4 to assert the clear input, CLR, of the shift register. The outputs of the shift register will then all be low. One of these lows will be coupled through a jumper and an inverter to pin 9 of the A15 NAND gate we discussed previously. This high on pin 9, together with a high on pin 11, will cause the RDY1 input of the 8284 to be pulled low. However, WAIT states will not be inserted unless RDY1 remains low long enough. Now, when $\overline{\text{RD}}$, $\overline{\text{WR}}$, or $\overline{\text{INTA}}$ goes low in the machine cycle, the $\overline{\text{CLR}}$ input of the 74LS164 shift register will go high, and the shift register will function normally. The highs on the INA and INB inputs will be loaded onto the QA output on the next positive edge of the clock. If the WAIT-state jumper is in the W27 position, then this high on the QA output will, through the inverter and NAND gate, cause the RDY1 input of the 8284 to go high again. For this case, the RDY1 input goes high soon enough that no WAIT states are inserted.

The high loaded into the 74LS164 shift register is shifted one stage to the right by each successive clock pulse. When the high reaches the jumper connected to the A25 inverter, it will cause the RDY1 input of the 8284 to go high. The 8086 will then exit from a WAIT state on the next clock pulse. The number of WAIT states inserted in a machine cycle is determined by how many stages the high has to be shifted before it reaches the installed jumper.

To summarize all this, the 8086 will insert the selected number of WAIT states in any machine cycle which accesses any device not addressed on the board or any

I/O device on the board. If jumper W39 is inserted, the selected number of WAIT states will be inserted for any onboard or off-board access. The purpose of inserting WAIT states is to give the addressed device more time to accept or output data.

How the 8088 Microprocessor Accesses Memory and Ports

Now that we have shown in detail how the 8086 accesses memory and port devices, we can show you how the 8088 does it.

In Chapter 2 we mentioned that the 8088 is the CPU used in the original IBM PC and the IBM PC/XT. The instruction set of the 8088 is identical to that of the 8086, and the registers of the two are the same, but there are two major differences between the two devices. First, the 8088 instruction byte queue is only 4 bytes long instead of 6. Second, and more important, the 8088 memory is not divided into two banks as the 8086 memory is; it consists of a single bank of up to 1,048,576 bytes, as shown in Figure 7-18.

As you can see, the 8088 has only an 8-bit data bus, D0–D7. All the memory devices and ports in an 8088 system are connected onto these eight lines. Address lines A0 through A19 are used with some decoders to select a desired byte in memory. The 8088 does not produce the $\overline{BHE}$ signal because it is not needed. This single bank structure means that an 8088 can read or write only a byte at a time. Therefore, an 8088 must always do two machine cycles to read or write a word. The 8088 was designed with an 8-bit data bus so that it would interface more easily with 8-bit memory devices and I/O devices.

8086 Timing Parameters

In previous sections of this chapter, we used generalized timing waveforms such as that in Figure 7-1b. These diagrams are sufficient to show the sequence of activities on the 8086 buses. However, they are not detailed enough to determine, for example, whether a memory device is fast enough to work in a given 8086 system. To allow you to make precise timing calculations, manu-

facturers' data books give detailed timing waveforms and lists of timing parameters for each microprocessor. Complete timing information for the 8086 is contained in the data sheet in Appendix A. Figure 7-19, pp. 198-9, shows some timing waveforms and parameters for an 8086 minimum-mode read machine cycle.

As you look at Figure 7-19a, remember the *5-minute freak-out rule.* Most of the time there are only a very few of these parameters that you need to worry about. In most systems, for example, you don't need to worry about the clock signal parameters, because an 8284 clock generator and a crystal will be used to produce the clock signal. The frequency of the clock signal from an 8284 is always one-third the resonant frequency of the crystal connected to it. The 8284 is designed to guarantee the correct clock period, clock time low, clock time high, etc., as long as the correct suffix number part is used. The 8284A, for example, can be used in an 8-MHz system, but a faster part, the 8284A-1, must be used for a system where a 10-MHz clock is desired.

The edges of the clock signal cause operations in the 8086 to occur; therefore, as you can see in Figure 7-19a, the clock waveform is used as a reference for other times. The timing values for when the 8086 puts out M/$\overline{IO}$, addresses, ALE, and control signals, for example, are all specified with reference to an appropriate clock edge.

As we mentioned earlier, one of the main things you use these diagrams and parameters for is to find out whether a particular memory or port device is fast enough to work in a system with a given clock frequency. Here's an example of how you do this.

If you look in zone C5 of sheet 2 of the SDK-86 schematics, you will see that if jumper W41 is installed, the 8086 will receive a 4.9-MHz clock signal from the 8284. If jumper W40 is installed, the 8086 will receive the 2.45-MHz PCLK signal from the 8284. Now, suppose that you want to determine whether the 2716 EPROMs on the SDK-86 board will work correctly with no WAIT states if you install jumper W41 to run the 8086 with the 4.9-MHz clock.

First, you look up the access times for the 2716 EPROM in the appropriate data book. According to an Intel data book, the 2716 has a maximum address to output access time, t_{ACC}, of 450 ns. This means that if the 2716 is already enabled and its output buffers are turned on, it will put valid data on its outputs no more than 450 ns after an address is applied to the address inputs. The 2716 data sheet also gives a chip enable to output access time, t_{CE}, of 450 ns. This means that if an address is already present on the address inputs of the 2716 and the output buffers are already enabled, the 2716 will put valid data on its outputs no later than 450 ns after the $\overline{CE}$ input is asserted low. A third parameter given for the 2716 in the data book is an output enable to output time, t_{OE}, of 120 ns maximum. This means that if the device already has an address on its address inputs, and its $\overline{CE}$ input is already asserted, valid data will appear on the output pins at most 120 ns after the $\overline{OE}$ pin is asserted low.

Now that you have these three parameters for the 2716, the next step is to check whether each one of

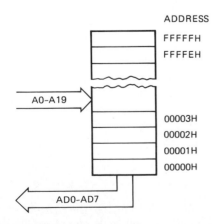

FIGURE 7-18   8088 memory structure.

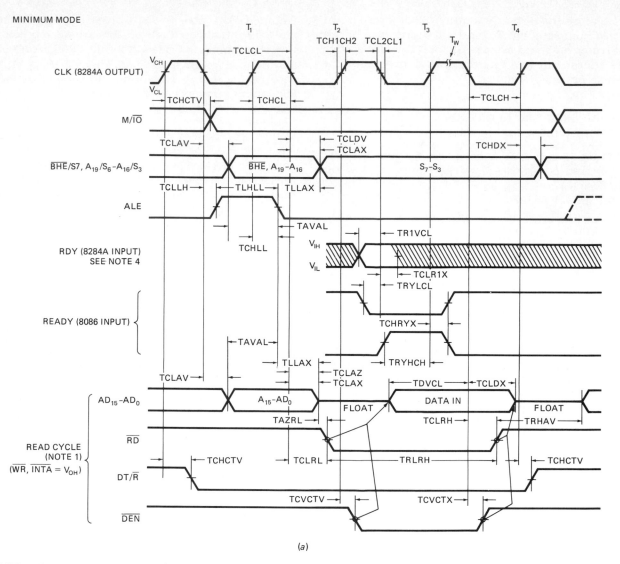

(a)

FIGURE 7-19 8086 minimum-mode timing waveforms and parameters. (a) Read waveforms. (*See also next page.*)

these times is short enough for the device to work with a 4.9-MHz 8086. In other words, does the 2716 put out valid data soon enough after it is addressed and enabled to satisfy the requirements of the 8086? To determine this, you need to look at both the 8086 timing parameters and how the 2716 is addressed and enabled on the SDK-86 board.

To make it easier for you to find the important parameters for these calculations, we show in Figure 7-19b a simplified version of the timing diagram in Figure 7-19a. You should try to do this simplification mentally whenever you are faced with a timing diagram. As shown by the timing diagram in Figure 7-19b, the 8086 sends out M/$\overline{\text{IO}}$, $\overline{\text{BHE}}$, and an address during T_1 of the machine cycle. Note on the AD15–AD0 lines of the timing diagram that the 8086 outputs this information within a time labeled TCLAV after the falling edge of the clock at the start of T_1. TCLAV stands for *time from clock low to address valid*. According to the 8086 column of the data sheet shown in Figure 7-19c, the maximum value of this time is 110 ns.

Now look further to the right on the AD15–AD0 lines. You should see that valid data must arrive at the 8086 from memory a time TDVCL before the falling edge of the clock at the end of T_3. TDVCL stands for *time data must be valid before clock goes low*. The data sheet gives a value of 30 ns for this parameter.

The time between the end of the TCLAV interval and the start of the TDVCL interval is the time available for getting the address to the memory and for the t_{ACC} of the memory device. You can determine this time by subtracting TCLAV and TDVCL from the time for three clock cycles. With a 4.9-MHz clock, each clock cycle will be 204 ns. Three clock cycles then total 612 ns. Subtracting a TCLAV of 110 ns and a TDVCL of 30 ns leaves 472 ns available for getting the address to the 2716 and for its t_{ACC}. To help you visualize these times, Figure 7-20a, p. 200, shows this operation in simplified diagram form.

If you look at sheets 1 and 3 of the SDK-86 schematics, you should see that the $\overline{\text{BHE}}$ signal and the A0–A11 address information go from the 8086 through the

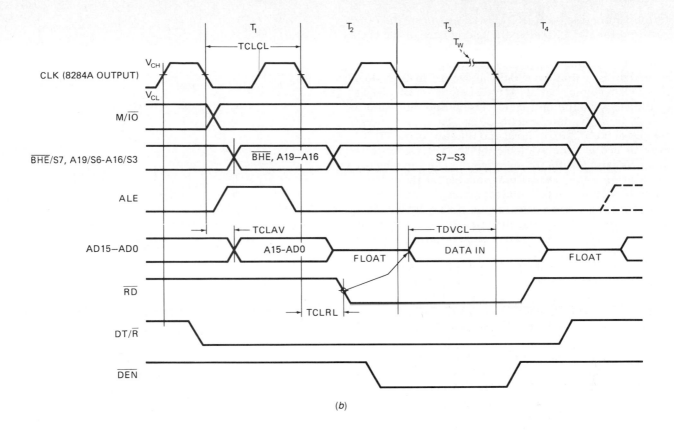

(b)

MINIMUM COMPLEXITY SYSTEM TIMING REQUIREMENTS

SYMBOL	PARAMETER	8086		8086-1 (Preliminary)		8086-2		UNITS
		MIN.	MAX.	MIN.	MAX.	MIN.	MAX.	
TCLCL	CLK Cycle Period	200	500	100	500	125	500	ns
TDVCL	Data in Setup Time	30		5		20		ns
TCLAV	Address Valid Delay	10	110	10	50	10	60	ns
TCLRL	$\overline{RD}$ Active Delay	10	165	10	70	10	100	ns

NOTE: Complete timing information in Appendix

(c)

FIGURE 7-19 (*continued*) (b) Simplified read waveforms. (c) Timing parameters. (*Intel Corporation*)

74S373 latches to get to the 2716s. The propagation delay of the 74S373s then must be subtracted from the 472 ns to determine how much time is actually available for the t_{ACC} of the 2716. The maximum delay of a 74S373 is 12 ns. As shown in Figure 7-20a, subtracting this from the 472 ns leaves 460 ns for the t_{ACC} of the 2716. Now, as we told you in a previous paragraph, the 2716 has a maximum t_{ACC} of 450 ns. Since 450 ns is less than the 460 ns available, you know that the t_{ACC} of the 2716 is acceptable for the SDK-86 operating with a 4.9-MHz clock. You still, however, must check if the values of t_{CE} and t_{OE} for the 2716 are acceptable.

If you look at sheet 1 of the SDK-86 schematics, you should see that the $\overline{CE}$ inputs of the 2716s are connected either to A0 or to $\overline{BHE}$. The timing for these signals is the same as that for the addresses in the preceding section. As shown in Figure 7-20a, the time available for t_{CE} of the 2716 will be 460 ns. Since the maximum

t_{CE} of the 2716 is 450 ns, you know that this parameter is also acceptable for an SDK-86 operating with a 4.9-MHz clock.

The final parameter to check is t_{OE} of the 2716. According to sheet 1 of the SDK-86 schematics, the $\overline{OE}$ signals for the 2716s are produced by the 3625 decoder. The signals coming to this decoder are A12 through A19, $M/\overline{IO}$, and $\overline{RD}$. Look at the 8086 timing diagram in Figure 7-19b to see if you can determine which of these signals arrives last at the 3625. You should find that addresses and $M/\overline{IO}$ are sent out during T_1, but $\overline{RD}$ is not sent out until T_2. As indicated by the arrow from the falling edge of the $\overline{RD}$ signal, $\overline{RD}$ going low causes the address decoder to send an $\overline{OE}$ signal to the 2716 EPROMs. Since $\overline{RD}$ is sent out so much later than addresses, it will be the limiting factor for timing. $\overline{RD}$ going low and the EPROM returning valid data must occur within the time of states T_2 and T_3. Now, according to the timing diagram, $\overline{RD}$ is sent out from the 8086 within a time TCLRL after the falling edge of the clock at the start of T_2. From the data sheet, the maximum value of TCLRL is 165 ns. As we discussed before, the 8086 requires that valid data arrive on AD0 through AD15 from memory a time TDVCL before the falling edge of the clock at the end of T_3. The minimum value of TDVCL from the data sheet is 30 ns. The time between the end of the TCLRL interval and the start of the TDVCL interval is the time available for the $\overline{OE}$ signal to be produced and for the $\overline{OE}$ signal to turn on the memory. To determine the actual time available for these operations, first compute the time for states T_2 and T_3. For a 4.9-MHz clock, each clock cycle or state will be 204 ns, so the two together total 408 ns. Then subtract the TCLRL of 165 ns and the TDVCL of 30 ns. As shown by the simple diagram in Figure 7-20b, this leaves 213 ns available for the decoder delay and the t_{OE} of the 2716. Checking a data sheet for the 3625 would show you that it has a maximum $\overline{CS2}$ to output delay of 30 ns. Subtract this from the available 213 ns to see how much time is left for the t_{OE} of the 2716. The result of this subtraction is 183 ns.

As we indicated in a previous paragraph, the 2716 has a maximum t_{OE} of 120 ns. Since this time is considerably less than the 183 ns available, the 2716 has an acceptable t_{OE} value for operating on the SDK-86 board with a 4.9-MHz clock.

All three times for the 2716 are less than those required by the 8086 for 5-MHz operation, so you know that the devices will work correctly at 4.9 MHz without inserting a WAIT state. You could use a logic analyzer as we described earlier in the chapter to verify the timing on an actual SDK-86 board.

Here's a final point about calculating the time available for t_{ACC}, t_{CE}, and t_{OE} of some device in a system. Suppose that you want to add another pair of 2716 EPROMs in the prototyping area of the SDK-86 board, and you want to enable the outputs of these added devices with the O3 output of the 3625 ROM decoder on sheet 1 of the schematics. The timing for these added devices will be the same as for the previously discussed 2716s, except that the data from the added devices must come back through the 8286 buffers shown on sheet 4 of the SDK-86 schematics. According to an 8286 data sheet, these buffers have a maximum delay of 30 ns. This 30 ns must be subtracted from the times available for t_{ACC}, t_{CE}, and t_{OE}. If you look back at our calculations of the time available for t_{ACC} in Figure 7-20a, for example, you will see that we ended up with 460 ns available for t_{ACC}. Subtracting the 30 ns of buffer delay from this leaves only 430 ns, which is considerably less than the maximum t_{ACC} of 450 ns for the 2716. This tells you that, because of the buffer delay, the added 2716s are not fast enough to operate on an SDK-86 board with a 4.9-MHz clock and no WAIT states. To take care of this problem, the SDK-86 is designed so that any access to a memory or I/O device "off board" will cause the selected number of WAIT states to be inserted in the machine cycle. For our example here, selecting one WAIT state with jumper W28 on sheet 2 will give another 204 ns for the data to get from the 2716s to the 8086. This is more than

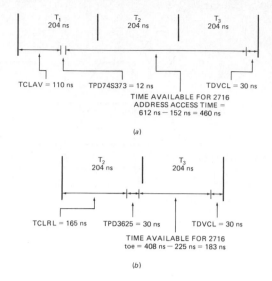

FIGURE 7-20 Calculations of maximum allowable access times for 4.9-MHz 8086. (a) Time for t_{ACC} and t_{RD}. (b) Time for t_{OE}.

enough time to compensate for the buffer delay, so the added 2716s will work correctly.

TROUBLESHOOTING A SIMPLE 8086-BASED MICROCOMPUTER

Now that you have some knowledge of the software and the hardware of a microcomputer system, we can start teaching you how to troubleshoot a simple microcomputer system such as an SDK-86 board. For this section assume that the microcomputer or microprocessor-based instrument previously worked. Later sections of this book will describe how the prototype of a microprocessor-based instrument is developed.

The following sections describe a series of steps that we have found effective in troubleshooting various microcomputer systems. The first point to impress on your mind about troubleshooting a microcomputer is that a systematic approach is almost always more effective than random poking, probing, and hoping. You don't, for example, want to spend 2 hours troubleshooting a system and finally find that the only problem is that the power supply is putting out only 3 V instead of 5 V. Use the following list of steps or a list of your own each time you have to troubleshoot a microcomputer: (1) Identify the symptoms, (2) make a careful visual and tactile inspection, (3) check the power supply, (4) do a "signal roll call," (5) systematically substitute socketed ICs, and (6) troubleshoot soldered-in ICs. The following paragraphs describe each step.

Identify the Symptoms

Make a list of the symptoms that you find or those that a customer describes to you. Find out, for example, whether the symptom is present immediately when the power is turned on or whether the system must operate for a while before the symptom shows up. If someone else describes the symptoms to you, check them yourself, or have that person demonstrate the symptoms to you. This allows you to check if the problem is with the machine or with how the person is attempting to use the machine.

Make a Careful Visual and Tactile Inspection

This step is good for preventive maintenance as well for finding a current problem. Check for components that have been or are excessively hot. When touching components to see if any are too hot, do it gently, because a bad IC can get hot enough to give a nasty burn if you keep your finger on it too long.

Check to see that all ICs are firmly seated in their sockets and that the ICs have no bent pins. Vibration can cause ICs to work loose in their sockets. A bent pin may make contact for a while, but after heating, cooling, and vibration, it may no longer make contact. Also, inexpensive IC sockets may oxidize with age and no longer make good contact.

Check for broken wires and loose connectors. A thin film of dust, etc., may form on printed-circuit-board edge connectors and prevent them from making dependable contact. The film can be removed by gently rubbing the edge connector fingers with a cleaning pad available for this purpose. If the microcomputer has ribbon cables, check to see if they have been moved around or stressed. Ribbon cables have small wires that are easily broken. If you suspect a broken conductor in a ribbon cable, you can later make an ohmmeter check to verify your suspicions.

Check the Power Supply

From the manual for the microcomputer, determine the power supply voltages. Check the supply voltage(s) directly on the appropriate pins of some ICs to make sure the voltage is actually getting there. Check with a scope to make sure the power supplies do not have excessive noise or ripple. One microcomputer that we were called on to troubleshoot had very strange symptoms caused by 2-V peak-to-peak ripple on the 5-V supply.

Do a Signal Roll Call

The next step is to make a quick check of some key signals around the CPU of the microcomputer. If the problem is a bad IC, this can help point you toward the one that is bad. First, check if the clock signal is present and at the right frequency. If not, perhaps the clock generator IC is bad. If the microcomputer has a clock but doesn't seem to be doing anything, use an oscilloscope to check if the CPU is putting out control signals such as $\overline{RD}$, $\overline{WR}$, and ALE. Also, check the least significant data bus line to see if there is any activity on the buses. If there is no activity on these lines, a common cause is that the CPU is stuck in a wait, hold, halt, or reset

condition by the failure of some TTL devices. To check this out, use the manual to help you predict what logic level should be on each of the CPU input control signals for normal operation. The RDY input of the 8086, for example, should be high for normal operation. If an external logic gate fails and holds RDY low, the 8086 will go on inserting WAIT states forever, and the buses will be held constant. If the 8086 HOLD input is stuck high or the RST input is held high, the 8086 address/data bus will be floating. Connecting a scope probe to these lines will pull them to ground, so you will see them as constant lows.

If there is activity on the buses, use an oscilloscope to see if the CPU is putting out control signals such as $\overline{RD}$ and $\overline{WR}$. Also, check with your oscilloscope to see if select signals are being generated on the outputs of the ROM, RAM, and port decoders as the system attempts to run its monitor or basic program. If no select signals are being produced, then the address decoder may be bad or the CPU may not be sending out the correct addresses.

After a little practice, you should be able to work through the previously described steps quite quickly. If you have not located the problem at this point, the next step for a system with its ICs in sockets is to systematically substitute known good ICs for those in the nonworking system.

Systematically Substitute Socketed ICs

The easiest case of substitution is that where you have two identical microcomputers, one that works and one that doesn't, and the ICs of both units are in sockets. For this case you can use the working system to test the ICs from the nonworking system. The trick here is to do this in such a way that you don't end up with two systems that do not work! Here's how you do it.

First of all, *do not remove or insert any ICs with the power on!* With the power off, remove the CPU from the good system and put it in a piece of conductive foam. Plug the CPU from the bad system into the now empty socket on the good board and turn on the power. If the good system still works, then the CPU is probably good. Turn off the power and put the CPU back in the bad system. If the good system does not work with the CPU from the bad system, then the CPU is probably bad. Remove it from the good system and bend the pins so that you know it is bad. If the CPU seems bad, you can try replacing it with the CPU you removed from the good system. If you do this, however, it is important that you keep track of which IC came from which system. To do this, we like to mark each IC from the good system with a wide-tip, water-soluble marking pen. We can then rebuild the good system by simply putting back all the marked ICs. The marks on the ICs can easily be removed with a damp cloth.

The procedure from here on is to keep testing ICs from the bad system until you find all the bad ICs. Make sure you turn the power off before you remove or insert any ICs. Be aware that more than one IC may be bad. It is not unusual, for example, for an AC power line surge to wipe out several devices in a system. We usually work our way out from the CPU to address latches, buffers, decoders, and memory devices. Often the specific symptoms point you to the problem group of ICs without your having to test every IC in the system. If, for example, the system accesses ROM but doesn't access RAM, suspect the RAM decoder. If a system uses buffers on the buses, suspect these devices. Buffers are high-current devices, and they often fail.

Troubleshoot Soldered-in ICs

The approach described in the preceding paragraphs works well if the system ICs are all in sockets and you have two identical systems. However, since sockets add to the cost and unreliability of a system, many small systems put only the CPU and ROMs in sockets. This makes your troubleshooting work harder but not impossible.

Again, if you have two identical systems, one that works and one that doesn't work, you can attempt to run the monitor or basic system program on each and compare signals on the two. A missing or wrong signal may point you to the bad IC or ICs.

If the system works enough to read some instructions from ROM and execute them, you can replace the monitor or basic system ROM with one that contains diagnostic programs which test RAM and I/O devices. A RAM test routine, for example, might attempt to write all 1's to each RAM location and then read each memory location to see if the data was written correctly to that location. If the data read back is not correct, the diagnostic program can stop and in some way indicate the address that it could not write to. If a write of all 1's is successful, then the test routine will try to write all 0's to each memory location. A port test routine might initialize a port for output and then write alternating 1's and 0's to the port over and over again. With an oscilloscope you can see if the port device is getting enabled and if the data is getting to the output of the port device. Another port test routine might try to read a byte of data in from a port over and over so that you can again see if the device is getting enabled and if the data is getting through the device to the system data bus. The technique of using program routines to test hardware is a very important one that you will use many times when you are working with microcomputer systems.

Now, suppose that you have localized the problem to a few ICs that are soldered in. If the problem is one that occurs when the unit gets hot, you might try spraying some cold spray on the ICs, one at a time, to see if you can determine which one has a problem. If this does not find the bad IC or the problem is not heat-related, what you do next is replace these ICs one at a time until the system works correctly. The point we want to stress here is that the cost of these few ICs is probably much less than the cost of the time it would take you to determine just which IC is bad, if you do not have specialized test equipment.

If you do not have special tools available to remove a "through-hole mounted" IC from a printed-circuit board, do not attempt to desolder pins with a hand-held solder

"slurper." Modern multilayer printed-circuit boards are quite fragile, and these tools can slip and knock a trace right off the board. Instead, use cutters with narrow tips to cut all the leads of the IC next to the body. Since you are going to throw it out anyway, you don't care if you destroy the IC. With the body of the IC out of the way, you can then gently heat each pin individually and use needle-nose pliers to remove it from the PC board. If the hole fills with solder, heat it gently and insert a small wooden toothpick until the solder cools. After you replace each IC, power up the system and see if it now works.

To remove "surface-mount" ICs, use a tool such as that shown in Figure 7-21. This tool sends out a directed blast of hot air which heats all the pins at the same time and allows the IC to be easily removed. To replace the IC, you put some solder paste on the PC board pads for the IC, place the IC carefully in position, and heat the pins with another blast of hot air.

The techniques described in the preceding sections will enable you to troubleshoot many microcomputer systems with a minimum of test equipment. However, specialized test equipment is available to speed up the process and help find complex problems. The following sections describe two of these instruments.

Equipment for Troubleshooting Microcomputers

LOGIC ANALYZER

A logic analyzer can be a powerful tool for debugging difficult problems, but it is important for you to have a perspective on when to use an analyzer in troubleshooting simple systems that previously worked. Generally you can use the techniques described in previous sec-

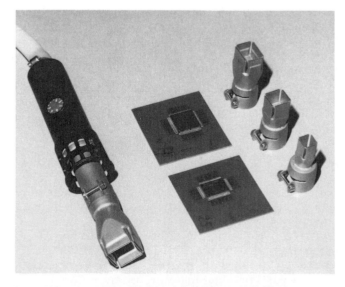

FIGURE 7-21   Leister-Labor S hot-air contactless desoldering and soldering tool for removing and replacing leaded and surface mount components on PC boards. (*Courtesy Brian R. White Co., Inc., Ukiah, California.*)

tions to find and fix a problem in less time than it would take you to connect the logic analyzer, figure out what you should see in a trace, and determine if the trace is correct.

One of the main problems is that in a repair setting you often don't have good documentation on an instrument, so it is difficult to determine what the correct trace should be. Analyzers such as the Tektronix 1230 allow you to store a trace from a functioning instrument in a reference memory. This trace can then be compared with a trace from a nonfunctioning instrument. We have found this feature very helpful in pointing to the source of a problem.

The disassembly feature found in some analyzers is also useful, because it allows you to determine if a microcomputer-based instrument is correctly fetching and executing its basic control program.

Despite the minor difficulties, don't hesitate to use an analyzer when the simple techniques don't seem to be getting you anywhere.

OTHER MICROCOMPUTER TROUBLESHOOTING EQUIPMENT

A logic analyzer is a very powerful troubleshooting tool, but to use it effectively, you need some detailed knowledge and a program listing for the system that you are trying to troubleshoot. If you are working as a repair technician and have to repair several different types of microcomputer systems with poor documentation to work from, most analyzers are not too useful. To make your life easier in this case, "smart" instruments such as the Fluke 9010A Microsystem troubleshooter have been created.

As you can see from the picture of the 9010A in Figure 7-22, it has a keyboard, a display, and an "umbilical" cable with an IC plug on the end. The unit also contains a minicassette tape recorder. For troubleshooting, the 9010A is used as follows.

The microprocessor in a fully functioning unit is removed, and the plug at the end of the cable is inserted in its place. The learn function of the 9010A is then executed. This function finds and maps ROM, RAM, and I/O registers that can be written into and read from. It also computes signatures (checksums) for blocks of ROM. All these parameters are stored in the 9010A's RAM and/or on a minicassette tape. The microprocessor on a malfunctioning unit is then removed and the plug at the end of the umbilical cable inserted in its place. An automatic test function is then executed. In this mode, the 9010A tests the buses, RAM, ROM, ports, power supply, and clock on the malfunctioning system. Any problem found, such as stuck nodes or adjacent trace short circuits, is indicated on the display. The results of this test give some good hints as to the source of the problem. Because of its built-in intelligence, the 9010A can be programmed to do other tests as well.

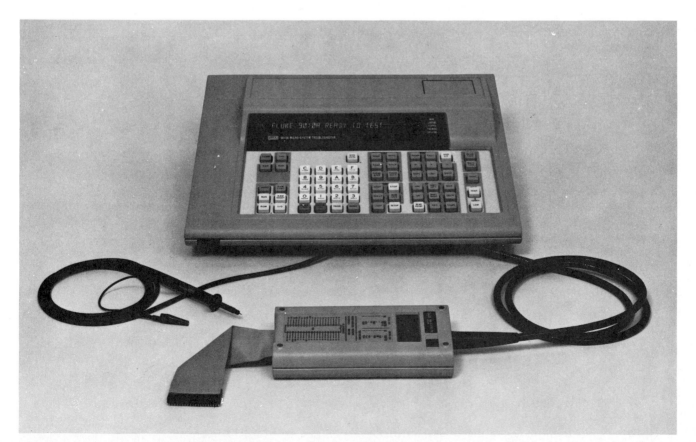

FIGURE 7-22   Fluke 9010A microsystem troubleshooter. (*John Fluke Mfg. Co., Inc.*)

The point of an instrument such as the 9010A is that with it you do not have to be intimately familiar with the programming language and hardware details of a simple microcomputer system in order to troubleshoot it.

CHECKLIST OF IMPORTANT TERMS AND CONCEPTS IN THIS CHAPTER

If you do not remember any of the terms or concepts in the following list, use the index to find them in the chapter.

Pin functions of 8086:
V_{CC}, $\overline{RD}$, $\overline{WR}$, CLK, ALE, M/$\overline{IO}$, $\overline{LOCK}$, MN/$\overline{MX}$, RESET, NMI, INTR, $\overline{BHE}$, $\overline{DEN}$, DT/$\overline{R}$

8086 RESET response

Maximum and minimum mode of 8086

8086 timing diagram interpretation

State, instruction cycle, machine cycle, WAIT state, RDY signal

Bus activities during read/write

Logic analyzer use: external clock, internal clock, word recognizer, trigger, trace

Bidirectional buffer

General functions: 8284, 8255A, 8251A, 8279, 2716, 2142

SDK-86 schematic: zones, plugs, jacks, resistor packs

Address decoding: ROM decoding, RAM decoding, port decoding

Memory-mapped and direct I/O

8086 memory banks

Timing parameters: t_{ACC}, t_{CL}, t_{OE}, t_{CE}, TCLAV, TCLRL, TDVCL

8086 typical clock frequencies

Troubleshooting steps for a simple 8086-based microcomputer

REVIEW QUESTIONS AND PROBLEMS

1. From what point on the clock waveform is the start of an 8086 state measured?

2. Why are latches required on the AD0–AD15 bus in an 8086 system?

3. What is the purpose of the ALE signal in an 8086 system?

4. Describe the sequence of events on the 8086 data/address bus, the ALE line, the M/$\overline{IO}$ line, and the $\overline{RD}$ line as the 8086 fetches an instruction word.

5. What logic levels will be on the 8086 $\overline{RD}$, $\overline{WR}$, and M/$\overline{IO}$ lines when the 8086 is doing a write to a memory location? A read from a port?

6. What is the major difference between an 8086 operating in minimum mode and an 8086 operating in maximum mode?

7. Describe the response an 8086 will make when its RESET (RST) input is asserted high.

8. Why are buffers often needed on the address, data, and control buses in a microcomputer system?

9. a. How is an 8086 entered into a WAIT state?
   b. At what point in a machine cycle does an 8086 enter a WAIT state?
   c. What information is on the buses during a WAIT state?
   d. How long is a WAIT state?

   e. How many WAIT states can be inserted in a machine cycle?
   f. Why would you want the 8086 to insert a WAIT state?

10. What are the functions of the 8086 DT/$\overline{R}$ and $\overline{DEN}$ signals?

11. What does an arrow going from a transition on one signal waveform to a transition on another tell you?

12. Draw a block diagram of a simple logic analyzer and briefly describe how it operates. Include in your answer the function of the clock and the function of the trigger.

13. What do you use for a logic analyzer clock when you want to make detailed timing measurements?

14. On what signal and what edge of that signal would you clock a logic analyzer, and on what word would you trigger to see each of the following in an 8086 system?
   a. The sequence of addresses output after a RESET.
   b. The sequence of instructions read in after a RESET. (Assume that the first instruction word is 9CEAH.)
   c. Both the addresses sent out and the words read in.

d. What clock qualifier would you use to see a trace of only data read in from ports?

15. How is it possible for a logic analyzer to display data that occurred before the trigger?

16. How are wire-wrap jumpers indicated on a schematic?

17. What is the meaning of /8 on a signal line in a schematic?

18. Describe the two purposes of address decoders in microcomputer systems.

19. A memory device has 15 address lines connected to it and 8 data outputs. What size words and how many words does the device store?

20. Briefly describe the function of the 8255, 8251A, and 8279 devices in the SDK-86 microcomputer system.

21. A group of signal lines in a schematic has the label 2ZB3 next to it. What is the meaning of this label?

22. What is the difference between a connector identified with a J and a connector identified with a P?

23. Describe the purpose of the many small capacitors connected between V_{CC} and ground on microcomputer printed-circuit boards.

24. A 74LS138 decoder has its three SELECT inputs connected to A12, A13, and A14 of the system address bus. It has $\overline{G2A}$ connected to A15, $\overline{G2B}$ connected to $\overline{RD}$, and G1 connected to +5 V. Use an address decoder worksheet to determine what eight ROM address blocks the decoder outputs will select. Why is $\overline{RD}$ used as one of the enables on a ROM decoder?

25. Show a memory map for the ROMs in Problem 24.

26. Use an address decoder worksheet to help you draw a circuit to show how another 74LS138 can be connected to select one of eight 1-Kbyte RAMs starting at address 8000H.

27. Why are there actually many addresses that will select one of the port devices connected to the port decoder in Figure 7-12*a*?

28. Describe memory-mapped I/O and direct I/O. Give the main advantage and main disadvantage of each.

29. *a.* Why is the 8086 memory set up as 2-byte-wide banks?
    b. What logic levels would you find on $\overline{BHE}$ and A0 when an 8086 is writing a byte to address 04274H? When it is writing a word to 04274H?
    c. Describe the 8086 bus operations required to write a word to address 04373H.

30. How does the circuitry on the SDK-86 make sure that you cannot accidentally write a byte or word to ROM?

31. Why is some ROM put at the top of the address space in an 8086 system?

32. *a.* Show the truth table you would use for a 3625 PROM decoder to produce $\overline{CS1}$ signals for 4K × 8 RAMs in an 8086 system. Assume the first RAM starts at address 00000H. Don't forget A0 and $\overline{BHE}$.
    b. Draw the circuit connections for the 3625 decoder PROM and for two of the 4K × 8 RAMs.

33. Use sheets 5 and 7 of the SDK-86 schematics to help you determine for the SDK-86 what logic levels will be on $\overline{BHE}$, A0 to A19, M/$\overline{IO}$, $\overline{RD}$, and $\overline{WR}$ when a word is read from ports FFF8H and FFF9H. Are these ports memory-mapped or direct? What instruction(s) would you use to do this read operation?

34. *a.* How is the $\overline{\text{OFF BOARD}}$ signal produced on the SDK-86 board?
    b. Describe the purpose of the $\overline{\text{OFF BOARD}}$ signal.

35. Describe how the 8088 memory is configured. Why doesn't the 8088 need a $\overline{BHE}$ signal?

36. By referring to the 8086 timing diagrams in Figure 7-19*a* and parameters in Appendix A, determine for the 8086-2:
    a. The maximum clock frequency.
    b. The time between CLOCK going low and $\overline{RD}$ going low.
    c. The time for which memory must hold data on the data bus after CLOCK goes low at the start of T_4.
    d. The time that the lower 16 address bits remain on the data bus after ALE goes low.

37. The 27128-25 is a 16K × 8 EPROM with a t_{ACC} of 250 ns maximum, a t_{CE} of 250 ns maximum, and a t_{OE} of 100 ns maximum. Will this device work correctly without WAIT states in an 8-MHz 8086-2 system with circuit connections such as those in the SDK-86 schematics? Assume the address latches have a propagation delay of 12 ns and the decoder has a delay of 30 ns.

38. List the major steps you would take to troubleshoot a microcomputer system such as the SDK-86 which previously worked. Assume all ICs are in sockets.

39. Why is it important to check power supplies with an oscilloscope?

40. Describe how you can keep from mixing up ICs from a good system with those from a bad system when substituting.

41. Write an 8086 routine to test the system RAM in addresses 00200H through 07FFFH.

42. Write a test routine to output alternating 1's and 0's to port FFFAH over and over. With this routine running, you could check with an oscilloscope to see if the port device is getting enabled and is outputting data.

43. Describe the symptoms that an SDK-86 would show for each of the following problems.

    a. Pin 8 of A15 in zone D5 of schematic sheet 2 is stuck low.

    b. The reset key is stuck on.

    c. None of the outputs of A29 in zone D7 of schematic sheet 6 ever goes low.

    d. Pin 6 of A3 in zone A5 of schematic sheet 5 is stuck low.

## CHAPTER 8

8086 Interrupts and Interrupt Applications

Most microprocessors allow normal program execution to be interrupted by some external signal or by a special instruction in the program. In response to an interrupt, the microprocessor stops executing its current program and calls a procedure which "services" the interrupt. An IRET instruction at the end of the interrupt-service procedure returns execution to the interrupted program. This chapter introduces you to the 8086 interrupt types, shows you how the microprocessors in the 8086 family respond to interrupts, teaches you how to write interrupt-service procedures, and describes how interrupts are used in a variety of applications.

OBJECTIVES

At the conclusion of this chapter, you should be able to:

1. Describe the interrupt response of an 8086 family processor.

2. Initialize an 8086 interrupt vector (pointer) table.

3. Write interrupt-service procedures.

4. Describe the operation of an 8254 programmable counter/timer and write the instructions necessary to initialize an 8254 for a specified application.

5. Describe the operation of an 8259A priority interrupt controller and write the instructions needed to initialize an 8259A for a specified application.

6. Call a BIOS procedure using a software interrupt.

8086 INTERRUPTS AND INTERRUPT RESPONSES

Overview

An 8086 interrupt can come from any one of three sources. One source is an external signal applied to the *nonmaskable interrupt* (NMI) input pin or to the *interrupt* (INTR) input pin. An interrupt caused by a signal applied to one of these inputs is referred to as a *hardware interrupt*.

A second source of an interrupt is execution of the Interrupt instruction, INT. This is referred to as a *software interrupt*.

The third source of an interrupt is some error condition produced in the 8086 by the execution of an instruction. An example of this is the divide-by-zero interrupt. If you attempt to divide an operand by zero, the 8086 will automatically interrupt the currently executing program.

At the end of each instruction cycle, the 8086 checks to see if any interrupts have been requested. If an interrupt has been requested, the 8086 responds to the interrupt by stepping through the following series of major actions.

1. It decrements the stack pointer by 2 and pushes the flag register on the stack.

2. It disables the 8086 INTR interrupt input by clearing the interrupt flag (IF) in the flag register.

3. It resets the trap flag (TF) in the flag register.

4. It decrements the stack pointer by 2 and pushes the current code segment register contents on the stack.

5. It decrements the stack pointer again by 2 and pushes the current instruction pointer contents on the stack.

6. It does an indirect far jump to the start of the procedure you wrote to respond to the interrupt.

Figure 8-1, p. 208, summarizes these steps in diagram form. As you can see, the 8086 pushes the flag register on the stack, disables the INTR input and the single-step function, and does essentially an indirect far call to the interrupt service procedure. An IRET instruction at the end of the interrupt service procedure returns execution to the main program. Now let's see how the 8086 actually gets to the interrupt procedure.

Remember from Chapter 5 that when the 8086 does a far call to a procedure, it puts a new value in the code segment register and a new value in the instruction pointer. For an indirect far call, the 8086 gets the new values for CS and IP from four memory addresses. Likewise, when the 8086 responds to an interrupt, it goes to four memory locations to get the CS and IP values for the start of the interrupt-service procedure. In an 8086 system, the first 1 Kbyte of memory, from 00000H to 003FFH, is set aside as a table for storing the starting addresses of interrupt service procedures. Since 4 bytes are required to store the CS and IP values

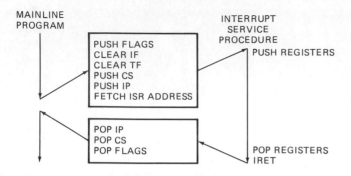

FIGURE 8-1 8086 interrupt response.

for each interrupt service procedure, the table can hold the starting addresses for up to 256 interrupt procedures. The starting address of an interrupt service procedure is often called the *interrupt vector* or the *interrupt pointer,* so the table is referred to as the *interrupt-vector table* or the *interrupt-pointer table.*

Figure 8-2 shows how the 256 interrupt vectors are arranged in the table in memory. Note that the instruction pointer value is put in as the low word of the vector, and the code segment register is put in as the high word of the vector. Each doubleword interrupt vector is identified by a number from 0 to 255. Intel calls this number the *type* of the interrupt.

The lowest five types are dedicated to specific interrupts, such as the divide-by-zero interrupt, the single-step interrupt, and the nonmaskable interrupt. Later in this chapter we explain the operation of these interrupts in detail. Interrupt types 5 to 31 are reserved by Intel

for use in more complex microprocessors, such as the 80286, 80386, and 80486. In a later chapter we discuss some of these interrupt types. The upper 224 interrupt types, from 32 to 255, are available for you to use for hardware or software interrupts.

As you can see in Figure 8-2, the vector for each interrupt type requires four memory locations. Therefore, when the 8086 responds to a particular type interrupt, it automatically multiplies the type by 4 to produce the desired address in the vector table. It then goes to that address in the table to get the starting address of the interrupt service procedure. We will show you later how you use instructions at the start of your program to load the starting address of a procedure into the vector table.

Now that you have an overview of how the 8086 responds to interrupts, we will discuss one type of interrupt in detail and show you how to write a procedure to service that interrupt.

An 8086 Interrupt Response Example—Type 0

Probably the easiest 8086 interrupt to understand is the divide-by-zero interrupt, identified as *type 0* in Figure 8-2. Before we get into the details of the type 0 interrupt response, let's refresh your memory about how the 8086 DIV and IDIV instructions work.

The 8086 DIV instruction allows you to divide a 16-bit unsigned binary number in AX by an 8-bit unsigned number from a specified register or memory location. The 8-bit result (quotient) from this division will be left in the AL register. The 8-bit remainder will be left in the AH register. The DIV instruction also allows you to divide a 32-bit unsigned binary number in DX and AX by a 16-bit number in a specified register or memory location. The 16-bit quotient from this division is left in the AX register, and the 16-bit remainder is left in the DX register. In the same manner, the 8086 IDIV instruction allows you to divide a 16-bit signed number in AX by an 8-bit signed number in a specified register or a 32-bit signed number in DX and AX by a 16-bit signed number from a specified register or memory location.

If the quotient from dividing a 16-bit number is too large to fit in AL or the quotient from dividing a 32-bit number is too large to fit in AX, the result of the division will be meaningless. A special case of this is where an attempt is made to divide a 32-bit number or a 16-bit number by zero. The result of dividing by zero is infinity (actually undefined), which is somewhat too large to fit in AX or AL. Whenever the quotient from a DIV or IDIV operation is too large to fit in the result register, the 8086 will automatically do a type 0 interrupt. In response to this interrupt the 8086 proceeds as follows.

The 8086 first decrements the stack pointer by 2 and copies the flag register to the stack. It then clears IF and TF. Next, it saves the return address on the stack. To do this, the 8086 decrements the stack pointer by 2, pushes the CS value of the return address on the stack, decrements the stack pointer by 2 again, and pushes the IP value of the return address on the stack. The 8086 then gets the starting address of the interrupt-service procedure from the type 0 locations in the

3FFH	TYPE 255 POINTER: (AVAILABLE)
3FCH	
	TYPE 33 POINTER: (AVAILABLE)
084H	
	TYPE 32 POINTER: (AVAILABLE)
080H	
07FH	TYPE 31 POINTER: (RESERVED)
	TYPE 5 POINTER: (RESERVED)
014H	
	TYPE 4 POINTER: OVERFLOW
010H	
	TYPE 3 POINTER: 1-BYTE INT INSTRUCTION
00CH	
	TYPE 2 POINTER: NON-MASKABLE
008H	
	TYPE 1 POINTER: SINGLE-STEP
004H	
	TYPE 0 POINTER: DIVIDE ERROR
000H	

AVAILABLE INTERRUPT POINTERS (224)

RESERVED INTERRUPT POINTERS (27)

DEDICATED INTERRUPT POINTERS (5)

CS BASE ADDRESS
IP OFFSET

— 16 BITS —

FIGURE 8-2 8086 interrupt-pointer table.

interrupt-vector table. As you can see in Figure 8-2, it gets the new value for CS from addresses 00002H and 00003H and the new value for IP from addresses 00000H and 00001H. After the starting address of the procedure is loaded into CS and IP, the 8086 then fetches and executes the first instruction of the procedure.

At the end of the interrupt-service procedure, an IRET instruction is used to return execution to the interrupted program.

The IRET instruction pops the stored value of IP off the stack and increments the stack pointer by 2. It then pops the stored value of CS off the stack and increments the stack pointer again by 2. Finally, it restores the flags by popping off the stack the values stored during the interrupt response and increments the stack pointer by 2. Remember from the previous paragraph that during its interrupt response, the 8086 disables the INTR and single-step interrupts by clearing IF and TF. If the INTR input and/or the trap interrupt were enabled before the interrupt, they will be enabled upon return to the interrupted program. The reason for this is that flags from the interrupted program were pushed on the stack before IF and TF were cleared by the 8086 in its interrupt response. To summarize, then, IRET returns execution to the interrupted program and restores IF and TF to the state they were in before the interrupt. Now that we have described the type 0 response, we can show you how to write a program to handle this interrupt.

An 8086 Interrupt Program Example

DEFINING THE PROBLEM AND WRITING THE ALGORITHM

In the last chapter we were working mostly with hardware, so instead of jumping directly into the program, let's use this example to review how you go about writing any program.

For the example program here, assume we have four word-sized hexadecimal values stored in memory. We want to divide each of these values by a byte-type scale factor to give a byte-type scaled value. If the result of the division is valid, we want to put the scaled value in an array in memory. If the result of the division is invalid (too large to fit in the 8-bit result register), we want to put 0 in the array for that scaled value. Figure 8-3 shows the algorithm for this program in pseudocode.

As shown in Figure 8-3a, the mainline part of this program gets each 16-bit value from memory in turn and divides that value by the 8-bit scale factor. If the result of the division is valid, it is stored in the appropriate memory location; else a 0 is stored in the memory location. Not indicated in the algorithm is how we determine whether the quotient is valid or not. With 8086 family microprocessors, a type 0 interrupt procedure is a handy way to do this.

Remember from the preceding discussion that if the result of the division is too large to fit in the quotient register, AL, then the 8086 will do a type 0 interrupt immediately after the divide instruction finishes. Figure 8-3b shows the algorithm for a procedure to service this type 0 interrupt. The main function of this procedure is to set a *flag* which will be checked by the mainline

```
INITIALIZATION LIST

REPEAT
  Get INPUT_VALUE
  Divide by scale factor
  If result valid THEN
    store result as scaled value
  ELSE store zero
UNTIL all values scaled
```
(a)

```
Save registers
Set error flag
Restore registers
Return to mainline
```
(b)

FIGURE 8-3   Algorithm for divide-by-zero program example. (a) Mainline program. (b) Interrupt-service procedure.

program. The flag in this case is not one of the flags in the 8086 flag register. The flag here is a bit in a memory location we set aside for this purpose. In the actual program, we give this memory location the name BAD_DIV_FLAG. At the end of the interrupt-service procedure, execution is returned to the interrupted mainline program.

After the divide operation in the mainline program, we check the value of the BAD_DIV_FLAG to determine if the result of the division is valid. If the result of the division was too large, then the 8086 will have done a type 0 interrupt, and the interrupt-service procedure will have set the BAD_DIV_FLAG to a 1. If the result of the division is valid, then the 8086 will not have done the type 0 interrupt, and the BAD_DIV_FLAG will be 0.

This sequence of operations is repeated until all the values have been scaled.

WRITING THE INITIALIZATION LIST

After you have worked out the data structure and the algorithm for a program, the next step is to make an initialization list such as the one shown in Chapter 3. Here is a list for this program.

1. Initialize the interrupt-vector table. In other words, the starting address of our type 0 interrupt service routine must be put in locations 00000H and 00002H.

2. Set up the data segment where the values to be scaled, the scale factor, the scaled values, and the BAD_DIV_FLAG will be put.

3. Initialize the data segment register to point to the base address of the data segment containing the values to be scaled.

4. Set up a stack to store the flags and return address.

5. Initialize the stack segment and stack pointer registers.

6. Initialize a pointer to the start of the data to be scaled, a counter to keep track of how many values have been scaled, and a pointer to the start of the array where the scaled values are to be written.

```
1                                       ;8086 MAINLINE PROGRAM F8-04A.ASM
2                                       ;ABSTRACT    : Program scales data values using division.
3                                       ;PORTS       : None used
4                                       ;REGISTERS   : Uses CS,DS,ES,SS,SP,SI,AX,BX,CS
5                                       ;PROCEDURES  : Uses BAD_DIV, a type 0 interrupt service procedure
6                                                   ; Link mailine F8-04A.OBJ with procedure F8-04B.OBJ
7
8  0000                                 DATA SEGMENT  WORD    PUBLIC
9  0000   0035 0855 2011 1359               INPUT_VALUES  DW 0035H, 0855H, 2011H, 1359H
10 0008   04*(00)                           SCALED_VALUES DB 4 DUP(0)  ; Answers = 05,ED,00,00
11 000C   09                                SCALE_FACTOR  DB 09
12 000D   00                                BAD_DIV_FLAG  DB 0
13 000E                                 DATA ENDS
14
15 0000                                 STACK_SEG  SEGMENT STACK
16 0000   64*(0000)                         DW   100 DUP (0)          ; Set up stack of 100 words
17                                          TOP_STACK  LABEL  WORD ; Pointer to top of stack
18 00C8                                 STACK_SEG  ENDS
19
20                                      PUBLIC   BAD_DIV_FLAG          ; Make flag available to other modules
21
22 0000                                 INT_PROC  SEGMENT  WORD   PUBLIC
23                                          EXTRN  BAD_DIV:FAR        ; Let assembler know procedure BAD_DIV
24 0000                                 INT_PROC  ENDS               ; is in another assembly module
25
26 0000                                 CODE SEGMENT WORD   PUBLIC
27                                          ASSUME CS:CODE, DS:DATA, SS:STACK_SEG
28 0000   B8 0000s                      START: MOV  AX, STACK_SEG     ; Initialize stack segment
29 0003   8E D0                                MOV  SS, AX            ; register
30 0005   BC 00C8r                              MOV  SP, OFFSET TOP_STACK ; Initialize stack pointer
31 0008   B8 0000s                              MOV  AX, DATA          ; Initialize data segment
32 000B   8E D8                                MOV  DS, AX            ; register
33                                      ;Store the address for the BAD_DIV routine at address 0000:0000
34                                      ;Address 00000-00003 is where type 0 interrupt gets interrupt
35                                      ;service procedure address. CS at 00002 & 00003, IP at 00000 & 00001
36 000D   B8 0000                               MOV  AX, 0000
37 0010   8E C0                                 MOV  ES, AX
38 0012   26: C7 06 0002 0000s                  MOV  WORD PTR ES:0002, SEG BAD_DIV
39 0019   26: C7 06 0000 0000e                  MOV  WORD PTR ES:0000, OFFSET BAD_DIV
40 0020   BE 0000r                              MOV  SI, OFFSET INPUT_VALUES  ; Initialize pointer for input values
41 0023   BB 0008r                              MOV  BX, OFFSET SCALED_VALUES ; Point BX at start of result array
42 0026   B9 0004                               MOV  CX, 0004          ; Initialize data value counter
43 0029   8B 04                        NEXT:  MOV  AX, [SI]           ; Bring a value to AX for divide
44 002B   F6 36 000Cr                         DIV  SCALE_FACTOR       ; Divide by scale factor
45 002F   80 3E 000Dr 01                       CMP  BAD_DIV_FLAG, 01   ; If divide produced valid result
46 0034   75 06                                JNE  OK                ; then go save scaled value
47 0036   C6 07 00                              MOV  BYTE PTR [BX], 00  ; else load 0 as scaled value
48 0039   EB 03 90                              JMP  SKIP
49 003C   88 07                        OK:    MOV  [BX], AL           ; Save scaled value
50 003E   C6 06 000Dr 00               SKIP:  MOV  BAD_DIV_FLAG, 0    ; Reset BAD_DIV_FLAG
51 0043   83 C6 02                              ADD  SI, 02            ; Point at next input value location
52 0046   43                                    INC  BX               ; Point at location for next result
53 0047   E2 E0                                 LOOP NEXT              ; Repeat until all values done
54 0049   90                           STOP:  NOP
55 004A                                 CODE   ENDS
56                                             END  START
```

(a)

FIGURE 8-4 8086 assembly language program for divide-by-zero example. (a) Mainline. (See also next page.)

Once you have the algorithm and the initialization list for a program, the next step is to start writing the instructions for the program, so now let's look at the assembly language program for this problem.

ASSEMBLY LANGUAGE PROGRAM AND INTERRUPT PROCEDURE

Figure 8-4 shows our 8086 assembly language program for the mainline and for the type 0 interrupt service procedure. You can use many parts from these examples

when you write your own interrupt programs. Also, to help refresh your memory of the PUBLIC and EXTRN directives, we have written the mainline program and the interrupt service procedure as two separate assembly modules.

At the start of the mainline program in Figure 8-4a, we declare a segment named DATA for the data that the program will be working with. The WORD in this statement tells the linker/locator to locate this segment on the first available even address. The PUBLIC in this statement tells the linker that this segment can be joined

```
 1                                  ;8086 PROCEDURE F8-04B.ASM called by the program F8-04A.ASM
 2                                  ;ABSTRACT: PROCEDURE BAD_DIV
 3                                           ; Services divide-by-zero interrupt (TYPE 0).
 4                                           ; Sets the LSB of a memory location called BAD_DIV_FLAG,
 5                                           ; enables INTR, and returns execution to the interrupted program
 6                                  ;DESTROYS: Nothing
 7
 8  0000                           DATA  SEGMENT WORD PUBLIC
 9                                    EXTRN  BAD_DIV_FLAG:BYTE      ; Let assembler know BAD_DIV_FLAG
10  0000                           DATA  ENDS                      ; is in another assembly module
11
12                                 PUBLIC  BAD_DIV                  ; Make procedure BAD_DIV available
13                                                                  ; to other assembly modules
14  0000                           INT_PROC SEGMENT WORD PUBLIC ; Segment for interrupt service procedure
15  0000                           BAD_DIV  PROC FAR               ; Procedure for type 0 interrupt
16                                   ASSUME CS:INT_PROC, DS:DATA
17  0000  50                          PUSH  AX                     ; Save AX of interrupted program
18  0001  1E                          PUSH  DS                     ; Save DS of interrupted program
19  0002  B8 0000s                     MOV   AX, DATA              ; Load Data Segment register value
20  0005  8E D8                        MOV   DS, AX                ; needed here
21  0007  C6 06 0000e 01               MOV   BAD_DIV_FLAG, 01      ; Set LSB of BAD_DIV_FLAG byte
22  000C  1F                          POP   DS                     ; Restore DS of interrupted program
23  000D  58                          POP   AX                     ; Restore AX of interrupted program
24  000E  CF                          IRET                         ; Return to next instruction in interrupted
25  000F                           BAD_DIV  ENDP                   ; program
26  000F                           INT_PROC ENDS
27                                            END
```

(b)

FIGURE 8-4 (continued) (b) Interrupt-service procedure.

together (concatenated) with segments of the same name from other assembly modules. The input values are words, so we use a DW directive to declare these four values. The scaled values will be bytes, so we use a DB directive to set aside four locations for them. Remember that the DUP(0) in the statement initializes the 4-byte locations to all 0's. As the program executes, the results will be written into these locations. SCALE_FACTOR DB 09H sets aside a byte location for the number by which we are going to be dividing the input values. The advantage of using a DB rather than an EQU directive to declare the scale factor is that with a DB the value of the scale factor can be held in RAM, where it can be changed dynamically in the program as needed. If you use a statement such as SCALE_FACTOR EQU 09H to set a value, you have to reassemble the program to change the value.

Part of the 8086 interrupt response is essentially a far call to the interrupt service procedure. In any program that calls a procedure, we have to set up a stack to store the return address and parameters passed to and from the procedure. The next section of the program declares a stack segment called STACK_SEG. It also establishes a pointer to the next location above the stack with the statement TOP_STACK LABEL WORD. Remember from the examples in Chapter 5 that this label is used to initialize the stack pointer to the next location after the top of the stack.

The next two parts of the program are necessary because we wrote the mainline program and the interrupt service procedure as two separate assembly modules. When the assembler reads through a source program, it makes a *symbol table* which contains the segment and offset of each of the names and labels used in the program. The statement PUBLIC_BAD_DIV_FLAG tells the assembler to identify the name BAD_DIV_FLAG

as public. This means that when the object module for this program is linked with some other object module that declares BAD_DIV_FLAG as EXTRN, the linker will be allowed to make the connection. Some programmers say that the PUBLIC directive "exports" a name or label.

The other end of this export operation is to "import" labels or names that are defined in other assembly modules. For example, the statement EXTRN BAD_DIV:FAR in our example program tells the assembler that BAD_DIV is a label of type far and that BAD_DIV is defined in some other assembly module. The INT_PROC SEGMENT WORD PUBLIC and INT_PROC ENDS statements tell the assembler that BAD_DIV is defined in a segment named INT_PROC. When the assembler reads these statements, it will make an entry in its symbol table for BAD_DIV and identify it as external. When the object module for this program is linked with the object module for the program where BAD_DIV is defined, the linker will fill in the proper values for the CS and IP of BAD_DIV.

For the actual instructions of our mainline program, we declare a code segment with the statement CODE SEGMENT WORD PUBLIC.

As usual, at the start of the code segment we use an ASSUME statement to tell the assembler what logical segments to use for code, data, and stack. After this come the familiar instructions for initializing the stack segment register, the stack pointer register, and the data segment register.

The next four instructions load the address of the BAD_DIV interrupt-service procedure in the type 0 locations of the interrupt-vector table. We load ES with 0000 so that we can use it as an imaginary segment at absolute address 00000H. Then we use the statement MOV WORD PTR ES:0000 OFFSET BAD_DIV to load the offset of the interrupt-service procedure in memory at 00000H and 00001H. The statement MOV WORD PTR ES:0000 SEG BAD_DIV is used to load the segment base address of BAD_DIV into memory at 00002H and 00003H. It is necessary to load the interrupt procedure addresses in this way if you are using an SDK-86 board or using the MASM and Link programs on an IBM PC-type machine.

Next, we initialize SI as a pointer to the first input value and initialize BX as a pointer to the first of the locations we set aside for the 8-bit scaled results. CX is initialized as a counter to keep track of how many values have been scaled.

Finally, after everything is initialized, we get to the operations we set out to do. The statement MOV AX,[SI] copies an input value from memory to the AX register, where it has to be for the divide operation. The DIV SCALE_FACTOR instruction divides the number in AX by 09H, the value we assigned to SCALE_FACTOR previously with a DB directive. The 8-bit quotient from this division will be put in AL, and the 8-bit remainder will be put in AH. If the quotient is too large to fit in AL, then the 8086 will automatically do a type 0 interrupt. For our program here, the 8086 will push the flags on the stack, reset IF and TF, and push the return address on the stack. It will then go to addresses 0000H and 0002H to get the IP and CS values for the start of BAD_DIV, the procedure we wrote to service a type 0 interrupt. It will then execute the BAD_DIV procedure. Now let's look at the procedure in Figure 8-4b and see how it works.

The BAD_DIV procedure starts by letting the assembler know that the name BAD_DIV_FLAG represents a variable of type byte and that this variable is defined in a segment called DATA in some other (EXTRN) assembly module. We also tell the assembler that the label BAD_DIV should be made available to other assembly modules (PUBLIC).

Next, we declare a logical segment called INT_PROC. We could have put this procedure in the segment CODE with the mainline program. However, in system programs where there are many interrupt-service procedures, a separate segment is usually set aside for them. The statement BAD_DIV PROC FAR identifies the actual start of the procedure and tells the assembler that both the CS and IP values for this procedure must be saved.

Now, an important operation to do at the start of any interrupt-service procedure is to push on the stack any registers that are used in the procedure. You can then restore these registers by popping them off the stack just before returning to the interrupted program. The interrupted program will then resume with its registers as they were before the interrupt. In the procedure in Figure 8-4b, we saved AX and DS. Since we use the same data segment, DATA, in the mainline and in the procedure, you may wonder why we saved DS. The point is that an interrupt-service procedure should be written so that it can be used at any point in a program. By saving the DS value for the interrupted program, this interrupt-service procedure can be used in a program section that does not use DATA as its data segment. The ASSUME statement tells the assembler the name of the segment to use as a data segment, but remember

that it does not load the DS register with a value for the start of that segment. The instructions MOV AX,DATA and MOV DS,AX do this in our procedure.

Finally, we get to the whole point of this procedure with the MOV BAD_DIV_FLAG,01 instruction. This instruction simply sets the least significant bit of the memory location we set aside with a DB directive at the start of the mainline program. Note that in order to access this variable by name, you have to let the assembler know that it is external, and you have to make sure that the DS register contains the segment base for the segment in which BAD_DIV_FLAG is located.

To complete the procedure, we pop the saved registers off the stack and return to the interrupted program. The IRET instruction, remember, is different from the regular RET instruction in that it pops the flag register and the return address off the stack. Note in the program in Figure 8-4b that the procedure must be "closed" with an ENDP directive, and the segment must as usual be closed with an ENDS directive.

Now let's look back in the mainline to see what it does with this BAD_DIV_FLAG. Immediately after the DIV instruction, the mainline checks to see if the BAD_DIV_FLAG is set by comparing it with 01. If the BAD_DIV_FLAG was not set by the type 0 interrupt-service procedure, then a jump is made to the MOV [BX],AL instruction. This instruction copies the result of the division in AL to the memory location in SCALED_VALUES pointed to by BX. If BAD_DIV_FLAG was set by a type 0 interrupt, then 0 is put in the memory location in SCALED_VALUES and a jump will be made to the MOV BAD_DIV_FLAG,00 instruction, which resets the BAD_DIV_FLAG. Since this jump passes over the MOV [BX],AL instruction, the invalid result of the division will not be copied into one of the locations in SCALED_VALUES.

After putting the scaled value or 0 in the array and resetting the flag, we get ready to operate on the next input value. The ADD SI,02 instruction increments SI by 2 so that it points to the next 16-bit value in INPUT_VALUES. The INC BX instruction points BX at the next 8-bit location in SCALED_VALUES. The LOOP instruction after these automatically decrements the CX register by 1 and, if CX is not then 0, causes the 8086 to jump to the specified label, NEXT.

The preceding section has shown you how to set up an interrupt-pointer table, how to write an interrupt-service procedure, and how the 8086 responds to a type 0 interrupt. Now we can discuss some of the other types of 8086 interrupts.

8086 Interrupt Types

The preceding sections used the type 0 interrupt as an example of how the 8086 interrupts function. In this section we discuss in detail the different ways an 8086 can be interrupted and how the 8086 responds to each of these interrupts. We discuss these in order, starting with type 0, so that you can easily find a particular discussion when you need to refer back to it. However, as you read through this section, you should not attempt to learn all the details of all the interrupt types at once.

Read through all the types to get an overview, and then focus on the details of the hardware-caused NMI interrupt, the software interrupts produced by the INT instruction, and the hardware interrupt produced by applying a signal to the INTR input pin.

DIVIDE-BY-ZERO INTERRUPT—TYPE 0

As we described in the preceding section, the 8086 will automatically do a type 0 interrupt if the result of a DIV operation or an IDIV operation is too large to fit in the destination register. For a type 0 interrupt, the 8086 pushes the flag register on the stack, resets IF and TF, and pushes the return address (CS and IP) on the stack. It then gets the CS value for the start of the interrupt-service procedure from address 00002H in the interrupt-pointer table and the IP value for the start of the procedure from address 00000H in the interrupt pointer-table.

Since the 8086 type 0 response is automatic and cannot be disabled in any way, you have to account for it in any program where you use the DIV or IDIV instruction. One way is to in some way make sure the result will never be too large for the result register. We showed one way to do this in the example program in Figure 5-27b. In that example, you may remember, we first make sure the divisor is not zero, and then we do the division in several steps so that the result of the division will never be too large.

Another way to account for the 8086 type 0 response is to simply write an interrupt-service procedure which takes the desired action when an invalid division occurs. The advantage of this approach is that you don't have the overhead of a more complex division routine in your mainline program. The 8086 automatically does the checking and docs the interrupt procedure only if there is a problem.

SINGLE-STEP INTERRUPT—TYPE 1

In a section of Chapter 3 on debugging assembly language programs, we discussed the use of the single-step feature found in some monitor programs and debugger programs. When you tell a system to single-step, it will execute one instruction and stop. You can then examine the contents of registers and memory locations. If they are correct, you can tell the system to go on and execute the next instruction. In other words, when in single-step mode, a system will stop after it executes each instruction and wait for further direction from you. The 8086 trap flag and type 1 interrupt response make it quite easy to implement a single-step feature in an 8086-based system.

If the 8086 trap flag is set, the 8086 will automatically do a type 1 interrupt after each instruction executes. When the 8086 does a type 1 interrupt, it pushes the flag register on the stack, resets TF and IF, and pushes the CS and IP values for the next instruction on the stack. It then gets the CS value for the start of the type 1 interrupt-service procedure from address 00006H and it gets the IP value for the start of the procedure from address 00004H.

The tasks involved in implementing single stepping are: Set the trap flag, write an interrupt-service procedure which saves all registers on the stack, where they can later be examined or perhaps displayed on the CRT, and load the starting address of the type 1 interrupt-service procedure into addresses 00004H and 00006H. The actual single-step procedure will depend very much on the system on which it is to be implemented. We do not have space here to show you the different ways to do this. We will, however, show you how the trap flag is set or reset, because this is somewhat unusual.

The 8086 has no instructions to directly set or reset the trap flag. These operations are done by pushing the flag register on the stack, changing the trap flag bit to what you want it to be, and then popping the flag register back off the stack. Here is the instruction sequence to set the trap flag.

```
PUSHF                   ; Push flags on stack
MOV BP,SP               ; Copy SP to BP for use as index
OR WORD PTR[BP+0],0100H
                        ; Set TF bit
POPF                    ; Restore flag register
```

To reset the trap flag, simply replace the OR instruction in the preceding sequence with the instruction AND WORD PTR [BP+0], OFEFFH.

> NOTE: We have to use [BP+0] because BP cannot be used as a pointer without a displacement. See Figure 3-8.

The trap flag is reset when the 8086 does a type 1 interrupt, so the single-step mode will be disabled during the interrupt-service procedure.

NONMASKABLE INTERRUPT—TYPE 2

The 8086 will automatically do a *type 2* interrupt response when it receives a low-to-high transition on its NMI input pin. When it does a type 2 interrupt, the 8086 will push the flags on the stack, reset TF and IF, and push the CS value and the IP value for the next instruction on the stack. It will then get the CS value for the start of the type 2 interrupt-service procedure from address 0000AH and the IP value for the start of the procedure from address 00008H.

The name *nonmaskable* given to this input pin on the 8086 means that the type 2 interrupt response cannot be disabled (masked) by any program instructions. Because this input cannot be intentionally or accidentally disabled, we use it to signal the 8086 that some condition in an external system must be taken care of. We could, for example, have a pressure sensor on a large steam boiler connected to the NMI input. If the pressure goes above some preset limit, the sensor will send an interrupt signal to the 8086. The type 2 interrupt-service procedure for this case might turn off the fuel to the boiler, open a pressure-relief valve, and sound an alarm.

Another common use of the type 2 interrupt is to save program data in case of a system power failure. Some external circuitry detects when the ac power to the system fails and sends an interrupt signal to the NMI input. Because of the large filter capacitors in most power supplies, the dc system power will remain for perhaps 50 ms after the ac power is gone. This is more than enough time for a type 2 interrupt-service procedure to copy program data to some RAM which has a battery backup power supply. When the ac power returns, program data can be restored from the battery-backed RAM, and the program can resume execution where it left off. A practice problem at the end of the chapter gives you a chance to write a simple procedure for this task.

BREAKPOINT INTERRUPT—TYPE 3

The *type 3* interrupt is produced by execution of the INT 3 instruction. The main use of the type 3 interrupt is to implement a breakpoint function in a system. In Chapter 4 we described the use of breakpoints in debugging assembly language programs. We hope that you have been using them in debugging your programs. When you insert a breakpoint, the system executes the instructions up to the breakpoint and then goes to the breakpoint procedure. Unlike the single-step feature, which stops execution after each instruction, the breakpoint feature executes all the instructions up to the inserted breakpoint and then stops execution.

When you tell most 8086 systems to insert a breakpoint at some point in your program, they actually do it by temporarily replacing the instruction byte at that address with CCH, the 8086 code for the INT 3 instruction. When the 8086 executes this INT 3 instruction, it pushes the flag register on the stack, resets TF and IF, and pushes the CS and IP values for the next mainline instruction on the stack. The 8086 then gets the CS value of the start of the type 3 interrupt-service procedure from address 0000EH and the IP value for the procedure from address 0000CH. A breakpoint interrupt-service procedure usually saves all the register contents on the stack. Depending on the system, it may then send the register contents to the CRT display and wait for the next command from the user, or in a simple system it may just return control to the user. In this case an Examine Register command can be used to check if the register contents are correct at that point in the program.

OVERFLOW INTERRUPT—TYPE 4

The 8086 overflow flag (OF) will be set if the signed result of an arithmetic operation on two signed numbers is too large to be represented in the destination register or memory location. For example, if you add the 8-bit signed number 01101100 (108 decimal) and the 8-bit signed number 01010001 (81 decimal), the result will be 10111101 (189 decimal). This would be the correct result if we were adding unsigned binary numbers, but it is not the correct signed result. For signed operations, the 1 in the most significant bit of the result indicates that the result is negative and in 2's complement form. The result, 10111101, then actually represents -67 decimal, which is obviously not the correct result for adding $+108$ and $+89$.

There are two major ways to detect and respond to an overflow error in a program. One way is to put the Jump if Overflow instruction, JO, immediately after the arithmetic instruction. If the overflow flag is set as a result of the arithmetic operation, execution will jump to the address specified in the JO instruction. At this address you can put an error routine which responds to the overflow in the way you want.

The second way of detecting and responding to an overflow error is to put the *Interrupt on Overflow* instruction, INTO, immediately after the arithmetic instruction in the program. If the overflow flag is not set when the 8086 executes the INTO instruction, the instruction will simply function as an NOP. However, if the overflow flag is set, indicating an overflow error, the 8086 will do a *type 4* interrupt after it executes the INTO instruction.

When the 8086 does a type 4 interrupt, it pushes the flag register on the stack, resets TF and IF, and pushes the CS and IP values for the next instruction on the stack. It then gets the CS value for the start of the interrupt-service procedure from address 00012H and the IP value for the procedure from address 00010H. Instructions in the interrupt-service procedure then perform the desired response to the error condition. The procedure might, for example, set a "flag" in a memory location as we did in the BAD_DIV procedure in Figure 8-4*b*. The advantage of using the INTO and type 4 interrupt approach is that the error routine is easily accessible from any program.

SOFTWARE INTERRUPTS—TYPES 0 THROUGH 255

The 8086 INT instruction can be used to cause the 8086 to do any one of the 256 possible interrupt types. The desired interrupt type is specified as part of the instruction. The instruction INT 32, for example, will cause the 8086 to do a *type 32* interrupt response. The 8086 will push the flag register on the stack, reset TF and IF, and push the CS and IP values of the next instruction on the stack. It will then get the CS and IP values for the start of the interrupt-service procedure from the interrupt-pointer table in memory. The IP value for any interrupt type is always at an address of 4 times the interrupt type, and the CS value is at a location two addresses higher. For a type 32 interrupt, then, the IP value will be put at 4×32 or 128 decimal (80H), and the CS value will be put at address 82H in the interrupt-vector table.

Software interrupts produced by the INT instruction have many uses. In a previous section we discussed the use of the INT 3 instruction to insert breakpoints in programs for debugging. Another use of software interrupts is to test various interrupt-service procedures. You could, for example, use an INT 0 instruction to send execution to a divide-by-zero interrupt-service procedure without having to run the actual division program. As another example, you could use an INT 2 instruction to send execution to an NMI interrupt-service procedure. This allows you to test the NMI procedure without needing to apply an external signal to the NMI input of the 8086. In a later section of the chapter, we show an example of another important application of software interrupts.

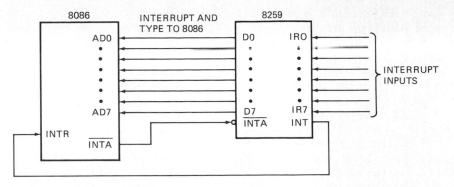

FIGURE 8-5   Block diagram showing an 8259 connected to an 8086.

INTR INTERRUPTS—TYPES 0 THROUGH 255

The 8086 INTR input allows some external signal to interrupt execution of a program. Unlike the NMI input, however, INTR can be masked (disabled) so that it cannot cause an interrupt. If the interrupt flag (IF) is cleared, then the INTR input is disabled. IF can be cleared at any time with the *Clear Interrupt* instruction, CLI. If the interrupt flag is set, the INTR input will be enabled. IF can be set at any time with the *Set Interrupt* instruction, STI.

When the 8086 is reset, the interrupt flag is automatically cleared. Before the 8086 can respond to an interrupt signal on its INTR input, you have to set IF with an STI instruction. The 8086 was designed this way so that ports, timers, registers, etc., can be initialized before the INTR input is enabled. In other words, this allows you to get the 8086 ready to handle interrupts before letting an interrupt in, just as you might want to get yourself ready in the morning with a cup of coffee before turning on the telephone and having to cope with the interruptions it produces.

Remember that the interrupt flag (IF) is also automatically cleared as part of the response of an 8086 to an interrupt. This is done for two reasons. First, it prevents a signal on the INTR input from interrupting a higher-priority interrupt-service procedure in progress. However, if you want another INTR input signal to be able to interrupt an interrupt procedure in progress, you can reenable the INTR input with an STI instruction at any time.

The second reason for automatically disabling the INTR input at the start of an INTR interrupt-service procedure is to make sure that a signal on the INTR input does not cause the 8086 to interrupt itself continuously. The INTR input is activated by a high level. In other words, whenever the INTR input is high and INTR is enabled, the 8086 will be interrupted. If INTR were not disabled during the first response, the 8086 would be continuously interrupted and would never get to the actual interrupt-service procedure.

The IRET instruction at the end of an interrupt-service procedure restores the flags to the condition they were in before the procedure by popping the flag register off the stack. This will reenable the INTR input. If a high-level signal is still present on the INTR input, it will cause the 8086 to be interrupted again. If you do not want the 8086 to be interrupted again by the same input signal, you have to use external hardware to make sure that the signal is made low again before you reenable INTR with the STI instruction or before the IRET from the INTR service procedure.

When the 8086 responds to an INTR interrupt signal, its response is somewhat different from its response to other interrupts. The main difference is that for an INTR interrupt, the interrupt type is sent to the 8086 from an external hardware device such as the 8259A *priority interrupt controller*, as shown in Figure 8-5. We discuss the 8259A in detail later in the chapter, but here's an introduction.

When an 8259A receives an interrupt signal on one of its IR inputs, it sends an interrupt request signal to the INTR input of the 8086. If the INTR input of the 8086 has been enabled with an STI instruction, the 8086 will respond as shown by the waveforms in Figure 8-6.

The 8086 first does two interrupt-acknowledge ma-

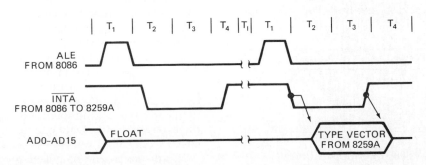

FIGURE 8-6   8086 interrupt-acknowledge machine cycles.

chine cycles, as shown in Figure 8-6. The purpose of these two machine cycles is to get the interrupt type from the external device. At the start of the first interrupt-acknowledge machine cycle, the 8086 floats the data bus lines, AD0–AD15, and sends out an interrupt-acknowledge pulse on its INTA output pin. This pulse essentially tells the 8259A to "get ready." During the second interrupt-acknowledge machine cycle, the 8086 sends out another pulse on its INTA output pin. In response to this second INTA pulse, the 8259A puts the interrupt type (number) on the lower eight lines of the data bus, where it is read by the 8086.

Once the 8086 receives the interrupt type, it pushes the flag register on the stack, clears TF and IF, and pushes the CS and IP values of the next instruction on the stack. It then uses the type it read in from the external device to get the CS and IP values for the interrupt-service procedure from the interrupt-pointer table in memory. The IP value for the procedure will be put at an address equal to 4 times the type number, and the CS value will be put at an address equal to 4 times the type number plus 2, just as is done for the other interrupts.

The advantage of having an external device insert the desired interrupt type is that the external device can "funnel" interrupt signals from many sources into the INTR input pin on the 8086. When the 8086 responds with INTA pulses, the external device can send to the 8086 the interrupt type that corresponds to the source of the interrupt signal. As you will see later, the external device can also prevent an argument if two or more sources send interrupt signals at the same time.

PRIORITY OF 8086 INTERRUPTS

As you read through the preceding discussions of the different interrupt types, the question that may have occurred to you is, What happens if two or more interrupts occur at the same time? The answer to this question is that the highest-priority interrupt will be serviced first, and then the next-highest-priority interrupt will be serviced. Figure 8-7 shows the priorities of the 8086 interrupts as shown in the Intel data book. Some examples will show you what these priorities actually mean.

As a first example, suppose that the INTR input is enabled, the 8086 receives an INTR signal during execution of a Divide instruction, and the divide operation produces a divide-by-zero interrupt. Since the internal interrupts—such as divide error, INT, and INTO — have higher priority than INTR, the 8086 will do a divide error (type 0) interrupt response first. Part of the type 0

interrupt response is to clear IF. This disables the INTR input and prevents the INTR signal from interrupting the higher-priority type 0 interrupt-service procedure. An IRET instruction at the end of the type 0 procedure will restore the flags to what they were before the type 0 response. This will reenable the INTR input, and the 8086 will do an INTR interrupt response. A similar sequence of operations will occur if the 8086 is executing an INT or INTO instruction and an interrupt signal arrives at the INTR input.

As a second example of how this priority works, suppose that a rising-edge signal arrives at the NMI input while the 8086 is executing a DIV instruction, and that the division operation produces a divide error. Since the 8086 checks for internal interrupts before it checks for an NMI interrupt, the 8086 will push the flags on the stack, clear TF and IF, push the return address on the stack, and go to the start of the divide error (type 0) service procedure. However, because the NMI interrupt request is not disabled, the 8086 will then do an NMI (type 2) interrupt response. In other words, the 8086 will push the flags on the stack, clear TF and IF, push the return address on the stack, and go execute the NMI interrupt-service procedure. When the 8086 finishes the NMI procedure, it will return to the divide error procedure, finish executing that procedure, and then return to the mainline program.

To finish our discussion of 8086 interrupt priorities, let's see how the single-step (trap, or type 1) interrupt fits in. If the trap flag is set, the 8086 will do a type 1 interrupt response after every mainline instruction. When the 8086 responds to any interrupt, however, part of its response is to clear the trap flag. This disables the single-step function, so the 8086 will not normally single-step through the instructions of the interrupt-service procedure. The trap flag can be set again in the single-step procedure if single-stepping is desired in the interrupt-service procedure.

Now that we have shown you the different types of 8086 interrupts and how the 8086 responds to each, we will show you a few examples of how the 8086 hardware interrupts are used. Other applications of interrupts will be shown throughout the rest of the book.

HARDWARE INTERRUPT APPLICATIONS

Simple Interrupt Data Input

One of the most common uses of interrupts is to relieve a CPU of the burden of polling. To refresh your memory, polling works as follows.

The strobe or data ready signal from some external device is connected to an input port line on the microcomputer. The microcomputer uses a program loop to read and test this port line over and over until the data ready signal is found to be asserted. The microcomputer then exits the polling loop and reads in the data from the external device. Data can also be output on a polled basis.

The disadvantage of polled input or output is that while the microcomputer is polling the strobe or data

INTERRUPT	PRIORITY
DIVIDE ERROR, INT n, INTO	HIGHEST
NMI	
INTR	
SINGLE-STEP	LOWEST

FIGURE 8-7 Priority of 8086 interrupts. (*Intel Corporation*)

ready signal, it cannot easily be doing other tasks. In systems where the microcomputer must be doing many tasks, polling is a waste of time, so interrupt input and output is used. In this case the data ready or strobe signal is connected to an interrupt input on the microcomputer. The microcomputer then goes about doing its other tasks until it is interrupted by a data ready signal from the external device. An interrupt-service procedure can read in or send out the desired data in a few microseconds and return execution to the interrupted program. The input or output operation then uses only a small percentage of the microprocessor's time.

For our example here, we will connect the key-pressed strobe to the NMI interrupt input of the 8086 on an SDK-86. The NMI input is usually reserved for responding to a power failure or some other catastrophic condition. However, since we are not expecting any catastrophic conditions to befall our SDK-86, we choose to use this input because it does not require an external hardware device to insert the interrupt type as does the INTR input.

Sheet 2 of the SDK-86 schematics in Figure 7-8 shows the circuitry normally connected to the NMI input. This circuitry is designed so that you can produce an NMI interrupt by pressing a key labeled INTR on the hex keypad. When this key is pressed, the input of the 74LS14 inverter will be made low, and the output of the inverter will go high. The low-to-high transition on the NMI input causes the 8086 to automatically do an NMI (type 2) interrupt response.

Figure 8-8 shows how we modified the circuitry for our example here. We removed R22, a 110-Ω resistor, and C33, a 1-μF capacitor, so that the keypad switch can no longer cause an interrupt. We then connected an active low strobe line from an ASCII-encoded keyboard directly to the input of A21, the 74LS14 inverter. When a key on the ASCII keyboard is pressed, the keyboard circuitry will send out the ASCII code for the pressed key on its eight parallel data lines and it will assert the key-pressed strobe line low. The key-pressed strobe going low will cause the NMI input of the 8086 to be asserted high. This will cause the 8086 to do a type 2 interrupt.

Now let's look at the software considerations for this interrupt example.

The software considerations are very similar to those for the divide-by-zero example in a previous section. As shown in Figure 8-9a, p. 218, the mainline program for this example consists mostly of a walk through an initialization list. First, assuming that you are going to read in the ASCII characters from the keyboard and put them in an array in memory, you need to set up a data segment for the array, set up the array, and declare any other variables you are going to use in the program. The statement ASCII_POINTER DW OFFSET ASCII_STRING in the data segment in Figure 8-9a sets aside a word location in memory and initializes that location with the offset of the start of the array we declared to put the ASCII characters in. In the procedure we get this pointer, use it to store a character, and increment it to point to the next location in the array. Since this pointer is stored in a named memory location, it can be accessed easily by the procedure, no matter when the interrupt occurs in the mainline program. KEYDONE is a flag which will be set by the interrupt procedure when 100 characters have been read in and stored.

Any interrupt response uses the stack, so next you need to set up a stack. Note that the PUBLIC and EXTRN directives are used so that the mainline program and the interrupt procedure can be in separate assembly modules.

In the code section of the mainline you need to initialize the stack segment register, the stack pointer register, and the data segment register. Finally, you need to initialize the interrupt-vector table by loading address 00008H with the IP value for the start of the type 2 procedure, and address 0000AH with the CS value for the start of the procedure.

The HERE:JMP HERE instruction at the end of the mainline program stimulates a complex mainline program that the 8086 might be executing. The 8086 will execute this instruction over and over until an interrupt occurs. When an interrupt occurs, the 8086 will service the interrupt and then return to execute the HERE:JMP HERE instruction over and over again until the next interrupt. Now let's consider the interrupt procedure.

The algorithm for the interrupt procedure can be simply stated as

IF 100 characters not read THEN
      Read character from port
      Mask parity bit
      Put character in array
      Increment array pointer
      Decrement character count
      Return
ELSE Return

Note that we used an IF-THEN-ELSE structure rather than a WHILE not 100 characters DO structure, because we want only one character to be read in for each call of the procedure.

Figure 8-9b, p. 219, shows the assembly language program for the interrupt-service procedure. After saving AX, BX, CX, and DX on the stack, we check to see if all

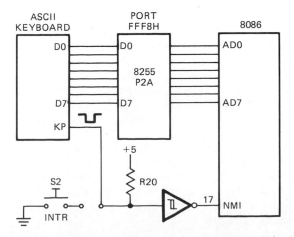

FIGURE 8-8   Circuit modifications for SDK-86 NMI input.

```
 1                              ;8086 PROGRAM F8-09A.ASM
 2                              ;ABSTRACT   : Mainline of program to read characters from a keyboard
 3                              ;           ; The mainline of this program initializes the interrupt
 4                              ;           ; table with the address of the procedure that reads
 5                              ;           ; characters from a keyboard on an interrupt basis.
 6                              ;PORTS      : Uses none in mainline. Uses FFF8H in procedure
 7                              ;REGISTERS : Uses CS,DS,SS,ES,SP,AX
 8                              ;PROCEDURES: Uses KEYBOARD
 9                              ;           : Link mainline F8-09A.OBJ with procedure F8-09B.OBJ
10
11 0000                        DATA SEGMENT   WORD   PUBLIC
12 0000  64*(00)                   ASCII_STRING    DB    100 DUP(0)          ; Store for characters
13 0064  0000r                     ASCII_POINTER   DW    OFFSET ASCII_STRING ; Pointer to ASCII_STRING
14 0066  64                        CHARCNT         DB    100                 ; Read 100 characters
15 0067  00                        KEYDONE         DB    0                   ; =1 if characters all read
16 0068                        DATA ENDS
17
18 0000                        STACK_SEG SEGMENT
19 0000  64*(0000)                 DW   100 DUP (0)                          ; Set up stack of 100 words
20                                  TOP_STACK LABEL   WORD                   ; Pointer to top of stack
21 00C8                        STACK_SEG     ENDS
22
23                             PUBLIC  ASCII_POINTER, CHARCNT, KEYDONE ; Make available to other modules
24                             EXTRN   KEYBOARD:FAR                    ; Procedure in another assembly module
25
26 0000                        CODE SEGMENT   WORD   PUBLIC
27                                  ASSUME CS:CODE, DS:DATA, SS:STACK_SEG
28 0000  B8 0000s              START: MOV  AX, STACK_SEG          ; Initialize stack segment register
29 0003  8E D0                        MOV  SS, AX
30 0005  BC 00C8r                     MOV  SP, OFFSET TOP_STACK    ; Initialize stack pointer
31 0008  B8 0000s                     MOV  AX, DATA                ; Initialize data segment register
32 000B  8E D8                        MOV  DS, AX
33                             ;Store the address for the KEYBOARD routine at address 0000:0008
34                             ;Address 00008-0000B is where type 2 interrupt gets interrupt
35                             ;service procedure address. CS at 0000A & 0000B, IP at 00008 & 00009
36 000D  B8 0000                      MOV  AX, 0000
37 0010  8E C0                        MOV  ES, AX
38 0012  26: C7 06 000A 0000s         MOV  WORD PTR ES:000AH, SEG KEYBOARD
39 0019  26: C7 06 0008 0000e         MOV  WORD PTR ES:0008H, OFFSET KEYBOARD
40                             ;Simulate larger program
41 0020  EB FE                HERE:  JMP  HERE
42 0022                        CODE   ENDS
43                                    END
```

(a)

FIGURE 8-9 Reading characters from an ASCII keyboard on interrupt basis.
(a) Initialization and mainline. (*See also next page.*)

characters have been read. If CHARCNT is 0, then we just pop the registers and return to the mainline program. If CHARCNT is not 0, we copy the array pointer from its named memory location, ASCII_POINTER, to BX. We then read in the ASCII character from the port that the keyboard is connected to and mask the parity bit of the ASCII character. The MOV [BX],AL instruction next copies the ASCII character to the memory location pointed to by BX. To get the pointer ready for the read and store operation, we increment the stored pointer with the INC ASCII_POINTER instruction. Finally, we restore DX, CX, BX, and AX, and return to the mainline program.

Sitting in a HERE:JMP HERE loop waiting for an interrupt signal may not seem like much of an improvement over polling the key-pressed strobe. However, in a more realistic program, the 8086 would be doing many other tasks between keyboard interrupts. With polling, the 8086 would not easily be able to do this.

Using Interrupts for Counting and Timing

COUNTING APPLICATIONS

As a simple example of the use of an interrupt input for counting, suppose that we are using an 8086 to control a printed-circuit-board-making machine in our computerized electronics factory. Further suppose that we want to detect each finished board as it comes out of the machine and to keep a count of finished boards so that we can compare this count with the number of boards fed in. This way we can determine if any boards were lost in the machine.

To do this count on an interrupt basis, all we have to do is detect when a board passes out of the machine and send an interrupt signal to an interrupt input on the 8086. The interrupt-service procedure for that input can simply increment the board count stored in a named memory location.

```
 1                        ;8086 PROCEDURE F8-09B.ASM called by program F8-09A.ASM
 2                        ;ABSTRACT  : PROCEDURE KEYBOARD
 3                        ;           ; This procedure reads in ASCII characters from an
 4                        ;           ; encoded keyboard on an interrupt basis and stores them
 5                        ;           ; in a buffer in memory.
 6                        ;DESTROYS  : Nothing
 7                        ;PORTS     : Uses input port FFF8H for the keyboard input.
 8
 9 0000                  DATA      SEGMENT    WORD    PUBLIC
10                          EXTRN     ASCII_POINTER:WORD, CHARCNT:BYTE, KEYDONE:BYTE
11 0000                  DATA      ENDS
12
13                       PUBLIC    KEYBOARD
14
15 0000                  CODE      SEGMENT PUBLIC
16 0000                  KEYBOARD  PROC    FAR
17                          ASSUME CS:CODE, DS:DATA
18 0000   FB                       STI                        ; Enable 8086 INTR so higher priority
19                                                            ; interrupts can be recognized
20 0001   50                       PUSH AX                    ; Save registers used
21 0002   53                       PUSH BX
22 0003   51                       PUSH CX
23 0004   52                       PUSH DX
24 0005   80 3E 0000e 00           CMP  CHARCNT, 00           ; See if all characters read in
25 000A   74 23                    JZ   EXIT                  ; Leave procedure if all done
26 000C   8B 1E 0000e              MOV  BX, ASCII_POINTER     ; Get pointer to buffer
27 0010   BA FFF8                   MOV  DX, 0FFF8H            ; Point at keyboard port
28 0013   EC                       IN   AL, DX                ; Read in ASCII code
29 0014   24 7F                    AND  AL, 7FH               ; Mask parity bit
30 0016   88 07                    MOV  [BX], AL              ; Write character to buffer
31 0018   FF 06 0000e              INC  ASCII_POINTER         ; Point to next buffer location
32 001C   FE 0E 0000e              DEC  CHARCNT               ; Reduce character count
33 0020   75 08                    JNZ  NOTDONE               ; If 100 chars not read, clear carry
34 0022   C6 06 0000e 01           MOV  KEYDONE, 01           ; else set flag to indicate done
35 0027   EB 06 90                 JMP  EXIT
36 002A   C6 06 0000e 00 NOTDONE:  MOV  KEYDONE, 00           ; More characters to read so zero flag
37 002F   5A            EXIT:      POP  DX                    ; Restore registers
38 0030   59                       POP  CX
39 0031   5B                       POP  BX
40 0032   58                       POP  AX
41 0033   CF                       IRET                       ; Return to interrupted program
42 0034                  KEYBOARD  ENDP
43 0034                  CODE      ENDS
44                                 END
```

(b)

FIGURE 8-9 (continued) (b) Interrupt-service procedure.

To detect a board coming out of the machine, we use an infrared LED, a phototransistor, and two conditioning gates, as shown in Figure 8-10, p. 220. The LED is positioned over the track where the boards come out, and the phototransistor is positioned below the track. When no board is between the LED and the phototransistor, the light from the LED will strike the phototransistor and turn it on. The collector of the phototransistor will then be low, as will the NMI input on the 8086. When a board passes between the LED and the phototransistor, the light will not reach the phototransistor, and it will turn off. Its collector will go high, and so will the signal to the NMI input of the 8086. The 74LS14 Schmitt trigger inverters are necessary to turn the slow-risetime signal from the phototransistor collector into a signal which meets the risetime requirements of the NMI input on the 8086.

When the 8086 receives the low-to-high signal on its NMI input, it will automatically do a type 2 interrupt response. As we mentioned before, all the type 2 interrupt-service procedure has to do in this case is increment the board count in a named memory location and return to running the machine. This same technique can be used to count people going into a stadium, cows coming in from the pasture, or just about anything else you might want to count.

TIMING APPLICATIONS

In Chapter 4 we showed how a delay loop could be used to set the time between microcomputer operations. In the example there, we used a delay loop to take in data samples at 1-ms intervals. The obvious disadvantage of a delay loop is that while the microcomputer is stuck in the delay loop, it cannot easily be doing other useful work. In many cases a delay loop would be a waste of the microcomputer's valuable time, so we use an interrupt approach.

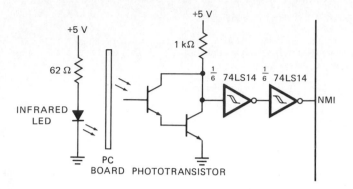

FIGURE 8-10   Circuit for optically detecting presence of an object.

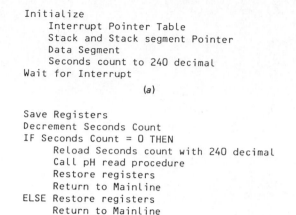

Initialize
   Interrupt Pointer Table
   Stack and Stack segment Pointer
   Data Segment
   Seconds count to 240 decimal
Wait for Interrupt

(a)

Save Registers
Decrement Seconds Count
IF Seconds Count = 0 THEN
      Reload Seconds count with 240 decimal
      Call pH read procedure
      Restore registers
      Return to Mainline
ELSE Restore registers
      Return to Mainline

(b)

FIGURE 8-12   Algorithm for pH read at 4-min intervals. (a) Initialization and mainline. (b) Interrupt-service procedure.

Suppose, for example, that in our 8086-controlled printed-circuit-board-making machine we need to check the pH of a solution approximately every 4 min. If we used a delay loop to count off the 4 min, either the 8086 wouldn't be able to do much else or we would have some difficult calculations to figure out at what points in the program to go check the pH.

To solve this problem, all we have to do is connect a simple 1-Hz pulse source to an interrupt input, as shown in Figure 8-11. This 555 timer circuit is not very accurate, but it is inexpensive, and it is good enough for this application. The 555 timer will send an interrupt signal to the 8086 NMI input approximately once every second. An interrupt procedure is used to keep a count of how many NMI interrupts have occurred. This count is equal to the number of seconds that have passed.

To help you visualize how this works, Figure 8-12 shows the algorithm for this mainline and procedure. In the mainline we set up stack and data segments. In the data segment, we set aside a memory location for the seconds count and initialize that location to the number of seconds that we want to count off. In this case we want 4 min, which is 240 decimal or F0H seconds. Then we initialize the data segment register, stack segment register, and stack pointer register as before.

Each time the 8086 receives an interrupt from the 555 timer, it executes the interrupt-service procedure

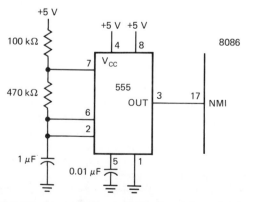

FIGURE 8-11   Inexpensive 1-Hz pulse source for interrupt timing.

for the NMI interrupt. In this procedure we decrement the seconds count in the named memory location and test to see if the count is down to zero yet. If the count is zero, we know that 4 min have elapsed, so we reload the seconds count memory location with 240 and call the procedure which reads the pH of the solution and takes appropriate action if the pH is not correct. If the seconds count is not zero, execution simply returns to the mainline program until the next interrupt from the 555 or from some other source occurs. The advantage of this interrupt approach is that the interrupt-service procedure takes only a few microseconds of the 8086's time once every second. The rest of the time the 8086 is free to run the mainline program.

USING AN INTERRUPT TO PRODUCE A REAL-TIME CLOCK

Another application using a 1-Hz interrupt input might be to generate a real-time clock of seconds, minutes, and hours. The time from this clock can then be displayed and/or printed out on timecards, etc. To generate the clock, a 1-Hz signal is applied to an interrupt input. A seconds count, a minutes count, and an hours count are kept in three successive memory locations. When an interrupt occurs, the seconds count is incremented by 1. If the seconds count is not equal to 60, then execution is simply returned to the mainline program. If the seconds count is equal to 60, then the seconds count is reset to 0 and the minutes count is incremented by 1. If the minutes count is not 60, then execution is simply returned to the mainline. If the minutes count is 60, then the minutes count is reset to 0 and the hours count is incremented by 1. If the hours count is not 13, then execution is simply returned to the mainline. If the hours count is equal to 13, then it is reset to 1 and execution is returned to the mainline. A problem at the end of the chapter asks you to write the algorithm and program for this real-time clock.

The interrupt-service routine for the real-time clock can easily be modified to also keep track of other time measurements such as the 4-min timer shown in the preceding example. In other words, the single interrupt-service routine can be used to keep track of several different time intervals. By counting a different number of interrupts or applying a different frequency signal to the interrupt input, this technique can be used to time many different tasks in a microcomputer system.

GENERATING AN ACCURATE TIME BASE FOR TIMING INTERRUPTS

The 555 timer that we used for the 4-min timer just described was accurate enough for that application, but for many applications—such as a real-time clock—it is not. For more precise timing, we usually use a signal derived from a crystal-controlled oscillator. The processor clock signal is generated by a crystal-controlled oscillator, so it is stable, but this signal is obviously too high in frequency to drive a processor interrupt input directly. The solution is to divide the clock signal down with an external counter device to the desired frequency for the interrupt input. Most microcomputer manufacturers have a compatible device which can be programmed with instructions to divide an input frequency by any desired number. Besides acting as programmable frequency dividers, these devices have many important uses in microcomputer systems. Therefore, the next section describes how an Intel 8254 Programmable Counter operates, how an 8254 can easily be added to an SDK-86 board, and how an 8254 is used in a variety of interrupt applications. Also in the next section, we use the 8254 discussion to show you the general procedure for initializing any of the programmable peripheral devices we discuss in later chapters.

8254 SOFTWARE-PROGRAMMABLE TIMER/COUNTER

Because of the many tasks that they can be used for in microcomputer systems, programmable timer/counters are very important for you to learn about. As you read through the following sections, pay particular attention to the applications of this device in systems and the general procedure for initializing a programmable device such as the 8254. Read lightly through the discussions of the different counter modes to become aware of the types of problems that the device can solve for you. Later, when you have a specific problem to solve, you can dig into the details of these discussions.

Another important point to make to you here is that the discussions of various devices throughout the rest of this book are not intended to replace the manufacturers' data sheets for the devices. Many of the programmable peripheral devices we discuss are so versatile that each requires almost a small book to describe all the details of its operations. The discussions here are intended to introduce you to the devices, show you what they can be used for, and show you enough details about them that you can do some real jobs with them. After you become familiar with the use of a device in some simple applications, you can read the data sheets to learn further "bells and whistles" that the devices have.

Basic 8253 and 8254 Operation

The Intel 8253 and 8254 each contain three 16-bit counters which can be programmed to operate in several different modes. The 8253 and 8254 devices are pin-for-pin compatible, and they are nearly identical in function. The major differences are as follows:

1. The maximum input clock frequency for the 8253 is 2.6 MHz; the maximum clock frequency for the 8254 is 8 MHz (10 MHz for the 8254-2).

2. The 8254 has a *read-back* feature which allows you to latch the count in all the counters and the status of the counter at any point. The 8253 does not have this read-back feature.

To simplify reading of this section, we will refer only to the 8254. However, you can assume that the discussion also applies to the 8253 except where we specifically state otherwise.

As shown by the block diagram of the 8254 in Figure 8-13, the device contains three 16-bit counters. In some ways these counters are similar to the TTL presettable counters we reviewed in Chapter 1. The big advantage of these counters, however, is that you can load a count in them, start them, and stop them with instructions in your program. Such a device is said to be software-programmable. To program the device, you send count bytes and control bytes to the device just as you would send data to a port device.

If you look along the left side of the block diagram in Figure 8-13, you will see the signal lines used to interface the device to the system buses. A little later we show how these are actually connected in a real system. The main points for you to note about the 8254 at the moment are that it has an 8-bit interface to the data bus, it has a $\overline{CS}$ input which will be asserted by an

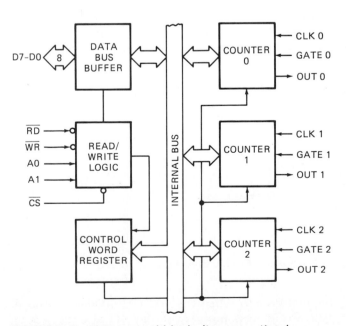

FIGURE 8-13   8254 internal block diagram.   (*Intel Corporation*)

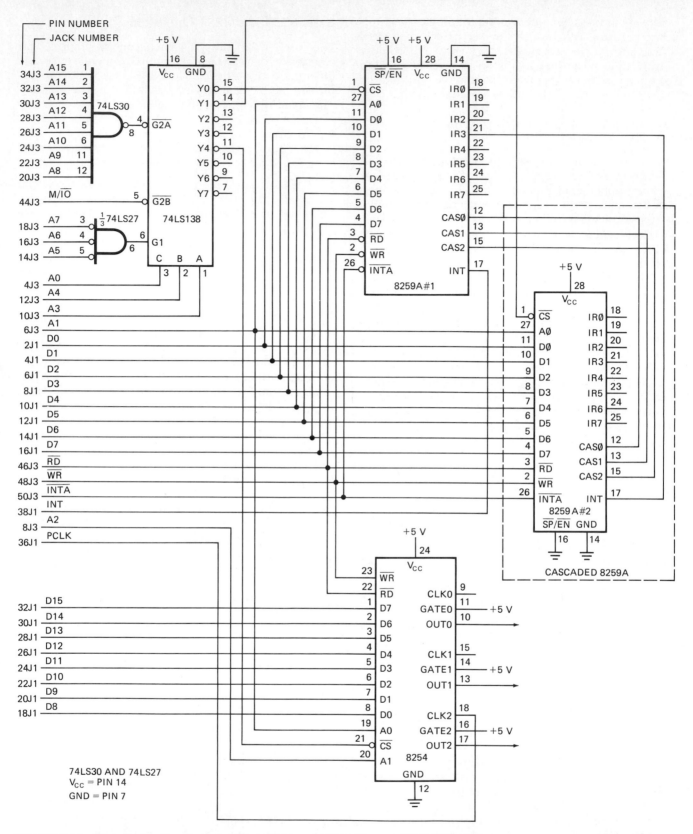

FIGURE 8-14   Circuit showing how to add an 8254 and 8259A(s) to an SDK-86 board.

address decoder when the device is addressed, and it has two address inputs, A0 and A1, to allow you to address one of the three counters or the control word register in the device.

The right side of the 8254 block diagram in Figure 8-13 shows the counter inputs and outputs. You can apply a signal of any frequency from dc to 8 MHz to each of the counter clock inputs, labeled CLK in the diagram.

The GATE input on each counter allows you to start or stop that counter with an external hardware signal. If the GATE input of a counter is high (1), then that counter is enabled for counting. If the GATE input is low, the counter is disabled. The output signal from each counter appears on its OUT pin. Now let's see how a programmable peripheral device such as the 8254 is connected in a system.

System Connections for an 8254 Timer/Counter

An 8254 is a very useful device to have in a microcomputer system, but, in order to keep the cost down, the SDK-86 was not designed with one on the board. Figure 8-14 shows the circuit connections for adding an 8254 Counter and an 8259A Priority Interrupt Controller to an SDK-86 board. We discuss the 8259A in a later section of this chapter.

If you use wire-wrap headers for connectors J1 and J3 on an SDK-86 board, the circuitry shown can easily be wire-wrapped on the prototyping area of the board. Install the WAIT-state jumper to insert one WAIT state. As explained in Chapter 7, a WAIT state is needed because of the added delay of the decoders and buffers.

The 74LS138 in Figure 8-14 is used to produce chip select (CS) signals for the 8254, the 8259A, and any other I/O devices you might want to add. Let's look first at the circuitry around this device to determine the system base address which selects each device.

In order for any of the outputs of the 74LS138 to be asserted, the G1, G2A, and G2B enable inputs must all be asserted. The G1 input will be asserted (high) if system address lines A5, A6, and A7 are all low. The G2A input will be asserted (low) if system address lines A8 through A15 are all high. As shown by the truth table in Figure 8-15, these two inputs therefore will be asserted for a system base address of FF00H. The G2B input of the 74LS138 will be asserted (low) if the M/IO line is low, as it will be for a port read or write operation.

Now, remember from Chapter 7 that only one of the Y outputs of the 74LS138 will ever be asserted at a time. The output asserted is determined by the 3-bit binary code applied to the A, B, and C select inputs. In the circuit in Figure 8-14, we connected system address line A0 to the C input, address line A4 to the B input, and address line A3 to the A input. The truth table in Figure 8-15 shows the system base addresses that will enable each of the 74LS138 Y outputs. As you will see a little later, system address lines A1 and A2 are used to select internal parts of the 8254 and 8259A.

We connected A0 to the C input so that half of the Y outputs will be selected by even addresses and half of the Y outputs will be selected by odd addresses. We did this so that loading on the two halves of the data bus will be equal as we add peripheral devices such as the 8254 and 8259A. To see how this works, note that the peripheral devices have only eight data lines. For an odd-addressed device we connect these data lines to the upper eight system data lines, and for an even-addressed device, we connect these to the lower eight system data lines. By alternating between odd- and even-selected outputs as we add peripheral devices, we equalize loading on the bus.

As shown by the truth table in Figure 8-15, the system base address of the added 8254 is FF01H. Other connections to the 8254 are the system RD and WR lines used to enable the 8254 for reading or writing; eight data lines, used to send control bytes, status bytes, and count values between the CPU and the 8254; and system address lines A1 and A2, used to select the control register or one of the three counters in the 8254. Now that you see how an 8254 is connected in a system, we will show you how to initialize an 8254 to do some useful work for you.

Initializing an 8254 Programmable Peripheral Device

When the power is first turned on, programmable peripheral devices such as the 8254 are usually in *undefined states.* Before you can use them for anything, you have to initialize them in the *mode* you need for your specific application. Initializing these devices is not usually difficult, but it is very easy to make errors if you do not do it in a very systematic way. To initialize any programmable peripheral device, you should always work your way through the following series of steps.

1. Determine the system base address for the device. You do this from the address decoder circuitry or the address decoder truth table. From the truth table

A8–A15	A5–A7	A4	A3	A2	A1	A0	M/$\overline{\text{IO}}$	Y OUTPUT SELECTED	SYSTEM BASE ADDRESS			DEVICE
1	0	0	0	X	X	0	0	0	F	F	0	0	8259A #1
1	0	0	1	X	X	0	0	1	F	F	0	8	8259A #2
1	0	1	0	X	X	0	0	2	F	F	1	0	
1	0	1	1	X	X	0	0	3	F	F	1	8	
1	0	0	0	X	X	1	0	4	F	F	0	1	8254
1	0	0	1	X	X	1	0	5	F	F	0	9	
1	0	1	0	X	X	1	0	6	F	F	1	1	
1	0	1	1	X	X	1	0	7	F	F	1	9	
ALL OTHER STATES								NONE					

FIGURE 8-15   Truth table for 74LS138 address decoder in Figure 8-14.

A1	A0	SELECTS
0	0	COUNTER 0
0	1	COUNTER 1
1	0	COUNTER 2
1	1	CONTROL WORD REGISTER

(a)

SYSTEM ADDRESS	8254 PART
F F 0 1	COUNTER 0
F F 0 3	COUNTER 1
F F 0 5	COUNTER 2
F F 0 7	CONTROL REG

(b)

FIGURE 8-16   8254 addresses. (a) Internal. (b) System.

D7	D6	D5	D4	D3	D2	D1	D0
SC1	SC0	RW1	RW0	M2	M1	M0	BCD

SC – SELECT COUNTER:

SC1	SC0	
0	0	SELECT COUNTER 0
0	1	SELECT COUNTER 1
1	0	SELECT COUNTER 2
1	1	READ–BACK COMMAND (SEE READ OPERATIONS)

RW – READ/WRITE:

RW1	RW0	
0	0	COUNTER LATCH COMMAND (SEE READ OPERATIONS)
0	1	READ/WRITE LEAST SIGNIFICANT BYTE ONLY.
1	0	READ/WRITE MOST SIGNIFICANT BYTE ONLY.
1	1	READ/WRITE LEAST SIGNIFICANT BYTE FIRST, THEN MOST SIGNIFICANT BYTE.

M – MODE:

M2	M1	M0	
0	0	0	MODE 0 – INTERRUPT ON TERMINAL COUNT
0	0	1	MODE 1 – HARDWARE ONE-SHOT
X	1	0	MODE 2 – PULSE GENERATOR
X	1	1	MODE 3 – SQUARE WAVE GENERATOR
1	0	0	MODE 4 – SOFTWARE TRIGGERED STROBE
1	0	1	MODE 5 – HARDWARE TRIGGERED STROBE

BCD:

0	BINARY COUNTER 16-BITS
1	BINARY CODED DECIMAL (BCD) COUNTER (4 DECADES)

NOTE: DON'T CARE BITS (X) SHOULD BE 0 TO INSURE COMPATIBILITY WITH FUTURE INTEL PRODUCTS.

FIGURE 8-17   8254 control word format.   (*Intel Corporation*)

in Figure 8-15, the system base address of the 8254 in our example here is FF01H.

2. Use the device data sheet to determine the internal addresses for each of the control registers, ports, timers, status registers, etc., in the device. Figure 8-16a shows the internal addresses for the three counters and the control word register for the 8254. A0 in this table represents the A0 input of the device, and A1 represents the A1 input of the device. Note in the schematic in Figure 8-14 that system address line A1 is connected to the A0 input of the 8254, and system address line A2 is connected to the A1 input. We could not use system address line A0 as one of these because, as described before, we used system address line A0 as one of the inputs to the address decoder.

3. Add each of the internal addresses to the system base address to determine the system address of each of the parts of the device. You need to do this so that you know the actual addresses where you have to send control words, timer values, etc. Figure 8-16b shows the system addresses for the three timers and the control register of the 8254 we added to the SDK-86 board. Note that the addresses all have to be odd because the device is connected on the upper half of the data bus.

4. Look in the data sheet for the device for the format of the control word(s) that you have to send to the device to initialize it. For different devices, incidentally, the control word(s) may be referred to as command words or mode words. To initialize the 8254, you send a control word to the control register for each counter that you want to use. Figure 8-17 shows the format for the 8254 control word.

5. Construct the control word required to initialize the device for your specific application. You construct this control word on a bit-by-bit basis. We have found it helpful to actually draw the eight little boxes shown at the top of Figure 8-17 so that we don't miss any bits. (An easy way to draw the eight boxes is to draw a long rectangle, divide it in half, divide

each resulting half in two, and finally divide each resulting quarter in two.) To help keep track of the meaning of each bit of a control word, write under each bit the meaning of that bit. A little later we show you how to do this for an 8254 control word. Documentation of this sort is very valuable when you are trying to debug a program or modify an old program for some new application.

6. Finally, send the control word(s) you have made up to the control register address for the device. In the case of the 8254, you also have to send the starting count to each of the counter registers.

Now that you have an overview of the initialization process, let's take a closer look at how you do the last two steps for an 8254.

A separate control word must be sent for each counter that you want to use in the device. However, according to Figure 8-16a, the 8254 has only one control register address. The trick here is that the control words for all three counters are sent to the same address in the device. As shown in Figure 8-17, you use the upper 2 bits of a control word to tell the 8254 which counter you want that control word to initialize. For example, if you are making up a control word for counter 0 in the 8254, you make the SC1 bit of the control word a 0 and the SC0 bit a 0. Later we will explain the meaning of the read-back command, specified by a 1 in each of these bits.

The 16-bit counters in the 8254 are down counters. This means that the number in a counter will be decremented by each clock pulse. You can program the 8254 to count down a loaded number in BCD (decimal) or in binary. If you make the D0 bit of the control word a 0, then the counter will treat the loaded number as a pure binary number. In this case the largest number that you can load in is FFFFH. If you make the D0 bit of the control word a 1, then the largest number you can load in the counter is 9999H, and the counter will count a loaded number down in decimal (BCD). Actually, because of the way the 8254 counts, the "largest" number you can load in for both cases is 0000, but thinking of FFFFH and 9999H makes it easier to remember the difference between the two modes.

Now let's take a brief look at the mode bits (M2, M1, and M0) in the control word format in Figure 8-17. The binary number you put in these bits specifies the effect that the gate input will have on counting and the waveform that will be produced on the OUT pin. For example, if you specify mode 3 for a counter by putting 011 in these 3 bits, the counter will be put in a square-wave mode. In this mode, the output will be high for the first half of the loaded count and low for the second half of the loaded count. When the count reaches 0, the original count is automatically reloaded and the count-down repeated. The waveform on the OUT pin in this mode will then be a square wave with a frequency equal to the input clock frequency divided by the count you wrote to the counter. A little later we will discuss and show applications for some of the six different modes. First, let's finish looking at the control word bits and see how you send the control word and a count to the device.

The RW1 and RW0 bits of the control word are used to specify how you want to write a count to a counter or to read the count from a counter. If you want to load a 16-bit number into a counter, you put 1's in both these bits in the control word you send for that counter. After you send the control word, you send the low byte of the count to the counter address and then send the high byte of the count to the counter address. In a later paragraph we show an example of the instruction sequence to do this. In cases where you only want to load a new value in the low byte of a counter, you can send a control word with 01 in the RW bits and then send the new low byte to the counter. Likewise, if you want to load only a new high byte value in the counter, you can send a control word with 10 in the RW bits, and then send only the new high byte to the counter.

You can read the number in one of the counters at any time. The usual way to do this is to first latch the current count in some internal latches by sending a control word with 00 in the RW bits. Send another control word with 01, 10, or 11 in the RW bits to specify how you want to read out the bytes of the latched count. Then read the count from the counter address.

As a specific example of initializing an 8254, suppose that we want to use counter 0 of the 8254 in Figure 8-14 to produce a stable 78.6-kHz square-wave signal for a UART clock by dividing down the 2.45-MHz PCLK signal available on the SDK-86 board. To do this, we first connect the SDK-86 PCLK signal to the CLK input of counter 0 and tie the GATE input of the counter high to enable it for counting. To produce 78.6 kHz from 2.45 MHz, we have to divide by 32 decimal, so this is the value that we will eventually load into counter 0. First, however, we have to determine the system addresses for the device, make up the control word for counter 0, and send the control word.

As shown in Figure 8-16b, the system address for the control register of this 8254 is FF07H. This is where we will send the control word. For our control word we want to select counter 0, so we make the SC1 and SC0 bits both 0's. We want the counter to operate in square-wave mode. This is mode 3, so we make the mode bits of the control word 011. Since we want to divide by 32 decimal, we tell the counter to count down in decimal by making the BCD bit of the control word a 1. This makes our life easier, because we don't have to convert the 32 to binary or hex. Finally, we have to decide how we want to load the count into the counter. Since the count that we need to load in is less than 99, we only have to load the lower byte of the counter. According to Figure 8-17, the RW1 bit should be a 0 and the RW0 bit a 1 for a write to only the lower byte (LSB). The complete control word then is 00010111 in binary. Here are the instructions to send the control word and count to counter 0 of the 8254 in Figure 8-14. Note how the bits of the control word are documented.

```
MOV AL,00010111B   ; Control word for counter 0
                   ; Read/write LSB only, mode 3, BCD countdown
                   ; 00 01 011 1
                   ;  |  |  |   |_____BCD countdown
                   ;  |  |  |_____Mode 3
                   ;  |  |_____R/W LSB only
                   ;  |_____Select counter 0
MOV DX,0FF07H      ; Point at 8254 control register
OUT DX,AL          ; Send control word
MOV AL,32H         ; Load lower byte of count
MOV DX,0FF01H      ; Point to counter 0 count register
OUT DX,AL          ; Send count to count register
```

Note that since we set the RW bits of the control word for read/write LSB only, we do not have to include instructions to load the MSB of the counter. Programmed in this way, the 8254 will automatically load 0's in the upper byte of the counter.

If you need to load a count that is larger than 1 byte, make the RW bits in the control word both 1's. Send the lower byte of the count as shown above. Then send the high byte of the count to the count register by adding the instructions

MOV AL,HIGH_BYTE_OF_COUNT ; Load MSB of count
OUT DX,AL   ; Send MSB to
                                        count register

Note that the high byte of the count is sent to the same address that the low byte of the count was sent.

For each counter that you want to use in an 8254, you repeat the preceding series of six or eight instructions with the control word and count for the mode that you want. Before going on with this chapter, review the six initialization steps shown at the start of this section to make sure these are firmly fixed in your mind. In the next section we discuss and show some applications of the different modes in which an 8254 counter can be operated, but we do not have space there to show all the steps for each of the modes.

8254 Counter Modes and Applications

As we mentioned previously, an 8254 counter can be programmed to operate in any one of six different modes. The Intel data book uses timing diagrams such as those in Figure 8-18 to show how a counter functions in each of these modes. Since these waveforms may not be totally obvious to you at first glance, we will work our way through some of them to show you how to interpret them. We will also show some uses of the different counter modes. As you read through this section, don't try to absorb all the details of the different modes. Concentrate on learning to interpret the timing waveforms and on the different types of output signals you can produce with an 8254.

MODE 0—INTERRUPT ON TERMINAL COUNT

First read the Intel notes at the bottom of Figure 8-18; then take a look at the top set of waveforms in the figure. For this first example, the GATE input is held high so that the counter is always enabled for counting. The first dip in the waveform labeled $\overline{WR}$ represents the control word for the counter being written to the 8254. CW = 10 over this dip indicates that the control word written is 10H. According to the control word format in Figure 8-17, this means that counter 0 is being initialized for binary counting, mode 0, and a read/write of only the LSB. After the control word is written to the control register, the output pin of counter 0 will go low. The next dip in the $\overline{WR}$ waveform represents a count of 4 being written to the count register of counter 0. Before this count can be counted down, it must be transferred from the count register to the actual counter. If you look at the count values shown under the OUT waveform in

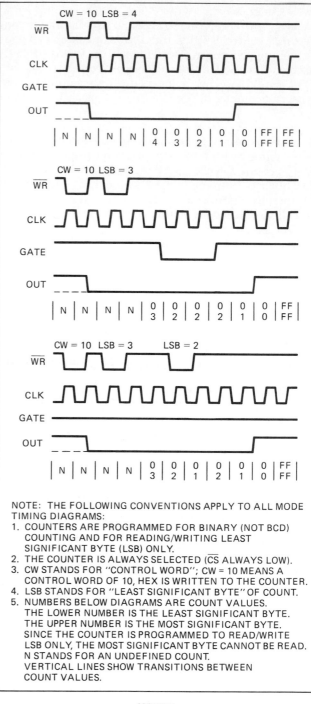

NOTE: THE FOLLOWING CONVENTIONS APPLY TO ALL MODE TIMING DIAGRAMS:
1. COUNTERS ARE PROGRAMMED FOR BINARY (NOT BCD) COUNTING AND FOR READING/WRITING LEAST SIGNIFICANT BYTE (LSB) ONLY.
2. THE COUNTER IS ALWAYS SELECTED (CS ALWAYS LOW).
3. CW STANDS FOR "CONTROL WORD"; CW = 10 MEANS A CONTROL WORD OF 10, HEX IS WRITTEN TO THE COUNTER.
4. LSB STANDS FOR "LEAST SIGNIFICANT BYTE" OF COUNT.
5. NUMBERS BELOW DIAGRAMS ARE COUNT VALUES. THE LOWER NUMBER IS THE LEAST SIGNIFICANT BYTE. THE UPPER NUMBER IS THE MOST SIGNIFICANT BYTE. SINCE THE COUNTER IS PROGRAMMED TO READ/WRITE LSB ONLY, THE MOST SIGNIFICANT BYTE CANNOT BE READ. N STANDS FOR AN UNDEFINED COUNT. VERTICAL LINES SHOW TRANSITIONS BETWEEN COUNT VALUES.

MODE 0

FIGURE 8-18   8254 MODE 0 example timing diagrams. (*Intel Corporation*)

the timing diagram, you should see that the count of 4 is transferred into the counter by the next clock pulse after $\overline{WR}$ goes high. Each clock pulse after this will decrement the count by 1. When the count is decremented to 0, the OUT pin will go high. If you write a count N to a counter in mode 0, the OUT pin will go high after N + 1 clock pulses have occurred. Note that the counter decrements from 0000 to FFFFH on the next clock pulse unless you load some new count into the

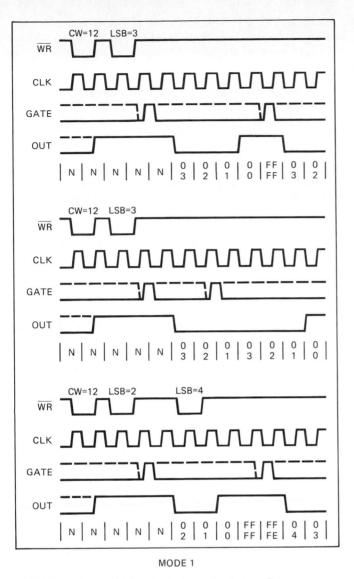

| | N | N | N | N | N | 0 3 | 0 2 | 0 1 | 0 0 | FF FF | 0 3 | 0 2 |

| | N | N | N | N | N | 0 3 | 0 2 | 0 1 | 0 3 | 0 2 | 0 1 | 0 0 |

| | N | N | N | N | N | 0 2 | 0 1 | 0 0 | FF FF | FF FE | 0 4 | 0 3 |

MODE 1

FIGURE 8-19   8254 MODE 1 example timing diagrams.
(*Intel Corporation*)

counter. If the OUT pin is connected to an 8259A IR input or the NMI interrupt input of an 8086, then the processor will be interrupted when the counter reaches 0 (terminal count).

The second set of waveforms in Figure 8-18 shows that if the GATE input is made low, the counter value will be held. When the GATE input is made high again, the counter continues to decrement by 1 for each clock pulse.

The third set of waveforms in Figure 8-18 shows that if a new count is written to a counter, the new count will be loaded into the counter on the next clock pulse. Following clock pulses will decrement the new count until it reaches 0.

As an example of what you can use this mode for, suppose that as one of its jobs you want to use an 8086 to control some parking lot signs around an electronics factory. The main parking lot can hold 1000 cars. When it gets full, you want to turn on a sign which directs people to another lot. To detect when a car enters the

lot, you can use an optical sensor such as the one shown in Figure 8-10. Each time a car passes through, this circuit will produce a pulse. You could connect the signal from this sensor directly to an interrupt input and have the processor count interrupts, as we did for the printed-circuit-board-making machine in a previous example. However, the less you burden the processor with trivial tasks such as this, the more time it has available to do complex work for you. Therefore, you let a counter in an 8254 count cars and interrupt the 8086 only when it has counted 1000 cars.

You connect the output from the optical sensor circuit to the CLK input of, say, counter 1 of an 8254. You tie the GATE input of counter 1 to +5 V so it will be enabled for counting and connect the OUT pin of counter 1 to an interrupt input on an 8259A or the NMI input on the 8086.

In the mainline program, you initialize counter 1 for mode 0, BCD counting, and read/write LSB then MSB with a control word of 01110001 binary. You want the counter to produce an interrupt after 1000 pulses from the sensor, so you will send a count of 999 decimal to the counter. The reason that you want to send 999 instead of 1000 is that, as shown in Figure 8-18, the OUT pin will go high N + 1 clock pulses after the count value is written to the counter. Since you initialized the counter for read/write LSB then MSB, you send 99H and then 09H to the address of counter 1. By initializing the counter for BCD counting, you can just send the count value as a BCD number instead of having to convert it to hex.

The service procedure for this interrupt will contain instructions which turn on the parking-lot-full sign, close off the main entrance, and return to the mainline program. For this example you don't have to worry that the counter decrements from 0000 to FFFFH, because after you shut the gate, the counter will not receive any more interrupts.

MODE 1—HARDWARE-RETRIGGERABLE ONE-SHOT

The basic principle of a *one-shot* is that when a signal is applied to the trigger input of the device, its output will be asserted. After a fixed amount of time the output will automatically return to its unasserted state. For a TTL one-shot such as the 74LS122, the time that the output is asserted is determined by the time constant of a resistor and a capacitor connected to the device. For an 8254 counter in one-shot mode, the time that the output is asserted low is determined by the frequency of an applied clock and by a count loaded into the counter. The advantage of the 8254 approach is that the output pulse width can be changed under program control and, if a crystal-controlled clock is used, the output pulse width can be very accurately specified.

Figure 8-19 shows some example timing waveforms for an 8254 counter in mode 1. Let's take a look at the top set of waveforms. Again, the first dip in the $\overline{WR}$ waveform represents the control word of 12H being sent to the 8254. Use Figure 8-17 to help you determine how this control word initializes the device. You should find that a control word of 12H programs counter 0 for binary count, mode 1, read/write LSB only. When the control word is written to the 8254, the OUT pin goes high.

The second dip in the $\overline{WR}$ waveform represents writing a count to the counter. Note that, because the GATE input is low, the counter does not start counting down immediately when the count is written, as it does in mode 0. For mode 1, the GATE input functions as a trigger input. When the GATE/trigger input is made high, the count will be transferred from the count register to the actual counter on the next clock pulse. Each following clock pulse will decrement the counter by 1. When the counter reaches 0, the OUT pin will go high again. In other words, if you load a value of N in the counter and trigger the device by making the GATE input high, the OUT pin will go low for a time equal to N clock cycles. The output pulse width is then N times the period of the signal applied to the CLK input. Incidentally, the dashed sections of the GATE waveforms in Figure 8-19 mean that the GATE/trigger input signal can go low again any time during that time interval.

The second set of waveforms in Figure 8-19 demonstrates what is meant by the term *retriggerable*. If another trigger pulse comes before the previously loaded count has been counted down to 0, the original count will be reloaded on the next clock pulse. The countdown will then start over and continue until another trigger occurs or until the count reaches 0. If trigger pulses continue to come before the count is decremented to 0, the OUT pin will remain low.

The bottom set of waveforms in Figure 8-19 shows that if you write a new count to a count register while the OUT pin is low, the new count will not be loaded into the counter and counted down until the next trigger pulse occurs.

For an example of the use of mode 1, we will show you how to make a circuit which produces an interrupt signal if the ac power fails. This circuit could be connected to the NMI input of an 8086 to call an interrupt procedure which saves parameters in battery-backed RAM when the ac power fails.

Figure 8-20 shows a circuit which uses an optical coupler (an LED and a phototransistor packaged together) to produce logic-level pulses at power line fre-

quency. The 74LS14 inverters sharpen the edges of these pulses so that they can be applied to the GATE/trigger input of an 8254. For a 60-Hz line frequency, a pulse will be produced every 16.66 ms. Now what we want to do here is to load the counter with a value such that the counter will always be retriggered by the power line pulses before the countdown is completed. As shown by the second set of waveforms in Figure 8-19, the OUT pin will then stay low and not send an interrupt signal to the NMI input of the 8086. If the ac power fails, no more pulses come in to the 8254 trigger input. The trigger input will be left high, and the countdown will be completed. The 8254 OUT pin will then go high and interrupt the 8086.

To determine the counter value for this application, you just calculate the number of input clock pulses required to produce a countdown time longer than 16.66 ms—for example, 20 ms. If you use the 2.4576-MHz PCLK signal on an SDK-86 board, 20 ms requires 49,152 cycles of PCLK, so this is the number you would load in the 8254 counter. Since this number is too large to load in as a BCD count, you put a 0 in the BCD bit of the control word to tell the 8254 to count the number down in binary. Then you send the count value of C000H to the count register.

MODE 2—TIMED INTERRUPT GENERATOR

In a previous section we described how a real-time clock of seconds, minutes, and hours could be kept in three memory locations by counting interrupts from a 1-Hz pulse source. We also described how the 1-Hz interrupts could be used to measure off other time intervals. The difficulty with using a 1-Hz interrupt signal is that the maximum resolution of any time measurement is 1 s. In other words, if you use a 1-Hz signal, you can only measure times to the nearest second. To improve the resolution of time measurements, most microcomputer systems use a higher-frequency signal such as 1 kHz for a real-time clock interrupt. With a 1-kHz interrupt signal, the time resolution is 1 ms. An 8254 counter operating in mode 2 can be used to produce a stable 1-kHz signal by dividing down the processor clock signal.

Figure 8-21 shows the waveforms for an 8254 counter operating in mode 2. Let's look at the top set of waveforms

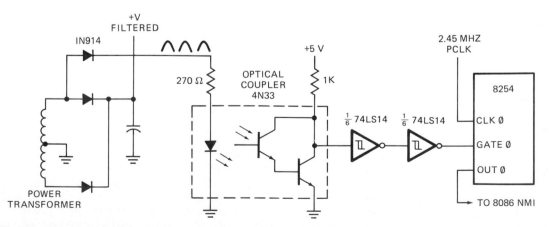

FIGURE 8-20   Circuit to produce logic-level pulses at power line frequency.

first. The two dips in the $\overline{\text{WR}}$ waveform represent a control word and the LSB of a count being written to the count register. The next clock pulse after the count is written will transfer the count from the count register to the actual counter. Since the GATE input is high, succeeding clock pulses will count down this value until it reaches 1. When the count reaches 1, the OUT pin, which was previously high, will go low for one clock pulse time. The falling edge of the next clock pulse will cause the OUT pin to go high again and the original count to be loaded into the counter again. Successive clock pulses will cause the countdown and load cycle to repeat over and over. If the counter is loaded with a number N, the OUT pin will go low for one clock cycle every N input clock pulses. The frequency of the output waveform then will be equal to the input clock frequency divided by N.

Now, for a specific example, suppose that you want to produce a 1-kHz signal for a real-time clock from an 8-MHz processor clock signal. To do this, you connect the processor clock signal to the CLK input on one of the 8254 counters and tie the GATE input of that counter high. You initialize that counter for BCD counting, mode 2, and read/write LSB then MSB. Since you want to divide the 8 MHz by 8000 decimal to get 1 kHz, you then write 00H to the counter as the LSB and 80H to the counter as the MSB.

A question that may occur to you at this point is, How do I count seconds if the interrupts are coming in every millisecond? The answer to the question is that you set aside a memory location as a milliseconds counter and initialize that location with 1000 decimal (3E8H). The interrupt-service procedure decrements this count each time an interrupt occurs and checks to see if the count is down to 0 yet. If the count is not 0, then execution is simply returned to the mainline. If the count is down to 0, 1000 interrupts or 1 s has passed. The milliseconds counter location is then reloaded with 3E8H, and the seconds-minutes-hours procedure is called to update the count of seconds, minutes, and hours. An exercise in the accompanying lab manual gives you a chance to develop a real-time clock in this way. Incidentally, the 1-kHz interrupt-service procedure can be used to measure off several different time intervals that are multiples of 1 ms.

The middle set of mode 2 waveforms in Figure 8-21 demonstrates that if the GATE input is made low while the counter is counting, counting will stop. If the GATE input is made high again, the original count will be reloaded into the counter by the next clock pulse. Succeeding clock pulses will decrement the loaded count.

The bottom set of mode 2 waveforms in Figure 8-21 shows that if a new count is written to the count register, this new count will not be transferred to the counter until the previously loaded count has been decremented to 1.

MODE 3—SQUARE-WAVE MODE

If an 8254 counter is programmed for mode 3 and an even number is written to its count register, the waveform on the OUT pin will be a *square wave*. The frequency of the square wave will be equal to the frequency of the input clock divided by the number written to the count register. If an odd number is written to a counter programmed for mode 3, the output waveform will be high for one more clock cycle than it is low, so the waveform will not be quite symmetrical. Figure 8-22, p. 230, shows some example waveforms for mode 3. By now these waveforms should look quite familiar to you.

The top set of waveforms shows that after a control word is written to the control register and a count is written to the count register, the count is transferred to the counter on the next clock pulse. As shown by the count sequence under the OUT waveform, each additional clock pulse decrements the counter by 2. When the count is down to 2, the OUT pin goes low and the original count is reloaded. The OUT pin stays low while the loaded count is again counted down by 2's. When the count is down to 2, the OUT pin goes high again and the original count is again loaded into the counter. The cycle then repeats.

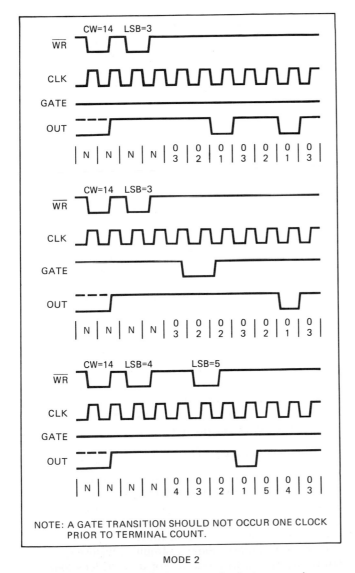

NOTE: A GATE TRANSITION SHOULD NOT OCCUR ONE CLOCK PRIOR TO TERMINAL COUNT.

MODE 2

FIGURE 8-21   8254 MODE 2 example timing waveforms. (*Intel Corporation*)

we used the counter to produce an interrupt when the parking lot was full, so we could shut the gate. Now further suppose that as part of a traffic flow study, we want to find out how many cars have come into the lot by 7:30 A.M. An interrupt-driven real-time clock procedure can, at 7:30 A.M., call a procedure which reads in the current count from the counter. Since the counter was initially loaded with 1000 decimal and is being counted down as cars come in, we can simply subtract the current count from 1000 to determine how many cars have come in.

The counters in an 8254 have latches on their outputs. When you read the count from a counter, what you are actually reading is the data on the outputs of these latches. These latches are normally enabled during counting so that the latch outputs just follow the counter outputs. If you try to read the count while the counter is counting, the count may change between reading the LSB and the MSB. This may give you a strange count. To read a correct count, then, you must in some way stop the counting or latch the current count on the output of the latches. There are three major ways of doing this.

The first is to stop counting by turning off the clock signal or making the GATE input low with external hardware. This method has the disadvantages that it requires external hardware and that a clock pulse which occurs while the clock is disabled will obviously not be counted.

The second way of reading a stable value from a counter is to latch the current count with a counter latch command and then read the latched count. A counter is latched by sending a control word to the control register address in the 8254. If you look at the format for the 8254 control word in Figure 8-17, you should see that a counter latch command is specified by making the RW1 and RW0 bits both 0. The SC1 and SC0 bits specify which counter we want to latch. The lower 4 bits of the control word are "don't cares" for a counter latch command word, so we usually make them 0's for simplicity. As an example, here is the sequence of instructions you would use to latch and read the LSB and MSB from counter 1 of the 8254 in Figure 8-14. We assume that the counter was already programmed for read/write LSB then MSB when the device was initialized. If the counter was programmed for only LSB or only MSB, then only that byte can be read.

```
MOV AL,01000000B   ; Counter 1 latch command
MOV DX,0FF07H      ; Point at 8254 control register
OUT DX,AL          ; Send latch command
MOV DX,0FF03H      ; Point at counter 1 address
IN AL,DX           ; Read LSB of latched count
MOV AH,AL          ; Save LSB of latched count
IN AL,DX           ; Read MSB of latched count
XCHG AH,AL         ; Count now in AX
```

When a counter latch command is sent, the latched count is held until it is read. When the count is read from the latches, the latch outputs return to following the counter outputs.

The third method of reading a stable count from a counter is to latch the count with a read-back command.

A0, A1 = 11 $\overline{CS}$ = 0 $\overline{RD}$ = 1 $\overline{WR}$ = 0

D7	D6	D5	D4	D3	D2	D1	D0
1	1	COUNT	STATUS	CNT 2	CNT 1	CNT 0	0

D5: 0 = LATCH COUNT OF SELECTED COUNTERS(S)
D4: 0 = LATCH STATUS OF SELECTED COUNTER(S)
D3: 1 = SELECT COUNTER 2
D2: 1 = SELECT COUNTER 1
D1: 1 = SELECT COUNTER 0
D0: RESERVED FOR FUTURE EXPANSION; MUST BE 0

FIGURE 8-26   8254 read-back control word format.

This method is available in the 8254 but not in the 8253. It is essentially an enhanced version of the counter latch command approach described in the preceding paragraphs.

Figure 8-26 shows the format for the 8254 counter read-back command word. It is sent to the same address that other control words are for a particular 8254. The 1's in bits D7 and D6 identify this as a read-back command word. To latch the count on a counter, you put a 0 in bit D5 of the control word and put a 1 in the bit position that corresponds to that counter in the control word. The advantage of this control word is that you can latch one, two, or all three counters by putting 1's in the appropriate bits. Once a counter is latched, the count is read as shown in the previous example program. After being read, the latch outputs return to following the counter outputs.

If a read-back command word with bit D4 = 0 is sent to an 8254, the status of one or more counters will be latched on the output latches. Consult the Intel data sheet for further information on this latched status.

The preceding sections have shown how 8254 counters can be used to do a wide variety of tasks around microcomputers. Many of these applications produce an interrupt signal which must be connected to an interrupt input on the microprocessor. In the next section we show how a *priority interrupt controller* device, the Intel 8259A, is used to service multiple interrupts.

8259A PRIORITY INTERRUPT CONTROLLER

Previous sections of this chapter show how interrupts can be used for a variety of applications. In a small system, for example, we might read ASCII characters in from a keyboard on an interrupt basis; count interrupts from a timer to produce a real-time clock of seconds, minutes, and hours; and detect several emergency or job-done conditions on an interrupt basis. Each of these interrupt applications requires a separate interrupt input. If we are working with an 8086, we have a problem here because the 8086 has only two interrupt inputs, NMI and INTR. If we save NMI for a power failure interrupt, this leaves only one interrupt input for all the other applications. For applications where we have interrupts from multiple sources, we use an external device called a *priority interrupt controller* (PIC) to "funnel" the interrupt signals into a single interrupt input on the processor. In this section, we show how a common PIC, the Intel 8259A, is connected in an 8086 system, how it is initialized, and how it is used to handle interrupts from multiple sources.

8259A Overview and System Connections

To show you how an 8259A functions in an 8086 system, we first need to review how the 8086 INTR input works. Remember from Figure 8-5 and a discussion earlier in this chapter that if the 8086 interrupt flag is set and the INTR input receives a high signal, the 8086 will

1. Send out two interrupt acknowledge pulses on its INTA pin to the INTA pin of an 8259A PIC. The INTA pulses tell the 8259A to send the desired interrupt type to the 8086 on the data bus.

2. Multiply the interrupt type it receives from the 8259A by 4 to produce an address in the interrupt vector table.

3. Push the flags on the stack.

4. Clear IF and TF.

5. Push the return address on the stack.

6. Get the starting address for the interrupt procedure from the interrupt-vector table and load that address in CS and IP.

7. Execute the interrupt-service procedure.

Now let's take a little closer look at how the 8259A functions during this process. To start, study the internal block diagram of an 8259A in Figure 8-27. In the figure, first notice the 8-bit data bus and control signal pins in the upper left corner of the diagram. The data bus allows the 8086 to send control words to the 8259A and read a status word from the 8259A. The RD and WR inputs control these transfers when the device is selected by asserting its chip select (CS) input low. The 8-bit data bus also allows the 8259A to send interrupt types to the 8086.

Next, in Figure 8-27, observe the eight interrupt inputs labeled IR0 through IR7 on the right side of the diagram. If the 8259A is properly enabled, an interrupt signal applied to any one of these inputs will cause the 8259A to assert its INT output pin high. If this pin is connected to the INTR pin of an 8086 and if the 8086 interrupt flag is set, then this high signal will cause the previously described INTR response.

The INTA input of the 8259A is connected to the INTA output of the 8086. The 8259A uses the first INTA pulse from the 8086 to do some activities that depend on the mode in which it is programmed. When it receives the second INTA pulse from the 8086, the 8259A outputs an interrupt type on the 8-bit data bus, as shown in Figure 8-6. The interrupt type that it sends to the 8086 is determined by the IR input that received an interrupt signal and by a number you send the 8259A when you initialize it. The point here is that the 8259A "funnels" interrupt signals from up to eight different sources into the 8086 INTR input, and it sends the 8086 a specified interrupt type for each of the eight interrupt inputs.

At this point the question that may occur to you is, What happens if interrupt signals appear at, for example, IR2 and IR4 at the same time? In the *fixed-priority mode* that the 8259A is usually operated in, the answer to this question is quite simple. In this mode, the IR0 input has the highest priority, the IR1 input the next highest, and so on down to IR7, which has the lowest priority. What this means is that if two interrupt signals occur at the same time, the 8259A will service the one with

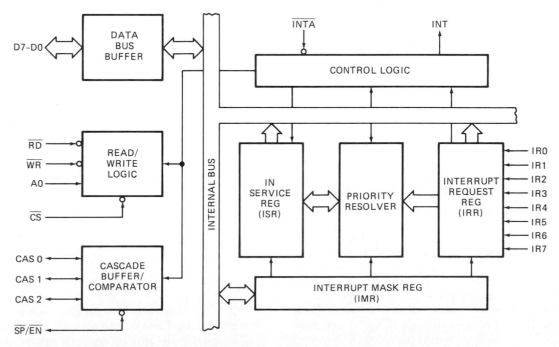

FIGURE 8-27 8259A internal block diagram. (*Intel Corporation*)

the highest priority first, assuming that both inputs are unmasked (enabled) in the 8259A.

Now let's look again at the block diagram of the 8259A in Figure 8-27 so we can explain in more detail how the device will respond to multiple interrupt signals. In the block diagram note the four boxes labeled *interrupt request register* (IRR), *interrupt mask register* (IMR), *in-service register* (ISR), and *priority resolver.*

The interrupt mask register is used to disable (mask) or enable (unmask) individual interrupt inputs. Each bit in this register corresponds to the interrupt input with the same number. You unmask an interrupt input by sending a command word with a 0 in the bit position that corresponds to that input.

The interrupt request register keeps track of which interrupt inputs are asking for service. If an interrupt input has an interrupt signal on it, then the corresponding bit in the interrupt request register will be set.

> NOTE: An interrupt signal must remain high on an IR input until after the falling edge of the first INTA pulse.

The in-service register keeps track of which interrupt inputs are currently being serviced. For each input that is currently being serviced, the corresponding bit will be set in the in-service register.

The priority resolver acts as a "judge" that determines if and when an interrupt request on one of the IR inputs gets serviced.

As an example of how this works, suppose that IR2 and IR4 are unmasked and that an interrupt signal comes in on the IR4 input. The interrupt request on the IR4 input will set bit 4 in the interrupt request register. The priority resolver will detect that this bit is set and check the bits in the in-service register (ISR) to see if a higher-priority input is being serviced. If a higher-priority input is being serviced, as indicated by a bit being set for that input in the ISR, then the priority resolver will take no action. If no higher-priority interrupt is being serviced, then the priority resolver will activate the circuitry which sends an interrupt signal to the 8086. When the 8086 responds with INTA pulses, the 8259A will send the interrupt type that was specified for the IR4 input when the 8259A was initialized. As we said before, the 8086 will use the type number it receives from the 8259A to find and execute the interrupt-service procedure written for the IR4 interrupt.

Now, suppose that while the 8086 is executing the IR4 service procedure, an interrupt signal arrives at the IR2 input of the 8259A. This will set bit 2 of the interrupt request register. Since we assumed for this example that IR2 was unmasked, the priority resolver will detect that this bit in the IRR is set and make a decision whether to send another interrupt signal to the 8086. To make the decision, the priority resolver looks at the in-service register. If a higher-priority bit in the ISR is set, then a higher-priority interrupt is being serviced. The priority resolver will wait until the higher-priority bit in the ISR is reset before sending an interrupt signal to the 8086 for the new interrupt input. If the priority resolver finds that the new interrupt has a higher priority

than the highest-priority interrupt currently being serviced, it will set the appropriate bit in the ISR and activate the circuitry which sends a new INT signal to the 8086. For our example here, IR2 has a higher priority than IR4, so the priority resolver will set bit 2 of the ISR and activate the circuitry which sends a new INT signal to the 8086. If the 8086 INTR input was reenabled with an STI instruction at the start of the IR4 service procedure, as shown in Figure 8-28a, then this new INT signal will interrupt the 8086 again. When the 8086 sends out a second INTA pulse in response to this interrupt, the 8259A will send it the type number for the IR2 service procedure. The 8086 will use the received type number to find and execute the IR2 service procedure.

At the end of the IR2 procedure, we send the 8259A a command word that resets bit 2 of the in-service register so that lower-priority interrupts can be serviced. After that, an IRET instruction at the end of the IR2 procedure sends execution back to the interrupted IR4 procedure. At the end of the IR4 procedure, we send the 8259A a command word which resets bit 4 of the in-service register so that lower-priority interrupts can be

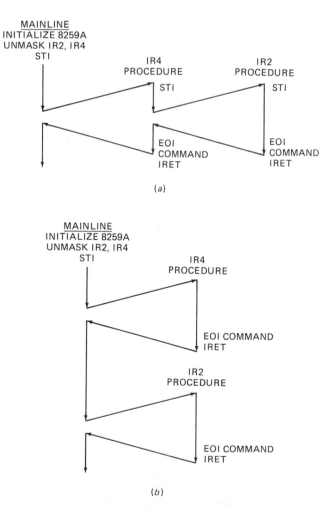

FIGURE 8-28   8259A and 8086 program flow for IR4 interrupt followed by IR2 interrupt. (*a*) Response with INTR enabled in IR4 procedure. (*b*) Response with INTR not enabled in IR4 procedure.

serviced. An IRET instruction at the end of the IR4 procedure returns execution to the mainline program. This all sounds very messy, but it is really just a special case of nested procedures. Incidentally, if the IR4 procedure did not reenable the 8086 INTR input with an STI instruction, the 8086 would not respond to the IR2-caused INT signal until it finished executing the IR4 procedure, as shown in Figure 8-28b.

We can't describe all the possible cases, but the main point here is that the 8086 and the 8259A can be programmed to respond to interrupt signals from multiple sources in almost any way you want them to. Now, before we can show you how to initialize and write programs for an 8259A, we need to show you more about how one or more 8259As are connected in a microcomputer system.

8259A System Connections and Cascading

Figure 8-14 shows how an 8259A can be added to an SDK-86 board. As shown by the truth table in Figure 8-15, the 74LS138 address decoder will assert the $\overline{CS}$ input of the 8259A when an I/O base address of FF00H is on the address bus. The A0 input of the 8259A is used to select one of two internal addresses in the device. This pin is connected to system address line A1, so the system addresses for the two internal addresses of the 8259A are FF00H and FF02H. The eight data lines of the 8259A are always connected to the lower half of the 8086 data bus because the 8086 expects to receive interrupt types on these lower eight data lines. $\overline{RD}$ and $\overline{WR}$ are connected to the system $\overline{RD}$ and $\overline{WR}$ lines. $\overline{INTA}$ from the 8086 is connected to $\overline{INTA}$ on the 8259A. The interrupt request signal, INT, from the 8259A is connected to the INTR input of the 8086. The multipurpose $\overline{SP}/\overline{EN}$ pin is tied high because we are using only one 8259A in this system. When just one 8259A is used in a system, the cascade lines (CAS0, CAS1, and CAS2) can be left open. The eight IR inputs are available for interrupt signals. Unused IR inputs should be tied to ground so that a noise pulse cannot accidentally cause an interrupt. In a later section we will show you how to initialize this 8259A, but first we need to show you how more than one 8259A can be added to a system.

The dashed box on the right side of Figure 8-14 shows how another 8259A could be added to the SDK-86 system to give a total of 15 interrupt inputs. If needed, an 8259A could be connected to each of the eight IR inputs of the original 8259A to give a total of 64 interrupt inputs. Note that since the 8086 has only one INTR input, only one of the 8259A INT pins is connected to the 8086 INTR pin. The 8259A connected directly into the 8086 INTR pin is referred to as the *master*. The INT pin from the other 8259A connects into an IR input on the master. This secondary, or *cascaded*, device is referred to as a *slave*. Note that the $\overline{INTA}$ signal from the 8086 goes to both the master and the slave devices.

Each 8259A has its own addresses so that command words can be written to it and status bytes read from it. For the cascaded 8259A in Figure 8-14, the two system I/O addresses will be FF08H and FF0AH.

The cascade pins (CAS0, CAS1, and CAS2) from the master are connected to the corresponding pins of the slave. For the master, these pins function as outputs, and for the slave device, they function as inputs. A further difference between the master and the slave is that on the slave the $\overline{SP}/\overline{EN}$ pin is tied low to let the device know that it is a slave.

Briefly, here is how the master and the slave work when the slave receives an interrupt signal on one of its IR inputs. If that IR input is unmasked on the slave and if that input is a higher priority than any other interrupt level being serviced in the slave, then the slave will send an INT signal to the IR input of the master. If that IR input of the master is unmasked and if that input is a higher priority than any other IR inputs currently being serviced in the master, then the master will send an INT signal to the 8086 INTR input. If the 8086 INTR is enabled, the 8086 will go through its INTR interrupt procedure and send out two $\overline{INTA}$ pulses to both the master and the slave. The slave ignores the first interrupt acknowledge pulse, but when the master receives the first $\overline{INTA}$ pulse, it outputs a 3-bit slave identification number on the CAS0, CAS1, and CAS2 lines. (Each slave in a system is assigned a 3-bit ID as part of its initialization.) Sending the 3-bit ID number enables the slave. When the slave receives the second $\overline{INTA}$ pulse from the 8086, the slave will send the desired interrupt type number to the 8086 on the lower eight data bus lines.

If an interrupt signal is applied directly to one of the IR inputs on the master, the master will send the desired interrupt type to the 8086 when it receives the second $\overline{INTA}$ pulse from the 8086.

Now that we have given you an overview of how an 8259A operates and how 8259As can be cascaded, the initialization command words for the 8259A should make some sense to you.

Initializing an 8259A

Earlier in this chapter, when we showed you how to initialize an 8254, we listed a series of steps you should go through to initialize any programmable device. To refresh your memory of these very important steps, we will work quickly through them again for the 8259A.

The first step in initializing any device is to find the system base address for the device from the schematic or from a memory map for the system. In order to have a specific example here, we will use the 8259A shown in Figure 8-14. The base address for the 8259A in this system is FF00H.

The next step is to find the internal addresses for the device. For an 8259A the two internal addresses are selected by a high or a low on the A0 pin. In the circuit in Figure 8-14, the A0 pin is connected to system address line A1, so the internal addresses correspond to 0 and 2.

Next, you add the internal addresses to the base address for the device to get the system address for each internal part of the device. The two system addresses for this 8259A then are FF00H and FF02H.

Next, look at Figure 8-29a for the format of the command words that must be sent to an 8259A to

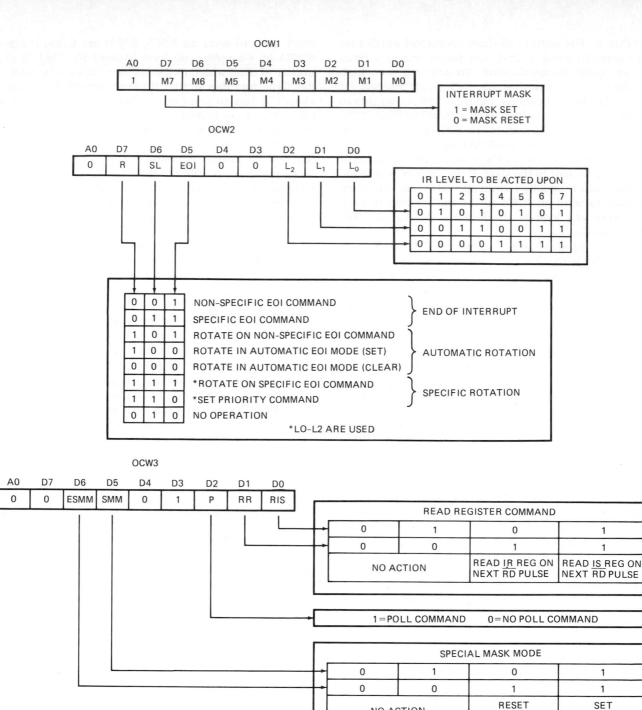

FIGURE 8-30   8259A operational command words.   (*Intel Corporation*)

which service one or more interrupts. This program initializes the SDK-86 system in Figure 8-14 for generating a real-time clock of seconds, minutes, and hours from a 1-kHz interrupt signal and for reading ASCII codes from a keyboard on an interrupt basis. This program assumes that the 2.4576-MHz PCLK signal on the board is connected to the CLK input of the 8254 counter 0, the GATE input of the 8254 counter 0 is tied high, and the OUT pin of counter 0 is connected to the IR0 input of the 8259A. The program further assumes

that the key-pressed strobe from the ASCII keyboard is connected to the IR2 input of the 8259A.

In the program, we first declare a segment called AINT_TABLE to reserve space for the vectors to the interrupt procedures. The statement TYPE_64 DW 2 DUP(0), for example, sets aside a word space for the offset of the type 64 procedure and a word for the segment base of the procedure. The statement TYPE_65 DW 2 DUP(0) sets aside a word for the offset of the type 65 procedure and a word space for the segment base

```
 1                               ;8086 PROGRAM F8-31.ASM
 2                               ; Program fragment to show the initialization of interrupt jump table,
 3                               ; 8259A priority interrupt controller, and 8254 programmable counter/timer
 4
 5 0000                          AINT_TABLE  SEGMENT  WORD  PUBLIC
 6 0000  02*(0000)                 TYPE_64   DW    2 DUP(0)    ;Reserve space for clock procedure address
 7 0004  02*(0000)                 TYPE_65   DW    2 DUP(0)    ;Not used in this program
 8 0008  02*(0000)                 TYPE_66   DW    2 DUP(0)    ;Reserve space for keyboard procedure address
 9 000C                          AINT_TABLE  ENDS
10
11 0000                          DATA SEGMENT WORD PUBLIC
12 0000  00                        SECONDS   DB    0
13 0001  00                        MINUTES   DB    0
14 0002  00                        HOURS     DB    0
15 0003  03E8                      INT_COUNT DW    03E8H          ;1 kHz interrupt counter
16 0005  64*(00)                   KEY_BUF   DB    100  DUP(0) ;Buffer for 100 ASCII characters
17 0069                          DATA ENDS
18
19 0000                          STACK_SEG   SEGMENT                ;No STACK directive used because
20 0000  64*(0000)                 DW          100   DUP(0)   ; will be using EXE2BIN
21                                  TOP_STACK LABEL WORD
22 00C8                          STACK_SEG   ENDS
23
24 0000                          CODE SEGMENT PUBLIC
25                                  ASSUME CS:CODE, DS:AINT_TABLE, SS:STACK_SEG
26 0000  B8 0000s                   MOV  AX, STACK_SEG            ;Initialize stack
27 0003  8E D0                      MOV  SS, AX                   ;segment register
28 0005  BC 00C8r                   MOV  SP, OFFSET TOP_STACK     ;Initialize stack pointer register
29 0008  B8 0000s                   MOV  AX, AINT_TABLE           ;Initialize data
30 000B  8E D8                      MOV  DS, AX                   ;segment register
31                               ;Define the addresses for the interrupt service procedures
32 000D  C7 06 0002r 0000s          MOV  TYPE_64+2, SEG CLOCK     ; Put in clock procedure address
33 0013  C7 06 0000r 004Er          MOV  TYPE_64,   OFFSET CLOCK
34 0019  C7 06 000Ar 0000s          MOV  TYPE_66+2, SEG KEYBOARD  ; Put in keyboard procedure address
35 001F  C7 06 0008r 0055r          MOV  TYPE_66,   OFFSET KEYBOARD
36                               ;Initialize data segment register
37                                  ASSUME DS:DATA
38 0025  B8 0000s                   MOV  AX, DATA
39 0028  8E D8                      MOV  DS, AX
40                               ;Initialize 8259A priority interrupt controller
41 002A  B0 13                      MOV  AL, 00010011B            ; Edge triggered, single, ICW4
42 002C  BA FF00                    MOV  DX, 0FF00H               ; Point at 8259A control
43 002F  EE                         OUT  DX, AL                   ; Send ICW1
44 0030  B0 40                      MOV  AL, 01000000B            ; Type 64 is first 8259A type
45 0032  BA FF02                    MOV  DX, 0FF02H               ; Point at ICW2 address
46 0035  EE                         OUT  DX, AL                   ; Send ICW2
47 0036  B0 01                      MOV  AL, 00000001B            ; ICW4, 8086 mode
48 0038  EE                         OUT  DX, AL                   ; Send ICW4
49 0039  B0 FA                      MOV  AL, 11111010B            ; OCW1 to unmask IR0 and IR2
50 003B  EE                         OUT  DX, AL                   ; Send OCW1
51                               ;Initialize 8254 counter 0
52 003C  B0 37                      MOV  AL, 00110111B            ; 1 kHz square wave, LSB then MSB, BCD
53 003E  BA FF07                    MOV  DX, 0FF07H               ; Point at 8254 control address
54 0041  EE                         OUT  DX, AL                   ; Send counter 0 command word
55 0042  B0 58                      MOV  AL, 58H                  ; Load LSB of count
56 0044  BA FF01                    MOV  DX, 0FF01H               ; Point at counter 0 data address
57 0047  EE                         OUT  DX, AL                   ; Send LSB of count
58 0048  B0 24                      MOV  AL, 24H                  ; Load MSB of count
59 004A  EE                         OUT  DX, AL                   ; Send MSB of count
60                               ;Enable interrupt input of 8086
61 004B  FB                         STI
62 004C  EB FE                   HERE:JMP  HERE                   ; wait for interrupt
63
64 004E                          CLOCK  PROC  FAR
65                               ;    :                           ; Clock procedure instructions
66 004E  B0 20                      MOV  AL, 00100000B            ; OCW2 for non-specific EOI
67 0050  BA FF00                    MOV  DX, 0FF00H               ; Address for OCW2
68 0053  EE                         OUT  DX, AL                   ; Send OCW2 for end of interrupt
69 0054  CF                         IRET
70 0055                          CLOCK  ENDP
```

FIGURE 8-31 Assembly language program showing initialization of 8086, 8259A, and 8254 for real-time clock and keyboard interrupt procedures. (*Continued on next page.*)

```
71
72 0055                          KEYBOARD PROC FAR                          ; Keyboard procedure instructions
73                               ;     :
74 0055  B0 20                        MOV   AL, 00100000B                  ; OCW2 for non-specific EOI
75 0057  BA FF00                      MOV   DX, 0FF00H                     ; Address for OCW2
76 005A  EE                           OUT   DX, AL                         ; Send OCW2 for end of interrupt
77 005B  CF                           IRET
78 005C                          KEYBOARD ENDP
79 005C                          CODE ENDS
80                               END
```

FIGURE 8-31 (continued).

address of the type 65 procedure, etc. As you will soon see, we use program instructions to load the actual starting addresses of the interrupt procedures in these locations.

NOTE: Because of the way the EXE2BIN program works, the AINT_TABLE segment must be first in your program so that it will be located at absolute address 0000:0100H, where it must be for the program to work correctly when downloaded to an SDK-86 board.

The next thing we do in our program is to declare a data segment and set aside some memory locations for seconds count, minutes count, hours count, and 100 characters read in from the keyboard. After the data segment, we set up a stack segment.

At the start of the mainline, we initialize the stack segment register and the stack pointer register. Then we initialize the DS register to point to the interrupt-vector table we set up at the start of the program.

The next four instructions load the addresses of the clock and keyboard procedures in the type 64 and type 66 locations in the interrupt-pointer table.

After we load the interrupt-vector table, we ASSUME DS:DATA and initialize DS to point to the data segment which contains the data for the clock and keyboard.

The next step is to initialize the 8259A as we described in the preceding section. The A0 bit next to ICW1 in Figure 8-29 is a 0, so ICW1 is sent to the lower of the two addresses for the 8259A, FF00H. For the example here we chose type 64 to correspond to an IR0 interrupt, so the needed ICW2 will be 01000000. The A0 bit next to ICW2 in Figure 8-29 is a 1, so ICW2 is sent to the higher of the two addresses for the 8259A, FF02H. Likewise, ICW4 and OCW1 are sent to system address FF02H.

The next section of the mainline program initializes counter 0 of the 8254 for mode 3, BCD countdown, and read/write LSB then MSB. To produce a 1-kHz signal from the 2.4576-MHz PCLK, we then write a count of 2458 to counter 0. This will not give exactly 1 kHz, but it is as close as we can get with this particular input clock frequency. The PCLK frequency for this board was chosen to make baud rate clock frequencies come out exact, not a 1-kHz real-time clock.

Finally, after the timer is initialized, we enable the 8086 INTR input with the STI instruction so that the 8086 can respond to INT signals from the 8259A, and wait for an interrupt with the HERE:JMP HERE instruction.

For the two interrupt-service procedures, we show just the skeletons and the End-of-Interrupt instructions. We leave it to you to write the actual procedures. Note that the interrupt procedures must be declared as far so that the assembler will load both the IP and the CS values in the interrupt-pointer table. Also note the End-of-Interrupt operation at the end of each procedure.

Remember from a previous discussion that when the 8259A responds to an IR signal, it sets the corresponding bit in the ISR. This bit must be reset at some time during or at the end of the interrupt-service procedure so that the priority resolver can respond to future interrupts of the same or lower priority. At the end of our procedures here we do this by sending an OCW2 to the 8259A. The OCW2 of 00100000 that we send tells the 8259A to reset the ISR bit for the IR level that is currently being serviced. This is a nonspecific End-of-Interrupt (EOI) instruction.

SOFTWARE INTERRUPT APPLICATIONS

In an earlier section of the chapter, we described how the 8086 software interrupt instruction INT N can be used to test any type of interrupt procedure. For example, to test a type 64 interrupt procedure without the need for external hardware such as we described in the preceding section, you can just execute the instruction INT 64.

Another important use of software interrupts is to call Basic Input Output System, or BIOS, procedures in an IBM PC-type computer. These procedures in the system ROMs perform specific input or output functions, such as reading a character from the keyboard, writing some characters to the CRT, or reading some information from a disk.

To call one of these procedures, you load any required parameters in specified registers and execute an INT N instruction. N in this case is the interrupt type which vectors to the desired procedure. You can read the BIOS section of the IBM PC technical reference manual to get all the details of these if you need them, but here's an example of how you might use one of them.

Suppose that, as part of an assembly language program that you are writing to run on an IBM PC-type computer, you want to send some characters to the printer. The INT 17H instruction can be used to call a procedure which will do this.

Figure 8-32 shows the header for the INT 17H procedure from the IBM PC BIOS listing. Note that the DX, AH, and AL registers are used to pass the required

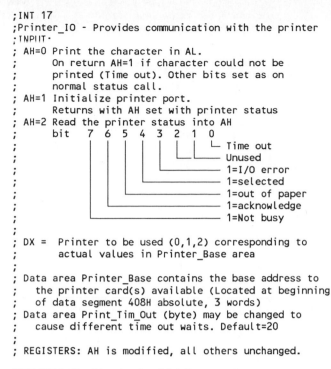

```
;INT 17
;Printer_IO - Provides communication with the printer
;INPUT:
; AH=0 Print the character in AL.
;       On return AH=1 if character could not be
;       printed (Time out). Other bits set as on
;       normal status call.
; AH=1 Initialize printer port.
;       Returns with AH set with printer status
; AH=2 Read the printer status into AH
;       bit  7 6 5 4 3 2 1 0
;                        └ Time out
;                        Unused
;                      1=I/O error
;                    1=selected
;                  1=out of paper
;                1=acknowledge
;              1=Not busy
;
; DX =  Printer to be used (0,1,2) corresponding to
;       actual values in Printer_Base area
;
; Data area Printer_Base contains the base address to
;   the printer card(s) available (Located at beginning
;   of data segment 408H absolute, 3 words)
; Data area Print_Tim_Out (byte) may be changed to
;   cause different time out waits. Default=20
;
; REGISTERS: AH is modified, all others unchanged.
```

FIGURE 8-32   Header for INT 17 procedure.
(*IBM Corporation*)

parameters to the procedure. Also note that the procedure is used for two different operations: initializing the printer port and sending a character to the printer. The operation performed by the procedure is determined by the number passed to the procedure in the AH register. AH = 1 means initialize the printer port, AH = 0 means print the character in AL, and AH = 2 means read the printer status and return it in AH. If an attempt to print a character was not successful for some reason, such as the printer not being turned on, not being selected, or being busy, 01 is returned in AH.

Now work your way through the program example in Figure 8-33 to see how the INT 17H procedure is called to initialize the printer and how it is called over and over to send a text string to the printer. Note that we sent a carriage return character and a linefeed character after the text string because the printer will not print a line until it receives a carriage return.

The main advantage of calling procedures with software interrupts is that you don't need to worry about the absolute address where the procedure actually resides or about trying to link the procedure into your program. All you have to know is the interrupt type for the procedure and how to pass parameters to the procedure. This means that a program you write for an IBM computer will work on a compatible COMPAQ computer, even though the BIOS printer driver procedures are

```
 1                              ;8086 PROGRAM F8-33.ASM
 2                              ;ABSTRACT  : This program sends a string of characters to a printer
 3                                         ; from an IBM type PC. To run this program, first assemble
 4                                         ; and use the LINK program to create the .EXE file. Then
 5                                         ; turn on your printer, & at the DOS prompt type F8-33.
 6                              ;REGISTERS : Uses CS, SS, DS, BX, AX, CX, DX
 7                              ;PORTS     : Uses printer port 0
 8                              ;PROCEDURES: Calls BIOS printer IO procedure INT 17
 9
10 0000                        STACK_SEG SEGMENT   STACK
11 0000  C8*(0000)                  DW        200     DUP(0)   ; Set aside 200 words for stack
12                                  STACK_TOP LABEL   WORD     ; Assign name to word above stack top
13 0190                        STACK_SEG ENDS
14
15     = 001E                  CHAR_COUNT EQU  30
16
17 0000                        DATA    SEGMENT
18 0000  48 45 4C 4C 4F 20 54 +     MESSAGE       DB   'HELLO THERE, HOW ARE YOU?'
19        48 45 52 45 2C 20 48 +
20        4F 57 20 41 52 45 20 +
21        59 4F 55 3F
22 0019  0D 0A 0D 0A                MESSAGE_END   DB   ODH, OAH, ODH, OAH        ; return & line feed
23 001D                        DATA    ENDS
24
25 0000                        CODE    SEGMENT
26                                  ASSUME CS:CODE, SS:STACK_SEG, DS:DATA
27 0000  B8 0000s              START: MOV  AX, STACK_SEG      ; Initialize stack segment register
28 0003  8E D0                        MOV  SS, AX
29 0005  BC 0190r                     MOV  SP, OFFSET STACK_TOP ; Initialize stack pointer register
30 0008  B8 0000s                     MOV  AX, DATA           ; Initialize data segment register
31 000B  8E D8                        MOV  DS, AX
32 000D  B4 01                        MOV  AH, 01             ; Set up registers to initialize printer
33 000F  BA 0000                      MOV  DX, 0              ; port 0
34 0012  CD 17                        INT  17H                ; Call procedure to intitialize printer port
35 0014  8D 1E 0000r                  LEA  BX, MESSAGE        ; Get to start of message
36 0018  B9 001E                      MOV  CX, CHAR_COUNT     ; Set up a count variable
37 001B  B4 00                 AGAIN: MOV  AH, 0              ; Load code for procedure to send character
```

FIGURE 8-33   8086 assembly language program for outputting characters to a printer. (*Continued on next page.*)

```
38 001D  8A 07                  MOV    AL, [BX]      ; Load character to be sent into AL
39 001F  CD 17                  INT    17H           ; Use BIOS routine to send character to printer
40 0021  80 FC 01               CMP    AH, 01H       ; If character not printed then returns AH =1
41 0024  75 04                  JNE    NEXT          ; IF character not printed THEN
42 0026  F9           NOT_RDY:  STC                  ; Set carry to indicate message not sent
43 0027  EB 05 90               JMP    EXIT          ; and leave loop
44 002A  F8           NEXT:     CLC                  ; ELSE Clear carry flag (character sent)
45 002B  43                     INC    BX            ; Move to address of next character
46 002C  E2 ED                  LOOP   AGAIN         ; Send the next character
47 002E  B8 4C00      EXIT:     MOV    AX, 4C00H     ; Graceful exit to DOS
48 0031  CD 21                  INT    21H           ; with function call 4CH
49 0033               CODE      ENDS
50                              END    START
```

FIGURE 8--33   (*continued*).

located at very different absolute addresses in the two machines. In later chapters we show more examples of using BIOS procedures.

This chapter has introduced you to interrupts and some interrupt applications. The following chapters will show you many more applications of interrupts because almost every microcomputer system uses a variety of interrupts.

CHECKLIST OF IMPORTANT TERMS AND CONCEPTS IN THIS CHAPTER

If you do not remember any of the terms in the following list, use the index to help you find them in the chapter for review.

8086 interrupt response

Interrupt-service procedure

Interrupt vector, interrupt pointer

Interrupt-vector table, interrupt-pointer table

Interrupt type

Divide-by-zero interrupt—type 0

Single-step interrupt—type 1

Nonmaskable interrupt—type 2

Breakpoint interrupt—type 3

Overflow interrupt—type 4

Software interrupts—INT types 0 through 255

INTR interrupts—types 0 through 255

Edge- and level-activated interrupt input

Interrupt priority

Programmable timer/counter devices—8253, 8254

Initialization steps for peripheral devices

Internal addresses

Control words, command words, mode words

8259A priority interrupt controller
    In-service register (ISR)
    Priority resolver
    Interrupt request register (IRR)
    Interrupt mask register (IMR)

BIOS

REVIEW QUESTIONS AND PROBLEMS

1. List and describe in general terms the steps an 8086 will take when it responds to an interrupt.

2. Describe the purpose of the 8086 interrupt-vector table.

3. What addresses in the interrupt-vector table are used for a type 2 interrupt?

4. The starting address for a type 4 interrupt-service procedure is 0010:0082. Show where and in what order this address should be placed in the interrupt-vector table.

5. Address 00080H in the interrupt-vector table contains 4A24H, and address 00082H contains 0040H.
    a. To what interrupt type do these locations correspond?
    b. What is the starting address for the interrupt-service procedure?

6. Briefly describe the condition(s) which cause the 8086 to perform each of the following types of interrupts: type 0, type 1, type 2, type 3, type 4.

7. Why is it necessary to PUSH all registers used in the procedure at the start of an interrupt-service procedure and to POP them at the end of the procedure?

8. Why must you use an IRET instruction rather than the regular RET instruction at the end of an interrupt-service procedure?

9. Show the assembler directive and instructions you would use to initialize the interrupt-pointer table locations for a type 0 procedure called DIV_0_ERROR and a type 2 procedure called POWER_FAIL.

10. a. Describe the main use of the 8086 type 1 interrupt.

b. Show the assembly language instructions necessary to set the 8086 trap flag.

11. In a system which has battery-backed RAM for saving data in case of a power failure, the stack is often put in the battery-backed RAM. This makes it easy to save registers and critical program data. Assume that the battery-backed RAM is in the address range of 08000H through 08FFFH. Write an 8086 power failure interrupt-service procedure which

Sets an external battery-backed flip-flop connected to bit 0 of port 28H to indicate that a power failure has occurred.

Saves all registers on the stack.

Saves the stack pointer value for the last entry at location 8000H.

Saves the contents of memory locations 00100H through 003FFH after the saved stack pointer value at the start of the battery-backed memory. (A string instruction might be useful for this.)

Halts.

When the power comes back on, the start-up routine can check the power fail flip-flop. If the flip-flop is set, the start-up procedure can copy the saved data back into its operating locations, initialize the stack segment register, and then get the saved SP value from address 08000H. Using this value, it can restore the pushed registers and return execution to where the power fail interrupt occurred. This is called a "warm start." If we don't want it to do a warm start, we can reset the flip-flop with an external RESET key so the system does a start from scratch, or "cold start."

12. *a.* Why is the 8086 INTR input automatically disabled when the 8086 is RESET?
b. How is the 8086 INTR input enabled to respond to interrupts?
c. What instruction can be used to disable the INTR input?
d. Why is the INTR input automatically disabled as part of the response to an INTR interrupt?
e. How is the INTR input automatically reenabled at the end of an INTR interrupt-service procedure?

13. Describe the response an 8086 will make if it receives an NMI interrupt signal during a division operation which produces a divide-by-zero interrupt.

14. The data outputs of an 8-bit analog-to-digital converter are connected to bits D0–D7 of port FFF9H, and the end-of-conversion signal from the A/D converter is connected to the NMI input of an 8086. Write a simple mainline program and an interrupt-service procedure which reads in a byte of data from the converter. If the MSB of the data is a 0, indicating that the value is in range, add the byte to a running total kept in two successive memory locations. If the MSB of data is 1, showing that the value is out of range, ignore the input. After 100 samples have been totaled, divide by 100 to get the average, store this average in another reserved memory location, and reset the total to 0.

15. Write the algorithm and the program for an interrupt-service procedure which turns an LED connected to bit D0 of port FFFAH on for 25 s and off for 25 s. The procedure should also turn a second LED connected to bit D1 of port FFFAH on for 1 min and off for 1 min. Assume that a 1-Hz interrupt signal is connected to the NMI input of an 8086 and that a high on a port bit turns on the LED connected to it.

16. Write the algorithms for a mainline program and an interrupt-service procedure which generate a real-time clock of seconds, minutes, and hours in three memory locations using a 1-Hz signal applied to the NMI input of an 8086. Then write the assembly language programs for the mainline and the procedure. If you are working on an SDK-86 board, there is a procedure in Figure 9-32 that you can add to your program to display the time on the data and address field LEDs of the board. You can use this procedure without needing to understand the details of how it works. To display a word on the data field, simply put the word in the CX register, put 00H in AL, and call the procedure. To display a word on the address field, put the word in CX, 01H in AL, and call the procedure. *Hint:* Clear carry before incrementing a count in AL so that DAA works correctly.

17. In Chapter 5 we discussed using breakpoints to debug programs containing procedures. List the sequence of locations where you would put breakpoints in the example program in Figure 8-9 to debug it if it did not work when you loaded it into memory.

18. Suppose that we add another 8254 to the SDK-86 add-on circuitry shown in Figure 8-14 and that the $\overline{CS}$ input of the new 8254 is connected to the Y5 output of the 74LS138 decoder.
a. What will be the system base address for this added 8254?
b. To which half of the 8086 data bus should the eight data lines from this 8254 be connected?
c. What will be the system addresses for the three counters and the control word register in this 8254?
d. Show the control word you would use to initialize counter 1 of this device for read/write LSB then MSB, mode 3, and BCD countdown.
e. Show the sequence of instructions you would use to write this control word and a count of 0356 to the counter.
f. Assuming that the GATE input is high, when does the counter start counting down in mode 3?

g. Assuming initialization as in parts *d* and *f*, and that a 712-kHz signal is applied to the CLK input of counter 1 in mode 3, describe the frequency, period, and duty cycle of the waveform that will be on the OUT pin of the counter.

h. Describe the effect that a control word of 10010000 sent to this 8254 will have.

19. Show the instructions you would use to initialize counter 2 of the 8254 in Figure 8-14 to produce a 1.2-ms-wide STROBE pulse on its OUT pin when it receives a trigger input on its GATE input.

20. Show the instructions needed to latch and read a 16-bit count from counter 1 of the 8254 in Figure 8-14.

21. Describe the sequence of actions that an 8259A and an 8086, as connected in Figure 8-14, will take when the 8259A receives an interrupt signal on its IR2 input. Assume only IR2 is unmasked in the 8259A and that the 8086 INTR input has been enabled with an STI instruction.

22. Describe the use of the CAS0, CAS1, and CAS2 lines in a system with a cascaded 8259A.

23. Describe the response that an 8259A will make if it receives an interrupt signal on its IR3 and IR5 inputs at the same time. Assume fixed priority for the IR inputs. What response will the 8259A make if it is servicing an IR5 interrupt and an IR3 interrupt signal occurs?

24. Why is it necessary to send an End-of-Interrupt (EOI) command to an 8259A at some time in an interrupt-service routine?

25. Show the sequence of command words and instructions that you would use to initialize an 8259A with a base address of FF10H as follows: edge-triggered; only one 8259A; 8086 system; interrupt type 40 corresponds to IR0 input; normal EOI; nonbuffered mode, not special fully nested mode; IR1 and IR3 unmasked.

26. What is the major advantage of calling BIOS procedures with software interrupts instead of calling them with absolute addresses?

CHAPTER 9

Digital Interfacing

The major goal of this chapter and the next is to show you the circuitry and software needed to interface a basic microcomputer with a wide variety of digital and analog devices. In each topic we try to show enough detail so that you can build and experiment with these circuits. Perhaps you can use some of them to control appliances around your house or to solve some problems at work.

In this chapter, we concentrate on the devices and techniques used to get digital data into and out of the basic microcomputer. Then, in the next chapter, we concentrate on analog interfacing.

OBJECTIVES

At the conclusion of this chapter, you should be able to:

1. Describe simple input and output, strobed input and output, and handshake input and output.

2. Initialize a programmable parallel-port device such as the 8255A for simple input or output and for handshake input or output.

3. Interpret the timing waveforms for handshake input and output operations.

4. Describe how parallel data is sent to a printer on a handshake basis.

5. Show the hardware connections and the programs that can be used to interface keyboards to a microcomputer.

6. Show the hardware connections and the programs that can be used to interface alphanumeric displays to a microcomputer.

7. Describe how an 8279 can be used to refresh a multiplexed LED display and scan a matrix keyboard.

8. Initialize an 8279 for a given display and keyboard format.

9. Show the circuitry used to interface high-power devices to microcomputer ports.

10. Describe the hardware and software needed to control a stepper motor.

11. Describe how optical encoders are used to determine the position, direction of rotation, and speed of a motor shaft.

PROGRAMMABLE PARALLEL PORTS AND HANDSHAKE INPUT/OUTPUT

Throughout the program examples in the preceding chapters, we have used port devices to input parallel data to the microprocessor and to output parallel data from the microprocessor. Most of the available port devices, such as the 8255A on the SDK-86 board, contain two or three ports which can be programmed to operate in one of several different modes. The different modes allow you to use the devices for many common types of parallel data transfer. First we will discuss some of these common methods of transferring parallel data, and then we will show how the 8255A is initialized and used in a variety of I/O operations.

Methods of Parallel Data Transfer

SIMPLE INPUT AND OUTPUT

When you need to get digital data from a simple switch, such as a thermostat, into a microprocessor, all you have to do is connect the switch to an input port line and read the port. The thermostat data is always present and ready, so you can read it at any time.

Likewise, when you need to output data to a simple display device such as an LED, all you have to do is connect the input of the LED buffer on an output port pin and output the logic level required to turn on the light. The LED is always there and ready, so you can send data to it at any time. The timing waveform in Figure 9-1a, p. 246, represents this situation. The crossed lines on the waveform represent the time at which a new data byte becomes valid on the output lines of the port. The absence of other waveforms indicates that this output operation is not directly dependent on any other signals.

SIMPLE STROBE I/O

In many applications, valid data is present on an external device only at a certain time, so it must be read in at that time. An example of this is the ASCII-encoded keyboard discussed in Chapter 4. When a key is pressed,

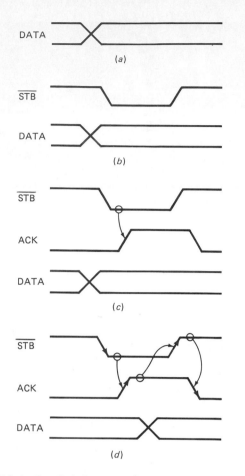

FIGURE 9-1 Parallel data transfer. (a) Simple output. (b) Simple strobe I/O. (c) Single handshake I/O. (d) Double handshake I/O.

read in data only when a strobe pulse tells you that the data is valid.

Figure 9-1b shows the timing waveforms which represent this type of operation. The sending device, such as a keyboard, outputs parallel data on the data lines, and then outputs an STB signal to let you know that valid data is present.

For low rates of data transfer, such as from a keyboard to a microprocessor, a simple strobe transfer works well. However, for higher-speed data transfer this method does not work, because there is no signal which tells the sending device when it is safe to send the next data byte. In other words, the sending system might send data bytes faster than the receiving system could read them. To prevent this problem, a *handshake* data transfer scheme is used.

SINGLE-HANDSHAKE I/O

Figure 9-2 shows the circuit connections and Figure 9-1c shows some example timing waveforms for a *handshake data transfer* from a peripheral device to a microprocessor. The peripheral outputs some parallel data and sends an STB signal to the microprocessor. The microprocessor detects the asserted STB signal on a polled or interrupt basis and reads in the byte of data. Then the microprocessor sends an Acknowledge signal (ACK) to the peripheral to indicate that the data has been read and that the peripheral can send the next byte of data. From the viewpoint of the microprocessor, this operation is referred to as a *handshake* or *strobed input*.

These same waveforms might represent a handshake output from a microprocessor to a parallel printer. In this case, the microprocessor outputs a character to the printer and asserts an STB signal to the printer to tell the printer, "Here is a character for you." When the printer is ready, it answers back with the ACK signal to tell the microprocessor, "I got that one; send me another." We will show you much more about printer interfacing in a later section.

The point of this handshake scheme is that the sending device or system is designed so that it does not send the next data byte until the receiving device or system indicates with an ACK signal that it is ready to receive the next byte.

DOUBLE-HANDSHAKE DATA TRANSFER

For data transfers where even more coordination is required between the sending system and the receiving

circuitry on the keyboard sends out the ASCII code for the pressed key on eight parallel data lines, and then sends out a strobe signal on another line to indicate that valid data is present on the eight data lines. As shown in Figure 4-19, you can connect this strobe line to an input port line and poll it to determine when you can input valid data from the keyboard. Another alternative, described in Chapter 8, is to connect the strobe line to an interrupt input on the processor and have an interrupt service procedure read in the data when the processor receives an interrupt. The point here is that this transfer is time dependent. You can

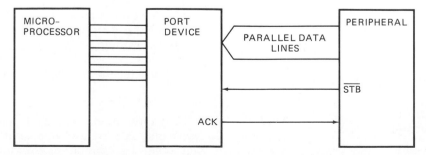

FIGURE 9-2 Signal directions for handshake input data transfer.

system, a *double handshake* is used. The circuit connections are the same as those in Figure 9-2. Figure 9-1d shows some example waveforms for a double-handshake input from a peripheral to a microprocessor. Perhaps it will help you to follow these waveforms by thinking of them as a conversation between two people. In these waveforms each signal edge has meaning. The sending device asserts its STB line low to ask, "Are you ready?" The receiving system raises its ACK line high to say, "I'm ready." The peripheral device then sends the byte of data and raises its STB line high to say, "Here is some valid data for you." After it has read in the data, the receiving system drops its ACK line low to say, "I have the data, thank you, and I await your request to send the next byte of data."

For a handshake output of this type, from a microprocessor to a peripheral, the waveforms are the same, but the microprocessor sends the STB signal and the data, and the peripheral sends the ACK signal. In the accompanying laboratory manual we show you how to interface with a speech-synthesizer device using this type of handshake system.

Implementing Handshake Data Transfer

For handshake data transfer, a microprocessor can determine when it is time to send the next data byte on a polled or on an interrupt basis. The interrupt approach is usually used, because it makes better use of the processor's time.

The STB or ACK signals for these handshake transfers can be produced on a port pin by instructions in the program. However, this method usually uses too much processor time, so parallel-port devices such as the 8255A have been designed to automatically manage the handshake operation. The 8255A, for example, can be programmed to automatically receive an STB signal from a peripheral, send an interrupt signal to the processor, and send the ACK signal to the peripheral at the proper times. The following sections show you how to connect, initialize, and use an 8255A for a variety of handshake and nonhandshake applications.

8255A Internal Block Diagram and System Connections

Figure 9-3, p. 248, shows the internal block diagram of the 8255A. Along the right side of the diagram, you can see that the device has 24 input/output lines. Port A can be used as an 8-bit input port or as an 8-bit output port. Likewise, port B can be used as an 8-bit input port or as an 8-bit output port. Port C can be used as an 8-bit input or output port, as two 4-bit ports, or to produce handshake signals for ports A and B. We will discuss the different modes for these lines in detail a little later.

Along the left side of the diagram, you see the signal lines used to connect the device to the system buses. Eight data lines allow you to write data bytes to a port or the control register and to read bytes from a port or the status register under the control of the RD and WR lines. The address inputs, A0 and A1, allow you to selectively access one of the three ports or the control

register. The internal addresses for the device are: port A, 00; port B, 01; port C, 10; control, 11. Asserting the CS input of the 8255A enables it for reading or writing. The CS input will be connected to the output of the address decoder circuitry to select the device when it is addressed.

The RESET input of the 8255A is connected to the system reset line so that, when the system is reset, all the port lines are initialized as input lines. This is done to prevent destruction of circuitry connected to port lines. If port lines were initialized as outputs after a power-up or reset, the port might try to output to the output of a device connected to the port. The possible argument between the two outputs might destroy one or both of them. Therefore, all the programmable port devices initialize their port lines as inputs when reset.

We discussed in Chapter 7 how two 8255As can be connected in an 8086 system. Take a look at Figure 7-8 (sheet 5) to refresh your memory of these connections. Note that one of the 8255As is connected to the lower half of the 8086 data bus, and the other 8255A is connected to the upper half of the data bus. This is done so that a byte can be transferred by enabling one device, or a word can be transferred by enabling both devices at the same time. According to the truth table for the I/O port address decoder in Figure 7-16, the A40 8255A on the lower half of the data bus will be enabled for a base address of FFF8H, and the A35 8255A will be enabled for a base address of FFF9H.

Another point to notice in Figure 7-8 is that system address line A1 is connected to the 8255A A0 inputs, and system address line A2 is connected to the 8255A A1 inputs. With these connections, the system addresses for the three ports and the control register in the A40 8255A will be FFF8H, FFFAH, FFFCH, and FFFEH, as shown in Figure 7-16. Likewise, the system addresses for the three ports and the control register of the A35 8255A are FFF9H, FFFBH, FFFDH, and FFFFH.

8255A Operational Modes and Initialization

Figure 9-4, p. 249, summarizes the different modes in which the ports of the 8255A can be initialized.

MODE 0

When you want to use a port for simple input or output without handshaking, you initialize that port in mode 0. If both port A and port B are initialized in mode 0, then the two halves of port C can be used together as an additional 8-bit port, or they can be used individually as two 4-bit ports. When used as outputs, the port C lines can be individually set or reset by sending a special control word to the control register address. Later we will show you how to do this. The two halves of port C are independent, so one half can be initialized as input, and the other half initialized as output.

MODE 1

When you want to use port A or port B for a handshake (strobed) input or output operation such as we discussed in previous sections, you initialize that port in mode 1.

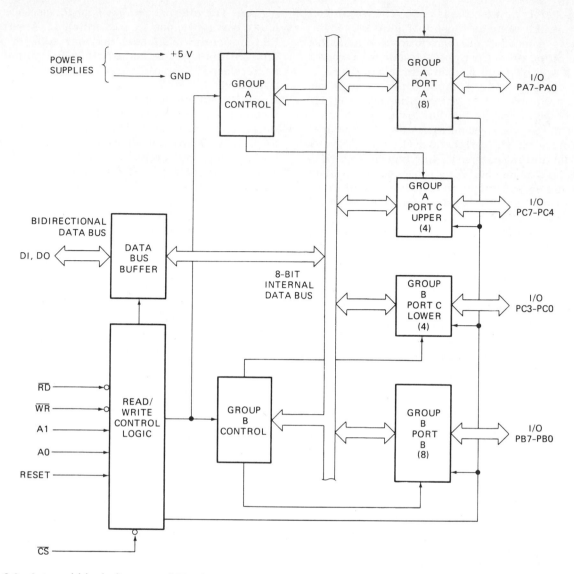

FIGURE 9-3   Internal block diagram of 8255A programmable parallel port device.   (*Intel Corporation*)

In this mode, some of the pins of port C function as handshake lines. Pins PC0, PC1, and PC2 function as handshake lines for port B if it is initialized in mode 1. If port A is initialized as a handshake (mode 1) input port, then pins PC3, PC4, and PC5 function as hand-shake signals. Pins PC6 and PC7 are available for use as input lines or output lines. If port A is initialized as a handshake output port, then port C pins PC3, PC6, and PC7 function as handshake signals. Port C pins PC4 and PC5 are available for use as input or output lines. Since the 8255A is often used in mode 1, we show several examples in the following sections.

MODE 2

Only port A can be initialized in mode 2. In mode 2, port A can be used for *bidirectional handshake* data transfer. This means that data can be output or input on the same eight lines. The 8255A might be used in this mode to extend the system bus to a slave microprocessor or to transfer data bytes to and from a floppy disk controller

board. If port A is initialized in mode 2, then pins PC3 through PC7 are used as handshake lines for port A. The other three pins, PC0 through PC2, can be used for I/O if port B is in mode 0. The three pins will be used for port B handshake lines if port B is initialized in mode 1. After you work your way through the mode 1 examples in the following sections, you should have little difficulty understanding the discussion of mode 2 in the Intel data sheet if you encounter it in a system.

Constructing and Sending 8255A Control Words

Figure 9-5 shows the formats for the two 8255A control words. Note that the MSB of the control word tells the 8255A which control word you are sending it. You use the *mode definition control word* format in Figure 9-5*a* to tell the device what modes you want the ports to operate in. You use the *bit set/reset control word* format in Figure 9-5*b* when you want to set or reset the output on a pin of port C or when you want to enable the

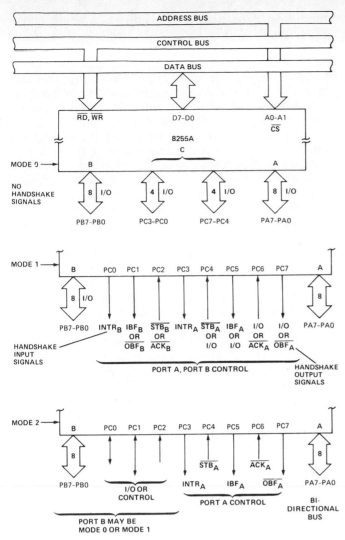

MODE 0 → NO HANDSHAKE SIGNALS

MODE 1 → HANDSHAKE INPUT SIGNALS — PORT A, PORT B CONTROL — HANDSHAKE OUTPUT SIGNALS

MODE 2 → PORT B MAY BE MODE 0 OR MODE 1 — PORT A CONTROL — BI-DIRECTIONAL BUS

FIGURE 9-4   Summary of 8255A operating modes. (*Intel Corporation*)

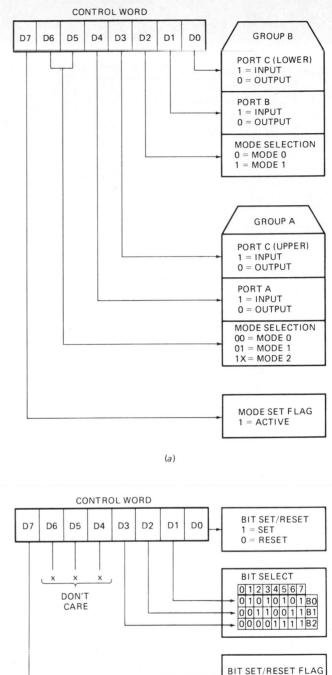

(a)

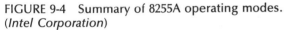

FIGURE 9-5   8255A control word formats. (*a*) Mode-set control word. (*b*) Port C bit set/reset control word.

interrupt output signals for handshake data transfers. Both control words are sent to the control register address of the 8255A.

As usual, initializing a device such as this consists of working your way through the steps we described in the last chapter. As an example for this device, suppose that you want to initialize the 8255A (A40) in Figure 7-8 as follows:

Port B as mode 1 input

Port A as mode 0 output

Port C upper as inputs

Port C bit 3 as output

As we said previously, the base address for the A40 8255A is FFF8H, and the control register address is FFFEH. The next step is to make up the control word by figuring out what to put in each of the little boxes, one bit at a time. Figure 9-6*a*, p. 250, shows the control word which will program the 8255A as desired for this example. The figure also shows how you should document

any control words you make up for use in your programs. Using Figure 9-5*a*, work your way through this word to make sure you see why each bit has the value it does.

To send the control word, you load the control word in AL with a MOV AL,10001110B instruction, point DX at the port address with the MOV DX,0FFFEH instruction, and send the control word to the 8255A control register with the OUT DX,AL instruction.

As an example of how to use the bit set/reset control

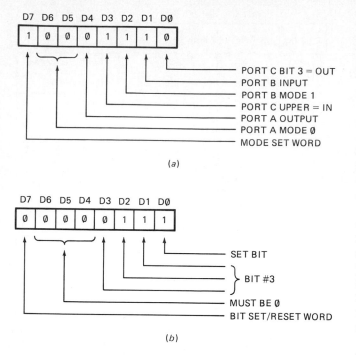

D7 D6 D5 D4 D3 D2 D1 D0
| 1 | 0 | 0 | 0 | 1 | 1 | 1 | 0 |

- PORT C BIT 3 = OUT
- PORT B INPUT
- PORT B MODE 1
- PORT C UPPER = IN
- PORT A OUTPUT
- PORT A MODE 0
- MODE SET WORD

(a)

D7 D6 D5 D4 D3 D2 D1 D0
| 0 | 0 | 0 | 0 | 0 | 1 | 1 | 1 |

- SET BIT
- BIT #3
- MUST BE 0
- BIT SET/RESET WORD

(b)

FIGURE 9-6   Control word examples for 8255A.
(a) Mode-set control word. (b) Port C bit set/reset
control word to set bit 3.

word, suppose that you want to output a 1 to (set) bit 3 of port C, which was initialized as an output with the mode set control word above. To set or reset a port C output pin, you use the bit set/reset control word shown in Figure 9-5b. Make bit D7 a 0 to identify this as a bit set/reset control word, and put a 1 in bit D0 to specify that you want to set a bit of port C. Bits D3, D2, and D1 are used to tell the 8255A which bit you want to act on. For this example you want to set bit 3, so you put 011 in these 3 bits. For simplicity and compatibility with future products, make the other 3 bits of the control word 0's. The result, 00000111B, is shown with proper documentation in Figure 9-6b.

To send this control word to the 8255A, simply load it into AL with the MOV AL,00000111B instruction, point DX at the control register address with the MOV DX,0FFFEH instruction if DX is not already pointing there, and send the control word with the OUT DX,AL instruction. As part of the application examples in the following sections, we will show you how you know which bit in port C to set to enable the interrupt output signal for handshake data transfer.

8255A Handshake Application Examples

INTERFACING TO A MICROCOMPUTER-CONTROLLED LATHE

All the machines in the machine shop of our computer-controlled electronics factory operate under microcomputer control. One example of these machines is a lathe which makes bolts from long rods of stainless steel. The cutting instructions for each type of bolt that we need to make are stored on a 3/4-in.-wide teletype-like metal

tape. Each instruction is represented by a series of holes in the tape. A tape reader pulls the tape through an optical or mechanical sensor to detect the hole patterns and converts these to an 8-bit parallel code. The microcomputer reads the instruction codes from the tape reader on a handshake basis and sends the appropriate control instructions to the lathe. The microcomputer must also monitor various conditions around the lathe. It must, for example, make sure the lathe has cutting lubricant oil, is not out of material to work on, and is not jammed up in some way. Machines that operate in this way are often referred to as *computer numerical control*, or *CNC, machines*.

Figure 9-7 shows in diagram form how you might use an 8255A to interface a microcomputer to the tape reader and lathe. Later in the chapter, we will show you some of the actual circuitry needed to interface the port pins of the 8255A to the sensors and the high-power motors of the lathe. For now, we want to talk about initializing the 8255A for this application and analyze the timing waveforms for the handshake input of data from the tape reader.

Your first task is to make up the control word which will initialize the 8255A in the correct modes for this application. To do this, start by making a list showing how you want each port pin or group of pins to function. Then put in the control word bits that implement those pin functions. For our example here,

Port A needs to be initialized for handshake input (mode 1) because instruction codes have to be read in from the tape reader on a handshake basis.

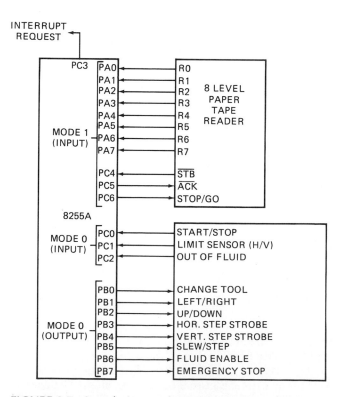

FIGURE 9-7   Interfacing a microprocessor to a tape reader and lathe.

Port B needs to be initialized for simple output (mode 0). No handshaking is needed here because this port is being used to output simple on or off control signals to the lathe.

Port C, bits PC0, PC1, and PC2 are used for simple input of sensor signals from the lathe.

Port C, bits PC3, PC4, and PC5 function as the handshake signals for the data transfer from the tape reader connected to port A.

Port C, bit PC6 is used for output of the STOP/GO signal to the tape reader.

Port C, bit PC7 is not used for this example.

Figure 9-8 shows the control word to initialize the 8255A for these pin functions. You send this word to the control register address of the 8255A as described above.

Before we go on, there is one more point we have to make about initializing the 8255A for this microcomputer-controlled lathe application. In order for the handshake input data transfer from the tape reader to work correctly, the interrupt request signal from bit PC3 has to be enabled. This is done by sending a bit set/reset control word for the appropriate bit of port C. Figure 9-9 shows the port C bit that must be set to enable the interrupt output signal for each of the 8255A handshake modes. For the example here, port A is being used for handshake input, so according to Figure 9-9, port C, bit PC4 must be set to enable the interrupt output for this operation. The bit set/reset control word to do this is 00001001B. You send this bit set/reset control word to the control address of the 8255A.

Handshake data transfer from the tape reader to the 8255A can be stopped by disabling the 8255A interrupt output on port C, pin PC3. This is done by resetting bit PC4 with a bit set/reset control word of 00001000. You will later see another example of the use of this interrupt enable/disable process in Figure 9-16.

As another example of 8255A interrupt output enabling, suppose that you are using port B as a handshake output port. According to Figure 9-9, you need to set bit PC2 to enable the 8255A interrupt output signal. The bit set/reset control word to do this is 00000101.

Now let's talk about how the program for this machine might operate and how the handshake data transfer actually takes place.

Port C		To Enable
Interrupt Signal		Interrupt Request
	Pin Number	Set Port C bit
MODE 1		
Port A IN	PC3	PC4
Port B IN	PC0	PC2
Port A OUT	PC3	PC6
Port B OUT	PC0	PC2
MODE 2		
Port A IN	PC3	PC4
Port A OUT	PC3	PC6

FIGURE 9-9   Port C bits to set to enable interrupt request outputs for handshake modes.

After initializing everything, you would probably read port C, bits PC0, PC1, and PC2 to check if the lathe was ready to operate. For any 8255A mode, you read port C by simply doing an input from the port C address. Then you output a start command to the tape reader on bit PC6. This is done with a bit set/reset command. Assuming that you want to reset bit PC6 to start the tape reader, the bit set/reset control word for this is 00001100. When the tape reader receives the Go command, it will start the handshake data transfer to the 8255A. Let's work our way through the timing waveforms in Figure 9-10, p. 252, to see how the data transfer takes place.

The tape reader starts the process by sending out a byte of data to port A on its eight data lines. The tape reader then asserts its $\overline{STB}$ line low to tell the 8255A that a new byte of data has been sent. In response, the 8255A raises its Input Buffer Full (IBF) signal on PC5 high to tell the tape reader that it is ready for the data. When the tape reader detects the IBF signal at a high level, it raises its $\overline{STB}$ signal high again. The rising edge of the $\overline{STB}$ signal has two effects on the 8255A. It first latches the data byte in the input latches of the 8255A. Once the data is latched, the tape reader can remove the data byte in preparation for sending the next data byte. This is shown by the dashed section on the right side of the data waveform in Figure 9-10. Second, if the interrupt signal output has been enabled, the rising edge of the $\overline{STB}$ signal will cause the 8255A to output an Interrupt Request signal to the microprocessor on bit PC3.

The processor's response to the interrupt request will be to go to an interrupt service procedure which reads in the byte of data latched in port A. When the $\overline{RD}$ signal from the microprocessor goes low for this read of port A, the 8255A will automatically reset its Interrupt Request signal on PC3. This is done so that a second interrupt cannot be caused by the same data byte transfer. When the processor raises its $\overline{RD}$ signal high again at the end of the read operation, the 8255A automatically drops its IBF signal on PC5 low again. IBF going low again is the signal to the tape reader that the data transfer is complete and that it can send the next byte of data. The time between when the 8255A sends the Interrupt Request signal and when the processor reads the data byte from port A depends on when the processor gets around to servicing that interrupt. The point here is that this time doesn't matter. The tape reader will not

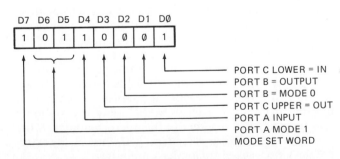

FIGURE 9-8   Control word to initialize 8255A for interface with tape reader and lathe.

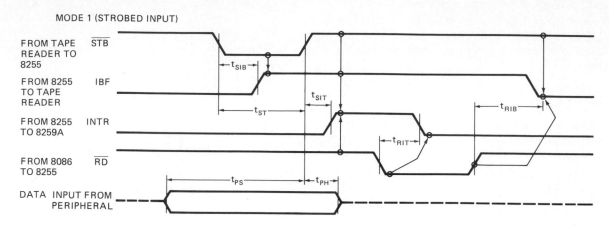

MODE 1 (STROBED INPUT)

FIGURE 9-10   Timing waveforms for 8255 handshake data input from a tape reader.

send the next byte of data until it detects that the IBF signal has gone low again. The transfer cycle will then repeat for the next data byte.

After the processor reads in the lathe control instruction byte from the tape reader, it will decode this instruction, and output the appropriate control byte to the lathe on port B of the 8255A. The tape reader then sends the next instruction byte. If the instruction tape is made into a continuous loop, the lathe will keep making the specified parts until it runs out of material. The unused bit of port C, PC7, could be connected to a mechanism which loads in more material so the lathe can continue.

The microcomputer-controlled lathe we have described here is a small example of automated manufacturing. The advantage of this approach is that it relieves humans of the drudgery of standing in front of a machine continually making the same part, day after day. We hope society can find more productive use for the human time made available.

PARALLEL PRINTER INTERFACE—HANDSHAKE OUTPUT EXAMPLE

At the end of Chapter 8, we showed you how to send a string of text characters to a printer by calling a BIOS procedure with a software interrupt. In this section we show you the hardware connections and software required to interface with a parallel printer in a system which does not have a BIOS procedure you can call to do the job.

For most common printers, such as the IBM PC printers, the Epson dot-matrix printers, and the Panasonic dot-matrix printers, data to be printed is sent to the printer as ASCII characters on eight parallel lines. The printer receives the characters to be printed and stores them in an internal RAM buffer. When the printer detects a carriage return character (0DH), it prints out the first row of characters from the print buffer. When the printer detects a second carriage return, it prints out the second row of characters, etc. The process continues until all the desired characters have been printed.

Transfer of the ASCII codes from a microcomputer to

a printer must be done on a handshake basis because the microcomputer can send characters much faster than the printer can print them. The printer must in some way let the microcomputer know that its buffer is full and that it cannot accept any more characters until it prints some out. A common standard for interfacing with parallel printers is the *Centronics Parallel Interface Standard,* named for the company that developed it. In the following sections, we show you how a Centronics parallel interface works and how to implement it with an 8255A.

Centronics Interface Pin Descriptions and Circuit Connections

Centronics-type printers usually have a 36-pin interface connector. Figure 9-11 shows the pin assignments and descriptions for this connector as it is used in the IBM PC printer and the Epson printers. Some manufacturers use one or two pins differently, so consult the manual for your specific printer before connecting it up as we show here.

Thirty-six pins may seem like a lot of pins just to send ASCII characters to a printer. The reason for the large number of lines is that each data and signal line has its own individual ground return line. For example, as shown in Figure 9-11, pin 2 is the LSB of the data character sent to the printer, and pin 20 is the ground return for this signal. Individual ground returns reduce the chance of picking up electrical noise in the lines. If you are making an interface cable for a parallel printer, these ground return lines should only be connected together and to ground at the microcomputer end of the cable, as shown in Figure 9-12, p. 254.

While we are talking about grounds, note that pin 16 is listed as logic ground and pin 17 is listed as chassis ground. In order to prevent large noise currents from flowing in the logic ground wires, these wires should only be connected together in the microcomputer. (This precaution is necessary whenever you connect any external device or system to a microcomputer.)

The rest of the pins on the 36-pin connector fall into two categories: signals sent to the printer to tell it what

SIGNAL PIN NO.	RETURN PIN NO.	SIGNAL	DIRECTION	DESCRIPTION
1	19	STROBE	IN	STROBE pulse to read data in. Pulse width must be more than 0.5 μs at receiving terminal. The signal level is normally "high"; read-in of data is performed at the "low" level of this signal.
2	20	DATA 1	IN	These signals represent information of the 1st to 8th bits of parallel data respectively. Each signal is at "high" level when data is logical "1" and "low" when logical "0."
3	21	DATA 2	IN	
4	22	DATA 3	IN	
5	23	DATA 4	IN	
6	24	DATA 5	IN	
7	25	DATA 6	IN	
8	26	DATA 7	IN	
9	27	DATA 8	IN	
10	28	ACKNLG	OUT	Approximately 5 μs pulse; "low" indicates that data has been received and the printer is ready to accept other data.
11	29	BUSY	OUT	A "high" signal indicates that the printer cannot receive data. The signal becomes "high" in the following cases: 1. During data entry. 2. During printing operation. 3. In "offline" state. 4. During printer error status.
12	30	PE	OUT	A "high" signal indicates that the printer is out of paper.
13	—	SLCT	OUT	This signal indicates that the printer is in the selected state.
14	—	AUTO FEED XT	IN	With this signal being at "low" level, the paper is automatically fed one line after printing. (The signal level can be fixed to "low" with DIP SW pin 2-3 provided on the control circuit board.)
15	—	NC		Not used.
16	—	OV		Logic GND level.
17	—	CHASIS-GND	—	Printer chasis GND. In the printer, the chassis GND and the logic GND are isolated from each other.
18	—	NC	—	Not used.
19-30	—	GND	—	"Twisted-Pair Return" signal; GND level.
31	—	INIT	IN	When the level of this signal becomes "low" the printer controller is reset to its initial state and the print buffer is cleared. This signal is normally at "high" level, and its pulse width must be more than 50 μs at the receiving terminal.
32		ERROR	OUT	The level of this signal becomes "low" when the printer is in "Paper End" state, "Offline" state and "Error" state.
33	—	GND	—	Same as with pin numbers 19 to 30.
34	—	NC	—	Not used.
35				Pulled up to +5 Vdc through 4.7 k-ohms resistance.
36	—	SLCT IN	IN	Data entry to the printer is possible only when the level of this signal is "low." (Internal fixing can be carried out with DIP SW 1-8. The condition at the time of shipment is set "low" for this signal.)

Notes: 1. "Direction" refers to the direction of signal flow as viewed from the printer.
2. "Return" denotes "Twisted-Pair Return" and is to be connected at signal-ground level.
   When wiring the interface, be sure to use a twisted-pair cable for each signal and never fail to complete connection on the return side. To prevent noise effectively, these cables should be shielded and connected to the chassis of the system unit.
3. All interface conditions are based on TTL level. Both the rise and fall times of each signal must be less than 0.2 μs.
4. Data transfer must not be carried out by ignoring the ACKNLG or BUSY signal. (Data transfer to this printer can be carried out only after confirming the ACKNLG signal or when the level of the BUSY signal is "low.")

FIGURE 9-11 Pin connections and descriptions for Centronics-type parallel interface to IBM PC and EPSON FX-100 printer. (*IBM Corporation*)

operation to do, and signals from the printer that indicate its status. The major control signals to the printer are INIT on pin 31, which tells the printer to perform its internal initialization sequence, and STROBE on pin 1, which tells the printer, "Here is a character for you." Two additional input pins, pin 14 and pin 36, are usually taken care of inside the printer.

The major status signals output from the printer are

1. The ACKNLG signal on pin 10, which, when low, indicates that the data character has been accepted and the printer is ready for the next character.

2. The BUSY signal on pin 11, which is high if, for some reason such as being out of paper, the printer is not ready to receive a character.

3. The PE signal on pin 12, which goes high if the out-of-paper switch in the printer is activated.

4. The SLCT signal on pin 13, which goes high if the printer is selected for receiving data.

5. The ERROR signal on pin 32, which goes low for a variety of problem conditions in the printer.

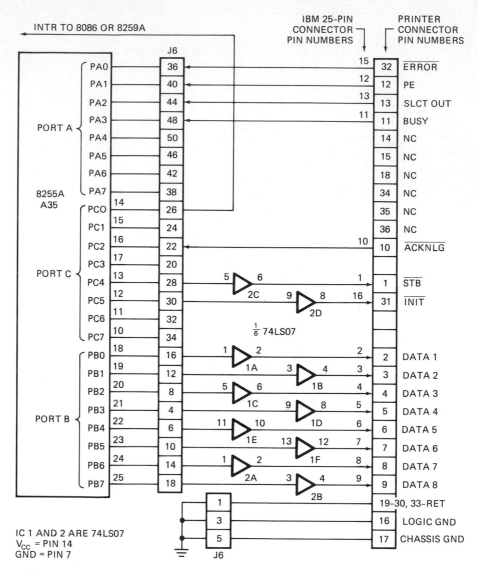

FIGURE 9-12   Circuit for interfacing Centronics-type parallel input printer to 8255A on SDK-86 board.

Figure 9-13 shows the timing waveforms for transferring data characters to an IBM printer using the basic handshake signals. Here's how this works.

Assuming the printer has been initialized, the BUSY signal is checked to see if the printer is ready to receive data. If this signal is low, indicating the printer is ready (not busy), an ASCII code is sent out on the eight parallel data lines. After at least 0.5 μs, the STROBE signal is asserted low to tell the printer that a character has been sent. The STROBE signal going low causes the printer to assert its BUSY signal high. After a minimum time of 0.5 μs, the STROBE signal can be raised high again. Note that the data must be held valid on the data lines for at least 0.5 μs after the STROBE signal is made high.

When the printer is ready to receive the next character, it asserts its ACKNLG signal low for about 5 μs. The rising edge of the ACKNLG signal tells the microcomputer that it can send the next character. At the same time as the rising edge of the ACKNLG signal, the printer also resets the BUSY signal. A low on BUSY is another

indication that the printer is ready to accept the next character. Some systems use the ACKNLG signal for the handshake, and some systems use the BUSY signal. Now let's see how you can do this handshake printer interface with an 8255A.

8255A CONNECTIONS AND INITIALIZATION

For this example, we disconnected our printer cable from the printer output and connected it to an 8255A on an SDK-86 board, as shown in Figure 9-12. The 74LS07 open-collector buffers are used on the signal and data lines from the 8255A because the 8255A outputs do not have enough current drive to charge and discharge the capacitance of the connecting cable fast enough. Pull-up resistors for the open-collector outputs of the 74LS07s are built into the printer.

Port B of the 8255A is used for the handshake output data lines. Therefore, as shown in Figure 9-4, bit PC0 functions as the interrupt request output to the 8086.

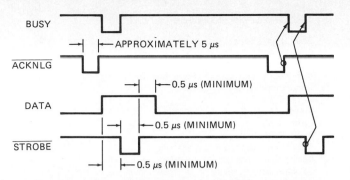

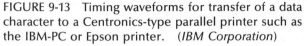

FIGURE 9-13 Timing waveforms for transfer of a data character to a Centronics-type parallel printer such as the IBM-PC or Epson printer. (*IBM Corporation*)

The $\overline{\text{ACKNLG}}$ signal from the printer is connected to the 8255A $\overline{\text{ACK}}$ input on bit PC2. The $\overline{\text{OBF}}$ signal on PC1 of the 8255A would normally be used as the strobe signal for this type of handshake data transfer. Unfortunately, however, it does not have the right timing parameters for this handshake, so it is left unconnected. Therefore, the $\overline{\text{STROBE}}$ input of the printer is connected to bit PC4. The $\overline{\text{STROBE}}$ signal will be generated by a bit set/reset of this pin.

The four printer status signals are connected to port A so the program can read them in to determine the condition of the printer.

Finally, the $\overline{\text{INIT}}$ input of the printer is connected to bit PC5 so that the printer can be initialized under program control.

Now, while the hardware configuration is fresh in your mind, let's look at the control words we have to send to the 8255A for this application.

Figure 9-14a shows the mode control word to initialize port B for mode 1 output, port A for mode 0 input, and

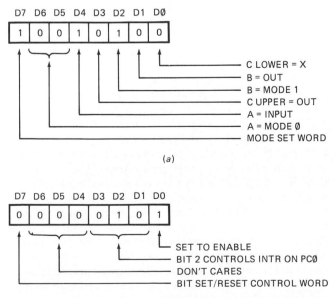

(a)

(b)

FIGURE 9-14 8255A control words for printer interface. (a) Mode control word. (b) Bit set/reset control word.

the upper 4 bits of port C as outputs. Figure 9-14b shows the bit set/reset control word necessary to enable the interrupt request signal on bit PC0 for the handshake. The addresses for the 8255A, A35, on the SDK-86 board are, as shown in Figure 7-16, port P1A—FFF9H; port P1B—FFFBH; port P1C—FFFDH; and control P1—FFFFH. For that system, then, both control words are output to FFFFH.

THE PRINTER DRIVER PROGRAM

Procedures which input data from or output data to peripheral devices such as disk drives, modems, and printers are often called *I/O drivers*. Here we show you one way to write the I/O driver procedure for our parallel printer interface.

The first point to consider when writing any I/O driver is whether to do it on a polled or on an interrupt basis. For the parallel Centronics interface here, the maximum data transfer rate is about 1000 characters/second. This means that there is about 1 ms between transfers. If characters are sent on an interrupt basis, many other program instructions can be executed while waiting for the interrupt request to send the next character. Also, when the printer buffer gets full, there will be an even longer time that the processor can be working on some other job while waiting for the next interrupt. This is another illustration of how interrupts allow the computer to do several tasks "at the same time." For our example here, assume that the interrupt request from PC0 of the 8255A is connected to the IR6 interrupt input of the 8259A shown in Figure 8-14. The higher-priority interrupt inputs on the 8255A are left for a clock interrupt and a keyboard interrupt.

Figure 9-15a, p. 256, shows the steps needed in the mainline to initialize everything and "call" the printer driver to send a string of ASCII characters to the printer.

At the start of the mainline some named memory locations are set aside to store parameters needed for transfer of data to the printer. The memory locations set aside for passing information between the mainline and the I/O driver procedure are often called a *control block*. In the control block, a named location is set aside for a pointer to the address of the ASCII character that is currently being sent. Another memory location is set aside to store the number of characters to be sent. The number in this location will function as a counter so you know when you have sent all the characters in the buffer. Instead of using this counter approach to keep track of how many characters have been sent, a *sentinel method* can be used. With the sentinel approach you put a *sentinel* character in memory after the last character to be sent out. MS/DOS, for example, uses a $ (24H) as a sentinel character for some of the I/O drivers. As you read each character in from memory, you compare it with the sentinel value. If it matches, you know all the characters have been sent. The sentinel approach and the counter approach are both widely used, so you should be familiar with both.

To get the hardware ready to go, you need to initialize the 8259A and unmask the IR inputs of the 8259A that are used. The 8086 INTR input must also be enabled. Next, the 8255A must be initialized by sending it the

```
MAINLINE ALGORITHM FOR PRINTER DRIVER              PRINTER DRIVER PROCEDURE ALGORITHM

  INITIALIZATION                                     Save registers
    Set up control block                             Enable 8086 INTR for higher priority interrupts
      Word for storing pointer to ASCII string       Get pointer to string
      Word for number of charaters in string         Get ASCII character from buffer
    Initialization control words to 8259A            Send character to printer
    Unmask 8259A IR6 and any other IR inputs used    Wait 5 μs
    Mode set word to 8255A                           Send STROBE low
    Unmask 8086 INTR input                           Wait 5 μs
    Send STROBE high to printer                       Send STROBE high
    Initialize printer (pulse INIT low)              Increment pointer to string
  TO SEND ASCII STRING                               Decrement character counter
    Read printer status from port                    IF character count = 0 THEN
    IF error THEN                                         Disable 8255A interrupt request output
          send message                               Send EOI command to 8259A
          exit, terminate program                    Restore registers
    Set print done status bit                        Return from interrupt procedure
    Load starting address of string into pointer store
    Load length of string into character counter
    Enable 8255A INTR output
    Wait for interrupt
```

(a)   (b)

FIGURE 9-15   Algorithm for printer mainline and interrupt-based printer driver
procedure. (a) Mainline steps. (b) Printer driver procedure steps.

mode control word shown in Figure 9-14a. A bit set/reset control word is then sent to the 8255A to make the STROBE signal to the printer high, because this is the unasserted level for the signal. When interfacing with hardware, you must always remember to put control and handshake signals such as this in known states.

Also, to make sure the printer is internally initialized, we pulse the INIT line to the printer low for a few microseconds.

When we reach a point in the mainline where we want to print a string, we first read the printer status from port A and check if the printer is selected, not out of paper, and not busy. In a more complete program, we could send a specific error message to the display indicating the type of error found. The program here just sends a general error message. If no printer error condition is found, the starting address of the string of ASCII characters is loaded into the control block location set aside for this, and the number of characters in the string is sent to a reserved location in the control block. Finally, the interrupt request pin on the 8255A is enabled so that printer interrupts can be output to the 8259A IR input. Note that this interrupt is not enabled until everything else is ready. To see how this algorithm is implemented in assembly language, work your way through Figure 9-16a. The JMP WT at the end of this program represents continued execution of the mainline program while waiting for an interrupt from the printer.

A high on the ACKNLG line from the printer will cause the 8255A to output an Interrupt Request signal. This Interrupt Request signal goes through the 8259A to the processor and causes it to go to the interrupt service procedure.

Figure 9-15b shows the algorithm for the procedure which services this interrupt and actually sends the characters to the printer. After some registers are pushed, the 8086 INTR input is enabled so that higher-priority interrupts such as a clock can interrupt this procedure. The string address pointer is then read in from the control block and used to read a character in from the memory buffer to AL. The character in AL is then output to port B of the 8255A.

From here on, the program follows the timing diagram in Figure 9-13. After sending the character, the program waits at least 0.5 μs, asserts the STROBE input low, waits at least another 0.5 μs, and raises the STROBE line high again. As we said before, the strobe signal must be generated with program instructions because the hardware strobe signal generated by the 8255A does not have the correct timing for this handshake. The data hold parameter in the timing diagram is satisfied because the data byte will be latched on the port B output pins until the next character is sent. Sending of the character is now complete, so the next step is to get ready to send another character.

To do this, the buffer pointer in the control block is incremented by 1, and the character counter in the control block is decremented by 1. If the character counter is not down to 0, there are more characters to send, so the EOI command is sent to the 8259A, the registers are popped off the stack, and execution is returned to the mainline to wait for the next interrupt. If the character counter in the control block is down to 0, all the characters have been sent, so the Interrupt Request output of the 8255A is disabled with a bit set/reset control word. This prevents further interrupt requests from the 8255A until we enable it again to send another buffer of characters to the printer. Work your way through Figure 9-16b to see how this algorithm is easily implemented. One part of the program that we do want to expand and clarify is the generation of the STROBE signal with bit PC3.

We could use external hardware to "massage" the OBF signal from the 8255A so it matches the timing and polarity requirements of the receiving device. However,

```
  1                            ;8086 MAINLINE PROGRAM F9-16A.ASM
  2                            ;ABSTRACT  : Printer-driver mainline initializes the 8259A and the 8255A
  3                            ;           on an SDK-86 board so that a message in a buffer can be sent
  4                            ;           to a printer. It also sets up a control block and initializes
  5                            ;           all variables used
  6                            ;REGISTERS : Uses CS,DS,SS,SP,AX,DX,CX,
  7                            ;PORTS     : SDK-86 port P1A (FFF9H) - used to input status of printer
  8                            ;              port P1B (FFFBH) - used to output a character
  9                            ;              port P1C used for handshake signals for port B
 10                            ;PROCEDURES: Uses PRINT_IT used to output characters
 11
 12 0000                      A_INT_TABLE      SEGMENT      WORD
 13 0000   0C*(0000)              TYPE_64_69 DW  12 DUP(0)    ; Reserved for IR0-IR5
 14 0018   02*(0000)              TYPE_70    DW   2 DUP(0)    ; IR6 interrupt
 15 001C   02*(0000)              TYPE_71    DW   2 DUP(0)    ; IR7 interrupt - not used
 16 0020                      A_INT_TABLE      ENDS
 17
 18 0000                      DATA SEGMENT WORD PUBLIC
 19 0000   54 68 69 73 20 69 73 +     MESSAGE_1    DB   'This is the message from the printer driver!'
 20        20 74 68 65 20 6D 65 +
 21        73 73 61 67 65 20 66 +
 22        72 6F 6D 20 74 68 65 +
 23        20 70 72 69 6E 74 65 +
 24        72 20 64 72 69 76 65 +
 25        72 21
 26 002C   0D 0A 0D                         DB   0DH, 0AH, 0DH     ; Return & line-feed for printer
 27  = 002F                    MESSAGE_LENGTH EQU ($-MESSAGE_1)    ; Compute length of message
 28 002F   00                  PRINT_DONE    DB  0
 29 0030   0000                POINTER       DW  00              ; Storage for pointer to MESSAGE_1
 30 0032   00                  COUNTER       DB  0               ; Counter for length of MESSAGE_1
 31 0033   00                  PRINTER_ERROR DB  0
 32 0034                      DATA ENDS
 33
 34                           PUBLIC  PRINT_DONE, POINTER, COUNTER, MESSAGE_1
 35                           EXTRN   PRINT_IT:FAR
 36
 37 0000                      STACK_SEG  SEGMENT
 38 0000   1E*(0000)                     DW      30 DUP(0)
 39                              STACK_TOP LABEL  WORD
 40 003C                      STACK_SEG  ENDS
 41
 42 0000                      CODE SEGMENT WORD PUBLIC
 43                             ASSUME CS:CODE, DS:A_INT_TABLE, SS:STACK_SEG
 44                           ;Initialize stack and data segment registers
 45 0000   B8 0000s                   MOV  AX, STACK_SEG           ; Initialize stack
 46 0003   8E D0                      MOV  SS, AX                  ; segment register
 47 0005   BC 003Cr                   MOV  SP, OFFSET STACK_TOP    ; Initialize top of stack
 48 0008   B8 0000s                   MOV  AX, A_INT_TABLE         ; Initialize data
 49 000B   8E D8                      MOV  DS, AX                  ; segment register
 50                           ;Set up interrupt table and put in address for printer interrupt subroutine
 51 000D   C7 06 001Ar 0000s          MOV  TYPE_70+2, SEG PRINT_IT
 52 0013   C7 06 0018r 0000e          MOV  TYPE_70,   OFFSET PRINT_IT
 53                           ;Initialize data segment register
 54                             ASSUME DS:DATA
 55 0019   B8 0000s                   MOV  AX, DATA
 56 001C   8E D8                      MOV  DS, AX
 57                           ;Initialize 8259A and unmask IR6
 58 001E   BA FF00                    MOV  DX, 0FF00H              ; Point at 8259A control address
 59 0021   B0 13                      MOV  AL, 00010011B           ; ICW1, edge triggered, single, 8086
 60 0023   EE                         OUT  DX, AL                  ; Send ICW1
 61 0024   BA FF02                    MOV  DX, 0FF02H              ; Point at ICW2 address
 62 0027   B0 40                      MOV  AL, 01000000B           ; Type 64 is first 8259A type
 63 0029   EE                         OUT  DX, AL                  ; Send ICW2
 64 002A   B0 01                      MOV  AL, 00000001B           ; ICW4, 8086 mode
 65 002C   EE                         OUT  DX, AL                  ; Send ICW4
 66 002D   B0 BF                      MOV  AL, 10111111B           ; OCW1 to unmask IR6
 67 002F   EE                         OUT  DX, AL                  ; Send OCW1
 68                           ;Initialize 8255A, P1A-mode1 input. P1B-mode0 output. Unused P1C bits-output
 69 0030   BA FFFF                    MOV  DX, 0FFFFH              ; Control address for 8255A
 70 0033   B0 94                      MOV  AL, 10010100B           ; Control word for above conditions
 71 0035   EE                         OUT  DX, AL                  ; Send control word
 72 0036   FB                         STI                         ; Unmask 8086 INTR interrupt
```

FIGURE 9-16   8086 assembly language program for driver. (a) Mainline.

(Continued)

```
73                                  ;Send strobe high to printer with bit set on PC4
74 0037  B0 09                             MOV   AL, 00001001B
75 0039  EE                                OUT   DX, AL
76                                  ;Initialize printer-pulse INIT low for > 50 useconds (on PC5)
77 003A  B0 0D                             MOV   AL, 00001011B          ; Bit set on PC5
78 003C  EE                                OUT   DX, AL                 ; Send INIT high
79 003D  B0 0C                             MOV   AL, 00001010B          ; Bit reset on PC5
80 003F  EE                                OUT   DX, AL                 ; Send INIT low
81 0040  B9 0017                           MOV   CX, 17H                ; Wait > 50 useconds
82 0043  E2 FE             PAUSE1:  LOOP   PAUSE1
83 0045  B0 0D                             MOV   AL, 00001101B          ; Bit set on PC5
84 0047  EE                                OUT   DX, AL                 ; Send INIT high again
85                                  ;Read printer status from port A, status OK - AL = XXXX0101
86                                  ;PA3-BUSY=0, PA2-SLCT=1, PA1-PE=0, PA0-ERROR=1
87 0048  C6 06 0033r 00                    MOV   PRINTER_ERROR, 0       ; Printer OK so far
88 004D  BA FFF9                           MOV   DX, 0FFF9H             ; Point at port A
89 0050  EC                                IN    AL, DX                 ; Get printer status
90 0051  24 0F                             AND   AL, 0FH                ; Upper 4 bits not used
91 0053  3C 05                             CMP   AL, 00000101B          ; If status OK then
92 0055  74 14                             JZ    SEND_IT                ; send it
93                                  ;else printer not ready, wait 20 ms and try again
94 0057  B9 16EA                           MOV   CX, 16EAH              ; Load count for 20 ms
95 005A  E2 FE             PAUSE:   LOOP   PAUSE                        ; and wait
96 005C  EC                                IN    AL, DX                 ; Repeat steps to read status
97 005D  24 0F                             AND   AL, 0FH
98 005F  3C 05                             CMP   AL, 00000101B
99 0061  74 08                             JZ    SEND_IT
100 0063 C6 06 0033r 01                    MOV   PRINTER_ERROR, 01      ; If printer not ready then
101 0068 EB 19 90                          JMP   FIN                    ; set error code and
102                                                                     ; terminate program
103 006B B8 0000r                  ;else set up pointer to message storage and say print not done yet
104 006E A3 0030r          SEND_IT:MOV   AX, OFFSET MESSAGE_1
105 0071 C6 06 002Fr 00            MOV   POINTER, AX
106 0076 C6 06 0032r 2F            MOV   PRINT_DONE, 00
107                                 MOV   COUNTER, MESSAGE_LENGTH
108 007B BA FFFF           ;Enable 8255A interrupt request output on PC0 by setting PC2
109 007E B0 05                     MOV   DX, 0FFFFH             ; Point at port control addr
110 0080 EE                        MOV   AL, 00000101B          ; Bit set word for PC0 intr
111                                 OUT   DX, AL
112 0081 EB FE            ;Wait for an interrupt from the printer
113 0083 90               WT:      JMP   WT
114 0084                  FIN:     NOP
115                       CODE     ENDS
                                   END
```

(a)

FIGURE 9-16 *(Continued)*   (a) Mainline.

here we generate the strobe directly under software control.

In the mainline we make the $\overline{\text{STROBE}}$ signal on PC4 high by sending a bit set/reset control word of 00001001 to the control register of the 8255A. In the printer driver procedure a character is sent to the printer with the OUT DX,AL instruction. According to the timing diagram in Figure 9-13, we then want to wait at least 0.5 μs before asserting the $\overline{\text{STROBE}}$ signal low. This is automatically done in the program because the instructions required to assert the strobe low take longer than 0.5 μs. The MOV AL,00001000B instruction requires 4 clock cycles, and the OUT DX,AL instruction requires 8 clock cycles to execute. Assuming a 5-MHz clock (0.2-μs period), these two instructions take 2.4 μs to execute, which is more than required.

Again referring to the timing diagram in Figure 9-13, the STROBE time low must also be at least 0.5 μs. The MOV AL,00001001B instruction takes 4 clock cycles, and the OUT DX,AL instruction takes 8 clock cycles. With a 5-MHz clock, this totals to 2.5 μs, which again

is more than enough time for $\overline{\text{STROBE}}$ low. In this case, creating the $\overline{\text{STROBE}}$ signal with software does not use much of the processor's time, so this is an efficient way to do it.

A FEW MORE POINTS ABOUT THE 8255A

Before leaving our discussion of the 8255A, we want to show you a little more about how port C can be used.

Any bits of port C which are programmed as inputs can be read by simply doing a read from the port C address. You can then mask out any unwanted bits of the word read in. If port A and/or port B is programmed in a handshake mode, then some of the bits of a byte read in from port C represent *status information* about the handshake signals. Figure 9-17, p. 260, shows the meaning of the bits read from port C for port A and/or port B in mode 1. Here's how you read this diagram. If port B is initialized as a handshake (mode 1) input port, then bits D0, D1, and D2 read from port C represent the status of the port B handshake signals. Bit D2 will

```
 1                            ;8086 PROCEDURE F9-16B.ASM use with mainline F9-16A.ASM
 2                            ;ABSTRACT    : Printer Driver procedure outputs a character from a buffer
 3                                          ; to a printer. If no characters are left in the buffer then
 4                                          , the interrupt to the 8086 on IR6 of the 8259A is disabled
 5                            ;PROCEDURES  : None used
 6                            ;PORTS       : Uses SDK-86 board Port P1B (FFFBH) to output characters
 7                                          ; and port P1C bits for handshake signals and printer intr
 8                            ;REGISTERS   : Destroys nothing
 9
10                            PUBLIC  PRINT_IT
11 0000                      DATA SEGMENT PUBLIC
12                                  EXTRN   COUNTER  :BYTE, POINTER    :WORD
13                                  EXTRN   MESSAGE_1:BYTE, PRINT_DONE:BYTE
14 0000                      DATA ENDS
15
16 0000                      CODE  SEGMENT WORD PUBLIC
17 0000                      PRINT_IT PROC FAR
18                                  ASSUME  CS:CODE, DS:DATA
19 0000  9C                        PUSHF                       ; Save registers
20 0001  50                        PUSH AX
21 0002  53                        PUSH BX
22 0003  52                        PUSH DX
23 0004  FB                        STI                         ; Enable higher interrupts
24 0005  BA FFFB                   MOV   DX, OFFFBH            ; Point at port B
25 0008  8B 1E 0000e               MOV   BX, POINTER           ; Load pointer to message
26 000C  8A 07                     MOV   AL, [BX]              ; Get a character
27 000E  EE                        OUT   DX, AL                ; Send the character to printer
28                          ;Send printer strobe on PC4 low then high
29 000F  BA FFFF                   MOV   DX, OFFFFH            ; Point at port control addr
30 0012  B0 08                     MOV   AL, 00001000B         ; Strobe low control word
31 0014  EE                        OUT   DX, AL
32 0015  B0 09                     MOV   AL, 00001001B         ; Strobe high control word
33 0017  EE                        OUT   DX, AL
34                          ;Increment pointer and decrement counter
35 0018  FF 06 0000e               INC POINTER
36 001C  FE 0E 0000e               DEC COUNTER
37 0020  75 08                     JNZ NEXT                    ; Wait for next character?
38                          ;No more characters-disable 8255A int request on PC0 by bit reset of PC2
39 0022  B0 04                     MOV   AL, 00000100B         ; Bit reset word for PC0 interrupt
40 0024  EE                        OUT   DX, AL
41 0025  C6 06 0000e 01            MOV PRINT_DONE, 1
42 002A  B0 20              NEXT:   MOV   AL, 00100000B         ; OCW2 for non-specific EOI
43 002C  BA FF00                   MOV   DX, OFF00H            ; Point at 8259A control addr
44 002F  EE                        OUT   DX, AL
45 0030  5A                        POP DX                      ; Restore registers
46 0031  5B                        POP BX
47 0032  58                        POP AX
48 0033  9D                        POPF
49 0034  CF                        IRET
50 0035                     PRINT_IT ENDP
51 0035                     CODE    ENDS
52                                  END
```

(b)

FIGURE 9-16 (Continued)   (b) Procedure.

be high if the port B interrupt request output has been enabled. Bit D2 is a copy of the level on the input buffer full (IBF) pin. Bit D3 is a copy of the interrupt request output, so it will be high if port B is requesting an interrupt.

In our previous application examples, we showed how to do handshake data transfer on an interrupt basis to make maximum use of the CPU time. However, in applications where the CPU has nothing else to do while waiting to, for example, read in the next character from some device, then you can save one interrupt input by reading data from the 8255A on a polled basis. To do this for a handshake input operation on port B, you simply loop through reading port C and checking bit D1

over and over until you find this bit high. The IBF pin being high means that the input data byte has been latched into the 8255A and can now be read. The timing waveforms for this case are the same as those in Figure 9-10, except that you are not using the interrupt request output from the 8255A.

Port C bits that are not used for handshake signals and programmed as outputs can be written to by sending bit set/reset control words to the control register. Technically, bits PC0 through PC3 can also be written to directly at the port C address, but we have found it safer to just use the bit set/reset control word approach to write to all leftover port C bits programmed as outputs.

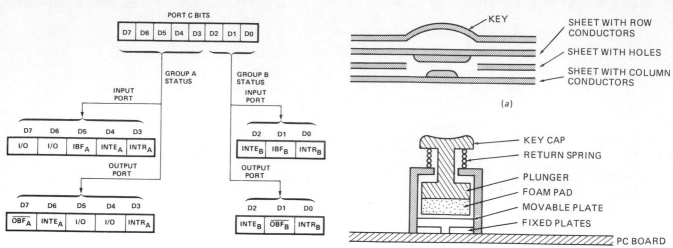

FIGURE 9-17   8255A status word format for mode 1 input and output operations.

INTERFACING A MICROPROCESSOR TO KEYBOARDS

Keyboard Types

When you press a key on your computer, you are activating a switch. There are many different ways of making these switches. Here's an overview of the construction and operation of some of the most common types.

MECHANICAL KEYSWITCHES

In mechanical-switch keys, two pieces of metal are pushed together when you press the key. The actual switch elements are often made of a phosphor-bronze alloy with gold plating on the contact areas. The keyswitch usually contains a spring to return the key to the nonpressed position and perhaps a small piece of foam to help damp out bouncing. Some mechanical keyswitches now consist of a molded silicone dome with a small piece of conductive rubber on the underside. When a key is pressed, the rubber foam shorts two traces on the printed-circuit board to produce the Key Pressed signal.

Mechanical switches are relatively inexpensive, but they have several disadvantages. First, they suffer from *contact bounce*. A pressed key may make and break contact several times before it makes solid contact. Second, the contacts may become oxidized or dirty with age so they no longer make a dependable connection. Higher-quality mechanical switches typically have a rated lifetime of about 1 million keystrokes. The silicone dome type typically last 25 million keystrokes.

MEMBRANE KEYSWITCHES

These switches are really just a special type of mechanical switch. They consist of a three-layer plastic or rubber sandwich, as shown in Figure 9-18a. The top layer has a conductive line of silver ink running under each row of keys. The middle layer has a hole under each key position. The bottom layer has a conductive line of silver ink running under each column of keys. When you press

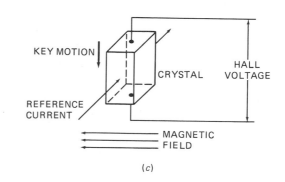

FIGURE 9-18   Keyswitch types. (a) Membrane. (b) Capacitive. (c) Hall effect.

a key, you push the top ink line through the hole to contact the bottom ink line. The advantage of membrane keyboards is that they can be made as very thin, sealed units. They are often used on cash registers in fast-food restaurants, on medical instruments, and in other messy applications. The lifetime of membrane keyboards varies over a wide range.

CAPACITIVE KEYSWITCHES

As shown in Figure 9-18b, a capacitive keyswitch has two small metal plates on the printed-circuit board and another metal plate on the bottom of a piece of foam. When you press the key, the movable plate is pushed closer to the fixed plate. This changes the capacitance between the fixed plates. Sense amplifier circuitry detects this change in capacitance and produces a logic-level signal that indicates a key has been pressed. The big advantage of a capacitive switch is that it has no mechanical contacts to become oxidized or dirty. A small disadvantage is the specialized circuitry needed to detect the change in capacitance. Capacitive keyswitches typically have a rated lifetime of about 20 million keystrokes.

HALL EFFECT KEYSWITCHES

This is another type of switch which has no mechanical contact. It takes advantage of the deflection of a moving

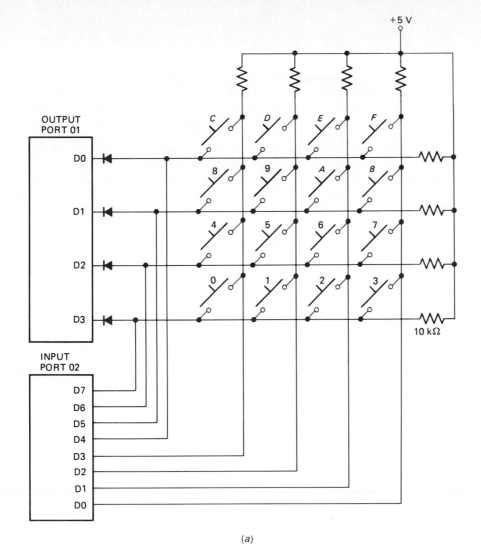

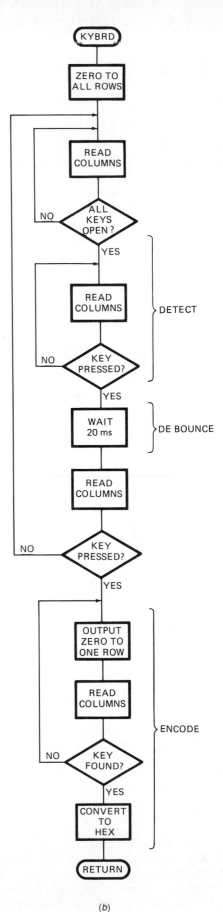

FIGURE 9-19 Detecting a matrix keyboard keypress, debouncing it, and encoding it with a microcomputer. (a) Port connections. (b) Flowchart for procedure.

charge by a magnetic field. Figure 9-18c shows you how this works. A reference current is passed through a semiconductor crystal between two opposing faces. When a key is pressed, the crystal is moved through a magnetic field which has its flux lines perpendicular to the direction of the current flow in the crystal. (Actually, it is easier to move a small magnet past the crystal.) Moving the crystal through the magnetic field causes a small voltage to be developed between two of the other opposing faces of the crystal. This voltage is amplified and used to indicate that a key has been pressed. (Hall effect sensors are also used to detect motion in many electrically controlled machines.) Hall effect keyboards are more expensive because of the more complex switch mechanisms, but they are very dependable and have typical rated lifetimes of 100 million or more keystrokes.

Keyboard Circuit Connections and Interfacing

In most keyboards, the keyswitches are connected in a matrix of rows and columns, as shown in Figure 9-19a.

We will use simple mechanical switches for our examples here, but the principle is the same for other types of switches. Getting meaningful data from a keyboard such as this requires the following three major tasks:

1. Detect a keypress.

2. Debounce the keypress.

3. Encode the keypress (produce a standard code for the pressed key).

The three tasks can be done with hardware, software, or a combination of the two, depending on the application. We will first show you how they can be done with software, as might be done in a microprocessor-based grocery scale where the microprocessor is not pressed for time. Later we describe some hardware devices which do these tasks.

Software Keyboard Interfacing

CIRCUIT CONNECTIONS AND ALGORITHM

Figure 9-19a shows how a hexadecimal keypad can be connected to a couple of microcomputer ports so the three interfacing tasks can be done as part of a program. The rows of the matrix are connected to four output-port lines. The column lines of the matrix are connected to four input-port lines. To make the program simpler, the row lines are also connected to four input lines.

When no keys are pressed, the column lines are held high by the pull-up resistors connected to +5 V. Pressing a key connects a row to a column. If a low is output on a row and a key in that row is pressed, then the low will appear on the column which contains that key and can be detected on the input port. If you know the row and the column of the pressed key, you then know which key was pressed, and you can convert this information into any code you want to represent that key. Figure 9-19b shows a flowchart for a procedure to detect, debounce, and produce the hex code for a pressed key. This procedure is another example of an I/O driver.

An easy way to detect if any key in the matrix is pressed is to output 0's to all the rows and then check the columns to see if a pressed key has connected a low to a column. In the algorithm in Figure 9-19b, we first output lows to all the rows and check the columns over and over until the columns are all high. This is done to make sure a previous key has been released before looking for the next one. In standard keyboard terminology, this is called *two-key lockout*. Once the columns are found to be all high, the program enters another loop, which waits until a low appears on one of the columns, indicating that a key has been pressed. This second loop does the detect task for us. A simple 20-ms delay procedure then does the debounce task.

After the debounce time, another check is made to see if the key is still pressed. If the columns are now all high, then no key is pressed and the initial detection was caused by a noise pulse or a light brushing past a key. If any of the columns are still low, then the assumption is made that it was a valid keypress.

The final task is to determine the row and column of the pressed key and convert this row and column information to the hex code for the pressed key. To get the row and column information, a low is output to one row and the columns are read. If none of the columns is low, the pressed key is not in that row, so the low is rotated to the next row and the columns are checked again. The process is repeated until a low on a row produces a low on one of the columns. The pressed key then is in the row which is low at that time. With the connections shown in Figure 9-19a, the byte read in from the input port will contain a 4-bit code which represents the row of the pressed key and a 4-bit code which represents the column of the pressed key. As we show later, a lookup table can be used to easily convert this row-column code to the desired hex value.

Figure 9-20 shows the assembly language program for this procedure. The detect, debounce, and row-detect parts of the program follow the flowchart very closely and should be easy for you to follow. Work your way down through these parts until you reach the ENCODE label; then continue with the discussion here.

CODE CONVERSION

There are two important ways of converting one code to another in a program. The ENCODE portion of this program uses a *compare* technique, which we will discuss in detail here. In a later section on keyboard interfacing with hardware, we will show you the other major code conversion technique, the *XLAT* method.

After the row which produces a low on one of the columns is found, execution jumps to the label ENCODE. The IN AL,DX instruction here reads the row and column codes from the input port. Since this 8-bit code read in represents the pressed key, all that has to be done now is to convert this 8-bit code to the hex code for that key. If we press the D key, for example, we want to exit from the procedure with 0DH in AL.

The conversion is done with the lookup table declared with DBs at the top of Figure 9-20. This table contains the 8-bit keypressed codes for each of the 16 keys. Note that the row-column codes are put in the table in the same order as the hex codes they represent. To convert a row-column code read in from the port, we compare it with each value in the table until we reach the value it matches. For several reasons, we start by comparing a row-column code with the highest entry in the table. A counter is used to keep track of how far down the table we have to go to find a match for a particular input code. Because the entries in the table are in numerical order, the counter will contain the hex code for the pressed key when a match is found. Let's look at the actual program instructions in Figure 9-20 to help you see how this works.

The BX register is used as a counter and as a pointer to one of the codes in the table, so to start we load 000FH in BX. The CMP AL,TABLE[BX] after this compares the code at offset [BX] in the table with the row-column code in AL. Initially, BX contains 000FH, so the row-column code in AL is compared with the row-column code at the highest location in the table. As shown in the data

```
1                              ;8086 PROGRAM F9-20.ASM
2                              ;ABSTRACT  : Program scans and decodes a 16-switch keypad.
3                              ;           It initializes the ports below and then calls a procedure
4                              ;           to input an 8-bit value from a 16-switch keypad and encode it.
5                              ;PORTS     : SDK-86 board Port P1A (FFF9H) - output, P1B (FFFBH) - input
6                              ;PROCEDURES: Calls KEYBRD to scan and decode 16-switch keypad
7                              ;REGISTERS : Uses CS,DS,SS,SP,AX,DX
8
9  0000                        DATA  SEGMENT WORD  PUBLIC
10                             ;          0    1    2    3    4    5    6    7
11 0000  77 7B 7D 7E B7 BB BD + TABLE DB    77H, 7BH, 7DH, 7EH, 0B7H, 0BBH, 0BDH, 0BEH
12        BE
13                             ;          8    9    A    B    C    D    E    F
14 0008  D7 DB DD DE E7 EB ED +    DB  0D7H, 0DBH, 0DDH, 0DEH, 0E7H, 0EBH, 0EDH, 0EEH
15        EE
16 0010                        DATA  ENDS
17 0000                        STACK_SEG SEGMENT
18 0000  1E*(0000)                   DW     30   DUP(0)   ; Set up stack of 30 words
19                                  TOP_STACK  LABEL WORD   ; Pointer to top of stack
20 003C                        STACK_SEG ENDS
21
22 0000                        CODE SEGMENT WORD PUBLIC
23                                  ASSUME  CS:CODE, DS:DATA, SS:STACK_SEG
24 0000  B8 0000s              START: MOV  AX, STACK_SEG      ; Initialize stack
25 0003  8E D0                        MOV  SS, AX             ; segment register and
26 0005  BC 003Cr                     MOV  SP, OFFSET TOP_STACK ; top of stack
27 0008  B8 0000s                     MOV  AX, DATA
28 000B  8E D8                        MOV  DS, AX
29                             ;Initialize ports, mode 0, Port A for output, Ports B & C for input
30 000D  BA FFFF                      MOV  DX, 0FFFFH         ; Put port control address in DX
31 0010  B0 8B                        MOV  AL, 10001011B      ; Code 8BH
32 0012  EE                           OUT  DX, AL             ; Send control word.
33 0013  E8 0001                      CALL KEYBRD
34 0016  90                           NOP
35                             ;Program will continue here with other tasks
36
37                             ;8086 PROCEDURE KEYBRD
38                             ;ABSTRACT  : Procedure gets a code from a 16-switch keypad and decodes it.
39                             ;           It returns the code for the keypress in AL and AH=00. If there
40                             ;           is an error in the keypress then it returns AH=01.
41                             ;PORTS     : Uses SDK-86 ports P1A (FFF9H) for output and P1B (FFFBH) for input
42                             ;INPUTS    : Keypress from port
43                             ;OUTPUTS   : Keypress code or error message in AX
44                             ;PROCEDURES: None used
45                             ;REGISTERS : Destroys AX
46
47 0017                        KEYBRD PROC NEAR
48 0017  9C                           PUSHF                   ; Save registers used
49 0018  53                           PUSH BX
50 0019  51                           PUSH CX
51 001A  52                           PUSH DX
52                             ;Send 0's to all rows
53 001B  B0 00                        MOV  AL, 00
54 001D  BA FFF9                      MOV  DX, 0FFF9H         ; Load output address
55 0020  EE                           OUT  DX, AL             ; Send 0's
56                             ;Read columns to see if all keys are open
57 0021  BA FFFB                      MOV  DX, 0FFFBH         ; Load input port address
58 0024  EC                   WAIT_OPEN:IN  AL, DX
59 0025  24 0F                        AND  AL, 0FH            ; Mask row bits
60 0027  3C 0F                        CMP  AL, 0FH            ; Wait until no keys pressed
61 0029  75 F9                        JNE  WAIT_OPEN
62                             ;Read columns to see if a key is pressed
63 002B  EC                   WAIT_PRESS:IN  AL, DX           ; Read columns
64 002C  24 0F                        AND  AL, 0FH            ; Mask row bits
65 002E  3C 0F                        CMP  AL, 0FH            ; See if keypressed
66 0030  74 F9                        JE   WAIT_PRESS
67                             ;Debounce keypress
68 0032  B9 16EA                      MOV  CX, 16EAH          ; Delay of 20 ms
69 0035  E2 FE                DELAY:   LOOP DELAY
70                             ;Read columns to see if key still pressed
71 0037  EC                           IN   AL, DX
```

FIGURE 9-20   Assembly language instructions for keyboard detect, debounce,
and encode procedure.

(Continued)

```
72 0038  24 OF                           AND    AL, OFH
73 003A  3C OF                           CMP    AL, OFH
74 003C  74 ED                           JE     WAIT_PRESS
75                              ;Find the key
76 003E  B0 FE                           MOV    AL, OFEH           ; Initialize a row mask with bit 0
77 0040  8A C8                           MOV    CL, AL             ; low and save the mask
78 0042  BA FFF9             NEXT_ROW:    MOV    DX, OFFF9H         ; Send out a low on one row
79 0045  EE                              OUT    DX, AL
80 0046  BA FFFB                          MOV    DX, OFFFBH         ; Read columns & check for low
81 0049  EC                              IN     AL, DX
82 004A  24 OF                           AND    AL, OFH            ; Mask out row code
83 004C  3C OF                           CMP    AL, OFH            ; If low in a column then
84 004E  75 06                           JNE    ENCODE             ; key column found, so encode it
85 0050  D0 C1                           ROL    CL, 01             ; else rotate mask
86 0052  8A C1                           MOV    AL, CL
87 0054  EB EC                           JMP    NEXT_ROW           ; and look at next row
88                              ;Encode the row/column information
89 0056  BB 000F             ENCODE:      MOV    BX, 000FH          ; Set up BX as a counter and
90 0059  EC                              IN     AL, DX             ; read row and column from port
91 005A  3A 87 0000r         TRY_NEXT:    CMP    AL, TABLE[BX]      ; Compare row/col code with table entry
92 005E  74 08                           JE     DONE               ; Hex code in BX
93 0060  4B                              DEC    BX                 ; Point at next table entry
94 0061  79 F7                           JNS    TRY_NEXT
95 0063  B4 01                           MOV    AH, 01             ; Pass an error code in AH
96 0065  EB 05 90                        JMP    EXIT
97 0068  8A C3              DONE:         MOV    AL, BL             ; Hex code for key in AL
98 006A  B4 00                           MOV    AH, 00             ; Put key-valid code in AH
99 006C  5A                 EXIT:         POP    DX                 ; Restore calling program
100 006D  59                              POP    CX                 ; registers
101 006E  5B                              POP    BX
102 006F  9D                              POPF
103 0070  C3                              RET
104 0071              KEYBRD    ENDP
105 0071              CODE      ENDS
106                             END
```

FIGURE 9-20 (*Continued*)

segment in Figure 9-20, the row-column code at this location in the table is the code for the F key. If the code in AL matches this code, we know the F key was pressed. BX contains 000FH, the hex code for this key. Since we need only the lower 8 bits of BX, the hex code in BL is copied to AL to pass it back to the calling program. AH is loaded with 00H to tell the calling program that this was a valid keypress, and a return is made to the calling program.

If the row-column code in AL doesn't match the table value on the first compare, we decrement BX to point to the code for the E key in the table and do another compare. If a match occurs this time, then we know that the E key was the key pressed and that the hex code for that key, 0EH, is in BL. If we don't get a match on this compare, we cycle through the loop until we get a match or until the row-column code for the pressed key has been compared with all the values in the table. As long as the value in BX is 0 or above after the DEC BX instruction, the Jump if Not Sign instruction, JNS TRY_NEXT, will cause execution to go back to the Compare instruction. If no match is found in the table, BX will decrement from 0 to FFFFH. Since the sign bit is a copy of the MSB of the result after the DEC instruction, the sign bit will then be set. Execution will fall through to an instruction which loads an error code of 01H in AH. We then return to the calling program. The calling program will check AH on return to determine if the contents of AL represent the code for a valid keypress.

ERROR TRAPPING

The concept of detecting some error condition such as "no match found" is called *error trapping*. Error trapping is a very important part of real programs. Even in this simple program, think what might happen with no error trap if two keys in the same row were pressed at exactly the same time and a column code with two lows in it was produced. This code would not match any of the row-column codes in the table, so after all the values in the table were checked, BX would be decremented from 0000H to FFFFH. On the next compare, AL would be compared with a value in memory at offset FFFFH. Since this location is not even in the table, the compare-decrement cycle would continue through 65,536 memory locations until, by chance, the value in a memory location matched the row-column code in AL. The contents of BL at that point would be passed back to the calling routine. The chances are 1 in 256 that this would be the correct value for one of the two pressed keys. Since these are not very good odds, you should put an error trap in a program wherever there is a chance for it to go off to "never-never land" in this way. An error/ no-error "flag" can be passed back to the calling program in a register as shown, in a dedicated memory location, or on the stack.

Keyboard Interfacing with Hardware

The previous section described how you can connect a keyboard matrix to a couple of microprocessor ports and perform the three interfacing tasks with program instructions. For systems where the CPU is too busy to be bothered doing these tasks in software, an external device is used to do them. One example of a MOS device which can do this is the General Instrument AY5-2376, which can be connected to the rows and columns of a keyboard switch matrix. The AY5-2376 independently detects a keypress by cycling a low down through the rows and checking the columns just as we did in software. When it finds a key pressed, it waits a debounce time. If the key is still pressed after the debounce time, the AY5-2376 produces the 8-bit code for the pressed key and sends it out to, for example, a microcomputer port on eight parallel lines. To let the microcomputer know that a valid ASCII code is on the data lines, the AY5-2376 outputs a strobe pulse. The microcomputer can detect this strobe pulse and read in the ASCII code on a polled basis, as we showed in Figure 4-20, or it can detect the strobe pulse on an interrupt basis, as we showed in Figure 8-9. With the interrupt method the

microcomputer doesn't have to pay any attention to the keyboard until it receives an interrupt signal, so this method uses very little of the microcomputer's time.

The AY5-2376 has a feature called *two-key rollover.* This means that if two keys are pressed at nearly the same time, each key will be detected, debounced, and converted to ASCII. The ASCII code for the first key and a strobe signal for it will be sent out; then the ASCII code for the second key and a strobe signal for it will be sent out. Compare this with two-key lockout, which we described previously in our discussion of the software method of keyboard interfacing.

DEDICATED MICROPROCESSOR KEYBOARD ENCODERS

Most computers and computer terminals now use detached keyboards with built-in encoders. Instead of using a hardware encoder device such as the AY5-2376, these keyboards use a dedicated microprocessor. Figure 9-21 shows the encoder circuitry for the IBM PC capaci-

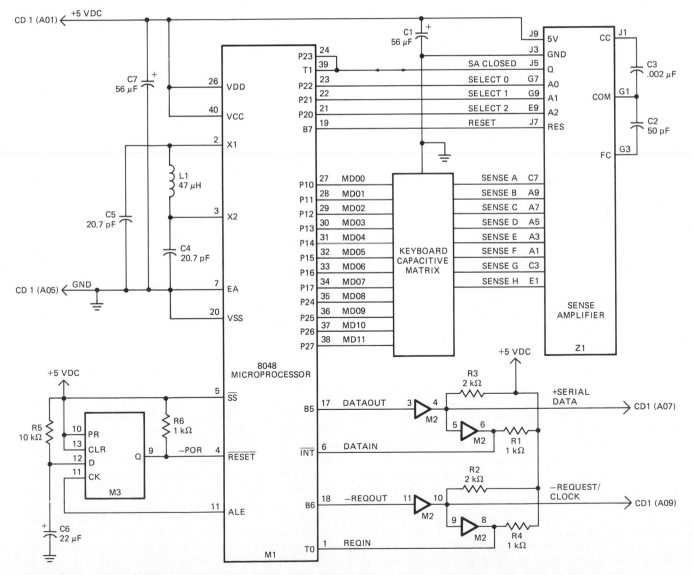

FIGURE 9-21 IBM PC keyboard scan circuitry using a dedicated microprocessor. (*IBM Corporation*)

tive-switch matrix keyboard. The 8048 microprocessor used here contains an 8-bit CPU, a ROM, some RAM, three ports, and a programmable timer/counter. A program stored in the on-chip ROM performs the three keyboard tasks and sends the code for a pressed key out to the computer. To cut down the number of connecting wires, the key code is sent out in serial form rather than in parallel form. Some keyboards send data to the computer in serial form using a beam of infrared light instead of a wire.

Note in Figure 9-21 that a sense amplifier is used to detect the change in capacitance produced when a key is pressed. Also note that the 8048 uses a tuned LC circuit rather than a more expensive crystal to determine its operating clock frequency.

One of the major advantages of using a dedicated microprocessor to do the three keyboard tasks is programmability. Special-function keys on the keyboard can be programmed to send out any code desired for a particular application. By simply plugging in an 8048 with a different lookup table in ROM, the keyboard can be changed from outputting ASCII characters to outputting some other character set.

The IBM keyboard, incidentally, does not send out ASCII codes, but instead sends out a hex "scan" code for each key when it is pressed and a different scan code when that key is released. This double-code approach gives the system software maximum flexibility because a program command can be implemented either when a key is pressed or when it is released.

CONVERTING ONE KEYBOARD CODE TO ANOTHER USING XLAT

Suppose that you are building up a simple microcomputer to control the heating, watering, lighting, and ventilation of your greenhouse. As part of the hardware, you buy a high-quality, fully encoded keyboard at the local electronics surplus store for a few dollars. When you get the keyboard home, you find that it works perfectly, but that it outputs EBCDIC codes instead of the ASCII codes that you want. Here's how you use the 8086 XLAT instruction to easily solve this problem.

First, look at Table 1-2, which shows the ASCII and EBCDIC codes. The job you have to do here is to convert each input EBCDIC input code to the corresponding ASCII code. One way to do this is the compare technique described previously for the hex-keyboard example. For that method you would first put the EBCDIC codes in a table in memory in the order shown in Table 1-2 and set up a register as a counter and pointer to the end of the table. Then you enter a loop which compares the EBCDIC character in AL with each of the EBCDIC codes in the table until a match is found. The counter would be decremented after each compare so that when a match was found, the count register would contain the desired ASCII code.

This compare technique works well, but since EBCDIC contains 256 codes, the program will, on the average, have to do 128 compares before a match is found. The compare technique then is often too time-consuming for long tables. The XLAT method is much faster.

The first step in the XLAT method is to make up a

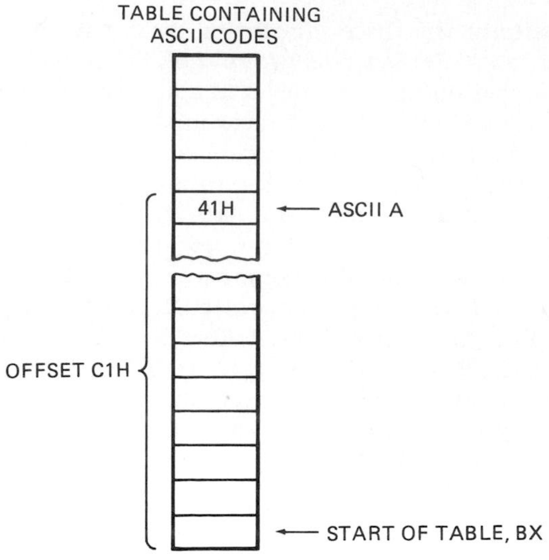

FIGURE 9-22 Memory table setup for using XLAT to convert EBCDIC keycode to ASCII equivalent.

memory table which contains all the ASCII codes. The trick here is to put each ASCII code in the table at a displacement from the start of the table equal to the value of the EBCDIC character. For example, the EBCDIC code for uppercase A is C1H, so you put the ASCII code for uppercase A, 41H, at offset C1H in the table, as shown in Figure 9-22. Since EBCDIC code is an 8-bit code, the table will require 256 memory locations. For EBCDIC values which have no ASCII equivalent, you can just put in 00H because these locations will not be accessed. You can use the DB assembler directive to set up the table, as we did with the row-column table in Figure 9-20.

To do the actual conversion, you simply load the BX register with the offset of the start of the table, load the EBCDIC character to be converted in the AL register, and do the XLAT instruction. When the 8086 executes the XLAT instruction, it internally adds the EBCDIC value in AL to the starting offset of the table in BX. Because of the way the table is made up, the result of this addition will be a pointer to the desired ASCII value in the table. The 8086 then automatically uses this pointer to copy the desired ASCII character from the table to AL. Later in the chapter we show you another example of the use of the XLAT instruction.

The advantage of the XLAT technique for this conversion is that, no matter where in the table the desired ASCII value is, the conversion only requires execution of two loads and one XLAT instruction. The question may occur to you at this point, If this method is so fast, why didn't we use it for the hex-keypad conversion described earlier? The answer is that since the row-column code from the hex keypad is an 8-bit code, the lookup table for the XLAT method would require 256 memory locations, but only 16 of these would actually be used. This would be a waste of memory, so the compare method is a better choice. Since code conversion is a commonly encountered problem in low-level programming, it is important for you to become familiar with both the compare and the XLAT methods so that you can use the one which best fits a particular application.

INTERFACING TO ALPHANUMERIC DISPLAYS

To give directions or data values to users, many microprocessor-controlled instruments and machines need to display letters of the alphabet and numbers. In systems where a large amount of data needs to be displayed, a CRT is usually used to display the data, so in Chapter 13 we show you how to interface a microcomputer to a CRT. In systems where only a small amount of data needs to be displayed, simple digit-type displays are often used. There are several technologies used to make these digit-oriented displays, but we have space here to discuss only the two major types. These are *light-emitting diodes* (LEDs) and *liquid-crystal displays* (LCDs). LCD displays use very low power, so they are often used in portable, battery-powered instruments. LCDs, however, do not emit their own light; they simply change the reflection of available light. Therefore, for an instrument that is to be used in low-light conditions, you have to include a light source for the LCDs or use LEDs, which emit their own light. Starting with LEDs, the following sections show you how to interface these two types of displays to microcomputers.

Interfacing LED Displays to Microcomputers

Alphanumeric LED displays are available in three common formats. For displaying only numbers and hexadecimal letters, simple 7-segment displays such as that shown in Figure 1-4a are used.

To display numbers and the entire alphabet, 18-segment displays such as that shown in Figure 9-23a or 5 by 7 dot-matrix displays such as that shown in Figure 9-23b can be used. The 7-segment type is the least expensive, most commonly used, and easiest to interface with, so we will concentrate first on how to interface with this type. Later we will show the modifications needed to interface with the other types.

DIRECTLY DRIVING LED DISPLAYS

Figure 9-24, p. 268, shows a circuit that you might connect to a parallel port on a microcomputer to drive a single 7-segment, common-anode display. For a common-anode display, a segment is turned on by applying a logic low to it. The 7447 converts a BCD code applied to its inputs to the pattern of lows required to display the number represented by the BCD code. This circuit connection is referred to as a *static display* because current is being passed through the display at all times. Here's how you calculate the value of the current-limiting resistors that have to be connected in series with each segment.

Each segment requires a current of between 5 and 30 mA to light. Let's assume you want a current of 20 mA. The voltage drop across the LED when it is lit is about

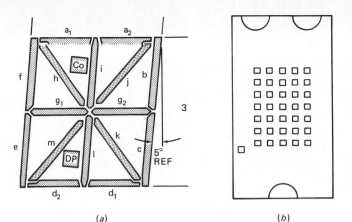

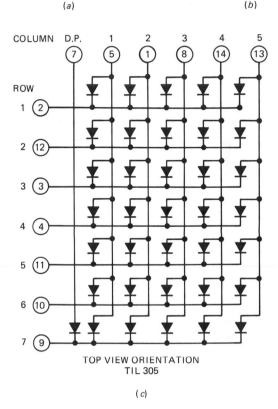

FIGURE 9-23   Eighteen-segment and 5 by 7 matrix LED displays. (a) 18-segment display. (b) 5 by 7 dot-matrix display format. (c) 5 by 7 dot-matrix circuit connections.

1.5 V. The output low voltage for the 7447 is a maximum of 0.4 V at 40 mA, so assume that it is about 0.2 V at 20 mA. Subtracting these two voltage drops from the supply voltage of 5 V leaves 3.3 V across the current-limiting resistor. Dividing 3.3 V by 20 mA gives a value of 168 Ω for the current-limiting resistor. The voltage drops across the LED and the output of the 7447 are not exactly predictable, and the exact current through the LED is not critical as long as we don't exceed its maximum rating. Therefore, a standard value of 150 Ω is reasonable.

SOFTWARE-MULTIPLEXED LED DISPLAYS

The circuit in Figure 9-24 works well for driving just one or two LED digits with a parallel output port. However, this scheme has several problems if you want

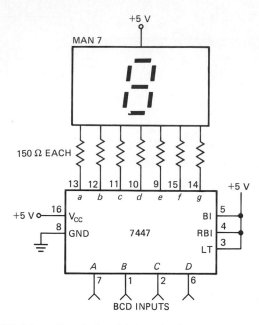

FIGURE 9-24   Circuit for driving single 7-segment LED display with 7447.

to drive, for example, eight digits. The first problem is power consumption. For worst-case calculations, assume that all 8 digits are displaying the digit 8, so all 7 segments are lit. Seven segments times 20 mA per segment gives a current of 140 mA per digit. Multiplying this by 8 digits gives a total current of 1120 mA, or 1.12 A, for the 8 digits! A second problem of the static approach is that each display digit requires a separate 7447 decoder, each of which uses, perhaps, another 13 mA. The current required by the decoders and the LED displays might be several times the current required by the rest of the circuitry in the instrument.

To solve the problems of the static display approach, we use a *multiplex* method. A circuit example is the easiest way to explain to you how this multiplexing works. Figure 9-25 shows a circuit you can add to a couple of microcomputer ports to drive some common-anode LED displays in a multiplexed manner. Note that the circuit has only one 7447 and that the segment outputs of the 7447 are bused in parallel to the segment inputs of all the digits. The question that may occur to you on first seeing this is: Aren't all the digits going to display the same number? The answer is that they would if all the digits were turned on at the same time. The trick of multiplexing displays is that only one display digit is turned on at a time. The PNP transistor in series with the common anode of each digit acts as an on/off switch for that digit. Here's how the multiplexing process works.

The BCD code for digit 1 is first output from port B to the 7447. The 7447 outputs the corresponding 7-segment code on the segment bus lines. The transistor connected to digit 1 is then turned on by outputting a low to the appropriate bit of port A. (Remember, a low turns on a PNP transistor.) All the rest of the bits of port A are made high to make sure no other digits are turned on. After 1 or 2 ms, digit 1 is turned off by outputting

all highs to port A. The BCD code for digit 2 is then output to the 7447 on port B, and a word to turn on digit 2 is output on port A. After 1 or 2 ms, digit 2 is turned off and the process is repeated for digit 3. The process is continued until all the digits have had a turn. Then digit 1 and the following digits are lit again in turn. We leave it to you as an exercise at the end of the chapter to write a procedure which is called on an interrupt basis every 2 ms to keep these displays refreshed with some values stored in a table.

With 8 digits and 2 ms per digit, you get back to digit 1 every 16 ms, or about 60 times a second. This refresh rate is fast enough that, to your eye, the digits will each appear to be lit all the time. Refresh rates of 40 to 200 times a second are acceptable.

The immediately obvious advantages of multiplexing the displays are that only one 7447 is required, and only one digit is lit at a time. We usually increase the current per segment to between 40 and 60 mA for multiplexed displays so that they will appear as bright as they would if they were not multiplexed. Even with this increased segment current, multiplexing gives a large saving in power and parts.

> NOTE: If you are calculating the current-limiting resistors for multiplexed displays with increased segment current, check the data sheet for the displays you are using to make sure you are not exceeding their maximum current rating.

The software-multiplexed approach we have just described can also be used to drive 18-segment LED devices and dot-matrix LED devices. For these devices, however, you replace the 7447 in Figure 9-25 with a ROM which generates the required segment codes when the ASCII code for a character is applied to the address inputs of the ROM.

Display and Keyboard Interfacing with the 8279

A disadvantage of the software-multiplexing approach shown here is that it puts an additional burden on the CPU. Also, if the CPU gets involved in doing some lengthy task which cannot be interrupted to refresh the display, only one digit of the display will be left lit. An alternative approach to interfacing multiplexed displays to a microcomputer is to use a *dedicated display controller* such as the Intel 8279. As we show you in the next section, an 8279 independently keeps a bank of 7-segment displays refreshed and performs the three tasks for a matrix keyboard at the same time.

8279 CIRCUIT CONNECTIONS AND OPERATION OVERVIEW

Sheets 7 and 8 of the SDK-86 schematics in Figure 7-8 show the circuit connections for the keypad and the multiplexed 7-segment displays. First let's look at the display circuitry on sheet 8. The displays there are common-anode, and each digit has a PNP transistor switch between its anode and the +5-V supply. A logic low is required to turn on one of these switches. Note

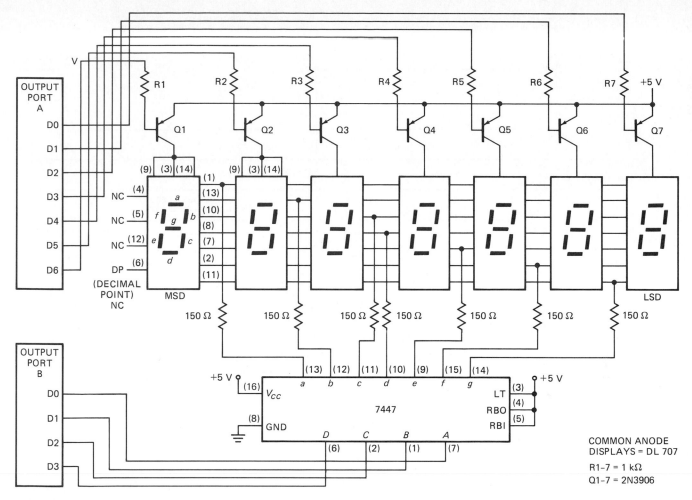

FIGURE 9-25   Circuit for multiplexing 7-segment displays with a microcomputer.

the 22-μF capacitor between +5 V and ground at the top of the schematic. This is necessary to filter out transients caused by switching the large currents to the LEDs off and on.

The segments of each digit are all connected on a common bus. Since these are common-anode displays, a low is needed to turn on a segment. Now let's look at sheet 7 in Figure 7-8 to see how these displays are driven.

The drive for the digit-switch transistors comes from a 7445 BCD-to-decimal decoder. This device is also known as a one-of-ten-low decoder. When a 4-bit BCD code is applied to the inputs of this device, the output corresponding to that BCD number will go low. For example, when the 8279 outputs 0100 or BCD 4, the 7445 output labeled 04 will go low. In the mode used for this circuit, the 8279 outputs a continuous count sequence from 0000 to 1111 over and over. This causes a low to be stepped from output to output of the 7445 in ring counter fashion, turning on each LED digit in turn. Only one output of the 7445 will ever be low at a time, so only one LED digit will be turned on at a time.

The segment bus lines for the displays are connected to the A3–A0 and B3–B0 outputs of the 8279 through some high-current inverting buffers in the ULN2003A.

Note that the 22-Ω current-limiting resistors in series with the segment lines are much smaller in value than those we calculated for the static circuit in Figure 9-24. There are two reasons for this. First, there is an additional few tenths of a volt drop across the transistor switch on each anode. Second, when multiplexing displays, we pass a higher current through the displays so that they appear as bright as they would if they were not multiplexed. Here's how the 8279 keeps these displays refreshed.

The 8279 contains a 16-byte display refresh RAM. When you want to display some letters or numbers on the LEDs, you write the 7-segment codes for the letters or numbers that you want displayed to the appropriate location in this display RAM. The 8279 then automatically cycles through sending out one of the segment codes, turning on the digit for a short time and then moving on to the next digit. The top five lines in Figure 9-26, p. 270, show this multiplex operation in timing diagram form.

The 8279 first outputs the binary number for the first digit to the 7445 on the SL0 to SL3 lines (Figure 7-8, sheet 7) to turn on the first of the digit-driver transistors. The lines SL0 and SL1 in Figure 9-26 represent the SL0 and SL1 lines from the 8279. During this time, the 8279

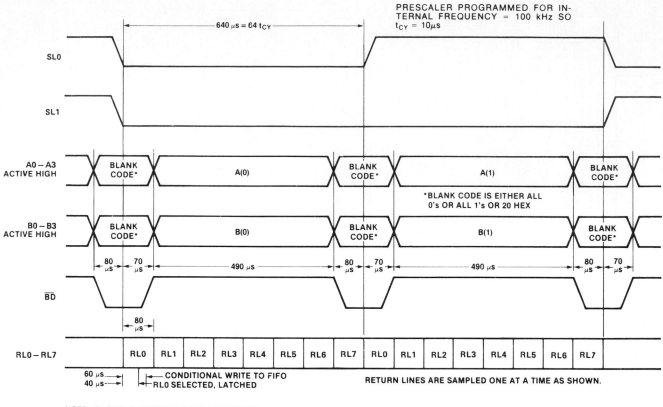

PRESCALER PROGRAMMED FOR IN-
TERNAL FREQUENCY = 100 kHz SO
$t_{CY} = 10\mu s$

640 μs = 64 t_{CY}

SL0

SL1

A0 – A3
ACTIVE HIGH — BLANK CODE* — A(0) — BLANK CODE* — A(1) — BLANK CODE*

*BLANK CODE IS EITHER ALL
0's OR ALL 1's OR 20 HEX

B0 – B3
ACTIVE HIGH — BLANK CODE* — B(0) — BLANK CODE* — B(1) — BLANK CODE*

80 μs / 70 μs / 490 μs / 80 μs / 70 μs / 490 μs / 80 μs / 70 μs

$\overline{BD}$

80 μs

RL0 – RL7 — RL0 RL1 RL2 RL3 RL4 RL5 RL6 RL7 RL0 RL1 RL2 RL3 RL4 RL5 RL6 RL7

60 μs
40 μs

CONDITIONAL WRITE TO FIFO
RL0 SELECTED, LATCHED

RETURN LINES ARE SAMPLED ONE AT A TIME AS SHOWN.

NOTE: SHOWN IS ENCODED SCAN LEFT ENTRY
S2-S3 ARE NOT SHOWN BUT THEY ARE SIMPLY S1 DIVIDED BY 2 AND 4

FIGURE 9-26   8279 display refresh timing and keyboard scan timing.   (*Intel Corporation*)

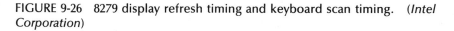

outputs on the A3–A0 and B3–B0 segment lines a code which turns off all the segments. For the circuit in Figure 7-8, sheet 7, this blanking code will be all zeros (00H). The display is blanked here to prevent "ghosting" of information from one digit to the next when the digit strobe is switched from one digit to the next.

After about 70 μs, the 8279 outputs the 7-segment code for the first digit on the A3–A0 and B3–B0 lines. This will light the first digit with the desired pattern. After 490 μs, the 8279 outputs the blanking code again. While the displays are blanked, the 8279 sends out the BCD code for the next digit to the 7445 to enable the driver transistor for digit 2. It then sends out the 7-segment code for digit 2 on the A3–A0 and B3–B0 lines. This lights the desired pattern on digit 2. After 490 μs, the 8279 blanks the display again and goes on to digit 3. The 8279 steps through all the digits and then returns to digit 1 and repeats the cycle. Since each digit requires about 640 μs, the 8279 gets back to digit 1 after about 5.1 ms for an 8-digit display and back to digit 1 after about 10.3 ms for a 16-digit display. The time it takes to get back to a digit again is referred to as the *scan time.*

The point here is that once you load the 7-segment codes into the internal display RAM, the 8279 automatically keeps the displays refreshed without any help from

the microprocessor. As we will show you later, the 8279 can be connected and initialized to refresh a wide variety of display configurations.

The 8279 can also automatically perform the three tasks for interfacing to a matrix keyboard. Remember from previous discussions that the three tasks involve putting a low on a row of the keyboard matrix and checking the columns of the matrix. If any keys are pressed in that row, a low will be present on the column which contains the key because pressing a key shorts a row to a column. If no low is found on the columns, the low is stepped to the next row and the columns checked again. If a low is found on a column, then, after a debounce time, the column is checked again. If the keypress was valid, a compact code representing the key is constructed. Take a look at the circuit on sheet 7 of Figure 7-8 to see how an 8279 can be connected to do this.

When connected as shown in Figure 7-8, sheet 7, the 74LS156 functions as a one-of-eight-low decoder. In other words, if you apply 011, the binary code for 3, to its inputs, the 74LS156 will output a low on its 2Y3 output. Now remember from the discussion of 8279 display refreshing that the 8279 is outputting a continuous counting sequence from 0000 to 1111 on its SL0–SL3 lines. Applying this count sequence to the inputs of the 74LS156 will cause it to step a low along its outputs. The 74LS156 then puts a low on one row of the keyboard at a time, as desired.

The column lines of the keyboard are connected to the return lines, RL0–RL7, of the 8279. As a low is put on each row by the scan-line counter and the 74LS156, the 8279 checks these return lines one at a time to see if any of them are low. The bottom line of the timing waveforms in Figure 9-26 shows when the return lines are checked. If the 8279 finds any of the return lines low, indicating a keypress, it waits a debounce time of about 10.3 ms and checks again. If the keypress is still present, the 8279 produces an 8-bit code which represents the pressed key. Figure 9-27 shows the format for the code produced. Three bits of this code represent the number of the row in which the 8279 found the pressed key, and another 3 bits represent the column of the pressed key. For interfacing to full typewriter keyboards the shift and control keys are connected to pins 36 and 37, respectively, of the 8279. The upper 2 bits of the code produced represent the status of these two keys.

After the 8279 produces the 8-bit code for the pressed key, it stores the byte in an internal 8-byte *FIFO* RAM. The term FIFO stands for first in, first out, which means that when you start reading codes from the FIFO, the first code you read out will be that for the first key pressed. The FIFO can store the codes for up to eight pressed keys before overflowing.

When the 8279 finds a valid keypress, it does two things to let you know about it. It asserts its interrupt request pin, IRQ, high, and it increments a FIFO count in an internal status register. You can connect the IRQ output to an interrupt input and detect when the FIFO has a character for you on an interrupt basis, or you can simply check the count in the status word to determine when the FIFO has a code ready to be read. The point here is that once the 8279 is initialized, you don't need to pay any attention to it until you want to send some new characters to be displayed, or until it notifies you that it has a valid keypressed code for you in its FIFO. Now that you have an overview of how the 8279 functions, we will show you how to initialize an 8279 to do all of these wondrous things and more.

INITIALIZING AND COMMUNICATING WITH AN 8279

As we have shown before, the first step in initializing a programmable device is to determine the system base address for the device, the internal addresses, and the system addresses for the internal parts. As an example here, we will use the 8279 on sheet 7 of the SDK-86

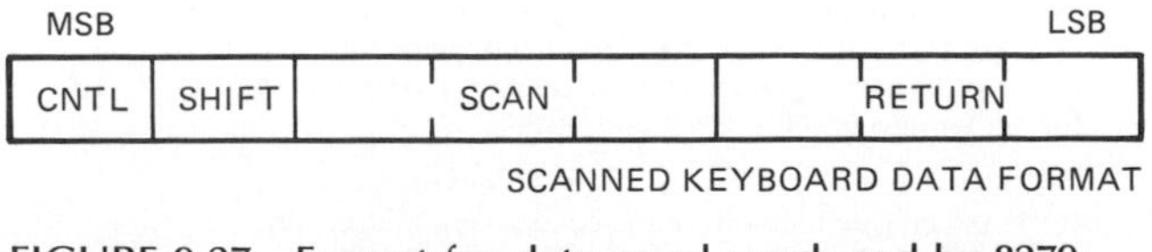

schematics in Figure 7-8. Figure 7-16b shows that the system base address for this device is FFE8H. The 8279 has only two internal addresses, which are selected by the logic level on its A0 input, pin 21. If the A0 input is low when the 8279 is selected, then the 8279 is enabled for reading data from it or writing data to it. A0 being high selects the internal control/status registers. For the circuit on sheet 7 of Figure 7-8, the A0 input is connected to system address line A1. Therefore, the data address for this 8279 is FFE8H and the control/status address is FFEAH.

After you have figured out the system addresses for a device, the next step is to look at the format for the control word(s) you have to send to the device to make it operate in the mode you want. Figure 9-28, p. 272, shows the format for the 8279 control words as they appear in the Intel data book. After you use up your 5-minute "freak-out" time, we will help you decipher these.

One question that may occur to you when you see all these control words is, If the 8279 only has one control register address, how am I going to send it all these different control words? The answer to this is that all the control words are sent to the same control register address, FFEAH for this example. The upper 3 bits of each control word tell the 8279 which control word is being sent. A pattern of 010 in the upper 3 bits of a control word, for example, identifies that control word as a Read FIFO/Sensor RAM control word. Keep Figure 9-28 handy as we discuss this and the other control words.

The first control word you send to initialize the 8279 is the *keyboard/display mode set* word. The bits labeled DD in the control word specify first of all whether you have 8 digits or 16 digits to refresh. If you have eight or fewer displays, make sure to initialize for 8 digits so the 8279 doesn't spend half its time refreshing nonexistent displays. The DD bits in this control word also specify the order in which the characters in the internal 16-byte display RAM will be sent out to the digits. In the left entry mode, the 7-segment code in the first address of the internal display RAM will be sent to the leftmost digit of the display. If you want to display the letters AbCd on the 4 leftmost digits of an 8-digit display, then you put the 7-segment codes for these letters in the first four locations of the display RAM, as shown in Figure 9-29a, p. 273. Codes put in higher addresses in the display RAM will be displayed on following digits to the right. In the right entry mode, the first code sent to the display RAM is put in the lowest address. This character will be displayed on the rightmost digit of the display. If a second character is written to the display RAM, it will be put in the second location in the RAM, as shown in Figure 9-29b. On the display, however, the new character will be displayed on the rightmost digit, and the previous character will be shifted over to the second position from the right. This is the way the displays of most calculators function as you enter numbers.

Now let's look at the KKK bits of the mode-set control word. The first choice you have to make here if you are using the 8279 with a keyboard is whether you want *encoded scan* or *decoded scan*. You know that for

MSB			LSB
CNTL	SHIFT	SCAN	RETURN

SCANNED KEYBOARD DATA FORMAT

FIGURE 9-27   Format for data word produced by 8279 keyboard encoding.

Keyboard/Display Mode Set

```
        MSB                     LSB
Code:   0 0 0 D D K K K
```

Where DD is the Display Mode and KKK is the Keyboard Mode.

DD

0 0   8 8-bit character display — Left entry

0 1   16 8-bit character display — Left entry*

1 0   8 8-bit character display — Right entry

1 1   16 8-bit character display — Right entry

For description of right and left entry, see Interface Considerations. Note that when decoded scan is set in keyboard mode, the display is reduced to 4 characters independent of display mode set.

KKK

0 0 0   Encoded Scan Keyboard — 2 Key Lockout*

0 0 1   Decoded Scan Keyboard — 2-Key Lockout

0 1 0   Encoded Scan Keyboard — N-Key Rollover

0 1 1   Decoded Scan Keyboard — N-Key Rollover

1 0 0   Encoded Scan Sensor Matrix

1 0 1   Decoded Scan Sensor Matrix

1 1 0   Strobed Input, Encoded Display Scan

1 1 1   Strobed Input, Decoded Display Scan

Program Clock

```
Code:   0 0 1 P P P P P
```

All timing and multiplexing signals for the 8279 are generated by an internal prescaler. This prescaler divides the external clock (pin 3) by a programmable integer. Bits PPPPP determine the value of this integer which ranges from 2 to 31. Choosing a divisor that yields 100 kHz will give the specified scan and debounce times. For instance, if Pin 3 of the 8279 is being clocked by a 2 MHz signal, PPPPP should be set to 10100 to divide the clock by 20 to yield the proper 100 kHz operating frequency.

Read FIFO/Sensor RAM

```
Code:   0 1 0 AI X A A A     X = Don't Care
```

The CPU sets up the 8279 for a read of the FIFO/Sensor RAM by first writing this command. In the Scan Keyboard Mode, the Auto-Increment flag (AI) and the RAM address bits (AAA) are irrelevant. The 8279 will automatically drive the data bus for each subsequent read ($A_0 = 0$) in the same sequence in which the data first entered the FIFO. All subsequent reads will be from the FIFO until another command is issued.

In the Sensor Matrix Mode, the RAM address bits AAA select one of the 8 rows of the Sensor RAM. If the AI flag is set (AI = 1), each successive read will be from the subsequent row of the sensor RAM.

Read Display RAM

```
Code:   0 1 1 AI A A A A
```

The CPU sets up the 8279 for a read of the Display RAM by first writing this command. The address bits AAAA select one of the 16 rows of the Display RAM. If the AI flag is set (AI = 1), this row address will be incremented after each following read *or write* to the Display RAM. Since the same counter is used for both reading and writing, this command sets the next read *or write* address and the sense of the Auto-Increment mode for both operations.

Write Display RAM

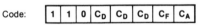
```
Code:   1 0 0 AI A A A A
```

The CPU sets up the 8279 for a write to the Display RAM by first writing this command. After writing the command with $A_0 = 1$, all subsequent writes with $A_0 = 0$ will be to the Display RAM. The addressing and Auto-Increment functions are identical to those for the Read Display RAM. However, this command does not affect the source of subsequent Data Reads; the CPU will read from whichever RAM (Display or FIFO/Sensor) which was last specified. If, indeed, the Display RAM was last specified, the Write Display RAM will, nevertheless, change the next Read location.

Display Write Inhibit/Blanking

```
            A  B  A  B
Code:   1 0 1 X IW IW BL BL
```

The IW Bits can be used to mask nibble A and nibble B in applications requiring separate 4-bit display ports. By setting the IW flag (IW = 1) for one of the ports, the port becomes marked so that entries to the Display RAM from the CPU do not affect that port. Thus, if each nibble is input to a BCD decoder, the CPU may write a digit to the Display RAM without affecting the other digit being displayed. It is important to note that bit B_0 corresponds to bit D_0 on the CPU bus, and that bit A_3 corresponds to bit D_7.

If the user wishes to blank the display, the BL flags are available for each nibble. The last Clear command issued determines the code to be used as a "blank." This code defaults to all zeros after a reset. Note that both BL flags must be set to blank a display formatted with a single 8-bit port.

Clear

```
Code:   1 1 0 CD CD CD CF CA
```

The C_D bits are available in this command to clear all rows of the Display RAM to a selectable blanking code as follows:

```
CD CD CD
     0  X    All Zeros (X = Don't Care)
     1  0    AB = Hex 20 (0010 0000)
     1  1    All Ones
— Enable clear display when = 1 (or by CA = 1)
```

During the time the Display RAM is being cleared (~160 μs), it may not be written to. The most significant bit of the FIFO status word is set during this time. When the Display RAM becomes available again, it automatically resets.

If the C_F bit is asserted ($C_F = 1$), the FIFO status is cleared and the interrupt output line is reset. Also, the Sensor RAM pointer is set to row 0.

C_A, the Clear All bit, has the combined effect of C_D and C_F; it uses the C_D clearing code on the Display RAM and also clears FIFO status. Furthermore, it resynchronizes the internal timing chain.

End Interrupt/Error Mode Set

```
Code:   1 1 1 E X X X     X = Don't care.
```

For the sensor matrix modes this command lowers the IRQ line and enables further writing into RAM. (The IRQ line would have been raised upon the detection of a change in a sensor value. This would have also inhibited further writing into the RAM until reset).

For the N-key rollover mode — if the E bit is programmed to "1" the chip will operate in the special Error mode. (For further details, see Interface Considerations Section.)

FIGURE 9-28   8279 command word formats and bit descriptions.   (*Intel Corporation*)

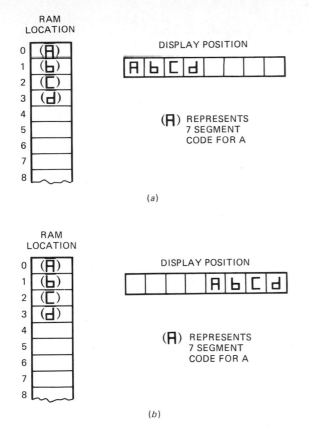

RAM LOCATION

0 (A)
1 (b)
2 (C)
3 (d)
4
5
6
7
8

DISPLAY POSITION

A b C d

(A) REPRESENTS
7 SEGMENT
CODE FOR A

(a)

RAM LOCATION

0 (A)
1 (b)
2 (C)
3 (d)
4
5
6
7
8

DISPLAY POSITION

A b C d

(A) REPRESENTS
7 SEGMENT
CODE FOR A

(b)

FIGURE 9-29   8279 RAM and display location relationships. (a) Left entry. (b) Right entry.

scanning a keyboard or turning on digit drivers, you need a pattern of stepping lows. In encoded mode the 8279 puts out a binary count sequence on its SL0–SL3 scan lines, and an external decoder such as the 7445 is used to produce the stepping lows. If you have only 4 digits to refresh, you can program the 8279 in decoded mode. In this mode, the 8279 directly outputs stepping lows on the four scan lines. The second choice you have to make for this control word is whether you want *two-key lockout* or *N-key rollover*. In the two-key mode, one key must be released before another keypress will be detected and processed. In the N-key rollover mode, if two keys are pressed at nearly the same time, both keypresses will be detected and debounced and their codes put in the FIFO RAM in the order the keys were pressed.

In addition to being used to scan a keyboard, the 8279 can also be used to scan a matrix of switch sensors, such as the metal strips and magnetic sensors you see on store windows and doors. In sensor matrix mode, the 8279 scans all the sensors and stores the condition of up to 64 switches in the FIFO RAM. If the condition of any of the switches changes, an IRQ signal is sent out on the IRQ pin. An interrupt service procedure can then sound an alarm and let the guard dogs loose. The return lines of the 8279 can also function as a strobed input port in much the same way as port A or B on an 8255A.

The SDK-86 initializes the 8279 for eight-character display, left entry, encoded scan, two-key lockout. See if

you can determine the mode-set control word for these conditions. You should get 00000000.

The next control word you have to send the 8279 is the *program-clock word*. The 8279 requires an internal clock frequency of about 100 kHz. A programmable divider in the 8279 allows you to apply some available frequency, such as the 2.45-MHz PCLK signal, to its clock input and divide this frequency down to the needed 100 kHz. The lower 5 bits of the program-clock control word simply represent the binary number you want to divide the applied clock by. For example, if you want to divide the input clock frequency by 24, you send a control word with 001 in the upper 3 bits and 11000 in the lower 5 bits.

The final control word needed for basic initialization is the *clear* word. You need to send this word to tell the 8279 what code to send to the segments to turn them off while the 8279 is switching from one digit to the next. (Refer to Figure 9-26 and its discussion.) In addition to telling the 8279 what blanking character to use during refresh, this control word can be used to clear the display RAM and/or the FIFO at any time. For now we are only concerned with the first function. The lower 2 bits, labeled C_D in the control word in Figure 9-28, specify the desired blanking code. The required code will depend on the hardware connections in a particular system. For the SDK-86 a high from the 8279 turns on a segment, so the required blanking code is all 0's. Therefore you can put 0's in the 2 C_D bits. The resultant control word is 11000000.

The three control words described so far take care of the basic initialization. However, before you can send codes to the internal display RAM, you have to send the 8279 a *write-display-RAM* control word. This word tells the 8279 that data sent to the data address later should be put in the display RAM, and it tells the 8279 where to put the data in the display RAM. The 8279 has an internal 4-bit pointer to the display RAM. The lower 4 bits of the write-display-RAM control word initialize the pointer to the location where you want to write a data byte in the RAM. If you want to write a data byte to the first location in the display RAM, for example, you put 0000 in these bits. If you put a 1 in the auto increment bit, labeled AI in the figure, the internal pointer will be automatically incremented to point to the next RAM location after each data byte is written. To start loading characters in the first location in the RAM and select auto increment, then, the control word is 10010000.

Figure 9-30, p. 274, shows the sequence of instructions to send the control words we have developed here to the 8279 on the SDK-86 board. Also shown are instructions to send a 7-segment code to the first location in the display RAM. Note that the control words are all sent to the control address, FFEAH, and the character going to the display RAM is sent to the data address, FFE8H. Also note from sheet 7 of Figure 7-8 that the D0 bit of the byte sent to the display RAM corresponds to segment output B0, and D7 of the byte sent to the display corresponds to segment output A3. This is important to know when you are making up a table of 7-segment codes to send to the 8279.

You now know how to initialize an 8279 and send

```
                       ;INITIALIZATION
  MOV DX, 0FFEAH       ; Point at 8279 control address
  MOV AL, 00000000B    ; Mode set word for left entry,
                       ; encoded scan, 2-key lockout
  OUT DX, AL           ; Send to 8279
  MOV AL, 00111000B    ; Clock word for divide by 24
  OUT DX, AL
  MOV AL, 11000000B    ; Clear display char is all zeros
  OUT DX, AL

                       ;SEND SEVEN SEGMENT CODE TO DISPLAY RAM
  MOV AL, 10010000B    ; Write display RAM, first location,
                       ;   auto increment
  MOV DX, 0FFEAH       ; Point at 8279 control address
  OUT DX, AL           ; Send control word
  MOV DX, 0FFE8H       ; Point at 8279 data address
  MOV AL, 6FH          ; Seven segment code for 9
  OUT DX, AL           ; Send to display RAM
  MOV AL, 5BH          ; Seven segment code for 2
  OUT DX, AL           ; Send to display RAM
  ; :
  ; :
                       ;READ KEYBOARD CODE FROM FIFO
  MOV AL, 01000000B    ; Control word for read FIFO RAM
  MOV DX, 0FFEAH       ; Point at 8279 control address
  OUT DX, AL           ; Send control word
  MOV DX, 0FFE8H       ; Point at 8279 data address
  IN  AL, DX           ; Read FIFO RAM
```

FIGURE 9-30   8086 instructions to initialize SDK-86 8279, write to display RAM, and read FIFO RAM.

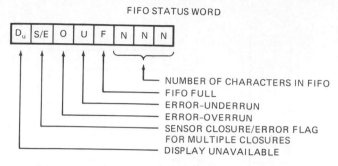

FIGURE 9-31   8279 status word format.

characters to its display RAM. Two additional points we need to show you are how to read keypressed codes from the FIFO RAM and how to read the status word. In order to read a code from the FIFO RAM, you first have to send a *read FIFO/sensor RAM* control word to the 8279 control address. Figure 9-28 shows the format for this word. For a read of the FIFO RAM, the lower 5 bits of the control word are don't cares, so you can just make them 0's. You send the resultant control word, 01000000, to the control register address and then do a read from the data address. The bottom section of Figure 9-30 shows this.

Now, suppose that the processor receives an interrupt signal from the 8279, indicating that one or more valid keypresses have occurred. The question then comes up, How do I know how many codes I should read from the FIFO? The answer to this question is that you read the status register from the control register address before you read the FIFO. Figure 9-31 shows the format for this status word. The lowest 3 bits of the status word indicate the number of valid characters in the FIFO. You can load this number into a memory location and count it down as you read in characters. Incidentally, if more than eight characters have been entered in the FIFO, only the last eight will be kept. The error-overrun bit, labeled O in the status word, will be set to tell you that characters have been lost.

Characters can be read from the 8279 on a polled basis as well as on an interrupt basis. To do this, you simply read and test the status word over and over again until bit 0 of the status word becomes a 1. Since the basic SDK-86 does not have an 8259A to receive interrupt inputs, the SDK-86 monitor uses this polling method to tell when the FIFO holds a keypressed code.

SDK-86 DISPLAY DRIVER PROCEDURE

Figure 9-32 shows an example of an I/O driver which will send the contents of the four nibbles in the CX register to four SDK-86 LED displays. You may have used this procedure for a variety of experiments; now you get to see how it works.

This procedure assumes the 8279 has already been initialized by the SDK-86 monitor program, or as shown in the first part of Figure 9-30. If AL is 0 when this procedure is called, the contents of CX will be displayed on the data field LEDs. If AL is not 0, then the contents of CX will be displayed on the address field LEDs. There are two main points for you to see in this procedure.

The first is the sending of the write-display-RAM control word to the 8279 so we can write to the desired locations in the display RAM. Note that for the data field we write a control word of 90H, which tells the 8279 to put the next data word sent into the first location in the display RAM. Since the 8279 is initialized for left entry, the first location should correspond to the leftmost display digit. However, if you look at sheet 8 of the SDK-86 schematics, you will see that digit 1 (leftmost as far as the 8279 is concerned) is actually the rightmost on the board. This means that for the SDK-86, the position of a 7-segment code in the display RAM corresponds to its position in the display starting from the right! All you have to do is send the 7-segment code for a number you want to display in a particular digit position to the corresponding location in the display RAM.

The next part of the display procedure to take a close look at is the instructions which convert the four hex nibbles in the CX register to the corresponding 7-segment codes for sending to the display RAM. To do this, we first shuffle and mask to get each nibble into a byte by itself. We then use a lookup table and the XLAT instruction to do the actual conversion. Note that when making up 7-segment codes for the SDK-86 board, a high turns on a segment, bit D0 of a display RAM byte represents the "a" segment, bit D6 represents the "g" segment, and bit D7 represents the decimal point. If you are displaying only BCD digits, you can replace the upper six values in the segment code table with values which allow you to blank a digit, display an A or P on a clock, etc. Work your way through the conversion section as a review of using the XLAT instruction.

```
1                              ;8086 PROCEDURE F9-32.ASM
2                              ;ABSTRACT  : Displays a 4-digit hex or BCD number on LEDs of the SDK-86.
3                              ;INPUTS    : Data in CX, control in AL
4                              ;           ; AL = 00H  data displayed in data-field of LEDs
5                              ;           ; AL <> 00H  data displayed in address field of LEDs.
6                              ;PORTS     : None used
7                              ;PROCEDURES: None used
8                              ;REGISTERS : Destroys nothing
9
10                             PUBLIC  DISPLAY_IT
11
12 0000                        DATA SEGMENT   WORD  PUBLIC
13                             ;        0    1    2    3    4    5    6    7
14 0000   3F 06 5B 4F 66 6D 7D + SEVEN_SEG DB  3FH, 06H, 5BH, 4FH, 66H, 6DH, 7DH, 07H
15      07
16                             ;        8    9    A    b    C    d    E    F
17 0008   7F 6F 77 7C 39 5E 79 +     DB   7FH, 6FH, 77H, 7CH, 39H, 5EH, 79H, 71H
18      71
19 0010                        DATA ENDS
20
21 0000                        CODE SEGMENT WORD PUBLIC
22                               ASSUME CS:CODE, DS:DATA
23 0000                        DISPLAY_IT PROC  FAR
24 0000  9C                           PUSHF                    ; Save flags
25 0001  1E                           PUSH DS                  ; Save caller's registers
26 0002  50                           PUSH AX
27 0003  53                           PUSH BX
28 0004  51                           PUSH CX
29 0005  52                           PUSH DX
30 0006  BB 0000s                     MOV  BX, DATA            ; Init DS as needed for procedure
31 0009  8E DB                        MOV  DS, BX
32 000B  BA FFEA                      MOV  DX, OFFEAH          ; Point at 8279 control address
33 000E  3C 00                        CMP  AL, 00H             ; If data field required then
34 0010  74 05                        JZ   DATFLD             ; load control word for data field
35 0012  B0 94                        MOV  AL, 94H            ; else load address-field control word
36 0014  EB 03 90                     JMP  SEND               ; Send control word
37 0017  B0 90             DATFLD: MOV  AL, 90H               ; Load control word for data field
38 0019  EE               SEND:   OUT  DX, AL                 ; Send control word to 8279
39 001A  BB 0000r                     MOV  BX, OFFSET SEVEN_SEG ; Pointer to seven-segment codes
40 001D  BA FFE8                      MOV  DX, OFFE8H          ; Point at 8279 display RAM
41 0020  8A C1                        MOV  AL, CL             ; Get low byte to be displayed
42 0022  24 0F                        AND  AL, 0FH            ; Mask upper nibble
43 0024  D7                           XLATB                   ; Translate lower nibble to 7-seg code
44 0025  EE                           OUT  DX, AL             ; Send to 8279 display RAM
45 0026  8A C1                        MOV  AL, CL             ; Get low byte again
46 0028  B1 04                        MOV  CL, 04             ; Load rotate count
47 002A  D2 C0                        ROL  AL, CL             ; Move upper nibble into low position
48 002C  24 0F                        AND  AL, 0FH            ; Mask upper nibble
49 002E  D7                           XLATB                   ; Translate 2nd nibble to 7-seg code
50 002F  EE                           OUT  DX, AL             ; Send to 8279 display RAM
51 0030  8A C5                        MOV  AL, CH             ; Get high byte to translate
52 0032  24 0F                        AND  AL, 0FH            ; Mask upper nibble
53 0034  D7                           XLATB                   ; Translate to 7-seg code
54 0035  EE                           OUT  DX, AL             ; Send to 8279 display RAM
55 0036  8A C5                        MOV  AL, CH             ; Get high byte to fix upper nibble
56 0038  D2 C0                        ROL  AL, CL             ; Move upper nibble into low position
57 003A  24 0F                        AND  AL, 0FH            ; Mask upper nibble
58 003C  D7                           XLATB                   ; Translate to 7-seg code
59 003D  EE                           OUT  DX, AL             ; 7-seg code to 8279 display RAM
60 003E  5A                           POP  DX                 ; Restore all registers and flags
61 003F  59                           POP  CX
62 0040  5B                           POP  BX
63 0041  58                           POP  AX
64 0042  1F                           POP  DS
65 0043  9D                           POPF
66 0044  CB                           RET
67 0045                        DISPLAY_IT ENDP
68 0045                        CODE    ENDS
69                                     END
```

FIGURE 9-32   Procedure to display contents of CX register on SDK-86 LED displays.

INTERFACING TO 18-SEGMENT AND DOT-MATRIX LED DISPLAYS

In the preceding examples we used an 8279 to refresh some 7-segment displays. The 7-segment codes for each digit were stored in successive locations in·the display RAM. To display ASCII codes on 18-segment LED displays, you can store the ASCII codes for each digit in the display RAM. (Remember that the A lines are driven from the upper nibble of the display RAM and the B lines are driven by the lower nibble.) An external ROM is used to convert the ASCII codes to the required 18-segment codes and send them to the segment drivers. Strobes for each digit driver are produced just as they are for the 7-segment displays in Figure 7-8. The refreshing of each digit then proceeds just as it does for the 7-segment displays.

Refreshing 5 by 7 dot-matrix LED displays is a little more complex because, instead of lighting an entire digit, you have to refresh one row or one column at a time in each digit. To solve this problem, Beckman Instruments, Hewlett-Packard, and several other companies make large integrated display/driver devices which require you to send only a series of ASCII codes for the characters you want displayed.

Liquid-Crystal Display Operation and Interfacing

LCD OPERATION

Liquid-crystal displays are created by sandwiching a thin (10- to 12-µm) layer of a liquid-crystal fluid between two glass plates. A transparent, electrically conductive film or backplane is put on the rear glass sheet. Transparent sections of conductive film in the shape of the desired characters are coated on the front glass plate. When a voltage is applied between a segment and the backplane, an electric field is created in the region under the segment. This electric field changes the transmission of light through the region under the segment film.

There are two commonly available types of LCD: *dynamic scattering* and *field-effect.* The dynamic scattering type scrambles the molecules where the field is present. This produces an etched-glass-looking light character on a dark background. Field-effect types use polarization to absorb light where the electric field is present. This produces dark characters on a silver-gray background.

Most LCDs require a voltage of 2 or 3 V between the backplane and a segment to turn on the segment. You can't, however, just connect the backplane to ground and drive the segments with the outputs of a TTL decoder, as we did the static LED display in Figure 9-24. The reason for this is that LCDs rapidly and irreversibly deteriorate if a steady dc voltage of more than about 50 mV is applied between a segment and the backplane. To prevent a dc buildup on the segments, the segment-drive signals for LCDs must be square waves with a frequency of 30 to 150 Hz. Even if you pulse the TTL decoder, it still will not work because the output low voltage of TTL devices is greater than 50 mV. CMOS gates are often used to drive LCDs.

Figure 9-33a shows how two CMOS gate outputs can be connected to drive an LCD segment and backplane. Figure 9-33b shows typical drive waveforms for the backplane and for the on and the off segments. The off (in this case unused) segment receives the same drive signal as the backplane. There is never any voltage between them, so no electric field is produced. The waveform for the on segment is 180° out of phase with the backplane signal, so the voltage between this segment and the backplane will always be +V. The logic for this is quite simple because you only have to produce two signals, a square wave and its complement. To the driving gates, the segment-backplane sandwich appears as a somewhat leaky capacitor. The CMOS gates can easily supply the current required to charge and discharge this small capacitance.

Older and/or inexpensive LCD displays turn on and off too slowly to be multiplexed the way we do LED displays. At 0°C, some LCDs may require as much as 0.5 s to turn on or off. To interface to these types we use a nonmultiplexed driver device. Newer, more expensive LCDs can turn on and off faster, so they are often multiplexed using a variety of techniques. In the following section we show you how to interface a nonmultiplexed LCD display to a microprocessor such as the SDK-86.

INTERFACING A MICROCOMPUTER TO NONMULTIPLEXED LCD DISPLAYS

Figure 9-34 shows how an Intersil ICM7211M can be connected to drive a 4-digit, nonmultiplexed, 7-segment

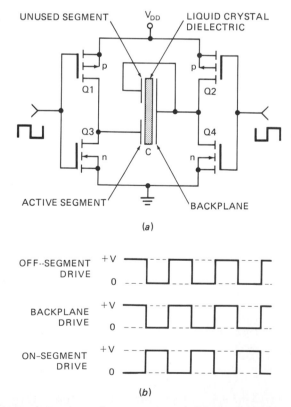

FIGURE 9-33 LCD drive circuit and drive waveforms. (a) CMOS drive circuits. (b) Segment and backplane drive waveforms.

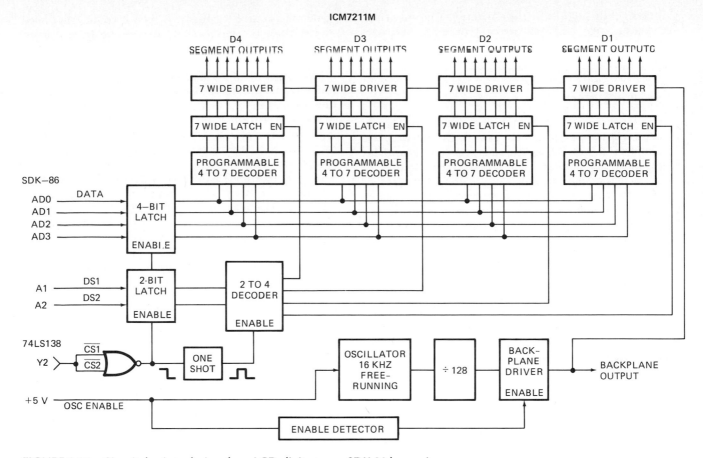

FIGURE 9-34   Circuit for interfacing four LCD digits to an SDK-86 bus using Intersil ICM7211M.

LCD display such as you might buy from your local electronics surplus store. The 7211M inputs can be connected to port pins or directly to microcomputer buses as shown. For our example here, we have connected the $\overline{CS}$ inputs to the Y2 output of the 74LS138 port decoder that we showed you how to add to an SDK-86 board in Figure 8-14. According to the truth table in Figure 8-15, the device will then be addressable as ports with a base address of FF10H. SDK-86 system address line A2 is connected to the digit-select input (DS2), and system address line A1 is connected to the DS1 input. This gives digit 4 a system address of FF10H. Digit 3 will be addressed at FF12H, digit 2 at FF14H, and digit 1 at FF16H. The data inputs are connected to the lower four lines of the SDK-86 data bus. The oscillator input is left open.

To display a character on one of the digits, you simply put the 4-bit hex code for that digit in the lower 4 bits of the AL register and output it to the system address for that digit. The ICM7211M converts the 4-bit hex code to the required 7-segment code. The rising edge of the $\overline{CS}$ input signal causes the 7-segment code to be latched in the output latches for the addressed digit. An internal oscillator automatically generates the segment and backplane drive waveforms shown in Figure 9-33b.

For interfacing with LCD displays which can be multiplexed, the Intersil ICM7233 can be used.

INTERFACING MICROCOMPUTER PORTS TO HIGH-POWER DEVICES

The output pins on programmable port devices can typically source only a few tenths of a milliampere from the +5-V supply and sink only 1 or 2 mA to ground. If you want to control some high-power devices such as lights, heaters, solenoids, and motors with a microcomputer, you need to use interface devices between the port pins and the high-power device. This section shows you a few of the commonly used devices and techniques.

Integrated-Circuit Buffers

One approach to buffering the outputs of port devices is with TTL buffers such as the 7406 hex inverting and 7407 hex noninverting devices. In Figure 9-12, for example, we show 74LS07 buffers on the lines from ports to a printer. In an actual circuit the 8255A outputs to the computer-controlled lathe in Figure 9-7 should also have buffers of this type. The 74LS06 and 74LS07 have open-collector outputs, so you have to connect a pull-up resistor from each output to +5 V. Each of the buffers in a 74LS06 or 74LS07 can sink as much as 40 mA to ground. This is enough current that you can easily drive an LED with each output by simply connecting the LED and a current-limiting resistor in series between the buffer output and +5 V.

Buffers of this type have the advantage that they come six to a package, and they are easy to apply. For cases where you need a buffer on only one or two port pins or you need more current, you can use discrete transistors.

Transistor Buffers

Figure 9-35 shows some single-transistor circuits you can connect to microprocessor port lines to drive LEDs or small dc lamps. We will show you how to quickly determine the parts values to put in these circuits for your particular application. First, determine whether you want a logic high on the output port pin to turn on the device or whether you want a logic low to turn on the device. If you want a logic high to turn on the LED, then use the NPN circuit. If you want a logic low to turn on the device, use the PNP circuit. Let's use an NPN for the first example.

Next, determine how much current you need to flow through the LED, lamp, or other device. For our example here, suppose that you want 20 mA to flow through an LED. You then look through your transistor collection to find an NPN transistor which can carry the required current, has a collector-to-emitter breakdown voltage (V_{BCEO}) greater than the applied supply voltage, and can dissipate the power generated by the current flowing through it. We usually keep some inexpensive 2N3904 NPNs and some 2N3906 PNPs on hand for low-current switch applications such as this. Some alternatives are the 2N2222 NPN and the 2N2907 PNP.

When you decide what transistor you are going to use, look up its current gain, h_{FE}, on a data sheet. If you don't have a data sheet, assume a value of 50 for the current gain of small-signal transistors such as these.

Remember, current gain, or β, as it is commonly called, is the ratio of collector current to the base current needed to produce that current. To produce a collector current of 20 mA in a transistor with a β of 50 requires a base current of 20 mA/50 or 0.4 mA. To drive this buffer transistor, then, the output port pin has to supply only the 0.4 mA.

The V_{OH}(PER) specification of the 8255A shows that an 8255A peripheral port pin can only source 200 μA (0.2 mA) of current and still maintain a legal TTL-compatible output voltage of 2.4 V! The outputs can source more than 0.2 mA, but if they source more than 0.2 mA, the output high voltage will drop below 2.4 V. You don't care about the output high voltage dropping below 2.4 V except in the unlikely case that you are trying to drive a logic gate input off the same port pin as the transistor. Let's assume an output voltage of 2.0 V for calculating the value of our current-limiting resistor, R_b. The value of this resistor is not very critical as long as it lets through enough base current to drive the transistor. The base of the NPN transistor will be at about 0.7 V when the transistor is conducting, and the output port pin will be at least 2.0 V. This leaves a voltage of 1.3 V across R_b. Dividing the 1.3 V across R_b by the desired base current of 0.4 mA gives an R_b value of 3.25 kΩ. A 2.7-kΩ or 3.3-kΩ resistor will work fine here.

If you chose to use the PNP circuit in Figure 9-35b, an output pin on an 8255A could easily sink enough current to drive the base of the transistor. The V_{OL}(PER) specification for an 8255A indicates that an output pin can sink at least 1.7 mA and still have an output low voltage no greater than 0.45 V. The base of the PNP transistor in Figure 9-35b will be at about +4.3 V when the transistor is on, and the output of the 8255A will be at about +0.3 V. This means that the R_b in Figure 9-35b has about 4 V across it. Dividing this voltage by the required 0.4 mA gives an R_b value of 10 kΩ.

When you need to switch currents larger than about 50 mA on and off with an output port line, a single transistor does not have enough current gain to do this dependably. One solution to this problem is to connect two transistors in a Darlington configuration, as shown in Figure 9-36. A circuit such as this might be used to drive a small solenoid valve which controls the flow of a chemical into our printed-circuit-board-making machine or a small solenoid in the print heads of a dot-matrix printer. The dotted lines around the two transistors in Figure 9-36 indicate that both devices are contained in the same package. Here's how this configuration works.

The output port pin supplies base current to transistor Q1. This base current produces a collector current β times as large in Q1. The collector current of Q1 becomes the base current of Q2 and is amplified by the current gain of Q2. The result of this is that the device acts like a single transistor with a current gain of β Q1 × β Q2 and a base-emitter voltage of about 1.4 V. The internal resistors help turn off the transistors. The TIP110 device we show here has a minimum β of 1000 at 1 A, so if we assume that we need 400 mA to drive the solenoid, then the worst-case current that must be supplied by the

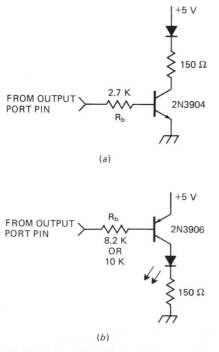

(a)

(b)

FIGURE 9-35   Transistor buffer circuits for driving LED from 8255A port pin. (a) NPN. (b) PNP.

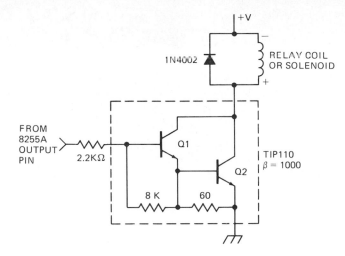

FIGURE 9-36 Darlington transistor used to drive relay coil or solenoid.

output port pin is about 400 mA/1000 or 0.4 mA. As we indicated before, a port pin can easily do this.

If the drive current required for the Darlington is too high for the port output, you can add, for example, a 3.3-kΩ resistor from the transistor base to +5 V to supply an additional milliampere of drive current. The port output can easily sink this additional milliampere of current when it is in the low state. Also, another transistor could be added as a buffer between the output pin and the Darlington input. Note that since the V_{BE} of the Darlington is about 1.4 V, a smaller R_b is needed here. Now let's check out the power dissipation.

According to the data sheet for the TIP110, it comes in a TO-220 package which can dissipate up to 2 W at an ambient temperature of 25°C with no heat sink. With 400 mA flowing through the device, it will have a collector-emitter saturation voltage of about 2 V. Multiplying the current of 400 mA times the voltage drop of 2 V gives us a power dissipation of 0.8 W for our circuit here. This is well within the limits for the device. A rule of thumb that we like to follow is, If the calculated power dissipation for a device such as this is more than half of its 25°C no-heat-sink rating, mount the device on the chassis or a heat sink to make sure it will work on a hot day. If mounted on the appropriate heat sink, the device will dissipate 50 W at 25°C.

One more important point to mention about the circuit in Figure 9-36 is the reverse-biased diode connected across the solenoid coil. You must remember to put in this diode whenever you drive an inductive load such as a solenoid, relay, or motor. Here's why. The basic principle of an inductor is that it fights a change in the current through it. When you apply a voltage to the coil by turning on the transistor, it takes a while for the current to start flowing. This does not cause any major problems. However, when you turn off the transistor, the collapsing magnetic field in the inductor keeps the current flowing for a while. This current cannot flow through the transistor, because it is off. Instead, this current develops a voltage across the inductor with the polarity shown by the + and − signs on the coil in

Figure 9-36. This induced voltage, sometimes called inductive "kick," will usually be large enough to break down the transistor if you forget to put in the diode. When the coil is conducting, the diode is reverse-biased, so it doesn't conduct. However, as soon as the induced voltage reaches 0.7 V, the diode turns on and supplies a return path for the induced current. The voltage across the inductor then is clamped at 0.7 V, the voltage across a conducting diode, so the transistor is saved.

Figure 9-37a shows how a device called a power MOSFET transistor can be used to drive a solenoid, relay, or motor winding. Power MOSFETS are somewhat more expensive than bipolar Darlingtons, but they have the advantage that they require only a voltage to drive them. The Motorola IRF130 shown here, for example, requires a maximum gate voltage of only 4 V to turn on a drain current of 8 A. Note that this MOSFET circuit also needs a reverse-biased diode across the solenoid to protect the transistor from inductive kick.

Figure 9-37b shows a power driver circuit using a newer device called an Isolated-Gate Bipolar Transistor (IGBT). In IGBT data books you may see the device referred to as an IGBT or as an MOSIGT. As you might expect from the schematic symbol, these devices are a compromise between bipolar transistors and MOSFETs. They have the high input impedance and fast switching speed of MOSFETs, and they have the low voltage drop and high current-carrying capacity of bipolar transistors. The Toshiba MG400H1US1, for example, has a collector-emitter breakdown voltage of 500 V and can

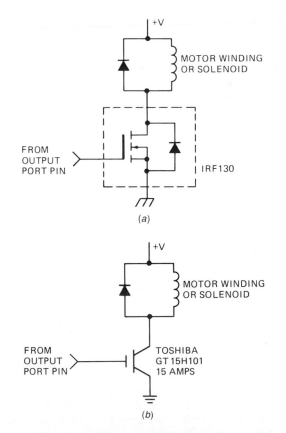

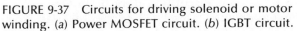

FIGURE 9-37 Circuits for driving solenoid or motor winding. (a) Power MOSFET circuit. (b) IGBT circuit.

switch a maximum current of 400 A. A driver device such as the National DS0026, Motorola MMH0026, or Silicon General SG1626 is used to convert the logic signal from an output port to the voltage and current levels required to rapidly switch high-power MOSFETs and IGBTs on and off.

Interfacing to AC Power Devices

To turn 110-V, 220-V, or 440-V ac devices on and off under microprocessor control, we usually use *mechanical* or *solid-state relays.* The control circuitry for both of these types of relay is electrically isolated from the actual switch. This is very important, because if the 110-V ac line gets shorted to the V_{CC} line of a microcomputer, it usually bakes most of the microcomputer's ICs.

Figure 9-38a shows a picture of a mechanical relay. This relay has both normally open and normally closed contacts. When a current is passed through the coil of the relay, the switch arm is pulled down, opening the top contacts and closing the bottom set of contacts. The contacts are rated for a maximum current of 25 A, so this relay could be used to turn on a 1- or 2-hp motor or a large electric heater in one of the machines in our electronics factory. When driven from a 12-V supply, the coil requires a current of about 170 mA. The Darlington circuit shown in Figure 9-36 could easily drive this relay coil from a microcomputer port line.

Mechanical relays, sometimes called contactors, are available to switch currents from milliamperes up to several thousand amperes. Mechanical relays, however, have several serious problems. First of all, when the contacts are opened and closed, arcing takes place between the contacts. This causes the contacts to oxidize and pit, just as the ignition points in older-style cars used to do. As the contacts become oxidized, they make a higher-resistance contact and may get hot enough to melt. Another disadvantage of mechanical relays is that they can switch on or off at any point in the ac cycle. Switching on or off at a high-voltage point in the ac cycle can cause a large amount of electrical noise, called electromagnetic interference (EMI). The solid-state relays discussed next avoid these problems to a large extent.

Figure 9-38b shows a picture of a solid-state relay which is rated for 25 A at 25°C if mounted on a suitable heat sink. Figure 9-38c shows a block diagram of the circuitry in the device and how it is connected from an output port to an ac load.

The input circuit of the solid-state relay is just an LED. A simple NPN transistor buffer and a current-limiting resistor are all that is needed to interface the relay to a microcomputer output port pin. To turn the relay on, you simply output a high on the port pin. This turns on the transistor and pulls the required 11 mA through the internal LED. The light from the LED is focused on a phototransistor connected to the actual output-control circuitry. Since the only connection between the input circuit and the output circuit is a beam of light, there are several thousand volts of isolation between the input circuitry and the output circuitry.

The actual switch in a solid-state relay is a triac. When

FIGURE 9-38 Relays for switching large currents. (*Potter and Brumfield*) (a) Mechanical. (b) Solid-state. (c) Internal circuitry for solid-state relay.

triggered, this device conducts on either half of the ac cycle. The zero-voltage detector makes sure that the triac is only triggered when the ac line voltage is very close to one of its zero-voltage crossing points. If you output a signal to turn on the relay, the relay will not actually turn on until the next time the ac line voltage crosses zero. This prevents the triac from turning on at a high-voltage point in the ac cycle, which would produce a burst of EMI. Triacs automatically turn off when the current through them drops below a small value called the holding current, so the triac automatically turns off at the end of each half-cycle of the ac power. If the control signal is on, the trigger circuitry will automatically retrigger the triac for each half-cycle. If you send a signal to turn off the relay, it will actually turn off the next time the alternating current drops to zero. In this type of solid-state relay, the triac is always turned on or off at a zero point on the ac voltage. Zero-point switching eliminates most of the EMI that would be caused by switching the triac on at random points in the ac cycle.

Solid-state relays have the advantages that they produce less EMI, they have no mechanical contacts to arc, and they are easily driven from microcomputer ports. Their disadvantages are that they are more expensive than equivalent mechanical relays and there is a voltage drop of a couple of volts across the triacs when they are on. Another potential problem with solid-state relays occurs when driving large inductive loads, such as motors. Remember from basic ac theory that the voltage waveform leads the current waveform in an ac circuit with inductance. A triac turns off when the current through it drops to near zero. In an inductive circuit, the voltage waveform may be at several tens of volts when the current is at zero. When the triac is conducting, it has perhaps 2 V across it. When the triac turns off, the voltage across the triac will quickly jump to several tens of volts. This large dV/dT may possibly turn on the triac at a point when you don't want it turned on. To keep the voltage across the triac from changing too rapidly, an *RC snubber* circuit is connected across the triac, as shown in Figure 9-38c. A system example in the next chapter uses a solid-state relay to control an electric heater.

Interfacing a Microcomputer to a Stepper Motor

A unique type of motor useful for moving things in small increments is a stepper motor. Instead of rotating smoothly around and around as most motors do, stepper motors rotate, or "step," from one fixed position to the next. If you have a dot-matrix printer such as an Epson FX, look inside and you should see one small stepper motor which is used to advance the paper to the next line position and another small stepper motor which is used to move the print head to the next character position. While you are in there, you might look for a small device containing an LED and a phototransistor which detects when the print head is in the "home" position. Stepper motors are also used to position the read/write head over the desired track of a floppy disk and to move the pen around on X-Y plotters.

Common step sizes for stepper motors range from 0.9° to 30°. A stepper motor is stepped from one position to the next by changing the currents through the fields in the motor. The two common field connections are referred to as two-phase and four-phase. We will discuss *four-phase steppers* here because their drive circuitry is much simpler.

Figure 9-39, p. 282, shows a circuit you can use to interface a small four-phase stepper such as the Superior Electric MO61-FD302, IMC Magnetics Corp. Tormax 200, or a similar, nominal 5-V unit to five microcomputer port lines. If you build up this circuit, bolt some small heat sinks on the MJE2955 transistors and mount the 10-W resistors where you aren't likely to touch them.

Since the 7406 buffers are inverting, a high on an output-port pin produces a low on a buffer output. This low turns on the PNP driver transistor and supplies current to a winding. Figure 9-39b shows the switching sequence to step a motor such as this clockwise or counterclockwise. (The directions assume you are facing the end of the motor shaft.) Here's how this works.

Suppose that SW1 and SW2 are turned on. Turning off SW2 and turning on SW4 will cause the motor to rotate one step of 1.8° clockwise. Changing to SW4 and SW3 on will cause the motor to rotate another 1.8° clockwise. Changing to SW3 and SW2 on will cause another step. After that, changing to SW2 and SW1 on again will cause another step clockwise. You can repeat the sequence until the motor has rotated as many steps clockwise as you want. To step the motor counterclockwise, you simply work through the switch sequence in the reverse direction. The motor is held in position between steps by the current through the coils. Figure 9-39c shows the switch sequence that can be used to rotate the motor half-steps of 0.9° clockwise or counterclockwise.

A close look at the switch sequence in Figure 9-39b shows an interesting pattern. To take the first step clockwise from SW2 and SW1 being on, the pattern of 1's and 0's is simply rotated one bit position around to the right. The 1 from SW1 is rotated around into bit 4. To take the next step, the switch pattern is rotated one more bit position. To step counterclockwise, the switch pattern is rotated left one bit position for each step desired. This rotating pattern can easily be produced with a sequence of 8086 instructions. Suppose that you initially load 00110011 into AL and output this to the switches. (Duplicating the switch pattern in the upper half of AL will make stepping easy.) To step the motor clockwise one step, you just rotate this pattern right one bit position and output it to the switches. To step counterclockwise one step, you rotate the switch pattern left one bit position and output it. You can repeat the rotate and output sequence as many times as needed to produce the desired number of steps.

After you output one step code, you must wait a few milliseconds before you output another step command because the motor can step only so fast. Maximum stepping rates for different types of steppers vary from a few hundred steps per second to several thousand steps per second. To achieve high stepping rates, the stepping rate is slowly increased to the maximum and then decreased as the desired number of steps is approached.

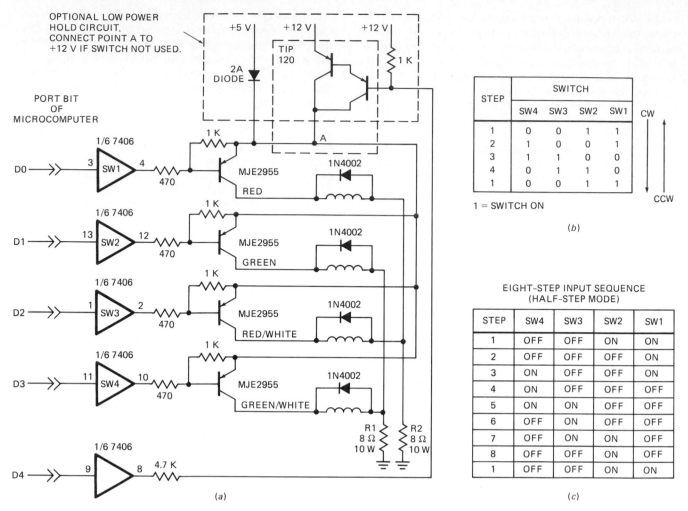

OPTIONAL LOW POWER
HOLD CIRCUIT.
CONNECT POINT A TO
+12 V IF SWITCH NOT USED.

PORT BIT
OF
MICROCOMPUTER

STEP	SWITCH				
	SW4	SW3	SW2	SW1	CW
1	0	0	1	1	
2	1	0	0	1	
3	1	1	0	0	
4	0	1	1	0	
1	0	0	1	1	CCW

1 = SWITCH ON

(b)

EIGHT-STEP INPUT SEQUENCE
(HALF-STEP MODE)

STEP	SW4	SW3	SW2	SW1
1	OFF	OFF	ON	ON
2	OFF	OFF	OFF	ON
3	ON	OFF	OFF	ON
4	ON	OFF	OFF	OFF
5	ON	ON	OFF	OFF
6	OFF	ON	OFF	OFF
7	OFF	ON	ON	OFF
8	OFF	OFF	ON	OFF
1	OFF	OFF	ON	ON

(a)

(c)

FIGURE 9-39 Four-phase stepper motor interface circuit and stepping waveforms. (a) Circuit. (b) Full-step drive signal order. (c) Half-step drive signal order.

When you step a stepper motor to a new position, it tends to oscillate around the new position before settling down. A common software technique to damp out this oscillation is to first send the pattern to step the motor toward the new position. When the motor has rotated part of the way to the new position, a word to step the motor backward is output for a short time. This is like putting the brakes on. The step-forward word is then sent again to complete the step to the next position. The timing for the damping command must be determined experimentally for each motor and load.

Before we go on, here are a couple of additional points about the circuit in Figure 9-39a, in case you want to add a stepper to your robot or some other project. First of all, don't forget the clamp diodes across each winding to save the transistors from inductive kick. Second, we need to explain the function of the current-limiting resistors, R1 and R2. The motor we used here has a nominal voltage rating of 5.5 V. This means that we could have designed the circuit to operate with a voltage of about 6.5 V on the emitters of the driver transistors (5.5 V for the motor plus 1 V for the drop across the transistor). For low stepping rates, this would work fine.

However, for higher stepping rates and more torque while stepping, we use a higher supply voltage and current-limiting resistors, as shown. The point of this is that by adding series resistance, we decrease the L/R time constant. This allows the current in the windings to change more rapidly. For the motor we used, the current per winding is 0.88 A. Since only one winding on each resistor is ever on at a time, 6.5 V/0.88 A gives a resistor value of 7.4 Ω. To be conservative, we used 8-Ω, 10-W resistors. The optional transistor switch and diode connection to the +5-V supply are used as follows. When the motor is not stepping, the switch to +12 V is off, so the motor is held in position by the current from the +5-V supply. Before you send a step command, you turn on the transistor to +12 V to give the motor more current for stepping. When stepping is done, you turn off the switch to +12 V, and drop back to the +5-V supply. This cuts the power dissipation.

In small printers, one or more dedicated microprocessors are used to control the various operations in the printer. In this case, the microprocessors have plenty of time to control the print-head and line-feed stepper motors in software, as we described above. For applications where the main microcomputer is too busy to be bothered with controlling a stepper directly, a smart stepper controller device, such as the Sprague UCN-5804B shown in Figure 9-40, can be used in place of the circuitry in Figure 9-39. This device is manufactured with a combination of CMOS and bipolar technology, so it has high input impedance and high output current drive capability. The device contains a shift resister to produce the step patterns, the power driver transistors, and the clamp diodes. Control inputs allow you to specify half-step or full-step operation, step direction, and type of motor. To step the motor, a pulse or series of pulses is applied to the STEP input. A programmable counter such as the 8254 we discussed earlier in the chapter could be programmed to send a desired number of pulses to the controller.

For applications where steps of 0.9° are not small enough, a technique called "microstepping" is used to produce as many as 25,000 steps per revolution. For microstep control, each winding is driven with the output of a D/A converter instead of with on/off switches. This means that the current through a winding can have a range of values instead of just zero or maximum. If the current ratios in the four windings are changed slightly, the motor will take a tiny step. Microstepping is much more complex to implement, but it produces very smooth and precise motion.

OPTICAL MOTOR SHAFT ENCODERS

In order to control the machines in our electronics factory, the microcomputers in these machines often need information about the position, direction of rotation, and speed of rotation of various motor shafts. The microcomputer, of course, needs this information in digital form. The circuitry which produces this digital information from each motor for the microcomputer is called a *shaft encoder*. There are two basic types of shaft encoders, *absolute* and *incremental*. Here's how these two types work.

Absolute Encoders

Absolute encoders have a binary-coded disk such as the one shown in Figure 9-41, p. 284, on the rotating shaft. Light sections of the disk are transparent, and dark sections are opaque. An LED is mounted on one side of each track, and a phototransistor is mounted on the other side of each track, opposite the LED. Outputs from the four phototransistors will produce one of the binary codes shown in Figure 9-41. The phototransistor outputs can be conditioned with Schmitt-trigger buffers and connected to input port lines. Each code represents an absolute angular position of the shaft in its rotation. With a 4-bit disk, 360° are divided up into 16 parts, so the position of the shaft can be determined to the nearest 22.5°. With an 8-bit disk, the position of the disk can be determined to the nearest 360°/256, or 1.4°.

Note that the codes in Figure 9-41 follow a *Gray-code* sequence rather than a normal binary count sequence. Using Gray code reduces the size of the largest possible error in reading the shaft position to the value of the least significant bit. If the disk used straight binary code, the largest possible error would be the value of the

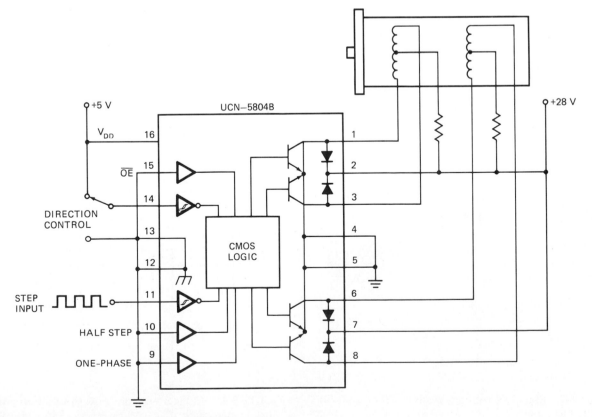

FIGURE 9-40   UCN-5804B stepper motor driver.

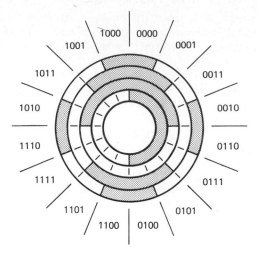

FIGURE 9-41   Gray-code optical-encoder dish used to determine angular position of a rotating shaft.

most significant bit. Look at the parallel listings of binary and Gray codes in Table 1-1 to help you see why this is the case.

To start, assume that a binary-encoded disk was used and that the disk was rotating from position 0111 (7) to position 1000 (8). Now suppose that the detectors pick up the change to 000 on the least significant 3 bits, but don't pick up the change to 1 on the most significant bit. The output code would then be 0000 instead of the desired 1000. This is an error equal to the value of the MSB. Now, while this is fresh in your mind, look across the table at the same position change for the Gray-code encoder. The Gray code for position 7 is 0100, and the Gray code for position 8 is 1100. Note that only 1 bit changes for this transition. If you look at the Gray-code table closely, you will see that this is the case for all the transitions. This means that if a detector fails to pick up the new bit value during a transition, the resulting code will always be the code for the preceding position. This represents a maximum error equal to the value of the LSB.

Absolute encoding using a Gray-code disk has the advantage that each position is represented by a specific code which can be directly read in by the microcomputer. Disadvantages of absolute encoding are the multiple detectors needed, the multiple lines required, and the difficulty keeping track of position during multiple rotations. Incremental encoders solve some of these problems.

Incremental Encoders

An incremental encoder produces a pulse for each increment of shaft rotation. Figure 9-42 shows an early version of the Rhino XR-2 robot arm, which uses incremental encoders to determine the position and direction of rotation for each of its motors. For this encoder, a metal disk with two tracks of slotted holes is mounted on each motor shaft. An LED is mounted on one side of each track of holes, and a phototransistor is mounted opposite the LED on the other side of the disk. Each phototransistor produces a train of pulses as the disk is rotated. The pulses are passed through Schmitt-trigger buffers to sharpen their edges.

The top part of Figure 9-43 shows a section of the encoder disk straightened out so it is easier to see the pulses produced as it rotates. The two tracks of slotted holes are 90° out of phase with each other, so as the disk is rotated, the waveforms shown at the bottom of Figure 9-43 will be produced by the phototransistors for rotation in one direction. Rotation in the other direction will shift the phase of the waveforms 180°, so that the B waveform leads the A waveform by 90° instead of lagging it by 90°. Now the question is, How do you get position, speed, and direction information from these waveforms?

You can determine the speed of rotation by simply counting the number of pulses from one detector in a fixed time interval, such as 1 s. As we described in Chapter 8, you can use a programmable timer and an

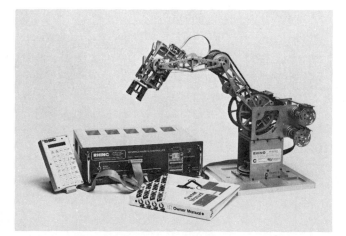

FIGURE 9-42   Rhino XR robotics system.   (*Rhino Robots Incorporated*)

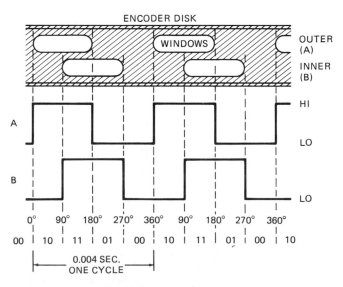

FIGURE 9-43   Optical-encoder disk slot pattern and output waveforms.

interrupt procedure to count off intervals of 1 s. If you connect the output of the detector to another interrupt input, you can use another interrupt procedure to count the number of holes that pass by in a 1-s interval. Each track has six holes, so six pulses will be produced for each revolution. Some simple arithmetic will give you the speed in revolutions per minute (rpm).

You can determine the direction of rotation with hardware or with software. For the hardware approach, connect the A signal to the D input of a D flip-flop and the B signal to the clock input of the flip-flop. The rising edge of the B signal will clock the level of the A signal at that point through the flip-flop to its Q output. If you look at the waveforms in Figure 9-43, you should see that the Q output will be high for rotation in the direction shown. You should also be able to convince yourself that the Q output will be low for rotation in the other direction.

To determine the direction of rotation with software, you can detect the rising edge of the B signal on a polled or an interrupt basis and then read the logic level on the A signal. As shown in the waveforms, the A signal being high when B goes high represents rotation in one direction, and the A signal being low when B goes high represents rotation in the opposite direction.

To determine the position of the motor shaft, you simply count off how many holes the motor has moved from some "home" position. On the Rhino robot arm a small mechanical switch on each axis is activated when the arm is in its starting, or home, position. When you turn on the power, the motor controller/driver box automatically moves the arm to this home position. To move the arm to some new position, you calculate the number of holes each motor must rotate to get the arm to that position. For each motor, you then send the controller a command which tells it which direction to rotate that motor and how many holes to rotate it. The controller will drive the motor the specified number of holes in the specified direction. If you then manually rotate the encoder wheel or some heavy load moves the arm and rotates the encoder disk, the controller will detect the change in position of the disk and drive the motor back to its specified position. This is an example of digital *feedback control*, which is easily done with a microcomputer. The Rhino controller uses an 8748 single-chip microcomputer to interpret and carry out the commands you send it. Commands are sent to the controller in the serial ASCII form described at the start of Chapter 13.

Incidentally, you may wonder at this point why the designers of the Rhino arm did not use stepper motors such as those we described in a previous section. The answers are: Stepper motors are much more expensive than the simple dc motors used, and if a stepper motor is forced back a step by a sudden load change, there is no way to know about it and correct for it unless it has an external encoder. Also, the dc motor-encoder approach better demonstrates the method used in large commercial robots.

In the Rhino robot arm, each motor drives its section of the arm through a series of gears. Gearing the motor down reduces the force that the motor has to exert and

makes the exact position of the motor shaft less critical. Therefore, for the Rhino, six sets of slots in the encoder disk are sufficient. However, for applications where a much more accurate indication of shaft position is needed, a self-contained shaft encoder such as the Hewlett-Packard HEDS-5000 is attached to the motor shaft. These encoders have two track-encoder disks with 500 tiny radial slits per track. The waveforms produced are the same as those shown for the Rhino encoder in Figure 9-43, but at a much higher frequency for the same motor speed.

Another common application for optical encoders is to produce digital information about the distance and direction that a computer mouse is moved. The Logictech™ mouse, for example, uses one optical encoder disk to produce pulses for vertical motion and another optical encoder disk to produce pulses for horizontal motion. As you move the mouse around on your desk, the rubber ball on the bottom of the mouse rotates the encoder disks. Data from the encoders is processed and sent to the microcomputer. The microcomputer uses the data from the mouse to move the on-screen cursor to the desired location.

Optical encoders in their many different forms are an important part of a large number of microcomputer-controlled machines.

CHECKLIST OF IMPORTANT TERMS AND CONCEPTS IN THIS CHAPTER

If you do not remember any of the terms in the following list, use the index to help you find them in the chapter for review.

Simple input and output

Strobed I/O

Single-handshake I/O

Double-handshake data transfer

8255A initialization
    Mode 0, mode 1, mode 2
    Mode definition control word
    Set/reset control word

Computer numerical control (CNC) machines

Centronics parallel printer standard

I/O driver
    Control block
    Sentinel

Keyswitches—mechanical, capacitive, Hall effect

Detect, debounce, and encode a keyboard

Two-key lockout, two-key rollover

Code conversion using compare method

Code conversion using XLAT method

Error trapping

LED interfacing
   Direct drive
   Software-multiplexed display
   8279 hardware display controller

8279 display and keyboard operation
   Encoded and decoded scan
   Keyboard/display mode set control word
   Clear control word
   Write-display control word

LCD interfacing
   Dynamic scattering display

Field-effect display
   Backplane drive

Relays
   Mechanical
   Solid-state
   Electromagnetic interference
   Zero-point switching
   RC snubber circuit

Four-phase stepper motor drive

Shaft encoders—absolute and incremental

REVIEW QUESTIONS AND PROBLEMS

1. Why must data be sent to a printer on a handshake basis?

2. For the double-handshake data transfer in Figure 9-1*d*,
   a. Indicate which signal is asserted by the sender and which signal is asserted by the receiver.
   b. Describe the meaning of each of the signal transitions.

3. Why are the port lines of programmable port devices automatically put in the input mode when the device is first powered up or reset?

4. An 8255A has a system base address of FFF9H. What are the system addresses for the three ports and the control register for this 8255A?

5. a. Show the mode set control word needed to initialize an 8255A as follows: Port A—handshake input; Port B—handshake output; Port C—bits PC6 and PC7 as outputs.
   b. Show the bit set/reset control word needed to initialize the port A interrupt request and the port B interrupt request.
   c. Show the assembly language instructions you would use to send these control words to the 8255A in problem 4.
   d. Show the additional instruction you need if you want the handshake to be done on an interrupt basis through the IR3 input of the 8259A in Figure 8-14.
   e. Show the instructions you would use to put a high on port C, bit PC6 of this device.

6. Describe the exchange of signals between the tape reader, 8255A, and 8086 in Figure 9-7 as a byte of data is transferred from the tape reader to the microprocessor.

7. When connecting peripheral devices such as printers, terminals, etc., to a computer, why is it very important to connect the logic ground and the chassis ground together only at the computer?

8. Describe the function and direction of the following signals in a Centronics parallel printer interface.
   a. STROBE
   b. ACKNLG
   c. BUSY
   d. INIT

9. Modify the printer driver procedure in Figure 9-16 so that it stops sending characters to the printer when it finds a sentinel character of 03H, instead of using the counter approach.

10. Would the software method of generating the STROBE signal to the printer in Figure 9-16 still work if you tried to run the program with an 8-MHz 8086?

11. Show the instructions you would use to read the status byte from the 8255A in Question 5.

12. Describe the three major tasks needed to get meaningful information from a matrix keyboard.

13. Describe how the compare method of code conversion in Figure 9-20 works.

14. Why is error trapping necessary in real programs? Describe how the error trap in the program in Figure 9-20 works.

15. Assume that the rows of the circuit shown in Figure 9-44 are connected to ports FFF8H and the 74148 is connected to port FFFAH of an SDK-86 board. The 74148 will output a low on its GS output if a low is applied to any of its inputs. The way the keyboard is wired, the A2, A1, and A0 outputs will have a 3-bit binary code for the column in which a low appears. Use the algorithm and discussion of Figure 9-20 to help you write a procedure which detects a keypress, debounces the keypress, and determines the row number and column number of the pressed key. The procedure should then combine the row code, column code, shift bit, and control bit into a single byte in the form: control, shift, row code, column code. The XLAT instruction can then be used to convert this code byte to ASCII for return to the calling program. *Hint:* Use a DB directive to make up the table of ASCII codes.
   Why is the XLAT approach more efficient than the compare technique for this case?

NOTE: For test purposes, the keyboard matrix can be simulated by building the diodes, resistors, and 74148 on a prototyping board and using a jumper wire to produce a "keypress."

16. a. Calculate the value of the current-limiting resistor needed in series with each segment of a 7-

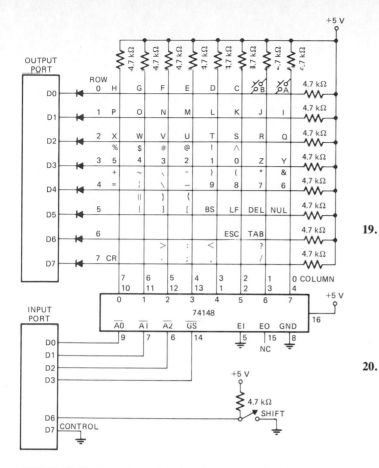

FIGURE 9-44   Interface circuitry for unencoded matrix keyboard for problem 15.

segment display driven by a 7447 if you want 40 mA per segment.

b. Approximately how much current is being pulsed through each LED segment on the SDK-86 board?

17. a. Write the algorithm for a procedure which refreshes the multiplexed LED displays shown in Figure 9-25. Assume that the procedure will be called every 2 ms by an interrupt signal to IR4 of an 8259A.

b. Write the assembly language instructions for the display refresh procedure. Since this procedure is called on an interrupt basis, all display parameters should be kept in named memory locations. If you have time, you can add the circuitry shown in Figure 9-25 to your microcomputer so you can test your program.

18. Figure 9-45, p. 288, shows a circuit for an 8 by 8 matrix of LEDs that you can connect to a couple of ports on your microcomputer to produce some interesting displays. The principle here is to output a 1 to port B for each LED you want turned on in the top row and then output a 1 to the D0 bit of port A to turn on that row. After 2 ms, you output the pattern you want in the second row to port B and a 1 to bit 1 of port A to turn on the second

row. The process is repeated until all rows are done and then started over.

The row patterns can be kept in a table in memory. If you want to display a sequence of letters, you can display the contents of one table for a few seconds and then switch to another table containing the second letter. Using the rotate instruction, you can produce some scrolled displays. *Hint:* The wiring required to build the LED matrix can be reduced by using an IC 5 by 7 dot-matrix LED display such as the Texas Instruments TIL305.

Write the algorithm and program for an interrupt procedure (called every 2 ms) to refresh these displays.

19. You are assigned the job of fixing several SDK-86 boards with display problems. For each of the following problems, describe a possible cause of the problem and tell where you would look with an oscilloscope to check out your theory. Use the circuit on sheet 7 of Figure 7-8 to help you.

a. A segment never lights.

b. The leftmost digit of the data field never lights.

c. All the displays show dim "eights."

20. a. Show the command words and assembly language instructions necessary to initialize an 8279 at address 80H and 82H as follows: 16-character display, left entry, encoded-scan keyboard, N-key rollover; 1-MHz input clock divided to 100 kHz; blanking character FFH.

b. Show the 8279 instructions necessary to write 99H to the first location in the display RAM and autoincrement the display RAM pointer.

c. Show the assembly language instructions necessary to read the first byte from the 8279 FIFO RAM.

d. Determine the 7-segment codes you would have to send to the SDK-86 8279 to display the letters HELP on the data field display. Remember that D0 of the byte sent = B0 and D7 of the byte sent = A3.

e. Show the sequence of instructions you can send to the 8279 of the SDK-86 board to blank the entire display.

21. Write a procedure which polls the LSB of the 8279 status register on the SDK-86 board until it finds a key pressed, then reads the keypressed code from the FIFO RAM to AL and returns.

22. Why must the backplane and segment-line signals be pulsed for LCD displays?

23. Draw a circuit you could attach to an 8255A port B pin to drive a 1-A solenoid valve from a +12-V supply. You want a high on the port pin to turn on the solenoid.

24. Why must reverse-biased diodes always be placed across inductive devices when you are driving them with a transistor?

25. a. Define the terms MOSFET and IGBT.

b. What is a major advantage of these devices over bipolar Darlingtons when driving a high-power load with a microcomputer port line?

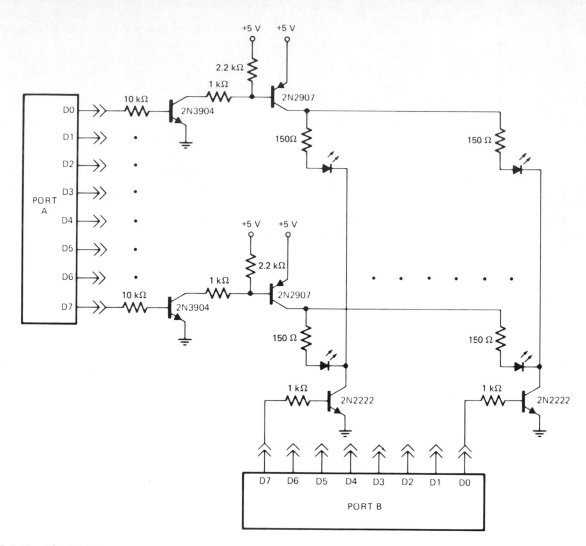

FIGURE 9-45   8 by 8 LED matrix circuitry for problem 18.

26.   *a.*   What are the major disadvantages of mechanical relays?

     b.   How do solid-state relays solve these problems?

27.   *a.*   How is electrical isolation between the control input and the output circuitry achieved in a solid-state relay?

     b.   Describe the function of the zero-crossing detector used in better-quality solid-state relays.

     c.   Why is a snubber circuit required across the triac of a solid-state relay when you are driving inductive loads?

28.   Write the algorithm and the program for an 8086 procedure to drive the stepper motor shown in Figure 9-39. Assume the desired direction of rotation is passed to the procedure in AL (AL = 1 is clockwise, AL = 0 is counterclockwise) and the number of steps is passed to the procedure in CX. Also assume full-step mode, as shown in Figure 9-39*b*. Don't forget to delay 20 ms between step commands!

29.   *a.*   Why is Gray code, rather than straight binary

code, used on many absolute-position shaft encoders?

     b.   If a Gray-code wheel has six tracks and each track represents 1 binary bit, what is its angular resolution?

30.   *a.*   Look at the encoder disk on the Rhino arm in Figure 9-42. Do the waveforms in Figure 9-43 represent clockwise or counterclockwise rotation of the motor shaft as seen from the gear end of the motor, which is what you care about?

     b.   Assume the A signal shown in Figure 9-43 is connected to bit D0 and the B signal is connected to bit D1 of port FFF8H. Write a procedure which determines the direction of rotation and passes a 1 back in AL for clockwise rotation and a 0 back in AL for counterclockwise rotation.

     c.   DC motors, such as those on the Rhino arms, are rotated clockwise by passing a current through them in one direction and rotated counterclockwise by passing a current through them in the opposite direction. Assume you have a motor controller that responds to a 2-bit control word as follows:

00 = hold 01 = rotate clockwise
11 = hold 10 = rotate counterclockwise

Write the algorithm and program for a procedure to rotate a motor. The number of holes is passed to the procedure in CX; the direction of rotation is determined by the value in AL. AL = 1 is clockwise; AL = 0 is counterclockwise.

CHAPTER 10

Analog Interfacing and Industrial Control

In order to control the machines in our electronics factory, medical instruments, or automobiles with microcomputers, we need to determine the values of variables such as pressure, temperature, and flow. There are usually several steps in getting electrical signals which represent the values of these variables and converting the electrical signals to digital forms the microcomputer can work with.

The first step involves a *sensor*, which converts the physical pressure, temperature, or other variable to a proportional voltage or current. The electrical signals from most sensors are quite small, so they must next be amplified and perhaps filtered. This is usually done with some type of operational-amplifier (op-amp) circuit. The final step is to convert the signal to digital form with an analog-to-digital (A/D) converter.

In this chapter we review some op-amp circuits commonly used in these steps, show the interface circuitry for some common sensors, and discuss the operation and interfacing of D/A converters. We also discuss the operation and interfacing of A/D converters and show how all of these pieces are put together in a microcomputer-based scale and a microcomputer-based machine-control system. As part of these examples, we discuss the tools and techniques used to develop microcomputer-based products. Finally, we discuss how an A/D converter, a microcomputer, and a D/A converter can be used to produce a digital filter.

OBJECTIVES

At the conclusion of this chapter, you should be able to:

1. Recognize several common op-amp circuits, describe their operation, and predict the voltages at key points in each.

2. Describe the operation and interfacing of several common sensors used to measure temperature, pressure, flow, etc.

3. Describe the operation of a D/A converter and define D/A data-sheet parameters, such as resolution, settling time, accuracy, and linearity.

4. Draw circuits showing how to interface D/A converters with any number of bits to a microcomputer.

5. Describe briefly the operation of flash, successive-approximation, and ramp A/D converters.

6. Draw circuits showing how A/D converters of various types can be interfaced to a microcomputer.

7. Write programs to control A/D and D/A converters.

8. Describe how feedback is used to control variables such as pressure, temperature, flow, motor speed, etc.

9. Describe the operation of a "time-slice" factory-control system.

10. Describe the tools and techniques currently used to develop a microcomputer-based product.

11. Draw a block diagram of a digital filter and briefly describe its basic operation.

REVIEW OF OPERATIONAL-AMPLIFIER CHARACTERISTICS AND CIRCUITS

Basic Operational-Amplifier Characteristics

Figure 10-1a shows the schematic symbol for an op amp. Here are the important points for you to remember about the basic op amp. First, the pins labeled +V and −V represent the power-supply connections. The voltages applied to these pins will usually be +15 V and −15 V, or +12 V and −12 V. The op amp also has two signal inputs. The input labeled with a − sign is called the inverting input, and the input labeled with a + sign is called the noninverting input. The + and − on these inputs have nothing to do with the power supply voltages. These signs indicate the phase relationship between a signal applied to that input and the result that signal produces on the output. If, for example, the noninverting input is made more positive than the inverting input, the voltage on the output will move in a positive direction. In other words, if a signal is applied to the noninverting input, the output signal will be in phase with the input signal. If the inverting input is made more positive than the noninverting input, the output signal will be inverted, or 180° out of phase with the input signal.

The ratio of the voltage out from an amplifier circuit to the input voltage is called *voltage gain*, A_V. In symbols,

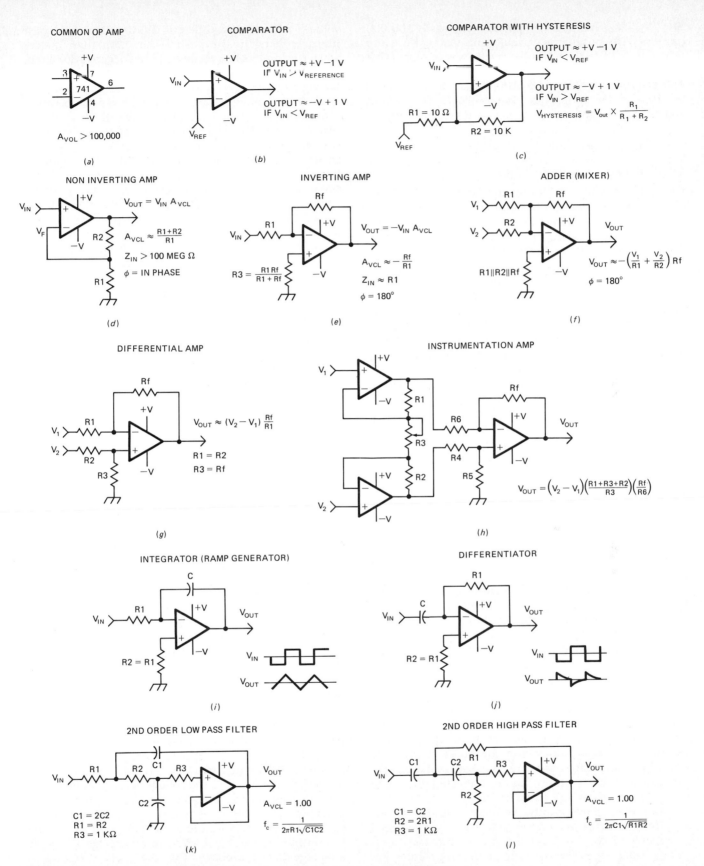

FIGURE 10-1 Overview of commonly used op-amp circuits. (a) Common op amp. (b) Comparator. (c) Comparator with hysteresis. (d) Noninverting amp. (e) Inverting amp. (f) Adder (mixer). (g) Differential amp. (h) Instrumentation amp. (i) Integrator (ramp generator). (j) Differentiator. (k) Second-order low-pass filter. (l) Second-order high-pass filter.

$A_V = V_{OUT}/V_{IN}$. The A_V for an op amp is typically 100,000 or more. (The number is variable with temperature and from device to device.) Another useful way of saying this is that an op amp amplifies the *difference* in voltage between these two inputs by 100,000 or more. Now let's see how much the output changes for a given input signal, and see how an op amp is used as a comparator.

Op-Amp Circuits and Applications

OP AMPS AS COMPARATORS

We said previously that an op amp amplifies the difference in voltage between its inputs by 100,000 or more. Suppose that you power an op amp with $+15$ V and -15 V, tie the inverting input of the op amp to ground, and apply a signal of $+0.01$ V dc to the noninverting input. The op amp will attempt to amplify this signal by 100,000 and produce the result on its output. An input signal of 0.01 V times a gain of 100,000 predicts an output voltage of 100 V. The maximum positive voltage the op-amp output can go to, however, is a volt or two less than the positive supply voltage, so this is as far as it goes. A common way of expressing this is to say the op-amp output "goes into saturation" at about $+13$ V.

Now suppose that you apply a signal of -0.01 V to the noninverting input. The output will now try to go to -100 V as fast as it can. The output, however, goes into saturation at about -13 V, so it stops there.

In this circuit the op amp effectively compares the input voltage with the voltage on the inverting input and gives a high or low output, depending on the result of the comparison. If the input is more than a few microvolts above the reference voltage on the inverting input, the output will be high ($+13$ V). If the input voltage is a few microvolts more negative than the reference voltage, the output will be low (-13 V). An op amp used in this way is called a *comparator*. Figure 10-1b shows how a comparator is usually labeled. The reference voltage applied to the inverting input does not have to be ground (0 V). An input voltage can be compared to any voltage within the input range specified for the particular op amp.

As you will see throughout this chapter, comparators have many applications. We might, for example, connect a comparator to a temperature sensor on the boiler in our electronics factory. When the voltage from the temperature sensor goes above the voltage on the reference input of the comparator, the output of the comparator will change state and send an interrupt signal to the microprocessor controlling the boiler. Commonly available comparators such as the LM319 have TTL-compatible outputs which can be connected directly to microcomputer ports or interrupt inputs.

Figure 10-1c shows another commonly used comparator circuit. Note in this circuit that the reference signal is applied to the noninverting input, and the input voltage is applied to the inverting input. This connection simply inverts the output state from those in the previous circuit. Note also in Figure 10-1c the positive-feedback resistors from the output to the noninverting input. This feedback gives the comparator a characteristic called *hysteresis*. Hysteresis means that the output

voltage changes at a different input voltage when the input is going in the positive direction than it does when the input voltage is going in the negative direction. If you have a thermostatically controlled furnace in your house, you have seen hysteresis in action. The furnace, for example, may turn on when the room temperature drops to 65° F and then not turn off until the temperature reaches 68° F. Hysteresis is the difference between the two temperatures. Without this hysteresis, the furnace would be turning on and off rapidly if the room temperature were near 68° F. Another situation where hysteresis saves the day is the case where you have a slowly changing signal with noise on it. Hysteresis prevents the noise from causing the comparator output to oscillate as the input signal gets close to the reference voltage.

To determine the amount of hysteresis in a circuit such as that in Figure 10-1c, assume $V_{REF} = 0$ V and $V_{OUT} = 13$ V. A simple voltage-divider calculation will tell you that the noninverting input is at about 13 mV. The voltage on the inverting input of the amplifier will have to go more positive than this before the comparator will change states. Likewise, if you assume V_{OUT} is -13 V, the noninverting input will be at about -13 mV, so the voltage on the inverting input of the amplifier will have to go below this to change the state of the output. The hysteresis of this comparator is 26 mV.

NONINVERTING AMPLIFIER OP-AMP CIRCUIT

When operating in open-loop mode (no feedback to the inverting input), an op amp has a very high, but unpredictable, gain. This is acceptable for use as a comparator, but not for use as a predictable amplifier. Figure 10-1d shows one way negative feedback is added to an op amp to produce an amplifier with stable, predictable gain. First of all, notice that the input signal in this circuit is applied to the noninverting input, so the output will be in phase with the input. Second, note that a fraction of the output signal is fed back to the inverting input. Now, here's how this works.

To start, assume that V_{IN} is 0 V, V_{OUT} is 0 V, and the voltage on the inverting input is 0. Now, suppose that you apply a $+0.01$-V dc signal to the noninverting input. Since the 0.1-V difference between the two inputs will be amplified by 100,000, the output will head toward $+100$ V as fast as it can. However, as the output goes positive, some of the output voltage will be fed back to the inverting input through the resistor divider. This feedback to the inverting input will decrease the difference in voltage between the two inputs. To make a long story short, the circuit quickly reaches a predictable balance point where the voltage on the inverting input, V_F, is very, very close to the voltage on the noninverting input, V_{IN}. For a 1.0-V dc output, this equilibrium voltage difference might be about 10 μV. If you assume that the voltages on the two inputs are equal, then predicting the output voltage for a given input voltage is simply a voltage-divider problem. $V_{OUT} = V_{IN} (R1 + R2)/R1$. If $R2 = 99$ kΩ and $R1 = 1$ kΩ, then $V_{OUT} = V_{IN} \times 100$. For a 0.01-V input signal, the output voltage will be 1.00 V.

The voltage gain of a circuit with feedback is called its *closed-loop gain*. The closed-loop gain, A_{VCL}, for this circuit is equal to the simple resistor ratio, $(R1 + R2)/R1$.

To see another advantage of feeding some of the output signal back to the inverting input, let's see what happens when the load connected to the output of the op amp changes and draws more current from the output. The output voltage will temporarily drop because of the increased load. Part of this voltage drop will be fed back to the inverting input, increasing the difference in voltage between the two inputs. The increased difference will cause the op amp to drive its output harder to correct for the increased load. The feedback then causes the op amp to at least partially compensate for the increased load on its output.

Feedback which causes an amplifier to oppose a change on its output is called *negative feedback*. Because of the negative feedback, the op amp will work day and night to keep its output stabilized and its two inputs at nearly the same voltage! This is probably the most important point you need to know to analyze or troubleshoot an op-amp circuit with negative feedback. Draw a box around this point in your mind so you don't forget it.

The noninverting circuit we have just discussed is used mostly as a *buffer* because it has a very high *input impedance*, Z_{IN}. This means that it will not load down a sensor or some other device you connect to its input. If it uses a bipolar-transistor input op amp, the circuit in Figure 10-1d will have an input impedance greater than 100 MΩ. If a FET input op amp such as the National LF356 is used, the input impedance will be about 10^{12} Ω.

INVERTING AMPLIFIER OP-AMP CIRCUIT

Figure 10-1e shows a somewhat more versatile amplifier circuit using negative feedback. Note that in this circuit, the noninverting input is tied to ground with a resistor, and the signal you want to amplify is applied to the inverting input through a resistor. Since the signal is applied to the inverting input, the output signal will be 180° out of phase with the input signal. For this circuit, resistor Rf supplies the negative feedback which keeps the two inputs at nearly the same voltage. Since the noninverting input is tied to ground, the op amp will sink or source whatever current is needed to hold the inverting input also at zero volts. Because the op amp holds the inverting input at zero volts, this node is referred to as a *virtual ground*.

The voltage gain of this circuit is also determined by the ratio of two resistors. The A_{VCL} for this circuit at low frequencies is equal to −Rf/R1. You can derive this for yourself by just thinking of the two resistors as a voltage divider with V_{IN} at one end, 0 V in the middle, and V_{OUT} on the other end. If V_{IN} is positive, then V_{OUT} must be negative because current cannot flow from positive to ground to positive again. The minus sign in the gain expression is another way of indicating that the output is inverted from the input. The input impedance Z_{IN} of this circuit is approximately R1 because the amplifier end of this resistor is held at 0 V by the op amp.

One additional characteristic of op-amp circuits that we need to refresh in your mind before going on to other op-amp circuits is *gain-bandwidth product*. As we indicated previously, an op amp may have an open-loop

dc gain of 100,000 or more. At higher frequencies, the gain decreases until, at some frequency, the open-loop gain drops to 1. Figure 10-2a shows an open-loop voltage gain versus frequency graph for a common op amp such as a 741. The frequency at which the gain is 1 is referred to on data sheets as the *unity-gain bandwidth* or the *gain-bandwidth product*. A common value for this is 1 MHz. The bandwidth of an amplifier circuit with negative feedback times the low-frequency closed-loop gain will be equal to this value. For example, if an op amp with a gain-bandwidth product of 1 MHz is used to build an amplifier circuit with a closed-loop gain of 100, the bandwidth of the circuit, f_c, will be about 1 MHz/100 or 10 kHz, as shown in Figure 10-2b.

The point here is that the gain-bandwidth product of the op amp limits the maximum frequency that an amplifier circuit can amplify.

OP-AMP ADDER CIRCUIT

Figure 10-1f shows a commonly used variation of the inverting amplifier described in the previous section. This circuit adds together or mixes two or more input signals. Here's how it works.

Remember from the previous discussion that in an inverting circuit, the op amp holds the inverting input at 0 V or virtual ground. The current through each of the input resistors will be the same as if it were connected

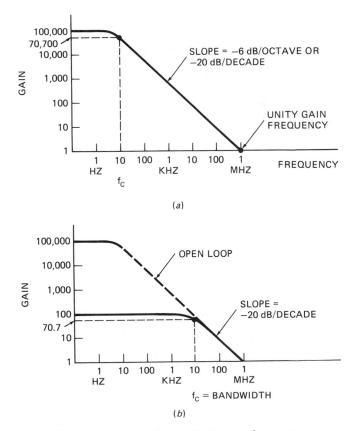

(a)

(b)

FIGURE 10-2   (a) Open-loop gain versus frequency response of 741 op amp. (b) Gain versus frequency response of 741 op-amp circuit with closed-loop gain of 100.

to ground. Input voltage V_1 produces a current through R1 to this point, and input voltage V_2 causes a current through R2 to this point. The two currents add together at the virtual ground. In this circuit the virtual ground is often called the *summing point*. The op amp pulls the sum of the two currents through resistor Rf to hold the inverting input at 0 V. The left end of Rf is at 0 V, so the output voltage is the voltage across Rf. This is equal to the sum of the currents times the value of Rf, or $V_1/R1 + V_2/R2 \times Rf$. A circuit such as this is used to "mix" audio signals and to sum binary-weighted currents in a D/A converter. Although the circuit in Figure 10-1f shows only two inputs, an adder can have any number of inputs.

SIMPLE DIFFERENTIAL-INPUT AMPLIFIER CIRCUIT

As we show later, many sensors have two output signal lines with a dc voltage of several volts on each signal line. The dc voltage present on both signal leads is referred to as a *common-mode voltage*. The actual signal you need to amplify from these sensors is a difference in voltage of a few millivolts between the two signal lines. If you try to use a standard inverting or noninverting amplifier circuit to do this, the large dc voltage will be amplified along with the small difference voltage you need to amplify. Figure 10-1g shows a simple circuit which, for the most part, solves this problem without using coupling capacitors to block the dc. The analysis of this circuit is beyond the space we have here, but basically the resistors on the noninverting input hold this input at a voltage near the common-mode dc voltage. The amplifier holds the inverting input at the same voltage. If the resistors are matched carefully, the result is that only the difference in voltage between V_2 and V_1 will be amplified. The output signal will consist of only the amplified difference in voltage between the input signals. We say that the common-mode signal has been *rejected*.

AN INSTRUMENTATION AMPLIFIER CIRCUIT

Figure 10-1h shows an op-amp circuit used in applications that need a greater rejection of the common-mode signal than is provided by the simple differential circuit in Figure 10-1g. The first two op amps in this circuit buffer the differential signals and give some amplification. The output op amp removes the common-mode voltage and provides further amplification. Another way of describing the function of the output op amp is to say that it converts the signal from a differential signal to a single-ended signal. Instrumentation amplifier circuits such as this are available in single packages.

AN OP-AMP INTEGRATOR CIRCUIT

Figure 10-1i shows an op-amp circuit that can be used to produce linear voltage ramps. A dc voltage applied to the input of this circuit will cause a constant current of $V_{IN}/R1$ to flow into the virtual-ground point. This current flows onto one plate of the capacitor. In order to hold the inverting input at ground, the op-amp output must pull the same current from the other plate of the capacitor. The capacitor then is getting charged by the constant current $V_{IN}/R1$. Basic physics tells you that the voltage across a capacitor being charged by a constant current is a *linear ramp*. Note that because of the inverting amplifier connection, a positive input voltage will cause the output to ramp negative. Also note that some provision must be made to prevent the amplifier output from ramping into *saturation*.

The circuit is called an *integrator* because it produces an output voltage proportional to the integral, or "sum," of the current produced by an input voltage over a period of time. The waveforms in Figure 10-1i show the circuit response for a pulse-input signal.

AN OP-AMP DIFFERENTIATOR CIRCUIT

Figure 10-1j shows an op-amp circuit which produces an output signal proportional to the rate of change of the input signal. With the input voltage to this circuit at 0 or some other steady dc voltage, the output will be at 0. If a new voltage is applied to the input, the voltage across the capacitor cannot change instantly, so the inverting input will be pulled away from 0 V. This will cause the op amp to drive its output in a direction to charge the capacitor and pull the inverting input back to zero. The waveforms in Figure 10-1j show the circuit response for a pulse-input signal. The time required for the output to return to zero is determined by the time constant of R1 and C.

OP-AMP ACTIVE FILTERS

In many control applications, we need to filter out unwanted low-frequency or high-frequency noise from the signals read in from sensors. This could be done with simple RC filters, but *active filters* using op amps give much better control over filter characteristics. There are many different filter configurations using op amps. The main points we want to refresh here are the meanings of the terms *low-pass* filter, *high-pass* filter, and *bandpass* filter and how you identify the type when you find one in a circuit you are analyzing.

A low-pass filter amplifies or passes through low frequencies, but at some frequency determined by circuit values, the output of the filter starts to decrease. The frequency at which the output is down to 0.707 of the low-frequency value is called the *critical frequency* or *breakpoint*. Figure 10-3a shows a graph of gain versus frequency for a low-pass filter with the critical frequency, f_C, labeled. Note that above the critical frequency the gain drops off rapidly. For a first-order filter such as a single R and C, the gain decreases by a factor of 10 for each increase of 10 times in frequency (-20 dB/decade). For a second-order filter, the gain decreases by a factor of 100 for each increase of 10 times in frequency.

Figure 10-1k shows a common op-amp circuit for a second-order low-pass filter. The way you recognize this as a low-pass filter is to look for a dc path from the input to the noninverting input of the amplifier. If the dc path is present, as it is in Figure 10-1k, you know that the amplifier can amplify dc and low frequencies. Therefore, it is a low-pass filter with a response such as that shown in Figure 10-3a.

For contrast, look at the circuit for the second-order high-pass filter in Figure 10-1k. Note that in this circuit,

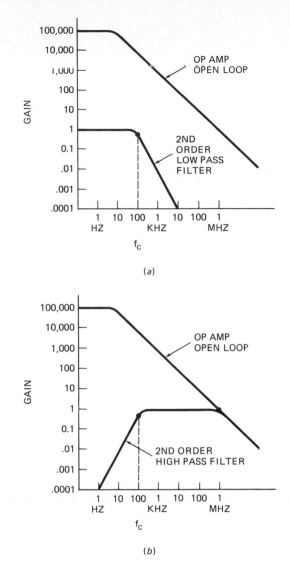

(a)

(b)

FIGURE 10-3 Gain versus frequency response for second-order low-pass and high-pass filters. (a) Low-pass. (b) High-pass.

the dc component of an input signal cannot reach the noninverting input, because of the two capacitors in series with that input. Therefore, this circuit will not amplify dc and low-frequency signals. Figure 10-3b shows the graph of gain versus frequency for a high-pass filter such as this. Note that the gain-bandwidth product of the op amp limits the high-frequency response of the circuit.

For the low-pass circuit in Figure 10-1k, the gain for the flat part of the response curve is 1, or unity, because the output is fed back directly to the inverting input. At the critical frequency, f_c, the gain will be 0.707, and above this frequency the gain will drop off. The critical frequency for the circuit is determined by the equation next to the circuit. The equation assumes that R1 and R2 are equal and that the value of C1 is twice the value of C2. R3 is simply a damping resistor. The positive feedback supplied by C1 is the reason the gain is only down to 0.707 at the critical frequency, rather than

down to 0.5 as it would be if we cascaded two simple RC circuits.

For the high-pass filter, the gain for the flat section of the response curve is also 1. Assuming that the two capacitors are equal and the value of R2 is twice the value of R1, the critical frequency is determined by the formula shown next to Figure 10-1l. Again, R3 is for damping.

A low-pass filter can be put in series with a high-pass filter to produce a bandpass filter which lets through a desired range of frequencies. There are also many different single-amplifier circuits which will pass or reject a band of frequencies.

Now that we have refreshed your memory of basic op-amp circuits, we will next discuss some of the different types of sensors you can use to produce electrical signals proportional to the values of temperatures, pressures, position, etc.

SENSORS AND TRANSDUCERS

It would take a book many times the size of this one to describe the operation and applications of all the different types of available sensors and transducers. What we want to do here is introduce you to a few of these and show how they can be used to get data for microcomputer-based machines in, for example, our electronics factory.

Light Sensors

One of the simplest light sensors is a light-dependent resistor such as the Clairex CL905 shown in Figure 10-4a. A glass window allows light to fall on a zigzag

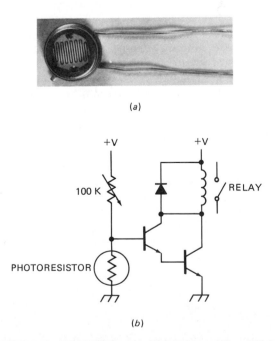

FIGURE 10-4 (a) Cadmium sulfide photocell. (Clairex Electronics) (b) Light-controller relay circuit using a photocell.

pattern of cadmium sulfide or cadmium selenide whose resistance depends on the amount of light present. The resistance of the CL905 varies from about 15 MΩ when in the dark to about 15 kΩ when in a bright light. Photoresistors such as this do not have a very fast response time and are not stable with temperature, but they are inexpensive, durable, and sensitive. For these reasons, they are usually used in applications where the light measurement need not be precise. The devices placed on top of streetlights to turn them on when it gets dark, for example, contain a photoresistor, a transistor driver, and a mechanical relay, as shown in Figure 10-4b. As it gets dark, the resistance of the photoresistor goes up. This increases the voltage on the base of the transistor until, at some point, it turns on. This turns on the transistor driving the relay, which in turn switches on the lamp.

Another device used to sense the amount of light present is a photodiode. If light is allowed to fall on the junction of a specially constructed silicon diode, the reverse leakage current of the diode increases linearly as the amount of light falling on it increases. A circuit such as that shown in Figure 10-5 can be used to convert this small leakage current to a proportional voltage. Note that in this circuit a negative reference voltage is applied to the noninverting input of the amplifier. The op amp will then produce this same voltage on its inverting input, reverse-biasing the photodiode. The op amp will pull the photodiode leakage current through Rf to produce a proportional voltage on the output of the amplifier. For a typical photodiode such as the HP 5082-4203 shown, the reverse leakage current varies from near 0 μA to about 100 μA, so with the 100-kΩ Rf, an output voltage of about 0 to 10 V will be produced. The circuit will work without any reverse bias on the diode, but with the reverse bias, the diode responds faster to changes in light. An LM356 FET input amplifier is used here because it does not require an input bias current.

A photodiode circuit such as this might be used to determine the amount of smoke being emitted from a smokestack. To do this, a gallium arsenide infrared LED is put on one side of the smokestack, and the photodetector circuit is put on the other. Since smoke absorbs light, the amount of light arriving at the photodetector is a measure of the amount of smoke present. An infrared LED is used here because the photodiode is most sensitive to light wavelengths in the infrared region.

Still another useful light-sensitive device is a solar cell. Common solar cells are simply large, very heavily doped silicon PN junctions. Light shining on the solar cell causes a reverse current to flow, just as in the photodiode. Because of the large area and the heavy doping in the solar cell, however, the current produced is milliamperes rather than microamperes. The cell functions as a light-powered battery. Solar cells can be connected in a series-parallel array to produce a solar power supply.

Light meters in cameras, photographic enlargers, and our printed-circuit-board-making machine use solar cells. The current from the solar cell is a linear function of the amount of light falling on the cell. A circuit such as the one in Figure 10-5 can be used to convert the output current to a proportional voltage. Because of the larger output current, the value of R_f is decreased to a much smaller value, depending on the output current of the cell. The noninverting input of the amplifier is connected to ground because reverse biasing is not needed with solar cells. The frequency response to light (spectral response) of solar cells has been tailored to match the output of the sun. Therefore, they are ideal in photographic applications where we want a signal proportional to the total light from the sun.

Temperature Sensors

Again, there are many types of temperature sensors. The four types we discuss in some detail here are semiconductor devices, thermocouples, RTDs, and thermistors.

SEMICONDUCTOR TEMPERATURE SENSORS

The two main types of semiconductor temperature sensors are temperature-sensitive voltage sources and temperature-sensitive current sources. An example of the first type is the National LM35, which we show the circuit connections for in Figure 10-6a. The voltage output from this circuit increases by 10 mV for each degree Celsius that its temperature is increased. If the output is connected to a negative reference voltage, V_s, as shown, the sensor will give a meaningful output for a temperature range of −55 to +150° C. The output is adjusted to 0 V for 0° C. The output voltage can be amplified to give the voltage range you need for a particular application. In a later section of this chapter, we show another circuit using the LM35 temperature sensor. The accuracy of this device is about 1° C.

Another common semiconductor temperature sensor is a temperature-dependent current source, such as the Analog Devices AD590. The AD590 produces a current of 1 μA/°K. Figure 10-6b shows a circuit which converts this current to a proportional voltage. In this circuit the current from the sensor, I_T, is passed through an approximately 1-kΩ resistor to ground. This produces a voltage which changes by 1mV/°K. The AD580 in the circuit is a precision voltage reference used to produce a reference voltage of 273.2 mV. With this voltage applied to the inverting input of the amplifier, the amplifier output will be at zero volts for 0° C. The advantage of a current-source sensor is that voltage drops in long

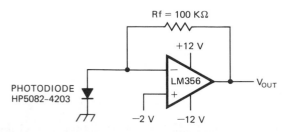

FIGURE 10-5   Photodiode circuit to measure light intensity.

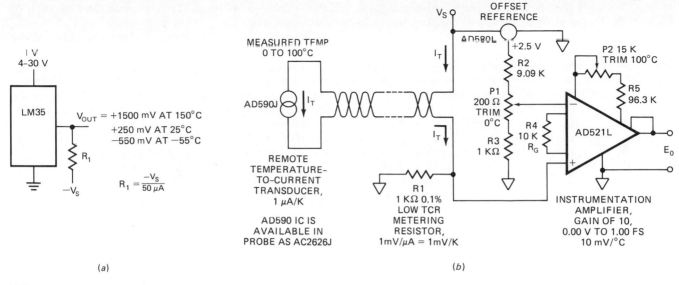

(a)   (b)

FIGURE 10-6   Semiconductor temperature-sensor circuits. (a) LM35 temperature-dependent voltage source. (b) AD590 temperature-dependent current source.   (*Analog Devices Incorporated*)

connecting wires do not have any effect on the output value. If the gain and offset are carefully adjusted, the accuracy of the circuit in Figure 10-6b is ±1° C using an AD590K part.

THERMOCOUPLES

Whenever two different metals are put in contact, a small voltage is produced between them. The voltage developed depends on the type of metals used and the temperature. Depending on the metals, the developed voltage increases between 7 and 75 µV for each degree Celsius increase in temperature. Different combinations of metals are useful for measuring different temperature ranges. A thermocouple junction made of iron and constantan, commonly called a type J thermocouple, has a useful temperature range of about − 184 to +760° C. A junction of platinum and an alloy of platinum and 13 percent rhodium has a useful range of 0 to about 1600° C. Thermocouples can be made small, rugged, and stable; however, they have three major problems which must be overcome.

The first of these is the fact that the output is very small and must be amplified a great deal to bring it up into range where it can, for example, drive an A/D converter.

Second, as shown in Figure 10-7, a reference junction made of the same metals must be connected in series with the junction being used to make the measurement. Note that the reference junction is connected in the reverse direction from the measuring junction. This is done so that the output connecting wires are both constantan. The thermocouples formed by connecting these wires to the copper wires going to the amplifier will then cancel out. The input voltage to the amplifier will be the difference between the voltages across the two thermocouples. If we simply amplify this voltage, however, there is a problem if the temperature of both

thermocouples is changing. The problem is that it is impossible to tell which thermocouple caused a change in output voltage. One cure for this is to put the reference junction in an ice bath or a small oven to hold it at a constant temperature. This solution is usually inconvenient, so instead a circuit such as that in Figure 10-7 is used to compensate electronically for changes in the temperature of the reference junction.

As we discussed in a previous section, the AD590 shown here produces a current proportional to its temperature. The AD590 is attached to the reference thermocouple so that they are both at the same temperature. The current from the AD590, when passed through the resistor network, produces a voltage which compensates for changes in the reference thermocouple with temperature. The signal to the amplifier then is propor-

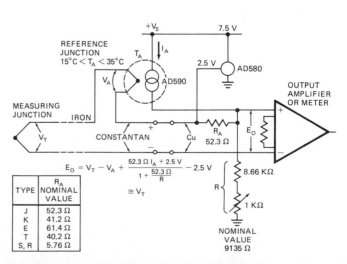

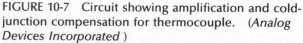

FIGURE 10-7   Circuit showing amplification and cold-junction compensation for thermocouple.   (*Analog Devices Incorporated*)

tional only to changes in the sensor thermocouple. Canceling out the effects of ambient temperature variations on the reference junction is referred to as *cold-junction compensation*. The table in Figure 10-7 shows the values of R_A which will provide cold-junction compensation for common types of thermocouples. An instrumentation amplifier such as that in Figure 10-1*h* is usually used for this application.

The third problem with thermocouples is that their output voltages do not change linearly with temperature. This can be corrected with analog circuitry which changes the gain of an amplifier according to the value of the signal. However, when a thermocouple is used with a microcomputer-based instrument, the correction can be easily done using a lookup table in ROM. An A/D converter converts the voltage from the thermocouple to a digital value. The digital value is then used as a pointer to a ROM location which contains the correct temperature for that reading.

RTDS AND THERMISTORS

Resistance temperature detectors (RTDs) and thermal sensitive resistors (thermistors) are two other commonly used types of temperature sensors. Both of these types are essentially resistors which change value with a change in temperature. RTDs consist of a wire or a thin film of platinum or a nickel wire. The response of RTDs is nonlinear, but they have excellent stability and repeatability. Therefore, they are often used in applications where very precise temperature measurement is needed. RTDs are useful for measures in the range of -250 to $+850°$ C. A circuit such as that in Figure 10-8 can be used to convert the change in resistance of the RTD to a proportional voltage. Op amp A1 in this circuit produces a precise reference voltage of -6.25 V. This voltage produces a precise current at the inverting input of A2. Op amp A2 pulls this current through the RTD to produce a voltage proportional to

the resistance of the RTD. The resistance of an RTD increases with an increase in temperature.

Thermistors consist of semiconductor material whose resistance decreases nonlinearly with temperature. Devices with 25° C resistance of tens of ohms to millions of ohms are available for different applications. Thermistors are relatively inexpensive, have very fast response times, and are useful in applications where precise measurement is not required. A circuit similar to that in Figure 10-8 can be used to produce a voltage proportional to the resistance of the thermistor.

Force and Pressure Transducers

To convert force or pressure (force/area) to a proportional electrical signal, the most common methods use *strain gages* or *linear variable differential transformers* (LVDTs). Both of these methods involve moving something. This why we refer to them as *transducers* rather than as sensors. Here's how strain gages work.

STRAIN GAGES AND LOAD CELLS

A strain gage is a small resistor whose value changes when its length is changed. It may be made of thin wire, thin foil, or semiconductor material. Figure 10-9*a* shows a simple setup for measuring force or weight with strain gages. One end of a piece of spring steel is attached to a fixed surface. A strain gage is glued on the top of the flexible bar. The force or weight to be measured is applied to the unattached end of the bar. As the applied force bends the bar, the strain gage is stretched, increasing its resistance. Since the amount that the bar is bent is directly proportional to the applied force, the change in resistance will be proportional to the applied force. If a current is passed through the strain gage, then the change in voltage across the strain gage will be proportional to the applied force.

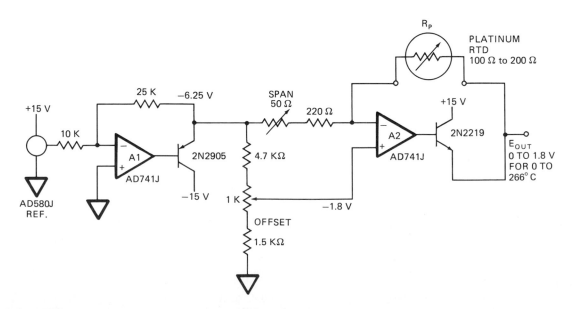

FIGURE 10-8   100-Ω RTD connected to perform temperature measurements in the range 0°C to 266°C.   (*Analog Devices Incorporated*)

Unfortunately, the resistance of the strain-gage element also changes with temperature. To compensate for this problem, two strain-gage elements mounted at right angles, as shown in Figure 10-9b, are often used. Both of the elements will change resistance with temperature, but only element A will change resistance appreciably with applied force. When these two elements are connected in a balanced-bridge configuration, as shown in Figure 10-9c, any change in the resistance of the elements due to temperature will have no effect on the differential output of the bridge. However, as force is applied, the resistance of the element under strain will change and produce a small differential output voltage. The full-scale differential output voltage is typically 2 or 3 mV for each volt of excitation voltage applied to the top of the bridge. For example, if 10 V is applied to the top of the bridge, the full-load output voltage will be 20 or 30 mV. This small signal can be amplified with a differential amplifier or an instrumentation amplifier.

Strain-gage bridges are used in many different forms to measure many different types of force and pressure. If the strain-gage bridge is connected to a bendable

beam structure, as shown in Figure 10-9a, the result is called a *load cell* and is used to measure weight. Figure 10-10 shows a 10-lb load cell that might be used in a microprocessor-controlled delicatessen scale or postal scale. Larger versions can be used to weigh barrels being filled or even trucks.

If a strain-gage bridge is mounted on a movable diaphragm in a threaded housing, the output of the bridge will be proportional to the pressure applied to the diaphragm. If a vacuum is present on one side of the diaphragm, then the value read out will be a measure of the absolute pressure. If one side of the diaphragm is open, then the output will be a measure of the pressure relative to atmospheric pressure. If the two sides of the diaphragm are connected to two different pressure sources, then the output will be a measure of the differential pressure between the two sides. Figure 10-11 shows a Sensym LX1804GBZ pressure transducer which measures pressures in the range of 0 to 15 lb/in^2. A transducer such as this might be used to measure blood pressure in a microcomputer-based medical instrument.

LINEAR VARIABLE DIFFERENTIAL TRANSFORMERS

An *LVDT* is another type of transducer often used to measure force, pressure, or position. Figure 10-12 shows the basic structure of an LVDT. It consists of three coils of wire wound on the same form and a movable iron core. An ac excitation signal of perhaps 20 kHz is applied to the primary. The secondaries are connected such that the voltage induced in one opposes the voltage induced in the other. If the core is centered, then the induced voltages are equal and cancel each other, so there is no net output voltage. If the coil is moved off center, coupling to one secondary coil will be stronger, so that the coil will produce a greater output voltage. The result will be a net output voltage. The phase relationship between the output signal and the input signal is an indication of which direction the core moved from the center position. The amplitude of the output signal is linearly proportional to how far the core moves from the center position.

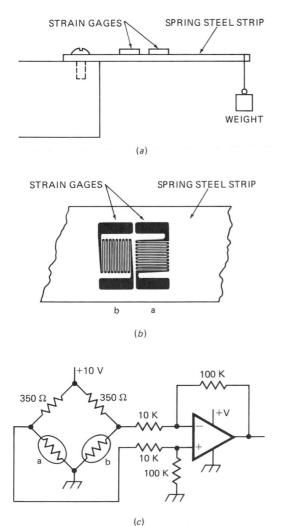

FIGURE 10-9   Strain gages used to measure force.
(a) Side view. (b) Top view (expanded).
(c) Circuit connections.

FIGURE 10-10   Photograph of load-cell transducer used to measure weight.   (*Transducers, Incorporated*)

FIGURE 10-11   LX1804GBZ pressure transducer.   (*Sensym, Incorporated*)

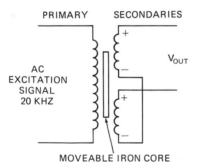

FIGURE 10-12   Linear variable differential transformer (LVDT) structure.

An LVDT can be used directly in this form to measure displacement or position. If you add a spring so that a force is required to move the core, then the voltage out of the LVDT will be proportional to the force applied to the core. In this form, the LVDT can be used in a load cell for an electronic scale. Likewise, if a spring is added and the core of the LVDT is attached to a diaphragm in a threaded housing, the output from the LVDT will be proportional to the pressure exerted on the diaphragm. We do not have the space here to show the ac-interface circuitry required for an LVDT.

Flow Sensors

If we are going to control the flow rate of some material in our electronics factory, we need to be able to measure it. Depending on the material, flow rate, and temperature, we use different methods.

One method used is to put a paddle wheel in the flow, as shown in Figure 10-13a. The rate at which the paddle wheel turns is proportional to the rate of flow of a liquid

or gas. An optical encoder can be attached to the shaft of the paddle wheel to produce digital information as to how fast the paddle wheel is turning.

A second common method of measuring flow is with a *differential pressure transducer,* as shown in Figure 10-13b. A wire mesh or screen is put in the pipe to create some resistance. Flow through this resistance produces a difference in pressure between the two sides of the screen. The pressure transducer gives an output proportional to the difference in pressure between the two sides of the resistance. In the same way that the voltage across an electrical resistor is proportional to the flow of current through the resistor, the output of the pressure transducer is proportional to the flow of a liquid or gas through the pipe.

Other Sensors

As we mentioned previously, the number of different types of sensors is very large. In addition to the types we have discussed, there are sensors to measure pH, concentration of various gases, thickness of materials, presence of an object (proximity), and just about anything else you might want to measure. Often you can use commonly available transducers in creative ways to solve a particular application problem you have. Suppose, for example, that you need to accurately determine the level of a liquid in a large tank. To do this, you could install a pressure transducer at the bottom of the tank. The pressure in a liquid is proportional to the height of the liquid in the tank, so you can easily convert a pressure reading to the desired liquid height. The point here is to check out what is available and then be creative.

4- to 20-mA Current Loops

In the preceding discussions, we showed how op amps can be used to convert output signals to voltages in a range that can be applied to the input of an A/D

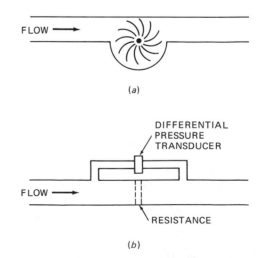

FIGURE 10-13   Flow sensors. (*a*) Paddle wheel. (*b*) Differential pressure.

converter. In many industrial applications where the sensor is a long distance from the A/D converter, however, the signals from the sensors or transducers are converted to currents instead of voltages. Sending a signal as a current has the advantages that the signal amplitude is not affected by resistance, induced-voltage noise, or voltage drops in a long connecting line. A common range of currents used to represent analog signals in industrial environments is 4 to 20 mA. A current of 4 mA represents a zero output, and a current of 20 mA represents the full-scale value. The reason the current range is offset from zero is so that a current of zero is left to represent an open circuit. At the receiving end of the line, a resistor or a simple op-amp circuit is used to convert the current to a proportional voltage which can be applied to the input of the A/D converter.

D/A CONVERTER OPERATION, INTERFACING, AND APPLICATIONS

In the previous sections of this chapter we have discussed how we use sensors to get electrical signals proportional to pressure, temperature, etc, and how we use op amps to amplify and filter these electrical signals. The next logical step would be to show you how to use an A/D converter to get these signals into digital form that a microcomputer can work with. However, since D/A converters are simpler and since several types of A/D converters have D/As as part of their circuitry, we will discuss D/As first.

D/A Converter Operation and Specifications

OPERATION

The purpose of a digital-to-analog converter is to convert a binary word to a proportional current or voltage. To see how this is done, let's look at the simple 4-input adder circuit in Figure 10-14.

Since the noninverting input of the op amp is grounded, the op amp will work day and night to hold the inverting input also at 0 V. Remember that the inverting input in this circuit is referred to as the summing point. When one of the switches is closed, a current will flow from −5 V (V_{REF}) through that resistor to the summing point. The op amp will pull the current on through the feedback resistor to produce a proportional output voltage. If you close switch D0, for example, a current of 0.05 mA will flow into the summing point. In

order to pull this current through the feedback resistor, the op amp must put a voltage of 0.05 mA × 10 kΩ or 0.5 V on its output. If you also close switch D1, it will send another 0.1 mA into the summing point. In order to pull the sum of the currents through the feedback resistor, the op amp has to output a voltage of 0.15 mA × 10 kΩ or 1.5 V.

The point here is that the binary-weighted resistors produce binary-weighted currents which are summed by the op amp to produce a proportional output voltage. The binary word applied to the switches produces a proportional output voltage. Technically the output voltage is "digital" because it can only have certain fixed values, just as the display on a digital voltmeter can. However, the output simulates an analog signal, so we refer to it as analog. Switch D3 in Figure 10-14 represents the most significant bit because closing it produces the largest current. Note that since V_{REF} is negative, the output will go positive as switches are closed.

As you see here, the heart of a D/A converter is a set of binary-weighted current sources which can be switched on or off according to a binary word applied to its inputs. Since these current sources are usually inside an IC, we don't need to discuss the different ways the binary-weighted currents can be produced. The op-amp circuit in Figure 10-14 converts the sum of the currents to a proportional voltage.

D/A CHARACTERISTICS AND SPECIFICATIONS

Figure 10-15 shows the circuit for an inexpensive IC D/A converter with an op-amp circuit as a current-to-

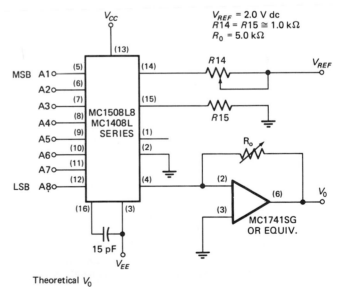

Theoretical V_0

$$V_0 = \frac{V_{REF}}{R14}(R_0)\left\{\frac{A1}{2} + \frac{A2}{4} + \frac{A3}{8} + \frac{A4}{16} + \frac{A5}{32} + \frac{A6}{64} + \frac{A7}{128} + \frac{A8}{256}\right\}$$

ADJUST V_{REF}, R14 OR R_0 SO THAT V_0 WITH ALL DIGITAL INPUTS AT HIGH LEVEL IS EQUAL TO 9.961 V

$$V_0 = \frac{2\,V}{1\,k\Omega}(5\,k\Omega)\left\{\frac{1}{2} + \frac{1}{4} + \frac{1}{8} + \frac{1}{16} + \frac{1}{32} + \frac{1}{64} + \frac{1}{128} + \frac{1}{256}\right\}$$

$$= 10\,V\left\{\frac{255}{256}\right\} = 9.961\,V$$

FIGURE 10-15   Motorola MC1408 8-bit D/A with current-to-voltage converter.

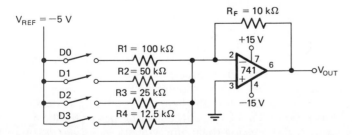

FIGURE 10-14   Simple 4-bit D/A converter.

voltage converter. We will use this circuit for our discussion of D/A characteristics.

The first characteristic of a D/A converter to consider is *resolution*. This is determined by the number of bits in the input binary word. A converter with 8 binary inputs, such as the one in Figure 10-15, has 2^8 or 256 possible output levels, so its resolution is 1 part in 256. As another example, a 12-bit converter has a resolution of 1 part in 2^{12} or 4096. Resolution is sometimes expressed as a percentage. The resolution of an 8-bit converter expressed as a percentage is $(1/256) \times 100$ percent or about 0.39 percent.

The next D/A characteristic to determine is the *full-scale output voltage*. For the converter in Figure 10-15, the current for all the switches is supplied by V_{REF} through R14. The current output from pin 4 of the D/A is pulled through R_o to produce the output voltage. The formula for the output voltage is shown under the circuit in Figure 10-15. In the equation the term A1, for example, represents the condition of the switch for that bit. If a switch is closed, allowing a current to flow, put a 1 in that bit. If a switch is open, put a 0 in that bit. As we also show in Figure 10-15, if all the switches are closed, the output will be 10 V $\times$ (255/256) or 9.961 V. Even though the output voltage can never actually get to 10 V, this is referred to as a *10-V output converter*. The maximum output voltage of a converter will always have a value 1 least significant bit less than the named value. As another example of this, suppose that you have a 12-bit, 10-V converter. The value of 1 LSB will be (10 V)/4096 or 2.44 mV. The highest voltage out of this converter when it is properly adjusted will then be $(10.0000 - 0.0024)$ V or 9.9976 V.

Several different binary codes, such as *straight binary*, BCD, and *offset binary*, are commonly used as inputs to D/A converters. We will show examples of these codes in a later discussion of A/D converters.

The accuracy specification for a D/A converter is a comparison between the actual output and the expected output. It is specified as a percentage of the full-scale output voltage or current. If a converter has a full-scale output of 10 V and ±0.2 percent accuracy, then the *maximum error* for any output will be 0.002×10.00 V or 20 mV. Ideally the maximum error for a D/A converter should be no more than $\pm\frac{1}{2}$ the value of the LSB.

Another important specification for a D/A converter is *linearity*. Linearity is a measure of how much the output ramp deviates from a straight line as the converter is stepped from no switches on to all switches on. Ideally, the deviation of the output from a straight line as the converter is stepped from no switches on to all switches on. Ideally, the deviation of the output from a straight line should be no greater than $\pm\frac{1}{2}$ the value of the LSB to maintain overall accuracy. However, many D/A converters are marketed which have linearity errors greater than that. National Semiconductor, for example, markets the DAC1020, DAC1021, DAC1022 series of 10-bit-resolution converters. The linearity specification for the DAC1020 is 0.05 percent, which is appropriate for a 10-bit converter. The DAC1021 has a linearity specification of 0.10 percent, and the DAC1022 has a specification of 0.20 percent. The question that may

occur to you at this point is, What good is it to have a 10-bit converter if the linearity is only equivalent to that of an 8- or 9-bit converter? The answer to this question is that for many applications, the resolution given by a 10-bit converter is needed for small output signals, but it doesn't matter if the output value is somewhat nonlinear for large signals. The price you pay for a D/A converter is proportional not only to its resolution, but also to its linearity specification.

Still another D/A specification to look for is *settling time*. When you change the binary word applied to the input of a converter, the output will change to the appropriate new value. The output, however, may overshoot the correct value and "ring" for a while before finally settling down to the correct value. The time the output takes to get within $\pm\frac{1}{2}$ LSB of the final value is called settling time. As an example, the National DAC1020 10-bit converter has a typical settling time of 500 ns for a full-scale change on the output. This specification is important because if a converter is operated at too high a frequency, it may not have time to settle to one value before it is switched to the next.

D/A Applications and Interfacing to Microcomputers

D/A converters have many applications besides those where they are used with a microcomputer. In a compact-disk audio player, for example, a 14- or 16-bit D/A converter is used to convert the binary data read off the disk by a laser to an analog audio signal. Most speech-synthesizer ICs contain a D/A converter to convert stored binary data for words into analog audio signals. Here, however, we are primarily interested in the use of a D/A converter with a microcomputer.

The inputs of the D/A circuit (A1 through A8) in Figure 10-15 can be connected directly to a microcomputer output port. As part of a program, you can produce any desired voltage on the output of the D/A. Here are some ideas as to what you might use this circuit for.

As a first example, suppose that you want to build a microcomputer-controlled tester which determines the effect of power supply voltage on the output voltage of some integrated-circuit amplifiers. If you connect the output of the D/A converter to the reference input of a programmable power supply or simply add the high-current buffer circuit shown in Figure 10-16 to the output of the D/A, you have a power supply which you can vary under program control. To determine the output voltage of the IC under test as you vary its supply voltage, connect the input of an A/D converter to the IC output, and connect the output of the A/D converter to an input port of your microcomputer. You can then read in the value of the output voltage on the IC.

Another application you might use a D/A and a power buffer for is to vary the voltage supplied to a small resistive heater under program control. Also, the speed of small dc motors is proportional to the amount of current passed through them, so you could connect a small dc motor to the output of the power buffer and control the speed of the motor with the value you output to the D/A. Note that without feedback control, the speed

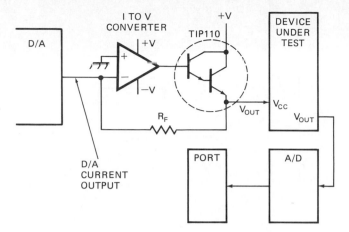

FIGURE 10-16   High-power buffer for D/A output.

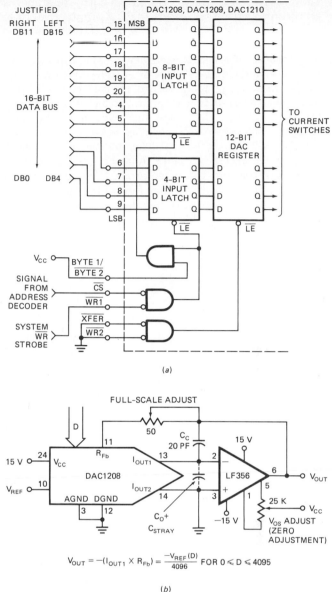

(a)

$$V_{OUT} = -(I_{OUT1} \times R_{Fb}) = \frac{-V_{REF}(D)}{4096} \quad FOR\ 0 \leqslant D \leqslant 4095$$

(b)

FIGURE 10-17   (a) National DAC1208 12-bit D/A input block diagram showing internal latches. (b) Analog circuit connections.

of the motor will vary if the load changes. Later in the chapter we show you how to add feedback control to maintain constant motor speed under changing loads.

So far we have talked about using an 8-bit D/A with a microprocessor. Interfacing an 8-bit converter involves simply connecting the inputs of the converter to an output port or, for some D/As, simply connecting the inputs to the buses as you would a port device. Now, suppose that for some application you need 12 bits of resolution, so you need to interface a 12-bit converter. If you are working with a system which has an 8-bit data bus, your first thought might be to connect the lower 8 inputs of the 12-bit converter to one output port and the upper four inputs to another port. You could send the lower 8 bits with one write operation and the upper 4 bits with another write operation. However, the time between the two writes introduces a potential problem in this approach.

Suppose, for example, that you want to change the output of a 12-bit converter from 0000 1111 1111 to 0001 0000 0000. When you write the lower 8 bits, the output will go from 0000 1111 1111 to 0000 0000 0000. When you write the upper 4 bits, the output will go back up to the desired 0001 0000 0000. The point here is that for the time between the two writes the output will go to an unwanted value. In many systems this could be disastrous. The cure for this problem is to put latches on the input lines. The latches can be loaded separately and then strobed together to pass all 12 bits to the D/A converter at the same time.

Many currently available D/A converters contain built-in latches to make this easier. Figure 10-17a shows a block diagram of the National DAC1230- and DAC1208-type 12-bit converters. Note the internal latches and the register. The DAC1230 series of parts has the upper 4 input bits connected to the lower 4 bits so that the 12 bits can be written with two write operations from an 8-bit port or data bus such as that of the 8088 microprocessor. The DAC1208 series of parts has the upper 4 data inputs available separately so they can be connected directly to the bus in a system which has a 16-bit data bus, as shown in Figure 10-17a. If, for example, you want to connect a DAC1208 converter to

an SDK-86 board, you can simply connect the DAC1208 data inputs to the lower 12 data bus lines, connect the $\overline{CS}$ input to an address decoder output, connect the $\overline{WR1}$ input to the system $\overline{WR}$ line, and tie the $\overline{WR2}$ and $\overline{XPER}$ inputs to the ground. The BYTE1/$\overline{BYTE}$ input is tied high. You then write words to the converter just as if it were a 16-bit port. The timing parameters for the DAC1208 are acceptable for an 8086 operating with a clock frequency of 5 MHz or less. For higher 8086 clock frequencies, you would have to add a one-shot or other circuitry that inserts a WAIT state each time you write to the D/A. Here are a few notes about the analog connections for these devices.

These D/A converters require a precision voltage reference. The circuit in Figure 10-17b uses a −10.000-V reference. The D/A converters have a current output, so an op amp is used to convert the D/A output current to a proportional voltage. A FET input amplifier is used here because the input bias current of a bipolar input amp might affect the accuracy of the output. The DAC1208 and DAC1230 have built-in feedback resistors which match the temperature characteristics of the internal current-divider resistors, so all you have to add externally is a 50-Ω resistor for "tweaking" purposes. With a −10.000-V reference as shown, the output voltage will be equal to (the digital input word/4096) × (+10.000 V). Note that the D/A has both a digital ground and an analog ground. To avoid getting digital noise in the analog portions of the circuit, these two should be connected together only at the power supply.

A/D CONVERTER SPECIFICATIONS, TYPES, AND INTERFACING

A/D Specifications

The function of an A/D converter is to produce a digital word which represents the magnitude of some analog voltage or current. The specifications for an A/D converter are very similar to those for a D/A converter. The resolution of an A/D converter refers to the number of bits in the output binary word. An 8-bit converter, for example, has a resolution of 1 part in 256. Accuracy and linearity specifications have the same meanings for an A/D converter as they do for a D/A converter. Another important specification for an A/D converter is its *conversion time*. This is simply the time it takes the converter to produce a valid output binary code for an applied input voltage. When we refer to a converter as *high-speed*, we mean that it has a short conversion time. There are many different ways to do an A/D conversion, but we have space here to review only three commonly used methods, which represent a wide variety of conversion times.

A/D Converter Types

PARALLEL COMPARATOR A/D CONVERTER

Figure 10-18 shows a circuit for a 2-bit A/D converter using *parallel comparators*. A voltage divider sets reference voltages on the inverting inputs of each of the comparators. The voltage at the top of the divider chain represents the full-scale value for the converter. The voltage to be converted is applied to the noninverting inputs of all the comparators in parallel. If the input voltage on a comparator is greater than the reference voltage on the inverting input, the output of the comparator will go high. The outputs of the comparators then give us a digital representation of the voltage level of the input signal. With an input voltage of 2.6 V, for example, the outputs of comparators A1 and A2 will be high.

The major advantage of a parallel, or *flash*, A/D converter is its speed of conversion, which is simply the propagation delay time of the comparators. The output code from the comparators is not a standard binary

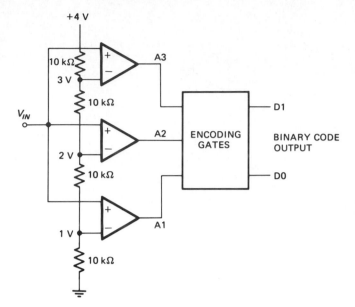

FIGURE 10-18   Parallel comparator A/D converter.

code, but it can be converted to any desired code with some simple logic. The major disadvantage of a flash A/D is the number of comparators needed to produce a result with a reasonable amount of resolution. The 2-bit converter in Figure 10-18 requires three comparators. To produce a converter with N bits of resolution, you need $(2^N - 1)$ comparators. For an 8-bit conversion, then, you need 255 comparators, and for a 10-bit flash converter, you need 1023 comparators. Single-package flash converters are available from TRW for applications in which the high speed is required, but they are relatively expensive. Flash converters which can do an 8-bit conversion in under 10 ns are currently available.

DUAL-SLOPE A/D CONVERTERS

Figure 10-19*a* shows a functional block diagram of a *dual-slope* A/D converter. This type of converter is often used as the heart of a digital voltmeter because it can give a large number of bits of resolution at a low cost. Here's how the converter in Figure 10-19 works.

To start, the control circuitry resets all the counters to zero and connects the input of the integrator to the input voltage to be converted. If you assume the input voltage is positive, then this will cause the output of the integrator to ramp negative, as shown in Figure 10-19*b*. As soon as the output of the integrator goes a few microvolts below ground, the comparator output will go high. The comparator output being high enables the AND gate and lets the 1-MHz clock into the counter chain. After some fixed number of counts, typically 1000, the control circuitry switches the input of the integrator to a negative reference voltage and resets all the counters to zero. With a negative input voltage, the integrator output will ramp positive, as shown in the right-hand side of Figure 10-19*b*. When the integrator output crosses 0 V, the comparator output will drop low and shut off the clock signal to the counters. The number of counts required for the integrator output to

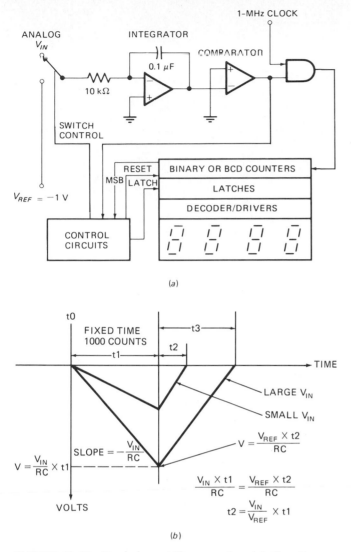

FIGURE 10-19 Dual-slope A/D converter. (a) Circuit. (b) Integrator output waveform.

In the figure (a), labels: ANALOG V_{IN}, INTEGRATOR, 1-MHz CLOCK, COMPARATOR, 0.1 µF, 10 kΩ, SWITCH CONTROL, $V_{REF} = -1$ V, RESET, MSB, LATCH, BINARY OR BCD COUNTERS, LATCHES, DECODER/DRIVERS, CONTROL CIRCUITS.

In figure (b): t0, FIXED TIME 1000 COUNTS, t1, t2, t3, TIME, LARGE V_{IN}, SMALL V_{IN}, VOLTS.

$$V = \frac{V_{IN}}{RC} \times t1$$

$$\text{SLOPE} = -\frac{V_{IN}}{RC}$$

$$V = \frac{V_{REF} \times t2}{RC}$$

$$\frac{V_{IN} \times t1}{RC} = \frac{V_{REF} \times t2}{RC}$$

$$t2 = \frac{V_{IN}}{V_{REF}} \times t1$$

get back to zero is directly proportional to the input voltage. For the circuit shown in Figure 10-19a, an input signal of $+2$ V, for example, produces a count of 2000. Because the resistor and the capacitor on the integrator are used for both the input voltage integrate and the reference integrate, small variations in their value with temperature do not have any effect on the accuracy of the conversion.

Complete slope-type A/D converters are readily available in single IC packages. One example is the Intersil ICL7136, which contains all the circuitry for a 3½-digit A/D converter and all the interface circuitry needed to drive a 3½-digit LCD. Another example is the Intersil ICL7135, which contains all the circuitry for a 4½-digit A/D converter and has a multiplexed BCD output. Note that, because of the usual use of this type of converter, we often express its resolution in terms of a number of digits. The full-scale reading for a 3½-digit converter is 1999, so the resolution corresponds to about 1 part in 2000. A two-chip set, the Intersil ICL8068 and ICL7104-16, contains all the circuitry for a slope-type 16-bit binary output A/D converter.

The main disadvantage of slope-type converters is their slow speed. A 4½-digit unit may take 300 ms to do a conversion.

SUCCESSIVE-APPROXIMATION A/D CONVERTERS

Figure 10-20, p. 306, shows a circuit for an 8-bit *successive-approximation* converter which uses readily available parts. The heart of this converter is a successive-approximation register (SAR) such as the MC14549, which functions as follows.

On the first clock pulse at the start of a conversion cycle, the SAR outputs a high on its most-significant bit to the MC1408 D/A converter. The D/A converter and the amplifier convert this to a voltage and apply it to one input of a comparator. If this voltage is higher than the input voltage on the other input of the comparator, the comparator output will go low and tell the SAR to turn off that bit because it is too large. If the voltage from the D/A converter is less than the input voltage, then the comparator output will be high, which tells the SAR to keep that bit on. When the next clock pulse occurs, the SAR will turn on the next most significant bit to the D/A converter. Based on the answer this produces from the comparator, the SAR will keep or reset this bit. The SAR proceeds in this way on down to the least significant bit, adding each bit to the total in turn and using the signal from the comparator to decide whether to keep that bit in the result. Only nine clock pulses are needed to do the actual conversion here. When the conversion is complete, the binary result is on the parallel outputs of the SAR, and the SAR sends out an end-of-conversion (EOC) signal to indicate this. In the circuit in Figure 10-20, the EOC signal is used to strobe the binary result into some latches, where it can be read by a microcomputer. If the EOC signal is connected to the start-conversion (SC) input as shown, then the converter will do continuous conversions. Note in the circuit in Figure 10-20 that the noninverting input of the op amp on the 1408 D/A converter is connected to -5 V instead of to ground. This shifts the analog input range to -5 V to $+5$ V instead of 0 V to $+10$ V so that sine waves and other ac signals can be input directly to the converter to be digitized.

The National ADC1280 is a single-chip 12-bit successive-approximation converter which does a conversion in about 22 µs. Datel and Analog Devices have several 12-bit converters with conversion times of about 1 µs.

Several commonly available successive-approximation A/D converters have analog multiplexers on their inputs. The National ADC0816, for example, has a 16-input multiplexer in front of the A/D converter. This allows the one converter to digitize any one of 16 input signals. The input channel to be digitized is determined by a 4-bit address applied to the address inputs of the device. An A/D converter with a multiplexer on its inputs is often called a *data acquisition system*, or DAS. Later in this chapter we show an application of a DAS in a factory control system.

Before we go on to discuss A/D interfacing, we need to make a few comments about common A/D output codes.

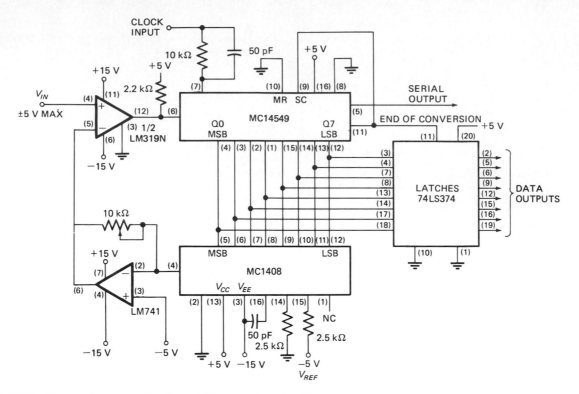

FIGURE 10-20   Successive-approximation A/D converter circuit.

A/D OUTPUT CODES

For convenience in different applications, A/D converters are available with several different, somewhat confusing, output codes. The best way to make sense out of these different codes is to see them all together with representative values, as shown in Figure 10-21. The values shown here are for an 8-bit converter, but you can extend them to any number of bits.

For an A/D converter with only a positive input range (*unipolar*), a straight binary code or inverted binary code is usually used. If the output of an A/D converter is going to drive a display, then it is convenient to have the output coded in BCD. For applications where the input range of the converter has both a negative and a positive range (*bipolar*), we usually use offset-binary coding. As you can see in Figure 10-21, the values of 00000000 to 11111111 are simply shifted downward so that 00000000 represents the most negative input value and 10000000 represents an input value of zero. This coding scheme has the advantage that the 2's complement representation can be produced by simply inverting the most significant bit. Some bipolar converters output the digital value directly in 2's complement form.

Interfacing Different Types of A/D Converters to Microcomputers

INTERFACING TO PARALLEL-COMPARATOR A/D CONVERTERS

In any application where a parallel comparator converter is used, the converter is most likely going to be producing digital output values much faster than a microcomputer

UNIPOLAR BINARY CODES

VALUE	10 VOLTS FULL SCALE	BINARY (BIN)	COMPLEMENTARY BINARY (CB)	INVERTED BINARY (IB)	INVERTED COMPLEMENTARY BINARY (ICB)
+FS −1 LSB +½ FS +½FS −1 LSB +1 LSB	9.9609 5.0000 4.9609 0.0391	1111 1111 1000 0000 0111 1111 0000 0001	0000 0000 0111 1111 1000 0000 1111 1110		
ZERO	0.0000	0000 0000	1111 1111	0000 0000	1111 1111
−1 LSB −½ FS + 1 LSB −½ FS − FS + 1 LSB	−0.0391 −4.9609 −5.0000 −9.9609			0000 0001 0111 1111 1000 0000 1111 1111	1111 1110 1000 0000 0111 1111 0000 0000

UNIPOLAR BINARY CODED DECIMAL CODES

VALUE	10 VOLTS FULL SCALE	BINARY CODED DECIMAL (BCD)	COMPLEMENTARY BINARY CODED DECIMAL (CBCD)	INVERTED BINARY CODED DECIMAL (IBCD)	INVERTED COMPLEMENTARY BINARY CODED DECIMAL (ICBCD)
+ FS −1 LSB +½ FS +1 LSB	9.9 5.0 0.1	1001 1001 0101 0000 0000 0001	0110 0110 1010 1111 1111 1110		
ZERO	0.0	0000 0000	1111 1111	0000 0000	1111 1111
−1 LSB −½ FS −FS +1 LSB	−0.1 −5.0 −9.9			0000 0001 0101 0000 1001 1001	1111 1110 1010 1111 0110 0110

BIPOLAR BINARY CODES

VALUE	10 VOLTS FULL SCALE RANGE	OFFSET BINARY (OB)	COMPLEMENTARY OFFSET BINARY (COB)	TWO'S COMPLEMENT (TC)
+FS +FS −1 LSB +1 LSB	5.0000 4.9609 0.0391	1111 1111 1000 0001	0000 0000 0111 1110	0111 1111 0000 0001
ZERO	0.0000	1000 0000	0111 1111	0000 0000
−1 LSB −FS +1 LSB −FS	−0.0391 −4.9609 −5.0000	0111 1111 0000 0001 0000 0000	1000 0000 1111 1110 1111 1111	1111 1111 1000 0001 1000 0000

FIGURE 10-21   Common A/D output codes.

could possibly read them in. Therefore, separate circuitry is used to bypass the microprocessor and load a set of samples from the converter directly into a series of memory locations. The microprocessor can later perform the desired operation on the samples. Bypassing the microprocessor in this way is called *direct memory access*, or DMA. The basic principle of DMA is that an external controller IC tells the microprocessor to float its buses. When the microprocessor does this, the DMA controller takes control of the buses and allows data to be transferred directly from the A/D converter to successive memory locations. We discuss DMA in detail in the next chapter.

INTERFACING TO SLOPE-TYPE A/D CONVERTERS

Most of the commonly available slope-type converters were designed to drive 7-segment displays in, for example, a digital voltmeter. Therefore, they usually output data in a multiplexed BCD or 7-segment form. Figure 10-23 shows how you can connect the multiplexed BCD outputs of an inexpensive 3½-digit slope converter, the MC14433, to a microprocessor port. In the section of the chapter where Figure 10-23 is located, we use this converter as part of a microcomputer-based scale. The BCD data is output from the converter on lines Q0 through Q3. A logic high is output on one of the digit strobe lines, DS1 through DS4, to indicate when the BCD code for the corresponding digit is on the Q outputs. The MC14433 converter shown in Figure 10-23 outputs the BCD code for the most significant digit and then outputs a high on the DS1 pin. After a period of time, it outputs the BCD code for the next most significant digit and outputs a high on the DS2 pin. After all 4 digits have been put out, the cycle repeats.

To read in the data from this converter, the principle is simply to poll the bit corresponding to a strobe line until you find it high, read in the data for that digit, and put the data in a reserved memory location for future reference. After you have read the BCD code for one digit, you poll the bit which corresponds to the strobe line for the next digit until you find it high, read the code for that digit, and put it in memory. Repeat the process until you have the data for all the digits. The A/D converter in Figure 10-23 is connected to do continuous conversions, so you can call the procedure to read in the value from the A/D converter at any time.

Frequency counters, digital voltmeters, and other test instruments often have multiplexed BCD outputs available on their back panel. With the connections and procedure we have just described, you can use these instruments to input data to your microcomputer.

INTERFACING A SUCCESSIVE-APPROXIMATION A/D CONVERTER

Successive-approximation A/D converters usually have outputs for each bit. The code output on these lines is usually straight binary or offset binary. You can simply connect the parallel outputs of the converter to the required number of input port pins and read in the converter output under program control. In addition to the data lines, there are two other successive-approximation A/D converter signal lines you need to interface to

the microcomputer for the data transfer. The first of these is a START CONVERT signal which you output from the microcomputer to the A/D to tell it to do a conversion for you. The second signal is an EOC signal which the A/D converter outputs to indicate that the conversion is complete and that the word on the outputs is valid. Here are the program steps you use to get a data sample from this type of converter.

First, you pulse the START CONVERT input for a time required by the particular converter. Then you detect the EOC signal going low on a polled or interrupt basis. You then read in the digitized value from the parallel outputs of the converter. In a later section of this chapter we show a detailed example of this for the National ADC0808 converter.

A MICROCOMPUTER-BASED SCALE

So far in this book we have shown you how a basic microcomputer functions and how to interface a wide variety of devices to the basic microcomputer. Now it's time to show you how some of these pieces are put together to make a microcomputer-based instrument. The first instrument we have chosen is a "smart" scale such as you might see at the checkout stand in your local grocery store.

Overview of Smart-Scale Operation

Figure 10-22, p. 308, shows a block diagram of our smart scale. A load cell converts the applied weight of, for example, a bunch of carrots to a proportional electrical signal. This small signal is amplified and converted to a digital value which can be read in by the microprocessor and sent to the attached display. The user then enters the price per pound with the keyboard, and this price per pound is shown on the display. When the user presses the compute key on the keyboard, the microprocessor multiplies the weight times the price per pound and displays the computed price. After holding the price display long enough for the user to read it, the scale goes back to reading in the weight and displaying it. To save the user from having to type the computed price into the cash register, an output from the scale could be connected directly into the cash register circuitry. Also, a speech synthesizer could be added to verbally tell the customer the weight, price per pound, and total price.

Smart scales such as this have many applications other than weighing carrots. A modified version of this scale is used in company mail rooms to weigh packages and calculate the postage required to send them to different postal zones. The output of the scale is usually connected to a postage meter, which then automatically prints out the required postage sticker. Another application of smart scales is to count coins in a bank or gambling casino. For this application the user simply enters the type of coin being weighed. A conversion factor in the program computes the total number of coins and the total dollar amount. Still another application of a scale such as this is in packaging items for sale. Suppose, for example, that we are manufacturing wood-

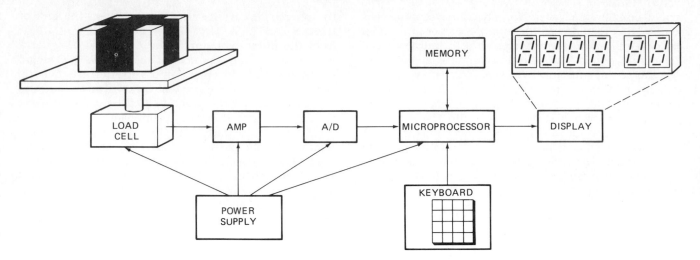

FIGURE 10-22   Block diagram of microcomputer-based smart scale.

screws and that we want to package 100 of them per box. We can pass the boxes over the load cell on a conveyor belt and fill them from a chute until the weight, and therefore the count, reaches some entered value. The point here is that the combination of intelligence and some simple interface circuitry gives you an instrument with as many uses as your imagination can come up with.

Smart-Scale Input Circuitry

Figure 10-10 shows a picture of the Transducers, Inc. Model C462–10#-10P1 strain-gage load cell we used when we built this scale. We added a piece of plywood to the top of the load cell to keep the carrots from falling off. This load cell has an accuracy of about 1 part in 1000, or 0.01 lb over the 0- to 10-lb range for which it was designed.

As shown in Figure 10-23, the load cell consists of four 350-Ω resistors connected in a bridge configuration. A stable 10.00-V excitation voltage is applied to the top of the bridge. With no load on the cell, the outputs from the bridge are at about the same voltage, 5 V. When a load is applied to the bridge, the resistance of one of the lower resistors will be changed. This produces a small differential output voltage from the bridge. The maximum differential output voltage for this 10-lb load cell is 2 mV per volt of excitation, so with 10.00 V excitation as shown, the maximum differential-output voltage is 20 mV.

To amplify this small differential signal, we use a National LM363 instrumentation amplifier. This device contains all the circuitry shown for the instrumentation amplifier in Figure 10-1h. The closed-loop gain of the amplifier is programmable with jumpers on pins 2, 3, and 4 for fixed values of 5, 100, and 500. We have jumpered it for a gain of 100 so that the 20-mV maximum signal from the load cell will give a maximum voltage of 2.00 V to the A/D converter input. A precision voltage divider on the output of the amplifier divides this signal in half so that a weight of 10.00 lb produces an output voltage of 1.000 V. This scaling simplifies the display of

the weight after it is read into the microprocessor. The 0.1-μF capacitor between pins 15 and 16 of the amplifier reduces the bandwidth of the amplifier to about 7.5 Hz. This removes 60 Hz and any high-frequency noise that might have been induced in the signal lines.

The MC14433 A/D converter used here is an inexpensive dual-slope device intended for use in 3½-digit digital voltmeters, etc. Because the load cell output changes slowly, a fast converter isn't needed here. The voltage across an LM329 6.9-V precision reference diode is amplified by IC4 to produce the 10.00-V excitation voltage for the load cell and a 2.000-V reference for the A/D. With a 2.000-V reference voltage, the full-scale input voltage for the A/D is 2.000 V. Conversion rate and multiplexing frequency for the converter are determined by an internal oscillator and R11. An R11 of 300 kΩ gives a clock frequency of 66 kHz, a multiplex frequency of 0.8 kHz, and about four conversions per second. Accuracy of the converter is ±0.05 percent and ± 1 count, which is comparable to the accuracy of the load cell. In other words, the last digit of the displayed weight may be off by 1 or 2 counts. As we described in a previous section, the output from this converter is in multiplexed BCD form.

An Algorithm for the Smart Scale

Figure 10-24 shows the flowchart for our smart scale. Note that, as indicated by the double-ended boxes in the flowchart, most major parts of the program are written as procedures. This is an example of the structured, modular programming approach we have stressed throughout the book. Here's how it all works.

The output of the A/D is in multiplexed BCD form. The converter outputs the BCD code for a digit on its Q0–Q3 lines and outputs the strobe for that digit on the corresponding digit strobe line, DS1–DS4. To read the data for a digit, that digit strobe is polled until it goes high; then the BCD code for that digit is read in. After the four BCD values are read in from the converter, a display procedure is called to display these values on the address field displays of the SDK-86. The letters "Lb" are displayed in the data field displays.

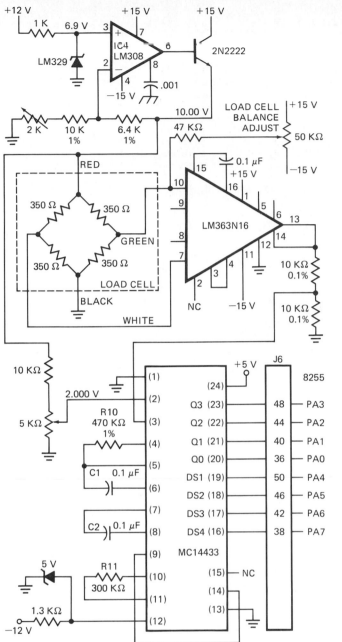

FIGURE 10-23 Circuit diagram for load-cell interface circuitry and A/D converter for smart scale.

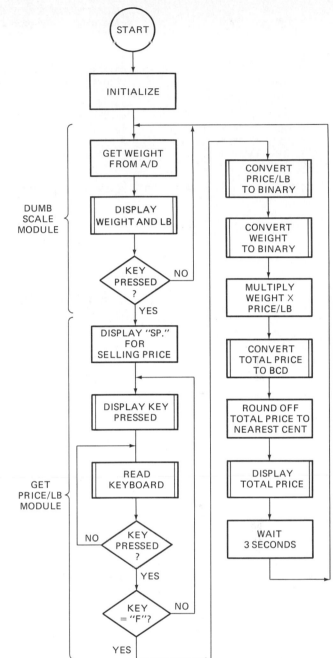

FIGURE 10-24 Flowchart for smart-scale program.

Next, a check is made to see if any keys have been pressed by the user. If a key has been pressed, the letters "SP," which represent selling price, are displayed in the address field. Keycodes are read from the 8279 as entered and displayed on the data field display. Keys can be pressed until the desired price per pound shows on the display. When a nonnumeric key is pressed, it is assumed that the entered price per pound is correct, and the program goes on to compute the total price.

Computing the price involves multiplying the weight in BCD form times the price per pound in BCD form. It is not easy to do a BCD × BCD multiply directly, so we took an alternate route to get there. We converted both the weight and the price per pound to their binary

equivalents and then multiplied the binary numbers. Another procedure converts the binary result of the multiplication to BCD. The BCD result is rounded to the nearest cent and displayed in the data field. The letters "Pr" are displayed in the address field to indicate that this is the total price. After a few seconds the program goes back to reading and displaying weight over and over, until a key is pressed.

The Microprocessor-Based Scale Program

Figure 10-25, p. 310–15, shows the complete program for our microprocessor-based scale. It is important for you not to be overwhelmed by a multipage program such

```
  1                          ;8086 PROGRAM F10-25.ASM
  2                          ;ABSTRACT  : Program for smart scale
  3                          ;PORTS     : Uses SDK-86 port P1A (FFF9H) for input
  4                          ;PROCEDURES: READ_KEY, DISPLAY_IT, PACK, EXPAND, CONVERT2BIN, BINCVT
  5
  6 0000                     DATA SEGMENT  WORD  PUBLIC
  7 0000  04*(00)            WEIGHT_BUFFER  DB  4 DUP(0)          ; Space for unpacked BCD weight
  8 0004  04*(00)            SELL_PRICE     DB  4 DUP(0)          ; Space for unpacked price/pound
  9 0008  04*(00)            PRICE_TOTAL    DB  4 DUP(0)          ; Space for total price to display
 10 000C  0000               BINARY_WEIGHT  DW  0                ; Space for converted weight
 11 000E  0B 10 14 14        LB             DB  0BH, 10H, 14H, 14H ; b, L, blank, blank
 12 0012  12 11 14 14        S_P            DB  12H, 11H, 14H, 14H ; P, S, blank, blank
 13 0016  13 12 14 14        PR             DB  13H, 12H, 14H, 14H ; r, P, blank, blank
 14
 15                          ;                0   1   2   3   4   5   6   7
 16 001A  3F 06 5B 4F 66 6D 7D +  SEVEN_SEG DB  3FH, 06H, 5BH, 4FH, 66H, 6DH, 7DH, 07H
 17       07
 18                          ;                8   9   A   b   C   d   E   F
 19 0022  7F 6F 77 7C 39 5E 79 +           DB  7FH, 6FH, 77H, 7CH, 39H, 5EH, 79H, 71H
 20       71
 21                          ;                L   S   P   r blank  H
 22 002A  38 6D 73 50 00 76               DB  38H, 6DH, 73H, 50H, 00H, 76H
 23 0030                     DATA ENDS
 24
 25 0000                     STACK_SEG SEGMENT
 26 0000  28*(0000)                    DW        40 DUP(0)
 27                            STACK_TOP     LABEL       WORD
 28 0050                     STACK_SEG     ENDS
 29
 30 0000                     CODE  SEGMENT WORD  PUBLIC
 31                              ASSUME CS:CODE, DS:DATA, SS:STACK_SEG
 32                          ;Initialize data & stack segment registers
 33 0000  B8 0000s           START:  MOV  AX, DATA
 34 0003  8E D8                      MOV  DS, AX
 35 0005  B8 0000s                   MOV  AX, STACK_SEG
 36 0008  8E D0                      MOV  SS, AX
 37 000A  BC 0050r                   MOV  SP, OFFSET STACK_TOP
 38                          ;8279 initialized at power-up of SDK-86 for 8 character display,
 39                          ; left entry encoded scan, 2-key lockout.
 40 000D  BA FFEA                    MOV  DX, 0FFEAH             ; Point at 8279 control address
 41 0010  B0 00                      MOV  AL, 00H                ; Control word for above conditions
 42 0012  EE                         OUT  DX, AL                 ; Send control word
 43 0013  B0 38                      MOV  AL, 00111000B          ; Clock word for divide by 24
 44 0015  EE                         OUT  DX, AL
 45 0016  B0 C0                      MOV  AL, 11000000B          ; Clear display character is all 0's
 46 0018  EE                         OUT  DX, AL
 47                          ;Dumb scale start
 48 0019  B9 0004            RDWT:   MOV  CX, 04H                ; Zero out weight buffer
 49 001C  BB 0000r                   MOV  BX, OFFSET WEIGHT_BUFFER
 50 001F  C6 07 00           NEXT1:  MOV  BYTE PTR[BX], 00H
 51 0022  43                         INC  BX
 52 0023  E2 FA                      LOOP NEXT1
 53 0025  B9 0004                    MOV  CX, 04H                ; Zero out price/pound buffer
 54 0028  BB 0004r                   MOV  BX, OFFSET SELL_PRICE
 55 002B  C6 07 00           NEXT2:  MOV  BYTE PTR[BX], 00H
 56 002E  43                         INC  BX
 57 002F  E2 FA                      LOOP NEXT2
 58                          ;Get weight from A/D converter and display.
 59 0031  BB 0003r                   MOV  BX,OFFSET WEIGHT_BUFFER+3; MSD Position in weight buffer
 60 0034  BA FFF9                    MOV  DX, 0FFF9H             ; Point at A/D port
 61 0037  EC                DS1:    IN   AL, DX                 ; Read byte from A/D
 62 0038  24 10                      AND  AL, 10H                ; Check for MSD strobe high
 63 003A  74 FB                      JZ   DS1                    ; Loop till high
 64 003C  EC                         IN   AL, DX                 ; Read MSD data from A/D
 65 003D  24 0F                      AND  AL, 0FH                ; Mask strobe bits
 66 003F  3C 04                      CMP  AL, 04H                ; See if MSD in bit 3 is a one
 67 0041  74 06                      JE   LOAD1                  ; Yes, go load 01H in buffer
 68 0043  C6 07 14                   MOV  BYTE PTR[BX], 14H      ; No, load code for blank
 69 0046  EB 04 90                   JMP  NXTCHR
 70 0049  C6 07 01           LOAD1:  MOV  BYTE PTR[BX], 01H
 71 004C  4B                NXTCHR: DEC  BX                     ; Point to next buffer location
 72 004D  EC                DS2:    IN   AL, DX                 ; Poll for digit 2 strobe
```

FIGURE 10-25   Assembly language program for smart scale. (*Continued on pages 311–15.*)

```
73 004E  24 20              AND   AL, 20H
74 0050  74 FB              JZ    DS2
75 0052  EC                 IN    AL, DX           ; Read digit 2 from A/D
76 0053  24 0F              AND   AL, OFH          ; Mask strobe bits
77 0055  88 07              MOV   [BX], AL         ; Digit 2 BCD to buffer
78 0057  4B                 DEC   BX               ; Point at next buffer location
79 0058  EC          DS3:   IN    AL, DX           ; Poll for digit 3 from A/D
80 0059  24 40              AND   AL, 40H
81 005B  74 FB              JZ    DS3
82 005D  EC                 IN    AL, DX           ; Read digit 3 from A/D
83 005E  24 0F              AND   AL, OFH          ; Mask strobe bits
84 0060  88 07              MOV   [BX],AL          ; Digit 3 to buffer
85 0062  4B                 DEC   BX               ; Point to next buffer location
86 0063  EC          DS4:   IN    AL, DX           ; Poll for digit 4 (LSD)
87 0064  24 80              AND   AL, 80H
88 0066  74 FB              JZ    DS4
89 0068  EC                 IN    AL, DX           ; Read digit 4 from A/D
90 0069  24 0F              AND   AL, OFH          ; Mask strobe bits
91 006B  88 07              MOV   [BX], AL         ; Digit 4 BCD to buffer
92                   ;Display weight on address field of SDK-86
93 006D  BB 0000r           MOV   BX, OFFSET WEIGHT_BUFFER   ; Point at stored weight
94 0070  B0 01              MOV   AL, 01H          ; Specifies address field
95 0072  B4 01              MOV   AH, 01H          ; Specifies decimal point
96 0074  E8 00CF            CALL  DISPLAY_IT
97 0077  BB 000Er           MOV   BX, OFFSET LB    ; Point at Lb string
98 007A  B0 00              MOV   AL, 00           ; Specifies data field
99 007C  B4 00              MOV   AH, 00           ; Specifies no decimal point
100 007E E8 00C5            CALL  DISPLAY_IT
101                  ;Check if key has been pressed
102 0081 BA FFEA            MOV   DX, OFFEAH       ; Point at 8279 status address
103 0084 EC                 IN    AL, DX           ; Read 8279 FIFO status
104 0085 24 01              AND   AL, 01H          ; See if FIFO has keycode
105 0087 75 02              JNZ   GETKEY           ; Yes, go read it
106 0089 EB 8E              JMP   RDWT             ; No, go get weight and display
107 008B B0 40       GETKEY: MOV  AL, 01000000B    ; Control word for read FIFO
108 008D EE                 OUT   DX, AL           ; Send to 8279
109 008E BA FFE8            MOV   DX, OFFE8H       ; Point at 8279 data address
110 0091 EC                 IN    AL, DX           ; Read code from FIFO
111 0092 3C 09              CMP   AL, 09H          ; Check if legal keycode (number)
112 0094 76 02              JBE   OK               ; Go on if below or equal 9
113 0096 EB 81              JMP   RDWT             ; Else ignore, read weight again
114                  ;Read in and display price/pound
115 0098 BB 0004r    OK:    MOV   BX, OFFSET SELL_PRICE  ; Point at price per pound buffer
116 009B 88 07              MOV   [BX], AL         ; Keycode to buffer
117 009D B0 00              MOV   AL, 00           ; Specify data field for display
118 009F B4 01              MOV   AH, 01           ; Specify decimal point
119 00A1 E8 00A2            CALL  DISPLAY_IT
120 00A4 BB 0012r           MOV   BX, OFFSET S_P   ; Point at SP string
121 00A7 B0 01              MOV   AL, 01           ; Specify address field
122 00A9 B4 00              MOV   AH, 00           ; Specify no decimal point
123 00AB E8 0098            CALL  DISPLAY_IT
124 00AE E8 0083    NXTKEY: CALL  READ_KEY         ; Wait for next keypress
125 00B1 3C 09              CMP   AL, 09H          ; See if more price or command
126 00B3 77 1F              JA    COMPUTE          ; Go compute total price
127 00B5 BB 0004r           MOV   BX, OFFSET SELL_PRICE  ; Point at price per pound buffer
128 00B8 8A 4F 02           MOV   CL, [BX+2]       ; Shift contents of buffer one
129 00BB 88 4F 03           MOV   [BX+3], CL       ; position left and insert new
130 00BE 8A 4F 01           MOV   CL, [BX+1]       ; keycode
131 00C1 88 4F 02           MOV   [BX+2], CL
132 00C4 8A 0F              MOV   CL, [BX]
133 00C6 88 4F 01           MOV   [BX+1], CL
134 00C9 88 07              MOV   [BX], AL
135 00CB B0 00              MOV   AL, 00           ; Specify data field
136 00CD B4 01              MOV   AH, 01           ; Specify decimal point
137 00CF E8 0074            CALL  DISPLAY_IT
138 00D2 EB DA              JMP   NXTKEY           ; Keep reading and shifting keys
139                                                ; until command key pressed
140                  ;Compute total price
141 00D4 BB 0000r    COMPUTE: MOV BX,OFFSET WEIGHT_BUFFER; Point at weight buffer for pack
142 00D7 80 7F 03 14        CMP   BYTE PTR[BX+3], 14H  ; See if MSD of weight = 0
143 00DB 75 04              JNE   NOTZER
144 00DD C6 47 03 00        MOV   BYTE PTR[BX+3], 00   ; Yes, load 0 in place of blank code
145 00E1 E8 009B     NOTZER: CALL PACK             ; Pack BCD weight into word
```

FIGURE 10-25 (*Continued*)

```
146 00E4  E8 00D8              CALL      CONVERT2BIN          ; Convert to 16 bit binary in AX
147 00E7  A3 000Cr             MOV       BINARY_WEIGHT, AX    ;   and save
148 00EA  BB 0004r             MOV       BX, OFFSET SELL_PRICE ; Point at price per pound for pack
149 00ED  E8 008F              CALL      PACK                 ; Pack BCD price into AX for convert
150 00F0  E8 00CC              CALL      CONVERT2BIN          ; Convert price to 16-bit binary in AX
151 00F3  F7 26 000Cr          MUL       BINARY_WEIGHT        ; Price per pound in AX x binary weight
152                                                           ;  total price result in DX:AX
153 00F7  8B D8                MOV       BX, AX               ; Prepare for convert to BCD
154 00F9  E8 0104              CALL      BINCVT               ; Packed BCD price result in DX:BX
155                  ;Round off price to nearest cent and display
156 00FC  80 FB 49             CMP       BL, 49H              ; Carry set if BL >49H
157 00FF  B0 00                MOV       AL, 00               ; Clear AL, keep carry
158 0101  12 C7                ADC       AL, BH               ; Add any carry to next digit
159 0103  27                   DAA                            ; Keep in BCD format
160 0104  8A D8                MOV       BL, AL               ; Save lower two digits of price
161 0106  B0 00                MOV       AL, 00               ; Clear AL, save carry
162 0108  12 C2                ADC       AL, DL               ; Propagate carry to upper digits
163 010A  27                   DAA                            ; Keep in BCD form
164 010B  8A E0                MOV       AH, AL               ; Position upper digits for EXPAND
165 010D  8A C3                MOV       AL, BL               ; Position lower digits for EXPAND
166 010F  BB 0008r             MOV       BX, OFFSET PRICE_TOTAL ; Point at buffer for expanded BCD
167 0112  E8 0084              CALL      EXPAND               ; Unpack BCD for DISPLAY_IT procedure
168 0115  B0 00                MOV       AL, 00               ; Display total price on data field
169 0117  B4 01                MOV       AH, 01               ;  with decimal point
170 0119  E8 002A              CALL      DISPLAY_IT
171 011C  BB 0016r             MOV       BX, OFFSET PR        ; Point at price/lb string
172 011F  B0 01                MOV       AL, 01               ; Display in address field
173 0121  B4 00                MOV       AH, 00               ; without decimal point
174 0123  E8 0020              CALL      DISPLAY_IT
175                  ;Delay a few seconds
176 0126  B9 FFFF              MOV       CX,0FFFFH            ; Delay a few seconds
177 0129  BB 000A      CNTDN1: MOV       BX, 000AH
178 012C  4B          CNTDN2:  DEC       BX
179 012D  75 FD                JNZ       CNTDN2
180 012F  E2 F8                LOOP      CNTDN1
181                  ;Go read next weight
182 0131  E9 FEE5              JMP       RDWT                 ; Jump back to dumb scale
183
184                  ;============== PROCEDURES USED IN SMART SCALE PROGRAM ====================
185
186                  ;====================== PROCEDURE READ_KEY ===============================
187                  ;ABSTRACT  :Reads the SDK-86 keyboard - polls the status register of the
188                  ;           8279 on the SDK-86 board until it finds a key pressed. It then
189                  ;           reads the keypressed code from the FIFO RAM to AL and exits
190                  ;REGISTERS: Destroys AL - returns with character read in AL
191
192 0134            READ_KEY PROC  NEAR
193 0134  52                   PUSH      DX
194 0135  BA FFEA              MOV       DX, 0FFEAH           ; Point at 8279 control address
195 0138  EC          NO_KEY:  IN        AL, DX               ; Get FIFO status
196 0139  24 01                AND       AL, 00000001B        ; Mask all but LSB, high if key in FIFO
197 013B  74 FB                JZ        NO_KEY               ; Loop until a key is pressed
198 013D  B0 40                MOV       AL, 01000000B        ; Control word for read FIFO
199 013F  EE                   OUT       DX, AL               ; Send control word
200 0140  BA FFE8              MOV       DX, 0FFE8H           ; Point at 8279 data address
201 0143  EC                   IN        AL, DX               ; Read character in FIFO ram
202 0144  5A                   POP       DX
203 0145  C3                   RET
204 0146            READ_KEY ENDP
205
206                  ;==================== PROCEDURE DISPLAY_IT =============================
207                  ;ABSTRACT: Displays characters on the SDK-86 display. The data is sent to
208                  ;INPUT   : AL=0 for data field
209                  ;           AL=1 for address field
210                  ;           AH=0 for no decimal point
211                  ;           AH=1 for decimal point between second & third digit
212                  ;           BX= offset of buffer containing 7-seg codes of the four
213                  ;               characters to be displayed
214 0146            DISPLAY_IT PROC  NEAR
215 0146  9C                   PUSHF                          ; Save flags and registers
216 0147  50                   PUSH      AX
217 0148  53                   PUSH      BX
218 0149  51                   PUSH      CX
```

FIGURE 10-25 (*Continued*)

```
219 014A  52                       PUSH DX
220 014B  56                       PUSH SI
221 014C  BA FFEA                  MOV  DX, OFFEAH        ; Point at 8279 control address
222 014F  3C 00                    CMP  AL, 00H           ; See if data field required
223 0151  74 05                    JZ   DATFLD            ; Yes, load control word for data field
224 0153  B0 94                    MOV  AL, 94H           ; No, load address-field control word
225 0155  EB 03 90                 JMP  SEND              ; Go send control word
226 0158  B0 90            DATFLD:  MOV  AL, 90H           ; Load control word for data field
227 015A  EE              SEND:    OUT  DX, AL            ; Send control word to 8279
228 015B  B1 04                    MOV  CL, 04H           ; Counter for number of characters
229 015D  8B F3                    MOV  SI, BX            ; Free BX for use with XLAT
230 015F  BB 001Ar                 MOV  BX, OFFSET SEVEN_SEG  ; Pointer to seven-segment codes
231 0162  BA FFE8                  MOV  DX, OFFE8H        ; Point at 8279 display RAM
232 0165  8A 04            AGAIN:   MOV  AL, [SI]          ; Get character to be displayed
233 0168  D7                       XLATB                  ; Translate to 7-seg code
234 0168  80 F9 02                 CMP  CL, 02H           ; See if digit that gets decimal point
235 016B  75 07                    JNE  MORE              ; No, go send digit
236 016D  80 FC 01                 CMP  AH, 01H           ; Yes, see if decimal point specified
237 0170  75 02                    JNE  MORE              ; No, go send character
238 0172  0C 80                    OR   AL, 80H           ; Yes, OR in decimal point
239 0174  EE              MORE:    OUT  DX, AL            ; Send 7-seg code to 8279 display RAM
240 0175  46                       INC  SI                ; Point to next character
241 0176  E2 ED                    LOOP AGAIN             ; until all four characters sent
242 0178  5E                       POP  SI
243 0179  5A                       POP  DX                ; Restore all registers and flags
244 017A  59                       POP  CX
245 017B  5B                       POP  BX
246 017C  58                       POP  AX
247 017D  9D                       POPF
248 017E  C3                       RET
249 017F          DISPLAY_IT ENDP
250
251              ;========================= PROCEDURE PACK ===============================
252              ;ABSTRACT: Converts four unpacked BCD digits pointed to by BX to
253              ;          four packed BCD digits in AX
254              ;DESTROYS: AX
255
256 017F          PACK     PROC NEAR
257 017F  9C               PUSHF                          ; Save flags and registers
258 0180  53               PUSH BX
259 0181  51               PUSH CX
260 0182  8A 07            MOV  AL, [BX]                  ; First BCD digit to AL
261 0184  B1 04            MOV  CL, 04H                   ; Counter for rotate
262 0186  D2 47 01         ROL  BYTE PTR[BX+1], CL        ; Position second BCD digit
263 0189  02 47 01         ADD  AL, [BX+1]                ; First 2 digits in AL
264 018C  8A 67 02         MOV  AH, [BX+2]                ; Third digit to AH
265 018F  D2 47 03         ROL  BYTE PTR[BX+3], CL        ; Position fourth digit
266 0192  02 67 03         ADD  AH, [BX+3]                ; Second two digits now in AH
267 0195  5B               POP  BX
268 0196  59               POP  CX
269 0197  9D               POPF
270 0198  C3               RET
271 0199          PACK     ENDP
272
273              ;============================ PROCEDURE EXPAND ========================
274              ;ABSTRACT: Expands a packed BCD number in AX to 4 unpacked BCD
275              ;          digits in a buffer pointed to by BX
276
277 0199          EXPAND   PROC NEAR
278 0199  9C               PUSHF
279 019A  50               PUSH AX
280 019B  53               PUSH BX
281 019C  51               PUSH CX
282 019D  88 07            MOV  [BX],AL                   ; Move first 2 BCD digits to buffer
283 019F  80 27 0F         AND  BYTE PTR[BX],0FH          ; Mask off upper digit
284 01A2  B1 04            MOV  CL, 04H                   ; Counter for rotates
285 01A4  D2 C8            ROR  AL, CL                    ; Position digit 2 in low nibble
286 01A6  24 0F            AND  AL, 0FH                   ; Mask upper nibble
287 01A8  88 47 01         MOV  [BX+1], AL                ; Digit 2 to buffer
288 01AB  88 67 02         MOV  [BX+2], AH                ; Second 2 BCD digits to buffer
289 01AE  80 67 02 0F      AND  BYTE PTR[BX+2],0FH        ; Mask off upper digit
290 01B2  D2 CC            ROR  AH, CL                    ; Position digit 4 in low nibble
291 01B4  80 E4 0F         AND  AH, 0FH                   ; Mask upper nibble
```

FIGURE 10-25 (*Continued*)

```
292  01B7  88 67 03            MOV    [BX+3], AH                    ; Digit 4 to buffer
293  01BA  59                  POP    CX
294  01BB  5B                  POP    BX
295  01BC  58                  POP    AX
296  01BD  9D                  POPF
297  01BE  C3                  RET
298  01BF              EXPAND  ENDP
299
300                    ;========================= PROCEDURE CONVERT2BIN =========================
301                    ;ABSTRACT: Converts a 4 digit BCD number in AX register into its binary
302                    ;          (HEX) equivalent. It returns the result in the AX register
303                    ;DESTROYS: AX register
304
305       = 03E8          THOU EQU   3E8H                            ; 1000 = 3E8H
306  01BF          CONVERT2BIN    PROC NEAR
307  01BF  9C                  PUSHF                                 ; Save flags and registers
308  01C0  53                  PUSH   BX
309  01C1  52                  PUSH   DX
310  01C2  51                  PUSH   CX
311  01C3  57                  PUSH   DI
312  01C4  8B D8               MOV    BX, AX                        ; Copy number into BX
313  01C6  8A C4               MOV    AL, AH                        ; Place for upper 2 digits
314  01C8  8A FB               MOV    BH, BL                        ; Place for lower 2 digits
315                    ;Split up numbers so that we have one digit in each register
316  01CA  B1 04               MOV    CL, 04                        ; Nibble count for rotate
317  01CC  D2 CC               ROR    AH, CL                        ; Digit 1 in correct place
318  01CE  D2 CF               ROR    BH, CL                        ; Digit 3 in correct place
319  01D0  25 0F0F             AND    AX, 0F0FH
320  01D3  81 E3 0F0F          AND    BX, 0F0FH                     ; Mask upper nibbles of each digit
321                    ;Copy AX into CX so that can use AX for multiplication
322  01D7  8B C8               MOV    CX, AX
323  01D9  B8 0000             MOV    AX, 0000H
324                    ;Now multiply each number by its place value
325  01DC  8A C5               MOV    AL, CH                        ; Multiply byte in AL * word
326  01DE  BF 03E8             MOV    DI, THOU                      ; No immediate multiplication
327  01E1  F7 E7               MUL    DI                            ; Digit 1 * 1000
328                    ;Result in DX and AX. Because BCD digit not >9 result in AX only
329                    ;Zero DX and add BL because that digit needs no multiplication for
330                    ;place value. Then add the result in AX for digit 4
331  01E3  BA 0000             MOV    DX, 0000H
332  01E6  02 D3               ADD    DL, BL                        ; Add digit 1
333  01E8  03 D0               ADD    DX, AX                        ; Add digit 4
334                    ;Continue with multiplications
335  01EA  B8 0064             MOV    AX, 0064H                     ; Byte * byte result in AX
336  01ED  F6 E1               MUL    CL                            ; Digit 2 * 100
337  01EF  03 D0               ADD    DX, AX                        ; Add digit 3
338  01F1  B8 000A             MOV    AX, 000AH                     ; Byte * byte result in AX
339  01F4  F6 E7               MUL    BH
340  01F6  03 D0               ADD    DX, AX                        ; Add digit 2
341  01F8  8B C2               MOV    AX, DX                        ; Put result in correct place
342  01FA  5F                  POP    DI
343  01FB  59                  POP    CX
344  01FC  5A                  POP    DX                            ; Restore registers
345  01FD  5B                  POP    BX
346  01FE  9D                  POPF
347  01FF  C3                  RET
348  0200          CONVERT2BIN    ENDP
349
350                    ;========================= PROCEDURE BINCVT =========================
351                    ;ABSTRACT: Converts a 24-bit binary number in DL and BX to a packed
352                    ;          BCD equivalent in DX:BX
353                    ;INPUTS:   DL, BX - 24 BIT BINARY NUMBER
354                    ;OUTPUTS:  DX, BX - PACKED BCD RESULT
355                    ;CALLS:    CNVT1
356                    ;DESTROYS: DX and BX
357
358  0200          BINCVT  PROC NEAR
359  0200  9C                  PUSHF                                 ; Save registers and flags
360  0201  50                  PUSH   AX
361  0202  51                  PUSH   CX
362  0203  B6 19               MOV    DH, 19H                       ; Bit counter for 24 bits
363  0205  E8 001B             CALL   CNVT1                         ; Produce 2 LS BCD digits in CH
364  0208  8A CD               MOV    CL, CH                        ; Save in CL
```

FIGURE 10-25 (*Continued*)

```
365 020A  B6 19              MOV    DH, 19H          ; Bit counter for 24 BITS
366 020C  E8 0014            CALL   CNVT1            ; Produce next 2 BCD digits in CH
367 020F  51                 PUSH   CX               ; Save lower 4 BCD digits on stack
368 0210  B6 19              MOV    DH, 19H          ; Bit counter for 24 bits
369 0212  E8 000C            CALL   CNVT1            ; Produce next 2 BCD digits in CH
370 0215  8A CD              MOV    CL, CH           ; Position in CL
371 0217  B6 19              MOV    DH,19H           ; Set bit counter for 24 bits
372 0219  E8 0007            CALL   CNVT1            ; Produce last 2 BCD digits in CH
373 021C  8B D1              MOV    DX,CX            ; Position 4 MS BCD DIGITS for return
374 021E  5B                 POP    BX               ; Four LS BCD digits back from stack
375 021F  59                 POP    CX               ; for return
376 0220  58                 POP    AX
377 0221  9D                 POPF
378 0222  C3                 RET
379 0223         BINCVT      ENDP
380
381                          ;========================= PROCEDURE CNVT1 =============================
382 0223         CNVT1       PROC   NEAR
383 0223  32 C0              XOR    AL, AL           ; Clear AL and carry as workspace
384 0225  8A E8              MOV    CH, AL           ; Clear CH
385 0227  32 C0  CNVT2:      XOR    AL, AL           ; Clear AL and CARRY
386 0229  FE CE              DEC    DH               ; Decrement bit counter
387 022B  75 01              JNZ    CONTINUE         ; Do all bits
388 022D  C3                 RET                     ; Done if DH down to zero
389 022E  D1 D3  CONTINUE:RCL  BX, 1                 ; BX left one bit, MSB to carry
390 0230  D0 D2              RCL    DL, 1            ; MSB from BX to LSB of DL, MSB of DL to carry
391 0232  8A C5              MOV    AL, CH           ; Move BCD digit being built to AL
392 0234  12 C0              ADC    AL, AL           ; Double AL and add carry from DL shift
393 0236  27                 DAA                     ; Keep result in BCD form
394 0237  8A E8              MOV    CH, AL           ; Put back in CH for next time through
395 0239  73 EC              JNC    CNVT2            ; No carry from DAA, continue
396 023B  83 D3 00           ADC    BX, 0000H        ; If carry, propagate to BX and DL
397 023E  80 D2 00           ADC    DL, 00H          ;  for future terms
398 0241  EB E4              JMP    CNVT2            ; Continue conversion
399 0243         CNVT1       ENDP
400 0243         CODE        ENDS
401                          END
```

FIGURE 10-25 (*Continued*)

as this. If you use the 5-minute rule and work your way through this program one module at a time, you should pick up some more useful programming techniques and procedures you can use in your programs.

Three 4-byte buffers set up at the start of the program are used to store the unpacked BCD values of the weight, the price per pound, and the computed total price. These buffers will be used to pass values to the display procedure. The SEVEN_SEG table in the data segment contains the 7-segment codes for BCD digits, hex digits, and some letters we use to indicate which value is being displayed. In the display procedure you will see how these codes are accessed.

After initializing everything, the program polls the digit strobe for the most significant digit from the A/D converter. Since this A/D converter is a $3\frac{1}{2}$-digit unit, the MSD can be only a 0 or a 1. The value for this digit is sent in the third bit (bit 2) of the 4-bit digit read in. If this bit is a 1, then 01 is loaded into the buffer location. If the bit is a 0, then the value which will access the 7-segment code for a blank (14H) is loaded into the buffer location. Each of the other digit strobes is then polled in turn, and the values for those digits are read in. When all the BCD digits for the weight are in the WEIGHT_BUFFER, the display procedure is called to show the weight on the address field.

To use the display procedure we wrote for this program, you first load a 0 or a 1 into AL to specify data field or address field and a 1 or a 0 in AH to specify a decimal point in the middle of the display or no decimal point. You then load BX with the offset of the memory buffer containing the unpacked codes for the digits to be displayed. A program loop in the display procedure uses the XLAT instruction and the SEVEN_SEG table to convert these codes to the required 7-segment values and send the values to the 8279 display RAM. For displaying the weight, BX is simply loaded with the offset of WEIGHT_BUFFER, AL is loaded with 01 to display the weight in the address field, and AH is loaded with 01 to insert a decimal point at the appropriate place.

To display the letters Lb in the data field, BX is loaded with the offset of the string named LB, and the display procedure is called. Again, the XLAT instruction loop converts the codes from the LB string to the required 7-segment codes and sends them out of the 8279 display RAM. The codes in the string named LB represent the offsets from the start of the SEVEN_SEG table for the desired 7-segment codes. For example, the 7-segment code for a P is at offset 12H in the SEVEN_SEG table. Therefore, if you want to display a P, you put 12H in the appropriate location in the character string in memory. The XLAT instruction will then use the value 12H to access the 7-segment code for P in the SEVEN_SEG table.

After displaying the weight, the program reads the

8279 status register to see if the operator has pressed a number key to start entering a price per pound. If no key has been pressed or if a nonnumeric key has been pressed, the program simply goes back and reads the weight again. If a number key has been pressed, the weight is removed from the address field and the letters SP (selling price) are displayed in the address field. The entered number is put in the SELL_PRICE buffer and displayed on the rightmost digit of the data field. The program then polls the 8279 status register until another keypress is detected. If the pressed key is a numeric key, then the code(s) for the previously entered number(s) will be shifted one location in the buffer to make room for the new number. The new number is then put in the first location in the buffer so that it will be displayed in the rightmost digit of the display. In other words, previously entered numbers are continuously shifted to the left as new numbers are entered. If a mistake is made, the operator can simply enter a 0 followed by the correct price per pound.

When a nonnumeric key is pressed, this is the signal that the displayed price per pound is correct and that the total price should now be computed. Before the weight and the price per pound can be multiplied, however, they must each be put in packed BCD form and converted to binary.

The PACK procedure converts four unpacked BCD digits in a memory buffer pointed to by BX to a 4-digit packed result in AX. This procedure is simply some masking and moving of nibbles. Once the weight and price per pound are packed in BCD form, the CONVERT2BIN procedure is used to convert each to its binary equivalent. The algorithm for this procedure is explained in detail in Chapter 5.

Unlike earlier processors, which required a messy procedure for multiplication, a single 8086 MUL instruction does the 16 × 16 binary multiply to produce the binary equivalent of the total price. The procedure BINCVT is used to convert the binary total price to the packed BCD form needed for the DISPLAY_IT procedure. Here's how the BINCVT procedure works.

In a binary number, each bit position represents a power of 2. An 8-bit binary number, for example, can be represented as:

$$b7 \times 2^7 + b6 \times 2^6 + b5 \times 2^5 + b4 \times 2^4$$
$$+ b3 \times 2^3 + b2 \times 2^2 + b1 \times 2^1 + b0$$

This can be shuffled around and expressed as

Binary number
$$= ((((((2b7 + b6) 2 + b5) 2 + b4) 2 + b3) 2 + b2) 2 + b1) 2 + b0$$

where b7 through b0 are the values of the binary bits. If we start with a binary number and do each operation in the nested parentheses in BCD with the aid of the DAA instruction, the result will be the BCD number equivalent to the original binary number.

The procedure in Figure 10-25 produces two BCD digits of the result at a time by calling the subprocedure CNVT1. Figure 10-26 shows a flowchart for the operation

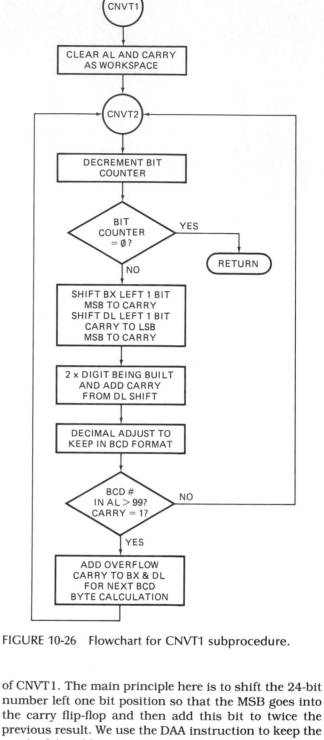

FIGURE 10-26   Flowchart for CNVT1 subprocedure.

of CNVT1. The main principle here is to shift the 24-bit number left one bit position so that the MSB goes into the carry flip-flop and then add this bit to twice the previous result. We use the DAA instruction to keep the result of the addition in BCD format. If the DAA produces a carry, we add this carry back into the shifted 24-bit number in DL and BX so that it will be propagated into higher BCD digits. After each run of CNVT1 (24 runs of CNVT2), DL and BX will be left with a binary number which is equal to the original binary number minus the value of the two BCD digits produced. You can adapt this procedure to work with a different number of bits by simply calling CNVT1 more or fewer times and by adjusting the count loaded into DH to be 1 more than the number of binary bits in the number to be converted.

The count has to be 1 greater because of the position of the decrement in the loop. The temperature-controller procedure in Figure 10-35 shows another example of this conversion.

The least significant two digits of the BCD value for the total price returned by BINCVT in BL represent tenths and hundredths of a cent. If the value of these two BCD digits is greater than 49H, then the carry produced by the compare instruction and the next two higher BCD digits in BH are added to AL. This must be done in AL, because the DAA instruction, used to keep the result in BCD format, only works on an operand in AL. Any carry from these two BCD digits is propagated on to the upper two digits of the result in DL. After this rounding off, the packed BCD for the total price is left in AX.

In order for the display procedure to be able to display this price, it must be converted to unpacked BCD form and put in four successive memory locations. Another "mask and move nibbles" procedure called EXPAND does this. The DISPLAY_IT procedure is then called to display the total price on the data field. The DISPLAY_IT procedure is called again to display the letters Pr in the address field.

Finally, after delaying a few seconds to give the operator time to read the price, execution returns to the "dumb-scale" portion of the program and starts over.

A question that may occur to you when reading a long program such as this is, How do you decide which parts of the program to keep in the mainline and which parts to write as procedures? There is no universal agreement on the answer to this question. The general guidelines we follow are to write a program section as a procedure if it is going to be used more than once in the program, it is reusable (could be used in other programs), it is so lengthy (more than 1 page) that it clutters up the conceptual flow of the main program, or it is an essentially independent section. The disadvantage of using too many procedures is the time and overhead required for each procedure call. As you write more programs, you will arrive at a balance that feels comfortable to you. The following section shows you another long program example which was written in a highly modular manner so that it can easily be expanded. This example should further help you see when and how to use procedures.

A MICROCOMPUTER-BASED INDUSTRIAL PROCESS-CONTROL SYSTEM

Overview of Industrial Process Control

One area in which microprocessors and microcomputers have had a major impact is *industrial process control.* Process control involves first measuring system variables such as motor speed, temperature, the flow of reactants, the level of a liquid in a tank, the thickness of a material, etc. The output of the controller then adjusts the value of each variable until it is equal to a predetermined value called a *set point.* The system controller must maintain each variable as close as possible to its set-point value, and it must compensate as quickly and accurately as

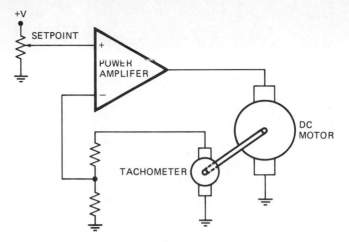

FIGURE 10-27   Circuit for controlling speed of dc motor using feedback from tachometer.

possible for any change in the variable caused by, for example, increased load on a motor. A simple example will show the traditional approach to control of a process variable and explain some of the terms used in control systems.

The circuit in Figure 10-27 shows an analog approach to controlling the speed of a dc motor. Attached to the shaft of the motor is a dc generator, or *tachometer,* which puts out a voltage proportional to the speed of the motor. The output voltage is typically a few volts per 1000 rpm. A fraction of the output voltage from the tachometer is fed back to the inverting input of the power amplifier driving the motor. A positive voltage is applied to the noninverting input of the amplifier as a set point. When the power is turned on, the motor accelerates until the voltage fed back from the tachometer to the inverting input of the amplifier is nearly equal to the set-point voltage.

If the load on the motor is increased, the motor will initially slow down, and the voltage output from the tachometer will decrease. This will increase the difference in voltage between the inputs of the amplifier and cause it to drive more current to the motor. The increased current will increase the speed of the motor to nearly the speed it had before the increased load was added. A similar reaction takes place if the load on the motor is decreased.

Using negative feedback to control a system such as this is often called *servo control.* A control loop of this type keeps the motor speed quite constant for applications where the load on the motor does not change much. Some hard-disk drive motors and high-quality phonograph turntables use this method of speed control.

For applications in which the load and/or the set point changes drastically, there are several potential problems. The first of these is overshoot when you change the set point. Figure 10-28a, p. 318, shows an example of this. In this case the variable—motor speed, for example—overshoots the new set point and bounces up and down for a while. The time it takes the bouncing to settle within a specified error range or error band is called the

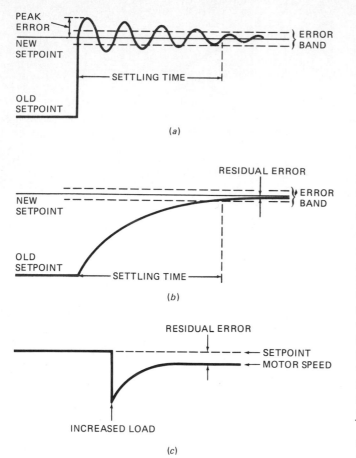

FIGURE 10-28   Overshoot and undershoot of system when set point or load is changed. (*a*) Overshoot. (*b*) Undershoot. (*c*) Load change.

settling time. This type of response is referred to as *underdamped* and is similar to the response that a car with bad shock absorbers will make when it hits a bump. The ringing can be prevented by adding damping to the system. However, if too much damping is added, the response to a change in set point may look like that shown in Figure 10-28*b*. This type response is referred to as an *overdamped response.* The difficulty with this type response is that it takes a long time for the variable to reach the new set point. For best performance, the damping must be custom designed for a particular system.

Another problem in any process control system is *residual error.* Figure 10-28*c* shows the response a control system such as the motor speed controller in Figure 10-27 will have when more load is added on the motor. The motor initially slows down, so the voltage out of the tachometer decreases. As we said before, this increases the voltage difference between the amplifier inputs and causes the amplifier output to increase. Increased amplifier output increases the speed of the motor and thereby the output from the tachometer. When the system reaches equilibrium, however, there is some noticeable difference between the set point and the voltage fed back from the tachometer. It is this difference or residual error which is amplified by the

gain of the amplifier to produce the additional drive for the motor. For stability reasons, the gain of many control systems cannot be too high. Therefore, even if you adjust the speed of a motor, for example, to be exactly at a given speed for one load, when you change the load there will always be some residual error between the set point and the actual output.

To help solve these problems, circuits with more complex feedback are used. Figure 10-29 shows a circuit which represents the different types of feedback commonly used. First note in this circuit that the output power amplifier is an adder with four inputs. The current supplied to the summing point of the adder by the set-point input produces the basic output drive current. The other three inputs do not supply any current unless there is a difference between the set point and the feedback voltage from the tachometer. Amplifier 1 is another adder whose function is to compare the set-point voltage with the feedback voltage from the tachometer. Let's assume the two input resistors, R1 and R2, are equal. Since the set-point voltage is negative and the voltage from the tachometer is positive, there will be no net current through the feedback resistor of the amplifier if the two voltages are equal in magnitude. In other words, if the speed of the motor is at its set-point value, the output of amplifier 1 will be zero, and amplifiers 2, 3, and 4 will contribute no current to the summing junction of the power amp.

Now, suppose that you add more load on the motor, slowing it down. The tachometer voltage is no longer equal to the set-point voltage, so amplifier 1 now has some output. This error signal on the output produces three types of feedback to the summing junction of the power amp.

Amplifier 1 produces simple dc feedback proportional to the difference between the set point and the tachometer output. This is exactly the same effect as the voltage divider on the tachometer output in Figure 10-27. *Proportional feedback*, as this is called, will correct for most of the effect of the increased load, but, as we discussed before, there will always be some residual error.

The cure for residual error is to use some *integral feedback.* Amplifier 3 in Figure 10-29 provides this type of feedback. Remember from a previous discussion that this circuit produces a ramp on its output whenever a voltage is applied to its input. For the example here, the integrator will ramp up or ramp down as long as there is any error signal present on its input. By ramping up and down just a tiny bit about the set point, the integrator can eliminate most of the residual error. Too much integral feedback, however, will cause the output to oscillate up and down. Also, feedback only slowly affects the output because the error signal must be present for some time before the integrator has much output.

To improve the response time of the system, amplifier 4 in Figure 10-29 supplies a third type of feedback called *derivative feedback.* Derivative feedback is a signal proportional to the rate of change of the error signal. If the load on the system is suddenly changed, the derivative amplifier circuit will give a quick shot of feedback

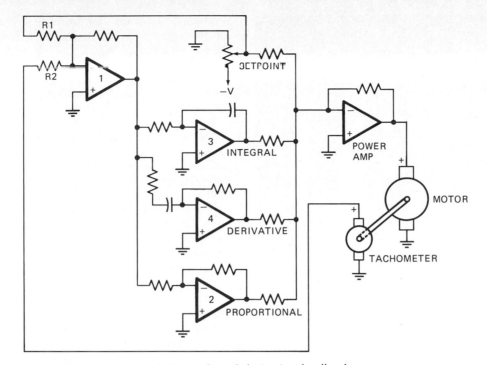

FIGURE 10-29   Circuit showing proportional, integral, and derivative feedback control.

to try to correct the error. When the error signal is first applied to the differentiator circuit, the capacitor in series with the input is not charged, so it acts like a short circuit. This initially lets a large current flow, so the amplifier has a sizable output. As the capacitor charges, the current decreases, so the feedback from the differentiator decreases. The differentiator essentially gives the amplifier a quick pulse of feedback to help correct for the increased load. Too much derivative feedback can cause the system to overshoot and oscillate.

The point here is that by using a combination of some or all of these types of feedback, a given feedback-controlled system can be adjusted for optimum response to changes in load or set point. Process control loops that use all three types of feedback are called *proportional integral derivative* or PID control loops. Because process variables change much more slowly than the microsecond operation of a microcomputer, a microcomputer with some simple input and output circuitry can perform all the functions of the analog circuitry in Figure 10-29 for several PID loops.

Figure 10-30 shows a block diagram of a microcomputer-based process-control system. Data acquisition systems convert the analog signals from various sensors to digital values that can be read in and processed by the microcomputer. A keyboard and display in the

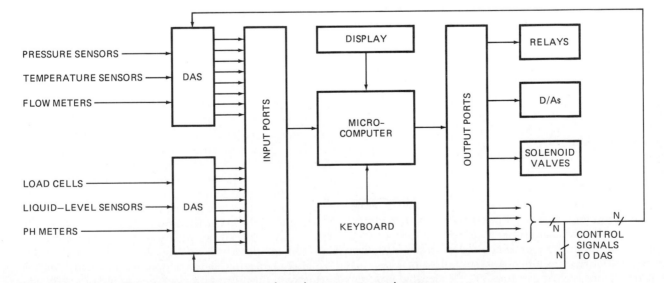

FIGURE 10-30   Block diagram of microcomputer-based process control system.

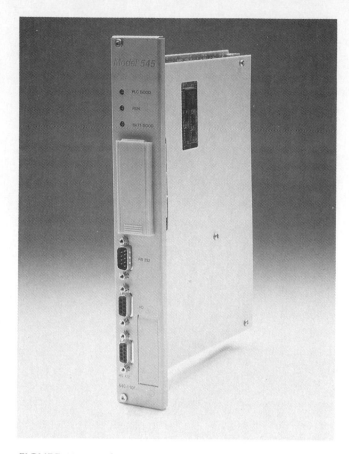

FIGURE 10-31 Photograph of Texas Instruments' programmable controller.

keyboard or a clock "tick" from the timer. The keyboard strobe signal and the clock signal are each connected to interrupt inputs.

When the microcomputer receives an interrupt from the timer, it goes to a procedure which determines whether it is time to service the next control loop. The interrupt procedure does this by counting interrupts in the same way as the real-time clock we described in Chapter 8 does. If you program the timer to produce a pulse every 1 ms, and you want the controller to service another loop every 20 ms, for example, you can simply have the interrupt procedure count 20 interrupts before going on to update the next loop. Once 20 interrupts have been counted down, the program falls into a decision structure which determines which loop is to be updated next. Every 20 ms a new loop is updated, so with eight loops, each loop gets updated every 160 ms. This system is an example of a *time-slice* system, because each loop gets a 20-ms "slice" of time every 160 ms.

An important point here is that the microcomputer services each loop at regular intervals instead of simply updating all eight loops, one loop right after another. This is done so that the timing for each loop is independent of the timing for the other loops. Therefore, a change in the internal timing for one loop will not affect the timing in the other loops.

Each PID loop is controlled by an independent procedure. For our example system here, we have space to show the implementation of only one loop, the control of the temperature of a tank of liquid in, perhaps, our printed-circuit-board-making machine. You could write other similar control-loop procedures to control pH, flow, light exposure timing, motor speed, etc.

Figure 10-32c shows the flowchart for our temperature-controller PID loop. Note that we use lower-level procedures to implement most steps in the basic PID procedure. These low-level operations are written as procedures so that they can be used in other PID loops. Also, using procedures here maintains the top-down program structure we have been trying to get you to use in your programs. Work your way through Figure 10-32 until you clearly see the program levels. After we look at the hardware of the system, we will dig into the details of the actual program.

system allow the user to enter set-point values, to read the current values of process variables, and to issue commands. Relays, D/A converters, solenoid valves, and other actuators are used to control process variables under program direction. A programmable timer in the system determines the rate at which control loops are serviced.

Microcomputer-based process-control systems range from a small programmable controller such as the one shown in Figure 10-31, which might be used to control a machine on a factory floor, to a large minicomputer used to control an entire fractionating column in an oil refinery. To show you how these microcomputer-based control systems work, here's an example system you can build and experiment with.

AN 8086-BASED
PROCESS-CONTROL SYSTEM

Program Overview

Figure 10-32 shows in flowchart form one way in which the program for a microcomputer-based control system with eight PID loops can be structured. After power is turned on, a mainline or *executive program* initializes ports, initializes the timer, and initializes process variables to some starting values. The executive program then sits in a loop waiting for a user command from the

Hardware for Control Systems and Temperature Controller

To build the hardware for this project, we started by adding an 8254 programmable timer and an 8259A priority interrupt controller to an SDK-86 board, as shown in Figure 8-14. The timer is initialized to produce 1-kHz clock ticks. The 8259A provides interrupt inputs for the clock-tick interrupts and for keyboard interrupts. We built the actual temperature sensing and detecting circuitry on a separate prototyping board and connected it to some ports on the SDK-86 with a ribbon cable. Figure 10-33, p. 322, shows this analog interface circuitry.

The temperature-sensing element in the circuit is an LM35 precision Celsius temperature sensor. The voltage between the output pin and the ground pin of this device will be 0 V at 0° C and will increase by 10 mV for

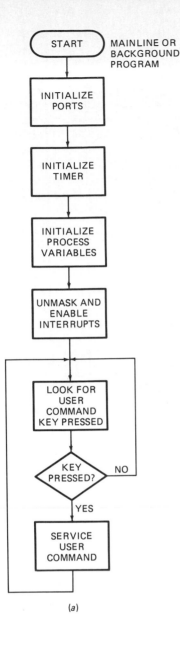

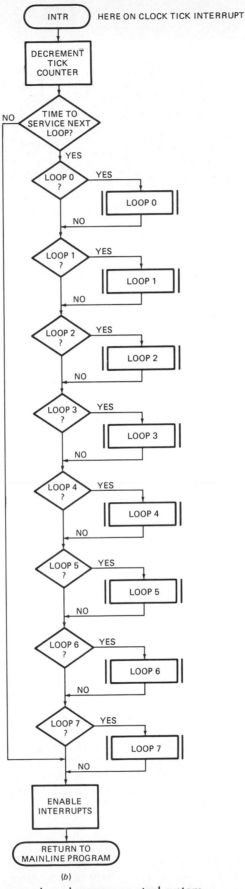

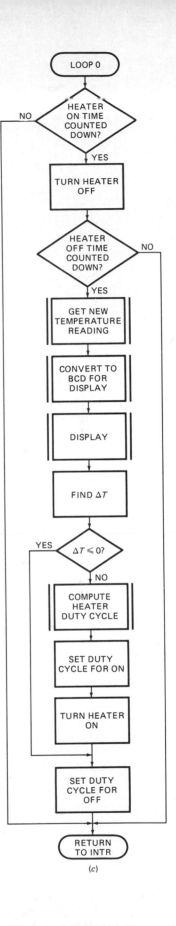

FIGURE 10-32 Flowchart for microcomputer-based process control system.
(a) Mainline or executive. (b) Loop selector. (c) Temperature-control loop.

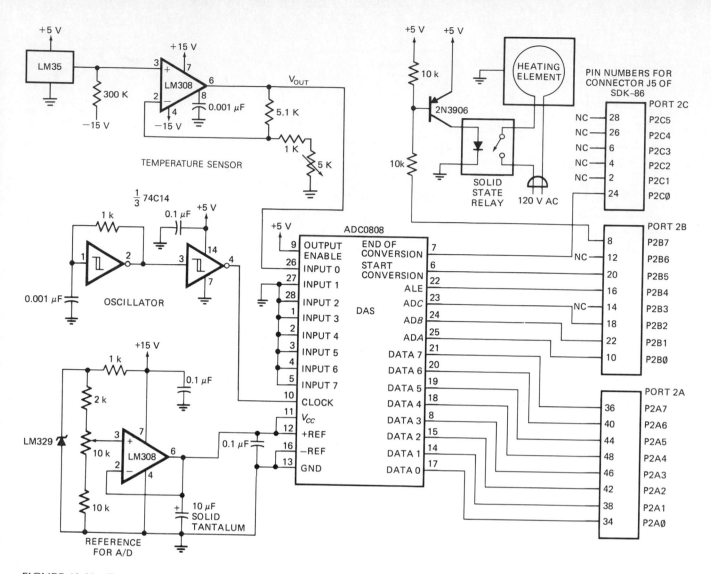

FIGURE 10-33   Temperature-sensing and heater-control circuitry for microcomputer-based controller.

each increase of 1° C above that. The 300-kΩ resistor connecting the output of the LM35 to − 15 V allows the output to go negative for temperatures below 0° C. (If you are operating with ±12-V supplies, use a 240-kΩ resistor.) This makes the circuit able to measure temperatures over the range of − 55 to + 150° C. For our application here, we use only the positive part of the output range, but we thought you might find this circuit useful for some of your other projects. An LM308 buffers and amplifies the signal from the sensor by 2 so that the signal uses a greater part of the input range of the A/D converter. This improves the noise immunity and resolution.

The ADC0808 A/D converter used here is an 8-input *data acquisition system*. You tell the device which input signal you want digitized with a 3-bit address you send to the ADC, ADB, and ADA inputs. This 8-input device was chosen so that other control loops could be added later. Some Schmitt-trigger inverters in a 74C14 are connected as an oscillator to produce a 300-kHz clock for the DAS. The voltage drop across an LM329 low-drift

zener is buffered by an LM308 amplifier to produce a V_{CC} and a V_{REF} of 5.12 V for the A/D converter. With this reference voltage, the A/D converter will have 256 steps of 20 mV each. Since the temperature sensor signal is amplified by 2, each degree Celsius of temperature change will produce an output change of 20 mV, or one step on the A/D converter. This gives us a resolution of 1° C, which is about equal to the typical accuracy of the sensor. The advantage of using V_{REF} as the V_{CC} for the device is that this voltage will not have the switching noise that the digital V_{CC} line has. The control inputs and data outputs of the A/D converter are simply connected to SDK-86 ports as shown.

Figure 10-34 shows the timing waveforms and parameters for the ADC0808. Note the sequence in which control signals must be sent to the device. The 3-bit address of the desired input channel is first sent to the multiplexer inputs. After at least 50 ns, the ALE input is sent high. After another 2.5μs, the START CONVERSION input is sent high and then low. Then the ALE input is brought low again. When the END OF CONVER-

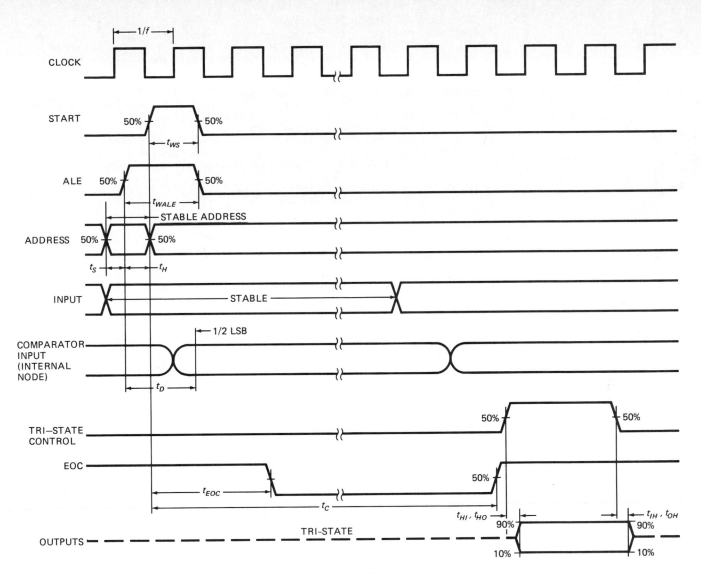

FIGURE 10-34 Timing waveforms for the ADC0808 data acquisition system.

SION signal from the A/D converter is found to be high, the 8-bit data value which represents the temperature can be read in.

To control the power delivered to the heater, we used a 25-A, 0-V turn-on, solid-state relay, such as the Potter Brumfield unit described in Chapter 9. With this relay we can control a 120- or 240-V ac-powered hot plate or immersion heater. To control the amount of heat put out by the heater, we vary the duty cycle of pulses sent to the relay.

For very low power applications, a D/A converter and a power amplifier could be used to drive the heater. However, in high-power applications this is not very practical because the power amplifier may dissipate as much or more power than the load. For example, an amplifier intended to control a 5000-W heater over its full range must be able to dissipate more than 5000 W. The D/A-converter approach has the added disadvantage that it cannot directly use the available ac line voltage.

The driver transistor on the input of the solid-state relay supplies the drive for the relay, isolates the port

pin from the relay, and holds the relay in the off position when the power is first turned on. Port pins, remember, are in a floating state after a reset, so some method must be used to hold external circuitry in a known state until the port is initialized and the desired value is output to the port. Now that you know how the hardware is connected, we can explain the operation of the controller program.

The Controller System Program

THE MAINLINE OR EXECUTIVE SECTION

Figure 10-35, pp. 324–29, shows the assembly language program for our controller system. Refer to the flowchart in Figure 10-32 as you work your way through this program. The mainline or executive part of the program starts by initializing port FFFAH for output, the 8259A to receive interrupt inputs from the timer and the keyboard, and the 8254 to produce a 1-kHz square wave on its counter 0 output. In Chapter 8 we described all

```
1                    ;8086 MAINLINE PROGRAM F10-35a.ASM       -    MODULE 1
2                    ;ABSTRACT: Program for controller system. Services eight process
3                    ;          control loops on a rotating basis. Program written to run on an
4                    ;          Intel SDK-86 board. Timing for the control loops is generated on
5                    ;          an interrupt basis by an on-board 8254 timer. Control-loop 0 in
6                    ;          the program controls the temperature of a water bath.
7                    ;PORTS:    Uses port P2B (FFFAH) as output
8                    ;          bits 7 = heater, bits 6,3 = not connected, bit 5 = start conversion
9                    ;          bit 4 = ALE,    bits 2,1,0 = channel address
10                   ;          Uses port P2A (FFF8H) as data input
11                   ;          Uses port P2C (FFFCH) as end-of-conversion input from A/D
12                   ;PROCEDURES: Uses CLOCK_TICK - interrupt service procedure
13                   ;            KEYBOARD   - interrupt service procedure (empty)
14
15 0000             INT_PROC   SEGMENT WORD      PUBLIC
16                       EXTRN  CLOCK_TICK:FAR, KEYBOARD:FAR
17 0000             INT_PROC   ENDS
18
19                   PUBLIC    COUNTER, TIMEHI, TIMELO, LOOPNUM, CURTEMP, SETPOINT
20
21 0000             AINT_TABLE    SEGMENT   WORD     PUBLIC
22 0000 02*(0000)       TYPE_64   DW     2 DUP(0)    ;Reserve space for clock-tick proc addr IR0
23 0004 02*(0000)       TYPE_65   DW     2 DUP(0)    ;Not used in this program - IR1
24 0008 02*(0000)       TYPE_66   DW     2 DUP(0)    ;Reserve space for keyboard proc addr - IR2
25 000C             AINT_TABLE    ENDS
26
27 0000             DATA SEGMENT   WORD  PUBLIC
28 0000 00              COUNTER   DB     00          ;Counter for number of interrupts
29 0001 01              TIMEHI    DB     01          ;Heater relay - time on
30 0002 01              TIMELO    DB     01          ;Heater relay - time off
31 0003 00              LOOPNUM   DB     00          ;Temp storage for loop counter
32 0004 00              CURTEMP   DB     00          ;Current temperature
33 0005 3C              SETPOINT  DB     60          ;Setpoint temperature
34 0006             DATA ENDS
35
36 0000             STACK_SEG  SEGMENT                ;No STACK directive because using EXE2BIN
37 0000 28*(0000)              DW 40      DUP(0)      ;so can then download code to SDK-86
38                       TOP_STACK LABEL     WORD
39 0050             STACK_SEG ENDS
40
41 0000             CODE SEGMENT WORD  PUBLIC
42                       ASSUME CS:CODE, DS:AINT_TABLE, SS:STACK_SEG
43                   ;Initialize stack segment, stack pointer, and data segment registers
44 0000 B8 0000s         MOV    AX, STACK_SEG
45 0003 8E D0            MOV    SS, AX
46 0005 BC 0050r         MOV    SP, OFFSET TOP_STACK
47 0008 B8 0000s         MOV    AX, AINT_TABLE
48 000B 8E D8            MOV    DS, AX
49                   ;Define the addresses for the interrupt service procedures
50 000D C7 06 0002r 0000s    MOV    TYPE_64+2, SEG CLOCK_TICK    ;Put in clock-tick proc addr
51 0013 C7 06 0000r 0000e    MOV    TYPE_64,   OFFSET CLOCK_TICK
52 0019 C7 06 000Ar 0000s    MOV    TYPE_66+2, SEG KEYBOARD      ;Put in keyboard proc addr
53 001F C7 06 0008r 0000e    MOV    TYPE_66,   OFFSET KEYBOARD
54                   ;Initialize data segment register
55                       ASSUME DS:DATA
56 0025 B8 0000s         MOV    AX, DATA
57 0028 8E D8            MOV    DS, AX
58                   ;Initialize port P2B (FFFA) as output - mode 0, P2A & P2C as inputs - mode 0
59 002A BA FFFE          MOV    DX, 0FFFEH              ;Point DX at port control addr
60 002D B0 99            MOV    AL, 10011001B           ;Mode control word for above conditions
61 002F EE               OUT    DX, AL                  ;Send control word
62                   ;Initialize 8259A, edge triggered, single, ICW4
63 0030 B0 13            MOV    AL, 00010011B
64 0032 BA FF00          MOV    DX, 0FF00H              ;Point at 8259A control
65 0035 EE               OUT    DX, AL                  ;Send ICW1
66 0036 B0 40            MOV    AL, 01000000B           ;Type 64 is first 8259A type (IR0)
67 0038 BA FF02          MOV    DX, 0FF02H              ;Point at ICW2 address
68 003B EE               OUT    DX, AL                  ;and send ICW2
69 003C B0 01            MOV    AL, 00000001B           ;ICW4, 8086 mode
70 003E EE               OUT    DX, AL                  ;Send ICW4
71 003F B0 FE            MOV    AL, 11111110B           ;OCW1 to unmask IR0 only leave IR2 masked
72 0041 EE               OUT    DX, AL                  ;because not used & send OCW1
```

FIGURE 10-35 8086 assembly language program for process control system (*continued on pp. 325–29*).
(a, pp. 324–5) Module 1—mainline. (b, pp. 325–6) Module 2—interrupt-service procedures.
(c, pp. 326–7) Module 3—loop service procedures. (d, pp. 327–29) Module 4—utility procedures.

```
73                                   ;Initialize 8254 counter 0 for 1-kHz output, LSB then MSB, square wave, BCD
74 0042  B0 37                       MOV     AL, 00110111B
75 0044  BA FF07                     MOV     DX, 0FF07H              ;Point 8254 control addr
76 0047  EE                          OUT     DX, AL                  ;Send counter 0 command word
77 0048  B0 58                       MOV     AL, 58H                 ;Load LSB of count
78 004A  BA FF01                     MOV     DX, 0FF01H              ;Point at counter 0 data addr
79 004D  EE                          OUT     DX, AL                  ;Send LSB of count
80 004E  B0 24                       MOV     AL, 24H                 ;Load MSB of count
81 0050  EE                          OUT     DX, AL                  ;Send MSB of count
82                                   ;Initialize variables
83 0051  C6 06 0005r 3C              MOV     SETPOINT, 3CH           ;Initialize final temp at 60°
84 0056  C6 06 0000r 14              MOV     COUNTER, 14H            ;Intialize time counter
85 005B  C6 06 0003r 00              MOV     LOOPNUM, 00H            ;Start at first loop
86 0060  C6 06 0001r 01              MOV     TIMEHI, 01H
87 0065  C6 06 0002r 01              MOV     TIMELO, 01H
88 006A  C6 06 0004r 00              MOV     CURTEMP, 00H
89                                   ;Enable interrupt input of 8086
90 006F  FB                          STI
91 0070  EB FE                HERE:JMP   HERE                       ; Wait for interrupt, if required,
92 0072  90                          NOP                             ; can put more instructions here
93 0073                       CODE ENDS
94                                   END
```

(a)

```
 1                                   ;8086 MODULE 2 PROCEDURES: F10-35B.ASM
 2                                   ;ABSTRACT: Module 2 contains the interrupt service subroutines for Module 1.
 3
 4                                   PUBLIC CLOCK_TICK, KEYBOARD
 5
 6 0000                       DATA SEGMENT   WORD    PUBLIC       ;Tell assembler where to find
 7 0000  00000000se           LOOP_ADDR_TABLE DD     LOOP0        ;loop addresses used in this module
 8 0004  00000000se                          DD     LOOP1
 9 0008  00000000se                          DD     LOOP2
10 000C  00000000se                          DD     LOOP3
11 0010  00000000se                          DD     LOOP4
12 0014  00000000se                          DD     LOOP5
13 0018  00000000se                          DD     LOOP6
14 001C  00000000se                          DD     LOOP7
15                           EXTRN      COUNTER:BYTE, LOOPNUM:BYTE
16 0020                       DATA ENDS
17
18                           ;Tell assembler where to find procedures used in this module
19 0000                       CODE SEGMENT WORD PUBLIC
20                           EXTRN      LOOP0:FAR, LOOP1:FAR, LOOP2:FAR, LOOP3:FAR
21                           EXTRN      LOOP4:FAR, LOOP5:FAR, LOOP6:FAR, LOOP7:FAR
22 0000                       CODE ENDS
23
24 0000                       INT_PROC SEGMENT WORD PUBLIC        ;Segment for interrupt service procedures
25                             ASSUME  CS:INT_PROC, DS:DATA
26
27                           ;8086 INTERRUPT PROCEDURE CALLED CLOCK_TICK
28                           ;ABSTRACT:   Services process control loops. Calls 1 of 8 process
29                           ;             control loops on a rotating basis.
30                           ;PORTS USED: None
31                           ;PROCEDURES: Calls LOOP0,LOOP1,LOOP2,LOOP3,LOOP4,LOOP5,LOOP6,LOOP7
32                           ;REGISTERS : Saves all
33
34 0000                       CLOCK_TICK PROC      FAR
35 0000  50                          PUSH    AX                      ;Save registers
36 0001  53                          PUSH    BX
37 0002  52                          PUSH    DX
38 0003  1E                          PUSH    DS                      ;Save DS of interrupted program
39 0004  FB                          STI                             ;Enable higher interrupts if any
40 0005  B0 20                       MOV     AL, 00100000B           ;OCW2 for nonspecific EOI
41 0007  BA FF00                     MOV     DX, 0FF00H              ;Load address for OCW2
42 000A  EE                          OUT     DX, AL
43 000B  B8 0000s                    MOV     AX, DATA                ;Load DS needed here
44 000E  8E D8                       MOV     DS, AX
45 0010  FE 0E 0000e                 DEC     COUNTER                 ;Decrement interrupt counter
46 0014  75 20                       JNZ     EXIT2                   ;Not zero yet, go wait
47 0016  C6 06 0000e 14              MOV     COUNTER, 20             ;If zero, reset tick counter to 20
48 001B  B7 00                       MOV     BH, 00                  ;Load BX with number of loop to
```

FIGURE 10-35 (Continued)

```
49 001D  8A 1E 0000e            MOV      BL, LOOPNUM               ;service and service that loop
50 0021  FF 9F 0000r            CALL     DWORD PTR LOOP_ADDR_TABLE[BX]
51 0025  80 06 0000e 04         ADD      LOOPNUM, 04               ;Point at next loop address
52 002A  80 3E 0000e 20         CMP      LOOPNUM, 20H              ;Was this the last loop?
53 002F  75 05                  JNE      EXIT2                     ;No, exit
54 0031  C6 06 0000e 00         MOV      LOOPNUM, 00               ;Yes, get back to first loop
55 0036  1F             EXIT2:POP       DS                         ;Restore registers
56 0037  5A                     POP      DX
57 0038  5B                     POP      BX
58 0039  58                     POP      AX
59 003A  CF                     IRET
60 003B                CLOCK_TICK     ENDP
61
62                     ;DUMMY INTERRUPT PROCEDURE TO SERVICE KEYBOARD
63 003B                KEYBOARD PROC FAR
64                     ;   :                                       ;Keyboard procedure intructions
65 003B  B0 20                  MOV      AL, 00100000B             ;OCW2 for non-specific EOI
66 003D  BA FF00                MOV      DX, 0FF00H                ;Load address for OCW2
67 0040  EE                     OUT      DX, AL                    ;and send OCW2 for end of interrupt
68 0041  CF                     IRET
69 0042                KEYBOARD       ENDP
70
71 0042                INT_PROC       ENDS
72                                     END
```

(b)

```
 1                     ;8086 MODULE 3 PROCEDURES: F10-35C.ASM
 2                     ;ABSTRACT: Module 3 contains the procedures to service each loop
 3
 4 0000                DATA SEGMENT WORD    PUBLIC
 5                            EXTRN   TIMEHI :BYTE, TIMELO  :BYTE  ;Imported into this
 6                            EXTRN   CURTEMP:BYTE, SETPOINT:BYTE  ;module from the mainline
 7 0000                DATA ENDS
 8
 9                     PUBLIC LOOP0, LOOP1, LOOP2, LOOP3, LOOP4, LOOP5, LOOP6, LOOP7
10
11 0000                CODE SEGMENT WORD PUBLIC
12                     EXTRN DISPLAY_IT  : NEAR                   ; These procedures can be
13                     EXTRN A_D_READ    : NEAR                   ; found in MODULE 4 which
14                     EXTRN BINCVT      : NEAR                   ; will be linked this module
15 0000                CODE ENDS                                 ; and MODULES 1 and 2
16
17 0000                CODE SEGMENT WORD PUBLIC
18                       ASSUME  CS:CODE, DS:DATA
19
20                     ;8086 PROCEDURE - LOOP0
21                     ;ABSTRACT :  This procedure services the temperature controller
22                     ;REGISTERS: Destroys none
23                     ;PORTS:      Uses bit 7 of P2B (FFFAH) as output port control heater.
24                     ;PROCEDURES: Uses DISPLAY_IT, A_D_READ, BINCVT from Module 4
25
26 0000                LOOP0 PROC     FAR
27 0000  9C                     PUSHF                             ;Save registers
28 0001  50                     PUSH     AX
29 0002  53                     PUSH     BX
30 0003  51                     PUSH     CX
31 0004  52                     PUSH     DX
32 0005  FE 0E 0000e            DEC      TIMEHI                    ;Decrement time for heater on
33 0009  75 50                  JNZ      EXIT                      ;Return to interrupt procedure
34 000B  C6 06 0000e 01         MOV      TIMEHI, 01                ;Reset time high to fall through value
35 0010  BA FFFA                MOV      DX, 0FFFAH                ;Point at output port P2B &
36 0013  B0 80                  MOV      AL, 80H                   ;turn off heater
37 0015  EE                     OUT      DX, AL
38 0016  FE 0E 0000e            DEC      TIMELO                    ;Decrement time for heater off
39 001A  75 3F                  JNZ      EXIT                      ;Return to interrupt procedure
40 001C  B3 00                  MOV      BL, 00                    ;Load channel address (0)
41 001E  E8 0000e               CALL     A_D_READ                  ;Do A/D conversion
42 0021  A2 0000e               MOV      CURTEMP, AL               ;Save current temperature
43 0024  E8 0000e               CALL     BINCVT                    ;Convert to BCD
44 0027  8A C8                  MOV      CL, AL                    ;Put result in CX to display
45 0029  B5 00                  MOV      CH, 00
46 002B  B0 00                  MOV      AL, 00                    ;temp in data field of SDK-86
```

FIGURE 10-35 (Continued)

```
47 002D E8 0000e                CALL   DISPLAY_IT
48 0030 A0 0000e                MOV    AL, SETPOINT      ;Get setpoint temperature
49 0033 2A 06 0000e             SUB    AL, CURTEMP       ;Get temperature & subtract from setpoint
50 0037 76 18                   JBE    DONE              ;Heater off if above or equal setpoint
51 0039 8A D0                   MOV    DL, AL            ;Save temperature difference
52 003B B8 0064                 MOV    AX, 0064H         ;Compute new TIMELO
53 003E F6 F2                   DIV    DL                ; 0064/error, quotient is value
54 0040 A2 0000e                MOV    TIMELO, AL        ; for new time low
55 0043 C6 06 0000e 04          MOV    TIMEHI, 04        ;Set time high for 4 loops
56 0048 B0 00                   MOV    AL, 00
57 004A BA FFFA                 MOV    DX, 0FFFAH        ;Point at output port
58 004D EE                      OUT    DX,AL             ;Turn on heater
59 004E EB 0B 90                JMP    EXIT
60 0051 C6 06 0000e 01  DONE:   MOV    TIMEHI, 01H       ;Fall through value for time high
61 0056 C6 06 0000e 7F          MOV    TIMELO, 7FH       ;Long off value for time low
62 005B 5A              EXIT:   POP    DX                ;Loop serviced - return to
63 005C 59                      POP    CX                ; interrupt service procedure
64 005D 5B                      POP    BX
65 005E 58                      POP    AX
66 005F 9D                      POPF
67 0060 CB                      RET
68 0061                 LOOP0 ENDP
69
70                      ;DUMMY PROCEDURES FOR OTHER LOOPS INSERTED HERE
71 0061                 LOOP1 PROC FAR
72                      ;      :                          ;Instructions for this loop
73 0061 CB                      RET
74 0062                 LOOP1     ENDP
75
76 0062                 LOOP2 PROC FAR
77                      ;      :                          ;Instructions for this loop
78 0062 CB                      RET
79 0063                 LOOP2 ENDP
80
81 0063                 LOOP3 PROC FAR
82                      ;      :                          ;Instructions for this loop
83 0063 CB                      RET
84 0064                 LOOP3 ENDP
85
86 0064                 LOOP4 PROC FAR
87                      ;      :                          ;Instructions for this loop
88 0064 CB                      RET
89 0065                 LOOP4 ENDP
90
91 0065                 LOOP5 PROC FAR
92                      ;      :                          ;Instructions for this loop
93 0065 CB                      RET
94 0066                 LOOP5 ENDP
95
96 0066                 LOOP6 PROC FAR
97                      ;      :                          ;Instructions for this loop
98 0066 CB                      RET
99 0067                 LOOP6 ENDP
100
101 0067                LOOP7 PROC FAR
102                     ;      :                          ;Instructions for this loop
103 0067 CB                     RET
104 0068                LOOP7 ENDP
105
106 0068                CODE   ENDS
107                            END
```

(c)

```
1                       ;8086 MODULE 4 PROCEDURES:   F10-35D.ASM
2                       ;ABSTRACT : Module 4 contains the service procedures needed by the loop modules
3
4                       PUBLIC DISPLAY_IT, A_D_READ, BINCVT ; Make procedures available to other modules
5
6 0000                  DATA SEGMENT WORD PUBLIC
7                       ;               0    1    2    3    4    5    6    7
8 0000 3F 06 5B 4F 66 6D 7D + SEVEN_SEG DB   3FH, 06H, 5BH, 4FH, 66H, 6DH, 7DH, 07H
9        07
```

FIGURE 10-35 (*Continued*)

```
 10                                            ;     8    9    A    b    C    d    E    F
 11 0008 7F 6F 77 7C 39 5E 79 +                     DB    7FH, 6FH, 77H, 7CH, 39H, 5EH, 79H, 71H
 12      71
 13 0010                                 DATA ENDS
 14 0000                                 CODE   SEGMENT WORD PUBLIC
 15                                         ASSUME CS:CODE, DS:DATA
 16
 17                                 ;8086 PROCEDURE DISPLAY_IT
 18                                 ;ABSTRACT:  Displays a 4-digit hex or BCD number on LEDs of the SDK-86
 19                                 ;INPUTS:    Data in CX, control in AL.
 20                                 ;           AL =  00H  data displayed in data-field of LEDs
 21                                 ;           AL <> 00H, data displayed in address field of LEDs.
 22                                 ;PORTS:     Uses none
 23                                 ;PROCEDURES:Uses none
 24                                 ;REGISTERS: Saves all registers and flags
 25
 26 0000                           DISPLAY_IT  PROC  NEAR
 27 0000 9C                                PUSHF                      ;Save flags
 28 0001 1E                                PUSH    DS                 ;Save caller's registers
 29 0002 50                                PUSH    AX
 30 0003 53                                PUSH    BX
 31 0004 51                                PUSH    CX
 32 0005 52                                PUSH    DX
 33 0006 BB 0000s                          MOV     BX, DATA           ;Initialize DS as needed for procedure
 34 0009 8E DB                             MOV     DS, BX
 35 000B BA FFEA                           MOV     DX, 0FFEAH         ;Point at 8279 control address
 36 000E 3C 00                             CMP     AL, 00H            ;See if data field required
 37 0010 74 05                             JZ      DATFLD             ;Yes, load control word for data field
 38 0012 B0 94                             MOV     AL, 94H            ;No, load address-field control word
 39 0014 EB 03 90                          JMP     SEND               ;Send control word
 40 0017 B0 90                 DATFLD:     MOV     AL, 90H            ;Load control word for data field
 41 0019 EE                    SEND:       OUT     DX, AL             ;Send control word to 8279
 42 001A BB 0000r                          MOV     BX, OFFSET SEVEN_SEG ;Pointer to seven-segment codes
 43 001D BA FFE8                           MOV     DX, 0FFE8H         ;Point at 8279 display RAM
 44 0020 8A C1                             MOV     AL, CL             ;Get low byte to be displayed
 45 0022 24 0F                             AND     AL, 0FH            ;Mask upper nibble
 46 0024 D7                                XLATB                      ;Translate lower nibble to 7-seg code
 47 0025 EE                                OUT     DX, AL             ;Send to 8279 display RAM
 48 0026 8A C1                             MOV     AL, CL             ;Get low byte again
 49 0028 B1 04                             MOV     CL, 04             ;Load rotate count
 50 002A D2 C0                             ROL     AL, CL             ;Move upper nibble into low position
 51 002C 24 0F                             AND     AL, 0FH            ;Mask upper nibble
 52 002E D7                                XLATB                      ;Translate 2nd nibble to 7-seg code
 53 002F EE                                OUT     DX, AL             ;Send to 8279 display RAM
 54 0030 8A C5                             MOV     AL, CH             ;Get high byte to translate
 55 0032 24 0F                             AND     AL, 0FH            ;Mask upper nibble
 56 0034 D7                                XLATB                      ;Translate to 7-seg code
 57 0035 EE                                OUT     DX, AL             ;Send to 8279 display RAM
 58 0036 8A C5                             MOV     AL, CH             ;Get high byte to fix upper nibble
 59 0038 D2 C0                             ROL     AL, CL             ;Move upper nibble into low position
 60 003A 24 0F                             AND     AL, 0FH            ;Mask upper nibble
 61 003C D7                                XLATB                      ;Translate to 7-seg code
 62 003D EE                                OUT     DX, AL             ;7-seg code to 8279 display RAM
 63 003E 5A                                POP     DX                 ;Restore all registers and flags
 64 003F 59                                POP     CX
 65 0040 5B                                POP     BX
 66 0041 58                                POP     AX
 67 0042 1F                                POP     DS
 68 0043 9D                                POPF
 69 0044 C3                                RET
 70 0045                           DISPLAY_IT   ENDP
 71
 72                                 ;8086 PROCEDURE A_D_READ
 73                                 ;ABSTRACT:  Controls A/D converter
 74                                 ;PORTS:     Uses Port P2A for input from A/D
 75                                 ;           Port P2B, bit 7 = heater, bit 5 = start conversion
 76                                 ;                    bit 4 = ALE    bits 2,1,0 = channel address
 77                                 ;           Port P2C  bit 0 = end of conversion
 78                                 ;INPUTS:    Channel address for A/D in BL
 79                                 ;OUTPUTS:   A/D data in AL
 80                                 ;REGISTERS: DESTROYS AL & BL
 81
 82 0045                           A_D_READ     PROC     NEAR
```

FIGURE 10-35 (Continued)

```
83 0045  9C                     PUSHF
84 0046  52                     PUSH    DX
85 0047  B0 80                  MOV     AL, 80H        ;Control for heater off
86 0049  0A C3                  OR      AL, BL         ;Combine with channel address
87 004B  BA FFFA                MOV     DX, 0FFFAH     ;Point at P2B, output port
88 004E  EE                     OUT     DX, AL         ; send
89 004F  B0 90                  MOV     AL, 90H        ;Send ALE, keep heater on
90 0051  0A C3                  OR      AL, BL         ;Keep channel address on
91 0053  EE                     OUT     DX, AL
92 0054  B0 B0                  MOV     AL, 0B0H       ;Send start of conversion
93 0056  0A C3                  OR      AL, BL         ;Keep channel address on
94 0058  EE                     OUT     DX, AL
95 0059  B0 80                  MOV     AL, 80H        ;Turn off ALE and start
96 005B  0A C3                  OR      AL, BL         ;Keep channel address
97 005D  EE                     OUT     DX, AL
98 005E  BA FFFC                MOV     DX, 0FFFCH     ;Point at port P2C
99 0061  EC           EOCL:     IN      AL, DX         ;Wait for end of conversion
100 0062 D0 D8                  RCR     AL, 01         ; to go low
101 0064 72 FB                  JC      EOCL
102 0066 EC           EOCH:     IN      AL, DX         ;Wait for end of conversion
103 0067 D0 D8                  RCR     AL, 01         ; to go high
104 0069 73 FB                  JNC     EOCH
105 006B BA FFF8                MOV     DX, 0FFF8H     ;Point at port P2A
106 006E EC                     IN      AL, DX         ;Read data from A/D
107 006F 5A                     POP     DX
108 0070 9D                     POPF
109 0071 C3                     RET
110 0072          A_D_READ      ENDP
111
112                            ;8086 PROCEDURE BINCVT
113                            ;ABSTRACT: Converts 8-bit binary number in AL to packed BCD equivalent in AL
114                            ;INPUTS:    AL - 8-bit binary number
115                            ;OUTPUTS:   AL - packed BCD result
116
117 0072          BINCVT PROC   NEAR
118 0072 9C                     PUSHF                  ;Save registers and flags
119 0073 51                     PUSH    CX
120 0074 B4 09                  MOV     AH,09H         ;Bit counter for 8 bits
121 0076 8A C8                  MOV     CL, AL         ;Save binary in CL
122 0078 B5 00                  MOV     CH, 00         ;Clear CH for use as buffer
123 007A 32 C0        CNVT2:    XOR     AL, AL         ;Clear AL and carry
124 007C FE CC                  DEC     AH             ;Decrement bit counter
125 007E 75 03                  JNZ     GO_ON          ;Do all bits
126 0080 EB 0C 90               JMP     HOME           ;Done if AH down to zero
127 0083 D0 D1        GO_ON:    RCL     CL,1           ;MSB from CL to carry
128 0085 8A C5                  MOV     AL, CH         ;Move BCD digit being built to AL
129 0087 12 C0                  ADC     AL, AL         ;Double AL and add carry from CL shift
130 0089 27                     DAA                    ;Keep result in BCD form
131 008A 8A E8                  MOV     CH, AL         ;Put back in CH for next time through
132 008C EB EC                  JMP     CNVT2          ;Continue conversion
133 008E 8A C5        HOME:     MOV     AL, CH         ;BCD in AL for return
134 0090 59                     POP     CX             ;Restore registers
135 0091 9D                     POPF
136 0092 C3                     RET
137 0093          BINCVT ENDP
138                                    ,
139 0093          CODE   ENDS
140                      END
```

(d)

FIGURE 10-35 (*Continued*)

these operations in detail, so we won't dwell on them here. Also in the mainline we initialize some process variables. We will explain these initializations later when they will have more meaning.

After enabling the 8086 INTR input with an STI instruction, the program then enters a loop and waits for an interrupt from the user via the keyboard, or an interrupt from the timer. The keyboard-interrupt procedure would normally contain a command recognizer and subprocedures to implement commands

which allow the user to change set points, stop a process, or examine the value of process variables at any time. Due to severe space limitations, we can't show here the implementation of the keyboard interrupt procedure, but we will show you how the timer interrupt procedure and the example PID loop procedure work.

THE CLOCK_TICK INTERRUPT HANDLER

As we said before, the 8254 is programmed to send a pulse to an interrupt input of the 8259A every millisecond. When a clock interrupt occurs, execution goes to the CLOCK_TICK procedure. At the start of this procedure, we simply decrement an interrupt "tick counter" kept in a memory location called COUNTER. In the initialization, this counter was set to 20 decimal or 14H. If the counter is not down to 0, execution is simply returned to the wait loop in the mainline. If the tick counter is now down to 0, the clock-tick counter is reset to 20, and one of the loop procedures is called to service the next loop. It is important that this clock-tick procedure be reentrant because if one of the loop procedures takes more than the time between clock ticks (1 ms), the CLOCK_TICK procedure will be reentered before its first use is completed. The procedure is made reentrant by pushing all registers used in the procedure and by immediately resetting the clock-tick counter to 20. If a loop procedure takes longer than 1 ms and the clock_tick procedure is called again, the tick counter will be decremented by 1 and execution returned to the interrupted loop procedure.

Selecting one of the loop procedures is an example of the CASE or nested IF-THEN-ELSE programming structure described in Chapter 3. To implement this structure, we use a powerful programming technique called a *call table*. Here's how it works.

The starting addresses of all the loop procedures are put in a table called LOOP_ADDR_TABLE, as shown at the start of module 2 in Figure 10-35b. The names LOOP0, LOOP1, LOOP2, etc., are the names of the procedures to service each of the loops. Since these procedures are FAR, the DD directive is used to reserve space for the IP and CS of each. When this program module is linked and loaded into memory, the instruction pointer and code segment addresses for each of the loop procedures will be loaded into this table.

To point to the desired loop procedure address in the table, we use a variable called LOOPNUM. During initialization LOOPNUM is loaded with 00H. When it is time to service the first loop, the value in LOOPNUM is loaded into BX. The CALL DWORD PTR LOOP_ADDR_TABLE [BX] instruction then gets the address of the LOOP0 procedure from the call table and goes to that address. For the first access to the table, BX is zero, so the first address in the table is used to call LOOP0 procedure.

When execution returns from the LOOP0 procedure to the interrupt handler, we add 4 to the LOOPNUM. This is done so that LOOP1 will be called the next time the tick counter is counted down to zero. LOOPNUM must be incremented by 4 because each address in the call table uses 4 bytes. When all loops have been serviced, LOOPNUM is set back to 0 so LOOP0 will be serviced again. Now let's look at the actual temperature-control loop.

THE TEMPERATURE-CONTROLLER PROCEDURE

As we said previously, the amount of heat output by the heater is controlled by the duty cycle of a pulse waveform sent to the solid-state relay. The time on for the output waveform to the solid-state relay is determined by counting down a value called TIMEHI. The time off for this waveform is determined by counting down a value called TIMELO. At start-up the mainline program initializes TIMEHI and TIMELO to 01H, so that the first time the LOOP0 procedure is called both of these are decremented to 0, and execution falls through to the A/D conversion procedure. This is done to get a temperature value which can be compared with the set-point value. The difference between the set-point value and the actual temperature will be used to set the value of TIMEHI and TIMELO for the next time the LOOP0 procedure is called.

The part of the program which controls the A/D converter is written as a separate procedure so that it can be used in other PID loops. The A/D converter has eight input channels, so as part of the interaction with the A/D converter, we have to tell it which channel to digitize. The number of the A/D channel that we want to digitize is passed to the A/D conversion procedure in the AL register. The procedure then sends out this channel number to the A/D converter and generates the control waveforms shown in Figure 10-34. Since the timing for these waveforms is in the range of microseconds, we chose to generate the waveforms with program instructions rather than use an 8255A in handshake mode. The binary value for the temperature is returned in AL.

Upon return, the binary value of the temperature is stored in a memory location called CURTEMP for future reference. For testing purposes, we wanted to display the temperature on the address field of the SDK-86 display. To do this, the binary value for the temperature is converted to a BCD value using a reduced version of the binary-to-BCD procedure from the scale program earlier in this chapter and the display routine from Chapter 9.

After the current temperature is displayed, it is compared with the set-point temperature to see if the heater needs to be turned on. If the temperature is at or above the set point, TIMEHI is loaded with fall-through value and TIMELO is loaded with a large number.

If the temperature is below the set point, we call a procedure, DUTY_CYCLE, which computes the correct values for TIMEHI and TIMELO based on the difference between the set point and the current temperature. In a more critical application, a complex PID algorithm might be used for this procedure. For our example here, however, we have used simple proportional feedback. To further simplify the calculations, a fixed value of 4 was used for TIMEHI. The thinking for the value of TIMELO then goes as follows.

If the difference in temperature is large, then TIMELO should be small so the heater is on for a longer duty cycle. If the difference in temperature is small, then the value of TIMELO should be large so the heater has a short duty cycle. Experimentally we found that a good first approximation for our system was (difference in temperature) × TIMELO = 100 decimal (64H). For example, if the difference in temperature is 20° (14H), then 64H/14H gives a value of 5 for TIMELO. The values for TIMEHI and TIMELO are returned in their named memory locations. Upon return to the main loop procedure, we send a control word which turns on the heater. Execution then jumps to EXIT.

When execution returns to loop 0 again after 160 ms,

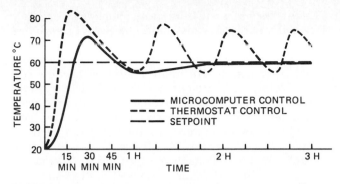

FIGURE 10-36 Temperature versus time responses for thermostat-controlled and microcomputer-controlled heaters.

TIMEHI will be decremented. If TIMEHI is not yet down to 0 after the decrement, then we simply adjust a few things and return. If TIMEHI is 0 after the decrement, the heater is turned off, and TIMELO is decremented. TIMELO is then decremented every time loop 0 is serviced (every 160 ms) until TIMELO reaches 0. When TIMELO gets counted down to 0, a new A/D conversion is done, and a new feedback value for TIMELO is calculated.

An important point here is that the part of the program that determines the feedback is separate from the rest of the program, so it can be easily altered without changing the rest of the program. All that needs to be changed in this procedure is the value of TIMEHI, the value of TIMELO, and the rate at which these change in response to a difference in temperature to produce proportional, integral, and derivative feedback control.

TEMPERATURE CONTROLLER RESPONSE

The dotted line in Figure 10-36 shows the temperature versus time response of our system with traditional thermostat control, which is often called *on-off control* or "bang-bang" control. As you can see, with thermostat control the temperature initially overshoots the set point a great deal and then oscillates over a wide range around the set point. The solid line in Figure 10-36 shows the response of the system operating with our temperature controller program. The initial overshoot was caused by the large thermal inertia of the hot plate we used. The overshoot and the residual error of about 1° could be eliminated by using a more complex feedback algorithm. This example should make you aware of the advantages of computer feedback control.

DEVELOPING THE PROTOTYPE OF A MICROCOMPUTER-BASED INSTRUMENT

The first step in developing a new instrument is to very carefully define exactly what you want the instrument to do. The next step is to decide which parts of the instrument you want to do in hardware and which parts you want to do in software. You then can decide how you want to do each of these.

For the software, you will break the overall programming job down into modules which can be individually

tested and debugged, as we have described previously. Likewise, the best way to develop the hardware is in small parts which can be individually tested and debugged. To give you a specific example of how to do this, here's how we developed the SDK-86-based factory-control system described in the preceding section.

The basic SDK-86 does not have a timer to produce 1-kHz clock ticks or a priority interrupt controller to handle keyboard and clock-tick interrupts. Therefore, we first added these two devices and some address decoder circuitry to the SDK-86, as shown in Figure 8-14. To test this circuitry we used a short program which wrote a byte to the starting address for the timer over and over again. We ran this test program with an emulator such as the Applied Microsystems ES1800 shown in Figure 3-17. With the program running, we used a scope to check if the $\overline{CS}$ input of the timer was getting asserted. It was, so we knew that the address decoding circuitry was working correctly.

We then connected the 2.45-MHz PCLK signal to the clock inputs of all three timers in the 8254 and wrote the instructions needed to initialize the three timers for 1-kHz square-wave outputs. Even though we need only one timer here, it was very little additional work to check the other two for future reference. Hurrah, the timers worked the first time; now on to the 8259A priority interrupt controller (PIC).

Testing the 8259A was a little more complex because we had to provide an interrupt signal, initialize the 8259A, initialize the interrupt vector table in low RAM, and provide a location for execution to go to when the PIC received an interrupt. We used the 1-kHz clock tick from the timer as the interrupt signal to the 8259A. For 8259A initialization and the interrupt jump table initialization, we used the instructions in the mainline program in Figure 10-35. For the test-interrupt procedure, we actually used a real-time clock and display procedure that we developed for examples in previous chapters. We used these so that we could see if the interrupt mechanism was working correctly by watching the displays on the SDK-86 count off seconds. This again shows the advantage of writing programs as separate, reusable modules. Note in the program in Figure 10-35 that we initialize the 8259A before we initialize and start the timer. When we first wrote a test program to test an 8259A and an 8254, we did this in the reverse order. When we ran the test program with the emulator, the system would accept only one interrupt and then hang up. We did a trace with the emulator and found that execution was returning from the interrupt procedure to the WAIT loop in the mainline program properly, but it was not recognizing the next interrupt. Careful reading of the 8259A data sheet showed us that we had to initialize the 8259A *before* we started sending it interrupt signals, or it would not respond correctly to the nonspecific EOI command that we used at the end of the interrupt procedure to reset the 8259A's in-service register.

After the interrupt mechanism was working correctly, we wrote the interrupt procedure which implements the decision structure shown in Figure 10-32b. Initially we made all eight loops dummy loops to test the basic structure. By inserting breakpoints with the emulator, we were able to see whether execution was getting to each of the eight loops. When all this was working, we went on to build and test the temperature-control section.

For the temperature-control section, we first built the analog circuitry and tested it. Then we wrote a small program to read the temperature from the A/D converter and display the result on the SDK-86 displays. Initially then, the loop 0 procedure simply read in the temperature, displayed it in binary (hex) form, and returned. This worked the first time, so we went on to add the binary-to-BCD conversion routine and run the result with the emulator. This was a previously written and tested module, and when it was added, the result worked fine.

Next we added a couple of instructions to turn the heater on during one execution of loop 0 and turn the heater off during the next time through loop 0. We then used an oscilloscope to check that the solid-state relay was getting turned on and off correctly.

Finally, we added the actual duty cycle and control instructions and sat back waiting for the system to heat up a big container of water for tea.

The actual development cycle will obviously be somewhat different for every instrument developed. The main points here are to develop and test both the hardware and the software in small modules. To speed up the debugging process, take the time to learn to use all or most of the power of the emulator and system you are working with.

ROBOTICS AND EMBEDDED CONTROL

In recent years the term *robot* has become a "buzzword" in the media and in many people's minds. Science fiction movies have helped us form an image of robots as mobile, rational companions. Robots, however, have many forms, and in operation they are simply a combination of feedback control systems such as we described in the previous section. This is why we have not included a chapter dedicated just to robotics. The controller for the Rhino robot arm shown in Figure 9-42, for example, uses optical encoders to detect the position of its different joints, motors (actuators) to move each joint to a desired position, and a microcomputer to control the motors based on feedback from the sensors. Large industrial robots such as those that weld or spray-paint cars may also use tactile or visual sensors, and the actuators may be hydraulic or pneumatic, but the control principle is the same. A microcomputer or several microcomputers use feedback from the various sensors to control one or more actuators.

Most of you have probably used some simple robots around your home without realizing it. One example is an electric garage door opener which starts to open or close when you tell it to and then stops when a sensor indicates that it is open or closed as desired. Common household examples of microcomputer-controlled robots are a microwave oven with a temperature probe, a programmable sewing machine, a remote-control stereo system, etc.

Smart machines such as these usually use specially designed microprocessors called *embedded controllers* instead of a general-purpose microprocessor such as the 8086 which we used in the scale and the factory controller examples. The main differences of these embedded controlled microprocessors is that they have additional functions included on the chip with the basic CPU and they have special instructions for working with individual bits in a word. In the following sections we give you an overview of a few common embedded controller families. Consult the appropriate Intel handbooks for additional details when you need them.

The Intel 8051 Embedded Controller Family

Figure 10-37a shows a block diagram of a basic 8051 family controller and Figure 10-37b summarizes some of the features of the members of the family. These controllers are 8-bit units which can address up to 64 Kbytes of memory. All of the family members have some RAM on the chip, and different members of the family have some ROM or EPROM also included on the chip. As shown in Figure 10-37b, members of this family also have programmable timers and priority interrupt controllers included on the chips.

If an application does not require any memory other than that included on the chip, then all four parts are available for use as input or output ports. If additional memory is needed, then port 0 and port 2 can be programmed to function as a multiplexed address/data bus. When used with external memory, two lines on port 3 are used to generate the $\overline{RD}$ and $\overline{WR}$ signals.

The devices in the 8051 family also contain serial data interface circuitry. When this feature is used, two pins on port 3 function as the RxD and TxD lines. Figure 10-37c shows the special uses of the port 3 pins.

The Intel 8096 Embedded Controller Family

Figure 10-38a, p. 334, shows a block diagram for the Intel 8096 family of 16-bit microcontrollers. One of the most important features of the members of this family is the 232-byte register file and the register ALU (RALU) shown in the center of Figure 10-38a. Instead of using a single accumulator register as the 8086 does, the ALU in the 8096 family devices can perform most operations on any of the registers in the register file. This structure is referred to as *register-to-register* architecture. The large number of registers makes it possible to have many data bytes in registers where they can be very quickly accessed. Also, since the contents of any register can be output to a port, the I/O "bottleneck" of 8086-type processors is eliminated. The 8086, remember, requires that data be output from or input to AL/AX.

Other features found in all the 8096 family devices are five ports which can be programmed for use in a variety of ways. In addition to their use as standard ports, ports 3 and 4 can be used as a multiplexed address/data bus to access external memory and ports. Port 2 can be programmed for use as a serial port and/ or an output for the pulse-width-modulated signal. The

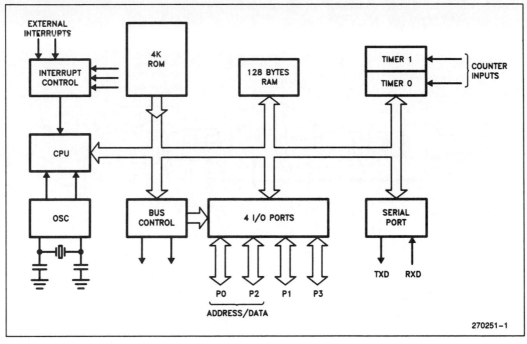

(a)

Device	Internal Memory		Timers/ Event Counters	Interrupts
	Program	Data		
8052AH	8K x 8 ROM	256 x 8 RAM	3 x 16-Bit	6
8051AH	4K x 8 ROM	128 x 8 RAM	2 x 16-Bit	5
8051	4K x 8 ROM	128 x 8 RAM	2 x 16-Bit	5
8032AH	none	256 x 8 RAM	3 x 16-Bit	6
8031AH	none	128 x 8 RAM	2 x 16-Bit	5
8031	none	128 x 8 RAM	2 x 16-Bit	5
8751H	4K x 8 EPROM	128 x 8 RAM	2 x 16-Bit	5
8751H-8	4K x 8 EPROM	128 x 8 RAM	2 x 16-Bit	5

(b)

Port 3 also serves the functions of various special features of the MCS-51 Family, as listed below:

Port Pin	Alternative Function
P3.0	RXD (serial input port)
P3.1	TXD (serial output port)
P3.2	$\overline{INT0}$ (external interrupt 0)
P3.3	$\overline{INT1}$ (external interrupt 1)
P3.4	T0 (Timer 0 external input)
P3.5	T1 (Timer 1 external input)
P3.6	$\overline{WR}$ (external data memory write strobe)
P3.7	$\overline{RD}$ (external data memory read strobe)

(c)

FIGURE 10-37   8051 family. (a) Block diagram. (b) Family features. (c) Port pin uses.   (*Intel Corporation*)

PWM signal is software programmable and can be used to control the speed of a small motor or the duty cycle of a heater, as we described earlier in the chapter. The 8096 family devices also have two programmable counters and 21 hardware and software interrupt types. Note that both the clock generator and the baud-rate generator are included in the basic architecture.

Figure 10-38b shows the numbering for the different members of the 8096 family so you can see the options available in different parts. As you can see, devices are available with 8 Kbytes of internal EPROM, 8 Kbytes of internal mask-programmed ROM, or no internal ROM. Also note that some members of the 8096 family contain a 10-bit successive-approximation A/D converter. As shown in Figure 10-38c, this A/D has a sample-and-hold and an 8-input analog multiplexer on its input. This allows it to digitize any of eight input signals under program control.

The 8096 instructions are designed for fast operations on registers and for easily working with individual bits in data words. The 8096 also has multiply and divide instructions. From the scale and temperature controller examples earlier in the chapter, you should see that these features optimize the devices for use in hardware control applications.

The 80186 and 80188 Microprocessors

The 8051 and 8096 embedded controllers we described in the preceding sections have different instruction sets and very different architectures from the 8086, which

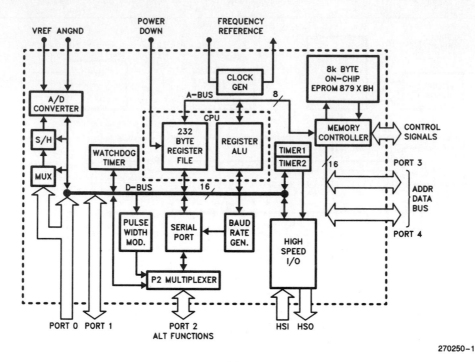

270250–1

(a)

The MCS® –96 Family Nomenclature

		Without A/D	With A/D
ROMless 809XBH	48 Pin		C8095BH - Ceramic DIP P8095BH - Plastic DIP
	68 Pin	A8096BH - Ceramic PGA N8096BH - PLCC	A8097BH - Ceramic PGA N8097BH - PLCC
ROM 839XBH	48 Pin		C8395BH - Ceramic DIP P8395BH - Plastic DIP
	68 Pin	A8396BH - Ceramic PGA N8396BH - PLCC	A8397BH - Ceramic PGA N8397BH - PLCC
EPROM 879XBH	48 Pin		C8795BH - Ceramic DIP
	68 Pin	A8796BH - Ceramic PGA R8796BH - Ceramic LCC	A8797BH - Ceramic PGA R8797BH - Ceramic LCC

(b)

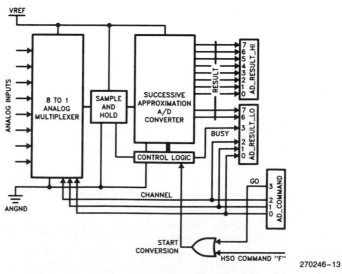

270246–13

(c)

FIGURE 10-38 8096 family. (a) Block diagram. (b) Family features.
(c) A/D converter diagram. (Intel Corporation)

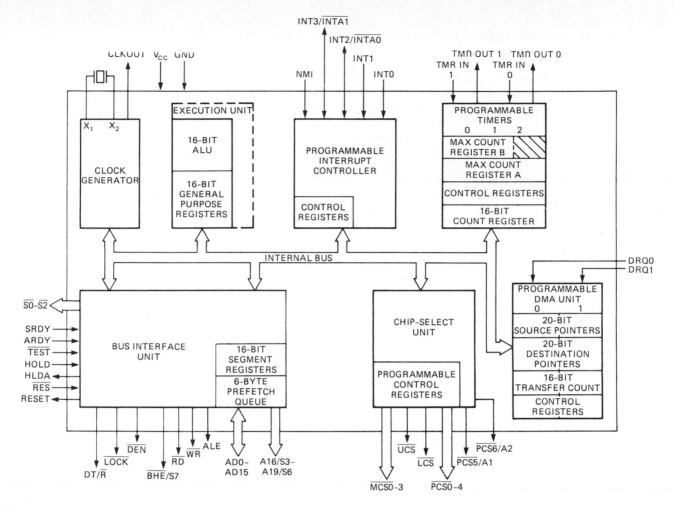

FIGURE 10-39   80186 Internal block diagram.   (*Intel Corporation*)

we have used for examples in this book. The 80186 and 80188 are 16-bit processors commonly used for embedded control applications, and they have basically the same instructions set as the 8086. However, as shown in Figure 10-39, they contain some peripheral functions as well as a CPU.

The architecture and instruction set of the 80188 are identical to those of the 80186 except that the 80188 has only an 8-bit data bus instead of the 16-bit data bus that the 80186 has. With this in mind, we will use the 80186 to represent both the 80186 and the 80188 in our discussions here.

The 80186 has the same bus-interface unit and execution unit as the 8086 which we discussed previously, so there is nothing new there for you. Unlike the 8086, however, the 80186 has the clock generator built in so that all you have to add is an external crystal. Also note that the 80186 does not have a pin labeled MN/$\overline{\text{MX}}$. The 80186 is packaged in a 68-pin leadless package, so it has enough pins to send out both the minimum-mode-type signals $\overline{\text{RD}}$ and $\overline{\text{WR}}$ and the S0–S3 status signals which can be connected to external bus controller ICs for maximum-mode systems. Now let's look at the four peripheral chip function blocks in the 80186.

First is a priority interrupt controller which has up to four interrupt inputs, INT0, INT1, INT2/$\overline{\text{INTA0}}$, and

INT3/$\overline{\text{INTA1}}$ as well as an NMI interrupt input. If the four INT inputs are programmed in their internal mode, then a signal applied to one of them will cause the 80186 to push the return address on the stack and vector directly to the start of the interrupt service procedure for that interrupt. The INT2/$\overline{\text{INTA0}}$ and INT3/$\overline{\text{INTA1}}$ pins can be programmed to be used as interrupt inputs, or they can be programmed to function as interrupt acknowledge outputs. This mode is used to interface with external 8259As. The interrupt request line from an external 8259A is connected to, for example, the 80186 INT0 input, and the 80186 INT2/$\overline{\text{INTA0}}$ pin is connected to the interrupt acknowledge input of the 8259A. When the 8259A receives an interrupt request, it asserts the INT0 input of the 80186. When the 8259A receives interrupt acknowledge signals from the INT2/$\overline{\text{INTA0}}$ pin, its sends the desired interrupt type to the 80186 on the data bus.

Next to look at in the block diagram is the built-in address decoder, referred to in the drawing as the chip select unit. This unit can be programmed to produce an active low chip select signal when a memory address in the specified range or a port address in a specified range is sent out. Six memory address chip select signals are available: $\overline{\text{LCS}}$, $\overline{\text{UCS}}$, and $\overline{\text{MCS0}}$ through $\overline{\text{MCS3}}$. The *lower-chip select* signal, $\overline{\text{LCS}}$, will be asserted by addresses between 00000H and some address which you specify in a control word. The specified ending address can be anywhere between 1K and 256K. The highest address that will assert the *upper-chip select* signal, UCS, is fixed at FFFFFH. The lowest address for this block of memory is again programmable by some bits you put in a control word. The size of the upper memory block can be anywhere between 1K and 256K. Finally, there are four *middle-chip select* lines, MCS0 through MCS3. Each of these four is asserted by an address in a block of memory in the middle range of memory. Both the starting address and the size of the four blocks can be specified for this middle-range block. The specified size of blocks can be anywhere from 2K to 128K.

In addition to producing memory chip select signals, the 80186 can be programmed to produce up to seven peripheral chip select signals on its PCS0 through PCS4, PCS5/A1, and PCS6/A2 pins. You program a base address for these I/O addresses in a control word. PCS0 will be asserted when this base address is output during an IN or an OUT instruction. The other PCS outputs will be asserted by addresses at intervals of 128 bytes above the base address.

Now let's look at the programmable DMA unit in the 80186. As you can see from the block diagram in Figure 10-39, the DMA unit has two DMA request inputs, DRQ0 and DRQ1. These inputs allow external devices such as disk controllers, CRT controllers, etc. to request use of the microcomputer address and data bus so that data can be transferred directly from memory to the peripheral or from the peripheral to memory without going through the CPU. In the next chapter we show you the details of how a DMA controller manages this transfer. For each DMA channel, the 80186 has a full 20-bit register to hold the address of the source of the DMA transfer, a 20-bit register to hold the destination address, and a 16-bit counter to keep track of how many words or bytes have been transferred. DMA transfers can be from memory to memory, from I/O to I/O, or between I/O and memory.

Finally, let's look at the three 16-bit programmable counter/timers in the 80186. The inputs and outputs of counters 0 and 1 are available on pins of the 80186. These two counters can be used to divide down the frequency of external signals, produce programmed-width pulses, etc., just as you do with the counters in an 8254. You can also internally direct the processor clock to the input of one of these counter inputs by clearing the appropriate bit in a control word. The input of the third number in the 80186 is internally connected to the processor clock.

As you can see from the preceding discussion, the 80186 contains many of the peripheral chip functions needed in a medium-complexity microcomputer system. In order to use these integrated peripherals, you have to initialize them just as you do external peripherals. If you have to work with an 80186, you can find the formats for these words in the 80186 data sheet, and work out the control words you need for your particular application on a bit-by-bit basis, just as you do for the separate peripherals. You may also find Intel Application Note 186, *Introduction to the 80186 Microprocessor*, helpful.

The 10 additional instructions that the 80186 has are as follows:

ENTER	—	Enter a procedure
LEAVE	—	Leave a procedure
BOUND	—	Check if an array index in a register is in range of array
INS	—	Input string byte or string word
OUTS	—	Output string byte or string word
PUSHA	—	Push all registers on stack
POPA	—	Pop all registers off stack
PUSH immediate	—	Push immediate number on stack
IMUL destination register, source, immediate	—	Immediate × source to destination
SHIFT/ROTATE destination, immediate	—	Shift register or memory contents specified immediate number of times

The 80960 Embedded Controller

The 80960 family controllers are 32-bit devices which are an evolutionary step up from the 8096 family. They are built with a register-to-register architecture for fast processing, and they contain code and data caches. In Chapter 11 we explain how these caches also help speed up program execution.

The devices in the 80960 family also contain a floating-point processor which performs mathematical operations on 80-bit floating-point numbers. In the next chapter we show you how a floating point processor such as this works.

DIGITAL SIGNAL PROCESSING AND DIGITAL FILTERS

The term *digital signal processing*, or *DSP*, is a very general term used to describe any system which takes samples of a signal with an A/D converter, processes the samples with a microcomputer, and outputs the computed results to a D/A converter or some other device. The process-control system and temperature controller we described earlier in the chapter is one example of digital signal processing. Other applications of DSP include antiskid braking and engine-control systems on automobiles, speech recognition and synthesis systems, and contrast enhancement of images sent back from satellites and planet probes. When most people think of DSP, however, the thought that probably comes to mind first is a special one called a *digital filter*.

A section at the start of this chapter showed how op amps can be used to build high-pass and low-pass filter circuits. In this section of the chapter, we show how filtering of a signal can also be done by taking samples of the signal with an A/D converter, performing mathematical operations on the samples with a microcomputer, and outputting the results to a D/A converter. This digital filter approach can easily produce a filter response which is difficult, if not impossible, to produce with analog circuitry. The digital approach has the further advantage that the filter response can be changed under program control.

To most people it is not intuitively obvious how an A/D converter, microcomputer, and D/A converter can produce the same effect on a signal as, for example, an RC low-pass filter. Before we can show you how digital filters work, we need to review some basic signal relationships and analog filter characteristics.

Time-Domain and Frequency-Domain View of a Square Wave

There are two ways of producing or describing a waveform such as the square wave. One way is with a circuit such as that in Figure 10-40a. If the switch is repeatedly flipped up for one-half the period and down for one-half the period, the output waveform will be a square wave centered around 0 V. This way of producing or describing a square wave is referred to as the *time-domain* method.

The second way of producing a square wave of a given frequency is by adding together a series of sine-wave signals which have just the right amplitude and phase relationships. This method of producing or describing a square wave is called the *frequency-domain* method. Figure 10-40b shows a circuit which generates a square wave by adding sine-wave signals.

Remember from basic electric circuits that when voltage sources are connected in series, the output voltage at any time is the sum of the individual voltages. The lowest-frequency sine-wave signal added here has the same frequency as the desired square-wave signal. Added to this is a signal with a frequency 3 times the frequency of the fundamental frequency, a signal with a frequency 5 times the frequency of the fundamental frequency, a signal with a frequency 7 times the fundamental frequency, etc. These multiples of the fundamental frequency are called *harmonics*. As we said before, the added harmonics must have the right amplitude and phase relationships to produce a square wave when added. Figure 10-40c shows the required phase and relative amplitude relationships.

To help you further visualize this addition process, Figure 10-40d shows the resultant waveform that will be produced by adding just the fundamental frequency and the third harmonic. It is somewhat difficult to show, but the more harmonics you add, the more the resultant waveform approaches a square wave.

Mathematically, the equation for this square wave can be expressed in terms of a fundamental frequency and harmonics as

$$v(t) = \frac{4}{\pi} \sin(2\pi ft) + \frac{1}{3}\sin 3(2\pi ft)$$

$$+ \frac{1}{5}\sin 5(2\pi ft) + \frac{1}{7}\sin 7(2\pi ft) + \cdots$$

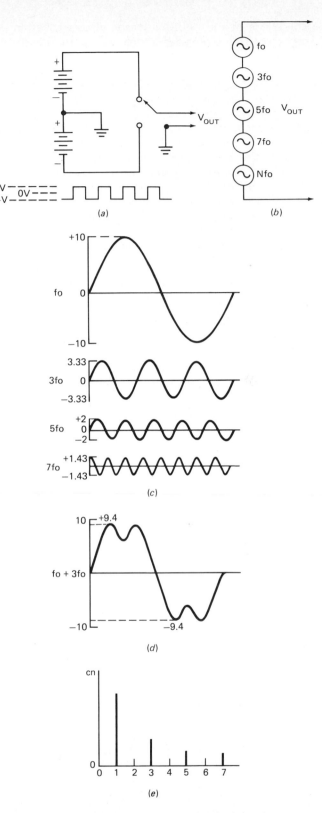

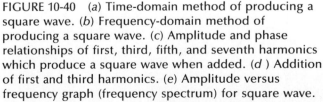

FIGURE 10-40 (a) Time-domain method of producing a square wave. (b) Frequency-domain method of producing a square wave. (c) Amplitude and phase relationships of first, third, fifth, and seventh harmonics which produce a square wave when added. (d) Addition of first and third harmonics. (e) Amplitude versus frequency graph (frequency spectrum) for square wave.

The terms in the right-hand side of this equation are referred to as a *Fourier series*. As it turns out, any periodic waveform can be described with a Fourier series, but for now, we will just stay with a square wave.

When we want to graphically represent the frequency components in a signal, it is very messy to draw waveforms such as those in Figure 10-40c. Therefore, we usually use an amplitude-versus-frequency graph, such as that in Figure 10-40e. From this graph you can easily see that the frequency components of our square wave are a fundamental frequency with a relative amplitude of 1, a third harmonic with a relative amplitude of $\frac{1}{3}$, a fifth harmonic with a relative amplitude of $\frac{1}{5}$, a seventh harmonic with a relative amplitude of $\frac{1}{7}$, etc. Later we will use this graph to help describe the effect of a low-pass filter on a square-wave signal.

Time-Domain View and Frequency-Domain View of a Low-Pass Filter

If a square wave is passed through the simple RC circuit shown in Figure 10-41a, the output waveform will look like that in Figure 10-41b. The time-domain explanation for this output waveform is that it takes time for the capacitor to charge through the resistor, so the risetime and falltime of the output signal will be increased. As you may remember, the 10% to 90% risetime for the output signal is $t_R = 2.2RC$.

Now, if you think of the square wave as a combination of harmonically related sine waves, as shown in Figure 10-40e, you can easily describe the operation of the circuit in the frequency domain. In the frequency domain, this circuit acts as a low-pass filter. This means that it passes the fundamental frequency but reduces the amplitude of the harmonics. As we showed you in Figure 10-40d, adding harmonics to the fundamental frequency is what produces the square wave, so reducing the amplitude of the harmonics will change the output waveform. For the simple RC circuit in Figure 10-41a, the critical frequency, or in other words the frequency at which a sine-wave input signal will be attenuated to 0.707 of its input value, is $f_C = 1/(2\pi RC)$. Above the critical frequency the output decreases by a factor of 10 for each increase of 10 in frequency. This means that the upper harmonics will be attenuated more than the lower harmonics, and mathematically it can be shown that the result is the waveform in Figure 10-41b.

You can pull the time-domain view of this circuit and the frequency-domain view into the same equation as follows:

$$t_R = 2.2RC \qquad \text{so } RC = \frac{t_R}{2.2}$$

$$f_C = \frac{1}{2\pi RC} \qquad \text{so } f_C = \frac{2.2}{2\pi t_R}$$

$$f_C = \frac{0.35}{t_R}$$

The point of the preceding discussions was to show you the two equivalent ways of describing the operation of a filter circuit. When we are designing analog filters, such as those made with simple resistors and capacitors, we usually think and work in the frequency domain. When we are designing digital filters, we usually think and work in the time domain. Now let's see how you can use an A/D, microcomputer, and D/A converter to function as a digital filter which modifies the waveform/frequency composition of a signal.

Digital Filters

The basic principle of a digital filter is to take continuous samples of the input waveform with the A/D converter, process the samples with the microcomputer, and output the processed results to the D/A converter. The processing done by the microcomputer determines the filter response.

If the samples are simply read in from the A/D converter and output directly to the D/A converter, then the output signal will be almost identical to the input signal. If the samples are read in from the A/D converter and held in memory for some time before being output to the D/A converter, then the output signal will simply be a delayed version of the input signal.

Now, to make it more interesting, suppose that we read in, for example, 100 samples from the A/D converter and use some mathematical algorithm to compute an output value based on these samples. When we take in the next sample from the A/D converter, we throw out the oldest sample and use the latest 100 samples to compute the next output value. The output value at any time then will be a sort of "average" of the last 100 samples. To help visualize this, you might think of the process as sliding a window of 100 samples along the waveform and using some algorithm to compute an "average" of the samples.

If the window is positioned so that all 100 samples come from a section of the square wave where the waveform is at $-V$, as shown in Figure 10-42a, then the computed output value will be $-V$. As the window slides to the right so that it includes some samples from the high section, as shown in Figure 10-42b, the "average" will increase, so the computed output value will increase. The risetime of the output or the rate at which the output value increases is determined by the weight given to new samples versus the weight given to old samples in computing the "average." Using a low-

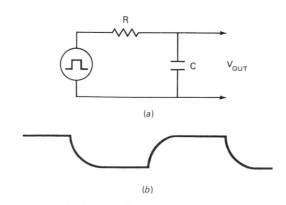

(a)

(b)

FIGURE 10-41   (a) Simple RC circuit. (b) Output waveform from RC circuit.

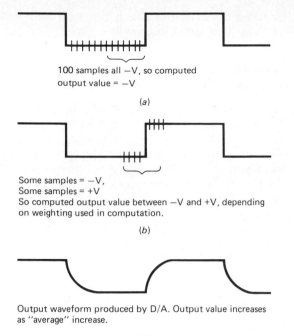

100 samples all −V, so computed
output value = −V

(a)

Some samples = −V,
Some samples = +V,
So computed output value between −V and +V, depending
on weighting used in computation.

(b)

Output waveform produced by D/A. Output value increases
as "average" increase.

(c)

FIGURE 10-42   Effective sample position on computed
output value.

pass filter weighting, the output waveform will look like
that in Figure 10-42c. The algorithm used to compute
the output values determines the characteristics of the
output waveform.

The two basic algorithms commonly used for computing the output values are the *finite impulse response* or
FIR type and the *infinite impulse response* or IIR type.
Figure 10-43a shows a functional diagram of the operation of an FIR-type filter. The box containing Z^{-1} repre-

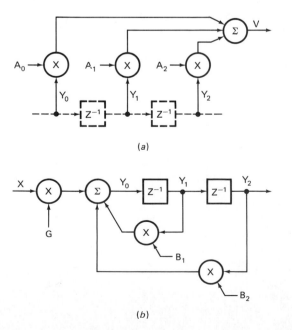

(a)

(b)

FIGURE 10-43   Digital filter algorithms. (a) FIR. (b) IIR.

sents a delay of one sample interval time. Circles containing an X represent a multiplication operation, and
the letters to the left of each circle represent the numbers
or coefficients that the term will be multiplied by. Y_0
represents the value of the current sample from the
A/D, Y_1 represents the value of the previous sample from
the A/D, and Y_2 represents the value of the sample before
that. Here's how this works. The output value V at any
time is produced by summing the (current sample ×
some coefficient) + (the previous sample × some coefficient) + (the sample before that × some coefficient),
etc. To do all this with a microprocessor requires the
simple operations of saving previous samples, multiplying, and adding.

Figure 10-43b shows a functional diagram for an
IIR digital filter. Here again the blocks containing Z^{-1}
represent a delay of one sample time. The value of the
current sample from the A/D converter is represented by
the X at the left of the diagram. The Y_0 point represents
the output from the microprocessor to the D/A converter.
Note that for an IIR filter, it is this output value which
is saved to be used in computing feedback terms for
future samples. In the FIR type, remember, the samples
from the A/D converter were saved directly for future
use. The output for an IIR type is produced by summing
(the current sample × a calculated coefficient) + (the
previous output value × a calculated coefficient) + (the
output value before that × a calculated coefficient), etc.

FIR filters are easier to design, but they may require
many terms to produce a given filter response. IIR filters
require fewer stages, but they have to be carefully
designed so that they do not become oscillators. After
we take a look at the special hardware commonly used to
implement digital filters, we will describe how computer-
based tools are used to calculate the coefficients for FIR
and IIR filters.

Digital Filter Hardware

As we said before, the basic parts of a digital filter are
an A/D converter, a microcomputer, and a D/A converter.
For very low-speed applications the microprocessor used
in the microcomputer can be a general-purpose device,
such as the 8086 we have used for other applications
throughout the book. For many real-time applications
such as digital speech processing, however, a general-
purpose microprocessor is not nearly fast enough. There
are several reasons for this.

1. The architecture of general-purpose machines is
    mostly memory-based, so most operands must be
    fetched from memory. The memory access time then
    adds to the processing time.

2. The Von Neuman architecture of general-purpose
    microprocessors uses the same bus for instructions
    and data. This means that data cannot be fetched
    until the code fetch is completed.

3. The multiply and add operations needed in most
    digital filter applications each require several clock
    cycles to execute in a general-purpose machine be-
    cause the internal hardware is not optimized for

these operations. Since many computations are needed to produce each output value, the time required for these instructions severely limits the sampling rate and the maximum frequency the filter can handle.

To solve these and other problems, several companies have designed microprocessors which have the specific features needed for digital signal processing applications. The leading examples of these types of processors are the TMS320CXX family devices from Texas Instruments. Currently the five generations in this family are the TMS320C1X, the TMS320C2X, the TMS320C3X, the TMS320C4X, and the TMS320C5X devices. These devices have a wide variety of features, but here are some of the common features.

1. Sizable amounts of on-chip registers, ROM, and RAM, so data and instructions can be accessed very quickly.

2. Separate buses for code words and for data words. This approach is commonly referred to as *Harvard architecture*. As you can see in Figure 10-44, the TMS320CXX devices' implementation of Harvard architecture has an address bus and a data bus for program words, an address bus and a data bus for data words, and even an address bus and a data bus for direct memory access (DMA) by an external device. These parallel buses allow instructions and data to be fetched at the same time.

3. An optimized multiplier which, depending on the specific device, can perform a 16 × 16- or a 32 × 32-bit multiply in one clock cycle. For the TMS320C50 device, a clock cycle can be as short as 35 ns.

4. A 32-bit barrel shifter which can shift an operand any number of bits in one clock cycle.

5. A 16-bit or a 32-bit CPU which maintains precision during the chain calculations needed in most digital filter applications.

6. An instruction set optimized for DSP applications. For example, the single TMS320C30 instruction MPYI3 <srcA>, <srcB>, <dst1> || ADDI3 <srcC>, <srcD>, <dst2> will multiply two specified operands (srcA × srcB) and add two different operands (srcC + srcD). Perhaps you can see how an instruction such as this would be useful in implementing the computations for an FIR filter such as we described before. The TMS320C30 also has a "zero-overhead" loop instruction which can be used to quickly repeat an operation some number of times.

7. Some devices in the family also have built-in floating-point processors which can directly perform operations on numbers in floating-point format. (In the next chapter we show you how the 8087 floating-point processor works.)

Figure 10-45 shows a block diagram of a complete digital filter system using one of the TMS320C25 family parts. Note that a simple analog low-pass filter is put in series with the input. Remember the *sampling theorem*, which states that the highest-frequency signal which can be digitized and reconstructed is one which contains two samples per cycle. If higher frequencies are digitized, alias frequencies will be generated when the signal is reconstructed with a D/A converter. This low-pass filter on the input helps prevent aliasing.

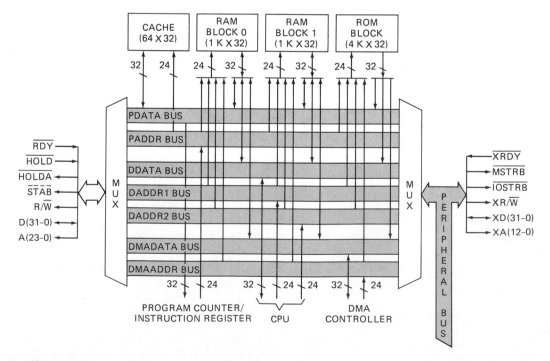

FIGURE 10-44 The TMS320CXX device's implementation of Harvard architecture. (*Texas Instruments Inc.*)

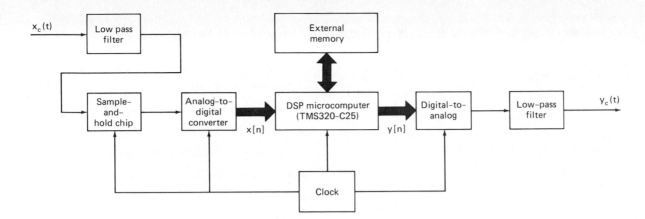

FIGURE 10-45 Block diagram of a TMS320C25 DSP-based filter.

After the anti-alias filter a sample-and-hold is used to keep the value on the input of the A/D constant during conversion. A simple low-pass analog filter is connected to the output of the D/A converter to "smooth" the output signal.

For development purposes and experimentation with a PC-type microcomputer, the DSP-16 board from Ariel Corp. has two 16-bit, 50-kHz A/D converters, a 40-MHz TMS320C25, and two 16-bit 50-kHz D/A converters. The dual channels allow two signals to be processed at the same time. Other boards allow different combinations of sampling rate and number of channels.

Digital Filter Software and Development Tools

As perhaps you can guess from the algorithms in Figure 10-43, developing the program for a digital filter involves two main tasks. The first task is to determine the coefficients by which the terms in the equation will be multiplied to implement the desired filter. The second task is to write a program which reads in values from the A/D converter, computes an output value, and sends the completed value to the D/A converter at the right time.

Several DOS-compatible software packages are available to help perform these tasks. Examples are the Digital Filter Design Package-2 (DFDP2) from Atlanta Signal Processors Inc. and the Filter Design and Analysis System (FDAS2) from Momentum Data Systems. When given the desired filter type, break frequencies, and attenuation rates, these packages tell you if the desired filter can be implemented and generate the required coefficients. After the coefficients are generated, another module in these software packages can be used to produce the assembly language program for the DSP microprocessor. To give you an example of how simple the actual program is, Figure 10-46 shows a procedure which implements a bandpass filter on the TMS320C25 in Figure 10-45. The RPTK 68 instruction in this procedure causes the following instruction to be repeated 68 times. The MACD FDATA+>FD00,*— that is repeated 68 times will multiply a data memory value by a program memory value, add the result to an accumulator, and decrement the pointer to point to the next operands. These two instructions then do most of the work of computing an output value.

Once the coefficients and program for a digital filter have been produced, the next step is to test the result.

```
DELAR     EQU       1                ★DELAY AR REGISTER
★
FILTER

          LARP      DELAR            ★POINT TO THE DELAY INDEX REGISTER
          LRLK      DELAR,Z000       ★INDEX POINTS TO Z-0 (INPUT)
          LAC       VSAMPL,15        ★GET & SCALE INPUT
          SACH      ★                ★SAVE SCALED INPUT

          MPYK      0                ★P = 0
          ZAC                        ★AC = 0
          LRLK      DELAR,ZLAST      ★INDEX POINTS TO Z-N
          RPTK      68
          MACD      FDATA+>FD00,★—   ★MULTIPLY,ACCUM.and DELAY
          APAC                       ★FORM RESULT
          SACH      VSAMPL,0         ★SAVE OUTPUT
          RET                        ★RETURN
★

          PEND
          END
```

FIGURE 10-46 TMS320C25 digital filter program. (*R.W. Schafer, "The Math Behind the MIPS: DSP Basics." Electronic Design, September 1988*)

One way to do this is with a PC-compatible board such as the Ariel unit described before. Another method is to use an emulator such as the Texas Instruments XDS1000. This emulator consists of a PC board which plugs into an IBM PC-compatible computer and a buffer pod which plugs into the prototype hardware. As with other emulators we have discussed, it allows you to load programs, set breakpoints, do traces, etc. A software package and an emulator allow you to quickly design, test, and debug a digital filter system.

Switched Capacitor Digital Filters

For simple filter designs, another type of digital filter called a *switched capacitor filter* implements digital filtering without the need for the A/D and D/A converters. An example of this type of device is the National MF10. In this type of filter an input signal is sampled on a capacitor. The signal is passed on to other capacitors, and fractions of the outputs from these capacitors are summed to produce an analog output signal directly. Switched capacitor filters are less expensive, but they do not give the degree of programmability that the microprocessor-based filters do.

CHECKLIST OF IMPORTANT TERMS AND CONCEPTS IN THIS CHAPTER

If you do not remember any of the terms in the following list, use the index to help you find them in the chapter for review.

Op amp

Comparator

Hysteresis

Noninverting amplifier

Inverting amplifier

Virtual ground

Gain-bandwidth product

Unity-gain bandwidth

Adder circuit—summing point

Differential amplifier

Common-mode signal, common-mode rejection

Instrumentation amplifier

Op-amp integrator circuit

Linear ramp
  Saturation

Op-amp differentiator

Op-amp active filters

Low-pass filter, high-pass filter, bandpass filter
  Critical frequency or breakpoint
  Second-order low-pass filter, second-order high-pass filter

Photodiode, solar cell

Temperature-sensitive voltage sources

Temperature-sensitive current sources

Thermocouples, cold-junction compensation

Force and pressure transducers

Strain gage, LVDT, load cell

Flow sensors—paddle wheel, differential pressure transducer

D/A converters
  Resolution
  Full-scale output voltage
  Maximum error
  Linearity
  Settling time

A/D converters
  Conversion time
  Sample and hold
  Sampling theorem
  Quantizing error

A/D conversion methods
  Parallel-comparator A/D converter
  Dual-slope A/D converter
  Successive-approximation A/D converter
  Data acquisition system

Direct memory access, DMA

Set point

Servo control

Settling time, underdamped and overdamped responses

Residual error

Proportional-integral-derivative control loop, PID

Time-slice system

On/off control

Robotics

Embedded controllers

80186, 80188

Digital signal processing

Time-domain and frequency-domain view of a square wave

Digital filter operation

Finite impulse response (FIR) filter algorithm

Infinite impulse response (IIR) filter algorithm

Switched capacitor filter

REVIEW QUESTIONS AND PROBLEMS

1. *a.* A comparator circuit such as the one in Figure
    10-1*b* is powered by ±15 V, the inverting input
    is tied to +5 V, and the noninverting input is
    at +5.3 V. About what voltage will be on the
    output of the comparator?

    b. An amplifier circuit, such as the one in Figure
    10-1*d*, has R1 = 10 kΩ and R2 = 190 kΩ.
    Calculate the closed-loop voltage gain for the
    circuit and the V_{out} that will be produced by a
    V_{in} of 0.030 V. What voltage would you measure
    on the inverting input? What would be the gain
    of the circuit if R2 = 0 Ω?

    c. An amplifier circuit, such as the one in Figure
    10-1*e*, is built with an R1 of 15 kΩ and an R_f
    of 75 kΩ. Calculate the closed-loop voltage gain
    for the circuit and the output voltage for an
    input voltage of 0.73 V. What voltage will you
    always measure on the inverting input of this
    circuit?

    d. A differential amplifier, such as the one in
    Figure 10-1*g*, is built with R1 = R2 = 100 kΩ
    and R_f = R = 1 MΩ. V_1 = 4.9 V, and V_2 = 5.1
    V. Calculate the output voltage and polarity.

    e. Describe the main advantage of the instrumen-
    tation amplifier in Figure 10-1*h* over the simple
    differential amplifier in Figure 10-1*g*.

    f. If the amplifier used in the circuit in part *b* has
    a gain-bandwidth product of 1 MHz, what will
    be the closed-loop bandwidth of the circuit?

2. Draw a circuit showing how a light-dependent
    resistor can be connected to a comparator so the
    output of the comparator changes state when the
    resistance of the LDR is 10 kΩ.

3. For the photodiode amplifier circuit in Figure 10-5,
    what voltage will you measure on the inverting
    input of the amplifier? Why is it important to use
    an FET input amplifier for this circuit? Which
    direction are electrons flowing through the photo-
    diode?

4. In what application might you use a temperature-
    dependent current device such as the AD590 rather
    than a temperature-dependent voltage device such
    as the LM35?

5. Why must thermocouples be cold-junction compen-
    sated in order to make accurate measurements?
    How can the nonlinearity of a thermocouple be
    compensated for?

6. Why are strain gages usually connected in a bridge
    configuration? Why do you use a differential ampli-
    fier to amplify the signal from a strain-gage bridge?

7. Calculate the full-scale output voltage for the simple
    D/A converter in Figure 10-14.

8. What is the resolution of a 13-bit D/A converter? If
    the converter has a full-scale output of 10.000 V,
    what is the size of each step? What will be the

actual maximum output voltage of this converter?
What accuracy should this converter have to be
consistent with its resolution?

9. Why must a 12-bit D/A converter have latches on
    its inputs if it is to be connected to 8-bit ports or
    an 8-bit data bus?

10. Describe the operation of a flash-type A/D converter.
    What are its main advantages and disadvantages?

11. For the dual-slope A/D converter in Figure 10-19,
    what will be the displayed count for an input voltage
    of 2.372 V? What is the resolution of a $4\frac{1}{2}$-digit
    slope-type A/D converter expressed in bits?

12. How many clock cycles does a 12-bit successive-
    approximation A/D converter take to do a conver-
    sion on a 0.1-V input signal? On a 5-V input signal?
    How does this compare with the number of clock
    cycles required for a 12-bit dual-slope type?

13. *a.* Assume the inputs of the MC1408 D/A converter
    in Figure 10-20 are connected to an output port
    on your microcomputer board and the output
    of the comparator is connected to bit D0 of an
    input port. Write the algorithm for a procedure
    to do an A/D conversion by outputting an
    incrementing count to the output port.

    b. Write an algorithm for a procedure to do the
    conversion by the successive-approximation
    method. Which method will produce a faster
    result? If the hardware is available, write the
    programs for these algorithms and compare the
    times by watching the comparator output with
    an oscilloscope.

14. Show the detailed algorithm for the procedure you
    would use to read in the data from a multiplexed
    BCD output A/D converter such as the MC14433
    in Figure 10-23 and assemble the value in a 16-bit
    register for display.

15. The data sheet for an A/D converter indicates that
    its output is in offset-binary code. If the converter
    is set up for a range of −5 to +5 V and the output
    code is 01011011, what input voltage does this
    represent? How could you convert this code to 2's
    complement form after you read the code into your
    microcomputer?

16. Write a procedure to round a 32-bit BCD number
    in DX:AX to a 16-bit BCD number in DX.

17. For the scale circuitry in Figure 10-23, what voltage
    should you measure on the inverting input of
    the LM308 amplifier? What voltages should you
    measure on the two inputs of the LM363 amplifier
    with no load on the scale? What voltage should you
    measure on the output of the LM363 with no load
    on the scale?

18. The section of the scale program following the label

NXTKEY in Figure 10-35 moves some bytes around in memory. Rewrite this section of the program using an 8086 string instruction to do the move operations. Which version seems more efficient in this case?

19. Describe how feedback helps hold the value of some variable, such as a motor speed, constant. Refer to Figure 10-27 in your explanation.

20. What problem in a control loop does integral feedback help solve? Why is derivative feedback sometimes added to a control loop?

21. What is the major advantage of a microcomputer-controlled loop over the analog approach shown in Figure 10-29?

22. Suppose that you want to control the speed of a small dc motor, such as the one in Figure 10-27, with LOOP1 of our microcomputer-based process controller.
   a. Show how you would connect the output from the motor's tachometer to the system in Figure 10-33. Also show how you would connect an 8-bit D/A to control the current to the motor.
   b. Write a flowchart for the LOOP1 procedure to control the speed of the motor.
   c. Describe how a lookup table could be used to determine the feedback value.

23. a. Describe how a square wave can be generated by the time-domain method.
   b. Describe how a square wave can be generated by the frequency-domain method.

24. a. Describe the basic operation of a digital filter.
   b. Describe the major difference in how an output value is computed in an FIR digital filter and how it is computed in an IIR filter.

25. a. Why is a general-purpose microprocessor such as the 8086 not suitable for most digital filter applications?
   b. Describe three features designed into a digital signal processing microprocessor such as a TMS320CXX device to speed up processing.

26. a. What is the minimum frequency that a sine-wave signal must be sampled with an A/D converter so that it can be reconstructed with a D/A converter?
   b. Why is an analog low-pass filter often put before the A/D in a digital filter?
   c. What is the purpose of the sample-and-hold circuit on the input of the A/D in Figure 10-45?

27. List the two tasks involved in writing the program for a digital filter.

CHAPTER 11

DMA, DRAMs, Cache Memories, Coprocessors, and EDA Tools

The major objective of the first six chapters of this book was to introduce you to structured programming and to writing 8086 assembly language programs. Chapters 7 through 10 introduced you to the hardware of an 8086 minimum-mode system, showed you how to interface a microcomputer to a wide variety of input and output devices, and finally demonstrated how all these pieces are put together to build a simple microcomputer-based instrument or control system. The major goal of the remaining chapters in the book is to show you the hardware and software of larger microcomputer systems.

As an example of what we mean by a larger system, look at Figure 11-1, which shows the component side of the main microprocessor board or "motherboard" for an IBM PC. As you can see, the board contains an 8088 microprocessor, ROM, and a large block of dynamic RAM. The board also has a socket for a special 8087 math auxiliary processor. Finally, note the system expansion slots in the upper left corner of Figure 11-1. These slots allow you to plug in additional boards which give the system the specific interface functions you need. For example, you may want to add a disk-controller board,

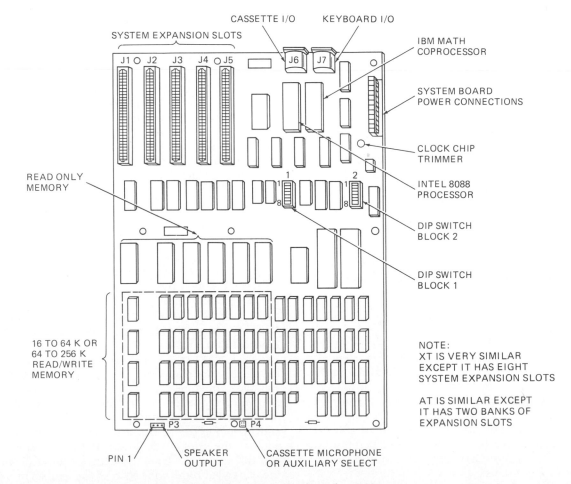

FIGURE 11-1 Component layout diagram for IBM PC motherboard. (*IBM Corporation*)

a serial-port board, a CRT controller board, a board with additional memory, an A/D-D/A board, or a board which allows your PC to function as a logic analyzer. This "open-system" approach lets you easily customize a system for your applications and financial state.

In later chapters we discuss the operation of peripheral boards such as CRT controller boards, disk-drive controller boards, and serial communication boards which plug into these expansion slots.

The first goal of this chapter is to show you how the circuitry on a microcomputer motherboard such as the one in Figure 11-1 works. A second goal of this chapter is to show you how computer-based tools are used to design, test, debug, and produce the hardware and software for a board such as this.

OBJECTIVES

At the end of this chapter you should be able to:

1. Show how an 8086 is connected with a controller device for operation in its maximum mode.

2. Show how a direct memory access (DMA) controller device can be connected in an 8086 system and describe how a DMA data transfer takes place.

3. Describe how large banks of dynamic RAM can be connected in a system.

4. Describe how a cache memory is used to reduce the number of wait states required in a system which has a large dynamic RAM main memory.

5. Describe how automatic error detecting-correcting circuitry works with memories.

6. Show how a coprocessor can be connected to an 8086 or 8088 operating in maximum mode.

7. Describe how an 8086 and an 8087 cooperate during the execution of a program which contains instructions for each.

8. Write a simple assembly language program for an 8087.

9. Describe how schematic capture programs, simulator programs, and other computer-based tools are now used to develop a microcomputer system.

INTRODUCTION

After much agonizing we finally decided to use the original IBM PC for some of the system examples in this chapter. Although the PC itself is somwhat outdated, it demonstrates well the concepts of DMA, DRAM interface, and coprocessors that we want to teach here. Almost all our discussion of PC operation is also valid for a PC/AT, and as you will see in later chapters, an understanding of the basic PC is a good starting point for understanding later generation systems.

To give you a more detailed idea of where we are going in this chapter and how it relates to what you have learned in previous chapters, let's take a look at Figure 11-2, which shows a block diagram of circuitry on an IBM PC motherboard. As you look at this diagram you should see many familiar parts and a few new ones. Start on the left side of the diagram and work your way across it from the 8088 CPU and the 8259A priority-interrupt controller. Under the 8088 main processor note the auxiliary processor socket which can be used for an 8087 math coprocessor.

The next vertical line of devices to the right in Figure 11-2 consists of the address bus buffers, the data bus buffers, and the 8288 bus controller chip. As we explain later, a bus controller chip is required to generate control bus signals when the 8088 is operated in its maximum mode. The buses from these devices go across the drawing and connect to the 62-pin peripheral board connectors so the 8088 can communicate with the boards in the peripheral expansion slots as well as with the ROM, RAM, and ports on board. Incidentally, the layout of the IBM PC/XT motherboard is very similar to this layout, but the XT has eight I/O slots instead of five.

Now find the ROM in the lower center, the keyboard logic, etc., in the middle right, and the dynamic RAM in the upper right. Finally, take a look at the column of devices which contains the 8237A-5 DMA controller. Starting at the bottom of this column you see an 8253-5 programmable timer which is nearly identical to the 8254 we described in Chapter 8. Just above this is the familiar 8255A-5 programmable port device. Now you are left to ponder just the three devices with DMA in their labels.

The major parts of this circuit that are new to you are the DMA section, the dynamic RAM section and its associated parity check/generator logic, and the auxiliary processor. In the following sections of the chapter we discuss each of these types of circuitry in detail. First, however, we will explain what we mean when we say that an 8086 or 8088 is operating in maximum mode because many of the circuits shown in this chapter and the following chapters use the devices in this mode.

THE 8086 MAXIMUM MODE

Figure 11-3a, p. 348, shows the pin diagram of the 8086 again. You may remember from our discussion in Chapter 7 that if pin 33, the MN/$\overline{\text{MX}}$ pin, is tied high, the 8086 operates in its minimum mode. In minimum mode the 8086 directly generates the control bus signals shown in parentheses next to pins 24 through 31 in Figure 11-3a.

If the MN/$\overline{\text{MX}}$ pin is tied low, the 8086 operates in its maximum mode and pins 24 through 31 generate the signals named next to the pins in Figure 11-3a. In maximum mode the control bus signals are sent out in coded form on the status lines, $\overline{\text{S0}}$, $\overline{\text{S1}}$, and $\overline{\text{S2}}$. As shown in Figure 11-3b, an external controller device such as the Intel 8288 is used to produce the required control bus signals from these lines. Figure 11-3b shows the expanded names for each of the control bus signals generated by the 8288. Note in Figure 11-3b that 8282 octal latches are used to demultiplex the address signals

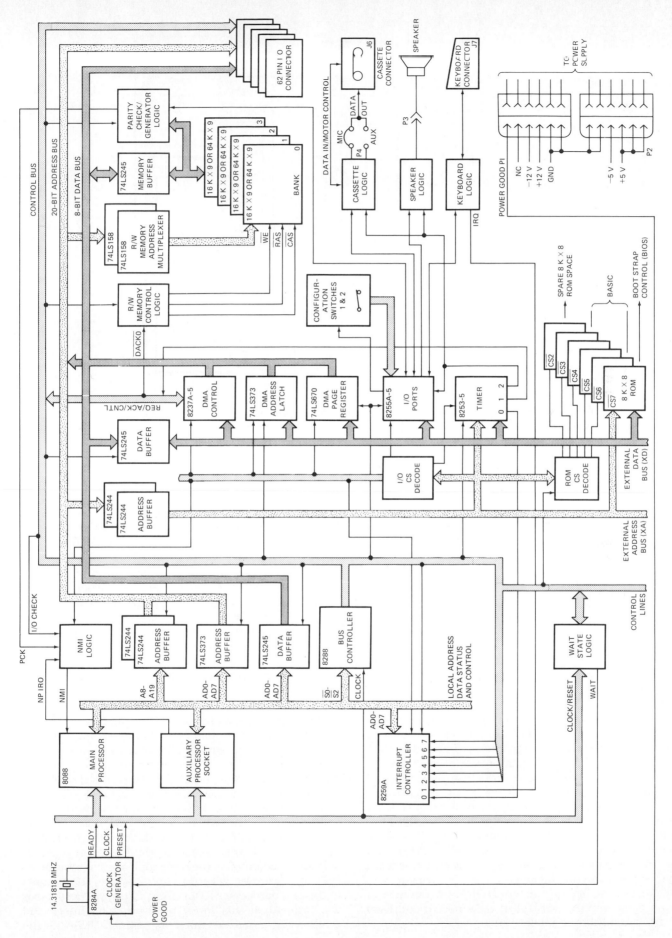

FIGURE 11-2 Block diagram of circuitry on IBM PC motherboard.   (*IBM Corporation*)

347

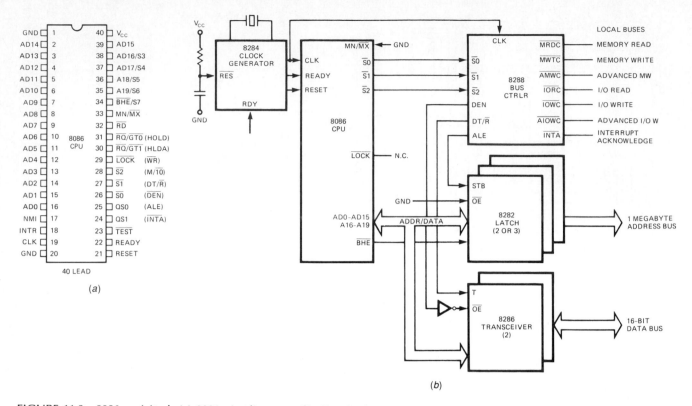

FIGURE 11-3   8086 revisited. (a) 8086 pin diagram. (b) Circuit showing 8086 connections for MAX mode operation.   (*Intel Corporation*)

and 8286 bidirectional drivers are used to buffer the data bus so that it can drive a boardful of devices.

Now we will show you some of the ways that a microprocessor can timeshare its buses in minimum mode and maximum mode.

DIRECT MEMORY ACCESS (DMA) DATA TRANSFER

DMA Overview

Up to this point in the book we have used program instructions to transfer data from ports to memory or from memory to ports. For some applications, such as transferring data bytes to memory from a magnetic or optical disk, however, the data bytes are coming in from the disk faster than they can be read in with program instructions. In a case like this we use a dedicated hardware device called a *direct memory access* or *DMA* controller to manage the data transfer. The DMA controller temporarily borrows the address bus, data bus, and control bus from the microprocessor and transfers the data bytes directly from the disk controller to a series of memory locations. Because the data transfer is handled totally in hardware, it is much faster than it would be if done by program instructions. A DMA controller can also transfer data from memory to a port. Some DMA devices even can do memory-to-memory transfers to implement fast block transfers. Here's an example of how a common DMA controller is connected and used in an 8086 minimum-mode system.

Circuit Connections and Operation of the Intel 8237 DMA Controller

We chose the 8237 DMA controller as the example for this section because it is a commonly used device; also, it is one of the devices you will find if you start poking around inside an IBM PC/XT or PC/AT. Before we dig into the actual connections and operation of an 8237 circuit, however, let's take a look at the block diagram in Figure 11-4 to get an overview of how a DMA transfer takes place. The main point to keep in your mind here is that the microprocessor and the DMA controller timeshare the use of the address, data, and control buses. The three switches in the middle of the block diagram are an attempt to show how control of the buses is transferred.

When the system is first turned on, the switches are in the up position, so the buses are connected from the microprocessor to system memory and peripherals. We initialize all the programmable devices in the system and go on executing our program until we need, for example, to read a file off a disk. To read a disk file we send a series of commands to the smart disk controller device, telling it to find and read the desired block of data from the disk. When the disk controller has the first byte of data from the disk block ready, it sends a *DMA request*, DREQ, signal to the DMA controller. If that input (channel) of the DMA controller is unmasked, the DMA controller will send a *hold-request*, HRQ, signal to the microprocessor HOLD input. The microprocessor will respond to this input by floating its buses and sending out a *hold-acknowledge* signal, HLDA, to the

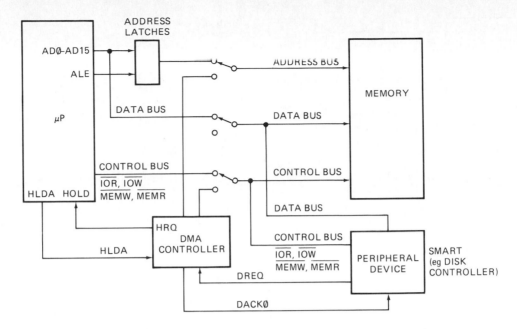

FIGURE 11-4 Block diagram showing how a DMA controller operates in a microcomputer system.

DMA controller. When the DMA controller receives the HLDA signal, it will send out a control signal which throws the three bus switches down to their DMA position. This disconnects the processor from the buses and connects the DMA controller to the buses.

When the DMA controller gets control of the buses, it sends out the memory address where the first byte of data from the disk controller is to be written. Next the DMA controller sends a *DMA-acknowledge*, DACK0, signal to the disk controller device to tell it to get ready to output the byte. Finally, the DMA controller asserts both the $\overline{\text{MEMW}}$ and the $\overline{\text{IOR}}$ lines on the control bus. Asserting the $\overline{\text{MEMW}}$ signal enables the addressed memory to accept data written to it. Asserting the $\overline{\text{IOR}}$ signal enables the disk controller to output the byte of data from the disk on the data bus. The byte of data then is transferred directly from the disk controller to the memory location without passing through the CPU or the DMA controller.

NOTE: For this type of transfer the disk controller chip select input does not have to be enabled by the port address decoding circuitry as it does for normal reading from and writing to registers in the device. In fact, the normal port-decoding circuitry is disabled during DMA operations to prevent the combination of $\overline{\text{IOR}}$ and the output memory address from turning on unwanted ports.

When the data transfer is complete, the DMA controller unasserts its hold-request signal to the processor and releases the buses. The switches in Figure 11-4 are effectively thrown back up to the CPU position. This lets the processor take over the buses again until another DMA transfer is needed. The processor continues executing from where it left off in the program.

A DMA transfer from memory to the disk controller proceeds in a similar manner except that the DMA controller asserts the memory-read control signal, $\overline{\text{MEMR}}$, and the output-write control signal, $\overline{\text{IOW}}$. DMA transfers may be done a byte at a time or in blocks.

Now, to give you more practice working your way through actual microprocessor circuits, let's look at Figure 11-5, p. 359, to see some of the circuitry we might add to an 8086 system so that we can do DMA transfers to and from a disk controller. This circuitry is simply a more detailed version of the block diagram in Figure 11-4.

The first thing to do in analyzing this schematic is to identify the major devices and relate their function, where possible, to the block diagram. The 8086 and 8284 should be old friends from your exploration of the SDK-86. The 8237 is, of course, the DMA controller, and the 8272 is the floppy-disk controller. We discuss the operation of a disk controller more in Chapter 13, but for now all you need to know about it is the overview of how it interacts with the 8237, as we described earlier. The 8282s in this circuit are octal latches with three-state outputs. They are used here to latch addresses output from either the 8086 or from the DMA controller. These devices are controlled by ALE from the 8086 and by AEN and ADSTB from the DMA controller.

When the power is first turned on, the *address-enable* signal, AEN, from the DMA controller is low. Devices U1, U2, and U4 are then enabled, and the ALE signal from the 8086 goes to the strobe inputs of all three devices. When the 8086 sends out an address and an ALE signal, these three devices will grab the address and send it out on the address bus lines, A19–A0. This is just as would be done in a simpler 8086 system. Now, when the DMA controller wants to take over the bus, it asserts its AEN output high. This does several things. First, it disables

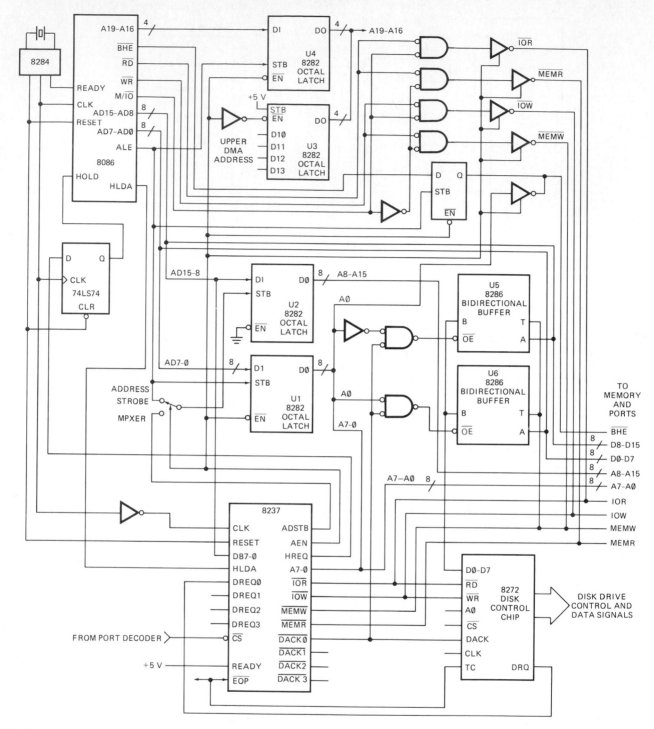

FIGURE 11-5 Schematic for 8086 system with 8237 DMA controller and 8272 floppy-disk controller.

device U1 so that address lines A7–A0 no longer come from the 8086 bus. The 8237 directly outputs the lower 8 bits of the memory address for the DMA transfer.

Second, AEN, going high, switches the strobe multiplexer so that the strobe for device U2 comes from the address strobe output of the 8237. To save pins, the 8237 outputs the upper 8 bits of the memory address for the DMA transfer on its data bus pins and asserts its ADSTB output high to let you know that this address

is present there. At the start of a DMA transfer, then, memory address bits A15–A8 will be sent out by the 8237 and latched on the outputs of U2.

Still another effect of AEN going high is to switch the source of address bits A19–A16 from device U4 to device U3. The DMA controller does not send out these address bits during a DMA transfer, so you have to produce them in some other way. You can either hard-wire the inputs of U3 to ground or +5 V to produce a fixed value for these bits, or you can connect these inputs to an output port so you can specify these address bits under program control.

Finally, AEN going high switches the source of the control bus signals from the outputs of the control bus decoder circuitry to the control bus signal outputs of the DMA controller. This is necessary because, during a DMA transfer, the 8237 generates the required control bus signals such as $\overline{MEMW}$ and $\overline{IOR}$. Incidentally, the NOR gate decoder circuitry in the upper right corner of the schematic is necessary to produce processor control bus signals compatible with those from the 8237.

The final part of the circuit in Figure 11-5 to analyze is the two 8286 octal bus transceivers. The disk controller has only an 8-bit data bus output. If we had connected these eight lines on the lower eight data bus lines of the 8086 system, the DMA controller would be able to transfer bytes only to even addresses. Likewise, if we had connected the disk controller data outputs on the upper eight data lines of the 8086 system, the DMA controller would be able to transfer bytes only to odd addresses in memory. To solve this problem, we connect the two 8286s as a switch which can route data to/from the disk controller from/to either odd or even addresses in memory. If you work through the glue logic, you should see that A0 determines which half of the data bus is connected to the eight data pins of the disk controller. $\overline{MEMW}$ determines whether the buffers are set to transfer data to or from the disk controller. Now let's look more closely at the signal flow and timing for this circuit.

A DMA Transfer Timing Diagram

Figure 11-6 shows the sequence of signals that will take place for a DMA transfer in a system such as that in Figure 11-5. Keep a copy of Figure 11-5 handy as you work your way down through these waveforms. The labels we have added to each signal should help you. We will pick up where the 8237 asserts AEN high and gains control of the buses. After the 8237 gains control of the bus, it sends out the lower 8 bits of the memory address on its A7–A0 pins and the upper 8 bits of the memory address on its DB0–DB7 pins. The 8237 pulses ADSTB high to latch these address bits in the 8282 and then removes these address bits from the data bus. At about the same time the 8237 sends a DACK signal to the disk controller to tell it to get ready for a data transfer.

Now that everything is ready, the 8237 asserts two control bus signals to enable the actual transfer. For a transfer from memory to the disk controller, it will assert $\overline{MEMR}$ and $\overline{IOW}$. For a transfer from the disk controller to memory, it will assert $\overline{MEMW}$ and $\overline{IOR}$. Note that the 8237 does not have to put out an I/O address to enable the disk controller for this transfer. When programmed in DMA mode, the disk controller needs only $\overline{IOR}$ or $\overline{IOW}$ to be asserted to enable it for the transfer. Also note that the 8237 will not output a new address on A8 through A15 when a second transfer is done, unless those bits have to be changed. This saves time during multiple-byte transfers.

When the programmed number of bytes have been transferred, the DMA controller pulses its end-of-proc-

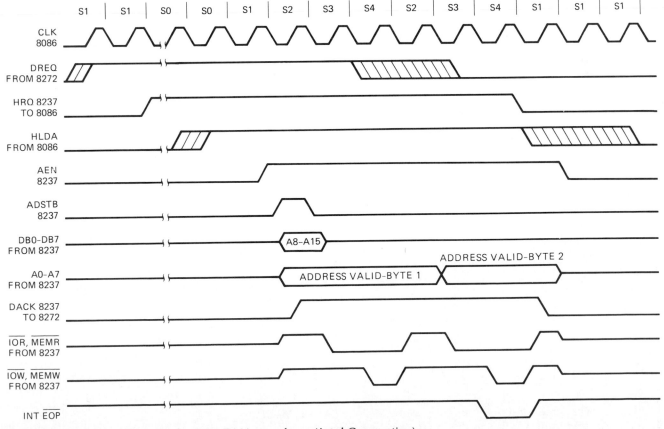

FIGURE 11-6 Timing diagram for 8237 DMA transfer. (*Intel Corporation*)

ess, $\overline{EOP}$, pin low, unasserts its hold request to the 8086, and drops its AEN signal low. This releases the buses back to the 8086. Now that you have an idea how an 8237 is connected and operates in a system, we will give you an overview of what is involved in initializing it.

8237 Initialization Overview

Initializing an 8237 is not difficult, but it does require a fairly large number of bytes. We do not have space to show you a complete initialization, but here is an overview.

The 8237 is connected in a system as a port device, so you write initialization words to it just as you would to any other port device. Incidentally, several 8237s can be cascaded in a master-slave arrangement to give more input channels and each device must be initialized.

As shown by the pin labels on the 8237 in Figure 11-5, the 8237 has four DMA request inputs or *channels*, as they are commonly called. For each channel you need to send a command word which specifies the general operation, mode words, the starting memory address, and the number of bytes to be transferred. Each channel of the 8237 can be programmed to transfer a single byte for each request, a block of bytes for each request, or to keep transferring bytes until it receives a wait signal on the $\overline{EOP}$ input/output. Consult the data sheet in an Intel data book to get the details of each command word.

DMA and the IBM PC

Now that you know how DMA operates, let's take a look back at the DMA section in the block diagram of the

IBM PC motherboard circuitry in Figure 11-2. The 8237A-5 is, of course, the DMA controller. The 74LS373 just under it is used to grab the upper 8 bits of the DMA address sent out on the data bus by the 8237A-5 during a transfer. This device has the same function as device U2 in Figure 11-5. The 74LS670 just below this is used to output bits A16–A19 of the DMA transfer address, the same function performed by U3 in the circuit in Figure 11-5.

In order that peripheral boards can interface with the motherboard circuitry on a DMA basis, the DMA signal lines are connected to the peripheral connectors shown in the upper right corner of Figure 11-2. To see how DMA and other signals go to the peripheral boards, take a look at the pin descriptions in Figure 11-7.

The signals shown in Figure 11-7a are bused to all five peripheral connectors in parallel so that any board can access them. Most of the signals on these connectors

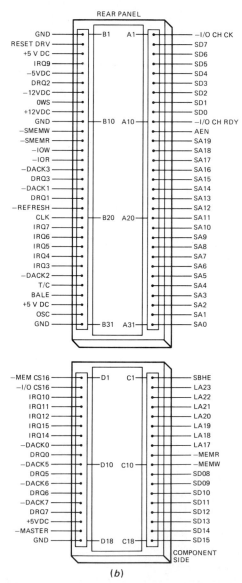

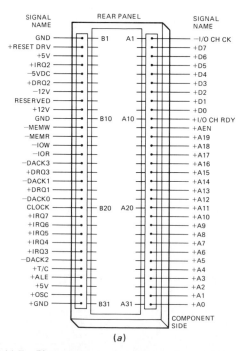

FIGURE 11-7 Pin names and numbers for peripheral slots. (a) On IBM PC motherboard. (b) On IBM PC/AT motherboard. (*IBM Corporation*)

should be easily recognizable to you. A + in front of a signal indicates that the signal is active high, and a − indicates that the signal is active low. A0 through A19 on the connectors are the 20 demultiplexed address lines, and D0 through D7 are the eight data lines. IRQ2 through IRQ7 are interrupt request lines which go to the 8259A priority-interrupt controller so that peripheral boards can interrupt the 8086 if necessary. Some other simple signals on the connectors are the power supply voltages; the standard ALE, −MEMW, −MEMR, −IOW, and −IOR control bus signals; and some clock signals. The I/O CH RDY pin on the connector can be asserted by a peripheral board to cause the 8086 to insert WAIT states until the peripheral board is ready.

Finally, we are down to the DMA signals on the expansion connectors. The DMA request pins DRQ1–DRQ3 allow peripheral boards to request use of the buses. A disk controller board, for example, might request a DMA transfer of a block of data from system memory. When the DMA controller gains control of the system buses, it lets the peripheral device or board know by asserting the appropriate −DACK0 through −DACK3 signal. The AEN signal on the connectors is used to gate the DMA address on the bus, as we described earlier. When the programmed number of bytes has been transferred, the T/C pin on the connector goes high to let the peripheral know that the transfer is complete.

To show you that it is a small step to understand another bus, Figure 11-7b shows the pin names for the I/O bus connectors on IBM PC/AT. The 80286 microprocessor used in the AT has 24 address lines which are sent out on the bus as SA0 through SA19 and LA20 through LA23. SD0 through SD15 are the 16 data lines for the bus. The AT motherboard uses two 8259A priority interrupt controllers to produce 15 interrupt inputs. The 11 interrupt inputs not used in the motherboard are connected to IRQ pins on the bus. The AT uses two 8237A DMA controllers to produce 7 DMA channels. The DREQ input signal for each channel and the DACK signal for each channel are present on the bus. Other DMA signals present are AEN and T/C. The next signals to look for in Figure 11-7b are the control bus signals, −SMEMW, −SMEMR, −IOW, −IOR, −MEMW, −MEMR, BALE, and SBHE, which should be fairly familiar to you from our previous discussions of the 8086. Now, all you have left are a few miscellaneous signals such as REFRESH, which is used to indicate a DRAM refresh operation is in process; −MEM CS16, which lets the motherboard know that the present data transfer is a 1 wait-state transfer; and −I/O CS16, which is used to let the motherboard know that the present data transfer is a 1 wait-state transfer. The 0WS line on the bus is used to tell the motherboard that no wait states are required to complete the current read or write cycle. RESET DRV is the system reset line, CLK is the 6.0-MHz system clock, and OSC is a high frequency clock signal which can be divided down and used on I/O boards. Finally, the −MASTER signal is used by another processor board to gain control of the bus.

Now that you know how DMA works in a microcomputer, the next block of circuitry to talk about is the RAM section.

INTERFACING AND REFRESHING DYNAMIC RAMs

Review of Dynamic RAM Characteristics

For small systems such as the SDK-86, where we only need a few kilobytes of RAM, we usually use static RAM devices because they are very easy to interface to. For larger systems, where we want several hundred kilobytes or megabytes of memory, we use dynamic RAMs, often called DRAMs. Here's why.

Static RAMs store each bit in an internal flip-flop which requires four to six transistors. In DRAMs a data bit is stored as a charge or no charge on a tiny capacitor. All that is needed in addition to the capacitor is a single transistor switch to access the capacitor when a bit is written to it or read from it. The result of this is that DRAMs require much less power per bit, and many more bits can be stored in a given size chip. This makes the cost per bit of storage much less. The disadvantage of DRAMs is that each stored data bit must be refreshed every 2 to 8 ms because the charge stored on the tiny capacitors tends to change due to leakage. When activated by an external signal, the refresh circuitry in the device checks the voltage level stored on each capacitor. If the voltage is greater than $V_{CC}/2$, then that location is charged to V_{CC}. If the voltage is less than $V_{CC}/2$, then that location is discharged to 0 V. Let's take a look at a typical DRAM to see how we read, write, and refresh it.

Figure 11-8a, p. 354, shows an internal block diagram for a Texas Instruments TMS44C256 CMOS DRAM. This device is a 256K × 4 device, so it stores 262,144 words of 4 bits each in its 20-pin package. You can connect two of these in parallel to store bytes or 4 in parallel to store 16-bit words. Since DRAMs are almost always connected in parallel, several companies now produce DRAM modules such as the TI TM4256FL8 256K × 8 device shown in Figure 11-8b. The 30-pin single in-line package (SIP) takes much less PC board space than the equivalent DIPs.

Now, according to the basic rules of address decoding, 18 address lines should be required to address one of the 256K or 2^{18} words stored in the MT44C256 DRAM. The diagram in Figure 11-8a, however, shows only nine address inputs, A0–A8. The trick here is that to save pins, DRAMs usually multiplex in the address one-half at a time. A look at the timing diagram for a read operation in Figure 11-8c should help you to see how this works.

To read a word from a bank of dynamic RAMs, a DRAM controller device or other circuitry asserts the write-enable, $\overline{W}$, pin of the DRAMs high to enable them for a read operation. It then sends the upper half of the address, called the row address or page address, to the nine address inputs of the DRAMs. The controller then asserts the *row-address-strobe*, $\overline{RAS}$, input of the DRAM low to latch the row address in the DRAM. After the proper timing interval, the controller removes the row address and outputs the lower half of the address, called the column address, to the nine address inputs of the DRAMs. The controller then asserts the *column-*

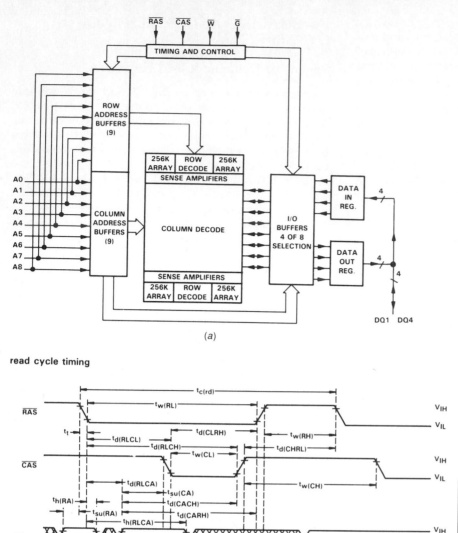

read cycle timing

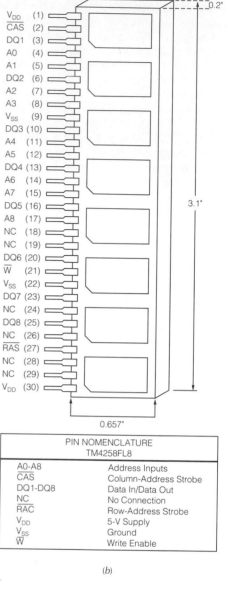

NOTE 18: Output may go from high impedance to an invalid data state prior to the specified access time.

(c)

FIGURE 11-8 TMS44C256 DRAM (a) Functional block diagram. (b) 30-pin SIP diagram. (c) Read-cycle timing. (*Texas Instruments Inc.*)

address-strobe, $\overline{CAS}$, inputs of the DRAMs low to latch the column address in the DRAMs. After a propagation delay, the data word from the addressed memory cells will appear on the data outputs of the DRAMs.

The timing diagram for a write cycle is nearly the same except that after it sends out the column address and $\overline{CAS}$, the controller asserts the write-enable, $\overline{W}$, input

low to enable the DRAMs for writing, and asserts a signal which is used to gate the data to be written onto the data inputs of the DRAMs.

To refresh a row in a DRAM, the row address is applied to the address inputs and the $\overline{RAS}$ input is pulsed low. For this particular device each row must be refreshed at least once every 8 ms. The refresh can be done in either a *burst* mode or in a *distributed* mode. In the burst mode all 512 rows are addressed and pulsed with a $\overline{RAS}$ strobe one right after the other every 8 ms. In the distributed mode a row is addressed and pulsed after every 8/512 ms or 15.6 μs. In a particular system you use the mode which least interferes with the operation of the system. Now that the operation of dynamic RAMs is fresh in your mind, we will show you how you interface banks of DRAMs to an 8086.

Overview of Interfacing DRAMs to a Microprocessor

As perhaps you can see from the preceding discussion, the following are the main tasks you have to do to interface a bank of DRAMs to a microprocessor:

1. Multiplex the two halves of the address into each device with the appropriate $\overline{RAS}$ and $\overline{CAS}$ strobes.

2. Provide a read/write control signal to enable data into or out of the devices.

3. Refresh each row at the proper interval.

4. Ensure that a read or write operation and a refresh operation do not take place at the same time.

There are many ways to do these tasks. For a start let's look at how it is done in an IBM PC or PC/XT type microcomputer.

DRAM Interfacing and Refreshing in the IBM PC

As you can see in Figure 11-2, the IBM PC has four banks of 64K × 1 DRAMs. Two 74LS158 multiplexer devices are used to separate the two halves of an address as needed by the DRAMs. Some simple control logic generates the $\overline{RAS}$, $\overline{CAS}$, and RD/$\overline{W}$ signals. To refresh the DRAMs on the PC and PC/XT, we use a dummy DMA read approach. Here's how it works.

An 8253 timer is programmed to produce a pulse every 15 μs. This pulse is connected into one of the DMA request inputs (DREQ0) of an 8237 DMA controller, which has been programmed to read from memory and write to a nonexistent port. When the 8237 DMA controller receives this pulse, it sends a hold request to the 8088 microprocessor. After the 8088 responds with an HLDA signal, the 8237 takes over the buses, sends out a memory address, sends out a memory-read signal, and sends out a DMA acknowledge (DACK0) signal. The lower 8 bits of the memory address it sends out go to the address inputs of all of the DRAMs. The DACK0 signal from the DMA controller generates a signal which pulses the $\overline{RAS}$ lines of all of the DRAM banks low at this time. After each DMA operation the current address register in the DMA controller will be automatically incremented or decremented, depending on how the device was programmed. In either case, the next DMA operation will refresh the next row in the DRAMs. If the 8237 is programmed for transfer of 64 Kbytes, start at address 0, increment count after DMA, and autoinitialize; the sequence of addresses sent out will refresh all

256 rows in the DRAMs over and over. One row in each of the banks then is refreshed every 15 μs. With the 4.77-MHz clock used in the basic IBM PC, a refresh DMA cycle takes about 820 ns every 15 μs, or about 5 percent of the processor's time.

The DRAM-refresh method used in IBM PC/AT-type microcomputers is not based on DMA, but it does put the microcomputer out of action for about 5 percent of the time. In a system where we don't want to sacrifice 5 percent of the processor's time for simply refreshing DRAMs, we use a dedicated controller device to do the refresh, etc. Here's an example of this type of device.

Using an 82C08 DRAM Controller IC with an 8086

In high-performance systems where we want DRAM refreshing to take up a minimum amount of the processor's time, we usually use a dedicated device which handles all of the refreshing chores without tying up the microprocessor or its buses as the DMA approach does. An example of this type of device is the Intel 82C08. Figure 11-9, p. 356, shows, in block diagram form, how an 82C08 can be connected with an 8086 in maximum mode to refresh and control 512 Kbytes of dynamic RAM. The 82C08 takes care of all of the addressing and refresh tasks we described before.

The memories here are the 256K × 4 devices shown in Figure 11-8a. As usual for an 8086 system, the memory is set up as 2-byte-wide banks. In this system each bank has two DRAM devices, so each bank has 256 Kbytes.

One important point to observe here is that the status signals, S0–S3, from the 8086 are connected directly to the control inputs of the 82C08. The 82C08 decodes these status signals to produce the read and write signals needed for the DRAMs. This advanced decoding means that, except when a refresh cycle is in progress, the 8086 will be able to read a byte or word from the DRAMs without WAIT states.

If you look closely at the 82C08 in Figure 11-9, you should find the port enable input, $\overline{PE}$. This input is asserted low to request access to the DRAM. If the 82C08 is not involved in a refresh operation when $\overline{PE}$ is asserted low, the 82C08 will multiplex the address from the address bus into the DRAMs with the appropriate $\overline{RAS}$ and $\overline{CAS}$ strobes. The 82C08 will also send out an AACK signal which clocks the 74LS74 flip-flops to transfer the A0 and $\overline{BHE}$ signals to the two memory banks. For a read operation the addressed byte or word will then be output on the data bus to the 8086. For a write operation the byte or word on the data bus will be written to the addressed locations in the DRAMs.

The output of an address decoder is connected to the $\overline{PE}$ input to assert it for the desired range of addresses. Because the DRAM banks in the circuit in Figure 11-9 are so large, the address decoding is very simple. Each bank in the circuit contains 256 Kbytes. Since $256K = 2^{18}$, 18 address lines are required to address one of the bytes in a bank. In most systems we connect system address lines A1 through A18 to the 82C08 address inputs and the 82C08 multiplexes these signals

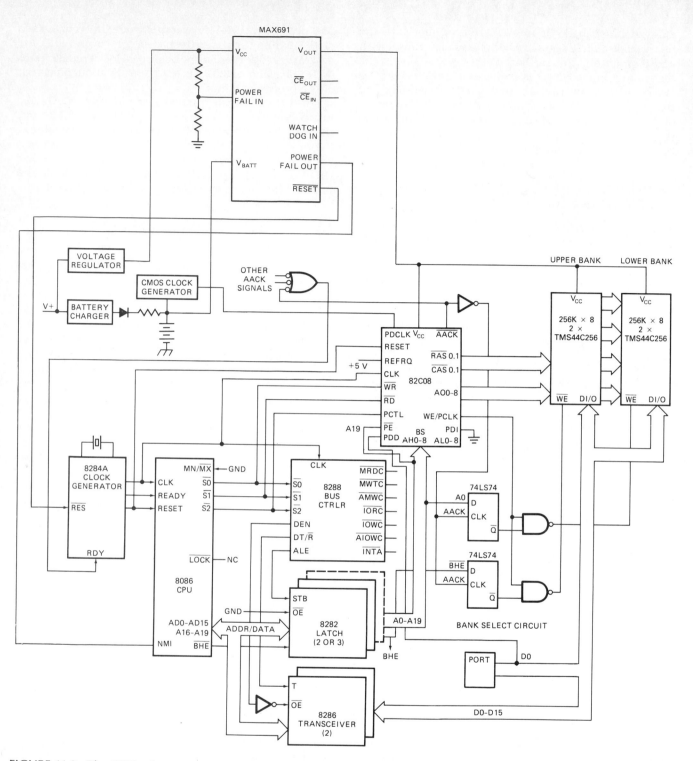

FIGURE 11-9 The 8086 microcomputer system using 82C08 DRAM controller.

into the DRAMs, nine at a time. Address line A0 is used along with the $\overline{BHE}$ signal to select the desired bank(s). This leaves only the A19 system address line unaccounted for. If we connect the A19 address line directly to the $\overline{PE}$ input of the 82C08, then $\overline{PE}$ will be asserted whenever the 8086 outputs a memory address with A19 low. In other words, the $\overline{PE}$ input will be asserted when the 8086 outputs any address between 00000H and 7FFFFH.

NOTE: The status signals from the 8086 are decoded in the 82C08, so it knows whether an address is intended for memory or an I/O port.

The address decoder here is simply a piece of wire or circuit trace which connects A19 to the $\overline{PE}$ input. This connection puts the RAM in the lower half of the 8086 address range, which is appropriate, because for an

8086 we want ROMs containing the startup program to be at the top of the address range.

The next point to consider in the system in Figure 11-9 is how the controller arbitrates the dispute that occurs if the CPU tries to read from or write to memory while the controller is doing a refresh cycle. If the 82C08 in Figure 11-9 happens to be in the middle of a refresh cycle when the 8086 tries to read a DRAM location, the 82C08 will hold its $\overline{AACK}$ high until it is finished with the refresh cycle. With the connections shown in Figure 11-9, this will cause the 8086 to insert one or more WAIT states while the 82C08 finishes its refresh cycle. In this system then, the occasional access conflict is arbitrated by the DRAM controller. Inserting a wait state now and then slows the 8086 down less than the DMA approach used in the IBM PC/XT-type computers.

Another interesting feature of the system in Figure 11-9 is the battery-backup circuitry. In Chapter 8 we discussed the use of an 8086 NMI interrupt procedure to save program data in the case of a power failure. In the few milliseconds between the time the ac power goes off and the time the dc power drops below operating levels, an interrupt procedure copies program data to a block of CMOS static RAM which has a battery-backup power supply. When the system is repowered, the saved data is copied back into the main RAM, and processing takes up where it left off. In larger systems there may not be time enough to copy all of the important data to another RAM, so we simply use a battery backup for the entire RAM array, as shown in Figure 11-9.

In this circuit we used CMOS DRAMs, because when these devices are not being accessed for reading, writing, or refreshing, they take only microwatts of power. During battery backup of the DRAMs they must still be refreshed, so the 82C08 DRAM controller is also connected to the battery power.

When the power supply voltage drops below a specified level, the PFO pin on the MAXIM 691 supervisor device sends a signal to the NMI input of the 8086. The NMI interrupt procedure saves parameters so the program can restart correctly when power returns and then sends a signal to the POWER DOWN DETECT (PDD) input of the 82C08. In response to this signal the 82C08 switches from the high-frequency system clock to a lower-frequency clock signal from the CMOS crystal oscillator. Reducing the clock frequency decreases the amount of current required by the DRAMs and by the 82C08 to perform refresh operations. Also, by using the CMOS oscillator, the high-current 8284 system clock generator does not need to be kept running.

When the power returns, the MAX691 generates a power-on-reset signal, $\overline{RESET}$, with the correct timing for the 8086. If a low is output to the PDD input of the 82C08 as part of the startup sequence, the 82C08 will automatically switch to using the system clock and operate normally for read, write, and refresh operations.

For the backup battery we use a nickel-cadmium or some other type which can stand the continuous recharging and supply the needed current. The diodes in the circuit prevent the power supply output and the battery from fighting with each other.

In applications where the entire system must be kept running during an ac power outage, we use a *noninterruptible power supply* or *NPS*. These power supplies contain large batteries, charging circuitry, and circuitry needed to convert the battery voltage to the voltages needed by the microcomputer.

Dynamic RAM Timing in Microcomputer Systems

In Chapter 7 we showed you how to determine if a memory device such as a ROM or RAM is fast enough to operate in an 8086 system with a given clock frequency. To make these calculations for a ROM or SRAM, you use its access times. For DRAMs, however, the limiting time is the read-cycle time, t_{RD}. Here's why.

If you take a close look at the read-cycle timing diagram for the TMS44C256 in Figure 11-8c, you should see that valid data will be present on the output a time $t_{a(R)}$ after $\overline{RAS}$ goes low. For the fastest current version of the device, this time is about 100 ns. Before another row in the device can be accessed, however, the $\overline{RAS}$ input has to be made high and held high for a time labeled $t_{w(RH)}$. This time of about 80 ns is required to *precharge* the DRAM so that it is ready to accept the next row address. (Reading data from a storage location in a row discharges that location somewhat and the internal circuitry in the DRAM "precharges" the location again before it allows access to another row.)

The precharge time effectively adds to the access time, so the time before a data bit from another row can be available on the output is considerably longer than the access time. The total time from the start of one read cycle to the start of the next is identified in Figure 11-8c as $t_{c(rd)}$. For the fastest version of the TMS44C256 the access time is only 100 ns, but the $t_{c(rd)}$ is 190 ns. For applications where the data words are rapidly being read from random rows, it is this $t_{c(rd)}$ that limits the rate at which words from random rows can be read. Let's see how this time fits in a microprocessor read cycle.

As shown in Figure 7-19, an 8086 requires four clock cycles for each memory access. If the 8086 is operated with a 10-MHz clock (100 ns per clock), a memory access cycle will take 400 ns. This means that if you are willing to pay the price, you can get DRAMs which will operate without wait states in a microcomputer using a 10-MHz 8086. However, as we discuss in Chapter 15, later-generation processors such as the 80386 require only two clock cycles for a memory access, and they are typically operated with a clock signal of 25 MHz or more. These factors drastically decrease the time available for memory access. If currently available DRAMs are used as the main memory in a microcomputer which has a clock frequency greater than about 15 MHz, one or more wait states must usually be inserted in every DRAM read or write cycle. However, the low cost per bit of DRAMs makes them attractive enough that several methods have been developed so they can be used without having to insert wait states in every memory access cycle. While the characteristics of DRAMs are fresh in your mind, we will introduce you to some of these techniques.

Page Mode and Static Column Mode DRAM Systems

Two of the most commonly used techniques to reduce the number of wait states needed with DRAMs are the *page mode* method and the *static column* method. Here's how they work.

Remember from our discussion of DRAMs in a previous section that a precharge time is required each time a new row (page) is accessed in a DRAM. This precharge time is the reason that the typical read and write cycle times are so much longer than the access times for DRAMs. If successive data words are read from or written to locations in the same page (row), however, no precharge time is required. Also, if successive data words are read from the same page, the row address is the same, so a new row address does not have to be sent out and strobed in with an RAS signal. With the proper DRAM controller these two factors make it possible to read data from a page or write data to a page without wait states. Some timing diagrams should help you see this.

Figure 11-10a shows the read timing waveforms for a Texas Instruments TMS44C256 DRAM which can be used for page mode access. For the first access in a row (page), the DRAM controller carries out a normal row address-RAS, column address-CAS sequence of signals. If the next address the controller sends out is in the same row, an external comparator will send a signal to the DRAM controller. In response to this "same-row" signal, the DRAM controller will hold RAS low, send out just the column address to the A0–A8 inputs of the DRAMs, and pulse CAS low. As long as the microprocessor continues to access memory locations in the same page (row), the controller will simply hold RAS low, send out the column part of the addresses to the DRAMs, and pulse CAS low for each new column address. These accesses within a page are much faster because they require no row address and RAS time, and because they require no precharge time.

To determine if a memory access is within the same page, a device such as the SN74ALS6310 is connected to the address bus. This device holds the page part of the previous address in a register and compares it to the page part of the new address. If the two address parts are the same, the 6310 signals the DRAM controller to do a page mode access such as that shown in Figure 11-10a. If the previous page address and the current page address are different, the controller will do a normal RAS and CAS access.

Figure 11-10b shows the read timing waveforms for a Texas Instruments TMS44C257 DRAM which is designed for static column mode operation. During the first access in a row, the DRAM controller carries out a normal row address-RAS, column address-CAS sequence of signals. If the next address the controller sends out is in the same row, an external comparator will signal the DRAM controller. In response to this "same-row" signal, the DRAM controller will hold RAS and CAS low and send out just the column address to the A0–A8 inputs of the DRAMs. As long as the microprocessor continues to access memory locations in the same page

(row), the controller will simply hold RAS and CAS low and send out the column part of the addresses to the DRAMs. The static column mode is more difficult to implement than the page mode, but it is faster than the page mode because it does not require CAS strobes and the associated setup and hold times.

In a high-speed microprocessor system, the static column decode technique can reduce the average number of wait states per memory access from 2 or 3 to perhaps 0.8. This is a considerable improvement, but it is not as much of an improvement as can be gained by using a cache system.

Cache Mode DRAM Systems

INTRODUCTION

Traditionally the term *cache*, which is pronounced "cash," refers to a hiding place where you put provisions for future use. As we describe how a cache memory system is implemented in a microcomputer, perhaps you can see why the term is used here.

Figure 11-11, p. 360, shows in block diagram form how a simple cache memory system is implemented in an 80386 based microcomputer system. In Chapter 15 we discuss the details of the 80386 microprocessor, but for this discussion all you need to know is that the 80386 has a 32-bit data bus and a 32-bit address bus. A 32-bit address bus allows the 80386 to address up to 4 Gbytes of memory and a 32-bit data bus allows the 80386 to read or write 4 bytes in parallel.

The cache in a system such as this consists of perhaps 32 or 64 Kbytes of high-speed SRAM. The main memory consists of a few megabytes or more of slower but cheaper DRAM. The general principal of a cache system is that code and data sections currently being used are copied from the DRAM to the high-speed SRAM cache, where they can be accessed by the processor with no wait states. A cache system takes advantage of the fact that most microcomputer programs work with only small sections of code and data at a particular time. The fancy term for this is "locality of reference." Here's how the system works.

When the microprocessor outputs an address, the cache controller checks to see if the contents of that address have previously been transferred to the cache. If the addressed code or data word is present in the cache, the cache controller enables the cache memory to output the addressed word on the data bus. Since this access is to the fast SRAM, no wait states are required.

If the addressed word is not in the cache, the cache controller enables the DRAM controller. The DRAM controller then sends the address on to the main memory to get the data word. Since the DRAM main memory is slower, this access requires one or two wait states. However, when a word is read from main memory, it not only goes to the microprocessor, it is also written to the cache. If the processor needs to access this data word again, it can then read the data directly from the cache with no wait states. The percentage of accesses where the microprocessor finds the code or data word it

enhanced page-mode read cycle timing

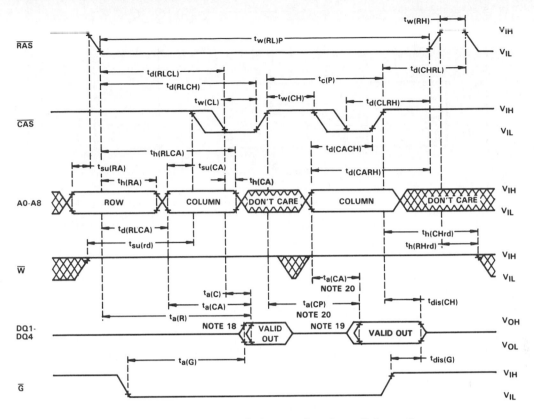

NOTES: 18. Output may go from high impedance to an invalid data state prior to the specified access time.
   19. A write cycle or read-modify-write cycle can be mixed with the read cycles as long as the write and read-modify-write timing
     specifications are not violated.
   20. Access time is $t_{a(CP)}$ or $t_{a(CA)}$ dependent.

(a)

static column decode mode read cycle timing

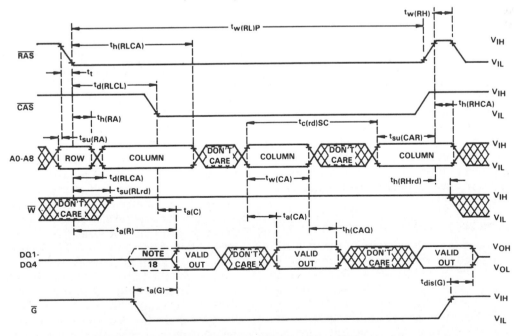

NOTE 18: Output may go from high impedance to an invalid data state prior to the specified access time.

(b)

FIGURE 11-10 TMS44C256 DRAM. (a) Page mode read-cycle operation.
(b) Static column read-cycle operation. (*Texas Instruments Inc.*)

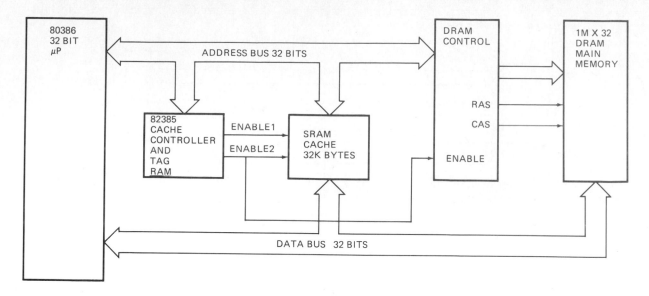

FIGURE 11-11   80386 microcomputer RAM memory system using high-speed SRAM cache.

needs in the cache is called the *hit rate.* Current systems have average hit rates greater than 90 percent.

For write to memory operations most cache systems use a *posted-write-through* method. If the cache controller determines that the addressed word is present in the cache, the controller will write the new word to the cache with no wait states and signal the 80386 that the write is complete. The controller will then write the data word to main memory. This write to the main memory is transparent to the main processor unless the main memory is still involved in a previous write operation.

To keep track of which main memory locations are currently present in the SRAM cache, the cache controller uses a *cache directory.* For the Intel 82385 cache controller shown in Figure 11-11, the cache directory RAM is contained in the controller. Each location in the cache is represented by an entry in the directory. The exact format for the directory entry depends on the particular cache scheme used. The three basic cache schemes are direct-mapped, two-way set associative, and fully associative. We don't have time here to do a detailed discussion of these three caching schemes, but we will give you an introduction to each so you will understand the terms if you see them in a computer magazine article or advertisement. We discuss cache systems further in Chapter 15.

A DIRECT MAPPED CACHE

Figure 11-12a shows a block diagram of how a direct-mapped 32 Kbyte cache can be implemented in an 80386 system with an 82385 controller. As we said before, an 80386 has a 32-bit address bus, so it can address 2^{32} bytes, or about 4 Gbytes, of memory. The 80386 also has a 32-bit data bus, so it can read up to 4 bytes at a time from memory. A group of four parallel bytes is commonly referred to as a line.

The cache memory for the 80386 system in Figure 11-12a is set up to hold 8K 4-byte lines or a total of 32 Kbytes. The 8K lines in the cache are organized as 1024

sets of 8 lines each. The cache controller treats the 4 Gbytes of main memory as 2^{17} or 131,072 pages of 32 Kbytes each. Each page in main memory then is the same size as the cache.

The term *direct mapped* here means that a particular numbered line from a page in main memory will always be copied to that same numbered line in the cache. For example, if line 1 from page 0 is in the cache, it will be stored in line 1 of the cache. If line 1 from page 131,070 is in the cache, it will be stored in line 1 of the cache.

The cache directory on the left of Figure 11-12a is used to keep track of which lines from the main memory currently have copies in the cache. As you can see, the directory contains a 26-bit entry for each set of 8 lines in the cache. The upper 17 bits of a directory entry are called a *tag.* The tag in a directory entry identifies the main memory page that a line or set of lines in the cache duplicates. Each directory entry also contains a *tag valid bit* and eight *line valid bits* (one for each line in the set). Here's how the 82385 uses this directory during a read operation.

When the 80386 sends out a 32-bit address to read a word from memory, address lines A15 through A31 represent a main memory page, address lines A5 through A14 identify the set containing a desired line, and address lines A2 through A4 identify the number of the line in the set containing the desired word. Figure 11-12b shows this in diagram form. The cache controller first uses address bits A5 through A14 to select the directory entry for the set that contains the addressed line. Then it compares the upper 17 bits of the address from the 80386 with the 17-bit tag stored in the directory entry. If the two are equal, the controller checks the tag valid bit to see if the tag is current. If the tag valid bit is set, the controller checks the line valid bit for the line addressed by address bits A2 through A4. If the tag matches and is valid and the line is valid, the line is in the cache. This is a cache *hit.* In this case the controller will apply address bits A2 through A14 to the cache

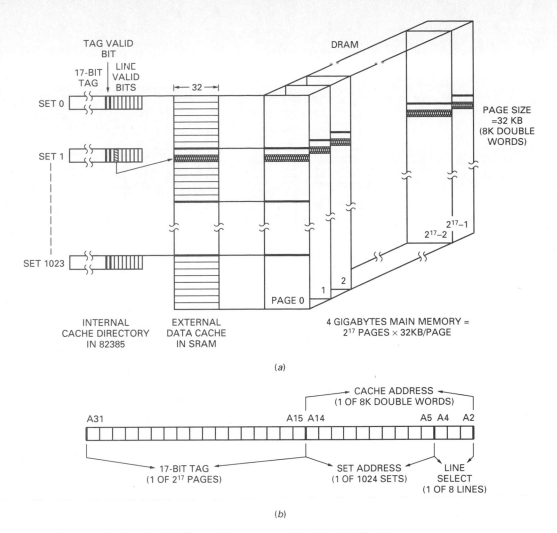

FIGURE 11-12   Cache organization for 32-Kbyte direct-mapped cache. (a) Block diagram. (b) Use of 32-bit address by 82385 cache controller.

memory and enable the cache memory to output the addressed word on the data bus.

If the upper 17 bits of the address from the 80386 are not the same as the tag in the directory, the tag bit is not valid, or the line bit for the addressed line is not valid, the read operation is a cache *miss*. In this case the 82385 will send the complete address from the 80386 along to the DRAM controller. The DRAM controller will cause the main memory to output the addressed line on the data bus. When this line appears on the data bus, the 82385 will enable the cache memory so that the line gets written to the cache as well as going to the 80386. The 82385 will also update the cache directory to indicate that this line is now in the cache. If this line or any part of it is needed again, it can be read directly from the cache.

When the 80386 writes a word to memory, the 82385 grabs the address and the data word then signals the 80386 that the transfer is complete. The controller then enables the main memory so that the word is written to the correct address in the main memory. If the data word is present in the cache, it is also written to the cache. This "posted write" process does not require any

wait states unless the memory is still busy with a previous write.

A TWO-WAY SET ASSOCIATIVE CACHE SYSTEM

One difficulty with the direct-mapped cache approach is that if a program happens to use the same numbered line from two memory pages at the same time, it will be swapping the two lines back and forth between main memory and the cache as it executes. This swapping back and forth is called *thrashing*. A scheme which helps avoid thrashing is the *two-way set associative cache* approach shown in Figure 11-13a, p. 362. In this approach two separate caches and two separate cache directories are set up so that the same lines from two different pages can be cached at the same time. Each cache is half the size of the direct-mapped cache we discussed in the previous section, so the controller treats memory as 262,144 pages of 4096 lines each. To identify one of these 262,144 pages, the tag in each cache directory entry contains 18 bits. Each directory entry in this system also contains a tag valid bit, eight line valid bits, and a *least recently used bit* or LRU. Here's how this system works during a read operation.

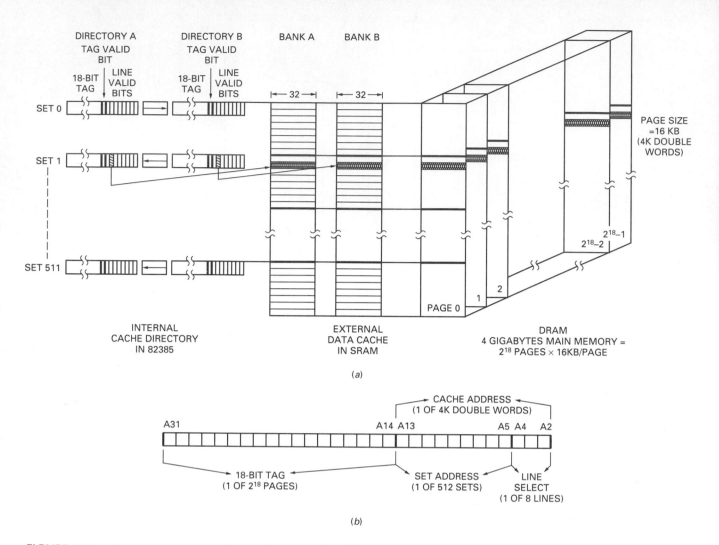

FIGURE 11-13 Two-way set-associative cache for 32-bit address bus system. (a) Block diagram. (b) Use of 32-bit address by 82385 cache controller.

When the 80386 outputs an address, the 82385 controller uses address bits A5 through A13 to select the appropriate entry in each cache directory. It then compares the upper 18 bits of the address from the 80386 with the tag in each of the selected directory entries. If one of the tags matches, the controller checks the tag valid bit in that directory entry. The controller also checks the line valid bit for the line specified by address bits A2 through A4. If these bits are set, the controller outputs address bits A2 through A13 to the cache associated with that directory and enables the cache to output the desired word on the data bus.

If the addressed data word is found in cache A, the LRU bit in the directory entry is set to indicate that the A cache was most recently used. If the data word is found in the B cache, the LRU bit is set to indicate that the B cache was most recently used. This mechanism is used to determine which cache should be used to hold a new line read in from main memory. When a read operation produces a cache miss, the 82385 will send the address and control signals to the main memory to read a line containing the desired word. When this line comes down the data bus, the 82385 will write it to the least recently

used cache and update the corresponding directory entry. If the controller finds that the tag for a read operation is correct but a line valid bit is invalid, it will read the line from main memory and write it in the cache whose directory contains the tag. This ensures that adjacent lines from a page in main memory end up in the same cache.

For a write operation this two-way set associative cache approach uses the same posted write-through method we described earlier. The controller always writes an output data word to the main memory, and if the word is present in one of the caches, it also updates the word in the cache.

Because of the two-tag RAMs, etc., this approach is somewhat more complex to implement, but it usually produces a better hit rate than a direct-mapped cache. The 25-MHz Compaq Deskpro 386/25 is an example of a system that uses an Intel 82385 cache controller and a two-way set associative cache to minimize wait states.

A FULLY ASSOCIATIVE CACHE SYSTEM

Still another type of cache that you may hear mentioned is the *fully associative* type. In this type a 4-byte block

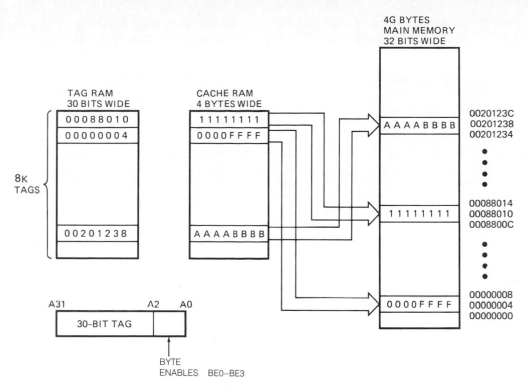

TAG RAM
30 BITS WIDE

| 00088010 |
| 00000004 |

8K
TAGS

| 00201238 |

CACHE RAM
4 BYTES WIDE

| 1 1 1 1 1 1 1 1 |
| 0 0 0 0 F F F F |

| A A A A B B B B |

4G BYTES
MAIN MEMORY
32 BITS WIDE

| A A A A B B B B | 0020123C
00201238
00201234

| 1 1 1 1 1 1 1 1 | 00088014
00088010
0008800C

| 0 0 0 0 F F F F | 00000008
00000004
00000000

A31   A2   A0

| 30-BIT TAG | |

BYTE
ENABLES   BE0–BE3

FIGURE 11-14   Fully associative 32-Kbyte cache for 32-bit address bus system.

or line from main memory can be written in any location in the cache. Figure 11-14 shows in block diagram form how this works.

The system has a 32-bit address bus, so it can address 4 Gbytes of memory. This corresponds to 1 Gbyte of 4-byte lines. Since 1 Gbyte is equal to 2^{30} bytes, a 30-bit tag is required to identify each block or line stored in the cache. Each entry in the directory then must contain 30 bits for the tag plus any additional bits used to keep track of how recently the line was used.

A fully associative cache has the advantage that it can hold the same numbered lines from several different pages at the same time. It has the disadvantage, however, that the upper 30 bits of each memory address sent out by the microprocessor must be compared with all of the tags in the directory to see if that line is present in the cache. This can be a time-consuming process. Also, when a fully associative cache is full, some algorithm must be used to determine which line to overwrite when a new line must be brought in from main memory. The most common algorithm replaces the least recently used line with the new line. The 82385, incidentally, is not designed to work with a fully associative cache system.

SUMMARY

The key point for you to remember about a cache is that by keeping the currently used code and data in a high-speed SRAM cache, the processor can use relatively inexpensive DRAM for its large main memory and still operate with few wait states. A cache controller device such as the 82385 automatically keeps the cache and the cache directory updated, so the process is essentially "invisible" to the microprocessor and to an executing program.

Error Detecting and Correcting in DRAM Arrays

PARITY GENERATION/CHECKING

Data read from DRAMs is subject to two types of errors, *hard errors* and *soft errors*. Hard errors are caused by permanent device failures. These may be caused by a manufacturing defect or simply random breakdown in the chip. Soft errors are one-time errors caused by a noise pulse in the system or, in the case of dynamic RAMs, perhaps an alpha particle or some other radiation causing the charge to change on the tiny capacitor where a data bit is stored. As the size of a RAM array increases, the chance of a hard or a soft error increases sharply. This increases the chance that the entire system will fail. It seems unreasonable that one fleeting alpha particle may cause an entire system to fail. To prevent or at least reduce the chances of this kind of failure, we add circuitry which detects and in some cases corrects errors in the data read out from DRAMs. There are several ways to do this, depending on the amount of detection and correction needed.

The simplest method for detecting an error is with a parity bit. This is the method used in the IBM PC circuit shown in Figure 11-2. Note in this circuit that the DRAM memory bank is 9 bits wide. Eight of these bits are the data byte being stored, and the ninth bit is a parity bit which is used to detect errors in the stored data. A 74LS280 parity generator/checker circuit generates a parity bit for each byte and stores it in the ninth location as each byte is written to memory. When the 9 bits are read out, the overall parity is checked by the parity generator checker circuit. If the parity is not correct, an error signal is sent to the NMI logic to interrupt the processor. When you first turn on the power to an IBM

PC or warm boot it by pressing the Ctrl, Alt, and Del keys at the same time, one of the self-tests that it performs is to write byte patterns to all of the RAM locations and check if the byte read back and the parity of that byte are correct. If any error is found, an error message is displayed on the screen so you don't try to load and run programs in defective RAM.

ERROR DETECTING AND CORRECTING CIRCUITS

One difficulty with a simple parity check is that two errors in a data word may cancel each other. A second problem with the simple parity method is that it does not tell you which bit in a word is wrong so that you can correct the error. More complex error detecting/correcting codes (ECCs), often called *Hamming codes* (after the man who did some of the original work in this area), permit you to detect multiple-bit errors in a word and to correct at least one bit error.

Figure 11-15*a* shows in block diagram form how a TI 74AS632 error detecting and correcting (EDAC) device can be connected in the data path between a 32-bit microprocessor and 16-Mbyte DRAM main memory. Note that the EDAC is connected in parallel with the DRAM refresh controller and in series with the SRAM cache. Here's how the EDAC device works.

When a data word is sent from the microprocessor to memory, it also goes to the EDAC. As the data word is read in by the EDAC, several *encoding* or *check* bits are generated and written in memory along with the data word. As shown in Figure 11-15*b*, the number of encoding bits, K, required is determined by the size of the data word, M, and the degree of detection/correction desired. The total number of bits required for a data word N is equal to M + K. For example, 5 encoding bits are required to detect and correct a single-bit error in a 16-bit data word, so a total of 21 bits have to be stored for each 16-bit word. To detect/correct a 1-bit error and detect 2 wrong bits in a 32-bit word requires 7 encoding bits, or a total of 39 bits. The encoding bits, incidentally, are not just tacked on to one end of the data word as a parity bit is. They are interspersed in the data word.

When the processor reads a data word from memory, the data word and the check bits from memory go to the EDAC. The EDAC calculates the check bits for the data word read out from memory and XORs these check bits with the check bits that were stored in memory with the data word. The result of this XOR operation is called a *syndrome word*. The syndrome word is decoded to determine if the data word has no errors, has a single-bit error, or has multiple-bit errors.

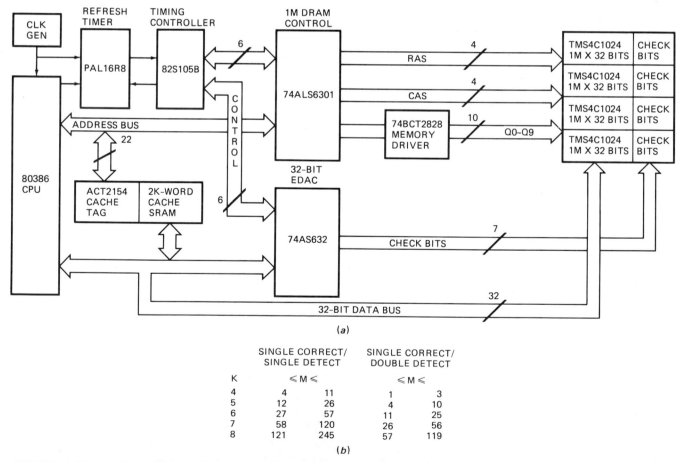

(a)

	SINGLE CORRECT/ SINGLE DETECT			SINGLE CORRECT/ DOUBLE DETECT	
K	≤ M ≤			≤ M ≤	
4	4	11		1	3
5	12	26		4	10
6	27	57		11	25
7	58	120		26	56
8	121	245		57	119

(b)

FIGURE 11-15 (a) Block diagram showing how error detecting and correcting circuitry is connected in a large DRAM system. (*Texas Instruments Inc.*) (b) Hamming-code data bits and encoding bits and number of encoding bits required for desired degree of detection/correction.

If the data word contains no errors, the 74AS632 EDAC will simply output the data word to the processor on the data bus. If the data word contains a single-bit error, the EDAC device uses the syndrome word to determine which bit is incorrect and simply inverts that bit to correct the bit. The EDAC then outputs the corrected data word to the processor on the data bus. If the data word contains multiple-bit errors, the EDAC device asserts a signal which is usually connected to an interrupt input on the processor. In the case of a multiple-bit error, the programmer must decide what action to take and write the appropriate interrupt-service procedure.

The 74AS632 EDAC in Figure 11-15a can also work with the 74ALS6301 DRAM controller to remove errors in stored data words during refresh operations as well as during normal read operations. This process is called *scrubbing*. Correcting errors during each refresh operation decreases the chance of multiple-bit errors accumulating between read operations.

For more information on DRAM error detecting/correcting, consult the data sheets for error detecting/correcting devices such as the Intel 8206, the Texas Instruments 74AS632, or the National DP8402A.

In the next section of this chapter we show you how a second processor can directly share the address, data, and control buses with the main processor in a microcomputer. Processors which share the local buses in this way are referred to as coprocessors. The example we use for this section is an Intel 8087 math coprocessor. As shown in Figure 11-2, the IBM PC and PC/XT have a socket for one of these devices.

A COPROCESSOR — THE 8087 MATH COPROCESSOR

Overview

Many microcomputer programs, such as those used for scientific research, engineering, business, and graphics, need to make mathematical calculations such as computing the square root of a number, the tangent of a number, or the log of a number. Another common need is to do arithmetic operations on very large and very small numbers. There are several ways to do all this.

One way is to write the number-crunching part of the program in a high-level language such as FORTRAN, compile this part of the program, and link in I/O modules written in assembly language. The difficulty with this approach is that programs written in high-level languages tend to run considerably slower than programs written in assembly language.

Another way is to write an assembly language program which uses the normal instruction set of the processor to do the arithmetic functions. Reference books which contain the algorithms for these are readily available. Our experience has shown that it is often time consuming to get from the algorithm to a working assembly language program.

Still another approach is to buy a library of floating-point arithmetic object modules from the manufacturer of the microprocessor you are working with or from an independent software house. In your program you just declare a procedure needed from the library as external, call the procedure as required, and link the library object code files for the procedures to the object code for your program. This approach spares you the labor of writing all the procedures.

In an application where you need a calculation to be done as quickly as possible, however, all the previous approaches have a problem. The architecture and instruction sets of general-purpose microprocessors such as the 8086 are not designed to do complex mathematical operations efficiently. Therefore, even highly optimized number-crunching programs run slowly on these general-purpose machines. To solve this problem, special processors with architectures and instruction sets optimized for number-crunching have been developed. An example of this type of number-crunching processor is the Intel 8087 math processor. An 8087 is used in parallel with the main microprocessor in a system, rather than serving as a main processor itself. Therefore, it is referred to as a *coprocessor*. The major principle here is that the main microprocessor, an 8088, for example, handles the general program execution and the 8087 coprocessor handles specialized math computations. An 8087 instruction may perform a given mathematical computation 100 times faster than the equivalent sequence of 8086 instructions.

An important point that we need to make about the 8087 is that it is an actual processor with its own, specialized instruction set. Instructions for the 8087 are written in a program as needed, interspersed with the 8088/8086 instructions. To you, the programmer, adding an 8087 to the system simply makes it appear that you have suddenly been given a whole new set of powerful math instructions to use in writing your programs. When your program is assembled, the opcodes for the 8087 instructions are put in memory right along with the codes for the 8086 or 8088 instructions. As the 8086 or 8088 fetches instruction bytes from memory and puts them in its queue, the 8087 also reads these instruction bytes and puts them in its internal queue. The 8087 decodes each instruction that comes into its queue. When it decodes an instruction from its queue and finds that it is an 8086 instruction, the 8087 simply treats the instruction as an NOP. Likewise, when the 8086 or 8088 decodes an instruction from its queue and finds that it is an 8087 instruction, the 8086 simply treats the instruction as an NOP or in some cases reads a data word from memory for the 8087. The point here is that each processor decodes all the instructions in the fetched instruction byte stream but executes only its own instructions. The first question that may occur to you is, How do the two processors recognize 8087 instructions? The answer is that all the 8087 instruction codes have 11011 as the most significant bits of their first code byte.

To start our discussion of the 8087 we will show you the data types, internal architecture, and programming of an 8087; then we will describe how an 8087 is connected and functions in a system. If you have an IBM PC or PC/XT type of computer, you can plug an

8087 chip in its auxiliary processor socket and run our example 8087 program or your own 8087 programs.

8087 Data Types

Figure 11-16 shows the formats for the different types of numbers that the 8087 is designed to work with. The three general types are binary integer, packed decimal, and real. We will discuss and show examples of each type individually.

BINARY INTEGERS

The first three formats in Figure 11-16 show different-length binary integer numbers. These all have the same basic format that we have been using to represent signed binary numbers throughout the rest of the book. The most significant bit is a sign bit which is 0 for positive numbers and 1 for negative numbers. The other 15 to 63 bits of the data word in these formats represent the magnitude of the number. If the number is negative, the magnitude of the number is represented in 2's complement form. Zero, remember, is considered a positive number in this format because it has a sign bit

of 0. Note also in Figure 11-16 the range of values that can be represented by each of the three integer lengths. When you put numbers in this format in memory for the 8087 to access, you put the least significant byte in the lowest address.

PACKED DECIMAL NUMBERS

The second type of 8087 data format to look at in Figure 11-16 is the packed decimal. In this format a number is represented as a string of 18 BCD digits, packed two per byte. The most significant bit is a sign bit which is 0 for positive numbers and 1 for negative numbers. The bits indicated with an X are don't cares. This format is handy for working with financial programs. Using this format you can represent a dollar amount as large as $9,999,999,999,999,999.99, which is probably about what the national debt will be by the year 2000. Again, when you are putting numbers of this type in memory locations for the 8087 to access, the least significant byte goes in the lowest address.

REAL NUMBERS

Before we discuss the 8087 real-number formats, we need to talk a little about real numbers in general.

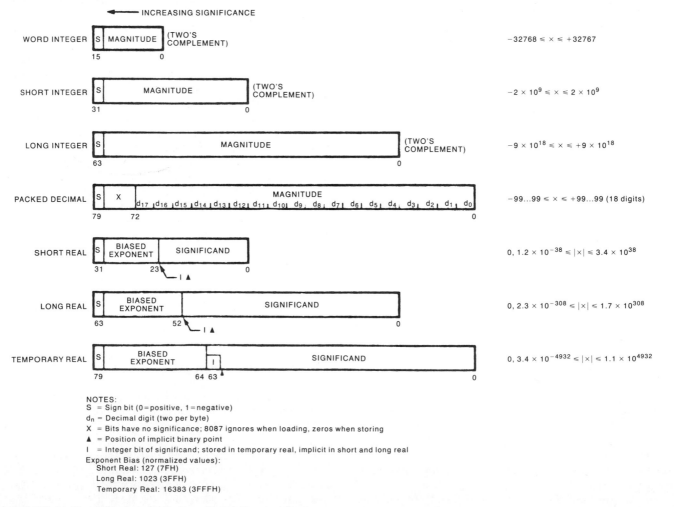

FIGURE 11-16   8087 data formats.   (*Intel Corporation*)

So far the computations we have shown in this book have used signed integer numbers or BCD numbers. These numbers are referred to as *fixed-point* numbers because they contain no information about the location of the decimal point or binary point in the number. The decimal or binary point is always assumed to be to the right of the least significant digit, so all numbers are represented in this form as whole numbers with no fractional part. A weight of 9.4 pounds, for example, is stored in a memory location simply as 10010100 BCD or 01011110 binary. A price of $0.29 per pound is stored in a memory location as 00101001 in BCD or 00011101 in binary. When the binary representation of the weight is multiplied by the price per pound to give the total price, the result is 101010100110 binary, or 2726 decimal. To give the desired display of $2.73, the programmer must round off the result and keep track of where to put the decimal point in the result. For simple numbers such as these from the scale program in Chapter 10, it is not too difficult to do this. However, for a great many applications we need a representation that automatically keeps track of the position of the decimal or binary point for us. In other words we need to be able to represent numbers which have both an integer part and a fractional part. Such numbers are called *real numbers*, or *floating-point numbers*.

There are several different formats for representing real numbers in binary form. The basic principle of all these, however, is to use one group of bits to represent the digits of the number and another group of bits to represent the position of the binary point with respect to these digits. This is very similar to the way numbers are represented in scientific notation, so as a lead-in we will refresh your memory about scientific notation.

To convert the number 27,934 to scientific notation, you move the decimal point four digit positions to the left and multiply the number by 10^4. The result, 2.7934×10^4, is said to be in scientific notation. As another example, you convert 0.00857 to scientific notation by moving the decimal point three digit positions to the right and multiplying by 10^{-3} to give 8.57×10^{-3}. The process of moving the decimal point to a position just to the right of the most significant nonzero digit is called *normalizing* the number. In these examples you can see the digit part, sometimes called the *significand* or the *mantissa*, and the *exponent* part of the representation. When you are working with a calculator or computer, the number of digits you can store for the significand determines the accuracy or *precision* of the representation. In most cases the real numbers you work with in your computer will be approximations because to "accurately" represent a number such as π would require an infinite number of digits. The point here is that more digits give more precision, or, in other words, a better approximation.

The number of digits you can store for the exponent of a number determines the range of magnitudes of numbers you can store in your computer or calculator. The sign of the exponent indicates whether the magnitude of the number is greater than 1 or less than 1. The sign of the significand or mantissa indicates whether the number itself is positive or negative. Now let's see how you represent real numbers in binary form so the 8087 can digest them.

First let's look at the short-real format shown in Figure 11-16. This format, which uses 32 bits to represent a number, is sometimes referred to as *single-precision* representation. In this format 23 bits are used to represent the magnitude of the number, 8 bits are used to represent the magnitude of the exponent, and 1 bit is used to indicate whether the number is negative or positive. The magnitude of the number is normalized so that there is only a single 1 to the left of the binary point. The 1 to the left of the binary point is not actually present in the representation; it is simply assumed to be there. This leaves more bits for representing the magnitude of the number. You can think of the binary point as being between the bits numbered 22 and 23. The exponent for this format is put in an *offset form*, which means that an offset of 127 (7FH) is added to the 2's complement value of the exponent. This is done so that the magnitude of two numbers can be compared without having to do arithmetic on the exponents first. The sign bit is 0 for positive numbers and 1 for negative numbers. To help make this clear to you, we will show you how to convert a decimal number to this format.

We chose the number 178.625 for this example because the fractional part converts exactly, and therefore we don't have to cope with rounding at this point. The first step is to convert the decimal number to binary, which gives 10110010.101, as shown in Figure 11-17. Next normalize the binary number so that only a single 1 is to the left of the binary point, and represent the number of bit positions you had to move the binary point as an exponent, as shown in Figure 11-17. The result at this point is 1.0110010101E7. If you now add the bias of 127 (7FH) to the exponent of 7, you get the biased exponent value of 86H that you need for the short-real representation. The final line in Figure 11-17 shows the complete short-real result. For the significand you put in the binary bits to the right of the binary point. Remember, the 1 to the left of the binary point is assumed. The biased exponent value of 86H or 10000110 binary is put in as bits 23 through 30. Finally, since the number is positive, a 0 is put in bit 31 as the sign bit. The complete result is then 01000011001100101010000000000000 or 4332A000H, which is lengthy but not difficult to produce.

The long-real format shown in Figure 11-16 uses 64 bits to represent each number. This format is often

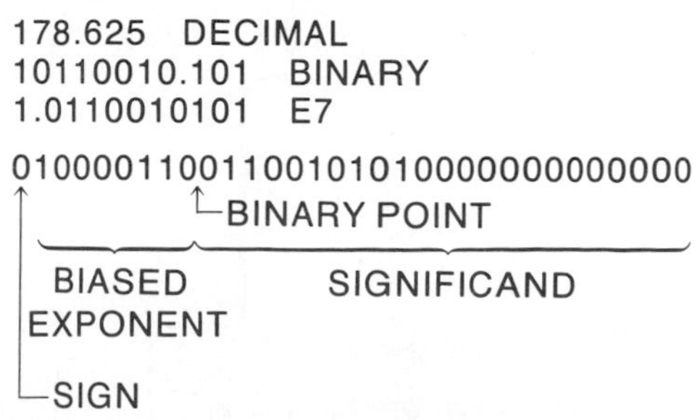

```
178.625  DECIMAL
10110010.101   BINARY
1.0110010101   E7

01000011001100101010000000000000
                └BINARY POINT
```

FIGURE 11-17 Converting a decimal number to short-real format.

referred to as *double-precision* representation. This format is basically the same as that of the short-real, except that it allows greater range and accuracy because more bits are used for each number. For long-real, 52 bits are used to represent the magnitude of the number. Again, the number is normalized so that only a single 1 is to the left of the binary point. You can think of the binary point as being between the bits numbered 51 and 52. The 1 to the left of the binary point is not actually put in as one of the 64 bits. For this format, 11 bits are used for the exponent, so the offset added to each exponent value is 1023 decimal or 3FFH. The most significant bit is the sign bit. Our example number of 178.625 is represented in this long-real or double-precision format as 4066540000000000H. Note in Figure 11-16 the range of numbers that can be represented with this format. This range should be large enough for most of the problems you want to solve with an 8087.

The final format in Figure 11-16 to discuss is the temporary-real format, which uses 80 bits to represent each number. This is the format that all numbers are converted to by the 8087 as it reads them in, and it is the format in which the 8087 works with numbers internally. The large number of bits used in this format reduces rounding errors in long chain calculations. To understand what this means, think of multiplying 1234×4567 in a machine that can store only the upper 4 digits of the result. The actual result of 5,635,678 will be truncated to 5,635,000. If you then divide this by 1234 to get back to the original 4567, you instead get 4566 because of the limited precision of the intermediate number.

As you can see in Figure 11-16, the temporary-real format has a sign bit, 15 bits for a biased exponent, and 64 bits for the significand. The offset or bias added to the exponent here is 16,383 decimal or 3FFFH. A major difference in the significand for this format from that for short-reals and long-reals is that the 1 to the left of the binary point after normalization is included as bit 63 in the significand. To express our example number of 178.625 in this form, then, we convert it to binary and normalize it as before to give 1.0110010101E7. This gives us the upper bits of the significand directly as 10110010101. We simply add enough 0's on the right of this to fill up the rest of the 64 bits reserved for the significand. To produce the required exponent, we add the bias value of 3FFFH to our determined value of 7. This gives 4006H or 100000000000110 binary as the value for the exponent. The sign bit is a 0 because the number is positive. Putting all these pieces together gives 4006B2A0000000000000H as the temporary-real representation of 178.625.

The 8087 Internal Architecture

Figure 11-18 shows an internal block diagram of the 8087. As we will discuss in detail later, the 8087 connects directly to the address, data, and status lines of the 8086 or 8088 so that it can track and decode instructions fetched by the 8086 or 8088 host. The 8087 has a control-word register and a status register. Control words are sent to the 8087 by writing them to a memory location and having the 8087 execute an instruction which reads in the control word from memory. Likewise, to read the status word from an 8087 you have it execute an instruction which writes the status word to memory where you can read or check it with an 8086 instruction. Figure 11-19 shows the formats for the 8087 control and status words. Take a look at these now so you have an overview of the meaning of the various bits of these words. We will discuss the meaning of most of these bits as we work our way through the following sections.

The 8087 works internally with all numbers in the 80-bit temporary-real format which we discussed in the

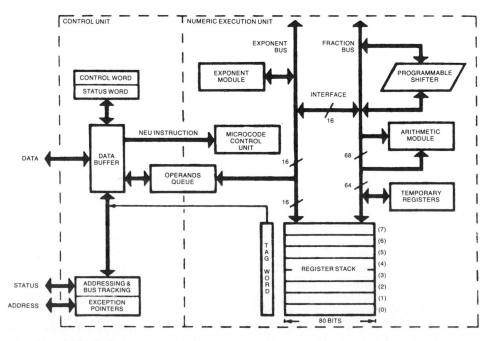

FIGURE 11-18 8087 internal block diagram. (*Intel Corporation*)

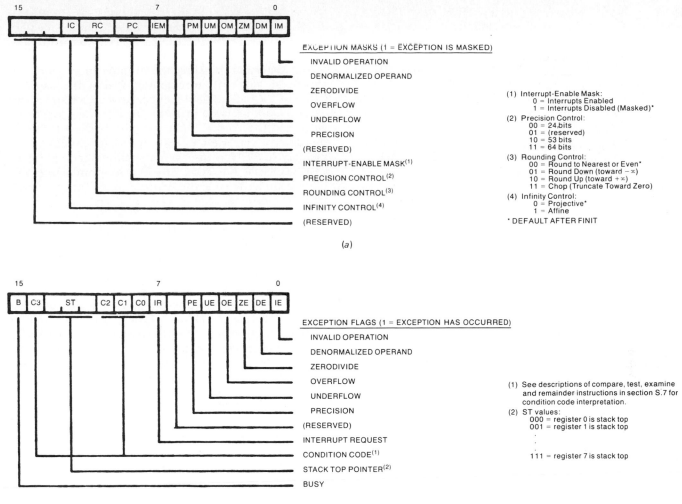

FIGURE 11-19   8087 control and status word formats. (a) Control.
(b) Status.   (*Intel Corporation*)

preceding paragraphs. To hold numbers being worked on, the 8087 has a register stack of eight 80-bit registers, labeled (0)–(7) in Figure 11-18. These registers are used as a last-in–first-out stack in the same way the 8086 uses a stack. The 8087 has a 3-bit stack pointer which holds the number of the register that is the current top-of-stack (TOS). When the 8087 is initialized, the 3-bit stack pointer in the 8087 is loaded with 000, so register 0 is then the TOS. When the 8087 reads in the first number that it is going to work on from memory, it converts the number to 80-bit temporary-real format if necessary. It then decrements the stack pointer to 111 and writes the temporary-real representation of the number in register number 111 (7). Figure 11-20a, p. 370, shows this in diagram form. As shown by the arrow in the figure, you can think of the stack as being wrapped around in a circle so that if you decrement 000 you get 111. From this diagram you can also see that if you push more than 8 numbers on the stack, they wrap around and write over previous numbers. After this write-to-stack operation, register 7 is now the TOS.

In the 8087 instructions the register that is currently

the TOS is referred to as ST(0), or simply ST. The register just below this in the stack is referred to as ST(1). By the register "just below," we mean the register that the stack pointer would be pointing to if we popped one number off the stack. For the example in Figure 11-20a, register 000 would be ST(1) after the first push.

To help you understand this concept, Figure 11-20b shows another example. In this example we have pushed three numbers on the stack after initializing. Register 101 is now the TOS, so it is referred to as ST(0), or just ST. The preceding number pushed on the stack is in register 110, so it is referred to as ST(1). Likewise, the location below this in the stack is referred to as ST(2). If you draw a diagram such as that in Figure 11-20b, it is relatively easy to keep track of where everything is in the stack as instructions execute. In a program you can determine which register is currently the ST by simply transferring the status word to memory and checking the bits labeled ST in the status-word format in Figure 11-19b. Now let's have a look at the 8087 instruction set.

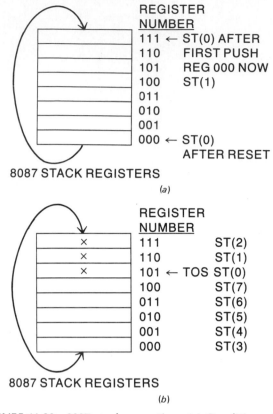

8087 STACK REGISTERS

(a)

8087 STACK REGISTERS

(b)

FIGURE 11-20   8087 stack operation. (a) Condition of stack after reset and one push. (b) Condition of stack after reset and three pushes.

8087 Instruction Set

8087 INSTRUCTION FORMATS

Before we work our way through the list of 8087 instructions, we will use one simple instruction to show you how 8087 instructions are written, how they operate, and how they are coded. The instruction we have chosen to use as an example here is the FADD instruction.

All the 8087 mnemonics start with an F, which stands for floating point, the form in which the 8087 works with numbers internally. If you look in the Intel data book, you will see this instruction represented as FADD // source/destination,source. This cryptic representation means that the instruction can be written in three different ways.

The // at the start indicates that the instruction can be written without any specified operands as simply FADD. In this case, when the 8087 executes the instruction, it will automatically add the number at the top of the stack, ST, to the number in the next location under it in the stack, ST(1). The 8087 stack pointer will be incremented by 1, so the register containing the result will be ST.

The word *source* by itself in the expression means that the instruction can be written as FADD source. The source specified here can be one of the stack elements or a memory location. For example, the instruction FADD ST(2) will add the number from two locations below ST to the number in ST and leave the result in

ST. As another example, the instruction FADD CORREC-TION_FACTOR will add a real number from the memory location named CORRECTION_FACTOR to the number in ST and leave the result in ST. The assembler will be able to determine whether the number in memory is a short-real, long-real, or temporary-real by the way that CORRECTION_FACTOR was declared. Short-reals, for example, are declared with the DD directive, long-reals with the DQ directive, and temporary-reals with the DT directive. If you want to add an integer number from memory to ST, you use an instruction such as FIADD CORRECTION_FACTOR. The I in the mnemonic tells the assembler to code the instruction so that the 8087 treats the number read in as an integer.

NOTE: The FIADD instruction only works for a source operand in memory.

The /destination,source in the representation of the FADD instruction means that you can write the instruction with both a specified source and a specified destination. The source can be one of the stack elements or a number from memory. The destination has to be one of the stack elements. The instruction FADD ST(2),ST(1), for example, will add the number one location down from ST to the number two locations down from ST and leave the result in ST(2). The instruction FADD ST(3),CORRECTION_FACTOR will add the real number from the memory location named CORRECTION_FAC-TOR to the contents of the ST(3) stack element.

Another form of the 8087 FADD instruction shown in the data book is FADDP. The P at the end of this mnemonic means POP. When the 8087 executes this form of the FADD instruction, it will increment the stack pointer by one after it does the add operation. This is referred to as "popping the stack." The instruction FADDP ST(1),ST(4), for example, will add the number at ST(4) to the number at ST(1) and put the result in ST(1). It will then pop the stack, or, in other words, increment the stack pointer so that what was ST(1) is now ST. This form of the instruction leaves the result at ST, where it can easily be transferred to memory. Now let's see how the different forms of this instruction are coded.

Coding 8087 Instructions

Common 8086 assemblers such as MASM and TASM accept 8087 mnemonics, and an assembler is the only practical way to produce codes for 8087 programs. However, to give you a feeling for how they are coded, we will show a few examples.

Figure 11-21 shows the coding templates for the 8087 FADD instructions as found in the Intel data book. Note that the figure shows coding for "8087" encoding and for "emulator" encoding. The 8087 encoding represents the codes required by an actual 8087 device. The emula-tor encoding represents the codes needed to call the FADD procedure from an available Intel library of 8086 procedures which perform the same functions as the 8087 instructions. The procedures in this library, writ-ten in 8086 code, run much slower, but they allow you

Type 1: Stack top and stack element

8087	10011011	11011 d 00	11000(i)
Emulator	11001101	00011 d 00	11000(i)

Type 2: Stack top and memory operand

8087	10011011	11011 m 00	mod 000 r/m
Emulator	11001101	00011 m 00	mod 000 r/m

m = 0 for short real operand; 1 for long real operand

Type 3: Pop stack

8087	10011011	11011110	11000(i)
Emulator	11001101	00011110	11000(i)

8087 Timing (clocks)	TYPICAL	RANGE
stack element and stack top	85	70-100
stack element, stack top + pop	90	75-105
short real memory and stack top	105+EA	90-120+EA
long real memory and stack top	110+EA	95-125+EA

FIGURE 11-21   8087 FADD coding templates.   (*Intel Corporation*)

to test an 8087 program without having an actual 8087 in the system. We will concentrate here on the codes for the actual 8087 device.

First let's look at the coding for the FADD instruction with no specified operands. This instruction, remember, will add the contents of ST to the contents of ST(1), put the results in ST(1), and then pop the stack so that the result is at ST. The first byte of the instruction code, 10011011, is the code for the 8086 WAIT instruction. As we explain in detail later, this instruction code is put here to make the 8086 and 8087 wait until the 8087 has completed this instruction before starting the next one. The second byte shown is actually the first byte of the 8087 FADD instruction. The 5 most significant bits, 11011, identify this as an 8087 instruction. The lower 3 bits of the first code byte and the middle 3 bits of the second code byte are the opcode for the particular 8087 instruction. The bit labeled d at the start of these 6 bits is a 0 if the destination for an FADD ST(N),ST(N)-type instruction is ST. The d bit is a 1 if the destination stack element is one other than ST, as it is for the FADD instruction with no specified operands. For the FADD instruction with no specified operands, these 6 bits will be 100 000. The two most significant (MOD) bits in the second code byte are 1's because this form of the FADD instruction does not read a number from memory. The least significant 3 bits of the second instruction byte, represented by an i in the template, indicate which stack element other than ST is specified in the instruction.

Since the simple FADD instruction uses ST(1) as a destination, 001 will be put in these bits. Putting all of this together for the FADD instruction with no specified source or destination gives 10011011 11011100 11000001 binary or 9BH DCH C1H as the code bytes.

For a little more practice with this, see if you can code the 8087 instruction FADD ST,ST(2). Most of the coding for this instruction is the same as that for the previous instruction. For this one, however, the d bit is a 0 because ST is the specified destination. Also, the R/M bits are 010, because the other register involved in the addition is ST(2). The answer is 9BD8C2H. Now let's try an example which uses memory as the source of an operand for FADD.

For an FADD instruction such as FADD CORRECTION_FACTOR, which brings in one operand from memory and adds it to ST, the memory address can be specified in any of the 24 ways shown in Figure 3-8. For the memory reference form of the FADD instruction, the MOD and R/M bits in the second code byte are used to specify the desired addressing mode. FADD CORRECTION_FACTOR represents direct addressing, so the MOD bits will be 00 and the R/M bits will be 110, as shown in Figure 3-8. Two additional code bytes will be used to put in the direct address, low byte first. Since we are not using any of the other stack elements other than ST for this instruction, we don't need the d bit to specify the other stack element. Instead, as shown in Figure 11-21, this bit is labeled m. A 0 in this bit is used to specify a short-real, and a 1 in this bit is used for a long-real. Assuming CORRECTION_FACTOR is declared as a long-real, the code bytes for our FADD CORRECTION_FACTOR instruction will then be 10011011 11011100 00000110 followed by the 2 bytes of the direct address.

Now that you have an overview of how 8087 instructions are written and coded, we briefly discuss each of the 8087 instructions.

8087 Instruction Descriptions

The 8087 instruction mnemonics all begin with the letter F, which stands for floating point and distinguishes the 8087 instructions from 8086 instructions. We have found that if we mentally remove the F as we read the mnemonic, it makes it easier to connect the mnemonic and the operation performed by the instruction. Here we briefly describe the operation of each of the 8087 instructions so that you can use some of them to write simple programs. As you read through these instructions the first time, don't try to absorb them all, or you probably won't remember any of them. Concentrate first on the instructions you need to get operands from memory into the 8087, simple arithmetic instructions, and the instructions you need to get results copied back from the 8087 to memory where you can use them. Then work your way through the example program in the next section. After that, read through the instructions again and pay special attention to the transcendental instructions which allow you to perform trigonometric and logarithmic operations.

The instructions are grouped here in six functional

groups so that you can more easily find the instruction which performs a desired operation.

If the 8087 detects an error condition, usually called an *exception*, while it is executing an instruction, it will set the appropriate bit in its status register. After the instruction finishes executing, the status register contents can be transferred to memory with another 8087 instruction. You can then use 8086 instructions to check the status bits and decide what action to take if an error has occurred. Figure 11-19b shows the format of the 8087 status word. The lowest 6 bits are the exception status bits. These bits will all be 0's if no errors have occurred. In the instruction descriptions following, we use the first letter of each exception type to indicate the status bits affected by each instruction.

If you send the 8087 a control word which unmasks the exception interrupts, as shown in Figure 11-19a, the 8087 will also send out a hardware interrupt signal when an error occurs. This signal can be used to send the 8086 directly to an exception handling procedure.

DATA TRANSFER INSTRUCTIONS

Real Transfers

FLD source—Decrements the stack pointer by one and copies a real number from a stack element or memory location to the new ST. A short-real or long-real number from memory is automatically converted to temporary-real format by the 8087 before it is put in ST. Exceptions: I, D.

EXAMPLES:

```
FLD ST(3)            ; Copies ST(3) to ST
FLD LONG_REAL[BX]    ; Number from memory copied
                     ; to ST
```

FST destination—Copies ST to a specified stack position or to a specified memory location. If a number is transferred to a memory location, the number and its exponent will be rounded to fit in the destination memory location. Exceptions: I, O, U, P.

EXAMPLES:

```
FST ST(2)               ; Copy ST to ST(2), and
                        ; increment stack pointer
FST SHORT_REAL[BX]      ; Copy ST to memory
                        ; at SHORT_REAL[BX]
```

FSTP destination—Copies ST to a specified stack element or memory location and increments the stack pointer by 1 to point to the next element on the stack. This is a stack pop operation. It is identical to FST except for the effect on the stack pointer.

FXCH //destination—Exchanges the contents of ST with the contents of a specified stack element. If no destination is specified, then ST(1) is used. Exception: I.

EXAMPLE:

```
FXCH ST(5)   ; Swap ST and ST(5)
```

Integer Transfers

FILD source—Integer load. Convert integer number from memory to temporary-real format and push on 8087 stack. Exception: I.

EXAMPLE:

```
FILD DWORD PTR [BX]   ; Short integer from memory
                      ; at [BX]
```

FIST destination—Integer store. Convert number from ST to integer form and copy to memory. Exceptions: I, P.

EXAMPLE:

```
FIST LONG_INT   ; ST to memory locations
                ; named LONG_INT
```

FISTP destination—Integer store and pop. Identical to FIST except that stack pointer is incremented after copy.

Packed Decimal Transfers

FBLD source—Packed decimal(BCD) load. Convert number from memory to temporary-real format and push on top of 8087 stack. Exception: I.

EXAMPLE:

```
FBLD MONEY_DUE   ; Ten byte BCD number from
                 ; memory to ST
```

FBSTP destination—BCD store in memory and pop 8087 stack. Pops temporary-real from stack, converts to 10-byte BCD, and writes result to memory. Exception: I.

EXAMPLE:

```
FBSTP TAX   ; ST converted to BCD, sent to memory
```

ARITHMETIC INSTRUCTIONS

Addition

FADD //source/destination, source—Add real from specified source to real at specified destination. Source can be stack element or memory location. Destination must be a stack element. If no source or destination is specified, then ST is added to ST(1) and the stack pointer is incremented so that the result of the addition is at ST. Exceptions: I, D, O, U, P.

EXAMPLES:

```
FADD ST(3), ST    ; Add ST to ST(3), result in ST(3)
FADD ST,ST(4)     ; Add ST(4) to ST, result in ST
FADD INTEREST     ; Real num from mem + ST
FADD              ; ST+ST(1), pop stack-result at ST
```

FADDP destination, source—Add ST to specified stack element and increment stack pointer by 1. Exceptions: I, D, O, U, P.

EXAMPLE:

FADDP ST(1)   ; Add ST(1) to ST. Increment stack
              ; pointer so ST(1) becomes ST

FIADD source—Add integer from memory to ST, result in ST. Exceptions: I, D, O, P.

EXAMPLE:

FIADD CARS_SOLD   ; Integer number from
                  ; memory + ST

Subtraction

FSUB //source/destination,source—Subtract the real number at the specified source from the real number at the specified destination and put the result in the specified destination. Exceptions: I, D, O, U, P.

EXAMPLES:

FSUB ST(2),ST   ; ST(2) becomes ST(2) − ST
FSUB CHARGE   ; ST becomes ST − real from memory
FSUB   ; ST becomes (ST(1) − ST)

FSUBP destination,source—Subtract ST from specified stack element and put result in specified stack element. Then increment stack pointer by 1. Exceptions: I, D, O, U, P.

EXAMPLES:

FSUBP ST(1)   ; ST(1) − ST. ST(1) becomes new ST.

FISUB source—Integer from memory subtracted from ST, result in ST. Exceptions: I, D, O, P.

EXAMPLE:

FISUB CARS_SOLD   ; ST becomes ST − integer
                  ; from memory

Reversed Subtraction

FSUBR //source/destination,source

FSUBRP //destination,source

FISUBR source—These instructions operate the same as the FSUB instructions described previously, except that these instructions subtract the contents of the specified destination from the contents of the specified source and put the difference in the specified destination. Normal FSUB instructions, remember, subtract source from destination.

Multiplication

FMUL //source/destination,source—Multiply real number from source by real number from specified destination and put result in specified stack element. See FADD instruction description for examples of specifying operands. Exceptions: I, D, O, U, P.

FMULP destination,source—Multiply real number from specified source by real number from specified destination, put result in specified stack element, and increment stack pointer by 1. See FADDP instruction for examples of how to specify operands for this instruction. With no specified operands FMULP multiplies ST(1) by ST and pops stack to leave result at ST. Exceptions: I, D, O, U, P.

FIMUL source—Multiply integer from memory times ST and put result in ST. Exceptions: I, D, O, P.

EXAMPLE:

FIMUL DWORD PTR [BX]

Division

FDIV //source/destination,source—Divide destination real by source real; result goes in destination. See FADD formats. Exceptions: I, D, Z, O, U, P.

FDIVP destination,source—Same as FDIV, but also increment stack pointer by 1 after DIV. See FADDP formats. Exceptions: I, D, Z, O, U, P.

FIDIV source—Divide ST by integer from memory, result in ST. Exceptions: I, D, Z, O, U, P.

Reversed Division

FDIVR //source/destination,source

FDIVP destination,source

FIDIVR source—These three instructions are identical in format to the FDIV, FDIVP, and FIDIV instructions, except that they divide the source operand by the destination operand and put the result in the destination.

Other Arithmetic Operations

FSQRT—Contents of ST are replaced with its square root. Exceptions: I, D, P.

EXAMPLE:

FSQRT

FSCALE—Scale the number in ST by adding an integer value in ST(1) to the exponent of the number in ST. Fast way of multiplying by integral powers of two. Exceptions: I, O, U.

FPREM—Partial remainder. The contents of ST(1) are subtracted from the contents of ST over and over again until the contents of ST are smaller than the contents of ST(1). FPREM can be used to reduce a large angle to less than $\pi/4$ so that the 8087 trig functions can be used on it. Exceptions: I, D, U.

EXAMPLE:

FPREM

FRNDINT—Round number in ST to an integer. The *round-control* (RC) bits in the control word determine how the number will be rounded. If the RC bits are set for down or chop, a number such as 205.73 will be rounded to 205. If the RC bits are set for up or nearest, 205.73 will be rounded to 206. Exceptions: I, P.

FXTRACT—Separates the exponent and the significand parts of a temporary-real number in ST. After the instruction executes, ST contains a temporary-real representation of the significand of the number and ST(1) contains a temporary-real representation of the exponent of the number. These two could then be written separately out to memory locations. Exception: I.

FABS—Number in ST is replaced by its absolute value. Instruction simply makes sign positive. Exception: I.

FCHS—Complements the sign of the number in ST. Exception: I.

COMPARE INSTRUCTIONS

The compare instructions with COM in their mnemonic compare contents of ST with contents of specified or default source. The source may be another stack element or real number in memory. These compare instructions set the condition code bits C3, C2, and C0 of the status word shown in Figure 11-19*b* as follows:

C3	C2	C0	
0	0	0	ST > source
0	0	0	ST < source
1	0	0	ST = source
1	1	1	numbers cannot be compared

You can transfer the status word to memory with the 8087 FSTSW instruction and then use 8086 instructions to determine the results of the comparison. Here are the different compares.

FCOM //source—Compares ST with real number in another stack element or memory. Exceptions: I, D.

EXAMPLES:

FCOM	; Compares ST with ST(1)
FCOM ST(3)	; Compares ST with ST(3)
FCOM MINIMUM_PAYMENT	; Compares ST with real ; from memory

FCOMP //source—Identical to FCOM except that the stack pointer is incremented by 1 after the compare operation. Old ST(1) becomes new ST.

FCOMPP—Compare ST with ST(1) and increment stack pointer by 2 after compare. This puts the new ST above the two numbers compared. Exceptions: I, D.

FICOM source—Compares ST to a short or long integer from memory. Exceptions: I, D.

EXAMPLE:

FICOM MAX_ALTITUDE

FICOMP source—Identical to FICOM except stack pointer is incremented by 1 after compare.

FTST—Compares ST with 0. Condition code bits C3, C2, and C0 in the status word are set as shown above if you assume the source in this case is 0. Exceptions: I, D.

FXAM—Tests ST to see if it is 0, infinity, unnormalized, or empty. Sets bits C3, C2, C1, and C0 to indicate result. See Intel data book for coding. Exceptions: None.

TRANSCENDENTAL (TRIGONOMETRIC AND EXPONENTIAL) INSTRUCTIONS

FPTAN—Computes the values for a ratio of Y/X for an angle in ST. The angle must be expressed in radians, and the angle must be in the range of $0 <$ angle $< \pi/4$.

> NOTE: FPTAN does not work correctly for angles of exactly 0 and $\pi/4$. You can convert an angle from degrees to radians by dividing it by 57.295779. An angle greater than $\pi/4$ can be brought into range with the 8087 FPREM instruction. The Y value replaces the angle on the stack, and the X value is pushed on the stack to become the new ST. The values for X and Y are created separately so you can use them to calculate other trig functions for the given angle. Exceptions: I, P.

FPATAN—Computes the angle whose tangent is Y/X. The X value must be in ST, and the Y value must be in ST(1). Also, X and Y must satisfy the inequality $0 < Y < X < \infty$. The resulting angle expressed in radians replaces Y in the stack. After the operation the stack pointer is incremented so the result is then ST. Exceptions: U, P.

F2XM1—Computes the function $Y = 2^x - 1$ for an X value in ST. The result, Y, replaces X in ST. X must be in the range $0 \le X \le 0.5$. To produce 2^X, you can simply add 1 to the result from this instruction. Using some common equalities, you can produce values often needed in engineering and scientific calculations.

EXAMPLES:

$$10^X = 2^{X(LOG_2 10)}$$
$$e^X = 2^{X(LOG_2 e)}$$
$$Y^X = 2^{X(LOG_2 Y)}$$

FYL2X—Calculates Y times the LOG to the base 2 of X or $Y(LOG_2 X)$. X must be in the range of $0 < X < \infty$ and Y must be in the range $-\infty < Y < +\infty$. X must initially be in ST and Y must be in ST(1). The result replaces Y

and then the stack is popped so that the result is then at ST. This instruction can be used to compute the log of a number in any base, n, using the identity $LOG_nX = LOG_n2(LOG_2X)$. For a given n, LOG_n2 is a constant which can easily be calculated and used as the Y value for the instruction. Exceptions: P.

FYL2XP1—Computes the function Y times the LOG to the base 2 of $(X + 1)$ or $Y(LOG_2(X + 1))$. This instruction is almost identical to FYL2X except that it gives more accurate results when computing the LOG of a number very close to 1. Consult the Intel manual for further detail.

INSTRUCTIONS WHICH LOAD CONSTANTS

The following instructions simply push the indicated constant onto the stack. Having these commonly used constants available reduces programming effort.

FLDZ—Push 0.0 on stack.

FLD1—Push +1.0 on stack.

FLDPI—Push the value of π on stack.

FLD2T—Push LOG of 10 to the base 2 on stack (LOG_210).

FLDL2E—Push LOG of e to the base 2 on stack (LOG_2e).

FLDLG2—Push LOG of 2 to the base 10 on stack ($LOG_{10}2$).

FLDLN2—Push LOG of 2 to the base e on stack (LOG_e2).

PROCESSOR CONTROL INSTRUCTIONS

These instructions do not perform computations. They are used to do tasks such as initializing the 8087, enabling interrupts, writing the status word to memory, etc.

Instruction mnemonics with an N as the second character have the same function as those without the N, but they put an NOP in front of the instruction instead of putting a WAIT instruction there.

FINIT/FNINT—Initializes 8087. Disables interrupt output, sets stack pointer to register 7, sets default status.

FDISI/FNDISI—Disables the 8087 interrupt output pin so that it cannot cause an interrupt when an exception (error) occurs.

FENI/FNENI—Enables 8087 interrupt output so it can cause an interrupt when an exception occurs.

FLDCW source—Loads a status word from a named memory location into the 8087 status register. This instruction should be preceded by the FCLEX instruction to prevent a possible exception response if an exception bit in the status word is set.

FSTCW/FNSTCW destination—Copies the 8087 control word to a named memory location where you can determine its current value with 8086 instructions.

FSTSW/FNSTSW destination—Copies the 8087 status word to a named memory location. You can check various status bits with 8086 instructions and base further action on the state of these bits.

FCLEX/FNCLEX—Clears all the 8087 exception flag bits in the status register. Unasserts BUSY and INT outputs.

FSAVE/FNSAVE destination—Copies the 8087 control word, status word, pointers, and entire register stack to a named, 94-byte area of memory. After copying all this, the FSAVE/FNSAVE instruction initializes the 8087 as if the FINIT/FNINIT instruction had been executed.

FRSTOR source—Copies a 94-byte named area of memory into the 8087 control register, status register, pointer registers, and stack registers.

FSTENV/FNSTENV destination—Copies the 8087 control register, status register, tag words, and exception pointers to a named series of memory locations. This instruction does not copy the 8087 register stack to memory as the FSAVE/FNSAVE instruction does.

FLDENV source—Loads the 8087 control register, status register, tag word, and exception pointers from a named area in memory.

FINCSTP—Increments the 8087 stack pointer by 1. If the stack pointer contains 111 and it is incremented, it will point to 000.

FDECSTP—Decrements the stack pointer by 1. If the stack pointer contains 000 and it is decremented, it will contain 111.

FFREE destination—Changes the tag for the specified destination register to empty. See the Intel manual for a discussion of the tag word. (You usually don't need to know about it.)

FNOP—Performs no operation. Actually copies ST to ST.

FWAIT—This instruction is actually an 8086 instruction which makes the 8086 wait until it receives a not-busy signal from the 8087 to its $\overline{\text{TEST}}$ pin. This is done to make sure that neither the 8086 nor the 8087 starts the next instruction before the preceding 8087 instruction is completed.

An 8087 Example Program — Pythagoras Revisited

As you may remember from back there somewhere in geometry, the Pythagorean theorem states that the hypotenuse (longest side) of a right triangle squared is equal to the square of one of the other sides plus the square of the remaining side. This is commonly written as $C^2 = A^2 + B^2$. For this example program we want to solve this for the hypotenuse C, so we take the square root of both sides of the equation to give $C = \sqrt{A^2 + B^2}$.

Figure 11-22, p. 376, shows a simple 8087 program you can use to compute the value of C for given values of A and B. We have shown the assembler listing for the program so you can see the actual codes that are generated for the 8087 instructions. Note, for example, that each of the codes for the 8087 instructions here starts with 9BH, the code for the WAIT instruction whose function we explained before.

At the start of the program we set aside some named memory locations to store the values of the three sides

```
1                          ;8087 PROGRAM F11-22.ASM
2                          ;ABSTRACT:  NUMERIC DATA PROCESSOR EXAMPLE PROGRAM
3                          ;           This program calculates the hypotenuse of a right
4                          ;           triangle, given SIDE A and SIDE B.
5
6                          .8087      ; This line tells TASM that the program contains 8087 instructions
7
8                          NAME    PYTHAG
9
10 0000                    DATA SEGMENT       WORD    PUBLIC
11 0000  40400000              SIDE_A      DD    3.0        ; Set aside space for Side A, short real
12 0004  40800000              SIDE_B      DD    4.0        ; Set aside space for Side B, short real
13 0008  00000000              HYPOTENUSE  DD    0          ; Set aside space for result, short real
14                                                          ; 5.0 normalized = 40A00000
15 000C  0000                  CONTROL_WORD DW   0          ; Space for control word
16 000E  0000                  STATUS_WORD  DW   0          ; Space for status  word
17 0010                    DATA ENDS
18
19 0000                    CODE SEGMENT WORD PUBLIC
20                              ASSUME CS:CODE, DS:DATA
21 0000  B8 0000s          START: MOV   AX, DATA            ; Initialize data segment register
22 0003  8E D8                    MOV   DS, AX
23 0005  9B DB E3                 FINIT                     ; Initialize 8087
24 0008  C7 06 000Cr 03FF         MOV   CONTROL_WORD, 03FFH ; Put control word in memory so 8087 can access
25                                                          ; it. Sets round to even & mask interrupts
26 000E  9B D9 2E 000Cr           FLDCW CONTROL_WORD        ; Load control to 8087
27 0013  9B D9 06 0000r           FLD   SIDE_A              ; Put value of SIDE_A on stack top
28 0018  9B D8 C8                 FMUL  ST, ST(0)           ; Square SIDE_A
29 001B  9B D9 06 0004r           FLD   SIDE_B              ; Put value of SIDE_B on stack top
30 0020  9B D8 C8                 FMUL  ST, ST(0)           ; Square SIDE_B
31 0023  9B D8 C1                 FADD  ST, ST(1)           ; (AxA + BxB), result at top of stack
32 0026  9B D9 FA                 FSQRT                     ; Take square root of ST, result in ST
33 0029  9B DD 3E 000Er           FSTSW STATUS_WORD         ; Copy status word to mem so 8086 can access it
34 002E  A1 000Er                 MOV   AX, STATUS_WORD     ; Bring status to AX to check for errors
35 0031  24 BF                    AND   AL, 0BFH            ; Mask unneeded bit
36 0033  75 05                    JNZ   STOP                ; Handle error if found
37 0035  9B D9 1E 0008r           FSTP  HYPOTENUSE          ; No error, copy result from 8087 to memory
38 003A  90               STOP:   NOP
39 003B                   CODE    ENDS
40                                 END   START
```

FIGURE 11-22   8087 program to compute the hypotenuse of a right triangle.

of our triangle, the control word we want to send the 8087, and the status word we will read from the 8087 to check for error conditions. Remember, the only way you can pass numbers to and from the 8087 is by using 8087 instructions to read the numbers from memory locations or write the numbers to memory locations. In this section of the example program the statement SIDE_A DD 3.0 tells the assembler to set aside two words in memory to store the value of one of the sides of the triangle. The decimal point in 3.0 tells the assembler that this is a real number. The assembler then produces the short-real representation of 3.0 (40400000) and puts it in the reserved memory locations. Likewise, the statement SIDE_B DD 4.0 tells the assembler to set aside two word locations and put the short-real representation of 4.0 in them. The statement HYPOTENUSE DD 0 reserves a double-word space for the result of our computation. When the program is finished, these locations will contain 40A00000, the short-real representation for 5.0.

You would normally write the actual code section of this program as a procedure so that you could call it as needed. To make it simple here we have written it as a stand-alone program. We start by initializing the data segment register to point to our data in memory. We

then initialize the 8087 with the FINIT instruction. The notations for the control word in Figure 11-19a show the default values for each part of the control word after FINIT executes. For most computations these values give the best results. However, just in case you might want to change some of these settings from their default values, we have included the instructions needed to send a new control word to the 8087. You first load the desired control word in a reserved memory location with the MOV CONTROL_WORD,03FFH instruction and then load this word into the 8087 with the FLDCW CONTROL_WORD instruction.

To perform the actual computation, we start at the inside of the equation and work our way outward. FLD SIDE_A brings in the value of the first side and pushes it on the 8087 stack. FMUL ST,ST(0) multiplies ST by ST and puts the result in ST, so $ST = A^2$. Next we bring in SIDE_B, push it on the 8087 stack with the FLD SIDE_B instruction, and square it with the FMUL ST,ST(0) instruction. ST now contains B^2 and ST(1) now contains A^2. We add these together and leave the result in ST with the FADD instruction. FSQRT takes the square root of the contents of ST and leaves the results in ST. To see if the result is valid, we copy the 8087 status word to the memory location we reserved for it with the FSTSW STATUS_WORD instruction. We then use 8086 instructions to check the six exception status bits to see if anything went wrong in the square root computation. If there were no exceptions (errors), these status bits will all be 0's, and the program will copy the result from ST to the memory location named HYPOTENUSE using the FSTP HYPOTENUSE instruction. We used the POP form of this instruction so that after this instruction, the stack pointer is back at the same register as it was when we started. This makes it easier to keep track of which register is ST, if necessary.

For the case where our test found an error had occurred, we could have program execution go to an error handling routine instead of simply to the STOP label as we did for this simple example.

Now that you know how it is programmed, let's look at how an 8087 is connected in a system and how it works with an 8086 or 8088 as it executes programs.

8087 Circuit Connections and Cooperation

Figure 11-23, p. 378, shows the first sheet of the schematics for the 256K version of the IBM PC. We chose this schematic not only to show you how an 8087 is connected in a system with an 8088 microprocessor, but also to show you another way in which schematics for microcomputers are commonly drawn.

First in Figure 11-23, note the numbers along the left and right edges of the schematic. These numbers indicate the other sheet(s) that the signal goes to. This is an alternative approach to the zone coordinates used in the schematics in Figure 7-8. In the schematic here the zone coordinates are not needed because all the input signal lines are extended to the left edge of the schematic, and all of the output signal lines are run to the right edge of the schematic. If you see that an output signal goes to sheet 10, then it is a simple task to scan down the left edge of sheet 10 to find that signal. The wide crosshatched strips in Figure 11-23 represent the address, data, and control buses. From the pin descriptions for the major ICs, you know where these signals are produced. You can then scan along the bus to see where various signals get dropped off at other devices. On this type of schematic the buses are always expanded to individual lines where they enter or leave a schematic. Now let's look at how the 8087 and 8088 are connected.

First note that the MIN/$\overline{\text{MX}}$ pin of the 8088 is grounded, so the 8088 is operating in its maximum mode. Remember that in maximum mode the 8088 sends out encoded control signals on the status lines S2, S1, and S0 and the queue status lines QS1 and QS0 instead of generating the control signals directly. In a maximum-mode system an external controller such as the 8288 at the bottom of Figure 11-23 decodes these status signals to produce the control signals. These status signals also go to the 8087 so that the 8087 can track the bus activity of the 8088.

Next observe that the multiplexed address/data lines, AD0–AD7, also go directly from the 8088 to the 8087. The 8088, remember, has the same instruction set as the 8086, but it has only an 8-bit data bus, so all read

and writes are byte operations. The upper address lines, A8–A19, also connect directly from the 8088 to the 8087. The 8087 receives the same clock and reset signals as the 8088.

Now look at Figure 11-23 to see if you can figure out that the request/grant signal, $\overline{\text{RQ/GT0}}$, from the 8087 is connected to the request/grant pin, $\overline{\text{RQ/GT1}}$, of the 8088. The way you figure this out from the schematic is to notice that the signal from the 8087 $\overline{\text{RQ/GT0}}$ pin is labeled just $\overline{\text{RQ/GT}}$ where it enters the crosshatched bus. Likewise, the label on the signal coming from the crosshatched bus to the $\overline{\text{RQ/GT1}}$ pin of the 8088 is also just labeled $\overline{\text{RQ/GT}}$. You know from the fact that the two lines have the same label they are connected together. For an 8086 or an 8088 operating in maximum mode, this bidirectional line is used for DMA request/acknowledge signals. The 8087 uses DMA to transfer data between memory and its internal registers.

When the 8086 or 8088 reads an 8087 instruction that needs data from memory or wants to send data to memory, the 8086 sends out the memory address coded in the instruction and sends out the appropriate memory-read or memory-write signals to transfer a word of data. In the case of a memory-read, the addressed word will be put on the data bus by the memory. The 8087 then simply reads in this word off the data bus. The 8086 or 8088 ignores the data word. If the 8087 needs only this one word of data, it can then go on and execute its instruction. However, many 8087 instructions need to read in or write out up to 80-bit words. In these cases the 8088 outputs the address of the first data word on the address bus and outputs the appropriate memory-read or memory-write control signal. The 8087 reads the data word put on the data bus by memory or writes a data word to memory on the data bus. The 8087 then grabs the 20-bit physical address that was output by the 8086 or 8088. To transfer additional words it needs to or from memory, the 8087 then takes over the buses from the 8086. To take over the bus the 8087 sends out a low-going pulse on its $\overline{\text{RQ/GT0}}$ pin, as shown in Figure 11-23. The 8086 or 8088 responds to this by sending another low-going pulse back to the $\overline{\text{RQ/GT0}}$ pin of the 8087 and by floating its buses. The 8087 then increments the address it grabbed during the first transfer and outputs the incremented address on the address bus. When the 8087 outputs a memory-read or memory-write signal, another data word will be transferred to or from the 8087. The 8087 continues the process until it has transferred all the data words required by the instruction to or from memory. When the 8087 is through using the buses for its data transfer, it sends another low-going pulse out on its $\overline{\text{RQ/GT0}}$ pin to let the 8086 or 8088 know it can have the buses back again. The key point here, then, is that the 8087 coprocessor can take over the buses from the *host* or *bus master* processor to transfer data when it needs to by pulsing the $\overline{\text{RQ/GT0}}$ input of the host processor.

Another important connection to observe in Figure 11-23 is that between the BUSY signal from the 8087 and the $\overline{\text{TEST}}$ input of the 8088. As we mentioned earlier in the chapter, this connection and the 8086 WAIT instruction are used to make sure the 8086 or 8088

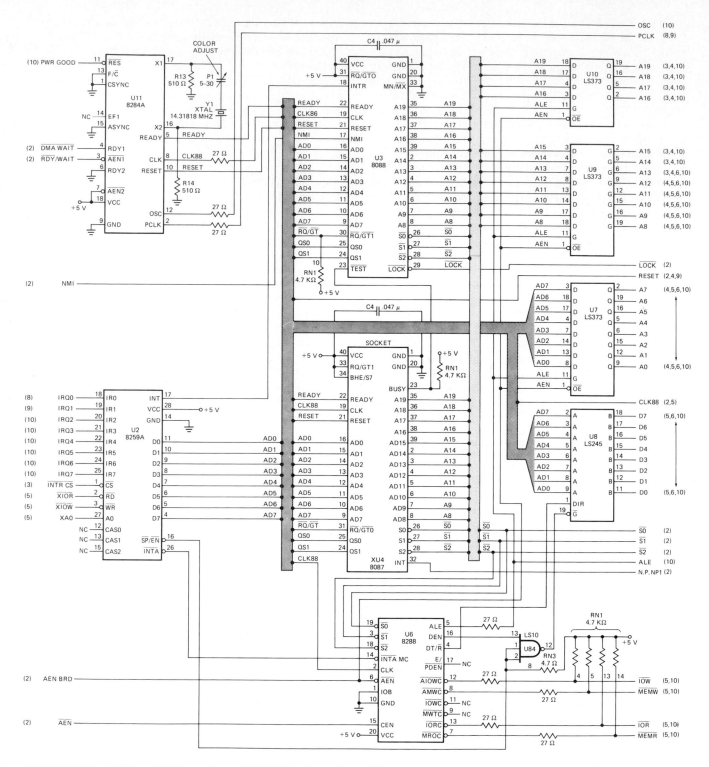

FIGURE 11-23   8088 and 8087 section of IBM PC schematic.   (*IBM Corporation*)

host does not attempt to execute the next instruction before the 8087 has completed an instruction. There are two possible problem situations here.

One problem situation is the case where the 8086 needs the data produced by execution of an 8087 instruction to carry out its next instruction. In the instruction sequence in Figure 11-22, for example, the 8087 must complete the FSTSW STATUS_WORD instruction before

the 8086 will have the data it needs to execute the MOV AX,STATUS_WORD instruction. Without some mechanism to make the 8086 wait until the 8087 completes the FSTSW instruction, the 8086 will go on and execute the MOV AX,STATUS_WORD instruction with erroneous data. This problem is solved by connecting the 8087 BUSY output to the TEST pin of the 8086 or 8088 and putting an 8086 WAIT instruction prefix,

9BH, before the 8087 FSTSW STATUS_WORD instruction in the program as shown in Figure 11-22. Here's how it works.

While the 8087 is executing an instruction, it asserts its BUSY pin high. The 8086 WAIT instruction prefix before the FSTSW STATUS_WORD instruction causes the 8087 to sit in a wait loop until its TEST pin is pulled low by the 8087 BUSY pin going low. The 8087 asserts its BUSY pin low when it completes the current instruction.

Another case where the host must be made to wait for the coprocessor is the case where a program has several 8087 instructions in sequence. The 8087 can obviously execute only one instruction at a time, so you have to make sure that the 8087 has completed one instruction before you allow the 8086 to fetch the next 8087 instruction from memory. Here again the BUSY-TEST connection and the FWAIT instruction prefix solve the problem.

As shown in the example program in Figure 11-22, an assembler will automatically insert the 8-bit code for the 8086 WAIT instruction, 10011011 binary (9BH), as the first byte of the code for each 8087 instruction. When the 8086 or 8088 fetches and decodes this code byte, it will enter on the internal loop and wait for the TEST input to go low before fetching and decoding the next 8087 instruction.

The final point we want to mention about the connections of the 8088 and 8087 in an IBM PC is that the INT output of the 8087 is connected to the nonmaskable interrupt (NMI) input of the 8088. This connection is made so that an error condition in the 8087 can interrupt the 8088 to let it know about the error condition. The signal from the 8087 INT output actually goes through some circuitry on sheet 2 of the schematics and returns to the input labeled NMI on the left edge of Figure 11-23. We do not have room here to show and explain all the circuitry on sheet 2. The main purposes of the circuitry between the INT output of the 8087 and the NMI input of the 8088 are to make sure that an NMI signal is not present during a reset, to make it possible to mask the NMI input, and to make it possible for other devices such as the parity checker to cause an NMI interrupt.

A couple of pins on the 8087 that we aren't concerned with in this system are the bus-high-enable (BHE) and request/grant1 (RQ/GT1) pins. When the 8087 is used with an 8086, the BHE pin is connected to the system BHE line to enable the upper bank of memory. The RQ/GT1 input is available so that another coprocessor can be connected in parallel with the 8087.

Next here we want to show you the tools and techniques currently used to design and test a microcomputer system such as the IBM PC shown in Figure 11-2.

COMPUTER-BASED DESIGN AND DEVELOPMENT TOOLS

In more and more companies the entire design, prototyping, manufacturing, and testing processes for an electronic product such as a microcomputer are being done with the help of a series of computer programs. The term *computer-aided engineering* (CAE) has been used in the past to describe the use of these tools, but now we commonly use the term *electronic design automation* or EDA instead of the more general term, CAE. The EDA term gives a better indication of the extent to which the currently available tools automate much of the design process. The following sections describe how a new microcomputer is designed and developed using design automation tools.

The Design Review Committee and Design Overview

The most important step in the design of any system is to think very carefully about what you want the system to do. In most companies a new product is now defined by a team consisting of design engineers, marketing/sales representatives, mechanical engineers, and production engineers. This team approach is necessary so that the product can be designed using current technology, manufactured and tested with minimal problems, and marketed successfully.

Once the specifications for the new product are agreed upon, the design engineers then think about how the circuit for it can be implemented. The next step in the design process is to partition the overall instrument design into major functional blocks or modules. Each module can then be individually designed and tested or even assigned to different designers.

Initial Design and Schematic Generation

The next step in the design process is to analyze each functional block to determine how it can best be implemented. After working out the basic design of each module, the design engineers draw a schematic for each module. In the old days (until about 5 years ago) we drew schematics on a large sheet of grid paper with a mechanical pencil and a plastic template. If we decided that a section of circuitry did not fit at a particular point on a schematic, we erased the block of circuitry with our electric eraser and started over again. The process was very time consuming and tedious. Just the remembrance of it makes me tired.

Now we use a *schematic capture* program to draw schematics on an engineering workstation such as the Apollo DN4500 shown in Figure 11-24, p. 380. Using a computer to draw schematics has the same advantage over hand drawing that using a word processor has over using a standard mechanical typewriter. Since the schematic is drawn on the computer screen, you don't have to erase anything on paper. You can move symbols around on the screen with a mouse, change connecting wires, add or delete symbols, and print out the result on a printer or plotter when the schematic looks just the way you want it to. If you change your mind about some part of the schematic, you can just edit the drawing on the screen and do a new printout.

A further advantage of the computer-aided drafting approach is that you usually don't even have to draw the symbols! Most schematic capture programs have

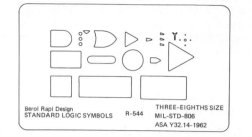

Berol Rapl Design
STANDARD LOGIC SYMBOLS   R-544   THREE-EIGHTHS SIZE
MIL-STD-806
ASA Y32.14-1962

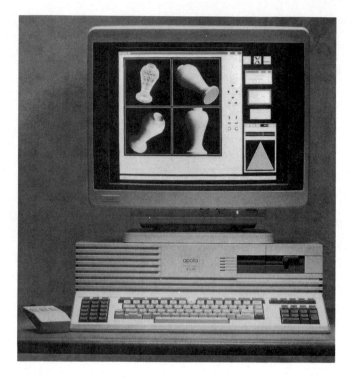

FIGURE 11-24   Apollo DN4500 workstation.   (*Apollo Computers—HP Inc.*)

large library files containing common device symbols, complete with pin numbers and electrical characteristics. All you have to do when you want to put a particular IC on a schematic is to pull the symbol for it from the library file. Once you have the IC symbols for a circuit on the screen, you can use a mouse to draw the connecting wires between them and then add junctions, connectors, labels, etc., to complete the drawing.

Schematic capture programs are available for most computers. The Ideaware programs from Mentor Graphics run on Hewlett-Packard/Apollo engineering workstations such as the one shown Figure 11-24. We used a workstation such as this and the Mentor Graphics Neted schematic capture program to draw the basic microcomputer system in Figure 11-25. Workstations such as this are used for designing large, complex digital systems or ICs. For small projects we often use an IBM PC/AT or a Macintosh-type computer. Schematic capture programs for IBM PC-type computers include CapFast from Phase Three Logic, Draft from OrCAD Systems Corporation, Schema II+ from Omation, Inc., and EE Designer II from Visionics. Schematic capture programs

available for the Macintosh include Schematic from Douglas Electronics Inc. and LogicWorks from Capilano Computing Systems Ltd.

When the schematic design file is completed, it is processed by a program called a *design rule checker* or *DRC*, which checks that there are no duplicate symbols, overlapped lines, or dangling lines. This step is similar to checking a text file with a spelling checker program.

After the schematic design file passes the DRC check, it is processed by a program called an *electrical rule checker* or *ERC*, which checks for wiring errors such as two outputs connected together or an output connected to V_{CC}.

When the schematic design file for a module passes the ERC test, a *netlist* program produces a netlist or wiring list for the design. A netlist is a file which lists all devices in the design and all the connections between devices.

Prototyping the Circuit — Simulation

After the design is polished, the next step is to prototype or "breadboard" the circuit design to make sure the logic and the timing in the circuit are correct. In the past this prototyping was usually done by soldering or wire-wrapping the circuit on a prototype board of some type. More and more we now use "software breadboarding" to test the operation of circuits of ICs. To do this we use a program called a *simulator.*

The simulator uses software *models* of the devices in the design to determine the response that the circuit will make to specified input signals. One big advantage of simulation or software breadboarding is that you don't have to order parts and wait for them to come in before you can test the operation of your design. Another big advantage of simulation is that you can change the design and resimulate the circuit in a matter of minutes to hours instead of waiting days for new parts to come in so you can modify a physical prototype and test it. Apollo Computer Corporation reportedly used simulation to cut several months from the prototype debug time for an engineering workstation such as the one shown in Figure 11-24.

Another advantage of simulation over traditional breadboarding is that you can simulate the circuit operation with worst-case timing parameters for all devices. This often discovers marginal timing problems that might not show up in a physical prototype because you can't vary the timing parameters of physical parts. We remember a case where a timing problem did not show up in the wire-wrapped prototype but caused a 40 percent failure rate in the first production run of the instrument.

As we said before, a simulator program uses models of the devices in the circuit to determine the effect that specified input signals will have on the outputs of the circuit. Most models are just software descriptions of the characteristics of the devices. These descriptions are usually written in a high-level programming language such as Pascal or C. As a simple example, part of the model for a basic, 3-input AND gate might look something like the following.

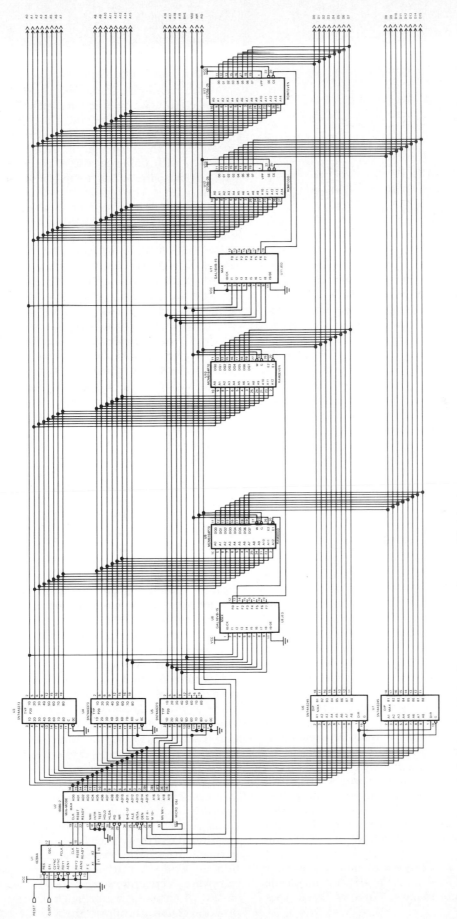

FIGURE 11-25 Schematic for simple 8086 microcomputer drawn with Mentor Graphic's Neted schematic capture program.

```
PROCEDURE ANDGATE   ;
   CONST       TPLH = 15;
               TPHL = 10;
   VAR IN1, IN2, IN3  :  INTEGER ;
       DELAY, OUT   :  INTEGER ;
   BEGIN
    IF (IN1 = 1) AND (IN2 = 1) AND (IN3 = 1)
        THEN BEGIN
               DELAY  : =   TPLH
               OUT    : =   1;
               END
                 ELSE BEGIN
                         DELAY  : =   TPHL
                         OUT    : =   0
                         END
   END;
```

This model is very primitive, but it should give you the idea. The constants represent the characteristics of the specific device being simulated (TPLH and TPHL). The variables represent the input logic levels (IN1–IN3), the output logic level (OUT), and the time between a change on the input and the corresponding change on the output (DELAY). Some simulators refer to these characteristics as *properties*. The schematic symbol is really part of the model for a device, so when you draw a schematic with a schematic capture program, you are actually creating a design file which contains the logical and timing characteristics of each device as well as the schematic symbols and connections.

When you set up the simulator to do a simulation run, you specify the signals you want applied to the inputs at a particular time, just as you connect signal generators to the inputs of a physical circuit. The simulator uses the model to determine the effects that the specified input signals will have on the output and schedules the output to change appropriately after the delay time for that device. As you can see, the model for the 3-input AND gate device tells the simulator program that if the input signals become all 1's, the output should be scheduled to change to a 1 after 15 ns. If the inputs change to a case where they are not all 1's, the output should be scheduled to change to a 0 after 10 ns.

The smallest increment of time used by a simulator is called its *time step.* You can think of the time step as the time resolution of the simulator. For simulating TTL and CMOS circuits, simulators usually use a time step of 1 ns or 0.1 ns because the delay times for these devices are a few ns. An important point here is that the 0.1-ns time step is simulator time, not real time. The simulator may take 20 minutes to determine the effects that some input signal changes produce on the outputs of a complex circuit. The physical circuit would respond to the same input changes in a real time of just a few nanoseconds. The simulator essentially exercises the circuit "in slow motion" and generates an output which *represents,* or "simulates," the real-time operation of the circuit.

Now that you have an overview of how a simulator uses models, we need to talk briefly about some of the commonly used types of models. Three of these types are:

Gate-level models

Behavioral models

Hardware models

As you may remember from a basic logic course, any digital circuit can be implemented with just basic gates. We didn't bother to show you, but even a complex device such as an 8086 or 80386 microprocessor can be modeled at the basic gate level for simulation. The difficulty with using gate-level models for complex devices is that simulation using these models requires a very long time. The reason for this is that the simulator must evaluate the effects of each signal change on all the intermediate circuit points *(nodes)* in the device.

If the complex device is a standard part, we usually know that all the internal circuitry works correctly, so we don't need to resimulate at the gate level of detail. To speed up the simulation of circuits containing complex devices, we often use *behavioral models.* Behavioral models simply describe the effects that input signals will have on the output signals and the signal delays between inputs and outputs. A behavioral model of a D flip-flop, for example, will indicate that 20 ns after a positive clock edge, the logic level on the D input will be transferred to the Q output if neither the Preset nor the Clear input is asserted. Behavioral models also contain properties such as setup times, hold times, and minimum pulse widths so the simulator can check for violations of these times by the signals propagating through the circuit. Sophisticated behavioral models such as the "SmartModels" from Logic Automation Inc. give detailed error messages to pinpoint a timing problem instead of making you work your way through a logic-analyzer-type display to find the problem.

For simulating microprocessors there are two types of behavioral models available. One type is called a *hardware verification model.* This type model is essentially a "black box" which will, for example, produce the correctly timed address and control bus signals for a memory-read cycle when given the proper *processor control language (PCL)* file. Hardware verification models are easy to use for checking system timing because all they need is a simple PCL file as a stimulus. However, hardware verification models do not allow simulation of actual microprocessor instructions. If we need this level of simulation, we use *full functional models,* which do allow the execution of instructions. The disadvantages of full functional models are that they operate more slowly than hardware verification models and you have to develop a file containing the actual object codes for the microprocessor instructions you want to execute.

In cases where a behavioral model of a device is not available and it is not practical to write a model or in cases where the simulation must interfere with external circuitry at real time speeds, we use *hardware modeling.* In this approach the devices to be simulated are plugged into an external unit such as the Mentor Graphics Hardware Modeling System (HML) shown in Figure 11-26. When using a unit such as this, the simulator program sends stimulus signals to the external devices,

FIGURE 11-26 Mentor Graphics HML box.

reads back the responses of the external devices, and includes these responses in the simulation.

To develop complex systems such as the engineering workstation shown in Figure 11-24 we use *multilevel* simulators. An example of a multilevel simulator is Mentor Graphics Quicksim, which can simulate combinations of gate, behavioral, and hardware models. Quicksim runs on engineering workstations such as the one in Figure 11-24. Another useful but somewhat less powerful, multilevel simulator is SUSIE from Aldec Corp. SUSIE runs on PC-type computers and is available to schools at a generous discount. Multilevel simulators such as this even allow the JEDEC files for PALs to be included in the simulation.

To simulate analog circuits, you can use an analog circuit simulator such as PSPICE from Microsim Corporation or Accusim from Mentor Graphics. For circuits such as A/D converters, which have both analog and digital circuitry, you can use a *mixed-mode simulator* such as SABER from Analogy, Inc. or LSIM from Mentor Graphics.

A Microcomputer Simulation Example

We drew the schematic for the basic 8086 based microcomputer in Figure 11-25 using Mentor Graphics Neted and Logic Automation Smartmodels. As you can see in the figure, the circuit uses SN74AS373s as address latches and SN74AS245s as data bus buffers. The ROM in this systems consists of two I27256 EPROMs, one for the even bank and one for the odd bank. A Lattice GAL16V8 EPLD is used as an address decoder for the ROMs. The RAM in this basic system consists of two MCM6164 static RAM devices, one for the even bank and one for the odd bank. A second Lattice GAL16V8 EPLD is used as an address decoder for the RAMs. Offpage connectors go to a second sheet which contains the ports, timers, etc. For this example we are interested only in the basic microprocessor and memory section of the system.

The Logic Automation Smartmodel for the 8086 processor in Figure 11-25 is a hardware verification type. As we said above, this type model allows us to verify that the signal connections, address decoding, and timing of the system are correct. To refresh your memory as to what is involved in the timing of a system such as this, take another look at Figure 7-13.

As you can see in Figure 7-13a, the 8086 and memories essentially form a loop. To read a word from memory the 8086 sends out an address and control signals, and after some propagation delay the memory sends the data word back to the 8086. In order for the data word to be accepted by the 8086, it has to get back to the 8086 within a certain time period. In Figure 7-20 and the accompanying discussion, for example, we showed you how to determine if the address access time of a 2716 EPROM was fast enough for the device to work in a 4.9-MHz 8086 system.

When you use Smartmodels to simulate a system such as that in Figure 11-25, the simulator will automatically perform all the memory timing computations and give you an error message if it finds any timing violations. You can then redesign the circuit and resimulate until you get no error messages.

To simulate the circuit you have to give the simulator several types of information in addition to the basic netlist produced from the schematic. These additional parts are put in files which the simulator will read out as it needs them. The process is really quite simple. Here is a list of the parts you need.

1. A fusemap or JEDEC file for each of the GAL16V8 EPLD address decoders. These can be produced with a PAL programming tool such as ABEL from Data I/O. Figure 11-27a, p. 384, shows an ABEL source file for the U11 ROM decoder.

2. A memory image file for each of the memory devices. These are simple test files which essentially initialize the memory devices with known contents so you will know if data is read back correctly. Figure 11-27b shows a memory image file which will initialize the first 100H locations of a memory device with 88H.

3. A processor control (PCL) file which tells the simulator the bus operations you want the processor to perform. For Logic Automation Smartmodels this file is written in C. Figure 11-27c shows an example of a PCL file for our 8086 system. The instructions in the first block write bytes to a sequence of RAM locations starting at address 00000H. After it is written, each byte is read back. After the simulation is run the results from this part help us determine if the address decoding, control signals, and timing are correct for the RAM part of the circuit. The next block in Figure 11-27c reads data words from a series of ROM locations to verify the address decoding, control signals, and timing of the ROM section of the circuit. If we were also simulating programmable peripheral devices, we would include a section in the PCL file to initialize the devices and exercise their functions.

4. A stimulus file which tells the simulator what signals

```
module rompal
title '8086 SYSTEM ROM DECODER - DOUG HALL 1988'

    U11                     DEVICE 'P16V8S';
    A0,BHE,MIO              PIN 2,3,4;
    A16,A17,A18,A19         PIN 6,7,8,9;
    ROMF_EVEN, ROMF_ODD     PIN 19,18;
    ROME_EVEN, ROME_ODD     PIN 17,16;

EQUATIONS

    !ROMF_EVEN = A19 & A18 & A17 &  A16 & !A0  & MIO;
    !ROMF_ODD  = A19 & A18 & A17 &  A16 & !BHE & MIO;
    !ROME_EVEN = A19 & A18 & A17 & !A16 & !A0  & MIO;
    !ROME_ODD  = A19 & A18 & A17 & !A16 & !BHE & MIO;
END rompal
```

(a)

```
0:100/88;
```

(b)

```
    #include <i8086min.cmd>
    int i,addr;
main( )
{
    trace_on( );
    set_trace_level(1);
    addr = 0x0000;

    for (i=0; i<=16; i++)
    {
    write(1,addr,i);
    read(1,addr);
    idle(5);
    addr++;
    }
    addr = 0xf0000;
        i = 0;
    for (i=0; i<=16; i++)
    {
    read(2,addr);
    addr++;
    addr++;
    }
}
```

(c)

```
CLOCK PERIOD 125
FORCE CLOCK 0 0    -R
FORCE CLOCK 1 62.5 -R
FORCE RESET 0 0
FORCE RESET 1 1000
```

(d)

FIGURE 11-27   Files required for simulating
microcomputer circuit in Figure 11-25. (a) ABEL source
file for PAL address decoder. (b) Memory image file.
(c) Processor control file. (d) Simulator stimulus file.

to apply to the signal inputs of the system so that it
runs through the operations in the PCL file. Figure
11-27d shows an example. The first three statements
generate an 8-MHz clock for the external clock input

of the 8284 clock generator. The next two statements
generate a RESET signal. Note that the numbers
such as 125, 62.5, and 1000 in these statements
represent times in nanoseconds.

Once you have generated the necessary files, all you
have to do is run the simulation. Figure 11-28 shows
the screen messages produced as Quicksim is invoked
and run on our microcomputer system design. As you
can see, Quicksim first loads the required files in memory. When the Quicksim prompt appears, we execute
the stimulus file in Figure 11-27d with D0 MICRO.DO
command. Then we run the simulator for 100,000 time
units of 1 ns with the RUN 100000 command.

When the simulator started running, it immediately
gave an error message indicating that we did not hold
the RESET input of the 8086 low for the four clock
periods required by the manufacturer's specifications.
The problem here is that in our force file shown in Figure
11-27d, we generated an 8-MHz clock on the external
clock input of the 8284 clock generator and held RESET
low for 1000 ns, or eight of these clock cycles. The 8284,
however, divides the external clock signal by 3 to produce
the clock signal actually applied to the processor. This
means that in actuality our reset stimulus was holding
the RESET input low for only a little more than two
cycles of the clock applied to the 8086, rather than the
required four. This is a good example of the intelligence
built into the models.

When we discovered this error, we stopped the simulation, corrected the stimulus file, and ran the simulation
again. The second time we ran the simulation it did not
show the RESET error. As directed by the trace settings
we put in the PCL file, the simulator produced a trace
of each state as the 8086 wrote to and read from memory.
The bottom few lines of Figure 11-28 show some examples of the type of information the trace gives you. Note
that the first operations the simulator carries out are to
write to and read back from RAM locations as specified
in the PCL file. A careful study of the trace showed that
values were written to memory and read back correctly.
This indicates that the address decoders are working
correctly and that the circuit connections are correct.
After we fixed the RESET problem described before, we
ran the simulator again and got no significant timing
warnings, so we felt reasonably sure the system would
work correctly when we designed and built a PC board
for it.

A very important point here is that it took only about
10 to 12 hours to design the system in Figure 11-25,
draw the schematic for the system, and completely
simulate it. Perhaps you can see that when designing a
more complex system such as the microcomputer system
in Figure 11-15a, simulation is the only practical way
to determine if all the timing requirements are met in
the design.

Design for Test

Once a system has passed simulation, the next step is
to design in some circuitry which allows the system to
be easily tested when it goes to production. Many

```
# Executing object named: '/idea/sys/lib/lsim_server.mod'
#   LOGIC SIMULATION SERVER V6.1_1.10 Monday, April 18, 1988 6:01:59 pm (PDT)
#   LAI Version: MG_A3_610_970_200  May 17, 1988
#   SmartModels: All pictorial, graphic, and audiovisual works, collective works
#                representations, compilations, and arrangements therof,
#                Copyright 1984-1988 Logic Automation Incorporated.
#
#   Note: Loading the PCL program from file "/user/doug/micro2/MICRO_OBJ".
#         Instance I$4(U2:I8086-2), sheet1 of micro2 at time 0.0
#
# ! Warning: Input pin MNMX is not allowed to change (will continue in MIN mode)
# !          Instance I$4(U2:I8086-2), sheet 1 of micro2 at time 0.0
#
#   Note: Loading the JEDEC file "/user/doug/micro2/U11.JED"
#         Instance I$62(U11:GAL16V8-15), sheet1 of micro2 at time 0.0
#         --- 173 fuses have been blown.
#
#   Note: Loading the JEDEC file "/user/doug/micro2/U8.JED"
#         Instance I$11(U8:GAL16V8-15), sheet1 of micro2 at time 0.0
#         --- 169 fuses have been blown.
#
#   Note: Loading the memory image file "/user/doug/micro2/RAMOEVEN"
#         Instance I$61(U10:MCM6164P70), sheet1 of micro2 at time 0.0
#         --- 257 values have been initialized.
#
#   Note: Loading the memory image file "/user/doug/micro2/RAMOODD"
#         Instance I$41(U9:MCM6164P70), sheet1 of micro2 at time 0.0
#         --- 257 values have been initialized.
#
#   Note: Loading the memory image file "/user/doug/micro2/RAMFEVEN"
#         Instance I$63(U13:I27256-25), sheet1 of micro2 at time 0.0
#         --- 257 values have been initialized.
#
#   Note: Loading the memory image file "/user/doug/micro2/RAMFODD"
#         Instance I$15(U12:I27256-25), sheet1 of micro2 at time 0.0
#         --- 257 values have been initialized.
     VIEw Sheet
QuickSim>
     DO MICRO.DO
     RUN 100000
#
# ! Warning: RESET did not last 4 Clock Cycles.
# !              Instance I$4(U2:I8086-2), sheet1 of micro2 at time 1562.5
#
#   Trace: Trace is turned on
#          Instance I$4(U2:I8086-2), sheet1 of micro2 at time 4812.5
#
#   Trace: Trace level is now set to 1 (internal timing states shown)
#          Instance I$4(U2:I8086-2), sheet1 of micro2 at time 4812.5
#
#   Trace: CPU state T1
#          Instance I$4(U2:I8086-2), sheet1 of micro2 at time 4937.5
#
#   Trace: Write Memory (1-byte) location 00000 with 0000
#          Instance I$4(U2:I8086-2), sheet1 of micro2 at time 4937.5
#
#   Trace: CPU state T2
#          Instance I$4(U2:I8086-2), sheet1 of micro2 at time 5312.5
#
#   Trace: CPU state T3
#          Instance I$4(U2:I8086-2), sheet1 of micro2 at time 5687.5
#
#   Trace: CPU state T4
#          Instance I$4(U2:I8086-2), sheet1 of micro2 at time 6062.5
#
#   Trace: CPU state T1
#          Instance I$4(U2:I8086-2), sheet1 of micro2 at time 6437.5
#
#   Trace: Read Memory (1-byte) location 00000
#          Instance I$4(U2:I8086-2), sheet1 of micro2 at time 6437.5
```

FIGURE 11-28 Screen messages during simulator invocation and run.

microcomputers now contain built-in-self-test (BIST) circuitry so that the unit does a complete internal test each time the power is turned on. If the unit fails any test, it sends a message to the CRT.

After the test circuitry is added, the circuit is simulated again to make sure the added test circuitry has not adversely affected the operation of the circuit.

Printed-Circuit-Board Design

In the old says we used a light table and large plastic sheets to develop the layout for a PC board. To produce "pads" for IC pins, transistor leads, resistor leads, etc., we stuck opaque "donuts" on the sheets. To produce traces between pads we used opaque tape. The plastic sheets were photographed and the resulting films were used to produce the desired patterns of traces on copper plated circuit boards.

Now we use automatic place-and-route programs such as Board Station from Mentor Graphics, Allegro from Valid Logic Systems, or Tango PCB from ACCEL Technologies, Inc., to lay out PC boards. These programs work with the netlist file and determine the best placement of components and the most efficient route for traces between components. The programs allow user interaction so that specific paths can be optimized if needed. For example, in designing a PC board for a very high speed system, you might determine the actual signal delays from an initial layout attempt and then resimulate the system with these delays. If the resimulation shows a problem, you can manually alter the layout to solve the problem before going on.

The file produced by the PC board layout program is sent to a laser printer to directly produce film negatives for each layer of the board. The negative is used to photographically produce the desired pattern on a copper-plated PC board. A chemical solution then etches copper from all the areas of the board except those where component pads, traces, ground planes, and power planes are desired. For a multilayer board, several individual boards are produced and then epoxied together under pressure to form a single board.

The board is then drilled under computer control. Finally, the plated-through holes and other *vias* which connect traces on different layers are electrochemically added to the board.

After manufacture, the "bare" PC boards are tested with a computer-based tester to check for shorts and opens. On a prototype PC board, minor problems can often be solved by, for example, drilling out a plated-through hole which accidentally got shorted to a power plane. A jumper wire can be added to make a missed connection.

Case Design

Once the PC board, power supply, and display have been designed for an instrument, the mechanical engineer can design the case for the system. A program such as the Mentor Graphics Package Station can be used to do much of this design. This program allows the designer

to draw a three-dimensional view of a case and the placement of the components in the case. The Package Station program also allows a designer to determine the temperature that will be present at each location in the prototype case for a specified ambient temperature and airflow. This feature allows the designer to determine if the airflow is great enough, the placement of the PC board(s) in the case is reasonable, and perhaps if devices which produce a large amount of heat are placed too close together on a PC board. Here is another example of "software breadboarding," which saves much work and materials because, if a problem is found, you can simply go back to the computer screen and try a new design instead of producing a new physical box and trying it.

Developing the System Software

In addition to designing the hardware of a microcomputer, you also have to develop the BIOS software which allows programs to interact with the hardware. As we said earlier, the logic automation hardware verification model for a processor such as the 8086 allows you to include statements in a PCL file to initialize the programmable peripheral device models, write data to them, and read data from them. This is a way to verify the address, operation, and timing of these devices. If a fully functional model is available for the microprocessor, you can write sections of actual code for the microprocessor and run the code as part of the simulation.

When a prototype PC board for the system becomes available, an emulator such as we described in Chapter 3 can be used to develop the more complex software procedures of the BIOS.

Production and Test

Once the prototype of a system is debugged and any necessary changes are made, the design is finalized and released to production. Many parts of the production, testing, and troubleshooting of the instrument are done with the aid of computer programs.

Programs are available to generate a parts list from the netlist for a design. Other available programs direct a robot to collect the needed parts from the warehouse for the production run. A computer program running on an automatic tester tests the bare PC boards for shorts and opens before parts are inserted. Another program controls the machine that automatically places the components on the printed circuit board. The machine which solders all the components on the board is most likely controlled by a microcomputer program. Still another computer program controls the machine which automatically tests the finished PC boards. The program for this automatic test system uses test vectors which were developed as part of the design process. If the product does not have a complete built-in self-test, the finished product is also tested with an automatic test system. The linking together of all the computer-based tools used in the production of a product is called computer integrated manufacturing, or CIM.

CHECKLIST OF IMPORTANT TERMS AND CONCEPTS IN THIS CHAPTER

If you do not remember any of the terms in the following list, use the index to help you find them in the chapter for review.

Motherboard and system expansion slots

8086 minimum mode and maximum mode

DMA operation

DMA channel

DRAM
  RAS and $\overline{\text{CAS}}$ strobes
  Refresh: burst and distributed modes
  82C08 DRAM controller IC
  Error detecting and correcting
    Hard and soft errors
    Parity check
    Hamming codes and syndrome word
  Page mode read/write access
  Static column read/write access
  Cache memory system
    Direct-mapped cache

Two-way set associative cache
Fully associative cache

8087 math coprocessor
  Data types and terms
    Word, short, and long integers
    Packed decimals
    Short-, long-, and temporary-reals
    Fixed-point numbers
    Floating-point numbers
    Normalizing
    Significand, mantissa, exponent, biased exponent
    Single- and double-precision representation

Electronic Design Automation
  Schematic capture
  Simulation
    Gate-level model
    Behavioral model
    Hardware model
    Time step
    Stimulus file
  Design for test
  PC board layout
  Case design
  Computer integrated manufacturing

REVIEW QUESTIONS AND PROBLEMS

1. Why are microcomputers such as the IBM PC designed with peripheral expansion slots instead of having functions such as a CRT controller designed into the motherboard?

2. Describe how the control bus signals are produced for an 8086 system operating in maximum mode.

3. Why is DMA data transfer faster than doing the same data transfer with program instructions?

4. Describe the series of actions that a DMA controller will perform after it receives a request from a peripheral device to transfer data from the peripheral device to memory.

5. Describe how the 20-bit memory address for a DMA transfer is produced by the circuit in Figure 11-5.

6. Describe the function and operation of devices U5 and U6 in Figure 11-5.

7. Sketch the sequence of signals that must occur to read a data word from a dynamic RAM such as the TMS44C256.

8. List the major tasks that must be done to support dynamic RAM in a microcomputer system.

9. How does a dynamic RAM controller in a system such as that in Figure 11-9 arbitrate the dispute that occurs when the CPU attempts to read from or write to a bank of dynamic RAMs while the controller is doing a refresh cycle?

10. *a.* What timing parameter limits the rate at which data words can be read from random rows (pages) in a DRAM?
    b. Explain how page mode operation of a bank of DRAMs makes it possible for a microprocessor to read data words without wait states.
    c. What is the main difference between page mode operation and static column mode operation of a bank of DRAMs?

11. *a.* Describe how an SRAM cache reduces the average number of wait states required by a microprocessor which uses DRAM for its main memory.
    b. How does a cache controller keep track of which blocks from the main memory are present in the cache?
    c. With a direct-mapped cache system, what does each entry in the cache tag RAM represent?
    d. In a direct-mapped cache system, only one block with a particular number can be present in the cache at a time. How does a two-way set associative cache overcome this problem?

12. Describe how parity is used to check for RAM data errors in microcomputers such as the IBM PC. What is a major shortcoming of the parity method of error detection?

13. When using a Hamming code error detection/correction scheme for DRAMs, how many encoding bits must be added to detect and correct a single-bit error in a 64-bit data word?

14. How can you tell from the schematic that the 8088 in Figure 11-23 is configured in maximum mode?

15. Device U7 in Figure 11-23 has a signal named AEN connected to its $\overline{OE}$ input. If, in troubleshooting this system, you find that this signal is not getting asserted, on which schematic sheet would you first look to see how this signal is produced?

16. In what ways are a standard microprocessor and a coprocessor different from each other?

17. *a.* Convert the decimal number 2435.5625 to binary, normalized binary, long-real, and temporary-real format.
    b. Why are most floating-point numbers actually approximations?

18. *a.* Which 8087 stack register is ST after a reset?
    b. Which 8087 stack register will be ST after one data item is read into the 8087?
    c. Describe the operation that will be done by the 8087 FADD ST(2),ST(3) instruction.
    d. How does the operation of the instruction FADDP ST(2),ST(3) differ from the operation of the instruction in 18c?

19. Describe the operation performed by each of the following 8087 instructions.
    a. FLD TAX_RATE
    b. FMUL INFLATION_FACTOR
    c. FSQRT
    d. FLDPI
    e. FSTSW CHECK_ANSWER
    f. FPTAN

20. Why does the assembler insert 9BH, the code for the 8086 WAIT instruction, before the code for most of the 8087 instructions?

21. Using the example program in Figure 11-24 as a guide, write an 8087 program which computes the volume of a sphere. The formula is $V = 4/3\pi R^3$.

22. *a.* When a coprocessor and a standard processor are connected together in a system such as that in Figure 11-23, why are the S2–S0 status lines, the QS1–QS0 lines, the address, and the data lines of the two devices connected directly together?
    b. Where does the 8087 coprocessor in Figure 11-23 get its instructions from?
    c. How does the main processor distinguish its instructions from those for the 8087 as it fetches instructions from memory?
    d. Describe how the 8087 and 8088 work together to load a long-real data item from memory to the 8087 ST.
    e. How does the 8087 in Figure 11-23 signal the 8088 that it needs to use the buses?
    f. How can you prevent the 8088 in Figure 11-23 from going on with its next instruction before the 8087 has completed an instruction? What hardware connection in Figure 11-23 is part of this mechanism?

23. *a.* Describe how a schematic is drawn using a schematic capture program.
    b. What are the major advantages of the schematic capture approach over the traditional drafting approach?

24. *a.* What is meant by the term *software breadboard*?
    b. Describe the major advantages of simulation over hardware prototyping.
    c. What information does the simulation model for a device contain?
    d. Briefly describe the steps involved in simulating a microcomputer such as the one in Figure 11-25.
    e. What information does simulation give you about a circuit such as the one in Figure 11-25?

25. Briefly describe the sequence of steps in the electronic design automation method of designing, debugging, and producing an electronic product such as a microcomputer.

CHAPTER 12

C, a High-level Language for System Programming

In the last chapter we introduced you to the operation of the motherboard hardware of a typical microcomputer system. Before we discuss the operation of system peripherals such as CRTs, hard disks, and telecommunications links, we need to introduce you to the languages and tools which are now commonly used to write application and system-level programs.

Up to this point in the book we have used assembly language for all the programming examples because we were working very close to the hardware. As we said earlier in the book, assembly language is appropriate for initializing peripheral devices, writing programs which manipulate a lot of hardware, or writing programs which have to execute very fast. Writing large system-level programs in assembly language is slow and tedious, so we usually write major parts of these programs in a high-level language such as Pascal or C.

As you are probably aware, there are many different high-level languages. For the high-level language programming examples throughout the rest of this book, we use the C language. We chose C because it is very widely used in industry, it is a good stepping-stone to a modern programming language called C++, and it is very easy to learn if you are already familiar with 8086-type assembly language programming.

To develop a system-level program, the overall design is broken down into a group of modules. A decision is then made whether each module can be written in a high-level language or must be written in assembly language. The high-level modules are written, debugged, and compiled to produce .OBJ files. Likewise, the assembly language modules are written, debugged, and assembled to .OBJ files. All the .OBJ files are then linked together to produce a .EXE file which can be run. This is basically the same process we described in Chapter 5 for writing multimodule assembly language programs. In this chapter we will first show you how to write some simple programs in C, and then we will show you how to write programs which contain both high-level language modules and assembly language modules.

OBJECTIVES

At the conclusion of this chapter, you should be able to:

1. Describe how the tools in an integrated programming environment such as Borland's Turbo C++

IDE are used to edit, compile, link, run, and debug C programs.

2. Describe the data types that are available in C.

3. Declare and initialize simple variables, arrays, and structures in C.

4. Implement standard programming structures such as IF-THEN-ELSE, SWITCH (CASE), WHILE-DO, DO-WHILE, and FOR-DO in C.

5. Declare, define, and call functions (procedures) in C programs.

6. Write C programs which implement simple algorithms.

7. Write simple programs which consist of C modules and assembly language modules.

INTRODUCTION—A SIMPLE C PROGRAM EXAMPLE

As we said before, it is very easy to learn the C programming language if you are already familiar with 8086 assembly language programming. To give you some feeling for how easy it is to make this transition and to give you an introduction to the general structure of a C program, we will first show how the cost-price array example program in Figure 4-23 can be written in C.

If you look back at the program in Figure 4-23, you will see that this program adds a profit of 15 to each of eight costs. More specifically, the program reads in a value from an array called COST, adds a profit of 15 to the value read in, and puts the computed price in the corresponding element of an array called PRICES.

Figure 12-1a on page 390 shows a simple C program which will perform basically the same operations and also write the results out on your computer screen. The first point to observe in this program is that any text enclosed between /* and */ is a comment, not part of the actual program. The next parts to look at in this program are the statements which define the data the program is going to work with. The statement int cost[ ]= {20,28,15,26,19,27,16,29,39,42}; declares an array of 10 integers called cost and initializes the 10 elements of the array with the specified values. This corresponds

```
/* C PROGRAM F12-01A.C */
/* COMPUTE THE SELLING PRICE OF 10 ITEMS */

#include <stdio.h>
#define PROFIT 15
#define MAX_PRICES 10

int cost[] = { 20,28,15,26,19,27,16,29,39,42 }; /* array of 10 costs */
int prices[10];                                  /* array to hold 10 prices */
int index;                                       /* variable to use as index */

main()
{
    for (index=0; index <MAX_PRICES; index++)    /* for loop to compute */
    prices[index] = cost[index] + PROFIT;        /* 10 prices */

    for (index=0; index <10; index++)            /* for loop to display results */
    printf("cost = %d, price = %d, \n", cost[index], prices[index]);

}
```

(a)

```
cost  =  20,  price  =  35,
cost  =  28,  price  =  43,
cost  =  15,  price  =  30,
cost  =  26,  price  =  41,
cost  =  19,  price  =  34,
cost  =  27,  price  =  42,
cost  =  16,  price  =  31,
cost  =  29,  price  =  44,
cost  =  39,  price  =  54,
cost  =  42,  price  =  57,
```

(b)

FIGURE 12-1   (a) Simple C program to add profit of 15 to each of 10 items.
(b) Printout of program results.

to the COST DB 20, . . . statement in the program of Figure 4-23. The statement int prices[10]; declares an array of 10 integers called prices. Since no values are given, the elements of this array are not initialized. Note that the C program statements are terminated with semicolons.

Program lines which begin with a # are *preprocessor directives*. These lines do not generate any code; they give instructions to the compiler. The #define PROFIT 15 line in Figure 12-1a, for example, tells the compiler to replace the name PROFIT with the constant 15 each time it finds PROFIT in the program. This is equivalent to the PROFIT EQU 15 line in the assembly language version in Figure 4-23. The #define MAX_PRICES 10 line in Figure 12-1a is another example. As we pointed out in our earlier discussions of assembly language programming techniques, it is very important to define constants at the start of a program in this way, rather than using "hard" numbers directly in the program. The reason is that if you have to change the number, you only have to change the value in the equ or the #define, instead of finding and changing the value each place it occurs in the program. Note that we always use upper-case letters for constants such as PROFIT, so that we

can tell them from variables, which we put in lowercase letters.

The int index; statement in Figure 12-1a declares a variable called index. The int at the start of the statement indicates that the variable can have only integer values. This index will be used to point to the array element being processed at a particular time and to keep track of how many elements have been processed. Now that you have an overview of the data, let's take a look at the action part of the program.

All the action statements in C programs, even those in the mainline part of a program, are written in functions. In Pascal and some other languages, a function is the name given to a procedure which returns some value(s) to the calling program. In C all procedures are referred to as functions whether they return a value or not.

Every C program must have a function, usually called main, which gets called when your program starts executing. Other functions are called from main as needed. As you can see, the main( ) function in Figure 12-1a contains a for structure and two statements. You use the "curly braces" { and } to enclose the parts of a function. The parentheses ( ) after the name of the function are used to contain parameters and the names of variables that you want passed to the function. Later we will show you examples of how to do this. Empty parentheses after a function name mean that no parameters are being passed to the function.

The statement for (index=0; index <MAX_PRICES; index++) implements a FOR-DO loop which executes the statements contained in the second set of curly braces 10 times (index values of 0 through 9). The index++ term in the parentheses means that the value of index will be incremented each time through the loop. The prices[index]=cost[index]+PROFIT statement and the printf statement will also be implemented each time through the loop.

As perhaps you can figure out, the prices[index]=cost[index]+PROFIT; statement reads an indexed location in the cost array, adds a PROFIT of 15 to the value read, and writes the result to the same indexed location in the prices array. Note how the variable index is used here to access the elements in each array and also to determine how many times the loop executes.

Each time through the loop the printf statement calls the predefined printf( ) function which sends the specified text and values to the screen. The parentheses after printf contain the parameters we are passing to the function. Characters enclosed in " " inside the parentheses are printed out as written until a % is encountered. A % indicates that the value of a variable is to be inserted at that point. The name of that variable is included in a list of variables after the second " in the print statement. In this example the first variable encountered after the second " is cost[index], so the value of this variable will be printed out after cost= is printed out. The d after the % tells the function to print the decimal value of cost[index]. When the function encounters the second %d in the parentheses, it will print the decimal value of prices[index], the next variable after cost[index] in the variables list. The \n in the statement stands for "newline" and tells the printf function to send a carriage-return character and a linefeed character. This will move the cursor to the start of the next line down on the screen. Figure 12-1b shows the printout produced by the printf function when this program was run.

As you can see in Figure 12-1a, the printf function is not present in our program. The printf function is found in a library of input/output functions that comes with the program development software. The #include <stdio.h> at the start of the program tells the preprocessor part of the compiler that the prototype for the printf function is in a file called stdio.h. The linker will use this prototype to get the object code for the printf function from a library file and link it with the object code for our price.c program so that it will be part of the final executable file. In a later section we will tell you more about predefined functions.

If you compare the number of statements in our C program with the number of statements needed to do the job in the assembly language version in Figure 4-23, you should immediately see one of the advantages of writing as many programs as possible in a high-level language. In the next section we discuss some software

tools you can use to develop your own C programs. Then in the following sections we show you much more of the structure and syntax of the C language.

PROGRAM DEVELOPMENT TOOLS FOR C

To develop a C program you need an editor to create a source program such as the one in Figure 12-1a, a compiler to convert the source program to an object code file, a linker to link the various object code modules of your program into an executable (.exe) file, and a powerful debugger to help you get the program working correctly. For the examples in this section we chose the Borland Turbo C++ Integrated Development Environment which has all these features and many more. As the name implies, the Turbo C++ tools also fully support AT&T C++ version 2.0 as well as ANSI standard C. We don't have the space or the need in this book to teach C++, but the Borland documentation contains a tutorial and many examples which will help you learn it if you want to later.

The term Integrated Development Environment means that you can access all the programming tools from one on-screen menu. We chose the Borland IDE system because it is very powerful but easy to use, the company has a generous educational pricing policy, and the company gives very good support if you encounter problems. Other available tool sets such as Programmer's Workbench from Microsoft are very similar, so you should have little trouble adapting the following discussion if you have some other set of programming tools.

The purpose of this section is not to make you an expert with the Borland tools but to show you enough about using tools such as these that you can enter, run, and experiment with the simple program examples in the later sections of the chapter. Even if you don't have tools such as these available, this section should show you how programs are developed in a modern programming environment and some of the features you should look for when you buy a toolset.

For the following discussions we assume your Borland Turbo C++ Integrated Environment tools and libraries are all installed in a hard-disk directory named C:\tc, as described in the Borland manual, and the path command in your autoexec.bat file contains C:\tc and c:\tc\bin. We further assume that your work disk is a floppy in the A drive. Here's how you use these tools to develop a program such as the SELL.C program in Figure 12-1a.

To bring up the turbo C environment you simply type tc and press the Enter key. After a short pause the main menu screen shown in Figure 12-2a, page 392, will appear. Each of the entries in the banner at the top of the display represents a pull-down menu of commands. To get to one of these menus you hold down the Alt key and press the letter key which corresponds to the first letter of the desired menu's name. If you have a mouse on your system, you can use the mouse to move the cursor to the desired menu box and click the left mouse key. Incidentally, almost all commands in the Turbo C environment can be executed by pressing a "hot key"

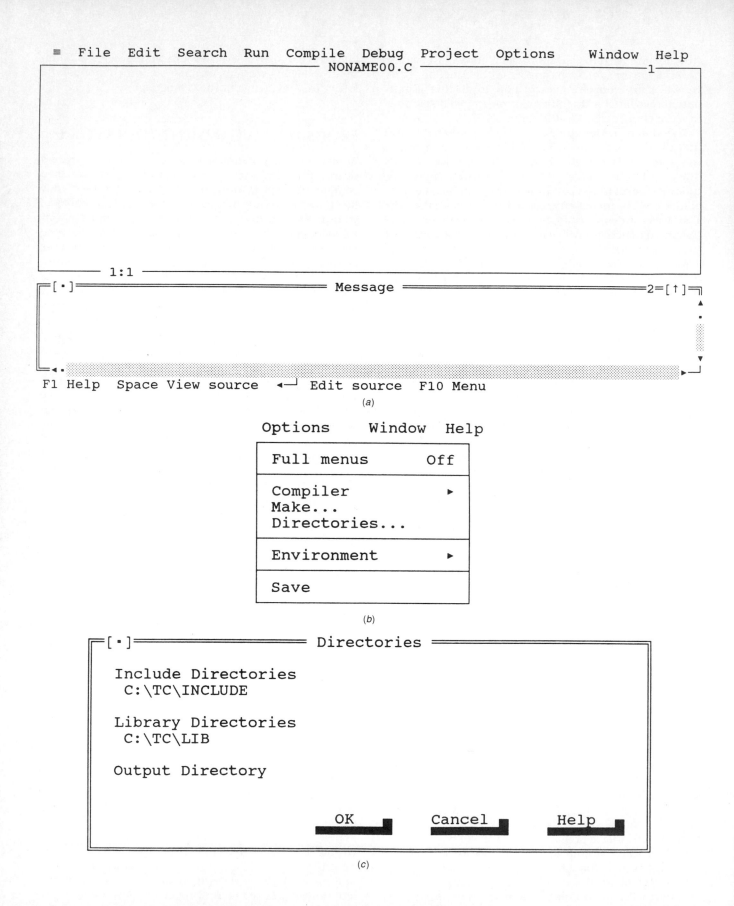

FIGURE 12-2 Borland Turbo C++ Integrated Development Environment
screen displays. (a) Main menu and edit window 2. (b) Options submenu.
(c) Directories submenu of Options submenu.

combination such as Alt-F1, which executes the command directly, or by working your way through a sequence of menus with a mouse or the arrow keys. When you are first learning a new system, the menu method helps you better learn the available features, so we will emphasize that approach. Here's an example of how you work your way through one of these menus.

One thing you have to do when you create a program is to tell the compiler, linker, etc., where to put the .obj and .exe files they create. You use a command in the Options menu to do this. To get to the Options menu you hold down the Alt key and press the O key. Figure 12-2b shows the Options menu that appears. The command you want in the Options menu is the Directories command. To get to the submenu for this command, you simply press the D key, and the window display shown in Figure 12-2c will appear. You want to assign an Output directory, so you hold the Alt key down and press the O key to get to that line.

Now, suppose that you don't understand just exactly what you are supposed to put in this line. If you hit the F1 key, the system will display an explanation of the command requirements and, in some cases, examples. In this case the help window tells you that the .obj, .exe, and .map files will be stored in the location you enter as the output directory. After you have read the help window, you press the Esc key to close it.

Since you want your output files to go to your work disk in the A drive, you just type A: and press the Enter key. We don't expect you to remember all this; we just used it as an example of how you work your way down through a sequence of menus to perform a desired operation and how to get help with a command if you need it.

The next step in developing a program is to use the editor to enter the source text for the program. For a new program you go to the File menu and press the N key. A blinking cursor will appear in the large window on the screen and you can type in the text of your source program. To work on an old file you go to the File menu and press the O key. When a list of files appears, you select the desired file from the list and the file will be loaded into the editor window. In either case you edit the program just as you would with any text editor. You may find it helpful to use spaces instead of tabs to format your programs, because the default tab setting of most printers is 8, and with this setting C programs do not usually fit easily on 8.5-in.-wide paper. Incidentally, the IDE editor accepts Wordstar commands such as Ctrl g to delete a character, Ctrl t to delete a word, and Ctrl y to delete a line, so if you are familiar with Wordstar you should find the editor very easy.

After you type in the source file you need to save it on your work disk. To do this go to the File menu, select the Save As line and press the Enter key. When a small window appears, you can type in a file name such as a:SELL.C and press the Enter key.

The next step is to compile the program to generate the .obj file. To do this go to the Compile menu and press the C key. If the compiler finds any errors, it will display a window with a flashing error message. When you press a key, the error message(s) will be displayed in the message window at the bottom of the screen. Figure 12-3 shows the error messages we produced

```
≡   File   Edit   Search   Run   Compile   Debug   Project   Options       Window   Help
┌──────────────────────────────── SELL.C ─────────────────────────────────1──┐
│/* COMPUTE THE SELLING PRICE OF 10 ITEMS */                                  │
│                                                                             │
│include <stdio.h>                                                            │
│                                                                             │
│int cost[]={20,28,15,26,19,27,16,29,39,42};/* array of 10 costs */           │
│int prices[10];                            /* array to hold 10 prices */     │
│int index;                                 /* variable to use as index */    │
│                                                                             │
│void main ()                                                                 │
│{                                                                            │
│    for (index=0; index <10; index++)         /* for loop to compute */      │
│    prices [index] = cost[index] + 15;        /* for 10 prices */            │
│                                                                             │
│    for (index=0; index <10; index++)    /* for loop to display results */   │
└─ 3:9 ───────────────────────────────────────────────────────────────────────┘
┌[•]══════════════════════════ Message ═══════════════════════════════2=[↑]┐
│ Compiling D:\TEMP\CH12\SELL.C:                                          ▲  │
│ Error D:\TEMP\CH12\SELL.C 3: Declaration syntax error                   ▒  │
│ Error D:\TEMP\CH12\SELL.C 12: Undefined symbol 'cost' in function main  •  │
│ Error D:\TEMP\CH12\SELL.C 15: Invalid indirection in function main      ▒  │
└◄•─────────────────────────────────────────────────────────────────►┘
F1 Help   Space View source   ◄┘ Edit source   F10 Menu
```

FIGURE 12-3 Compiler error messages generated by omitting # in #include<stdio.h> directive.

when we intentionally left out the # sign in front of the include directive in SELL.C. A highlighted line in the source program indicates the statement which caused the error highlighted in the message window. You can press the Enter key to switch from the message window to the edit window and correct the error. For this error all we had to do was insert the missing # before the include directive. A major error such as this will cause many errors throughout the program, so when you find one of these it is a good idea to compile the program again before you start chasing down the other indicated errors.

To recompile the program all you have to do is go to the Compile menu and press the C key. Once the compile is successful, you should always save your source file before continuing. To do this just go to the File menu and press the S key. This is important, because if your program locks up the machine when you run it, your program will be lost.

The next step in developing a program is to generate an executable file which you can run. For this example the file will be given the name sell.exe by the linker which generates it. There are two ways to generate the .exe file. One way is to go to the Compile menu and press the M key to make a .EXE file. The second way to generate the .exe file is to go to the Run menu and press the R key to run the program. This sequence of commands generates the .exe file and also runs it. For a single-module program, this second method is obviously the easiest.

When the program has finished running, the display will return to your source program. If you wrote a program such as sell.c which outputs to the screen, this display will be left in an alternate screen buffer. To see the output of your program hold down the Alt key and press the F5 key. To toggle back to the IDE screen, hold down the Alt key and press the F5 key again.

Now, suppose that your program doesn't work correctly the first time you run it. The Turbo C++ IDE contains a powerful "source-level" debugger. A source-level debugger allows you to view your source program on the screen and single-step through it one statement at a time or run to a breakpoint you placed on a statement and watch the values of variables change as program statements execute. The debugger is integrated with the editor, compiler, and linker, so when you find an error, you can just go back to the edit window, fix the error, compile the program, and run the program again, all from the same main menu. In most cases this integrated approach is much more efficient than the independent tools approach. Here's a short example of how you might watch the values of some variables change as you single step your way through our example program, sell.c.

NOTE: For this process to work as described, the program must have been just compiled and linked so the debugger has the needed "hooks."

As a first step let's assume that you want to observe the values of index, cost[index], and prices[index] change as you single-step through the program. To get ready to

single-step you go to the Run menu and press the T key to Trace into the program. A highlighted bar will then appear on the first line of your program. To put a "watch" on each of the desired variables, you go to the Debug menu and press the W key to bring up the Watch submenu. Then press the A key to add a watch. When a small window appears, type in the name of the first variable you want to watch and press the Enter key. The name of the variable that you placed a watch on should appear in the Watch window at the bottom of the screen. You can repeat the procedure to put watches on other variables.

To execute the first line of the program, you press the F7 key. The highlighted bar will move to the next statement, and the values of the variables in the Watch window will be updated to show the results of executing that instruction. Figure 12-4 shows the result after stepping through the for loop in sell.c a couple of times.

If you want to determine the value of some variable that you did not put in the Watch window, you go to the Debug menu and then press the I key to execute the Inspect command. When a small window appears, you type in the name of the variable that you want to look at and press the Enter key. The current value of the specified variable will be returned in the Inspect window. You press the Esc key to get back to stepping through the program.

If you find an error as you step through your program, you can just edit the source code version. After you save the new version you can run the program again by simply going to the Run menu and pressing the T key. In this case the IDE tools will detect that the source program has been modified, and they will automatically compile, link, and put the highlighted bar on the first line of your program. You can then single-step through the program by just pressing the F7 key.

Again, the point here is not for you to remember all this key pressing, but to see how easy it is to use a source-level debugger and an integrated environment such as IDE to write and debug your C programs.

Before we leave this section, there is one additional point we want to mention. Modern compilers such as the one in the Turbo C++ IDE allow you specify how you want the generated object code to be optimized. In its default mode the compiler compiles your program to a binary instruction sequence which uses minimum memory. An alternative is to tell the compiler to produce code which is optimized for speed. You can also tell the compiler to make maximum use of registers to hold variables and to rearrange the code so that loops and other jumps are optimized.

We usually leave the compiler optimization in its default mode when debugging a program, and then when we know the program works correctly, we recompile it with speed, register, and jump optimizations "on" to produce the final version of the program. The reason we initially leave these optimizations off is that it is very difficult to step through a program which has been highly optimized unless you are familiar with the algorithms used by the compiler.

Now that you have an overview of the tools used to develop C programs, we will show you more of the

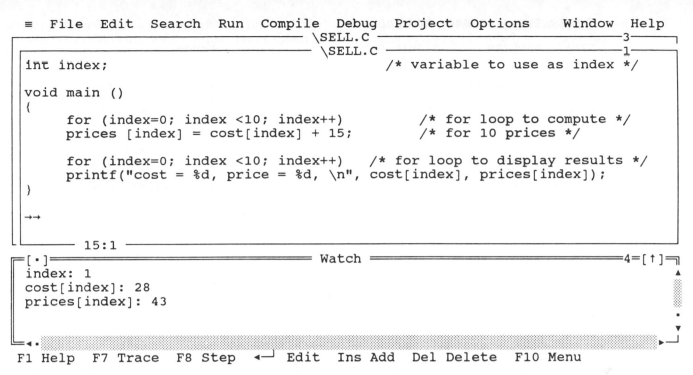

```
≡  File  Edit  Search  Run  Compile  Debug  Project  Options     Window  Help
┌───────────────────────────── \SELL.C ──────────────────────────────────3──┐
│                         ┌──── \SELL.C ──────────────────────────────────1─┐│
│int index;                                    /* variable to use as index */││
│                                                                            ││
│void main ()                                                                ││
│{                                                                           ││
│     for (index=0; index <10; index++)        /* for loop to compute */     ││
│     prices [index] = cost[index] + 15;       /* for 10 prices */           ││
│                                                                            ││
│     for (index=0; index <10; index++)   /* for loop to display results */  ││
│     printf("cost = %d, price = %d, \n", cost[index], prices[index]);        ││
│}                                                                           ││
│→→                                                                          ││
│└──── 15:1 ──────────────────────────────────────────────────────────────┘ │
├─[•]═══════════════════════════ Watch ═══════════════════════════════4=[↑]═┐│
│ index: 1                                                                  ▲ ││
│ cost[index]: 28                                                             ││
│ prices[index]: 43                                                          ││
│                                                                          ▼ ││
│└◄•▓▓▓▓▓▓▓▓▓▓▓▓▓▓▓▓▓▓▓▓▓▓▓▓▓▓▓▓▓▓▓▓▓▓▓▓▓▓▓▓▓▓▓▓▓▓▓▓▓▓▓▓▓▓▓▓▓▓▓▓▓▓▓▓▓►┘    │
└────────────────────────────────────────────────────────────────────────────┘
  F1 Help   F7 Trace   F8 Step   ◄┘ Edit   Ins Add   Del Delete   F10 Menu
```

FIGURE 12-4   Debugger screen display showing watch values.

structure and syntax of the C language so you can write some programs of your own.

PROGRAMMING IN C

Introduction

One reason it is easy to learn a second programming language is that you already know what features to look for. When you have to learn a new language, we suggest a "bottom-up" approach, roughly as follows.

1. First explore the data types that are available in the language and how these data types are represented. In 8086 assembly language, for example, you have worked with bytes, words, double words, and ASCII characters.

2. Then look at how basic statements such as variable declarations are written in the language. The DB, DW, DD, and array declaration statements are examples of this in 8086 assembly language.

3. Next, find out what logical, mathematical, and bit "operators" are available in the language. This is equivalent to looking at available 8086 instructions such as AND, ADD, INC, RCR, etc. It is best to just skim through these and pick out some commonly used ones. Don't try to remember them all the first time through.

4. Since you should always try to write programs in a structured way, the next step is to see how standard programming structures such as IF-THEN-ELSE, CASE, REPEAT-UNTIL, WHILE-DO, and FOR-NEXT

are implemented in the language. Look for examples of these such as the 8086 assembly language examples we showed you in Chapter 4.

5. Most programs contain many procedures, so next find out how procedures are defined and called in the language and how parameters are passed to procedures. Look for some examples such as the assembly language examples we showed you in Chapter 5.

6. The final step in the discovery process is to use the new language to write some simple programs that you have written successfully in another language. Since the algorithms are already very familiar, all you have to do is determine the syntax needed to express the algorithms in the new language. You are really just translating each program from one language to another. The simple program in Figure 12-1*a* is an example of translating a familiar algorithm to C.

In the following sections we will lead you through the C language along the path described in the preceding steps. If you have some C programming tools available, we suggest that you work your way through the exercises at the end of the chapter and those in the accompanying lab manual to develop some skill in C.

C Data Types

In the first 10 chapters of this book you worked with integer data types such as bytes, words, double words, and ASCII character codes. Then in Chapter 11 you met a variety of floating-point data types. Figure 12-5 shows

int represents a signed value, ffffH is actually equal to −1. If you want to declare a variable and initialize it with a value of +ffffH, you can use a statement such as "unsigned int hex_value = 0xffff;."

The int i = 10, j = 20, k = 30; example in Figure 12-7 shows how you can declare and initialize three or more variables of the same type in a single statement to make your program more compact.

The following two examples declare arrays. These examples should be very familiar to you from the program in Figure 12-1a. The int prices[10]; statement declares an array of 10 words and leaves the 10 locations uninitialized. The int cost[ ] = {20,28,15,26,19,27,16,29,39,42}; declares an array of 10 words and initializes the 10 locations with the specified values. Note that you do not have to include the length of the array in the [ ] for the cost declaration, because the compiler counts the number of specified values and makes the array long enough to hold that number.

The last two int examples in Figure 12-7 show how to declare two- and three-dimensional arrays. A two-dimensional array consists of rows and columns. An instructor's grade roster is an example of a two-dimensional array. The rows represent the names of the students and the columns represent the scores on tests, quizzes, and labs. The statement int test_scores[25][4]; declares a two-dimensional array that might be used to store 4 test scores for each of 25 students. The 25 in this declaration represents the number of rows and the 4 represents the number of columns. We did not initialize this array, because a program that uses this array would probably prompt the instructor to enter the values for the array from the keyboard. To see how to initialize a two-dimensional array as part of the declaration, see the array declarations under the float type in Figure 12-8.

You can think of the three-dimensional array declared by the int av_temp[5][12][31]; statement in Figure 12-7 as consisting of 5 "pages" with 12 horizontal rows and 31 vertical columns on each page. This array represents the form in which the average temperature values for a 5-year period might be stored. The program that uses this array would probably compute the value for each element in the array using maximum and minimum values entered by a friendly weatherperson. Later we show you how to access elements in multidimensional arrays such as this.

FLOAT VARIABLES

As shown in Figure 12-5, the three floating-point number types available in C are float, double, and long double. The basic format of float-type declarations is the same as that for int type declarations, so we have just shown a couple of examples of this type in Figure 12-8. The first example again shows how you can declare and initialize several variables in a single statement. The second example shows how you can declare and initialize a two-dimensional array of real numbers. Note how the inner curly braces are used to set off the rows and the outer curly braces are used to enclose all the rows. The final float example in Figure 12-8 shows how to declare a long-double-type variable. I suppose that we will have to create a new floating-point type when the national debt becomes too large to be represented with a long-double-type variable.

Declaring, Initializing, and Using Pointers in C

INTRODUCTION

People who have not worked with an 8086-type assembly language often have trouble understanding pointers when they are first learning C. By now you have several chapters of experience with 8086 assembly language pointer instructions such as MOV AX,[BX] and MOV AL,COST[BX], so if we do our job well, you should have little trouble with C pointers.

To help you with the transition to C, we will not only show you how to declare and initialize pointers, we will show you how they are used in simple programs. To further help you, we will show the 8086 assembly language equivalents for some of the C examples we use. Read through this section until you thoroughly understand it, because much of the power of the C language is based on the use of pointers.

A SIMPLE INT POINTER

The first statement in the pointer example in Figure 12-9a declares an integer-type variable called headcount and initializes the variable with a value of 5. The second statement in this example declares a pointer named present and initializes the pointer with the address of

```
/* Examples of declaring and initializing float type variables */

long double national_debt;              /* 80-bit floating point number */
                                        /* extern, anybody can access */
void main()
{
float side_a = 3.0, side_b = 4.0, side_c;  /* Init side_a and side_b, but not side_c*/
float max_min_temp[2][7]=
    {{37.3,42.0,42.9,46.0,51.7,44.2,40.0},
     {29.4,32.2,30.1,34.2,37.2,36.1,32.3}}; /* declare and initialize 2 dimensional
                                        array of 2 rows and 7 columns */

}
```

FIGURE 12-8 Declaring and initializing float variables in C.

```
/* declaring and initializing a simple int pointer */

#include <stdio.h>
void main()
{
  int headcount = 5;                    /* declare variable and initialize to 5 */
  int *present = &headcount;            /* declare pointer named present and initialize
                                           the pointer with the address of headcount */


  printf(" headcount= %d \n &headcount = %d \n present = %d \n"
       " *present = %d \n &present = %d \n", headcount, &headcount,
          present, *present, &present);


  *present = *present + 10;

  printf("\nheadcount= %d \n &headcount = %d \n present = %d \n"
       " *present = %d \n &present= %d \n", headcount, &headcount,
          present, *present, &present);
}
```

(a)

```
Turbo Assembler  Version 1.0       04-04-90 22:08:54        Page 1
APX-9B.ASM


   1                              ;8086 assembly language program to demonstrate int pointers
   2
   3 0000                         data segment
   4 0000  0005                       headcount dw 5
   5 0002  0000r                      present dw offset headcount
   6 0004                         data ends
   7
   8 0000                         code segment
   9                                  assume cs:code, ds:data
  10 0000  B8 0000s               start:  mov ax, data          ; initialize ds register
  11 0003  8E D8                           mov ds, ax
  12 0005  8B 1E 0002r                     mov bx, present       ; copy pointer to bx register
  13 0009  8B 07                           mov ax, [bx]          ; use pointer to copy value
  14                                                             ;   of headcount to ax
  15 000B                         code ends
  16                                  end start
```

(b)

```
headcount  = 5
&headcount = 404
present    = 404
*present   = 5
&present   = 406
```

(c)

FIGURE 12-9   (a) Declaring and initializing a simple int pointer. (b) Assembly
language example of initializing and using int pointer. (c) Results produced by
printf statement in Figure 12-9a.

the variable headcount. There are three points to store
in your mind from this example.

First, the type for a pointer is the type of the data
pointed to. Second, the * in front of the name present
in the declaration tells the complier that present is a
pointer. Third, the & in front of headcount is the
"address of" operator. This operator tells the compiler
that you want to initialize the pointer present with "the
address of" the variable headcount. To summarize then,
this statement declares a pointer-type variable named
present and initializes it with the address of the int
variable called headcount.

To help you relate all this to your previous experience,
the DATA SEGMENT in Figure 12-9b shows the 8086
assembly language equivalent for these two C declarations. As you can see by the comments, the first DW
statement sets aside a word of storage for (declares)
HEADCOUNT and initializes headcount with 5. The
second DW statement sets aside a word of storage for
(declares) a variable named PRESENT and initializes it
with the OFFSET of the variable HEADCOUNT. Since
the offset of a variable is its address within a segment,
PRESENT is then a pointer to HEADCOUNT. To access
HEADCOUNT you can copy the pointer into BX with the

instruction MOV BX,PRESENT and then copy the value of HEADCOUNT into AX with the instruction MOV AX,[BX].

The thought that probably comes to mind now is, Why didn't you just MOV AX,HEADCOUNT to get the value of HEADCOUNT into AX instead of using the indirect method? The answer is that for this case you can use the direct approach, but for other cases we show you later, you can't. To make sure you understand what is pointed to and what is doing the pointing in the declarations in Figure 12-9a, let's look at the actual values produced by the terms in the C declarations.

Figure 12-9c shows the results produced by the printf statement in Figure 12-9a. Work your way carefully through these so you see the two ways of representing the value of headcount and the two ways of expressing the address of headcount in programs.

You can refer to the value of headcount directly by name or with the *present representation. When used in a program statement, the * in front of a pointer name means "the contents of the memory location pointed to by that pointer." The *present term in the printf statement then means the value of the variable pointed to by present. The standard programming jargon for using a * in front of a pointer to refer to the value pointed to by the pointer is *dereferencing the pointer*. As you can see in our example here, present points to headcount, so the value printed for *present is the same as that printed for headcount. The only confusion here is that in a pointer declaration the * is used to indicate that the declared variable is a pointer, and in other program statements the * means the value of the variable pointed to by the pointer named after the *. The * in this context means the same thing as the [ ] in an assembly language statement such as MOV AX,[BX]. Remember how we told you to read these [ ] as "the contents of the memory location(s) pointed to by the value in the BX register."

The output of the printf function in Figure 12-9c also shows that you can represent the address where headcount is stored in two ways. One way is with the "address of" operator, &. The term &headcount is a shorthand way of saying "the address where the variable headcount is stored in memory." In its default mode the compiler assigns the same segment base address to your data segment, stack segment, and extra segment, so the address produced by printf for &headcount is just the offset of headcount in the segment. The second way to refer to the address of headcount is with the pointer, present. In the int *present = &headcount; statement, we declared present as a pointer and "pointed it" at headcount. As shown by the printout, the value of present then is the same as the value of &headcount.

Finally, in the printf output note the value produced by &present. This value represents the memory address where the compiler decided to store the pointer present. If you take another look at the assembly language equivalent of this program in Figure 12-9b, you can see how this corresponds to the offset where PRESENT is stored in the data segment.

Now that you know a little about C pointers, we want to take a moment to show you one reason why they are important.

When you call a C function you often want to pass parameters (arguments) to the function. The statement printf("%d", sum);, for example, calls the printf function and passes it a variable called sum. What is actually passed to the function is a *copy* of the variable sum. The function then is given the value of the variable sum but is not given access to the actual variable itself. The technical term for this method is *passing by value*. If only the value of a variable is passed to a function, then the function cannot modify the actual variable. For a function such as printf this is no problem, because printf is not intended to change the values of variables.

However, if you call a function which is intended to change the value of a variable, you must pass the address of the variable to the function. The function can then use the address it receives to access and change the value of the variable. As an example of this, the C statement scanf("%d", &headcount); calls the predefined function scanf to read a decimal value from the keyboard and assign the value to a variable called headcount. The &headcount in this statement passes the address of headcount to scanf so that scanf can write the new value in headcount. If present has been previously declared and initialized as a pointer to headcount with int *present = &headcount; statement, then another way to write the scanf statement is scanf("%d", present);.

In a later section we discuss C functions in great detail, but to give you a head start you might store in your mind the fact that when you call a C function to change the value of a variable, you must pass the address of the variable to the function instead of passing the value of the variable. The technical term for this is *passing by reference*. For a simple variable such as headcount, you can use &headcount to represent the address of the variable headcount. However, for many applications, declaring a separate pointer is a much more versatile technique. In the following section we show you how to declare and use pointers with simple, one-dimensional arrays. Throughout the rest of the book we will show many more examples of how you use pointers in programs.

USING POINTERS WITH INT ARRAYS

The program in Figure 12-10a shows three different ways to add a profit to each of 10 costs from an array of ints. As in the example in Figure 12-1a, we first declare an int array called cost, initialize the cost array with 10 values, and declare an empty array of 10 elements to hold the computed prices. In the third line of declarations we declare a simple variable called index and declare two pointers. The *cpntr = cost term declares a pointer called cpntr and initializes the pointer with the address of the first element in the array cost. The *ppntr = prices term in the third line declares a pointer called ppntr and initializes it with the address of the first element in the prices array. Now let's look at the three methods of accessing the elements in these arrays.

The first method shown in Figure 12-10a is the array-index method we showed you in Figure 12-1a. When you declare an array such as cost[ ], C treats the name cost as a pointer to the first element in the array.

```c
/* C PROGRAM F12-10A.C - COMPUTE THE SELLING PRICE OF 10 ITEMS */
#include <stdio.h>
#define PROFIT 15
#define MAX_PRICES 10

void main()
{
 int cost[] = { 20,28,15,26,19,27,16,29,39,42 };
 int prices[10];
 int index, *cpntr = cost, *ppntr = prices;

 /* array index method */
      for (index=0; index <MAX_PRICES; index++)
      {
      prices[index] = cost[index] + PROFIT;
      printf("cost = %d, price = %d, \n", cost[index],
             prices[index]);
      }
 /* pointer method */
      for (index =0; index<MAX_PRICES; index++)
      {
      *ppntr = *cpntr + PROFIT;
      printf("cost = %d, price = %d,\n",*cpntr,*ppntr);
      cpntr++; ppntr++;
      }
 /* pointer arithmetic method */
      for (index =0; index<10; index++)
      {
      *(prices +index) = *(cost +index) + PROFIT;
      printf("cost = %d, price = %d, \n",
      *(cost + index), *(prices + index));
      }
}
```
(a)

```asm
;8086 PROGRAM F12-10B.ASM
;ABSTRACT : Assembly language program to add profit to costs using pointers
          ; Program adds a profit factor to each element in a
          ; COST array and puts the result in an PRICES array.

PROFIT   EQU     15H          ; profit = 15 cents
ARRAYS   SEGMENT
         COST    DB  20H,28H,15H,26H,19H,27H,16H,29H,39H,42H
         PRICES  DB  10 DUP(0)
         CPNTR   DW OFFSET COST
         PPNTR   DW OFFSET PRICES
ARRAYS   ENDS

CODE     SEGMENT
         ASSUME  CS:CODE, DS:ARRAYS
START:   MOV  AX, ARRAYS ; Initialize data segment
         MOV  DS, AX     ; register
         MOV  CX, 0010   ; Initialize counter

DO_NEXT: MOV  BX, CPNTR  ; Load cost pointer in BX
         MOV  SI, PPNTR  ; Load price pointer in SI
         MOV  AL, [BX]   ; Get element pointed to by CPNTR
         ADD  AL, PROFIT ; Add the profit to value read
         DAA             ; Decimal adjust result
         MOV  [SI], AL   ; Store result at location pointed
                         ;  to by PPNTR in PRICES
         INC  CPNTR      ; Increment pointers
         INC  PPNTR
         LOOP DO_NEXT    ; If not last element, do again
CODE     ENDS
         END  START
```
(b)

FIGURE 12-10 (a) C program which uses pointers to compute selling prices.
(b) 8086 assembly language equivalent of program in 12-10a.

This pointer, however, is a constant, so it cannot be incremented to access the other elements in the array. To access the other elements in the array, you have to in some way add an index to cost. The term cost[index] in the array-index example in Figure 12-10a tells the compiler to generate the effective address by adding the value of index to the address represented by the name cost. Likewise the term prices[index] tells the compiler to generate the effective address of the variable by adding the value of index to the address represented by the name prices. The first time through the for loop, index will have a value of zero, so the first element in each array will be accessed when the prices[index] = cost[index] + profit; statement is executed. The second time through the for loop, index will have a value of 1, so the second element in each array will be accessed.

The method described for this C example is exactly the same method we used to access the array elements in the assembly language program in Figure 4-23. If you look back at that program, you will see that we loaded the index in BX, used the instruction MOV AL,COST[BX] to copy an element from the cost array to AL, and used the instruction MOV PRICES[BX],AL to copy the computed price back to the indexed location in the PRICES array.

The second method of accessing the elements in our arrays uses the pointers, cpntr and ppntr, that we declared. The statement *ppntr = *cpntr + profit; says read the value pointed to by cpntr, add a profit of 15 to the value, and write the result at the location pointed to by ppntr. In the initial declarations we initialized cpntr with the address of the first element in cost and ppntr with the address of the first element in prices. Therefore, the first execution of the for loop will read the first element in cost, perform the specified computation, and write the result in the first element of prices. The cpntr and ppntr pointers are variables, so they can be incremented, decremented, added to, subtracted from, etc., to access other elements in the arrays. The cpntr + +; statement increments cpntr to point to the next element in cost, and the ppntr + +; statement increments ppntr to point to the next element in prices.

NOTE: Both cpntr and ppntr were declared as pointers to int type variables, so the compiler automatically generates instructions which increment the pointers as needed to access the next elements in the two arrays. Since int variables take 2 bytes, the compiler will generate instructions which add 2 to the value of cpntr and add 2 to the value of ppntr. The next time through the for loop then, cpntr will point to the second element in cost and ppntr will point to the second element in prices. With this pointer method you do not need [index] to identify the desired elements in the arrays, because the pointers are incremented to point to the desired elements. The printf( ) statement in the pointer method example in Figure 12-10a also uses the *cpntr notation to represent "the contents of the memory location(s) pointed to by cpntr" and *ppntr to represent "the contents of the memory location pointed to by ppntr." We

didn't bother to show you, but this second method produces the same printout as that shown in Figure 12-1b.

To help you further understand how this pointer version of the program works, Figure 12-10b shows how you could write it in 8086 assembly language. The program in Figure 12-10b actually generates machine code very close to that generated by the compiler for the C pointer example we have just discussed except that it works with bytes instead of words, and it obviously does not produce the code for the printf function.

In this assembly language example you can see that we first use a DW statement to declare and initialize a pointer to the first element in cost and another DW statement to declare and initialize a pointer to the first element in prices. Then in the code section of the program we load CPNTR into BX and PPNTR into SI so we can use them to access the arrays. We use MOV AL,[BX] to read in an element from cost and MOV [SI],AL to copy the result to prices. We then increment the pointers so they point to the next elements in the arrays and loop back to do the next add and store operation.

The third method of accessing the elements in the two arrays is the pointer arithmetic method shown in Figure 12-10a. As we said before, the name of an array such as cost is a pointer to the first element in the array. To access the other elements in the array you need to add an offset to the value of cost. One way to indicate this addition is with an expression such as cost[index] that we showed you in the first array-access method. Another way to indicate this addition is with an expression such as (cost + index). Putting a * in front of this expression gives *(cost + index), which translates to "the value in memory pointed to by the sum of cost + index." The expression *(cost + index) is exactly equivalent to the expression cost[index] and the compiler generates the same code for each expression. Note that since cost is a pointer to an int-type array, the compiler generates instructions which add two times the value of index to cost when it translates the expression (cost + index).

Now that you have seen the three methods of accessing an array, the question that may occur to you is, Which one is best? The answer is that usually you can use any of them. The array-index method is probably more intuitive when you are first learning about arrays, but most experienced C programmers use the direct pointer or the pointer arithmetic method because they generate considerably more efficient machine code. If for no other reason, you should use these last two methods in your programs so that you can easily follow them in other people's programs.

Another point we want to briefly make about the program in Figure 12-10a is the format in which the data is stored and manipulated. Cost is declared as type int, so according to Figure 12-5, 2 bytes are set aside for each element in cost. The compiler converts the decimal value supplied for each element to a 16-bit signed equivalent. When the program is loaded into memory to be run, these 16-bit signed values are loaded in the memory locations allocated for cost. When the program is run, the binary equivalent of 15 is added to

FORMAT SPECIFIER SYMBOL	PRINT
%d	decimal integer
%u	unsigned integer
%ld	long decimal integer
%p	pointer value
%f	floating point format
%6.2f	floating point format round off to two digits of decimal point, total of six digits
%e	exponential format floating point
%c	ASCII character for value
%s	string
%x or %X	hex value of integer

FIGURE 12-11 C format specifiers for use in printf, scanf, and other library functions.

each value from cost and the 16-bit signed result is put in the appropriate location in prices. The %d format specifiers in the printf( ) statement cause the printf function to convert the *cpntr and *ppntr values to their decimal equivalents before sending the values to the screen. The result is the decimal printout shown in Figure 12-1b. For reference Figure 12-11 shows the formats for some of the specifiers you can use with printf, scanf, and other predefined functions.

A FLOAT POINTER EXAMPLE

By now you are probably getting tired of the cost-price example, but we will use it one more time to quickly show you a few useful techniques that make the program more realistic.

Figure 12-12, page 404, shows the new "improved" version. The first improvement is to make the program able to work with floating-point numbers instead of just integers. We did this by declaring the two arrays as type float instead of type int.

The second improvement is to make it easy to change the program so it can work with some number of values other than 10. Note how we use the preprocessor directive #define MAX_PRICES 10 at the start of the program to declare a constant called MAX_PRICES and then use MAX_PRICES in the for loops and every time we refer to the number of elements in the arrays. If we want to change the number of elements in the arrays, all we have to do is change the value of MAX_PRICES in the #define and recompile the program. The compiler will automatically replace each occurrence of MAX_PRICES with the new value. This shows the advantage of using defined constants instead of hard numbers in a program.

A third improvement in the program is to add a section which allows you to enter any desired values instead of using just the fixed values we put in cost for the previous examples. To do this we declare the array cost as shown, but we do not initialize the array with fixed values. After using the predefined function printf to send a prompt message to the user, we use another predefined function called scanf and a for loop to read in 10 values entered on the keyboard.

The actual code for the scanf function is contained in a library file. The #include <stdio.h> preprocessor directive at the start of the program tells the compiler to look in the file stdio.h for the prototype of the scanf( ) function. When the program is linked, the code for scanf( ) and printf( ) functions will be linked with the code for the rest of the program to generate the executable (.exe) file.

The scanf("%f", cpntr) statement in the program calls the function and passes the parameters needed by the function. The scanf function needs to know what type of data you want it to read and where you want it to put the data. As with the printf function we used before, you use a format specifier to indicate the type of data you want it to read. In this program we want scanf to read floating-point values, so we pass a %f to scanf by putting it first in the ( ). As we said earlier, the scanf function requires that you pass it a pointer to tell it where to put the data read. We want the data values to be put in the cost array, so we pass the pointer cpntr that we initialized with the starting address of the cost array. Each time through the for loop, cpntr will be incremented so that it points to the next element in cost.

This is a good time to show you why the type of each variable is important. According to Figure 12-5, a float-type variable uses 4 bytes of memory, so the elements of cost are at intervals of 4 in memory. Since cost is an array of floats, we declared cpntr as a type float pointer. When the compiler translates the cpntr + + statement, it automatically generates an 8086 instruction which adds 4 to the value of cpntr so it points to the next element in cost.

When this first section of the program runs, it will send the "Enter 10 costs..." message to the screen and wait for you to enter a value. After you enter a value and press the space bar or the Enter key, the program will put the value in the array and wait for you to enter the next value.

After all 10 values are read in, the cpntr pointer is reset to point at the start of the cost array with the cpntr = cost; statement, so we can process the 10 values read. To process the 10 values we use a for loop, as in the previous examples. Now let's see how we compute each cost.

In the previous examples we added a fixed profit of 15 to each cost, but this is not very realistic. A more realistic approach is to compute profit as a percentage of the cost and add the computed profit to the initial cost for each item. The statement *ppntr = *cpntr + 0.25*(*cpntr); does this. In more English-like terms it says, "get the cost pointed to by cpntr, multiply that value by 0.25, add the value pointed to by cpntr to the result, and write

```
/* C PROGRAM F12-12.C */
/* float pointers and reading data from the keyboard */

#include<stdio.h>
#define MAX_PRICES 10
void main ()
{
    float cost[MAX_PRICES], prices[MAX_PRICES];
    float *cpntr = cost, *ppntr = prices;
    int i;

    printf("Enter %d costs. After each cost press "
            "space or enter.\n", MAX_PRICES);
    for(i=0; i < MAX_PRICES; i++)
    {
        scanf("%f", cpntr);
        cpntr++;
    }
    cpntr = cost;  /* reset cost pointer to start of array */
    for(i=0; i < MAX_PRICES; i++)
    {
        *ppntr = *cpntr + .25 * (*cpntr);
        printf("cost= %6.2f, price= %6.2f \n",*cpntr,*ppntr);
        cpntr++; ppntr++;
    }
}
```

FIGURE 12-12   Program using float pointers and the scanf function.

the result to the memory locations pointed to by ppntr."
Note that the * symbol is used to represent the multiplication operation as well as to represent the "contents of the memory location pointed to by" a pointer. The meaning of a * in a statement is usually clear from how it is used.

After we compute each selling price, we call printf to display the entered costs and the computed prices on the screen. Since we want to print floating-point values, we use %f format specifiers. The 2 between the % and the f indicates that we want the values rounded off to two digits to the right of the decimal point. This is appropriate for money values. The 6 between the % and the f indicates that the values will have a maximum of 6 digits, including the two to the right of the decimal point. This number is optional. Note that we use *cpntr to pass the current cost value to printf and *ppntr to pass the current price value to printf. We then increment the two pointers, cpntr and ppntr, so they point to the next locations in their arrays.

Now that you have some experience with int and float pointers, let's take a look at some char pointers which work just a little bit differently.

CHAR POINTERS AND CHARACTER STRINGS

Some programming languages such as BASIC have a string data type which is used for ASCII code sequences. In C you just use an array of type char to store strings. The last two examples in Figure 12-6 show how to declare char arrays. The next-to-last example in Figure 12-6 shows how you can initialize a char array with a desired string of ASCII codes. Remember that when you initialize a char array in this way, the compiler

automatically includes a null character as a sentinel at the end of the string.

As with int and float arrays, the name of a char array is a pointer to the first element in the array, but again, this pointer is a constant, so it cannot be incremented, etc. It is often useful to declare a variable pointer to the start of a char array and use this pointer to access the array. Figure 12-13 shows you how to declare char pointers and some of the different ways to work with character strings in C programs.

At the top of Figure 12-13 note that you can use the #define preprocessor directive to declare a constant string. Whenever the compiler finds the identifier exitmess, it will substitute the constant string "password incorrect." Since this string is a constant, it cannot be modified in the program.

The first char example in Figure 12-13 does several jobs. It declares a char-type pointer called greeting and sets aside 2 bytes of memory to store the pointer. It allocates 14 bytes of memory and initializes these bytes with the ASCII codes for the string "Good Morning" and a null character. Finally, it initializes the pointer, greeting, with the address of the first character in the string.

The printf("%s\n", greeting); statement in main shows how you can get this message printed out on the screen. To let printf know that you are passing it a string, you use the %s format specifier. To identify the string you want to send to the screen, you simply use the name of the pointer to the string. Note that you do not have to put a * in front of the name of the pointer as we did for the float pointer in the printf( ) statement in Figure 12-11. For string operations the compiler assumes that the name of the pointer refers to the whole string. Since the

```
/* examples of declaring and using char type pointers */

#include <stdio.h>
#define exitmess "password incorrect"

void main()
{
char *greeting = "Good morning, ";    /* pointer to type char location, initialized with string */
char wakeup[20] = "Good morning\n";    /* array of 20 char initialized with string shown */
char *message;                         /* declare pointer named message,
                                          but allocate no storage */

char name[20];

printf("%s\n", exitmess);

printf("%s\n", greeting);
printf("%s\n", wakeup);

message = "Hello there.";              /* allocate storage and load string into locations
                                          starting where pointer message points */
printf("The message is, %s\n", message);

printf("Please type in your name and press the Enter key.\n");
gets(name);
printf("%s%s\n", greeting, name);
}
```

FIGURE 12-13   Declaring and using char type pointers.

pointer greeting initially points to the first element in the string, a term such as *greeting would refer only to the first element in the string rather than to the whole string. Don't make this overly complicated in your mind. Just remember that you don't use a * in front of a pointer to a string unless you want to refer to just the first character in the string or individual elements in the string.

The char wakeup[ ]="Good morning.\n"; statement in Figure 12-13 declares an array of characters and initializes the elements of the array with the ASCII codes for the specified string. An ASCII null character, 00H, will automatically be inserted as a sentinel at the end of the string. As we said before, the name of an array is a pointer to the first element in the array, so you can print this message with a statement such as printf("%s \n", wakeup);. Note that here again you do not have to use a * in front of wakeup to tell printf that you want to print the contents of string named wakeup.

The char *message; declaration in Figure 12-13 declares a char-type pointer and sets aside a couple of memory locations for the pointer. However, this statement does not assign any value to the pointer, and it does not allocate any memory for storing a string. When the compiler reads the message="Hello there."; statement in main, it will allocate some memory locations for the string "Hello there." and store the ASCII codes for the string in the allocated memory bytes. The compiler will also initialize the pointer named message with the starting address of the memory allocated for the string. Note again that we referred to the string simply with the name message. The compiler is smart enough to know that message refers to the entire string.

The char name[20]; statement in Figure 12-13 allocates 20 bytes of memory for an array of characters but does not initialize these bytes. The last three statements in main show how you can read a string in from the keyboard and put it in this array.

The printf( ) statement at the start of this section simply prompts the user to enter his or her name and press the Enter key. The second line in this section of the program uses the predefined function gets( ) to read characters entered on the keyboard. You tell gets( ) where to put the characters by passing it a pointer to some char-type locations. In this example, name is a pointer to the array we declared, so we just pass name to gets( ) by including it in the ( ). Gets( ) keeps reading ASCII codes from the keyboard and putting them in the array until it reads the code for a carriage return. When it reads a carriage return, gets( ) puts a null character at the end of the stored string and returns to main. The final printf( ) statement sends the declared string "Good morning," to the screen and then sends the string read in from the keyboard to the screen.

As you look at this last example the question that may occur to you is, Why didn't we use the scanf( ) function that we showed you in Figure 12-12 to read in the string? The answer to this is that scanf terminates when it finds a space, a tab, or a carriage return. Therefore, the space between a first name and a last name would terminate scanf, and only the first name would be read in and put in the array. The scanf function with a %s format specifier works fine if you want to read in only a single character or a single word.

Two important points to remember when working with character arrays or strings are as follows:

1. Use just the name of the array or the name of the pointer to refer to the array. You don't need an * in front of the name unless you want to refer to just the first character in the array or individual elements in the string.

2. You must tell the compiler to allocate storage for a string with a statement such as char name[20]; before you can read in a string from the keyboard. You cannot just declare a pointer with char *message; and then gets(message); because the char *message declaration doesn't allocate any space to put the characters read from the keyboard. It just declares a pointer.

Now that you know how to declare different C data types, how to send messages to the screen, and how to read strings from the keyboard, you should be able to write some simple programs to entertain your friends. To make your programs more interesting, you need some more instructions in your toolbox. In the next sections we show you the different C "instructions" or operators you can use to perform computations, etc., in your programs.

C Operators

THE ASSIGNMENT OPERATOR

The assignment operator in C is simply the = sign. We have already used the assignment operator in the preceding program examples without bothering to give it a name. A statement such as side_a = 3.0;, for example, assigns a value of 3.0 to the variable side_a. This corresponds to an assembly language instruction such as MOV SIDE_A,3.

The = sign says "evaluate the expression to the right of the = and write the result in the variable to the left of the =." The statement prices[index] = cost[index] + 15;, for example, adds 15 to an element from the cost array and puts the result in the corresponding element in the prices array.

In 8086 assembly language you used MOV instructions to copy the contents of one memory location to another. One way to do this in C is with a simple assignment statement. If you have two variables such as maxval and curval of the same type, you can copy the value of curval to maxval with the statement maxval = curval;.

ARITHMETIC OPERATORS

Operation	Symbol	Examples	
Addition	+	a = c + d;	
Subtraction	−	a = c − d;	
Multiplication	*	a = 4*b	
Division	/	a = c/d;	
Modulus	%	a = c%d;	/* a = remainder of c/d */
Increment	+ +	index + +;	/* increment index by one */
		a = a + b + +;	/* postfix increment */
			/* add b to a, then inc b */
		a = a + + +b;	/* prefix increment */
			/* inc b, add result to a */
Decrement	− −	count − −;	/* decrement count by one */
		a = a − b − −;	/* postfix decrement */
			/* subtract b from a, decrement b */
		a = a + − −b;	/* prefix decrement */
			/* decrement b, then add b to a */

BITWISE OPERATORS

These operators correspond to assembly language instructions such as AND, OR, XOR, NOT, ROL, and ROR. As with the assembly language instructions, they perform the specified operation on a bit-by-bit basis.

The AND operator, for example, logically ANDs each bit of one operand with the corresponding bit of the other operand. For reference, here are the C bit operators and some examples of each.

Operation	Symbol	Examples	
AND	&	a = a & b;	/* each bit of b ANDed with corresponding bit in a, result in a */
		a = a & 0xff;	/* mask upper 8 bits of int a */
OR	|	a = a | b;	/* each bit of b ORed with corresponding bit in a, result in a */
		a = a | 0x8000;	/* set MSB of int in a */
XOR	^	a = a ^ b;	/* each bit in b is XORed with corresponding bit in a, result in a */
		a = a ^ 0x000f;	/* invert low nibble int a */
NOT	~	a = ~a;	/* invert bits in a, result in a */

Operation	Symbol	Examples	
Shift-left	<<	a = a << 4;	/* shift bits in a 4 bit positions left around loop. This corresponds to 8086 assembly language sequence MOV CL, 04H, ROL a, CL.
Shift-right	>>	a = a >> 8;	/* shift bits in 8 bit positions right around loop. This corresponds to 8086 assembly language sequence MOV CL,08H, ROR a, CL. It effectively swaps the bytes of a if a is type int.

COMBINED OPERATORS

It seems that many experienced C programmers have a habit of trying to pack as much action as possible in a single program statement. This often makes the statement somewhat difficult to decipher. As we go through the rest of the book we will try to show you some of the more common shortcuts so that you can use them or at least recognize them when you see them. To start we will show how expressions using the operators in the previous sections are commonly written in shortened form. Again, the best way to do this seems to be with a list of examples that you can easily refer to. Once you see the pattern of these, you will find them quite easy.

Operation	Standard Form	Combined Form
Addition	a = a + b;	a + = b;
Subtraction	a = a − b;	a − = b;
Multiplication	a = a * b;	a * = b;
Division	a = a/b;	a / = b;
Modulus	a = a%b;	a % = b;
AND	a = a&b;	a & = b;
OR	a = a|b;	a	= b;
XOR	a = a^b;	a ^ = b;
Shift-left	a = a<<b;	a << = b;
Shift-right	a = a>>b;	a >> = b;

RELATIONAL OPERATORS

Relational operators are used in expressions to compare the values of two operands. If the result of the comparison is true, then the value of the expression is 1. If the result of the comparison is false, then the value of the expression is 0. These comparisons are usually used to determine which of two actions to take. You will see many more examples in a later section which discusses how the standard program structures are implemented in C, but a simple example here using the "greater than or equal to" operator should help you see how these are used.

Remember in Chapter 4 we showed you how to implement an algorithm which turned on a light if the temperature in a printed-circuit-board-making machine was equal to or greater than a preset value. To implement this decision we used a compare instruction and a conditional jump instruction. In C you might implement this action with a couple of statements such as:

```
if (current_temp >= run_temp)
{
    heater (off);
    green_light (on);
}
```

We assume here that the value of current_temp was read from an A/D converter by calling an assembly language procedure before the if statement. (Later in the chapter we show you how to do this.) If the value of current_temp is not equal to or greater than the predeclared value of run_temp, then the comparison is false, and the statements in the curly braces will be skipped over. If the expression in ( ) evaluates to true, then the two statements in the curly braces will be executed. In the first of these statements we call a function called heater and pass it a value which will turn the heater off. Likewise, in the second statement we call a function called green_light and pass it a value to turn on the green light. The heater function and the green_light function would most likely call assembly language procedures to manipulate the actual hardware.

Here is a list of the C relational operators. As you read each of these, mentally insert them in a statement such as "if (a == b) { }," to help you remember how they are used. Note that the == used here has a very different meaning from the single = used for assignment.

Operator	Symbol
Equal to	==
Not equal to	!=
Greater than	>
Greater than or equal to	>=
Less than	<
Less than or equal to	<=

LOGICAL OPERATORS

In the last section we showed you how the relational operators are used to choose between two actions in, for example, an IF-THEN-ELSE structure. The C logical operators allow you to include two or more conditions in a decision such as this. The three logical operators and the symbols which represent them are as follows.

Operator	Symbol	Examples

AND	&&	if (curtemp < maxtemp && curpress < maxpress)
		{
		green_light(on);
		}
		/* green light on only if both conditions true */

OR	||	if (curtemp > maxtemp || curpress > maxpress)
		{
		   red_light(on);
		}
		/* red light on if either condition met */

NOT	!	if (!a)
		{
		  statements;
		}
		/* do statements if a is false (= 0)
		   skip over statements if a is true (= 1) */

OPERATOR PRECEDENCE

In the preceding sections we have shown you most of the C operators. We will show you the few remaining operators in later program examples where they may make more sense. The next topic we have to discuss here is the priority or precedence of the C operators. To properly evaluate or write an expression which has several operators, you have to know the order in which the operations are done. As an example of this, in the statement *prices = *cost + 0.25*(*cost);, how did we know that the 0.25 would first be multiplied by *cost and then the result added to *cost? The answer to this is that the multiplication operator has a higher priority or precedence than the addition operator, so the multiplication gets done before the addition.

As another simple example of this, suppose you have an expression such as a/b + c/d. From ordinary algebra you know that division also has a higher precedence than addition, so the two divisions will be done first, and then the results of the two divisions will be added together.

Shown below in descending order is the precedence of the C operators. For reference we have included some operators that we haven't discussed yet, so don't worry if you don't recognize all of these. To help you identify the different operators, we have included simple examples of each. In the paragraphs following this list we show you some more examples to help stick the important ones in your mind.

NOTE: All the operators in a group have the same priority.

Operator	Example	
( )	4*(9 + 2)	/* operation in parentheses done first */
[ ]	cost [3]	/* fourth element in array cost */
.	class.ssnmbr	/* pointer to ssnmbr member of structure */
− >		/* indirect structure operator */
−	a = −23;	/* negation */
+	a = +28;	/* positive value */
˜	a = ˜a ;	/* invert each bit in a */
*	*cpntr	/* contents of location pointed to by cpntr */
&	&headcount	/* address of headcount */
+ +	index + +	/* increment operator */
− −	count − −	/* decrement operator */
sizeof	count = sizeof cost;	/* determine # of bytes in cost */
*	a * b	/* multiplication */
/	a/b	/* division */
%	a%b	/* modulus-remainder from division */
+	a+b	/* addition */
−	a−b	/* subtraction */
<<	a<<4	/* shift bits of a left 4 bit positions */
>>	a>>8	/* shift bits of a right 8 bit positions */

Operator	Example	
<	if (a<10)	/* less than */
>	if (temp> 30)	/* greater than */
<=	if (a<=10)	/* less than or equal to */
>=	if (temp>=5)	/* greater than or equal to */
==	if (a==b)	/* relational equal */
!=	if (a!=b)	/* relational not equal */
&	a & 0xfff0	/*AND a with fff0H to mask lowest nibble*/
|	a | 0x8000	/* OR a with 8000H to set MSB */
^	a ^ 0x000f	/* XOR a with 000fH to invert 4 LSBs
&&	If (condition 1 && condition 2)	/* both 1 AND 2 */
||	If (condition 1 || condition 2)	/* 1 OR 2 */

simple assignment
=   a=4;   /* simple assignment */

combined assignment (see previous examples)
*= /= %= += −= <<= >>= &= |= ^=

As we showed before, the precedence of C arithmetic operators is basically the same as in ordinary algebra, so you should have little trouble with these. In an expression such as 3+4*a, the multiplication will be done before the addition, because multiplication has a higher precedence than addition. If you want the addition to be done first, you can write the expression as (3+4)*a. Parentheses have a higher precedence than multiplication, so any operations within parentheses will be done first. If there is any possibility of misinterpreting an expression, you should use parentheses to make it clear.

The only case where you may initially need a little help to understand the precedence of operators is with the increment and decrement operators, so we will discuss these.

If you use the increment operator, ++, in a simple statement such as index++;, you can write the ++ after index or in front of it. In other words, the statement ++index; and the statement index++; will each increment the value of index by 1. When ++ or −− is used in more complex expressions, however, the placement of the operator is important.

In a statement such as Y=(a+ ++b)/10;, for example, the value of b will first be incremented by 1 and the result added to a. The sum of a and the incremented b is then divided by 10 and the result assigned (copied) to the variable y. Incrementing or decrementing a variable before it is used in the expression is often referred to as a *prefix* operation.

If you write the statement as Y=(a+ b++)/10;, the current value of b will be added to a. Next the result of this addition will be divided by 10 and assigned to Y. Finally, the value of b will be incremented by 1. Using a variable and then incrementing or decrementing it is often referred to as a *postfix* operation.

The simple rules here then are: Put the ++ or −− operator in front of the variable name if you want the variable incremented or decremented before it is used to evaluate the expression. Put the ++ or −− operator after the variable name if you want the current value of the variable used to evaluate the expression.

Statements such as those shown in the preceding paragraphs are usually quite straightforward, once you understand the prefix and postfix concept. Another situation where you will often see the increment and decrement operators is in conditional expressions such as while (a++ <20), which might be used at the start of a WHILE-DO structure. The ++ is after the variable a, so you know that the current value of a is used to evaluate the expression, and then a is incremented. The expression then says "compare the current value of a to 20 and then increment a." If the value of a is less than 20, do the statements following the while.

To see if you understand how this works, try interpreting the statement while (−−b >0) { }. The −− is before the variable b, so b will be decremented and the decremented value of b compared with 0. If the decremented value is greater than 0, the statements following the while will be executed. If the decremented value of b is equal to 0, execution will go to the next statement in the program after the while block.

Throughout the preceding discussions we have given you little glimpses of how the standard programming structures are implemented in C. In the next section we take a closer look at these.

Implementing Standard Program Structures in C

As we tried to show you in Chapter 3, the most successful way to write any program is to solve the problem mentally; write the algorithm for the solution using the basic IF-THEN-ELSE, CASE, REPEAT-UNTIL, WHILE-DO, and FOR-DO structures shown in Figure 3-3; and finally translate the algorithm to an appropriate programming language. The C implementation of these structures is very close to the pseudocode for them, so the translation is usually quite easy. In this section we discuss each of these and show you some more C programming techniques.

IF-THEN AND IF-THEN-ELSE IMPLEMENTATION

The general format of the IF-THEN-ELSE structure in C is:

```
if   (condition)
{
        statement;
        statement;
}
else
{
        statement;
        statement;
}
```

Condition in this format represents some expression such as currtemp = = maxtemp. If the condition expression evaluates to 1 or any nonzero value, the block of statements under the if will be executed. If the condition expression evaluates to 0, the block of statements under the else will be executed. The else block can be omitted if you want just an IF-THEN instead of an IF-THEN-ELSE. Note that the curly braces are not needed for the case where the if block contains only one statement. Likewise, the curly braces are not needed in the else block if it contains only one statement.

The program section in Figure 12-14 shows a simple IF-ELSE structure and introduces you to getch( ), another predefined function which you will probably want to use in your programs. This example also gives you a little more practice with operator precedence.

At the start of the program we declare a char-type variable and give it the traditional name ch. After printing a couple of prompt messages, we use an IF-ELSE to determine a course of action based on the user's response. To evaluate an expression such as the if condition in Figure 12-14, you start with the innermost parentheses and work your way out. The getch( ) part of the if expression calls the predefined function getch( ). The getch( ) function sits in a loop until the user presses a key on the keyboard. When the user presses a key, getch( ) terminates and returns the ASCII code for the key pressed. In this example the ch = getch( ) means that the returned ASCII value will be assigned (copied) to the variable named ch. This completes the action in the inner parentheses. The value produced by these actions is the ASCII code stored in ch.

The = = 'n' next in the expression compares the value in ch with the ASCII code for a lowercase n. If the values are the same, the entire expression is true (evaluates to 1) and the statements in the if block will be executed. If the value in ch is not equal to the value of the ASCII code for a lowercase n, the || ch = = 'N' part of the expression compares the value of ch with the ASCII code for an uppercase N. Remember that the || symbol represents the logical OR operation, so the overall expression is true if ch = n OR ch = N. If the entered character was an N, the statements in the if block will be executed. If the character was not an n or an N, the entire expression evaluates to 0, and statements in the else block will be executed.

NOTE: The expression for the if statement is evaluated from left to right, so the (ch = getch( )) is done first and the result compared with n. For the second comparison you just write ch = 'N', because ch already has the value read in from the keyboard. If we had used (ch = getch( )) = = 'N' here, execution would sit in getch( ) until the user pressed another key! Incidentally, if you want the key pressed by the user to be echoed to the CRT, you can use the getche( ) function instead of the getch( ) function.

The exit( ); statement in the if block calls a predefined function which terminates the program and returns control to the operating system (DOS prompt).

In the else block we display a message to let the user know that something is happening, then we use the "goto start" statement to send execution to the beginning of the program. The goto statement in C corresponds to the unconditional JMP instruction in assembly lan-

```
/* C PROGRAM F12-14.C */
#include <stdio.h>
void main()
{
  char ch;
  start:    printf("Game over.\n");
            printf("Enter y to play another game, n to quit.\n");
        if ((ch = getch()) == 'N' || ch == 'n')
            {
            printf("Goodbye.\n");
            exit();
            }
        else
            {
            printf("Here we go again.\n");
            goto start;
            }

    }
```

FIGURE 12-14   Basic if-else example.

guage. As in assembly language, the name start represents a label which you place in front of the instruction statement that you want execution to go to. In C you write a : after the label, just as you do in assembly language. In this example we put the start label next to the first printf statement, just to show you how to write labels.

> NOTE: The label for a goto must be in the same function as the goto statement.

Some structured programming fanatics say that you should never use even a single goto in a program. This attitude is probably a reaction to the way goto statements were abused in old BASIC programs. To us, however, using a simple goto to rerun the entire program is the clearest way to do it. In reality, even if you hide the action in some other structure, the compiler will usually generate an unconditional jump instruction to implement the action.

The program fragment in Figure 12-14 has a minor problem. It thoroughly tests to see if the user entered an n or an N and exits if either of these was entered. However, if any other key is pressed, the else-block statements start the game over again. Figure 12-15 shows how you can use a nested if-else structure to provide three alternative actions based on the key pressed. For an n or N the statements in the first if block will be executed. For a y or a Y the statements in the second if block will be executed. For any other key the statements after the final else will be executed. In a later example we show you how a "real C programmer" might write this program segment to avoid the direct goto statement in the final else block.

MULTIPLE CHOICES—THE SWITCH STATEMENT

To implement algorithms with more than three choices, you can nest additional if-else sections, but often a more efficient way to do this is with the *switch* structure. The C switch structure is essentially the same as the CASE structure we showed you in Figure 3-3. The general format for the switch statement is:

```
switch (variable)
        {
        case value1:
        {
        statements;
        break;
        }
        case value2: statement(s); break;
        case value3: statement(s); break;
        default: statement;              /* optional */
```

Variable in this statement must be some quantity such as an int or char which can be evaluated as an integer. Value1 in the first case line represents some value of the variable used to make the decision. After each case line you write the statement(s) you want executed if the variable has that value. If, for example, the value of variable is equal to value1, the statements after case value1: will be executed. The break statement at the end of this block of statements will cause execution to skip over the rest of the choices in the structure. If you leave out the break statement, the actions for the next case after the selected case will be executed. The optional default directive at the end of the switch structure allows you to specify the action(s) you want taken if the value of variable does not match any of the specified values.

```
/* C PROGRAM F12-15.C */
#include <stdio.h>
void main()
{
        char ch;
        printf("Game over.\n");

prompt:    printf("Enter y to play another game, n to quit.\n");
        if ((ch = getch()) == 'N' || ch == 'n')
                {
                printf("Goodbye.\n");
                exit();
                }
        else if (ch == 'Y'|| ch == 'y')
                {
                printf("Here we go again.\n");
                /* goto start; */
                }
        else
                {
                ch = getchar(); /* clear buffer */
                goto prompt;
                }
        }
```

FIGURE 12-15   Nested if-else example.

Figure 12-16 shows how you might use the switch statement to implement a "command recognizer" in one of your programs. This example is modeled after the commands available at the highest menu level in the Borland TC development environment we discussed earlier in the chapter. To get to the main menu in TC, you press the F10 key. To select the desired submenu you then press the key which corresponds to the first letter in the name of the submenu. The choices are F, E, R, C, P, O, D, and B. Each of these options brings up a lower-level menu or carries out a command.

In the program in Figure 12-16 we use our new friend getch( ) to read a character from the keyboard. We then use a switch structure to evaluate the character and decide what action to take. To simplify the basic structure of this example, we call a function to implement each of the desired actions. Actually, for this example we show the function calls as comments, because we did not want to declare and define all these functions. When execution returns from the called function, the break statement at the end of that line will cause execution to skip to the next statement after the switch structure. If the key pressed by the user does not match any of the choices, the default: edit_window( ); statement at the end of the block sends execution back to the edit operation. You can have only one value in each case evaluation, so if you want the program to accept lower- or uppercase letters, you have to put case lines in for each. The line case 'F': followed by the line case 'f': file( ); break;, for example, will call the file function if the user enters either a lower- or uppercase f. A more versatile alternative is to write a small function which converts all entered characters to lowercase before entering the switch structure. We leave this for you to do as an exercise at the end of the chapter.

THE WHILE AND DO-WHILE IMPLEMENTATIONS

In Chapter 3 we showed you how the WHILE-DO and the REPEAT-UNTIL structures are used to loop through a series of statements. In C these two structures are called the while and the do-while, respectively. The major difference between the two structures is when the exit test is done. For comparison, Figure 12-17 shows how the two are implemented in C.

As you can see, in the while loop in Figure 12-17a, the condition is evaluated before any statements are executed. If the condition expression initially evaluates to 0, execution will simply bypass the block of statements under while and go on with the rest of the program. In this case none of the statements in the while block will be executed. If the condition expression initially evaluates to a nonzero value, the statements in the while block will be executed once. Then the condition expression will be evaluated again, and if the result of the evaluation is still nonzero, the statements in the while block will be executed again. Looping will continue until the condition expression evaluates to 0.

The key point of a while loop is that the condition is tested before any statements are executed. In most cases this "look before you leap" approach is the best one, and most loop algorithms can be written in this way.

For those cases where you want the loop statements to be executed once before the condition is checked, C has the do-while structure shown in Figure 12-17b. In this structure the statements in the do-while block are executed once, and then the specified condition expression is evaluated. If the condition expression evaluates to 0, the do-while terminates and execution goes on to the rest of the program. With this structure, then, the statements in the do-while block will always be executed at least once. If the condition expression evaluates to a nonzero value after executing these statements, the statements in the do-while block will be executed again and the condition expression evaluated again. Looping will continue until the condition expression evaluates to 0. Note that in this structure there is a semicolon at the end of the while line.

Figure 12-18a shows how you can use a while loop to make a user enter a Y or an N in response to a prompt. This approach avoids using a goto such as the goto prompt; statement in Figure 12-15. The declaration statement for ch at the start of the program gives it a null value, so the first time the condition for the while

```
#include<stdio.h>
void main()
{
 char ch;
 ch=getchar();
 switch (ch) {
 case 'F':
 case 'f': /* file_menu();    */ break;
 case 'e': /* edit_window();  */ break;
 case 'r': /* run_menu();     */ break;
 case 'c': /* compile_menu(); */ break;
 case 'p': /* project_menu(); */ break;
 case 'o': /* options_menu(); */ break;
 case 'd': /* debug_menu();   */ break;
 case 'b': /* break_menu();   */ break;
 default : /* edit_window();  */ ;
             }
}
```

FIGURE 12-16   Example of C switch structure.

```
/* while format */

while(condition)
        {
        statement(s);
        }
        (a)

/* do-while format */
do
        {
        statement(s);
        }
while(condition);
        (b)
```

FIGURE 12-17   (a) Basic format of C while structure.
(b) Basic format of C do-while structure.

```
/* while example */
#include <stdio.h>
void main()
{
char ch = 0x00;  /* assign initial value to ch */
while(ch!='n'&& ch!='N'&& ch!='y'&& ch!='Y')
      {
      printf("Enter y to play another game, n to quit.\n");
      ch=getch();
      }
if (ch=='n'|| ch=='N')
      {
      printf("Goodbye.\n");
      exit();
      }
else
      {
      printf("Here we go again.\n");
      /* goto start */
      }
}
```
(a)

```
/* do-while example */
#include <stdio.h>
void main()
{
     char ch;
     do
     {
     printf("Enter y to play another game, n to quit.\n");
     ch=getch();
     }
while(ch!='n'&& ch!='N'&& ch!='y'&& ch!='Y');
if (ch=='n'|| ch=='N')
      {
      printf("Goodbye.\n");
      exit();
      }
else
      {
      printf("Here we go again.\n");
      /* goto start */
      }
}
```
(b)

FIGURE 12-18   (a) Example of C while structure. (b) Example of C do-while structure.

statement is tested, the result is false. Therefore, the ch=getch( ); statement part of the while is executed. When getch( ) returns a new value to ch, the condition expression for the while will be checked again. Execution will stay in this while loop until getch( ) returns a y, Y, n, or N. After it exits the loop, execution goes to the if-else section of the program to determine the actions to take based on the value returned by getch( ) and assigned to ch.

Figure 12-18b shows how the same program section can be implemented as a do-while. In this example we did not need to give ch an initial value, because the ch=getch( ); statement at the start of the do-while gives ch a value before any tests are made. The ch=getch( ) statement will be repeated until the value of ch matches one of the values in the condition test part of the do-while.

It is not obvious in the examples shown in Figure 12-18, but in most cases the while structure is a better choice than the do-while, because the condition is checked before any action is done.

THE FOR LOOP

As we showed you in several previous program examples, a for loop can be used to do a sequence of statements a specified number of times. The general format of a for loop is:

```
for (initialization(s); test; modify)
{
statement(s)
}
```

To refresh your memory, Figure 12-19 shows a simple example of a for loop. The initialization in this example assigns a value of 0 to the variable count. If you want to, you can include more than one initialization here. You might, for example, include two initialization statements such as count = 0; b = 23; to initialize a variable called b with a value of 23 as well as initialize the loop variable count.

The test part of this example compares the value of count with the terminal value. If the value of count is not equal to the terminal value, the statements in the loop will be repeated.

The count − − in our example represents the "modify" part of the for. This is where you specify what you want to change each time around the loop so that the loop eventually terminates. In some C programs you may see more than one action statement in the modify section of the for( ). You might, for example, see something such as "count + +, index = index + 4;" in the modify section. These two statements will increment count by 1 and increment index by 4 each time through the loop. Our personal feeling is that the program is more readable if you put only the loop variable initialization and loop variable modification in the for parentheses.

To give you a little more challenging example of a for loop and teach you more about arrays, the first part of the program in Figure 12-20a shows how you can use nested for loops to read maximum and minimum temperature values from the keyboard and put the values in a two-dimensional array. The last section of the program uses another for loop to compute the average temperature for each day and display all the results.

The int temps[7][3]; statement at the start of the program declares an array of seven rows and three columns. To help you visualize this, Figure 12-20b shows the array in diagram form. As you can see, there is one row for each of the 7 days of the week. Also, there is one column for the daily maximum temperatures, one column for the daily minimum temperatures, and one column for the averages that will be calculated. The arrow looping through the array shows the sequence that the array values are stored in memory. As you can see, the three elements in the first row are stored in the

three lowest memory locations, the three elements in the next row are stored in the next three memory locations, etc.

The elements of the array are stored in sequence in memory, so you could access the elements in this array as if it were a one-dimensional array of 21 elements. In other words, you could set up a pointer to the first element in the array and then keep incrementing the pointer to access the other elements in the array. The problem with this method is that you lose the row and column information.

A much more versatile way to access the elements in this array is with row and column index values. The index for an array starts from zero, so the term temps[0][0] is a way to refer to the element in the first row of the first column. Likewise, the term temps[0][1] is a way to refer to the element in the second column of the first row, and the term temps[6][2] is a way to refer to the value of the third element of the seventh row.

In the program in Figure 12-20a we use the variable i to index a desired row and the variable j to index a desired column in the array. The inner for loop in the program uses j to access the elements in a row. The first time the inner loop executes it will put the value returned by scanf in the first element in the row. The second time the inner for loop executes, it will put the value returned by scanf in the second element in the row. Since the inner loop is set to terminate for $j < 2$, the inner loop will then terminate and execution will go back to the outer for loop.

The outer for loop uses i to access the desired row in the array. The first time through the outer loop $i = 0$, so the first row in the array will be accessed. The next time through the loop i has been incremented to 1, so the second row in the array will be accessed. This process is essentially the same as the nested delay loops that you met in earlier chapters.

The scanf function requires that you pass it a format specifier to tell it what type of data it will be reading and that you pass it the address of the location where you want the data put. You use the %d specifier to indicate that you want the data treated as a decimal value, and you use the term &temps[i][j] to pass the address of the desired element in the array to scanf. Remember that temps[i][j] is a way to refer to the value of an element in the array, so &temps[i][j] is a simple way to refer to the address of that element. Note that we used $i + 1$ for the value of the day instead of just i. An array index starts from zero, but we want the days to be numbered 1 through 7.

After all fourteen temperature values are read in and put in the appropriate locations in the array, we use a single for loop to compute the average temperature for each day and put the computed results in the appropriate row of the third column in the array. The temps[i][j + 2] = (temps[i][j] + temps[i][j + 1])/2 statement shows how you can add a constant to the j index value to access the different elements in a row. Likewise, in the last printf statement in Figure 12-20a, we add constants to the j index to access the three elements in a row. Textbooks often refer to this as "pointer arithmetic."

Now that you know the array-index method of ac-

```
#include<stdio.h>
int count;
void main()
{
        int count;
        for (count=10; count>0; count--)
        {
        printf("%d\n ", count);
        }
        printf("blastoff!");
}
```

FIGURE 12-19   Example of simple count-down for loop.

```
/* C PROGRAM F12-20A.C */
/*Program to read max and min temperatures, then compute average */

#include <stdio.h>
int temps[7][3];                /* extern so other modules can access */

void main()
{
    int i, j;
    for (i=0; i<7; i++)
        {
            printf("Enter max temp for day %d,"
                "then min temp.\n", i+1);
            for(j=0; j<2; j++) /* read max, then min */
            scanf ("%d", &temps[i][j]);
        }
    j=0;  /* reset column index */
    for(i=0; i<7; i++)
    {
    temps[i][j+2] = (temps[i][j] + temps[i][j+1])/2;
    printf("For day %d max = %d min = %d av = %d \n",
            (i+1), temps[i][j], temps[i][j+1], temps[i][j+2]);
    }
}
```

(a)

(b)

(c)

FIGURE 12-20   (a) Program showing index method of accessing elements in two-dimensional array. (b) Two-dimensional array of 7 rows and 3 columns used to store maximum, minimum, and average temperatures for 7 days. NOTE: Arrow shows order that values are stored in memory, going from lowest to highest memory address. (c) Two-dimensional array shown as 7-element array of one-dimensional 3-element arrays. (*See also next page.*)

```
/* C PROGRAM F12-20D.C */
/*Program to read max and min temperatures, then compute average */

#include <stdio.h>
int temps[7] [3];
void main()
{
    int i, j;
    for (i=0; i<7; i++)                          /* read values entered */
        {
          printf("Enter max temp for day %d,"
              "then min temp.\n", i+1);
          for(j=0; j<2; j++)                     /* read max, then min */
          scanf ("%d", (*(temps+i)+j));
        }
    for(i=0; i<7; i++)              /* compute averages and print all values */
    {
    *(*(temps+i)+2) = (*(*(temps+i)+0) + *(*(temps+i)+1))/2;
    printf("For day %d max = %d min = %d av = %d \n",
      (i+1), *(*(temps+i)+j), *(*(temps+i)+1), *(*(temps+i)+2));
    }
}
```

(d)

For day 1 max = 98 min = 68 av = 83
For day 2 max = 89 min = 65 av = 77
For day 3 max = 87 min = 59 av = 73
For day 4 max = 90 min = 67 av = 78
For day 5 max = 86 min = 58 av = 72
For day 6 max = 78 min = 68 av = 73
For day 7 max = 83 min = 69 av = 76

(e)

FIGURE 12-20 (*Continued*) (d) Program in Figure 12-20a rewritten using pointer notation.
(e) Results produced by program in 12-20a or 12-20d.

cessing the elements in a two-dimensional array such as this, we will briefly show you the direct pointer method, which is very commonly used by experienced C programmers. Even if you don't choose to use this pointer method yourself, you should understand it well enough to follow it in other peoples' programs.

As we said before, one way of thinking about the array temps[7][3] is as a two-dimensional array with seven rows and three columns. Another common way of thinking of the array named temps is as seven one-dimensional arrays of three elements each. In this view shown in Figure 12-20c, temps[0] is the name of the first three-element array, temps[1] is the name of the second three-element array, and temps[6] is the name of the last three-element array.

The key to understanding how you work with this form is to remember that *the name of an array is a pointer to the first element in the array.* The name temps then is a pointer to the first element in the array of arrays. In this view the first element in the array is the subarray temps[0], so temps is a pointer to temps[0]. One way to represent this relationship in C syntax is temps = &temps[0]. The other way to represent this relationship is *temps = temp[0].

Now, temp[0] is the name of an array of three ints, so temp[0] is a pointer to the first element in the array temps[0]. You can refer to the value of the first element in temps[0] with the expression *temps[0]. This expression simply says "the value pointed to by the pointer temps[0]." In the last paragraph we showed you that *temps = temps[0], so with a little substitution the expression *temps[0] can be written as **temps. The **temps expression, which is the pointer form we wanted to get to, means "the contents of the memory location pointed to by the contents of the memory location pointed to by temps." This is easier to understand if you mentally put parentheses around *temps and think of it as a pointer to the first subarray, temps[0].

The result of all this is that the three equivalent ways to refer to the value of the first element in the first subarray of temps are:

temps[0][0] = *temps[0] = **temps

The expression temps[0][0] is the two-dimensional array method we showed you in Figure 12-20a. The expression *temps[0] takes advantage of the fact that temps[0] is a pointer to the first subarray and *temps[0] represents the value pointed to. The expression **temps is just an indirect way to point to temps[0] and then to the value pointed to by temps[0]. The two-dimensional-array form is probably the most intuitive, but most compilers convert it to the pointer form to produce the actual machine code. Therefore, many programmers write array expressions directly in the pointer form.

If you follow that **temps is a valid way to refer to the first element in the first subarray or row of temps, the question that may occur to you is, How do you access the other elements in the array using the pointer form? The answer to this question is that you add index values to the pointer to access the desired element. If you use *i* as the row or subarray index and *j* as the column index as we did in Figure 12-20*a*, then

$$\text{temps[i][j]} = *(*(\text{temps} + i) + j)$$

The *(temps + i) in the second expression points to the desired subarray. Adding *j* to this changes the value of the pointer to point to the desired element in the subarray. For reference, Figure 12-20*d* shows how the program in Figure 12-20*a* can be written using the pointer notation we have just shown you. If you work your way through this example, you should be well on your way to understanding C pointers. Note that we used the numbers 0, 1, and 2 to index the desired column in the statement which computes the average and in the printf statement. The +0 is not needed in the second term, but we included it to emphasize the position of the column index in the term. Figure 12-20*e* shows the results produced by either the program in 12-20*a* or the one in 12-20*d*.

C Functions

DECLARING, DEFINING, AND CALLING C FUNCTIONS

As we have told you many times before, often the best way to write a large program is to break it down into manageable modules and write each module as a tion or a series of functions. The C functions we used in the preceding program examples are all "predefined." The code for these functions is contained in library files. All you have to do to use one of these functions is to put #include<> at the start of your program to tell the compiler the name of the file which contains the prototype of the function, call the function by name, and in some cases pass some parameters to the function. Now we need to show you how to write and use your own C functions.

To create and use a function in a program, you must declare the function, define the function, and call the function. Figure 12-21*a*, page 418; shows a template or model of how you do each of these, and Figure 12-21*b* shows a simple program example. To help you understand the terms in the templates, we suggest that you look at the corresponding parts in the example program as we discuss the templates. Don't worry about the details of the example program, because after we work through the templates we will discuss the example program more thoroughly. The three templates in Figure 12-21*a* are shown in the order that they appear in programs, but we will discuss them in the order that you usually construct them as you write a program.

The first step in writing a function is to define the actual function. Functions are always defined outside of main( ), because you cannot define one function within another. To actually write the function you will probably work from the inside out. In other words, you will probably first write the data declarations and the action statements which implement the algorithm for the body of the function. Note that the statement block for the function is enclosed in curly braces. After you write the body of the function, you can then decide what values have to be passed to the function and what value, if any, will be returned from the function to the calling program. When you arrive at these decisions you can write the header for the function.

As shown in Figure 12-21*a*, the function header starts with a type such as int, float, char, etc. The type in this case represents the type of the variable returned from the function to the calling program. A C function can return the value of only one variable to the calling program. If the function does not directly return a value to the calling program, you give the function a type void.

NOTE: Most programmers don't bother to assign a type to the main function, but the Turbo C++ compiler will give a warning if no type is given. You can either make main type void or ignore the warning.

After the function name, you enclose in parentheses the type and name for each function variable that will receive values passed from the calling program. These variables declared in the function header are often called *formal arguments* or *formal parameters*. The trick here is that you usually use different names for particular variables in the calling program and in the function. This makes the function "generic," because you can then pass any variables of the same types to the function in place of the "local" variables declared in the function definition header. Later, when we discuss the details of the example program in Figure 12-21*b*, you will better see how this works.

As an example of a function header, the function header int c2f(int c) in Figure 12-21*b* declares a function called c2f which returns an int value and requires an int value to be passed to it. The int value passed to the function will be automatically assigned to the int variable called c in the function. Also in Figure 12-21*b* the function header void get_temp(int *ptr) defines a function called get_temp which does not return a value, but requires that a pointer to an int type variable be passed to it. Note that function header lines do not have semicolons after them.

After you write the function definition, the next step is to declare the function by writing a *prototype* for the function. This declaration is equivalent to declaring a variable at the start of your program. Note in Figure 12-21*a* that the function prototype declaration at the start of the program has the same format as the function definition header, but it is followed by a ;. This prototype lets the compiler know the name of the function and the types of data to be passed to the function. The compiler uses this information to make sure that the correct data

TEMPLATES FOR DECLARING, CALLING AND DEFINING C FUNCTIONS

<u>DECLARATION</u> (PROTOTYPE)

```
type        function_name(variable list);
  ↑                          ↑
type of data            type and formal parameter (dummy)
returned by function    name for each variable to be passed
```

<u>CALL</u>

```
void main()
{
        function_name(actual arguments);
                          ↑
                      names of variables or pointers
                      to be passed to function this call
}
```

<u>DEFINITION</u>

```
type     function_name(formal arguments)
  ↑                        ↑              ↑
  |                        |           note: no ;
  |                        |
type of data         types and names of local
returned by          variables which correspond to
function             actual variables passed to function

    {
    statements;

    return(variable);
           ↑
        name of variable returned to
        calling function
    }
```

(a)

FIGURE 12-21   Declaring, calling, and defining C functions. (a) Template. (See also next page.)

types are passed to the function when it is called. In large programs the function prototypes are put in a separate header file and pulled into the program at compile time with a #include<> directive. This reduces the "clutter" at the start of the main program.

As shown in the CALL section of Figure 12-21a, you call a function with its name and a set of parentheses which enclose the name(s) of the variables being passed to the function. If no variables are passed to the function, you put the term void in the parentheses after the function name.

The variables named in the function call are commonly called *actual arguments* or *actual parameters*. Remember from a previous discussion that when you pass a variable to a function in C, you pass just the value of the variable, or—in other words—just a copy of the variable. If you want the function to be able to access and change the actual value of a variable, you must pass the function a pointer to the variable. Now that you have an overview of the three tasks, let's take a little closer look at the example program in Figure 12-21b.

In this example program we first declare an int variable named tempc which will hold the value of a Celsius temperature entered by the user and an int variable called tempf which will hold the value of a Fahrenheit temperature calculated by a function in the program.

The int c2f(int c); statement next in the program is the function prototype declaration for the c2f function. As you should be able to tell from the statement, the c2f function returns an int value and expects to receive a single int value from the calling program. Before we look at the next function prototype, let's work our way through the call and execution of the c2f function.

We call the c2f function with the statement tempf = c2f(tempc); statement. This statement will pass the value of tempc to the function and assign the value returned by the function to tempf. This second effect is the same as you met earlier in statements such as ch = getch( ).

Note that the variable name tempc does not appear in the c2f function block. As we said before, the actual argument passed in the function call is given to the corresponding formal argument identified in the function header. In this case the only formal argument in the header is c, so the value of the actual argument tempc will be assigned to the variable c in the function. In a case where several arguments are being passed to the function, each actual argument will be assigned to the corresponding numbered formal argument.

In the c2f function we declare an additional int variable named f and then we use a familiar formula to calculate the equivalent Fahrenheit temperature for the Celsius

```
/* Declaring, calling, and defining functions */

#include<stdio.h>

int tempc, tempf;        /* external (global) variables */
int c2f(int c);          /* declare function c2f which returns an int value */

void get_temp(int *ptr); /* declare function which modifies a value
                            pointed to, but does not directly return a value */

void main()
{
    get_temp(&tempc);        /* call function get_temp.
                                get_temp writes directly to tempc */

    tempf = c2f(tempc);      /* call c2f function, pass value
                                of tempc to function. Returned value
                                assigned to tempf */

    printf("The temperature in Celsius is %d\n", tempc);
    printf("The temperature in Fahrenheit is %d\n",tempf);
}  /* end of main */

int c2f(int c)              /* define function c2f. Note no ; at end */
    {
    int f;                  /* automatic (local) variable */
    f = 9*c/5 + 32;
    return (f);
    }

void get_temp(int *ptr)     /* define function get_temp */
    {
    printf("Please enter the Celsius temperature.\n");
    scanf("%d",ptr);
    }
```

(b)

FIGURE 12-21 (*Continued*) (b) Examples in a program.

value passed to the function. The operator precedence rules we showed you earlier in the chapter tell you that c will first be multiplied by 9 and the result divided by 5. Then 32 will be added to the quotient and the result assigned to the variable f. The return(f); statement at the end of the function returns execution to the calling program and passes back the value of f. As we said before, this value is assigned to tempf in the calling program. Incidentally, the parentheses after the return statement can contain any expression which evaluates to an int. You could, for example, write the return statement as return(9*c/5 + 32);. For your first programs, however, it is probably better to keep the action "spread out" as we did in the example so you can follow it more easily. Now let's work through the second function in Figure 12-21b.

The void get_temp(int *ptr); prototype declaration tells you that the function get_temp does not directly return a value and that the function expects to receive a pointer to an int type variable when called. We call the function with the statement get_temp(&tempc), so the address of the variable tempc is passed to the function. In the get_temp function header, we declared a pointer named ptr with the (int *ptr) after the function name, so the address of tempc will be assigned to ptr when it is passed to the function. In other words, ptr = &tempc.

In the get_temp function we send a prompt message to the user and then use scanf to read the user's response. As you may remember from previous examples, the predefined scanf function requires a format specifier and a pointer to the location where you want it to put the data read from the keyboard. In this call to scanf we pass ptr to it, so the result read from the keyboard will be written to the location pointed to by ptr. Since ptr = &tempc, the value read from the keyboard will be written to tempc. This function has no return statement, because no value is returned to the calling program, but when the scanf("%d",ptr) call is finished, execution will return to the calling program.

Now that you know more about C functions, we need to talk again about the difference between variables declared in a function and variables declared outside any function.

EXTERN, AUTOMATIC, STATIC, AND REGISTER STORAGE CLASSES

Any variable or function declared in a program has two properties, which are sometimes referred to as lifetime and visibility or scope. These terms are best explained by some examples. As we mentioned in an earlier section, variables declared outside of main are by default *extern*, or—in other words—global. This means that they are visible to or accessible from anywhere in the source file where they are defined or from other files which will be linked with that file. Extern variables are created in memory when the program is loaded and remain there or "live" as long as the program is running. In Figure 12-21b tempc and tempf are examples of variables which are extern by default.

We also mentioned earlier that variables declared in a function are by default *automatic*. An automatic variable is "local," which means that it is accessible or visible only within the function where it is declared. Each time you call a function which contains an automatic variable, a temporary storage space is allocated on the stack for that variable. When the function returns execution to the calling program, this storage space is deallocated. An automatic variable then only lives during the execution of the function block where it is declared. In Figure 12-21b the variables ptr, c, and f are examples of automatic variables.

Now, suppose that you want to declare a variable within a function so the whole world can't access it, but you want the variable to keep its value from one call of the function to the next. You can do this by putting the word *static* in front of the variable declaration. For example, if the declaration "static int count;" is located in a function, count will be visible only in the function but will hold its value of "live" all the time that the program is running. If you put the word static in front of a variable declaration that is outside of main, the effect is to make the variable accessible or visible only in the source file where it is declared.

Another useful storage class for variables is *register*. You might, for example, declare a variable in a function with a statement such as "register int index;." The term register at the start of this declaration asks the compiler to assign this variable to one of the 8086 registers. The reason for doing this is that it is much faster to, for example, increment the contents of a register than it is to increment the contents of a memory location dynamically allocated to an automatic variable. If all registers are in use, the compiler will ignore the register storage request and treat the variable as a normal automatic variable.

Functions also have storage classes. By default, functions are extern or global. This means that they can be accessed from other files. To access a function from another file, you write a copy of the function prototype in that file and put the word extern in front of it.

If you give a function the storage class static, the function is accessible only from within the file where it is defined.

To summarize the different storage classes and their characteristics, Figure 12-22 shows examples of each. You can use these examples to help you decide which storage class to use for particular applications in your programs.

FUNCTIONS AND ARRAYS

One of the main reasons to learn about C pointers is so that you can use them with functions. As we said before, if you want a function to modify the value of a variable, you must pass the function a pointer to the variable. In Figure 12-21b we showed you how to pass a simple variable pointer and in Figure 12-12 we showed you how to pass an array pointer to the predefined scanf function. Now we need to show you how to pass array pointers to functions you write.

Figure 12-23 shows how you can declare, define, and call a function to add profit to costs instead of doing the operations in main as we did in previous examples. The first section of main prompts the user and then calls scanf to read in 10 costs and put the 10 values in a float array called cost. Remember that scanf requires a format specifier and a pointer to where you want to put the value read. In Figure 12-12 we used a declared pointer as the argument for scanf, but here we use the expression (cost + i) as a pointer to the desired element in cost. Cost is a pointer to the first element in the array, and as we explained earlier, (cost + i) is a pointer to element i in the array. When the compiler performs pointer arithmetic on the expression (cost + i), it automatically multiplies i times the number of bytes in the data type so that the computed pointer accesses the desired element.

After all the values are read into the cost array, we call the function add_profit to compute the selling price for each and print the results. The add_profit function is type void, because it does not return a value directly to main. The expression in the parentheses of the add_profit function header declares a float pointer called

VARIABLE EXAMPLE	LIFETIME	ACCESSIBILITY
int tempf;	program	all source files
static int tempc;	program	this file only
extern int book_total	program	defined in another file
int c2f(inc c);	program	all source files
static int f2c(intf)	program	this source file only
void main () {		
int count;	block	block and sub blocks after declared
static int interrupt_cnt;	program	block and sub blocks after declared
register int index	block	block and sub blocks after declared

FIGURE 12-22   Examples of variable and function storage classes.

```
/* C PROGRAM F12-23.C */

/* Passing array pointers to functions */

float cost[10], prices[10];              /* array declarations */
                                         /* function declaration or prototype */

void  add_profit(float *pp, float *cp, int count);

void main ()
{
    int i;
    int number=10;
    printf("Enter %d costs. After each cost press enter.\n",number);

    for(i=0; i < number; i++)            /* read in costs */
      scanf("%f", (cost+i));

    add_profit(prices, cost, number); /* function call */
}  /* end of main */


/* function definition */

void add_profit(float *pp, float *cp, int count)
    {
    int i;
    for(i=0; i < count; i++)
      {
      *(pp+i) = *(cp+i) + .25 * *(cp+i);
      printf("cost=%6.2f, price=%6.2f \n",*(cp+i),*(pp+i));
      }
    }
```

FIGURE 12-23   Program showing how to pass array pointers to functions.

pp that will be used to receive a pointer to prices and a float pointer called cp that will be used to receive a pointer to cost. The header also declares an int which will receive the number of elements in the array. Here's why we declared these three.

The procedure reads a value from the array cost, computes the selling price, and puts the result in the array prices. Since we are changing values in the prices array, we have to pass the function a pointer to prices. For this simple example, however, we are not modifying the values in cost, so we did not actually have to pass a pointer to cost. The array cost could have been accessed directly from the function. (Remember, cost is declared outside of main, so it is extern and accessible globally.)

If you refer to cost directly in the function, then the function will work only with values from the array cost. We passed both the source and the destination pointers to the function so that the function will work with any array of costs and any array of prices. Likewise, we pass the number of elements in the array to the function. The for loop in the function uses this passed number instead of a fixed number to determine how many elements to process. The function then can process arrays with any number of elements up to the limit of int, which is +32,767.

In a more realistic program you might declare the arrays large enough to hold 1000 or more elements and then get the value for number by counting how many costs a user actually entered before entering an EOF character (Ctrl Z). The main point we are trying to make here is that by passing pointers and lengths to functions instead of passing directly named variables, you make the function more universally useful or "portable."

Since the name prices is a pointer to the prices array and the name cost is a pointer to the cost array, the actual call of add_profit in Figure 12-23 passes prices to pp, cost to cp, and number to count.

The example we have just discussed shows you how to write a function which accesses two one-dimensional arrays. Figure 12-24, page 422, shows how you can declare, define, and call a function which accesses the elements in a two-dimensional array. Specifically, the function in this program converts each Celsius temperature in a two-dimensional array of temperatures to its Fahrenheit value. This program is simply an extension of the program in Figure 12-20a.

In Figure 12-24 the first for loop in main reads the max and min Celsius temperatures for 7 days and puts them in the first two columns of a 7 × 3 array. The second for loop in main computes the average temperature for each day and writes the result in the third column of the appropriate row in the array.

Once all the Celsius values are in place, we call the function c2f to convert each Celsius value to its

```
/* C PROGRAM F12-24.C */
/* Program to read max and min Celsius temperatures, compute average,
   convert all values to Fahrenheit, and display results */

#include <stdio.h>
int ctemps[7][3];
int ftemps[7][3];
void c2f(int ct[][3], int ft[][3], int rows);     /* function declaration */

void main()
{
    int days = 7;
    int i, j;                         /* note i and j separate variables in main and c2f */
    for (i=0; i<days; i++)
       {
        printf("Enter max Celsius temp for day %d,"
            "then min Celsius temp for day %d.\n", i+1,i+1);
        for(j=0; j<2; j++)                                      /* read max, then min */
        scanf ("%d", &ctemps[i][j]);
       }

    for(i=0; i<days; i++)
       {
       ctemps[i][2] = (ctemps[i][0] + ctemps[i][1])/2; /* average */
       printf("Celsius temperatures for day %d: max = %d min = %d "
          "av = %d \n", (i+1), ctemps[i][0], ctemps[i][1], ctemps[i][2]);
       }
       c2f(ctemps,ftemps, days);               /* call c2f function */
       for(i=0; i<days; i++)
       printf("Fahrenheit temperatures for day %d: max = %d min = %d "
           "av = %d \n", i+1,
           ftemps[i][0], ftemps[i][1], ftemps[i][2]);
}  /* end of main */

    /* define c2f function */
void c2f(int ct[][3], int ft[][3], int rows)
   {
   int i, j;                              /* note these variables different from I,J in main */
   for(i=0; i < rows; i++)
       for(j=0; j<3; j++)
       ft[i][j] = 9*ct[i][j]/5 + 32;
   }
```

FIGURE 12-24   Program using pointers and functions with a two-dimensional array.

Fahrenheit equivalent and put the results in an array called ftemps. As with the previous example, we want to pass pointers to the two arrays and pass the length of the arrays so that the function is as versatile as possible.

The expression int ct[ ][3] in the c2f function header in Figure 12-24 shows one way to declare the pointer needed to receive a pointer to a two-dimensional array. The empty brackets between ct and [3] indicate that ct is a pointer to an array of three elements. When we call the c2f function, we pass ctemps as the actual argument. As shown in Figure 12-20c, the name ctemps is a pointer to the first three-element array, temps[0], so the call gives the c2f access to the first three-element array. In the c2f function a nested for loop is used to access the elements in ctemps[0], ctemps[1], ctemps[2], etc.

In the same way the int ft[ ][3] expression in the c2f function header declares another pointer to an array of

three elements. This formal parameter is used to receive a pointer to ftemps during the call. Incidentally, you can declare a pointer to a three-dimensional array with an expression such as float hrs_worked[ ][12][31]. The trick here is to simply leave the first set of brackets after the array name empty.

Another method of declaring the formal argument for passing the ctemps pointer to the function is with the expression int (*ct)[3]. This expression likewise declares ct as a pointer to a three-element array. The parentheses around *ct are required to indicate that you are declaring a pointer to an array. The expression int *ct[3] declares an array of three pointers which each point to int-type variables.

To summarize the operation of all this, the c2f(ctemps, ftemps, days) statement in Figure 12-24 calls the function. The ctemps in the function call passes a pointer to the ctemps array to the function pointer variable ct. The ftemps in the function call passes a pointer to the ftemps array to the function pointer variable ft. The days in the function call passes the value of the variable days to the function variable called rows. The function uses these passed values and a nested for loop to read an element from ctemps, compute the Fahrenheit equivalent, and write the result to the same element in ftemps. Note that since the number of rows is a variable in the function, the function can be called to process any number of three-element arrays.

DECLARING AND USING POINTERS TO FUNCTIONS

In the preceding sections we have shown you how to declare pointers to simple variables and pointers to arrays. You can also declare and initialize a pointer to a function. This is an advanced technique and it is unlikely that you will use pointers to functions in your initial programs. However, we want to show you a couple of examples so that you will recognize them in someone else's programs. Here is how you could declare a pointer to the c2f function in Figure 12-21c and call the function using the pointer instead of using a direct call.

```
int c2f(int c);            /* declare the function c2f */
int (*convert) (int c);    /* declare a pointer to a function */
convert = c2f;             /* initialize the pointer to point
                              to c2f */
tempf = (*convert)         /* call c2f with pointer and pass */
   (tempc);                /* value of temp c to the function */
int c2f(int c)             /* c2f function definition header */
```

The basic function declaration and definition here are the same as those in Figure 12-21b. The second statement declares a pointer called convert that points to a function. The key to recognizing that convert is a pointer to a function is the double set of parentheses in the declaration. The int at the start of the declaration indicates that the function pointed to returns an int value. The int c in the second set of parentheses indicates that the function pointed to expects to receive an int value. The parentheses around the name of the function pointer are required to indicate that convert is a pointer to a function. The statement int *convert(int c);, which does not have these parentheses, declares a function that returns a pointer to an int value.

The tempf = (*convert)(tempc); statement calls the c2f function using the pointer called convert. The term *convert represents the contents of convert, which we initialized with the address of the c2f function. The value of tempc is passed to the function, and the int value returned by c2f is assigned to tempf.

Now that you know much more about functions, in the next section we will take a closer look at some of the predefined functions available to you in libraries.

C Library Functions

INTRODUCTION

Throughout this chapter we have used predefined functions such as printf( ), scanf( ), and getch( ) in many of the example programs. The functions we have used are just a small sample of those available. Turbo C++ comes with a *Run Time Library* containing over 450 predefined functions and macros. These library functions allow you to perform I/O operations with a variety of devices, dynamically allocate memory in a program, produce graphics displays, read from and write to disk files, perform complex mathematical computations, etc. For many applications you can use one of these predefined functions instead of writing your own function. The source code for all these functions is available from Borland, so if the predefined function does not quite fit your application, you can modify a copy of the source code for the function to produce a custom version which does.

The declarations or prototypes for the predefined functions are contained in files called header files or include files. These files have names such as stdio.h, string.h, math.h, graphics.h, and alloc.h. The preprocessor #include directive tells the compiler which header files to search for the predefined functions you use in a program. The directive #include<stdio.h>, for example, tells the compiler to look in the header file called stdio.h to find the prototypes for functions such as printf( ), scanf( ), and getch( ).

The actual codes for the predefined functions are contained in library (.lib) files. When you call a function, the object code for the function gets linked with the code for the rest of your program when the .exe file is created.

In the following sections of the chapter we review the functions we have used previously and show some more functions and examples that you may find useful in your programs. In later chapters we show you how to use other predefined functions for graphics, disk file, and communications programs. To help you refer to the examples here, we have separated them according to the type of operation they perform. For discussions of all 450+ functions and macros consult the Turbo C++ Reference Guide.

KEYBOARD INPUT FUNCTIONS

Function   Prototypes in stdio.h

Function		
getch( )	int getch(void)	/* read char as soon as pressed */
getche( )	int getche(void)	/* read char and echo to CRT */
getchar( )	int getchar(void)	/* wait for Enter, read char */
gets( )	char *gets(char *s)	/* reads characters from keyboard until Enter and writes string to location pointed to by s. Reads spaces and tabs.*/
scanf( )	int scanf(const char *format,[address, . . .])	

Scanf reads characters from the keyboard until it reads a blank, a tab, or an Enter. Data read in is formatted according to the format specifier in the call and written to the address passed in the call. The three dots after address indicate that the number of arguments to be passed to scanf is variable. This means that you can include several format specifiers and several addresses in one scanf call to read in multiple values.

Scanf normally returns the number of values read and stored. If the first entered character that scanf reads cannot be converted to the specified format, scanf will not store the value, and it will return a value of 0. For example, if the scanf call statement contains a %f format specifier and you accidentally enter a T, scanf will terminate and return a 0.

The input loop in Figure 12-12 can be rewritten as follows to make sure that the pointer does not get incremented if no value was written to one of the elements in the array:

```
for(i=0;i<10; i++)
{
        if((scanf("%f",cpntr))==0)
        {
        i--;                     /* correct index value */
        fflush(stdin);           /* clear unread characters from
                                    keyboard buffer */
        continue;                /* skip rest of loop actions */
        }
        else cpntr++;
}
```

The continue statement here will cause the cpntr++ to be skipped over in this trip through the loop if the value returned by scanf is zero.

NOTE: This cure does not work if an illegal character is entered in any but the first digit position.

OUTPUT FUNCTIONS

Function   Prototype in stdio.h

putchar( )   int putchar   /* outputs   passed
             (int c)   character to screen.
                                  Returns −1 (EOF) if
                                  error. */

puts( )   int puts(const
             char *s)

Puts sends a null terminated string pointed to by s to the screen. If an error occurs, puts returns a value of −1 (EOF). For outputting simple strings, puts uses much less memory and time than printf.

printf( )   int printf(const char *format, [argument,
             . . .]);

As shown by the many examples in the preceding programs, the format here consists of text and format specifiers. The arguments are a list of variables, one for each format specifier. The general form of the format specifiers is as follows:

% flags width . precision [F,N, h, l, L] type

>   flags = output justification, numeric signs and other
>   − = left justify printed digits
>   + = print + or minus sign in front of value

blank = positive values start with blank instead of +
width = total number of digits left of decimal point
[F,N,h,l,L] = override default size of argument with
         F = far pointer, N = near pointer, h = short int,
         l = long, L = long double
type = conversion specifier as shown in Figure 12-11

Consult the Turbo C++ Reference Manual for a complete explanation of the print controls in printf.

fprintf( )   int fprintf (FILE *stream, constant char
              *format [,argument, . . .])

With the proper setup fprintf( ) will send program output to the printer instead of to the CRT screen. As we discuss further in a later chapter, we often think of data going to or coming from a disk file as a "stream." The same term can be used to refer to data going to the CRT. The fprintf( ) function allows a stream of data to be sent to the printer. Figure 12-25 shows how this function can be used to send the output of our old prices program to the printer.

Before you can call the fprintf( ) function, you must use the predefined setmode( ) function to tell the compiler that you are going to send a text file to the printer. The 0004 in this call is a "handle" which identifies the printer, and the O_TEXT is a predefined term for text mode. The prototype for setmode( ) is in fcntl.h, so we put #include<fcntl.h> at the top of the program.

The fprintf( ) function call is the same as a call to printf, except that we include the term stdprn before the usual printf arguments. The term stdprn tells fprintf to direct the data stream to the standard printer device. Incidentally, the \f in the final fprintf statement is a formfeed character, which tells the printer to advance to the top of the next page.

STRING FUNCTIONS

Function   Prototype in string.h

strcat( )   char *strcat(char *dest, cons char *src)

Strcat( ) adds a copy of string pointed to by src to the string pointed to by dest. and returns a pointer to the start of the combined string.

strchr( )   char *strchr(const char *s, int c);

Strchr scans a string pointed to by s for the first occurrence of c. Strchr returns a pointer to the first occurrence of c or returns a null if c was not found in the string.

strlen( )   size_t strlen(const char *s);

Strlen returns length of string pointed to by s.

strcmp( )   int strcmp(const char *s1, const char *s2);

Strcmp compares each character in s1 with the corresponding character in s2. Strcmp( ) returns 0 if the two strings are equal, a positive number if s1 is greater than s2, and a negative number if s2 is greater than s1. The

```
/* C PROGRAM F12-25.C   */
/* Sending program output to a printer */

#include <stdio.h>
#include <fcntl.h>

int cost[] = { 20,28,15,26,19,27,16,29,39,42 };   /* array of 10 costs */
int prices[10];                                    /* array to hold 10 prices */

void main()
{
    int index;
    setmode(0004, O_TEXT);
    for (index=0; index <10; index++)              /* for loop to compute */
    prices[index] = cost[index] + 15;              /* 10 prices */

    for (index=0; index <10; index++)              /* for loop to display results */
      fprintf(stdprn,"cost = %d, price = %d, \n",
                        cost[index], prices[index]);
    fprintf(stdprn,"\f");
}
```

FIGURE 12-25 Program using predefined fprintf function to send program output to a printer instead of to the CRT.

stricmp( ) function is the same as strcmp( ), except that it ignores the case of the characters in the strings. Figure 12-26 shows how you can use the stricmp( ) function to implement an improved version of the password check program from Figure 5-3.

At the start of the program we declare the required character arrays and a counter. Then we prompt the user and use gets( ) to read the response. The while loop compares the value returned by stricmp with 0 to see if

```
/* C PROGRAM F12-26.C    */
/* Password program in C */

#include<stdio.h>
#include<string.h>

void main()
{
 char password[] = "failsafe";
 char input_word[8];
 int try = 0;
 printf("Please enter your password.\n");
 gets(input_word);
 while(stricmp(password,input_word) != 0 && try++ <2)
  {
  printf("Entered password is incorrect,try again.\n");
  gets(input_word);
  }
 if(stricmp(password,input_word) != 0)
  {
  printf("This computer does not know you!");
  /* alarm() *//* call ASM function to sound alarm */
  exit();
  }
 printf("Welcome, what can I do for you?");
}
```

FIGURE 12-26 Program using predefined string function to compare passwords.

the entered password is correct. If the password is correct, execution exits the while loop and goes on to the if structure. If the entered password is incorrect, the while loop gives the user two more tries to enter the correct password before going on to the if structure.

If the value returned by stricmp( ) is equal to zero, execution will simply fall through the if structure and print the welcome message. If the user did not get the password correct in three tries, then the if structure prints a message, sounds an alarm, and exits. In a more realistic program you would probably call a function which locks up the machine at this point instead of doing a simple exit.

MATH FUNCTIONS

Function   *Prototype in math.h*

sqrt( )   double sqrt (double x);

Sqrt( ) returns the positive square root of x. If x is negative, sqrt returns zero. We don't have space here to discuss the prototypes for the many 8087 type math functions found in math.h. However, to keep a promise we made earlier, Figure 12-27, page 426, shows how the Pythagoras program from Chapter 11 can be written in C.

Remember, this program calculates the value of the hypotenuse of a right triangle by taking the square root of the sum of the squares of the two legs. In the program in Figure 12-27 we call the predefined function sqrt( ) to take the square root. We pass sqrt a value which is equal to side_a squared+side_b squared. Sqrt returns the square root of the sum and assigns it to side_c. Note that we wrote a #include<math.h> directive at the start of the program to tell the compiler where to look for the prototype of the sqrt( ) function.

When the compiler compiles this program, it will use the default mode of "emulator" for the instructions

```
/* C PROGRAM F12-27.C */
/*PYTHAGORAS REVISITED */

#include <stdio.h>
#include <math.h>
void main (  )
{
   float side_a, side_b, side_c;
   side_a = 3.0;
   side_b = 4.0;

   side_c = sqrt (side_a * side_a + side_b * side_b);
   printf("side a = %2.2f side b = %2.2f
           side C = %2.2f\n", side_a, side_b, side_c);
}
```

FIGURE 12-27   C version of 8086/8087 Pythagoras program in Figure 11-22.

which act on floating-point numbers. When you run the program, a predefined function determines if your system contains an 8087 or 80287. If an 8087 is present, the program will use 8087 instructions to implement floating-point operations in the program. If your system does not contain an 8087, the program will use floating-point library functions which emulate the 8087 instructions. If you are sure that a floating-point program will be run only on systems which have 8087s present, you can work your way through the menu path Options->Compiler->Code generation in the Turbo C++ IDE and toggle the Floating-point line to 8087/80287. This will shorten the length of the .exe program produced, because the emulation functions do not have to be included.

Writing Programs Which Contain C and Assembly Language

INTRODUCTION

The C language is very useful for writing user-interface programs, but code produced by a C compiler does not execute fast enough for applications such as drawing a complex graphics display on a CRT. Therefore, system programs are often written with a combination of C and assembly language functions. The main user interface may be written in C and specialized, high-speed functions written in assembly language. These assembly language functions are simply called from the C program as needed.

Also, when writing a program that is mostly assembly language, you may find it useful to call one of the predefined C functions to do some task that you don't want to take the time to implement in assembly language.

The main points you have to consider when interfacing C with assembly language are

1. How do you call a desired function?

2. How do you pass parameters to the called function?

3. How are parameters passed back to the calling program from the function?

4. How do you declare code and data segments in the function so that they are compatible with those in the calling program?

The easiest way to answer these questions is to look closely at how the compiler does each one. Here's how you get a look at how a compiler treats a C program.

Earlier in the chapter we described how you can use the Turbo C++ IDE to compile, run, and debug programs. In addition to the compiler in the IDE, the Turbo C++ toolset has a separate compiler called tcc. The tcc compiler has a few advanced features that the integrated compiler doesn't have. The tcc compiler, for example, will compile a C program to its assembly language equivalent. The command tcc −S 12-28a.c, for example, will produce a file called 12-28a.asm which contains the assembly language equivalent for the specified C source file. The C source program statements are included as comments in the .asm file.

THE ASSEMBLY LANGUAGE EQUIVALENT OF A C PROGRAM

Figure 12-28a shows a simplified version of the temperature conversion program in Figure 12-21b, and Figure 12-28b shows an edited version of the .asm program produced from it by tcc. To make the program easier to follow, we removed all the debug information normally put in by the compiler, shortened the list of DBs at the end of the program, and added some comments. Read the C program in Figure 12-28a, skim through the .asm version in Figure 12-28b to see how much you can intuitively understand, and then come back to the discussion here to get more details. The analysis of this

```
/* C PROGRAM F12-28A.C /*
/* Simple temperature conversion function
   definition and call */

#include<stdio.h>
int tempc = 25, tempf;/* external (global) variables*/

int c2f(int c);      /* declare function c2f which
                        returns an int value */
void main()
{
 tempf = c2f(tempc);  /* call c2f function, pass value
                        of tempc to function. Returned
                        value assigned to tempf */

 printf("Celsius = %d,Fahrenheit=%d \n", tempc,tempf);
} /* end of main */

int c2f(int c)       /* define function c2f.
                        Note no ; at end */
   {
   int f;            /* automatic (local) variable */
   f = 9*c/5 + 32;
   return (f);
   }
```

(a)

FIGURE 12-28   (a) Simplified version of Figure 12-21b.

```
;8086 PROGRAM F12-28B.ASM
_TEXT       SEGMENT     BYTE PUBLIC 'CODE'
DGROUP      GROUP       _DATA,_BSS          ; Assign same start to segments
            ASSUME      CS:_TEXT, DS:DGROUP, SS:DGROUP
_TEXT       ENDS


_DATA       SEGMENT WORD PUBLIC 'DATA' ; Initialized variables here
_TEMPC      LABEL   WORD               ; Declare and init TEMPC
            DW      25
_DATA       ENDS


_TEXT       SEGMENT BYTE PUBLIC 'CODE' ; Code always in _TEXT segment
_MAIN       PROC    NEAR
    PUSH    WORD PTR DGROUP:_TEMPC      ; Pass value of TEMPC on stack
    CALL    NEAR PTR _C2F              ; Call C2F function
    POP     CX                         ; Increment SP over TEMPC arg
    MOV     WORD PTR DGROUP:_TEMPF,AX  ; Save TEMPF returned in AX
    PUSH    WORD PTR DGROUP:_TEMPF     ; Put value of TEMPF on stack
    PUSH    WORD PTR DGROUP:_TEMPC     ; Put value of TEMPC on stack
    MOV     AX,OFFSET DGROUP:S@        ; Put pointer to text string
    PUSH    AX                         ;      on stack
    CALL    NEAR PTR _PRINTF           ; Call PRINTF fucntion
    ADD     SP,6                       ; Increment SP over three passed arguments
    RET                                ; Return from main
_MAIN       ENDP


_C2F        PROC       NEAR            ; C2F function definition
    PUSH    BP                         ; Save old BP
    MOV     BP,SP                      ; Copy of SP To BP
    PUSH    SI                         ; Save SI reg because used here
    MOV     AX,WORD PTR [BP+4]         ; Get value of TEMPC from stack
    MOV     DX,9                       ; prepare to multiply by 9
    MUL     DX                         ; Multiply value of TEMPC by 9
    MOV     BX,5                       ; Prepare to divide result by 5
    CWD
    IDIV    BX                         ; Do division, int result in AX
    MOV     SI,AX                      ; SI used for local variable F
    ADD     SI,32                      ; Add 32 to F
    MOV     AX,SI                      ; Value of F returned in AX
    POP     SI                         ; Restore SI
    POP     BP                         ; Restore old BP value
    RET                                ; Return to main
_C2F        ENDP
_TEXT       ENDS


_BSS        SEGMENT WORD PUBLIC 'BSS' ; Uninitialized variables here
_TEMPF      LABEL   WORD              ; Declare TEMPF
            DB      2 DUP (?)
_BSS        ENDS
```

(b)

FIGURE 12-28 (*Continued*)   (b) Assembly language equivalent of C program
in 12-28a produced by tcc compiler with -S switch. (*Continued on next page.*)

```
_DATA     SEGMENT WORD PUBLIC 'DATA'    ; Text string and format
S@        LABEL      BYTE                ; Specifiers for PRINTF here
          DB    67
          DB    101
          :                             ; List shortened to save space
          DB    116
          DB    32
          DB    61
          DB    100
          DB    32
          DB    10
          DB    0
_DATA     ENDS


_TEXT     SEGMENT       BYTE PUBLIC 'CODE'
          EXTRN      _PRINTF:NEAR        ; Let compiler know PRINTF()
_TEXT     ENDS                          ; function is external

          PUBLIC     _TEMPF             ; Make extern variables and
          PUBLIC     _MAIN              ; functions public
          PUBLIC     _TEMPC
          PUBLIC     _C2F
          END
```

(b)

FIGURE 12-28 (*Continued*)   (b) Assembly language equivalent of C program
in 12-28a produced by tcc compiler with -S switch.

program should help you better understand some of the earlier discussions of passing arguments to functions and variable storage classes.

The C program in Figure 12-28a calls our c2f function to compute the Fahrenheit equivalent of 25°C and calls the predefined printf function to display the result. The first feature we need to talk about in the assembly equivalent for this program is how the segments are defined and grouped.

Turbo C allows you to compile a program for any of six *memory models*. The six memory models are tiny, small, medium, compact, large, and huge. The memory model used determines the location of segments in memory and the size pointers used to refer to code and data. Here is a short discussion of each.

Tiny—All four segment registers are set to the same physical address, so only 64 Kbytes are available for all code and data. Since everything is in one 64-Kbyte space, near pointers are used for all code and data references. The tiny model is used to generate .com-type programs which automatically get loaded into memory at 100H.

Small—This model uses one 64-Kbyte code segment. One 64-Kbyte segment is shared by the data segment, the stack segment, and the extra segment, so these segments all start at the same address. This memory model is the default for the Turbo C++ compilers. Near pointers are used for all code and data references.

Medium—Far pointers are used for references in code, so code references can be anywhere in the 1-Mbyte address space. The data segment, extra segment, and stack segment share one 64-Kbyte space, so near pointers are used for data references.

Compact—This model uses one 64-Kbyte code segment, so near pointers are generated for code references. Far pointers are generated for data references, so data can be accessed anywhere in the 1-Mbyte range.

Large—Far pointers are used for both code and data references, so both have a 1-Mbyte range. If a program has a code file or a data file larger than 64 Kbytes, however, the file must be broken into files smaller than 64 Kbytes and the resulting files linked.

Huge—Huge is similar to the large model, except that the far pointers are always normalized. A far pointer is normalized by generating the 20-bit physical address from the segment and offset and then using the upper 4 nibbles of the physical address as the segment and the lower nibble of the physical address as the offset. A pointer reference of 4057:3244 produces a 20-bit address of 437B4 and a normalized pointer value of 437B:0004. The advantage of normalized pointers is that they can be accurately compared in expressions using the ==, !=, =, >=, <, and <= operators.

We used the default memory model to compile the program in Figure 12-28a, so the data, stack, and extra segments all share one 64-Kbyte address space. The DGROUP GROUP _DATA, _BSS statement at the top of Figure 12-28b groups the logical segments _DATA and _BSS together in a group called DGROUP. The ASSUME statement just after this indicates that DS will be initialized to point to DGROUP and SS will also be initialized to point to DGROUP.

Note that the assembly language for this program does not show any instructions for initializing the segment registers and the stack pointer register. These instructions are contained in a special startup section of code that is linked with your program when the .exe file is created.

If you look again at Figure 12-28b, you can see that the _TEXT segment is used to hold program instructions. The _DATA segment is used to hold initialized extern variables and text strings such as those used in printf statements. The _BSS segment is used to hold uninitialized extern variables. You should use these same conventions when you write an assembly language function to be called from a C program.

The next point to consider here is how C passes arguments to a function. If you call an .asm function from a C program, this is the way the arguments will be passed to the function. If you call a C function from an .asm program, this is how you have to pass arguments to the C function.

C passes almost all arguments to functions by pushing them on the stack. The first instruction in main in Figure 12-28b pushes the value of TEMPC on the stack to pass to C2F. As we said earlier, this call just passes a copy of CTEMP to the function, so the function cannot change the actual value of CTEMP. Remember, if you want a function to change the value of a variable, you pass the offset of the variable to the function.

Now let's look at how the function accesses the CTEMPS value passed to it on the stack. The process here is the same one we introduced you to in Figure 5-17. We first save the old value of BP by pushing it on the stack and then copy the value of SP to BP so that BP is a second pointer to the stack. As we told you in Chapter 5, the easiest way to keep track of where everything is in the stack is with a simple stack map such as that in Figure 12-29. We pushed ctemps on the stack in main, the return address (IP) got pushed on the stack during the call, and BP got pushed on the stack at the start of the C2F function. The BP register then points to the stack at the location where the old value of BP is stored. You can access any value on the stack by simply adding a displacement to BP. The value of CTEMPS is in the stack at [BP+4], so the instruction MOV AX,WORD PTR[BP+4] will copy the value of CTEMPS to AX. The 8086 arithmetic instructions after this perform the specified computations.

Note that the compiler assigned the local variable named f in the C program to the SI register, even though we did not tell it to make f a register variable. If you declare more than two automatic or register variables, the compiler will allocate space for them on the stack below BP, as shown in Figure 12-29. Since they are dynamically allocated on the stack, automatic variables are re-created each time a function is called.

Stack map			
stack pointer		stack	
before push	→		
after push	→	ctemps	← [BP+4]
after call	→	IP	← [BP+2]
after push BP	→	BP	← [BP]
after push SI	→	SI	← [BP-2]
automatic variable	→	—	← [BP-4]
automatic variable	→	—	← [BP-6]

FIGURE 12-29 Stack map showing use of BP to access arguments passed to a function on the stack.

The computed value of f is returned to the calling program in the AX register. If the function were returning a 32-bit value, it would return the high word in DX and the low word in AX.

If you look at the stack map in Figure 12-29 again, you should see that when execution returns to main from the procedure, SP will be pointing to the value of ctemps in the stack. The POP CX instruction in main will "clean up" the stack by incrementing SP to its initial value. Since C doesn't use the CX register for anything special, we don't care about the value put in CX by the POP CX instruction.

The next part of the program pushes the specified arguments on the stack and then calls printf to display the results of the computation. The C compiler pushes arguments on the stack in the reverse order from the order they are written in the function call parentheses. For our example here, then, the value of ftemp will be pushed on the stack first. Next the value of ctemp will be pushed on the stack. Finally, a pointer to the text string in the printf( ) call will be pushed on the stack. This final step is done with the two instructions MOV AX,OFFSET DGROUP:S@ and PUSH AX.

The printf( ) function is obviously not present in this source module. The statement EXTRN _PRINTF: near the bottom of Figure 12-28b indicates that the code for this function will be linked later. When execution returns from the printf function, the ADD SP,6 instruction cleans up the stack by incrementing it up over the three arguments passed to printf on the stack.

Finally in Figure 12-28b, note that the variables and functions declared outside of main are made public so that they can be accessed from other source modules. As we showed you in Chapter 5, if you want to access one of these from another source module, you have to declare it extrn in that module.

Now that you have some ideas about how a C compiler "thinks," let's talk about how you can use this to write assembly language functions you can call from your C programs and how you can call C functions from your assembly language programs.

A PROGRAM WITH C AND ASSEMBLY LANGUAGE MODULES

Figure 12-28b shows you almost everything you need to know to interface C and assembly language, but to make it a little clearer, Figure 12-30 shows a C program which calls two assembly language functions and also shows the two assembly language functions. To show a C function call from assembly language, one of the assembly language functions calls the predefined C function, printf( ).

In the C program in Figure 12-30a, we put the term extern in the two function declarations to let the compiler know that these functions are in another source module. We then call the functions by name and pass any required arguments, just as we would call C functions.

In the assembly language part of the program in Figure 12-30b, we declare segments using the names shown in Figure 12-28b. Note that you put underscores (_) in front of all segment names, function names, and variable names in the assembly language module. This is required for compatibility with the C compiler conventions.

The c2f function in Figure 12-30b is exactly the same as that produced by the compiler in Figure 12-28b. It is very common practice to write a function in C, compile the function to its assembly language equivalent, and then "hand optimize" the .asm equivalent for maximum efficiency in the specific application. As we will show you, the .asm file can be assembled and the resulting object file linked with the object file for the mainline program.

The show function in Figure 12-30b calls printf to display the Celsius temperature, the Fahrenheit temperature, and appropriate text. We declare the text in the data segment with a simple DB statement. The 0AH at the end of the declaration represents a carriage return, and the 00H is a NULL character required as a terminator on the string. From the string you can see that we need to pass three arguments to printf, just as we did in Figure 12-28a. The three arguments are a pointer to the string, the value of tempc, and the value of tempf. The three push statements in Figure 12-30b put these arguments on the stack in reverse order as required by the C calling convention. When execution returns from printf, we add six to SP to increment it up over the three arguments we passed to printf.

A very important point to observe in Figure 12-30 is the use of the extern or extrn directives and the use of the public directive. In the C program we use the extern directive to tell the compiler that c2f and show are in another source module. In the assembly module in Figure 12-30b we use the public directive to make the procedures c2f and show accessible to other source modules. Note that the public declarations are put in the code segment. Also in Figure 12-30b use the extrn directive to tell the assembler that the variables tempf and tempc are defined in another source module. Note that the extrn directives are put in the segments where the named variables are found.

As we told you in Chapter 5, the rules here are very simple. You declare a function or variable public in the module where it is defined if you want other modules to be able to access it. You use the extern or extrn directive to tell the assembler/compiler that a function or variable is located in some other source module.

SIMPLIFIED SEGMENT DIRECTIVES

Newer versions of TASM and MASM allow you to use a simplified set of segment directives in assembly language programs. You can use these simplified segment directives in many stand-alone assembly language programs, but their main use is in writing assembly language modules which interface with high-level language program modules.

Figure 12-30c shows in skeleton form how the assembly language module from Figure 12-30b can be written using these simplified directives. The DOSSEG directive at the start tells the linker to put the segments in an order which is compatible with DOS and high-level languages. Basically the order is code segment, data segment containing initialized variables, data segment containing uninitialized variables, and stack segment.

The .MODEL directive tells the assembler to use the SMALL memory model, which consists of one 64-Kbyte code segment and one 64-Kbyte data segment. This is the default model for the Turbo C++ compiler.

The .CODE directive sets up the code segment. With this directive the assembler automatically gives the code segment the name required by the memory model used and generates the required ASSUME directive. For the small memory model the code segment will be assigned the name _TEXT, as shown in Figure 12-30b.

In a similar way the .DATA directive declares a segment for initialized variables and the .DATA? directive declares a segment for uninitialized variables. In a small model program the assembler will automatically "group" these two segments, as we described for the standard segment directive version in Figure 12-30b. Incidentally, you do not need to declare a stack or initialize the stack

```
/* C PROGRAM F12-30A.C */
/* Temperature conversion function */

#include<stdio.h>
int tempc = 25, tempf; /* external (global) variables*/
int extern c2f(int c); /* declare function c2f which */
                       /* returns an int value */
void extern show(void);/* function show is in
                         another module */
void main()
{
 tempf = c2f(tempc);   /* call c2f function, pass
                         value of tempc to function.
                         Returned value assigned
                         to tempf */

 show();
}/* end of main */
```

(a)

FIGURE 12-30   Program with C and assembly language modules. (a) C mainline module. (See also pp. 431–2.)

```
; 8086 PROGRAM F12-30B.ASM

_TEXT       SEGMENT     BYTE PUBLIC 'CODE'
DGROUP      GROUP       _DATA,_BSS
            ASSUME      CS:_TEXT,DS:DGROUP,SS:DGROUP
_TEXT       ENDS


_DATA       SEGMENT WORD PUBLIC 'DATA'
S@      DB 'CELSIUS = %D, FAHRENHEIT = %D',0AH, 00H ; PRINTF STRING
_DATA       ENDS


_TEXT       SEGMENT     BYTE PUBLIC 'CODE'
PUBLIC _C2F
PUBLIC _SHOW
EXTRN _PRINTF:NEAR


_C2F        PROC        NEAR                ; C2F function definition
            PUSH        BP                  ; Save old BP
            MOV         BP,SP               ; Copy of SP to BP
            PUSH        SI                  ; Save SI
            MOV         AX,WORD PTR [BP+4]   ; Get TEMPC from stack
            MOV         DX,9
            MUL         DX
            MOV         BX,5
            CWD
            IDIV        BX
            MOV         SI,AX
            ADD         SI,32
            MOV         AX,SI               ; Return value of F in AX
            POP         SI
            POP         BP                  ; Restore old BP
            RET
_C2F        ENDP


_SHOW PROC NEAR
            PUSH        WORD PTR DGROUP:_TEMPF ; Put value of TEMPF on stack
            PUSH        WORD PTR DGROUP:_TEMPC ; Put value of TEMPC on stack
            MOV         AX,OFFSET DGROUP:S@    ; Put offset of string on stack
            PUSH        AX
            CALL        NEAR PTR _PRINTF        ;
            ADD         SP,6                ; Increment SP over arguments
            RET
_SHOW ENDP
_TEXT       ENDS


_BSS        SEGMENT WORD PUBLIC 'BSS'
            EXTRN _TEMPF:WORD
_BSS        ENDS


_DATA SEGMENT WORD PUBLIC 'DATA'
            EXTRN _TEMPC:WORD
_DATA ENDS
            END
```

(b)

FIGURE 12-30 *(Continued)* (*b*) Assembly language functions. (*See also next page.*)

```
        DOSSEG
         .MODEL SMALL

         .CODE

        PUBLIC _C2F
        PUBLIC _SHOW
        EXTRN _PRINTF:NEAR
        _C2F           PROC            NEAR
                        .
                        .
                        .
                       RET
        _C2F           ENDP

        _SHOW PROC NEAR
                        .
                        .
                        .
                       RET
        _SHOW ENDP

         .DATA
        S@ DB 'CELSIUS = %D, FAHRENHEIT = %D'
           DB 0AH, 00H ; PRINTF STRING
           EXTRN _TEMPC:WORD

         .DATA?
                   EXTRN _TEMPF:WORD

                   END
                         (c)
```

FIGURE 12-30 (*Continued*) (c) Assembly language module using simplified segment directives.

pointer in a program intended to run on a PC type computer, because this is done by DOS and/or the C startup code. If you are writing a program for some other environment, you can declare a stack and initialize the stack pointer with a simple directive such as .STACK 200H.

We showed you the standard segment directive version of an assembly language module first, so that you could see how all the pieces fit together, but the simplified directives are obviously easier to use in your programs. Now that you know how to write C and assembly language modules that interface with each other, we will outline how you produce an executable program from these modules.

PRODUCING A .EXE FILE FOR MULTIMODULE PROGRAMS

If you are using the Turbo C++ environment, the steps in producing a .exe file from a multimodule program such as the one in Figure 12-30 are as follows. If you are using some other environment, the steps are very similar.

1. Create the C module using the editor. Don't forget any required extern directives.

2. Compile the module and repeat the edit-compile cycle until the compile is successful.

3. Create the assembly language module with the editor. Don't forget to include any required public and extrn directives. Save the module in a file with a .asm extension.

4. Press the Alt key and the spacebar to get to the menu containing Turbo Assembler. Move the highlighted box to the TurboAssembler line and press the Enter key.

5. Repeat the edit-assemble loop until the assemble is successful.

6. Go to the Project menu and select Open Project. When the dialog box appears, type in some appropriate name for your project and give it a .prj extension.

7. Use the Add Item line in the Project menu to add the name(s) of the C source (.C) files and the names of your assembly language object (.obj) files to the project file. Press the Esc key to get back to the project window.

8. Go to the Options menu and select Linker. In this menu go to the case sensitive link and press the Enter key to turn it off. TASM produces uppercase for all names, and this toggle will prevent link errors caused by uppercase/lowercase disagreements.

9. Go to the Compile menu, select build all, and press the Enter key. This tells the IDE tools to do a "make" on the files specified in the project list. Make checks the times and dates on the .obj files and the associated source files. If the times are different, the source modules are automatically recompiled. The resulting object files are linked with object files from .asm modules and object modules from libraries to produce the final .exe file.

10. Go to the Run menu and press the R key to run the program.

NOTE: For complex multimodule programs, you may want to use the separate tcc compiler and Tlink linker, which have some options not available in the integrated environment. We don't have space here to describe the operation of tcc.

In this chapter we used your knowledge of assembly language to quickly teach you about the C programming language. In the following chapters we will show you how C can be used for graphics, file handling, and communications programming.

CHECKLIST OF IMPORTANT TERMS AND CONCEPTS IN THIS CHAPTER

If you do not remember any of the terms in the following list, use the index to help you find them in the chapter for review.

Integrated program development environment

Compiler optimizations

C language
  Variable types
  Variable declarations
  Simple pointers
  Array pointers
  Dereferencing a pointer
  Passing a parameter by value
  Passing a parameter by reference
  Preprocessor directives
  Assignment operator, =
  Arithmetic operators +, −, *, /, %, ++, −−
  Bitwise operators &, |, ^, ~, <<, >>
  Combined operators
  Relational operators ==, !=, >, >=, <, <=
  Logical operators &&, ||, !
  Operator precedence

If-else
Switch and break statements
Goto statement
While and do-while loops
For loops
Function prototype, function declaration
Function definition
Function call
Formal arguments
Actual arguments
Return statement
Extern, automatic, static, and register storage classes
Lifetime and visibility of variables
Passing pointers to functions
Pointers to functions
Predefined library functions
Turbo C++ memory models
Cleaning up the stack
Simplified segment directives

REVIEW QUESTIONS AND PROBLEMS

1. *a.* What is the index value for the first element in the cost array in Figure 12-1a?
    b. Which element in the cost array is accessed by the term cost[index] during the second execution of the for loop?
    c. What is the purpose of the #include<stdio.h> line at the top of the program in Figure 12-1a?
    d. What does the word printf in the statement in Figure 12-1a refer to?

2. *a.* Describe the advantages of an integrated program environment such as the Turbo C++ IDE over the separate tools approach.
    b. How does the IDE compiler let you know if it finds any errors when it compiles your program?
    c. What is meant by the term watch in the IDE?

3. Give the range of values that can be represented by each of the following C data types.
    a. Char
    b. Int
    c. Unsigned int
    d. Long
    e. Float

4. Write C declaration statements for each of the following variables:
    a. An integer named total_boards.
    b. A character named no, initialized with the ASCII code for lowercase n.
    c. A floating-point variable named body_temp, initialized with 98.6.
    d. A five-element integer array called scores.
    e. A six-element integer array called scores and initialized with the values 95, 89, 84, 93, and 92 (last element uninitialized).
    f. A pointer called ptr which points to the array declared in e.
    g. A two-dimensional character array called screen which has 25 rows and 40 columns.
    h. A three-dimensional character array called screen_buffer which has 4 pages of 25 rows and 80 columns.
    i. An integer called monitor_start, initialized with +FE00H.
    j. A character pointer named answer.
    k. A pointer named ptr, initialized with the address of an integer variable called setpoint.
    l. A pointer named wptr, initialized with the start of the array declared with the statement float net_weights[100];.

5. Describe the operation or sequence of operations performed by each of the following expressions:
    a. 5−4*7/9
    b. (a+4)*17−B/2+6
    c. x+y++
    d. x− −−Y
    e. count += 4;
    f. strobe_val & 0×0001
    g. y=a>>4;
    h. a=4;
        b=39%a;
    i. if (ch == 'Y' || ch == 'y')
        goto start;

6. Write printf statements which
    a. Print the decimal value of an integer named count.
    b. Print a prompt message which tells the user to enter his or her weight.
    c. Print the value of a float variable named conversion_factor with 4 decimal places and a total of 10 digits.
    d. Print the value of a float variable called average_lunar_distance in exponential format.

7. Given the array declared by int nums[ ]={45, 65, 38, 72};, write a program which computes the average and prints the result.

8. Use Figure 12-12 to help you write a program which

   Declares a six-element array of integers.

   Reads five test scores entered by a user into the array.

   Computes the average of the five scores and puts the computed average in the sixth element in the array.

   Prints out the scores and the average with appropriate text.

9. Write a program which

   Declares an array for 25 characters.

   Prompts the user to enter his or her name.

   Reads an entered name into the array.

   Determines the number of characters in the name.

   Prints out appropriate text and the number of letters.

10. a. Write a program section which calls the predefined exit function if the user enters a q or a Q on the keyboard.

    b. The predefined character constant called EOF has a value of −1 (FFH). To produce this character on the keyboard, you hold the Ctrl key down and press the Z key. Write a program which

       Declares an array for up to 1000 characters.

       Reads characters from the keyboard and puts them in the array until the array is full or until the user enters an EOF character Ctrl Z.

       Prints a "buffer full" message if 1000 characters entered.

       Prints a "goodbye" message and exits to DOS if the EOF character is entered.

11. The character display on a CRT screen can be thought of as an array of 25 rows and 80 columns. Write a program which

    Declares a character array of 25 rows and 80 columns.

    Declares a character array initialized with your name.

    Uses a nested for loop to write the ASCII code for a blank, 20H, to each element in the array.

    Writes your name in the array elements which approximately correspond to the center of the screen.

12. Use the array-index method as shown in Figure 12-20a to write a program which

    Declares a two-dimensional array of 7 rows and 3 columns.

    Reads in the maximum temp and minimum temp for each of 7 days and puts the values in the array.

    Computes the average temperature for each day and puts the result in the appropriate position in the third column of the array.

    Computes the average maximum temperature for the week.

    Computes the average minimum temperature for the week.

    Computes the average temperature for the entire week.

    Prints out the results with appropriate labeling.

13. Rewrite the program in problem 12 using pointer notation instead of array-index notation.

14. Explain the difference between formal arguments and actual arguments.

15. Write the declaration, definition, and call for a function which converts a Fahrenheit temperature to its Celsius equivalent. The formula is $F = 9C/5 + 32$.

16. Write a program which reads characters from the keyboard until an EOF (Ctrl Z) is entered, uses a function to detect and convert the ASCII codes for uppercase letters to their lowercase equivalents, and writes the codes in an array.

17. Given the array declared by int nums[ ]= 45,65,38,72;, write a function which computes the average of the four values and passes the average back to the calling program to print out.

18. Rewrite the answer to problem 12 so that it uses a function to compute the desired averages and print the result.

19. Give the lifetime and accessibility of each of the variables and functions declared here.

    a. int scale_factor = 12;

    b. char *text;

    c. float tax(float income, float deductions);

    d. static double debts;

    main( )
    {

    e. static weight = 145;

    f. register count = 23;

    g. int tare;

    }

20. Modify problem 11 to read in two sets of row, column coordinates from a user, store these values, and then call a function which ORs each element in the array between the specified coordinates with 80H.

21. What are the main advantages and the main disadvantages of using predefined C library functions?

22. Rewrite the Pythagoras program in Figure 12-27 so that it allows a user to enter values for side_a and side_b, does the computation, and sends the results to a printer.

23. What are the main points you have to consider when you want to write assembly language functions that will be called from a C program?

24. a. Name the six Turbo C++ memory models.

    b. What are the main features which distinguish one memory model from another?

    c. Describe the default memory model for the Turbo C++ compiler.

    d. Show the simplified segment directives you would use for a small model assembly language module that contains only code and initialized variables.

25. Briefly describe the process used to develop a program which consists of assembly language modules and C modules.

26. Given the array declared with int screen[25][80];, write a C mainline which calls an assembly language function to write 20H in the low byte of each element and 07H in the high byte of each element.

CHAPTER 13

Microcomputer System Peripherals

In Chapter 11 we discussed the circuitry commonly found on the motherboard of a microcomputer. Included in this discussion was a section on the I/O connectors that allow you to plug in boards which interface with system peripherals. In this chapter we discuss the hardware and software of system peripherals such as keyboards, CRT displays, disk drives, printers, and speech I/O devices. Then in the next chapter we discuss serial data communication and network peripherals.

One important goal of this chapter is to help you understand the terminology of displays, disk drives, and printers so you feel comfortable with these when you read your BYTE magazine or when you walk into a computer store. Another important goal is to show you how to interface with displays, disk drives, and printers in your programs. For most of the examples in this and the following chapters we use IBM PC- and PS/2-type microcomputers.

OBJECTIVES

At the conclusion of this chapter, you should be able to:

1. Read and interpret data from the keyboard of an IBM PC- or PS/2-type microcomputer.

2. Describe the operation of basic hardware needed to produce raster scan text or graphics CRT displays.

3. Calculate the frequencies, frame buffer memory requirements, and memory access rate for a given-resolution raster scan display.

4. Describe how a video adapter such as a VGA displays 256 colors from a palette of 256K colors.

5. Use BIOS calls to display a text message on the CRT display of an IBM PC-compatible computer.

6. Use BIOS calls to produce graphics displays on the CRT display of an IBM PC-compatible computer.

7. Write simple C programs which use predefined functions to produce graphics displays on a CRT.

8. Describe how text and graphics displays are produced on large LCDs and plasma displays.

9. Show in general terms the formats in which digital data is stored on magnetic and optical disks.

10. Describe the operation of disk controller circuitry.

11. Use DOS function calls and C function calls to open, read, write, and close disk files.

12. Describe the print mechanism used in several common types of computer printers.

13. Describe how computer vision systems produce an image that can be stored in a digital memory.

14. Briefly describe how phoneme, formant filters, and linear predictive coding synthesizers produce human-sounding speech from a computer.

15. Briefly describe the basic principle used in speech-recognition systems.

16. Describe the operation and significance of a Digital Video Interactive system.

SYSTEM-LEVEL KEYBOARD INTERFACING

In Chapter 9 we discussed the tasks involved in getting meaningful data from a keyboard and in Figure 9-22 we showed you the hardware typically used to do these tasks in an IBM PC-type computer. Now we will show you how to read and interpret keyboard data in system-level programs.

When you press a key on an IBM PC-type computer, a type 9 interrupt is executed. The procedure for this interrupt reads the scan codes generated by the keyboard circuitry and determines the action to take, based on the code read. For certain special key combinations such as Shift-Print Screen or Ctrl-Alt-Del, the type 9 procedure will call other procedures to carry out the specified action. For standard keys the type 9 procedure will convert the scan codes to an ASCII equivalent code and put the ASCII code in a buffer. For special keys such as function keys and cursor-move keys the procedure generates *extended ASCII codes*.

To read the ASCII or extended ASCII codes from the buffer at the assembly language level, you use the BIOS INT 16H procedure. Perhaps you remember from the discussion of software interrupts in Chapter 8 that the ROMS in a microcomputer contain procedures for many input and output operations. Figure 8-9, for example, showed how you load some parameters in AH and AL

PARAMETERS FOR BIOS INT 16H KEYBOARD PROCEDURE

```
input:    AH = 0
function: Wait for next key pressed, return code
return:   key code in AL, scan code in AH


input:    AH = 1
function: Determine if character ready in buffer
return:   Zero flag = 1 - no character in buffer
          Zero flag = 0 - character in buffer


input:    AH = 2
function: Return status of Alt, Shift, Ctrl keys
return:   shift status in AL
```

FIGURE 13-1   Parameters for BIOS INT 16H BIOS procedure.

then execute the INT 17H instruction to send a character to a printer.

Figure 13-1 shows the format for the INT 16H procedure which you can use to read characters from the keyboard of an IBM PC- or PS/2-type computer. If you call the procedure with AH=0, execution will sit in a loop until a key is pressed. When a key is pressed, the procedure will return a value in AX. If the value returned in AL is not 0, then the value in AL is the ASCII code for the corresponding key or key combination shown in Figure 13-2a. Note that you can generate any desired hex value in AL by pressing the Alt key and the equivalent sequence of decimal digits on the numeric keypad. If the value returned in AL is zero, then the value in AH represents the extended ASCII code for one of the special keys or key combinations shown in Figure 13-2b.

If you call the INT 16H procedure with 1 in AH, the procedure will return with the carry flag set if there is no character in the buffer waiting to be read. If the

Value				Value			Value			Value			Value		
Hex	Dec	Symbol	Keystrokes	Hex	Dec	Keystrokes	Hex	Dec	Keystrokes	Hex	Dec	Keystrokes	Hex	Dec	Keystrokes
00	0	Blank (Null)	Ctrl 2	18	24	Ctrl X	2F	47	/	4A	74	J	65	101	e
01	1	☺	Ctrl A	19	25	Ctrl Y	30	48	0	4B	75	K	66	102	f
02	2	☻	Ctrl B	1A	26	Ctrl Z	31	49	1	4C	76	L	67	103	g
03	3	♥	Ctrl C	1B	27	Ctrl [, Esc, Shift Esc, Ctrl Esc	32	50	2	4D	77	M	68	104	h
04	4	♦	Ctrl D				33	51	3	4E	78	N	69	105	i
05	5	♣	Ctrl E				34	52	4	4F	79	O	6A	106	j
06	6	♠	Ctrl F	1C	28	Ctrl \	35	53	5	50	80	P	6B	107	k
07	7	•	Ctrl G	1D	29	Ctrl]	36	54	6	51	81	Q	6C	108	l
08	8	◘	Ctrl H, Backspace, Shift Backspace	1E	30	Ctrl 6	37	55	7	52	82	R	6D	109	m
				1F	31	Ctrl —	38	56	8	53	83	S	6E	110	n
09	9	○	Ctrl I	20	32	Space Bar, Shift Space, Ctrl Space, Alt Space	39	57	9	54	84	T	6F	111	o
0A	10	◎	Ctrl J, Ctrl ↵				3A	58	:	55	85	U	70	112	p
0B	11	♂	Ctrl K	21	33	!	3B	59	;	56	86	V	71	113	q
0C	12	♀	Ctrl L	22	34	"	3C	60	<	57	87	W	72	114	r
0D	13	♪	Ctrl M, ↵, Shift ↵	23	35	#	3D	61	=	58	88	X	73	115	s
0E	14	♫	Ctrl N	24	36	$	3E	62	>	59	89	Y	74	116	t
0F	15	☼	Ctrl O	25	37	%	3F	63	?	5A	90	Z	75	117	u
10	16	►	Ctrl P	26	38	&	40	64	@	5B	91	[	76	118	v
11	17	◄	Ctrl Q	27	39	'	41	65	A	5C	92	\	77	119	w
12	18	↕	Ctrl R	28	40	(	42	66	B	5D	93	]	78	120	x
13	19	‼	Ctrl S	29	41	)	43	67	C	5E	94	^	79	121	y
14	20	¶	Ctrl T	2A	42	*	44	68	D	5F	95	—	7A	122	z
15	21	§	Ctrl U	2B	43	+	45	69	E	60	96	`	7B	123	{
16	22	▬	Ctrl V	2C	44	'	46	70	F	61	97	a	7C	124	¦
17	23	↨	Ctrl W	2D	45	–	47	71	G	62	98	b	7D	125	}
				2E	46	.	48	72	H	63	99	c	7E	126	~
							49	73	I	64	100	d	7F	127	Ctrl –

(a)

FIGURE 13-2   IBM PC keys and keycodes. (a) Standard key codes returned in AL. (*Continued on next page.*)

Second Code	Function
3	Nul Character
15	←
16–25	Alt Q, W, E, R, T, Y, U, I, O, P
30–38	Alt A, S, D, F, G, H, J, K, L
44–50	Alt Z, X, C, V, B, N, M
59–68	F1 to F10 Function Keys Base Case
71	Home
72	↑
73	Page Up and Home Cursor
75	←
77	→
79	End
80	↓
81	Page Down and Home Cursor
82	Ins(Insert)
83	Del(Delete)
84–93	F11 to F20 (Uppercase F1 to F10)
94–103	F21 to F30 (Ctrl F1 to F10)
104–113	F31 to F40 (Alt F1 to F10)
114	Ctrl PrtSc (Start/Stop Echo to Printer)
115	Ctrl ← (Reverse Word)
116	Ctrl → (Advance Word)
117	Ctrl End [Erase to End of Line (EOL)]
118	Ctrl PgDn [Erase to End of Screen (EOS)]
119	Ctrl Home (Clear Screen and Home)
120–131	Alt 1, 2, 3, 4, 5, 6, 7, 8, 9, 0, -, = (Keys 2–13)
132	Ctrl PgUp (Top 25 Lines of Text and Home Cursor)

(b)

SHIFT STATUS BYTE RETURNED BY BIOS INT 16H

BIT   MEANING IF BIT IS A ONE

d0   Right shift key pressed

d1   Left shift key pressed

d2   Control key pressed

d3   Alt key pressed

d4   Scroll lock active

d5   Numeric lock active

D6   Caps lock active

D7   Insert state active

(c)

FIGURE 13-2 (*Continued*) (*b*) Extended ASCII codes returned in AH. (*c*) Status byte returned in AL with AH = 2 during call.

procedure returns with the carry flag = 0, the buffer contained a character, and that character has been read into AX as described before. This option allows you to check if a key has been pressed without having to sit in a loop until a key is pressed.

Finally, if you call the INT 16H procedure with a 2 in AH, the procedure will return the status of the Shift, Alt, and Ctrl keys, as shown in Figure 13-2c.

From the preceding discussion you can see that to interface with the keyboard from an assembly language program all you have to do is load the desired subfunction number (0, 1, or 2) in AH and execute the INT 16H instruction. The next question to answer is, How do you interface with the keyboard from a C program?

In the last chapter we showed you how to use predefined C functions such as scanf, getche, and gets to read characters from the keyboard. The problem with these functions is that they do not allow you to read anything but the standard ASCII codes (00–7FH). In many system programs you want to use the function keys, arrow keys, or other special keys to specify some course of action, so you need to be able to read in codes for these. The Turbo C++ run time libraries contain two predefined functions which you can call to read in key codes directly. Both of these use the BIOS INT 16H procedure.

The predefined function int bioskey (int cmd) will call the INT 16H procedure and pass it the subprocedure specified as cmd in the call. The statement key = bioskey(0);, for example, will wait until a key is pressed and assign the value returned in AX to key. You can then manipulate the value in key to determine which key was pressed.

The second way to read the keyboard is with the int86() function. The example program in Figure 13-3, page 438, shows how you can use this function to call the BIOS INT 16H procedure, but this function can be used to call any of the BIOS procedures. The key to using this function is to understand how the register values are passed to the function and how register values are returned to the calling program. The technique used to do this is a C data structure called a *union*. In simple terms a union is a memory location assigned to two or more variables, so that the contents can be accessed in two different ways. You might, for example, create a union of an integer and an unsigned character so that you could access either the entire 16 bits or the two 8-bit halves.

The header file dos.h contains the prototype for a union called REGS. This union is composed of two structures which represent the register set of the 8086. One structure represents the registers as 8-bit values. The other structure represents the registers as 16-bit values. This allows you to initialize an 8-bit register or a 16-bit register and read a value from an 8-bit register or from a 16-bit register.

In the example program in Figure 13-3, we declare a union of type REGS called rg. The statement rg.h.ah = 0; then initializes the ah element in the structure with a value of 0. The .h in the reference to the union indicates that we want to access the structure of 8-bit registers. To initialize the DX register with a value of 0, we would use a statement such as rg.x.dx = 0;.

The prototype for the int86 function is int86(int intno, union REGS *inregs, union REGS *outregs). What all this means is that you pass the INT number, a pointer to the union which contains the register values to pass to the function, and a pointer to the union which will receive the register values passed back to the calling program. In the program in Figure 13-3 we use the same union, rg, for the inregs and the outregs. The statement ch = rg.h.al copies the value placed in the al element of the rg union to the variable named ch.

The rest of the example in Figure 13-3 shows you how to examine the value returned by INT 16H to determine the action to take. If the value returned in AL is not zero, then the code is in the range of 00–FFH. We use

```
/* C PROGRAM F13-03.C */
#include<dos.h>
#include<stdio.h>
#include<conio.h>
#include<ctype.h>
void show_it(char c);

void main ()
{
    int count = 0;
    char ch; char *bptr;
    bptr = malloc(10000);         /* allocate memory for text buffer */
do
{
    union REGS rg;                /* declare union called rg */
        rg.h.ah = 0;              /* initialize ah element with 0 */
    int86(0x16, &rg, &rg);        /* call BIOS INT16H procedure */
    if((ch=rg.h.al) !=0)          /* standard ASCII if AL !=0 */
      {
      if(isprint(ch))             /* if ch is a printable character, */
        {
        *bptr =ch;                /* write to buffer   */
        putchar(ch);              /* write to screen   */
        bptr++; count++;          /* increment counter, pointer */
        }
        else                      /* if control code, decide action */
        {
        switch (ch){
           case 0x0d:             /* example, insert linefeed after CR */
             {
             *bptr =ch;           /* write CR to buffer   */
             putchar(ch);         /* write CR to screen   */
             bptr++; count++;     /* increment counter, pointer */
             ch = 0x0a;           /* code for linefeed */
             *bptr =ch;           /* write LF to buffer   */
             putchar(ch);         /* write LF to screen   */
             bptr++; count++;     /* increment counter, pointer */
             break;
             }
                }
        }
      }
    else                          /* character is extended ASCII */
     {
    ch = rg.h.ah;                 /* scan code returned in AH */
    switch (ch) {
        case 0x43: {
        show_it(ch); break;       /* F9 key */
                }
        case 0x44: {
        show_it(ch); exit();      /* F10 key */
                }
            }
     }
}
while(count<10000);
}
void show_it(char c)             /* display ASCII equivalent */
{                                /* for scan code */
    putchar(c);
}
```

FIGURE 13-3   C program showing how to use int86( ) function call to read
keyboard and decode the value read.

the predefined function isaprint() to determine if the code is a printable ASCII code, and if it is we write it to a buffer and send it to the screen. If it is not a printable code, we use a switch structure to determine what action to take. For the example here we showed you how to insert a linefeed character after a carriage return. You can add more case statements to perform the desired action for other special keys such as backspace.

If the value returned in AL is zero, the rg.h.ah element of the union will contain the scan code for the pressed key according to the values shown in Figure 13-2b. In the example in Figure 13-3 we show you how to use another switch structure to choose some action based on the code returned.

Now that you know more about reading characters from a microcomputer keyboard, let's dig into how character and graphics displays are produced.

MICROCOMPUTER DISPLAYS

Currently there are several different technologies used to display characters and graphics for a microcomputer. The most common type display is still the *cathode-ray tube* (CRT), so we will start the chapter with a discussion of the hardware and software for these displays. Later in the chapter we will discuss large *liquid-crystal displays* (LCDs) and plasma displays which are often used on laptop microcomputers.

Raster Scan Character Displays

RASTER SCAN BASICS

A CRT is basically a large, bottle-shaped vacuum tube. An electron gun at the rear of the tube produces a beam of electrons, which is directed toward the front of the tube by a high voltage. The inside surface of the front of the tube is coated with a phosphor substance which gives off light when it is struck by electrons. The color of the light given off is determined by the particular phosphor used.

The most common method of producing images on a CRT screen is to sweep the electron beam back and forth from left to right across the screen. When the beam reaches the right side of the screen, it is turned off (blanked) and retraced rapidly back to the left side of the screen to start over. If the beam is slowly swept from the top of the screen to the bottom of the screen as it is swept back and forth horizontally, the entire screen appears lighted. When the beam reaches the bottom of the screen, it is blanked and rapidly retraced back to the top to start over. A display produced in this way is referred to as a *raster scan* display. To produce an image, the electron beam is turned on or off as it sweeps across the screen. The trick here is to get the beam intensity or *video information* synchronized with the horizontal and vertical sweeping so the display is stable.

For a first example, Figure 13-4 shows the scanning used to produce pictures on a TV set and displays on some computer monitors. To get better picture resolu-

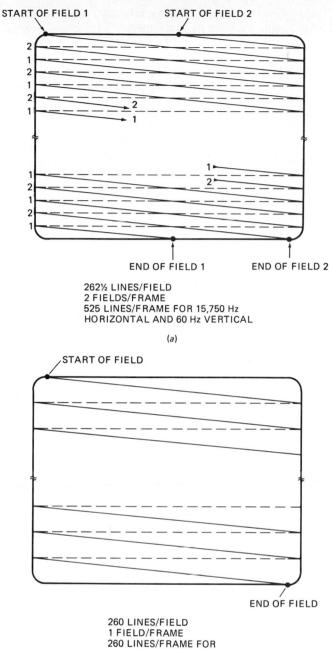

262½ LINES/FIELD
2 FIELDS/FRAME
525 LINES/FRAME FOR 15,750 Hz
HORIZONTAL AND 60 Hz VERTICAL

(a)

260 LINES/FIELD
1 FIELD/FRAME
260 LINES/FRAME FOR
15,600 Hz HORIZONTAL AND
60Hz VERTICAL

(b)

FIGURE 13-4   CRT scanning methods. (a) Interlaced. (b) Noninterlaced.

tion and avoid flicker, TVs use *interlaced scanning*. As shown in Figure 13-4a, this means the scan lines for one sweep of the beam from the top of the screen to bottom (field) are offset and interleaved with those of the next field. After every other field the scan lines repeat. Therefore, two fields are required to make a complete picture or frame. To give you some numbers for reference, black-and-white TVs in the United States use a horizontal sweep frequency of 15,750 Hz and a vertical sweep frequency of 60 Hz. Sixty fields per second are then swept out. Since each complete picture or frame consists of two fields, the frame rate is 30 frames/second. This is fast enough to avoid flicker. The beam sweeps horizontally 15,750 times per second, so during the $\frac{1}{60}$ s required for the beam to go from the top of the screen to the bottom, the beam will have swept out 15,750/60 or 262.5 horizontal scan lines. A complete frame therefore consists of 525 horizontal scan lines.

Some computer monitors use *noninterlaced scanning* such as that shown in Figure 13-4b. In this case the beam traces out the same path on each trip from the top of the screen to the bottom. For a noninterlaced display the frame rate and the field rate are the same. A horizontal sweep rate of 15,600 Hz and a vertical sweep rate of 60 Hz gives 15,600/60 or 260 horizontal sweep lines per field.

The three basic circuits required to produce a display on a CRT are the vertical oscillator, which produces the vertical sweep signal for the beam; the horizontal oscillator, which produces the horizontal sweep signal for the beam; and the video amplifier, which controls the intensity of the electron beam. A *CRT* or *video monitor* contains just a CRT and this basic drive circuitry. A CRT *terminal* contains this basic drive circuitry plus a keyboard, memory, communication circuitry, and a dedicated microprocessor to control all these parts.

The basic control circuitry for a *monochrome* (one-color) CRT monitor requires three input signals to operate properly. It must have horizontal sync pulses to keep the horizontal oscillator synchronized, vertical sync pulses to keep the vertical oscillator synchronized, and video information that controls the intensity of the beam as it sweeps across the screen. It is important that these three signals be synchronized with each other so that a particular dot of video information is displayed at the same point on the screen during each frame. If you have seen a TV picture rolling or a TV picture with jagged horizontal lines in it, you have seen what happens if the horizontal, vertical, and video information get out of synchronization. Now let's see how we generate these three signals to display characters on a CRT screen.

OVERVIEW OF CHARACTER DISPLAY CONTROL SYSTEM

Characters or graphics are generated on a CRT screen as a pattern of light and dark dots. The dots are created by turning the electron beam on and off as it sweeps across the screen. Figure 13-5 shows how the letters P

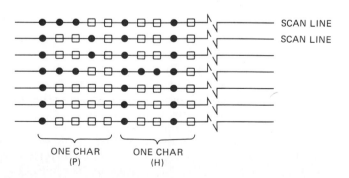

FIGURE 13-5 Producing a character display on a CRT screen with dots.

and H can be displayed in the upper-left corner of the screen in this way. The round dots in the figure represent the beam on, and the square boxes represent the beam off. As you can see, in this example the dot matrix for each character is 5 dots wide and 7 dots high. Other common dot-matrix sizes for character displays are 7 by 9, and 7 by 12, and 9 by 14.

Figure 13-6 shows a block diagram of the circuitry needed to keep the pattern of dots for a page of text displayed on the screen of a CRT monitor. For this example assume that the display has 25 rows of characters with 80 characters per row.

The ASCII codes for the characters to be displayed on the screen are stored in a RAM. This RAM is often referred to as the *frame buffer* or the *display refresh RAM*. The RAM must contain at least one byte location for each character to be displayed. A display size of 25 rows with 80 characters in each row then requires 25 × 80 or about 2 Kbytes RAM. In an actual circuit this RAM is set up so that the microprocessor can access it to change the stored characters, or the display refresh circuitry can access it to keep the display refreshed on the screen.

The dot patterns for each scan line of each character to be displayed are stored in a ROM called a *character generator* ROM. Figure 13-7 shows the matrix for a typical character-generator ROM. This ROM uses a 7 by 9 matrix for the actual character, but the total dot space for each character is a 9 by 14 dot matrix. The extra dots are included to leave space between characters and between rows of characters. Also, the extra space allows lowercase letters to be dropped in the matrix so that descenders are shown correctly. Each dot row in Figure 13-7 represents the pattern of dots for a horizontal scan line of the character.

To start the display in the upper left corner, the character counter and the character row counter outputs are all 0's so the ASCII code for the first character in the display RAM is addressed. The ASCII code from the addressed location is output by the RAM to the address inputs of the character-generator ROM. These inputs essentially tell the character generator which character is to be displayed.

To keep track of which line in a character row is currently being swept out, we use a scan line counter. For our example here each row of characters has 14 dot rows or scan lines, so the scan line counter is a modulo-14 counter. The outputs of this counter are connected to four additional address inputs on the character generator ROM.

Given an ASCII code and a dot row count, the character-generator ROM will output the 9-bit dot pattern for one dot row in the character. For the first scan across the screen, the counter will output 0000, so the dot pattern output will be that for dot row 0000 of the character.

The output from the character generator is in parallel form. In order to turn the beam on and off at the correct time as it sweeps across the screen, this dot pattern must be converted to serial form with a parallel-in, serial-out shift register. The high-frequency clock used to clock this shift register is called the *dot clock* because it

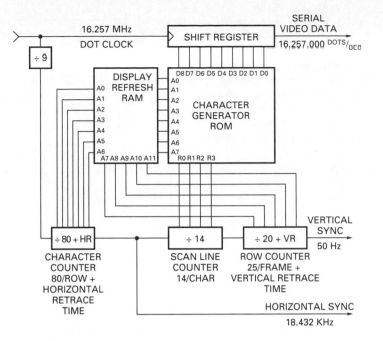

FIGURE 13-6 Block diagram of circuitry to produce dot-matrix character display on CRT.

controls the rate at which dot information is sent out to the video amplifier. As you can see in Figure 13-6, we used a dot clock frequency of 16.257 MHz for this example.

After the nine dots for the first scan line of the first character are shifted out, the character counter is incremented by 1. The outputs of the character counter are connected to some of the address inputs of the display refresh RAM, so when this count is incremented, the ASCII code for the next character in the top row is addressed in the refresh RAM. The ASCII code for this second character will be output to the character-generator ROM. Since the dot line counter inputs to the

ROM are still 0000, the ROM will output the 9-bit dot pattern for the top scan line of the second character in the top row of characters on the screen. When all the dots for the top scan line of this character are all shifted out, the character counter will be incremented by 1 again, and the process will be repeated for the third character in the top row of characters. The process continues until the first scan line for all 80 characters in the top row of characters is traced out.

A horizontal sync pulse is then produced to cause the beam to sweep back to the left side of the screen. After the beam retraces to the left, the character counter is rolled back to zero to point to the ASCII code for the first

CAPITAL OR UPPERCASE

DOT ROW									
0000	0	0	0	0	0	0	0	0	0
0001	0	1	1	1	1	1	1	0	0
0010	0	1	0	0	0	0	0	1	0
0011	0	1	0	0	0	0	0	1	0
0100	0	1	0	0	0	0	0	1	0
0101	0	1	1	1	1	1	1	0	0
0110	0	1	0	0	0	0	0	0	0
0111	0	1	0	0	0	0	0	0	0
1000	0	1	0	0	0	0	0	0	0
1001	0	1	0	0	0	0	0	0	0
1010	0	0	0	0	0	0	0	0	0
1011	0	0	0	0	0	0	0	0	0
1100	0	0	0	0	0	0	0	0	0
1101	0	0	0	0	0	0	0	0	0

SMALL OR LOWERCASE

0	0	0	0	0	0	0	0	0
0	0	0	0	0	0	0	0	0
0	0	0	0	0	0	0	0	0
0	0	0	0	0	0	0	0	0
0	1	0	1	1	1	0	0	0
0	1	1	0	0	0	1	0	0
0	1	0	0	0	0	1	0	0
0	1	0	0	0	0	1	0	0
0	1	1	0	0	0	1	0	0
0	1	0	1	1	1	0	0	0
0	1	0	0	0	0	0	0	0
0	1	0	0	0	0	0	0	0
0	0	0	0	0	0	0	0	0
0	0	0	0	0	0	0	0	0

FIGURE 13-7 Dot matrix for 9 × 14 character-generator ROM.

character in the row again. The dot line counter (R0–R3) is incremented to 0001 so that the character generator will now output the dot patterns for the second scan line of each character. After the dot pattern for the second scan line of the first character in the row is shifted out to the video amplifier, the character counter is incremented to point to the ASCII code for the second character in the display RAM. The process repeats until all the scan lines for one row of characters have been scanned.

The character row counter is then incremented by 1. The outputs of the character counter and the character row counter now point to the display RAM address where the ASCII code for the first character of the second row of characters is stored. The process we described for the first row will be repeated for the second row of characters. After the second row of characters is swept out, the process will go on to the third row of characters, and then on to the fourth, and so on until all 25 rows of characters have been swept out.

When all the character rows have been swept out, the beam is at the lower right corner of the screen. The counter circuitry then sends out a horizontal sync pulse to retrace the beam to the left side of the screen and a vertical sync pulse to retrace the beam to the top of the screen. When the beam reaches the top left corner of the screen, the whole *screen-refresh* process that we have described will repeat. As we mentioned before, the entire screen must be scanned (refreshed) 30 to 75 times a second to avoid a blinking display. For the example in Figure 13-6 we used 50 Hz for the frame-refresh rate. Now let's look at a simple example of an actual CRT controller.

THE IBM PC MONOCHROME ADAPTER

Figure 13-8 shows a block diagram for the IBM PC monochrome display adapter board. This adapter is somewhat obsolete, but it is a good next step from the generic circuit in Figure 13-6. Take a look at Figure 13-8 and see what parts you recognize from our previous discussions. You should quickly find the CRT controller, character generator, and dot shift register. Next, find the 2-Kbyte memory where the ASCII codes for the characters to be displayed are stored. To the right of this memory is another 2-Kbyte memory used to store an *attribute* code for each character. An attribute code specifies whether the character is to be displayed normally, with an underline, with increased or decreased intensity, blinking, etc. You may have observed, for example, that it is common practice to display a screen menu at reduced intensity so it does not distract from the main text on the screen. For future reference Figure 13-9 shows the meaning of the bits in the attribute byte. If the B bit is a 1, the displayed character will blink. If the I bit is a 1, the character will be highlighted; in other words, it will have increased intensity. These bits give you several choices for how you want each character displayed on the screen.

As we discussed in a preceding section, ASCII codes from the display refresh RAM go to the character generator. Also going to the character generator are four address lines which specify the dot line of the character

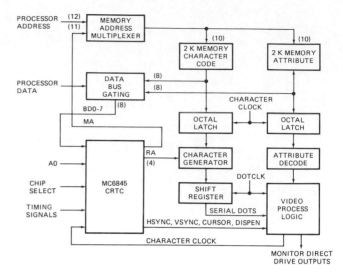

FIGURE 13-8   Block diagram of IBM PC monochrome adapter board.

scanned. The counter which generates this address is contained in the MC6845 CRT controller device. The output from the character generator goes to a shift register to be converted to serial form for the video amplifier. The shift register is clocked by the 16.257-MHz dot clock. Circuitry in the video process logic section divides this dot clock signal by 9 to produce the character clock signal of 1,787,904 Hz. This character clock signal pulses each time a new ASCII character needs to be fetched from the display refresh RAM and a new attribute from the attribute RAM.

Next observe that there is a multiplexer in series with the address lines going to the character and attribute memories. This multiplexer is connected so that either the CPU or the CRT controller can access the display refresh RAM.

To keep the display refreshed, the 6845 CRT controller device sends out the memory address for a character code and an attribute code. The character clock signal

DISPLAY–CHARACTER CODE BYTE								ATTRIBUTE BYTE							
7	6	5	4	3	2	1	0	7	6	5	4	3	2	1	0

EVEN ADDRESS   ODD ADDRESS

(a)

ATTRIBUTE FUNCTION	ATTRIBUTE BYTE							
	7	6	5	4	3	2	1	0
	B	R	G	B	I	R	G	B
	FG	BACKGROUND				FOREGROUND		
NORMAL	B	0	0	0	I	1	1	1
REVERSE VIDEO	B	1	1	1	I	0	0	0
NONDISPLAY (BLACK)	B	0	0	0	I	0	0	0
NONDISPLAY (WHITE)	B	1	1	1	I	1	1	1

I = HIGHLIGHTED FOREGROUND (CHARACTER)
B = BLINKING FOREGROUND (CHARACTER)

(b)

FIGURE 13-9   Data storage format for IBM PC character displays. (a) Character byte and attribute byte in word. (b) Attribute byte format.

latches the code from memory for the character generator and the attribute code for the attribute decode circuitry. The character clock also increments the address counter in the 6845 to point to the next character code in memory. The next character clock transfers the next codes to the character generator and attribute decoder. The process cycles through all of the characters on the page and then repeats.

Now, when you want to display some new characters on the screen, you simply have the CPU execute some instructions which write the ASCII codes for the new characters to the appropriate address in the display RAM. When the address decoding circuitry detects a display RAM address, it produces a signal which toggles the multiplexers so that the CPU has access to the display RAM. The question that probably occurs to you at this point is, What happens if the 6845 and the CPU both want to access the display RAM at the same time? There are several solutions to this problem. One solution is to allow the CPU to access the RAM only during horizontal and/or vertical retrace times. Another solution is to interleave 6845 accesses and CPU accesses. This is how it is done on the IBM monochrome board.

The CPU is allowed to access the RAM during one-half of the character clock signal and the 6845 is allowed to access the RAM during the other half of the character clock signal. If the CPU tries to access the display RAM during the controller's half of the character clock cycle, a not-ready signal from the CRT controller board will cause the processor to insert WAIT states until the half of the character clock signal when it can access the display refresh RAM.

The 6845 CRT controller in Figure 13-8 contains the chain of counters shown in Figure 13-6 and other circuitry needed to produce horizontal blanking pulses, vertical blanking pulses, a cursor, scrolling, and highlighting for a CRT display. Several manufacturers offer CRT controller ICs that contain different amounts of the required circuitry. The Motorola MC6845 is used in both the monochrome and the color/graphics adapter boards for the IBM PC.

CRT DISPLAY TIMING AND FREQUENCIES

There are many different horizontal, vertical, and dot clock frequencies commonly used in raster scan CRT displays. The horizontal sweep frequency is usually in the range of 15 to 50 kHz, the vertical sweep frequency is usually 50 or 60 Hz, and the dot clock frequency is usually in the range of 10 to 100 MHz. As a first example, let's look a little closer at the frequencies used in the IBM PC monochrome adapter we discussed in the preceding section.

To refresh your memory, the IBM PC monochrome display adapter produces a display of 25 rows of 80 characters/row. Each character is produced as a 7 by 9 matrix of dots in a 9 by 14 dot space. This means that because clear space is left around each actual character, each character actually uses 9 dot spaces horizontally and 14 scan lines vertically.

The active horizontal display area then is 9 dots/character × 80 characters/line or 720 dots per line. The active vertical display area is 25 rows × 14 scan lines/row or 350 scan lines.

Now, according to the IBM Technical Reference Manual, the monochrome adapter uses a dot clock frequency of 16.257 MHz. This means that the video shift register is shifting out 16,257,000 dots/second. The manual also indicates that the board uses a horizontal sweep frequency of 18,432 lines/second. Dividing 16,257,000 dots per second by 18,432 lines per second tells you that the board is shifting out 882 dots/line. Just above we showed you that the active display area of a line is only 720 dots. The extra 162 dot times actually present give the beam time to get from the right edge of the active display to the right edge of the screen, retrace to the left edge of the screen, and sweep to the left edge of the active display area. The large number of extra dot times is necessary because most monitors have a large amount of *overscan*. Overscan means that the beam is actually swept far off the left and right sides of the screen. This is done so that the portion of the sweep actually displaying the characters is linear and the characters do not run off the edges of the screen.

The manual for the monochrome display adapter also indicates that the frame rate is 50 Hz. In other words, the beam sweeps from the top of the screen to the bottom and back again 50 times/s. To see how many horizontal lines are in each frame, you can divide the 18,432 lines/s by 50 frames/s to give 369 scan lines/frame. As we showed before, the active vertical display area is 350 lines. The 19 extra scan line times give the beam time to get to the bottom of the screen, retrace to the top of the screen, and get to the start of the active display area again.

Another point it is appropriate to mention here concerns the bandwidth required by the video amplifier in the monitor. In order to produce a sharp display the video amplifier in the monitor must be able to turn on and off fast enough so that dots and undots don't smear together. For our example here, the dot clock frequency is 16.257 MHz. This means that the dot shift register is shifting out 16,257,000 dots/s. If alternating dots and undots are being shifted out, then the waveform on the serial output pin of the shift register will be a square wave with a frequency of half that of the dot clock or 8.1285 MHz. In order to produce a clear display with this many dots per line, then, the video amplifier in the monitor connected to the display adapter must have a bandwidth of at least 8 MHz.

This bandwidth requirement is the reason that normal TV sets connected to computers cannot display high-resolution 80-character lines for word processing, etc. In order to filter out the 4.5-MHz sound subcarrier signal and the 3.58-MHz color subcarrier, the bandwidth of TV video amplifiers is limited to 3 MHz or less.

A final point we want to make about CRT timing is how often the display-refresh RAM has to be accessed. As the circuitry scans one line of the display, it has to access a new character in RAM after each 9 dots are shifted out, assuming 9 dots horizontally per character. Dividing the dot clock frequency of 16,257,000 dots per second by 9 dots/character tells you that characters are read from RAM at a rate of about 1,806,333 characters/

s, or one character every 553 ns! As we discussed in the last section, the CRT controller device accesses the display refresh RAM during one half of this time, and the microprocessor accesses the frame buffer RAM during the other half of this time. Only about 200 ns are actually available for access to the RAM during each half of the character clock time. As we show later, higher resolution and color displays require even faster memory access.

Raster Scan Graphics Displays

MONOCHROME GRAPHICS

As we discussed previously, characters can be displayed on a CRT screen by sending out a series of dots and undots to the video amplifier. The ASCII codes for the characters to be displayed are stored in a display-refresh RAM. As shown in Figure 13-6, the character-generator ROM uses an ASCII code from RAM and a 4-bit code from the dot row counter to produce the dot pattern for the specified scan line in the character.

Now, suppose that the character generator is left out of this circuit and the outputs of the RAM are connected directly to the inputs of an 8-bit dot shift register. And further suppose that instead of storing the ASCII codes for characters in the RAM, we store in successive memory locations the dot patterns we want for each 8 dots of a scan line.

When a byte is read from the RAM and loaded into the shift register, the stored dot pattern will be shifted out to the CRT beam to produce the desired pattern for 8 dots along a section of a scan line on the screen. When the next RAM byte is transferred to the shift register, it will produce the next 8 dots along the scan line. The process is continued until all the dot positions on the screen have been refreshed. The entire screen then can be thought of as a matrix of dots. Each dot can be programmed to be on or off by putting a 1 or a 0 in the corresponding bit location in RAM. A graphics display produced in this way is known as a *bit-mapped raster scan display*. Each dot or, in some cases, block of dots on the screen is called a *picture element*. Most people shorten this to *pixel* or *pel*. For our discussions here let's assume a pixel is 1 dot.

Now, suppose that we want a monochrome graphics display of 640 pels horizontally by 200 pels vertically. This gives a total of 200 × 640 or 128,000 dots on the screen. Since each dot corresponds to a bit location in memory, this means that we have to have at least 128,000 bits or 16 Kbytes of RAM to hold the pel information for just one display screen. Compare this with the 4 Kbytes needed to hold the ASCII codes and attributes for an 80 by 25 character display. As we will show you a little later, producing a color graphics display with a large number of pels requires even more memory.

Monochrome graphics displays get boring after a while, so let's see how you can get some color in the picture.

COLOR MONITORS AND COLOR GRAPHICS

The screen of a monochrome CRT is coated with a single type phosphor, which produces a color specific to that phosphor when bombarded with electrons from the single electron gun at the rear of the tube. To produce a color CRT display, we apply dots or bars of red, green, and blue phosphors to the inside of the CRT. One very common approach is to have dots of the three phosphors in a line pattern as shown in Figure 13-10. The dots are close enough together so that to your eye they appear as a single dot or pixel. Three separate electron beams are used to bombard the three different phosphors. A "shadow mask" just behind the screen of the CRT helps prevent electrons intended for one color phosphor from falling on the other color phosphors. The distance between the holes in the shadow mask of a color CRT or the distance between pixels on the screen is referred to as its *pitch*. The pitch of commonly available CRTs is in the range of 0.21 mm to 0.66 mm. Smaller pitch and smaller dots mean that more dots can be put on the screen and therefore the screen has better resolution. The trade-off, however, is that as the pitch and dot size are made smaller, the beam current must be increased to get acceptable intensity. A large percentage of the beam current hits the shadow mask, and if this current is too high, it may overheat and warp the shadow mask and permanently distort the image on the screen.

A CRT monitor designed to produce color displays is commonly referred to as an *RGB monitor* or an *RGBI monitor*. In addition to red, green, and blue signal inputs, an RGB monitor has a horizontal sync input, a vertical sync input, and—in some cases—an intensity input. An RGB monitor must be designed to work with the display format and sync frequencies of the circuitry in the microcomputer. Fortunately, some monitors such as the NEC MultiSync, the Sony Multiscan, and the Magnavox MVX9CM will work correctly with a wide range of display formats and sync frequencies.

The apparent color of a pixel to your eye is determined by the intensity ratio of the three electron beams and the total intensity of the three beams. Figure 13-11

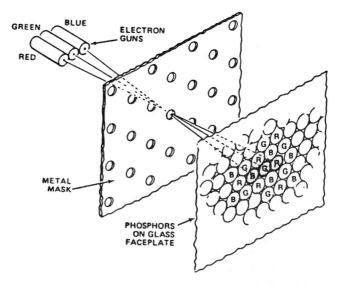

FIGURE 13-10 Three-color phosphor dot pattern used to produce color pixels on a CRT screen.

I	R	G	B	COLOR
0	0	0	0	BLACK
0	0	0	1	BLUE
0	0	1	0	GREEN
0	0	1	1	CYAN
0	1	0	0	RED
0	1	0	1	MAGENTA
0	1	1	0	BROWN
0	1	1	1	WHITE
1	0	0	0	GRAY
1	0	0	1	LIGHT BLUE
1	0	1	0	LIGHT GREEN
1	0	1	1	LIGHT CYAN
1	1	0	0	LIGHT RED
1	1	0	1	LIGHT MAGENTA
1	1	1	0	YELLOW
1	1	1	1	HIGH INTENSITY WHITE

FIGURE 13-11   Sixteen colors produced by different on and off combinations of red, green, and blue beams at normal and increased intensity.

shows 16 colors that can be produced when different combinations of on and off signals are applied to the three beams and to an overall intensity input. A 1 in the I bit means that the overall intensity of the beam is increased to lighten the color, as shown. If all three beams are off, the dot is, of course, black. If the beams are all turned on, then the dot will appear white. Other combinations give the other 14 shades shown.

To give a greater range of colors, newer monitors are designed to accept analog RGB signals instead of just digital RGB signals. The signals for these analog inputs are produced with D/A converters. Using a 2-bit D/A converter to produce each color signal, for example, gives $4 \times 4 \times 4$ or 64 colors. However, as we discuss in the next section, increasing the number of colors increases the amount of memory needed in the frame buffer and the rate at which the memory must be accessed.

PALETTES, PIXEL PLANES, AND VRAMS

For a monochrome graphics display, the data for each pixel is stored in a single bit in the display-refresh RAM. Color displays require more than 1 bit per pixel, because the red, green, and blue data for each pixel must be stored. For example, 2 bits are required to specify one of 4 colors, 3 bits are required to specify one of 8 colors, 8 bits are required to specify one of 256 colors, etc. The number of colors we want to produce on a display then has a direct impact on the amount of memory required for the frame buffer. As an example of this, suppose that we want a 640×480 pixel display with 256 colors on an 8086 system. The total number of pixels in the display is 640×480, or 307,200. To specify one of 256 colors, 8 bits (1 byte) are required for each pixel. The total amount of frame buffer memory needed then is 307,200 bytes. Aside from the cost, this is an excessive

amount of memory to devote to the display in a system that can address a total of only 1 Mbyte of memory.

To reduce the number of bits required for storing pixel data and still be able to display a wide range of colors, we use a *palette* scheme. The term palette is used here in about the same way an artist uses the term. An artist's palette holds the paint colors that he or she has available. The artist, for example, may have 16 colors on the palette, but for a particular painting he or she may use only 4 of the colors. We might say, then, that the artist has chosen 4 colors from a palette of 16.

As a first graphics example of this, the IBM Color Graphics Adapter board (CGA) can display medium resolution (320×200 pixel) graphics with 4 colors from a palette of 16 colors. Since only 4 colors are used at a time, only 2 bits of memory are required to hold the data for each pixel.

As a second example of a graphics palette, we might for our 640×480 pixel system decide to display 16 colors from a palette of 256, instead of all 256 colors. Only 4 bits are required to store the pixel data for 1 of 16 colors, so the frame buffer can be half the size it would be for a direct 256-color display. A little later we will take a look at how different systems implement the palette approach in hardware.

Another limiting factor in the design of a high-resolution color graphics system is the rate at which pixel data can be read from the frame buffer. For example, suppose that we want a 640×480 pixel display with 256 colors. As we said before, this requires 1 byte of memory per pixel, or a total of 307,200 bytes of memory. Assuming a frame rate of 50 Hz, each byte would have to be read from memory 50 times per second. This corresponds to 15,360,000 bytes per second, or 1 byte every 65 ns. (The time is actually shorter than this because all 307,200 accesses must occur during the active display time.) As we explained in Chapter 11, the read cycle times for common DRAMs is considerably longer than 65 ns. This means that we can't use DRAMs for the frame buffer unless we can find some way to allow more time for each access. There are several ways to do this.

The first step we take to give more time for the refresh controller access to the frame buffer is to allow the microprocessor to access the buffer only during horizontal and vertical retrace times. This gives all the time between characters or pixels to the controller instead of timesharing as we described for the monochrome adapter board.

A second way to reduce the required memory access rate is to use the palette scheme to reduce the number of bits required to store the data for each pixel. As we showed before, reducing a display to 16 colors from a palette of 256 instead of a direct 256-color display cuts the size of the display memory in half. Since only 4 bits are required to specify one of 16 colors, the data for 4 pixels can be packed in a single word, as shown in Figure 13-12a, page 446. Each memory access then reads in the data for 4 pixels.

A third method of reducing the access rate for the frame buffer is to set the memory up as parallel planes. Figure 13-12b attempts to show this in diagram form for a system which requires 4 bits per pixel. As you can

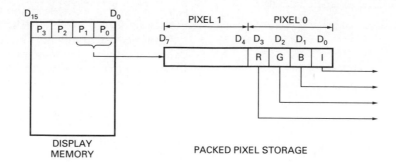

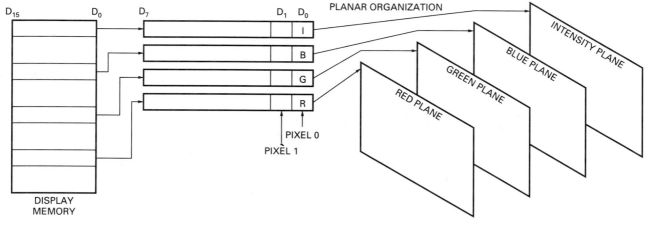

FIGURE 13-12 Frame buffer memory configurations. (a) Packed pixel. (b) Planar.

see, the 4 data bits for a pixel are stored at the same bit position in four different memory locations. When the controller transfers a word from each of the four memory locations to its internal registers, it has all the data it needs for 16 pixels. During the time that these 16 pixels are being swept out, the DRAMs will recover and can be accessed again. Additional planes can be added in parallel to store more bits per pixel.

Still another method of solving the memory access rate problem is to build the frame buffer with special DRAMs called *video RAMs* or *VRAMs*. Figure 13-13 shows a block diagram of the TI TMS44C251 VRAM. The DRAM section of the device consists of four arrays, which each store 256 Kbits. To the DRAM controller and the microprocessor circuitry, this device functions as a 256K × 4 device for read and write operations. The DRAM controller will supply RAS, CAS, multiplexed address, and refresh signals to it just as it would to any other DRAM.

To output data to a video controller, however, the 512 bits stored in each row in a DRAM array are transferred in parallel to a 512-bit register. The outputs of the register are connected to a 512-input multiplexer, which routes one of the register outputs to an SDQ output. As the multiplexer is stepped through its 512 positions, it outputs the 512 data bits one after the other to the SDQ output. The point here is that a VRAM can rapidly shift

out the data for 512 pixels. A TMS44C251, for example, can shift out bits at up to 33 MHz, which is more than fast enough for a 800 × 512 pixel display. (Not counting overscan, this calculation is: (800 × 512 pixels/frame) × 60 frames/s = 24,576,000 pixels/s).

VRAMs can be used to store data in packed pixel

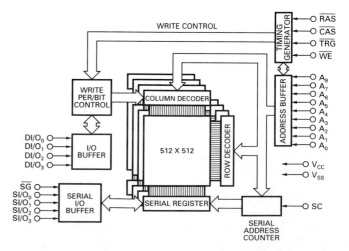

FIGURE 13-13 Block diagram of TI TMS44C251 video RAM (VRAM). (*Courtesy Texas Instruments Inc.*)

format or in planar format. Probably the easiest format to visualize is the planar. A single TMS44C251 can store four complete bit planes for a 512 × 512 pixel display. The devices can be cascaded to give scan lines longer than 512 pixels, or more than 4 bit planes. VRAMS are somewhat more expensive than standard DRAMS, but they make it relatively easy to implement a high-resolution display.

Now that you have a general awareness of how color graphics are produced, let's look at some specific examples.

Common Microcomputer Display Formats and Hardware

INTRODUCTION

There are an almost unbelievably large number of hardware configurations and formats for microcomputer displays. Figure 13-14 is an attempt to show the major display formats available on various IBM-type microcomputers. Reading the table from top to bottom essentially traces the development steps for IBM personal computer graphics during the last 10 years.

The IBM PC, the PC/XT, and the PC/AT do not have built-in graphics capability. For these computers you choose the text/graphics capability you want, buy the appropriate adapter board, plug it into one of the I/O slots in the motherboard, and connect a compatible monitor.

As we described in the preceding section, the IBM monochrome adapter board produces an 80 × 25 character display, but it does not produce graphics. An improvement on the basic monochrome adapter was the Hercules, Inc. monochrome adapter, which can display monochrome text or graphics in a 720 × 348 pixel format.

ADAPTER	MODE	RESOLUTION	COLORS PALETTE	SIGNAL	COMPUTERS
CGA	ALPHA	25x80	4/16	DIGITAL	PC,XT,AT
	LOW RES	160x100	4/16	DIGITAL	PC,XT,AT
	MED RES	320x200	4/16	DIGITAL	PC,XT,AT
	HI RES	640x400	2/16	DIGITAL	PC,XT,AT
HERCULES	MONO	720x348	2	DIGITAL	PC,XT,AT
	COLOR	720x348	16/64	DIGITAL	PC,XT,AT
EGA		640x350	16/64	DIGITAL	PC,XT,AT
MGA		320x200	256	ANALOG	PS2-25,30
		640x480	2	ANALOG	PS2-25,30
VGA	11H	640x480	2	ANALOG	PS2-50,80
	12H	640x480	16/256K	ANALOG	
	13H	640x200	256/256K	ANALOG	
SUPER VGA		640x480	256/256K	ANALOG	ADAPTER
8514/A		1024x768	256/256K	ANALOG	ADAPTER

FIGURE 13-14 Major display formats available on various IBM-type microcomputers.

The most commonly used graphics format on the IBM Color Graphics Adapter (CGA) adapter is the medium-resolution (320 × 200 pixel) graphics mode, which displays 4 colors from a palette of 16 colors. A CGA adapter also has an alphanumeric or character mode, but in this mode it uses only an 8 × 8 dot matrix for each character. This makes its text display unpleasant to look at for long periods of time.

To solve this problem IBM developed the Enhanced Graphics Adapter (EGA) board. The EGA board has 25 × 80 text mode, which uses an 8 × 14 dot matrix for characters so text is more readable than that produced by a CGA card. The EGA board can operate in the CGA graphics modes and other graphic modes such as a 640 × 350 display with 16 colors from a palette of 64. To be able to display all the 64 colors in this mode, the monitor used must have a red-intensified input, a green-intensified input, and a blue-intensified input in addition to the standard red, green, and blue inputs.

Further improvement came with the IBM PS/2 line of microcomputers, which have CRT controllers included on their motherboards. The Multicolor Graphics Array (MCGA) found on the PS/2 Models 25 and 30 gives these machines all the display modes of an EGA and several others. Among the additional display modes are a 320 × 200 pixel display mode with 256 colors and a 640 × 480 pixel two-color display mode.

In the PS/2 models 50, 60, 70, and 80, a video graphics array (VGA) device produces a wide variety of display modes. In addition to EGA-compatible modes, a VGA has a 640 × 480 graphics display with 16 colors from a palette of 256K, a 320 × 200 graphics mode with 256 colors from a palette of 256K, and 25 × 80 text mode which uses an 8 × 16 dot matrix for characters.

To achieve 256 colors the MCGA and VGA circuits generate analog red, green, and blue signals instead of the digital RGB signals produced by EGA and earlier display adapters. The monitor for an MCGA or VGA system must be able to accept the analog color signals. Incidentally, VGA and other high-resolution graphics boards are availble for PC-, PC/XT-, and PC/AT-type computers.

In addition to built-in VGA capability, the PS/2 models 60, 70, and 80 have an I/O slot especially designed for a high-resolution graphics board such as the 8514/A. The 8514/A uses a custom two-chip set to provide graphics modes with up to 1024 × 768 pixels and 256 from a palette of 256K.

Obviously we can't describe here all the details of all the graphics adapters and modes shown in Figure 13-14. In the following sections we will briefly discuss the hardware used to implement a CGA adapter, an EGA adapter, and a VGA adapter. In a later section we show you how to write characters or dots of a desired color to each of these basic display types.

THE IBM PC COLOR GRAPHICS ADAPTER BOARD

Figure 13-15, page 448, shows a block diagram of the IBM PC Color Graphics Adapter (CGA) board. This board again uses the Motorola MC6845 CRT controller device to do the overall display control. As we described in a

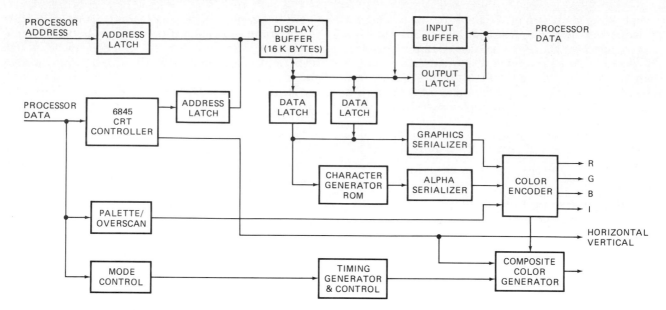

FIGURE 13-15   The block diagram of the IBM PC Color Graphics Adapter (CGA) board.

previous section, the 6845 produces the sequential addresses required for the display-refresh RAM, the horizontal sync pulses, and the vertical sync pulses. As you can see by the signals shown in the lower right corner of Figure 13-15, the adapter board is designed to drive either a monitor with separate red, green, and blue inputs or a *composite video color monitor*, which has all the required signals combined on a single line. The 16-Kbyte display-refresh RAM on the CGA board is *dual-ported* so that it can be accessed by either the system processor or the CRT controller.

This adapter board can operate in either a character mode or a graphics mode. In the character mode it uses a character-generator ROM and shift registers (alpha serializer) to produce the serial dot information for the RGB outputs. In the character or alphanumeric mode each character is represented by 2 bytes in the display-refresh RAM in the format shown in Figure 13-9a. The even-addressed or lower byte contains the 8-bit ASCII code for the character to be displayed. The odd-addressed or upper byte contains an attribute code, as shown in Figure 13-9b. The lower 4 bits of this attribute byte use the codes shown in Figure 13-11 to specify the color of the displayed characters. Bits 4–7 of the attribute byte allow you to specify the background color from among the first eight choices shown in Figure 13-11. The B bit in the attribute byte allows you to specify that the character will blink. Only 4 Kbytes are needed to hold the character and attribute codes for an 80-character by 25-row display, so the codes for up to four pages can be present in the 16-Kbyte display RAM.

As a preview of video programming, perhaps you can see how you can display a character at a particular location on the screen of a CGA system by directly writing to the display RAM. The frame buffer in a CGA system starts at absolute address B8000H and 2 bytes are required to hold the character code and attribute for each character. You can just count up by 2 from B8000H

to get the address which corresponds to a particular character position on the screen. You then use a MOV instruction to write the ASCII code for the character to that address and the attribute byte to the next higher address.

When operating in a color graphics mode, a CGA board uses separate shift registers (graphics serializer) to produce the dot information for each of the color guns and for the overall intensity. The pixel data for the graphics serializer comes directly from the display-refresh RAM.

For displaying graphics, a CGA adapter board can be operated in low-resolution mode, medium-resolution mode, or high-resolution mode. The low-resolution mode is not of much interest, because the display has only 100 rows of pels with 160 pels in each row. The high-resolution mode displays 200 rows with 640 pels in each row, but it can produce only monochrome graphics displays.

In the medium-resolution mode the display consists of 200 rows of pels with 320 pels in each row, or a total of 64,000 pels. The 16 Kbytes of display-refresh RAM corresponds to 16 Kbits $\times$ 8 or 128 Kbits. Dividing the number of pels into the number of bits available for storage tells you that in this mode there are only 2 bits per pel available to store color information. With 2 bits you can specify only one of four colors for each pel.

Figure 13-16a shows how the 2 bits for each pel are positioned in display-refresh RAM bytes. Figure 13-16b shows the codes used to specify the color desired for a pixel. The 2 bits for each pel specify whether that pel is to have the background color or a color from one of two color sets. Figure 13-16c shows the two available color sets. The desired color set can be selected by outputting a control byte through port 3D9H to the palette circuit shown on the left edge of Figure 13-15. As we show you later in the section on video programming, an easier way to do it is with the BIOS INT 10H procedure.

7	6	5	4	3	2	1	0
C1	C0	C1	C0	C1	C0	C1	C0
FIRST DISPLAY PEL		SECOND DISPLAY PEL		THIRD DISPLAY PEL		FOURTH DISPLAY PEL	

(a)

C1	C0	FUNCTION
0	0	DOT TAKES ON THE COLOR OF 1 of 16 PRESELECTED BACKGROUND COLORS
0	1	SELECTS FIRST COLOR OF PRESELECTED COLOR SET 1 OR COLOR SET 2
1	0	SELECTS SECOND COLOR OF PRESELECTED COLOR SET 1 OR COLOR SET 2
1	1	SELECTS THIRD COLOR OF PRESELECTED COLOR SET 1 OR COLOR SET 2

(b)

COLOR SET 1	COLOR SET 2
COLOR 1 IS GREEN COLOR 2 IS RED COLOR 3 IS BROWN	COLOR 1 IS CYAN COLOR 2 IS MAGENTA COLOR 3 IS WHITE

(c)

FIGURE 13-16   CGA 320 × 200 pixel storage formats. (a) Position of pel bits in memory byte. (b) Codes used to specify the color desired for a pixel. (c) Two-color sets.

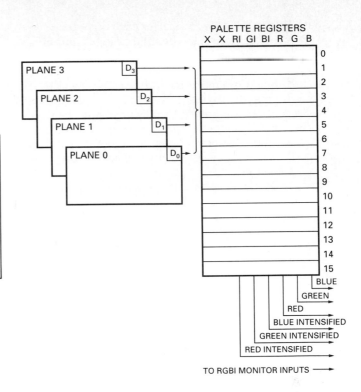

FIGURE 13-17   Functions of the frame buffer and palette registers for the most commonly used EGA display modes.

You can write dots directly to a CGA screen by writing the byte for each 4 pixels on a line to the appropriate memory location. A CGA adapter uses interlaced scanning, so the pixel codes for the even scan lines are put in memory starting at B8000H and the pixel codes for the odd scan lines are put in memory starting at BA000H. You can count up from these starting addresses to find the memory location that corresponds to a given pixel location on the screen. In a later section we show you how to use the BIOS INT 10H procedure to write dots to the screen.

ENHANCED GRAPHICS ADAPTER (EGA) HARDWARE

The Enhanced Graphics Adapter has a programmable CRT controller which allows you to set the display mode much as you do with the MC6845 on a CGA board. However, the key parts of EGA hardware that we need to talk about are the frame buffer and the palette registers. We can't show you how all the different EGA display modes use these, but Figure 13-17 shows how they function for the most commonly used format, a 640 × 350 pixel display with 16 colors from a palette of 64.

In this mode the frame buffer memory is configured as four planes. Each plane holds one of the 4 bits required to specify the color of each pixel. A 4-bit value read from the four planes is used to address one of the sixteen 8-bit palette registers. The lowest 6 bits from the addressed palette register are output to the color monitor.

NOTE: To work with this mode the monitor must have red-intensified, green-intensified, and blue-intensified inputs as well as standard red, green, and blue inputs.

There are 64 possible combinations for the 6-bit value in each palette register, but since there are only 16 palette registers, only 16 of the 64 possible combinations can be stored at a time. The 16 values in the palette registers at any particular time then specify 16 colors from a palette of 64. During bootup the palette registers in an EGA are initialized with values which correspond to the 16 colors available on a CGA system, but you can load the palette registers with values which produce your favorite colors.

VIDEO GATE ARRAY (VGA) DISPLAY HARDWARE

A proprietary gate array CRT controller device in a VGA based system allows you to select the dot clock frequency, the number of horizontal scan lines, the vertical refresh rate, the amount of overscan, etc. You can program a VGA system to operate in the previously described CGA modes, in the various EGA modes, or in several other modes. One of the standard display modes of a VGA allows you to display up to 256 colors at a time from a palette of 262,144 colors. In order to produce 256 colors, a VGA system generates analog red, green, and blue signals instead of the digital RGB signals used by previously described CRT adapters. As shown in Figure 13-18a (page 450), a 6-bit D/A converter, commonly called a *video DAC*, is used to produce each of the color signals. With a 6-bit D/A converter each signal can have 2^6 or 64 possible values, so the total possible number of combinations for the three signals is $64 \times 64 \times 64$ or 262,144, which we refer to as 256K.

As also shown in Figure 13-18a, the 18-bit values for the colors to be displayed are stored in 256 color registers. Since there are only 256 color registers, the maximum number of colors that you can display at a time is 256. Incidentally, several companies produce ICs called *RAMDACs*, which contain both the color registers and the D/A converters.

For each pixel an 8-bit value is used to select the color register which drives the D/A converters. This 8-bit value is produced in several different ways, depending on the selected display mode.

The left side of Figure 13-18a shows how this 8-bit color register "address" is generated for a $320 \times 200 \times 256$ color display. The 8-bit values for four successive pixels are stored in four memory planes as shown. When an 8-bit pixel value is read from one of the memory planes, the upper 4 bits of the pixel value are used directly as part of the color register address. The lower 4 bits of the pixel value from the memory plane are used to address one of 16 palette registers. (These palette

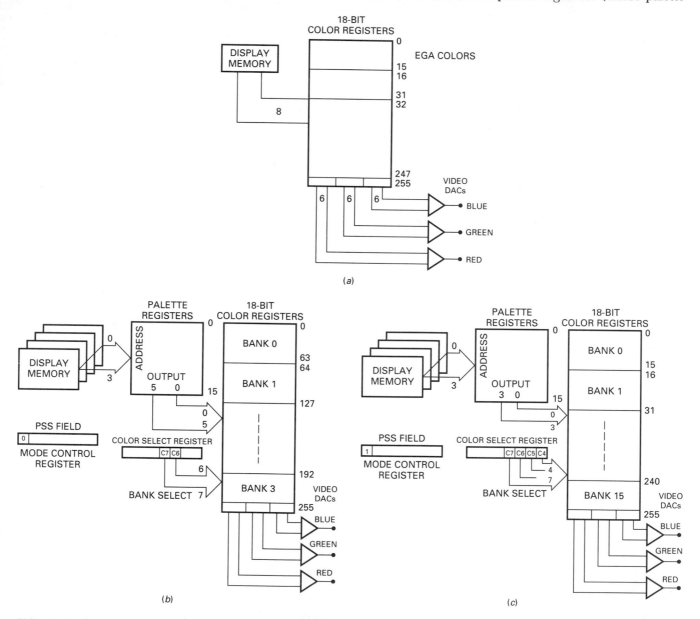

(a)

(b)

(c)

FIGURE 13-18 Hardware configurations for common VGA display modes. (a) $320 \times 200 \times 256$ color—8 bits per pixel directly select one of 256 color registers. (b) $640 \times 480 \times 16$ color—2 bits from color-select register select one of four banks of 64 color registers. Four bits from color planes select one of 16 palette registers. Six-bit value from palette register selects one of the 18-bit color registers. (c) Alternative $640 \times 480 \times 16$ color—4 bits from color-select register select a bank of 16 color registers. Lower 4 bits from palette register value select one of 16 color registers in that bank.

registers were included for downward compatibility with EGA graphics modes.) The lower 4 bits of the value from the addressed palette register are used as the lower 4 bits of the color register address.

Figure 13-18b shows one way the VGA hardware is configured for a 640 × 480 pixel display with 16 colors. The 4-bit pixel values are stored in four bit-mapped planes. To the CRT controller each of these bit planes has the same address, so the controller reads out all the bits for a pixel at the same time. The 4 bits read from the four memory planes are used to address one of the 16 palette registers. The lower 6 bits from the addressed palette register are used as the lower 6 bits of the 8-bit address for the color registers. A 6-bit value from the palette register can address any one of 64 color registers. However, since there are only 16 palette registers, only 16 of the 64 color registers can be accessed at a time. This means that the display can only have 16 colors at a time.

The upper 2 bits of the address for the color registers come from bits C7 and C6 of a special register called the Color Select Register. These bits are user programmable. You can think of these bits as selecting one of four banks of 64 colors in the 256 color registers. You can change these bits to rapidly change from one set of 16 colors to another.

Figure 13-18c shows another way the VGA hardware can be configured for a 640 × 480 pixel display with 16 colors. In this configuration the 4 bits from the memory planes select one of the 16 palette registers, but only the lower 4 bits of the 6 bits from the palette register are used to address the color registers. The other four bits of the color register address come from the Color Select Register. You can think of these four bits as selecting one of 16 banks of colors in the 256 color registers. Again, the advantage of this approach is that you can very quickly switch from one set of 16 colors to another.

After reading through the preceding discussions of the CGA, EGA, and VGA adapters the question that probably occurs to you is, With all these different pixel storage formats, palette registers, and color registers, how on earth do I put text or graphics to the screen as part of a program? In the next section of the chapter we show you some ways to do this.

Video Programming

INTRODUCTION

There are three major methods of writing programs to control the video hardware we have described in the preceding sections. One method is to use assembly language instructions to write the required values directly to the CRT controller registers, the palette registers, the frame buffer, etc. A program written at this level usually runs faster than one written at a higher level, but programming at this level is quite complex because you have to keep track of many register bits, memory addresses, pixel storage formats, etc. Also, when programming at this register level it is easy to forget to restore some register to the correct value at the end of an operation. This may cause the display to "hang."

The next-higher level of CRT programming is to use the BIOS INT 10H procedures. In some cases the INT 10H procedures execute very slowly, but they are easy to use and programs written using them have a high degree of portability to different systems.

Still another level of video programming is to use a high-level language such as C. The advantage of this high-level-language approach, of course, is that you do not have to "reinvent the wheel." You can simply call library functions to draw lines and boxes, create windows, move images on the screen, etc. The Turbo C graphics functions manipulate the display hardware directly rather than using the BIOS INT 10H procedure, so they are quite fast. Our choice is to use C wherever possible, but your choice will depend on the programming environment you have available. To give you choices we will first show you how to use the BIOS INT 10H procedures to initialize a graphics adapter, write characters to the screen, and write pixels of a desired color to the screen. Then we will show you how to write pixel data directly to the frame buffer of an EGA or VGA system. Finally, we will show you how to use some of the Turbo C graphics functions.

USING BIOS INT 10H PROCEDURE FOR VIDEO PROGRAMMING

Figure 13-19, page 452, shows you the different subprocedures or functions of the BIOS INT 10H procedure and the registers used to pass parameters to these functions. Some of these functions are: set display mode, set cursor position, scroll page up, scroll page down, write dot, and write character to screen. An important point here is that the BIOS procedures on an EGA system are a "superset" of the BIOS procedures for a CGA system. The INT 10H procedure in an EGA system simply has additional subprocedures to access the palette registers, etc. on an EGA system. Likewise, the VGA BIOS INT 10H procedures are a superset of the BIOS procedures for CGA and EGA systems. The significance of this is that a VGA system, for example, can be programmed to operate as an EGA system or as a CGA system so that programs written for those systems can be run without problems.

The first step in a video program is to set the system to the desired display mode. An INT 10H procedure call is an easy way to do this. As a simple example of this, the following instructions use the BIOS INT 10H to initialize a CGA, EGA, or VGA adapter to a color text mode with 80 columns × 25 rows.

```
MOV AH, 00    ; Call set mode function of INT 10H
MOV AL, 03    ; Code for 80 × 25 color text mode
INT 10H       ; Call BIOS procedure
```

To put a system in some other mode you simpy put the display mode number from Figure 13-19 in AL instead of the 03H used for this example.

Once you get the adapter or system in the desired display mode, the next step is to write characters or dots to the desired positions on the screen. The following instructions use the BIOS INT 10H procedure to put the

AH   FUNCTION
00H   Set display mode using value in AL
        AL = 0   40 x 25 BW
        AL = 1   40 x 25 COLOR
        AL = 2   80 x 25 BW
        AL = 3   80 x 25 COLOR
        AL = 4   320 x 200 COLOR
        AL = 5   320 x 200 BW
        AL = 6   640 x 200 x 2 COLOR
        AL = 7   80 x 25 BW
        AL = D   320 x 200 x 16 COLOR
        AL = E   640 x 200 x 16 COLOR
        AL = F   640 x 350 BW
        AL = 10 640 x 350 x 16 COLOR
        AL = 11 640 x 480 x 2 COLOR
        AL = 12 640 x 480 x 16 COLOR
        AL = 13 320 x 200 x 256 COLORS

01   Set cursor type

        CH = bottom line number for cursor
        CL = top line number for cursor

02   Set cursor position
        DH = row, DL = column, BH = page

03   Read cursor position
        BH = page
        Returns: DH = row, DL = column
                 CH, CL = cursor mode

04   Read light pen position
        Returns: AH = light pen active
                 DH = character row of pen
                 DL = character column of pen
                 CH = raster scan line #
                 BX = pixel column number

05   Select active display page
        AL = desired page

06   Scroll active page up, blanks at bottom
        AL = number of lines to scroll
        AL = 0 blanks entire window
        CH = row, CL = column of upper left
        corner of scroll. DH = row, DL = column
        of lower right corner of scroll.
        BH = attribute to be used on blanked lines

07   Scroll active page down, blank top line
        AL = number of lines to scroll
        AL = 0 blanks entire window
        CH = row, CL = column of upper
        left corner of scroll
        DH = row, DL = column of lower right
        corner of scroll
        BH = attribute to be used on blanked lines

AH   FUNCTION
08   Read character and attribute at cursor
        BH = display page
        Returns: AH = attribute, AL = character

09   Write character and attribute at cursor
        BH = display page, CX = number of characters
        AL = character,   BL = attribute

0AH   Write just character at cursor position
        BH = display page, CX = number of characters
        AL = character

0BH   Set CGA color palette
        BH = 0 - set background color
        BL = color
        BH = 1 - select color set
        BL = color set - 0 or 1

0CH   Write pixel at graphics cursor
        DX = row, CX = column, AL = color

0DH   Read pixel value
        DX = row, CX = column
        Returns AL = pixel value

0EH   Write character and advance cursor
        AL = character, BH = page(text mode)
        BL = color(graphics modes)

0FH   Get current video state
        Returns: AL = current video mode
        AH = number of character columns
        BH = current display page

10H   Set EGA/VGA palette registers
        AL = 00 - program a single palette reg
        AL = 01 - program border color register
        AL = 02 - program all palette registers
        AL = 03 - enable blink or intensify
        AL = 07 - read a single palette register
        AL = 08 - read the border color register
        AL = 09 - read all palette registers
        AL = 10H - program a single VGA color reg
        AL = 12H - program several VGA color regs
        AL = 13H - select color subset
        AL = 15H - read a single VGA color reg
        AL = 17H - read several VGA color regs
        AL = 1AH - get color page state
        AL = 1BH - convert color register set to
                   gray scale values

11H   Load Character generator
        Subfunction number determines character set.
        For example, if AL = 3, value in BL
        determines which of four EGA character sets
        is loaded.

FIGURE 13-19   BIOS INT 10H subprocedures and parameters.

cursor at position 24 in row 7 and write a blinking A to the screen at that position.

```
MOV AH,02H   ; Load subfunction number for set cur-
                 sor position
MOV DH,07    ; load row number of cursor position
MOV DL,24    ; load column number of cursor position
MOV BH,00    ; load display page number
INT 10H      ; call BIOS video procedure
             ; write character at cursor position
MOV AH,09    ; subfunction # for write character/attri-
                 bute at cursor position
MOV BH,00    ; load display page number
MOV CX,01    ; load number of characters to send
MOV AL,41H   ; ASCII code for A
MOV BL,      ; Attribute code for blinking,
   10001001B ; black background, light blue character
             ; See Figure 13-9 for attribute byte format
INT 10H      ; Call BIOS video procedure
```

The first call of the INT 10H puts the cursor in the desired location on the screen. Note that as part of the setup for this call, we loaded the desired display page in the BH register. As we pointed out earlier, an 80 × 25 character display requires only 4 Kbytes of frame buffer memory. The IBM CGA board has a 16-Kbyte frame buffer, so with one of these boards you can have up to four pages stored in the frame buffer at a time. You can use subfunction 5 of the INT 10H procedure to flip the display from one page to another.

The second call of the INT 10H procedure simply sends the character and attribute bytes to the correct locations in the frame buffer. The character code to be sent is put in AL and the attribute byte is put in BL. If CX contains a 1, the character will be written to just the location where the cursor is located. After the write the cursor will not be advanced to the next position. If CX contains a number other than 1, the same character will be written to the number of sequential locations contained in CX. The cursor will be left on the last character written.

If you want to write a sequence of characters to the display, function 14 of the INT 10H procedure is more efficient because it automatically advances the cursor to the next position after a write. To call this function you load 14 in AH, load the ASCII code for the character to be sent in AL, and execute the INT 10H instruction.

The obvious advantage of using the BIOS procedure here is that you don't have to figure out the memory location which corresponds to the position of the character on the screen.

Incidentally, a CGA system has only one text font and the character generator for that font is in ROM, as shown in Figure 13-15. On an EGA or VGA system the character generator is located in RAM. The default character generator data for a specified mode is loaded into RAM when the system is put in that mode with an INT 10H function. However, you can use subfunction 17 of the INT 10H procedure to load one of several available character fonts or a custom character font.

Now that you know how to display characters on the screen, let's take a look at how you can produce a graphics display. Earlier we mentioned that you could write a dot on the screen by writing the appropriate pixel code directly to the corresponding memory location. An easier way to do this is with the BIOS INT 10H procedure.

The program in Figure 13-20, p. 454, shows you how to put an EGA or VGA system in 640 × 350 × 16 color mode, set the background color for light blue, draw a magenta window near the center of the screen, and write a message in the window. The first major step in the program is to use the INT 10H procedure to put the system in mode 10H, which according to Figure 13-19 is the 640 × 350 × 16 color graphics mode. The next step in the program is to set the background color to light blue. For an EGA or VGA in this mode, the background color is the color code stored in palette register zero. To change the background color, then, all you have to do is use subfunction 16 of the INT 10H procedure to load the code for the desired color in palette register 0.

The next part of the program uses a nested loop and the "write dot" subfunction of INT 10H to draw a magenta window on the screen. The window is produced by drawing horizontal lines. You can draw a window of any size by simply changing the start and stop coordinates in this loop.

The final section of the program in Figure 13-20 uses function 2 of INT 10H to position the cursor in the window and then uses function 14 to write a message at the cursor position. We included this last section to show you that you can use the INT 10H text functions to write characters to the screen even though you are in graphics mode. After writing the message to the screen we load AX with 4C00H and use software interrupt 21H to return execution to the DOS prompt.

A DIRECT WRITE VIDEO GRAPHICS EXAMPLE

The program in Figure 13-20 takes about 10 s just to draw the small window on the screen of a 25-MHz 80386-based microcomputer. For some applications this may be an unreasonably long time, so we decided to show you how to do the job by directly manipulating the controller registers and writing to the video RAM.

The program in Figure 13-21, p. 455, puts an EGA or VGA system in the 640 × 350 × 16 color graphics mode and draws a magenta window just as the program in Figure 13-20 does, but to save paper we did not show the write message portion. This program draws the window in less than 1 s. The program would be much faster, except for the fact that when an EGA or VGA system is operating in a high-resolution graphics mode, the processor can access the video RAM only about 20 percent of the time.

After we initialize the system to the desired mode and set the background color with the INT 10H procedure, we use three custom procedures to set the controller registers, write dots to draw the window, and restore the controller registers to their initial values. We don't have space here to discuss all the details of the EGA and VGA controller registers, but we will try to give you

```
                    ; 8086 PROGRAM F13-20.ASM
                    ;ABSTRACT : This program use the BIOS INT 10H procedure to put
                    ;           an EGA or VGA system in 640 x 350 x 16 color graphics
                    ;           mode, set the background to light blue, draw a magenta
                    ;           window and display a message in the window

            DATA SEGMENT
                TEXT  DB 'GRAPHICS PROGRAMMING IS FUN',24h
            DATA ENDS

            CODE SEGMENT
                ASSUME CS:CODE, DS:DATA
            START: MOV AX, DATA              ; Initialize DS
                   MOV DS, AX
                   MOV AL, 10H               ; Set up for 640 x 350
                   MOV AH, 0                 ;    graphics mode
                   INT 10H
                   MOV AH, 10H               ; Set background color light blue
                   MOV AL, 0                 ;   with subprocedure 10H of BIOS
                   MOV BL, 0                 ;   INT 10H. AL = palette function
                   MOV BH, 09                ;   BL = reg #, BH = color
                   INT 10H
                   MOV  BX, 0005H            ; Display page and color for window
                   MOV  CX, 160              ; start column number for window
                   MOV  DX, 100              ; start row number for window
            L1:    MOV  AH, OCH              ; INT 10H write dot sub function
                   MOV  AL, BL               ; color from store
                   INT  10H                  ; video BIOS routine
                   INC  CX                   ; Increment column count
                   CMP  CX, 480              ; check for end of row
                   JB   L1                   ; No, write another dot
                   INC  DX                   ; Yes, increment row count
                   CMP  DX, 250              ; Check if all rows done
                   JE   DONE                 ; Yes, go write message
                   MOV  CX, 160              ; No, point at start of line
                   JMP  L1                   ; Draw next dot row
            DONE:  MOV AH, 02                ; Set cursor position
                   MOV DH, 12                ; Load character row number
                   MOV DL, 27                ; Load character column number
                   MOV BL, 0                 ; Display page number
                   INT 10H
            ; Write messsage in window
                   MOV DX, 00                ; Use DX to hold pointer
                   MOV BL,OFH                ; BL contains desired character color
            NXTCHR:MOV SI, DX                ;   SI destroyed in INT 10H
                   MOV AH, 14                ; Write character at cursor and
                   MOV AL, TEXT[SI]          ;   increment cursor position
                   CMP AL, 24H               ; Check if sentinel character
                   JE EXIT
                   INT 10H
                   INC DX                    ; Point to next character in string
                   JMP NXTCHR
            EXIT:  MOV AX, 4C00H             ; return to DOS
                   INT 21H
            CODE   ENDS
                   END START
```

FIGURE 13-20   Program using BIOS INT 10H to draw a window on an EGA
or VGA.

enough information so you can comfortably use parts of Figure 13-21 in your own programs. For further details consult one of the EGA/VGA programming books listed in the Bibliography.

As the name implies, the SETUP procedure gets the attention of the video controller device and puts some of its registers in the required mode. EGA and VGA controllers each have an incredible number of registers

```
; 8086 PROGRAM F13-21.ASM
; ABSTRACT: This program puts an EGA or VGA in 640 x 350 x 16 color
            ; graphics mode, sets the background light blue, then
            ; uses direct controller writes to draw a magenta window.

CODE      SEGMENT
     ASSUME CS:CODE
START:
     MOV AL, 10H              ; Put system in 640 x 350
     MOV AH, 0                ; graphics mode
     INT 10H                  ;
     MOV AH, 10H              ; INT 10 H subprocedure #
     MOV AL, 0                ; Write to single palette register
     MOV BL, 0                ; Palette register number
     MOV BH, 09H              ; Code for light blue
     INT 10H
     CALL SETUP               ; Set up graphics controller for set/reset
                              ; mode of writing to display buffer

     MOV  BX, 160             ; start column number for window
     MOV  AX, 100             ; start row number for window
L1: CALL WRITE_DOT            ; Fast write pixel procedure
    INC  BX
    CMP  BX, 480              ; check for end of row
    JB   L1
    INC  AX                   ; Increment row count
    CMP  AX, 250              ; Check if all rows done
    JE   EXIT                 ; Yes, done
    MOV  BX, 160              ; No, point at start of line
    JMP  L1                   ;   Draw next dot row
EXIT:CALL RESTORE
     MOV AX, 4C00H            ; return to DOS
     INT 21H


PROC SETUP
     MOV DX, 03CEH            ; Address of controller reg
     MOV AX, 0005h            ; Enable Write Mode 0. AH-write mode, AL-index
     OUT DX, AX
     MOV AH, 05              ; Load Set/Reset register with
     MOV AL, 0               ; code for magenta,  AL - index
     OUT DX, AX
     MOV AX, 0F01h           ; Enable all four color planes
     OUT DX,AX               ;   AH - enable bits, AL - index
     RET
ENDP


PROC WRITE_DOT
; The Video Controller must be set for Write Mode 0, and have the
; Map Mask Set for the desired color outputs.
     PUSH AX
     PUSH BX
     PUSH CX
     PUSH DX
; Compute address of pixel in video buffer. Pixel address = row x 80 + column/8
     MOV DX, 80
     MUL DX                   ; AX now = row * 80
     MOV CX, BX               ; Save column for later use
     SHR BX, 1
     SHR BX, 1
     SHR BX, 1                ; BX = col / 8
     ADD BX, AX               ; BX = row * 80 + col / 8
     MOV AX, 0A000h           ; Point ES at video buffer base
     MOV ES, AX
```

FIGURE 13-21   Program using direct controller write to draw a window.

```
              AND CL, 7                      ; Use lowest 3 bits in column
                                             ; to determine pixel # in byte
              MOV AX, 8008h                  ;  generate and set the BitMask
              SHR AH, CL                     ;   in graphics controller, so
              MOV DX, 03CEh                  ;   so don't write color to all
              OUT DX, AX                     ;    8 pixels in byte
              OR ES:BX, AL                   ; Write the Pixel - (Contents of AL ignored).
              POP DX
              POP CX
              POP BX
              POP AX
              RET
        ENDP

        PROC RESTORE
              MOV DX, 03CEH
              MOV AX, 0000H                  ; Default Set/Reset register value
              OUT DX, AX
              MOV AX, 0001H                  ; Default Enable Set/Reset value
              OUT DX, AX
              MOV AX, 0FF08H                 ; Default bit mask value
              OUT DX, AX
              RET
        ENDP
        CODE ENDS
              END START
```

FIGURE 13-21 (*Continued*)

that are used to hold the values of parameters for various display modes, etc. To reduce the number of I/O addresses required to access all these registers, an index system is used. Here's how it works.

Each group of registers in the controller has two I/O addresses. As an example, the group of registers we access in this program uses the addresses 03CEH and 03CFH. The lower address is used to send the index number for the register we want to access, and the upper address is used to write the desired value to the selected register or read a value from the selected register. To speed up write operations, the index and the value can be sent with a single 16-bit OUT instruction.

There are several ways to write pixel values to the memory planes of an EGA or VGA system. For this example we chose the "set/reset" method, because it is very efficient for drawing lines or filling regions of the screen. To give you an overview before we get into the details, the major steps in this method are

1. Put the video controller in write mode 0 so that the set/reset write mode will work.

2. Enable the planes we want affected by the color value we will load into the set/reset register.

3. Load set/reset register with the desired color value.

4. Generate and send a mask byte so that only the desired pixel bits in the display memory bytes are set or reset.

5. Activate the controller to set/reset the desired bits in the display memory.

The first group of instructions in the SETUP procedure enables the controller for Write Mode 0 so the set/reset operation will work. The second MOV and OUT group of instructions in the SETUP procedure is used to enable the desired color planes in the video RAM for a write. In this case we want to write to all four planes, so we put 1's in the lower 4 bits of the data word in AH. The SETUP procedure needs to be done only once before a series of dots is written.

The next procedure to look at in Figure 13-21 is the WRITE_DOT procedure. The first task of the WRITE_DOT procedure is to compute the video RAM address which corresponds to the desired pixel coordinates. As shown in Figure 13-17, the pixel data for this display mode is stored in four parallel planes. The 4-bit value for each pixel is stored as the same numbered bits in the four planes. Each byte in one of the planes then contains 1 bit of the pixel data for 8 pixels, so it takes 80 bytes of memory in each plane to store the pixel data for one line of 640 dots on the screen. From the microprocessor's standpoint the four planes all occupy the same system address space, starting at address 0A000H. The offset of the byte which contains the bit for a particular pixel then can be calculated with the simple expression Offset = (row × 80) + column/8. In the WRITE_DOT procedure in Figure 13-21, we used the MUL instruction to multiply the row number by 80, but for the divide instruction we used a shift-right operation because it is faster than DIV.

The next step in the WRITE_DOT procedure is to generate a mask which will be used to make sure a new pixel code is written only to the desired bit in each of the display planes. The number of a bit in a byte is represented by the lowest three bits of the column number. The MOV CX,BX instruction in the procedure saves the column number in CX, so the AND CL,07H instruction gives the number of the bit in the memory byte. To actually generate the mask word, we load 80H in AH and shift this value CL times to the right. The 1 in the data word in AH will be left in the bit position we want to write to in the RAM byte. (As we show you in a problem at the end of the chapter, it is sometimes useful to set all the bits in this mask so that the pixel data is written to all 8 bits in a byte at the same time.) Once the mask is generated we send it and the index of 08H in AL out to the controller.

As we mentioned before, the four planes of the video buffer RAM all occupy the same address space, starting at 0A000H. For the write mode we have chosen, this means that we have to send pixel codes to the RAM through the controller rather than writing them directly. Remember that in the WINDOW procedure, we sent the pixel code to the Set/Reset (color) register of the controller. The first step in this indirect process is to point ES at the base of the Video RAM segment. The next step is to tell the controller to write the pixel code to the desired address with the OR ES:[BX],AL instruction.

Normally, the OR memory, register instruction reads a byte from memory, ORs AL with this word, and writes the result back to the specified memory location. In this program the read part of the operation causes the controller to read a byte from each of the display planes into four latches in the controller. The controller then sets or resets the unmasked bits in each of these registers with the new pixel code. During the write part of the OR operation the updated bytes are written back to the specified address in the planes. The byte in AL is ignored during this operation.

The RESTORE procedure at the end of the program is used to return all the registers in the video controller to their default values. We wanted to show you how to do this, but in most cases it is not really necessary, because other procedures will usually put the controller in the mode needed for that procedure.

DRAWING DIAGONAL LINES ON THE SCREEN

The program in Figure 13-21 uses the WRITE_DOT procedure to draw horizontal lines across the screen. Perhaps you can see that the WRITE_DOT procedure could easily be used to draw a vertical line on the screen. However, drawing a diagonal line is much more difficult, because most of the pixel positions do not fall exactly on the desired line. As an example of this, Figure 13-22c shows the pixels which best approximate a line from coordinates (0, 0) to (10, 4). For each horizontal pixel position a calculation must be done to determine which of two vertical positions more closely approximates the desired line. To compute the "best-fit" pixel locations, we usually use Bresenham's algorithm. This algorithm determines the closer pixel by determining whether a point halfway between the pixels is above or below the actual line. A couple of examples should help you see how this works.

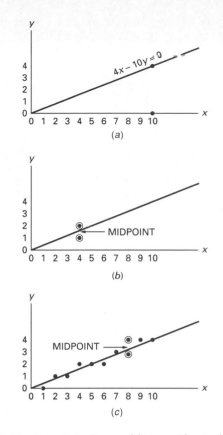

FIGURE 13-22 Drawing diagonal lines with pixels. (a) Graph of 4X × 10Y = 0. (b) Method to determine pixel to use for an X value of 4. (c) Method to determine pixel for X = 8 and best-fit pixels for entire line.

The equation for the line in Figure 13-22a is $4X - 10Y = 0$. Figure 13-22b shows how we determine which pixel to use for an X value of 4. The two choices for the pixel are the $Y = 1$ pixel and the $Y = 2$ pixel. To determine which pixel, we first compute the value of the function at the midpoint between these two. For this example the midpoint is at (4, 1.5), so the function is $4 \times 4 - 10 \times 1.5 = +1$. A positive result here indicates that the midpoint value is not large enough to make the function equal to zero; in other words, the midpoint is below the line. This means that the pixel at (4, 2) is closer to the actual line. In this case, all we do is increment the X value from that for the previous pixel, increment the Y value from that for the previous pixel, and write the pixel to the video RAM.

Figure 13-22c shows the results this technique produces for the pixel at X = 8. The midpoint here is (8, 3.5), so the function at this point is $4 \times 8 - 10 \times 3.5 = -3$. The negative result tells you that the midpoint is above the line. This means that the pixel at (8, 3) is closer to the line than the pixel at (8, 4). In this case we increment the X value from that of the preceding pixel, keep the Y value the same as that of the preceding pixel, and write the pixel to the video RAM.

The example in Figure 13-22 assumes the line is in the first octant of a standard graph, but the basic principle can be extended to a line in any octant. To draw a line in the second octant, you increment the Y value by one and compute appropriate pixel value for X instead of incrementing X and computing Y. To draw a line in the third octant, you reverse the starting and ending points so the line is drawn left to right instead of right to left. We don't have space here to show you an assembly language program for this algorithm, but almost every graphics book has at least one.

One point we hope you gained from the preceding discussion is that it takes considerable computing just to draw a sequence of lines on the screen. Another type of graphics programming that requires considerable computation is the creation and manipulation of windows. The programs in Figures 13-20 and 13-21 showed you how to draw simple graphics windows by writing pixel data to locations in the frame buffer, but in most real applications there is considerably more to do than just draw the window.

Suppose, for example, that in a program you are writing you want to have a pull-down menu window which lists a series of commands that a user can select from, similar to the menus in the tc integrated environment. When you create a window, you write over the old pixel values in the frame buffer. Therefore, you must save the pixel codes for the region where you are going to put the window so that you can restore the original display when you close the window. The transfer of pixel codes from the frame buffer to another buffer, from the buffer back to the frame buffer, or from one location to another in the frame buffer is commonly called a bit-aligned block transfer or BITBLT (pronounced bit blit).

Diagonal lines and BITBLT operations are required in almost every graphics program, so predefined C functions have been developed to implement these and other graphics functions. In the next section we show you how to use some of the Turbo C predefined graphics functions.

USING C GRAPHICS FUNCTIONS

Almost every C compiler comes with a library of graphics functions. Also, several other companies market packages of graphics functions which provide capabilities beyond those of the basic graphic functions that come with the compilers. One difficulty with all these is that the names, operations, and prototypes for these functions vary widely from company to company. For our discussions here we use just the graphics functions that come with Turbo C version 2.0. If you have some other compiler, you should be able to find similar functions in the libraries for it.

Figure 13-23 shows a C program which uses Turbo C library functions to initialize the graphics adapter, draw an eight-segment "pie" graph on the screen, open a graphics window, draw some figures in the window, and close the window on user command.

To get an overview of how the program works, read just the comments in Figure 13-23; then read the discussion here to get the details of how the described action is done. You should then be able to use these functions to produce some interesting displays.

After we declare some variables, the first action in

main is to call the initgraph function to initialize the display adapter. The arguments you pass this function are the address of a variable containing the desired graphics driver, the address of a variable containing the desired mode, and a pointer to a string containing the path to the specified graphics driver (.BGI) file. For this example we used the predefined constant VGA for the graphics driver and the predefined constant VGAHI for the display mode. These values produce a 640 × 480 16-color display. On an EGA system you could use the constants EGA and EGAHI to initialize the adapter for a 640 × 350 16-color display. Note in the string containing the path to the graphics drivers you have to insert the \ twice to get the compiler to accept a \.

The setbkcolor function next in the program sets the background color to the predefined constant LIGHTBLUE. The choices here are BLACK, BLUE, GREEN, CYAN, RED, MAGENTA, BROWN, LIGHTGRAY, DARKGRAY, LIGHTBLUE, LIGHTGREEN, LIGHTCYAN, LIGHTRED, LIGHTMAGENTA, YELLOW, and WHITE.

The for loop next in the program draws eight different-colored pie slices on the screen. The pie is centered at pixel coordinates X = 320 and Y = 175 and has a radius of 100 pixels. The starting point for the first slice is the 3 o'clock position. The angles are incremented so that the other slices are added in a counterclockwise direction. The predefined colors in the previous paragraph are really an enumerated list, where BLACK has a value of 0, BLUE has a value of 1, GREEN has a value of 2, etc. The color value of i + 1 that is passed to the setfillstyle function starts with blue, then goes to green, then cyan, etc. as the loop executes.

After we draw the pie slices, we change the drawing color to white, draw a couple of white circles around the pie, and move the current position of the graphics cursor to the upper left corner of the screen for future reference.

NOTE: The graphics cursor is normally invisible, so you have to keep track of where it is or, perhaps, on the screen draw an arrow which points to the current position.

The demo_window function called next in the program contains some really important programming points. As we mentioned, before you draw a window on the screen you have to first save everything from the current display so you can restore it when you close the window. This is equivalent to pushing registers on the stack when you call a procedure in assembly language.

The first data you need to save is the current position of the graphics cursor. The getx and gety functions determine the coordinates of the cursor and store them in the local variables X and Y.

The next data you have to save is the pixel data for the section of the screen where you are going to draw the window. The first step in this process is to call the imagesize function to determine how many bytes of memory are needed to store the pixel data. The value returned by imagesize is then passed to the function malloc. Malloc (memory allocate) creates a buffer of the requested size in an area of memory called *the heap*.

```c
/* C PROGRAM F13-23.C */
/* Program to demonstrate Turbo C graphics functions and windows */

#include<stdlib.h>
#include<stdio.h>
#include<graphics.h>

void main()
{
int driver = VGA, mode = VGAHI;              /* 640 x 480 x 16 color */
int i, start_angl = 0, end_angl = 45;
void demo_window(void);                      /* function declaration */

initgraph(&driver,&mode, "c:\\tc");          /* initialize adapter */
setbkcolor(LIGHTBLUE);                        /* set background color */

for(i=0; i<8; i++)                           /* draw 8 pie wedges */
{
setfillstyle(SOLID_FILL, i+1);               /* change drawing color for each */
pieslice(320,175,start_angl,end_angl,100);   /* center, angls, radius */
start_angl = start_angl + 45;                /* increment angles */
end_angl = end_angl + 45;
}
setcolor(WHITE);                             /* change drawing color to white */
circle(320,175,101);                         /* draw circles around pie */
circle(320,175,102);

moveto(0,0);                                 /* set cursor to home position */
demo_window();                               /* call window demo function */
exit(0);                                     /* return to DOS */
}

void demo_window(void)
{
int x,y,i;
unsigned window_size;
void * window_buffer;

x=getx(); y=gety();                          /* get and save current cursor position */
                                             /* determine size of image to store */
window_size = imagesize(160,100,480,250);    /* find # bytes for image */
window_buffer = malloc(window_size);         /* dynamically allocate memory*/
getimage(160,100,480,250,window_buffer);     /* store bit map under window */
setviewport(160,100,480,250,1);              /* create window */
setcolor(RED);                               /* change drawing color */
for(i=0; i<150; i++)                         /* paint window red */
line(0,i,319,i);
setcolor(WHITE);                             /* change drawing color */
circle(25,25,10);                            /* draw circle in window */
rectangle(160,75,320,150);                   /* draw rectangle to show clipping */
while(getchar()!='e')                        /* wait for e to exit */
   continue;
setviewport(0,0,639,349,1);                  /* restore to full screen */
putimage(160,100,window_buffer,0);           /* restore original display */
free(window_buffer);                         /* release allocated memory */
moveto(x,y);                                 /* put cursor back in position
                                                where it was before call */

}
```

FIGURE 13-23   C program which uses Turbo C library functions to initialize the graphics adapter, draw an eight-segment pie graph on the screen, open a graphics window, draw some figures in the window, and close the window on user command.

The heap is above the normal data area and below the stack. If there is not memory left in the heap for the requested buffer, malloc returns an error code of 00. Since this is such a small program, we did not bother to check for an error condition, but in a larger program you should. If malloc succeeds, it returns a pointer to the start of the buffer. Once you have the buffer set up, you use the getimage function to copy the pixel data from the display refresh RAM to the buffer. The arguments passed to getimage are: the X and Y coordinates of the upper-left corner of the area, the X and Y coordinates of the lower-right corner of the area, and a pointer to the buffer created by malloc. Now you are ready to actually create the window.

The setviewport function is used to create the window. The first four arguments passed to setviewport are the coordinates of the upper-left and the lower-right corners of the window. The final argument in the setviewport call is the clip flag. If this flag is set and you attempt to draw a figure which would extend outside the window, the figure will be clipped so it stops at the edge of the window.

The setviewport function creates the window and moves the graphics cursor to the upper left corner of the window. However, the created window has the same background color as the main screen, so it is not visible. To make the window visible we set the drawing color to red and draw the window full of lines. There are other ways to fill a rectangle, but this method gave us an excuse to show you how to draw lines.

Just for fun we drew a small circle and a rectangle in the window. Note that the coordinates for the circle are relative to the upper left corner of the window, not the upper left corner of the screen as they were for the preceding circles. Also note that the coordinates given for the rectangle would cause it to extend outside the window. We set the clip flag in the setviewport call, so the rectangle will not be allowed to extend outside the window. This is important, because anything drawn outside the window would not be replaced by the original display when you close the window.

When the user presses the e key and then the Enter key, we close the window and restore everything. The setviewport call here sets up the whole screen as the window again. The putimage function copies the pixel data from the window_buffer back to the display refresh RAM. The free(window_buffer) function call releases the memory allocated for the window_buffer by malloc. This step is very important, because if the memory is not put back in the heap when you are done with it, the heap will grow up until it runs into the stack. The principle here is the same as cleaning up the stack when returning from a function call.

The final step before returning to main is to put the graphics cursor back in the location where it was before the call. The moveto function puts the graphics cursor at the X and Y coordinates passed to it.

The C library functions we used in this program are obviously much easier to work with than the assembly language equivalents. They write directly to the video hardware instead of using the INT 10H procedures, so they are quite fast. However, they are still relatively low level. More advanced graphics packages such as Windows from Microsoft, DGIS from Graphic Software Systems, and GEM from Digital Research contain all the basic procedures needed to create and move windows. Also, they contain tools needed to draw text and graphics in windows. Packages such as this better insulate an applications programmer from the hardware details.

HIGH-RESOLUTION GRAPHICS AND GRAPHICS PROCESSORS

In the preceding sections we mostly discussed CGA, EGA, and VGA systems so that you could experiment with the examples on your own system. For many applications such as advanced CAD (computer-aided drafting), CAE (computer-aided engineering), or EDA (electronic design automation), however, the resolution of even a VGA screen is not nearly enough. For these applications a screen resolution of 1024×768 or greater is required. There are several problems in producing these high-resolution displays.

First, it is nearly a full-time job keeping the display refreshed and the display RAM refreshed. Second, manipulating complex images on the screen requires a great many computations. As we discussed earlier, even drawing a diagonal line or a circle on the screen requires considerable computation to determine the pixel values. Drawing a three-dimensional view of an airplane model on the screen, for example, requires several hundred thousand floating-point computations. Rotating the image to see a slightly different view requires hundreds of thousands of floating-point computations. Manufacturers have attempted to solve these problems in a number of ways.

As shown in Figure 13-14, IBM's next step up from the VGA is the 8514/A adapter, which plugs into a special slot in PS/2-type computers. This adapter uses a two-chip graphics processor to produce a display of 1024×768 pixels. One part of the 8514/A chip set keeps the display and the frame buffer RAM refreshed. The graphic processor part has hard-wired instructions to draw lines, perform BITBLT operations, and generate addresses for pixel coordinates. The 8514/A graphics processor, however, does not have instructions for drawing arcs and other more complex shapes, so the burden for these operations is still left with the main processor.

Another common example of a "hard-wired" graphic processor is the Intel 82786 Graphics coprocessor, which works with the main processor in about the same way that 8087 math coprocessor we described in Chapter 11 works with the main processor. The 82786 contains circuitry to refresh DRAMs as well as circuitry to refresh the screen. The 82786 has hard-wired instructions to draw lines, draw polygons, perform BITBLT operations, create multiple windows, and manipulate windows. The advantages of these hard-wired instructions are that they execute very rapidly and they require very little main processor overhead. The disadvantage of the 82786 is that if the desired operation is not one of the hard-wired instructions, you have to implement it with main processor instructions.

Still other common examples of graphics processors

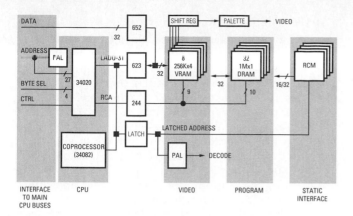

FIGURE 13-24 A TMS34020 ("three-forty-twenty") subsystem which can be connected to the main processor buses to control a 1024 × 1024 × 8-bit/pixel display.

are the Texas Instruments TMS34010 and TMS34020. Figure 13-24 shows how a TMS34020 ("three-forty-twenty") subsystem can be connected to the main processor buses to control a 1024 × 1024 × 8 bits/pixel display. As we explained earlier, the VRAM is used for the actual video buffer, because it can get data out fast enough to refresh pixels. The outputs of the VRAMs go to the palette registers, and the outputs of the palette registers go to D/A converters, which produce the analog RGB signals for the monitor. The standard DRAM and ROM in this subsystem are used to hold the programs and data for the graphics coprocessor. Note that a TMS34082 floating-point graphics coprocessor can be connected in the system to handle floating-point computations.

The major advantage and the major disadvantage of a TMS34020 system is its programmability. The device has basic graphics instructions such as draw line, pixel move, and area fill, and it can be programmed to implement much more complex graphics functions than common hard-wired devices, but the programmer has the burden of developing the required programs. To make this easier TI has a development system and an extensive library of programs for common operations.

Another step that Texas Instruments has taken to make the programmer's job easier is to develop the Texas Instruments Graphics Architecture (TIGA) standard and release this standard to the industry. TIGA establishes a standard interface between PC applications and the TMS34010 or TMS34020 hardware. What this means is that an applications programmer developing, for example, a drafting program can write his or her program to interface with TIGA and not worry about the actual hardware underneath it. TIGA does, however, allow the developer to write custom extensions if needed.

A still-higher level of graphics hardware is the Intel i860™, whose architectural block diagram is shown in Figure 13-25. This device is intended for use as the CPU in an engineering workstation which has advanced 3-dimensional imaging capability. As we discussed before, this requires a great many floating-point computations. With a 40-MHz clock the i860™ can perform at a peak rate of 80 *million floating point operations per second*

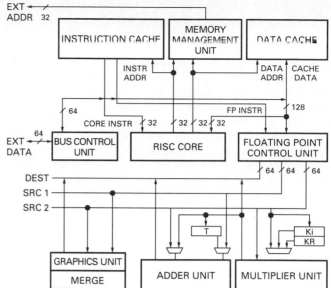

FIGURE 13-25 Block diagram of the Intel's i860™.

(*MEGAFLOPS* or *MFLOPS*). The i860™ achieves this speed by putting many functions on a single chip and by doing many operations in parallel, rather then serially.

As you can see in Figure 13-25, the device contains a RISC processor core, an integer processor, a floating-point processor, and a graphics processor. The device also contains an instruction cache and a data cache. The separate caches mean that instructions and data can be read at the same time by a processor. Also, the 64-bit external data bus allows a 32-bit data word and a 32-bit instruction word to be read in at the same time.

The main processor in the i860™ is a *reduced instruction set computer* or *RISC*. As the name implies, this type processor has a very simple set of instructions which operate very fast. A RISC processor typically has only logical, simple arithmetic, shift, load, store, and jump instructions. When programming a RISC processor you use these simple instructions to "custom make" the more complex operations you need for a specific application. The advantage of a RISC approach over the *complex instruction set computer* or *CISC* approach of a processor such as the 8086 is that you don't have the overhead of, for example, string instructions which you may never use. RISC instructions typically execute in one or two clock cycles. Another advanced feature integrated in the i860™ is a complete memory-management unit shown at the top of Figure 13-25. In Chapter 15 we describe the operation of memory-management units.

Other Display Technologies

ALPHANUMERIC/GRAPHICS LCD DISPLAYS

In Chapter 9 we discussed the operation, advantages, and interfacing of LCD for displaying individual numbers and letters as individual digits. Because of their light weight, thin profile, and low power dissipation, LCD displays are commonly used in laptop computers. To make a screen-type display the liquid-crystal elements are constructed in a large X-Y matrix of dots. The elements in each row are connected together, and the elements in each column are connected together. An individual element is activated by driving both the row and the column that contain that element. LCD elements cannot be turned on and off fast enough to be scanned one dot at a time in the way that a CRT display is scanned. Therefore, the data for one dot line of one character or for an entire line across the screen is applied to the X axis of the matrix, and that dot row or line is activated. After a short time, that line is deactivated. The data for the next dot row is applied to the X axis, and the Y line for that dot line is activated. The process is continued until the bottom of the screen is reached and then the process starts over at the top of the screen. For large LCDs the matrix may be divided into several blocks of perhaps 40 dot lines each. Since each block of dot rows can be refreshed individually, this reduces the speed at which each liquid-crystal element must be switched in order to keep the entire display refreshed. Large LCDs usually come with the multiplexing circuitry built in so that all you have to do is send the display data to the unit in the format specified by the manufacturer for that unit.

Most laptop computers in the past have used reflective type LCD displays because these displays use very low power. However, reflective displays have the disadvantages that they have low contrast, a relatively narrow viewing angle, and only monochrome displays. A common method of improving these displays has been to display different colors as different shades of gray. The shade of gray is determined by the duty cycle for which the pixel is activated. A device such as the 82C455 graphics controller from Chips and Technologies contains all the circuitry needed to interface with a VGA, EGA, or CGA LCD display with gray scaling.

To produce color displays some portable computers now use transmission-type LCD displays. In this type display the light from a strong fluorescent backlight is passed through the LCD elements and some filters to produce the desired display. As with color CRTs, a triad consisting of a red element, a green element, and a blue element makes up each pixel. The color of the pixel is determined by the relative intensity of the three elements.

In addition to their use as direct display devices transmission type LCD displays can be used to display the output of a computer on an overhead projector. A transparent frame containing the LCD panel and the interface electronics is simply placed on the overhead projector in place of the usual plastic overhead transparency. An example of this type unit is the PC Viewer from In Focus Systems; it produces a 640 × 480 × 16 color display.

The major disadvantages of the transmission-type LCDs currently are their high cost and the relatively large amount of power used by the backlight. The backlight power limits their use in battery-powered laptops.

PLASMA DISPLAYS

Another type display commonly used in portable computers is the plasma type. Plasma displays take advantage of the fact that some gases give off light when an electric current is passed through them. You have no doubt seen neon signs, which use this same principle.

A CRT plasma display consists of an X-Y matrix of pixels which contain neon gas between two electrodes in a tiny glass envelope. When a voltage is applied to both the X and the Y electrodes for a pixel, the pixel will light. A line on the display can be refreshed by applying the data to the X inputs for that line and applying a voltage to the Y input for that line.

Most plasma displays are orange because of the neon gas used, but different shades are commonly used to represent different colors. Color plasma displays are under development. Plasma displays typically have better contrast than reflective LCD, but they also require more power.

COMPUTER MICE AND TRACKBALLS

Figure 13-26*a* shows a common three-button mouse and Figure 13-26*b* shows a common trackball. As we're sure you know, devices such as these are commonly used to move the cursor around on a CRT screen to make drawings or execute commands by selecting a command from a menu. On the bottom of most mice there is a ball which rotates as you move the mouse around on your desk. As the ball rotates, it turns two optical encoder disks. One disk detects mouse motion in the X, or horizontal, direction and the other encoder detects motion in the Y, or vertical, direction. A trackball is essentially a mouse turned upside down so that you rotate the ball directly, instead of moving the mouse around to rotate the ball. The output data from a mouse or trackball consists of the condition of the switches and the amount of motion in the X and Y direction.

There are three major ways that mice and trackballs are interfaced to a computer. Serial mice connect to an RS-232-type serial port such as COM1 on the computer. Bus mice use an interface board which plugs into a slot in the motherboard of the computer. PS/2-type computers have a direct rear panel input especially designed for mice and other "pointer"-type devices.

When you buy a mouse or trackball, it usually comes with a diskful of programs and a fairly large instruction manual. Included on the disk for a mouse are two "drivers," typically called MOUSE.COM and MOUSE.SYS. You install one of these drivers to allow application programs to interface with the mouse. To install the standard mouse driver, MOUSE.COM, you simply copy the file to the DOS subdirectory on your hard disk and insert the command MOUSE in your AUTOEXEC.BAT file. To use the alternate driver, MOUSE.SYS, you copy this file to the DOS subdirectory on your hard disk and insert the statement device = mouse.sys in your CONFIG.SYS file. Either of these methods will load the mouse driver automatically when you boot up the system.

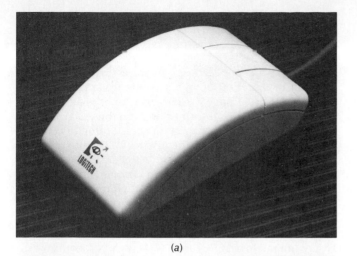

(a)

(b)

FIGURE 13-26 (a) Three-button mouse. (b) Trackball. (LOGITECH.)

In addition to the mouse drivers, the disk that comes with the mouse also contains a program which allows you to create pop-up menus containing a list of commands. To execute one of the commands in a pop-up menu, you move the mouse until a highlighted box appears on the desired command and then press a specified mouse key. For many people this sequence of operations is easier than typing in a command at the DOS prompt. To develop a menu you can choose from one of several menu templates supplied on the disk, or you can generate a custom menu format.

The question that may occur to you at this point is, How do I read mouse data to use in a program? If you are programming at the assembly language level, then the answer is to use the INT 33H procedure which is loaded into RAM as part of the mouse driver. As an introduction, Figure 13-27 shows some of the INT 33H subprocedures, the registers you use to pass parameters to these procedures, and the parameters that are passed back by the procedure. For more information on these consult the IBM Technical Reference Manual for the PS/2 Model 80 Microcomputer.

For high-level-language interfacing with a mouse, some mouse manufacturers supply a library of mouse

```
INTRODUCTION TO INT 33H MOUSE INTERFACE SUBPROCEDURES
AX      FUNCTION
1       Show visible pointer
2       Hide visible pointer

3       Get position and button status
        Returns: BX bit 0 = 1 - left
                 BX bit 1 = 1 - right
                 BX bit 2 = 1 - center
                 CX = X coordinate
                 DX = Y coordinate

4       Set pointer position
        CX = new horizontal position
        DX = new vertical position

11      Read mouse motion counters
        Returns: CX = horizontal mickeys count
                 DX = vertical mickeys count

15      Set mickey/pixel ratio (sensitivity)
        CX = horizontal #mickeys/8 pixels
        DX = vertical #mickeys/8 pixels
```

FIGURE 13-27 Some INT 33H mouse-interface subprocedures.

functions which you can call from your programs. The disk which comes with the Mouse systems mouse, for example, includes the file MSMOUSE.LIB, which contains a C function called mousec(). To use the mousec() function, you first declare four integer variables named m1, m2, m3, and m4 and then load these variables with the values that you want to pass to the AX, BX, CX, and DX registers, respectively, in the INT 33H procedure. You then call the function with the statement mousec (&m1, &m2, &m3, &m4);. The mousec function will put the mouse data in these variables in the same order that it would be returned in 8086 AX, BX, CX, and DX registers for a direct INT 33H call.

If you are programming in C and you do not have the library file containing the mousec function, you can use a function such as the Turbo C int86() to directly call the INT 33H procedure. The keyboard interface program in Figure 13-3 showed you an example of how to use the int86() function.

COMPUTER VISION

For many applications a microcomputer needs to be able to "see" its environment or perhaps a part that the machine it controls is working on. As part of a microcomputer-controlled security system, for example, we might want the microcomputer to "look" down a corridor to see if any intruders are present. In an automated factory application, we might want a microcomputer-controlled robot to "look" in a bin of parts, recognize a specified part, pick up the part, and mount the part on an engine being assembled. There are several mechanisms that can be used to allow a computer to see.

Cameras used in TV stations and for video recorders

use a special vacuum tube called a *vidicon*. A light-sensitive coating on the inside of the face of the vidicon is swept horizontally and vertically by a beam of electrons. The beam is swept in the same way as the beam in a TV set displaying the picture will be swept. The amount of beam current that flows when the beam is at a particular spot on the vidicon is proportional to the intensity of the light that falls on that spot. The output signal from the vidicon for each scan line then is an analog signal proportional to the amount of light falling on the points along that scan line. In order to get this analog video information into a digital form that a computer can store and process, we have to pass it through an A/D converter. For a color camera we need an A/D converter on each of the three color signals. Each output value from an A/D converter then represents a dot of the picture. The number of bits of resolution in the A/D converter will determine the number of intensity levels stored for each dot.

Standard video cameras and the associated digitizing circuitry are relatively expensive, so they are not cost-effective for many applications. In cases where we don't need the resolution available from a standard video camera, we often use a CCD camera.

Charge-coupled devices or CCDs are constructed as long shift registers on semiconductor material. Figure 13-28 shows the structure for a CCD shift register section. As you can see, the structure consists of simply a *P*-type substrate, an insulating layer, and isolated gates. If a gate is made positive with respect to the substrate, a "potential well" is created under that gate. What this means is that if a charge of electrons is injected into the region under the gate, the charge will be held there. By applying a sequence of clock signals to the gates, this stored charge can be shifted along to the region under the next gate. In this way a CCD can function as an analog or a digital shift register.

To make an image sensor, several hundred CCD shift registers are built in parallel on the same chip. A photodiode is doped in under every other gate. When all the gates with photodiodes under them are made positive, potential wells are created. A camera lens is used to focus an image on the surface of the chip. Light shining on the photodiodes causes a charge proportional to the light intensity to be put in each well which has a diode. These charges can be shifted out to produce the dot-by-dot values for the scan lines of a picture. Improved performance can be gained by alternating nonlighted shift registers with the lighted ones. Information for a scan line is shifted in parallel from the lighted register to the dark and then shifted out serially.

The video information shifted out from a CCD register is in discrete samples, but these samples are analog because the charge put in a well is simply a function of the light shining on the photodiode. To get the video information into a form that can be stored in memory and processed by a microcomputer, it must be passed through an A/D converter or in some way converted to digital. For many robot and surveillance applications, a black-and-white image with no gray tones is all we need. In this case the video information from the CCD registers can simply be passed through a comparator to produce a 1 or a 0 for each dot of the image. CCD cameras have the advantages that they are smaller in size, more rugged, more sensitive, less expensive, and easier to interface to computer circuitry than vidicon-based cameras. For these reasons CCD cameras were used in the space telescope recently placed in orbit.

Plug-in boards are available to interface inexpensive CCD cameras to IBM PC- and PS/2-type microcomputers. With one of these boards installed, you can display images on the CRT screen, adjust display parameters under program control, and save images on a disk. Once you get the bit pattern for an image into memory, you can then experiment with programs which attempt to recognize, for example, a bolt in the image.

Another example of the use of computer vision is in *optical scanners*. These devices read text from a piece of paper or some other source and convert the text to a string of ASCII codes which can be displayed, edited, and written to a file.

On a more whimsical note, Figure 13-29 shows an

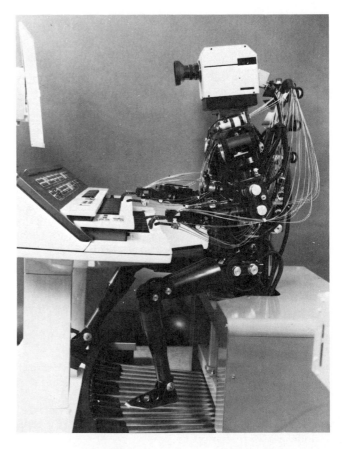

FIGURE 13-29 Sumitomo Electric Company robot playing an organ.

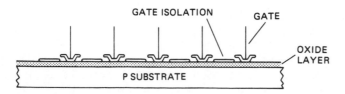

FIGURE 13-28 Structure for a CCD shift-register section.

example of what a little vision can do for a robot. The Sumitomo Electric Company robot shown here can play an organ using both hands on the keys and both feet on the pedals. It can press up to 15 keys per second. The robot can play selections from memory when verbally told to do so. Using its vision it can read and play songs from standard sheet music. The robot uses seventeen 16-bit microprocessors and fifty 8-bit controllers to control all its activities.

If you think some about what is involved in recognizing complex visual shapes—in any of their possible orientations—with a computer program, it should give you a new appreciation for the pattern recognition capabilities of the human eye-brain system.

Another area where the human brain excels is in that of data storage. Only very recently have the devices used to store computer data approached the capacity of the human brain. In the next section we look at how some of these mass data storage systems operate and how they are interfaced to microcomputers.

MAGNETIC-DISK DATA-STORAGE SYSTEMS

The most common devices used for mass data storage are magnetic tape, floppy magnetic disks, hard magnetic disks, and optical disks. Magnetic tapes are used mostly for backup storage, because the access time to get to data stored in the middle of the tape is usually too long to be acceptable for general computing. Therefore, in this section we will concentrate mostly on the three types of disk storage.

Floppy-Disk Overview

Common sizes for floppy disks are 8, $5\frac{1}{4}$, and $3\frac{1}{2}$ in. Figure 13-30a shows the flexible protective envelope used for 8 and $5\frac{1}{4}$-in. disks and Figure 13-30b shows the rigid plastic package used for the $3\frac{1}{2}$-in. disks.

The disk itself is made of Mylar and coated with a magnetic material such as iron oxide or barium ferrite. The Mylar disk is only a few thousandths of an inch thick, thus the name floppy. When the disk is inserted in a drive unit, a spindle clamps in the large center hole or in the center hub and spins the disk at a constant speed of perhaps 300 or 360 rpm.

Data is stored on the disk in concentric, circular tracks. There is no standard number of tracks for any size disk. Older 8-in. disks have about 77 tracks/side, common $5\frac{1}{4}$-in. disks about 40 tracks/side, and the new $3\frac{1}{2}$-in. disks about 80 tracks/side. Early single-sided drives recorded data tracks on only one side of the disk. Current double-sided disk drives store data on both sides of the disk.

Data is written to or read from a track with a read/write head such as that shown diagrammatically in Figure 13-31, page 466. During read and write operations the head is pressed against the disk through a slot in the envelope.

To write data on a track a current is passed through the coil in the head. This creates a magnetic flux in the iron core of the head. A gap in the iron core allows the magnetic flux to spill out and magnetize a section of the magnetic material along the track. Once a region on the track is magnetized in a particular direction, it retains that magnetism. The polarity of the magnetized region

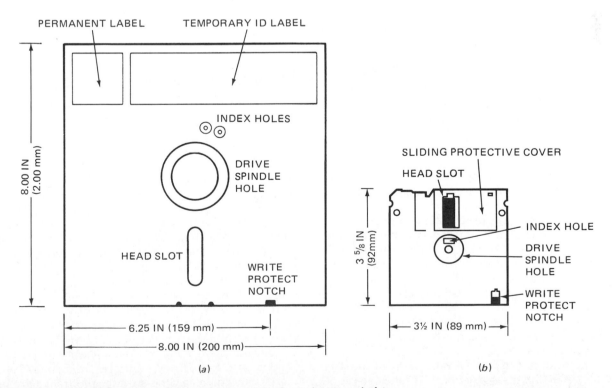

FIGURE 13-30 Common floppy-disk packages. (a) Package for 8- and $5\frac{1}{4}$-in. disks. (b) Hard plastic package used for $3\frac{1}{2}$-in. disks.

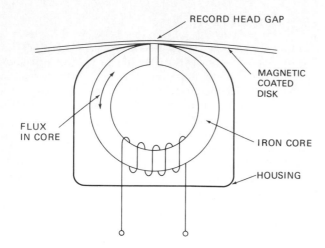

FIGURE 13-31   Diagram of read/write head used for magnetic-disk recording.

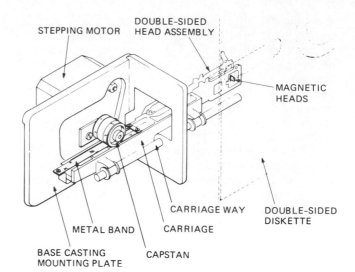

FIGURE 13-32   Common head-positioning mechanism for floppy-disk drive units.

is determined by the direction of the current through the coil. We will say more about this later.

Data can be read from the disk with the same head. Whenever the polarity of the magnetism along the track changes as the track passes over the gap in the read/write head, a small pulse of typically a few millivolts is induced in the coil. An amplifier and comparator convert this small signal to a standard logic level pulse.

The write-protect notch in a floppy disk envelope can be used to protect stored data from being written over, as do the knock-out plastic tabs on video tape cassettes. An LED and a phototransistor in the drive unit determine if the notch is present and enable the write circuits if it is.

On 8-in. and 5¼-in. disks, an index hole punched in the disk indicates the start of the recorded tracks. An LED and a phototransistor are used to detect when the index hole passes as the disk rotates. On 3½-in. disks the start of a track is indicated by the position of the hub in the center of the disk.

The motor used to spin the floppy disk is usually a dc motor whose speed is precisely controlled electronically. It takes about 250 ms for the motor to start up after a start-motor command.

One common method of positioning the read/write head over a desired track on the disk is with a stepper motor. A lead screw or a let-out-take-in steel band such as that shown in Figure 13-32 converts the rotary motion of the stepper motor to the linear motion needed to position the head over the desired track on the disk. As the stepper motor in Figure 13-32 rotates, the steel band is let out on one side of the motor pulley and pulled in on the other side. This slides the head along its carriage.

To find a given track, the motor is usually stepped to move the head to track zero near the outer edge of the disk. Then the motor is stepped the number of steps required to move the head to the desired track. It usually takes a few hundred milliseconds to position the head over a desired track.

Once the desired track is found, the head must be pressed against the disk or *loaded*. It takes about 50 ms to load the head and allow it time to settle against the disk.

If you add the time to start the motor, position the head over the desired track, and load the head, you can see that these operations take 100 to 500 ms, depending on the particular drive. When referring to disk drives, two different access times are usually given. One access time is the time required to get the head to the required track. This time is often called the *seek time*. The other access time is the time required to get to the first byte of a desired block of data on a track. This time is commonly called the *latency time*. For comparing the performance of drives, the average seek time is added to the average latency time to give an *average access time*. Average access times for currently available floppy disk drives range from 100 to 500 ms.

Magnetic Hard-Disk Overview

The floppy disks that we discussed in the previous section have the advantage that they are inexpensive and removable. However, because the disks are flexible, the data tracks cannot be put too close together, and the rate at which data can be read off a disk is limited by the fact that a floppy disk can be rotated at only 300 or 360 rpm. To solve these problems, we use a hard-disk system such as that shown in Figure 13-33.

The disks in a hard-disk system are made of a metal alloy, coated on both sides with a magnetic material. Common hard-disk sizes are 3½, 5¼, 8, 10½, 14, and 20 in. Most hard disks are permanently fastened in the drive mechanism and sealed in a dust-free package, but some systems do have removable disk packages. To increase the amount of storage per drive, several disks or "platters," as they are sometimes called, may be stacked with spacers between as shown in the Conner Peripherals' drive in Figure 13-33. A separate read-write head is used for each disk surface. On disk drives with more than one recording surface, the tracks are often called *cylinders* because if you mentally connect same numbered tracks on the two sides of a disk or on

FIGURE 13-33   Cutaway photo of Conner Peripherals'
CP3100 3-in., 100-Mbyte hard-disk drive.

different disks, the result is a cylinder. The cylinder number then is the same as the track number.

Hard disks are more dimensionally stable than floppies, so they can be spun faster. Large hard disks are rotated at about 1000 rpm and smaller hard disks are rotated at about 3600 rpm. Because the rotational speed is about 10 times that of a floppy disk, data is read out 10 times as fast, about 5 to 10 M*bits*/s.

The dimensional stability of hard disks also means that tracks and the bits on the tracks can be put closer together. There are no standards for the number of tracks on a hard disk, but typically there are several hundred tracks on each side of a disk. The high rotational speed and the closely spaced tracks on a hard disk also produce much faster access times than those of floppy disks. The fastest currently available hard disks have average access times of less than 20 ms.

The high rotational speed of hard disks not only makes it possible to read and write data faster, it creates a thin cushion of air that floats the read-write head 10 to 100 μin. off the disk. Unless the head *crashes*, it never touches the recorded area of the disk, so disk and head wear are minimized. Hard disks must be kept in a dust-free environment because the diameter of dust and smoke particles may be 10 times the distance the head floats off the disk. If dust does get into a hard-disk system, the result will be the same as that which occurs when a plane does not fly high enough to get over a mountain. The head will crash and often destroy the data stored on the disk. When power to the drive is turned off, most hard disk drives retract the head to a *parking zone* where no data is recorded and lock the head in that position until power is restored.

In some early hard-disk drives the read-write heads were positioned over the desired track by a stepper motor and a band actuator, as shown in Figure 13-32. Most current hard-disk drives, however, use a *linear voice coil* mechanism or a *rotary voice coil* mechanism such as that shown in Figure 13-33 to position the read-write heads. This mechanism is essentially a linear motor. A feedback system adjusts the position of the

head over the desired track until the strength of the signal read from the track is at its maximum.

Incidentally, hard-disk drives are sometimes called "Winchesters." Legend has it that the name came from an early IBM dual-drive unit with a planned storage of 30 Mbytes per drive. The 30-30 configuration apparently reminded someone of the famous rifle, and the name stuck.

Magnetic Disk Data Bit Formats

On a magnetic disk a "1" data bit is represented as a change in the polarity of the magnetism on the track. A "0" bit is represented as no change in the polarity of the magnetism. This form of recording is often called *nonreturn-to-zero* or NRZ recording because the magnetic field is never zero on a recorded track. Each point on the track is always magnetized in one direction or the other. The read head produces a signal when a region where the magnetic field changes passes over it.

Clock pulses are usually recorded along with the data bits on a track. The clock pulses read from the track are used to synchronize a phase-locked loop circuit. The output of the phase-locked loop is used to clock a D flip-flop at the center of the bit cell time where the data bits are written. The phase-locked loop is required to synchronize the read out circuits because the actual distance, and therefore time, between data bits read from an outer track is longer than it is for data bits read from an inner track. The phase-locked loop adjusts its frequency to that of the clock transitions and produces a signal which clocks the D flip-flop at the center of each bit time, regardless of the data rate. Recording clock information along with data information not only makes it possible to accurately read data from different tracks, but it also reduces the chances of a read error caused by small changes in disk speed.

Figure 13-34, page 468, shows the three common methods used to code data bits on magnetic disks. The top waveform in the figure shows how the example data bits are represented in a format called *frequency modulation, FM, F2F,* or *single-density* recording. Note the clock transition labeled C at the start of each bit cell in this format. These transitions represent the basic frequency. If the data bit in a cell time is a 1, the magnetic flux is changed again at the center of that bit time. If the data bit in a cell time is a 0, the magnetic flux is left the same at the center of that bit time. Putting in the 1 data transitions modifies the frequency, thus the name frequency modulation or F2F.

One major factor which determines how many data bits can be stored on a track is how close flux changes can be without interfering with each other. A disadvantage of standard F2F recording is that two transitions may be required to represent each data bit. A format which uses only half as many transitions to represent a given set of data bits is the *modified frequency modulation, MFM,* or *double-density* recording format shown as the second waveform in Figure 13-34. The basic principle of this format is that both clock transitions and 1 data transitions are used to keep the phase-locked loop and read circuitry synchronized. Clock transitions are not put in

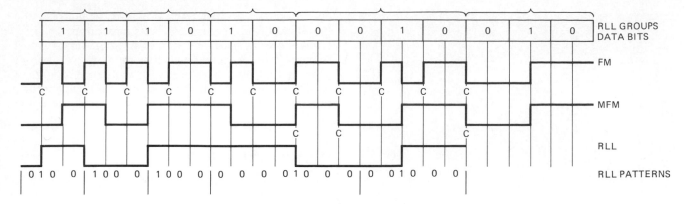

FIGURE 13-34   Comparison of FM, MFM, and RLL coding used for magnetic recording of digital data.

unless 1 transitions do not happen to come often enough in the data to keep the phase-locked loop synchronized. A clock transition will be put in at the start of the bit cell time only if the current data bit is a 0 and the previous data bit was a 0. If you work your way across the second waveform in Figure 13-34, you should see that where two 0's occur in the data sequence, a clock transition is written at the start of the bit cell for the second 0. The MFM waveform in Figure 13-34 is shown on the same scale as the F2F waveform, but since it contains only half as many transitions as the F2F waveform for the same data string, it can be written in half as much distance on a track. This means that twice as much data can be written on a track and explains why this coding is often called double density.

A still more efficient coding for recording data on floppy disks is the *RLL 2,7* format shown as the third waveform in Figure 13-34. In this format groups of data bits are represented by specific patterns of recorded transitions, as shown in Figure 13-35. The two 1's at the start of our data string, for example, are represented by the pattern 0100. To convert a data string to this coding, the data string is separated into groups chosen from the possibilities in the data column of Figure 13-35. The transition pattern which corresponds to that data bit combination is then written on the track. In MFM format there is at most one 0 between transitions, but in RLL 2,7 there are between two and seven 0's between transitions, depending on the sequence of data bits. As you can see in Figure 13-34, RLL requires considerably fewer transitions than MFM to represent the example data string. Fewer transitions mean that the data string

can be written in a shorter section of the track or, in other words, more data can be stored on a given track. RLL coding typically increases the storage capacity about 40 percent over MFM coding.

Most of the magnetic floppy and hard disks of the last 15 years have used longitudinal recording. This means that the magnetic regions are oriented parallel to the disk surface along the track. Advances in read/write head design have made it possible to orient the magnetized regions vertically along the track. Vertical recording makes it possible to store several times as much data per track as can be stored with longitudinal recording. Toshiba and several other companies now market a disk drive which uses vertical recording to store 4 Mbytes of data on a single $3\frac{1}{2}$-in. floppy disk such as that in Figure 13-30b. Some hard disks now available use vertical recording to store over a gigabyte of data in a single drive unit and transfer data at a rate of 3 Mbytes per second.

Magnetic-Disk Track Formats and Error Detection

In the preceding section we described the coding schemes commonly used to record data bits on floppy-disk or hard-disk tracks. The next level up from this is to show you the format in which blocks of data bytes are recorded along a track.

There are many slightly different formats commonly used to organize the data on a track, so we can't begin to show you all of them. However, to give you a general idea, Figure 13-36 shows an old standard, the IBM 3740 format, which is the basis of most current formats.

Each track on the disk is divided into sectors. In the 3740 format a track has three types of fields. An *index field* identifies the start of the track. *ID fields* contain the track and sector identification numbers for each of the 26 data sectors on the track. Each of the 26 sectors also contains a *data field* which consists of 128 bytes of data plus 2 bytes for a CRC error checking code. As you can see, besides the bytes used to store data, many bytes are used for track and sector identification, synchronization, error checking, and buffering between sectors. *Address marks* shown at several places in this

DATA BIT GROUP	RLL 2, 7 CODE
1 0	1 0 0 0
1 1	0 1 0 0
0 0 0	1 0 0 1 0 0
0 1 0	0 0 1 0 0 0
0 1 1	0 0 0 1 0 0
0 0 1 0	0 0 0 0 1 0 0 0
0 0 1 1	0 0 1 0 0 1 0 0

FIGURE 13-35   RLL 2, 7 data bit groups.

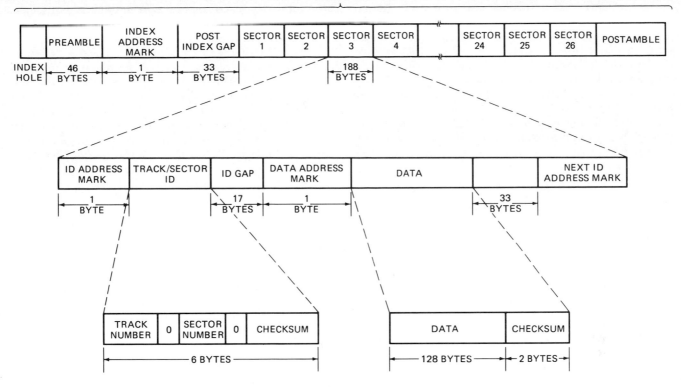

FIGURE 13-36   IBM 3740 floppy-disk soft-sectored track format.

format, for example, are used to identify the start of a field. Address marks, incidentally, have an extra clock pulse recorded with their D2 data bit so they can be distinguished from data bytes.

Two bytes at the end of each ID field and 2 bytes at the end of each data field are used to store *cyclic redundancy characters*. These are used to check for errors when the ID and the data are read out. One way the 2 CRC bytes can be produced is to treat the 128 data bytes as a single large binary number and divide this number by a constant. The 16-bit remainder from this division is written in after the data bytes as the CRC bytes. When the data bytes and the CRC bytes are read out, the CRC bytes are subtracted from the data string. The result is divided by the original constant. Since the original remainder has already been subtracted, the result of the division should be zero if the data was read out correctly. Higher-quality systems usually write data to a disk and immediately read it back to see if it was written correctly. If an error is detected, then another attempt to write can be made. If 10 write attempts are unsuccessful, then an error message can be sent to the CRT or the write can be directed to another sector on the disk.

The IBM 3740 format shown in Figure 13-36 is set up for single-density recording. An 8-in. disk in this format has one index track and 76 data tracks. Since each track has 26 sectors with 128 data bytes in each sector, the total is about 250 Kbytes. If double-density recording is used, the capacity increases to about 500 Kbytes. Using both sides of the disk increases the storage to about 1 Mbyte per disk. For reference, Figure 13-37 shows the

number of tracks, number of sectors, and some other information for floppy disks commonly used with IBM PC and PS/2 computers. There are no real standards for the number of tracks and sectors on hard disks, but later we will give you a few examples.

Magnetic Disk Hardware Interfacing

AN 8272 FLOPPY DISK INTERFACE

As you can probably tell from the preceding discussion, writing data to a floppy disk and reading the data back requires coordination at several levels. One level is the drive motor and head-positioning signals. Another level is the actual writing and reading to the disk at the bit level. Still another level is interfacing with the rest of the circuitry of a microcomputer. Doing all this

	3 1/2-INCH DISKS		5 1/4-INCH DISKS	
	1.44MB HD	720K LD	1.2MB HD	360K DSDD
SECTORS PER TRACK	18	9	15	9
TOTAL NUMBER OF SECTORS	2,880	1,440	2,400	720
NUMBER OF TRACKS	80	80	80	40
SECTORS PER CLUSTER	1	2	1	2
ALLOWABLE ENTRIES IN ROOT DIRECTORY	224	112	224	112

FIGURE 13-37   Comparison of common floppy-disk tracks and sectors.

coordination is a full-time job, so we use a specially designed floppy-disk controller device to do it. As our example device here we will use the Intel 8272A controller, which is equivalent to the NEC μPD765A device used in many disk controller boards for IBM PC-type computers. We chose the 8272A because data sheets and application notes for it are available in Intel Microprocessor and Peripheral Handbook if you want more information than we have space for here.

Figure 11-5 showed you how an 8272A controller can be connected in an 8086-based microcomputer system to transfer data to and from a disk on a DMA basis. Now we want to take a closer look at the controller itself to show you the types of signals it produces and the operations it can perform.

To start, take a look at the block diagram of the 8272A in Figure 13-38. The signals along the left side of the diagram should be readily recognizable to you. The data bus lines, $\overline{RD}$, $\overline{WR}$, A0, RESET, and $\overline{CS}$ are the standard peripheral interface signals. The DRQ, $\overline{DACK}$, and INT signals are used for DMA transfer of data to and from the controller. To refresh your memory from Chapter 11, here's a review of how the DMA works for a read operation.

When a microcomputer program needs some data off the disk, it sends a series of command words to registers inside the controller. The controller then proceeds to find the specified track and sector on the disk. When the controller reads the first byte of data from a sector, it sends a DMA request, DRQ, signal to the DMA controller. The DMA controller sends a hold request signal to the HOLD input of the CPU. The CPU floats its buses and sends a hold-acknowledge signal to the DMA controller. The DMA controller then sends out the first transfer address on the bus and asserts the $\overline{DACK}$ input of the 8272 to tell it that the DMA transfer is underway. When the number of bytes specified in the DMA controller initialization has been transferred, the DMA controller asserts the TERMINAL COUNT input of the 8272. This causes the 8272 to assert its interrupt output signal, INT. The INT signal can be connected to a CPU or 8259A interrupt input to tell the CPU that the requested block of data has been read in from the disk to a buffer in memory. The process would proceed in a similar manner for a DMA write-to-disk operation.

Now let's work our way through the drive control signals shown in the lower right corner of the 8272 block diagram in Figure 13-38. Reading through our brief descriptions of these signals should give you a better idea of what is involved in the interfacing to the disk drive hardware. Note the direction of the arrow on each of these signals.

The READY input signal from the disk drive will be high if the drive is powered and ready to go. If, for

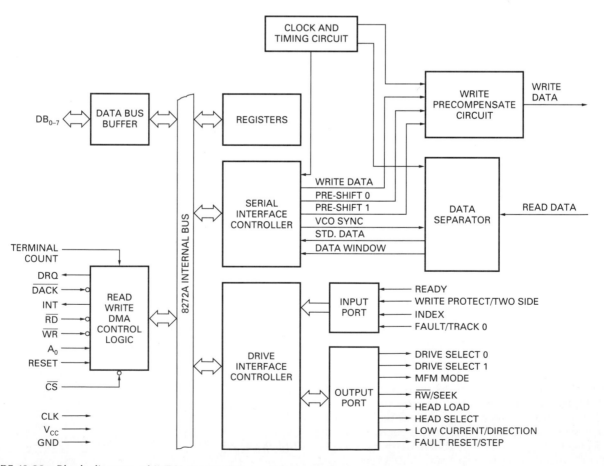

FIGURE 13-38 Block diagram of INTEL 8272A floppy-disk controller system. (*Intel Corporation.*)

example, you forget to close the disk-drive door, the READY signal will not be asserted.

The WRITE PROTECT/TWO SIDE signal indicates whether the write protect notch is covered when the drive is in the read or write mode. When the drive is operating in track-seek mode, this signal indicates whether the drive is two-sided or one-sided.

The INDEX signal will be pulsed when the index hole in the disk passes between the LED and phototransistor detector.

The FAULT/TRACK 0 signal indicates some disk-drive problem condition during a read/write operation. During a track-seek operation this signal will be asserted when the head is over track 0, the outermost track on the disk.

The DRIVE SELECT output signals, DS0 and DS1, from the controller are sent to an external decoder which uses these signals to produce an enable signal for one to four drives.

The MFM output signal will be asserted high if the controller is programmed for modified frequency modulation and low if the controller is programmed for standard frequency modulation (FM).

The $\overline{RW}$/SEEK signal is used to tell the drive to operate in read-write mode or in track-seek mode. Remember, some of the other controller signals have different meanings in the read-write mode than they do in the seek mode.

The HEAD LOAD signal is asserted by the controller to tell the drive hardware to put the read/write head in contact with the disk. When interfacing to a double-sided drive, the HEAD SELECT from the controller is used along with this signal to indicate which of the two heads should be loaded.

During write operations on inner tracks of the disk, the LOW CURRENT/DIRECTION signal is asserted by the controller. Because the bits are closer together on the inner tracks, the write current must be reduced to prevent recorded bits from splattering over each other. When executing a seek-track command this signal pin is used to tell the drive whether to step outward toward the edge of the disk or inward toward the center.

The FAULT RESET/STEP output signal is used to reset the fault flip-flop after a fault has been corrected when doing a read or write command. When the controller is carrying out a track-seek command, this pin is used to output the pulses which step the head from track to track.

Now that we have led you quickly through the drive interface signals, let's take a look at the 8272A signals used to read and write the actual clock and data bits on a track. To help with this, the upper right corner of Figure 13-38 shows a block diagram of the circuitry between these pins and the read/write head.

Remember from our discussion of FM, MFM, and RLL data formats that a phase-locked-loop circuit is required to tell the controller when to sample data bits in the input data stream. The V_{co} SYNC signal from the controller tells an external phase-locked-loop circuit to synchronize its frequency with that of the clock and/data pulses being read off the disk. The output from the phase-locked-loop circuitry is a DATA WINDOW signal. This signal is sent to the controller to tell it where to find the data pulses in the data stream coming in on the READ DATA input.

For writing pulses to the disk, the story is a little more complex. External circuitry supplies a basic WR CLOCK signal. On its WR DATA pin the 8272 outputs the serial stream of clock bits and data bits that are to be written to the disk. During a write operation the 8272 asserts its WR ENABLE signal to turn on the external circuitry that actually sends this serial data to the read/write head. However, data bits written on a disk will tend to shift in position as they are read out. A 1 bit, for example, will tend to shift toward an adjacent 0 bit. This shift could cause errors in readout unless it were compensated for. The PRE-SHIFT 0 and PRE-SHIFT 1 signals from the controller go to external circuitry which shifts bits forward or backward as they are being written. The bits will then be in the correct position when read out.

8272 COMMANDS

The 8272 can execute 15 different commands. Each of these commands is sent to the data register in the controller as a series of bytes. After a command has been sent to the 8272, it carries out the command and returns the results to status registers in the 8272 and/or to the data register in the 8272. In programs you will almost always be interfacing with disks on a much higher level, but to give you an idea of the kinds of operations the 8272A controller can do, we list them here with a short description for each.

SENSE INTERRUPT STATUS—Return interrupt status information.

SPECIFY—Initialize head load time, head step time, DMA/non-DMA.

SENSE DRIVE STATUS—Return drive status information.

SENSE INTERRUPT STATUS—Poll the 8272 interrupt signal.

SEEK—Position read/write head over specified track.

RECALIBRATE—Position head over track 0.

FORMAT TRACK—Write ID field, gaps, and address marks on track.

READ DATA—Load head, read specified amount of data from sector.

READ DELETED DATA—Read data from sectors marked as deleted.

WRITE DATA—Load head, write data to specified sector.

WRITE DELETED DATA—Write deleted data address mark in sector.

READ TRACK—Load head, read all sectors on track.

READ ID—Return first ID field found on track.

SCAN EQUAL—Compare sector of data bytes read from disk with data bytes sent from CPU or DMA controller until strings match. Set bit in status register if match occurs.

SCAN HIGH OR EQUAL—Set flag if data string from disk sector is greater than or equal to data string from CPU or DMA controller.

SCAN LOW OR EQUAL—Set flag if data string from disk sector is less than or equal to data string from CPU or DMA controller.

Working out a series of commands for a disk controller such as the 8272 on a bit-by-bit basis is quite tedious and time-consuming. Fortunately, you usually don't have to do this, because in most systems, you can use higher-level procedures to read from and write to a disk. In a later section we show you some of the software used to interface to disk drives.

ST-506, ESDI, AND SCSI HARD-DISK INTERFACES

The hardware interface for a hard disk is very similar to that for a floppy disk. Data is transferred to and from main memory on a DMA basis, as we described previously. However, in an attempt to maximize the rate of data transfer to and from the disk, several interface standards have developed. In order to understand these standards you first need to have an overview of how a hard disk is connected to microcomputer buses. The block diagram in Figure 13-39a shows how the hard disk in PC-type computers is usually connected. A board containing the hard-disk controller plugs into one of the expansion slots in the motherboard and a ribbon cable connects the controller to the hard disk.

One of the first standards for the interface connections between the controller card and the disk drive was the Seagate Technologies ST-506. This standard specified data and handshake signals very similar to those shown for the floppy interface in Figure 13-38. Standard 5.25-in. ST-506 hard disks use MFM recording with 17 sectors per track, 512 bytes per sector, and a rotation speed of 60 revolutions per second. The maximum rate at which data bits can be read from the track then is 60 tracks/s × 17 sectors/track × 512 bytes/sector × 8 bits/byte = 4,177,920 bits/s, or about 5 Mbits/s. The clocking of the ST-506 is set up to transfer data at a maximum rate of 5 Mbits/s, and this rate was more than adequate for early PC-type computers. In fact, it was necessary to use an *interleave factor* when writing data to the disk and reading data from the disk because the microprocessor and controller circuitry was not fast enough to read and transfer one sector directly after another. If the controller is programmed for an interleave factor of three, it will read a sector, skip over two sectors, and then read another sector. The skipped sectors give the controller time to transfer the data read from the first sector to main memory. Unfortunately, an interleave factor of three reduces the data transfer rate by a factor of three. As processors and controllers have become faster, it has become possible to decrease the interleave factor so that now an interleave factor of 1 is common. The limiting factor for data transfer then becomes the ST-506 transfer rate and the rate at which data bits can be read off the disk.

As we explained earlier, RLL encoding allows more data bits to be written on a track, so if RLL encoding is

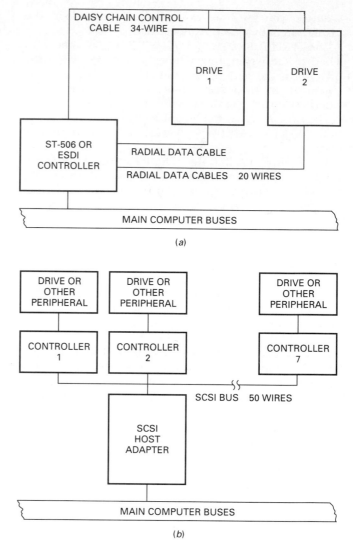

FIGURE 13-39 Common hard-disk controller interface connections. (a) ST-506 or ESDI controller. (b) SCSI I/O bus.

used, more sectors can be put on a track and the maximum data transfer rate increases to about 7.5 Mbits/s for an ST-506/RLL interface.

The next evolutionary hard disk interface step was the *enhanced small device interface* (ESDI) standard. As shown in Figure 13-39a, an ESDI controller interfaces the system bus with hard-disk drives similarly to the way an ST-506 controller does. However, an ESDI controller can access up to seven hard drives using a daisy-chained control cable and individual data cables. Also, an ESDI controller sends higher-level commands to the drive than ST-506, so the drive must have more built-in "intelligence" to interpret these commands. A 10-MHz clock is used for the controller, so the maximum data transfer rate is 10 Mbits/s or 1.25 Mbytes/s. The ESDI standard allows communication with hard disks with maximums of 4096 cylinders, 16 heads, 256 sectors per track, and 4096 bytes per sector. The IBM PS/2 Model 80 uses an ESDI controller.

Another interface standard which was developed about the same time as ESDI is the small computer systems interface (SCSI), which is commonly pronounced "scuzzy." As shown in Figure 13-39b, this standard is very different from the ST-506 and ESDI, because it defines a separate I/O bus. Many different I/O devices such as hard disks, streaming tape drives, optical disk drives, and printers can be connected on this I/O bus. The SCSI host adapter converts operating system commands into SCSI bus commands. These commands are interpreted and carried out by the individual peripheral controllers. An ESDI controller, for example, might be used to interface the SCSI bus with a couple of hard drives. The question that may immediately come to mind here is, Why would anyone want to put the extra layer of hardware between the microcomputer bus and the hard drive controller? The answer to this question is that with a separate I/O bus, many data transfers can take place with very little effort on the part of the main microprocessor. For example, data can be transferred directly from a hard disk to a streaming tape backup on the SCSI bus without having to pass though the main microcomputer data bus. SCSI is designed to allow data transfer at up to 32 Mbits (4 Mbytes) per second. A newer standard, SCSI-II, is designed to allow data transfers at greater than 80 Mbits (10 Mbytes) per second. A still newer standard called enhanced intelligent peripheral interface (EIPI) is designed to allow data transfer at up to 50 Mbytes/s.

Disk Formatting

FLOPPY-DISK FORMATTING

As you probably well know by now, before you can store data on a new floppy disk you have to format it. To do this you use the DOS FORMAT command. The first operation this command performs is to establish a track and sector format such as that in Figure 13-36 on the disk. The second operation performed by the FORMAT command is to set up a boot record, file allocation table, and directory on the disk. Figure 13-40 shows how these are arranged, starting from track 0, sector 0.

The boot record in the first sector of the first track indicates whether the disk contains the DOS files needed to load DOS into RAM and run it. Loading DOS and running it are commonly referred to as "booting" the system.

The directory on the disk contains a 32-byte entry for

---

each file. Let's take a quick look at the use of these bytes to get an overview of the directory information stored for each file.

Byte number
(decimal)

0–7	Filename
8–10	Filename extension
11	File attribute
	01H—read only
	02H—hidden file
	04H—system file
	08H—volume label in first 11 bytes, not filename
	10H—file is a subdirectory of files in lower level of hierarchical file tree
	20H—file has been written to and closed
12–21	Reserved
22–23	Time the file was created or last updated
24–25	Date the file was created or last updated
26–27	Starting cluster number –
28–31	Size of the file in bytes

Most of these parameters should be familiar to you, but the term *cluster* may be new. DOS allocates disk space in clusters of one or more sectors. As shown in Figure 13-37, the number of sectors per cluster depends on the disk size and format. The file allocation table or FAT put on the disk during the FORMAT operation contains an entry for each cluster. The code stored in a FAT entry indicates whether the cluster is available, used, or defective. When you tell DOS to write a file to disk, it searches through the FAT until it finds a cluster which is marked as unused, writes the data to the cluster, and writes the code for used in the FAT entry. If the file is larger than one cluster, DOS searches the FAT until it finds another unused cluster, writes data to the cluster, and writes a used code in the FAT entry for the cluster. To establish a link with the first cluster of the file, DOS writes the number for the second cluster in the FAT entry for the first. The process continues until enough clusters are allocated to contain the file. To summarize, then, the file is stored as a chain of clusters and the FAT entry for each cluster contains the number of the next cluster in the chain. When DOS finishes writing the file to the disk, it updates the directory entry for the file with the time, date, and the number of the starting cluster for the file. Incidentally, DOS actually maintains two identical FATs to provide a backup in case one is damaged.

Also notice in the directory entry format shown here that an entry can represent a file or the name of a subdirectory. Each subdirectory can also refer directly to program or data files, or it can refer to a lower subdirectory. The point here is that this "tree" structure allows you to group similar files together and to avoid going through a long list of filenames to find a particular file you need. To get to a file in a lower-level directory, you simply specify the *path* to that file. The path is simply the series of directory names that you go through to get to that file.

```
┌─────────────────────────────────────────┐
│  Boot record—variable size               │
├─────────────────────────────────────────┤
│  First copy of file allocation           │
│  table—variable size                     │
├─────────────────────────────────────────┤
│  Second copy of file allocation          │
│  table—variable size                     │
├─────────────────────────────────────────┤
│  Root directory—variable size            │
├─────────────────────────────────────────┤
│  Data area                               │
└─────────────────────────────────────────┘
```

FIGURE 13-40 DOS organization of boot record, FATs, directory, and data starting from track 0.

HARD-DISK FORMATTING

Formatting a hard disk usually now involves three different operations, low-level formatting, partitioning, and high-level formatting. To do the low-level format you use DEBUG to execute a program supplied by the manufacturer of the hard-disk controller card. The low-level format operation involves telling the controller the coding, the number of tracks, the number of sectors, the number of data bytes per sector, etc. In a low-level format you also specify the location(s) of any bad sector(s) on the disk. These bad sectors then will not be listed as available. Still another important value you specify in a low-level format is the interleave factor. As we explained before, the interleave factor is the number of sectors between consecutively numbered sectors on a track.

An important point about low-level formatting is that the format generated by a controller card from one manufacturer may not be the same as the format generated by one from another one. This means that if you move a hard disk from one controller card to another, you usually have to do a low-level format with the new controller before you can write to the disk.

To partition a hard disk, you use the DOS FDISK command. This command allows you to divide a large hard disk into as many as four logical drives. Each partition is assigned a drive identifier such as C:, D:, E:, etc. DOS versions before 4.0 limited the maximum size of each partition to 32 Mbytes, but later versions allow partitions of up to 2 Tbytes each. A sector called the partition table at the very start of the disk stores the start and stop cylinder numbers for each partition and a pointer to the partition that the system should boot from when the power is turned on.

To perform high-level formatting on a hard disk, you execute the DOS FORMAT command for each partition. The FORMAT command sets up the boot record, FAT, and directory for that partition in the same way as we described previously for a floppy. If the /s option is specified with the FORMAT command, the two system files needed to load the operating system from disk to RAM will automatically be copied to the disk. When the formatting is done, the rest of the DOS files are copied to the boot partition.

Disk-Drive Interface Software

BIOS-LEVEL INTERFACING

There are several different software levels at which you can interact with a disk drive. You can program directly at the controller level, but this is very tedious. Another approach is to use the BIOS INT 13H procedures to interface with a hard or floppy disk. The difficulty with this procedure is that you have to specify the particular track and sector(s) that you want to read or write and several other parameters. DOS function calls are much easier to use.

USING DOS FUNCTION CALLS

A large part of an operating system such as DOS is a collection of procedures which perform tasks such as formatting disks, creating disk files, writing data to files, reading data from files, and communicating with system peripherals such as modems and printers. DOS allows you to call these procedures from your programs with an INT 21H instruction, similar to the way you call BIOS procedures.

Each DOS function (procedure) has an identification number. To call a DOS function you put the function number in the AH register, put any required parameters in the specified registers, and then execute the INT 21H instruction. As a first example, DOS function call 40H can be used to print a string. To use this procedure, set up the registers as follows:

1. Load the function number, 40H, into the AH register.

2. Load the DS register with the segment base of the segment which contains the string.

3. Load the DX register with the offset of the start of the string.

4. Load the CX register with the number of bytes in the string.

5. Load the BX register with 0004H, the fixed "file handle" for the printer.

Then, to call the DOS procedure, execute the INT 21H instruction. Note that the DOS function allows you to send an entire string to the printer, rather than just a single character at a time as the BIOS INT 17H does.

As another example, the DOS 0AH function will read in a string from the keyboard and put the string in a buffer pointed to by DS:DX. Characters will also be displayed on the CRT as they are entered on the keyboard. The function terminates when a carriage return is entered. To use this function, first set up a buffer in the data segment with the DB directive. The first byte of the buffer must contain the maximum number of bytes the buffer can hold. The 0AH call will return the actual number of characters read in the second byte. The function does not require you to pass it a file handle, because the file handle is implied in the function.

You can also exit from one of your programs and return to the DOS command level using the DOS 4AH function. To do this, load AL with 00 and AH with 4CH and then execute the INT 21H instruction.

The main feature of DOS function calls that we want to discuss here, however, is working with disk files. Many disk operating systems and earlier versions of PC DOS require you to construct a *file control block* or FCB in order to access disk files from your programs. The format of a file control block differs from system to system, but basically the FCB must contain, among other things, the name of the file, the length of the file, the file attribute, and information about the blocks in the file. Version 2.0 and later versions of PC DOS simplify calling DOS file-handling procedures by letting you refer to a file with a single 16-bit number called a *file handle* or *token*. You simply put the file handle for a file you want to access in a specified register and call the DOS procedure which performs the desired action on that file. DOS then constructs the FCB needed to access the file. The question that may occur to you at this point is, How do I know what the file handle is for a file I want to access on a disk? The answer is that to get the file handle for a disk file, you simply call a DOS procedure which returns the file handle in a register. You can then pass the file handle to the procedure that you want to call to access the file. The point here is that file handles make it easy for you to access files.

DOS extends the concept of a file to include any device that can input or output data. DOS treats external devices such as printers, the keyboard, and the CRT as files for read and write operations. These devices are assigned fixed file handles by DOS as follows: 0000—keyboard, 0001—CRT, 0002—error output to CRT, 0003—serial port, 0004—printer. The significance of this is that you can use the same DOS function call to write the data in a buffer to a disk file, to the CRT screen, or to a printer. Also, a stream of data can be *redirected* from one file (device) to another. The DOS command DIR A: > LPT1, for example, will redirect the stream of data produced by the DIR command to the printer instead of sending it to the CRT, which is the normal output device for the DIR command.

As a final example here, Figure 13-41 shows you how DOS function calls can be used to open a file, read data from a file into a buffer in memory, and close the file. Opening a file means copying the file parameters from the directory to a file control block in memory and marking the file as open. Closing a file means updating the directory information for the file and marking the file closed. To open a file and get the file handle, we use DOS function call 3DH. For this call DS:DX must point to the start of an *ASCIIZ* string which contains the disk drive number, the path, and the filename. An ASCIIZ string is a string of ASCII characters which has a byte

of all 0's as its last byte. Also, AL must contain an access code which indicates the type of operation that you want to perform on the file. Use an access code of 00 for read only, 01 for write only, and 02 for read and write. Again, to actually call the function, you load 3DH into AH and execute the INT 21H instruction. The handle for the opened file is returned in the BX register. The first part of Figure 13-41 shows how these pieces are put together.

To read a file we use function call 3FH. For this call BX must contain the file handle and CX the number of bytes to read from the file. DS:DX must point to the buffer location in RAM that the data from the file will be read into. To do the actual call we load 3FH into AH and do an INT 21H instruction. After the file is read, AX contains the number of bytes actually read from the file.

To close the file we load function number 3EH into AH, load the file handle into BX, and execute the INT 21H instruction. The last half of Figure 13-41 shows the instructions you can use to read and close a file. Consult the IBM DOS Technical Reference Manual for the details of all of the available function calls.

DISK INTERFACING IN C

Interfacing with disk drives in C is in some ways very similar to using the DOS function calls as we described in the preceding section. In C as in DOS any device that can input or output data is referred to as a file. To make it easy for programmers to interface with this variety of files ANSI C buffers the files, similar to the way DOS does. Remember that DOS function calls buffer you from the track and sector details by allowing you to refer to a file with a simple file handle. The buffering also produces a uniform data stream regardless of the physical device characteristics. As we said above, this means that you can use the same DOS function call to send the data stream to any one of several different devices.

The predefined C functions for buffered I/O also allow you to work with a data stream in your programs instead of having to worry about the characteristics of the actual physical device or file. To refer to a file C uses a special pointer of type FILE. Type FILE is defined in stdio.h as a pointer to a data structure which is essentially the template for a file control block. To declare a file pointer for use in your program, you use a statement such as FILE *fp;. When you open a file you associate the pointer fp with the file, and for any further interactions with the file you can use fp, just as you use the file handle in DOS function calls. To give you a better idea of how this works, Figure 13-42, page 476, shows a program which opens a file for write, writes a line of text to the file, and then closes the file. The program then opens the file for read, writes the contents of the file to the screen, writes the contents of the file to the printer, and again closes the file. Note that this program requires very few statements to do a considerable amount of work.

To get you used to the way professional C programmers write code, we have included a few statements which contain several actions. The key to interpreting statements such as these, remember, is to start with the innermost parentheses and work your way out from there.

```
;8086 PROGRAM FRAGMENT
;ABSTRACT : This code shows how to use DOS functions
         ; to open a file, read the file contents
         ; into a buffer in memory, and close the file
; Point at start of buffer containing file name
MOV  DX, OFFSET FILE_NAME
MOV  AL, 00              ; open file for read
MOV  AH, 3DH             ; and get file handle
INT  21H
MOV  BX, AX              ; save file handle in BX
PUSH BX                  ; and push for future use
MOV  CX, 2048            ; set up maximum read
MOV  DX, OFFSET FILE_BUF ; point at memory buffer
                         ; reserved for disk file
                         ; contents
MOV  AH, 3FH             ; read disk file
INT  21H
POP  BX             ; get back file handle for close
PUSH AX             ; save file length returned by
                    ; 3FH function call
MOV  AH, 3EH        ; close disk file
INT  21H
; use the file now stored in memory
```

FIGURE 13-41   Using DOS function calls to open and read a file.

```
/* C PROGRAM F13-42.C */

#include<stdio.h>
#include<dos.h>
#include<conio.h>

main()
{
FILE *fp;
char filename[32];
char ch;
char textbuf[100];
char *tp =textbuf;
int count;

/* Open file, write line of text to it, close file */

printf("\n Please enter name of file you want to create.\n");
gets(filename);
if((fp=fopen(filename, "wt"))==0) /* fopen returns 0 if error */
        {
        perror(filename);    /* if error, print error message */
        exit();
        }
printf("Enter a line of text.\n");
gets(tp);                       /* read string into edit buffer */
count = strlen(tp);             /* determine number of bytes */
fwrite(tp,1,count,fp);          /* copy buffer to file */
fclose(fp);                     /* close file */

/* Open file for read and display file contents on screen */

if((fp=fopen(filename,"rt"))==0) /* open for read, check for error */
        {
        perror(filename);  /* if error, print error message */
        exit();
        }
while(!feof(fp))                    /* while not end of file, read */
        fputc(fgetc(fp),stdout); /* file and send to screen */

/* Send contents of file to printer */

rewind(fp);     /* reset file pointer to start of file buffer */

while(!feof(fp))  /* send characters from buffer to printer */
        fprintf(stdprn, "%c", fgetc(fp));

fprintf(stdprn, "\n"); /* carriage return to printer */

fclose(fp);     /* close file */
exit();
}
```

FIGURE 13-42   C program which uses predefined functions to perform file operations.

The program in Figure 13-42 first declares a FILE pointer, as we described earlier, and then declares an array to contain a user-entered file name, and an array to contain a user entered line of text. The program then prompts the user to enter a file name and reads the entered filename into the array named filename. After this the action gets more interesting.

The fp = fopen(filename, "wt") part of the if statement opens the file named filename for write text operations and initializes the file pointer fp to point to the file control block for that file. In programming jargon we say that we have opened a stream named fp. The if(= =0) part of this statement compares the value assigned to fp with 00. A value of 0 for fp indicates that some error occurred when the attempt was made to open the file. The drive door, for example, might have been open.

If an error occurred, we call the perror function, which determines the error that occurred and prints an appropriate error message to the screen. The exit function then returns execution to DOS.

If the file was opened without errors, we then prompt the user to enter a line of text and read the text into the array pointed to by tp. We then use the strlen function to determine how many bytes are in the entered string, so that we can pass this value to the fwrite function. The arguments you pass to the fwrite() function are a pointer to the array you want to write to the disk, the number of bytes in each data item in the array, the number of elements in the array, and the file pointer which identifies the file. The fwrite function actually writes the contents of the array to a buffer maintained by the buffering software, and this software takes care of actually writing the data to the disk. The fclose(fp) function closes the stream to this buffer, writes any data remaining in the buffer to the file, and closes the file.

In the next section of the program we open the file for read by passing the "rt" string to the fopen function. Again we print an error message if the file-open operation was unsuccessful. We then use a while loop to read characters from the fp stream and send them to the stdout stream until the end of file character is detected. The fgetc(fp) function reads a character from the fp stream. The character returned by fgetc() is passed to the fputc() function, along with the destination stream of stdout. Stdout is one of the predefined streams that is opened automatically by the C startup code. The predefined streams are stdin, stdout, errout, and stdaux, which refer to the CRT, and stdprn, which refers to the default printer. Now let's look at how we can send the contents of the file to the printer.

To keep track of the current location in a stream, the C buffering system maintains a stream pointer. After reading the characters in from the file and sending the characters to the CRT, the stream pointer for fp will be pointing at the end of the file. Before we can perform any other operation on this stream, we have to reset the stream pointer to the start of the file. The rewind(fp) function call does this.

The final part of the program in Figure 13-42 uses another while loop to read characters from the fp stream and send them to the printer until the end of file character is found. The arguments you pass to the fprintf() function are the destination stream, a format specifier, and the value of the variable you want to print. In this call the value to be printed is the value returned from the fp stream by the fgetc(fp) function call. Finally, we close the stream and the file with the fclose() function. An exercise in the accompanying lab manual gives you a further chance to work with these operations.

RAM DISKS

The VDISK command found in DOS versions 3.3 and later allows you to set aside an area of RAM in such a way that it appears to DOS as simply another disk drive. In a computer that has actual drives A:, B:, and C:, you can create a RAM or virtual drive which you access as D:. You can copy files to and from this RAM disk by name just as you would for any other drive. Here's an example of why you might want to set up a virtual drive.

When you load a large program such as Wordstar into memory to run it, the basic program and some commands are loaded, but some of the program remains on disk. This is done so that the program will run in systems that do not have a large amount of memory. When you execute a command that has not been loaded into memory, the code for that command is read from the disk and executed. If you have enough memory in your system, you can create a RAM drive and copy all the Wordstar files to that drive. The commands can then be accessed much faster because there is no mechanical access time as there is with an actual disk. The advantage of configuring the RAM as a disk drive is that the software can access it just as if it were on an actual disk.

DISK CACHES

Another commonly seen term in current computer periodicals is *disk cache*. A disk cache functions similarly to the RAM cache we discussed in Chapter 11. The principle of a RAM cache, remember, is to keep often-used sections of code and data in a fast SRAM cache where it can be accessed without wait states.

The DOS *BUFFERS command*, which you usually put in your CONFIG.SYS file with a statement such as BUFFERS = 20, sets aside RAM to hold data read in from disk files. Each buffer created with this command contains 528 bytes. The problem with this approach is that if you create too many buffers, the overhead of determining if a desired file section is present becomes too long and performance actually decreases. Another problem with the BUFFERS approach is that only the requested data is read into the buffers.

Programs such as IBMCACHE which come with the PS/2 50, 60, and 80 computers allow you to set up a separate block of 16 Kbytes to 512 Kbytes as a cache for data read from disk. When disk read occurs, all or at least a large part of the file can be read into the disk cache. This reduces the number of disk accesses required and makes "disk-intensive" programs execute two or three times faster. When a program writes data to a file that is in the cache, the data is written to the cache and to the actual file on the disk, so that the data will not be lost in case of a power failure.

Hard-Disk Backup Storage

To prevent data loss in the event of a head crash, hard disk files are backed up on some other medium such as floppy disks or magnetic tape. The difficulty with using floppy disks for backup is the number of disks required. Backing up a 70-Mbyte hard disk with 1.2-Mbyte floppies requires about 60 disks and considerable time shoving disks in and out. Most systems with large hard disks now use a high-speed magnetic tape system for backup. A typical *streaming tape* system, as these high-speed systems are often called, can dump or load the entire contents of a large hard disk to a single tape in a few minutes.

OPTICAL DISK DATA STORAGE

The same optical disk technology used to store audio on compact disks can be used to store very large quantities of digital data for computers. One unit now available, the Maxtor Tahiti I, for example, stores up to a total of 1 Gbyte (1000 Mbytes) of data on a single, removable $5\frac{1}{4}$-in. disk. This amount of storage corresponds to about 400,000 pages of text. Besides their ability to store large amounts of data, optical disks have the advantages that they are relatively inexpensive and immune to dust, and most are removable. Also, since data is written on the disk and read off the disk with the light from a tiny laser diode, the read/write head does not have to touch the disk. The laser head is held in position about 0.1 in. away from the disk, so there is no disk wear. Also, the increased head spacing means that the head will not crash on small dust particles and destroy the recorded data as it can with magnetic hard disks.

The disk sizes now available in different systems are 3.5, 4.72 (the compact audio disc size), 5.25, 12, and 14 in. Data storage per disk ranges from 60 Mbytes to several gigabytes. The actual drive and head-positioning mechanisms for optical disk drives are very similar to those for magnetic hard-disk drives. A feedback system is used to precisely control the speed of the motor which rotates the disk. Some units spin the disk at a constant angular velocity (CAV) in the range of 700 to 3000 rpm. Other systems such as those based on the compact audio (CD) format adjust the rotational speed of the disk so that the track passes under the head with a constant linear velocity (CLV). With CLV the disk is rotated slower when reading outer tracks.

Some optical disk systems record data in concentric circular tracks as magnetic disks do. Other systems, such as the CD disk systems, record data on a single spiral track in the same way a phonograph record does. A linear voice coil mechanism with feedback control is used to precisely position the read head over a desired track. The head positioning must be very precise, because the tracks on an optical disk are very narrow and very close together. The tracks are typically about 20 μin. wide and about 70 μin. between centers. This spacing allows tens of thousands of tracks to be put on a disk.

Optical disk systems are available in three basic types: read only, write once/read many, and read/write.

Read-only systems allow only prerecorded disks to be read out. A disk which can only be read from is often called an *optical ROM* or *OROM*. Examples of this type are the 4.7-in. compact audio disks and the optical disk encyclopedias.

Write once/read many or *WORM* systems allow you to write data to a disk, but once the data is written, it cannot be erased or changed. The stored data can be read out as many times as desired.

Erasable optical or *EO* systems allow you to erase recorded data and write new data on a disk. The recording materials and the recording methods are different for these different types of systems.

Disks used for read only and write once/read many systems are coated with a substance which is altered when a high-intensity laser beam is focused on it with a lens. The principle here is similar to using a magnifying glass to burn holes in paper, as you may have done in your earlier days. In some systems the focused laser light produces tiny pits along a track to represent 1's. In other systems a special metal coating is applied to the disk over a plastic polymer layer. When the laser beam is focused on a spot on the metal, heat is transferred to the polymer, causing it to give off a gas. The gas given off produces a microscopic bubble at that spot on the thin metal coating to represent a stored 1. Both of these recording mechanisms are irreversible, so once written, the data can only be read. Data can be read from this type of disk using the same laser diode used for recording, but at reduced power. A system might for example use 25 mW for writing, but only 5 mW for reading.

To read the data from the disk, the laser beam is focused on the track and a photodiode is used to detect the beam reflected from the data track. A pit or bubble on the track will spread out the laser beam light so that very little of it reaches the photodiode. A spot on the track with no pit or bubble will reflect light to the photodiode. Read-only and write-once systems are less expensive than read/write systems, and for many data-storage applications the inability to erase and rerecord is not a major disadvantage. One example of a WORM optical drive is the Control Data Corporation LaserDrive 510, which stores 654 Mbytes on a removable ANSI/ISO standard $5\frac{1}{4}$-in. disk cartridge.

Most current read/write optical disk systems use disks coated with an exotic metal alloy which has the required magnetic properties. The read/write head in this type of system has a laser diode and a coil of wire. A current is passed through the coil to produce a magnetic field perpendicular to the disk. At room temperature the applied vertical magnetic field is not strong enough to change the horizontal magnetization present on the disk. To record a 1 at a spot in a data track, a pulse of light from the laser diode is used to heat up that spot. Heating the spot makes it possible for the applied magnetic field to flip the magnetic domains around at that spot and create a tiny vertical magnet. This is called *magneto-optical* or *MO recording*.

To read data from this magneto-optical type disk, polarized laser light is focused on the track. When the polarized light reflects from one of the tiny vertical magnets representing a 1, its plane of polarization is rotated a few degrees. Special optical circuitry can detect this shift and convert the reflections from a data track to a data stream of 1's and 0's. A bit is erased by turning off the vertical magnetic field and heating the spot corresponding to that bit with the laser. When heated with no field present, the magnetism of the spot will flip around in line with the horizontal field on the disk. One example of a currently available read/write optical drive that uses MO recording is the Maxtor Corporation Tahiti I, which stores about 600 Mbytes on an ANSI/ISO standard $5\frac{1}{4}$-in. disk cartridge or 1 Gbyte on a special $5\frac{1}{4}$-in. cartridge. The Tahiti I has an average access time of 30 ms, which compares favorably with the 16- to 25-ms access times of the fastest current hard-disk drives.

The maximum data transfer rate for the Tahiti I is 10 Mbits/s, which is the same order of magnitude as the transfer rate for the leading hard disk units. Incidentally, most optical disk drives use the SCSI interface we described previously.

The amount of data storage on one optical disk is impressive, but to store even more data there are now available several "jukebox" optical disk systems, which can hold up to 256 removable disks. Typically, it takes only a few seconds to load a desired disk into the actual drive so it can be accessed. Optical disks have the further advantage that the disk cartridge is easily removable and can be locked away for safety and security purposes.

The potentially low cost of a few cents per megabyte and the hundreds of gigabytes of data storage possible for optical disk systems may change the whole way our society transfers and processes information. The contents of a sizable library, for example, can be stored on a few disks. Likewise, the entire financial records of a large company can be kept on a single disk. "Expert" systems for medical diagnosis or legal defense can use a massive data base stored on disk to do a more thorough analysis. Engineering workstations can use optical disks to store data sheets, drawings, graphics, or IC-mask layouts. The point here is that optical disks bring directly to your desktop computer a massive data base that previously was available only through a link to large mainframe computers or, in many cases, was not available at all. The large data storage capacity of optical disks also make them useful for a system called Digital Video Interactive, which we discuss in the last section of this chapter.

PRINTER MECHANISMS AND INTERFACING

Many different mechanisms and techniques are used to produce printouts or "hard" copies of programs and data. This section is intended to give you an overview of the operation and trade-offs of some of the common printer mechanisms. We start with those that mechanically hit the paper in some way.

Dot-Matrix Impact Print Mechanisms

Figure 13-43 shows an impact-type dot-matrix print head. Thin print wires driven by solenoids at the rear of the print head hit the ribbon against the paper to produce dots. The print wires are arranged in a vertical column so that characters are printed out one dot column at a time as the print head is moved across a line of characters. As we mentioned in an earlier chapter, a stepper motor is commonly used to move the print head across the paper, and another stepper motor is used to advance the paper to the next character row.

Early dot-matrix print heads had only seven print wires, so print quality of these units was not too good. Currently available dot-matrix printers use 9, 14, 18, or even 24 print wires in the print head. Using a large number of print wires and/or printing a line twice, with

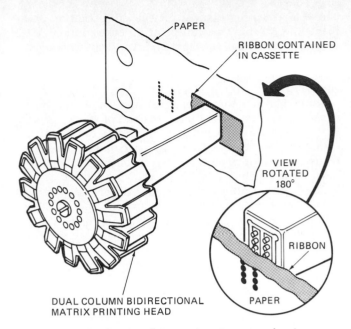

FIGURE 13-43 Impact dot-matrix printer mechanism. (*Courtesy DATAPRODUCTS Corporation.*)

the dots for the second printing offset slightly from those of the first, produces "letter-quality" print. Dot-matrix printers can also print graphics. To do this the dot pattern for each column of dots is sent out to the print-head solenoids as the print head is moved across the paper. The principle is similar to the way we produce bit-mapped raster graphics on a CRT screen. By using different-color ribbons and making several passes across a line, some dot-matrix impact printers allow you to print color graphics. Most dot-matrix printers now contain one or more microprocessors to control all this.

Print speeds for dot-matrix impact printers range up to 350 cps. Some units allow you to use a low-resolution mode of 200 cps for rough drafts, a medium resolution mode of 100 cps for finish copy, or 50 cps for near-letter-quality printing. The advantages of dot-matrix impact printers are their relatively low cost and their ability to change fonts or print graphics under program control.

Dot-Matrix Thermal Print Mechanisms

Most thermal printers require paper which has a special heat-sensitive coating. When a spot on this special paper is heated, the spot turns dark. Characters or graphics are printed with a matrix of dots. There are two main print-head shapes for producing the dots. For one of these the print head consists of a 5 by 7 or 7 by 9 matrix of tiny heating elements. To print a character the head is moved to a character position and the dot-sized heating elements for the desired character are turned on. After a short time the heating elements are turned off and the head is moved to the next character position. Printing then is done one complete character at a time.

The second print-head configuration for thermal dot-matrix printers has the heating elements along a metal bar which extends across the entire width of the paper.

There is a heating element for each dot position on a print line, so this type can print an entire line of dots at a time. The metal bar removes excess heat. Characters and graphics are printed by stepping the paper through the printer one dot line at a time. A few thermal printers can print up to 400 lines/min.

Some of the newer thermal printers have the heat-sensitive material on a ribbon instead of on the paper. When a spot on the ribbon is heated, a dot of ink is transferred to the paper. This approach makes it possible to use standard paper and, by switching ribbons, to print color graphics as well as text.

The main advantage of thermal printers is their low noise. Their main disadvantages are: the special paper or ribbon is expensive, printing carbon copies is not possible, and most thermal printers with good print quality are slow.

Laser and Other Page Printers

These printers operate on the same principle as most office copiers. The basic approach is to first form an image of the page that is to be printed on a photosensitive drum in the machine. Powdered ink, or "toner," is then applied to the image on the drum. Next the image is electrostatically transferred from the drum to a sheet of paper. Finally the inked image on the paper is "fused" with heat.

In an office copy machine a camera lens is used to produce an image of the original on the photo-sensitive drum. In page printers used with computers, there are three common methods of producing the image on the drum. The most common method and the one that gives us the name laser printer is with a laser, as shown in Figure 13-44. A rotating mirror sweeps a laser beam across the photosensitive drum as it rotates. The laser beam is turned on and off as it is swept back and forth

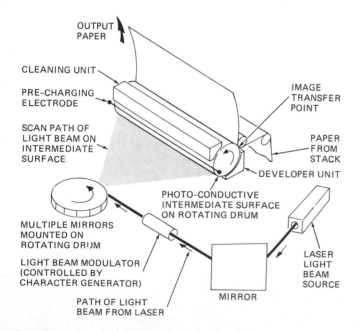

FIGURE 13-44 Laser printer mechanism. (*Courtesy DATAPRODUCTS Corporation.*)

across the drum to produce an image in about the same way that an image is produced on a raster scan CRT. After the image on the drum is inked and transferred to the paper, the drum is cleaned and is ready for the next page.

A second way of producing the dots on the photosensitive drum is with a linear array of tiny LEDs. The image is generated one line at a time as the drum rotates. This approach has less moving parts than the laser approach, but if an LED burns out, it will leave a blank streak through the printout.

The third common method of producing the image on the drum is with a linear array of tiny liquid-crystal "shutters." When the shutter is opened, the light from a bright backlight exposes a spot on the drum. As with the other methods, the image is produced on the drum one line at a time.

One major advantage of laser and other page printers is their high print quality. Commonly available lower-priced units have a resolution of 300 dots per inch, and the next generation will probably extend this to 600 dots per inch. For comparison, 1200 to 2400 dots per inch are commonly used for high-quality typesetting. Print speeds are in the range of 10 to 12 pages per minute for text and 1 to 4 pages per minute for graphics.

The control circuitry in, for example, a laser page printer is much more complex than that in an impact-type dot-matrix printer because the image is developed as a large dot matrix with many dots. To generate complex images as rapidly as possible, these printers often use a high-speed microprocessor with a graphics processor, similar to the CRT system shown in Figure 13-23. The dot patterns for several different character fonts are usually included in the ROMs in the controller so that you are not restricted to just one character set. Some of these printers also allow you to download custom character fonts to RAM in the printer. Several megabytes of RAM are needed in the printer to hold the data for complex graphics images.

To produce graphics and page layouts you write a program using a *printer control language* or *PCL*. The three most common languages are HP's PCL-4, Cannon's CaPCL, and Adobe's Postscript. These languages allow you to specify where to draw lines on the page, the scale factor for characters, gray shading, and many other page features.

Ink-Jet Printers

Still another type of printer that uses a dot-matrix approach to produce text and graphics is the ink-jet. Early ink-jet printers used a pump and a tiny nozzle to send out a continuous stream of tiny ink globules. These ink globules were passed through an electric field, which left them with an electrical charge. The stream of charged ink globules was then electrostatically deflected to produce characters on the paper in the same way that the electron beam is deflected to produce an image on a CRT screen. Excess ink was deflected to a gutter and returned to the ink reservoir. Ink-jet printers are relatively quiet, and some of these electrostatically deflected ink-jet printers can print up to 45,000 lines/min. Several disadvantages, however, prevented them from being used more widely. They tend to be messy and difficult to keep working well. Print quality at high speeds is poor and multiple copies are not possible.

Newer ink-jet printers use a variety of approaches to solve these problems. Some, such as the HP Thinkjet, use ink cartridges which contain a column of tiny heaters. When one of these tiny heaters is pulsed on, it causes a drop of ink to explode onto the paper. Others, such as the IBM Quietwriter, for example, use an electric current to explode microscopic ink bubbles from a special ribbon directly onto the paper. These last two approaches are really hybrids of thermal and ink-jet technologies. They can produce very near letter-quality print at speeds comparable to those of slower dot-matrix impact printers. A disadvantage of some ink-jet printers is that they require special paper for best results.

SPEECH SYNTHESIS AND RECOGNITION WITH A COMPUTER

In a great many cases it is very convenient for a computer to communicate verbally with a user. Some examples of the use of computer-created speech are talking games, talking cash registers, and text-to-speech machines used by blind people. Other examples are medical monitor systems that give verbal warnings and directions when some emergency condition exists. This use demonstrates some of the major advantages of speech readout. The verbal signal attracts more attention than a simple alarm, and the user does not have to search through a series of readouts to determine the problem.

Adding speech recognition circuitry to a computer so that it can interpret verbal commands from a user also makes the computer much easier to use. The pilot of a rocket ship or space shuttle, for example, can operate some controls verbally while operating other controls manually. (It probably won't be too long before we eliminate the verbal/manual link and control the whole ship directly from the brain, but that is another story, perhaps in the next book.) Voice entry systems are also useful for handicapped programmers and other computer users. We will first describe for you the different methods used to create speech with a computer and then describe some speech-recognition methods.

Speech-Synthesis Methods

There are several common methods of producing speech from a computer. The trade-offs between the different methods are speech quality and the number of bits that must be stored for each word. In other words, the higher the speech quality you want, the more bits you have to store in memory to represent each word and the faster you have to send bits to the synthesizer circuitry. All the common methods of speech synthesis fall into two general categories: waveform modification and direct digitization. In order to explain how the waveform-modification approaches work, we need to talk briefly about how humans produce sounds.

WAVEFORM-MODIFICATION SPEECH SYNTHESIS

Some speech sounds, called voiced sounds, are produced by vibration of the vocal cords as air passes from the lungs. The frequency of vibration or *pitch*, the position of the tongue, the shape of the mouth, and the position of the lips determine the actual sound produced. The vowels A and E are examples of voiced sounds. Another type of sound, called unvoiced sound, is produced by modifying the position of the tongue and the shape of the mouth as a constant stream of air comes from the lungs. The letter S is an example of this type of sound. A third type of sound, the nasal sounds—called *fricatives*—consist of a mixture of voiced and unvoiced sounds. In electronic terms then, the human vocal system consists of a variable-frequency signal generator as the source for voiced sounds, a "white" noise signal source for unvoiced sounds, and a series of filters which modify the outputs from the two signal sources to produce the desired sounds. Figure 13-45 shows this in block diagram form.

The three main approaches to implementing this model electronically are *linear predictive coding* or LPC, *formant filtering*, and *phoneme synthesis*. These methods differ mostly in the type of filter used and in how often the filter characteristics are updated.

LPC synthesizers, such as that in the Texas Instruments "Speak and Spell," use a digital filter such as we described in Chapter 10 to modify the signals from a pulse and a white noise source. For this type of filter the parameters that must be sent from the microcomputer are the coefficients for the filter and the pitch for the pulse source. Remember from the discussion in Chapter 10 that for a digital filter, the current output value is computed or "predicted" as the sum of the current input value and portions of previous input values. A high-quality LPC synthesizer may require as many as 16 Kbits/s. An example of a currently available LPC speech chip is the TI TSP50C10. For further information about LPC synthesis, consult the data sheet for this device.

The formant filter speech-synthesis approach uses several resonant or *formant* filters to massage the signals from a variable-frequency signal source and a white noise source. Figure 13-46, page 482, shows how the frequencies of these formant filters might be arranged for a male and for a female voice. For this type of system the parameters that must be sent from the computer are the pitch of the variable-frequency signal, the center frequency for each formant filter, and the bandwidth of each formant filter. The data rate for direct formant

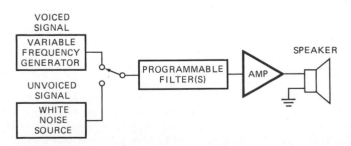

FIGURE 13-45 Electronic model of human vocal tract.

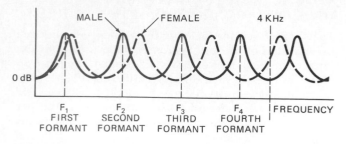

FIGURE 13-46 Filter responses for formant speech synthesizer.

synthesis is only about 1 Kbit/s, but the parameters must be determined with complex equipment. It is not easy to develop a custom vocabulary for a specific application. A phoneme approach solves this problem and requires a still lower data rate at the expense of lower speech quality.

Phonemes are fragments of words. An example of a phoneme speech synthesizer is the Artic Technologies 263A, which can be interfaced with a microcomputer port or in some cases interfaced directly to microprocessor buses. Words are produced by sending a series of 6-bit phoneme codes to the device. Five internal 8-bit registers also allow you to control parameters such as speech rate, pitch, amplitude, articulation rate, and vocal tract filter response. Inside the 263A the 6-bit phoneme code is used to control the characteristics of some formant filters, as described in the previous paragraph. Since only one code is sent out for a relatively long period of speech, the required bit rate is only about 70 bits/s. However, the long period between codes gives less control over waveform details and, therefore, sound quality. A phoneme synthesizer has a mechanical sound. One big advantage of phoneme synthesizers is that you can make up any message you want by simply putting together a sequence of phoneme codes.

DIRECT DIGITIZATION SPEECH SYNTHESIS

Direct digitation speech synthesis produces the highest-quality speech, because it is essentially just a playback of digitally recorded speech. To start, the word you want the computer to speak is spoken clearly into a microphone. The output voltage from the microphone is amplified and applied to the input of perhaps a 12-bit A/D converter. One approach at this point might be to simply store the A/D samples for the word in a ROM and read the values out to a D/A converter when you want the computer to speak the word. The difficulty with this approach is that if the samples are taken often enough to produce good speech quality, a lot of memory is required to store the samples for a word. To reduce the amount of memory required, several speech-compression algorithms are used. These algorithms are too complex to discuss here, but the basic principles involve storing repeated waveforms only once, taking advantage of symmetry in waveforms, and not storing values for silent periods. Even with compression, however, direct digital speech requires considerable memory and a bit rate as high as 64 Kbits/s. To further reduce the memory

required for direct digital speech, some systems use differential or *delta* modulation. In these systems only a 3-bit or 4-bit code, representing how much a sample has changed from the last sample, is stored in memory instead of storing the complete 12-bit value. This system works well for audio signals, since they change slowly.

The OKI Semiconductor MSM6388 device contains much of the circuitry needed to digitize and reproduce speech using adaptive-differential pulse code modulation (ADPCM). This device contains a microphone pre-amplifier, A/D converter, D/A converter, and some low-pass filters. The digital values produced by the A/D converter are stored in external memory. About 260 s of speech can be stored in 4 Mbits of external memory.

Another example of a direct digital synthesis system is the National Semiconductor *Digitalker*. For further information, consult the data sheets for these devices.

Speech Recognition

Speech recognition is considerably more difficult than speech synthesis. The process is similar to trying to recognize human faces with a computer vision system. With most speech-recognition systems the first step is to train the system or, in other words, produce templates for each of the words that the system needs to recognize and store these templates in memory. To produce a template for a word, the intended user speaks the word several times into a microphone connected to the system. The system then determines several parameters or *features* for each repetition of the word and averages them to produce the actual template.

Different systems extract different parameters to form the template. One of the most common methods uses a set of formant filters with their center frequencies adjusted to match those of the average speaker. The output amplitude of each formant filter is averaged to produce a signal proportional to the energy in that frequency band. Also used are one or more zero-crossing detectors to give basic frequency information. The pulse train from the zero-crossing detector is converted to a proportional voltage, so it can be digitized along with the outputs from the formant averagers.

When a word is spoken, samples of each of the features are taken and digitized at evenly spaced intervals of 10 to 20 ms during the duration of the word. The features are stored in memory. If this is a training run, the set of samples will be averaged with others to form the template for the word. If this is a recognition run, this set of features will be compared with the templates stored in memory. The best match is assumed to be the correct word. Currently none of the available voice-recognition systems is 100 percent accurate, but they are improving.

The best current example of speech recognition is probably the Dragon Systems Inc. DragonDictate which consists of a PC- or PS/2-compatible plug-in board and software. This system has a built-in vocabulary of 25,000 words and allows the user to define up to 5000 more words. This unit is intended for use in speech-to-text applications such as generating reports. When a user speaks a word, the system looks up the most likely match and sends the match word to the screen. If the word is incorrect, the user can correct the word verbally or with the keyboard. The system is adaptive, so its recognition rate improves with continued use. Incidentally, the DragonDictate system uses a TMS32010 digital signal processor device we described in Chapter 10 to filter the input signal.

A less expensive PC-compatible speech-recognition unit is the VPC 2000 from VOTAN Inc. In addition to recognizing words or phrases, this unit also has a built-in voice-activated telephone dialing and answering service. Another PC-compatible unit, the VocaLink from Interstate Voice Products, permits the programming of up to 240 spoken commands to control standard PC software such as word processors and business programs. Perhaps the HAL 9000 is not too far away.

DIGITAL VIDEO INTERACTIVE

In this chapter we have shown you how text and graphics images are produced on a CRT; how text, speech, and graphics data are stored on magnetic or optical disks; and how a computer can be used to recognize and generate speech. To us the most exciting applications of all these technologies are compact digital-interactive (CD-I) and digital video interactive (DVI). CD-I was developed by Phillips and DVI was developed by the David Sarnoff Research Center and later purchased by Intel Corporation, which is continuing its development. The systems are very similar, but we will concentrate on DVI for this discussion.

The Intel DVI system consists of some very powerful software and two circuit boards which plug into a PC- or PS/2-type computer. This system allows up to 72 min of full-motion video images and stereo sound to be produced on the computer from a single $5\frac{1}{4}$-in. optical disk. There are two very significant points about this.

First, the system is interactive. This means that the image and sound output at any particular time depends on the input that you supply with the keyboard, a mouse, or perhaps a joystick. One example called Design and Decorate, which was developed to demonstrate DVI, allows you to place furniture in a room, move the furniture around in the room, and even reupholster the furniture with different fabrics. Another DVI demonstration allows you to fly a plane around "real" landscapes. Another demo allows you to landscape an image of your house and see how it will look as the plants mature. Still another demo teaches you how to use a camera. This demo allows you to focus the camera and see the effect of f-stop on depth of field, etc. Perhaps you can see from these brief discussions that DVI has great potential for individualized education, entertainment, and marketing.

The technique that makes DVI possible is audio and video compression. As we explained in a previous section on digitizing speech signals, adaptive-differential pulse code modulation can be used to reduce the amount of data required to store a digitized audio signal. This technique is based on the fact that audio signals change relatively slowly, so instead of storing a value for the entire amplitude at each point on the signal, only a value for the change from the previous data point is stored.

Most of the time video images also change relatively slowly. The amount of data required to store a sequence of video images can be drastically reduced by storing the data for the first frame in the sequence and then just storing changes from that frame for the rest of the frames in the sequence. Further reduction can be accomplished by taking advantage of the fact that the resolution of the human eye is not as fine for color images as it is for monochrome images. The DVI system stores the color data for every fourth pixel and interpolates to get the color values for the pixels in between these.

To give you an idea of how important this video compression is, remember from the discussions earlier in the chapter that about 153 Kbytes of memory are required to store the pixel data for one frame of a 640 $\times$ 480 $\times$ 16 color display. With a refresh rate of 60 frames/s, a 648-Mbyte optical disk could hold only about 70 s of video frames. The DVI system requires an average of only about 5 Kbytes to store the data for a frame.

The steps involved in developing an application using the DVI system are as follows:

1. Use the edit level video (ELV) editor that comes with the system to digitize the basic video image sequence and reduce the resolution of the images to 256 $\times$ 240 pixels.

2. Digitize the audio signal.

3. Use ELV editor to select the desired video and audio sequences.

4. Add text, graphics images, and control programming.

5. Send the original video and the editor output to Intel or some other vendor who will use a high-speed parallel computer to produce the compressed video and audio data. This output is called presentation level video (PLV).

6. Combine the PLV with the ELV editor output and use the result to program a WORM or EO disk.

For further information on developing DVI applications, see the references in the Bibliography.

Once the DVI disk is programmed, it can be "played" on a compatible optical disk drive and run with the DVI software. The DVI boards decompress the video image data, decompress the audio and data, and interact with the user. Perhaps in the not-too-distant future, systems such as this will let you pilot the "Enterprise" through an adventure of your own.

CHECKLIST OF IMPORTANT TERMS AND CONCEPTS IN THIS CHAPTER

If you do not remember any of the terms in the following list, use the index to help you find them in the chapter for review.

REVIEW QUESTIONS AND PROBLEMS

1.   *a.* Why are the predefined functions such as scanf and getche not always suitable for reading keycodes from a PC- or PS/2-type computer?

  b. Use the program in Figure 13-3 to help you write a C program section which calls the BIOS INT 16H procedure to wait until a key is pressed, and then returns the code for the pressed key (assume only standard ASCII).

2. With the help of a simple drawing, explain how a noninterlaced raster is produced on a CRT.

3. Use a simple drawing to help you describe how a display of the letter X is produced by the electron beam on a noninterlaced raster-scan CRT display.

4. Refer to Figure 13-6 to help you answer the following questions.

  a. What is the purpose of the RAM in this circuit?

  b. At what point(s) in displaying a frame do the address inputs of this RAM get changed?

  c. At what point(s) in displaying a frame do the R0-R3 address inputs of the character-generator ROM get changed?

  d. What is the purpose of the shift register on the output of the character generator ROM?

  e. At what point(s) in displaying a frame are horizontal sync pulses produced?

  f. At what point(s) in displaying a frame are vertical sync pulses produced?

5. A CRT display is designed to display 24 character rows with 80 characters in each row. The system uses a 7 by 9 character generator in a 9 by 12 dot matrix. Assuming a 60-Hz noninterlaced frame rate, three additional character times for horizontal overscan, and 120 additional scan lines for vertical overscan, find the following values.

  a. Total number of character times/row

  b. Total number of scan lines/frame

  c. Horizontal frequency (number of lines/second)

  d. Dot-clock frequency (dots/second)

  e. Minimum bandwidth required for video amplifier

  f. Time between RAM accesses

6. The IBM PC color adapter board uses a 14-MHz dot

clock frequency, a 15.750-kHz horizontal scan rate, and a 60-Hz frame rate. Characters are produced in an 8 by 8 dot matrix. There are 80 characters/row and 25 rows/frame.

  a. What is the total number of dot times per scan line?
  b. How many dot times then are left for horizontal overscan?
  c. What is the total number of scan lines per frame including overscan?
  d. How many scan lines then are left for vertical overscan?

7. How does the CRT display system in Figure 13-5 arbitrate the dispute that occurs when the 6845 CRT controller and the microprocessor both want to access the display RAM at the same time?

8. Write a program which uses the IBM BIOS procedures to read a string of characters entered from the keyboard, put the key codes in a buffer in memory, and display the characters for the pressed keys on the CRT.

9. How much memory is required to store the pel data for a bit-mapped monochrome 640 by 480 display?

10. Describe how three electron beams are used to produce all possible colors on a color CRT screen.

11. a. How many memory bits are required to store the data for a pixel that can be any one of 256 colors?
  b. How much memory is required to store the pel data for a 1024 by 768 display where each pel can be any one of 16 colors?
  c. Use diagrams to help you explain the difference between packed pixel storage and planar pixel storage.

12. Use a diagram to help you explain how an EGA system uses palette registers to produce a display of 16 colors from a palette of 64 colors.

13. Mode 13H of a VGA system produces a display of 256 colors from a palette of 256K possible colors.
  a. How many bits are required to specify one of 256K colors?
  b. Why is it currently impractical to store the pixel data for a direct display of 256K colors?
  c. Draw a diagram showing how the VGA color registers and palette registers are used to specify one of 256 colors out of a palette of 256K.
  d. Describe how the actual red, green, and blue drive signals are produced from the color register values in a VGA system.

14. a. Write assembly language instructions which use the BIOS INT 10H procedure to initialize a VGA adapter for $320 \times 200 \times 256$ color mode.
  b. Add instructions which position the cursor approximately in the center of the screen and write your name at that location.

15. Explain the purpose of the following statements or groups of statements in the C graphics program in Figure 13-23.
  a. Initgraph(&driver,&mode,"c:\\tc\\BGI");
  b. window_size = imagesize(160,100,480 ,250); window_buffer = malloc (window_size);
  c. getimage(160,100,480,250);
  d. putimage(160,100,window_buffer,0);
  e. free(window_buffer)

16. a. Why do many microcomputers now use a dedicated graphics processor instead of having the main processor compute pixel values for graphics images?
  b. Why is a math coprocessor often included in the design of a graphics processor system?

17. What are the major advantages of LCD displays over CRT displays for use in portable microcomputers?

18. The vector graphics approach is an alternative to the raster scan approach of producing graphics displays on a CRT screen. In a vector graphics display system the beam is directly moved from point to point on the CRT screen to trace out images. The most common way to direct the beam is by connecting a D/A converter to the X axis drive and another D/A converter to the Y axis drive. For this problem, assume the inputs of an 8-bit D/A converter are connected to port FFF8H of a microcomputer and the output of the D/A converter is connected to the X axis of an oscilloscope. The inputs of another 8-bit D/A converter are connected to port FFFAH of a microcomputer, and the output of this D/A is connected to the Y axis of the oscilloscope. Write a program which uses these D/A converters to display a square on the screen of the oscilloscope. Then modify the program so that the square enlarges after each 100 refreshes.

19. Describe how a CCD camera produces pixel data which can be stored in computer memory.

20. a. Describe the mechanical mechanisms used to move the read/write head to the desired track on a floppy or hard disk.
  b. Explain why a magnetic hard disk can store much more data than a floppy disk and why data can be read from a hard disk much faster than it can from a floppy.
  c. Explain why a phase-locked loop is used as part of the interface circuitry for a floppy or hard disk drive.
  d. What is the major advantage of RLL 2,7 encoding over MFM encoding for recording data on magnetic disks?

21. a. What is the main improvement of an ESDI hard disk interface over the older ST-506 interface?
  b. Draw a diagram to help explain how an SCSI I/O bus is connected in a system and how it operates.

22. a. Describe the purpose of the CRC bytes included with each block of data recorded on the disk.

b. Describe how you format a floppy disk on a DOS-based system.
c. Describe the three steps involved in formatting and partitioning a blank magnetic hard disk.

23. a. Describe the purpose of the file allocation table written on a disk by DOS.
b. If a data file requires several clusters on a disk, how does a DOS keep track of where the pieces of the file are located?
c. List the major types of information contained in the directory entry for each file in a DOS system.

24. Write a program which uses the IBM PC DOS function calls to read in a string containing your name from the keyboard to a buffer in memory and sends the string to a printer. Remember to use the DOS 4CH function call to return to DOS at the end of the program.

25. Write a program which uses DOS function calls to read a line of text from the keyboard to a buffer in memory and then, when the carriage return key is pressed, opens a file and writes the text to the file.

26. Explain the operation performed in Figure 13-42 by each of the following C statements or group of statements more thoroughly than the comments.
a. FILE *fp;
b. if((fp = open(filename,"wt")) = = 0)
   {
   perror(filename)
   }
c. fclose();
d. while(!feof(fp))
   fputc(fgetc(fp),stdout);

27. a. Describe the operation of a RAM disk and explain how it speeds up the execution of some programs.

b. Explain the operation of a disk cache and explain how it is different from a RAM disk.

28. a. Describe how stored data is read from optical disks and describe the advantages this readout method has over that used for hard magnetic disks.
b. List the major advantages of optical disk data storage over magnetic hard disk data storage.
c. Describe how data bits are recorded in magneto-optic erasable optical (EO) disk systems.

29. A human brain can store about 10^{10} bits of data and has an access time in the order of about a second. Compare these parameters with those of an optical disk system such as the Maxtor Tahiti I discussed in the text.

30. Describe the operation of the print mechanism for each of the following types of printer. Also give an advantage and a disadvantage for each type.
a. Impact-type dot-matrix
b. Thermal
c. Laser
d. Ink-jet

31. What are the major differences between an LPC speech synthesizer and a formant speech synthesizer?

32. Describe the operation of a direct-digitization speech synthesizer. As part of the description give the major advantage and the major disadvantage of this type speech synthesis.

33. a. Digital video interactive systems allow up to 72 min of full motion video and sound to be recorded on a single 5-in. optical disk. Describe the techniques used to store this immense amount of data on the disk.
b. Describe how a DVI system might be used to teach you how to fly a space shuttle.

CHAPTER 14

Data Communication and Networks

In Chapter 2 we discussed "computerizing" an electronics factory. What this means is that computers are integrated into all the operations of the factory and that each person in the company has access to a computer. The company may have a large centrally located mainframe computer, several minicomputers that serve groups of users, individual computer engineering workstations, and portable computers spread around the world with its salespeople. In order for all these computers to work together, they must be able to communicate with each other in an organized manner. In this chapter we show you some of the devices, signal standards, and systems used for communication with and between computers.

In the first section of the chapter we discuss the hardware and low-level software required to interface microcomputer buses to serial data communication lines. Then we discuss how the serial data signals are transmitted from one place to another. This discussion includes RS-232C-type standards, modems, and fiber-optic cables. The next section of the chapter shows you how to write programs which perform simple serial data communication. As an example in this section we use a program which allows you to download programs from a PC- or PS/2-type computer to an SDK-86 board. In the final sections of the chapter we discuss the operation of several common computer networks.

OBJECTIVES

At the end of this chapter, you should be able to:

1. Show and describe the meaning of the bits in the format used for sending asynchronous serial data.

2. Initialize a common UART for transmitting serial data in a specified format.

3. Describe several voltage, current, and light (fiber-optic) signal methods used to transmit serial data.

4. Describe the function of the major signals in the RS-232C standard.

5. Show how to connect RS-232C equipment directly or with a "null-modem" connection.

6. Describe the different types of modulation commonly used by modems.

7. Use the IBM PC BIOS, DOS, and C procedures to send and receive serial data.

8. Show the formats for a byte-oriented protocol and for a bit-oriented protocol used in synchronous serial data transmission.

9. Draw diagrams to show the common computer network topologies.

10. Describe the operation of an Ethernet system.

11. Describe the operation of a token-passing ring system.

12. Show the major signal groups for the GPIB (IEEE 488) bus, describe how bus control is managed, and describe how data is transferred on a handshake basis for the GPIB.

INTRODUCTION TO ASYNCHRONOUS SERIAL DATA COMMUNICATION

Overview

Serial data communication is a somewhat difficult subject to approach, because you need pieces of information from several different topics in order for each part of the subject to really make sense. To make this approach easier, we will first give an overview of how all the pieces fit together and then describe the details of each piece later in specific sections. A problem with this subject is that it contains a great many terms and acronyms. To help you absorb all of these, you may want to make a glossary of terms as you work your way through the chapter.

Within a microcomputer data is transferred in parallel, because that is the fastest way to do it. For transferring data over long distances, however, parallel data transmission requires too many wires. Therefore, data to be sent long distances is usually converted from parallel form to serial form so that it can be sent on a single wire or pair of wires. Serial data received from a distant source is converted to parallel form so that it can easily be transferred on the microcomputer buses. Three terms often encountered in literature on serial data systems are *simplex*, *half-duplex*, and *full-duplex*. A simplex data line can transmit data only in one direction. An earthquake sensor sending data back from Mount St.

Helens or a commercial radio station are examples of simplex transmission. Half-duplex transmission means that communication can take place in either direction between two systems, but can only occur in one direction at a time. An example of half-duplex transmission is a two-way radio system, where one user always listens while the other talks because the receiver circuitry is turned off during transmit. The term full-duplex means that each system can send and receive data at the same time. A normal phone conversation is an example of a full-duplex operation.

Serial data can be sent *synchronously* or *asynchronously*. For synchronous transmission, data is sent in blocks at a constant rate. The start and end of a block are identified with specific bytes or bit patterns. In a later section of the chapter we discuss synchronous data transmission in detail. For asynchronous transmission, each data character has a bit which identifies its start and 1 or 2 bits which identify its end. Since each character is individually identified, characters can be sent at any time (asynchronously), in the same way that a person types on a keyboard.

Figure 14-1 shows the bit format often used for transmitting asynchronous serial data. When no data is being sent, the signal line is in a constant high or *marking* state. The beginning of a data character is indicated by the line going low for 1 bit time. This bit is called a *start* bit. The data bits are then sent out on the line one after the other. Note that the least significant bit is sent out first. Depending on the system, the data word may consist of 5, 6, 7, or 8 bits. Following the data bits is a parity bit, which—as we explained in Chapter 11—is used to check for errors in received data. Some systems do not insert or look for a parity bit. After the data bits and the parity bit, the signal line is returned high for at least 1 bit time to identify the end of the character. This always-high bit is referred to as a *stop bit*. Some older systems use 2 stop bits. For future reference note that the efficiency of this format is low, because 10 or 11 bit times are required to transmit a 7-bit data word such as an ASCII character.

The term *baud rate* is used to indicate the rate at which serial data is being transferred. Baud rate is defined as 1/(the time between signal transitions). If the signal is changing every 3.33 ms, for example, the baud rate is 1/(3.33 ms), or 300 Bd. There is an almost unavoidable, but incorrect, tendency to refer to this as 300 bits/s. In some cases, the two do correspond, but in other cases 2 or more actual data bits are encoded in one signal transition, so data bits per second and baud

do not correspond. Common baud rates are 300, 600, 1200, 2400, 4800, 9600, and 19,200.

To interface a microcomputer with serial data lines, the data must be converted to and from serial form. A parallel-in-serial-out shift register and a serial-in-parallel-out shift register can be used to do this. Also needed for some cases of serial data transfer is handshaking circuitry to make sure that a transmitter does not send data faster than it can be read in by the receiving system. There are available several programmable LSI devices which contain most of the circuitry needed for serial communication. A device such as the National INS8250, which can only do asynchronous communication, is often referred to as a *universal asynchronous receiver-transmitter* or UART. A device such as the Intel 8251A, which can be programmed to do either asynchronous or synchronous communication, is often called a *universal synchronous-asynchronous receiver-transmitter* or USART.

Once the data is converted to serial form, it must in some way be sent from the transmitting UART to the receiving UART. There are several ways in which serial data is commonly sent. One method is to use a current to represent a 1 in the signal line and no current to represent a 0. We discuss this *current-loop* approach in a later section. Another approach is to add line drivers on the output of the UART to produce a sturdy voltage signal. The range of each of these methods, however, is limited to a few thousand feet.

For sending serial data over long distances, the standard telephone system is a convenient path, because the wiring and connections are already in place. Standard phone lines, often referred to as *switched lines* because any two points can be connected together through a series of switches, have a bandwidth of only about 300 to 3000 Hz. Therefore, for several reasons, digital signals of the form shown in Figure 14-1 cannot be sent directly over standard phone lines.

NOTE: Phone lines capable of carrying digital data directly can be leased, but these are somewhat costly and are limited to the specific destination of the line.

The solution to this problem is to convert the digital signals to audio-frequency tones, which are in the frequency range that the phone lines can transmit. The device used to do this conversion and to convert transmitted tones back to digital information is called a *modem*. The term is a contraction of modulator-

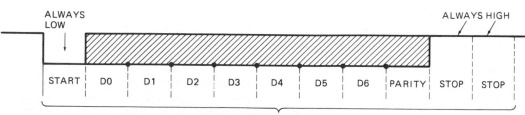

FIGURE 14-1 Bit format used for sending asynchronous serial data.

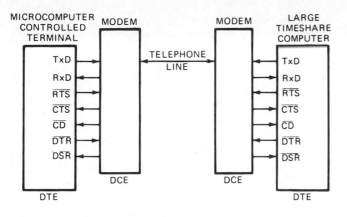

MICROCOMPUTER
CONTROLLED
TERMINAL

MODEM

MODEM

LARGE
TIMESHARE
COMPUTER

TxD

RxD

RTS

CTS

CD

DTR

DSR

DCE

DTE

TELEPHONE
LINE

TxD

RxD

RTS

CTS

CD

DTR

DSR

DCE

DTE

DTE = DATA TERMINAL EQUIPMENT
DCE = DATA COMMUNICATION EQUIPMENT

FIGURE 14-2   Digital data transmission using modems and standard phone lines.

demodulator. In a later section of this chapter we discuss the operation of some common types of modems. For now, take a look at Figure 14-2, which shows how two modems can be connected to allow a remote terminal to communicate with a distant mainframe computer over a phone line. Modems and other equipment used to send serial data over long distances are known as *data communication equipment* or DCE. The terminals and computers that are sending or receiving the serial data are referred to as *data terminal equipment* or DTE.

The data and handshake signal names shown in Figure 14-2 are part of a serial data communications standard called RS-232C, which we discuss in detail in a later section. For now you just need enough of an overview of these signals so that the initialization of the 8251A UART in the next section makes sense to you. Note the direction arrowheads on each of these signals. Here is a sequence of signals that might occur when a user at a terminal wants to send some data to the computer.

After the terminal power is turned on and the terminal runs any self-checks, it asserts the *data-terminal-ready* (DTR) signal to tell the modem it is ready. When it is powered up and ready to transmit or receive data, the modem will assert the *data-set-ready* (DSR) signal to the terminal. Under manual control or terminal control, the modem then dials up the computer.

If the computer is available, it will send back a specified tone. Now, when the terminal has a character actually ready to send, it will assert a *request-to-send* (RTS) signal to the modem. The modem will then assert its *carrier-detect* (CD) signal to the terminal to indicate that it has established contact with the computer. When the modem is fully ready to transmit data, it asserts the *clear-to-send* (CTS) signal back to the terminal. The terminal then sends serial data characters to the modem. When the terminal has sent all the characters it needs to, it makes its RTS signal high. This causes the modem to unassert its CTS signal and stop transmitting. A similar handshake occurs between the modem and the computer at the other end of the data link. The important

point at this time is that a set of handshake signals is defined for transferring serial data to and from a modem.

Now that you have an overview of asynchronous serial data, modems, and handshaking, we will describe the operation of a device commonly used to interface a microcomputer to a modem or other device which requires serial data.

An Example USART—The Intel 8251A

SYSTEM CONNECTIONS AND SIGNALS

As we showed you in Chapter 7, an 8251A is used as the serial port on SDK-86 boards. It is also used on the IBM PC synchronous communication board and on many other boards, so we chose to use it as an example here.

Figure 14-3, page 490, shows a block diagram and the pin descriptions for the 8251A, and Figure 7-6, sheet 9, shows how an 8251A is connected on the SDK-86 board. Keep copies of these two handy as you work your way through the following discussion.

As shown in the SDK-86 schematic, the eight parallel lines, D7–D0, connect to the system data bus so that data words and control/status words can be transferred to and from the device. The *chip select* (CS) input is connected to an address decoder so the device is enabled when addressed. The 8251A has two internal addresses, a control address, which is selected when the C/D input is high, and a data address, which is selected when the C/D input is low. For the SDK-86 the control/status address is FFF2H and the data read/write address is FFF0H. The RESET, RD, and WR lines are connected to the system signals with the same names. The clock input of the 8251A is usually connected to a signal derived from the system clock to synchronize the internal operations of the USART with the processor timing. In the case of the SDK-86 the clock input is connected to the 2.45-MHz PCLK signal, which is derived from the processor clock but has a frequency the 8251A can handle.

The signal labeled TxD on the upper right corner of the 8251A block diagram is the actual *serial-data* output. The pin labeled RxD is the *serial-data* input. The additional circuitry connected to the TxD pin on the SDK-86 board is needed to convert the TTL logic levels from the 8251A to current loop or RS-232C signals. The circuitry connected to the RxD pin performs the opposite conversion. We will discuss current loop and RS-232C signal standards a little later.

The shift registers in the USART require clocks to shift the serial data in and out. TxC is the *transmit shift-register clock* input, and RxC is the *receive shift-register clock* input. Usually these two inputs are tied together so they are driven by the same signal. If you look at Figure 7-6, sheet 9, you should see how some wire-wrap jumpers are used to select the desired clock frequency from one of the outputs of a counter. The frequency of the signal you choose for TxC and RxC must be 1, 16, or 64 times the transmit and receive baud rate, depending on the mode in which the 8251A is initialized. Using a clock frequency higher than the

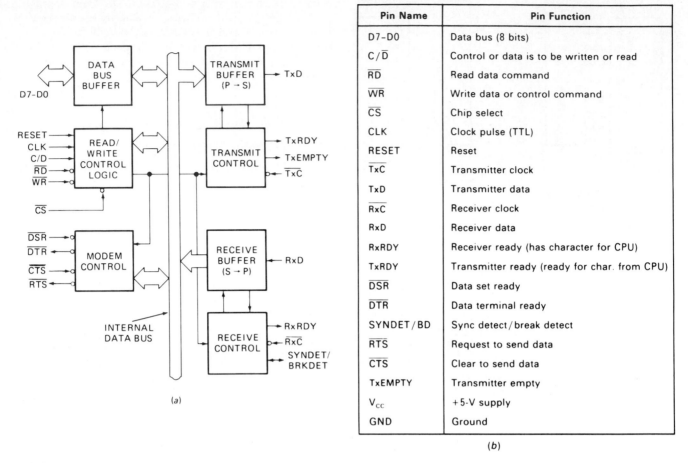

Pin Name	Pin Function
D7–D0	Data bus (8 bits)
C/$\overline{\text{D}}$	Control or data is to be written or read
$\overline{\text{RD}}$	Read data command
$\overline{\text{WR}}$	Write data or control command
$\overline{\text{CS}}$	Chip select
CLK	Clock pulse (TTL)
RESET	Reset
$\overline{\text{TxC}}$	Transmitter clock
TxD	Transmitter data
$\overline{\text{RxC}}$	Receiver clock
RxD	Receiver data
RxRDY	Receiver ready (has character for CPU)
TxRDY	Transmitter ready (ready for char. from CPU)
$\overline{\text{DSR}}$	Data set ready
$\overline{\text{DTR}}$	Data terminal ready
SYNDET/BD	Sync detect/break detect
$\overline{\text{RTS}}$	Request to send data
$\overline{\text{CTS}}$	Clear to send data
TxEMPTY	Transmitter empty
V_{cc}	+5-V supply
GND	Ground

(b)

FIGURE 14-3   Block diagram and pin descriptions for the Intel 8251A USART.
(a) Block diagram. (b) Pin descriptions.

baud rate allows the receive shift register to be clocked at the center of the bit times rather than at leading edges. This reduces the chance of signal noise at the start of the bit time causing a read error.

The 8251A is *double-buffered*. This means that one character can be loaded into a holding buffer while another character is being shifted out of the actual transmit shift register. The TxRDY output from the 8251A will go high when the holding buffer is empty, and another character can be sent from the CPU. The TxEMPTY pin on the 8251A will go high when both the holding buffer and the transmit shift register are empty. The RxRDY pin of the 8251A will go high when a character has been shifted into the receiver buffer and is ready to be read out by the CPU. Incidentally, if a character is not read out before another character is shifted in, the first character will be overwritten and lost.

The *sync-detect/break-detect* (SYNDET/BD) pin has two uses. When the device is operating in asynchronous mode, which we are interested in here, this pin will go high if the serial data input line, RxD, stays low for more than 2 character times. This signal then indicates an intentional break in data transmission, or a break in the signal line. When programmed for synchronous data transmission, this pin will go high when the 8251A finds a specified sync character(s) in the incoming string of data bits.

The four signals connected to the box labeled MODEM CONTROL in the 8251A block diagram are handshake signals, which we described in the previous section.

INITIALIZING AN 8251A

To initialize an 8251A you must send first a mode word and then a command word to the control register address for the device. Figure 14-4 shows the formats for these words and for the 8251A status word which is read from the same address. Baud rate factor, specified by the two least significant bits of the mode word, is the ratio between the clock signal applied to the $\overline{\text{TxC}}$-$\overline{\text{RxC}}$ inputs and the desired baud rate. For example, if you want to use a $\overline{\text{TxC}}$ of 19,200 Hz and transmit data at 1200 Bd, the baud rate factor is 19,200/1200 or 16×. If bits D0 and D1 are both made 0's, the 8251A is programmed for synchronous data transfer. In this case the baud rate will be the same as the applied $\overline{\text{TxC}}$ and $\overline{\text{RxC}}$. The other three combinations for these 2 bits represent asynchronous transfer. A baud rate factor of 1 can be used for asynchronous transfer only if the transmitting system and the receiving system both use the same $\overline{\text{TxC}}$

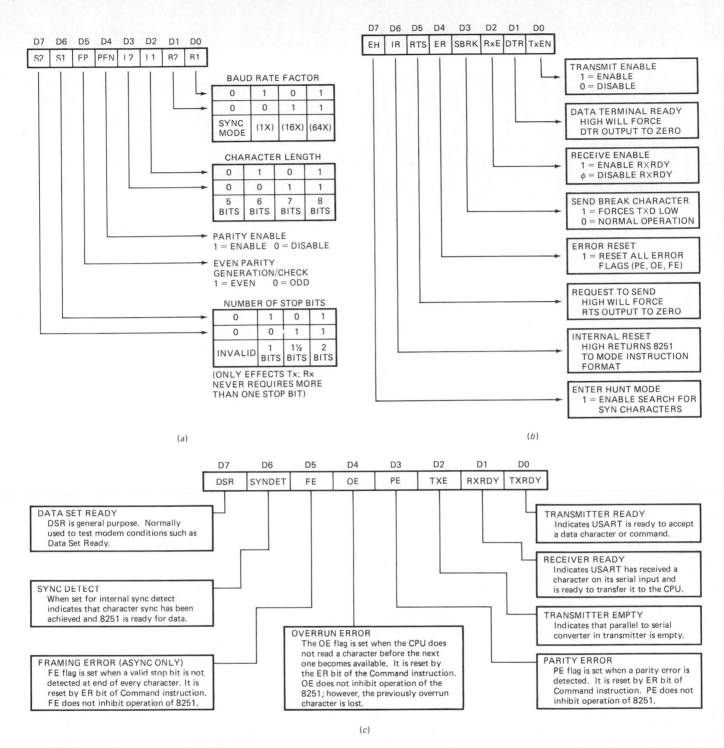

FIGURE 14-4 Formats of 8251A mode, command, and status words. (*a*) Mode word. (*b*) Command word. (*c*) Status word. (*Intel Corporation*)

and $\overline{\text{RxC}}$. The character length specified by bits D2 and D3 in the mode word includes only the actual data bits, not the start bit, parity bit, or stop bit(s). If parity is disabled, no parity bit is inserted in the transmitted bit string. If the 8251A is programmed for 5, 6, or 7 data bits, the extra bits in the data character byte read from the device will be 0's.

After you send a mode word to an 8251A, you must then send it a command word. A 1 in the least significant bit of the command word enables the transmitter section of the 8251A and the TxRDY output. When enabled, the 8251A TxRDY output will be asserted high if the $\overline{\text{CTS}}$ input has been asserted low, and the transmitter holding buffer is ready for another character from the CPU. The TxRDY signal can be connected to an interrupt input on the CPU or an 8259A, so that characters to be transmitted can be sent to the 8251A on an interrupt basis. When a character is written to the 8251A data address, the TxRDY signal will go low and remain low until the holding buffer is again ready for another character. Putting a 1 in bit D1 of the command word will cause the $\overline{\text{DTR}}$ output of the 8251A to be asserted low. As we explained before, this signal is used to tell a modem that a terminal or computer is operational. A 1 in bit D2 of the command word enables the RxRDY output pin of the 8251A. If enabled, the RxRDY pin will go high when the 8251A has a character in its receiver buffer ready to be read. This signal can be connected to an interrupt input so that characters can be read in on an interrupt basis. The RxRDY output is reset when a character is read from the 8251A.

Putting a 1 in bit D3 of the command word causes the 8251A to output a character of all 0's, which is called a break character. A break character is sometimes used to indicate the end of a block of transmitted data. Sending a command word with a 1 in bit D4 causes the 8251A to reset the parity, overrun, and framing error flags in the 8251A status register. The meanings of these flags are explained in Figure 14-4c. A 1 in bit D5 of the command word will cause the 8251A to assert its request-to-send ($\overline{\text{RTS}}$) output low. This signal, remember, is sent to a modem to ask whether the modem and the receiving system are ready for a data character to be sent.

Putting a 1 in bit D6 of the command word causes the 8251A to be internally reset when the command word is sent. After a software reset command is sent in this way, a new mode word must be sent. Later we will show you how this is used.

The D7 bit in the command word is only used when the device is operating in synchronous mode. A command word with a 1 in this bit position tells the 8251A to look for specified sync character(s) in a stream of bits being shifted in. If the 8251A finds the specified sync character(s), it will assert its SYNDET/BD pin high. We will discuss this more in the synchronous data communication section of this chapter.

Figure 14-5 shows an example of the instruction sequence you can use to initialize an 8251A. This sequence is somewhat lengthy for two reasons. First, the 8251A does not always respond correctly to a hardware reset on power-up. Therefore, a series of software commands must be sent to the device to make sure it is reset properly before the desired mode and command words are sent. The device is put into a known state by writing 3 bytes of all 0's to the 8251A control register address, and then it is reset by sending a control word with a 1 in bit D6. After this reset sequence the desired mode and control words can be sent to 8251A. The 8251A distinguishes a command word from a mode word by the order in which they are sent to the device. After reset, a mode word must be sent to the command address. Any words sent to the command address after the mode word will be treated as command words until the device is reset.

The second factor which lengthens this initialization is the *write-recovery* time T_{RV} of the 8251A. According to the data sheet, the 8251A requires a worst-case recovery time of 16 cycles of the clock signal connected to the CLK input. On the SDK-86 board the PCLK signal,

```
; 8086 instructions to initialize the 8251A on an
; SDK-86 board

      MOV  DX, 0FFF2H  ; point at command register address
      MOV  AL, 00H     ; send 0's to guarantee device is
      OUT  DX, AL      ; in the command instruction format
      MOV  CX, 2       ; before the RESET command is
D0:LOOP D0             ; issued and delay after sending
      OUT  DX, AL      ; each command instruction
      MOV  CX, 2
D1:LOOP D1
      OUT  DX, AL
      MOV  CX, 2
D2:LOOP D2
      MOV  AL, 40H     ; Sent internal reset command to
      OUT  DX, AL      ; return device to idle state
      MOV  CX, 2       ; Load delay constant
D3:LOOP D3             ; and delay
      MOV  AL,11001110B; Load mode control word & send it
      OUT  DX, AL
; 1 1 0 0 1 1 1 0      Mode Word
; \ \ \ \ \ \ \ \_\____baud rate factor of 16x
;   \ \ \ \ \ _____character length of 8 bits
;     \ \ \_\ _____parity disabled
;         _____2 stop bits

      MOV  CX, 2       ; and delay
D4:LOOP D4
      MOV  AL,00110111B ; Load command word and send it
      OUT  DX, AL
; 0 0 1 1 0 1 1 1      Command word
; \ \ \ \ \ \ \ _____Transmit enable
; \ \ \ \ \ \ _____Data terminal ready, DTR will
; \ \ \ \ \ \          output 0
; \ \ \ \ \ _____Receive enable
; \ \ \ \ _____Normal operation
; \ \ \ _____Reset all error flags
; \ \ _____RST output 0, request to send
; \ _____Do not return to mode
;  \                   instruction form
;   _____Disable hunt mode
```

FIGURE 14-5 Instruction sequence for 8251A initialization.

which is the same as the processor clock frequency, is connected to the CLK input of the 8251A. Therefore, for the SDK-86 board, the required write-recovery time corresponds to 16 processor clock cycles. What all this means is that you have to delay this many clock cycles between successive initialization byte writes to the 8251A. A simple way to produce the required delay and a margin of safety is to load CX with 0002 and count it down with the LOOP instruction. The MOV CX,0002 instruction takes 4 clock cycles, the first execution of the LOOP instruction takes 17 clock cycles, and the last execution of the LOOP instruction takes 5 cycles. The 8 cycles required for the OUT instruction, which writes the control words, also count as part of the time between writes, so the sum of all these is more than enough. When writing data characters to an 8251A, you don't have to worry about this recovery time, because a new character will not be written to the 8251A until the previous character has been shifted out. This shifting, of course, requires much more time than T_{RV}.

The comments in Figure 14-5 explain the meanings of the bits in the mode and control words used in this example. Once the 8251A is initialized as shown, new control words can be sent at any time to, for example, reset the error flags. Now let's look at how characters are sent to and read from an 8251A.

SENDING AND RECEIVING CHARACTERS WITH AN 8251A

Data characters can be sent to and read from the 8251A on an interrupt basis or on a polled basis. To send characters on an interrupt basis, the TxRDY pin of the 8251A is connected to an interrupt input on the processor of an 8259A priority-interrupt controller. The transmitter and the TxRDY output are enabled by putting a 1 in bit D1 of the control word sent to the 8251A during initialization. When the $\overline{\text{CTS}}$ input of the 8251A is asserted low and the 8251A buffer is ready for a character, the TxRDY pin will go high. If the processor and 8259A interrupt path is enabled, the processor will go to an interrupt-service procedure, which writes a data character to the 8251A data address. Writing the data character causes the 8251A to reset its TxRDY output until the buffer is again ready to receive a character. A counter can be used to keep track of how many characters have been sent.

In a similar manner characters can be read from an 8251A on an interrupt basis. In this case the RxRDY output of the 8251A is connected to an interrupt input of the processor or an 8259A, and this output is enabled by putting a 1 in bit D2 of the command word sent during initialization. When a character has been shifted into the 8251A and the character is in the receiver buffer ready to be read, the RxRDY pin will go high. If the interrupt chain through the 8259A and the processor is enabled, the processor will go to an interrupt procedure which reads in the data character. Reading a data character from the 8251A causes it to reset the RxRDY output signal. This signal will stay low until another character is ready to be read.

To send characters to an 8251A on a polled basis, the 8251A status register is read and checked over and over until the TxRDY bit (D0) is found to be a 1. In most systems you also want to check bit D7 of the status register to make sure the $\overline{\text{DSR}}$ input of the 8251A has been asserted by a signal from, for example, a modem. When the required bit(s) of the status register are all high, a data character is then written to the 8251A data address. Figure 14-6a shows the instruction sequence needed to do this. Note that the status register has the same internal address as the control register. Also note that both an AND and a CMP operation must be done to determine when the two desired bits are both high. Writing a data character to the 8251A resets the TxRDY bit in the status register.

Reading a character from the 8251A on a polled basis is a similar process, except that the RxRDY bit (D1) of the status register is polled to determine when a character is ready to be read. When bit D1 is found high, a character is read in from the 8251A data address. Figure 14-6b

```
; Instructions for transmitting data using an
; SDK-86 8251A using polling method

    MOV DX, 0FFF2H       ; Point at control register
TEST1:                   ; address
    IN  AL, DX           ; Read status
    AND AL, 10000001B    ; and check status of
;             _____data set ready & transmit ready
    CMP AL, 10000001B    ; Is it ready?
    JNE TEST1            ; Continue to poll if not ready
    MOV DX, 0FFF0H       ; otherwise point at data address
    MOV AL, DATA_TO_SEND ; Load data to send
    OUT DX, AL           ; and send it
```

(a)

```
; Instructions for receiving data with an
; SDK-86 8251A using polling method

    MOV DX, 0FFF2H       ; Point at control register
TEST2:                   ; address
    IN  AL, DX           ; Read status
    AND AL, 00000010B    ; and check status of RxRdy
    JZ  TEST2            ; Continue to poll if not ready
    MOV DX, 0FFF0H       ; otherwise point at data
    IN  AL, DX           ; address and get data
```

(b)

FIGURE 14-6   Instruction sequences for transmitting and receiving with an 8251A on a polled basis. (a) Transmit. (b) Polled.

shows the instruction sequence for this. Status register bits D3, D4, and D5 can be checked to see if a parity error, overrun error, or framing error has occurred. If an error has occurred, a message to retransmit the data can be sent to the transmitting system.

The next step in our journey into serial-data communications is to discuss the signal standards used to connect the serial inputs and outputs of UARTS to modems and other serial devices.

SERIAL-DATA TRANSMISSION METHODS AND STANDARDS

In the last section we showed you how a UART or USART is used to interface microcomputer buses with serial-data communication lines. The TTL signals output by a USART, however, are not suitable for transmission over long distances, so these signals are converted to some other form to be transmitted. In this section of the chapter we discuss devices and signal types commonly used to send serial-data signals over long distances.

Aside from drum beats in the jungle, one of the earliest forms of serial-data communication was the telegraph. In a telegraph, pressing a key at one end of a signal line causes a current to flow through the line. When this current reaches the receiving end of the line, it activates a solenoid (sounder), which produces a sound. Letters and numbers are sent using the familiar Morse code or some other convenient code. After a hundred years or so, the telegraph key and sounder evolved into the teletypewriter. A teletypewriter terminal has a typewriter-style keyboard so that the user can simply press a key to send a desired letter or number code. A teletype terminal also has a print mechanism which prints out characters as they are received. Most teletypes use a current to represent a 1 and no current to represent a 0. We start this section by briefly describing the old current-loop standards; then we go on to newer methods.

20- AND 60-mA CURRENT LOOPS

In teletypewriters or other current-signal systems, some manufacturers use a nominal current of 20 mA to represent a 1, or mark, and no current to represent a space, or 0. Other manufacturers use a nominal current of 60 mA to represent a 1 and no current to represent a 0. The actual current in a specific system may be considerably different from the nominal value.

Sheet 9 of Figure 7-8 shows circuitry which can be used to interface current type signals with the TTL input and output of an 8251A USART on the SDK-86 board. With the jumpers in place as shown, a high on the TxD output of the 8251A will produce a low on the PNP transistor. This will turn the transistor on and cause a positive current to flow out the TTY TX line. Inside a teletypewriter this current flows through an electromagnet and back to the TTY TX RET. To send a data bit, the teletypewriter opens or closes a switch in a current path. The current for this path in the SDK-86 circuitry is supplied from +5 V through R10 to the TTY RX RET line. Think of the key mechanism of the teletypewriter as a simple switch connected between pins 24 and 12 of J7 on the circuit. When the switch is closed the current flows back on the TTY RX line and through R3 to −12 V. The current flowing through R3 will produce a legal TTL high logic level on the input of the 74LS14 inverter. This high signal passes through two inverters and produces a high on the RxD input of the 8251A.

RS-232C Serial Data Standard

OVERVIEW

In the 1960s as the use of timeshare computer terminals became more widespread, modems were developed so that terminals could use phone lines to communicate with distant computers. As we stated earlier, modems and other devices used to send serial data are often referred to as *data communication equipment* or DCE. The terminals or computers that are sending or receiving the data are referred to as *data terminal equipment* or DTE. In response to the need for signal and handshake standards between DTE and DCE, the Electronic Industries Association (EIA) developed EIA standard *RS-232C*. This standard describes the function of 25 signal and handshake pins for serial-data transfer. It also describes the voltage levels, impedance levels, rise and fall times, maximum bit rate, and maximum capacitance for these

signal lines. Before we work our way through the 25 pin functions, we will take a brief look at some of the other hardware aspects of RS-232C.

RS-232C specifies 25 signal pins, and it specifies that the DTE connector should be a male and the DCE connector should be a female. A specific connector is not given, but the most commonly used connectors are the DB-25P male shown in Figure 14-7a. For systems where many of the 25 pins are not needed, a 9-pin DIN connector such as the DE-9P male connector shown in Figure 14-7b is used. When you are wiring up these connectors, it is important to note the order in which the pins are numbered.

The voltage levels for all RS-232C signals are as follows. A logic high, or mark, is a voltage between −3 V and −15 V under load (−25 V no load). A logic low or space is a voltage between +3 V and +15 V under load (+25 V no load). Voltages such as ±12 V are commonly used.

RS-232C TO TTL INTERFACING

Obviously a USART such as the 8251A is not directly compatible with RS-232C signal levels. Sheet 9 of the SDK-86 schematics in Figure 7-8 shows one way to interface TTL signals of the 8251A to RS-232C signal levels. If the jumpers shown are removed and the jumpers shown in the jumper table under CRT are inserted, the circuit will produce and accept RS-232C signals.

> NOTE: This is the jumpering needed to prepare the SDK-86 board for downloading programs from an IBM PC or other computer. Here's how it works.

With a jumper between the points numbered 7 and 8, a high on the TxD output of the 8251A produces a high on the base of the transistor, which turns it off. With points numbered 9 and 10 jumpered, the CR TX line will then be pulled to −12 V, which is a legal high or marking condition for RS-232C. A low on the TxD output of the 8251A will turn on the transistor and pull the CR TX line to +5 V, which is a legal low or space condition for RS-232C.

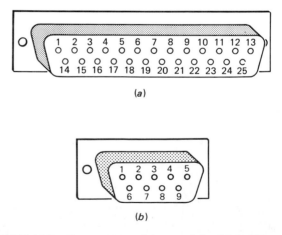

FIGURE 14-7 Connectors often used for RS-232C connections. (a) DB-25P 25-pin male. (b) DE-9P 9-pin male DIN connector.

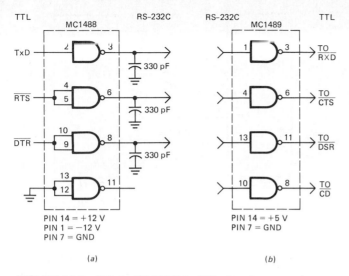

PIN 14 = +12 V
PIN 1 = −12 V
PIN 7 = GND

(a)

PIN 14 = +5 V
PIN 7 = GND

(b)

FIGURE 14-8   TTL to RS-232C to TTL signal conversion.
(a) MC1488 used to convert TTL to RS-232C. (b) MC1489
used to convert RS-232C to TTL.

Another, more standard way to interface between RS-232C and TTL levels is with MC1488 quad TTL-to-RS-232C drivers and MC1489 quad RS-232C-to-TTL receivers shown in Figure 14-8. The MC1488s require + and − supplies, but the MC1489s require only +5 V. Note the capacitor to ground on the outputs of the MC1488 drivers. To reduce cross talk between adjacent wires, the rise and fall times for RS-232C signals are limited to 30 V/μs. Also note that the RS-232C handshake signals such as $\overline{RTS}$ are active low. Therefore, if one of these signals is asserted, you will find a positive

voltage on the actual RS-232C signal line when you check it during troubleshooting. Now let's look at the RS-232C pin descriptions.

RS-232C SIGNAL DEFINITIONS

Figure 14-9 shows the signal names, signal direction, and a brief description for each of the 25 pins defined for RS-232C. For most applications only a few of these pins are used, so don't get overwhelmed. Here are a few additional notes about these signals.

First note that the signal direction is specified with respect to the DCE. This convention is part of the standard. We have found it very helpful to put arrowheads on all signal lines, as shown in Figure 14-2, when we are drawing circuits for connecting RS-232C equipment.

Next observe that there is both a chassis ground (pin 1) and a signal ground (pin 7). To prevent large ac-induced ground currents in the signal ground, these two should be connected together only at the power supply in the terminal or the computer.

The TxD, RxD, and handshake signals shown with common names in Figure 14-9 are the ones most often used for simple systems. We gave an overview of their use in the introduction to this section of the chapter and will discuss them further in a larger section of the chapter on modems. These signals control what is called the *primary* or *forward* communications channel of the modem. Some modems allow communication over a *secondary* or *backward* channel, which operates in the reverse direction from the forward channel and at a much lower baud rate. Pins 12, 13, 14, 16, and 19 are the data and handshake lines for this backward channel.

Pins 15, 17, 21, and 24 are used for synchronous data

PIN NUMBERS FOR 9 PINS	PIN NUMBERS FOR 25 PINS	COMMON NAME	RS-232C NAME	DESCRIPTION	SIGNAL DIRECTION ON DCE
	1		AA	PROTECTIVE GROUND	—
3	2	TXD	BA	TRANSMITTED DATA	IN
2	3	RXD	BB	RECEIVED DATA	OUT
7	4	$\overline{RTS}$	CA	REQUEST TO SEND	IN
8	5	$\overline{CTS}$	CB	CLEAR TO SEND	OUT
6	6	$\overline{DSR}$	CC	DATA SET READY	OUT
5	7	GND	AB	SIGNAL GROUND (COMMON RETURN)	—
1	8	$\overline{CD}$	CF	RECEIVED LINE SIGNAL DETECTOR	OUT
	9		—	(RESERVED FOR DATA SET TESTING)	—
	10		—	(RESERVED FOR DATA SET TESTING)	—
	11			UNASSIGNED	—
	12		SCF	SECONDARY RECEIVED LINE SIGNAL DETECTOR	OUT
	13		SCB	SECONDARY CLEAR TO SEND	OUT
	14		SBA	SECONDARY TRANSMITTED DATA	IN
	15		DB	TRANSMISSION SIGNAL ELEMENT TIMING (DCE SOURCE)	OUT
	16		SBB	SECONDARY RECEIVED DATA	OUT
	17		DD	RECEIVER SIGNAL ELEMENT TIMING (DCE SOURCE)	OUT
	18			UNASSIGNED	—
	19		SCA	SECONDARY REQUEST TO SEND	IN
4	20	$\overline{DTR}$	CD	DATA TERMINAL READY	IN
	21		CG	SIGNAL QUALITY DETECTOR	OUT
9	22		CE	RING INDICATOR	OUT
	23		CH/CI	DATA SIGNAL RATE SELECTOR (DTE/DCE SOURCE)	IN/OUT
	24		DA	TRANSMIT SIGNAL ELEMENT TIMING (DTE SOURCE)	IN
	25			UNASSIGNED	—

FIGURE 14-9   RS-232C pin names and signal directions.

communication. We will tell you a little more about these in the section of the chapter on modems. Next we want to show you some of the tricks in connecting RS-232C-"compatible" equipment.

CONNECTING RS-232C-COMPATIBLE EQUIPMENT

A major point we need to make right now is that you can seldom just connect together two pieces of equipment, described by their manufacturers as RS-232C compatible, and expect them to work the first time. There are several reasons for this. To give you an idea of one of the reasons, suppose that you want to connect the terminal in Figure 14-2 directly to the computer rather than through the modem-modem link. The terminal and the computer probably both have DB-25-type connectors so that, other than a possible male-female mismatch, you might think you could just plug the terminal cable directly into the computer. To see why this doesn't work, hold your fingers over the modems in Figure 14-2 and refer to the pin numbers for the RS-232C signals in Figure 14-9. As you should see, both the terminal and the computer are trying to output data (TxD) from their number 2 pins to the same line. Likewise, they are both trying to input data (RxD) from the same line on their number 3 pins. The same problem exists with the handshake signals. RS-232C drivers are designed so that connecting the lines together in this way will not destroy anything, but connecting outputs together is not a productive relationship. A solution to this problem is to make an adapter with two connectors so that the signals cross over, as shown in Figure 14-10a. This crossover connection is often called a *null modem*. We have again put arrowheads on the signals in Figure 14-10a to help you keep track of the direction for each. As you can see in the figure, the TxD from the terminal now sends data to the RxD input of the computer. Likewise, the TxD from the computer now sends data to the RxD input of the terminal as desired. The handshake signals also are crossed over so that each handshake output signal is connected to the corresponding input signal.

A second reason that you can't just plug RS-232C-compatible equipment together and expect it to work is that a partial implementation of RS-232C is often used to communicate with printers, plotters, and other computer peripherals besides modems. These other peripherals may be configured as DCE or as DTE. Also, they may use all, some, or none of the handshake signals. As an example of this, suppose that you want to connect the RS-232C port on the IBM PC asynchronous communication board to the serial port on the SDK-86 so that you can download object-code programs.

The IBM PC asynchronous board is configured as DTE, so TxD is on pin 2, RxD is on pin 3, $\overline{\text{RTS}}$ is on pin 4, $\overline{\text{CTS}}$ is on pin 5, $\overline{\text{DTR}}$ is on pin 20, $\overline{\text{DSR}}$ is on pin 6, and carrier detect ($\overline{\text{CD}}$) is on pin 8. In order for the IBM board to be able to transmit and receive, its $\overline{\text{CTS}}$, $\overline{\text{DSR}}$, and $\overline{\text{CD}}$ inputs must be asserted. The BIOS software asserts the $\overline{\text{DTR}}$ and $\overline{\text{RTS}}$ outputs.

Now take another look at sheet 9 of the SDK-86 schematics in Figure 7-6 to see how the data and handshake signals are connected there. For communi-

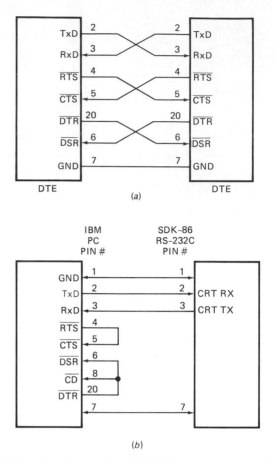

FIGURE 14-10 Nonmodem RS-232C connections. (a) Null modem for connecting two RS-232C data terminal–type devices. (b) IBM PC or PS/2 serial port to SDK-86 serial port connection.

cating with RS-232C-type equipment, the SDK-86 board is jumpered as shown in the jumper table column labeled "stand-alone CRT." The output data on CRT TX then connects to pin 3 of connector J7, a DB-25S-type connector. This corresponds to the RxD on the IBM connector, so no crossover is needed. Likewise, the CRT RX of the SDK corresponds to the TxD of the IBM board, so this is also a straight-through connection. The handshake signals here are another story.

The $\overline{\text{RTS}}$ of the SDK-86 is simply looped into the $\overline{\text{CTS}}$, so $\overline{\text{CTS}}$ will automatically be asserted when $\overline{\text{RTS}}$ is asserted by the 8251A. Therefore, neither of these signals is available for external handshaking. The $\overline{\text{DTR}}$ output of the 8251A on the SDK board is used for a teletypewriter function and does not connect to the normal RS-232C $\overline{\text{DTR}}$ pin number, so it is not available either. The $\overline{\text{DSR}}$ input of the 8251A is connected to the RxD input so that it will be asserted when a start bit comes in on the serial-data line, but this line is also not available for handshaking with external devices. Therefore, the problem here is that the SDK-86 is not set up to supply the handshake signals needed by the IBM PC serial board. Figure 14-10b shows the connections you make to solve this problem so the PC can talk to the SDK-86. The PC $\overline{\text{RTS}}$ line on pin 4 is jumpered on the connector to its $\overline{\text{CTS}}$ line on pin 5, so that $\overline{\text{CTS}}$ will automatically be asserted when $\overline{\text{RTS}}$ is asserted. Pins 6, 8, and 20 are also jumpered together on the connector so that when the PC asserts its $\overline{\text{DTR}}$ output on pin 20, the $\overline{\text{DSR}}$ input and the $\overline{\text{CD}}$ input will automatically be asserted. These connections do not provide for any hardware handshaking. They are necessary just to get the PC and the SDK-86 to talk to each other.

The point here is that whenever you have to connect RS-232C-compatible devices such as terminals, serial printers, etc., get the schematic for each and work your way through the connections one pin at a time. Make sure that an output on one device goes to the appropriate input on the other device. Sometimes you have to look at the actual drivers and receivers on the schematic to determine which pins on the connector are outputs and which are inputs. This is necessary because some manufacturers label an output pin connected to pin 3 as RxD, indicating that this signal goes to the RxD input of the receiving system.

If you do not have schematics for the RS-232C equipment you are trying to connect, you can often use a *breakout box* to determine the correct connections. You insert the breakout box in series with the connecting cable and LEDs on the box indicate which lines are outputs and which lines are inputs. By throwing switches on the box, you can try different connection combinations until data transfers correctly.

RS-423A and RS-422A

RS-423

A major problem with RS-232C is that it can only transmit data reliably for about 50 ft (16.4 m) at its maximum rate of 20,000 Bd. If longer lines are used, the transmission rate has to be drastically reduced. This limitation is caused by the open signal lines with a single common ground that are used to RS-232C.

Another EIA standard which is an improvement over RS-232C is *RS-423A*. This standard specifies a low-impedance single-ended signal which can be sent over 50-Ω coaxial cable and partially terminated at the receiv-

ing end to prevent reflections. Figure 14-11 shows how an MC3487 driver and MC3486 receiver can be connected to produce the required signals. A logic high in this standard is represented by the signal line being between 4 and 6 V negative with respect to ground, and a logic low is represented by the signal line being 4 to 6 V positive with respect to ground.

The RS-423 standard allows a maximum data rate of 100,000 Bd over a 40-foot line or a maximum baud rate of 1000 Bd on a 4000-foot line.

RS-422A

A still-newer standard for serial data transfer, *RS-422A* specifies that each signal will be sent differentially over two adjacent wires in a ribbon cable or a twisted pair of wires, as shown in Figure 14-12a, page 498.

The term differential in this standard means that the signal voltage is developed between the two signal lines rather than between a signal line and ground as in RS-232C and RS-423. In RS-422A a logic high is transmitted by making the "b" line more positive than the "a" line. A logic low is transmitted by making the a line more positive than the b line. The voltage difference between the two lines must be greater than 0.4 V but less than 12 V. Typical drivers such as the MC3487 shown in Figure 14-12a produce a differential voltage of about 2 V. The center or common-mode voltage on the lines must be between -7 V and $+7$ V. RS-422A specifies signal rise and fall times of 20 ns or 0.1 multiplied by the time for 1 bit, whichever is greater.

Figure 14-12b shows the relationship between maximum cable length and baud rate for RS-422A line. As we hope you can see in this graph, the maximum data rate for RS-422A lines ranges from 10 million Bd on a line 40 ft long to 100,000 Bd on a 4000-foot line. The reason that the data rates are so much higher than for RS-423 lines is that the differential line functions as a fully terminated transmission line. Common 24-gage twisted-pair wire has a Z_0 of about 100 Ω, so the line can be terminated with a matching 100-Ω resistor connected between the signal lines. A more common termination method, however, is to use a 50-Ω resistor from each signal line to ground as shown in Figure

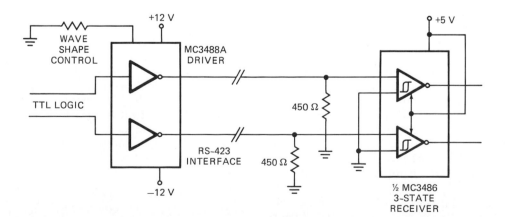

FIGURE 14-11 MC3488A driver and MC3486 receiver used for RS-423 signal transmission.

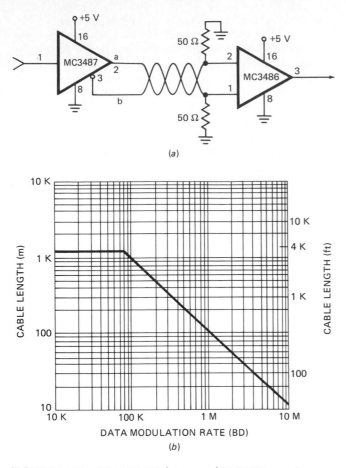

FIGURE 14-12 (a) MC3487 driver and MC3486 receiver used for RS-422A differential signal. (b) Maximum line length versus baud rate for RS-422A signal lines.

14-12a. This method helps keep the two signal lines balanced.

A further advantage of differential signal transmission is that any electrical noise induced in one signal line will be induced equally in the other signal line. A differential line receiver such as the MC3486 shown in Figure 14-12a responds only to the voltage difference between its two inputs, so any noise voltage that is induced equally on the two inputs will not have any effect on the output of the differential receiver.

The RS-422A and RS-423A standards do not specify connector pin numbers or handshake signals the way the RS-232C does. An additional EIA standard called *RS-449* does this for the two. RS-449 specifies 37 signal pins on a main connector and 9 additional pins on an optional connector. The signals on these connectors are a superset of the RS-232C signals so adapters can be used to interface RS-232C equipment with RS-449 equipment.

Now that we have discussed the signals commonly used to interface a computer to a modem, let's take a closer look at how modems transmit signals over standard phone lines.

Modems

INTRODUCTION

As we described in a previous section, a modulator-demodulator, or modem, sends digital 1's and 0's over standard phone lines as modulated tones. The frequency of the tones is within the bandpass of the lines. Two organizations are responsible for most of the current standards for modem modulation methods and transmissions rates. Older modems in the United States were based on de facto standards from Bell Telephone Company. Examples of these standards are the Bell types 103, 202, 308, and 212A. In the United States modem standards are now handled by the Telecommunications Industry Association, which works very closely with the *Comité Consultatif Internationale Téléphonique et Télégraphique* (CCITT), which is part of the International Telecommunications Union. CCITT standards which relate to modems start with a V. Examples are the V.22 bis, which is a 2400-bit/s modem standard, and the V.29, which is a 9600-bit/s modem standard. As we discuss modem modulation techniques in the following section, we will describe these and other standards in greater detail.

INTRODUCTION TO MODEM MODULATION

To represent digital 1's and 0's a modulator changes some characteristic of an audio signal which has a frequency within the bandwidth of the phone lines. An important point to keep in mind as you read through the following section is that the maximum rate at which the audio tone can be modulated is one-half the bandwidth of the transmission line. If, for example, we assume that the worst-case bandwidth of a two-wire phone line is 2400 Hz, then the maximum modulation rate for a half-duplex signal on the line is 1200 Bd. For full-duplex communication, half the bandwidth is used for transmission in each direction, so the maximum modulation rate for each direction on a two-wire phone line is 600 baud. In a 4-wire phone line which has separate wires for each direction, the maximum modulation rate for each direction is 1200 Bd. One of the goals of this section is to show you the modulation techniques that are used to overcome these basic limitations.

The major forms of modulation used are *amplitude*, *frequency-shift keying* (FSK), *phase-shift keying* (PSK), and *multiple carrier*.

As the name implies, amplitude modulation changes the amplitude of the transmitted tone. One common way of doing this is to turn a 387-Hz tone on to represent a 1 and turn the tone off to represent a turn the tone off to represent a 0, as shown in Figure 14-13. In other systems that we discuss later, the tone is always present, but its amplitude is changed between two or more values. Amplitude modulation is used only for very low speed reverse-channel transmission or in conjunction with some other type modulation such as phase modulation.

FREQUENCY-SHIFT KEYING MODULATION

Frequency-shift keying or FSK modulation uses one tone to represent a 0 and another tone to represent a 1, as

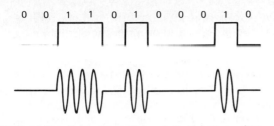

FIGURE 14-13 Representation of digital 1's and 0's with amplitude-modulated sine waves.

shown in Figure 14-14. In order to allow full-duplex communication, four different frequencies are often used. An old standard, the Bell 103A, 300-Bd FSK modem, for example, uses 2025 Hz for a 0 and 2225 Hz for a 1 in one direction, and 1070 Hz for a 0 and 1270 Hz for a 1 in the other direction. Another standard, the Bell 202 modem, permits half-duplex communication at 1200 baud. The 202 uses 1200 Hz to represent a 0 and 1700 Hz to represent a 1 for the main channel. Different versions of the 202 may also have either a 5-bit/s amplitude-modulated back channel or a 150-bit/s FSK back channel which uses 387 Hz for a 0 and 487 Hz for a 1.

As we discussed before, simple modulation such as FSK is limited to half-duplex operation at 1200 Bd on two-wire phone lines or 1200 Bd full-duplex on four-wire phone lines. For higher bit rates some type of phase-shift modulation is used.

PHASE-SHIFT MODULATION VARIATIONS

In the simplest form of phase-shift modulation called *differential phase-shift modulation* or DPSK, the phase of a constant-frequency sine-wave carrier of perhaps 1700 Hz is shifted by 180° to represent a change in the data from a 1 to a 0 or a change in the data from a 0 to a 1. Figure 14-15a shows an example of this. As the digital data changes from a 0 to a 1, near the left edge of the figure, the phase of the signal is shifted by 180°. When data changes from a 1 to a 0, the phase of the carrier is again shifted by 180°. For the next section of the digital data where the data stays 0 for 3 bit times, the phase of the carrier is not changed. Likewise, in a later section of the waveform where the data remains at a one level for 2 bit times, the phase of the carrier is not changed. The phase of the carrier then is shifted by 180° only when the data line changes from a 1 to a 0 or from a 0 to a 1.

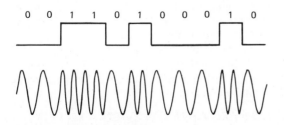

FIGURE 14-14 Representation of digital 1's and 0's with two different frequencies (FSK).

The simple phase-shift modulation shown in Figure 14-15a has no real advantage over FSK as far as maximum bit rate is concerned. However, by using additional phase angles besides 180°, 2 or more data bits can be sent with one phase change. Figure 14-15b shows how the value of 2 bits can be represented by four different phase shifts. If, for example, the value of a *dibit*, or 2 bits taken together, is 00, the phase of the carrier will be shifted 90° to represent that dibit. The trick here is that the phase of the carrier only has to shift once for each group of 2 transmitted bits.

Remember from a previous discussion that the baud rate limitation we are trying to overcome is the rate at which the carrier is changing. In this case the number of data bits per second is twice the baud rate. Bell 212A- and CCITT V.22-type modems use this scheme to transmit 1200 bits/s at an effective baud rate of only 600 Bd. Two carrier frequencies, 1200 Hz and 2400 Hz, are used to permit full-duplex operation at this rate.

A more complex phase-shift modulation scheme called *quaternary amplitude modulation* or QAM enables V.22-bis-type modems to transmit full-duplex data at 2400 bit/s over two-wire phone lines. V.29-type modems also use this type modulation to transmit half-duplex 9600-bit/s data from facsimile (FAX) machines. QAM uses 12 different phase angles and three different amplitudes to encode 4 data bits in each modulation change. Each group of 4 data bits is referred to as a *quadbit*. A phase-amplitude graph such as that shown in Figure 14-16, page 500, is often used to represent the phase and amplitude values for each of the 16 possible quadbits. Incidentally, the pattern of phase-amplitude points in

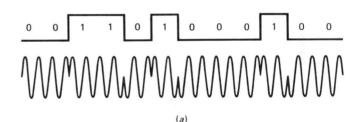

(a)

GRAY CODE DIBIT VALUE	DEGREES OF PHASE SHIFT
0 0	0
0 1	90
1 1	180
1 0	270

(b)

GRAY CODE TRIBIT VALUE	DEGREES OF PHASE SHIFT
0 0 1	22.5
0 0 0	67.5
0 1 0	112.5
0 1 1	157.5
1 1 1	202.5
1 1 0	247.5
1 0 0	292.5
1 0 1	337.5

(c)

FIGURE 14-15 Phase-shift modulation. (a) Waveforms for simple phase-shift modulation. (b) Set of phase shifts used to represent four possible dibit combinations. (c) Set of phase shifts used to represent eight possible tribit combinations.

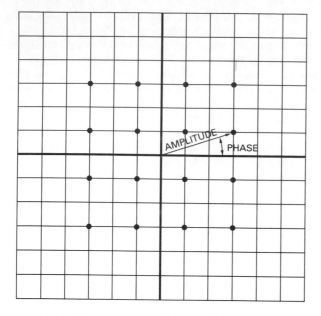

FIGURE 14-16   Phase-amplitude graph showing constellation for quaternary amplitude modulation (QAM).

a graph such as this is commonly referred to as a constellation.

Dibit and QAM phase-shift modulation permit higher data rates on phone lines, but correctly demodulating this type of phase-encoded data presents some unique problems. To illustrate the first problem, remember from our previous discussion that in a dibit system the value of a dibit is represented by shifting the phase of a carrier signal some specified number of degrees from a reference phase. In order to detect the amount of phase shift, the receiver and the transmitter must be using the same reference phase. This would be easy if we could just run another wire to carry a synchronizing clock signal. However, since this is not easily done, the synchronizing signal must in some way be included with the data. The carrier signal itself cannot be used directly, because that is the signal whose phase must be detected.

The solution to this problem is to use transitions in the transmitted signal to synchronize a phase-locked loop oscillator in the receiver. In order for this to work, two factors must be included in the transmitted data. First of all, the system must be operated synchronously rather than asynchronously, so that data, sync, or null characters are always being received by the receiver. Secondly, the transmitted data must have enough transitions at regular intervals to keep the phase-locked loop locked in the desired phase. The serial data stream from the USART may not have enough transitions in it to satisfy this second condition, so a special circuit called a *scrambler* is included in the transmitter part of the modem. The scrambler, which usually consists of a shift register with feedback, puts in extra signal transitions as needed. The output from the scrambler is then used to modulate the phase of the carrier. When the carrier signal reaches the receiver, the signal is demodulated to produce a signal of 1's and 0's. This signal is then

passed through a descrambler, which reverses the scrambling process and outputs the original data.

A second problem encountered in high-speed data transmission with modems is error detection/correction. One method used to decrease the error rate is called *trellis coding*. Trellis coding uses a constellation with more points than the minimum required to represent the number of data bit combinations in the group. The information needed to decode each data bit is spread over several transmitted values rather than being encoded in just one as in straight QAM. This scheme makes it possible for the receiver to detect illegal values caused by errors. V.32-type modems use trellis coding to allow full-duplex 9600-bit/s transmission on a two-wire phone line with 2400-Bd modulation.

Note that this modulation rate is higher than we told you was possible for a phone line bandwidth of 2400 Hz. The actual bandwidth of the phone lines is usually 3000 or somewhat more, so it is common practice to "push" the bandwidth limits to get higher data transmission rates. Most modems are designed to work with several different transmission rates and modulation so that they can communicate with a variety of modems. The software controlling the modem usually attempts communication at the highest available data rate, and if the particular phone connection will not support that rate, it "falls back" to a lower data rate where it can successfully transmit and receive. V.32-type modems also contain echo cancellation circuitry to reduce errors caused by interference between the signal being sent out and the signal coming in.

Other techniques being used to increase the rate at which modems can transfer data on standard phone lines are error correcting and data compression. CCITT standard V.42 specifies an error detection/correction algorithm that is independent of the data transmission speed and modulation method. CCITT standard V.42 bis specifies data compression algorithms that can be implemented in modems independently of the data transmission rate and the modulation method. The algorithm in this standard allows up to a 4:1 data compression, depending on the amount of redundancy in the data being transmitted. An average increase of about 60% in the actual data transmission rate is common with this algorithm.

Still another technique used to increase the data rate on phone lines is Telebit Corporation's Dynamically Adaptive Multicarrier Quadrature Amplitude Modulation (DAMQAM). This scheme uses up to 512 different carrier frequencies within the bandwidth of the phone lines. Data transmission is spread out over a large number of these channels, so the transmission on any one channel can be a very low rate, even with an overall transmission rate of 19,200 bits/s.

Now that you know more than you may want to about the modulation schemes used in modems, let's take a look at how a high-speed modem can be interfaced with microcomputer buses.

MODEM HARDWARE OVERVIEW

Figure 14-17 shows a block diagram for a combination FAX and data modem which interfaces directly to the

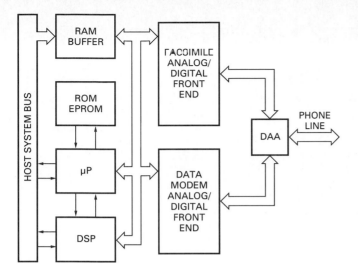

FIGURE 14-17 Block diagram of combination FAX and data modem.

main buses in a microcomputer. As you can see, the modem contains a dedicated microprocessor to control the operations of the modem. This processor manages handshaking, data formatting, dialing, etc. The ROM or EPROM stores the program for the microprocessor and the RAM stores blocks of data ·received by the modem and blocks of data waiting to be sent.

As we described before, high-speed data transmission on phone lines requires precisely detecting the amplitude of signals, precisely detecting the phase of signals, noise filtering, and echo cancellation. In current modems these tasks are accomplished with the digital signal processing techniques we described in Chapter 10. As you can see, the modem in Figure 14-17 contains a dedicated digital signal processor to do all this.

The modem in Figure 14-17 contains a FAX front end and a data front end. The reason for this is that a FAX typically uses V.29 type half-duplex 9600-bit/s transmission, and the corresponding data communication uses V.22 bis full-duplex 2400-bit/s transmission.

The box labeled DAA in Figure 14-17 is the *data access arrangement* circuitry which actually interfaces the signals with the phone lines. This circuitry must conform to the provisions of FCC rules, Section 68.

LSI has made it possible to build a modem with very few parts. A device such as the Advanced Micro Devices AM7910, for example, can be used to produce a 1200-Bd FSK modem. The EXAR Corp. XR-2901 and 2902 chip set contains a major part of the circuitry needed to implement a modem which can send or receive facsimile (FAX) data at 9600 bits/s or send and receive full-duplex modem data at 2400 bits/s.

MODEM HANDSHAKING

Earlier in this chapter we gave an overview of the handshake process between a terminal and a remote computer through modems and the phone lines. Now that you know more about modems, we can take a closer look at the handshake sequence.

Most of the currently available modems contain a dedicated microprocessor. The built-in intelligence allows these units to automatically dial a specified number with either tones or pulses, and redial the number if it is busy or doesn't answer. When a smart modem makes contact with another modem, it will automatically try to set its transmit circuitry to match the baud rate of the other modem. Many modems can be set to automatically answer a call after a programmed number of rings so that you can access your computer from a remote location. Some units allow the user to establish a voice contact and then switch over to modem operation.

After a modem dials up another modem, a series of handshake signals takes place. The handshake signals may be generated by hardware in the modem or by software in the system connected to the modem. Figure 14-18, page 502, shows an example of the data and handshake waveforms for a modem built with the AM7910 single-chip FSK modem. Other modems may use a slightly different sequence, but the principles are the same.

The modem which makes a call is usually referred to as the *originate* modem, and the modem which receives the call is usually referred to as the *answer* modem. In the following discussion we will use the terms *calling modem* and *called modem*, respectively, to agree with the labels on the waveforms in Figure 14-18.

At the left side of the waveforms, a call is being made from one modem to another. Assuming that the $\overline{\text{DTR}}$ of the called modem is asserted, the ringing signal on the line will cause the DAA circuitry to assert the *ringing input* $\overline{\text{RI}}$ of the 7910. In response to this the 7910 will send out a silent period of about 2s to accommodate billing signals, and then it will send out an answer tone of 2025 Hz to the calling modem for 2 s. If the $\overline{\text{DTR}}$ and the $\overline{\text{RTS}}$ of the calling modem are asserted, indicating that data is ready to be sent, the calling modem then puts a tone of 2225 Hz (mark) on the line for 8 ms to let the called modem know that contact is complete. In response to this mark, the called modem asserts its *carrier-detect* output $\overline{\text{CD}}$ to enable the receiving UART. The calling modem then sends data until its $\overline{\text{RTS}}$ input is released by the computer or terminal sending the data. While it is receiving data on the main channel, the called modem can send data to the calling modem on the 5-bit/s back channel. Releasing $\overline{\text{RTS}}$ causes the modem to release $\overline{\text{CTS}}$ to the sending computer and remove the carrier from the line. The called modem senses the loss of the carrier and unasserts its carrier detect ($\overline{\text{CD}}$) signal.

Now, if the called system is to send some data back to the calling system on the main channel, it asserts the $\overline{\text{RTS}}$ input to its modem. The called modem sends a marking tone to the calling modem for 8 ms. The calling modem asserts its $\overline{\text{CD}}$ output to its UART. The called modem then sends data to the calling modem on the main channel until its $\overline{\text{RTS}}$ input is unasserted by the called system, indicating no more data to send. While the called modem is transmitting on the main channel, the calling modem can transmit over the back channel if necessary. The handshake is similar for a full-duplex system, but the data rates are equal in both directions.

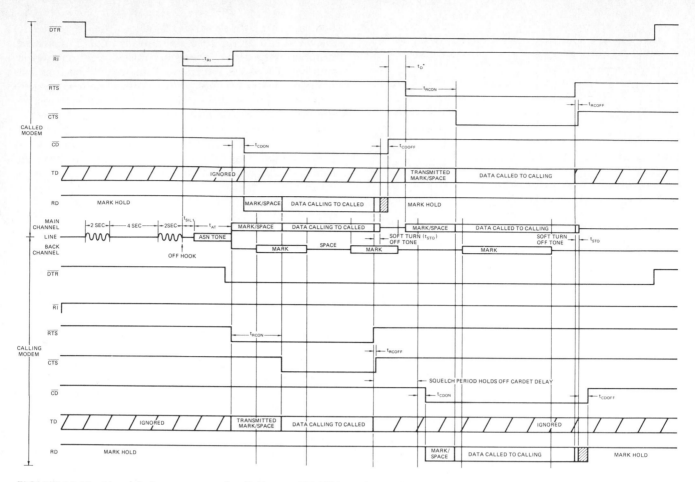

FIGURE 14-18   Handshake sequence for Bell-type 202 FSK modem using
AM7910 modem chip.   (*Copyright Advanced Micro Devices, Inc. (1982)
Reprinted with permission of copyright owner. All rights reserved.*)

CODECs, PCM, TDM, and ISDN

In the previous sections we described how modems
produce signals which are suitable for transmission over
standard phone lines. Now we want to briefly discuss
how telephone companies actually transmit the signals
output by modems and some new developments which
hopefully will eliminate the need for modems as we know
them.

Digital signals have much better noise immunity than
analog signals, so as soon as a phone company receives
a voice or modem signal in its local branch office, the
signal is converted to digital form. A D/A converter
at the destination uses the received binary codes to
reconstruct a replica of the original analog signal. Sending analog signals such as phone signals as a series of
binary codes is called *pulse-code modulation* or PCM.
The A/D converter that produces the binary codes in
this application is usually called a *coder* and the D/A
converter that reconstructs the analog signal from the
pulse codes is referred to as a *decoder.* Since both a
coder and a decoder are needed for two-way communication, they are often packaged in the same IC. This
combined coder and decoder is called a *codec.* A common
example of a codec is the Intel 2910A. This device
contains a sample-and-hold circuit on the analog input,

an 8-bit A/D converter, an 8-bit D/A converter, and
appropriate control circuitry.

Normal A/D converters are linear, which means that
the steps are the same size over the full range of the
converters. The A/D converters used in codecs are
nonlinear. They have small steps for small signals and
large steps for large signals. In other words, for signals
near the zero point of the A/D converter, it takes only a
small change in the signal to change the code on the
output of the A/D. For a signal near the full scale of the
converter, a large change in the input signal is required
to produce a change in the output binary code. This
nonlinearity of the A/D converter is said to *compress* the
signal, because it reduces the dynamic range of the
signal. Compression in this way greatly improves the
accuracy for small signals where it is needed, without
going to a converter with more bits of resolution. The
D/A in the codec is nonlinear in the reverse manner, so
that when the binary pulse codes are converted to
analog, the result is *expanded* to duplicate the original
waveform. A codec which has this intentional nonlinearity is often referred to as a *compander* or a *companding
codec.* Consult the Intel 2910A data sheet for more
information about this.

In most systems the output of the codec A/D is not
simply sent on a wire by itself, it is multiplexed with the

outputs of many other codecs in a manner known as *time-division multiplexing* or TDM. There are several different formats used. A simple one will give you the idea of how it's done.

One of the first TDM systems was the T1 or DS-1 system, which multiplexes 24 PCM voice channels onto a single wire. For this system an 8-bit codec on each channel samples and digitizes the input signal at an 8-kHz rate. The 8-bit codes from the codecs are sent to a multiplexer which sends them out serially, one after the other. One set of bits from each of the 24 codecs plus a framing bit is referred to as a frame. Figure 14-19 shows the format of a frame for this system. The framing bit at the start of each frame toggles after each frame is sent. It is used to keep the receiver and the transmitter synchronized and for keeping track of how many frames have been sent. After it sends the framing bit, the multiplexer sends out the 8-bit code from the first codec, then sends out the 8-bit code from the next codec, and so on until the codes for all 24 have been sent out. At specified intervals the multiplexer sends out a frame which contains synchronization information and signaling information. This does not seriously affect the quality of the transmitted data.

Since the multiplexer is sending out 193-bit frames at a rate of 8000 per second, the data rate on the wire is 193 × 8000, or 1.544 Mbits/s. A newer system, known as T4M or DS-4, multiplexes 4032 channels onto a single coaxial cable or optic fiber. The bit rate for this system is 274.176 Mbits/s.

The question that should come to your mind about now is, If the phone company transmits data in high-speed digital form, why do I have to send data as modulated audio tones? The answer to this question is that the circuitry between your phone and the local branch office is a relic from a bygone analog era. This circuitry creates a "bottleneck" in the communications link.

One attempt to eliminate this bottleneck is a wideband digital connection system known as the *integrated services digital network* or ISDN. As shown in Figure 14-20a, page 504, ISDN replaces the analog connections between your home and the telephone company branch office with relatively high speed digital connections. An ISDN basic-rate service connection gives two 64-kbit/s voice/data channels and a 16-Kbit/s data/control channel in each direction. The voice/data channels are referred to as B1 and B2. The data/control channel is referred to as the D channel.

Figure 14-20b shows how the B1, B2, D, framing, and other bits are packed in a 48-bit frame for transmission.

Note that a B channel has four times as many bits per frame as the D channel, so the bit rate for the B channel is four times the bit rate for the D channel. A 48-bit frame is transmitted every 250 μs, so the basic bit rate on the single line is 192 Kbits/s. Only 16 of the 48 data bits represent one of the B channels, so the transmission rate for a B channel is 64 Kbits/s.

For voice communication a codec in the telephone converts voice signals to a sequence of 8-bit codes which are then put in, for example, the B1 channel slots in the 48-bit frames. The codec also converts the codes for received voice signals back to analog form to drive a speaker. Some advantages of ISDN for standard telephone communications are that it gives better sound quality and allows identification of the number that a call is coming from.

For data communications an adapter in the computer formats the data to be transmitted in the required frames and adds the framing bits, etc. Since both B channels can be used, the effective data rate is the sum of that for the two channels, or 128K bits/s. In some cases the D channel can also be used for data, and the effective rate becomes the 144K bits/s.

In a large building with many telephones and computers, each phone and computer will communicate with the PBX in the building using a basic ISDN 2B +D service line such as we just described. The PBX will then use a higher-frequency multiplexed line such as the T1 system we described earlier to communicate with the telephone company's central office.

As you can see by the transmission rates for ISDN, it is a big improvement over the old analog connections. As of this writing ISDN is still available only in some major cities and a few other areas. It is slowly spreading to other areas, but if you want to communicate with many different locations, you will probably be stuck with an analog modem for some time. This is unfortunate, because high-speed data communication is required for interactive graphic user interfaces. In other words, if you want to rapidly transmit high-resolution color images, you need a high-speed communications link. In the next section we discuss fiber-optic systems, which allow the very high speed data transfer needed for this.

Fiber-Optic Data Communication

INTRODUCTION

All of the data communication methods we have discussed so far use metallic conductors. *Fiber-optic* systems use very thin glass or plastic fibers to transfer data as pulses of light. Some of the advantages of fiber-optic links are that they are immune to electrical noise, they can transfer data at very high rates, and they can transfer data over long distances without amplification.

Figure 14-21, page 505, shows the connections for a basic fiber-optic data link you can build and experiment with. This type of link might be used to transmit data from a sensor in an electrically noisy environment such as a factory. The light source here is a simple infrared LED. Higher-performance systems use an *infrared injection laser diode* (ILD) or some other laser driven by a high-speed, high-current driver. Digital data is sent over

FIGURE 14-19 Frame format for telephone company T1 digital data transmission.

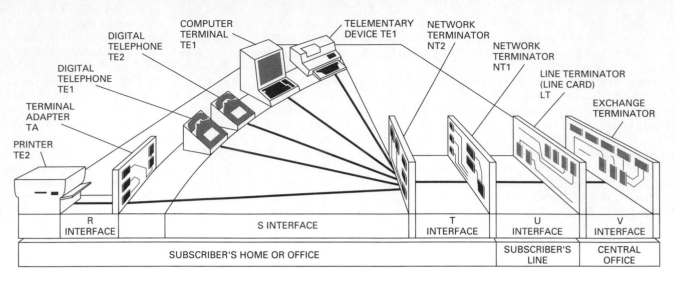

(a)

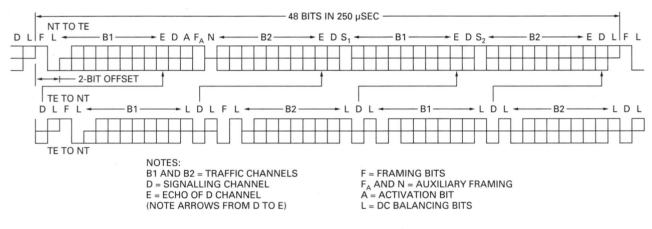

NOTES:
B1 AND B2 = TRAFFIC CHANNELS   F = FRAMING BITS
D = SIGNALLING CHANNEL   F_A AND N = AUXILIARY FRAMING
E = ECHO OF D CHANNEL   A = ACTIVATION BIT
(NOTE ARROWS FROM D TO E)   L = DC BALANCING BITS

(b)

FIGURE 14-20   Integrated services digital network (ISDN). (*a*) Line connections
and interfaces. Reprinted from EDN, April 27, 1989, © 1989 CAHNERS
PUBLISHING COMPANY, a Division of Reed Publishing USA. (*b*) Example S
interface frame format showing how B1, B2, and D channel bits are packaged
for transmission. NOTE: Frames sent from network termination to terminal
equipment are offset 2 bits from frames sent from terminal equipment to
network termination.

the fiber by turning the light beam on for a 1 and off for
a 0.

> NOTE: If you are working on a fiber-optic system
> you should never look directly into the end of the
> fiber to see if the light source is working, because
> the light beam from some laser diodes is powerful
> enough to cause permanent eye damage. Use a
> light meter, or point the cable at a nonreflective
> surface to see if the light source is working.

To convert the light signal back into an electrical
signal at the receiving end, Darlington photodetectors
such as the MFOD73 shown in Figure 14-21, PIN FET
devices, or avalanche photodiodes (APDs) are used. APDs

are more sensitive and operate at higher frequencies,
but the circuitry for them is more complex. A Schmitt
trigger is usually used on the output of the detector to
"square up" the output pulses.

The fiber used in a cable is made of special plastic or
glass. Fiber diameters used range from 2 to 1000 μm.
Larger-diameter plastic fibers are used for short-dis-
tance, low-speed transmission, and small-diameter glass
fibers are used for high-speed applications such as long-
distance telephone transmission lines. As shown in
Figure 14-22*e*, page 506, the fiber-optic cable consists
of three parts. The optical-fiber core is surrounded by a
cladding material which is also transparent to light. An
outer sheath protects the cladding and prevents external
light from entering.

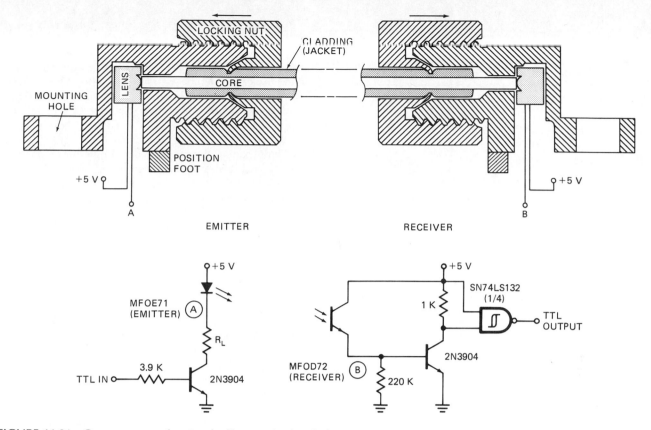

FIGURE 14-21   Components of a simple fiber-optic data link.

Now that you have an overview of an optical-fiber link, let's take a look at how the light actually propagates through the fiber and the trade-offs with different fibers.

THE OPTICS OF FIBERS

The path of a beam of light going from a material with one optical density to a material of different optical density depends on the angle at which the beam hits the boundary between the two materials. Figure 14-22 shows the path that will be taken by beams of light at various angles going from an opticaly dense material such as glass to a less dense material such as a vacuum or air. If the beam hits the boundary at the right angle, it will go straight through, as shown in Figure 14-22a. When a beam hits the boundary at a small angle away from the perpendicular or *normal*, it will be bent away from the normal when it goes from the more dense to the less dense, as shown in Figure 14-22b. A light beam going in the other direction would follow the same path. A quantity called the *index of refraction* is used to describe the amount that the light beam will be bent. Using the angle identifications shown in Figure 14-22b, the index of refraction, n, is defined as the (sine of angle B)/(sine of angle A). A typical value for the index of refraction of glass is 1.5. The larger the index of refraction, the more the beam will be bent when it goes from one material to another.

Figure 14-22c shows a unique situation that occurs when a beam going from a dense material to a less dense material hits the boundary at a special angle called the *critical angle*. The beam will be bent so that it travels parallel to the boundary after it enters the less dense material.

A still more interesting situation is shown in Figure 14-22d. If the beam hits the boundary at an angle greater than the critical angle, it will be totally reflected from the boundary at the same angle on the other side of the normal. This is somewhat like skipping stones across water. In this case the light beam will not leave the more dense material.

To see how all this relates to optical fibers, take a look at the cross-sectional drawing of an optical fiber in Figure 14-22e. If a beam of light enters the fiber parallel to the axis of the fiber, it will simply travel through the fiber. If the beam enters the fiber so that it hits the glass-cladding layer boundary at the critical angle, it will travel through the fiber-optic cable in the cladding layer as shown for beam Y in Figure 14-22e. However, if the beam enters the cable so that it hits the glass-cladding layer boundary at an angle greater than the critical angle, it will bounce back and forth between the walls of the fiber as shown for beam X in Figure 14-22e. The glass or plastic used for fiber-optic cables has very low absorption, so the beam can bounce back and forth along the fiber for several feet or miles without excessive attenuation. Most systems use light with wavelengths of 0.85μm, 1.3 μm, or 1.500 μm, because absorption of light by the optical fibers is minimum at these wavelengths.

If an optical fiber has a diameter many times larger than the wavelength of the light being used, then beams

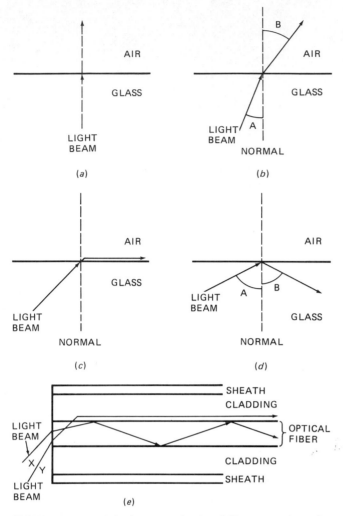

FIGURE 14-22 Light-beam paths for different angles of incidence with the boundary between higher optical density and lower optical density materials. (*a*) Right angle. (*b*) Angle less than critical angle. (*c*) At critical angle. (*d*) At angle greater than critical angle. (*e*) At angle greater than critical angle in optical fiber.

which enter the fiber at different angles will arrive at the other end of the fiber at slightly different times. The different angles of entry for the beams are referred to as *modes*. A fiber with a diameter large enough to allow beams with several different entry angles to propagate through it is called a *multimode* fiber. Since multimode fibers are larger, they are easier to manufacture, are easier to manually work with, and can use inexpensive LED drivers. However, the phase difference between the output beams in multimode fibers causes problems at high data rates. One partial solution to this problem is to dope the glass of the fiber so that the index of refraction decreases toward the outside of the fiber. Light beams travel faster in the region where the index of refraction is lower, so beams which take a longer path back and forth through the faster outer regions tend to arrive at the end of the fiber at the same time as those that take a shorter path through the slower center region.

A better solution to the phase problems of the multimode fiber is to use a fiber that has a diameter only a few times the wavelength of the light being transmitted. Only beams very nearly parallel to the axis of the fiber can then be transmitted. This is referred to as *single-mode* operation. Single-mode systems currently available can transmit data a distance of over 60 km at a rate greater than 1 Gbit/s. An experimental system developed by AT&T multiplexes 10 slightly different wavelength laser beams onto one single-mode fiber. The system can transmit data at an effective rate of 20 Gbit/s over a distance of 68 km without amplification.

One of the main problems with single-mode fibers is the difficulty in making low-loss connections with the tiny fibers. Another difficulty is that in order to get enough light energy into the tiny fiber, relatively expensive laser diodes or other lasers rather than inexpensive LEDs must be used.

FIBER-OPTIC CABLE USES

Fiber-optic transmission has the advantages that the signal lines are much smaller than the equivalent electrical signal lines, signals can be sent much longer distances without repeater amplifiers, and very high data rates are possible. One of the first major uses of fiber-optic transmission systems has been for carrying large numbers of phone conversations across oceans and between cities. A single 12-fiber, $\frac{1}{2}$-in. diameter optical-fiber cable can transmit 1,000,000 simultaneous telephone conversations. These specifications are impressive, but relatively primitive as compared to the possibilities shown by laboratory research. In the future it is possible that the high data rate of fiber-optic transmission may make picture phones a household reality, replace TV cables, replace satellite communication for many applications, replace modems, and provide extensive computer networking.

ASYNCHRONOUS COMMUNICATION SOFTWARE ON THE IBM PC

In a previous section of this chapter we discussed how asynchronous serial data can be sent or received with an 8251A on a polled or an interrupt basis. Any serial communication at some point has to get down to that level of hardware interaction. However, as we tried to show you in Chapter 13, you should write programs at the highest language level you have available without excessively sacrificing execution speed, the amount of memory used, or ease of use. In this section we show examples of serial data communication using direct UART interaction, BIOS function calls, DOS function calls, and C function calls, so that you can write programs at any level.

As a first example we will show you how we developed a simple terminal emulator program; then as a second example we will show you how we developed a program which downloads object code files from the IBM PC to an SDK-86 board.

A Terminal Emulator Using DOS Function Calls and BIOS Calls

As a first step in developing the SDK download program, we decided to write a simple terminal emulator program. A terminal emulator program, when run, makes the PC act like a dumb CRT terminal. Characters typed on the keyboard are sent out on an RS-232C line to a modem or some other RS-232C-compatible equipment, and characters coming into the PC on an RS-232C line are displayed on the CRT.

Whenever you want to write a system program such as this, you should first write the algorithm in a standard form as we taught you in Chapter 3. Figure 14-23 shows an algorithm for our simple terminal emulator.

The next step is to decide what language you want to work in and translate the algorithm to that language. For this example we decided to use DOS function calls and BIOS function calls. If you are programming at this level you should first see what DOS function calls are available to do each part of the algorithm for you. There are several reasons for this approach. First, DOS function calls are usually very easy to use because they do not require you to have extensive knowledge of the hardware details. Second, programs written at the DOS level are much more likely to run correctly on another "compatible" system. If you are going to be writing system programs for the IBM PC or PS/2, you should get a copy of the *DOS Technical Reference Manual*.

If you need some operation that is not provided by a DOS function call, then the next step is to check the available BIOS procedures in the IBM PC or PS/2 *Technical Reference Manual*. Finally, if neither DOS or BIOS has the functions you need, you invoke the 5-minute rule, and then dig into the Technical Reference Manual to find the pieces you need to write the functions yourself.

The relevant DOS function calls are as follows.

Function Call 2—The character in DL is sent to the CRT and the cursor is advanced one position.

Function Call 3—Waits for a character to be received in the serial port and then returns with character in AL.

Function Call 4—The character in DL is output to the serial port.

Function Call 8—Waits for a key to be pressed on the keyboard and then returns the ASCII code for the key in AL.

```
INIT COM1
REPEAT
    IF CHARACTER READY IN UART THEN
        READ CHARACTER
        SEND TO CRT
    IF KEYPRESSED ON IBM KEYBOARD THEN
        READ KEY
        SEND TO SERIAL PORT
UNTIL FOREVER
```

FIGURE 14-23   Algorithm for simple terminal emulator program.

Function call 2 looks useful for sending a character to the CRT, and function call 4 looks useful for sending a character to the serial port. However, the keyboard call and the serial-read call will not work because they both sit in loops waiting for input. In other words, if you call function 8, execution will not return from that function until a key is pressed on the keyboard. If execution is in the function 8 loop, characters coming into the serial port will not be read. What is needed here are procedures which allow polling to go back and forth between the keyboard and the serial port receiver. Also needed is the least painful way to initialize the serial port. Let's see what BIOS has to offer.

Figure 14-24 shows the subfunctions and parameter passing registers for the IBM PC BIOS INT 14H procedure. This procedure will do one of four functions,

```
BIOS INT 14H SUBPROCEDURES AND PARAMETERS

AH        FUNCTION

0         Initialize communications port
          DX = port number - 0 = com1, 1 = com2
          AL = comm port mode word as follows
          baud rate        parity    stop    data bits
          7 6 5              4 3       2       1 0
          0 0 0  110       X0-none   0-1     10-7
          0 0 1  150       01-odd    1-2     11-8
          0 1 0  300
          0 1 1  600
          1 0 0  1200
          1 0 1  2400
          1 1 0  4800
          1 1 1  9600

1         Send the character in AL out comm port
          DX = port number - 0 = com1, 1 = com2
          Returns line status in AH as shown
          below for AH = 3 call.

2         Read character from com port
          DX = port number - 0 = com1, 1 = com2
          Returns character in AL, status in AH.
          If AH bit 7 = 1, unable to read char.
          If AH bit 7 = 0, bits 3,2,1 flag errors.
          If AH = 0, char read with no errors.

3         Read line and modem status.
          DX = port number - 0 = com1, 1 = com2
          Returns: AH = line status
            bit 7 = time out
            bit 6 = transmit shift register empty
            bit 5 = transmit hold register empty
            bit 4 = break detect
            bit 3 = framing error
            bit 2 = parity error
            bit 1 = overrun error
            bit 0 = received character ready
                AL = modem signal status
            bit 7 = receive line signal detect
            bit 6 = ring indicator
            bit 5 = data set ready asserted
            bit 4 = clear to send asserted
            bit 3 = delta receive line detect
            bit 2 = trailing edge ring detect
            bit 1 = delta data set ready
            bit 0 = delta clear to send
```

FIGURE 14-24   Subprocedures and parameter passing registers for IBM PC BIOS INT 14H procedure.

depending on the value passed to it in the AH register. If AH = 0 when the procedure is called, the byte in AL is used to initialize the serial port device as shown. If AH = 1, then the character in AL will be sent out from the serial port. Likewise, if AH = 2, then a character will be read in from the serial port and left in AL. Finally, if AH = 3 when the procedure is called, the status of the serial port will be returned in AH and AL. The first of these four options solves the initialization problem. The last (AH = 3) supplies most of the solution for the problem of determining when the UART has a character ready to be read. Bit 0 of the status byte returned in AH will be set if the UART contains a character ready to be read. If a character is ready, it can be read in and sent to the CRT. If no character is present, the program can go check to see if a key on the keyboard has been pressed.

Figure 13-1 shows the subprocedures and parameter-passing registers for the IBM PC BIOS INT 16H procedure which accesses the keyboard. Remember from the discussion at the start of the last chapter that this procedure performs one of three different functions, depending on the value passed to it in AH. If AH = 0, the procedure will wait for a keypress and return the code for the pressed key in AL or AH. If AH = 1, the function will return with the zero flag = 0 if a key has been pressed and the code is available to be read. If AH = 2, the shift status will be returned in AL.

Calling the INT 16 procedure with AH = 1 solves the problem of polling the keyboard without sitting in a loop the way the DOS function call does. The zero flag can simply be checked upon return from the INT 16 procedure, and if no key is ready, execution can go check the UART again. If a key code is ready, it can be read in with a DOS call or another INT 16 call and sent to the UART.

Figure 14-25 shows a simple terminal emulator program which uses the procedures we have described. The program follows the algorithm almost line by line. Remember from previous chapter examples that BIOS procedures are called directly by an INT (number) instruction, and DOS calls are done by putting the function number in AH and doing an INT 21H instruction.

You can connect the serial port on an IBM PC- or PS/2-compatible to the serial port of an SDK-86 board as shown in Figure 14-10b and use this program to communicate with the board at 300 or 600 Bd. However, if you try to use the program at 1200 or 2400 Bd, the first character of each line of characters received from the SDK-86 or other source will be lost. It took some work to figure out why this is the case, because even with a 4.77-MHz 8088, the computer should be more than fast enough to handle 4800-Bd communciation with no trouble. The problem is in the INT 10H procedure which we used to send characters to the CRT. After a carriage return is sent to the CRT, the display on the screen is scrolled up one line. To avoid flicker, however, the screen is not scrolled until the next frame update. Since the frame rate for the monochrome display is 50 Hz, the return from the display procedure may take as long as 20 ms. Any characters that come into the UART during this time will be lost. The next section shows

how we solved this problem to produce a download program which works correctly at 4800 baud.

IBM PC to SDK-86 Download Program

The main purpose of the program described in this section is to allow the binary codes for programs developed on an IBM PC- or PS/2-compatible computer to be downloaded through an RS-232C link to an SDK-86 board. The program also functions as a dumb terminal so that downloaded programs can be run, memory contents displayed, and registers examined by using the SDK-86 serial monitor commands. These commands are implemented by simply typing the appropriate keys on the computer keyboard.

Figure 14-26, page 510, shows the overall algorithm for the program. The main difference between this algorithm and the one for the dumb terminal in Figure 14-24 is the addition of the actions when the letter Q or the letter L is typed. However, we implemented the algorithm in a different way in order to solve the speed problem described in the previous section, to give you some more exposure to the C programming language, and to show you some very important programming techniques. Incidentally, the 1986 version of this program, written entirely in assembly language, required six pages. This version, written mostly in C, requires only four pages. It would be shorter still except that we left two procedures in assembly language so you can more easily work your way through them if you want.

Figure 14-27, page 511, shows the complete program. The main part of the program is only a little over a page long. Main calls six functions: INIT, SERIAL_IN, CHK_N_DISPLAY, xmit, convert_and_send, and shutdown to do most of the work. After we give an overview, we will explain in detail how each of these functions work.

OVERVIEW

As you can see from the algorithm in Figure 14-26, this program spends most of the time running around a loop which waits for the user to press a key or a character to be received in a buffer from the SDK-86. In our program the two statements while (!bioskey(1)) and CHK_N_DISPLAY () implement this loop.

The bioskey (1) part of this calls the BIOS INT 16H procedure to determine if a key has been pressed. If a key has been pressed, we call bioskey again to read in the code for the pressed key and use a switch structure to determine the action to take for that key code. If no key has been pressed, the bioskey (1) function call returns a 0 and the while loop repeats.

When the CHK_N_DISPLAY function is called, it determines if a buffer contains any characters read in from the UART connected to the SDK-86. If the buffer contains no characters, execution simply returns to the while loop. If the buffer contains a character, the character is sent to the CRT. Here's how this program solves the timing problem suffered by the program in Figure 14-25.

Remember from the discussion in the previous section

```
;8086 PROGRAM F14-25.ASM
;TERMINAL EMULATOR PROGRAM FOR SDK-86
;  This program sends characters entered on the IBM PC to the COM1
;  serial port at 600 baud, and displays characters received from the
;  COM1 serial port on the CRT.
PAGE,132


STACK_HERE      SEGMENT     STACK
                DW 100 DUP(0)
                STACK_TOP LABEL WORD
STACK_HERE      ENDS


CODE_HERE       SEGMENT
      ASSUME CS:CODE_HERE, SS:STACK_HERE


START: MOV  AX, STACK_HERE       ; Initialize stack segment
       MOV  SS, AX
       MOV  SP, OFFSET STACK_TOP ; Initialize stack pointer
       MOV  AH, 00               ; Initialize COM1
       MOV  DX, 0000             ; Point at COM1
       MOV  AL, 01100111B        ; 600 Bd, no parity, 2 stop,8-bit
       INT  14H                  ; via BIOS INT 14H
       STI                       ; Enable interrupts
CHKAGN:MOV  DX, 0000             ; Point at COM1
       MOV  AH, 03               ; Check for character from SDK
       INT  14H
       TEST AH, 01H              ; See if char waiting in UART
       JNZ  RDCHAR               ; If char, read it
       JMP  KYBD                 ; else, go look for keypress
RDCHAR:MOV  AH, 02               ; Read character
       INT  14H                  ; from UART to AL
       MOV  DL, AL               ; Character to DL for DOS call
       MOV  AH, 02H              ; DOS call number for CRT display
       INT  21H                  ; Do DOS call
KYBD:  MOV  AH, 1                ; Check if key has been pressed
       INT  16H                  ;  using BIOS call
       JNZ  RDKY                 ; If keypress, read key code
       JMP  CHKAGN               ; else look for more from SDK
RDKY:  MOV  AH, 0                ; Read key code
       INT  16H                  ; using BIOS call
       MOV  DX, 0000H            ; Point at COM1 serial port
       MOV  AH, 01
       INT  14H                  ; Send character to UART with BIOS
       JMP  CHKAGN               ; Go look for another char from UART
                                 ; or from keyboard

CODE_HERE  ENDS
       END START
```

FIGURE 14-25   Simple terminal emulator program using DOS and BIOS
function calls.

that if the program in Figure 14-25 is operated at over 600 Bd, characters which come into the UART while the INT 10H procedure is scrolling the CRT display are missed. In this program we read characters from the UART on an interrupt basis and put them in a buffer. Even if the PC is in the middle of the INT 10H procedure or some other procedure when the UART has a character ready, the interrupt procedure will read the character from the UART and put it in the buffer. When execution loops back around to the CHK_N_DISPLAY procedure again, the character will be read from the buffer and sent to the display. SERIAL_IN is the interrupt procedure which reads characters from the UART and puts them in the buffer. Now let's take a closer look at the switch structure which executes when the user presses a key on the PC keyboard.

If the user presses a Q key, we call the shutdown function to put the system back in its initial state and exit to DOS. If the user presses an L key, we first prompt the user for the path and name of a .BIN or .COM file to be downloaded to the SDK-86. After reading in the name of the file, we open the file if possible and send the

```
INITIALIZE EVERYTHING
   REPEAT
      IF KEY PRESSED THEN
         READ KEY
         IF KEY = Q THEN
            QUIT
         ELSE IF KEY = L THEN
            DOWNLOAD BINARY FILE FROM DISK TO SDK-86
         ELSE SEND CHARACTER FOR PRESSED KEY TO SDK-86
      IF UART BUFFER HAS CHARACTER THEN
         SEND CHARACTER TO CRT
   UNTIL QUIT
```

(a)

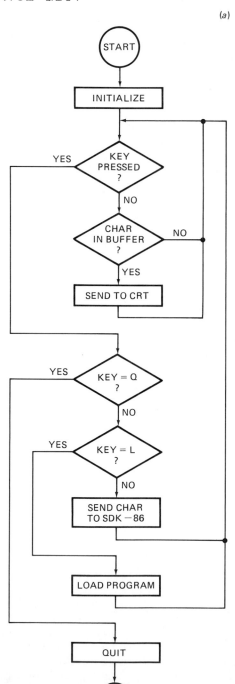

(b)

FIGURE 14-26 Algorithm for SDKCOM1 download program. (*a*, top) Pseudocode. (*b*, left) Flowchart.

Substitute command to the SDK-86. The while loop starting with while (!feof(fp)) reads a data byte from the file stream and then calls the convert_and_send function to convert the data byte to the format required by the SDK-86 and send it to the UART for transmission to the SDK-86. We then load numchar with the number of characters and call the CHK_N_DISPLAY procedure to send the SDK-86 response to the CRT.

Note that we have to use the feof () function to detect the end of this file rather than using the EOF character method we showed you for text files in the last chapter. The reason for this is that in a binary file such as a .BIN or .COM file, the EOF character, FFH, is a valid data byte and cannot be used as an end-of-file marker.

After all the data bytes are sent, we use the xmit function to send a carriage return to the SDK-86. This executes the SDK-86 Substitute command. Finally, we close the file before breaking from the switch structure.

If the key pressed by the user is not a Q or an L, the default part of the switch structure calls the xmit function to simply send the code for the pressed key on to the SDK-86.

The goto again; statement after the switch statement sends execution back to the while loop, which waits for a keypress or a character received in the buffer. Now let's dig a little deeper into the major parts of the program.

INITIALIZATION

The UART used on the IBM asynchronous communications adapter board is an INS8250. If the board is configured as system serial port COM1, the interrupt output from this device is connected to the IR4 input of an 8259A priority-interrupt controller on the main PC board of the IBM computer. The major part of the initialization here involves getting the 8250 initialized and setting up the interrupt mechanism. Remember from previous discussions that when an 8259A receives an interrupt on an IR input that is unmasked, it sends a specified interrupt type to the processor. The 8259A is initialized by the BIOS so that type 8 will be sent for an IR0 input. Therefore, for an IR4 signal from the UART, the 8259A will send type 0CH to the processor.

```
/* C PROGRAM F14-27A.C */
#include<stdio.h>
#include<dos.h>
#include<bios.h>
#include<stdlib.h>
extern void init(void);                  /* assembly language */
extern int chk_n_display(void);          /* assembly language */
extern void interrupt serial_in(void);   /* assembly language */
void convert_and_send(char binval);
void xmit(char ascval);
void shutdown(void);
void interrupt (*oldcomrxint)();         /* pointer to interrupt function */
int numchar = 0;                                     /* counter for chk_and_display function */

main()
{
FILE *fp;
char filename[40], ch;
char sdksub[] = "S 0000:0100,";         /* SDK substitute command */
char *ptr, val, mask;
int count;
                                                     /* ACTION STARTS HERE */
puts("SDK-86 Interface Program by Douglas V. Hall, 1990. \n\n");
puts("Press Caps Lock key on computer.\n");
puts("Enter - GO FE00:0 PERIOD on SDK-86 keypad to activate SDK-86.\n");
puts("In addition to monitor commands the following are available:\n");
puts("L- Load binary file and send to SDK-86\n");
puts("Q- Quit and return to DOS. \n");

oldcomrxint = getvect(12);              /* save old interrupt vector for RxRDY */
setvect(12, serial_in);                 /* load vector for custom RxRDY data read */
init();                                         /* initialize 8250 UART and 8259A PIC */

again:
  while(! bioskey(1))                                   /* loop until key pressed */
          chk_n_display();                              /* display characters read by UART if any */

ch = bioskey(0);                                        /* Read keycode and decide action */
switch (ch) {
  case 'Q':                                     /* If Q, the quit and return to DOS */
          shutdown();
          break;
  case 'L':                                     /* Download .bin or .com file to SDK-86 */
    puts("Please enter drive, path, and
          name of .bin or .com file.\n");
    gets(filename);
                if((fp=fopen(filename,"rb"))==0)
                    {
                        perror(filename);         /* print err message */
                        puts("\n Enter new command letter.\n");
                        goto again;               /* get new user command */
                    }
          ptr = sdksub;                           /* point at Substitute command string */
          while(*ptr != NULL)                     /* send Substitute command to SDK-86 */
                    {
                          xmit(*ptr);
                          ptr++;
                    }
          numchar = 17;                        /* number of characters sent by sdk */
          while(numchar >0)
                  chk_n_display();               /* echo sdk response to screen */
```

FIGURE 14-27   C and assembly language source program for SDKCOM1
program. (a) C mainline. (b) Assembly language modules. (*Continued on*
pp. 512–14.)

DATA COMMUNICATION AND NETWORKS   **511**

```
                while(!feof(fp))                                    /* process bytes until end of file */
                    {
                    val=getc(fp);                       /* read character from file stream */
                    if(!feof(fp))
                        {
                        convert_and_send(val);/* ASCII values to SDK-86 */
                        numchar = 14;                       /* characters returned by SDK-86 */
                        while(numchar >0)
                           chk_n_display();             /* send sdk echo in */
                                                                /*  ring buffer to CRT */

                        }
                    }
            val = 0x0d;                                 /* send terminator character to SDK-86 */
            xmit(val);
            fclose(fp);                                  /* close file */
            break;                                       /* go get next user command */
    default:                                             /* not Q or L, just send to SDK-86 */
            xmit(ch);
            break;
    }
    goto again;
}                                                                   /* end of main */

void convert_and_send(char binval)
{
  char hold;
  hold = binval;                                        /* Save copy of binary value */
  binval = binval >>4;                           /* upper four bits to lower */
  binval = binval & 0x0f;                      /*mask upper four bits */
  if(binval >= 0x0A)                                /* convert nibble to ASCII */
          binval = binval + 0x37;          /* add 37H if letter */
  else
          binval = binval + 0x30;          /* add 30H if number */
  xmit(binval);                                           /* send to SDK-86 */
  binval = hold;                                        /* get original value of binval */
  binval = binval & 0x000f;                  /* mask upper nibble */
  if(binval >= 0x0A)                                /* convert lower nibble to ASCII */
          binval = binval + 0x37;       /* add 37H if hex letter */
  else
          binval = binval + 0x30;          /* add 30H if hex number */
  xmit(binval);
  binval = 0x2c;                                          /* load code for comma */
  xmit(binval);
}                                                            /* send to SDK-86 */

void xmit(char ascval)
{
  while((bioscom(3,0,0)& 0x2000)==0)
            ;                                                       /* wait for UART xmit buffer ready */
  outportb(0x3f8, ascval);                 /* send ASCII character to UART */
}

void shutdown(void)
{
                                                                    /* shut everything down and return to DOS */
  unsigned char mask;
  mask = inportb(0x21);                      /* mask 8259 IR4 interrupt input */
  mask = mask | 0x10;
  outportb(0x21,mask);
  setvect(12, oldcomrxint);                       /* restore BIOS interrupt vector */
  exit(0);                                                   /* automatically closes any open files */
}
```

FIGURE 14-27 (*Continued*)

```
;8086 PROGRAM F14-27B.ASM
_TEXT       SEGMENT      BYTE PUBLIC 'CODE'
    DGROUP      GROUP      DATA
    ASSUME      CS:_TEXT,DS:DGROUP,SS:DGROUP
_TEXT       ENDS


_DATA       SEGMENT WORD PUBLIC 'DATA'
    QUEUE DB 1000 DUP(0)            ; Declare ring buffer
    HEAD_POINTER DW 0               ; Pointer to read location in buffer
    TAIL_POINTER DW 0               ; Pointer to write location in buffer
    TIME_OUT_MESS DB 'TRANSMIT TIMEOUT - CHECK HARDWARE',0DH, 0AH
    EXTRB    _NUMCHAR:WORD
_DATA       ENDS


_TEXT       SEGMENT      BYTE PUBLIC 'CODE'
    PUBLIC _INIT
    PUBLIC _SERIAL_IN
    PUBLIC _CHK_N_DISPLAY

 _INIT PROC NEAR
                            ; Unmask 8259A IR4
    IN   AL, 21H            ; Read 8259A IMR
    AND  AL, 0ECH           ; Unmask IR4
    OUT  21H, AL
;Initialize 8250 UART baud rate,etc.
    MOV  AH, 00             ; Initialize COM1
    MOV  DX, 0000           ; Point at COM1
    MOV  AL, 11000111B      ; 4800 Bd,No parity,2 stop,8-bit
    INT  14H               ;  via BIOS INT 14H
;Enable 8250 RxRDY interrupt
    MOV  DX, 03FBH          ; Point at 8250 line control port
    IN   AL, DX             ; Read in line control word
    AND  AL, 7FH            ; Set DLAB = 0
    OUT  DX, AL             ; Send line control word back out
    MOV  AL, 01H            ; Value to enable RxRDY interrupt
    MOV  DX, 03F9H          ; Point at interrupt enable register
    OUT  DX, AL             ; Enable RxRDY interrupt
    MOV  AL, 0BH            ; Assert 8250 OUT2, RTS, DTR byte
    MOV  DX, 03FCH          ; Point at modem control reg in 8250
    OUT  DX, AL             ; Send to 8250
    RET
 _INIT ENDP

 _SERIAL_IN PROC FAR
    STI                     ; Interrupts back on for clock, etc.
    PUSH AX
    PUSH BX
    PUSH DX
    PUSH DI
    PUSH DS
    MOV  AX, DGROUP         ; Load current DS register value
    MOV  DS, AX
    MOV  DX, 03F8H          ; Receiver buffer address for 8250
    IN   AL, DX             ; Read character
    MOV  DI, TAIL_POINTER   ; Get current tail pointer value
    INC  DI                 ; Point to next storage location
    CMP  DI, 1000           ; Compare with max to see if time
                            ;  to wrap around
    JNE  FULCHK             ; No, go check if queue full
    MOV  DI, 00             ; Yes, set DI for wraparound to start
```

FIGURE 14-27 (*Continued*)

```
        FULCHK:
            CMP  DI, HEAD_POINTER      ; Check for full queue
            JE   NO_MORE               ; Full, do not write char
            MOV  BX, TAIL_POINTER      ; Not full, point at write loc
            MOV  QUEUE[BX], AL         ; Character to circular buffer
            MOV  TAIL_POINTER, DI      ; Save new tail pointer value
        NO_MORE:

            MOV  AL, 20H               ; Non-specific EOI command
            OUT  20H, AL               ;   to 8259A
            POP  DS
            POP  DI
            POP  DX
            POP  BX
            POP  AX
            IRET
        _SERIAL_IN ENDP


        _CHK_N_DISPLAY PROC NEAR
            PUSH DI
            IN   AL, 21H
            OR   AL, 10H               ; Disable 8259A IR4 in critical region
            OUT  21H, AL               ;   by masking bit 4 of IMR
            MOV  DI, HEAD_POINTER
            CMP  DI, TAIL_POINTER      ; Is queue empty ?
            JE   NOCHAR                ; Yes, just return
            MOV  AL, QUEUE[DI]         ; No, get char from queue to AL
            INC  DI                    ; Point DI at next byte in queue
            CMP  DI, 1000              ; See if time to wrap pointer around
            JNE  OK                    ; No, go on
            MOV  DI, 0                 ; Yes, wrap pointer around to start
        OK:
            MOV  HEAD_POINTER, DI      ; Store new pointer value
            PUSH AX                    ; Save character in AL on stack
            IN   AL, 21H
            AND  AL, OECH              ; Enable IR4 interrupt so new char in 8250
            OUT  21H, AL               ;   can interrupt INT 10H
            POP  AX                    ; Get character back from stack
            MOV  AH, 14                ; Use BIOS INT 10H to send to CRT
            MOV  BH, 0
            INT  10H
            DEC  _NUMCHAR              ; Dec number char sent to CRT
            JMP  DONE
        NOCHAR:
            IN   AL, 21H
            AND  AL, OECH              ; End of critical region. Enable IR4 by
                                       ;   unmasking bit 4 in IMR of 8259A so
            OUT  21H, AL               ;   new char in UART can interrupt
        DONE:
            POP  DI
            RET
        _CHK_N_DISPLAY ENDP

        _TEXT     ENDS
            END
```

FIGURE 14-27 (*Continued*)

The processor multiplies the type number by 4 and goes to that address in the interrupt-vector table to get the starting address of the service procedure for that interrupt. In your program you must in some way put the starting address of your interrupt-service procedure in the correct address in the interrupt-vector table.

The setvect(12, serial_in); statement near the start of our program calls a predefined function to initialize the int 12 location in the vector table with the starting address of our SERIAL_IN procedure. In a simple application such as this, the setvect statement is all that is needed, but we used the opportunity to show you an important technique that is used in "terminate and stay resident" programs, which we discuss more in the next chapter.

The point here is that whenever you write a program which changes some basic system parameter such as the contents of the interrupt-vector table, you should save the initial values of the parameters so you can restore them when your program finishes executing. There are three steps in saving and restoring an interrupt vector. The first step is to declare a pointer to an interrupt function with a statement such as void interrupt (oldcomrxint) () ;. In this statement interrupt is a special pointer type and oldcomrxint is the name we gave to the pointer. The second step in the process is to save the initial contents of the interrupt vector table with the oldcomrxint-getvect(12); statement. In this statement the predefined function getvect () copies the interrupt vector to the location pointed to by oldcomrxint. The final step is to restore the initial vector when our program terminates. We do this with the setvect (12,oldcomrxint); statement in our shutdown function. As we will show you later, the point of all this is that you can "intercept" a system interrupt such as the keyboard interrupt, use it for your own program, and then restore the system interrupt vector when your program finishes.

To do the rest of the initialization for this program we call the assembly language program INIT, so take a look at it now. The 8259A itself is mostly initialized by the BIOS when the system is turned on. However, since the UART is connected to IR4 of the 8259A, that input has to be unmasked. To do this the current contents of the 8259A interrupt mask register are read in from address 21H. The bit corresponding to IR4 is then ANDed with a 0 to unmask the interrupt, and the result is sent back to the interrupt mask register. Using this approach saves the system environment. It is important to do this rather than just sending out a control word directly, so that you don't disable other system functions. In this system, for example, the system clock tick is connected to IR0 and the keyboard is connected to IR1, so these would be disabled if you accidentally put 1's in these bits of the control word.

Initializing the 8250 UART is next. Figure 14-28, page 516, shows the internal addresses and the bit formats for the control words we need here. The first part of the initialization involves the baud rate, parity, and stop bits. Since this step requires several words to be sent, we simply used the BIOS INT 14H procedure to do it.

NOTE: We initialize the 8250 here for 4800 Bd, so the baud rate jumper on the SDK-86 must be set for this baud rate.

The next task we do here is enable the desired interrupt circuitry in the 8250. In order to do this, the DLAB bit of the line control word must first be made a 0. Note that this is done by reading in the line control word, resetting the desired bit, and sending the word out again. This preserves the previous state of the rest of the bits in the line control register. As shown in Figure 14-28b, with DLAB = 0, a control word which enables the enable-receive line status interrupt can be sent to the interrupt enable register at address 03F9H. As shown in Figure 14-28b, the 8250 has four different conditions which can be enabled to assert the interrupt output when true. In cases where multiple interrupts are used, the interrupt identification register can be read to determine the source of an interrupt. For this application we are using only the enable receive line status interrupt, so a 1 is put in that bit. The final step in the 8250 initialization is to assert the $\overline{\text{RTS}}$, $\overline{\text{DTR}}$, and $\overline{\text{OUT2}}$ output signals. As shown by the circuit connections in Figure 14-10b, asserting $\overline{\text{RTS}}$ is necessary to assert the $\overline{\text{CTS}}$ input so the UART can transmit. Likewise, asserting $\overline{\text{DTR}}$ is necessary to assert the $\overline{\text{DSR}}$ and $\overline{\text{CD}}$ inputs of the UART. The $\overline{\text{OUT2}}$ signal from the 8250 must be asserted in order to enable a three-state buffer which is in series with the interrupt signal from the 8250 to the 8259A.

When you are working out an initialization sequence such as this, read the data sheet carefully and check out the actual hardware circuitry for the system you are working on. We missed the $\overline{\text{OUT2}}$ connection the first time through, but a second look at the schematic for the communications board showed that it was necessary to assert this signal. Now let's see how the procedure which reads characters from the UART works.

THE SERIAL_IN PROCEDURE

The purpose of the SERIAL_IN interrupt procedure is to read characters in from the UART and put them in a buffer. Note that since this is an interrupt procedure which can occur at any time, it is important to save the DS register of the interrupted program and load the DS register with DGROUP, the value needed for this procedure.

The buffer used here is a special type of queue called a *circular buffer* or *ring buffer*. Figure 14-29, page 517, attempts to show how this works. One pointer, called the TAIL_POINTER, is used to keep track of where the next byte is to be written to the buffer. Another pointer called the HEAD_POINTER is used to keep track of where the next character to be read from the buffer is located. The buffer is circular because when the tail pointer reaches the highest location in the memory space set aside for the buffer, it is "wrapped around" to the beginning of the buffer again. The head pointer follows the tail pointer around the circle as characters are read from the buffer. Two checks are made on the tail pointer before a character is written to the buffer.

First the tail pointer is brought into a register and incremented. This incremented value is then compared with the maximum number of bytes the buffer can hold. If the values are equal, the pointer is at the highest address in the buffer, so the register is reset to zero. After the current character is put in the buffer, this value will be loaded into TAIL_POINTER to wrap around to the lowest address in the buffer again.

Second, a check is made to see if the incremented value of the tail pointer is equal to the head pointer. If the two are equal, it means that the current byte can be written, but that the next byte would be written over the byte at the head of the queue. In this case we simply

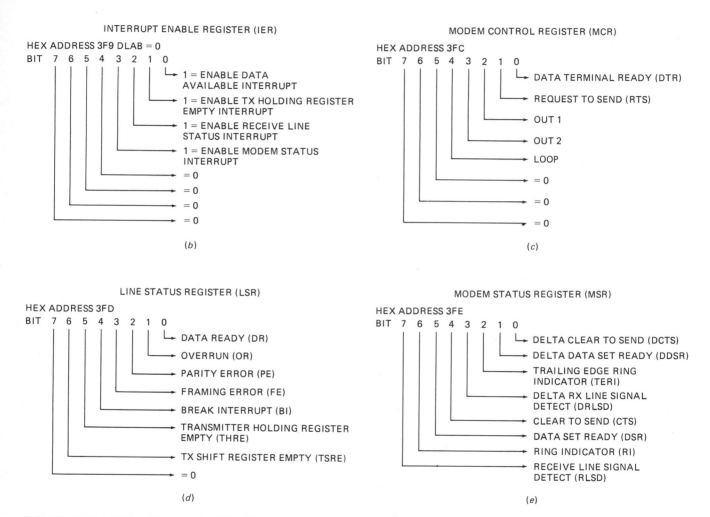

I/O DECODE (IN HEX)		REGISTER SELECTED	DLAB STATE
PRIMARY ADAPTER	ALTERNATE ADAPTER		
3F8	2F8	TX BUFFER	DLAB=0 (WRITE)
3F8	2F8	RX BUFFER	DLAB=0 (READ)
3F8	2F8	DIVISOR LATCH LSB	DLAB=1
3F9	2F9	DIVISOR LATCH MSB	DLAB=1
3F9	2F9	INTERRUPT ENABLE REGISTER	DLAB=X
3FA	2FA	INTERRUPT IDENTIFICATION REGISTERS	DLAB=X
3FB	2FB	LINE CONTROL REGISTER	DLAB=X
3FC	2FC	MODEM CONTROL REGISTER	DLAB=X
3FD	2FD	LINE STATUS REGISTER	DLAB=X
3FE	2FE	MODEM STATUS REGISTER	DLAB=X

(a)

INTERRUPT ENABLE REGISTER (IER)
HEX ADDRESS 3F9 DLAB = 0
BIT 7 6 5 4 3 2 1 0
- 1 = ENABLE DATA AVAILABLE INTERRUPT
- 1 = ENABLE TX HOLDING REGISTER EMPTY INTERRUPT
- 1 = ENABLE RECEIVE LINE STATUS INTERRUPT
- 1 = ENABLE MODEM STATUS INTERRUPT
- = 0
- = 0
- = 0
- = 0

(b)

MODEM CONTROL REGISTER (MCR)
HEX ADDRESS 3FC
BIT 7 6 5 4 3 2 1 0
- DATA TERMINAL READY (DTR)
- REQUEST TO SEND (RTS)
- OUT 1
- OUT 2
- LOOP
- = 0
- = 0
- = 0

(c)

LINE STATUS REGISTER (LSR)
HEX ADDRESS 3FD
BIT 7 6 5 4 3 2 1 0
- DATA READY (DR)
- OVERRUN (OR)
- PARITY ERROR (PE)
- FRAMING ERROR (FE)
- BREAK INTERRUPT (BI)
- TRANSMITTER HOLDING REGISTER EMPTY (THRE)
- TX SHIFT REGISTER EMPTY (TSRE)
- = 0

(d)

MODEM STATUS REGISTER (MSR)
HEX ADDRESS 3FE
BIT 7 6 5 4 3 2 1 0
- DELTA CLEAR TO SEND (DCTS)
- DELTA DATA SET READY (DDSR)
- TRAILING EDGE RING INDICATOR (TERI)
- DELTA RX LINE SIGNAL DETECT (DRLSD)
- CLEAR TO SEND (CTS)
- DATA SET READY (DSR)
- RING INDICATOR (RI)
- RECEIVE LINE SIGNAL DETECT (RLSD)

(e)

FIGURE 14-28 8250 addresses in IBM PC, registers, and control words.
(a) System addresses. (b) Interrupt enable register. (c) Modem control register.
(d) Line status register. (e) Modem status register.

return to the interrupted program without writing the current character into the buffer. Actually this wastes a byte of buffer space, but it is necessary to do this so that the pointers have different values for this buffer-full condition than they do for the buffer-empty condition. The buffer-empty condition is indicated when the head pointer is equal to the tail pointer. If the buffer is not full, the character read in from the UART is written

to the buffer, and the pointer to the next available location in the buffer is transferred from the register to the memory location called TAIL_POINTER. Finally, before returning, an end-of-interrupt command must be sent to the 8259A to reset bit 4 of the interrupt service register.

To summarize the operation of a circular buffer, then, bytes are put in at the tail pointer location and read out

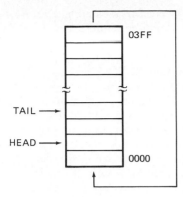

FIGURE 14-29 Diagram showing how ring buffer pointers wrap around at the top of the allocated buffer space.

from the head pointer location. The buffer is considered full when the tail pointer reaches one less than the head pointer. The buffer is empty when the head pointer is equal to tail pointer.

THE CHK_N_DISPLAY PROCEDURE

The main purpose of the CHK_N_DISPLAY procedure is to read a character from the circular buffer and send it to the CRT with the BIOS INT 10H procedure. In order to make sure the procedure operates correctly under all conditions, however, we mask the IR4 interrupt in the 8259A right at the start so that an interrupt from the UART cannot call the SERIAL_IN procedure while CHK_N_DISPLAY is using the head and tail pointers. This is necessary to prevent the SERIAL_IN procedure from altering the values of the pointers in the middle of CHK_N_DISPLAY's use of them and causing the CHK_N_DISPLAY procedure to make the wrong decisions about whether the buffer is empty, for example. The group of instructions which you need to protect from interruption is called a *critical region*. It is important to keep critical regions as short as possible so that interrupts need not be masked for unnecessarily long times. Note that we masked the IR4 interrupt input of the 8259A rather than disable the processor interrupt. This was done so that the keyboard and the timer interrupts, which have nothing to do with the critical region in this procedure, can keep running.

Once the critical region is safe, a check is made to see if there are any characters in the buffer. If not, the 8259A IR4 input is unmasked, and execution returned to the calling program. If a character is available in the buffer, the character is read out and the head pointer updated to point to the next available character. If the pointer is at the top of space allotted for the buffer, the pointer will be wrapped around to the start of the buffer again. As soon as the character is read out from the buffer and the pointers updated, an interrupt from the UART cannot do any damage, so we unmask IR4. The BIOS INT 10H procedure is then used to send the character to the CRT. If a UART interrupt occurs during the INT 10H procedure, the SERIAL_IN procedure will read the character from the UART and return execution to the INT 10H procedure. This short interrup-

tion produces no noticeable effect on the operation of the INT 10H procedure, and it makes sure no characters from the UART are missed. After the INT 10H procedure finishes, a character-sent counter called NUMCHAR is decremented and execution is returned to the calling program. This counter counts the number of characters actually sent to the CRT rather than just the number of times the CHK_N_DISPLAY procedure is called. This allows the procedure to be called over and over again until a given number of characters are received from the SDK-86 and sent to the CRT.

THE XMIT FUNCTION

After first checking to see if the UART transmitter buffer is ready, the XMIT procedure sends a character to the 8250 UART. To determine if the UART transmitter buffer is empty, we use the predefined bioscom () function, which is just a simple way to call the BIOS INT 14H procedure. The first argument in the bioscom parentheses is the BIOS INT 14H subfunction number. The second argument is the value you want to pass to the BIOS INT 14H procedure in AL. The third argument in the parentheses is the COM port number, 0 for COM1 and 1 for COM2. As you can see in Figure 14-24, if you call the BIOS INT 14H procedure with AH = 3, the status of the UART will be returned in AX. Our while loop repeats until the transmitter holding register bit, bit 13, becomes a 1. Normally, you should also check that CTS in bit 4 and DSR in bit 5 are also asserted. For this program, however, these signals are asserted by jumpers on the connector, so we didn't bother to check them.

To send the character to the UART we did a direct write to the UART transmitter holding register with the outportb(0x3fc, ascval) statement. Normally we avoid direct writes such as this and use BIOS procedures, DOS function calls, or C function calls so the program is more likely to run on a variety of systems. However, when we tried to use the statement bioscom(1,ascval,0) to send a character to the UART, the program would no longer read characters sent to the UART by the SDK-86. A careful reading of the BIOS INT 14H procedure in the IBM Technical Reference Manual showed that the Transmit subprocedure of the BIOS INT 14H procedure turns off the OUT2 signal. As we described in the initialization section, this signal must be asserted so that receiver-ready interrupt signals can get from the UART to the 8259A and call the SERIAL-IN procedure. The only real cure we found for the problem was to do the direct write to the UART as shown. Incidentally, the bioscom() function works fine if you are both sending and receiving characters on a polled basis.

THE CONVERT_AND_SEND FUNCTION

The SDK-86 requires that each nibble of a program code byte be sent in as the corresponding ASCII character. The code byte 3AH, for example, must be sent as 33H (ASCII 3), followed by 41H (ASCII A). We converted this procedure to C to show you how you can do bit operations in C. You can work your way through this section with an example data byte to see how it works. After the ASCII characters for each code byte are sent, the ASCII code for a comma is sent, as required by the SDK-86, and execution is returned to the L section of the switch structure. There the SDK-86 response is sent to the CRT.

THE SHUTDOWN FUNCTION

As we said earlier, you should always put everything back in its initial state when your program finishes executing. The shutdown function here remasks the IR4 input of the 8259A by reading the current value, ORing that value with 10H to set bit 4, and sending the result back to the 8259A. The setvect(12,oldcomrxint) function call restores the initial interrupt vector to the INT 12 location in the vector table. Finally, the exit (0) function call closes any open files and returns execution to DOS.

CONCLUSION

This program was written to do a specific job and to demonstrate such important programming concepts as installing an interrupt vector in a C program, interacting with a UART, working with a ring buffer, reading binary files, and preserving the system environment. Space limitations prevented us from making the program as "friendly" as we would have liked it to be. Perhaps you can see how the program could easily be modified to, for example, let the user enter the desired communications port number and the desired baud rate.

SYNCHRONOUS SERIAL-DATA COMMUNICATION AND PROTOCOLS

Introduction

Most of the discussion of serial-data transfer up to this point in the chapter has been about asynchronous transmission. For asynchronous serial transmission, a start bit is used to identify the beginning of each data character, and at least one stop bit is used to identify the end of each data character. The transmitter and the receiver are effectively synchronized on a character-by-character basis. With a start bit, 1 stop bit, and 1 parity bit, a total of 10 bits must be sent for each 7-bit ASCII character. This means that 30 percent of the transmission time is wasted. A more efficient method of transferring serial data is to synchronize the transmitter and the receiver and then send a large block of data characters one after the other with no time between characters. No start or stop bits are then needed with individual data characters, because the receiver automatically knows that every 8 bits received after synchronization represents a data character. When a block of data is not being sent through a synchronous data link, the line is held in a marking condition. To indicate the start of a transmission, the transmitter sends out one or more unique characters called *sync characters* or a unique bit pattern called a *flag*, depending on the system being used. The receiver uses the sync characters or the flag to synchronize its internal clock with that of the receiver. The receiver then shifts in the data following the sync characters and converts them to parallel form

so they can be read in by a computer. As we said in the discussions of modems and ISDN, high-speed modems and digital communication channels use synchronous transmission.

Now, remember from a previous section that a hardware level set of handshake signals is required to transmit asynchronous or synchronous digital data over phone lines with modems. In addition to this handshaking, a higher level of coordination, or *protocol*, is required between transmitter and receiver to assure the orderly transfer of data. A protocol in this case is an agreed set of rules concerning the form in which the data is to be sent. There are many different serial data protocols. The two most common that we discuss here are the IBM *binary synchronous communications protocol*, or BISYNC, and the *high-level data link control protocol*, or HDLC.

Binary Synchronous Communication Protocol—BISYNC

BISYNC is referred to as a *byte-controlled protocol* (BCP), because specified ASCII or EBCDIC characters (bytes) are used to indicate the start of a message and to handshake between the transmitter and the receiver. Incidentally, even in a full-duplex system, BISYNC protocol only allows data transfer in one direction at a time.

Figure 14-30 shows the general message format for BISYNC. For our first cycle through this we will assume that the transmitter has received a message from the receiver that it is ready to receive a transmission. If no message is being sent, the line is an "idle" condition with a continuous high on the line. To indicate the start of a message, the transmitting system sends two or more previously agreed upon sync characters. For example, a sync character might be the ASCII 16H. As we said before, the receiver uses these sync characters to synchronize its clock with that of the transmitter. A header may then be sent if desired. The header contents are usually defined for a specific system and may include information about the type, priority, and destination of the message that follows. The start of the header is indicated with a special character called *start-of-header* (SOH), which in ASCII is represented by 01H.

After the header, if present, the beginning of the text portion of the message is indicated by another special character called *start-of-text* (STX), which in ASCII is represented by 02H. To indicate the end of the text portion of the message, an *end-of-text* (ETX) character or an *end-of-block* (ETB) character is sent. The text portion may contain 128 or 256 characters (different systems use different-size blocks of text). Immediately following the ETX, character 1 or 2 block check charac-

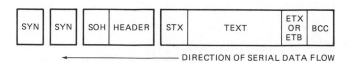

DIRECTION OF SERIAL DATA FLOW

FIGURE 14-30 General message format for binary synchronous communication (BISYNC).

ters (BCC) are sent. For systems using ASCII, the BCC is a single byte which represents complex parity information computed for the text of the message. For systems using EBCDIC, a 16-bit *cyclic redundancy check* is performed on the text part of the message and the 16-bit result sent as 2 BCCs. The point of these BCCs is that the receiving system can recompute the value for them from the received data and compare the results with the BCCs sent from the transmitter. If the BCCs are not equal, the receiver can send a message to the transmitter, telling it to send the message again. Now let's look at how messages are used for data transfer handshaking between the transmitter and the receiver.

To start let's assume that we have a remote "smart" terminal connected to a computer with a half-duplex connection. Further, let's assume that the computer is in the receive mode. Now, when the program in the terminal determines that it has a block of data to send to the computer, it first sends a message with the text containing only the single character ENQ (ASCII 05H), which stands for *enquiry*. The terminal then switches to receive mode to await the reply from the computer. The computer reads the ENQ message, and, if it is not ready to receive data, it sends back a text message containing the single character for *negative acknowledge*, NAK (ASCII 15H). If the receiver is ready, it sends a message containing the *affirmative acknowledge*, ACK, character (ASCII 06H). In either case, the computer then switches to receive mode to await the next message from the terminal. If the terminal received a NAK, it may give up, or it may wait a while and try again. If the terminal received an ACK, it will send a message containing a block of text and ending with a BCC character(s). After sending the message, the terminal switches to receive mode and awaits a reply from the computer as to whether the message was received correctly. The computer meanwhile computes the BCC for the received block of data and compares it with the BCC sent with the message. If the two BCCs are not equal, the computer sends a NAK message to the terminal. This tells the terminal to send the message again, because it was not received correctly. If the two BCCs are equal, then the computer sends an ACK message to the terminal, which tells it to send the next message or block of text. In a system where multiple blocks of data are being transferred, an ACK 0 message is usually sent for one block, an ACK 1 message sent for the next, and an ACK 0 again sent for the next. The alternating ACK messages are a further help in error checking. In either case, after the message is sent the computer switches to receive mode to await a response from the terminal.

A variation of BISYNC commonly used to transfer binary files in the PC environment and between Unix systems and PCs is called *XMODEM*. An XMODEM block consists of a SOH character, a block number, 128 bytes of data (padded if necessary to fill the block), and an 8-bit checksum. A transmission starts with the receiver sending a NAK character to the sender. The sender then sends a block of data. If the data is received correctly, the receiver sends back an ACK and the sender sends the next block of data. If the data is not received correctly, the receiver sends a NAK and the sender sends the block

again. The transmission is completed when the sender sends an end-of-transmission (EOT) character and the receiver replies with an ACK.

One major problem with a BISYNC type protocol is that the transmitter must stop after each block of data is transferred and wait for an ACK or NAK signal from the receiver. Due to the wait and line turnaround times, the actual data transfer rate may be only half of the theoretical rate predicted by the physical bit rate of the data link. The HDLC protocol discussed in a later section greatly reduces this problem. Next we want to return to the Intel 8251A USART which is used on the IBM PC Synchronous Communication Adapter and give you a brief look at how it is used for BISYNC communication.

USING THE INTEL 8251A USART FOR BISYNC COMMUNICATION

As shown in Figure 14-5, we initialize an 8251A by first getting its attention, sending it a mode word, and then sending it a command word. To initialize the 8251A for synchronous communication, 0's are put in the least significant 2 bits of the mode word. The rest of the bits in the mode word then have the meanings shown in Figure 14-31*a*, page 520. Most of the bit functions should be reasonably clear from the descriptions in the figure, but a couple need a little more explanation.

Bit 6 of the mode word specifies the SYNDET pin on the 8251A to be an input or an output. The pin is programmed to function as an input if external circuitry is used to detect the sync character in the data bit stream. When programmed as an output, the pin will go high when the 8251A has found one or more sync characters in the data bit stream.

Bit 7 of the mode word is used to specify whether 1 sync character or a sequence of 2 different sync characters is to be looked for at the start of a message.

To initialize an 8251A for synchronous operation:

1. Send a series of nulls and a software reset command to the control address as shown at the start of Figure 14-5.

2. Send a mode word based on the format in Figure 14-31*a* to the control address.

3. Send the desired sync character for that particular system to the control address of the 8251A.

4. If a second sync character is needed, send it to the control address.

5. Finally, send a command word to the control address to enable the transmitter, enable the receiver, and enable the device to look for sync characters in the data bit stream coming in the RxD input.

The format for the command word is shown in Figure 14-31*b*. Now, let's examine how the 8251A participates in a synchronous data transfer. As you work your way through this section, try to keep separate in your mind the parts of the process that are done by the 8251A and the parts that are done by software at one end of the link or the other.

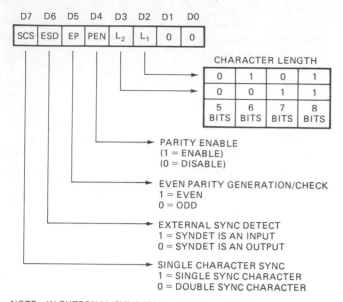

CHARACTER LENGTH

0	1	0	1
0	0	1	1
5 BITS	6 BITS	7 BITS	8 BITS

PARITY ENABLE
(1 = ENABLE)
(0 = DISABLE)

EVEN PARITY GENERATION/CHECK
1 = EVEN
0 = ODD

EXTERNAL SYNC DETECT
1 = SYNDET IS AN INPUT
0 = SYNDET IS AN OUTPUT

SINGLE CHARACTER SYNC
1 = SINGLE SYNC CHARACTER
0 = DOUBLE SYNC CHARACTER

NOTE: IN EXTERNAL SYNC MODE, PROGRAMMING DOUBLE
CHARACTER SYNC WILL AFFECT ONLY THE Tx.

(a)

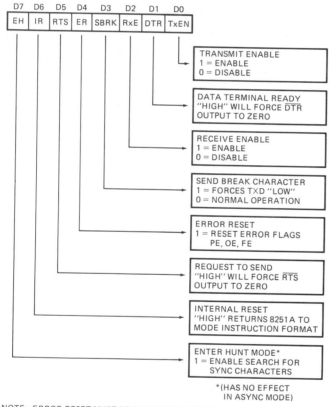

TRANSMIT ENABLE
1 = ENABLE
0 = DISABLE

DATA TERMINAL READY
"HIGH" WILL FORCE $\overline{\text{DTR}}$
OUTPUT TO ZERO

RECEIVE ENABLE
1 = ENABLE
0 = DISABLE

SEND BREAK CHARACTER
1 = FORCES TXD "LOW"
0 = NORMAL OPERATION

ERROR RESET
1 = RESET ERROR FLAGS
PE, OE, FE

REQUEST TO SEND
"HIGH" WILL FORCE $\overline{\text{RTS}}$
OUTPUT TO ZERO

INTERNAL RESET
"HIGH" RETURNS 8251A TO
MODE INSTRUCTION FORMAT

ENTER HUNT MODE*
1 = ENABLE SEARCH FOR
SYNC CHARACTERS

*(HAS NO EFFECT
IN ASYNC MODE)

NOTE: ERROR RESET MUST BE PERFORMED WHENEVER RxENABLE
AND ENTER HUNT ARE PROGRAMMED.

(b)

FIGURE 14-31 8251A synchronous mode and command word formats. (a) Mode word. (b) Command word. (Intel)

To start, let's assume the 8251A is in a terminal which has blocks of data to send to a computer, as we described earlier in this section. Further assume that the computer is in receive mode waiting for a transmission from the terminal and that the 8251A in the terminal has been

initialized and is sending out a continuous high on the TxD line.

An I/O driver routine in the terminal will start the transfer process by sending a sync character(s), SOH character, header characters, STX character, ENQ character, ETX character, and BCC byte to the 8251A, one after the other. The 8251A sends the characters out in synchronous serial format (no start and stop bits). If, for some reason such as a high-priority interrupt, the CPU stops sending characters while a message is being sent, the 8251A will automatically insert sync characters until the flow of data characters from the CPU resumes.

After the ENQ message has been sent, the CPU in the terminal awaits a reply from the computer through the RxD input of the 8251A. If the 8251A has been programmed to enter hunt mode by sending it a control word with a 1 in bit 7, it will continuously shift in bits from the RxD line and check after each shift if the character in the receive buffer is a sync character. When it finds a sync character, the 8251A asserts the SYNDET pin high, exits the hunt mode, and starts the normal data read operation. When the 8251A has a valid data character in its receiver buffer, the RxRDY pin will be asserted, and the RxRDY bit in the status register will be set. Characters can then be read in by the CPU on a polled or an interrupt basis.

When the CPU has read in the entire message, it can determine whether the message was a NAK or an ACK. If the message was an ACK, the CPU can then send the actual data message sequence of characters to the 8251A. Handshake and data messages will be sent back and forth until all the desired block of data has been sent to the computer. In the next section we discuss another protocol used for synchronous serial-data transfer.

High-level Data Link Control (HDLC) and Synchronous Data Link Control (SDLC) Protocols

The BISYNC-type protocols which we discussed in the previous section work only in half-duplex mode; except for XMODEM, they have difficulty transmitting pure 8-bit binary data such as object code for programs; and they are not easily adapted to serving multiple units sharing a common data link. In an attempt to solve these problems, the *International Standards Organization* (ISO) proposed the *high-level data link control protocol* (HDLC) and IBM developed the *synchronous data link control protocol* (SDLC). The standards are so nearly identical that, for the discussion here, we will treat them together under the name HDLC and indicate any significant differences as needed.

As we said previously, BISYNC is referred to as a byte-controlled protocol because character codes or bytes such as SOH, STX, and ETX are used to mark off parts of a transmitted message or act as control messages. HDLC is referred to as a *bit-oriented protocol* (BOP) because messages are treated simply as a string of bits rather than a string of characters. The group of bits which make up a message is referred to as a *frame*. The three types of frames used are information or *I frames*, supervisory control sequences or *S frames*, and command/response or *U frames*. The three types of frames all have the same basic format.

Figure 14-32*a* shows the format of an HDLC frame. Each part of the frame is referred to as *field*. A frame starts and ends with a specific bit pattern, 01111110, called a *flag* or *flag field*. When no data is being sent, the line idles with all 1's, or continuous flags. Immediately after the flag field is an 8-bit address field which contains the address of the destination unit for a control or information frame and the source of the response for a response frame.

Figure 14-32*b* shows the meaning of the bits in the 8-bit control field for each of the three types of frames. We don't have the space or the desire to explain here the meaning of all of these. A little later we will, however, explain the use of the Ns and Nr bits in the control byte for an information frame.

The information field, which is present only in information frames, can have any number of bits in HDLC protocol, but in SDLC the number of bits has to be a multiple of 8. In some systems as many as 10,000 or 20,000 information bits may be sent per frame. Now, the question may occur to you, What happens if the data contains the flag bit pattern, 01111110? The answer to this question is that a special hardware circuit modifies the bit stream between flags so that there are never more than five 1's in sequence. To do this the circuit monitors the data stream and automatically stuffs in a 0 after any series of five 1's. A complementary circuit in the receiver removes the extra zeros. This scheme allows character codes or binary data to be sent without the problems BISYNC has in this area.

The next field in a frame is the 16-bit *frame check sequence* (FCS). This is a cyclic redundancy word derived from all the bits between the beginning and end flags, but not including 0's inserted to prevent false flag bytes. This CRC value is recomputed by the receiving system to check for errors.

Finally, a frame is terminated by another flag byte. The ending flag for one frame may be the starting flag for another frame.

In order to describe the HDLC data transfer process, we first need to define a couple of terms. HDLC is used for communication between two or more systems on a data link. One of the systems or *stations* on the link will always be set up as a controller for the link. This station is called the *primary station*. Other stations on the link are referred to as *secondary stations.*

Now, suppose that a primary station—a computer, for example—wants to send several frames of information to a secondary station such as another computer or terminal. Here's how a transfer might take place.

The primary station starts by sending an S frame containing the address of the desired secondary station and a control word which inquires if the receiver is ready. The secondary station then sends an S frame which contains the address of the primary station and a control word which indicates its ready status. If the secondary station receiver was ready, the primary station then sends a sequence of information frames. The information frames contain the address of the secondary station, a control word, a block of information, and the FCS words. For all but the last frame of a sequence of information frames, the P/F bit in the control byte will be a 0. The 3 Ns bits in the control byte will contain the number of the frame in the sequence.

Now, as the secondary station receives each information frame, it reads the data into memory and computes the frame-check sequence for the frame. For each frame in a sequence that the secondary station receives correctly, it increments an internal counter. When the primary station sends the last frame in a sequence of up to seven frames, it makes the P/F bit in the control byte a 1. This is a signal to the secondary station that the primary station wants a response as to how many frames were received correctly. The secondary station responds with an S frame. The Nr bits in the control word of this S frame contain the sequence number of the last frame that was received correctly plus 1. In other words, Ns represents the number of the next expected frame. The primary station compares Ns = 1 with the number of frames sent in the sequence. If the two numbers do not agree, the primary station knows that it must retransmit some frames, because they were not all received correctly. The Nr number tells the primary station which frame number to start the retransmission from. For example, if Nr is 3, the primary station will retransmit the sequence of frames starting with frame 3. If the sequence of frames was received correctly, another series of frames can be sent if desired. Actually, since HDLC operates in full-duplex, the receiving station can be queried after each frame is sent to see if the

BEGINNING FLAG 01111110 8 BITS	ADDRESS 8 BITS	CONTROL 8 BITS	INFORMATION ANY NUMBER OF BITS	FRAME CHECK 16 BITS	ENDING FLAG 01111110 8 BITS

(a)

BITS IN CONTROL FIELD

HDLC FRAME FORMAT	7	6	5	4	3	2	1	0
I-FRAME (INFORMATION TRANSFER COMMANDS/RESPONSES)	Nr	Nr	Nr	P/F	Ns	Ns	Ns	0
S-FRAME (SUPERVISORY COMMANDS/RESPONSES)	Nr	Nr	Nr	P/F	S	S	0	1
U-FRAME (UNNUMBERED COMMANDS/RESPONSES)	M	M	M	P/F	M	M	1	1

SENDING ORDER - BIT 0 FIRST, BIT 7 LAST

NS   THE TRANSMITTING STATION SEND SEQUENCE NUMBER, BIT 2 IS THE LOW-ORDER BIT.

P/F   THE POLL BIT FOR PRIMARY STATION TRANSMISSIONS, AND THE FINAL BIT FOR SECONDARY STATION TRANSMISSIONS.

Nr   THE TRANSMITTING STATION RECEIVE SEQUENCE NUMBER, BIT 6 IS THE LOW-ORDER BIT.

S   THE SUPERVISORY FUNCTION BITS

M   THE MODIFIER FUNCTION BITS

(b)

FIGURE 14-32   (*a*) Format of HDLC frame. (*b*) Meaning of bits in 8-bit control field of frame.

previous frame was received correctly. A similar series of actions takes place when a secondary station transmits to a primary station or to another secondary station.

One advantage of this HDLC scheme is that a large number of bits can be sent in a frame so the framing bit percentage is low. Another advantage is that the transmitter does not have to stop after every short message for an acknowledge as it does in BISYNC protocol. True, several frames may have to sent again in case of an error, but in low-error-rate systems, this is the exception. HDLC is often used with high-speed modems, and as we will show in the next section, HDLC is used along with some higher-level protocols for network communication between a wide variety of systems.

A final point to discuss here is how HDLC protocol is implemented with a microcomputer. At the basic hardware level, a standard USART cannot be used because of the need to stuff and strip 0 bits. Instead, specially designed parts such as the Intel 8273 HDLC/SDLC protocol controller are used. Devices such as this automatically stuff and strip the required 0 bits, generate and check frame-check sequence words, and produce the interface signals for RS-232C. The devices interface directly to microcomputer buses.

The actual control of which station uses the data link at a particular time and the formatting of frames is done by the system software. The next section discusses how several systems can be connected together, or "networked," so they can communicate with each other.

LOCAL AREA NETWORKS

Introduction

The objective of this section is to show you how several computers can be connected together to communicate with each other and to share common peripherals such as printers, large disk drives, FAX machines, etc. We will start with simple cases and progress to the type of network that might be used in the computerized electronics factory we described in an earlier chapter.

To communicate between a single terminal and a nearby computer, a simple RS-232C connection is sufficient. If the computer is distant, then a modem and phone line or a leased phone line is used, depending on the required data rate. Now, for a more difficult case, suppose that we have in a university building 100 terminals that need to communicate with a distant computer. We could use 100 phone lines with modems, but this seems quite inefficient. One solution to this problem is to run wires from all of the terminals to a central point in the building and then use a multiplexer or *data concentrator* of some type to send all the communications over one wideband line. Either time-domain multiplexing or frequency-division multiplexing can be used. A demultiplexer at the other end of the line reconstructs the original signals.

As another example of computer communication,

suppose that we have several computers in one building or in a complex of buildings and that the computers need to communicate with each other. Our computerized electronics factory is an example of this situation. What is needed in this case is a high-speed network, commonly called a *local area network* or *LAN*, connecting the computers together. We start our discussion of LANs by showing you some of the basic ways that the systems on a network are connected together.

LAN Topologies

The different ways of physically connecting devices on a network with each other are commonly referred to as *topologies*. Figure 14-33 shows the five most common topologies and some other pertinent data about each, such as examples of commercially available systems which use each type.

In a *star topology* network, a central controller coordinates all communication between devices on the network. The most familiar example of how this works is probably a private automatic branch exchange, or PABX, phone system. In a PABX all calls from one phone on the system to another or to an outside phone are routed through a central switchboard. The new digital PABX systems allow direct communication between computers within a building at rates up to perhaps 100K bits/s.

In the *loop topology*, one device acts as a controller. If a device wants to communicate with one or more other devices on the loop, it sends a request to the controller.

TOPOLOGY	TYPICAL PROTOCOLS	TYPICAL NO. OF NODES	TYPICAL SYSTEMS
STAR	RS-232C OR COMPUTER	TENS	PABX, COMPUTER-μC CLUSTERS STARLAN
LOOP	SDLC	TENS	CPIB IBM 3600/3700, μC CLUSTERS
COMMON BUS	CSMA/CD OR CSMA WITH ACKNOWLEDGMENT	TENS TO HUNDREDS PER SEGMENT	ETHERNET, 3COM OMNINET, Z-NET μC CLUSTERS
RING	SDLC HDLC (TOKEN PASSING)	TENS TO HUNDREDS PER CHANNEL	PRIMENET, DOMAIN, OMNILINK μC CLUSTERS
OTHER SERVICES BROADBAND BUS	CSMA/CD RS-232C & OTHERS PER CHANNEL	TWO TO HUNDREDS PER CHANNEL	WANGNET, LOCALNET M/A-COM

- • TERMINAL
- ▮ DISTRIBUTED CONTROL
- Ⓒ LOCAL CONTROLLER
- ⊚ MULTINETWORK CONTROLLER
- FDM FREQUENCY DIVISION MULTIPLEX

FIGURE 14-33 Summary of common computer network topologies.

If the loop is not in use, the controller enables the one device to output and the other device(s) to receive. The GPIB or IEEE 488 bus described in the last section of this chapter is an example of this topology.

In the *common-bus topology*, control of the bus is spread among all the devices on the bus. The connection in this type of system is simply a wire (usually but not always a coaxial cable), which any number of devices can be tapped into. Any device can take over the bus to transmit data. Data is transmitted in fixed-length blocks called *packets*. One common scheme to prevent two devices from transmitting at the same time is called *carrier sense, multiple access with collision detection*, or CSMA/CD. We discuss the details of CSMA/CD in a later section on Ethernet.

In a *ring network*, the control is also distributed among all the devices on the network. Each device on the ring functions as a repeater, which means that it simply takes in the data stream and passes the data stream on to the next device on the ring if it is not the intended receiver for the data. Data always circulates around the ring in one direction. Any device can transmit on the ring. A *token* is one common way used to prevent two or more devices from transmitting at the same time. A token is a specific lone byte such as 01111111 which is circulated around the ring when no device is transmitting. A device must possess the token in order to transmit. When a device needs to transmit, it removes the token from the bus, thus preventing any other devices from transmitting. After transmitting one or more packets of data, the transmitting device puts the token back on the ring so another device can grab it and transmit. We discuss this more in a later section.

The final topology we want to discuss here is the *tree* structured network, which often uses broadband transmission. Before we can really explain this one, we need to introduce you to a couple of terms commonly used with networks. In some networks such as Ethernet, data is transmitted directly as digital signals at rates of up to 10 Mbits/s. With this type of signal, only one device can transmit at a time. This form of data transmission is often referred to as *baseband* transmission, because only one basic frequency is used. The other common form of data transmission on a network is referred to as *broadband* transmission. Broadband transmission is based on a frequency-division multiplexing scheme such as that used for community antenna television (CATV) systems. The radio-frequency spectrum is divided up into 6-MHz-bandwidth channels.

A single device or group of devices can be assigned one channel for transmitting and another for receiving. Each channel or pair of channels is considered a branch on the tree. Special modems are used to convert digital signals to and from the modulated radio-frequency signals required. The multiple channels and the 6-MHz bandwidth of the channels in a broadband network allow voice, data, and video signals to be transmitted at the same time throughout the network. This is an advantage over baseband systems, which can transmit only one digital data signal at a time, but the broadband system is much more expensive.

Network Protocols

In order for different systems on a network to communicate effectively with each other, a series of rules or protocols must be agreed upon and followed by all of the devices on the network. The International Standards Organization, in an attempt to bring some order to the chaos of network communication, has developed a set of standards called the *open systems interconnection* (OSI) model. This model is more of a recommendation than a rigid standard, but to increase compatibility more and more manufacturers are attempting to follow it. The OSI model is a seven-layer hierarchy of protocols as shown in Figure 14-34. This layered approach structures the design tasks and makes it possible to change, for example, the actual hardware used to transmit the data without changing the other layers. We will use a common network operation, electronic mail, to explain to you the function of the upper-layers model.

Electronic mail allows a user on one system on a network to send a message to another user on the same system or on another system. The message is actually sent to a "mailbox" in a hard-disk file. Each user on the network periodically checks a personal mailbox to see if it contains any messages. If any messages are present, they can be read out and then deleted from the mailbox.

The *application layer* of the OSI model specifies the general operation of network services such as electronic mail, file management, program-to-program communication, and peripheral sharing. For our electronic mail example, this layer of the protocol would specify the format for invoking the electronic mail function.

The *presentation layer* of the OSI protocol governs the programs which convert messages to the code and format that will be understood by the receiver. For our electronic mail message, this layer might involve translating the message from ASCII codes to EBCDIC codes and formatting the message into packets or frames such as those we described for HDLC in a previous

	LAYER NUMBER	FUNCTION
APPLICATION	7	SELECTS APPROPRIATE SERVICE FOR APPLICATIONS
PRESENTATION	6	PROVIDES CODE CONVERSION, DATA REFORMATTING
SESSION	5	COORDINATES INTERACTION BETWEEN END-APPLICATION PROCESSES
TRANSPORT	4	PROVIDES END-TO-END DATA INTEGRITY AND QUALITY OF SERVICE
NETWORK	3	SWITCHES AND ROUTES INFORMATION
DATA LINK	2	TRANSFERS UNITS OF INFORMATION TO OTHER END OF PHYSICAL LINK
PHYSICAL	1	TRANSMITS BIT STREAM TO MEDIUM

FIGURE 14-34 International Standards Organization open systems interconnect (OSI) model for network communications.

section a standard file format. Data compression and encryption also fall in this layer of the protocol.

The *session layer* of the OSI protocol establishes and terminates logical connections on the network. This layer is responsible for opening and closing named files, for translating a user name into a physical network address, and checking passwords. Electronic mail allows you to specify the intended receiver of a message by name. It is the responsibility of this layer of the protocol to make the connection between the name and the network address of the named receiver.

The *transport layer* of the protocol is responsible for making sure a message is transmitted and received correctly. An example of the operation of this protocol layer is the ACK or NAK handshake used in BISYNC transmission after the receiver has checked to see if the data was received correctly. For electronic mail, the message can be written to the addressed mailbox and then read back to make sure it was sent correctly.

The *network layer* of the protocol is used only in multichannel networks. It is responsible for finding a path through the network to the desired receiver by switching between channels. The function of this layer is similar to the function of postal mail routing, which finds a route to get a letter from your house to the addressed destination. Another example of the function performed by this layer is the telephone switching system, which finds a route to connect a phone call.

The *data link layer* of the OSI model is responsible for the transmission of packets or blocks from sender to receiver. At this level the BCC characters or CRC characters are generated and checked, zeros are stuffed in the data, and flags and addresses are added to data frames. The HDLC data transmission protocol described earlier in this chapter is an example of the type of factors involved in this layer.

The *physical layer* of the OSI model is the lowest level. This layer is used to specify the connectors, cables, voltage levels, bit rates, modulation methods, etc. RS-232C is an example of a standard which falls in this layer of the model.

We don't have space here to discuss all the different networks listed as examples in Figure 14-33, but we will discuss a few of the most common ones. To start we will take a more detailed look at the operation of a very widespread "common-bus" network, Ethernet. Ethernet is a trademark of Xerox Corporation.

Ethernet

The *Ethernet network standard* was originally developed by Xerox Corporation. Later Xerox, DEC, and Intel worked on defining the standard sufficiently so that commercial products for implementing the standard were possible. It has now been adopted, with slight changes, as the IEEE 802.3 standard.

Physically, Ethernet is implemented in a common-bus topology with a single 50-Ω coaxial cable. Data is sent over the cable using baseband transmission at 10 Mbits/s. Data bits are encoded using Manchester coding, as shown in Figure 14-35. The advantage of this coding is that each bit cell contains a signal transition. A system that wants to transmit data on the network first checks for these transitions to see if the network is currently busy. If the system detects no transitions, then it can go ahead and transmit on the network.

Figure 14-36 shows how a very simple Ethernet is set up. The backbone of the system is the coaxial cable. Terminations are put on each end of the cable to prevent signal reflections and each unit is connected into the cable with a simple tee-type tap. A transmitter-receiver, or *transceiver*, sends out data on the coax, receives data from the coax, and detects any attempt to transmit while the coax is already in use. The transceiver is connected to an interface board with a 15-pin connector and four twisted-wire pairs. The transceiver cable can be as long as 15 m. The interface board, as the name implies, performs most of the work of getting data on and off the network in the correct form. The *interface board* assembles and disassembles data frames, sends out source and destination addresses, detects transmission errors, and prevents transmission while some other unit on the network is transmitting.

The method used by a unit to gain access to the network is *CSMA/CD*. Before a unit attempts to transmit on the network, it looks at the coax to see if a carrier (Manchester code transitions) is present. If a carrier is present, the unit waits some random length of time and then tries again. When the unit finds no carrier on the line, it starts transmitting. While it is transmitting, it also monitors the line to make sure no other unit is transmitting at the same time. The question may occur to you at this point, If a unit cannot start transmitting until it finds no carrier on the coax, how can another unit be transmitting at the same time? The answer to this question involves propagation delay. Since transceivers can be as much as 2500 m apart, it may take as long as 23 μs for data transmitted from one unit to reach another unit. In other words, one unit may start transmitting before the signal from a transmitter that started earlier reaches it. A situation where two units transmit at the same time is referred to as a *collision*. When a unit detects a collision, it will keep transmitting until all transmitting stations detect that a collision

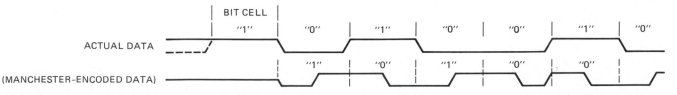

FIGURE 14-35 Manchester coding used for Ethernet data communication. Note that encoded data has a transition at center of each bit time.

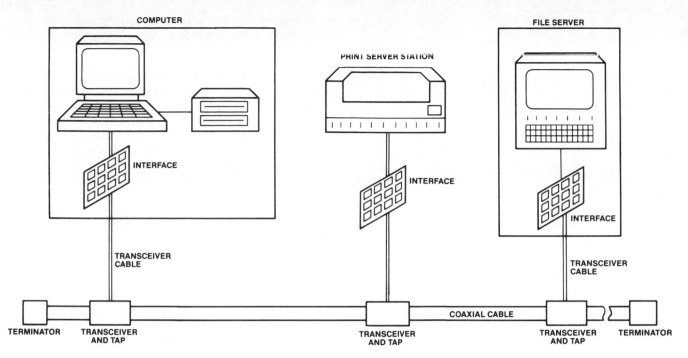

COMPUTER

FILE SERVER

PRINT SERVER STATION

INTERFACE

INTERFACE

INTERFACE

TRANSCEIVER
CABLE

TRANSCEIVER
CABLE

TERMINATOR   TRANSCEIVER
AND TAP

COAXIAL CABLE

TRANSCEIVER
AND TAP

TRANSCEIVER
AND TAP

TERMINATOR

FIGURE 14-36   Block diagram of very simple Ethernet system.   (*Intel Corporation*)

has occurred and then stop transmitting. Any other transmitting units will also stop transmitting and try again after a random period of time. The term "multiple access" in the CSMA/CD name means that any unit on the network can attempt to transmit. The network has no central controller to control which unit has use of the network at a particular time. Access is gained by any unit using the mechanism we have just described.

The maximum number of units that can be connected on a single Ethernet is 1024. For further information about how an interface board is built, consult the data sheets for the Intel 82586 LAN coprocessor and the data sheets for the Intel 82501 Ethernet serial interface.

One problem with standard Ethernet is the coax cable used to connect units on the network. This cable is expensive and somewhat difficult to get through wiring conduits in existing buildings. To solve these problems, a new Ethernet standard called *thin Ethernet* or *10BaseT* was developed. The 10 in this name indicates 10-M bits/s transmission and the T in the name stands for twisted-pair telephone wire. By limiting the maximum distance between units to 100m rather than the 2500-m maximum for standard Ethernet, a 10BaseT network can use standard telephone-type wiring, which is often already installed or can easily be installed. The basic operation of the 10BaseT network is basically the same as that of the standard Ethernet we described previously.

Another problem with Ethernet is that as the amount of traffic on the network increases, the time that a unit on the end of the network has to wait before it can transmit may become very long. As the number of units increases, the number of collisions and the amount of time spent waiting for a "clear shot" increases. This degrades the performance of the network. In the next section we discuss token-passing ring networks, which

solve the access problem in a way which degrades less under heavy traffic load.

Token-Passing Rings

IEEE standard 802.5 defines the physical layer and the data link layer for a *token-passing ring network*. As the name implies, systems on a token-passing ring are connected in series around a ring. To simplify wiring, however, token rings are often connected as shown in Figure 14-37, page 526. The multistation access unit or MAU is put in a wiring closet or some readily accessible place. Unlike the passive taps used in an Ethernet system, each active station or node on a token ring receives data, examines it to see if the data is addressed to it, and retransmits the data to the next station on the ring. A bypass relay in the MAU will automatically shunt data around defective or inactive nodes. Data always travels in one direction around the ring. Data is transmitted as HDLC or SDLC frames. Early token-ring network adapter cards transmitted data at 4 Mbits/s, but 16-Mbits/s network adapter cards are now becoming widely available.

Token-passing ring networks solve the multiple-access problem in an entirely different way from the CSMA/CD approach described for Ethernet. A token is a byte of data with an agreed-upon, unique bit pattern such as 01111111. If no station is transmitting, this token is circulated continuously around the ring. When a station needs to transmit, it withdraws the not-busy token, changes it to a busy token of perhaps 01111110, and sends the busy token on around the ring. The transmitting unit then sends a frame of data around the ring to the intended receiver(s). When the transmitting

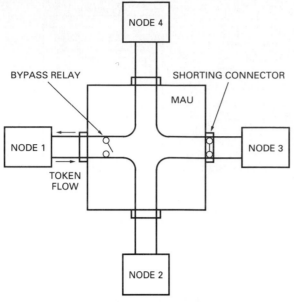

NOTE: MAU = MULTISTATION ACCESS UNIT

FIGURE 14-37   Block diagram of a token ring network system showing multistation access unit (MAU).

station receives the busy token and the data frame back again, it reads them in and removes them from the ring. It then sends out the not-busy token again. As soon as a transmitting station sends out the not-busy token again, the next station on the loop can grab the token and transmit on the network. The first station that transmitted cannot transmit again until the not-busy token works its way around the ring. This gives all units on the network a chance to transmit in a "round-robin" manner.

> NOTE: Some token-ring networks use tokens with priority bits so that a high-priority station can transmit again if necessary before a lower-priority station gets a turn.

Two questions occurred to us the first time we read about token-passing rings; perhaps these same two questions may have occurred to you. The first question is, How does a station on the network tell the bit pattern for a token from the same bit pattern in the data frame? The answer to this question is bit-stuffing, the same technique that is used to prevent the flag bit pattern from being present in the data section of an HDLC frame. A hardware circuit in the transmitter alters the data stream so that certain bit patterns are not present. Another hardware circuit in the receiver reconstructs the original data.

The second question is, What happens if the not-busy token somehow gets lost going around the ring? A couple of different approaches are used to solve this problem. One approach uses a timer in each station. When a station has a frame to transmit, it starts a timer. If the station does not detect a token in the data stream before the timer counts down, it assumes that the token was lost and sends out a new token. Another approach

used by IBM sets up one station as a network monitor. If this station does not detect a token within a prescribed time, it clears any leftover data from the ring and sends out a new not-busy token.

The Texas Instruments TMS380 chip set can be used to implement a node on a 4-Mbits/s token-ring network. Consult the data sheets for these devices to get more information about the operation of a token-ring network.

Token-passing ring networks have the disadvantage that more complex hardware is required where each station connects to the network, but as we said earlier, under heavy traffic loads they are more efficient than Ethernets. Also, the receive and transmit circuitry at the connection acts as a repeater, which helps maintain signal quality throughout the network. Since signals travel in only one direction around the ring, this topology is ideally suited for fiber-optic transmission.

A new standard called the Fiber Distributed Data Interface (FDDI) or ANSI X3T9.5 describes a fiber-optic token ring network which transmits data at 100 Mbits/s. The FDDI ring actually consists of a fiber which transmits data in one direction around the ring and another fiber which transmits data in the other direction around the ring. This dual-fiber approach allows data transmission to continue if one fiber path is broken or interrupted in some way. Nodes on FDDI can be as far as 2 km from each other, up to 500 nodes can be connected on the ring, and the maximum circumference of the ring can be much as 100 km. The Advanced Micro Devices' Supernet chip set or the National Semiconductor FDDI chipset can be used along with a microcontroller, buffer memory, and an electro-optical interface to build an FDDI node. Consult the data sheets for these devices to get more information about FDDI operation.

Figure 14-38 shows how an FDDI network can serve as a *backbone* which allows high speed communication between other networks. Circuits called *bridges* or *gateways* interface Ethernets, multiplexed Ethernets, or even T1 type signals with the FDDI. The Pentagon uses a network such as this.

A transmission rate of 100 Mbits/s may at first seem like "overkill," but as we move more and more toward high-resolution interactive video, computer simulations, and massive data storage, this rate is not nearly fast enough. Work is currently underway on fiber-optic networks that transmit data at 250 Mbits/s and 500 Mbits/s and allow nodes to be as much as 50 km apart.

A Network Application Example and LAN Software Overview

As an example of how you put all the pieces of a network together, suppose that you have the job of designing and setting up a general purpose computer room at a college. The lab is to be used for computer-aided drafting (CAD) with AutoCAD; programming in Pascal, C and assembly language; mechanical engineering simulations; word processing; and other unspecified applications. All programs that will be run require an IBM PC- or PS/2-type computer. The computer room is to have 24 workstations, a large plotter, a laser printer, and two letter-quality dot-matrix printers.

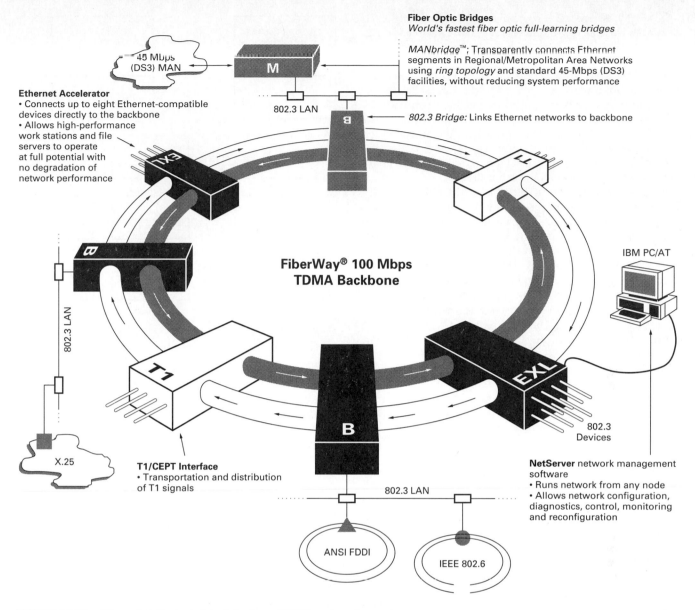

Fiber Optic Bridges
World's fastest fiber optic full-learning bridges

MANbridge™: Transparently connects Ethernet segments in Regional/Metropolitan Area Networks using *ring topology* and standard 45-Mbps (DS3) facilities, without reducing system performance

45 Mbps (DS3) MAN

M

802.3 LAN

B

802.3 Bridge: Links Ethernet networks to backbone

Ethernet Accelerator
• Connects up to eight Ethernet-compatible devices directly to the backbone
• Allows high-performance work stations and file servers to operate at full potential with no degradation of network performance

EXL

T1

FiberWay® 100 Mbps TDMA Backbone

IBM PC/AT

802.3 LAN

T1

802.3 Devices

EXL

X.25

T1/CEPT Interface
• Transportation and distribution of T1 signals

B

802.3 LAN

NetServer network management software
• Runs network from any node
• Allows network configuration, diagnostics, control, monitoring and reconfiguration

ANSI FDDI

IEEE 802.6

FIGURE 14-38   Fiber distributed data interface (FDDI) network used as "backbone" for different types of networks.   (*ARTEL Communications.*)

The drafting and mechanical engineering instructors indicate that they need the speed of an 80386-based machine and display resolution of 1024 × 768 pixels. These specifications require that each of 24 workstations be an 80386-based machine with an 8514/A-type video adapter. Some of the programs that they plan to run are very memory hungry, so the basic workstations need 2 Mbytes or more of RAM.

The systems need to run a very wide variety of programs, so a large amount of hard-disk storage is needed. One alternative is to install a large hard disk in each workstation and install a set of the required programs on each disk. One problem with this approach is the cost of the 24 large hard disks. A second problem with this approach is that it is difficult to maintain the software on all these separate machines. Updating is tedious and time-consuming. Still another problem is

that on these individual machines it is difficult to protect the application programs from accidental or mischievous corruption by users.

All these problems can be solved by connecting the workstations on a network which includes a fast file server. A single copy of the application programs can be installed on the file server and accessed from each workstation as needed. If the hard disk on the server is large enough, user files can also be stored on it. The plotter and printers can also be connected on the file server so that they are accessible from any workstation.

The file server and its hard disk need to be fast so that they do not create a bottleneck in the system. You might choose an 80486-based microcomputer for the file server and equip it with a 250-Mbyte, 16-ms hard disk. If your budget permits, you might also include an optical disk drive in the server so that programming classes could access the Microsoft Programmer's Library which is available on CD ROM. The server will also need a 1.2-Mbyte floppy drive and a 1.44-Mbyte floppy drive to transfer software from floppies to the hard disk.

The next step is to decide on the software you want to use to manage the network and to provide the file server and print server functions. The best approach for this is to choose the network software which will do the best job and then choose network hardware which is compatible with that software. As we write this discussion, the best choice seems to be Novell's Netware 386, so we will use it as an example.

Netware 386 works with Ethernet, ARCnet, and IBM's Token Ring boards. Since the workstations in this lab are physically all in the same room, you might consider using the 10BaseT or thin ethernet network we described earlier, because it is the cheapest of these alternatives. Remember that this type network transmits data at 10 Mbits/s over standard twisted-pair phone wire for distances up to 100 m. Synoptics, 3Com, and several other companies make adapter boards which interface PC or PS/2 buses to a 10BaseT network.

Netware requires a minimum 2 Mbytes of memory in the server, and it works better with 8M or 10M, so you should include this in the bid specifications for the server.

While you are waiting for hardware bids to come in, purchase orders to go out, and the hardware to arrive, we will give you an overview of how network software works so you will have some idea how to install and use it.

Part of the network software resides in each workstation and part of it resides in the server. Let's start with the workstation part. To refresh your memory, Figure 14-39a shows the software hierarchy for a DOS-based workstation operating in stand-alone mode. In this mode an application program such as a word processor uses DOS function calls to access system peripherals. The DOS function calls use BIOS procedures to interact with the actual hardware.

Figure 14-39b shows the software hierarchy when the workstation is operating in network mode. When the application program attempts to access a disk file, for example, the "interceptor" part of the resident network software determines whether the file is located on the workstation hard disk or on the server hard disk. If the file is on the workstation hard disk, the interceptor simply passes the request on to DOS and the access proceeds through DOS and BIOS as it would in stand-alone operation. If the file is on the server, the request goes to the request translator to get assembled in the proper packet format for transmission over Ethernet. The output from the request translator then goes to the network communications driver, which sends it to the server over the network. A standard set of network communication drivers written by Microsoft is called *NETBIOS*. Other companies which write network control programs either license NETBIOS from Microsoft or write their own compatible network drivers.

The server reads the requested file, converts it to packets, and sends it to the workstation. The appropriate driver reads the packets into the workstation.

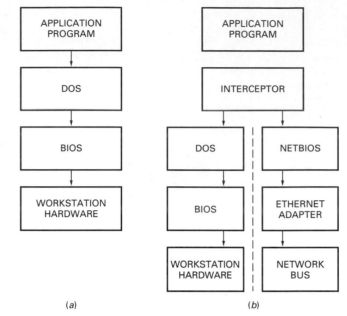

FIGURE 14-39   Software hierarchy on a workstation. (*a*) Nonnetworked. (*b*) Networked.

The reply translator part of the software converts the packets to DOS file format and loads the file in memory so the application can work with it.

The network software that resides in the server is a complete operating system in itself. To install Netware 386 on the server, you first format a small partition on the server hard disk in DOS format. You then load DOS in this partition so the system is bootable from it and load some of the basic Netware files here so you can install the rest of Netware. After you boot the system, the installation consists of working your way through a relatively simple sequence of steps outlined in the installation procedure.

Once installed, the network operating system is set up so that only the system administrator can access and change its operation. The system administrator sets up user accounts, assigns passwords, and sets the access rights for files. Application program files are usually specified as read-only so that users cannot accidentally or maliciously modify them. For files that are intended to be accessed and written to by any one of several users, Netware 386 has a default feature called *file locking*, which prevents one user from accessing the file until a previous user has finished with it. In this case the critical region is the file, and file locking provides a way to protect it.

Netware 386 uses several techniques to speed up disk access. First, it formats its partition of the hard disk differently from the way DOS formats it to make for more efficient access to the parts of a file. Second, it uses disk caches such as those we described in the last chapter to hold large blocks of data read from files. This reduces the number of read operations required to access a large file. Finally, Netware uses "elevator seeking" to reduce the amount the heads move to read a requested set of files for users. Just as an elevator moves sequentially from floor to floor instead of moving from floor to floor as requested, the head is moved to access files in the sequence they are located on disk tracks rather than strictly in the sequence they were requested.

In addition to allowing users to store and access files, the network operating system has many other useful features. It sets up a queue of files waiting to be printed or plotted so that users can just enter a print command and go on with their work. Most networks have electronic mail, which allows the system administrator to communicate with all users and users to communicate with each other. Most electronic mail systems are set up so you can define a group of users and direct mail messages to just that group.

For the reasons that we have discussed, it is likely that in the near future almost all computers will in some way be networked with other computers through telephone lines or direct connections. In the last section of the chapter we discuss a different type of computer network which is often used in a factory environment to build a "smart" test system.

THE GPIB, HPIB, IEEE488 BUS

The preceding sections of the chapter discussed networks which allow microcomputers to communicate with each other and to share peripherals such as printers. The *general-purpose interface bus* (GPIB), also known as the *Hewlett-Packard interface bus* and the *IEEE488 bus* that we discuss here is not intended for use as a computer network in the same way that the Ethernet and token rings are used. It was developed by Hewlett-Packard to interface smart test instruments with a computer.

The standard describes three types of devices that can be connected on the GPIB. First is a *listener*, which can receive data from other instruments or from the controller. Examples of listeners are printers, display devices, programmable power supplies, and programmable signal generators. The second type of device defined is a *talker*, which can send data to other instruments. Examples of talkers are tape readers, digital voltmeters, frequency counters, and other measuring equipment. A device can be both a talker and a listener. The third type of device on the bus is a *controller*, which determines who talks and who listens on the bus.

Physically the bus consists of a 24-wire cable with a connector such as that shown in Figure 14-40a, page 530, on each end. Actually, each end of the cable has both a male connector and a female connector, so that cables can daisy-chain from one unit to the next on the bus. Instruments intended for use on a GPIB usually have some switches which allow you to select the 5-bit address that the instrument will have on the bus. Standard TTL signal voltage levels are used.

As shown in Figure 14-40b, the GPIB has eight bidirectional data lines. These lines are used to transfer data, addresses, commands, and status bytes among as many as 8 or 10 instruments.

The GPIB also has five bus management lines which function basically as follows. The *interface clear* line (IFC), when asserted by the controller, resets all devices on the bus to a starting state. It is essentially a system reset. The *attention* (ATN) line, when asserted (low), indicates that the controller is putting a universal command or an address-command such as "listen" on the data bus. When the ATN line is high, the data lines contain data or a status byte. *Service request* (SRQ) is similar to an interrupt. Any device that needs to transfer data on the bus asserts the SRQ line low. The controller then polls all the devices to determine which one needs service. When asserted by the system controller, the *remote enable* (REN) signal allows an instrument to be controlled directly by the controller rather than by its front-panel switches. The *end or identify* (EOI) signal is usually asserted by a talker to indicate that the transfer of a block of data is complete.

Finally, the bus has three handshake lines that coordinate the transfer of data bytes on the data bus. These are *data valid* (DAV), *not ready for data* (NRFD), and *not data accepted* (NDAC). These handshake signals allow devices with very different data rates to be connected together in a system. A little later we will show you how this handshake works. First we will give you an overview of general bus operation.

Upon power-up the controller takes control of the bus and sends out an IFC signal to set all instruments on the bus to a known state. The controller then proceeds to use the bus to perform the desired series of measurements or tests. To do this the controller sends out a series of commands with the ATN line asserted low. Figure 14-40c shows the formats for the combination command-address codes that a controller can send to talkers and listeners. Bit 8 of these words is a don't care, bits 7 and 6 specify which command is being sent, and bits 5 through 1 give the address of the talker or listener to which the command is being sent. For example, to enable (address) a device at address 04 as a talker, the controller simply asserts the ATN line low and sends out a command-address byte of X1000100 on the data bus. A listener is enabled by sending out a command-address byte of $X01A_5A_4A_3A_2A_1$, where the lower 5 bits contain the address that the listener has been given in the system. When a data transfer is complete, all listeners are turned off by the controller sending an unlisten command, X0111111. The controller turns off the talker by sending an untalk command, X1011111. *Universal commands* sent by the controller with bits 7, 6, and 5 all 0's will go to all listeners and talkers. The lower 4 bits of these words specify one of 16 universal commands.

Periodically while it is using the bus, the controller checks the SRQ line for a service request. If the SRQ line is low, the controller polls each device on the bus one after another (serial) or all at once (parallel) until it finds the device requesting service. A talker such as a DVM, for example, might be indicating that it has completed a series of conversions and has some data to send to a listener such as a chart recorder. When the controller determines the source of the SRQ, it asserts the ATN line low and sends listener address commands to each listener that is to receive the data and a talk address command to the talker that requested service. The controller then raises the ATN line high, and data

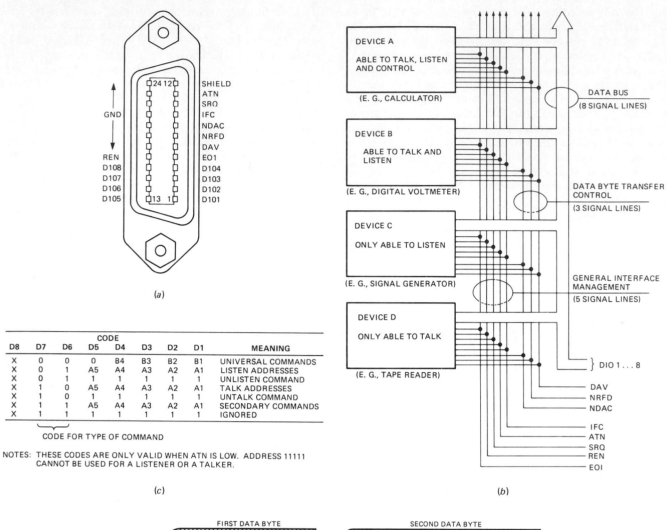

(a)

CODE								MEANING
D8	D7	D6	D5	D4	D3	D2	D1	
X	0	0	0	B4	B3	B2	B1	UNIVERSAL COMMANDS
X	0	1	A5	A4	A3	A2	A1	LISTEN ADDRESSES
X	0	1	1	1	1	1	1	UNLISTEN COMMAND
X	1	0	A5	A4	A3	A2	A1	TALK ADDRESSES
X	1	0	1	1	1	1	1	UNTALK COMMAND
X	1	1	A5	A4	A3	A2	A1	SECONDARY COMMANDS
X	1	1	1	1	1	1	1	IGNORED

CODE FOR TYPE OF COMMAND

NOTES: THESE CODES ARE ONLY VALID WHEN ATN IS LOW. ADDRESS 11111 CANNOT BE USED FOR A LISTENER OR A TALKER.

(c)

(b)

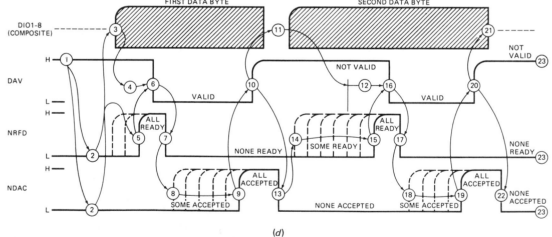

(d)

FIGURE 14-40   GPIB pins, signals, and handshake waveforms. (a) Connector. (b) Bus structure. (c) Command formats. (d) Data transfer handshake waveforms.

is transferred directly from the talker to the listeners using a double-handshake-signal sequence.

Figure 14-40d shows the sequence of signals on the handshake lines for a transfer of data from a talker to several listeners. The DAV, NRFD, and NDAC lines are all open-collector. Therefore, any listener can hold NRFD low to indicate that it is not ready for data or hold NDAC low to indicate that it has not yet accepted a data byte. The sequence proceeds as follows. When all listeners have released the NRFD line (5 in Figure 14-40d), indicating that they are ready (not not-ready), the talker asserts the DAV line low to indicate that a valid data byte is on the bus. The addressed listeners then all pull NRFD low and start accepting the data. When the slowest listener has accepted the data, the NDAC line will be released high (9 in Figure 14-40d). The talker senses NDAC becoming high and unasserts its DAV signal. The listeners pull NDAC low again, and the sequence is repeated until the talker has sent all the data bytes it has to send. The rate of data transfer is determined by the rate at which the slowest listener can accept the data.

When the data transfer is complete, the talker pulls the EOI line in the management group low to tell the controller that the transfer is complete. The controller then takes control again and sends an untalk command to the talker. It also sends an unlisten command to turn off the listeners and continues to use the bus according to its internal program.

A standard microprocessor bus can be interfaced to the GPIB with dedicated devices such as the Intel 8291 GPIB talker-listener and 8292 GPIB controller. The importance of the GPIB is that it allows a microcomputer to be connected with several test instruments to form an integrated test system.

CHECKLIST OF IMPORTANT TERMS AND CONCEPTS IN THIS CHAPTER

If you do not remember any of the terms in the following list, use the index to help you find them in the chapter for review.

Serial-data communication
  Simplex, half-duplex, full-duplex
  Synchronous, asynchronous
  Marking state, spacing state
  Start bit, stop bit
  Baud rate

UART, USART, DTE, DCE

20- and 60-mA current loops

RS-232C, RS-422A, RS-423A, RS-449 serial-data standards

CODECs, TDM, and PCM

ISDN

Modems

Amplitude Modulation, FSK, PSK
  Quaternary amplitude modulation (QAM)
  Scrambler, descrambler

Fiber-optic data communication
  Critical angle
  Multimode and single-mode fibers

Terminal emulator

Circular buffer, ring buffer
  Head pointer, tail pointer

Critical region

Binary synchronous communications protocol (BISYNC)
  Byte-controlled protocol (BCP)
  Cyclic redundancy check
  XMODEM protocol

HDLC, SDLC protocols
  Bit-oriented protocol (BOP)
  Frame, field, flag
  Frame check sequence (FCS)

Local area network (LAN)

Topologies—star, loop, ring, common-bus, broadband-bus (tree)

Electronic mail

Open system interconnection model (OSI)
  Presentation, session, transport, network, data link
  Physical layers

Ethernet
  Transceiver
  Collision
  CSMA/CD
  10 BaseT

Token-passing rings

Fiber distributed data interface (FDDI)

File server, print server

GPIB, HPIB, IEEE 488 bus standard
  Listener, talker, controller

REVIEW QUESTIONS AND PROBLEMS

1. Draw a diagram showing the bit format used for asynchronous serial data. Label the start, stop, and parity bits. Number the data bits to show the order of transmission.

2. A terminal is transmitting simple asynchronous serial data at 1200 Bd.
   a. How much time is required to transmit 1 bit?
   b. Assuming 7 data bits, a parity bit, and 1 stop bit, how long does it take to transmit one character?

3. What is the main difference between a UART and a USART?

4. Define the term *modem* and explain why a modem is required to send digital data over standard switched phone lines.

5. Describe the functions of the $\overline{DSR}$, $\overline{DTR}$, $\overline{RTS}$, $\overline{CTS}$, TxD, and RxD signals exchanged between a terminal and a modem.

6. What frequency transmit clock (TxC) is required by an 8251A in order for it to transmit data at 4800 Bd with a baud rate factor of 16?

7. *a.* Show the bit pattern for the mode word and the command word that must be sent to an 8251A to initialize the device as follows: baud rate factor of 64, 7 bits/character, even parity, 1 stop bit, transmit interrupt enabled, receive interrupt enabled, $\overline{DTR}$ and $\overline{RTS}$ asserted, error flags reset, no hunt mode, no break character.

   b. Show the sequence of instructions required to initialize an 8251A at addresses 80H and 81H with the mode and command words you worked out in part *a.*

   c. Show the sequence of instructions that can be used to poll this 8251A to determine when the receiver buffer has a character ready to be read.

   d. How can you determine whether a character received by an 8251A contains a parity error?

   e. What frequency transmit and receive clock will this 8251A require in order to send data at 2400 Bd?

   f. What other way besides polling does the 8251A provide for determining when a character can be sent to the device for transmission? Describe the additional hardware connections required for this method.

8. Give the signal voltage ranges for a logic high and for a logic low in the RS-232C standard.

9. *a.* Describe the problem that occurs when you attempt to connect together two RS-232C devices that are both configured as DTE.

   b. Draw a diagram which shows how this problem can be solved.

10. *a.* Why are the two ground pins on an RS-232C connector not just jumpered together?

    b. What symptom will you observe if the wire connected to pin 5 of an RS-232C terminal is broken?

11. Explain why systems which use the RS-422A or RS-423A signal standards can transmit data over longer distances and at higher baud rates than RS-232C systems.

12. *a.* How does an FSK modem represent digital 1's and 0's in the signal it sends out on a phone line?

    b. How does an FSK modem perform full-duplex communication over standard phone lines?

    c. Approximately what is the maximum bit rate for FSK data transmission on standard switched telephone lines?

13. *a.* Draw a waveform to show the signal that a simple phase-shift keying (PSK) modem will send out to represent the binary data 011010100.

    b. Describe how phase shift modulation can be used to transmit 2 data bits with only one carrier change.

    c. Describe how quaternary amplitude modulation transmits 4 data bits with only one carrier change.

14. *a.* Why do telephone companies transmit signals over long distances in digital form rather than in analog form?

    b. Describe the operation of a codec.

    c. Why are codecs designed with nonlinear response?

    d. Explain how telephone companies commonly transmit many phone signals on a single wire or channel.

15. *a.* Briefly describe the operation of the integrated services digital network.

    b. Explain the significance ISDN has for data communication between computers.

16. *a.* Draw a diagram which shows the construction of a fiber-optic cable, and label each part.

    b. Identify two types of devices which are used to produce the light beam for a fiber-optic cable and two devices which are commonly used to detect the light at the receiving end of the fiber.

    c. Why should you never look into the end of a fiber optic cable to see if light is getting through?

    d. Describe the difference between a multimode fiber and a single-mode fiber. Give a major advantage and a major disadvantage of each type.

    e. What are the major advantages of fiber-optic cables over metallic conductors?

17. Using IBM PC BIOS and DOS calls, write an assembly language program which reads characters from the keyboard and puts them in a buffer until a carriage return is entered. The characters should be displayed on the CRT as entered. When a carriage return is entered, the contents of the buffer should be sent out the COM1 serial port.

18. The SDK-86 will accept only uppercase letters as commands. The SDK-86 emulator program in Figure 14-25 would be friendlier if you did not have to remember to press the caps lock key on the IBM. Write an assembly language routine that will convert a letter entered in lowercase to uppercase without affecting entered uppercase letters or numbers and describe where you would insert this section of code in the program in Figure 14-25.

19. Describe the operation of a circular or ring buffer. Include in your answer the function of the tail pointer, the head pointer, and how the buffer-full and buffer-empty conditions are detected.

20. Why is it necessary to disable the UART interrupt input of the 8259A during part of the CHK_N_ DISPLAY procedure in Figure 14-27*b*?

21. *a.* When changing a bit in a control word or interrupt mask word, why should you not alter the other bits in the word?

b. Show the assembly language instructions you would use to unmask IR5 of an 8259A at base address 80H without changing the interrupt status of any other bits.

22. Why is synchronous serial data communication much more efficient than asynchronous communication?

23. *a.* If an 8251A is being used in synchronous mode for a BISYNC data link, what additional initialization word(s) must be sent to the device?
    b. How does the 8251A detect the start of a message?
    c. How does the 8251A indicate that it has found the start of a message?
    d. How does the receiving station in a BISYNC link indicate that it found an error in the received data?

24. *a.* How is the start of a message frame indicated in a bit-oriented protocol such as HDLC?
    b. How does an HDLC system prevent the flag bit pattern from appearing in the data part of the message?
    c. How does the receiver in an HDLC system tell the transmitter that an error was found in a transmitted frame?

25. *a.* Draw simple diagrams which show the five common network topologies.
    b. For each topology identify one commercially available system which uses it.

26. What is the difference between a baseband network and a broadband network?

27. *a.* List the seven layers of the ISO open systems model.
    b. Which of these layers is responsible for assembling messages into frames or packets?
    c. Which layer is responsible for making sure the message was transmitted and received correctly?

28. *a.* Describe the topology, physical connections, and signal type used in Ethernet.
    b. Describe the method used by a unit on an Ethernet to gain access to the network for transmitting a message.
    c. What response will a transmitting station make if it finds that another station starts transmitting after it starts?
    d. What is the term used to refer to this condition?

29. *a.* Describe the method used by a unit on a token-passing ring to take control of the network for transmitting a message frame.
    b. What is the advantage of this scheme over the method used in Ethernet?
    c. How can a token ring network recover if the token is lost while being passed around the ring?

30. *a.* Describe how the software on a network node responds when the user enters a command which accesses the hard disk in the workstation.
    b. Describe how the software on a network node responds when the user enters a command which accesses the hard disk on the file server.
    c. Describe how the file server software protects application program files from being modified by users.
    d. Describe how the file server software protects user files from access by other users.

31. *a.* For what purpose was the GPIB designed?
    b. Give the names for the three types of devices which the GPIB defines.
    c. List and briefly describe the function of the three signal groups of the GPIB.
    d. Describe the sequence of handshake signals that take place when a talker on a GPIB transfers data to several listeners. How does this handshake scheme make it possible for talkers and listeners with very different data rates to operate correctly on the bus?

CHAPTER 15

The 80286, 80386, and 80486 Microprocessors

For most of the examples up to this point in the book, we have used the 8086/8088 microprocessor, because it is the simplest member of this family of Intel processors and is therefore a good starting point. Now it is time to look at the evolutionary offspring of the 8086. To give you an overview, here are a few brief notes about the members of this family.

The 80186 processor is basically an 8086 with an on-chip priority-interrupt controller, programmable timer, DMA controller, and address decoding circuitry. This processor has been used mostly in industrial control applications.

The 80286, another 16-bit enhancement of the 8086, was introduced at the same time as the 80186. Instead of the integrated peripherals of the 80186, it has virtual memory-management circuitry, protection circuitry, and a 16-Mbyte addressing capability. The 80286 was the first family member designed specifically for use as the CPU in a multiuser microcomputer.

The 80386, the next evolutionary step in the family, is a 32-bit processor with a 32-bit address bus. The 32-bit ALU allows the 80386 to process data faster, and the 32-bit address bus allows the 80386 to address up to 4 Gbytes of memory. Another enhancement of the 80386 is that segments can be as large as 4 Gbytes instead of only 64 Kbytes. The memory-management circuitry and protection circuitry in the 80386 are improved over that in the 80286, so the 80386 is much more versatile as the CPU in a multiuser system.

The latest current member of this family, the 80486, has the same CPU as the 80386, so it has the same addressing capability, memory-management, and protection features as the 80386. The main new features included in the 80486 are a built-in 8-Kbyte code/data cache and a 32-bit floating-point-unit, similar to the 8087 we discussed in Chapter 11.

As perhaps you can see from the preceding brief discussions, the 80286, 80386, and 80486 were designed for use as the CPU in a multitasking microcomputer system. To help you better understand the operation and design rationale of these processors, we start the chapter with a discussion of the problems that must be solved in writing a multitasking/multiuser operating system. We then discuss the 80286, 80386, and 80486 microprocessors in detail and explain how the features designed in these processors help solve the problems involved in implementing a multitasking operating sys-

tem. After that we discuss how you develop real mode and protected mode programs for systems using these devices.

Finally in the chapter we discuss some of the directions in which microcomputer evolution seems to be heading. Included in this section are discussions of RISC processors, parallel processors, artificial intelligence, "fuzzy" logic, and neural networks.

OBJECTIVES

At the conclusion of this chapter, you should be able to:

1. Describe the difference between time-slice scheduling and preemptive priority-based scheduling.

2. Define the terms blocked, task queue, deadlock, deadly embrace, critical region, semaphore, kernel, memory-management unit, and virtual memory.

3. Describe how "expanded" memory is used to increase the amount of memory available in a microcomputer.

4. Describe how virtual memory gives a computer much more "logical" address space than the physical memory actually present in the system.

5. Describe the types of protection that should be implemented in a multitasking operating system.

6. Describe two methods that can be used to protect a critical region of code.

7. List the major hardware and software features that the 80286 microprocessor has beyond those in the 8086.

8. Show how the 80286 constructs physical addresses in its real address mode and in its protected virtual address mode.

9. List the evolutionary advances that the 80386 has over the 80286.

10. Describe how the 80386 produces a physical address when it is operating in paged mode.

11. Describe how segment-based protection is implemented in an 80386 system operating in protected mode.

534

12. Describe how an 80386 call gate is used to allow application programs to access operating systems procedures.

13. Describe how an 80386 performs a task switch.

14. Explain the term virtual 8086 mode for an 80386.

15. List the major advances that the 80486 has over the 80386.

16. Describe how system programs are developed for an 80386 or 80486 protected-mode system.

17. Describe how application programs are developed for 80386 or 80486 systems.

18. Describe the operation of the Microsoft Windows multitasking environment.

19. Define the terms RISC, CISC, artificial intelligence, expert system, neural network, and fuzzy logic.

MULTIUSER/MULTITASKING OPERATING SYSTEM CONCEPTS

Introduction

The basic principle of a timeshare system is that the CPU runs one user's program for a few milliseconds, then runs the next user's program for a few milliseconds, and so on until all of the users have had a turn. It cycles through the users over and over, fast enough that each user seems to have the complete attention of the CPU. An operating system which coordinates the actions of a timeshare system such as this is referred to as a *multiuser* operating system. The program or section of a program for each user is referred to as a *task* or *process*, so a multiuser operating system is also commonly referred to as *multitasking*. Multitasking operating systems are also used to control the operation of machines in industrial manufacturing environments. The factory controller program in Figure 10-35 is an example of a very simple multitasking operating system.

In this section we discuss some of the major problems encountered in building a multitasking operating system; then in later sections of the chapter we show you how the features of the 80286, 80386, and 80486 help solve these problems.

Scheduling

TSR PROGRAMS AND DOS

MS DOS is designed as a single-user, single-task operating system. This means that DOS can usually execute only one program at a time. The only exception to this in the basic DOS is the print program, print.com. You may have noticed that when you execute the print command, DOS returns a prompt and allows you to enter another command before the printing is completed. The print program starts printing the specified file and then returns execution to DOS. However, the print program continues to monitor DOS execution. When DOS is

sitting in a loop waiting for a user command or some other event, the print program borrows the CPU for a short time and sends more data to the printer. It then returns execution to the interrupted DOS loop.

The DOS print command then is a limited form of multitasking. Products such as Borland's Sidekick use this same technique in DOS systems to provide pop-up menus of useful functions such as a calculator, an appointment book, and a notepad. The first time you run a program such as Sidekick, it is loaded into memory as other programs are. However, unlike other programs, Sidekick is designed so that when you terminate the program, it stays "resident" in memory. You can execute the program and pop up the menu again by simply pressing some hot key combination such as Ctrl-Alt. Programs which work in this way are called *terminate-and-stay-resident* or TSR programs. Because TSRs are so common in the PC world, we thought you might find it interesting to see how they work before we get into discussions of the scheduling techniques used in full-fledged multitasking operating systems.

When you boot up DOS, the basic 640 Kbytes of RAM are set up as shown in Figure 15-1a. Starting from absolute address 00000, the first section of RAM is reserved for interrupt vectors. The main part of the DOS program is loaded into the next-higher section of RAM. After this come device drivers such as ANSI.SYS, MOUSE.SYS, etc. The DOS command processor program, command.com, gets loaded into RAM at boot time. This program, which processes user commands and executes programs, has two parts. The resident part of the command processor is loaded in memory just above the device drivers and the transient part is loaded in at the very top of RAM. When you tell DOS to execute a

COMMAND PROCESSOR (TRANSIENT PORTION)	COMMAND PROCESSOR (TRANSIENT PORTION)
TRANSIENT PROGRAM AREA (TPA)	TRANSIENT PROGRAM AREA (TPA)
	TSR PROGRAM #2
	TSR PROGRAM #1
COMMAND PROCESSOR (RESIDENT PORTION)	COMMAND PROCESSOR (RESIDENT PORTION)
DEVICE DRIVERS	DEVICE DRIVERS
DOS	DOS
INTERRUPT VECTORS	INTERRUPT VECTORS
(a)	(b)

FIGURE 15-1   (a) DOS memory map without TSRs. (b) DOS memory map with TSRs.

.exe program, the program will be loaded into the transient program area of RAM and, if necessary, into the RAM where the transient part of the command processor was loaded. (The transient part of the command processor wiill be reloaded when the program terminates.)

Normally, when a program terminates all the transient program area is deallocated, so that another program can be loaded in it to be run. TSR programs, however, are terminated in a special way so that they are left resident in memory, as shown in Figure 15-1*b*. The transient program area is simply reduced by the size of the TSR program(s). When another program is loaded to be run, it is put in RAM above the TSRs.

One question that might occur to you at this point is, How do I make a program resident? To make the program stay resident when it terminates, you use the 31H subfunction of the DOS INT 21H function call. Specifically, you load AH with 31H, load AL with 00H, load DX with the length of the TSR program, and execute the INT 21H instruction. When the program is run from the command line or the AUTOEXEC.BAT file, it will be loaded into RAM, terminated, and left resident.

The next question that might occur to you then is, How does the TSR program get executed after it is resident? The answer to this question is that TSRs are executed as part of interrupt procedures. The exact mechanism depends on whether the TSR is active or passive.

An example of a passive TSR is the switch.com program which I use on my computer. The purpose of this program is to switch the functions of the Caps Lock key and the Ctrl key so that I don't have to retrain my finger to the key positions on my new keyboard. When DOS finds the statement "switch" in my AUTOEXEC.BAT file, it executes the switch.com program. The switch.com program terminates and remains resident. To accomplish the desired switch action, the program "intercepts" the BIOS keyboard interrupt, 09H, as shown in Figure 15-2*a*. You may remember that we showed you how to intercept interrupts at the start of the SDKCOM1 program in Figure 14-27. The result of this interception is that whenever a key is pressed, execution goes first to the switch TSR program. The switch program then calls the BIOS INT 09H procedure to read in codes from the keyboard. If the key code read from the keyboard represents a Caps Lock, it is replaced with the code for a Ctrl, and if the key code represents a Ctrl, it is replaced with the code for a Caps Lock. Other key codes are simply passed on as received. To DOS, then, the switch TSR is simply an interrupt procedure which is executed automatically when a key on the keyboard is pressed.

An example of an active TSR is Borland's Sidekick program, which pops up a menu of command options when you press the Ctrl key and the Alt key. As we mentioned before, Sidekick allows you to temporarily pause during some other program and write a note in a notebook file, perform a calculation on a screen-based calculator, check your appointment schedule, or any one of several other functions. To terminate Sidekick and return to the previously executing program, you press the Esc key. As with the passive switch.com TSR,

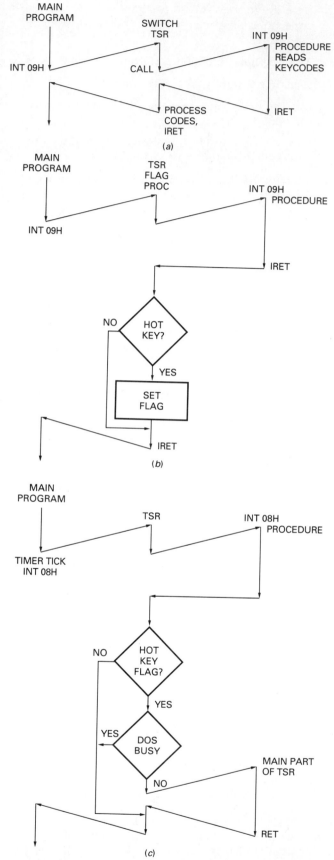

FIGURE 15-2 (*a*) Program flow for switch.com passive TSR. (*b*) Program flow for flag set part of active TSR. (*c*) Program flow for main part of TSR.

you make Sidekick resident by running it from the command line or as part of the AUTOEXEC.BAT file. Figure 15-2b and c show how an active TSR such as Sidekick is commonly executed when a hot key combination is pressed.

As shown in Figure 15-2b, the first part of the TSR intercepts the keyboard interrupt and immediately calls the BIOS keyboard procedure to read in the scan code from the keyboard. When execution returns from the BIOS INT 09H procedure, the TSR checks the returned key code to determine if a hot key was pressed. If a hot key was not pressed, execution simply returns to the interrupted program. If a hot key was pressed, the TSR procedure sets a global flag in memory before returning to the interrupted program. Another section of the TSR will check this flag at periodic intervals to determine if the main part of the TSR should be executed.

The part of the TSR which checks the hot key flag is often connected with the clock tick interrupt procedure, as shown in Figure 15-2c. The normal clock tick interrupt vector is replaced with the starting address of this section of the TSR. When a clock tick interrupt occurs (about every 18 ms for a PC- or PS/2-type computer), execution will then go to this section of the TSR. The TSR resets the hot key flag and immediately calls the normal BIOS clock procedure. This call is necessary because the clock procedure updates the system clock and controls the timing of many other system operations. When execution returns to the TSR from the BIOS clock procedure, a check is made to see if a hot key was pressed. If not, execution is simply returned to the program that was interrupted by the clock tick.

If a hot key was pressed, this section of the TSR usually has to determine if DOS or BIOS is executing any procedures before transferring execution to the main part of the TSR. The problem here is that for the most part, DOS and BIOS procedures are not reentrant. This means that the system would probably "lock up" if the TSR happened to call a DOS or BIOS procedure that was executing when the clock tick interrupt occurred. We don't have space to show you the details here, but the DOS INT 28H function can be used to determine if it is safe to run a TSR which uses DOS function calls to access disk files, etc.

If a DOS or BIOS function was in process when the clock tick occurred, execution is simply returned to the interrupted program. When the next clock tick occurs, this middle section of the TSR will again check if DOS is available. If no DOS or BIOS functions were executing when the interrupt occurred, execution will go to the main part of the TSR. When the main part of the TSR finishes, execution is returned to the interrupted main program. Note that the hot key flag was previously reset, so that if another clock tick interrupt occurs while the main part of the TSR is executing, the BIOS clock procedure will be executed, but the main part of the TSR will not be called again.

If you want to experiment with TSRs, the Bibliography lists a couple of references which have detailed examples of how to write TSRs.

As you can perhaps see from the preceding discussion, the TSR scheme allows a microcomputer to do limited multitasking, but it is not useful for controlling a multiuser system. In the next section we discuss the scheduling method commonly used in multiuser operating systems.

TIME-SLICE SCHEDULING

In a full-fledged multitasking or multiuser operating system, the part of the operating system which determines when it is time to switch from one task to another is called the *scheduler*, *dispatcher*, or *supervisor*. The most common method of scheduling task switches is the *time-slice* method which we discussed previously. In a simple round-robin implementation of this approach, the CPU executes one task for perhaps 20 ms and then switches to the next task. After all tasks have had their turn, execution returns to the first. In the program in Figure 10-35 we showed you how a programmable timer, priority-interrupt controller, and interrupt-service procedure can be used to implement this type of scheduling. The UNIX operating system and the OS/2 operating system use a more complex time-slice scheduling approach to implement multitasking. The advantage of the time-slice approach in a multiuser system is that all users are serviced at approximately equal time intervals. As more users are added, however, each user gets serviced less often, so each user's program takes longer to execute. This is referred to as *system degradation*. For industrial control operating systems, this variable scheduling is often not appropriate, so a different scheduling method is used.

PREEMPTIVE PRIORITY-BASED SCHEDULING

In a system which uses *preemptive priority-based scheduling*, an executing low-priority task can be interrupted by a higher-priority task. When the high-priority task finishes executing, execution returns to the low-priority task. This approach is well suited to some control applications because it allows the most important tasks to be done first. Priority-interrupt controllers such as the 8259A are often used to set up and manage the task service requests. The Intel RMX 86 operating system uses priority-based scheduling.

Preserving the Environment

The registers, data, pointers, etc., used by an executing task are referred to as its *environment*, *state*, or *context*. When a task switch occurs, the environment of the interrupted task must be saved so that the task can be restarted properly when it receives another time slice. The usual way of preserving the environment is to keep it in a special memory segment or on a stack. Some operating systems keep a separate stack for each task. In either case, when a task switch occurs the operating system saves the environment of the interrupted task and a pointer to the saved environment. When it is time to switch back to that task, the operating system uses the pointer to access the environment it saved. This process is commonly called "context switching."

A less obvious point in a multitasking system is that any global procedures have to be reentrant. This is necessary so that if one task is executing a procedure and its time slice ends, other tasks can use the procedure, and the procedure will still complete correctly when execution returns to the first task. Refer to Figure 5-20 if you need a refresher on reentrancy.

Accessing Resources

Another problem encountered in a multitasking system is assuring that tasks have orderly access to resources such as printers, disk drives, etc. As one example of this, suppose that a user at a terminal needs to read a file from a hard disk and print it on the system printer. Obviously the file cannot be read in from the disk and printed in one of the 20-ms time slices allotted to that user, so several provisions must be made to gain access to the resources and hang on to them long enough to get the job done properly. A flag or *semaphore* in memory is used to indicate whether the disk drive is in use by another task or not. Likewise, another semaphore is used to indicate whether the printer is in use. If a task cannot access a resource because it is busy, the task is said to be *blocked*. Now, rather than making the user type in a print command over and over until the disk drive or the printer is available, most operating systems of this type set up queues of tasks waiting for each resource. When one task finishes with a resource, it resets the semaphore for that resource. The next task in the queue can set the semaphore to indicate the resource is busy and then use the resource.

The Need for Protection

An interesting problem can occur in a multitasking operating system when two or more users attempt to read and change the contents of a memory location at the same time. As an example, suppose that an airline ticket-reservation system is operating on a time-slice basis. Now, further suppose that just before the end of his or her time slice, one user examines the memory location which represents a seat on a plane and finds the seat empty. Another user on the system can then, in his or her time slice, examine the same memory location, find it empty, mark it full, and print out a reservation confirmation on the CRT. When execution returns to the first user, his or her program has already checked the seat during its previous time slice, so it marks the seat full, and prints out a reservation confirmation on the CRT. The two people assigned to the same seat may make nasty remarks about computers unless this problem is solved.

The section of a program where the value of a variable is being examined and changed must be protected from access by other tasks until the operation is complete. The section of code which must be protected is called a *critical region* or *critical section*. A technique called *mutual exclusion* is used to prevent two tasks from accessing a critical region at the same time. In the CHK_N_DISPLAY procedure in Figure 14-27 we showed how a critical region can be protected from an interrupt procedure by simply masking the interrupt. In a time-slice system, however, a semaphore is used to provide mutual exclusion.

Figure 15-3 shows how this can be done with 8086 assembly language instructions. The instruction sequence is the same for each task. If task 1 needs to enter a critical section of code, it first loads the semaphore value for critical-region-busy into AL. The single instruction XCHG AL, SEMAPHORE then swaps the byte in AL with the byte in the memory location named SEMAPHORE. It is important to do this in one instruction so that the time-slice mechanism cannot switch to another task halfway through the exchange and cause our airline problem.

After the semaphore is read in Figure 15-3, it is compared with the busy value. If the critical region is busy, execution will remain in a wait loop for as many time slices as are required for the critical region to become free. If the semaphore value is a 0, indicating not busy, then execution enters the critical region. The XCHG instruction has already set the semaphore to indicate the critical region is busy. After execution of

```
;Instructions for accessing critical region of code protected by semaphore - USER 1
        MOV  AL, 01          ; Load semaphore value for region busy
HOLD: XCHG AL, SEMAPHORE ; Swap and set semaphore
        CMP  AL, 01          ; Check if region is busy
        JE   HOLD            ; Yes, loop until not busy. No enter critical region of code.
;       Instructions which access critical region are inserted here
        MOV  SEMAPHORE, 00 ; Reset semaphore to make critial region available to others.


;Instructions for accessing critical region of code protected by semaphore - USER 2
        MOV  AL, 01          ; Load semaphore value for region busy
HOLD: XCHG AL, SEMAPHORE ; Swap and set semaphore
        CMP  AL, 01          ; Check if region is busy
        JE   HOLD            ; Yes, loop until not busy. No enter critical region of code.
;       Instructions which access critical region are inserted here
        MOV  SEMAPHORE, 00 ; Reset semaphore to make critial region available to others.
```

FIGURE 15-3 8086 assembly language sequences showing how a flag or semaphore can be used to provide mutual exclusion for a critical region of code.

the critical region finishes, the MOV SEMAPHORE, 00 instruction resets the semaphore to indicate that the critical region is no longer busy. Task 2 can then swap the semaphore and access the critical region when needed. The semaphore functions in the same way as the "occupied" sign on a restroom of a plane or train. If you mentally try interrupting each sequence of instructions at different points, you should see that there is no condition where both tasks can get into the critical region at the same time.

Another region that requires protection is the operating system code. Most single-user operating systems such as DOS do little to prevent user programs from corrupting the operating system code and data areas. The usual results of this and Murphy's law are that an incorrect address in a user program may cause it to write over critical sections of the operating system. The system then "locks up" and the only way to get control again is to reboot the system. In a multitasking system this is intolerable, so several methods are used to protect the operating system.

The major method is to construct the operating system in two or more *layers*. Figure 15-4 shows an "onionskin" diagram for a two-layer operating system. The basic principle here is that the inner circle represents the code and data areas used by the operating system. The outer layer represents the code and data areas of user programs or tasks that are being run under control of the operating system. The inner layer is protected because user programs can only access operating system resources through very specific mechanisms rather than a simple, accidental call or jump. Devices in the Motorola

MC68000 family of microprocessors, for example, are designed to accommodate a two-level structure such as this. The MC68000 family devices have two modes of operation, user and supervisory. Certain privileged instructions which affect the operating system can only be executed when the processor is in supervisory mode. As we discuss in great detail later, the Intel 80286, 80386, and 80486 microprocessors have hardware features which allow up to four levels of protection to be built into a system. The 80286, 80386, and 80486 microprocessors also provide a hardware mechanism which can be used to protect tasks from each other.

Memory Management

INTRODUCTION

There are two major reasons why memory must be specifically managed in a multitasking operating system. The first reason is that the physical memory is usually not large enough to hold the operating system and all of the application programs that are being executed by the different users. The second reason is to make sure that executing tasks do not access protected areas of memory. Some memory management can be done by the operating system software, but complete memory management and protection require the aid of hardware called a *memory-management unit* or MMU. Before we get into the operation of an MMU, we want to give you a little background on other methods used to solve the limited memory problem.

OVERLAYS

A common problem, even in older, single-user systems, is that the physical memory is not large enough to hold, for example, an assembler and the program being assembled. The traditional solution to this problem is to write the assembler in modules and use an *overlay* scheme. When the assembler is invoked, the executive module of the assembler is loaded into memory, and an additional block of memory space called the *overlay area* is reserved for the assembler. The first module of the assembler is loaded into this overlay area. When the assembler reaches a point where it needs the next module, it reads that module, referred to as an *overlay*, from disk into the overlay area reserved in memory. When the assembler reaches a point where it needs another overlay, it reads that overlay from disk and loads it into the same overlay area in memory. The overlay approach is commonly used with assemblers, compilers, word processors, and spreadsheet programs. Incidentally, the Borland Turbo C++ tools we introduced you to in Chapter 12 can be used to develop an overlay type program.

BANK SWITCHING, EXPANDED MEMORY, AND EXTENDED MEMORY

Another approach traditionally used to expand the available memory in a microcomputer is *bank switching*. Early microprocessors such as the Intel 8085 have only 16 address lines, so they can directly address only 64 Kbytes of memory. Figure 15-5 shows how the amount

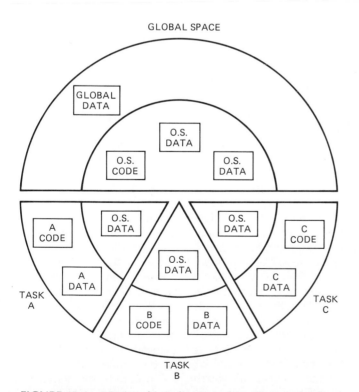

FIGURE 15-4 "Onionskin" diagram showing two-level-protection scheme for multitasking operating system. (*Intel Corporation*)

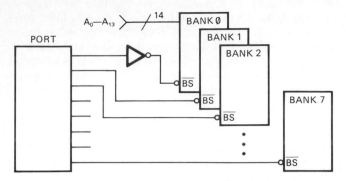

FIGURE 15-5 Block diagram showing how microcomputer memory can be expanded with bank switching.

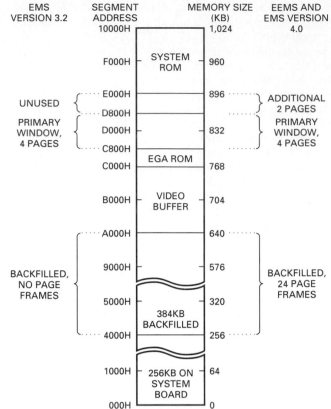

FIGURE 15-6 Memory maps for LIM/EMS 3.2 and LIM/EMS 4.0 expanded memory standards.

of memory accessible in a system such as this can be expanded beyond the address limit. The hardware is configured so that when the power is first turned on, the 16-Kbyte bank labeled bank 0 is enabled. Let's assume that this bank occupies system address space 4000H–7FFFH and that system address lines A0–A13 are used to address the bytes in this bank.

To switch to bank 1, a byte which turns off bank 0 and turns on bank 1 is output to the selection port. The bank 1 devices now occupy the address space 4000H–7FFFH and system address lines A0–A13 are used to address the bytes in this bank. Any of the other banks can be switched into the 4000H–7FFFH memory window by simply sending the appropriate word to the control port. As you can see, this bank-switching scheme allows the processor to access 8 banks of 16 Kbytes each or a total of 128 Kbytes through a 16-Kbyte window in the processor address space. Let's see how this scheme is used in IBM PC- and PS/2-type microcomputers.

The 8086 or 8088 processor used in PC-type microcomputers can address up to 1 Mbyte of memory. At the time the IBM PC was developed, it seemed inconceivable that anyone would ever need more than 640 Kbytes of memory for application programs, so all the address space above 640 Kbytes was reserved for the system BIOS, the video frame buffer, and system uses, as shown in Figure 15-6. Also, since the processor could address only 1 Mbyte of memory, DOS was designed to directly address only 1 Mbyte.

As the memory needs of application programs such as spreadsheets and databases banged into the 640-Kbyte limit, designers again looked to bank switching as a means to overcome this limit. The result was the Lotus-Intel-Microsoft Expanded Memory Standard, LIM/EMS 3.2. This combination hardware-software standard has been widely implemented.

The hardware for this expanded memory is often implemented as a plug-in board which contains up to 8 Mbytes of 16-Kbyte pages (banks) and bank-switch registers. The bank-switch registers are used to control which pages from the expanded memory are selected. As shown along the left side of Figure 15-6, in a LIM/EMS 3.2 system the four 16-Kbyte pages selected from the expanded memory at a particular time are mapped into the system address space between C800H and D7FFH. This address space was chosen for the expanded

memory window because it is not usually used for system functions. The newer LIM/EMS 4.0 standard allows 16-Kbyte pages to be mapped into any system address space that is not populated with ROM or RAM, and it allows the expanded memory to contain up to 32 Mbytes. As shown along the right side of Figure 15-6, LIM/EMS 4.0 allows pages above the 640-Kbyte boundary and additional pages in the 384-Kbyte region below the boundary.

The software part of either EMS standard includes a driver program called EMM.SYS. This driver program is installed in memory by including the statement device = emm.sys in the CONFIG.SYS program which runs when you boot your system. The EMM.SYS driver contains the functions which allow application programs to allocate and access expanded memory. The expanded memory functions are called with a software INT 67H. The value in AH determines the specific function that is called. The complete list of expanded memory functions is extensive, but to give you an idea of some of what is available, Figure 15-7 shows a few of the functions. Basically, an application program must use these functions to allocate enough expanded memory for its code and data, switch in pages as needed, and deallocate the expanded memory when it terminates so that the memory is available for the next program. Incidentally, MS DOS versions 4.0 and later support LIM/EMS 4.0.

As we discuss in detail later, the 80286, 80386, and 80486 microprocessors have more address lines than

EXPANDED MEMORY FUNCTION	CALL WITH	RETURNS
GET STATUS	AH = 40H	AH = STATUS
GET PAGE FRAME ADDRESS	AH = 41H	AH = STATUS BX = PAGE FRAME SEGMENT
GET NUMBER OF EXPANDED MEMORY PAGES	AH = 42H	AH = STATUS BX = AVAILABLE PAGES DX = TOTAL PAGES
ALLOCATE EXPANDED MEMORY PAGES	AH = 43H BX = NO. OF PAGES	AH = STATUS DX = EMM HANDLE
MAP EXPANDED MEMORY PAGE	AH = 44H AL = PHYSICAL PAGE BX = LOGICAL PAGE DX = EMM HANDLE	AH = STATUS
RELEASE EXPANDED MEMORY PAGES	AH = 45H DX = EMM HANDLE	AH = STATUS
GET EMM VERSION	AH = 46H	AH = STATUS AL = VERSION

FIGURE 15-7   Examples of EMM functions called through INT 67H.

an 8086 and can directly address considerably more memory. Memory located in the address space above 1 Mbyte is commonly referred to as *extended memory* or *XMS memory*. If a system using one of these processors is running under a version of DOS before 5.0, however, it still has the 1-Mbyte memory limit imposed by DOS. In other words, the extended memory in a system is invisible to DOS and will not be used for programs. There are three common cures for this problem.

One solution is to use a memory-management-device driver program which allows the extended memory to function as expanded memory. Another solution is to use a "DOS extender" program such as Phar Lap Software's 386/DOS extender or A.I. Architect's OS/x86. These programs operate under DOS, so they use the familar DOS commands, but they allow programs to take advantage of the advanced features of the 80286, 80386, and 80486 processors. The third solution to the DOS memory limit is to switch to an operating system such as Microsoft's OS/2, which is designed to take advantage of the addressing range and other features of the newer processors.

The expanded memory scheme we described in the preceding section makes more memory available to a program, but it has several disadvantages. One disadvantage is that the system must contain enough expanded memory for the largest program to be run. With today's large programs this could be a major expense. A second disadvantage of expanded memory is that application programs must manage the switching of pages in and out of the expanded memory window. This adds overhead to the execution time, and if a program is modified, the switching points may have to be changed. Still another disadvantage is that operating system and user-task protection are not easily implemented. The virtual memory scheme we discuss next helps solve these problems.

VIRTUAL MEMORY AND MMUs

Virtual memory is basically an extension of the memory caching scheme we discussed in Chapter 11. To refresh your memory of a cache system, take another look at Figure 11-11. The virtual memory scheme simply adds a hard-disk drive to the memory hierarchy. The hard-

disk drive becomes the main program and data memory, the DRAM functions as an intermediate cache, and the SRAM cache functions as a high-speed cache for the DRAM. In a virtual memory system the code and data segments currently being used for program execution are loaded from the disk into DRAM and accessed by the cache controller as needed. If an executing program needs a segment that is not currently in DRAM, the required segment is read in from the disk to the DRAM main memory. If the DRAM is full, one of the segments in the DRAM is swapped out to the disk to make room, and the required segment is swapped into DRAM.

There are three different ways of setting up the code and data blocks to be swapped in and out of DRAM. One scheme is to swap segments. The advantage of segment swapping is that segments correspond to the code and data structures in the program. The disadvantage of the segment scheme is that with processors such as the 80386 and 80486, segments can be very large. The time required to swap in a large segment would appreciably slow down the execution of a program. Also, it is often hard to fit variable-sized segments in memory. A second swapping scheme uses fixed-length pages of typically 4 Kbytes each. These small pages can be quickly swapped in and out of memory, but they don't correspond to the logical structure of the program. A third approach, implemented in the 80386 and 80486 microprocessors, allows a programmer to write a program using logical segments and divide the segments into 4-Kbyte pages for swapping in and out of physical memory.

The term virtual here refers to memory space that appears to be present from a programmer's viewpoint but is not physically present in the DRAM main memory. In other words, if you are writing a program for a system with virtual memory, you can create segments as if you had, for example, a gigabyte of memory space, even though the system has only perhaps 4 Mbytes of physical memory. The virtual memory space can be much larger than the physical memory, because all of the logical segments are not present in physical memory at any one time. As with the SRAM cache scheme, a virtual memory system works because most programs only need small sections of code and data at a particular time.

Virtual memory can be managed totally by the operating system, but most microcomputer systems use a hardware device called a *memory-management unit* or MMU to assist in the process. The Intel 80286, 80386, and 80486 and the Motorola MC68030 and MC68040 have a complete MMU integrated on the chip with the CPU. Separate MMUs are available for use with other processors. In either case the MMU is functionally positioned between the processor and the actual memory. Figure 15-8, page 542, shows an overview of how the MMUs in the 286, 386, and 486 processors manage segment-based virtual memory. The first step in explaining this is to clarify the terms logical address and physical address.

When you write an assembly language program, you usually refer to addresses by name. The addresses you work with in a program are called *logical addresses*, because they indicate the logical positions of code and data. An example of this is the 8086 instruction JNZ

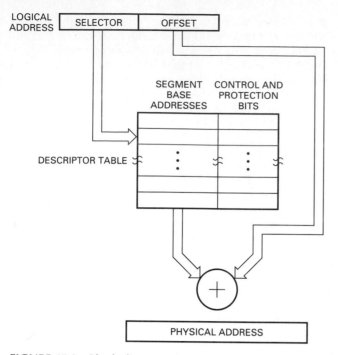

LOGICAL
ADDRESS

| SELECTOR | OFFSET |

SEGMENT
BASE
ADDRESSES

CONTROL AND
PROTECTION
BITS

DESCRIPTOR TABLE

$+$

PHYSICAL ADDRESS

FIGURE 15-8   Block diagram showing how segment-based virtual memory is implemented in 80286, 80386, and 80486 processors.

NEXT. The label NEXT represents a logical address that execution will go to if the zero flag is not set. When an 8086 program is assembled, each logical address is represented with a 16-bit offset and a 16-bit segment base. The 8086 BIU then produces the actual physical memory address by simply adding these two parts together, as explained many times previously.

When a program is assembled or compiled to run on a system with an MMU, each logical or virtual address is also represented by two components, but the components function differently. In a segment-oriented system such as an 80286, the upper 16-bit component is referred to as a *segment selector*, and the lower component is referred to as the *offset*. As shown in Figure 15-8, the MMU uses the segment selector to access a *descriptor* for the desired segment in a table of descriptors in memory. A descriptor is a series of memory locations that contain the physical base address for a segment, the privilege level of the segment, and some control bits.

The selectors for the 80286, 80386, and 80486 have 14 address bits and 2 privilege-level bits. The 14 address bits in the selector can select any one of 16,384 descriptors in the descriptor table. Since each descriptor represents a segment, this means that a program can access up to 16,384 segments. For an 80286 the offset part of the virtual address is 16 bits, so each segment can contain up to 64 Kbytes. The logical or virtual address space accessible by an 80286 then is 16,384 segments × 65,536 bytes/segment, or about 1 Gbyte. What this means is that the operating system and other programs can function as if a gigabyte of memory were available.

The physical memory is the amount of RAM and ROM actually present in the system. For this example let's assume that the MMU has 24 address lines so it can address 16 Mbytes of physical memory. Remember from our previous discussion that the physical memory, whatever its actual size, is simply a holding place for the segments currently being used by the operating system and user programs.

When the MMU receives a logical address from the CPU, it checks to see if that segment is currently in the physical memory. If the segment is present in physical memory, the MMU adds the offset component of the address to the segment base component of the address from the segment descriptor to form the physical address. It then outputs the physical address to memory on the memory address bus. The addressed code or data word is returned to the CPU on the data bus.

If the MMU finds that the segment specified by the selector part of the logical address is not in memory, it sends an interrupt signal to the CPU. In response to the interrupt, the operating system executes an interrupt procedure which reads the desired code or data segment from disk and loads it into the physical memory. The MMU then computes and outputs the physical address as described before. The operation is semiautomatic, so other than a slight delay, the user is not aware that the segment had to be loaded. In a well-structured system with a reasonably large amount of physical memory, the *hit rate* may be 90 to 95 percent.

When the CPU or smart MMU wants to load a segment from disk into physical memory, it must first make space for it in the physical memory. Depending on the system, it may do this by compacting the segments already present and changing the descriptors to point to the new physical locations or by swapping the segment being brought in with one currently in physical memory. To help in deciding which segment to swap back to memory, many systems use an *accessed* bit in the descriptor to keep track of how many times the segment has been used. A low-use segment is the most likely candidate to swap back to disk. Some virtual memory systems also have a *dirty* bit in each descriptor. This bit will be set if the contents of a segment have been changed. If the dirty bit is set, a segment must be written back to disk when its space is needed. If the dirty bit is not set, then the segment has not been altered, and the copy of the segment on disk is current. In this case the segment can just be overwritten by the new segment. This check saves the time that would be required to write the segment to disk.

The use of a descriptor table to translate logical addresses to physical addresses has another major advantage besides making virtual memory possible. The selector component of each logical address contains 2 bits which represent the privilege level of the program section requesting access to a segment. The descriptor for each segment contains 2 bits which represent the privilege level of that segment. When an executing program attempts to access a segment, the MMU compares the privilege level in the selector with the privilege level in the descriptor. If the segment selector has the same or a greater privilege level, then the MMU allows the segment to be accessed. If the selector privilege level is lower than the privilege level in the descriptor, the MMU refuses the access and sends an interrupt signal to the CPU indicating a privilege-level violation. As you can see, privilege bits and this indirect method of producing physical addresses provides a mechanism for protecting segments such as those containing the operating system kernel from application programs.

To summarize then, an MMU is used to manage virtual memory. The MMU uses a descriptor table to translate logical or virtual program addresses to physical addresses. This indirect approach makes possible a virtual address space much larger than the physical address space. The indirect approach also makes it possible to protect a memory segment from access by a program section with a lower privilege level. You will meet all these concepts again in the following sections, where we discuss the 80286, 80386, and 80486 microprocessors which have integrated MMUs.

THE INTEL 80286 MICROPROCESSOR

Introduction

The needs of a multitasking/multiuser operating system include environment preservation during task switches, operating system and user protection, and virtual memory management. The Intel 80286 was the first 8086 family processor designed to make implementation of these features relatively easy. The 80286 was used as the CPU in the IBM PC/AT and its clones, in the IBM PS/2 Model 50, and in the IBM PS/1. Although the 80286 has to a large extent been superseded by the 80386, the 80386SX, and the 80486, there are still many 80286-based systems in use and more 80286 systems being sold. Therefore, we will use a little space to tell you about the basic operation of an 80286.

80286 Architecture, Signals, and System Connections

As you can see in the block diagram in Figure 15-9, an 80286 contains four separate processing units.

The *bus unit* (BU) in the device performs all memory and I/O reads and writes, prefetches instruction bytes, and controls transfer of data to and from processor extension devices such as the 80287 math coprocessor.

The *instruction unit* (IU) fully decodes up to three prefetched instructions and holds them in a queue, where the execution unit can access them. This is a further example of how modern processors keep several instructions "in the pipeline" instead of waiting to finish one instruction before fetching the next.

The *execution unit* (EU) uses its 16-bit ALU to execute instructions it receives from the instruction unit. When operating in its real address mode, the 80286 register set is the same as that of an 8086 except for the addition of a 16-bit machine status word (MSW) register, which we will discuss later.

The *address unit* (AU) computes the physical addresses that will be sent out to memory or I/O by the BU. The 80286 can operate in one of two memory address modes, *real address mode* or *protected virtual address mode*. If the 80286 is operating in the real address mode, the address unit computes addresses using a segment base and an offset just as the 8086 does. The familiar CS, DS, SS, and ES registers are used to hold the base addresses for the segments currently in use. The maximum physical address space in this mode is 1 Mbyte, just as it is for the 8086.

If an 80286 is operating in its *protected virtual address mode* (protected mode), the address unit functions as a complete MMU. In this address mode the 80286 uses all 24 address lines to access up to 16 Mbytes of physical memory. In protected mode it also provides up to a gigabyte of virtual memory using the descriptor table scheme shown in Figure 15-8.

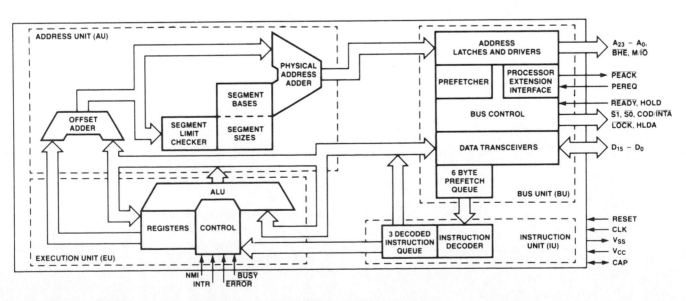

FIGURE 15-9   80286 internal block diagram.   (*Intel Corporation*)

Figure 15-10 shows the 68-pin package that is usually used for an 80286, and Figure 15-11 shows how an 8086 is connected with some other components to form a simple system. Keep these figures handy as we work our way around the major pins of the 80286. Many of the signals of the 80286 should be familiar to you from our discussion of the 8086 signals in Chapter 7.

The 80286 has a 16-bit data bus and a 24-bit nonmultiplexed address bus. The 24-bit address bus allows the processor to access 16 Mbytes of physical memory when operating in protected mode. Memory hardware for the 80286 is set up as an odd bank and an even bank, just as it is for the 8086. The even bank will be enabled when A0 is low, and the odd bank will be enabled when $\overline{BHE}$ is low. To access an aligned word, both A0 and $\overline{BHE}$ will be low. External buffers are used on both the address and the data bus.

From a control standpoint, the 80286 functions similarly to an 8086 operating in maximum mode. Status signals $\overline{S0}$, $\overline{S1}$, and $M/\overline{IO}$ are decoded by an external 82288 bus controller to produce the control bus, read, write, and interrupt-acknowledge signals.

The HOLD, HLDA, INTR, $\overline{INTA}$, (NMI), $\overline{READY}$, and LOCK and RESET pins function basically the same as they do on an 8086. An external 82284 clock generator is used to produce a clock signal for the 80286 and to synchronize RESET and $\overline{READY}$ signals.

The final four signal pins we need to discuss here are used to interface with processor extensions (coprocessors) such as the 80287 math coprocessor. The *processor extension request* (PEREQ) input pin will be asserted by a coprocessor to tell the 80286 to perform a data transfer to or from memory for it. When the 80286 gets around to do the transfer, it asserts the *processor extension acknowledge* ($\overline{PEACK}$) signal to the coprocessor to let it know the data transfer has started. Data transfers are done through the 80286 in this way so that the coprocessor uses the protection and virtual

memory capability of the MMU in the 80286. The $\overline{BUSY}$ signal input on the 80286 functions the same as the $\overline{TEST1}$ input does on the 8086. When the 80286 executes a WAIT instruction, it will remain in a WAIT loop until it finds the $\overline{BUSY}$ signal from the coprocessor high. If a coprocessor finds some error during processing, it will assert the $\overline{ERROR}$ input of the 80286. This will cause the 80286 to automatically do a type 16H interrupt call. An interrupt-service procedure can be written to make the desired response to the error condition.

The machine cycle waveforms for the 80286 are very similar to those of the 8086 that we showed and discussed in earlier chapters. You should be able to work your way through them in the Intel 80286 data sheets if you need that type of information.

As we mentioned before, the 80286 is used as the CPU in the IBM PC/AT and its clones. These AT-type machines use the AT/ISA bus shown in Figure 11-7b to interface with a CRT controller card, disk controller cards, and other peripheral cards.

80286 Real Address Mode Operation

After the 80286 is reset, it starts executing in its real address mode. This mode is referred to as real because physical memory addresses are produced by directly adding an offset to a segment base, just as they are in an 8086. In this mode the 80286 can address up to 1 Mbyte of physical memory and functions essentially as a "souped-up" 8086. Due to the extensive pipelining and other hardware improvements, the 80286 will execute most programs several times faster than an 8086 with the same-frequency clock signal.

When operating in real address mode, the interrupt-vector table of the 80286 is located in the first 1 Kbyte of memory, just as it is for an 8086, and the response to an interrupt is the same as that of an 8086. As shown in Figure 15-12 the 80286 has several additional built-in interrupt types. Some of these types will not make much sense until we dig a little deeper into the operations of the 80286 and the 80386, but while we are here we will introduce you to a few new terms used in Figure 15-12.

The 80186 and later processors separate interrupts into two categories, interrupts and exceptions. Asynchronous external events which affect the processor through the INTR or NMI input are referred to as interrupts. An exception-type interrupt is generated by some error condition that occurred during the execution of an instruction. Dividing by zero is an example of an operation that will cause an exception. Software interrupts produced by the INT n instruction are classified as exceptions, because they are synchronous with the processor.

Exceptions are further divided into faults and traps. Faults are exceptions that are detected and signaled before the faulting instruction is executed. The segment-not-present exception is an example of a fault. Traps are exceptions which are reported after the instruction which caused the exception executes. The divide-by-zero exception and the INT n interrupts are examples of traps.

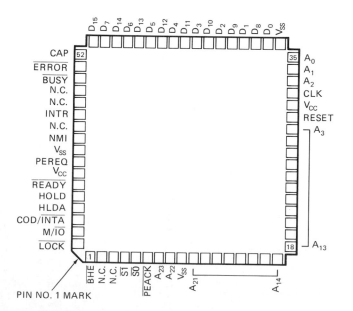

FIGURE 15-10 Pin diagram for 80286 microprocessor. (*Intel Corporation*)

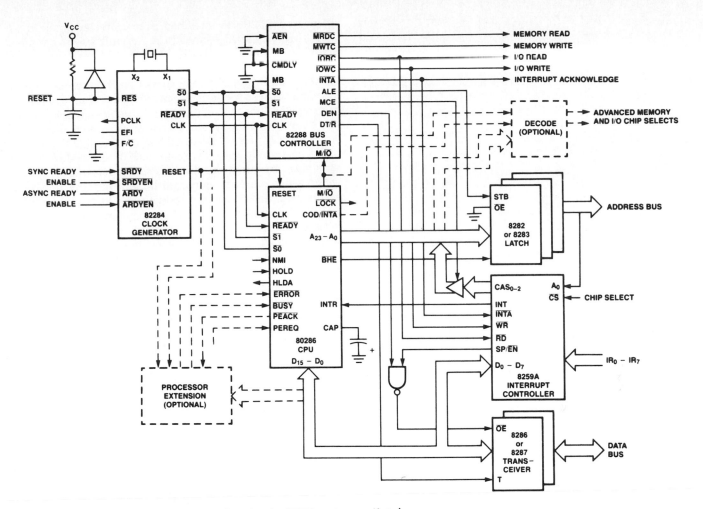

FIGURE 15-11   Circuit connections for simple 80286 system.   (*Intel Corporation*)

FUNCTION	INTERRUPT NUMBER
DIVIDE ERROR EXCEPTION	0
SINGLE STEP INTERRUPT	1
NMI INTERRUPT	2
BREAKPOINT INTERRUPT	3
INTO DETECTED OVERFLOW EXCEPTION	4
BOUND RANGE EXCEEDED EXCEPTION	5
INVALID OPCODE EXCEPTION	6
PROCESSOR EXTENSION NOT AVAILABLE EXCEPTION	7
INTERRUPT TABLE LIMIT TOO SMALL	8
PROCESSOR EXTENSION SEGMENT OVERRUN INTERRUPT	9
INVALID TASK STATE SEGMENT	10
SEGMENT NOT PRESENT	11
STACK SEGMENT OVERRUN OR NOT PRESENT	12
SEGMENT OVERRUN EXCEPTION	13
RESERVED	14,15
PROCESSOR EXTENSION ERROR INTERRUPT	16
RESERVED	17-31
USER DEFINED	32-255

FIGURE 15-12   80286 interrupt types.   (*Intel Corporation*)

80286 Protected-Mode Operation

As we said before, after a reset the 80286 operates in real address mode. On an 80286-based system running under MS DOS or a similar operating system, the 80286 is left in real address mode because current versions of DOS are not designed to take advantage of the protected-mode features of the 80286. If an 80286-based system is running an operating system such as Microsoft's OS/2, which uses the protected mode, the real mode will be used to initialize perhipheral devices, load the main part of the operating system from disk into memory, load some registers, enable interrupts, set up descriptor tables, and switch the processor to protected mode. The first step in switching an 80286 to protected mode is to set the protection enable bit in the *machine status word* (MSW) register in the 80286. Figure 15-13*a*, page 546, shows the format for the MSW. Bits 1, 2, and 3 of the MSW are for the most part used to indicate whether a processor extension (coprocessor) is present in the system or not. Bit 0 of the MSW is used to switch the 80286 into protected mode. To change bits in the MSW you load the desired word in a register or memory location and execute the *load machine status word* (LMSW) instruction. The final step to get the 80286 operating

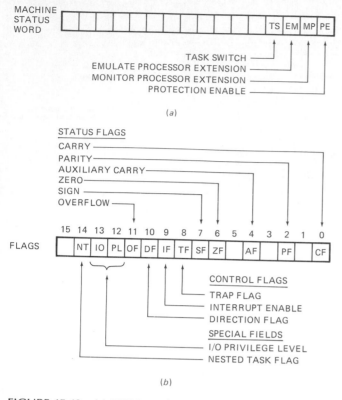

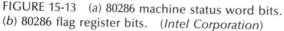

FIGURE 15-13 (a) 80286 machine status word bits.
(b) 80286 flag register bits. (*Intel Corporation*)

in protected mode is to execute an intersegment jump to the start of the main system program. This jump is necessary to flush the instruction byte queue because in protected mode the queue functions differently from the way it does in real mode.

Switching an 80286 to protected mode enables the integrated MMU to provide virtual memory and protection. As we described in an earlier section on virtual memory, a 286 virtual address consists of a 16-bit selector and a 16-bit offset. The MMU uses 14 bits of the selector to access a descriptor for the desired segment in a table of descriptors. The descriptor contains the 24-bit physical base address, the privilege level, and some control bits for the segment. If the privilege level contained in the selector is as high as or higher than the privilege level contained in the descriptor, then access to the segment will be allowed. If not, an exception will be generated. The MMU also checks the "P" bit in the descriptor to determine if the segment is present in physical memory. If not, the MMU will generate a segment-not-present exception. The service procedure for this exception will load the segment in memory and return to the interrupted program. If the memory access meets the privilege level test and the segment is present in physical memory, the MMU will add the 16-bit offset from the logical address to the 24-bit base address from the descriptor to produce the 24-bit physical address for the desired byte or word in the segment. Remember that in protected mode an 80286 uses all 24 address lines, so it can address 16 Mbytes of memory instead of just the 1 Mbyte addressable in real mode.

Once an 80286 is switched into protected mode by executing the LMSW instruction, the only way to get an 80286 back to its real address mode is by resetting the system. The 80286 was designed this way so that a "clever" programmer could not switch the system back into real address mode to defeat the protection schemes in protected mode. Unfortunately, this design also prevents an operating system running in protected mode on an 80286 from easily switching back to real mode to run a section of an 8086 real-mode program during a time slice. In other words, an 80286 operating in protected mode cannot easily multitask a mixture of programs with 8086 segment-offset-type addressing and 80286 selector-offset-type addressing. For this and other reasons, relatively little software has been written to take advantage of the memory-management and protection features available in the 80286 protected mode. The designs of the 80386 and 80486 processors solved the 80286 problems and added other features which make multitasking easier to implement. Much of the new software written during the lifetime of this book will utilize the advanced features of the 386 and 486. Therefore, we decided that the limited space we have available is better used to discuss the details of how the 386 and 486 manage virtual memory and provide protection. The protected mode operation of the 386 is very similar to that of the 80286, so if you have to work on a protected-mode 80286 system, you should have little difficulty "going back."

80286 New and Enhanced Instructions

From a software standpoint the 80286 was designed to be upward-compatible from the 8086 so that the huge amount of software developed for the 8086/8088 could be easily transported to the 80286. The instruction set of the 80286 and later processors are "supersets" of the 8086 instructions. Here's a brief description of the new and enhanced instructions available on the 80286.

Real- or protected-mode instructions

INS—Input string.

OUTS—Output string.

PUSHA—Push eight general-purpose registers on stack.

POPA—Pop eight general-purpose registers from stack.

PUSH immediate—Push immediate number on stack.

SHIFT/ROTATE destination, immediate—Shift or rotate destination register or memory location specified number of bit positions.

IMUL destination, immediate—Signed multiply destination by immediate number.

IMUL destination, multiplicand, immediate multiplier—Signed multiply, result in specified destination.

ENTER—Set up stack frame in procedure. Saves BP, points BP to TOS, and allocates stack space for local variables.

LEAVE—Undo ENTER actions before RET in procedure.

BOUND—Causes a type 5 execution if value in specified register is not within the specified range for an array.

LMSW—Load machine status word (LMSW) is used to switch the 80286 from real mode to protected mode.

Protected-mode instructions

NOTE: We postponed much of the discussion of protected mode to a later section on the 386 processor, so many of these instructions will be much more understandable to you after you read that section.

CTS—Clear task-switched flag in machine status word.

LGDT—Load global descriptor table register from memory.

SGDT—Store global descriptor table register contents in memory.

LIDT—Load interrupt descriptor table register from memory.

LLDT—Load selector and associated descriptor into LDTR.

SLDT—Store selector from LDTR in specified register or memory.

LTR—Load task register with selector and descriptor for TSS.

STR—Store selector from task register in register or memory.

LMSW—Load machine status register from register or memory.

SMSW—Store machine status word in register or memory.

LAR—Load access rights byte of descriptor into register or memory.

LSL—Load segment limit from descriptor into register or memory.

ARPL—Adjust requested privilege level of selector (down only).

VERR—Determine if segment pointed to by selector is readable.

VERW—Determine if segment pointed to by selector is writeable.

THE INTEL 80386 32-BIT MICROPROCESSOR

Introduction

Some of the limitations of the 80286 microprocessor are that it has only a 16-bit ALU, its maximum segment size is 64 Kbytes, and it cannot easily be switched back and forth between real and protected modes. The Intel 80386 microprocessor was designed to overcome these limits, while maintaining software compatibility with the 80286 and earlier processors. The 80386 has a 32-bit ALU, so it can operate directly on 32-bit data words. 80386 segments can be as large as 4 Gbytes and a program can have as many as 16,384 segments. The virtual address space then is 16,384 segments × 4 Gbytes, or about 64 Tbytes (terabytes). A 32-bit address bus allows an 80386 to address up to 4 Gbytes of physical memory. The 80386 has a "virtual 8086" mode, which allows it to easily switch back and forth between 80386 protected-mode tasks and 8086 real-mode tasks. Later we will discuss 80386 memory addressing, protection, and operating modes, but for now we want to discuss the hardware operation and system connections.

80386 Architecture, Pins, and Signals

The 80386 processor is available in two different versions, the 386DX and the 386SX. The 386DX has a 32-bit address bus and a 32-bit data bus. It is packaged in the 132-pin ceramic pin grid array package shown in Figure 15-14a, page 548. The 386SX, which is packaged in the 100-pin flatpack shown in Figure 15-14b, has the same internal architecture as the 386DX, but it has only a 24-bit address bus and a 16-bit data bus. The lower cost package and the ease of interfacing to 8-bit and 16-bit memory and peripherals make the 386SX suitable for use in lower cost systems. The trade-off here, of course, is that the 386SX address range and memory transfer rate are lower than those of the 386DX. Any reference to the 386 in the rest of this chapter will mean the 386DX unless specifically indicated otherwise.

Figure 15-15, page 548, shows the major signal groups for a 386DX. Most of these signals should be familiar to you from the discussions of earlier processors. Let's work our way around the device to pick up the new ones.

The clock signal applied to the 386 CLK2 input is internally divided by 2 to produce the clock signal which actually drives processor operations. For 33-MHz operation then, a 66-MHz signal is applied to the CLK2 input by an external clock generator such as the 82384.

The 386 address bus consists of the A2–A31 address lines and the byte enable lines BE0#–BE3#. The BE0#–BE3# lines are decoded from internal address signals A0 and A1 and function very similarly to the way A0 and BHE function in an 8086 or 80286 system. The 386 has a 32-bit data bus, so memory can be set up as four byte-wide banks. The BE0#–BE3# signals function as enables for the four banks. These individual enables allow the 386 to transfer bytes, words, or double words to and from memory. Incidentally, the # symbol after the BE signal names indicates that these signals are active low.

The bus cycle definition signals identify the type of operation that is occurring during a bus cycle. The WR/R# signal indicates whether a read or write operation is taking place and the D/C# indicates whether the bus operation is a data read/write or a control-word transfer such as an op-code fetch. M/IO# indicates whether the operation is a memory or a direct input/output operation. Incidentally, the 386 direct I/O port structure

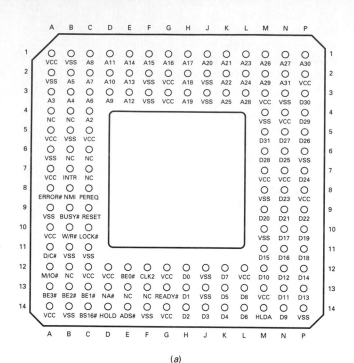

(a)

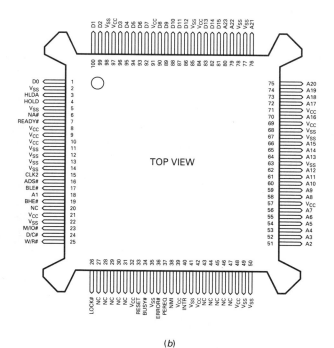

(b)

FIGURE 15-14 (a) Pin diagram for 386DX processor view from pin side. (b) Top view pin diagram for 386SX processor. (*Intel Corporation*)

address, a 386 can access up to 64K 8-bit ports, 32K 16-bit ports, or 8K 32-bit ports.

The PEREQ signal is output by a coprocessor such as an 80387 floating point processor to tell the 386 to fetch the first part of a data word for the coprocessor. The coprocessor will then take over the buses and read the rest of the data word, as we described for the 8087 in Chapter 11. As we also described in Chapter 11, the BUSY# signal is used by the coprocessor to prevent the 386 from going on with its next instruction before the coprocessor is finished with the current instruction. If the ERROR# signal is asserted by a coprocessor, the 386 will perform a type 16 exception.

Regarding the V_{cc} and ground connections, note in Figure 15-15 that the 386 has a large number of V_{cc} pins. It also has a large number of ground connections labeled V_{ss}. These pins are all connected to the appropriate power plane in the PC board.

The RESET, NMI, INTR, HOLD, and HLDA inputs function similarly to the way they do in earlier processors. In a later section we will describe how the 386 handles interrupts while operating in protected mode.

The final group of 386 signals to discuss is the bus control group. The READY# signal is used to insert wait states in bus cycles as needed to interface with slow memory and IO devices.

The BS16# input allows the 386 to work with a 16-bit and/or a 32-bit data bus. If BS16# is asserted, the 386 will transfer data only on the lower half of the 32-bit data bus. If BS16# is asserted and a 32-bit operand is being read from a 16-bit-wide memory, the 386 will automatically generate a second bus cycle to read the second word. For misaligned transfers the 386 will also generate the required number of bus cycles if BS16# is asserted.

The ADS# signal will be asserted when valid addresses, BE signals, and bus cycle definition signals are present on the buses. The 386 address bus is not multiplexed, so an 8086-type ALE signal is not needed. However, in some 386 systems the ADS# signal is used to transfer the address to the outputs of external latches for a

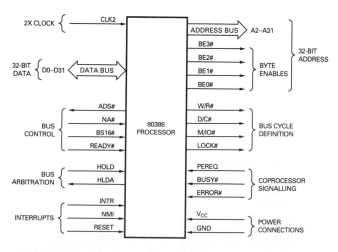

FIGURE 15-15 Signal groups of 386DX. (*Intel Corporation*)

is simply an extension of the 8086 and 80286 port structure to include 32-bit ports. Simple 32-bit I/O ports can be constructed by connecting 8-bit I/O port devices such as the 8255A in parallel. A 386 can use an IN or OUT instruction followed by an 8-bit port address to address up to 256 8-bit ports, 128 16-bit ports or 64 32-bit ports. Using the DX register to hold a 16-bit port

scheme called *address pipelining*. The principle of address pipelining is that if an address is held on the outputs of external latches, the 386 can remove the old address from its address pins and output the address for the next operation earlier in the bus cycle. External control circuitry asserts the next address signal, NA#, to tell the 386 when to output the address for the next operation. Pipelined addressing is not usually necessary in a system with an SRAM cache, because the SRAM cache is fast enough that no wait states are needed.

To help you understand the relationship of some 386 signals, Figure 15-16 shows some 386 nonpipelined read cycles. As you can see, each read operation requires two states, T1 and T2. Note that READY# is made low during T2 so that no wait states are inserted. If the device being read is not fast enough to output data during T2 as required, READY# would be held high longer by external circuitry and a wait state would be inserted in the read cycle after T2.

Incidentally, the 386 contains a large amount of built-in self-test (BIST) circuitry. If the 386 BUSY# input is held low while RESET is held low, the processor will automatically test about 60 percent of its internal circuitry. The self-test requires about 2^{20} CLK2 cycles. If the 386 passes all tests, a "signature" of all 0's will be left in the EAX register.

Now that you have had a short trip around the 386 pins, the next step is to discuss how a 386 can be connected in a system.

386 System Connections and Interface Buses

THE URDA SDK-386 BOARD

A relatively low cost 386 system useful for prototyping 386-based instruments is the SDK-386 shown in Figure 15-17. This board is similar to the SDK-86 board we discussed in Chapter 7. Both boards are available from University Research and Development, Inc. in Pittsburgh, PA. The SDK-386 board contains a 12-MHz 386, 16 Kbytes of EPROM, 32 Kbytes of static RAM, a keyboard, and a 40-character LCD display. The board also has a serial port and software which allows programs to be developed on a PC-type computer and downloaded to the board for testing and debugging.

This board is useful as a simple, protected-mode learning tool, because the monitor program in ROM on the board runs the 386 in protected mode. The monitor runs as one task and user programs run as another task. A simple keypress allows the user to switch from the user task to the monitor. This feature is very useful for debugging programs and hardware. The documentation for the board shows how the descriptor tables, etc. are set up, and how user programs can call monitor procedures to interface with the keyboard and the display.

386 FULL SYSTEMS

Examples of more complex 386 systems are the IBM PS/2 Model 80, the Compaq SYSTEMPRO 386/33, and

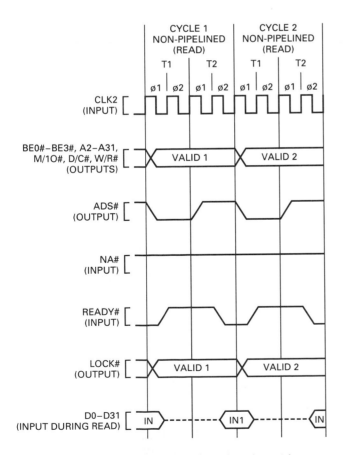

FIGURE 15-16   386 nonpipelined read cycles without wait states.   (*Intel Corporation*)

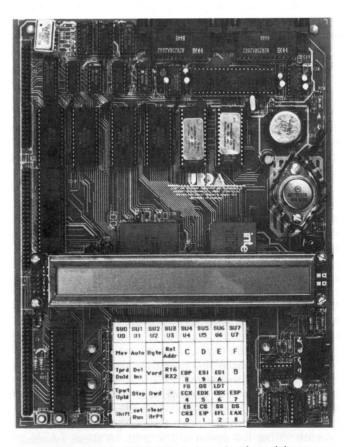

FIGURE 15-17   The SDK-386 prototyping board from University Research and Development Associates.

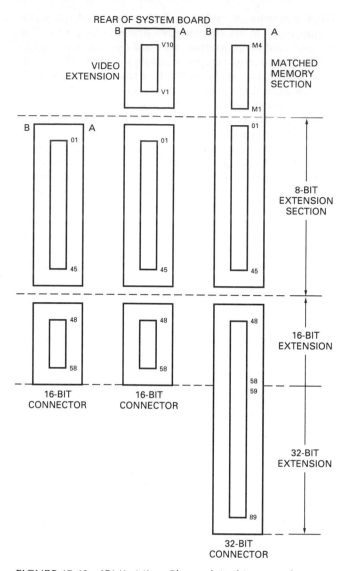

REAR OF SYSTEM BOARD

VIDEO
EXTENSION

MATCHED
MEMORY
SECTION

8-BIT
EXTENSION
SECTION

16-BIT
EXTENSION

16-BIT
CONNECTOR

16-BIT
CONNECTOR

32-BIT
EXTENSION

32-BIT
CONNECTOR

FIGURE 15-19   IBM's MicroChannel Architecture bus
connector types.

the PREEMPT line to the central control circuitry low.
At the appropriate time the control circuitry drives the
ARB/GNT line high. The arbiter on each master then
asserts its arbitration code on the ARB0–ARB3 lines. If
an arbiter sees a code that is lower than its code, it
removes its arbitration signals. This means that the
master with the lower arbitration code assumes control
of the bus. To signal the arbitration is complete, the
central control point asserts the ARB/GNT signal low.
Incidentally, the interrupt lines on the MCA bus are
level-triggered.

Now that you have had a brief introduction to the
system connections and buses used in 386 systems,
let's take a look at the internal architecture of the device
and talk about the different 386 operating modes.

Real Operating Mode

A 386 can operate in real mode, protected mode, or a
variation of protected mode called *virtual 8086* mode.

After a reset the 386 operates in real address mode. In
this mode it functions basically as a fast 8086 or real-
mode 80286. The register set for the 386 in real mode
in a superset of the 8086 and 80286 real-mode register
sets. As shown in Figure 15-20, the 32-bit general-
purpose registers are referred to as extended AX or EAX,
EBX, ECX, EDX, etc. Instructions can, for example,
refer to AL, AH, AX, or EAX. The assembler automatically
codes the instruction for the register size referred to in
an instruction.

The 386 in real mode computes memory addresses
using the same segment base and offset mechanism
used by the 8086. For this mode only the selectors or
visible parts of the segment registers are used. Note that
the 386 has two additional data segment registers, FS
and GS, so programs can have up to four data segments.
The length of segments in 386 real mode is fixed at 64
Kbytes, and any attempt to access a location outside a
segment will cause a type 13 exception.

The address range of 386 real mode is limited to 1
Mbyte, so address lines A20–A31 are normally all low.
The only exception to this is that during a reset these
address lines are all made high to access the boot ROM
at the highest locations in the 32-bit address space of
the 386. As soon as the boot-ROM code does a far jump
or call, the A20–A31 lines will go low and stay low as
long as the 386 is in real mode. A 386 in real mode uses
the address space 00000–003FFH for the interrupt-
vector table and services interrupts in the same way as
an 8086 does.

One new feature of the 386 is the debug registers
shown in Figure 15-20. A software debugger can load
breakpoint addresses in these registers to aid in debugging. A 386 can be instructed to "break" when the
address unit in the processor computes a linear address
which matches one of the addresses in the debug
registers. The older method of setting a breakpoint
involved replacing an instruction with a breakpoint
instruction such as INT 3. This method, of course, cannot be used to debug code in ROM, but the breakpoint
register method can because it does not depend on
modifying code bytes.

The 32-bit EFLAGS register in the 386 is an extension
of the 16-bit registers in the 8086 and 80286. For future
reference the upper right corner of Figure 15-20 shows
the names of the bits in the EFLAGS register, but in
real mode only the lower 16 bits have meaning.

The final real-mode registers to note in Figure 15-20
are the control registers CR0–CR3. The lower 16 bits of
CR0 correspond to the machine status word (MSW) of
the 80286. As with an 80286, a 386 is switched to
protected-mode operation by setting the LSB of this
register to a 1. Register CR1 is reserved by Intel, and
registers CR2 and CR3 are used for paged mode functions, which we discuss later.

386 Protected-Mode Operation

INTRODUCTION

The real power of a 386 lies in its protected-mode and
virtual 8086-mode features. These features are designed
in a very versatile way, so that almost any conceivable

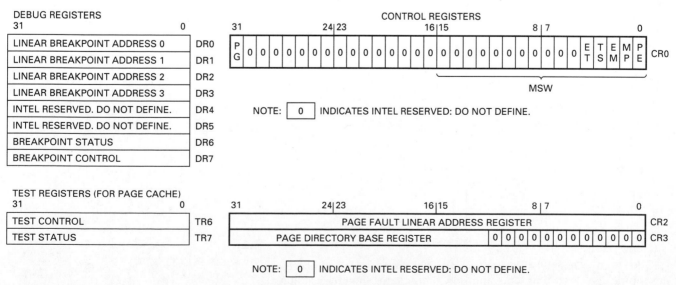

FIGURE 15-20   Intel 386 microprocessor register set.   (*Intel Corporation*)

operating system or program can be implemented on a 386. The problem with this versatility is that it leads to an almost unbelievable amount of detail in a complete description of how the 386 operates in these modes. In reality, unless you are writing a 386-based operating system, you can probably live a very happy life without knowing all these details. In the following sections we have tried to give just enough details so that you can understand the basic protected-mode operation of a 386, how its features fit the needs of a multiuser/ multitasking operating system, and how programs are written for a 386. If you need to know all the minute details, consult the Intel 80386 Programmer's Reference Manual and the Intel 80386 System Software Writer's Guide.

As you read through the following sections, the key concepts you should try to fix in your mind are: how a 386 computes physical addresses in segments-only mode and in paged mode, how a 386 provides protection for operating system code and protection for user tasks, the basic operation of a gate, the protected-mode interrupt response, the task switch process, and the operation of the "flat" system model.

SEGMENTATION AND VIRTUAL MEMORY

As we said in the preceding section, a 386 is switched from real mode to protected mode by setting the LSB of the CR0 register. The virtual memory addressing scheme of a 386 in protected mode is very similar to that of the 80286 we described earlier, except that 386 segments can be much larger and an optional paging mechanism allows segments to be divided into 4-Kbyte pages for faster swapping in and out of physical memory.

In protected mode each 386 address consists of a 16-bit segment selector and a 32-bit offset. As we described earlier in a section on virtual memory, the selector points to a descriptor for the segment in a table of descriptors and the offset specifies the location of the desired code or data in the segment. Using a 32-bit offset value means that segments can be anywhere from 1 byte in length to 2^{32} or about 4 Gbytes in length.

Figure 15-21 shows the format for 386 segment selectors and how these selectors are used to access a descriptor in a descriptor table. The 13-bit index part of this selector is multiplied by 8 and used as a pointer to the desired descriptor in a descriptor table. The index value is multiplied by 8 because each descriptor requires 8 bytes in the descriptor table. Among other things the descriptor contains the physical base address for the segment. The MMU adds the base address from the descriptor to the effective address or offset part of the logical address from the instruction to produce the physical memory address.

There are two major categories of descriptor table in

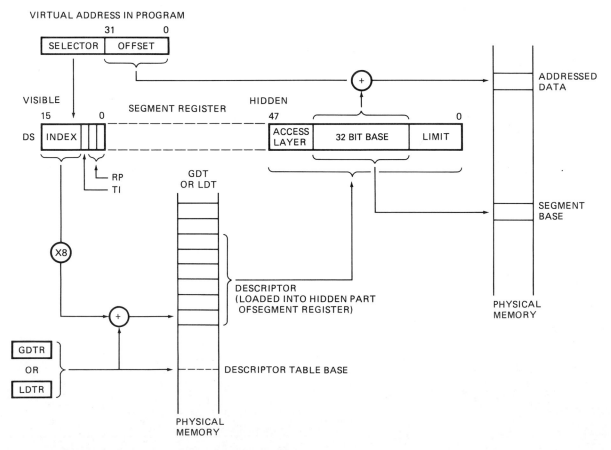

FIGURE 15-21   Diagram showing how the 386 uses a selector to access a descriptor in a descriptor table and how it computes the physical (linear) address.   (*Intel Corporation*)

a 386 system, global and local. A system has only one *global descriptor table* or GDT. The GDT contains, among other things, the segment descriptors for the operating system segments and the descriptors for segments which need to be accessed by all user tasks. A *local descriptor* table or LDT is set up in the system for each task or closely related group of tasks. Figure 15-22 shows, in diagram form, how this works. Tasks share a global descriptor table and the memory area defined by the descriptors in it. Each task can have its own local descriptor table and memory area defined by the descriptors in it. Setting up individual LDTs protects tasks from each other because one task cannot access the LDT of another task.

If the *table indicator* bit (bit 2) of a segment selector is a 0, then the upper 13 bits will index a segment descriptor in the global descriptor table. If the TI bit of the selector is a 1, then the upper 13 bits of the selector will index a segment descriptor in a local descriptor table.

The least significant 2 bits of a segment selector, the *requested privilege level* or RPL bits, are part of the 386's built-in protection features, which we discuss later. For now, let's take a closer look at segment descriptors.

Figure 15-23a and Figure 15-23b show the formats for the 386 segment descriptors and the access rights byte of the descriptors. First notice in the descriptor that 32 bits are set aside for the segment's physical base address and 20 bits are set aside for the size or limit of the segment. If you remember that we said 386 segments can be up to 2^{32} bytes long, you may wonder why only 20 bits are set aside here for the size of the segment. The answer to this is that if the granularity or G bit in the descriptor is a 0, the 20-bit limit value represents the length of the segment in bytes. With a 0 value in the

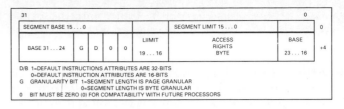

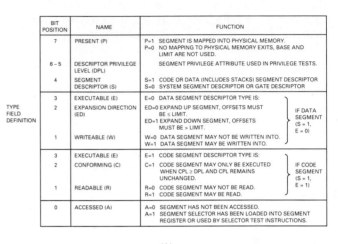

(b)

FIGURE 15-23 (a) 386 descriptor format. (b) Access rights byte format for code and data segment descriptors. (*Intel Corporation*)

G bit, then, a segment can be up to 1 Mbyte in length. If the G bit in the descriptor is a 1, the 20-bit limit value represents the length of the segment in 4-Kbyte blocks. The maximum limit value of 1,048,576 blocks × 4 Kbytes/block then gives a maximum segment length of 4 Gbytes. If an attempt is made to access a location outside the specified limit for a segment, a type 5 exception will be produced. This mechanism prevents a program from accessing memory outside its defined segments.

Byte 5 of a descriptor, the access byte, contains information about the privilege level, access, and type of the segment. To give you an idea of the kind of information contained in the access byte of a descriptor, Figure 15-23b summarizes the meanings of the bits in the access bytes of code segment and data segment descriptors. Skim through the descriptions to get an overview. Note the P bit, which is used to indicate whether the segment is present in physical memory, the privilege-level bits, which specify the privilege level that a program must have to access the segment, and the A bit, which is set if the segment has been accessed. The operating system can periodically read and reset the A bit to determine how often the segment has been accessed. A segment which has not been recently used can be swapped out to disk when space for a new segment is needed.

When a program attempts to access a segment, the selector for the segment is loaded into the visible part of the segment register. To access a data segment, for

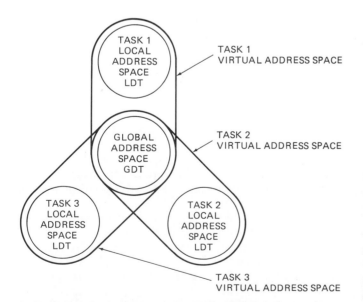

FIGURE 15-22 Diagram showing how tasks can be isolated from each other by having separate local descriptor tables but can share a common global descriptor table. (*Intel Corporation*)

example, the selector might be loaded into the visible part of the DS, ES, FS, or GS register. When the selector is loaded into the visible part of the segment register, the descriptor for the segment is automatically loaded into the hidden part of the segment register or segment descriptor cache, as it is commonly called. If the privilege level of the selector and the privilege level of the current code segment is not as high (or is higher than) the privilege level of the descriptor, an exception will be produced and the access will not be allowed. If the privilege level is high enough, the P bit in the descriptor will be checked to see if the segment is present in physical memory. If the segment is not present, a segment-not-present (type 11) exception will be generated and the exception handler will read the segment in from disk to physical memory. Once the segment is in physical memory, the address unit computes the physical addresses as needed to access the data words in the segment. As shown in Figure 15-21, the offset from the original address is added to the segment base address from a descriptor to form a linear address. For a 386 operating in segments-only mode, this linear address is the physical address that will be output on the address and BE lines to memory.

To complete the general picture of how a 386 manages virtual segments, we simply need to show you how it keeps track of where the descriptor tables are in memory. The 386 keeps the base addresses and limits for GDT and LDT descriptor tables currently being used in internal registers. The *global descriptor table register* (GDTR) shown in the middle of Figure 15-20 is used to hold the 32-bit base address and limit for the global descriptor table. This register is initialized with a load global descriptor table register (LGDT) instruction when the system is booted. The *local descriptor table register* (LDTR) shown in Figure 15-20 is used to hold the base address and limit of the local descriptor table for the task currently being executed. The LLDT instruction is used to load this register. The LLDT instruction can be executed only by programs executing at the highest privilege level. Therefore, unless a task is operating at the highest privilege level, it cannot intentionally or maliciously access the local descriptor table of another task. Task switching is usually handled by the operating system kernel, which operates at the highest-priority level.

386 SEGMENT PRIVILEGE LEVELS AND PROTECTION

When an attempt is made to access a segment by loading a segment selector into the visible part of a segment register, the 386 automatically makes several checks. First of all, it checks to see if the descriptor table indexed by the selector contains a valid descriptor for that selector. If the selector attempts to access a location outside the limit of the descriptor table or the location indexed by the selector in the descriptor table does not contain a valid descriptor, then an exception is produced.

The 386 also checks to see if the segment descriptor is of the right type to be loaded into the specified segment register cache. The descriptor for a read-only data seg-

ment, for example, cannot be loaded into the SS register, because a stack must be able to be written to. A selector for a code segment which has been designated "execute only" cannot be loaded into the DS register to allow reading the contents of the segment.

If all these protection conditions are met, the limit, base, and access rights byte of the segment descriptor are copied into the hidden part of the segment register. The 386 then checks the P bit of the access byte to see if the segment for that descriptor is present in physical memory. If it is not present, a type 11 exception is produced. The exception-handler procedure for this exception will swap the segment into physical memory, set the P bit in the descriptor, and restart the interrupted instruction.

After a segment selector and descriptor are loaded into a segment register, further checks are made each time a location in the actual segment is accessed. An attempt to write to a code segment or a read-only data segment, for example, will cause an exception. Also, the limit value contained in the segment descriptor is used to check that an address produced by program instructions does not fall outside the limit defined for the segment.

User tasks can be protected from each other in a 386 system by giving each task its own local descriptor table. The LDT register, which points to a user's local descriptor table, can only be changed with the LDTR instruction or by a task switch. The LDTR instruction can be executed only at the highest privilege level, which is usually reserved for the operating system. Likewise, a switch from one user task to another is done by the operating system at the highest privilege level, so user tasks operating at lower privilege levels cannot cause switches to other user tasks. Also, because of limit checking, a task cannot accidentally or intentionally access descriptors in another task's local descriptor table.

System software, such as the operating system kernel, is protected from corruption in several ways. One way we have already mentioned is that code segments can be made "execute only" so that they cannot be written to. The second and most important way that the operating system can be protected is with privilege levels. Figure 15-24 illustrates how a 386 protected-mode system can be set up with four privilege levels. As we mentioned before, the operating system kernel is assigned the highest privilege level, which is privilege level 0. System services such as BIOS procedures might be run at privilege level 1, and custom device drivers, etc. might operate at privilege level 2. Application programs and user tasks are usually operated at the privilege level 3, the lowest level.

The privilege level for a segment is represented by bits 5 and 6 of the access byte in the segment descriptor. (See Figure 15-23*b* for access byte format.) These 2 bits are referred to as the *descriptor privilege level* or DPL. This privilege level is established when the program is built.

The privilege level of an executing task is represented by the DPL bits in the access byte of the descriptor currently in the CS descriptor cache. This privilege level is referred to as the *current privilege level* or CPL.

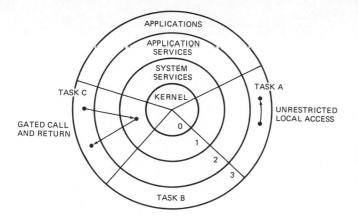

FIGURE 15-24 Diagram showing how a 386 system can be set up with four privilege levels. (*Intel Corporation*)

When a program needs to access a data segment, it does so by loading a segment selector into, for example, the visible part of the DS register. The privilege level encoded in the least significant bits of this selector is referred to as the *requesting privilege level* or RPL.

To successfully access a segment, both the RPL and the CPL must be a number less than or equal to the DPL of the segment. In other words, the privilege level of the currently executing task and the privilege level of the requesting selector must both be greater than or the same as the privilege level of the desired segment in order for access to be granted. If these conditions are not met, then an exception will be generated. The point here is that normally a task cannot directly access a segment which has a higher DPL.

CALL GATES

The question that might come to mind at this point is, If a task cannot access a segment with a more privileged DPL, how can user programs access the operating system kernel, BIOS, or utility procedures in segments which have more privileged DPLs? The answer to this is that a procedure located in a segment which has a higher privilege level can be called indirectly through a special structure called a *gate*. There are four types of gates: call, trap, interrupt, and task. For now, we will just describe how a call gate operates.

A gate is simply a special type of descriptor. Gate descriptors are put in the GDT or in an LDT, just as segment and other descriptors are. When a program does a call to a procedure in another segment, the selector for that segment's call gate is loaded into the CS register, and the call gate descriptor is loaded into the hidden part of the CS register. The call gate descriptor contains a selector which points to the descriptor for the segment where the procedure is actually located. The call gate descriptor also contains the offset of the called procedure in its segment.

If the call is determined to be valid, then the selector from the call gate and the corresponding segment descriptor will be loaded into the CS register. The processor then uses the base address from the segment descriptor

and the offset value from the call gate descriptor to compute the physical address of the called procedure. Therefore, the call is done indirectly, through the call gate descriptor, rather than directly through a segment descriptor.

This indirect access has two major advantages. First, this approach permits another level of privilege checking before access to the procedure in the higher-privileged segment is allowed. The privilege level of the calling program is compared with the privilege level specified in the call gate. If the privilege level of the calling program is lower than the privilege level specified in the call gate, the access will not be allowed. If, for example, the DPL in the call gate descriptor is 2, a level 2 program can use the call gate to call a privilege level 1 procedure, but a level 3 program cannot.

Another advantage of the indirect call gate approach is that user programs cannot accidentally enter higher-privileged segments at just any old point. If they are going to enter at all, they must enter at the specific offsets contained in the call gate descriptors. This is similar to the type of protection provided by using software interrupts to call BIOS and DOS functions instead of calling them directly.

I/O PRIVILEGE LEVELS

When a 386 is operating in protected mode, the 386 has two mechanisms for protecting I/O ports. The first mechanism involves the I/O privilege-level bits in the 386 EFLAGS register shown in Figure 15-20. Only the operating system or a procedure operating at a privilege level 0 can set these IOPL bits. In order to execute the IN, INS, OUT, OUTS, CLI, and STI instructions, the CPL of a procedure or task must be the same or a lower number than IOPL represented by these bits. If a procedure does not meet the IOPL test, a privilege-level exception will be generated.

The second mechanism for protecting ports from unauthorized access is an optional I/O permission bit map which allows ports to be associated only with specific tasks. If this feature is used, a map is set up for each task. Each bit in the map represents a byte-wide port address, so 16-bit ports use 2 bits each and 32-bit ports use 4 bits each. A 0 in a map bit means the port is available to the task.

When a task attempts to access a port, the 386 first compares the CPL of the task with the IOPL. If the access passes the IOPL test and an I/O bit map is in force, the 386 will then check the map bits corresponding to the addressed port. If the map has a 0 in the bit(s) for that port, access will be granted. If not, an exception will be generated. Incidentally, when a 386 is operating in real address mode, none of the port protection mechanisms are in effect.

INTERRUPT AND EXCEPTION HANDLING

For operation in protected mode, gate descriptors for the interrupt and exception procedures are kept in a special descriptor table called the interrupt descriptor table or IDT. This table can be located anywhere in memory. During initialization the base address and limit for the interrupt descriptor table are loaded into the *interrupt descriptor table register* (IDT) shown in Figure 15-20 with an LIDT instruction.

When an interrupt or exception occurs, its type is multiplied by 8 and added to the IDT base address in the IDT register. The result is a pointer to a gate descriptor in the interrupt descriptor table. The gate here can be an interrupt gate, a trap gate, or a task gate.

An interrupt gate, for example, contains a selector for the segment where the interrupt procedure is located, not the base address of the segment. The reason for this is so that the privilege level can be checked before access to the interrupt procedure is granted. If the CPL is high enough, then the selector from the gate will be loaded into the CS register and used to access the descriptor for the segment containing the interrupt procedure. The segment descriptor can be in the LDT or GDT. The 32-bit offset from the gate will be added to the base address from the descriptor to produce the linear address for the actual interrupt procedure. This is basically the same mechanism we described previously for the operation of a call gate, except that at the end of the procedure an IRET instruction is used instead of an RET. Incidentally, an interrupt procedure that needs to be accessible from any privilege level is put in a code segment that is made "conforming" by setting bit 2 in the access byte of its descriptor.

TASK SWITCHING

In a multiuser operating system each user's program can be set up as a separate task. When a user's time slice is up, the operating system switches execution from the current user's task to the next user's task. A similar process takes place in a single-user system which is operating in a multitasking mode. As we pointed out earlier, one of the main concerns in a multitasking system is saving the state or context of a task so that it will continue execution properly when it gets another time slice.

Each task in a 386 protected-mode system is assigned a *task state segment* or TSS. Figure 15-25 shows the format for a 386 TSS. As you can see, the TSS holds copies of all registers and flags, the selector for the task's LDT, and a link to the task state segment of the previously executing task. Descriptors for the task state segments are kept in the global descriptor table, where they can be accessed by the operating system during a task switch. The *task register* (TR) in the 386 holds the selector and the descriptor for the task state segment of the currently executing task. The *load task register* (LTR) instruction can be used to load the task register with the selector and segment descriptor for a specific task, but during a task switch the task register is automatically loaded with the selector and descriptor for the new task.

A task switch may be done in any one of four ways:

1. A long jump or call instruction contains a selector which points at a task state segment descriptor. The call instruction is used if a return to the previously executing task is desired. A jump instruction is used if a return to the previously executing task is not

31	15	0		
0000000000000000	LINK	0		
ESP0		4		STACKS
0000000000000000	SS0	8		FOR
ESP1		C		CPL
0000000000000000	SS1	10		0, 1, 2
ESP2		14		
0000000000000000	SS2	18		
CR3		1C		
EIP		20		
EFLAGS		24		
EAX		28		
ECX		2C		
EDX		30		
EBX		34		
ESP		38		
EBP		3C		CURRENT
ESI		40		TASK
ED1		44		STATE
0000000000000000	ES	48		
0000000000000000	CS	4C		
0000000000000000	SS	50		
0000000000000000	DS	54		
0000000000000000	FS	58		
0000000000000000	GS	5C		
0000000000000000	LDT	60		
AVAILABLE	T	64		
AVAILABLE TO USER		68		

TSS LIMIT

FIGURE 15-25   386 task state segment format. (*Courtesy Intel Corporation*)

desired. This is the simplest method and can be easily implemented by the operating system kernel at the end of a time slice.

2. The selector in a long jump or call instruction points to a task gate. In this case the selector for the destination TSS is in the task gate. The indirect mechanism here is similar to that we described above for call gates and has the same advantages regarding privilege levels and protection.

3. An interrupt occurs, and the interrupt selector points to a task gate in the interrupt descriptor table. The task gate contains the selector for the new task state segment. If the access passes all the privilege level tests, the selector and descriptor for the interrupt task will be loaded into the task register. The nested task (NT) bit in the EFLAGS register will be set.

4. An IRET instruction is executed with the NT bit in the EFLAGS register set. Complex interrupt procedures are often written and managed as separate tasks. The IRET instruction uses the back link selector in the task state segment to return execution to the interrupted task. This is similar to the way the IRET instruction works in real-mode operation.

We don't have space or inclination to explain the details of all the possible task switch scenarios, but we will make a few comments about the CALL/JMP method.

When a far CALL or JMP is executed to switch tasks, the privilege levels are first checked. As with any far call or far jump instruction, the RPL of the CALL selector and the CPL of the executing program must both be less than or equal to the DPL of the desired segment, or an exception will be produced.

Assuming proper privilege levels, the 386 will check if the task state segment for the new task is present in physical memory and generate a not-present exception if it is not. If necessary, the exception handler will load the TSS for the new task.

The 386 then copies all the register values for the current task to its task state segment. The value copied for the EIP is the offset of the next instruction after the one that caused the task switch.

At this point the old TSS is no longer needed, so the 386 loads the task register with the selector and the descriptor for the TSS of the new task. The 386 then automatically copies all the values for the new task from its TSS to the 386 registers. Execution then continues using the segment and offset values copied from the TSS.

In a multiuser/multitasking system, the operating system might use a JMP instruction to switch from the operating system task to a user task. A clock tick will interrupt the processor at the end of the time slice. If the interrupt descriptor table contains a task gate which points to the operating system task, then the state of the current task will be saved in its TSS, and execution will switch to the operating system task. The operating system can use another JMP instruction to switch to the next user's task.

PAGING MODE

The protected-mode segmentation and virtual memory scheme we described for the 386 in the preceding section is essentially the same as that for the 80286. The main difference is that 386 segments can be as large as 4 Gbytes, instead of only 64 Kbytes. The designers of the 386 realized that the time required to swap very large segments in and out of physical memory would be too long, so they added an optional paging mechanism to the design of the 386. The paging mechanism allows segments to be divided into 4-Kbyte pages for faster swapping.

The 386 is switched into paging mode by setting the MSB of the CR0 register with a simple MOV CR0, EAX-type instruction. In this mode the paging unit in the 386 uses the linear address, computed by the segmentation unit as described above, to produce the physical address. Figure 15-26 shows how this paging scheme works. To help fix it in your mind, we will first explain the paging scheme from the bottom up and then from the top down.

The Intel data sheets refer to each 4-Kbyte page in physical memory as a *page frame*. The least significant 12 bits of the linear address from the segmentation unit represent the offset of the desired data word within a 4-Kbyte page frame. The 32-bit base addresses and some other information for up to 1024 page frames are kept in a *page table* in memory. For future reference Figure 15-27a shows the details of the 4-byte entry placed in a

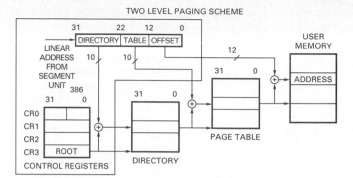

FIGURE 15-26 Diagram showing how a 386 computes physical addresses when paging mode is enabled.

page table for each page frame. The 10 address bits, A12–A21, from the linear address are used to select the desired entry in one of the page tables.

A system can contain up to 1024 page tables. The 32-bit base addresses and some other information for the page tables are kept in another table called the *page directory*. The format for the 4-byte entries in the page directory is the same as the format shown for a page table entry in Figure 15-27a. The 10 address bits, A22–A31, are used to select the desired entry in the page directory. The 32-bit base address for the page directory is kept in control register 3 (CR3) in the 386.

Looking at this from the top down then, CR3 points to the base of the page directory and linear address bits A22–A31 point to one of 1024 possible entries in the page directory. The selected entry in the page directory points to the base address of one of up to 1024 page tables, and linear address bits A12–A21 point to one of the entries in the selected page table. The selected entry in the page table contains the 32-bit base address of the desired 4-Kbyte page frame. Linear address bits A0–A11 are used to access the desired code or data word in the selected page frame. These bits are added to the base address from the page table entry to produce the physical

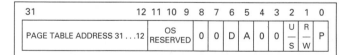

31		12	11 10 9	8	7	6	5	4	3	2	1	0
PAGE TABLE ADDRESS 31 . . .12			OS RESERVED	0	0	D	A	0	0	U–S	R–W	P

(a)

U/S	R/W	PERMITTED LEVEL 3	PERMITTED ACCESS LEVELS 0, 1, OR 2
0	0	NONE	READ/WRITE
0	1	NONE	READ/WRITE
1	0	READ-ONLY	READ/WRITE
1	1	READ/WRITE	READ/WRITE

(b)

FIGURE 15-27 (a) Format for 386-page directory and page table entries. (b) Access rights produced by combinations of R/W and U/S bits in 386-page table entries.

address that will be output to memory. The maximum amount of memory represented by this structure is 1024 page tables × 1024 pages/page table × 4096 bytes/page, or about 4 Gbytes, the full 32-bit address space of the 386. A system can be set up with just one page directory, but a more common practice is to give each task its own page directory and, thereby, its own set of page tables. Later we show you how the 386 task switch mechanism makes provisions for easily switching page directories.

As we said before, the page directory is located in memory and the page tables are located in memory. To avoid having to read page directory entries and page table entries from memory tables during each memory access, the 386 maintains a special cache called a *translation lookaside buffer* or TLB. The TLB is a four-way set-associative cache which holds the page table entries for the 32 most recently used pages. (Refer to the discussion of caches in Chapter 11 if the term set-associative is a little rusty in your mind.) When the 386 generates a linear address, the upper 20 bits of that address are compared with the tags for the 32 entries in the TLB. If there is a match, the page table entry for the desired page is in the TLB. The base address from this entry is used to compute the physical address. If there is no match, the 386 reads the page table entry from memory and puts it in the TLB. If the P bit in the page table entry is a 1, indicating that the page is present in physical memory, then the physical address will be computed and the desired word in the page accessed. If the P bit in the page table entry is a 0, indicating that the page is not present in physical memory, the processor will generate a page fault exception (type 14). After the page fault exception handler swaps the page into physical memory, the paging unit will compute and output the physical address for the desired word.

When the 386 paging mode is enabled, the U/S and R/W bits in the page directory entries and the page table entries can be used in place of or in addition to the segmentation protection mechanisms. The U/S bit in a directory or page table entry is used to specify one of two privilege levels, user or supervisor. A 0 in the U/S bit specifies the user privilege level, which corresponds to segment privilege level 3, the lowest level. A 1 in the U/S bit specifies supervisor privilege level, which corresponds to segment privilege levels 0, 1, and 2.

The R/W bit in a page directory or page table entry can be used to establish read-write access rights for pages or page tables. Figure 15-27b shows the access rights produced by various combinations of U/S and R/W. Note that for these bits 11 represents the most privilege and 00 the least privilege. If the access rights specified in a page directory entry are different from the access rights specified in a page table entry, the least privileged of these determines the access rights.

SUMMARY OF MEMORY MODELS

The memory in a 386 or 486 system can be set up using the segments-only model, the segmented-paged model, the simple flat model, or the paged flat model.

We thoroughly described the segments-only model in a previous section. This is the only protected-mode memory model available on an 80286. Versions 1.1 and 1.2 of Microsoft's OS/2 protected-mode operating system were designed to run on an 80286 system, so they use this model.

As we explained before, 386 segments can be too large to be conveniently swapped in and out of memory, so the 386 allows a paging mechanism to be switched in after the segmentation unit. The paging unit divides segments into 4-Kbyte pages for swapping in and out of physical memory. This segmented-paged model allows a programmer to think in terms of logical segments and the virtual memory hardware to think in terms of easily moved pages. However, one problem with this combined approach is that the amount of time required to manage all the descriptor tables, segments, page tables, and pages in a complex system becomes too large. A second problem is that developing the software to manage all this is a complex task. Also, the amount of memory used by all the tables can become excessively large. For these and other reasons, Microsoft's OS/2 for the 386, Novell's Netware 386, and many other programs for 386 and 486 systems use the flat memory model, which effectively removes segmentation.

The 386 does not have a way to turn off segmentation, but you can effectively eliminate segmentation by initializing all the segment registers with the same base address and initializing the segment limits for 4 Gbytes. Each segment then corresponds to the 4-Gbyte physical address space of the 386. The 32-bit offset or effective address part of each memory address is large enough to access any location in this 4-Gbyte space. The different parts of programs are simply located at different offsets in the address space.

This memory mode is referred to as the *simple flat system model* and is useful for dedicated control applications that need the fastest possible task switching and don't need all the segment-based protection features. The SDK-386 board we discussed earlier uses the simple flat model, and as we show later, this makes program development for it quite easy. Also, the flat system model makes it easy to transport software written for nonsegmented devices such as those in the Motorola 68000 family devices to a 386.

Paged flat model systems enable the 386 paging mechanism to provide virtual memory-management and protection features. The present (P) bit in a page directory entry indicates whether the requested page table is present in memory and the P bit in the page table entry indicates whether the requested page is present in memory. The accessed (A) bit in a page table entry indicates whether the page has been accessed. The operating system can periodically check and reset this bit to determine how often the page is being used. If the page has not been used lately, it can be replaced when the operating system needs space for a new page. The dirty (D) bit in a page table entry will be set if data has been written to the page. In this case the operating system must write the modified page out to disk before swapping a new page into its space. As we discussed earlier, the user/supervisor (U/S) bit in the page directory entries and the page table entries provide two privilege levels. The read/write (R/W) bit in a page table entry allows a page to be marked as read only or read/write. The I/O permission bit map which we mentioned earlier can provide protection for I/O ports.

The point of all this is that the paged flat memory model provides fast virtual memory capability and a degree of protection adequate for most applications.

386 Virtual 8086-Mode Operation

As we pointed out in an earlier discussion, it is difficult to switch a 286 processor back and forth between real and protected mode. This limitation makes a 286 hard to use for a multitasking system, which must run a mixture of tasks that use segment-offset addressing and protected-mode tasks that use descriptors. The 386 virtual 8086 mode solves this problem. A 386 operating in protected mode can easily switch to virtual 8086 mode to execute a time slice of an 8086-type program and then easily switch back to protected mode to execute a time slice of a protected-mode task. This means that some users in a multiuser system can be running programs under protected mode UNIX V and other users can be running real-mode DOS programs.

When a 386 operating in protected mode does a task switch, it examines the VM bit in the EFLAGS register. If this bit is set, the 386 will enter virtual 8086 mode to execute the new task. If the VM bit is not set, the 386 will execute the new task as a normal protected mode task.

In virtual 8086 mode the 386 computes physical addresses using the segment-offset mechanism used by an 8086. Therefore, the address range of a virtual 8086 mode task is 1 Mbyte. For a single virtual 8086 task this address range is in the lowest 1 Mbyte in the processor address space. If a system needs to run several different 8086 type tasks, then the 386 is operated in paging mode so that each 8086 task can be given a different page table and a different set of pages in physical memory. A side benefit of using the paging mode is that the U/S and R/W bits in the page directory entries and the page table entries provide protection that is normally not available in real mode.

In order to run virtual 8086 mode tasks, the operating system must have a section of privilege level 0 code called a *virtual machine monitor*. The main purpose of this monitor is to intercept interrupts, exceptions, and INT n instructions which occur during the execution of the 8086 task. Figure 15-28 shows how this works for an INT n instruction.

As you well know from previous chapters, most 8086 system programs use INT n software interrupts to access BIOS and DOS I/O procedures. In virtual 8086 mode the INT n instruction can be executed only at privilege level 0, the highest privilege level. Since an 8086 task always operates at level 3, the lowest privilege level, the 386 will generate an exception whenever the 8086 program executes an INT n instruction. The handler for this exception is in the virtual machine monitor, so the monitor effectively takes over execution at this point.

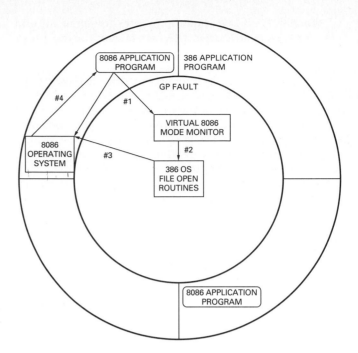

8086 APPLICATION MAKES "OPEN FILE CALL" → CAUSES GENERAL PROTECTION FAULT (ARROW #1)
VIRTUAL 8086 MONITOR INTERCEPTS CALL. CALLS 386 OS (ARROW #2)
386 OS OPENS FILE RETURNS CONTROL TO 8086 OS (ARROW #3)
8086 OS RETURNS CONTROL TO APPLICATION. (ARROW #4)
TRANSPARENT TO APPLICATION

FIGURE 15-28   Operation of virtual machine monitor when 8086 virtual mode application program makes DOS call to open a file.   (*Courtesy Intel Corporation*)

During the task switch to the monitor, the state of the 8086 task is saved in its TSS. Also the VM bit in the EFLAGS register is reset, so the monitor can operate in normal protected mode.

If the call was to a function such as the DOS "open file" command, the monitor will call the equivalent procedure in the 386 protected-mode operating system to open the file. This mechanism maintains all the protection built into the main 386 operating system. When the file has been opened, execution is returned to the DOS operating system. The IRET instruction used to return to the virtual 8086 DOS program restores the 8086 task state. As part of this, the VM bit in the EFLAGS register is restored to a 1 so that the 8086 program restarts in the virtual 8086 mode. For other DOS function calls which do not involve I/O, the monitor may return execution to DOS to perform the function. After the function is completed, DOS returns execution to the 8086 program.

In virtual 8086 mode interrupts are also intercepted by the monitor. In most cases the monitor will transfer execution to the 386 protected mode operating system to service the interrupt. To service interrupts the 386 operating system uses the interrupt descriptor table and gate scheme we described previously, so protection is maintained. If protection is not an issue, the monitor may return execution to DOS or to the 8086 program to service the interrupt.

When a clock tick interrupt occurs to signal the end of a time slice, execution will switch from the 8086 task to the monitor task. The monitor task through an IDT gate will switch to the 386 operating system scheduler. The scheduler will then switch to the next user task. The VM bit in the EFLAGS register image of the TSS for the new task will determine whether the task is executed in virtual 8086 mode or 386 protected mode. The point here is that the 386 provides a relatively simple mechanism to alternate between 8086-type programs and 386 protected-mode programs.

Now, before we dig into 386 instruction set enhancements and programming, let's summarize what we have found out about the 386 so far.

Summary of 386 Hardware and Operating Modes

The 386 is a 32-bit processor which is upward compatible from the 8086, 80186, and 80286. In real address mode the 386 functions as a fast 8086 and uses the segment-offset address mechanism to address 1 Mbyte of memory.

In its protected mode a 386 can address 4 Gbytes of physical memory and 64 Terabytes of virtual memory. Each protected-mode address consists of a 16-bit selector and a 32-bit offset or effective address. The 32-bit offset component means that segments can be as large as 4 Gbytes. An optional paging mechanism allows segments to be broken into 4 Kbytes pages for faster swapping in and out of memory. The 386 uses the 16-bit selector to access the descriptor for the segment in the global descriptor table or in a local descriptor table. The segment base address from the descriptor is added to the 32-bit offset to produce the linear address. In segments-only mode, the linear address is the physical address. If paging is enabled, the paging unit uses the linear address, a page directory, and a page table to produce the physical address.

The 386 contains several mechanisms to protect OS code from user tasks and user tasks from each other. One of these mechanisms is privilege levels. The operating system code is given a privilege level of 0, the highest privilege level, and user code is given a lower privilege level. Any direct attempt by a program to access a code or a data segment with a higher privilege level will generate an exception. Programs can, however, access procedures at a higher privilege level through an indirect method called a gate. The gate allows a second check on the privilege level of the access and makes sure the access is to the correct location in the procedure. A second protection mechanism is bounds checking. Any attempt to access a location outside the limit specified for a segment in its descriptor will generate an exception.

For a 386 operating in protected mode, interrupts are vectored through gates in the interrupt descriptor table. This indirect approach allows interrupt procedures to be protected.

In a 386 system using the flat memory model, the entire physical memory is treated as a single large segment. All segments are given the same base address and limit, so they share this segment. The 32-bit offset contained in every memory address is large enough to access any location in the 4-Gbyte physical address space of the 386. In a larger system using the flat memory model, paging is enabled so that virtual memory and protection can be implemented.

When the 386 does a protected-mode task switch, it automatically copies the state of the current task to a task state segment created for that task and loads the state of the new task from its TSS. If the 386 finds the VM bit of the EFLAGS register set when it does a task switch, the 386 goes to virtual 8086 mode. In this mode the 386 can directly execute 8086 type programs which use segment-offset addressing. The interrupt at the end of a time slice will cause the 386 to switch back to full protected mode so the operating system can switch to the next task using protected-mode features.

386 Instruction Set Additions and Enhancements

A SECOND LOOK AT THE 386 REGISTER SET

In Figure 15-20 we showed you that the 386 register set is a superset of the 8086 and 80286 register sets. The 386 register-type instructions allow you to specify 8-bit registers and 16-bit registers as you do in 8086 instructions or to specify 32-bit registers. In 386 instructions you can specify, for example, AH, AL, AX or EAX as an operand. The instruction MOV EAX,EBX, for example, will copy the 32-bit number in the extended BX register to the extended AX register. You cannot copy an 8-bit part of a register to a 32-bit register with an instruction such as MOV EBX,AL. Also, you cannot directly access just the upper 16 bits of a 32-bit register. If you need to copy just the upper 16 bits of, for example, the EAX register into the BX register, you can first rotate the upper 16 bits of EAX into the lower 16 bits with the ROR EAX,16 instruction and then use MOV BX,AX. If you need to put EAX back in its initial condition, you just do another ROR EAX,16 instruction. The 386 contains a "barrelshifter," which can shift an operand any number of bits in one clock pulse, so these rotates do not appreciably slow the overall operation. Incidentally, even a 386 real-mode program which uses 16-bit segments can use the 32-bit extended registers for data operations.

For real-mode programs only the lower 16 bits of the extended instruction pointer (EIP) are used, because only 16 bits are needed to access any location in a 64-Kbyte real-mode segment. In a protected-mode program a code segment can be specified as 16-bit or 32-bit. To specify a code segment as 16-bit, you simply write the term USE16 after SEGMENT in the segment declaration line. The line CODE SEGMENT USE16, for example, declares a 16-bit segment named CODE. A segment is specified as 32-bit by putting the term USE32 after SEGMENT in the segment declaration. If the segment is specified as a USE16 segment, then the maximum segment limit is 64 Kbytes, and only the lower 16 bits of EIP will be used to access instruction bytes. If the segment is specified as USE32, then the maximum segment limit is 4 Gbytes, and all 32 bits of EIP are used to hold the offset of an instruction byte.

The 386 contains two new segment registers, FS and GS, which can be used as additional data segments. None of the 386 instructions use these segments as their default segment, so you usually have to use a segment override prefix on an instruction which accesses a data item in one of these segments. We will show you how to do this in a later program example.

NEW ADDRESSING MODES AND SCALING

When an 8086 executes the instruction MOV AX,PATIENT_RECORD [BX] [DI], it computes the effective address of the memory operand by adding a displacement represented by the name PATIENT_RECORD, an offset contained in the BX register, and an index value contained in the DI register. For an 8086 only BX and BP can be used as base registers in this way, and only SI and DI can be used as index registers. A 386 can use any of the eight 32-bit, general-purpose registers as a base register, and it can use any of the 32-bit, general-purpose registers except ESP as an index register. When a 386 executes the instruction MOV BX, [EAX + EDX], for example, it will compute the effective address of the memory operand by adding the 32-bit number in EAX to the 32-bit number in EDX. Note that these new addressing modes work only with the 32-bit extended registers. You can't, for example, use just AX as a base pointer.

The 386 also has another powerful addressing feature called *index scaling*, which is useful for accessing successive elements in an array of words, double words, or quad words. Index scaling allows the value contained in an index register to be automatically multiplied by a specified scale factor of 2, 4, or 8 when an instruction executes. If a 386 executes the instruction MOV EAX, [EBX + EDI*4], for example, it will multiply the index value in EDI by a scale factor of 4 and add the result to the value from the EBX register to produce the effective address. The double word pointed to in DS by this effective address will be copied into the EAX register. If this instruction is part of a loop which processes an array of double words, then all that you have to do to get ready for the next trip around the loop is to increment the index value in EDI. When the MOV instruction is executed again, the new index value will automatically be multiplied by the scale factor in computing the effective address.

Even though real-mode data segments can be only 64 Kbytes long, you can still use index scaling and these new 32-bit addressing as long as the effective address produced does not exceed 16 bits. In a later section we show you an example program which demonstrates how to do this.

NEW INSTRUCTIONS

The 386 instruction set includes all the 8086/80186/80286 instructions and extends these instructions to work with 32-bit data words and 32-bit offsets. The 386 also includes several new instructions. In this section we briefly explain the functions of these new instructions and give you an example of each. Then we make a few comments about 8086 instructions that have been enhanced in the 386.

Bit Scan and Test Instructions

BSF—Bit scan to the left until nonzero bit is found.

EXAMPLE:

BSF CX, DX   ; Scan DX to left until nonzero bit,
             ; leave bit number in CX
             ; Zero flag set if all DX = 0

BSR—Bit scan to the right until nonzero bit is found.

EXAMPLE:

BSR CX, DX   ; Scan DX to right until nonzero bit,
             ; leave bit number in CX
             ; Zero flag set if all DX = 0

BT—Bit test and put specified bit in carry flag.

EXAMPLE:

BT EBX, 4   ; Copy bit 4 of EBX to carry flag

BTC—Bit test and complement.

EXAMPLE:

BT EBX, 7   ; Copy complement of bit 7 to CF

BTR—Bit test and reset.

EXAMPLE:

BTR WORD PTR [BX], 3 ; Bit 3 of [BX] to CF
                        ; Reset bit 3 of [BX]

BTS—Bit test and set.

EXAMPLE:

MOV CL, 4
BTS EAX, CL   ; Copy bit 4 of EAX to CF
               ; Set bit 4 of EAX

Data-type conversions

CDQ—Convert signed double word in EAX to quadword in EDX:EAX.

CWDE—Converts signed word in AX to double word in extended EAX.

Segment load instructions

These instructions are similar to LDS and LES instructions described in Chapter 6.

LFS—Load FS segment register and specified base register with values from specified memory locations.

EXAMPLE:

LFS BX, DWORD PTR [DI]
        ; Load FS and BX with
        ; DWORD from memory at [BX]

EXAMPLE:

LFS EBX, FWORD PTR [DI]
        ; Load FS with 16 bit
        ; selector and EBX with 32-bit
        ; offset for memory at [DI]

LGS—Load GS segment register and specified register from specified memory locations.

LSS—Load SS segment register and specified register from specified memory locations.

Move and expand instructions

MOVSX—Move and sign extend to fill destination register.

EXAMPLE:

MOVSX CX, BL   ; Copy BL to CL, extend sign bit of
               ; BL through all of CH

MOVZX—Move and zero extend to fill destination register.

EXAMPLE:

MOVZX CX, BL   ; Copy BL to CL, fill CH with zeros

Set memory flag word instruction

SETxx—Set all bits in specified byte if condition xx is met. xx here can be any condition from conditional jump mnemonics.

EXAMPLE:

SETC TooBig   ; Set all bits in flag TooBig if
             ; Carry flag set

Shifts between words

SHLD—Shift specified number of bits left from one operand into another.

EXAMPLE:

SHLD EAX, EBX, 8 ; Shift upper 8 bits from EBX
                 ; into lower 8 bits of EAX
                 ; EBX unchanged

SHRD—Shift specified number of bits right from one operand into another.

EXAMPLE:

SHRD EAX, EBX, 8 ; Shift lower 8 bits from EBX
                 ; into upper 8 bits of EAX.
                 ; EBX unchanged

INSTRUCTION ENHANCEMENTS

Several of the 386 instructions have significant improvements over the 8086/80186/80286 versions. Here are a few notes about these improvements.

1. The 386 string instructions work with double-word operands as well as with word and byte operands. A "B" at the end of an instruction mnemonic specifies byte operands, a W specifies word operands, and a D specifies double-word operands. Examples are CMPSB, CMPSW, and CMPSD.

2. The destination for a 386 conditional jump can be anywhere in the segment containing the jump instruction. Conditional far jumps must still be done by changing the jump condition and using an unconditional far jump as we showed you for the 8086 in Chapter 4.

3. The LOOP instructions can use the CX register or the ECX register as a counter. If you want CX to be used, write the instructions as LOOPW, LOOPWE, and LOOPWNE. If you want the ECX register to be used as the counter, write the instructions as LOOPD, LOOPDE, and LOOPDNE.

4. PUSHFD pushes the 32-bit EFLAGS register and POPFD restores it.

5. PUSHAD pushes the 8 general-purpose 32-bit registers on the stack, and POPAD restores these registers except for the value of ESP which is ignored.

6. IRETD pops the double word EIP, a double word for CS, and the EFLAGS register off the stack. The high word of the value popped for CS is discarded.

7. The IMUL instruction can now perform signed multiplication on any general-purpose register and a memory location or another general-purpose register.

8. In addition to the protected-mode instructions inherited from the 80286, the 386 instructions used to move data to/from the control registers (CR0–CR3), the debug registers (DR0–DR7), and the test registers (TR0–TR7) can be executed only in protected mode at privilege level 0. These instructions are simple MOV register, register instructions.

386 Programming

INTRODUCTION

The tools and techniques used to write a program for a 386 or a 486 depend very much on whether it is a system program or an application program and whether it utilizes protected mode or not. The tools and techniques are also determined by whether the program is going to execute in a graphical user-interface environment such as Microsoft's Windows 3.0 or OS/2. In this section we give you an introduction to writing 386 programs for five different programming environments.

386 PROGRAMS FOR MS DOS–BASED SYSTEMS

Current versions of DOS are designed to run on 8086/8088, real-mode 80286, or real-mode 386/486 systems. If you want a program to be able to run under DOS on any one of these systems, then you have to write it for the "weakest link" in the group, the 8086. The 8086 and C programming examples throughout this book were in fact compiled and run on a 386-based system. If you are writing a program that you are sure will only be run under DOS on a 386- or 486-based machine, you can write the program to take advantage of the 32-bit processing capability, addressing modes, and enhanced instructions of the 386. Assuming that you are using the MASM or TASM assembler, you tell the assembler to accept 386 instructions by putting the .386 directive at the top of your source program, as shown in Figure 15-29a.

If you are using the simplified segment directives, make sure to put the .386 directive after the .MODEL directive, as shown in Figure 15-29b. This order tells the assembler to create 16-bit segments which are compatible with real-mode operation. If you put the .386 directive before the .MODEL directive, the assembler will create 32-bit code and data segments which can be used only in protected mode.

Even though 386 real-mode programs are limited to 64-Kbyte segments and unless bank switching is implemented, to a 640-Kbyte address space, you can still use the 32-bit extended registers, addressing modes, and new instructions of the 386. The simple example program in Figure 15-29a shows some of the possibilities. The main points we included in this example are: how to declare segments; how to access data in the new segments, FS and GS; and how to use the 32-bit addressing modes and scaling.

First note that the code and data segments are specified as 16-bit with USE16 directives. The USE16 on the data segment directive specifies a maximum segment length of 64 Kbytes as required for real-mode operation. The USE16 on the CODE SEGMENT line tells the assembler to compute all memory addresses using the segment base and 16-bit offset method.

Next in the example note that we assume and initialize the FS register, just as we did the DS, ES, and SS registers in earlier program examples. The first action of the program then shows you how to read a double word from this segment to the 32-bit EAX register. A segment override prefix must always be used for references to the FS or GS segment, because there is no default as there is with DS. The ROR EAX,16 instruction rotates the 32-bit EAX register around 16 bits to the right. As we said earlier, if execution is limited to a 386 system, the 32-bit registers can be used for data operations, even in real mode.

The next section of the example in Figure 15-29a shows how the 32-bit addressing modes can be used to help process an array of words. The instruction MOV

```
; Some 386 addressing modes and instructions

      .386
DATA  SEGMENT USE16
      BIGVAL  DD 12345678H
      TABLE   DW 4235H, 7590H, 4968H, 3817H
DATA  ENDS

CODE  SEGMENT USE16
      ASSUME CS:CODE; FS:DATA

START: MOV  AX, DATA              ; Initialize FS
       MOV  FS, AX                ;   register
;Read 32-bit operand from memory
       MOV  EAX,FS:BIGVAL         ; Get double word
       ROR  EAX, 16               ; Swap word order
       MOV  FS: BIGVAL, EAX       ; Put back result
;Process table
       MOV  CX, 04
       MOV  EDI, 0
NEXT:  MOV  DX,FS:[TABLE+EDI*2]   ; Word from array to DX
                                  ; Scan from left for
       BSF  AX, DX                ; first zero bit
       JNZ  MORE                  ; Skip if all zeros
       MOV  FS:[TABLE+EDI*2],AX   ; Store number of
                                  ;   first zero bit
MORE:  INC  EDI                   ; Increment index
       LOOP NEXT
       MOV  AX, 4C00H             ; Return to DOS
       INT  21H
CODE  ENDS
      END START
```

(a)

```
;Simplified segment directives example
; for 16-bit segments

DOSSEG
 .MODEL large
 .386
 .DATA

 TABLE DW 4235H, 7590H, 4968H, 3817H

 .CODE
 START: MOV  AX, DATA         ; Initialize FS register
        MOV  FS, AX
```

(b)

FIGURE 15-29 (a) 386 real-mode program using traditional segment directives. (b) Simplified segment directives for generating 16-bit 386 segments.

DX,FS:[TABLE + EDI*2] copies a word from the array to DX. The effective address for this instruction is computed by multiplying the contents of EDI by 2 and adding the result to the displacement represented by the name TABLE. The first time through the loop EDI contains 0, so the effective address is just TABLE, the offset of the first word in the array. Before the loop executes again EDI is incremented to 1. During the next execution of the MOV DX,FS: [TABLE + EDI*2] instruction the effective address will be TABLE + 2, the offset of the second word in the array. An important point here is that in real-mode operation an exception will be generated if the effective address produced by an instruction is greater than 64 Kbytes.

Within the loop we use one of the new 386-bit instructions to process the word read in from memory. The BSF AX, DX instruction will scan the DX register starting from the left until it finds a nonzero bit. The number of the first nonzero bit will be loaded into AX. If all bits in DX are zeros, the zero flag will be cleared. In this case we just leave the word of all zeros in the array and process the next word. If the word is not all zeros, we write the number of the first nonzero bit in the memory word and then process the next word.

Finally, in the example program we use a familiar DOS function call to return execution to DOS. This is not a particularly significant program, but it does show you a little of what you can do with the added features of the 386 if you are willing to sacrifice 8086 downward capability.

386 PROGRAMS FOR THE SDK-386

As we told you earlier, you can download the binary programs from a PC- or PS/2-type computer to an URDA SDK-386 board through an RS-232C link. The SDK-386 board operates in protected mode using the simple flat memory model, so you can use it to experiment with a simple, dedicated 386 system such as those in Chapter 10.

During initialization the monitor program sets up a global descriptor table, a local descriptor table, and an interrupt descriptor table. The GDT, LDT, and IDT registers in the 386 are loaded with the base addresses and limits for these tables. The monitor also sets up a system task state segment and a user task state segment. As part of the initialization the selector for the user task state segment is loaded into the backlink field of the system TSS. When a user presses the RUN or the STEP key, an IRET instruction causes a task switch to the user task. This executes the user program. If the user presses the BREAK key, an NMI interrupt will be generated. This causes a task switch to the system task so that registers, memory locations, etc. can be examined. The BRPT key can be used to load up to four breakpoint addresses in the 386 debug registers. As we explained earlier, the 386 checks each memory address and will break if it finds any of the specified breakpoint addresses.

You have considerable flexibility in how you write a program for the SDK-386 board. The simplest approach is to use a format slightly modified from that in Figure 15-29a. The flat model memory mode used by this board means that all segments start from absolute address 00000000H, and all the segment registers contain the same base address. System and user programs use 32-bit offsets to access code and data words in this shared segment. The contents of the segment registers then do not have to be changed during a switch from the system task to the user task. This has important implications for how you write a program to run on the board.

The D bit in the code segment descriptor determines whether the 386 uses 16-bit effective addresses or 32-bit effective addresses. If the D bit is a 0, then 16-bit effective addresses are produced and if D = 1, 32-bit addresses are produced. The monitor program in the board sets the D bit of the code segment descriptor to a 1, so this means that 32-bit addressing is assumed. To make your program compatible, you make the code segment a USE32 type so that the assembler will produce 32-bit offsets. Your data segments should also be made USE32 type to be compatible with the segments set up by the monitor. Incidentally, you don't have to initialize data segments as part of your program, because the monitor loads the selectors and descriptors for these, and they are not changed when execution switches to the user task.

The user area of RAM on the board begins at 300H, so you should include an ORG 300H directive before the code segment in your program. The program will then be assembled to run in this address space in RAM. After the program is assembled and linked, it can be downloaded to the board and run.

For a more complex program the board allows you to use the segment-based protection features of the 386. The global descriptor table contains four user-definable descriptors and the local descriptor table contains six user-definable descriptors. The interrupt descriptor table also contains a user-definable descriptor for the USER INTERRUPT key on the board and another user-definable descriptor. We don't have a space here to show you how, but you can use these descriptors to define custom segments for your programs.

WRITING A 386 PROTECTED-MODE OPERATING SYSTEM

In the unlikely case that you should have to write a 386 protected-mode operating system or monitor program, you should be aware of Intel's 386 Relocation, Linkage, and Library (RLL) tools which run on IBM PC/AT or newer microcomputers. This tool set contains a *binder*, which is a high-powered linker that can combine object modules compiled from different languages into tasks, combine segments, resolve PUBLIC/EXTERNAL references, assign virtual addresses, and generate a file which can be loaded into RAM for debugging. The tool set also contains utilities for working with library functions. Another important part of the tool set is the *builder*, which allows a programmer to assign physical addresses to segments; set segment access rights and limits; create gates; create global, local, and interrupt descriptor tables; create task state segments; and set up the boot process.

Incidentally, the Intel 80386 System Software Writer's Guide shows a simple example of a flat system and a simple example of a segmented system.

MICROSOFT'S OS/2 2.0 OPERATING SYSTEM

As we told you earlier, MS DOS is for the most part a single-user, single-task operating system and does not take advantage of the virtual memory and multitasking capabilities of the 286/386/486 processors. The probable successor to DOS is Microsoft's OS/2, which is a single-user, multitasking operating system. Microsoft's OS/2 version 1.0 was an early attempt at a multitasking operating system for the 80286 processor. OS/2 1.0 and the later versions of OS/2 for the 80286 can multitask several protected mode tasks and one real mode task. The real-mode task is run in a "DOS compatibility box." The reason that only one real mode task can run is the difficulty in switching an 80286 from protected mode to real mode and back. The user interface for OS/2 1.0 was a typed command line similar to DOS.

The next version of OS/2, OS/2 1.1 introduced a new graphical user interface (GUI) called the *Presentation Manager* or PM. PM is similar to the screen-based interface you may have seen on Apple Macintosh computers. In PM you execute commands by using a mouse to move a cursor to a desired command in a menu of commands or to an *icon* which represents the command. You then execute the command by clicking a key on the mouse. PM also allows you to have multiple "windows" open on the screen. You can "cut" something from one window and "paste" it into another window. The file manager in PM allows you to display a directory tree on the screen, select a file from the tree, and perform some action on the file by just moving cursor around on the screen and clicking the mouse key at the appropriate points.

OS/2 1.2 kept Presentation Manager and added the High Performance File System (HPFS). Instead of the FAT used by the DOS file system, the HPFS uses a different system which allows much faster file access. Another obvious improvement in HPFS is that filenames can be longer than 8 characters. HPFS also sets up an "extended attribute" block for each file. The operating system or an application program can use this block to describe and control use of the file.

OS/2 version 2.0, designed to run only on 386 and 486 systems, uses the virtual 8086 mode of these processors to implement Multiple Virtual DOS Machines (MVDM) capability. In addition to the features of earlier versions, OS/2 2.0 can multitask any mixture of DOS programs, applications written for earlier versions of OS/2, and applications written specifically for version 2.0. OS/2 2.0 uses the flat paged memory model that we described earlier for the 386.

In the preceding chapters we showed you how to use DOS function calls to open files, read files, etc. in your programs. In OS/2 2.0 there are three different *application program interfaces* (APIs) or sets of functions which can be called to perform these functions. One is the real-mode DOS compatible API which is used by the programs operating in a DOS compatibility box. The functions in this API are called with software interrupts such as INT 21H. The second API contains the 16-bit functions that are compatible with OS/2 1.x application programs. To use one of these functions the required parameters are first pushed on the stack, and then the procedure is called by name. The third API contains the 32-bit functions used for OS/2 2.0 applications. The functions in this API are also called by name after pushing the required parameters on the stack. Unlike the 16-bit API calls, the parameters for these calls are pushed on the stack in the same order as parameters for C function calls are pushed. In fact, the 32-bit API

is in some ways like an extension of the C Run Time Library you met in Chapter 12. One major difference between the 32 bit API and the C RTL is in the way the functions are connected to the .exe program.

When a C program is linked, the object code files for library functions are linked with the object code for the compiled C program modules to make the .exe program. The OS/2 APIs are dynamic link libraries (DLLs). When a program containing an API call is linked, a reference to the function is put in the .exe file instead of the object code for the called function. When the program is loaded into memory to be run, the library containing the function is loaded into memory where the program can access it. This approach may seem strange at first, but it has several advantages. First, the .exe programs are much smaller, because they do not contain the large library functions. This means that the .exe files take less space on a hard disk. Also, the API functions are reentrant, so a library can be shared by multiple tasks on a multitasking system. This saves memory, because each task does not have to have a copy of the library in memory. Still another advantage of the DLL approach is that by updating the library you can update all programs that use the library, without having to relink each program.

You can write DOS type programs for an OS/2-based system using the programming tools we described in earlier chapters. For simple protected-mode programs you can use Microsoft's C 5.2 32-bit C compiler and the latest version of Microsoft's Macroassembler (MASM). To develop a 32-bit OS/2 application which utilizes PM, you use Microsoft's OS/2 2.0 Software Developer's Kit which contains all the needed tools.

MICROSOFT WINDOWS 3.0

Microsoft's Windows 3.0 is a relatively inexpensive bridge between the DOS world and the high-powered OS/2 2.0 operating system we discussed briefly in the preceding section. As the name implies, this program uses a graphical user interface (GUI) very similar to Presentation Manager. Windows 3.0 is essentially a very flexible DOS extender which can take advantage of the protected-mode features of the 80286, 386, and 486 processors. It can be operated in any one of three different modes, depending on the processor and memory available in the system. On an 8086/8088-based system, Windows 3.0 must be operated in its real mode. On an 80286-based system with at least 1 Mbyte of extended memory, Windows 3.0 can be run in standard mode, which takes advantage of the protected mode features of the 80286. In real mode and standard mode, only one DOS type task can be run at a time.

On a 386- or 486-based system with at least 2 Mbytes of extended memory, Windows 3.0 can be run in its 386 enhanced mode. In this mode, which is the one we are interested in here, it uses the 386's virtual 8086 mode to run multiple 8086 tasks, and it implements paged virtual memory so it can run programs that require more memory than is physically present in the system.

When you run Windows 3.0 the program manager window shown in Figure 15-30, page 568, appears on the screen. The icons along the bottom of this window

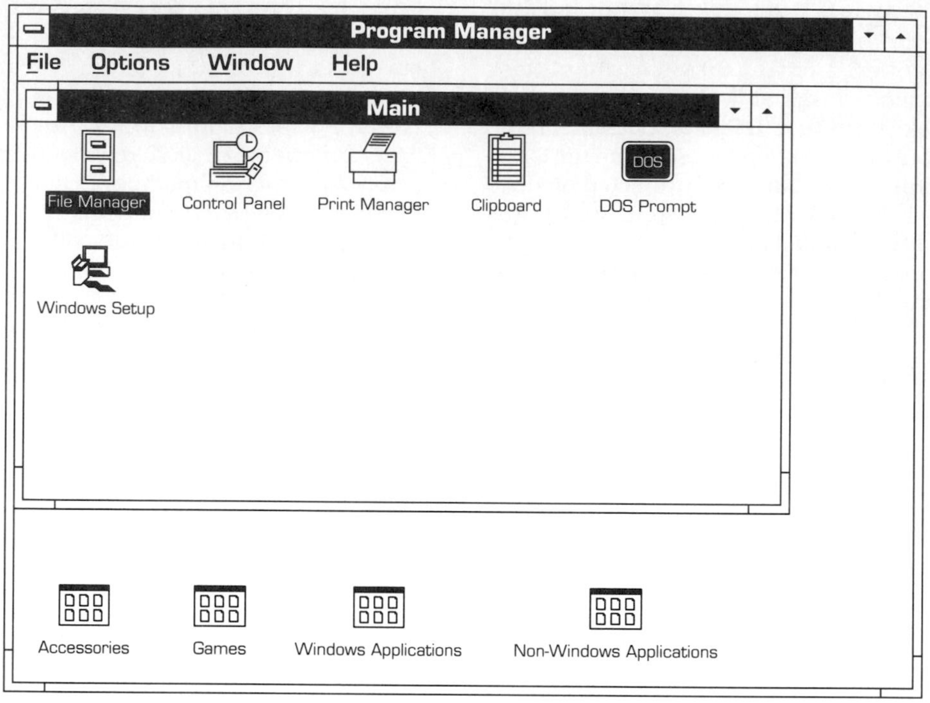

FIGURE 15-30   Microsoft Windows 3.0 Program Manager window display.

represent groups of programs you can execute. If you move the cursor to one of these icons and double-click the left mouse key, another window containing a menu of the programs in that group will appear. You can execute a program in the group by just double-clicking on the name of the program in the menu. If you want to start another program running at the same time, you can "minimize" the window for the running program to put that program in the background and then start another program running. The background program continues running after you start the new program in the foreground. Windows even allows you to specify the percentages of time you want the processor to spend on the background task and on the foreground task. Windows 3.0 keeps a task list of the currently running tasks. You can switch a task from background to foreground by bringing up the task list and clicking on the desired task.

One of the program icons in the program manager window is the file manager. When you double-click on this icon, it opens a file window and shows you a tree of the files and subdirectories in your current directory. In this window you can use the mouse to perform the usual file operations such as copy, delete, rename, etc. The point of all this is that instead of typing in commands, you can perform almost any operation by just moving the cursor to the appropriate location on the screen and clicking the mouse key. Windows 3.0 also has a very versatile on-screen help system which you can pop up as needed.

Windows 3.0 separates programs into two categories, windows applications and nonwindows applications. During setup Windows 3.0 scans your disk drive(s) and puts the programs it finds into the correct category.

Programs not specifically written for 3.0 will be classified as nonwindows applications. In the real and standard mode, nonwindows applications are run in full-screen mode similar to the way they would run in a pure DOS environment. Windows applications take advantage of the GUI. Among the windows application-type programs that come with Windows 3.0 are a word processor, notepad, paintbrush, calendar, clock, print spooler, and a card file.

To write a simple Windows 3.0 application program you can use the Asymetrix Corp *Toolbook* which comes with Windows 3.0. Toolbook includes some impressive demonstrations. To develop more complex Windows 3.0 applications, you need tools such as version 2.0 of Borland's C++ or the Microsoft Windows 3.0 Software Development Kit. The programming guide that comes with this tool set contains a sequence of templates that you can use to develop a custom application. We had hoped to rewrite the SDKCOM1 program from Chapter 14 as an example windows application program, but we ran out of space and time. Maybe we can include this in the next book.

THE INTEL 80486 MICROPROCESSOR

The 32-bit 486 is the next evolutionary step up from the 386. The basic processor unit used in the 486 is the same as that used in the 386, so all of the preceding discussion of the 386 applies to the 486. All we have to discuss here are the additions and enhancements that designers were able to add by increasing the number of transistors on the die from 300,000 to about 1,200,000.

As you can see in Figure 15-31, one of the most obvious features included in a 486 is a built-in math

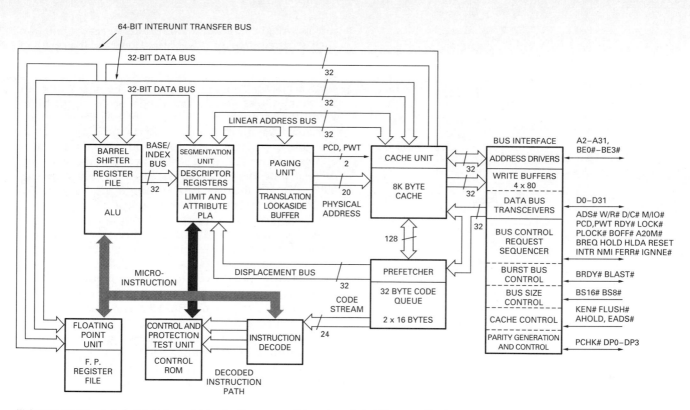

FIGURE 15-31   Intel 486 internal block diagram.   (*Courtesy Intel Corporation*)

coprocessor. This coprocessor is essentially the same as the 387 processor used with a 386, but being integrated on the chip allows it to execute math instructions about three times as fast as a 386/387 combination.

Another fairly obvious feature included in a 486 is an 8-Kbyte code and data cache. This four-way set-associative cache works in basically the same manner as the external caches we described in Chapter 11. One difference is that a "line" for this cache is 16 bytes instead of 4 bytes.

A less obvious 486 improvement is the five-stage instruction pipeline scheme that allows it to execute instructions much faster than a 386. This scheme, commonly used in RISC processors, allows several instructions to be "in the pipeline" at a time. The 486 will fetch several instructions ahead of time, and while it is executing one instruction, it will decode and as soon as possible, start the execution of the next instruction. The 486 may actually be executing parts of several instructions at the same time. For example, suppose the 486 is given the meaningless sequence of instructions:

MOV AX, MEMORY_LOCATION
ADD CX, BX
SHR AX, 1
MOV MEMORY_LOCATION, CX

A few clock cycles before it gets to the first of these instructions, the 486 will have prefetched all these simple instructions and started decoding them. As the MOV AX, MEMORY_LOCATION instruction executes, decoding of the ADD instruction will be completed. Since the ADD instruction does not uses the buses or the data

read in from memory by the MOV instruction, it can be executed before the MOV AX instruction is complete. Likewise, decoding of the SHR instruction will be completed while the ADD CX, BX instruction is executing, and on the next clock cycle the SHR instruction will be executed. During the clock cycle that the SHR instruction executes, the decoding of the MOV MEMORY_LOCATION, CX instruction will be completed, and the address of the memory location will be output on the address bus. On the next clock cycle the word in AX will be output on the data bus. This extensive overlapping of operations makes it possible for the 486 to execute many of its commonly used instructions in, effectively, a single clock cycle. The fetching, decoding, and executing of each of these instructions actually takes several clock cycles, but since these operations are overlapped with the decoding and execution of other instructions, the net time for each of the instructions is only one clock cycle. As an example of this, a 16-bit memory-write operation that takes 22 clock cycles to execute on an 8088 and 4 clock cyles to execute on a 386 takes only 1 clock cycle to execute on a 486. The conditional jump instructions have also benefited greatly from the pipelining in the 486. When the 486 decodes a conditional jump instruction, it automatically prefetches one or more instructions from the jump destination address just in case the jump is taken. If the branch is taken, then the 486 does not have to wait through a bus cycle for the first instruction at the branch address. A conditional jump instruction which takes 16/4 clock cycles on an 8088 and 8/3 clock cycles on a 386 takes only 3/1 clock cycles on a 486.

Most of the other improvements included in the 486

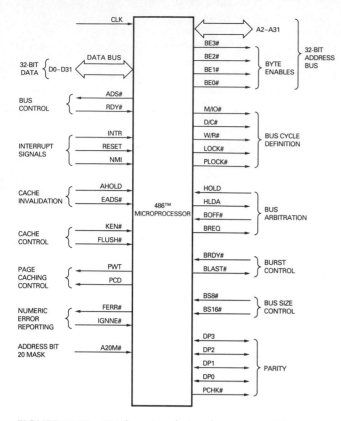

FIGURE 15-32   486 functional signal groups.   (*Courtesy Intel Corporation*)

involve hardware signals and interfacing. To make room for the additional signals, the 486 is packaged in a 168-pin pin grid array package instead of the 132-pin PGA used for the 386. Figure 15-32 shows the 486 signals in functional groups. We will briefly work our way through some of these to give you an overview of the major new features.

The 486 data bus, address bus, byte enable, ADS#, RDY#, INTR, RESET, NMI, M/IO#, D/C#, W/R#, LOCK#, HOLD, HLDA, and BS16# signals function as we described for the 386, so these hold no surprises. The 486 requires a 1 × clock instead of 2 × clock required by the 386.

A new signal group on the 486 is the parity group, DP0–DP3, and PCHK#. These signals allow the 486 to implement parity detection/generation for memory reads and writes. During a memory write operation, the 486 generates an even parity bit for each byte and outputs these bits on the DP0–DP3 lines. As we described for the IBM PC in Chapter 11, these bits will be stored in a separate parity memory bank. During a read operation the stored parity bits will be read from the parity memory and applied to the DP0–DP3 pins. The 486 checks the parities of the data bytes read and compares them with the DP0–DP3 signals. If a parity error is found, the 486 asserts the PCHK# signal.

Another new signal group consists of the burst ready signal, BRDY#, and the burst last signal, BLAST#. These signals are used to control burst-mode memory reads and writes. Here's how this works. A normal 486

memory-read operation to, for example, read a line into the cache requires 2 clock cycles. However, if a series of reads is being done from successive memory locations, the reads can be done in burst mode with only 1 clock cycle per read. To start the process the 486 sends out the first address and asserts the BLAST# signal high. When the external DRAM controller has the first data word ready on the data bus, it asserts the BRDY# signal. The 486 reads the data word and outputs the next address. Since the data words are at successive addresses, only the lower address bits need to be changed. If the DRAM controller is operating in the page or the static column modes we described in Chapter 11, then it will only have to output a new column address to the DRAM. In this mode the DRAM will be able to output the new data word within 1 clock cycle. (If the DRAM is not fast enough for a high-speed 486, then two DRAM banks can be interleaved to gain the required speed.) When the processor has read the required number of data words, it asserts the BLAST# signal low to terminate the burst mode.

The final signals we want to discuss here are the bus request output signal, BREQ; the back-off input signal, BOFF#; the HOLD signal; and the hold-acknowledge signal, HLDA. These signals are used to control sharing the local 486 bus by multiple processors (bus masters). When a master on the bus needs to use the bus, it asserts its BREQ signal. An external priority circuit will evaluate requests to use the bus and grant bus use to the highest-priority master. To ask the 486 to release the bus, the bus controller asserts the 486 HOLD input or BOFF# input. If the HOLD input is asserted, the 486 will finish the current bus cycle, float its buses, and assert the HLDA signal. To prevent another master from taking over the bus during a critical operation, the 486 can assert its LOCK# or PLOCK# signal.

Because of all the possible variations, we don't have space here to discuss the operation of the 486 cache control signals. Consult the 486 data sheet if you need to know about these and the few other signals we didn't get around to.

The 486 has six additional instructions beyond those of the 386. INVD and WBINVD invalidate the cache, and INVLPG invalidates a TLB entry. The BSWAP instruction swaps the order of the bytes in a 32-bit register. This is useful in interfacing with, for example, an IBM mainframe which stores the least significant byte in the upper bits of a data word. The XADD and CMPXCHG instructions are used to work with semaphores such as those we showed you in Figure 15-3.

NEW DIRECTIONS

Microprocessor and microcomputer evolution has been proceeding very rapidly in the last few years, and the rate of evolution seems to be increasing. As we have shown in the preceding chapters, the overall direction of this evolution is toward microcomputers with greater screen resolution, more memory capability, larger data words, higher processing speeds, and network communication. David House of Intel recently revealed Intel's current plans for evolution beyond the 486. The 586, expected in 1992, will contain about 2 million transistors, and the 686, expected in 1996, will contain about 5 million transistors. The added transistors, of course, will allow larger caches and many new functions to be implemented on the chips. The 786, to be available some time in the late 1990s, is projected to contain a 2-Mbyte cache, six separate integer and floating-point processors, and a complete digital video interactive or similar user interface. The 786 will maintain compatibility with the 386/486 instruction set and operate with a 250-MHz clock.

Throughout this book we have discussed the operation and evolution of primarily one processor family, the Intel 8086 family. We did this so that we could develop some depth rather than just an overview of all the different processors. To finish the book, however, we want to briefly discuss some other types of microcomputer systems that you should be aware of.

RISC Machines

High-performance engineering workstations often use a *reduced instruction set computer* or RISC-type processor. The term RISC is not precisely defined, but some of the main characteristics often associated with a RISC processor are the following:

1. The instruction set is limited to simple arithmetic-, logic-, load-, and store-type instructions. Fewer instructions and limited addressing modes mean a simpler and faster instruction decoder.

2. Extensive pipelining is used to achieve one-clock-cycle instruction execution. The 486 is a CISC processor, but as we described in a previous section, it uses a four-stage pipeline to achieve one-clock-cycle execution for many instructions. The assembler/compilers used for developing RISC programs are designed to put instructions in an order which will keep the pipeline full as much of the time as possible. To further overlap operations, some RISC machines use a *Harvard architecture*, which has separate data buses for code fetches and for data read/write operations.

3. Execution of conditional jump instructions is delayed to allow time to load the pipeline with instructions from the jump destination, or instructions from the jump destination are fetched ahead of time, as we described for the 486 in a previous section.

4. The CPU contains a large number of on-chip registers to give improved access to data operands.

One example of a current RISC implementation standard is the Scalable Processor Architecture RISC computer (SPARC) developed by Sun Microsystems and implemented in their SPARC stations. Fujitsu and Cypress Semiconductor have produced chip sets for this standard. Other common RISC chip sets are the Motorola 88000, the MIPS R3000, and the AMD 29000. A single-chip RISC processor now available is the Intel i860™.

The 1.2 million–transistor i860 contains a 64-bit RISC-based core with Harvard architecture, a floating-point coprocessor, and a graphics coprocessor with 3-D graphics capability. The processors in the i860™ operate relatively independently of each other, so they can all be working in parallel. With a 40-MHz clock an i860™, can perform at peak rate of 80 million floating-point operations per second (MFLOPS), or 85,000 drystones. (The drystone rating represents the relative performance of a computer executing a standard "benchmark" program.) Incidentally, the i860 does not use segmentation, but it does allow 386-type virtual memory paging. The data sheets for this device are a good source of information about RISC implementation.

Parallel Processing

Some computer applications such as analyzing weather data, simulating aircraft designs, or creating the graphics for high-tech science fiction movies require massive amounts of computing. The microcomputers we have discussed in this book so far do not operate nearly fast enough to be practical for many of these applications, so *supercomputers* are used. The peak execution speeds of the fastest current supercomputers are in the range of a few gigaFLOPS.

Most supercomputers are built by connecting several processing elements in parallel. One connection scheme, commonly called a *farm*, allows multiple processors to access a single large memory with a common bus. The difficulty with a simple bus structure such as this is that processors compete for shared resources. If one processor is using the bus, others must wait. This slows down the overall processing speed.

One of the more efficient multiprocessor architectures is the hypercube topology developed by Seitz and Fox at Caltech. A diagram of this topology is shown in Figure 15-33. Each node in the system consists of a complete processing unit which has the ability to communicate with other units. Each processor unit is typically connected to communicate with its nearest neighbors as

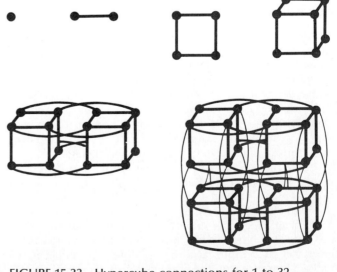

FIGURE 15-33 Hypercube connections for 1 to 32 processor nodes.

shown. The number of nodes can be expanded to give the power and speed needed to handle the problem the computer is being used to solve.

Intel Supercomputing Systems Division (ISSD) has produced the iPSC family of commercial products based on the hypercube topology. One of these, the iPSC/i860™ can be configured with up to 128 nodes, each containing a complete i860™-based microcomputer with high-speed network-type communication capability. The advantage of this structure is that each processor has enough memory to operate relatively independently, and communication between processors can take any one of several routes, instead of being limited to a single bus. Peak execution rates for the iPSC/i860™ range from 480 MFLOPS to 7.5 gigaFLOPS, depending on the number of processing units. These rates compare favorably with Cray Research Y-MP supercomputer's maximum execution rate of about 8 gigaFLOPS. However, because the iPSC/i860™ uses a larger number of common LSI components instead of a single or small number of very high speed processors made with gallium arsenide technology, the cost is less.

To program parallel computers such as these, new programming languages have had to be developed. A couple of these that you may be hearing more about are Scientific Computing Associates' C-Linda language and AIL Ltd.'s STRAND 88 language.

Expert Systems, Neural Networks, and Fuzzy Logic

INTRODUCTION

Artificial Intelligence or AI is the general term used to describe computers or computer programs which solve problems with "intuitive" or "best-guess" methods often used by humans instead of the strictly quantitative methods usually used by computers. Expert systems, neural networks, and fuzzy logic are the most common types of AI currently in use. These three are in relatively early stages of development and implementation, but they all have extensive implications for our lives.

EXPERT SYSTEMS

Probably the most developed area of AI at present is the area of *expert systems*. An expert-system program consists of a large data base and a set of rules for searching the data base to find the best solution for a particular type of problem. The data base and rules are developed by questioning "experts" in that particular problem area. The data base for a medical diagnosis expert system, for example, is built up by extensive questioning of experts in each medical specialty.

Unlike most computer programs, which require complete information to make a decision, expert system programs are designed to make a best guess, based on the available data, just as a human expert would do. A medical diagnosis expert system, for example, will indicate the illness that most likely corresponds to a given set of symptoms and test data. To enable it to make a better guess, the system may suggest additional tests to perform.

One advantage of a system such as this is that it can make the knowledge of many experts readily available to a physician anywhere in the world via a modem connection. Another advantage is that the data base and set of rules can be easily updated as new research results and drugs become available. Other examples of expert system programs are those used to lay out PC boards and those used to lay out ICs.

NEURAL NETWORKS

Programs for some problems such as image recognition, speech recognition, weather forecasting, and three-dimensional modeling are not easily or accurately implemented on fixed-instruction-set computers such as 386/i486-based systems. For applications such as these, a new computer architecture, modeled after the human brain, shows considerable promise.

As you may remember from a general science class, the brain is composed of billions of neurons. The output of each neuron is connected to the inputs of several thousand other neurons by synapses. If the sum of the signals on the inputs of a neuron is greater than a certain threshold value, the neuron "fires" and sends a signal to other neurons. The simple op-amp circuit in Figure 15-34a may help you see how a neuron works. Let's assume the output of the comparator is initially low. If the sum of the input signals to the adder produces an output voltage more negative than the comparator threshold voltage, the output of the comparator will go high. This is analogous to the neuron firing. The weight or relative influence of an input is determined by the value of the resistor on that input. Figure 15-34b shows a symbol commonly used to represent a neuron in neural network literature and Figure 15-34c shows a simple mathematical model of a neuron.

As with the neurons in the human brain, the neurons in a neural network are connected to many other neurons. Figure 15-34d shows a simple three-layer neural network. This network configuration is referred to as "feedforward," because none of the output signals are connected back to the inputs. In a "feedback" or "resonance" configured network, some intermediate or final output signals are connected back to network inputs. Researchers are currently experimenting with many different network configurations to determine the one that works best for each type of application.

Neural network based computing can be implemented in several ways. One way is to use a dedicated processor

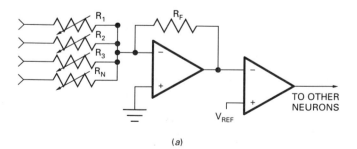

(a)

FIGURE 15-34 (a) Op-amp model of a neuron. (*See also next page.*)

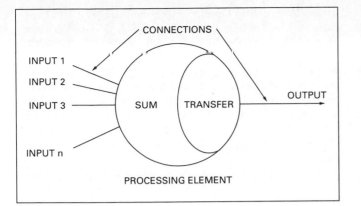

PROCESSING ELEMENT

(b)

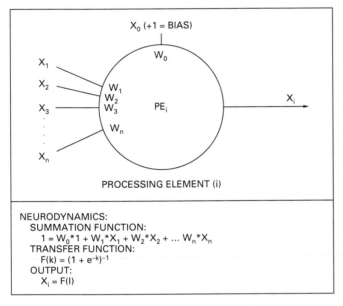

PROCESSING ELEMENT (i)

NEURODYNAMICS:
SUMMATION FUNCTION:
$$1 = W_0*1 + W_1*X_1 + W_2*X_2 + \ldots W_n*X_n$$
TRANSFER FUNCTION:
$$F(k) = (1 + e^{-k})^{-1}$$
OUTPUT:
$$X_i = F(I)$$

(c)

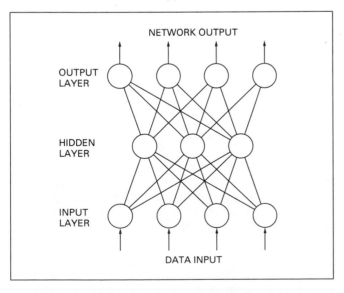

(d)

FIGURE 15-34 *(Continued)* *(b)* Neural network processing element. *(c)* Mathematical representation of processing element. *(d)* Simple three-layer neural network. *(Courtesy NeuralWare, Inc.)*

for each neuron. The large number of neurons usually makes this impractical, and most applications don't need the speed capability. An alternative approach is to use a single processor and simulate neurons with lookup tables. The lookup table for each neuron contains the connections, input weight values, and output equation constants. Hecht-Nielsen Neurocomputers markets a PC/AT-compatible coprocessor board which uses this approach.

A neural network can also be implemented totally in software. NeuralWare, Inc. markets neural net simulation programs for both PC and Macintosh type computers. These packages can be used to learn about neural nets or develop actual applications which do not have to operate in real time. Another interesting neural network program is BrainMaker from California Scientific Software.

Neural network computers are not programmed in the way that digital computers are, they are trained. Instead of being programmed with a set of rules the way a classic expert system is, a neural network computer learns the desired behavior. The learning process may be supervised, unsupervised, or self-supervised.

In the supervised method a set of input conditions and the expected output conditions are applied to the network. The network learns by adjusting or "adapting" the weights of the interconnections until the output is correct. Another input-output set is then applied, and the network is allowed to learn this set. After a few sets the network will have learned or generalized its response so that it can give the correct response to most applied input data.

The scheme used to adapt the network is called the learning rule. As an example, one of the simplest learning rules that can be used is the Hebbean Learning Law. This law decrees that each time the input of a neuron contributes to the firing, its weight should be increased, and each time an input does not contribute, its weight should be decreased. This is somewhat analogous to a positive-negative reinforcement scheme often used in human behavior modification. In the case of the network the result is that these successive "nudges" adapt the network output to the desired result.

The major advantages of neural networks are these:

1. They do not need to be programmed; they can simply be taught the desired response. This eliminates most of the cost of programming.

2. They can improve their response by learning. A neural network designed to evaluate loan applications, for example, can automatically adapt its criteria based on loan-failure feedback data.

3. Input data does not have to be precise, because the network works with the sum of the inputs. A neural network image-recognition system, for example, can recognize a person even though he or she has a somewhat different hairstyle than when the "learning" image was taken. Likewise, a neural network-based speech-recognition system can recognize words spoken by different people. Traditional digital techniques have a very hard time with these tasks.

4. Information is not stored in a specific memory location the way it is in a normal digital computer; it is stored *associatively* as a network of interconnections and weightings. The result of this is that the "death" of a few neurons will usually not seriously degrade the operation of the system. This characteristic is also fortunate for us humans!

Software-based neural networks can be used for non-realtime applications such as forecasting the weather or the stock market. For realtime applications such as image recognition and speech recognition, the software methods are obviously not fast enough. University researchers and companies such as TRW and Texas Instruments are working on ICs which implement neural networks in hardware. In the not-too-distant future these ICs should allow you to talk to your computer instead of using a mouse, allow your computer to read typed messages to you, and allow your car to drive itself down the freeway.

FUZZY LOGIC

Consumer products such as video camcorders, cameras, refrigerators, washing machines, and automobiles are increasingly using fuzzy logic control circuits. Linking the term fuzzy, which here means "not precisely defined," with the term logic may seem to create an oxymoron like "work party," but the concept is very real. The original work on fuzzy logic was done by Professor Lofti A. Zadeh at U.C. Berkeley in the mid-1960s, but Japanese companies have been the main ones to patent the technology and implement it in products.

A fuzzy logic controller is programmed with rules as is an expert system, but the rules are very flexible. Figure 15-35 shows the graphic method Professor Bart Kosko of the University of Southern California uses to illustrate the difference between traditional fixed value logic and fuzzy logic. Each corner of the cube represents one of the eight possibilities for a three-variable digital logic function. For this example, let's assume that the function is true for the 010, 001, and 100 combinations shown. In a traditional digital logic system the variables can only have values of 0 or 1, so the only values that will produce a true output are these three. In a fuzzy logic system the variables can have values other than 1 or 0, so the set of all the possible values that will produce a true output is represented by the triangular plane formed by the three points. One way to look at this is that traditional digital logic is just a special case of fuzzy logic.

One advantage of fuzzy logic systems is that they can work with imprecise terms such as cold, warm, hot, or near boiling that humans commonly use. In hardware terms this means that a fuzzy logic system often doesn't need precise A/D converters. The Sanyo Fisher Corp. Model FVC-880 camcorder, for example, uses fuzzy logic to directly process the outputs from six sensors and set the camera lens for best possible focusing and exposure.

Fuzzy logic can provide very smooth control of mechanical systems. The fuzzy logic-controlled subway in Sendai, Japan, is reportedly so smooth in operation that standing riders do not use the hand straps during starts and stops.

In the United States, Togai InfraLogic, Inc. in Irvine, California, has developed a Digital Fuzzy Processor chip. They have also developed a Fuzzy-C compiler which can be used to write a program containing the rules and knowledge base for the processor.

SUMMARY

The three AI approaches we have discussed in this section will obviously not replace standard digital computers for most applications, especially those that involve numerical processing, but they do give some new choices for difficult applications. The most likely scenario for the future is that a combination of these techniques will be used to design a system which best fits the particular application. The results should be very exciting.

EPILOGUE

This book has been able to show you only a small view of current microcomputers and the directions in which they seem to be evolving. Hopefully we have given you enough of a start that you can continue learning on your own and play a part in the evolution. Whenever you feel overwhelmed by the amount of new material there is to learn, remember the 5-minute rule and the old saying "Grapevines and people bear the best fruit on new growth."

CHECKLIST OF IMPORTANT TERMS AND CONCEPTS IN THIS CHAPTER

If you do not remember any of the terms in the following list, use the index to help you find them in the chapter for review.

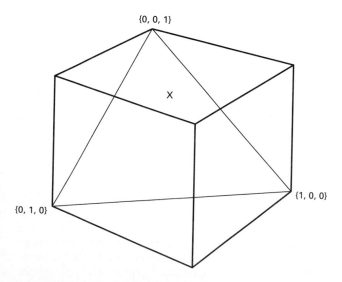

FIGURE 15-35 Comparison of binary logic values and fuzzy logic values for a 3-input function.

Multiuser, multitasking

TSR program

Time-slice and preemptive priority-based scheduling

Semaphore

Deadlock

Critical region

Overlay

Bank switching

Expanded memory

Extended memory

Descriptor table

Virtual memory

Memory-Management Unit

80286
   Real address mode
   Protected virtual address mode
   Interrupt, exception, fault, trap

80386
   Architecture, pins, and signals
   System connections and interface buses
      ISA bus standard
      EISA bus standard
      MicroChannel Architecture Bus
   Real-mode operation

Protected-mode operation
   Segmentation and virtual memory
   Segment privilege levels and protection
   Call gate
   I/O privilege levels
   Interrupt and exception handling
   Task switching and task state segment
   Paging mode
   Flat system memory model
Virtual 8086 mode operation
Virtual machine monitor
Index scaling
OS/2
Microsoft windows

80486
   Pipelining
   Cache
   Floating-point processor

Parallel processing
   Hypercube topology

RISC machine

Artifical intelligence

Expert system

Neural network

Fuzzy logic

5-minute rule

Grapevines and new growth

REVIEW QUESTIONS AND PROBLEMS

1.   a.   Describe the basic operation of a TSR program and draw a memory map to show how a TSR program is loaded in a DOS based system.
     b.   Use a diagram to help explain how a passive TSR gets executed after it is installed.

2.   Briefly describe the two types of scheduling commonly used in multiuser/multitasking operating systems.

3.   Suppose that two users in a time-share computer system each want to print out a file. How can the system be prevented from printing lines from one file between lines of the other file?

4.   Define the term deadlock and describe one way it can be prevented.

5.   Define the term critical region and show with 8086 assembly language instructions how a semaphore can be used to protect a critical region.

6.   Describe how an overlay scheme is used to run programs such as compilers which are too large to be loaded into physical memory all at once.

7.   a.   Describe how bank switching is implemented in a microcomputer system.

     b.   Describe how LIM 4.0-type expanded memory works in a DOS-based system.
     c.   How is extended memory different from expanded memory?

8.   a.   Define the term virtual memory and use Figure 15-8 to help you briefly describe how a logical address is converted to a physical address by a memory management unit.
     b.   What action will the MMU take if it finds that a requested segment is not present in physical memory?
     c.   What is another major advantage of the indirect addressing provided by descriptor tables, besides the ability to address a large amount of virtual memory?

9.   List the four major processing units in an 80286 microprocessor and briefly describe the function of each.

10.   Describe how the real-mode operation of an 80286 is different from protected-mode operation.

11.   Define the terms interrupt, exception, fault, and trap.

12. Explain how an 80286 is switched from real address mode to protected virtual address mode and how it is switched back to real address mode operation.

13. a. Show the computations which tell how much virtual memory an 80286 can address.
    b. What factors determine how much physical memory an 80286 can address?

14. a. List three major advances that the 80386 microprocessor has over the 80286.
    b. What is the main difference between the 386DX processor and the 386SX processor?
    c. What is the purpose of the 386DX BE0-BE3 signals?

15. a. How is the EISA bus different from the ISA bus?
    b. If you found an interface board lying on the bench, what is one way you could tell whether it came from an EISA-based system or from a MicroChannel Architecture system?
    c. Briefly compare the EISA and MCA methods of arbitrating bus requests from multiple masters or DMA slaves.

16. a. Show the computations which tell how much virtual memory a 386 can address.
    b. How much physical memory can a 386 address in real mode and in protected mode?

17. a. Give the names of the two parts of a 386 protected-mode address.
    b. Using Figure 15-21 to help, describe how a 32-bit virtual address for a data segment location in a task's local memory is translated to the actual 32-bit physical address for a 386 operating in segments only protected mode.
    c. How would the discussion in part b differ if the desired memory location were in the global memory area?
    d. How does a 386 keep track of where the global descriptor table and the currently used local descriptor table are located in memory?
    e. Why is the length of the segment included in the descriptor for a segment?

18. How are tasks in a 386 system protected from each other?

19. How can operating system kernel procedures and data be protected from access by application programs in a 386 system?

20. In a 386 system a task operating at a level 2 privilege can in a special way call a procedure at a higher privilege level. Describe briefly the mechanism that is used to make this access.

21. a. A 386 maintains a task state segment for each active task in a system. How are these task state segments accessed?
    b. Briefly describe how a 386 does a task switch using a FAR JMP or a FAR CALL instruction.

22. a. Use Figure 15-26 to help you explain how a 386 computes a physical address when its paging mode is enabled.
    b. What is the advantage of paged-based virtual memory over segments only based virtual memory?
    c. Define the term simple flat memory model and the term paged flat memory model for a 386.

23. a. How is a 386 switched into virtual 8086 mode during a task switch?
    b. Briefly describe the response of the virtual machine monitor when a real-mode 8086 program executes an INT 21H instruction.

24. Using the program in Figure 15-29a as a model, write a program which uses some of the new 386 instruction features to treat the four words in table as a 64-bit word, and rotate it 8 bits to the left.

25. Describe three major additions or improvements that the 486 processor has over the 386 processor.

26. List three major features characteristic of a RISC-based computer and describe how each of these features helps produce faster execution.

27. What are the major advantages of using parallel processors with, for example, a hypercube connection architecture over using a single fast processor?

28. a. Describe the basic operation of a neuron in a neural computer.
    b. How is the "programming" of a neural network computer different from the programming of a standard, fixed-instruction-set computer?
    c. List some advantages of a neural network–type computer.
    d. For what types of applications are neural network–type computers best suited?

29. a. How is a fuzzy logic control system different from a traditional digital logic control system?
    b. What are some advantages of fuzzy logic?

BIBLIOGRAPHY

Because of the technical level of this book, the major sources of further information on the topics discussed are manufacturer's data books, application notes, and articles in current engineering periodicals. With the foundation you get from this book you should be able to comfortably read these materials. Listed below, by chapter, are some materials that will give you more details for many of the topics we discuss in the book. Following the chapter listings is a list of periodicals which we have found to be particularly helpful in keeping up with the latest advances in microcomputer evolution and applications.

Chapter 1

Hall, Douglas V., *Digital Circuits and Systems*, McGraw-Hill, Inc., New York, 1989.

Chapters 2–8

Mick, John, and Jim Brick; *Bit-Slice Microprocessor Design*, McGraw-Hill, Inc., New York, 1980.

A History of Microprocessor Development at Intel, Intel Article Reprint/AR-173, Intel Corporation, Santa Clara, Calif.

Microprocessors, Intel Corporation, Santa Clara, Calif., latest edition (Databook).

Turbo Assembler User's Guide, Borland International, Scotts Valley, Calif., 1988.

Macro Assembler User's Guide, Microsoft Corp., Bellingham, Wash., 1989.

Peripherals, Intel Corporation, Santa Clara, Calif., latest edition (Databook).

SDK-86 MCS-86 System Design Kit User's Guide, Intel Corporation, Santa Clara, Calif., 1981.

8086 System Design, Application Note, Intel Corporation/AP-67, Intel Corporation, Santa Clara, Calif.

Chapters 9–10

Peripherals, Intel Corporation, Santa Clara, Calif., latest edition (Databook).

IBM PC TECHNICAL REFERENCE MANUAL, IBM Corp., Boca Raton, Fla., 1983.

Dorf, Richard C., *Robotics and Automated Manufacturing*, Reston Publishing Company, Reston, Va. 1983.

AMF Potter & Brumfield Catalog, Potter & Brumfield, Princeton, Ind., latest edition.

Optoelectronics Designer's Catalog, Hewlett-Packard, Palo Alto, Calif., latest edition.

Interfacing Liquid Crystal Displays in Digital Systems, Application Note AN-8, Beckman Instruments, Inc., Scottsdale, Ariz., latest edition.

Optoelectronics Device Data Book, DL118R1, Motorola Semiconductor Products Inc., Phoenix, Ariz., latest edition.

Sandhu, H. S., Hands-On Introduction to ROBOTICS—

The Manual for the XR-Series Robots, Rhino Robots, Champaign, Ill., latest edition.

Slo-Syn DC Stepping Motors Catalog, DCM1078, Superior Electric Company, Bristol, Conn., latest edition.

Auslander, David M., and Paul Sagues, *Microprocessors for Measurement and Control*, Osborne/McGraw-Hill, Berkeley, Calif., 1981.

Allocca, John A., and Allen Stuart, *Transducers Theory and Applications*, Reston Publishing Company, Inc., Reston, Va., 1984.

Seippel, Robert G., *Transducers, Sensors and Detectors*, Reston Publishing Company, Inc., Reston, Va., 1983.

Johnson, Curtis D., *Process Control Instrumentation Technology*, John Wiley & Sons, New York, latest edition.

Sheingold, Daniel H. (ed.), *Transducer Interfacing Handbook — A Guide to Analog Signal Conditioning*, Analog Devices, Inc., Norwood, Mass., latest edition.

Analog Devices Industrial Control Series Data Sheet, Analog Devices, Inc., Norwood, Mass., latest edition.

Texas Instruments, Inc. *Third Generation TMS320 User's Guide*, Dallas, Tex., latest edition.

Chassaing, Rulph, and Darell W. Horning, *Digital Signal Processing with the TMS320C25*, John Wiley & Sons, New York, 1990.

Chapter 11

Peripherals, Intel Corporation, Santa Clara, Calif., latest edition (Databook).

Microprocessors, Intel Corporation, Santa Clara, Calif., latest edition (Databook).

IBM PC Technical Reference Manual, IBM Corp., Boca Raton, Fla., 1983.

IBM PC/AT Technical Reference Manual, IBM Corp., Florida, 1984.

8086 Macro Assembly Language Reference Manual for 8086-Based Development Systems, Intel Corporation, Santa Clara, Calif., latest edition.

Error Detecting and Correcting Codes, Application Note AP-46, Intel Corporation, Santa Clara, Calif., 1979.

Getting Started With the Numeric Data Processor, Application Note AP-113, Intel Corporation, Santa Clara, Calif., 1981.

Hall, Douglas V., *Digital Circuits and Systems*, McGraw-Hill, Inc., New York, 1989. (Chapter 15 on Electronic Design Automation.)

Chapter 12

Turbo C++ User's Manual; Turbo C++ Programmer's Guide; Turbo C++ Library Reference, Borland International, Scotts Valley, Calif., 1990.

Microsoft C 6.0 Optimizing Compiler, Language Reference, Codeview, and Utilities, Microsoft Corporation, Bellingham, Wash., 1987.

Schildt, Herbert, *Turbo C: The Complete Reference*, Borland-Osborne/McGraw-Hill, Berkeley, Calif., 1988.

Waite, Michael, and Stephen Prata, *New C Primer Plus*, Howard W. Sams & Company, Carmel, Ind., 1990.

Chapter 13

Peripherals, Intel Corporation, Santa Clara, Calif., latest edition (Databook).

Lesea, Austin, and Rodnay Zaks, *Microprocessor Interfacing Techniques*, Sybex Inc., Berkeley, Calif., latest edition.

An Intelligent Data Base System Using the 8272, Application Note AP-116, Intel Corporation, Santa Clara, Calif., 1981. (Old, but good basics.)

Sutty, George, and Steve Blair, *Programmer's Guide to the EGA/VGA*, Brady Books, New York, NY, 1988.

Stevens, Roger T., *Fractal Programming in C*, M&T Books, Redwood City, Calif., 1989. (Demo disk comes with book and provides much fun.)

DOS Technical Reference Manual, Microsoft Corporation, Bellingham, Wash., latest edition.

Jamsa, Kris, *DOS—The Complete Reference*, Osborne/McGraw-Hill, Berkeley, Calif., 1987.

Jamsa, Kris, *DOS Power User's Guide*, Osborne/McGraw-Hill, Berkeley, Calif., 1988.

Luther, Arch, *Digital Video in the PC Environment*, McGraw-Hill, New York, NY, 1989.

Phillips International, Inc. *Compact Disk-Interactive, A Designer's Overview*, McGraw-Hill, New York, NY, 1989.

Chapter 14

Microcommunications Handbook, Intel Corporation, Santa Clara, Calif., latest edition. (Two-volume databook with many application notes.)

Stallings, William D., *Local Networks, an Introduction*, Macmillan, New York, NY, 1984. (Older, but good, clear basics.)

Friend, George E., et al., *Understanding Data Communications*, Howard W. Sams, Indianapolis, Ind., 1987. (Good basics.)

Fike, John L., and George E. Friend, *Understanding Telephone Electronics*, Howard W. Sams, Indianapolis, Ind., 1984. (Good basics.)

Schatt, Stan, *Understanding Local Area Networks*, Howard W. Sams, Indianapolis, Ind., 1989. (Good basics.)

McNamara, John E., *Technical Aspects of Data Communication*, Digital Equipment Corporation, Maynard, Mass., latest edition.

EIA Standard RS-422, Electrical Characteristics of Balanced Voltage Digital Interface Circuits, Electronic Industries Association, Engineering Department, Washington, D.C., 1975.

EIA Standard RS-232-C, Interface Between Data Terminal Equipment and Data Communication Equipment Employing Serial Binary Data Interchange, Electronic Industries Association, Engineering Department, Washington, D.C., 1969.

Sterling, Donald J., *Technician's Guide to Fiber Optics*, Delmar Publishers Inc, Albany, NY, 1987. (Good basics with emphasis on cables, connectors, and couplers.)

Chapter 15

Stevens, Al, *Turbo C Memory Resident Utilities, Screen I/O, and Programming Techniques*, MIS Press, Portland, Ore., 1987.

Kaisler, Stephen H., *The Design of Operating Systems for Small Computer Systems*, John Wiley & Sons, Inc., New York, 1983.

Microprocessors, Intel Corporation, Santa Clara, Calif., latest edition (Databook).

ASM386 Assembly Language Reference Manual, Intel Corporation, Santa Clara, Calif., 1986.

80386 System Software Writer's Guide, Intel Corporation, Santa Clara, Calif., 1987.

386 Microprocessor Hardware Reference Manual, Intel Corporation, Santa Clara, Calif., 1988.

80386 Programmer's Reference Manual, Intel Corporation, Santa Clara, Calif., 1986.

Pappas, Chris H., and William H. Murray, *Inside the Model 80*, Osborne/McGraw-Hill, Berkeley, Calif., 1988.

Microsoft Windows User's Guide, Microsoft Corporation, Bellingham, Wash., 1990.

Klimasausskas, Casimir C., *Teaching Your Computer to Learn*, NeuralWare, Inc., Pittsburgh, Penn., 1988 (Booklet).

Periodicals

BYTE. ISSN 0360-5280. Byte Publications, Inc., 70 Main Street, Peterborough, NH 03458.

EDN. ISSN 0012-7515. Cahners Publishing Co., 221 Columbus Avenue, Boston, MA 02116.

Electronic Design. USPS-172-080. Hayden Publishing Co., Inc., 50 Essex Street, Rochelle Park, NJ 07662.

Electronics. ISSN 0013-5070. McGraw-Hill, Inc., 1221 Avenue of the Americas, New York, NY 10020.

Instruments & Control Systems. ISSN 0164-0089. Chilton Company, Chilton Way, Radnor, PA 19089.

Electronic Engineering Times. ISSN 0192-1541. Electronic Engineering Times, 600 Community Drive, Manhasset, NY 11030.

iAPX 86/10
16-BIT HMOS MICROPROCESSOR
8086/8086-2/8086-1

- **Direct Addressing Capability 1 MByte of Memory**
- **Architecture Designed for Powerful Assembly Language and Efficient High Level Languages.**
- **14 Word, by 16-Bit Register Set with Symmetrical Operations**
- **24 Operand Addressing Modes**
- **Bit, Byte, Word, and Block Operations**
- **8 and 16-Bit Signed and Unsigned**

- **Arithmetic in Binary or Decimal Including Multiply and Divide**
- **Range of Clock Rates:**
  5 MHz for 8086,
  8 MHz for 8086-2,
  10 MHz for 8086-1
- **MULTIBUS™ System Compatible Interface**
- **Available in EXPRESS**
  – Standard Temperature Range
  – Extended Temperature Range

The Intel iAPX 86/10 high performance 16-bit CPU is available in three clock rates: 5, 8 and 10 MHz. The CPU is implemented in N-Channel, depletion load, silicon gate technology (HMOS), and packaged in a 40-pin CerDIP package. The iAPX 86/10 operates in both single processor and multiple processor configurations to achieve high performance levels.

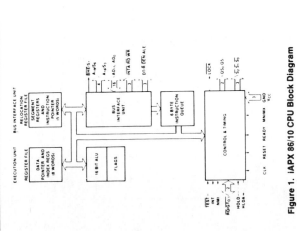

Figure 1. iAPX 86/10 CPU Block Diagram

Table 1. Pin Description

The following pin function descriptions are for iAPX 86 systems in either minimum or maximum mode. The "Local Bus" in these descriptions is the direct multiplexed bus interface connection to the 8086 (without regard to additional bus buffers).

Symbol	Pin No.	Type	Name and Function
AD_{15}–AD_0	2-16, 39	I/O	**Address Data Bus:** These lines constitute the time multiplexed memory/IO address (T_1) and data (T_2, T_3, T_W, T_4) bus. A_0 is analogous to $\overline{BHE}$ for the lower byte of the data bus, pins D_7–D_0. It is LOW during T_1 when a byte is to be transferred on the lower portion of the bus in memory or I/O operations. Eight-bit oriented devices tied to the lower half would normally use A_0 to condition chip select functions. (See $\overline{BHE}$.) These lines are active HIGH and float to 3-state OFF during interrupt acknowledge and local bus "hold acknowledge."
A_{19}/S_6, A_{18}/S_5, A_{17}/S_4, A_{16}/S_3	35-38	O	**Address/Status:** During T_1 these are the four most significant address lines for memory operations. During I/O operations these lines are LOW. During memory and I/O operations, status information is available on these lines during T_2, T_3, T_W, and T_4. The status of the interrupt enable FLAG bit (S_5) is updated at the beginning of each CLK cycle. A_{17}/S_4 and A_{16}/S_3 are encoded as shown. | A_{17}/S_4	A_{16}/S_3	Characteristics
---	---	---
0 (LOW)	0	Alternate Data
0	1	Stack
1 (HIGH)	0	Code or None
1	1	Data
S_6 is 0 (LOW)			 This information indicates which relocation register is presently being used for data accessing. These lines float to 3-state OFF during local bus "hold acknowledge."
$\overline{BHE}/S_7$	34	O	**Bus High Enable/Status:** During T_1 the bus high enable signal ($\overline{BHE}$) should be used to enable data onto the most significant half of the data bus, pins D_{15}–D_8. Eight-bit oriented devices tied to the upper half of the bus would normally use $\overline{BHE}$ to condition chip select functions. $\overline{BHE}$ is LOW during T_1 for read, write, and interrupt acknowledge cycles when a byte is to be transferred on the high portion of the bus. The S_7 status information is available during T_2, T_3, and T_4. The signal is active LOW, and floats to 3-state OFF in "hold." It is LOW during T_1 for the first interrupt acknowledge cycle. | $\overline{BHE}$	A_0	Characteristics
---	---	---
0	0	Whole word
0	1	Upper byte from/to odd address
1	0	Lower byte from/to even address
1	1	None	
$\overline{RD}$	32	O	**Read:** Read strobe indicates that the processor is performing a memory or I/O read cycle, depending on the state of the S_2 pin. This signal is used to read devices which reside on the 8086 local bus. $\overline{RD}$ is active LOW during T_2, T_3 and T_W of any read cycle, and is guaranteed to remain HIGH in T_2 until the 8086 local bus has floated. This signal floats to 3-state OFF in "hold acknowledge."
READY	22	I	**READY:** is the acknowledgement from the addressed memory or I/O device that it will complete the data transfer. The READY signal from memory/IO is synchronized by the 8284A Clock Generator to form READY. This signal is active HIGH. The 8086 READY input is not synchronized. Correct operation is not guaranteed if the setup and hold times are not met.
INTR	18	I	**Interrupt Request:** is a level triggered input which is sampled during the last clock cycle of each instruction to determine if the processor should enter into an interrupt acknowledge operation. A subroutine is vectored to via an interrupt vector lookup table located in system memory. It can be internally masked by software resetting the interrupt enable bit. INTR is internally synchronized. This signal is active HIGH.
$\overline{TEST}$	23	I	**TEST:** input is examined by the "Wait" instruction. If the $\overline{TEST}$ input is LOW execution continues, otherwise the processor waits in an "Idle" state. This input is synchronized internally during each clock cycle on the leading edge of CLK.

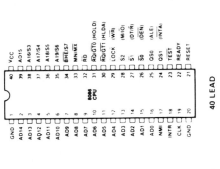

Figure 2. iAPX 86/10 Pin Configuration

579

Table 1. Pin Description (Continued)

Symbol	Pin No.	Type	Name and Function
NMI	17	I	Non-maskable interrupt: an edge triggered input which causes a type 2 interrupt. A subroutine is vectored to via an interrupt vector lookup table located in system memory. NMI is not maskable internally by software. A transition from a LOW to HIGH initiates the interrupt at the end of the current instruction. This input is internally synchronized.
RESET	21	I	Reset: causes the processor to immediately terminate its present activity. The signal must be active HIGH for at least four clock cycles. It restarts execution, as described in the Instruction Set description, when RESET returns LOW. RESET is internally synchronized.
CLK	19	I	Clock: provides the basic timing for the processor and bus controller. It is asymmetric with a 33% duty cycle to provide optimized internal timing.
V_{CC}	40		V_{CC}: + 5V power supply pin.
GND	1, 20		Ground
MN/$\overline{MX}$	33	I	Minimum/Maximum: indicates what mode the processor is to operate in. The two modes are discussed in the following sections.

The following pin function descriptions are for the 8086/8288 system in maximum mode (i.e., MN/$\overline{MX}$ = V_{SS}). Only the pin functions which are unique to maximum mode are described; all other pin functions are as described above.

Symbol	Pin No.	Type	Name and Function
$\overline{S}_2$, $\overline{S}_1$, $\overline{S}_0$	26-28	O	Status: active during T_4, T_1, and T_2 and is returned to the passive state (1,1,1) during T_3 or during T_W when READY is HIGH. This status is used by the 8288 Bus Controller to generate all memory and I/O access control signals. Any change by $\overline{S}_2$, $\overline{S}_1$, or $\overline{S}_0$ during T_4 is used to indicate the beginning of a bus cycle, and the return to the passive state in T_3 or T_W is used to indicate the end of a bus cycle. These signals float to 3-state OFF in "hold acknowledge." These status lines are encoded as shown.

$\overline{S}_2$	$\overline{S}_1$	$\overline{S}_0$	Characteristics
0 (LOW)	0	0	Interrupt Acknowledge
0	0	1	Read I/O Port
0	1	0	Write I/O Port
0	1	1	Halt
1 (HIGH)	0	0	Code Access
1	0	1	Read Memory
1	1	0	Write Memory
1	1	1	Passive

Symbol	Pin No.	Type	Name and Function
$\overline{RQ}/\overline{GT}_0$, $\overline{RQ}/\overline{GT}_1$	30, 31	I/O	Request/Grant: pins are used by other local bus masters to force the processor to release the local bus at the end of the processor's current bus cycle. Each pin is bidirectional with $\overline{RQ}/\overline{GT}_0$ having higher priority than $\overline{RQ}/\overline{GT}_1$. $\overline{RQ}/\overline{GT}$ has an internal pull-up resistor so may be left unconnected. The request/grant sequence is as follows (see Figure 9):

1. A pulse of 1 CLK wide from another local bus master indicates a local bus request ("hold") to the 8086 (pulse 1).

2. During a T_4 or T_1 clock cycle, a pulse 1 CLK wide from the 8086 to the requesting master (pulse 2), indicates that the 8086 has allowed the local bus to float and that it will enter the "hold acknowledge" state at the next CLK. The CPU's bus interface unit is disconnected logically from the local bus during "hold acknowledge."

3. A pulse 1 CLK wide from the requesting master indicates to the 8086 (pulse 3) that the "hold" request is about to end and that the 8086 can reclaim the local bus at the next CLK.

Each master-master exchange of the local bus is a sequence of 3 pulses. There must be one dead CLK cycle after each bus exchange. Pulses are active LOW.

If the request is made while the CPU is performing a memory cycle, it will release the local bus during T_4 of the cycle when all the following conditions are met:

1. Request occurs on or before T_2.
2. Current cycle is not the low byte of a word (on an odd address).
3. Current cycle is not the first acknowledge of an interrupt acknowledge sequence.
4. A locked instruction is not currently executing.

Table 1. Pin Description (Continued)

If the local bus is idle when the request is made the two possible events will follow:

1. Local bus will be released during the next clock.
2. A memory cycle will start within 3 clocks. Now the four rules for a currently active memory cycle apply with condition number 1 already satisfied.

Symbol	Pin No.	Type	Name and Function
$\overline{LOCK}$	29	O	LOCK: output indicates that other system bus masters are not to gain control of the system bus while LOCK is active LOW. The LOCK signal is activated by the "LOCK" prefix instruction and remains active until the completion of the next instruction. This signal is active LOW, and floats to 3-state OFF in "hold acknowledge."
QS_1, QS_0	24, 25	O	Queue Status: The queue status is valid during the CLK cycle after which the queue operation is performed. QS_1 and QS_0 provide status to allow external tracking of the internal 8086 instruction queue.

QS_1	QS_0	CHARACTERISTICS
0 (LOW)	0	No Operation
0	1	First Byte of Op Code from Queue
1 (HIGH)	0	Empty the Queue
1	1	Subsequent Byte from Queue

The following pin function descriptions are for the 8086 in minimum mode (i.e., MN/$\overline{MX}$ = V_{CC}). Only the pin functions which are unique to minimum mode are described; all other pin functions are as described above.

Symbol	Pin No.	Type	Name and Function
M/$\overline{IO}$	28	O	Status line: logically equivalent to S_2 in the maximum mode. It is used to distinguish a memory access from an I/O access. M/$\overline{IO}$ becomes valid in the T_4 preceding a bus cycle and remains valid until the final T_4 of the cycle (M = HIGH, IO = LOW). M/$\overline{IO}$ floats to 3-state OFF in local bus "hold acknowledge."
$\overline{WR}$	29	O	Write: indicates that the processor is performing a write memory or write I/O cycle, depending on the state of the M/$\overline{IO}$ signal. $\overline{WR}$ is active for T_2, T_3 and T_W of any write cycle. It is active LOW, and floats to 3-state OFF in local bus "hold acknowledge."
$\overline{INTA}$	24	O	$\overline{INTA}$ is used as a read strobe for interrupt acknowledge cycles. It is active LOW during T_2, T_3 and T_W of each interrupt acknowledge cycle.
ALE	25	O	Address Latch Enable: provided by the processor to latch the address into the 8282/8283 address latch. It is a HIGH pulse active during T_1 of any bus cycle. Note that ALE is never floated.
DT/$\overline{R}$	27	O	Data Transmit/Receive: needed in minimum system that desires to use an 8286/8287 data bus transceiver. It is used to control the direction of data flow through the transceiver. Logically DT/$\overline{R}$ is equivalent to $\overline{S}_1$ in the maximum mode, and its timing is the same as for M/$\overline{IO}$. (T = HIGH, R = LOW.) This signal floats to 3-state OFF in local bus "hold acknowledge."
$\overline{DEN}$	26	O	Data Enable: provided as an output enable for the 8286/8287 in a minimum system which uses the transceiver. $\overline{DEN}$ is active LOW during each memory and I/O access and for INTA cycles. For a read or $\overline{INTA}$ cycle it is active from the middle of T_2 until the middle of T_4, while for a write cycle it is active from the beginning of T_2 until the middle of T_4. $\overline{DEN}$ floats to 3-state OFF in local bus "hold acknowledge."
HOLD, HLDA	31, 30	I/O	HOLD: indicates that another master is requesting a local bus "hold." To be acknowledged, HOLD must be active HIGH. The processor receiving the "hold" request will issue HLDA (HIGH) as an acknowledgement in the middle of a T_1 clock cycle. Simultaneous with the issuance of HLDA the processor will float the local bus and control lines. After HOLD is detected as being LOW, the processor will LOWer the HLDA, and when the processor needs to run another cycle, it will again drive the local bus and control lines. The same rules as for $\overline{RQ}/\overline{GT}$ apply regarding when the local bus will be released. HOLD is not an asynchronous input. External synchronization should be provided if the system cannot otherwise guarantee the setup time.

FUNCTIONAL DESCRIPTION

GENERAL OPERATION

The internal functions of the iAPX 86/10 processor are partitioned logically into two processing units. The first is the Bus Interface Unit (BIU) and the second is the Execution Unit (EU) as shown in the block diagram of Figure 1.

These units can interact directly but for the most part perform as separate asynchronous operational processors. The bus interface unit provides the functions related to instruction fetching and queuing, operand fetch and store, and address relocation. This unit also provides the basic bus control. The overlap of instruction pre-fetching provided by this unit serves to increase processor performance through improved bus bandwidth utilization. Up to 6 bytes of the instruction stream can be queued while waiting for decoding and execution.

The instruction stream queuing mechanism allows the BIU to keep the memory utilized very efficiently. Whenever there is space for at least 2 bytes in the queue, the BIU will attempt a word fetch memory cycle. This greatly reduces "dead time" on the memory bus. The queue acts as a First-In-First-Out (FIFO) buffer, from which the EU extracts instruction bytes as required. If the queue is empty (following a branch instruction, for example), the first byte into the queue immediately becomes available to the EU.

The execution unit receives pre-fetched instructions from the BIU queue and provides un-relocated operand addresses to the BIU. Memory operands are passed through the BIU for processing by the EU, which passes results to the BIU for storage. See the Instruction Set description for further register set and architectural descriptions.

MEMORY ORGANIZATION

The processor provides a 20-bit address to memory which locates the byte being referenced. The memory is organized as a linear array of up to 1 million bytes, addressed as 00000(H) to FFFFF(H). The memory is logically divided into code, data, extra data, and stack segments of up to 64K bytes each, with each segment falling on 16-byte boundaries. (See Figure 3a.)

All memory references are made relative to base addresses contained in high speed segment registers. The segment types were chosen based on the addressing needs of programs. The segment register to be selected is automatically chosen according to the rules of the following table. All information in one segment type share the same logical attributes (e.g. code or data). By structuring memory into relocatable areas of similar characteristics and by automatically selecting segment registers, programs are shorter, faster, and more structured.

Word (16-bit) operands can be located on even or odd address boundaries and are thus not constrained to even boundaries as is the case in many 16-bit computers. For address and data operands, the least significant byte of the word is stored in the lower valued address location and the most significant byte in the next higher address location. The BIU automatically performs the proper number of memory accesses, one if the word operand is on an even byte boundary and two if it is on an odd byte boundary. Except for the performance penalty, this double access is transparent to the software. This performance penalty does not occur for instruction fetches, only word operands.

Physically, the memory is organized as a high bank ($D_{15}-D_8$) and a low bank (D_7-D_0) of 512K 8-bit bytes addressed in parallel by the processor's address lines $A_{19}-A_1$. Byte data with even addresses is transferred on the D_7-D_0 bus lines while odd addressed byte data (A_0 HIGH) is transferred on the $D_{15}-D_8$ bus lines. The processor provides two enable signals, $\overline{BHE}$ and A_0, to selectively allow reading from or writing into either an odd byte location, even byte location, or both. The instruction stream is fetched from memory as words and is addressed internally by the processor to the byte level as necessary.

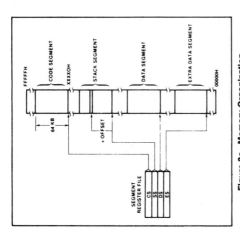

Figure 3a. Memory Organization

In referencing word data the BIU requires one or two memory cycles depending on whether or not the starting byte of the word is on an even or odd address, respectively. Consequently, in referencing word operands performance can be optimized by locating data on even address boundaries. This is an especially useful technique for using the stack, since odd address references to the stack may adversely affect the context switching time for interrupt processing or task multiplexing.

Certain locations in memory are reserved for specific CPU operations (see Figure 3b.) Locations from address FFFF0H through FFFFFH are reserved for operations including a jump to the initial program loading routine. Following RESET, the CPU will always begin execution at location FFFF0H where the jump must be. Locations 00000H through 003FFH are reserved for interrupt operations. Each of the 256 possible interrupt types has its service routine pointed to by a 4-byte pointer element

---

consisting of a 16-bit segment address and a 16-bit offset address. The pointer elements are assumed to have been stored at the respective places in reserved memory prior to occurrence of interrupts.

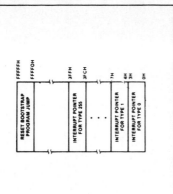

Figure 3b. Reserved Memory Locations

MINIMUM AND MAXIMUM MODES

The requirements for supporting minimum and maximum iAPX 86/10 systems are sufficiently different that they cannot be done efficiently with 40 uniquely defined pins. Consequently, the 8086 is equipped with a strap pin (MN/$\overline{MX}$) which defines the system configuration. The definition of a certain subset of the pins changes dependent on the condition of the strap pin. When MN/$\overline{MX}$ pin is strapped to GND, the 8086 treats pins 24 through 31 in maximum mode. An 8288 bus controller interprets status information coded into $\overline{S_0},\overline{S_1},\overline{S_2}$ to generate bus timing and control signals compatible with the MULTIBUS™ architecture. When the MN/$\overline{MX}$ pin is strapped to V_{CC}, the 8086 generates bus control signals itself on pins 24 through 31, as shown in parentheses in Figure 2. Examples of minimum mode and maximum mode systems are shown in Figure 4.

Memory Reference Need	Segment Register Used	Segment Selection Rule
Instructions	CODE (CS)	Automatic with all instruction prefetch.
Stack	STACK (SS)	All stack pushes and pops. Memory references relative to BP base register except data references.
Local Data	DATA (DS)	Data references when: relative to stack, destination of string operation, or explicitly overridden.
External (Global) Data	EXTRA (ES)	Destination of string operations: Explicitly selected using a segment override.

BUS OPERATION

The 86/10 has a combined address and data bus commonly referred to as a time multiplexed bus. This technique provides the most efficient use of pins on the processor while permitting the use of a standard 40-lead package. This "local bus" can be buffered directly and used throughout the system with address latching provided on memory and I/O modules. In addition, the bus can also be demultiplexed at the processor with a single set of address latches if a standard non-multiplexed bus is desired for the system.

Each processor bus cycle consists of at least four CLK cycles. These are referred to as T_1, T_2, T_3 and T_4 (see Figure 5). The address is emitted from the processor during T_1, and data transfer occurs on the bus during T_3 and T_4. T_2 is used primarily for changing the direction of the bus during read operations. In the event that a "NOT READY" indication is given by the addressed device, "Wait" states (T_W) are inserted between T_3 and T_4. Each inserted "Wait" state is of the same duration as a CLK cycle. Periods can occur between 8086 bus cycles. These are referred to as "Idle" states (T_I) or inactive CLK cycles. The processor uses these cycles for internal housekeeping.

During T_1 of any bus cycle the ALE (Address Latch Enable) signal is emitted (by either the processor or the 8288 bus controller, depending on the MN/MX strap). At the trailing edge of this pulse, a valid address and certain status information for the cycle may be latched.

Status bits $\overline{S_0}$, $\overline{S_1}$, and $\overline{S_2}$ are used, in maximum mode, by the bus controller to identify the type of bus transaction according to the following table:

$\overline{S_2}$	$\overline{S_1}$	$\overline{S_0}$	CHARACTERISTICS
0 (LOW)	0	0	Interrupt Acknowledge
0	0	1	Read I/O
0	1	0	Write I/O
0	1	1	Halt
1 (HIGH)	0	0	Instruction Fetch
1	0	1	Read Data from Memory
1	1	0	Write Data to Memory
1	1	1	Passive (no bus cycle)

Status bits S_3 through S_7 are multiplexed with high-order address bits and the $\overline{BHE}$ signal, and are therefore valid during T_2 through T_4. S_3 and S_4 indicate which segment register (see Instruction Set description) was used for this bus cycle in forming the address, according to the following table:

S_4	S_3	CHARACTERISTICS
0 (LOW)	0	Alternate Data (extra segment)
0	1	Stack
1 (HIGH)	0	Code or None
1	1	Data

S_5 is a reflection of the PSW interrupt enable bit, $S_6=0$ and S_7 is a spare status bit.

I/O ADDRESSING

In the 86/10, I/O operations can address up to a maximum of 64K I/O byte registers or 32K I/O word registers. The I/O address appears in the same format as the memory address on bus lines A_{15}-A_0. The address lines A_{19}-A_{16} are zero in I/O operations. The variable I/O instructions which use register DX as a pointer have full address capability while the direct I/O instructions directly address one or two of the 256 I/O byte locations in page 0 of the I/O address space.

I/O ports are addressed in the same manner as memory locations. Even addressed bytes are transferred on the D_7-D_0 bus lines and odd addressed bytes on D_{15}-D_8. Care must be taken to assure that each register within an 8-bit peripheral located on the lower portion of the bus be addressed as even.

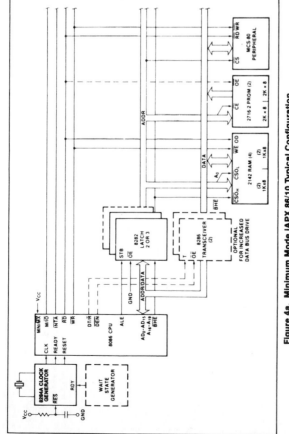

Figure 4a. Minimum Mode iAPX 86/10 Typical Configuration

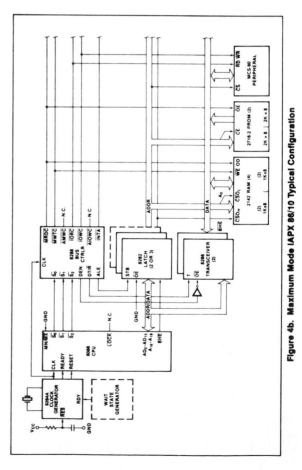

Figure 4b. Maximum Mode iAPX 86/10 Typical Configuration

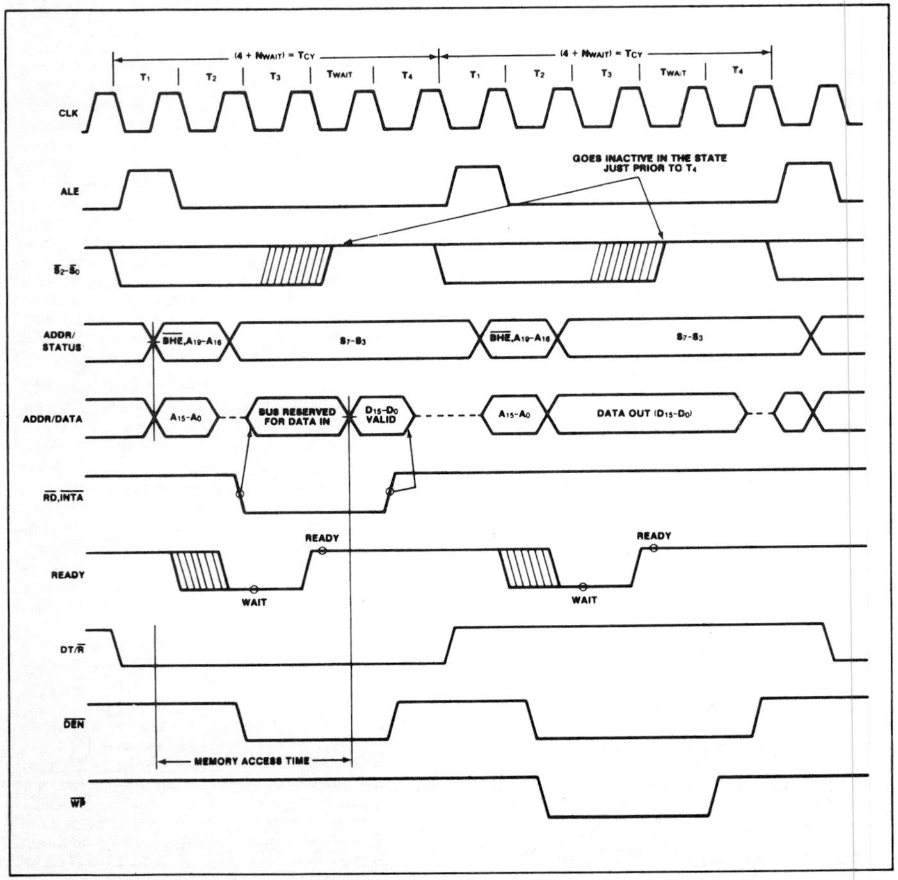

Figure 5. Basic System Timing

sequence, which is used to "vector" through the appropriate element to the new interrupt service program location.

EXTERNAL INTERFACE

PROCESSOR RESET AND INITIALIZATION

Processor initialization or start up is accomplished with activation (HIGH) of the RESET pin. The 8086 RESET is required to be HIGH for greater than 4 CLK cycles. The 8086 will terminate operations on the high-going edge of RESET and will remain dormant as long as RESET is HIGH. The low-going transition of RESET triggers an internal reset sequence for approximately 10 CLK cycles. After this interval the 8086 operates normally beginning with the instruction in absolute location FFFF0H (see Figure 3B). The details of this operation are specified in the Instruction Set description of the MCS-86 Family User's Manual. The RESET input is internally synchronized to the processor clock. At initialization the HIGH-to-LOW transition of RESET must occur no sooner than 50 μs after power-up, to allow complete initialization of the 8086.

NMI may not be asserted prior to the 2nd CLK cycle following the end of RESET.

INTERRUPT OPERATIONS

Interrupt operations fall into two classes: software or hardware initiated. The software initiated interrupts and software aspects of hardware interrupts are specified in the Instruction Set description. Hardware interrupts can be classified as non-maskable or maskable.

Interrupts result in a transfer of control to a new program location. A 256-element table containing address pointers to the interrupt service program locations resides in absolute locations 0 through 3FFH (see Figure 3b), which are reserved for this purpose. Each element in the table is 4 bytes in size and corresponds to an interrupt "type". An interrupting device supplies an 8-bit type number, during the interrupt acknowledge

NON-MASKABLE INTERRUPT (NMI)

The processor provides a single non-maskable interrupt pin (NMI) which has higher priority than the maskable interrupt request pin (INTR). A typical use would be to activate a power failure routine. The NMI is edge-triggered on a LOW-to-HIGH transition. The activation of this pin causes a type 2 interrupt. (See Instruction Set description.)

NMI is required to have a duration in the HIGH state of greater than two CLK cycles, but is not required to be synchronized to the clock. Any high-going transition of NMI is latched on-chip and will be serviced at the end of the current instruction or between whole moves of a block-type instruction. Worst case response to NMI would be for multiply, divide, and variable shift instructions. There is no specification on the occurrence of the low-going edge; it may occur before, during, or after the servicing of NMI. Another high-going edge triggers another response if it occurs after the start of the NMI procedure. The signal must be free of logical spikes in general and be free of bounces on the low-going edge to avoid triggering extraneous responses.

MASKABLE INTERRUPT (INTR)

The 86/10 provides a single interrupt request input (INTR) which can be masked internally by software with the resetting of the interrupt enable FLAG status bit. The interrupt request signal is level triggered. It is internally synchronized during each clock cycle on the high-going edge of CLK. To be responded to, INTR must be present (HIGH) during the clock period preceding the end of the current instruction or the end of a whole move for a block-type instruction. During the interrupt response sequence further interrupts are disabled. The enable bit is reset as part of the response to any interrupt (INTR, NMI, software interrupt or single-step), although the

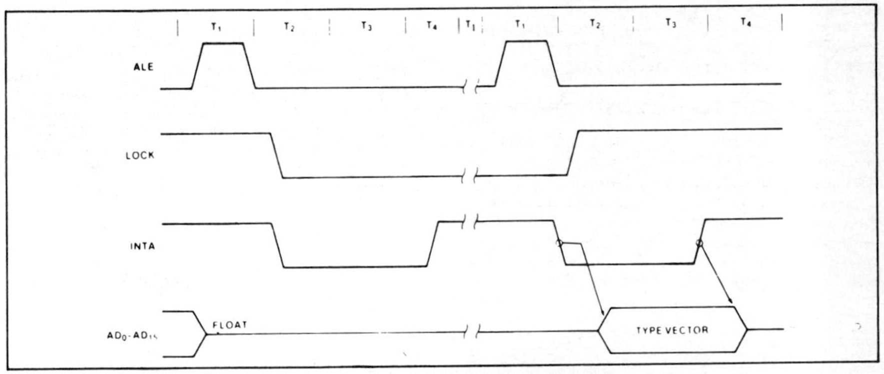

Figure 6. Interrupt Acknowledge Sequence

FLAGS register which is automatically pushed onto the stack reflects the state of the processor prior to the interrupt. Until the old FLAGS register is restored the enable bit will be zero unless specifically set by an instruction.

During the response sequence (figure 6) the processor executes two successive (back-to-back) interrupt acknowledge cycles. The 8086 emits the LOCK signal from T_2 of the first bus cycle until T_2 of the second. A local bus "hold" request will not be honored until the end of the second bus cycle. In the second bus cycle a byte is fetched from the external interrupt system (e.g., 8259A PIC) which identifies the source (type) of the interrupt. This byte is multiplied by four and used as a pointer into the interrupt vector lookup table. An INTR signal left HIGH will be continually responded to within the limitations of the enable bit and sample period. The INTERRUPT RETURN instruction includes a FLAGS pop which returns the status of the original interrupt enable bit when it restores the FLAGS.

HALT

When a software "HALT" instruction is executed the processor indicates that it is entering the "HALT" state in one of two ways depending upon which mode is strapped. In minimum mode, the processor issues one ALE with no qualifying bus control signals. In Maximum Mode, the processor issues appropriate HALT status on $\bar{S}_2, \bar{S}_1, \bar{S}_0$ and the 8288 bus controller issues one ALE. The 8086 will not leave the "HALT" state when a local bus "hold" is entered while in "HALT". In this case, the processor reissues the HALT indicator. An interrupt request or RESET will force the 8086 out of the "HALT" state.

READ/MODIFY/WRITE (SEMAPHORE) OPERATIONS VIA LOCK

The LOCK status information is provided by the processor when directly consecutive bus cycles are required during the execution of an instruction. This provides the processor with the capability of performing read/modify/write operations on memory (via the Exchange Register With Memory instruction, for example) without the possibility of another system bus master receiving intervening memory cycles. This is useful in multi-processor system configurations to accomplish "test and set lock" operations. The LOCK signal is activated (forced LOW) in the clock cycle following the one in which the software "LOCK" prefix instruction is decoded by the EU. It is deactivated at the end of the last bus cycle of the instruction following the "LOCK" prefix instruction. While LOCK is active a request on a RQ/GT pin will be recorded and then honored at the end of the LOCK.

EXTERNAL SYNCHRONIZATION VIA TEST

As an alternative to the interrupts and general I/O capabilities, the 8086 provides a single software-testable input known as the TEST signal. At any time the program may execute a WAIT instruction. If at that time the TEST signal is inactive (HIGH), program execution becomes suspended while the processor waits for TEST

to become active. It must remain active for at least 5 CLK cycles. The WAIT instruction is re-executed repeatedly until that time. This activity does not consume bus cycles. The processor remains in an idle state while waiting. All 8086 drivers go to 3-state OFF if bus "Hold" is entered. If interrupts are enabled, they may occur while the processor is waiting. When this occurs the processor fetches the WAIT instruction one extra time, processes the interrupt, and then re-fetches and re-executes the WAIT instruction upon returning from the interrupt.

BASIC SYSTEM TIMING

Typical system configurations for the processor operating in minimum mode and in maximum mode are shown in Figures 4a and 4b, respectively. In minimum mode, the MN/MX pin is strapped to V_{CC} and the processor emits bus control signals in a manner similar to the 8085. In maximum mode, the MN/MX pin is strapped to V_{SS} and the processor emits coded status information which the 8288 bus controller uses to generate MULTIBUS compatible bus control signals. Figure 5 illustrates the signal timing relationships.

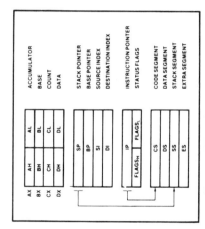

Figure 7. IAPX 86/10 Register Model

to a HIGH level, the addressed device will again 3-state its bus drivers. If a transceiver (8286/8287) is required to buffer the 8086 local bus, signals DT/R and DEN are provided by the 8086.

A write cycle also begins with the assertion of ALE and the emission of the address. The M/IO signal is again asserted to indicate a memory or I/O write operation. In the T_2 immediately following the address emission the processor emits the data to be written into the addressed location. This data remains valid until the middle of T_4. During T_2, T_3, and T_W the processor asserts the write control signal. The write (WR) signal becomes active at the beginning of T_2 as opposed to the read which is delayed somewhat into T_2 to provide time for the bus to float.

The BHE and A_0 signals are used to select the proper byte(s) of the memory/IO word to be read or written according to the following table:

BHE	A0	CHARACTERISTICS
0	0	Whole word
0	1	Upper byte from/ to odd address
1	0	Lower byte from/ to even address
1	1	None

I/O ports are addressed in the same manner as memory location. Even addressed bytes are transferred on the D_7-D_0 bus lines and odd addressed bytes on D_{15}-D_8.

The basic difference between the interrupt acknowledge cycle and a read cycle is that the interrupt acknowledge signal (INTA) is asserted in place of the

read (RD) signal and the address bus is floated. (See Figure 6.) In the second of two successive INTA cycles, a byte of information is read from bus lines D_7-D_0 as supplied by the interrupt system logic (i.e., 8259A Priority Interrupt Controller). This byte identifies the source (type) of the interrupt. It is multiplied by four and used as a pointer into an interrupt vector lookup table, as described earlier.

BUS TIMING—MEDIUM SIZE SYSTEMS

For medium size systems the MN/MX pin is connected to V_{SS} and the 8288 Bus Controller is added to the system as well as an 8282/8283 latch for latching the system address, and a 8286/8287 transceiver to allow for bus loading greater than the 8086 is capable of handling. Signals ALE, DEN, and DT/R are generated by the 8288 instead of the processor in this configuration although their timing remains relatively the same. The 8086 status outputs ($\bar{S}_2$, $\bar{S}_1$, and $\bar{S}_0$) provide type-of-cycle information and become 8288 inputs. This bus cycle information specifies read (code, data, or I/O), write (data or I/O), interrupt acknowledge, or software halt. The 8288 thus issues control signals specifying memory read or write, I/O read or write, or interrupt acknowledge. The 8288 provides two types of write strobes, normal and advanced, to be applied as required. The normal write strobes have data valid at the leading edge of write. The advanced write strobes have the same timing as read strobes, and hence data isn't valid at the leading edge of write. The 8286/8287 transceiver receives the usual T and OE inputs from the 8288's DT/R and DEN.

The pointer into the interrupt vector table, which is passed during the second INTA cycle, can derive from an 8259A located on either the local bus or the system bus. If the master 8259A Priority Interrupt Controller is positioned on the local bus, a TTL gate is required to disable the 8286/8287 transceiver when reading from the master 8259A during the interrupt acknowledge sequence and software "poll".

SYSTEM TIMING — MINIMUM SYSTEM

The read cycle begins in T_1 with the assertion of the Address Latch Enable (ALE) signal. The trailing (low-going) edge of this signal is used to latch the address information, which is valid on the local bus at this time, into the 8282/8283 latch. The BHE and A_0 signals address the low, high, or both bytes. From T_1 to T_4 the M/IO signal indicates a memory or I/O operation. At T_2 the address is removed from the local bus and the bus goes to a high impedance state. The read control signal is also asserted at T_2. The read (RD) signal causes the addressed device to enable its data bus drivers to the local bus. Some time later valid data will be available on the bus and the addressed device will drive the READY line HIGH. When the processor returns the read signal

iAPX 86/10

A.C. CHARACTERISTICS

(8086: T_A = 0°C to 70°C, V_{CC} = 5V ± 10%)
(8086-1: T_A = 0°C to 70°C, V_{CC} = 5V ± 5%)
(8086-2: T_A = 0°C to 70°C, V_{CC} = 5V ± 5%)

MINIMUM COMPLEXITY SYSTEM TIMING REQUIREMENTS

Symbol	Parameter	8086 Min	8086 Max	8086-1 (Preliminary) Min	8086-1 (Preliminary) Max	8086-2 Min	8086-2 Max	Units	Test Conditions
TCLCL	CLK Cycle Period	200	500	100	500	125	500	ns	
TCLCH	CLK Low Time	118		53		68		ns	
TCHCL	CLK High Time	69		39		44		ns	
TCH1CH2	CLK Rise Time		10		10		10	ns	From 1.0V to 3.5V
TCL2CL1	CLK Fall Time		10		10		10	ns	From 3.5V to 1.0V
TDVCL	Data in Setup Time	30		5		20		ns	
TCLDX	Data in Hold Time	10		10		10		ns	
TR1VCL	RDY Setup Time into 8284A (See Notes 1, 2)	35		35		35		ns	
TCLR1X	RDY Hold Time into 8284A (See Notes 1, 2)	0		0		0		ns	
TRYHCH	READY Setup Time into 8086	118		53		68		ns	
TCHRYX	READY Hold Time into 8086	30		20		20		ns	
TRYLCL	READY Inactive to CLK (See Note 3)	-8		-10		-8		ns	
THVCH	HOLD Setup Time	35		20		20		ns	
TINVCH	INTR, NMI, TEST Setup Time (See Note 2)	30		15		15		ns	
TILIH	Input Rise Time (Except CLK)		20		20		20	ns	From 0.8V to 2.0V
TIHIL	Input Fall Time (Except CLK)		12		12		12	ns	From 2.0V to 0.8V

iAPX 86/10

ABSOLUTE MAXIMUM RATINGS*

Ambient Temperature Under Bias........0°C to 70°C
Storage Temperature.............−65°C to +150°C
Voltage on Any Pin with
  Respect to Ground............. −1.0 to +7V
Power Dissipation...................2.5 Watt

*NOTICE: Stresses above those listed under "Absolute Maximum Ratings" may cause permanent damage to the device. This is a stress rating only and functional operation of the device at these or any other conditions above those indicated in the operational sections of this specification is not implied. Exposure to absolute maximum rating conditions for extended periods may affect device reliability.

D.C. CHARACTERISTICS

(8086: T_A = 0°C to 70°C, V_{CC} = 5V ± 10%)
(8086-1: T_A = 0°C to 70°C, V_{CC} = 5V ± 5%)
(8086-2: T_A = 0°C to 70°C, V_{CC} = 5V ± 5%)

Symbol	Parameter	Min.	Max.	Units	Test Conditions
V_{IL}	Input Low Voltage	−0.5	+0.8	V	
V_{IH}	Input High Voltage	2.0	V_{CC}+0.5	V	
V_{OL}	Output Low Voltage		0.45	V	I_{OL}=2.5 mA
V_{OH}	Output High Voltage	2.4		V	I_{OH}= −400 μA
I_{CC}	Power Supply Current: 8086		340	mA	T_A=25°C
	8086-1		360		
	8086-2		350		
I_{LI}	Input Leakage Current		±10	μA	0V ≤ V_{IN} ≤ V_{CC}
I_{LO}	Output Leakage Current		±10	μA	0.45V ≤ V_{OUT} ≤ V_{CC}
V_{CL}	Clock Input Low Voltage	−0.5	+0.6	V	
V_{CH}	Clock Input High Voltage	3.9	V_{CC}+1.0	V	
C_{IN}	Capacitance of Input Buffer (All input except AD_0 – AD_{15}, $\overline{RQ}/\overline{GT}$)		15	pF	fc = 1 MHz
C_{IO}	Capacitance of I/O Buffer (AD_0 – AD_{15}, $\overline{RQ}/\overline{GT}$)		15	pF	fc = 1 MHz

intel   iAPX 86/10

A.C. CHARACTERISTICS (Continued)

TIMING RESPONSES

Symbol	Parameter	8086 Min.	8086 Max.	8086-1 (Preliminary) Min.	8086-1 (Preliminary) Max.	8086-2 Min.	8086-2 Max.	Units	Test Conditions
TCLAV	Address Valid Delay	10	110	10	50	10	60	ns	
TCLAX	Address Hold Time	10		10		10		ns	
TCLAZ	Address Float Delay	TCLAX	80	TCLAX	40	TCLAX	50	ns	
TLHLL	ALE Width	TCLCH–20		TCLCH–10		TCLCH–10		ns	
TCLLH	ALE Active Delay		80		40		50	ns	
TCHLL	ALE Inactive Delay		85		45		55	ns	
TLLAX	Address Hold Time to ALE Inactive	TCHCL–10		TCHCL–10		TCHCL–10		ns	
TCLDV	Data Valid Delay	10	110	10	50	10	60	ns	*CL = 20–100 pF for all 8086 Outputs (In addition to 8086 self-load)
TCHDX	Data Hold Time	10		10		10		ns	
TWHDX	Data Hold Time After WR	TCLCH–30		TCLCH–25		TCLCH–30		ns	
TCVCTV	Control Active Delay 1	10	110	10	50	10	70	ns	
TCHCTV	Control Active Delay 2	10	110	10	45	10	60	ns	
TCVCTX	Control Inactive Delay	10	110	10	50	10	70	ns	
TAZRL	Address Float to READ Active	0		0		0		ns	
TCLRL	RD Active Delay	10	165	10	70	10	100	ns	
TCLRH	RD Inactive Delay	10	150	10	60	10	80	ns	
TRHAV	RD Inactive to Next Address Active	TCLCL–45		TCLCL–35		TCLCL–40		ns	
TCLHAV	HLDA Valid Delay	10	160	10	60	10	100	ns	
TRLRH	RD Width	2TCLCL–75		2TCLCL–40		2TCLCL–50		ns	
TWLWH	WR Width	2TCLCL–60		2TCLCL–35		2TCLCL–40		ns	
TAVAL	Address Valid to ALE Low	TCLCH–60		TCLCH–35		TCLCH–40		ns	
TOLOH	Output Rise Time		20		20		20	ns	From 0.8V to 2.0V
TOHOL	Output Fall Time		12		12		12	ns	From 2.0V to 0.8V

NOTES:
1. Signal at 8284A shown for reference only.
2. Setup requirement for asynchronous signal only to guarantee recognition at next CLK.
3. Applies only to T2 state. (8 ns into T3).

intel   iAPX 86/10

A.C. TESTING INPUT, OUTPUT WAVEFORM

INPUT/OUTPUT

2.4 ⟩ 1.5 ← TEST POINTS → 1.5 ⟨ 0.45

A.C. TESTING INPUTS ARE DRIVEN AT 2.4V FOR A LOGIC "1" AND 0.45V FOR A LOGIC "0". TIMING MEASUREMENTS ARE MADE AT 1.5V FOR BOTH A LOGIC "1" AND "0".

A.C. TESTING LOAD CIRCUIT

DEVICE UNDER TEST ── C_L = 100 pF

C_L INCLUDES JIG CAPACITANCE

WAVEFORMS

MINIMUM MODE

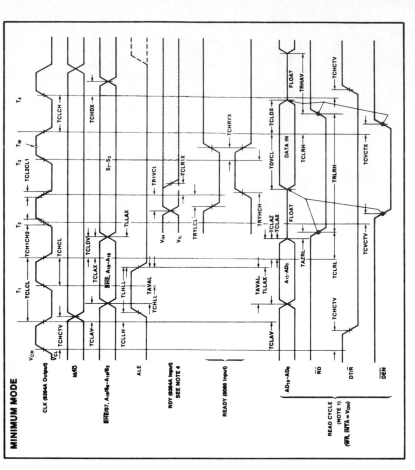

586   APPENDIX A

WAVEFORMS (Continued)

MINIMUM MODE (Continued)

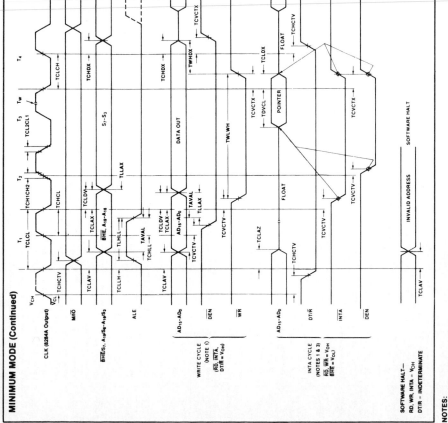

SOFTWARE HALT —
RD, WR, INTA = V$_{OH}$
DT/R̄ = INDETERMINATE

NOTES:
1. All signals switch between V$_{OH}$ and V$_{OL}$ unless otherwise specified.
2. RDY is sampled near the end of T$_2$, T$_3$, T$_W$ to determine if T$_W$ machines states are to be inserted.
3. Two INTA cycles run back-to-back. The 8086 LOCAL ADDR/DATA BUS is floating during both INTA cycles. Control signals shown for second INTA cycle.
4. Signals at 8284A are shown for reference only.
5. All timing measurements are made at 1.5V unless otherwise noted.

A.C. CHARACTERISTICS

MAX MODE SYSTEM (USING 8288 BUS CONTROLLER) TIMING REQUIREMENTS

Symbol	Parameter	8086		8086-1 (Preliminary)		8086-2 (Preliminary)		Units	Test Conditions
		Min.	Max.	Min.	Max.	Min.	Max.		
TCLCL	CLK Cycle Period	200	500	100	500	125	500	ns	
TCLCH	CLK Low Time	118		53		68		ns	
TCHCL	CLK High Time	69		39		44		ns	
TCH1CH2	CLK Rise Time		10		10		10	ns	From 1.0V to 3.5V
TCL2CL1	CLK Fall Time		10		10		10	ns	From 3.5V to 1.0V
TDVCL	Data in Setup Time	30		5		20		ns	
TCLDX	Data in Hold Time	10		10		10		ns	
TR1VCL	RDY Setup Time into 8284A (See Notes 1, 2)	35		35		35		ns	
TCLR1X	RDY Hold Time into 8284A (See Notes 1, 2)	0		0		0		ns	
TRYHCH	READY Setup Time into 8086	118		53		68		ns	
TCHRYX	READY Hold Time into 8086	30		20		20		ns	
TRYLCL	READY Inactive to CLK (See Note 4)	-8		-10		-8		ns	
TINVCH	Setup Time for Recognition (INTR, NMI, TEST) (See Note 2)	30		15		15		ns	
TGVCH	RQ/GT Setup Time	30		12		15		ns	
TCHGX	RQ Hold Time into 8086	40		20		30		ns	
TILIH	Input Rise Time (Except CLK)		20		20		20	ns	From 0.8V to 2.0V
TIHIL	Input Fall Time (Except CLK)		12		12		12	ns	From 2.0V to 0.8V

NOTES:
1. Signal at 8284A or 8288 shown for reference only.
2. Setup requirement for asynchronous signal only to guarantee recognition at next CLK.
3. Applies only to T3 and wait states.
4. Applies only to T2 state (8 ns into T3).

A.C. CHARACTERISTICS (Continued)

TIMING RESPONSES

Symbol	Parameter	8086 Min.	8086 Max.	8086-1 (Preliminary) Min.	8086-1 (Preliminary) Max.	8086-2 (Preliminary) Min.	8086-2 (Preliminary) Max.	Units	Test Conditions
TCLML	Command Active Delay (See Note 1)	10	35	10	35	10	35	ns	
TCLMH	Command Inactive Delay (See Note 1)	10	35	10	35	10	35	ns	
TRYHSH	READY Active to Status Passive (See Note 3)		110		45		65	ns	
TCHSV	Status Active Delay	10	110	10	45	10	60	ns	
TCLSH	Status Inactive Delay	10	130	10	55	10	70	ns	
TCLAV	Address Valid Delay	10	110	10	50	10	60	ns	
TCLAX	Address Hold Time	10		10		10		ns	
TCLAZ	Address Float Delay	TCLAX	80	TCLAX	40	TCLAX	50	ns	
TSVLH	Status Valid to ALE High (See Note 1)		15		15		15	ns	
TSVMCH	Status Valid to MCE High (See Note 1)		15		15		15	ns	C_L = 20-100 pF for all 8086 Outputs (in addition to 8086 self-load)
TCLLH	CLK Low to ALE Valid (See Note 1)		15		15		15	ns	
TCLMCH	CLK Low to MCE High (See Note 1)		15		15		15	ns	
TCHLL	ALE Inactive Delay (See Note 1)		15		15		15	ns	
TCLMCL	MCE Inactive Delay (See Note 1)		15		15		15	ns	
TCLDV	Data Valid Delay	10	110	10	50	10	60	ns	
TCHDX	Data Hold Time	10		10		10		ns	
TCVNV	Control Active Delay (See Note 1)	5	45	5	45	5	45	ns	
TCVNX	Control Inactive Delay (See Note 1)	10	45	10	45	10	45	ns	
TAZRL	Address Float to Read Active	0		0		0		ns	
TCLRL	RD Active Delay	10	165	10	70	10	60	ns	
TCLRH	RD Inactive Delay	10	150	10	60	10	80	ns	
TRHAV	RD Inactive to Next Address Active	TCLCL-45		TCLCL-35		TCLCL-40		ns	
TCHDTL	Direction Control Active Delay (See Note 1)		50		50		50	ns	
TCHDTH	Direction Control Inactive Delay (See Note 1)		30		30		30	ns	
TCLGL	GT Active Delay	0	85	0	45	0	50	ns	
TCLGH	GT Inactive Delay	0	85	0	45	0	50	ns	
TRLRH	RD Width	2TCLCL-75		2TCLCL-40		2TCLCL-50		ns	
TOLOH	Output Rise Time		20		20		20	ns	From 0.8V to 2.0V
TOHOL	Output Fall Time		12		12		12	ns	From 2.0V to 0.8V

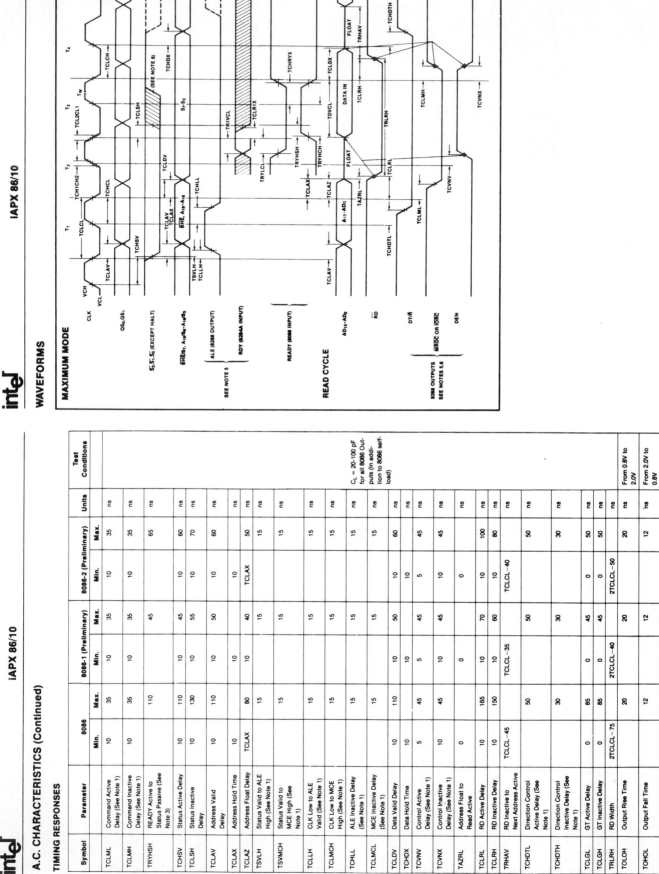

WAVEFORMS

MAXIMUM MODE

READ CYCLE

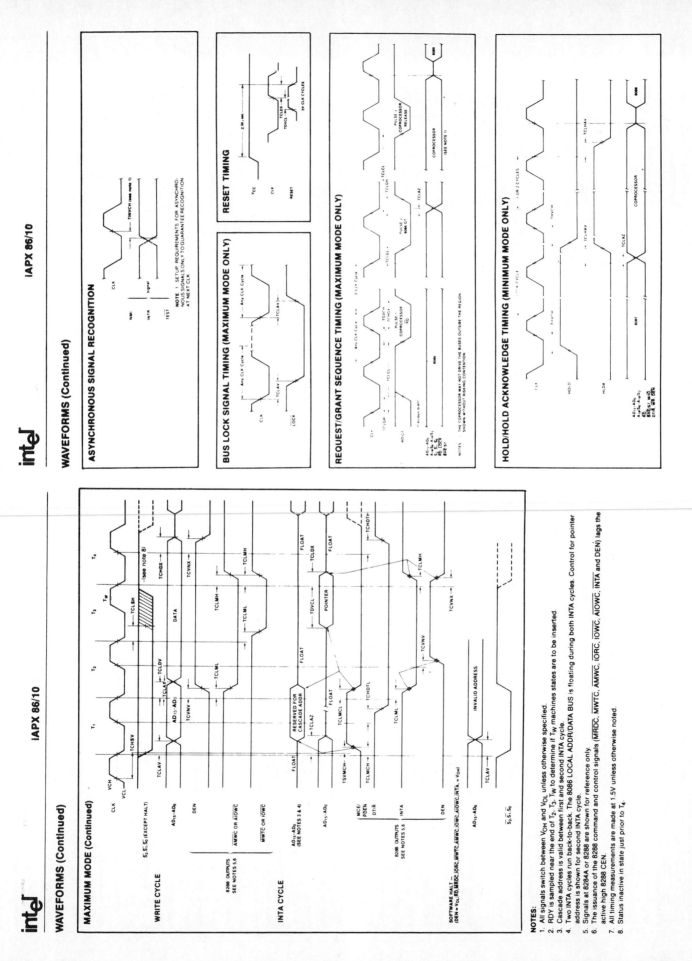

NOTES:

1. All signals switch between V_{OH} and V_{OL} unless otherwise specified.
2. RDY is sampled near the end of T_2, T_3, T_w to determine if T_w machines states are to be inserted.
3. Cascade address is valid between first and second INTA cycle.
4. Two INTA cycles run back-to-back. The 8086 LOCAL ADDR/DATA BUS is floating during both INTA cycles. Control for pointer address is shown for second INTA cycle.
5. Signals at 8284A or 8288 are shown for reference only.
6. The issuance of the 8288 command and control signals (MRDC, MWTC, AMWC, IORC, IOWC, AIOWC, INTA and DEN) lags the active high 8288 CEN.
7. All timing measurements are made at 1.5V unless otherwise noted.
8. Status inactive in state just prior to T_4.

Table 2. Instruction Set Summary

1. DATA TRANSFER

Mnemonic and Description	Instruction Code			
MOV = Move:	76543210	76543210	76543210	76543210
Register/Memory to/from Register	100010dw	mod reg r/m		
Immediate to Register/Memory	1100011w	mod 0 0 0 r/m	data	data if w = 1
Immediate to Register	1011w reg	data	data if w = 1	
Memory to Accumulator	1010000w	addr-low	addr-high	
Accumulator to Memory	1010001w	addr-low	addr-high	
Register/Memory to Segment Register	10001110	mod 0 reg r/m		
Segment Register to Register/Memory	10001100	mod 0 reg r/m		
PUSH = Push:				
Register/Memory	11111111	mod 1 1 0 r/m		
Register	01010 reg			
Segment Register	000 reg 110			
POP = Pop:				
Register/Memory	10001111	mod 0 0 0 r/m		
Register	01011 reg			
Segment Register	000 reg 111			
XCHG = Exchange:				
Register/Memory with Register	1000011w	mod reg r/m		
Register with Accumulator	10010 reg			
IN = Input from:				
Fixed Port	1110010w	port		
Variable Port	1110110w			
OUT = Output to:				
Fixed Port	1110011w	port		
Variable Port	1110111w			
XLAT = Translate Byte to AL	11010111			
LEA = Load EA to Register	10001101	mod reg r/m		
LDS = Load Pointer to DS	11000101	mod reg r/m		
LES = Load Pointer to ES	11000100	mod reg r/m		
LAHF = Load AH with Flags	10011111			
SAHF = Store AH into Flags	10011110			
PUSHF = Push Flags	10011100			
POPF = Pop Flags	10011101			
ARITHMETIC				
ADD = Add:				
Reg./Memory with Register to Either	000000dw	mod reg r/m		
Immediate to Register/Memory	100000sw	mod 0 0 0 r/m	data	data if s: w = 01
Immediate to Accumulator	0000010w	data	data if w = 1	
ADC = Add with Carry:				
Reg./Memory with Register to Either	000100dw	mod reg r/m		
Immediate to Register/Memory	100000sw	mod 0 1 0 r/m	data	data if s: w = 01
Immediate to Accumulator	0001010w	data	data if w = 1	
INC = Increment:				
Register/Memory	1111111w	mod 0 0 0 r/m		
Register	01000 reg			

2.

Mnemonic and Description	Instruction Code			
	76543210	76543210	76543210	76543210
AAA = ASCII Adjust for Add	00110111			
DAA = Decimal Adjust for Add	00100111			
SUB = Subtract:				
Reg./Memory and Register to Either	001010dw	mod reg r/m		
Immediate from Register/Memory	100000sw	mod 1 0 1 r/m	data	data if s w = 01
Immediate from Accumulator	0010110w	data	data if w = 1	
SSB = Subtract with Borrow				
Reg./Memory and Register to Either	000110dw	mod reg r/m		
Immediate from Register/Memory	100000sw	mod 0 1 1 r/m	data	data if s w = 01
Immediate from Accumulator	000111w	data	data if w = 1	
DEC = Decrement:				
Register/memory	1111111w	mod 0 0 1 r/m		
Register	01001 reg			
NEG = Change sign	1111011w	mod 0 1 1 r/m		
CMP = Compare:				
Register/Memory and Register	001110dw	mod reg r/m		
Immediate with Register/Memory	100000sw	mod 1 1 1 r/m	data	data if s w = 01
Immediate with Accumulator	0011110w	data	data if w = 1	
AAS = ASCII Adjust for Subtract	00111111			
DAS = Decimal Adjust for Subtract	00101111			
MUL = Multiply (Unsigned)	1111011w	mod 1 0 0 r/m		
IMUL = Integer Multiply (Signed)	1111011w	mod 1 0 1 r/m		
AAM = ASCII Adjust for Multiply	11010100	00001010		
DIV = Divide (Unsigned)	1111011w	mod 1 1 0 r/m		
IDIV = Integer Divide (Signed)	1111011w	mod 1 1 1 r/m		
AAD = ASCII Adjust for Divide	11010101	00001010		
CBW = Convert Byte to Word	10011000			
CWD = Convert Word to Double Word	10011001			
LOGIC				
NOT = Invert	1111011w	mod 0 1 0 r/m		
SHL/SAL = Shift Logical/Arithmetic Left	110100vw	mod 1 0 0 r/m		
SHR = Shift Logical Right	110100vw	mod 1 0 1 r/m		
SAR = Shift Arithmetic Right	110100vw	mod 1 1 1 r/m		
ROL = Rotate Left	110100vw	mod 0 0 0 r/m		
ROR = Rotate Right	110100vw	mod 0 0 1 r/m		
RCL = Rotate Through Carry Flag Left	110100vw	mod 0 1 0 r/m		
RCR = Rotate Through Carry Right	110100vw	mod 0 1 1 r/m		
AND = And:				
Reg./Memory and Register to Either	001000dw	mod reg r/m		
Immediate to Register/Memory	1000000w	mod 1 0 0 r/m	data	data if w = 1
Immediate to Accumulator	0010010w	data	data if w = 1	
TEST = And Function to Flags, No Result:				
Register/Memory and Register	1000010w	mod reg r/m		
Immediate Data and Register/Memory	1111011w	mod 0 0 0 r/m	data	data if w = 1
Immediate Data and Accumulator	1010100w	data	data if w = 1	

3

Mnemonic and Description	Instruction Code			
OR = Or:	76543210	76543210	76543210	76543210
Reg./Memory and Register to Either	000010dw	mod reg r/m		
Immediate to Register/Memory	1000000w	mod 0 0 1 r/m	data	data if w = 1
Immediate to Accumulator	0000110w	data	data if w = 1	
XOR = Exclusive or:				
Reg./Memory and Register to Either	001100dw	mod reg r/m		
Immediate to Register/Memory	1000000w	mod 1 1 0 r/m	data	data if w = 1
Immediate to Accumulator	0011010w	data	data if w = 1	
STRING MANIPULATION				
REP = Repeat	1111001z			
MOVS = Move Byte/Word	1010010w			
CMPS = Compare Byte/Word	1010011w			
SCAS = Scan Byte/Word	1010111w			
LODS = Load Byte/Wd to AL/AX	1010110w			
STOS = Stor Byte/Wd from AL/A	1010101w			
CONTROL TRANSFER				
CALL = Call:				
Direct within Segment	11101000	disp-low	disp-high	
Indirect within Segment	11111111	mod 0 1 0 r/m		
Direct Intersegment	10011010	offset-low	offset-high	
		seg-low	seg-high	
Indirect Intersegment	11111111	mod 0 1 1 r/m		
JMP = Unconditional Jump:				
Direct within Segment	11101001	disp-low	disp-high	
Direct within Segment-Short	11101011	disp		
Indirect within Segment	11111111	mod 1 0 0 r/m		
Direct Intersegment	11101010	offset-low	offset-high	
		seg-low	seg-high	
Indirect Intersegment	11111111	mod 1 0 1 r/m		
RET = Return from CALL:				
Within Segment	11000011			
Within Seg Adding Immed to SP	11000010	data-low	data-high	
Intersegment	11001011			
Intersegment Adding Immediate to SP	11001010	data-low	data-high	
JE/JZ = Jump on Equal/Zero	01110100	disp		
JL/JNGE = Jump on Less/Not Greater or Equal	01111100	disp		
JLE/JNG = Jump on Less or Equal/Not Greater	01111110	disp		
JB/JNAE = Jump on Below/Not Above or Equal	01110010	disp		
JBE/JNA = Jump on Below or Equal/Not Above	01110110	disp		
JP/JPE = Jump on Parity/Parity Even	01111010	disp		
JO = Jump on Overflow	01110000	disp		
JS = Jump on Sign	01111000	disp		
JNE/JNZ = Jump on Not Equal/Not Zero	01110101	disp		
JNL/JGE = Jump on Not Less/Greater or Equal	01111101	disp		
JNLE/JG = Jump on Not Less or Equal/Greater	01111111	disp		

4

Mnemonic and Description	Instruction Code			
	76543210	76543210	76543210	76543210
JNB/JAE = Jump on Not Below/Above or Equal	01110011	disp		
JNBE/JA = Jump on Not Below or Equal/Above	01110111	disp		
JNP/JPO = Jump on Not Par/Par Odd	01111011	disp		
JNO = Jump on Not Overflow	01110001	disp		
JNS = Jump on Not Sign	01111001	disp		
LOOP = Loop CX Times	11100010	disp		
LOOPZ/LOOPE = Loop While Zero/Equal	11100001	disp		
LOOPNZ/LOOPNE = Loop While Not Zero/Equal	11100000	disp		
JCXZ = Jump on CX Zero	11100011	disp		
INT = Interrupt				
Type Specified	11001101	type		
Type 3	11001100			
INTO = Interrupt on Overflow	11001110			
IRET = Interrupt Return	11001111			
PROCESSOR CONTROL				
CLC = Clear Carry	11111000			
CMC = Complement Carry	11110101			
STC = Set Carry	11111001			
CLD = Clear Direction	11111100			
STD = Set Direction	11111101			
CLI = Clear Interrupt	11111010			
STI = Set Interrupt	11111011			
HLT = Halt	11110100			
WAIT = Wait	10011011			
ESC = Escape (to External Device)	11011xxx	mod x x x r/m		
LOCK = Bus Lock Prefix	11110000			

NOTES:

AL = 8-bit accumulator
AX = 16-bit accumulator
CX = Count register
DS = Data segment
ES = Extra segment
Above/below refers to unsigned value
Greater = more positive;
Less = less positive (more negative) signed values
if d = 1 then "to" reg; if d = 0 then "from" reg
if w = 1 then word instruction; if w = 0 then byte instruction
if mod = 11 then r/m is treated as a REG field
if mod = 00 then DISP = 0*, disp-low and disp-high are absent
if mod = 01 then DISP = disp-low sign-extended to 16 bits, disp-high is absent
if mod = 10 then DISP = disp-high; disp-low
if r/m = 000 then EA = (BX) + (SI) + DISP
if r/m = 001 then EA = (BX) + (DI) + DISP
if r/m = 010 then EA = (BP) + (SI) + DISP
if r/m = 011 then EA = (BP) + (DI) + DISP
if r/m = 100 then EA = (SI) + DISP
if r/m = 101 then EA = (DI) + DISP
if r/m = 110 then EA = (BP) + DISP*
if r/m = 111 then EA = (BX) + DISP
DISP follows 2nd byte of instruction (before data if required)
*except if mod = 00 and r/m = 110 then EA = disp-high; disp-low.

Mnemonics © Intel, 1978

if s w = 01 then 16 bits of immediate data form the operand and
if s w = 11 then an immediate data byte is sign extended to form the 16-bit operand
if v = 0 then "count" = 1; if v = 1 then "count" in (CL)
x = don't care
z is used for string primitives for comparison with ZF FLAG

SEGMENT OVERRIDE PREFIX

0 0 1 reg 1 1 0

REG is assigned according to the following table:

16-Bit (w = 1)		8-Bit (w = 0)		Segment	
000	AX	000	AL	00	ES
001	CX	001	CL	01	CS
010	DX	010	DL	10	SS
011	BX	011	BL	11	DS
100	SP	100	AH		
101	BP	101	CH		
110	SI	110	DH		
111	DI	111	BH		

Instructions which reference the flag register file as a 16-bit object use the symbol FLAGS to represent the file:
FLAGS = X:X:X:X:(OF):(DF):(IF):(TF):(SF):(ZF):X:(AF):X:(PF):X:(CF)

APPENDIX B

8086/8088 Instructions
Notes for 8086/8088 Instructions

The individual instruction descriptions are shown by a format box such as the following:

Opcode	m/op/r/m				Data		

These are byte-wise representations of the object code generated by the assembler and are interpreted as follows:

- Opcode is the 8-bit opcode for the instruction. The actual opcode generated is defined in the "Opcode" column of the instruction table that follows each format box.
- m/op/r/m is the byte that specifies the operands of the instruction. It contains a 2-bit mode field (m), a 3-bit register field (op), and a 3-bit register or memory (r/m) field.
- Dashed blank boxes following the m/op/r/m box are for any displacement required by the mode field.
- Data is for a byte of immediate data.
- A dashed blank box following a Data box is used whenever the immediate operand is a word quantity.

Operand Summary

"reg" field Bit Assignments:

Word Operand	Byte Operand	Segment
000 AX	000 AL	00 ES
001 CX	001 CL	01 CS
010 DX	010 DL	10 SS
011 BX	011 BL	11 DS
100 SP	100 AH	
101 BP	101 CH	
110 SI	110 DH	
111 DI	111 BH	

Second Instruction Byte Summary

mod xxx r/m

mod	Displacement
00	DISP = 0*, disp-low and disp-high are absent
01	DISP = disp-low sign-extended to 16-bits, disp-high is absent
10	DISP = disp-high: disp-low
11	r/m is treated as a "reg" field

r/m	Operand Address
000	(BX) + (SI) + DISP
001	(BX) + (DI) + DISP
010	(BP) + (SI) + DISP
011	(BP) + (DI) + DISP
100	(SI) + DISP
101	(DI) + DISP
110	(BP) + DISP*
111	(BX) + DISP

DISP follows 2nd byte of instruction (before data if required).

*except if mod = 00 and r/m = 110 then EA = disp-high: disp-low.

Flags

```
AF: AUXILIARY CARRY — BCD
CF: CARRY FLAG
DF: DIRECTION FLAG (STRINGS)
IF: INTERRUPT ENABLE FLAG
OF: OVERFLOW FLAG (CF  SF)
PF: PARITY FLAG
SF: SIGN FLAG
TF: TRAP (SINGLE STEP FLAG)
ZF: ZERO FLAG
```

Instructions that reference the flag register file as a 16-bit object use the symbol FLAGS to represent the file:

15								8							0
X	X	X	X	OF	DF	IF	TF	SF	ZF	X	AF	X	PF	X	CF

X = Don't Care

Segment Override Prefix

0 0 1 reg 1 1 0

Timing: 2 clocks

Use of Segment Override

Operand Register	Default	With Override Prefix
IP (code address)	CS	Never
SP (stack address)	SS	Never
BP (stack address or stack marker)	SS	BP + DS or ES, or CS
SI or DI (not incl. strings)	DS	ES, SS, or CS
SI (implicit source addr for strings)	DS	ES, SS, or CS
DI (implicit dest addr for strings)	ES	Never

Operand Address (EA) Timing (Clocks):

Add 4 clocks for word operands at ODD ADDRESSES.
Immed Offset = 6
Base (BX, BP, SI, DI) = 5
Base + DISP = 9
Base + Index (BP + DI, BX + SI) = 7
Base + Index (BP + SI, BX + DI) = 8
Base + Index (BP + DI, BX + SI) + DISP = 11
Base + Index (BP + SI, BX + DI) + DISP = 12

AAA = ASCII Adjust for Addition

Opcode

Opcode	Clocks	Operation
37	4	adjust AL, flags, AH

AAD = ASCII Adjust for Division

Long——Opcode

Opcode	Clocks	Operation
D5,0A	60	Adjust AL, AH prior to division

AAM = ASCII Adjust for Multiplication

Long——Opcode

Opcode	Clocks	Operation
D4,0A	83	Adjust AL, AH after multiplication

AAS = ASCII Adjust for Subtraction

Opcode

Opcode	Clocks	Operation
3F	4	adjust AL, flags, AH

ADC = Integer Add with Carry

Memory/Reg + Reg

Opcode	mod reg r/m				

	Opcode	Clocks	Operation
Byte	12	3	Reg8 ← CF + Reg 8 + Reg8
	12	9 + EA	Reg8 ← CF + Reg8 + Mem8
	10	16 + EA	Mem8 ← CF + Mem8 + Reg8
Word	13	3	Reg16 ← CF + Reg16 + Reg16
	13	9 + EA	Reg16 ← CF + Reg16 + Mem16
	11	16 + EA	Mem16 ← CF + Mem16 + Reg16

Immed to AX/AL

Opcode	Data		

	Opcode	Clocks	Operation
Byte	14	4	AL ← CF + AL + Immed8
Word	15	4	AX ← CF + AX + Immed16

Immed to Memory/Reg

Opcode	mod 010 r/m			Data

	Opcode	Clocks	Operation
Byte	80	4	Reg8 ← CF + Reg8 + Immed8
	80	17+EA	Mem8 ← CF + Mem8 + Immed8
Word	81	4	Reg16 ← CF + Reg16 + Immed16
	81	17+EA	Mem16 ← CF + Mem16 + Immed16
	83	4	Reg16 ← CF + Reg16 + Immed8
	83	17+EA	Mem16 ← CF + Mem16 + Immed8

ADD = Integer Addition

Memory/Reg + Reg

Opcode	mod reg r/m		

	Opcode	Clocks	Operation
Byte	02	3	Reg8 ← Reg8 + Reg8
	02	9+EA	Reg8 ← Reg8 + Mem8
	00	16+EA	Mem8 ← Mem8 + Reg8
Word	03	3	Reg16 ← Reg16 + Reg16
	03	9+EA	Reg16 ← Reg16 + Mem16
	01	16+EA	Mem16 ← Mem16 + Reg16

Immed to AX/AL

Opcode	Data	

Opcode	Clocks	Operation
04	4	AL ← AL + Immed8
05	4	AX ← AX + Immed16

Immed to Memory/Reg

Opcode	mod 000 r/m			Data	

	Opcode	Clocks	Operation
Byte	80	4	Reg8 ← Reg8 + Immed8
	80	17+EA	Mem8 ← Mem8 + Immed8
Word	81	4	Reg16 ← Reg16 + Immed16
	81	17+EA	Mem16 ← Mem16 + Immed16
	83	4	Reg16 ← Reg16 + Immed8
	83	17+EA	Mem16 ← Mem16 + Immed8

AND = Logical AND

Memory/Reg with Reg

Opcode	mod reg r/m		

	Opcode	Clocks	Operation
Byte	22	3	Reg8 ← Reg8 AND Reg8
	22	9+EA	Reg8 ← Reg8 AND Mem8
	20	16+EA	Mem8 ← Mem8 AND Reg8
Word	23	3	Reg16 ← Reg16 AND Reg16
	23	9+EA	Reg16 ← Reg16 AND Mem16
	21	16+EA	Mem16 ← Mem16 AND Reg16

Immed to AX/AL

Opcode	Data	

	Opcode	Clocks	Operation
Byte	24	4	AL ← AL AND Immed8
Word	25	4	AX ← AX AND Immed16

Immed to Memory/Reg

Opcode	mod 100 r/m			Data	

	Opcode	Clocks	Operation
Byte	80	4	Reg8 ← Reg8 AND Immed8
	80	17+EA	Mem8 ← Mem8 AND Immed8
Word	81	4	Reg16 ← Reg16 AND Immed16
	81	17+EA	Mem16 ← Mem16 AND Immed16

CALL = Call

Within segment or group, IP relative

Opcode	DispL	DispH

Opcode	Clocks	Operation
E8	19	IP ← IP + Disp16—(SP) ← return link

Within segment or group, Indirect

Opcode	mod 010 r/m		

Opcode	Clocks	Operation
FF	16	IP ← Reg16—(SP) ← return link
FF	21+EA	IP ← Mem16—(SP) ← return link

Inter-segment or group, Direct

Opcode	offset	offset	segbase	segbase	segbase

Opcode	Clocks	Operation
9A	28	CS ← segbase IP ← offset

Inter-segment or group, Indirect

Opcode	mod 011 r/m		

Opcode	Clocks	Operation
FF	37+EA	CS ← segbase IP ← offset

CBW = Convert Byte to Word

Opcode

Opcode	Clocks	Operation
98	2	convert byte in AL to word in AX

CLC = Clear Carry Flag

Opcode

Opcode	Clocks	Operation
F8	2	clear the carry flag

CLD = Clear Direction Flag

Opcode

Opcode	Clocks	Operation
FC	2	clear direction flag

CLI = Clear Interrupt Enable Flag

Opcode	Clocks	Operation
FA	2	clear interrupt flag

CMC = Complement Carry Flag

Opcode

Opcode	Clocks	Operation
F5	2	complement carry flag

CMP = Compare Two Operands

Memory/Reg with Reg

Opcode	mod reg r/m		

	Opcode	Clocks	Operation
Byte	38	3	flags ← Reg8 - Reg8
	38	9+EA	flags ← Reg8 - Mem8
	3A	9+EA	flags ← Mem8 - Reg8
Word	39	3	flags ← Reg16 - Reg16
	39	9+EA	flags ← Reg16 - Mem16
	3B	9+EA	flags ← Mem16 - Reg16

Immed to AX/AL

Opcode	Data	

	Opcode	Clocks	Operation
Byte	3C	4	flags AL - Immed8
Word	3D	4	flags AX - Immed16

Immed to Memory/Reg

Opcode	mod 111 r/m			Data	

	Opcode	Clocks	Operation
Byte	80	4	flags←Reg8 - Immed8
	80	10+EA	flags←Mem8 - Immed8
Word	81	4	flags←Reg16 - Immed16
	81	10+EA	flags←Mem16 - Immed16
	83	4	flags←Reg16 - Immed8
	83	10+EA	flags←Mem16 - Immed8

CWD = Convert Word to Doubleword

Opcode

Opcode	Clocks	Operation
99	5	convert word in AX to doubleword in DX:AX

DAA = Decimal Adjust for Addition

Opcode

Opcode	Clocks	Operation
27	4	adjust AL, flags, AH

DAS = Decimal Adjust for Subtraction

Opcode

Opcode	Clocks	Operation
2F	4	adjust AL, flags, AH

DEC = Decrement by 1

Word Register

Opcode + reg

Opcode	Clocks	Operation
48+reg	2	Reg16←Reg16 - 1

Memory/Byte Register

Opcode	mod 001 r/m			

	Opcode	Clocks	Operation
Byte	FE	3	Reg8←Reg8 - 1
	FE	15+EA	Mem8←Mem8 - 1
Word	FF	15+EA	Mem16←Mem16 - 1

DIV = Unsigned Division

Memory/Reg with AX or DX:AX

Opcode	mod 110 r/m			

	Opcode	Clocks	Operation
Byte	F6	80-90	AH,AL←AX / Reg8
	F6	(86-96)+EA	AH,AL←AX / Mem8
Word	F7	144-162	DX:AX←DX:AX / Reg16
	F7	(150-168)+EA	DX:AX←DX:AX / Mem16

ESC = Escape

Opcode + i	mod xxx r/m			

	Opcode	Clocks	Operation
	D8+i	8+EA	data bus←(EA)
	D8+i	2	data bus←(EA)

HLT = Halt

Opcode

Opcode	Clocks	Operation
F4	2	halt operation

IDIV = Signed Division

Memory/Reg with AX or DX:AX

Opcode	mod 111 r/m			

	Opcode	Clocks	Operation
Byte	F6	101-112	AH,AL←AX / Reg8
	F6	(107-118)+EA	AH,AL←AX / Mem8
Word	F7	165-184	DX,AX←DX:AX / Reg16
	F7	(171-190)+EA	DX,AX←DX:AX / Mem16

IMUL = Signed Multiplication

Memory/Reg with AL or AX

Opcode	mod 101 r/m			

	Opcode	Clocks	Operation
Byte	F6	80-98	AX←AL*Reg8
	F6	(86-104)+EA	AX←AL*Mem8
Word	F7	128-154	DX:AX←AX*Reg16
	F7	(134-160)+EA	DX:AX←AX*Mem16

IN = Input Byte, Word

Fixed port

Opcode	Port

	Opcode	Clocks	Operation
Byte	E4	10	AL←Port8
	E5	10	AX←Port8

Variable port

Opcode

	Opcode	Clocks	Operation
Word	EC	8	AL←Port16(in DX)
	ED	8	AX←Port16(in DX)

INC = Increment by 1

Word Register

Opcode+reg

	Opcode	Clocks	Operation
	40+reg	2	Reg16←Reg16 + 1

Memory/Byte Register

Opcode	mod 000 r/m			

	Opcode	Clocks	Operation
Byte	FE	3	Reg8←Reg8 + 1
	FE	15+EA	Mem8←Mem8 + 1
Word	FF	15+EA	Mem16←Mem16 + 1

INT / INTO = Interrupt

Opcode	type

Opcode	Clocks	Operation
CC	52	Interrupt 3
CD	51	Interrupt 'type
CE	53 or 4	Interrupt4 if FLAGS.OF = 1 else NOP

IRET = Return from Interrupt

Opcode

Opcode	Clocks	Operation
CF	24	Return from interrupt

Jcond = Jump on Condition

Operation

if condition is true then do;
  sign-extend displacement to 16 bits;
  IP←IP + sign-extended displacement;
  end if;

Format

Opcode	Disp

Opcode	Clocks	Operation	cond =
77	16 or 4	jump if above	JA
73	16 or 4	jump it above or equal	JAE
72	16 or 4	jump if below	JB
76	16 or 4	jump if below or equal	JBE
72	16 or 4	jump if carry set	JC
74	16 or 4	jump if equal	JE
7F	16 or 4	jump if greater	JG
7D	16 or 4	jump if greater or equal	JGE
7C	16 or 4	jump if less	JL
7E	16 or 4	jump if less or equal	JLE
76	16 or 4	jump if not above	JNA
72	16 or 4	jump if neither above nor equal	JNAE
73	16 or 4	jump if not below	JNB
77	16 or 4	jump if neither below nor equal	JNBE
73	16 or 4	jump if no carry	JNC
75	16 or 4	jump if not equal	JNE
7E	16 or 4	jump if not greater	JNG
7C	16 or 4	jump if neither greater nor equal	JNGE
7D	16 or 4	jump if not less	JNL
7F	16 or 4	jump if neither less nor equal	JNLE
71	16 or 4	jump if no overflow	JNO
7B	16 or 4	jump if no parity	JNP
79	16 or 4	jump if positive	JNS
75	16 or 4	jump if not zero	JNZ
70	16 or 4	jump if overflow	JO
7A	16 or 4	jump if parity	JP
7A	16 or 4	jump if parity even	JPE
7B	16 or 4	jump if parity odd	JPO
78	16 or 4	jump if sign	JS
74	18 or 6	jump if zero	JZ
E3	18 or 6	jump if CX is zero (does not test flags)	JCXZ

JMP = Jump

Within segment or group, IP relative

Opcode	DispL	DispH

Opcode	Clocks	Operation
E9	15	IP → IP + Disp16
EB	15	IP → IP + Disp8 (Disp8 sign-extended)

Within segment or group, Indirect

Opcode	mod 100 r/m

Opcode	Clocks	Operation
FF	11	IP → Reg16
FF	18+EA	IP → Mem16

Inter-segment or group, Direct

Opcode	offset	offset	segbase	segbase

Opcode	Clocks	Operation
EA	15	CS → segbase IP → offset

Inter-segment or group, Indirect

Opcode	mod 101 r/m

Opcode	Clocks	Operation
FF	24+EA	CS → segbase IP → offset

LAHF = Load AH from Flags

Opcode

Opcode	Clocks	Operation
9F	4	copy low byte of flags word to AH

LDS/LES = Load Pointer to DS/ES and Register

Opcode	mod reg r/m

Opcode	Clocks	Operation
C4	16+EA	dword pointer at EA goes to reg16 (1st word) and ES (2nd word)
C5	16+EA	dword pointer at EA goes to reg16 (1st word) and DS (2nd word)

LEA = Load Effective Address

Opcode	mod reg r/m

Opcode	Clocks	Operation
8D	2+EA	Reg16 → EA

LOCK = Assert Bus Lock

Opcode

Opcode	Clocks	Operation
F0	2	assert the bus lock next instruction

LOOPxx = Loop Control

Opcode	Disp

Opcode	Clocks	Operation	xx =
E1	18 or 6	dec CX; loop if equal and CX not 0	LOOPE
E0	19 or 5	dec CX; loop if not equal and CX not 0	LOOPNE
E1	18 or 6	dec CX; loop if zero and CX not 0	LOOPZ
E0	19 or 5	dec CX; loop if not zero and CX not 0	LOOPNZ
E2	17 or 5	dec CX; loop if CX not 0	LOOP

MOV = Move Data

Memory/Reg to or from Reg

Opcode	mod reg r/m

	Opcode	Clocks	Operation
Byte	88	9+EA	Mem8 → Reg8
	88	2	Reg8 → Reg8
	8A	8+EA	Reg8 → Mem8
Word	89	9+EA	Mem16 → Reg16
	89	2	Reg16 → Reg16
	8B	8+EA	Reg16 → Mem16

Direct-Addressed Memory to or from AX/AL

Opcode	AddrL	AddrH

	Opcode	Clocks	Operation
Byte	A0	10	AL → Mem8
	A2	10	Mem8 → AL
Word	A1	10	AX → Mem16
	A3	10	Mem16 → AX

Immed to Reg

Opcode	Data

	Opcode	Clocks	Operation
Byte	B0+reg	4	Reg 8 → Immed8
Word	B8+reg	4	Reg16 → Immed16

Immed to Memory/Reg

Opcode	mod 000 r/m		Data

	Opcode	Clocks	Operation
	C6	4	Reg8 → Immed8
	C6	10+EA	Mem8 → Immed8
	C7	4	Reg16 → Immed16
	C7	10+EA	Mem16 → Immed16

Memory/Reg to or from SReg

Opcode	mod sreg r/m

	Opcode	Clocks	Operation
Word	8C	9+EA	Mem16 → SReg
	8C	2	Reg16 → SReg
	8E	8+EA	SReg → Mem16
	8E	2	SReg → Reg16

MUL = Unsigned Multiplication

Memory/Reg with AL or AX

Opcode	mod 100 r/m

	Opcode	Clocks	Operation
Byte	F6	70-77	AX → AL*Reg8
	F6	(76-83)+EA	AX → AL*Mem8
Word	F7	118-133	DX:AX → AX*Reg16
	F7	(124-139)+EA	DX:AX → AX*Mem16

NEG = Negate an Integer

Memory/Reg

Opcode	mod 011 r/m			

Opcode	Clocks	Operation
F6	3	Reg8 ← 00H - Reg 8
F7	3	Reg16 ← 0000H - Reg16
F6	16+EA	Mem8 ← 00H - Mem8
F7	16+EA	Mem16 ← 0000H - Mem16

NOP = No Operation

Opcode

Opcode	Clocks	Operation
90	3	no operation

NOT = Form One's Complement
Memory/Reg

Opcode	mod 010 r/m			

	Opcode	Clocks	Operation
Byte	F6	3	Reg8 ← 0FFH - Reg8
	F6	16+EA	Mem8 ← 0FFH - Mem8
Word	F7	3	Reg16 ← 0FFFFH - Reg16
	F7	16+EA	Mem16 ← 0FFFFH - Mem16

OR = Logical Inclusive OR
Memory/Reg with Reg

Opcode	mod reg r/m			

	Opcode	Clocks	Operation
Byte	0A	3	Reg8 ← Reg8 OR Reg8
	0A	9+EA	Reg8 ← Reg8 OR Mem8
	08	16+EA	Mem8 ← Mem8 OR Reg8
Word	0B	3	Reg16 ← Reg16 OR Reg 16
	0B	9+EA	Reg16 ← Reg16 OR Mem16
	09	16+EA	Mem16 ← Mem16 OR Reg16

Immed to AX/AL

Opcode	Data		

Opcode	Clocks	Operation
0C	4	AL ← AL OR Immed8
0D	4	AX ← AX OR Immed16

Immed to Memory/Reg

Opcode	mod 001 r/m			Data		

	Opcode	Clocks	Operation
Byte	80	4	Reg8 ← Reg8 OR Immed8
	80	17+EA	Mem8 ← Mem8 OR Immed8
Word	81	4	Reg16 ← Reg16 OR Immed16
	81	17+EA	Mem16 ← Mem16 OR Immed16

OUT = Output Byte, Word
Fixed port

Opcode	Port

	Opcode	Clocks	Operation
Byte	E6	10	Port8 ← AL
	E7	10	Port8 ← AX

Variable port

Opcode

	Opcode	Clocks	Operation
Word	EE	8	Port16 (in DX) ← AL
	EF	8	Port16 (in DX) ← AX

POP = Pop a Word from the Stack
Word Memory

Opcode	mod 000 r/m			

Opcode	Clocks	Operation
8F	17+EA	Mem16 ← (SP) + +

Word Register

Opcode + reg

Opcode	Clocks	Operation
58+reg	8	Reg16 ← (SP) + +

Segment Register

Opcode + SReg

Opcode	Clocks	Operation
07+SReg	8	SReg ← (SP) + +

POPF = Pop the TOS into the Flags

Opcode

Opcode	Clocks	Operation
9D	8	FLAGS ← (SP) + +

PUSH = Push a Word onto the Stack
Memory/Reg

Opcode	mod 110 r/m			

Opcode	Clocks	Operation
FF	16+EA	—(SP) ← Mem16

Word Register

Opcode + reg

Opcode	Clocks	Operation
50+reg	11	—(SP) ← Reg16

Segment Register

Opcode + SReg

Opcode	Clocks	Operation
06+SReg	10	—(SP) ← SReg

PUSHF = Push the Flags to the Stack

Opcode

Opcode	Clocks	Operation
9C	10	—(SP) ← FLAGS

RCL = Rotate Left Through Carry
Memory or Reg by 1

Opcode	mod 010 r/m			

	Opcode	Clocks	Operation
Byte	D0	2	rotate Reg 8 by 1
	D0	15+EA	rotate Mem8 by 1
Word	D1	2	rotate Reg 16 by 1
	D1	15+EA	rotate Mem16 by 1

Memory or Reg by count in CL

Opcode	mod 010 r/m			

	Opcode	Clocks	Operation
Byte	D2	8+4/bit	rotate Reg8 by CL
	D2	20+EA+4/bit	rotate Mem8 by CL
Word	D3	8+4/bit	rotate Reg16 by CL
	D3	20+EA+4/bit	rotate Mem16 by CL

RCR = Rotate Right Through Carry
Memory or Reg by 1

Opcode	mod 011 r/m			

	Opcode	Clocks	Operation
Byte	D0	2	rotate Reg8 by 1
	D0	15+EA	rotate Mem8 by 1
Word	D1	2	rotate Reg16 by 1
	D1	15+EA	rotate Mem16 by 1

Memory or Reg by count in CL

Opcode	mod 011 r/m			

	Opcode	Clocks	Operation
Byte	D2	8+4/bit	rotate Reg8 by CL
	D2	20+EA+4/bit	rotate Mem8 by CL
Word	D3	8+4/bit	rotate Reg16 by CL
	D3	20+EA+4/bit	rotate Mem16 by CL

REPx = Repeat Prefix

Opcode

Opcode	Clocks	Operation	REPx =
F3	2	repeat next instruction until CX=0	REP
F3	2	repeat next instruction until CX=0 or ZF=0	REPE REPZ
F2	2	repeat next instruction until CX=0 or ZF=1	REPNE REPNZ

RET = Return from Subroutine

Opcode

Opcode	Clocks	Operation
C3	8	intra-segment return
CB	18	inter-segment return

Return and add constant to SP

Opcode	DataL	DataH

Opcode	Clocks	Operation
C2	12	intra-segment ret and add
CA	17	inter-segment ret and add

ROL = Rotate Left
Memory or Reg by 1

Opcode	mod 000 r/m				

	Opcode	Clocks	Operation
Byte	D0	2	rotate Reg8 by 1
	D0	15 + EA	rotate Mem8 by 1
Word	D1	2	rotate Reg16 by 1
	D1	15 + EA	rotate Mem16 by 1

Memory or Reg by count in CL

Opcode	mod 000 r/m				

	Opcode	Clocks	Operation
Byte	D2	8 + 4/bit	rotate Reg8 by CL
	D2	20 + Ea + 4/bit	rotate Mem8 by CL
Word	D3	8 + 4/bit	rotate Reg16 by CL
	D3	20 + EA + 4/bit	rotate Mem16 by CL

ROR = Rotate Right
Memory or Reg by 1

Opcode	mod 001 r/m				

	Opcode	Clocks	Operation
Byte	D0	2	rotate Reg8 by 1
	D0	15 + EA	rotate Mem8 by 1
Word	D1	2	rotate Reg16 by 1
	D1	15 + EA	rotate Mem16 by 1

Memory or Reg by count in CL

Opcode	mod 001 r/m				

	Opcode	Clocks	Operation
Byte	D2	8 + 4/bit	rotate Reg8 by CL
	D2	20 + EA + 4/bit	rotate Mem8 by CL
	D3	8 + 4/bit	rotate Reg16 by CL
	D3	20 + EA + 4/bit	rotate Mem16 by CL

SAHF = Store AH in Flags

Opcode

Opcode	Clocks	Operation
9E	4	copy AH to low byte of flags word

SAL/SHL = Arithmetic/Logical Left Shift
Memory or Reg by 1

Opcode	mod 100 r/m				

	Opcode	Clocks	Operation
Byte	D0	2	shift Reg8 by 1
	D0	15 + EA	shift Mem8 by 1
Word	D1	2	shift Reg16 by 1
	D1	15 + EA	shift Mem16 by 1

Memory or Reg by count in CL

Opcode	mod 100 r/m				

	Opcode	Clocks	Operation
Byte	D2	8 + 4/bit	shift Reg8 by CL
	D2	20 + EA + 4/bit	shift Mem8 by CL
Word	D3	8 + 4/bit	shift Reg16 by CL
	D3	20 + EA + 4/bit	shift Mem16 by CL

SAR = Arithmetic Right Shift
Memory or Reg by 1

Opcode	mod 111 r/m				

	Opcode	Clocks	Operation
Byte	D0	2	shift Reg8 by 1
	D0	15 + EA	shift Mem8 by 1

Word	D1	2	shift Reg16 by 1
	D1	15 + EA	shift Mem16 by 1

Memory or Reg by count in CL

Opcode	mod 111 r/m				

	Opcode	Clocks	Operation
Byte	D2	8 + 4/bit	shift Reg8 by CL
	D2	20 + EA + 4/bit	shift Mem8 by CL
Word	D3	8 + 4/bit	shift Reg16 by CL
	D3	20 + EA + 4/bit	shift Mem16 by CL

SBB = Integer Subtraction with Borrow
Memory/Reg with Reg

Opcode	mod reg r/m				

	Opcode	Clocks	Operation
Byte	1A	3	Reg8 ← Reg8 - Reg8 - CF
	1A	9 + EA	Reg8 ← Reg8 - Mem8 - CF
	18	16 + EA	Mem8 ← Mem8 - Reg8 - CF
Word	1B	3	Reg16 ← Reg16 - Reg16 - CF
	1B	9 + EA	Reg16 ← Reg16 - Mem16 - CF
	19	16 + EA	Mem16 ← Mem16 - Reg16 - CF

Immed from AX/AL

Opcode	Data		

Opcode	Clocks	Operation
1C	4	AL ← AL - Immed8 - CF
1D	4	AX ← AX - Immed16 - CF

Immed from Memory/Reg

Opcode	mod 011 r/m			Data	

Opcode	Clocks	Operation
80	4	Reg8 ← Reg8 - Immed8 - CF
80	17 + EA	Mem8 ← Mem8 - Immed8 - CF
81	4	Reg16 ← Reg16 - Immed16 - CF
81	17 + EA	Mem16 ← Mem16 - Immed16 - CF
83	4	Reg16 ← Reg16 - Immed8 - CF
83	17 + EA	Mem16 ← Mem16 - Immed8 - CF (Immed8 is sign-extended before subtract)

SHR = Logical Right Shift
Memory or Reg by 1

Opcode	mod 101 r/m				

	Opcode	Clocks	Operation
Byte	D0	2	shift Reg8 by 1
	D0	15 + EA	shift Mem8 by 1
Word	D1	2	shift Reg16 by 1
	D1	15 + EA	shift Mem16 by 1

Memory or Reg by count in CL

Opcode	mod 101 r/m				

	Opcode	Clocks	Operation
Byte	D2	8 + 4/bit	shift Reg8 by CL
	D2	20 + Ea + 4/bit	shift Mem8 by CL
Word	D3	8 + 4/bit	shift Reg16 by CL
	D3	20 + EA + 4/bit	shift Mem16 by CL

STC = Set Carry Flag

Opcode

Opcode	Clocks	Operation
F9	2	set the carry flag

STD = Set Direction Flags

Opcode

Opcode	Clocks	Operation
FD	2	set direction flag

STI = Set Interrupt Enable Flag

Opcode

Opcode	Clocks	Operation
FB	2	set interrupt flag

String = String Operations

Opcode

Opcode	Clocks	Operation		String =
A6	22	flags ← (SI) - (DI)		CMPS

A7	22	flags ← (SI) - (DI)	CMPS
A4	18	(DI) ← (SI)	MOVS
A5	18	(DI) ← (SI)	MOVS
AE	15	flags ← (DI) - AL	SCAS
AF	15	flags ← (DI) - AX	SCAS
AC	12	AL ← (SI)	LODS
AD	12	AX ← (SI)	LODS
AA	11	(DI) ← AL	STOS
AB	11	(DI) ← AX	STOS

SUB = Integer Subtraction

Memory/Reg with Reg

Opcode	mod reg r/m		

	Opcode	Clocks	Operation
Byte	2A	3	Reg8 ← Reg8 - Reg8
	2A	9 + EA	Reg8 ← Reg8 - Mem8
	28	16 + EA	Mem8 ← Mem8 - Reg8
Word	2B	3	Reg16 ← Reg16 - Reg16
	2B	9 + EA	Reg16 ← Reg16 - Mem16
	29	16 + EA	Mem16 ← Mem16 - Reg16

Immed to AX/AL

Opcode	Data	

	Opcode	Clocks	Operation
Byte	2C	4	AL ← AL - Immed8
Word	2D	4	AX ← AX - Immed16

Immed to Memory/Reg

Opcode	mod 101 r/m			Data	

	Opcode	Clocks	Operation
Byte	80	4	Reg8 ← Reg8 - Immed8
	80	17 + EA	Mem8 ← Mem8 - Immed8
Word	81	4	Reg16 ← Reg16 - Immed16
	81	17 + EA	Mem16 ← Mem16 - Immed16
	83	4	Reg16 ← Reg16 - Immed8
	83	17 + EA	Mem16 ← Mem16 - Immed8

TEST = Logical Compare

Memory/Reg with Reg

Opcode	mod reg r/m		

	Opcode	Clocks	Operation
Byte	84	3	flags ← Reg8 AND Reg8
	84	9 + EA	flags ← Reg8 AND Mem8
Word	85	3	flags ← Reg16 AND Reg16
	85	9 + EA	flags ← Reg16 AND Mem16

Immed to AX/AL

Opcode	Data	

	Opcode	Clocks	Operation
Byte	A8	4	flags ← AL AND Immed8
Word	A9	4	flags ← AX AND Immed16

Immed to Memory/Reg

Opcode	mod 000 r/m			Data	

	Opcode	Clocks	Operation
Byte	F6	5	flags ← Reg8 AND Immed8
	F6	11 + EA	flags ← Mem8 AND Immed8
Word	F7	5	flags ← Reg16 AND Immed16
	F7	11 + EA	flags ← Mem16 AND Immed16

WAIT = Wait While TEST Pin Not Asserted

Opcode

	Opcode	Clocks	Operation
	9B	3 + 5n	none

XCHG = Exchange Memory/Register with Register

Memory/Reg with Reg

Opcode	mod reg r/m		

	Opcode	Clocks	Operation
Byte	86	4	Reg8 ↔ Reg8
	86	17 + EA	Mem8 ↔ Reg8
Word	87	4	Reg16 ↔ Reg16
	87	17 + EA	Mem16 ↔ Reg16

Word Register with AX

Opcode + Reg

	Opcode	Clocks	Operation
	90 + Reg	3	AX ↔ Reg16

XLAT
XLATB = Table Look-up Translation

Opcode

	Opcode	Clocks	Operation
	D7	11	replace AL with table entry

XOR = Logical Exclusive OR

Memory/Reg with Reg

Opcode	mod reg r/m		

	Opcode	Clocks	Operation
Byte	32	3	Reg8 ← Reg8 XOR Reg8
	32	9 + EA	Reg8 ← Reg8 XOR Mem8
	30	16 + EA	Mem8 ← Mem8 XOR Reg8
Word	33	3	Reg16 ← Reg16 XOR Reg16
	33	9 + EA	Reg16 ← Reg16 XOR Mem16
	31	16 + EA	Mem16 ← Mem16 XOR Reg16

Immed to AX/AL

Opcode	Data	

	Opcode	Clocks	Operation
	34	4	AL ← AL XOR Immed8
	35	4	AX ← AX XOR Immed16

Immed to Memory/Reg

Opcode	mod 110 r/m			Data	

	Opcode	Clocks	Operation
Byte	80	4	Reg8 ← Reg8 XOR Immed8
	80	17 + EA	Mem8 ← Mem8 XOR Immed8
Word	81	4	Reg16 ← Reg16 XOR Immed16
	81	17 + EA	Mem16 ← Mem16 XOR Immed16

186 INSTRUCTIONS

Notes for iAPX 186 Instructions

These instructions can be used only if the MOD186 control is specified. When MOD186 is specified, clocks for all instructions are as stated under "Clocks for MOD186 Operation."

BOUND = Check Array Against Bounds

Opcode	ModRM			

Opcode	Operation
62	if Reg16 < Mem16 at EA, or Reg16 > Mem16 at EA + 2 then INTERRUPT 5

ENTER = High Level Procedure Entry

Opcode	DataL	DataH	Level

Opcode	Operation
C8	build new stack frame

IMUL = Signed Multiplication

Mem/Reg* Immediate to Reg

Opcode	ModRM			Data	

Opcode	Operation
6B	Reg 16 ← Reg 16 * Immed 8
6B	Reg 16 ← Reg 16 * Immed 8
6B	Reg 16 ← Mem 16 * Immed 8
69	Reg 16 ← Reg 16 * Immed 16
69	Reg 16 ← Reg 16 * Immed 16
69	Reg 16 ← Mem 16 * Immed 16

LEAVE = High Level Procedure Exit

Opcode

Opcode	Operation
C9	release current stack frame and return to prior frame.

POPA = Pop All Registers

Opcode

Opcode	Operation
61	restore registers from stack

PUSH = Push a Word onto the Stack

Word Immediate

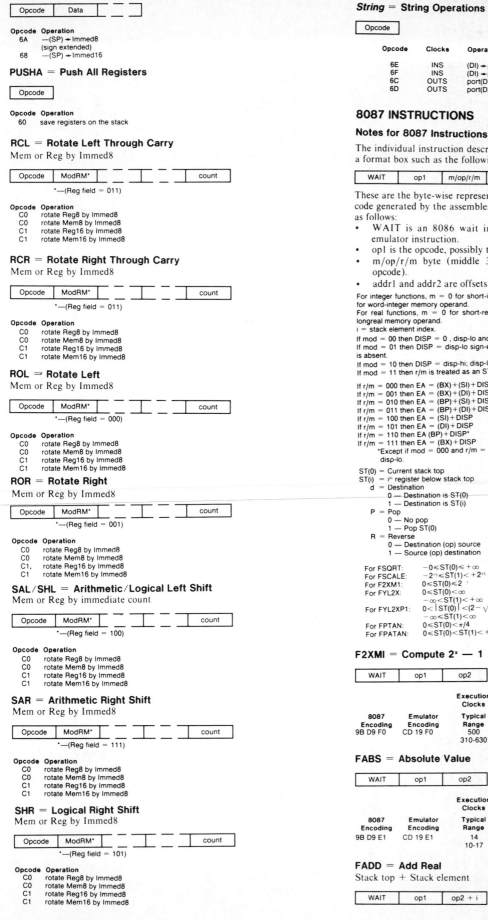

[Opcode | Data | - - -]

Opcode Operation
6A —(SP) ← Immed8
    (sign extended)
68 —(SP) ← Immed16

PUSHA = Push All Registers

[Opcode]

Opcode Operation
60   save registers on the stack

RCL = Rotate Left Through Carry
Mem or Reg by Immed8

[Opcode | ModRM* | — — | | — — | count]

*—(Reg field = 011)

Opcode Operation
C0 rotate Reg8 by Immed8
C0 rotate Mem8 by Immed8
C1 rotate Reg16 by Immed8
C1 rotate Mem16 by Immed8

RCR = Rotate Right Through Carry
Mem or Reg by Immed8

[Opcode | ModRM* | — — | | — — | count]

*—(Reg field = 011)

Opcode Operation
C0 rotate Reg8 by Immed8
C0 rotate Mem8 by Immed8
C1 rotate Reg16 by Immed8
C1 rotate Mem16 by Immed8

ROL = Rotate Left
Mem or Reg by Immed8

[Opcode | ModRM* | — — | | — — | count]

*—(Reg field = 000)

Opcode Operation
C0 rotate Reg8 by Immed8
C0 rotate Mem8 by Immed8
C1 rotate Reg16 by Immed8
C1 rotate Mem16 by Immed8

ROR = Rotate Right
Mem or Reg by Immed8

[Opcode | ModRM* | — — | | — — | count]

*—(Reg field = 001)

Opcode Operation
C0   rotate Reg8 by Immed8
C0   rotate Mem8 by Immed8
C1, rotate Reg16 by Immed8
C1   rotate Mem16 by Immed8

SAL/SHL = Arithmetic/Logical Left Shift
Mem or Reg by immediate count

[Opcode | ModRM* | — — | | — — | count]

*—(Reg field = 100)

Opcode Operation
C0 rotate Reg8 by Immed8
C0 rotate Mem8 by Immed8
C1 rotate Reg16 by Immed8
C1 rotate Mem16 by Immed8

SAR = Arithmetic Right Shift
Mem or Reg by Immed8

[Opcode | ModRM* | — — | | — — | count]

*—(Reg field = 111)

Opcode Operation
C0 rotate Reg8 by Immed8
C0 rotate Mem8 by Immed8
C1 rotate Reg16 by Immed8
C1 rotate Mem16 by Immed8

SHR = Logical Right Shift
Mem or Reg by Immed8

[Opcode | ModRM* | — — | | — — | count]

*—(Reg field = 101)

Opcode Operation
C0 rotate Reg8 by Immed8
C0 rotate Mem8 by Immed8
C1 rotate Reg16 by Immed8
C1 rotate Mem16 by Immed8

String = String Operations (INS/OUTS)

[Opcode]

Opcode	Clocks	Operation
6E	INS	(DI) ← port(DX)
6F	INS	(DI) ← port(DX:DX+1)
6C	OUTS	port(DX) ← (SI)
6D	OUTS	port(DX:DX+1) ← (SI)

8087 INSTRUCTIONS

Notes for 8087 Instructions

The individual instruction descriptions are shown by a format box such as the following:

[WAIT | op1 | m/op/r/m | addr1 | addr2]

These are the byte-wise representations of the object code generated by the assembler and are interpreted as follows:

- WAIT is an 8086 wait instruction, NOP or emulator instruction.
- op1 is the opcode, possibly taking two bytes.
- m/op/r/m byte (middle 3-bits is part of the opcode).
- addr1 and addr2 are offsets of either 8 or 16 bits.

For integer functions, m = 0 for short-integer memory operand; 1 for word-integer memory operand.
For real functions, m = 0 for short-real memory operand; 1 for longreal memory operand.
i = stack element index.
If mod = 00 then DISP = 0 , disp-lo and disp-hi are absent.
If mod = 01 then DISP = disp-lo sign-extended to 16 bits, disp-hi is absent.
If mod = 10 then DISP = disp-hi; disp-lo.
If mod = 11 then r/m is treated as an ST(i) field.

If r/m = 000 then EA = (BX)+(SI)+DISP
If r/m = 001 then EA = (BX)+(DI)+DISP
If r/m = 010 then EA = (BP)+(SI)+DISP
If r/m = 011 then EA = (BP)+(DI)+DISP
If r/m = 100 then EA = (SI)+DISP
If r/m = 101 then EA = (DI)+DISP
If r/m = 110 then EA (BP)+DISP*
If r/m = 111 then EA = (BX)+DISP
  *Except if mod = 000 and r/m = 110 then EA = disp-hi; disp-lo.

ST(0) = Current stack top
ST(i) = i^{th} register below stack top
d = Destination
  0 — Destination is ST(0)
  1 — Destination is ST(i)
P = Pop
  0 — No pop
  1 — Pop ST(0)
R = Reverse
  0 — Destination (op) source
  1 — Source (op) destination

For FSQRT: $-0 \leq ST(0) \leq +\infty$
For FSCALE: $-2^{15} \leq ST(1) < +2^{15}$ and ST(1) integer
For F2XM1: $0 \leq ST(0) \leq 2^{-1}$
For FYL2X: $0 \leq ST(0) < \infty$
             $-\infty < ST(1) < +\infty$
For FYL2XP1: $0 < |ST(0)| < (2-\sqrt{2})/2$
             $-\infty < ST(1) < \infty$
For FPTAN: $0 \leq ST(0) < \pi/4$
For FPATAN: $0 \leq ST(0) < ST(1) < +\infty$

F2XMI = Compute 2^x — 1

[WAIT | op1 | op2]

8087 Encoding	Emulator Encoding	Execution Clocks Typical Range	Operation
9B D9 F0	CD 19 F0	500 / 310-630	ST ← 2ST-1

FABS = Absolute Value

[WAIT | op1 | op2]

8087 Encoding	Emulator Encoding	Execution Clocks Typical Range	Operation
9B D9 E1	CD 19 E1	14 / 10-17	ST ← |ST|

FADD = Add Real
Stack top + Stack element

[WAIT | op1 | op2 + i]

8087 Encoding	Emulator Encoding	Execution Clocks Typical Range	Operation
9B D8 C0+i	CD 18 C0+i	85 / 70-100	ST ← ST + ST(i)
9B DC C0+i	CD 1C C0+i	85 / 70-100	ST(i) ← ST + ST(i)

Stack top + memory operand

| WAIT | op1 | mod 000 r/m | addr1 | addr2 |

8087 Encoding	Emulator Encoding	Execution Clocks Typical Range	Operation
9B D8 m0rm	CD 18 m0rm	105+EA / (90-120)+EA	ST ← ST + mem-op (short-real)
9B DC m0rm	CD 1C m0rm	110+EA / (95-125)+EA	ST ← ST + mem-op (long-real)

FADDP = Add Real and Pop

Stack top + Stack Element

| WAIT | op1 | op2 + i |

8087 Encoding	Emulator Encoding	Execution Clocks Typical Range	Operation
9B DE C1	CD 1E C1	90 / 75-105	ST(1) ← ST + ST(1) pop stack
9B DE C0+i	CD 1E C0+i	90 / 75-105	ST(i) ← ST + ST(i) pop stack

FBLD = Packed Decimal (BCD) Load

| WAIT | op1 | mod 100 r/m | addr1 | addr2 |

8087 Encoding	Emulator Encoding	Execution Clocks Typical Range	Operation
9B DF m4rm	CD 1F m4rm	300+EA / (290-310)+EA	push stack ST ← mem-op

FBSTP = Packed Decimal (BCD) Store and Pop

| WAIT | op1 | mod 110 r/m | addr1 | addr2 |

8087 Encoding	Emulator Encoding	Execution Clocks Typical Range	Operation
9B DF m6rm	CD 1F m6rm	530+EA / (520-540)+EA	mem-op ← ST pop stack

FCHS = Change Sign

| WAIT | op1 | op2 |

8087 Encoding	Emulator Encoding	Execution Clocks Typical Range	Operation
9B D9 E0	CD 19 E0	15 / 10-17	ST ← -ST

FCLEX / FNCLEX = Clear Exceptions

| WAIT | op1 | op2 |

8087 Encoding	Emulator Encoding	Execution Clocks Typical Range	Operation
9B DB E2	CD 1B E2	5 / 2-8	clear 8087 exceptions
90 DB E2	CD 1B E2	5 / 2-8	clear 8087 exceptions (no wait)

FCOM = Compare Real

Compare Stack top and Stack element

| WAIT | op1 | op2 + i |

8087 Encoding	Emulator Encoding	Execution Clocks Typical Range	Operation
9B D8 D1	CD 18 D1	45 / 40-50	ST - ST(1)
9B D8 D0+i	CD 18 D0+i	45 / 40-50	ST - ST(i)

Compare Stack top and memory operands

| WAIT | op1 | mod 010 r/m | addr1 | addr2 |

8087 Encoding	Emulator Encoding	Execution Clocks Typical Range	Operation
9B D8 m2rm	CD 18 m2rm	65+EA / (60-70)+EA	ST - memop (short-real)
9B DC m2rm	CD 1C m2rm	70+EA / (65-75)+EA	ST - memop (long-real)

FCOMP = Compare Real and Pop

Compare Stack top and Stack element and pop

| WAIT | op1 | op2 + i |

8087 Encoding	Emulator Encoding	Execution Clocks Typical Range	Operation
9B D8 D9	CD 18 D9	47 / 42-52	ST - ST(1) pop stack
9B D8 D8+i	CD 18 D8+i	47 / 42-52	ST - ST(i) pop stack

Compare Stack top and memory operand and pop

| WAIT | op1 | mod 011 r/m | addr1 | addr2 |

8087 Encoding	Emulator Encoding	Execution Clocks Typical Range	Operation
9B D8 m3rm	CD 18 m3rm	68+EA / (63-73)+EA	ST - mem-op pop stack (short-real)
9B DC m3rm	CD 1C m3rm	72+EA / (67-77)+EA	ST - mem-op pop stack (long-real)

FCOMPP = Compare Real and Pop Twice

| WAIT | op1 | op2 |

8087 Encoding	Emulator Encoding	Execution Clocks Typical Range	Operation
9B DE D9	CD 1E D9	50 / 45-55	ST - ST(1) pop stack pop stack

FDECSTP = Decrement Stack Pointer

| WAIT | op1 | op2 |

8087 Encoding	Emulator Encoding	Execution Clocks Typical Range	Operation
9B D9 F6	CD 19 F6	9 / 6-12	stack pointer ← stack pointer 1

FDISI / FNDISI = Disable Interrupts

| WAIT | op1 | op2 |

8087 Encoding	Emulator Encoding	Execution Clocks Typical Range	Operation
9B DB E1	CD 1B E1	5 / 2-8	Set 8087 interrupt mask
90 DB E1	CD 1B E1	5 / 2-8	Set 8087 interrupt mask (no wait)

FDIV = Divide Real

Stack top and Stack element

| WAIT | op1 | op2 + i |

8087 Encoding	Emulator Encoding	Execution Clocks Typical Range	Operation
9B D8 F0+i	CD 18 F0+i	198 / 193-203	ST ← ST/ST(i)

9B DC F8+i   CD 1C F8+i   198   193-203   ST(i) ← ST(i)/ST

Stack top and memory operand

| WAIT | op1 | mod 110 r/m | addr1 | addr2 |

8087 Encoding	Emulator Encoding	Execution Clocks Typical Range	Operation
9B D8 m6rm	CD 18 m6rm	220+EA (215-225)+EA	ST ← ST/mem-op (short-real)
9B DC m6rm	CD 1C m6rm	225+EA (220-230)+EA	ST ← ST/mem-op (long-real)

FDIVP = Divide Real and Pop

| WAIT | op1 | op2 + i |

8087 Encoding	Emulator Encoding	Execution Clocks Typical Range	Operation
9B DE F9	CD 1E F9	202 197-207	ST(1) ← ST(1)/ST pop stack
9B DE F8+i	CD 1E F8+i	202 197-207	ST(i) ← ST(i)/ST pop stack

FDIVR = Divide Real Reversed
Stack top and Stack element

| WAIT | op1 | op2 + i |

8087 Encoding	Emulator Encoding	Execution Clocks Typical Range	Operation
9B D8 F8+i	CD 18 F8+i	199 194-204	ST ← ST(i)/ST
9B DC F0+i	CD 1C F0+i	199 194-204	ST(i) ← ST/ST(i)

Stack top and memory operand

| WAIT | op1 | mod 111 r/m | addr1 | addr2 |

8087 Encoding	Emulator Encoding	Execution Clocks Typical Range	Operation
9B D8 m7rm	CD 18 m7rm	221+EA (216-226)+EA	ST ← mem-op/ST (short-real)
9B DC m7rm	CD 1C m7rm	226+EA (221-231)+EA	ST ← mem-op/ST (long-real)

FDIVRP = Divide Real Reversed and Pop

| WAIT | op1 | op2 + i |

8087 Encoding	Emulator Encoding	Execution Clocks Typical Range	Operation
9B DE F1	CD 1E F1	203 198-208	ST(1) ← ST/ST(1) pop stack
9B DE F0+i	CD 1E F0+i	203 198-208	ST(i) ← ST/ST(i)

FENI FNENI = Enable Interrupts

| WAIT | op1 | op2 |

8087 Encoding	Emulator Encoding	Execution Clocks Typical Range	Operation
9B DB E0	CD 1B E0	5 2-8	clear 8087 interrupt mask
90 DB E0	CD 1B E0	5 2-8	clear 8087 interrupt mask (no wait)

FFREE = Free Register

| WAIT | op1 | op2 + i |

8087 Encoding	Emulator Encoding	Execution Clocks Typical Range	Operation
9B DD C0+i	CD 1D C0+i	11 9-16	TAG(i) masked empty

FIADD = Integer Add

| WAIT | op1 | mod 000 r/m | addr1 | addr2 |

8087 Encoding	Emulator Encoding	Execution Clocks Typical Range	Operation
9B DA m0rm	CD 1A m0rm	125+EA (108-143)+EA	ST ← ST + mem-op (short integer)
9B DE m0rm	CD 1E m0rm	120+EA (102-137)+EA	ST ← ST + mem-op (word integer)

FICOM = Integer Compare

| WAIT | op1 | mod 010 r/m | addr1 | addr2 |

8087 Encoding	Emulator Encoding	Execution Clocks Typical Range	Operation
9B DA m2rm	CD 1A m2rm	85+EA (78-91)+EA	ST — mem-op (short integer)
t9B DE m2rm	CD 1E m2rm	80+EA (72-86)+EA	ST — mem-op (word integer)

FICOMP = Integer Compare and Pop

| WAIT | op1 | mod 011 r/m | addr1 | addr2 |

8087 Encoding	Emulator Encoding	Execution Clocks Typical Range	Operation
9B DA m3rm	CD 1A m3rm	87+EA (80-93)+EA	ST — mem-op pop stack (short integer)
9B DE m3rm	CD 1E m3rm	82+EA (74-88)+EA	ST — mem-op pop stack (word integer)

FIDIV = Integer Divide

| WAIT | op1 | mod 110 r/m | addr1 | addr2 |

8087 Encoding	Emulator Encoding	Execution Clocks Typical Range	Operation
9B DA m6rm	CD 1A m6rm	236+EA (230-243)+EA	ST ← ST/mem-op (short integer)
9B DE m6rm	CD 1E m6rm	230+EA (224-238)+EA	ST ← ST/mem-op (word integer)

FIDIVR = Integer Divide Reversed

| WAIT | op1 | mod 111 r/m | addr1 | addr2 |

8087 Encoding	Emulator Encoding	Execution Clocks Typical Range	Operation
9B DA m7rm	CD 1A m7rm	237+EA (231-245)+EA	ST ← mem-op/ST (short integer)
9B DE m7rm	CD 1E m7rm	230+EA (225-239)+EA	ST ← mem-op/ST (word integer)

FILD = Integer Load
Word Integer or Short Integer

| WAIT | op1 | mod 000 r/m | addr1 | addr2 |

8087 Encoding	Emulator Encoding	Execution Clocks Typical Range	Operation
9B DB m0rm	CD 1B m0rm	56+EA (52-60)+EA	push stack ST ← mem-op (short integer)
9B DF m0rm	CD 1F m0rm	50+EA (46-54)+EA	push stack ST ← mem-op (word integer)

Long Integer

| WAIT | op1 | mod 101 | addr1 | addr2 |

8087 Encoding	Emulator Encoding	Execution Clocks Typical Range	Operation
9B DF m5rm	CD 1F m5rm	64+EA (60-68)+EA	push stack ST ← mem-op (long integer)

FIMUL = Integer Multiply

WAIT	op1	mod001 r/m	addr1	addr2

8087 Encoding	Emulator Encoding	Execution Clocks Typical Range	Operation
9B DA m1rm	CD 1A m1rm	136 + EA (130-144) + EA	ST ← ST * mem-op (short integer)
9B DE m1rm	CD 1E m1m	130 + EA (124-138) + EA	ST ← ST * mem-op (word integer)

FINCSTP = Increment Stack Pointer

WAIT	op1	op2

8087 Encoding	Emulator Encoding	Execution Clocks Typical Range	Operation
9B D9 F7	CD 19 F7	9 6-12	stack pointer ← stack pointer + 1

FINIT FNINIT = Initialize Processor

WAIT	op1	op2

8087 Encoding	Emulator Encoding	Execution Clocks Typical Range	Operation
9B DB E3	CD 1B E3	5 2-8	initialize 8087
90 DB E3	CD 1B E3	5 2-8	initialize 8087 (no wait)

FIST = Integer Store

WAIT	op1	mod 010 r/m	addr1	addr2

8087 Encoding	Emulator Encoding	Execution Clocks Typical Range	Operation
9B DB m2rm	CD 1B m2rm	88 + EA (82-92) + EA	mem-op ← ST (short integer)
9B DF m2rm	CD 1F m2rm	86 + EA (80-90) + EA	mem-op ← ST (word integer)

FISTP = Integer Store and Pop
Short Integer or Word Integer

WAIT	op1	mod 011 r/m	addr1	addr2

8087 Encoding	Emulator Encoding	Execution Clocks Typical Range	Operation
9B DB m3rm	CD 1B m3rm	90 + EA (84-94) + EA	mem-op ← ST pop stack (short integer)
9B DF m3rm	CD 1F m3rm	88 + EA (82-92) + EA	mem-op ← ST pop stack (word integer)

Long Integer

WAIT	op1	mod 111	addr1	addr2

8087 Encoding	Emulator Encoding	Execution Clocks Typical Range	Operation
9B DF m7rm	CD 1F m7rm	100 + EA (94-105) + EA	mem-op ← ST pop stack (long integer)

FISUB = Integer Subtract

WAIT	op1	mod 100 r/m	addr1	addr2

8087 Encoding	Emulator Encoding	Execution Clocks Typical Range	Operation
9B DA m4rm	CD 1A m4rm	125 + EA (108-143) + EA	ST ← ST — mem-op (short integer)
9B DE m4rm	CD 1E m4rm	120 + EA (102-137) + EA	ST ← ST — mem-op (word integer)

FISUBR = Integer Subtract Reversed

WAIT	op1	mod 101 r/m	addr1	addr2

8087 Encoding	Emulator Encoding	Execution Clocks Typical Range	Operation
9B DA m5rm	CD 1A m5rm	125 + EA (109-144) + EA	ST ← mem-op — ST (short integer)
9B DE m5rm	CD 1E m5rm	120 + EA (103-139) + EA	ST ← mem-op — ST (word integer)

FLD = Load Real
Stack element to Stack top

WAIT	op1	op2 + i

8087 Encoding	Emulator Encoding	Execution Clocks Typical Range	Operation
9B D9 C0 + i	CD 19 C0 + i	20 17-22	T, ← ST(i) push stack ST ← T,

Memory operand to Stack top
Short Integer or Long Integer

WAIT	op1	mod 000 r/m	addr1	addr2

8087 Encoding	Emulator Encoding	Execution Clocks Typical Range	Operation
9B D9 m0rm	CD 19 m0rm	43 + EA (38-56) + EA	push stack ST ← mem-op (short integer)
9B DD m0rm	CD 1D m0rm	46 + EA (40-60) + EA	push stack ST ← mem-op (long integer)

Temp Real

WAIT	op1	mod 101	addr1	addr2

8087 Encoding	Emulator Encoding	Execution Clocks Typical Range	Operation
9B DB m5rm	CD 1B m5rm	57 + EA (53-65) + EA	push stack ST ← mem-op (temp real)

FLD1 = Load + 1.0

WAIT	op1	op2

8087 Encoding	Emulator Encoding	Execution Clocks Typical Range	Operation
9B D9 E8	CD 19 E8	18 15-21	push stack ST ← 1.0

FLDCW = Load Control Word

WAIT	op1	mod 101 r/m	addr1	addr2

8087 Encoding	Emulator Encoding	Execution Clocks Typical Range	Operation
9B D9 m5rm	CD 19 m5rm	10 + EA (7-14) + EA	processor control word ← mem-op

FLDENV = Load Environment

WAIT	op1	mod 100 r/m	addr1	addr2

8087 Encoding	Emulator Encoding	Execution Clocks Typical Range	Operation
9B D9 m4rm	CD 19 m4rm	40 + EA (35-45) + EA	8087 environment ← mem-op

FLDL2E = Load Log₂e

WAIT	op1	op2

8087 Encoding	Emulator Encoding	Execution Clocks Typical Range	Operation
9B D9 EA	CD 19 EA	18 15-21	push stack ST ← log,e

FLDL2T = Load Log₂10

	WAIT	op1	op2

8087 Encoding	Emulator Encoding	Execution Clocks Typical Range	Operation
9B D9 E9	CD 19 E9	19 16-22	push stack ST ← log.10

FLDLG2 = Load Log₁₀2

	WAIT	op1	op2

8087 Encoding	Emulator Encoding	Execution Clocks Typical Range	Operation
9B D9 EC	CD 19 EC	21 18-24	push stack ST ← log₁₀2

FLDPI = Load π

	WAIT	op1	op2

8087 Encoding	Emulator Encoding	Execution Clocks Typical Range	Operation
9B D9 EB	CD 19 EB	19 16-22	push stack ST ← π

FLDZ = Load + 0.0

	WAIT	op1	op2

8087 Encoding	Emulator Encoding	Execution Clocks Typical Range	Operation
9B D9 EE	CD 19 EE	14 11-17	push stack ST ← 0.0

FMUL = Multiply Real

Stack top and Stack element

	WAIT	op1	op2 + i

8087 Encoding	Emulator Encoding	Execution Clocks Typical Range	Operation
9B D8 C8+i	CD 18 C8+i	138 130-145	ST ← ST * ST(i)
9B DC C8+i	CD 1C C8+i	138 130-145	ST(i) ← ST(i) — ST

Stack top and memory operand

	WAIT	op1	mod 001 r/m	addr1	addr2

8087 Encoding	Emulator Encoding	Execution Clocks Typical Range	Operation
9B D8 m1rm	CD 18 m1rm	118+EA (110-125)+EA	ST ← ST * mem-op (short real)
9B DC m1rm	CD 1C m1rm	161+EA (154-168)+EA	ST ← ST * mem-op (long real)

FMULP = Multiply Real and Pop

	WAIT	op1	op2 + i

8087 Encoding	Emulator Encoding	Execution Clocks Typical Range	Operation
9B DE C9+i	CD 1E C9+i	142 134-148	ST(i) ← ST(i) * ST pop stack

FNOP = No Operation

	WAIT	op1	op2

8087 Encoding	Emulator Encoding	Execution Clocks Typical Range	Operation
9B D9 D0	CD 19 D0	13 10-16	ST ← ST

FPATAN = Partial Arctangent

	WAIT	op1	op2

8087 Encoding	Emulator Encoding	Execution Clocks Typical Range	Operation
9B D9 F3	CD 19 F3	650 250-800	T ← arctan (ST(1)/ST) pop stack ST ← T,

FPREM = Partial Remainder

	WAIT	op1	op2

8087 Encoding	Emulator Encoding	Execution Clocks Typical Range	Operation
9B D9 F8	CD 19 F8	125 15-190	ST ← REPEAT (ST — ST(1))

FPTAN = Partial Tangent

	WAIT	op1	op2

8087 Encoding	Emulator Encoding	Execution Clocks Typical Range	Operation
9B D9 F2	CD 19 F2	450 30-540	Y/X ← TAN (ST) ST ← Y push stack ST ← X

FRNDINT = Round to Integer

	WAIT	op1	op2

8087 Encoding	Emulator Encoding	Execution Clocks Typical Range	Operation
9B D9 FC	CD 19 FC	45 16-50	ST ← nearest integer (ST)

FRSTOR = Restore Saved State

	WAIT	op1	mod 100 r/m	addr1	addr2

8087 Encoding	Emulator Encoding	Execution Clocks Typical Range	Operation
9B DD m4rm	CD 1D m4rm	202+EA (197-207)+EA	8087 state ← mem-op

FSAVE FNSAVE = Save State

	WAIT	op1	mod 110 r/m	addr1	addr2

8087 Encoding	Emulator Encoding	Execution Clocks Typical Range	Operation
9B DD m6rm	CD 1D m6rm	202+EA (197-207)+EA	mem-op ← 8087 state
90 DD m6rm	CD 1D m6rm	202+EA (197-207)+EA	mem-op ← 8087 state (no wait)

FSCALE = Scale

	WAIT	op1	op2

8087 Encoding	Emulator Encoding	Execution Clocks Typical Range	Operation
9B D9 FD	CD 19 FD	35 32-38	ST ← ST * $2^{ST(1)}$

FSQRT = Square Root

	WAIT	op1	op2

8087 Encoding	Emulator Encoding	Execution Clocks Typical Range	Operation
9B D9 FA	CD 19 FA	183 180-186	ST ← √ST

FST = Store Real

Stack top to Stack element

WAIT	op1	op2 + i

		Execution Clocks	
8087 Encoding	Emulator Encoding	Typical Range	Operation
9B DD D0+i	CD 1D D0+i	18 15-22	ST(i) ← ST

Stack top to memory operand

WAIT	op1	mod 010 r/m	addr1	addr2

		Execution Clocks	
8087 Encoding	Emulator Encoding	Typical Range	Operation
9B D9 m2rm	CD 19 m2rm	87+EA (84-90)+EA	mem-op ← ST (short-real)
9B D0 m2rm	CD 1D m2rm	100+EA (96-104)+EA	mem-op ← ST (long-real)

FSTCW / FNSTCW = Store Control Word

WAIT	op1	mod 111 r/m	addr1	addr2

		Execution Clocks	
8087 Encoding	Emulator Encoding	Typical Range	Operation
9B D9 m7rm	CD 19 m7rm	15+EA (12-18)+EA	mem-op ← processor control word
90 D9 m7rm	CD 19 m7rm	15+EA (12-18)+EA	mem-op ← processor control word (no wait)

FSTENV / FNSTENV = Store Environment

WAIT	op1	mod 110 r/m	addr1	addr2

		Execution Clocks	
8087 Encoding	Emulator Encoding	Typical Range	Operation
9B D9 m6rm	CD 19 m6rm	45+EA (40-50)+EA	mem-op ← 8087 environment
90 D9 r6rm	CD 19 m6rm	45+EA (40-50)+EA	mem-op ← 8087 environment (no wait)

FSTP = Store Real and Pop

Stack top to Stack element

WAIT	op1	op2 + i

		Execution Clocks	
8087 Encoding	Emulator Encoding	Typical Range	Operation
9B DD D8+i	CD 1D D8+i	20 17-24	ST(i) ← ST pop stack

Stack top to memory operand

WAIT	op1	mod 011 r/m	addr1	addr2

Long Real or Short Real

		Execution Clocks	
8087 Encoding	Emulator Encoding	Typical Range	Operation
9B D9 m3rm	CD 19 m3rm	89+EA (86-92)+EA	mem-op ← ST pop stack (short-real)
9B DB m3rm	CD 1B m3rm	102+EA (98-106)+EA	mem-op ← ST pop stack (long-real)

Temp Real

WAIT	op1	mod 111 r/m	disp-lo	disp-hi

		Execution Clocks	
8087 Encoding	Emulator Encoding	Typical Range	Operation
9B DD m7rm	CD 1D m7rm	55+EA (52-58)+EA	mem-op ← ST pop stack (temp-real)

FSTSW / FNSTSW = Store Status Word

WAIT	op1	mod 111 r/m	addr1	addr2

		Execution Clocks	
8087 Encoding	Emulator Encoding	Typical Range	Operation
9B DD m7rm	CD 1D m7rm	15+EA (12-18)+EA	mem-op ← 8087 status word
90 DD m7rm	CD 1D m7rm	15+EA (12-18)+EA	mem-op ← 8087 status word (no wait)

FSUB = Subtract Real

Stack top and Stack element

WAIT	op1	op2 + i

		Execution Clocks	
8087 Encoding	Emulator Encoding	Typical Range	Operation
9B D8 E0+i	CD 18 E0+i	85 70-100	ST ← ST — ST(i)
9B DC E8+i	CD 1C E8+i	85 70-100	ST(i) ← ST(i) — ST

Stack top and memory operand

WAIT	op1	mod 100 r/m	addr1	addr2

		Execution Clocks	
8087 Encoding	Emulator Encoding	Typical Range	Operation
9B D8 m4rm	CD 18 m4rm	105+EA (90-120)+EA	ST ← ST — mem-op (short-real)
9B DC m4rm	CD 1C m4rm	110+EA (95-125)+EA	ST ← ST — mem-op (long-real)

FSUBP = Subtract Real and Pop

WAIT	op1	op2 + i

		Execution Clocks	
8087 Encoding	Emulator Encoding	Typical Range	Operation
9B DE E9	CD 1E E9	90 75-105	ST(1) ← ST(1) — ST pop stack
9B DE E8+i	CD 1E E8+i	90 75-105	ST(i) ← ST(i) — ST pop stack

FSUBR = Subtract Real Reversed

Stack top and Stack element

WAIT	op1	op2 + i

		Execution Clocks	
8087 Encoding	Emulator Encoding	Typical Range	Operation
9B D8 E8+i	CD D8 E8+i	87 70-100	ST ← ST(i) — ST
9B DC E0+i	CD 1C E0+i	87 70-100	ST(i) ← ST — ST(i)

Stack top and memory operand

WAIT	op1	mod 101 r/m	addr1	addr2

		Execution Clocks	
8087 Encoding	Emulator Encoding	Typical Range	Operation
9B D8 m5rm	CD 18 m5rm	105+EA (90-120)+EA	ST ← mem-op — ST (short-real)
9B DC m5rm	CD 1C m5rm	110+EA (95-125)+EA	ST ← mem-op — ST (long-real)

FSUBRP = Subtract Real Reversed and Pop

WAIT	op1	op2 + i

		Execution Clocks	
8087 Encoding	Emulator Encoding	Typical Range	Operation

| 9B DE E1 | CD 1E E1 | 90 75-105 | ST(1)←ST — ST(1) pop stack |
| 9B DE E0+i | CD 1E E0+i | 90 75-105 | ST(i)←ST — ST(i) pop stack |

FTST = Test Stack Top Against + 0.0

WAIT	op1	op2

8087 Encoding	Emulator Encoding	Execution Clocks Typical Range	Operation
9B D9 E4	CD 19 E4	42 38-48	ST←ST — 0.0

FWAIT = (CPU) Wait While 8087 Is Busy

WAIT

8087 Encoding	Emulator Encoding	Execution Clocks Typical Range	Operation
9B	90	3+5n 3+5n	8086 wait instruction

FXAM = Examine Stack Top

WAIT	op1	op2

8087 Encoding	Emulator Encoding	Execution Clocks Typical Range	Operation
9B D9 E5	CD 19 E5	17 12-23	set condition code

FXCH = Exchange Registers

WAIT	op1	op2 + i

8087 Encoding	Emulator Encoding	Execution Clocks Typical Range	Operation
9B D9 C8	CD 19 C8	12 10-15	T_1←ST(1) ST(1)←ST ST←T_1
9B D9 C8+i	CD 19 C8+i	12 10-15	T_1←ST(i) ST(i)←ST ST←T_1

FXTRACT = Extract Exponent and Significand

WAIT	op1	nn?

8087 Encoding	Emulator Encoding	Execution Clocks Typical Range	Operation
9B D9 F4	CD 19 F4	50 27-55	T_1←exponent (ST) T_2←significand (ST) ST←T_1 push stack ST←T_2

FYL2X = Compute Y · Log$_2$ X

WAIT	op1	op2

8087 Encoding	Emulator Encoding	Execution Clocks Typical Range	Operation
9B D9 F1	CD 19 F1	950 900-1100	T_1←ST(1) · log$_2$ (ST) pop stack ST←T_1

FYL2XP1 = Compute Y · Log$_2$ (X + 1)

WAIT	op1	op2

8087 Encoding	Emulator Encoding	Execution Clocks Typical Range	Operation
9B D9 F9	CD 19 F9	850 700-1000	T_1←ST + 1 T_2←ST(1) · log$_2$ T_1 pop stack ST←T_2

INDEX